TOP 10
MILAN
AND THE LAKES

Top 10 Milan and the Lakes Highlights

The Top 10 of Everything

CONTENTS

Milan and the Lakes Area by Area

Streetsmart

Within each Top 10 list in this book, no hierarchy of quality or popularity is implied. All 10 are, in the editor's opinion, of roughly equal merit.

Title page, front cover and spine Galleria Vittorio Emanuele II, the world's oldest shopping mall in Milan
Back cover clockwise from top left Arco della Pace, Milan; town of Menaggio, Lake Como; a street in Bellagio; Galleria Vittorio Emanuele II; scenic road on the coast of Lake Garda

The information in this DK Eyewitness Top 10 Travel Guide is checked regularly. Every effort has been made to ensure that this book is as up-to-date as possible at the time of going to press. Some details, however, such as telephone numbers, opening hours, prices, gallery hanging arrangements and travel information are liable to change. The publishers cannot accept responsibility for any consequences arising from the use of this book, nor for any material on third-party websites, and cannot guarantee that any website address in this book will be a suitable source of travel information. We value the views and suggestions of our readers very highly. Please write to: DK Eyewitness Travel Guides, Dorling Kindersley, 80 Strand, London WC2R 0RL, Great Britain, or email travelguides@dk.com

Welcome to
Milan and
the Lakes

The capital of Italy's north, Milan is a world leader in the fields of design. Behind the city's frenetic public face, lies the cultural heritage of Milan, while just beyond its borders lie the tranquil jewels of the Italian lakes. With Eyewitness Top 10 Milan and the Lakes, it's all yours to explore.

World-class museums and stunning architecture; top restaurants and traditional trattorias; chic boutiques and bustling markets; grand opera and hot night spots – Milan has it all. And whether you are gazing in awe at **Leonardo's Last Supper** or looking out across the city from the roof of the **Duomo**, Milan is a sightseeing paradise. As befits a city with fashion at its heart, no mere shopping mall can compete with the grand and glorious **Galleria Vittorio Emanuele II**, while, for culture vultures, the **Pinacotera di Brera, Pinacoteca Ambrosiana** and the museums of **Castello Sforzesco** offer an unequalled guided tour through the entire history of Western art.

The Italian lakes make an idyllic contrast to busy Milan. **Lake Como** and **Lake Maggiore,** with their villas and gardens, are the nearest, while laid-back **Lake Iseo** and beautiful **Lake Garda** are easily reached as well. The historic and cultural gems of **Bergamo** and **Mantua** are also close enough to merit a day's exploration.

Whether you're visiting for a weekend or a week, our Top 10 guide brings together the best of everything Milan and the Lakes have to offer, from futuristic **Porta Nuova** to arty **Brera**, from the **Navigli** district's waterways to the **Isole Borromee**. The guide has useful tips throughout, from seeking out what's free to avoiding the crowds, plus nine easy-to-follow itineraries designed to tie together a clutch of sights in a short space of time. Add inspiring photography and detailed maps, and you've got the essential pocket-sized travel companion. **Enjoy the book, and enjoy Milan and the Lakes**.

Clockwise from top: Galleria Vittorio Emanuele II in Milan, spires of Milan's Duomo, Piazza delle Erbe in Mantua, Varenna, Rocca di Angera frescoes, Triennale Design Museum, Lake Garda

Exploring Milan and the Lakes

Milan's city districts are many and varied, and each has its own well-defined character; moving from one to another can be a kaleidoscopic experience. The city's main monuments, galleries and shopping areas are relatively close together, however, within the compact and walkable historic centre.

Milan's Duomo affords magnificent city views from its Gothic-spired rooftop.

Two Days in Milan

Day ❶
MORNING
Start the day at Piazza Duomo to marvel at the Gothic **Duomo** *(see pp14–15)* and ascend to the roof for views as far as the Alps. Then it's just a hop to the **Quadrilatero d'Oro** *(see p71)* for window-shopping among the temples of fashion and coffee at historic **Cova** *(see p88)*.
AFTERNOON
Cross Piazza Duomo to browse the **Galleria Vittorio Emanuele II** *(see p83)* and stamp on the "lucky bull".

Galleria Vittorio Emanuele II is Milan's unique, spectacular shopping arcade.

Spend time exploring the **Pinacoteca di Brera** *(see pp16–19)* before dinner at **Latteria San Marco** *(see p97)*.

Day ❷
MORNING
Castello Sforzesco *(see pp20–21)* is your first destination, followed by a stroll through **Parco Sempione** *(see p92)*. From here walk along stylish Corso Como to the futuristic **Piazza Gae Aulenti** *(see p94)* and visit the bohemian Isola district just beyond. Have lunch at **Ratanà** *(see p97)*.
AFTERNOON
Head to **Navigli** *(see pp28–9)* for a boat trip and an evening enjoying the canalside bars for happy hour and then dinner at **El Brellin** *(see p103)*.

Four Days in and Around Milan

Day ❶
Arrive at **Santa Maria delle Grazie** *(see p92)* for an early reservation to see Leonardo's Last Supper *(see pp12–13)* then stroll to the basilica **Sant'Ambrogio** *(see pp26–7)* and the **Pinacoteca Ambrosiana** *(see pp24–5)*. Following a quick lunch at **Princi** *(see p88)* head to Piazza Duomo to visit the stunning **Duomo** *(see pp14–15)* and wander among the pinnacles

Key
— Two-day itinerary
— Four-day itinerary

METRO M2

from Bergamo

Gioia metro station

Milano Centrale Station

Ratanà

Piazza Gae Aulenti

Corso Como

Mantua via Centrale Station

METRO M3

Latteria San Marco

Turati metro station

Parco Sempione

Pinacoteca di Brera

Quadrilatero d'Oro

Castello Sforzesco

Cova

Santa Maria delle Grazie

Galleria Vittorio Emanuele II

Pinacoteca Ambrosiana

Princi

Duomo

METRO M2

Sant' Ambrogio

Piazza Duomo

0 metres 800
0 yards 800

Porta Genova station

El Brellin

Premiata Pizzeria

Navigli

Lake Maggiore is easily reached from Milan, and offers many lovely sights.

Around Milan

Lake Maggiore

Bergamo

Lake Garda

Milan

Mantua

Po

0 km 50
0 miles 50

on the roof. Stroll through the Brera to **Castello Sforzesco** (see pp20–21) and the adjacent **Parco Sempione** (see p92) and spend the evening among the exclusive bars and eateries of nearby Corso Como.

Day ❷
Make an early start at the **Pinacoteca di Brera** (see pp16–19) to enjoy more artistic marvels before leaving the city to spend the rest of the day in **Mantua** (see pp34–5). Explore the churches and piazzas of the historic centre then hire a bicycle or join a boat tour to enjoy the city's lakes.

Day ❸
Today, head for **Bergamo** (see pp32–3). Explore the sights of this lovely old town and take the funicular up to the ruined Castello di San Vigilio. Get back to Milan for sunset over the **Navigli** canals (see pp28–9) and dinner at **Premiata Pizzeria** (see p103).

Day ❹
Say goodbye to Milan and set off for **Lake Maggiore** (see pp106–11), taking the ferry from Stresa to the **Isole Borromee** (see pp30–31). Stop first at Isola Bella for its extravagant gardens and the **Borromeo Palace** (see pp30–31) then cross to Isola Madre for more exotic gardens and end up on pretty Isola dei Pescatori. Return to Stresa for dinner at **Osteria degli Amici** (see p111).

Bergamo combines culture and charm.

Top 10 Milan and the Lakes Highlights

The city of Milan viewed from the
roof of its magnificent Duomo

⏂10 Milan and the Lakes Highlights

Milan is Italy's stylish economic powerhouse, backed by an impressive cultural heritage of galleries, museums and ancient churches. Yet, just a 40-minute train ride away lie azure lakes, lined with fishing villages, villas and laid-back resorts.

1 Leonardo's Last Supper
One of the most impressive works created by the ultimate Renaissance Man. It is sadly in an advanced state of deterioration now *(see pp12–13)*.

2 Milan's Duomo
The world's largest Gothic cathedral took over 400 years to complete. It's a forest of pinnacles, flying buttresses and statues, with fantastic views from its roof *(see pp14–15)*.

3 Pinacoteca di Brera
Northern Italy's greatest gallery displays masterpieces by Mantegna, Giovanni Bellini, Piero della Francesca, Raphael and Caravaggio *(see pp16–19)*.

[Map of central Milan showing numbered locations 1, 4, 6, 7 and street names including Parco Sempione, Via Vincenzo, Foro Buonaparte, Piazza Castello, Largo Cairoli, Via G. Boccaccio, Via Meravigl, C. Magenta, Via G. Carducci, Via Cappuccio, Via Torino, Via Olona, Via Edmondo De Amicis, Piazza Resistenza Partigiana, Viale Papiniano, Corso Genova, Via Molino delle Ari, Porta Genova, Viale Carlo D'Annunzio, Darsena, Porta Ticinese, Viale Gian Galeazzo, Via Valenza, Naviglio Grande, Piazza XXIV Maggio]

| 0 metres | 800 |
| 0 yards | 800 |

4 Castello Sforzesco
This sprawling 15th-century castle is now home to a wide range of collections, which include Michelangelo's final work, the *Rondanini Pietà* *(see pp20–21)*.

5 Pinacoteca Ambrosiana
This cultural study centre, founded in the 17th century, contains works by Leonardo, Botticelli, Raphael and Caravaggio *(see pp24–5)*.

6 Sant'Ambrogio
This is one of the oldest churches in Milan, founded by the city's patron saint Ambrose in 379, with mosaics and carvings dating from the 4th century *(see pp26–7)*.

7 Navigli
Milan's picturesque canal district offers a vibrant evening scene. Boat trips and cycle paths offer an escape route from the busy city *(see pp28–9)*.

8 Isole Borromee, Lake Maggiore
Three verdant islands, one still a fishing village, the other two clad in the sumptuous villas and ornate gardens *(see pp30–31)*.

Around Milan

Lugano · Varenna · Breno · Riva del Garda
Varese · Lecco · Lovere
Arona · Como · Bergamo · Iseo · Salò
Rho · Monza · Brescia · Lago di Garda
Milan · Montichiari
Vercelli · Vigevano · Lodi
0 km   50
0 miles   50   Cremona · Po · Mantua 10

9 Bergamo
The perfect balance of small town charm and sophisticated culture, ancient streets and chic boutiques *(see pp32–3)*.

10 Mantua
Ringed on three sides by shallow lakes, the ancient seat of the Gonzaga dukes boasts Renaissance palaces by the likes of Mantegna and Romano *(see pp34–5)*.

TOP 10 ★ Leonardo's Last Supper

The Last Supper, Leonardo da Vinci's 1495–7 masterpiece, is a touchstone of Renaissance painting. Since the day it was finished, art students have journeyed to Milan to view the work, which takes up a refectory wall in a Dominican convent next to the church of Santa Maria delle Grazie. When writer Aldous Huxley called it "the saddest work of art in the world", he was referring not to the impact of the scene but to the fresco's fragile state of deterioration.

Leonardo da Vinci's remarkable depiction of the Last Supper

1 Light
Note the brilliant effects of the interaction between the three sources of light – from the refectory itself, from windows painted in the background, and from the windows on the refectory's left wall.

2 Coats of Arms Above Painting
The lunettes, above the fresco, were also painted by Leonardo. It seems he was as happy painting perfect leaves around the Sforza coats of arms as he was composing the vast scene below.

3 Example of Ageing
Montorfano's *Crucifixion* was painted in true *buon fresco*, but the now barely visible kneeling figures to the sides were added later on dry plaster – the same method Leonardo used.

NEED TO KNOW

MAP J3 ■ Visitor info: Piazza S Maria delle Grazie 2/Corso Magenta, Milan ■ 02-9280-0360 ■ www.vivaticket.it (tickets)

Open 8:15am–6:45pm Tue–Sun

Adm €10; reduction EU citizens 18–25 €2; free for under 18s; €2 booking fee; guided tours €3.50

■ Book well in advance, especially if visiting during the holidays.

■ Guided tours in English are at 9:30am and 3:30pm.

■ The informative audio guide will help explain why such a deteriorated fresco is so important.

■ On Via Magenta at Via Carducci 13, Bar Magenta *(see p66)* is a pleasing blend of Art Deco café and Guinness pub.

5 Judas
Previously Judas **(left)** was often painted across the table from everyone else. However, Leonardo's approach is more subtle, and instead he places the traitor right in the midst of the other disciples, snugly between Andrew and Peter.

6 Groupings
Leonardo studied the effects of sound and physical waves. The groups of figures reflect the triangular Trinity concept (with Jesus at the centre) as well as the effect of a metaphysical shock wave, emanating out from Jesus and reflecting back from the walls as he reveals there is a traitor in their midst.

7 Reflections
The colours of the disciples' robes are reflected in the glasses and pewter plates on the table, heightening the illusion of reality.

A VANISHING FRESCO

Rather than paint in *buon fresco* (applying pigment to wet plaster so the colours bind with the base), Leonardo used oil paint on semi-dry plaster, causing it to deteriorate while still in progress. Napoleon's troops used the fresco for target practice, and World War II bombs blew off the roof. Restoration has removed centuries of over-painting and filled gaps with a pale wash.

4 Crucifixion on Opposite Wall
Most people spend so much time gazing at *The Last Supper* that they don't notice the 1495 fresco **(below)** by Donato Montorfano on the opposite wall, rich in colour and detail.

8 The Table
The table probably has the same sort of cloth and settings that the monks would have used, reinforcing the illusion that they were sharing their meals with Jesus and the Apostles.

9 "Halo" of Jesus
The medieval taste for halos is satisfied without sacrificing Renaissance realism: Christ **(above)** is set in front of a window, giving him the requisite nimbus without looking as if he's wearing a plate for a hat.

10 Perspective
The walls of the room in the painting appear to be continuations of the walls of the room you are in. The lines zoom in on Christ at the centre, which draws your eye towards his, helping to heighten the drama.

Milan's Duomo

From its inception in 1386 to the finishing touches in 1813, Milan's cathedral took almost 430 years to be completed, during which the builders stuck to the Gothic style. It is the fifth-largest church in the world, with over 3,500 exterior statues, and is held up inside by 52 huge columns.

Façade 1
It wasn't until 1805–13 that the Neo-Gothic frontage **(right)**, with its bronze doors and reliefs, was finally built. The impressive central bronze door is by the Milanese sculptor Ludovico Pogliaghi.

3 Stained-Glass Windows
Dozens of stained-glass windows **(left)** create splashes of coloured light in the otherwise gloomy interior. The oldest, on the right aisle, date from 1470; the newest from 1988.

2 Ascent to Roof
Climb or take the lift to the roof *(see p51)* to see the cathedral's remarkable Gothic crown of spires, gargoyles and statues – and for the views.

Floorplan of Duomo

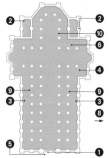

NEED TO KNOW

MAP M4 ■ Piazza del Duomo ■ 02-7202-2656 ■ www.duomomilano.it

Cathedral: open 8am–7pm daily (last adm 6pm); adm €3; 6–12-year-olds €2

Roof: open 9am–7pm (to 10pm May–mid-Sep) daily (last adm one hour before); adm €14 by elevator, €10 by stairs (reduction)

Museo del Duomo: open 10am–6pm Thu–Tue (last adm 5pm) €3 (reduction)

■ On clear days, the view from the roof stretches as far as the Alps.

■ You cannot enter if your shoulders are bare or your shorts or skirt rise above mid-thigh; bring a light shawl or two.

■ You're spoiled for café choices, but nothing beats a Campari at the historic Zucca *(see p88)*.

④ Funerary Monument to Gian Giacomo Medici

Leone Leoni created the 1560–63 tomb of a local mercenary general, including a life-sized bronze of him dressed in centurion armour.

⑧ Museo del Duomo

Here you will find stained-glass windows and tapestries removed from the Duomo for safety as well as *The Infant Christ among the Doctors* by Tintoretto; and wooden models of the Duomo.

⑩ Ambulatory and Crypt

The ambulatory is now open only to worshippers, but you can see a lovely example of a 14th-century Lombard sacristy door. Stairs nearby lead down into the crypt, where the body of St Charles Borromeo rests in a crystal coffin, and to the treasury, which is filled with elegant reliquaries and liturgical devices.

⑤ Battistero Paleocristiano

A stairway near the entrance leads down to excavations, which have uncovered traces of Roman baths dating from the 1st century BC, a baptistry from AD 287 and the remains of a 4th-century basilica.

⑨ Naves

The lofty interior **(above)** is a thicket of 52 pilasters ringed with statues of saints tucked into niches. The Gothic "tracery" on the vaulting of the four outer naves is actually ingenious *trompe l'oeil* paintings dating from the 16th century.

⑥ St Bartholomew Flayed

Marco d'Agrate's grisly carving of 1562 shows the unfortunate saint **(right)** with muscles and veins exposed and his flayed skin thrown jauntily over one shoulder.

⑦ La Madonnina

At the top of the Duomo's central spire, 108 m (354 ft) above ground level, the gilded copper "Little Madonna" has surveyed Milan's best panorama since 1774. Until 1995 she remained as the highest point in the city.

LA FABBRICA DEL DUOMO

There is no better example of Milanese tenacity than the fact that their cathedral is a totally unspoiled example of the pure Gothic style, in spite of it taking a full 427 years to build. The generations of builders somehow ignored the siren calls of every new style that came along, from the Renaissance, then Baroque, to Neo-Classical. It is for this reason that the phrase *la fabbrica del Duomo* – "the building of the Duomo", in Milanese dialect – is still used to this day to refer to any job or enterprise that seems to take forever to complete.

TOP 10 ⭐ Pinacoteca di Brera

Milan's Brera is unique among Italy's major art galleries in that it isn't founded on the riches of the church or a noble family, but the policies of Napoleon, who suppressed churches across the region and took their treasures off to galleries and academies. Over the next two centuries, the collections grew to take in some of the best Renaissance-era paintings from Northern Italy, representatives of the Venetian school and several giants of central Italy, including Raphael and Piero della Francesca.

① Umberto Boccioni's Riot in the Galleria

In this painting **(below)** of 1911, the Milanese are depicted dashing for the doors of Zucca *(see p66)*. A companion work of 1910, *The City Rises*, is also here.

② Tintoretto's Finding the Body of St Mark

Tintoretto uses his mastery of drama and light in this work of the 1560s to highlight the finding of the body of St Mark by Venetian merchants at the time of the Crusades.

③ Bellini's Virgin and Child

The Brera has two very different versions of Bellini's *Virgin and Child* **(above)**. One is almost a Flemish-style portrait, painted when Bellini was 40. The other is a luminous scene of colour and light, from 40 years later.

NEED TO KNOW

MAP M2 ■ Via Brera 28, Milan ■ 02-722-631; booking line 02-9280-0361 ■ www.pinacotecabrera.org

Open 8:30am–7:15pm Tue–Sun (last adm 6:30pm)

Adm €12; 18–25-year-olds €2; free for EU citizens under 18 and over 65

■ Make sense of the works on display with the excellent audio guides.

■ Affordable guided tours are available on weekdays. Book 2–3 days ahead.

■ Try Bar Radetzky *(see p96)* in the Brera district for a post-gallery apéritif.

Floorplan of Pinacoteca di Brera

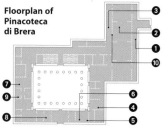

- ③
- ②
- ①
- ⑩
- ⑦
- ⑨
- ⑥
- ④
- ⑧
- ⑤

④ Gentile Fabriano's Valle Romita Polyptych

The Brera worked hard to reconstitute this altarpiece of 1410. The five main panels came with Napoleon; the other four were tracked down later.

8 Caravaggio's Supper at Emmaus

This 1605 work was Caravaggio's second painting of the Supper. The deep-black shadows and bright highlights create mood and tension.

9 Canaletto's Bacino di San Marco

The undisputed master of 18th-century Venetian cityscapes, Canaletto painted at least seven versions of this scene of St Mark's bell tower and the Doge's Palace.

10 Mantegna's Dead Christ

Mantegna was one of the Renaissance's greatest perspective virtuosos – this is his remarkable foreshortened master-piece **(below)**, which was painted in about 1500.

5 Piero della Francesca's Montefeltro Altarpiece

This 1472 scene **(above)** shows Piero's patron, the Duke of Montefeltro, kneeling in front of the Virgin and Child. Just a few months earlier, the duke's beloved wife had given birth to a male heir, but the child had trag-ically died within weeks.

6 Raphael's Marriage of the Virgin

In this early painting from 1504, depicting the Virgin Mary's terrestrial marriage to Joseph, Raphael took the idea and basic layout from his Umbrian master Perugino. He tweaked it with a perfected single-point perspective based on mathematical rules.

7 Francesco Hayez's The Kiss

This much-loved 1859 scene **(left)** – painted when Hayez was 68 – was intended by the artists as an allegory of the passionate struggle for independence at the time of the Risorgimento.

THE PALACE OF BRERA

Built from 1591 to 1658 as a Jesuit college, the late-Baroque Palazzo di Brera was not finished until 1774. The palace's vast courtyard centres around a bronze statue of Napoleon presented in the guise of Mars. The statue, commissioned in 1807, was installed 52 years later in 1859.

The Brera Collections

Coronation of the Virgin Polyptych by Andrea di Bartolo e Giorgio di Andrea

① 13th-Century Paintings (Rooms II–IV)

Italian art simply wouldn't be the same without the naturalism, bright colours and emotive qualities that Giotto brought to the world of painting, and his influence is clear in works such as *Three Scenes from the Life of St Columba* by Giovanni Baronzio of Rimini. Other works here trace the Gothic style from Central Italy (Ambrogio Lorenzetti and Andrea di Bartolo) to Venice (Lorenzo Veneziano and Jacopo Bellini). The best works are Ambrogio Lorenzetti's *Virgin and Child* and Gentile da Fabriano's *Crucifixion*.

Floorplan of the Brera Collections

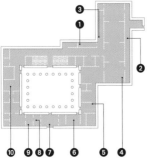

② Jesi Collection of 20th Century Art (Room X)

When Maria Jesi donated her impressive art hoard in 1976, the Brera became the first major museum in Italy to acquire a significant 20th-century collection. Boccioni's *Riot in the Galleria* is highlighted on p16; other master-works are by Morandi, Severini, Modigliani, Picasso and Braque.

Modigliani's Portrait of Moisè Kisling

③ Venetian Renaissance (Rooms VI; IX; XIV; XIX)

It is the art of Venice that steals the show at the Brera: Mantegna's *Dead Christ (see p17)* and numerous superlative works by his brother-in-law Giovanni Bellini. It all culminates in the brushy, stormy, wondrously lit and intriguingly coloured scenes of Venice's High Renaissance trio: Tintoretto, Titian and Paolo Veronese.

④ Lombard Renaissance (Rooms XII; XV)

The stars of the Lombard section are the 16th-century Campi clan from Cremona, painters inspired by Raphael and, above all Leonardo da Vinci. Tiny Room XIX is devoted to the heirs of the Leonardo revolution: Il Bergognone and Bernardino Luini.

Madonna della Candeletta by Carlo Crivelli

5 Marchese Renaissance (Rooms XXI–XIII; XXII)

Flemish-inspired artists and 15th-century painters from the central Marches province are featured in these rooms. The latter took local art from the post-Giotto Gothicism into a courtly Early Renaissance style, exemplified by Carlo Crivelli in his painting *Madonna della Candeletta*, which is rich with decorative elements.

6 Tuscan Renaissance (Rooms XXIV–XXVII)

The few paintings here are stunners: Piero's *Montefeltro Altarpiece* and Raphael's *Marriage of the Virgin (see p17)*, alongside works by Bramante, Signorelli and Bronzino.

The Chanter by Bramante

7 17th-Century Bolognese Renaissance (Room XXVIII)

As Florence and Rome got swept away with Mannerist fantasies and experiments, Bolognese artists held the line on Classical Renaissance ideals. In this room we see Ludovico Caracci, Il Guercino and Guido Reni engaged in an ever more crystalline and reductive naturalistic style.

Abraham casting out Hagar and Ishmael by Guercino

8 Caravaggio and his Followers (Room XXIX)

Caravaggio's use of harsh contrast in paintings such as the *Supper at Emmaus (see p17)* influenced a generation of painters. The works of some of the best of them – Mattia Preti, Jusepe de Ribera and Orazio Gentilleschi – are on display here too.

9 Baroque and Rococo (Rooms XXX–XXXVI)

In the late 16th century, Italy moved from Renaissance naturalism to the more ornate style of the Baroque, with Daniele Crespi and Pietro da Cortona to the fore. The Baroque fed off its own overblown conventions until it became Rococo, a lavish style that was heralded by Tiepolo and Giuseppe Maria Crespi.

10 19th-Century Painting (Rooms XXXVII; XXXVIII)

There's not so much of interest in these final rooms, save Francesco Hayez's monumental scenes and the pseudo-Impressionist Macchiaioli school (Fattori, Segantini and Lega).

🔟 ⭐ Castello Sforzesco

This massive, rectangular bastion in Milan is actually a complex of fortresses, castles and towers begun in 1451 for Francesco Sforza. Largely restored in 1893–1904, and again after massive World War II damage, its many collections include art and sculpture from the early Middle Ages to the 18th century, decorative arts, musical instruments, Oriental art and archaeology.

3 Bellini's Madonna and Child

This is an early Bellini **(left)**, painted in 1468–70, with touching detail. Mary wears a pearl-trimmed pink shawl, and Jesus gazes at a lemon.

4 Bellini's Poet Laureate

The attribution of this portrait, painted in 1475, has wavered between Bellini and Antonella da Messina.

1 Michelangelo's Rondanini Pietà

Michelangelo started his career with a *Pietà* carved at the age of 25 (now in St Peter's, Rome). He was famous for not finishing his statues, but in this case it was not his fault. At the age of 89 he had a stroke while working on this piece.

5 Mantegna's Madonna in Glory

Bellini's brother-in-law painted this magnificent altarpiece for a Verona church in 1497, making it one of his final works. Age and experience combine to yield a solid, naturalistic approach.

2 Parco Sempione

This 1893 public park **(below)** northwest of the castle is central Milan's largest green space. Many of its structures are fine early Art Nouveau *(see p92)*.

Floorplan of Castello Sforzesco

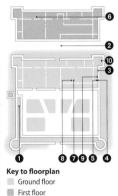

Key to floorplan
- Ground floor
- First floor

8 Cappella Ducale

The Ducal Chapel has frescoes **(left)** painted in 1472 by Stefano de Fedeli and Bonifacio Bembo for Galeazzo Maria Sforza, including a *Resurrection* and an *Annunciation*.

TOMB OF GASTON DE FOIX

In 1510, King Francis I ordered a tomb for the hero. Bambaia sculpted an effigy of the warrior, lying in state. When the French pulled out of Milanese affairs in 1522, work on it stopped and pieces were sold off, winding up here, in the Ambrosiana (*see p24*), in Turin and in London.

10 Sala delle Asse

The "Plank Hall" was decorated in 1498 by Leonardo da Vinci with a trompe l'oeil of intricate vines on the vaulted ceiling. The only bit we can be sure is original is a monochrome sketch of a twisting root, on the wall between two windows.

NEED TO KNOW

MAP K2

Castello Sforzesco: Piazza Castello, Milan; 02-8846-3700; open 7am–7:30pm daily (to 6pm in winter); www.milanocastello.it

Musei Civici: 02-8846-3703; open 9am–5:30pm Tue–Sun; adm €5; 18–25-year-olds and over 65 €3 (free from 2pm 1st and 2nd Tue of the month, from 4:30pm Wed–Sun and for under-18s)

■ Ask about special tours that explore many non-museum sections of the castle and are usually closed to the public.

■ Snack vans on-site are overpriced. Head down Via Dante to the café at No. 15, where you can enjoy panini and gelato.

6 Trivulzio Tapestries

The *Tapestries of the Twelve Months* **(above)** were designed by Bramantino in 1503 and named for the man who commissioned them, Gian Giacomo Trivulzio.

9 Bronzino's Lorenzo Lenzi

A Mannerist painter at the Medici court in Florence, Bronzino's delicate portrait shows a sensitivity to his subject's youthful restlessness.

7 Funerary Monument for Gaston de Foix

The ruler of the French Milan Duchy, Gaston de Foix was also the posthumous hero of the 1512 Battle of Ravenna. His tomb **(above)** was broken up and sold.

TOP 10 ★ Pinacoteca Ambrosiana

Local Cardinal Federico Borromeo founded this library (of about 36,000 manuscripts and over 750,000 prints) and painting gallery in Milan in 1603 after a formative time spent in Rome's artistic circles. It was, and remains, a place in which to study theological issues via academic tomes and works of art, a truly Renaissance mix of religion, intellectualism and aesthetics. There are paintings by such greats as Tiepolo, Francesco Hayez and Jan Brueghel.

4 Bassano's Rest on the Flight into Egypt

The Venetian master Jacopo Bassano was turning to a densely coloured palette, rich in contrasting tones, when he produced this work (**left**) in 1547.

5 Bambaia's Detail from the Tomb of Gaston de Foix

The Milanese sculptor carved this series of small marble panels (**below**) with figures surrounded by military accoutrements and mythological creatures, all in extraordinary high relief. Most of the monument is in the Castello Sforzesco (see pp20–21).

1 Titian's Adoration of the Magi

This courtly tumble of the three kings kissing the toes of baby Jesus in his manger was part of Federico Borromeo's original collection, a complex work from 1560 that the cardinal described as "a school for painters".

2 Leonardo's Portrait of a Musician

This portrait, which is quasi-Flemish in pose and detail, yet glowing with a sense of human psychology that is typical of Leonardo has been said to depict various individuals. However, it most likely represents a musician of the Sforza court. Almost certainly, it is a work of Leonardo, but has probably been retouched over the years.

3 Botticelli's Madonna del Padiglione

Angels are depicted pulling back a rich canopy to reveal a scene of Mary and Jesus in a pastoral setting. This work dates from the 1490s, after Botticelli's religious crisis turned him from the mythological scenes of his youth.

6 Raphael's Cartoon for School of Athens

This is the preparatory drawing for Raphael's famous fresco of Greek philosophers, which features the faces of Renaissance artists.

NEED TO KNOW

MAP L4 ▪ Piazza Pio XI 2, Milan ▪ 02-806-921 ▪ www.ambrosiana.it

Open 10am–6pm Tue–Sun (last adm 5:30pm)

Adm €15, €10 (reduction)

▪ Just round the corner, on Via Spadari, you will find Gastronomia Peck (see p87), one of Italy's best food emporia and oversized *tavole calde* (snack bars/cafés).

Previous pages Visitors in front of the ornate façade of Milan's Duomo

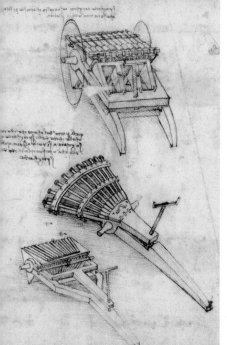

Floorplan of Pinacoteca Ambrosiana

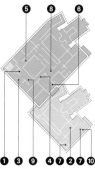

Key to floorplan
▢ Ground floor
▢ First floor

⑦ Leonardo's Codex Atlantico

Reproductions of pages from these oversized tomes **(above)** are on display. They are filled with Leonardo da Vinci's sketches.

⑧ Bril's Landscape with St Paul

This is quite the most dramatic of the over half-dozen Bril works on display, showcasing how Bril managed to work with the early 17th-century's most popular sacred scenes but set them in his intricately executed landscape form.

⑨ Luini's Holy Family

If this looks familiar, it is because, especially early on, Luini was almost slavishly devoted to the manner of his master Leonardo da Vinci, and this painting is based on a famous drawing by him.

⑩ Caravaggio's Basket of Fruit

This still life **(below)** shows how Caravaggio was, even at the age of 25, perfecting the hyper-realism he would soon apply to large canvases and more complex scenes.

TOP 10 ⭐ Sant'Ambrogio

One of Milan's oldest basilicas, Sant'Ambrogio was founded by St Ambrose in 379. It served as a model for most of the city's early medieval churches. It was enlarged in the 9th century, and what we see today dates largely from 1080 (albeit with later reconstructions). It instantly became Milan's most beloved house of worship when the wildly popular – and future patron saint – Ambrose was buried here in 397.

1 Golden Altar

The master goldsmith Volvinio crafted the magnificent "golden altar" (left) in 835. The Life of Christ is in gold leaf on the front, and the Life of St Ambrose in gilded silver is on the back.

2 Façade

The austere but balanced façade (right) consists of five arches fitted under the peaked roofline. It is flanked by two mismatched towers: the Monks' Tower on the right, dating from the 9th century, and the Canons' Tower on the left from 1144.

NEED TO KNOW

MAP K4

Sant'Ambrogio: Piazza Sant'Ambrogio 15; 02-8645-0895; open 7:30am–12:30pm & 2:30–7pm Mon–Sat, 7:30am–1pm & 3–8pm Sun

Sacello di San Vittore, Ciel d'Oro: open 9:30–11:45am & 2:30–6pm daily; adm €2

Museo della Basilica: open 10am–noon, 2:30–5:30pm daily, (no access during Mass); adm €2

■ Treasury objects are on display in the Museo Diocesano (see p100).

■ Eat at the café-pub Bar Magenta (see p66).

■ Avoid going to basilica during mass. Visit between 10am–noon & 2:30–6pm Mon–Sat, Sun 3–5pm.

3 Sarcophagus of Stilicho

This late Roman-era sarcophagus preceded the pulpit, which was built around it. The tomb is aligned with the original walls, while the pulpit aligns itself with the nave.

4 Bergognone's Redeemer

This striking and limpid late 15th-century Renaissance scene of the Risen Christ (right) was originally positioned on the wall to the right of the altar (where its painted trompe l'oeil architecture was far more suited). It was later moved to the first chapel on the left.

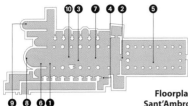

Floorplan of Sant'Ambrogio

5 Atrium

The elongated atrium **(below)** between the entrance and the church, was built from 1088 to 1099 using columns with 6th-century capitals of fantastical scenes.

9 Sacello di San Vittore in Ciel d'Oro

Sant'Ambrogio was built next to a Paleochristian cemetery and a chapel decorated in the 5th century with a dome of gold mosaics. The basilica eventually grew to include the chapel.

10 Pulpit

This composite of 11th- and early 12th-century Romanesque relief panels was saved after the church ceiling collapsed in 1196 and reconstructed into this magnificent pulpit.

6 Ciborium

This altar canopy sits at the centre of the presbytery. Its four ancient Roman columns support a canopy of four 10th-century Lombard stucco reliefs.

7 Serpent Column

Just on the inside of the third pier on the left stands a short column topped by a curlicue of a bronze serpent, a 10th-century Byzantine work (although local legend says it's the serpent cast by Moses).

8 Apse Mosaics

The vast, colourful mosaic **(above)** depicting Christ Pantocrater was pieced together between the 4th and 8th centuries, though bits were touched up or redone between the 17th and 20th centuries.

TOP 10 ⭐ Navigli

Colourful bars and restaurants make Milan's Navigli canal district one of the city's favourites for an evening out. In the past, however, the area was a bustling transport hub with links to lakes Maggiore and Como. Dating from the 12th century, Milan's system of canals is Europe's most ancient – even Leonardo da Vinci contributed by coming up with an ingenious system of locks to solve the problem of water-level changes. Today, tranquil canalside paths lead from Navigli out of town through the countryside and to nearby villages.

① Cycle Paths

Canalside paths **(below)** are perfect for a relaxed cycle ride. Hire a bike and explore the Navigli district or keep going along the canal to leave the city behind and discover nearby villages such as pretty Gaggiano.

③ Boat Trips

A 55-minute trip takes in most of the main sights of the Naviglio Grande and the docks. Other itineraries include NavigarMangiando, which includes dinner at an out-of-town canalside trattoria.

④ Vicolo dei Lavandai

Canal water fills the picturesque roofed washerwomen's area, still fitted with stone washboards, at this charming corner of Naviglio Grande. The adjacent building, now the El Brellin restaurant *(see p103)*, once sold brushes and soap.

② Santa Maria delle Grazie al Naviglio

This imposing Neo-Gothic church **(below)** offers an oasis of peace at the heart of the lively bars and restaurants of the Naviglio Grande. It was built at the start of the 20th century over a previous one.

⑤ Arts and Crafts

As you walk along the canals you'll come across a stimulating selection of Bohemian-chic boutiques, design studios and arts and crafts workshops, many based in picturesque interior courtyards.

⑥ Naviglio Martesana

Only two of Milan's canals (Naviglio Grande and Pavese) meet here. Naviglio Martesana, with a lovely canalside path, starts just northeast of the centre, ending at Trezzo sull'Adda *(see pp58–9)*, a pretty town on the banks of the Adda.

⑧ San Cristoforo sul Naviglio

Two churches, built side-by-side and dating from the 12th and 15th centuries, have been annexed to make up this attractive complex situated by the bridge of the same name. The walls feature several frescoes **(left)**, both internally and externally.

NAVIGLIO GRANDE

Naviglio Grande is the oldest of Milan's canals. Work began in 1177 and was completed 100 years later. It links the historic centre to the Ticino River and on to Lake Maggiore as well as Switzerland. The curious iron footbridge between Paoli and Via Casale dates from 1905.

Canalside scene in the lovely Navigli district

⑦ Aperitivo Time

The bars of Navigli have their own character but they all lay out a rich feast of bar snacks every evening at *aperitivo* time. Buy a drink and dip into the buffet.

⑨ Darsena

Restoration work at Milan's former docks has uncovered previously hidden canals. There are street food stalls in summer and a Christmas market in winter.

NEED TO KNOW

MAP J6–K6

Santa Maria delle Grazie al Naviglio: Alzaia Naviglio Grande 34

Boat Trips: www.navigli lombardi.it

San Cristoforo sul Naviglio: Via San Cristoforo 3

Antiques Market: www. navigliogrande.mi.it

■ The El Brellin restaurant *(see p103)* also has a bar; its aperitivo time starts at 6pm each evening and there's often live jazz performance in summer.

■ Happy hour in Milan does not mean you'll get discounted drinks – on the contrary, prices are often higher than usual, but the buffet of bar snacks is included.

⑩ Antiques Market

A treasure trove of items **(above)** from yesteryear fills the multitude of stalls which set up along the Naviglio Grande canal on the last Sunday of each month. Other regular open-air events include a canalside art show that takes place in mid-May.

TOP 10 ⭐ Isole Borromee, Lake Maggiore

This cluster of islands near Stresa has been shaped by the Borromeo family. In the 16th and 17th centuries they turned Bella and Madre into vast garden-and-palace complexes; Isola Bella is the most striking, while Isola Madre, the largest, has landscaped botanical gardens that are a joy to explore. The third island, Isola dei Pescatori, is an authentic fishing village, while the tiny Scoglio della Malghera has little more than a beach.

④ Kashmir Cypress, Isola Madre

Europe's largest cypress spreads its 200-year-old, weeping Oriental strands of needles over a Villa Borromeo courtyard.

① Tapestries in the Palace, Isola Bella

This detail-rich series **(above)** of 16th-century Flemish works is based on that popular theme for medieval tapestries: the unicorn (which is also a Borromeo heraldic totem).

⑤ Grottoes, Isola Bella

Artificial caves **(below)** were all the rage in the 18th century. They were decorated with intricate pebble-work in black-and-white patterns.

② Borromeo Tombs, Isola Bella

The "Private Chapel" was built in 1842–4 as a mausoleum for a pair of late Gothic/early Renaissance family tombs as well as the 1522 Monument to the Birago Brothers, carved by Renaissance master Bambaia.

③ Borromeo Palace, Isola Bella

The vast palace **(below)** and its grounds dominate the island. Largely 17th century, it wasn't finished until 1959. The sumptuous rooms have stucco ceilings and are filled with Murano chandeliers and fine art.

6 Sala di Musica in the Palace, Isola Bella

In April 1935, Mussolini met in this room with Laval of France and Ramsay MacDonald of Britain in an attempt to stave off World War II.

7 Isola dei Pescatori

The Borromei largely left this island alone when they were converting its neighbours, leaving a working fishing village. Wander the cobbled lanes, visit the 11th-century church and stop at one of the many eateries.

8 Gardens, Isola Bella

This pyramid of terraces (above) is topped by a unicorn, the edges lined by ornate, statue-laden balustrades. White peacocks strut over the clipped lawns.

9 Botanical Gardens, Isola Madre

The lush and extensive gardens around the Villa Borromeo are filled with exotic flora. Since the 19th century they have been famed for the flowering of many azaleas, rhododendrons and camellias.

10 Villa Borromeo, Isola Madre

This summer villa was built largely between 1518 and 1585. Today it is a museum with mannequins in Borromeo livery and paraphernalia from puppet theatres.

NEED TO KNOW

MAP A2 ■ Access is from the ferry docks at Stresa ■ www. isoleborromee.it

Isola Bella: 0323-30-556; open late Mar–Oct: 9am–5:30pm daily; adm €17, under-16s €9

Isola Madre: 0323-31-261; open late Mar–Oct: 9am–5:30pm daily (exact dates vary annually; check website); adm €13.50, under-16s €7

■ Buy discounted island admission tickets with your ferry ticket at the Stresa docks (see p109).

■ Isola Bella's gardens remain open all day and access is via the palazzo.

■ There are many cafés on Isola Bella's quay. Café Lago serves good panini, snacks, coffee, beer and wine.

4 9 10 2 km (1.2 miles)

7

Isola dei Pescatori

Scoglio della Malghera

Map of Isole Borromee, Lake Maggiore

1 3 6
5
2
8

Isola Bella

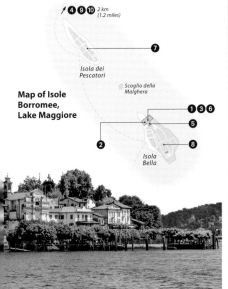

🔟 ⭐ Bergamo

One of Northern Italy's surprising gems, Bergamo mixes medieval charm with cultural sophistication. Bergamo has been a split-level town since Roman times, when a *civitas* (today's medieval Upper Town) perched on top of the hill and a *suburbia* (the now modernized Lower Town) spread into the plain.

① Galleria dell' Accademia Carrara

This gallery **(above)**, set in a Neo-Classical building, has over 1,800 works of art including Mantegna's *Madonna and Child* and Raphael's *Saint Sebastian*.

② Castello di San Vigilio

Constructed by the town's Venetian lords in the 16th and 17th centuries, the castle of San Vigilio has been reduced to romantic ruins. The garden boasts fine views.

③ Piazza Vecchia

In the Upper Town (Città Alta), one of Northern Italy's most theatrical squares **(right)** is surrounded by retro-medieval stone buildings, Renaissance palaces, a 12th-century tower and several historic cafés.

④ Galleria d'Arte Moderna e Contemporanea

Bergamo's modern art gallery features changing exhibitions alongside a permanent collection with works by Italy's key 20th-century painters.

⑤ Via Colleoni

The main drag of Bergamo's Upper Town is lined with shops and bars, modest medieval palaces and churches and tiny squares. It's closed to most traffic, and busy every evening.

NEED TO KNOW

MAP D3

Tourist Information: IAT Lower Town, Piazzale Papa Giovanni XXIII, 57, 035-210-204; IAT Upper Town, Viale Gombito 13, 035-242-226; www.visitbergamo.net

Castello di San Vigilio: open 7am–9pm daily (Nov–Mar: 8am–5pm)

Galleria d'Arte Moderna e Contemporanea: open 10am–6pm Wed–Mon; adm €6

Museo del 500 Veneto: open 9:30am–1pm, 2:30–6pm Tue–Sun (Jun–Sep: all day Sat, Sun & hols; last adm 5pm); adm €5, €3 (reduction), free for under-18s

Museo Donizettiano: open 10am–1pm Tue–Sun

(3–6pm Sat & Sun); adm €5, €3 (reduction), free for under-18s

Galleria dell'Accademia Carrara: open 9:30am–5:30pm Wed–Mon; adm €10

Basilica di Santa Maria Maggiore: open 9am–6pm Mon–Sun (closed 12:30pm–2:30pm Mon–Wed)

■ A funicular connects the upper and lower towns.

Map of Bergamo

⑨ Museo Donizettiano

The museum's collection here contains the original sheet music, piano **(below)** and other memorabilia of Bergamo's famous composer Gaetano Donizetti (1797–1848). He died of syphilis in the very bed that's on display here.

⑥ Museo del 500 Veneto

This museum in the Palazzo Podesta explores life in the 16th century, taking the visitor on a virtual journey from Venice to Bergamo.

⑦ Basilica di Santa Maria Maggiore

Inside the basilica **(left)**, every inch of ceiling is covered with frescoes. The gorgeous, early 16th-century, inlaid wood panels fronting the choir are by Lorenzo Lotto.

⑧ Piazza del Duomo

This square is dominated by elaborate Bergamasco architecture: Santa Maria Maggiore, the Capella Colleoni and a fanciful 1340 baptistry.

⑩ Cappella Colleoni

The anchor of the twinned Piazza Vecchia and Piazza del Duomo is this magnificent Renaissance chapel devoted to Bergamo's warrior-lord Bartolomeo Colleoni. In pink-and-white patterned marble, it is covered with reliefs and Rococo frescoes.

TOP 10 ★ Mantua

Known for its fine palaces and masterpieces by Mantegna and Giulio Romano, this town is surrounded by wide, shallow, swamp-edged lakes on three sides. These man-made lakes make the area humid in summer and rather damp and chilly in winter, creating a slight air of melancholy. The city makes up for this, however, with its cobbled lanes, attractive squares and cultural history – it was the birthplace of the poet Virgil and the setting of Verdi's opera *Rigoletto*.

1 Duomo

The cathedral has an 18th-century façade **(below)**, and its interior, reconstructed from the Gothic original by Giulio Romano, is an imitation of Paleochristian basilicas.

3 Palazzo Ducale

Delights in the Gonzagas' rambling fortress-palace include tapestries by Raphael and Mantegna's *Camera degli Sposi* frescoes (1465–74).

Map of Mantua

2 Casa del Mantegna

Mantua's most famous artist, Andrea Mantegna (1431–1506), custom-built this house and studio in 1465–74. It includes a circular courtyard and a portrait of himself by his fellow-artist and friend, Titian.

4 Piazza Broletto

Just north of the arcaded Piazza delle Erbe is this tiny square, hemmed in by medieval buildings including the 1227 *broletto* (town hall).

5 Basilica di Sant'Andrea

Lord Lodovico Gonzaga commissioned this basilica in 1470 from Leon Battista Alberti. Its façade is a highly original take on Classicism. The tomb of Mantegna is in the first chapel on the left.

6 Teatro Scientifico Bibiena

This jewel-box of a late Baroque theatre **(above)** is named after the architect who designed it, and was inaugurated in 1770 with a concert by Mozart, then a 13-year-old prodigy.

7 Piazza delle Erbe

Piazza delle Erbe **(below)** is a lively urban space, lined by arcades, filled with a food market each morning, and ringed by fascinating ancient buildings.

9 Palazzo d'Arco

This Renaissance *palazzo*, later remodelled in Neo-Classical style, includes the exquisite 1520 Sala dello Zodiaco, frescoed with astrological signs, in an original 15th-century wing.

10 Palazzo Te

Giulio Romano's Mannerist masterpiece is an ingenious interplay of spacious open courts, sweeping wings and discreet gardens. Built in 1525, it was frescoed largely by Romano.

8 Rotonda di San Lorenzo

This rotund church is a relic from an earlier age, built in 1082 and retaining scraps of medieval fresco in its otherwise pleasantly bare brick interior.

Mantua, viewed from across a lake

BOAT TOURS

The Gonzagas widened the Mincio River, setting their city within three defensive lakes. Now the protected homes of waterfowl and of Italy's highest concentration of fish, they're at their best in May and June. Boat tours are available.

NEED TO KNOW

MAP H6

Visitor Information: Piazza Mantegna 6; www.comune.mantova.gov.it

Duomo: open 7am–noon & 3–7pm daily

Casa del Mantegna: open 10am–12:30pm & 3–6pm Tue & Wed

Palazzo Ducale: open 8:15am–7:15pm Tue–Sun; adm €12 (free first Sun of the month)

Basilica di Sant'Andrea: open 8am–noon & 3–7pm daily

Teatro Scientifico Bibiena: open 10am–1pm & 3–6pm Tue–Fri, 10am–6pm Sat, Sun & hols; adm €2

Rotonda di San Lorenzo: open 10am–1pm & 3–6pm Mon–Fri, 10am–7pm Sat & Sun; donation

Palazzo d'Arco: open 9:30am–1pm & 2:30–6pm Tue–Sun; adm €8

Palazzo Te: open 9am–6:30pm Tue–Sun, 1–6pm Mon; adm €12

Boat Tours: Motonavi Andes Negrini, 0376-322-875; Navi Andes, 0376-324-506

The Top 10 of Everything

**Opulent interior of the historic
La Scala opera house in Milan**

Moments in History

1 298–283 BC: Third Samnite War

The Po Valley and land to the north, once called Cisalpine Gaul, was a Celtic province that often found itself up against Rome. Its alliance with the Samnites failed, and Rome then pushed its boundary north of the Po.

2 AD 313: Edict of Milan

During Rome's decline Milan became the capital of the Western Roman Empire. Constantine, holding court here in 313, made Christianity the official religion, setting a new course for European history.

3 572: Fall of Pavia to Lombards

In the 5th century barbarian tribes overran the disintegrating Roman Empire. The Germanic Lombards took Pavia in 572 and settled in the Po Valley, expanding across the north. The Byzantines and Charlemagne eventually trounced them, and the region dissolved into a network of city-states that lasted throughout the Middle Ages.

4 1176: Lombard League Defeats Barbarossa

When Swabian Emperor Frederick I (Barbarossa) levelled Milan and set up his own puppet mayors, the area's city-states banded together as the Lombard League and, with papal support, forced Barbarossa to reinstate their autonomy.

Fresco showing the Battle of Desio

5 1277: Ottone Visconti Defeats the Torriani

Archbishop Visconti overthrew the leading Torriani family at the Battle of Desio in 1277. Under 160 years of Visconti rule, Milan extended its hegemony over much of the north.

6 1450: Francesco Sforza Comes to Power

The last Visconti died in 1447. His illegitimate daughter couldn't inherit the title but was married to Francesco Sforza. Milan hired Sforza to defend it from Venetian power-grabbers, but he cut a deal with Venice, split up the territory and made himself duke.

Lombard League battles Barbarossa

7 1499: The Sforza Cede Milan to France

Francesco's son Galeazzo Maria was murdered in 1476, and power passed to Galeazzo's brother Lodovico. He ushered the Renaissance into Milan, inviting the likes of Leonardo da Vinci to his court, but ceded control to Louis XII in 1499. Milan changed many hands until Austria took over in 1706.

8 1848: Cinque Giornate Revolt

The 19th-century Risorgimento (unification movement) inspired the Milanese to rise up, on 18 March, for five days, with their victory triggering the demise of Austrian rule. By 1859 King Vittorio Emanuele II controlled Lombardy; he sent General Garibaldi off to conquer the rest of the peninsula, forming a new kingdom – Italy.

Cinque Giornate riots in Milan

9 1945: Mussolini Executed

Mussolini's Fascist regime ended after his alliance with Hitler put Italy on the losing side of World War II. As the Allies drew closer, Mussolini fled with his mistress. They were caught by partisans and their bodies were strung up on Milan's Piazzale Loreto.

10 1990: Lombard League Wins Local Elections

Northern resentment of sharing wealth with the poorer south led to the Lombard League, which came to prominence in 1990. Re-dubbed the Northern League, it gained power in 2001 as part of the Forza Italia coalition (now known as Popolo della Libertà) led by Silvio Berlusconi.

TOP 10 HISTORICAL FIGURES

Coronation of Gian Galeazzo Visconti

1 St Ambrose (334–97)
Milan's bishop and patron saint put down the Arian heresy and helped establish Church autonomy.

2 St Augustine (354–430)
St Ambrose's star pupil, Augustine of Hippo was an African-born philosopher.

3 Theodolinda (500s)
Lombard queen who converted her populace to orthodox Christianity.

4 Gian Galeazzo Visconti (1378–1402)
This conqueror of vast territories was the first Milan ruler to be honoured with the title of Duke of the city.

5 Lodovico "Il Moro" Sforza (1452–1508)
"The Moor" ruled Milan's Renaissance court but ceded to France, later siding against the French and being exiled.

6 St Charles Borromeo (1538–84)
The crusading anti-heretic archbishop carried out often brutal Counter-Reformation ideals in the north.

7 Antonio Stradivari (1644–1737)
The greatest luthier (violin maker) who ever lived learned his craft in his birthplace city of Cremona.

8 Alessandro Volta (1745–1827)
This Como physicist invented the battery in 1800 and gave his name to the electrical unit.

9 Benito Mussolini (1883–1945)
Known as "Il Duce" (the Leader), Mussolini founded the Fascist Party in Milan in 1919, and ruled Italy from 1922 until 1943.

10 Giò Ponti (1891–1979)
Ponti was an important architect (Pirelli Tower, Torre Branca), industrial designer and furniture designer.

⚑ Churches

Santa Maria delle Grazie's lofty nave

① Santa Maria delle Grazie, Milan

Each year, hundreds of thousands of people visit Leonardo da Vinci's *Last Supper* fresco *(see pp12–13)* in the adjacent refectory, but only a few bother with the lovely church *(see p92)* itself. Make the effort, though, if you can. Its architecture shows the stylistic changeover, from austere Gothic to Classical Renaissance, that marked the end of the 15th century. The art here is among Milan's best, including the rare *sgraffito* (etched designs) restored in the tribune.

② Basilica di Sant'Andrea, Mantua

Built to house a vial of Christ's blood, this basilica *(see pp34–5)* was created by some of Italy's finest architectural talents. Leon Battista Alberti, the great Renaissance theorist, designed it in 1470; Giulio Romano, a founder of

Mannerism, enlarged it in 1530; and Baroque master Filippo Juvarra added the magnificent dome in 1732. Lovely frescoes cover the barrel-vaulted interior.

③ San Lorenzo Maggiore, Milan

Dating from the 4th century, this church *(see p99)* is still pretty much Roman in its rotund design, although it was rebuilt several times in the Middle Ages. Roman columns line the front, and within are some of the oldest and best-preserved examples of post-Roman art in Northern Italy: 1,600-year-old Paleochristian mosaics.

④ Sant'Ambrogio, Milan

St Ambrose himself, Milan's 4th-century bishop, inaugurated this church *(see pp26–7)*, which was over-hauled in the 11th and 12th centuries. Highlights include a quiet entry atrium, Dark Age mosaics glittering in the apse, and medieval features.

⑤ Duomo, Milan

Milan's most famous landmark is the fifth-largest church *(see pp14–15)* in the world and a testament to Milanese persistence. The cathedral's most startling feature is its extraordinary roof, which boasts 135 spires, innumerable statues and gargoyles, and from which there are views of the Alps on a clear day.

Milan's Duomo

6 Sant'Eustorgio, Milan

The church *(see p100)* behind the 19th-century façade was founded in the 4th century. Behind the altar is the Cappella Portinari. It was designed locally, but so superbly did it embody early Renaissance Florentine ideals that it was for a long time attributed to Brunelleschi or Michelozzo. The chapel's masterpieces are the 1486 frescoes by Vicenzo Foppa.

7 Certosa di Pavia

MAP C5 ■ Via del Monumento 4, Pavia ■ 0382-925-613 ■ Open Apr: 9–11:30am & 2:30–5:30pm Tue–Sun (May–Sep: to 6pm); Oct–Mar: 9–11:30am & 2:30–6pm Tue–Sat (to 5pm Sun)

Gian Galeazzo Visconti had this vast, gorgeous Charterhouse built in 1396 as a lavishly decorated home for a group of Carthusian monks, but more importantly to ensure his ruling clan would have a grand family burial chapel of extravagant artistic merit.

8 Cappella Colleoni, Bergamo

Condottiere Bartolomeo Colleoni was a redoubtable mercenary general who, as a reward for his services, received Bergamo as his own fiefdom. Colleoni demolished a church sacristy to make his own tomb *(see p32)*, hiring the sculptor Giovanni Antonio Amadeo to decorate it with a complex allegory of biblical and Classical reliefs plus a horse-mounted effigy of himself for the sepulchre inside.

9 Santa Maria presso San Satiro, Milan

Though the main entrance is on Via Torino, walk up Via Speronari to see an 11th-century bell tower and the exterior of a tiny Renaissance chapel *(see p81)*. Turn right on Via Falcone for the Renaissance-meets-Baroque rear façade from 1871. Within are 15th-century decorations.

Altar, Santa Maria presso San Satiro

10 Duomo, Como

Como's cathedral *(see p113)* is devoted to Sant'Abbondio, whose life is depicted in the giant gilt altarpiece of 1509–14. Other Renaissance tapestries and paintings grace the interior, including one by Leonardo's protégé Bernardino Luini.

🔟 Notable Milanese Buildings

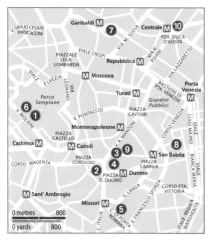

1771), once hosted the city's main market. The relief on the façade depicts the 13th-century mayor Oldrado da Tresseno on horseback. Inside, the Salone dei Giudici has its original frescoes.

3 Palazzo Marino

MAP M3 ▪ Piazza della Scala/Piazza S Fedele ▪ No public access

Milan's city hall has two distinct façades: a 1553 Mannerist one on Piazza S Fedele, and an 1886–92 Neo-Classical one facing La Scala theatre. The former was built by Galeazzo Alessi (who also designed the lovely main courtyard) in 1558; the latter dates to 1860.

1 Triennale (Palazzo dell'Arte)

On the outskirts of Parco Sempione, the Triennale houses Italy's first Design Museum (see p94), with regular architecture and design exhibitions. The DesignCafé is worth a visit.

2 Palazzo della Ragione

The arcade that occupies the ground level of this Lombard Romanesque palace (see p81), built in 1228–33 (the top floor dates from

4 Galleria Vittorio Emanuele II

High-class Italian elegance embraced the Industrial Age in such marvels as this four-storey steel-and-glass-canopied arcade (see p83), built in 1864–8 by Giuseppe Mengoni. He fell to his death from its scaffolding days before the King arrived to open the galleria and lend it his name.

Glorious glass-domed shopping arcades of Galleria Vittorio Emanuele II

The 1950s Torre Velasca skyscraper

5 Torre Velasca

When Nathan Rogers, Lodovico Belgioioso and Enrico Peressutti constructed this brick-red, 106-m (348-ft) tower block *(see p84)* in 1956–8, they showcased their post-war engineering talents by extending the top nine floors beyond the lower ones on struts, much like a medieval tower. Unfortunately, the maintenance costs have proved to be too much.

6 Torre Branca

MAP J2 ▪ Parco Sempione
▪ Open mid-May–mid-Sep: Tue–Sun; mid-Sep–mid-May: Wed, Sat & Sun ▪ Adm

This tapering 108-m (354-ft) steel tower was designed by the internationally acclaimed local architect Gio Ponti, and inaugurated in 1933 as part of the fifth edition of the Triennale design exhibition. There's a lift inside to whisk visitors up to the panoramic viewing floor. Formerly called the Torre Littoria, it now takes its name from the Fratelli Branca distillery, which provided funds for the restoration work.

7 Porta Nuova

MAP N1

This area has undergone massive redevelopment to become Milan's most futuristic district. Piazza Gae Aulenti *(see p94)* is dominated by the Unicredit tower – Italy's tallest, measuring over 230 m (750 ft). The Bosco Verticale (meaning "vertical forest") residential towers and a striking tubular sculpture are among other highlights. There is also a big green area called the Biblioteca degli Alberi (meaning "the library of trees").

8 Villa Necchi Campiglio

This perfectly preserved and restored 1930s villa *(see p94)* has technology that was revolutionary for its time, including a heated pool and an internal phone system, testimony to the elegant Milanese interwar lifestyle. It houses two important art collections: one of early 20th-century works; the other of 18th-century decorative arts.

Telamones on Casa degli Omenoni

9 Casa degli Omenoni

Renaissance sculptor Leone Leoni, whose works grace Milan's Duomo and Madrid's El Escorial, built this palazzo *(see p84)* in 1565, lining the lower level of the façade with eight giant telamones – columns in the form of a male figure.

10 Stazione Centrale

MAP S2 ▪ Piazza Duca D'Aosta

Milan's massive railway station is often considered a remarkable example of Fascist-era architecture, though its design (of 1912) predates this period and owes more to the Liberty style. Finally completed in 1931, the station is encased in gleaming white Aurisina stone and decorated with reliefs, statues and murals too often overlooked.

🔟 Museums

1 Museo Nazionale della Scienza e della Tecnologia – Leonardo da Vinci, Milan

Had Leonardo possessed more technological ambition, we might have had working versions of his helicopters, water screws, Gatling guns, parachutes and siege engines over four centuries ago. As it is, we can make do with the (modern) wooden mock-ups on display at this science and technology museum (see p99), alongside instructive exhibits on physics and antique autos and aeroplanes.

Museo Nazionale della Scienza

2 Museo Teatrale alla Scala, Milan

If it has anything to do with the opera in Milan, it's on display here (see p84), from costumes worn by Nureyev or Callas to historic instruments, or Verdi's death mask to Toscanini's batons. The second floor hosts temporary exhibitions, cultural activities, as well as the theatre archive.

3 Castello Sforzesco, Milan

Here (see pp20–21) you'll find paintings by Bellini and Mantegna, a cycle of 16th-century tapestries, archaeological collections and, its greatest piece, Michelangelo's unfinished *Rondanini Pietà*. Entrance to the castle is free, but there is an entry fee for the Musei Civici within.

4 Galleria d'Arte Moderna – Villa Belgiojoso Bonaparte, Milan

This fine collection of art, housed in the handsome Villa Belgiojoso Bonaparte (see p92), includes Neo-Classicism and Romanticism works from the beginning of the 20th century plus the Vismara and Grassi collections. Italian 20th-century works can be seen in the Museo del Novecento, which is housed in the Palazzo Reale (see p81).

5 Pinacoteca Ambrosiana, Milan

This formidable mix of Old Masters was started by Cardinal Federico Borromeo as an adjunct to the Ambrosiana Library. Famously, the library (see pp24–5) is home to the *Codex Atlantico*, which contains the lion's share of Leonardo's drawings and sketches – photocopied pages from it are displayed in the Pinacoteca. Elsewhere, you'll find paintings by the likes of Botticelli, Titian and Caravaggio, as well as Raphael's giant preparatory sketch for the *School of Athens*.

Leonardo, Pinacoteca Ambrosiana

Mantegna, Lotto, Caravaggio, Giovanni Bellini, Piero della Francesca, Tintoretto, El Greco Veronese, Correggio, Carpaccio, Tiepolo, and Rembrandt.

9 Galleria dell'Accademia Carrara, Bergamo

Count Giacomo Carrara, a collector of and expert on literature and art, left his collection to his native Bergamo on his death in 1796. The gallery *(see p32)* houses about 1,800 paintings, including works by Botticelli, Mantegna, Bellini and Raffaello. There is also a significant collection of prints and sketches, sculpture and china.

Above all, though, come to admire the emotion-filled Renaissance paintings of a Venetian painter, Lorenzo Lotto, who settled in Bergamo in 1513.

10 Museo di Santa Giulia, Brescia

Although you will find Romanesque carvings and detached frescoes galore in the cloisters, chapels and chambers of this medieval monastery, *(see p53)* the real focus here is on Brescia's great era as a Roman colony, and the archaeological works on display, including a magnificent bronze Winged Victory, are astoundingly beautiful and well preserved.

Interior of the Museo Poldi Pezzoli

6 Museo Poldi Pezzoli, Milan

Poldi Pezzoli's mansion *(see p83)* is preserved as a monument to his collections, from Persian tapestries, ancient arms and armour to historic jewellery and, above all, art. In one room alone, there are works by Piero della Francesca, Giovanni Bellini, Mantegna and Botticelli.

7 Museo del Violino, Cremona

MAP E6 ▪ Piazza Marconi 5 ▪ Open 10am–6pm Tue–Sun ▪ Adm ▪ www.museodelviolino.org

For centuries Cremona has been the world capital of violin-making thanks, among others, to the 17th-century master of the art, Antonio Stradivari. The museum includes fascinating displays – many of which are interactive – on the history, techniques and development of violins, and there are regular performances by soloists on a historic Stradivarius.

Museo di Santa Giulia bronze

8 Pinacoteca di Brera, Milan

One of Lombardy's most important galleries *(see pp16–19)* of paintings, displaying works by

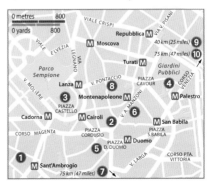

🔟 Books and Films Set in Lombardy

1 I Promessi Sposi (The Betrothed)

Written in the 1800s, Alessandro Manzoni's novel is a window into life in Lombard in the 1600s, set in Milan and Manzoni's Lake Como – home town of Lecco during Spanish rule. It is required reading for all Italian schoolchildren and has been translated into many languages.

Manzoni, author of *The Betrothed*

2 A Month by the Lake

This gentle romantic comedy, based on a short story by H E Bates, is set in 1937 on the shores of Lake Como. Vanessa Redgrave, Edward Fox and Uma Thurman head up the cast of the 1995 movie by John Irvin. Much of it was filmed in and around Varenna and Bellagio (see p117).

3 Casino Royale

The beautiful grounds of Villa Balbianello (see p114) on Lake Como featured in this James Bond film in 2006. Fans can also check out the famous Villa Gaeta, the location for the last scene in the movie. This private house, in Art Nouveau style, lies between Menaggio and Dongo, and is best seen from the ferry boat.

4 Theorem

Pier Paolo Pasolini's usual mix of sex, homosexuality and a communist critique on the emptiness of bourgeois life defines this 1968 film. Enigmatic stranger Terence Stamp raises the libidos of a Milanese family, then further stirs up their lives by disappearing.

5 Miracle in Milan

Vittorio de Sica's 1951 fable of a magical dove that grants wishes to the inhabitants of a Milan slum uses an early version of "special effects", bridging the popular Neo-Realistic style of Italy's post war cinema with the era of magical realism in Italian film-making that Fellini would make famous.

6 A Traveller in Italy

H V Morton who, in his youth, scooped the story of Tutankhamun's tomb discovery in the 1920s, became one of the 20th-century's finest, if little-known, travel writers. His 1950s journey through Italy is an erudite combination of travelogue, history and wonderful prose, much of it surprisingly undated.

7 The Spider's Stratagem

Before gaining international fame, Bernardo Bertolucci made this 1969 story of a dysfunctional family haunted by the Fascist past. He set this psychological drama in the quirky town of Sabbioneta.

Scene from *The Spider's Stratagem*

Monica Vitti in Antonioni's *La Notte*

⑧ La Notte

Film director Michelangelo Antonioni sets the slow death of affection between a couple, played by Marcello Mastroianni and Jeanne Moreau, against a backdrop of rapidly industralizing Milan in 1960.

1957 film of *A Farewell to Arms*

⑨ A Farewell to Arms

Ernest Hemingway's World War I novel (written in 1929), *A Farewell to Arms*, tells the story of a wounded American soldier reuniting with his love in Stresa on Lake Maggiore. They stay at the Grand Hôtel des Iles Borromées, where Hemingway himself often stayed, then flee by boat across the lake to Swiss Locarno.

⑩ Twilight in Italy

The first place D H Lawrence and his lover Frieda settled during their European travels was on Lake Garda, during the winter of 1912–13. In 1916 he compiled this travelogue.

TOP 10 LA SCALA PREMIERES

1 L'Europa Riconosciuta (1778)
Antonio Salieri's bellicose but light-hearted opera was first performed at La Scala on 3 August 1778.

2 La Pietra del Paragone (1812)
Rossini's work signalled La Scala's shift from comic opera and Neo-Classical works to Romantic melodrama.

3 Chiara e Serafina (1822)
The first of many fun-loving Donizetti premieres was this lively piratical tale.

4 Norma (1831)
Of Bellini's three La Scala premieres, the most famous is Norma, a Druid-Roman love triangle that ends badly.

5 Nabucco (1842)
Verdi would become La Scala's greatest home-grown composer, but he suffered two flops before this hit.

6 Mefistofele (1868)
Boito's first great success led to a collaboration with Verdi that produced Otello in 1887 and Falstaff in 1893.

7 Aïda (1872)
After a long absence from La Scala, Verdi offered this Egyptian melodrama.

8 Madama Butterfly (1904)
Puccini's tale of enduring love between a Japanese geisha and an American soldier was received badly at first.

9 Turandot (1926)
Over a year after his death, Puccini's final and unfinished opera premiered at La Scala, conducted by Toscanini.

10 The Rake's Progress (1951)
Under Toscanini's direction, La Scala started opening up to foreign works, including this Stravinsky classic.

Interior of La Scala opera house

🔟 Artists Working in Lombardy

Fresco of the Court of Gonzaga, by Mantegna, in Mantua

1 Andrea Mantegna (1431–1506)

Mantegna's classical mode of High Renaissance painting differed from, but was as beautiful as, that of his brother-in-law Giovanni Bellini. In 1460 he became court painter to the Gonzagas of Mantua, where he left masterful frescoes on the walls of the Palazzo Ducale *(see pp34–5)*. Milan's Pinacoteca di Brera houses his masterpiece, *Dead Christ (see p17)*.

2 Bramante (1444–1514)

The great architect of the High Renaissance travelled from Urbino to Rome, leaving churches in his wake, and even doing a stint as chief architect of St Peter's in Rome.

Sketches by Leonardo da Vinci

3 Leonardo da Vinci (1452–1519)

The ultimate Renaissance Man was a genius painter, inventor and scientist. His inventions – which included helicopters, machine guns and water systems – were centuries ahead of their time but mostly confined to sketches, though working models have been built at Milan's technical museum *(see p99)*.

4 Bernardino Luini (1475–1532)

This apprentice of Leonardo was so taken with his master's talents that he spent his life painting in the style of Leonardo without ever really developing one of his own.

5 Il Bergognone (1480–1523)

With the Renaissance going on all around him, Il Bergognone remained firmly a late Gothic artist, painting lovely but staid devotional works rooted in the style of his Milanese predecessor Vincenzo Foppa.

6 Giulio Romano (1499–1546)

Raphael's protégé helped finish his master's commissions after his death, but his fame as a frescoist was soon eclipsed by his architectural technique. Both came to the attention of the Gonzagas in Mantua, who commissioned from him the Palazzo Te *(see p35)* and other buildings. Only failing health kept him from returning to Rome to become chief architect of St Peter's.

7 Giuseppe Arcimboldo (1527–93)

This Milanese Mannerist may have been a gimmick artist, but he was very good at it. He churned out many allegorical "portraits" that are in fact collages: of flowers, fruit, weapons, fish, animals or even flames.

8 Caravaggio (1571–1609/10)

The Baroque master, who influenced an entire generation, used peasant models and a technique of heavy chiaroscuro, playing harsh light off deep black shadows to create dramatic scenes with brilliant realism. He often introduced an iconoclastic secularism to religious works. His painting *The Flight to Egypt* portrays a sexualized angel and has a very realisitic depiction of trees.

Caravaggio's *The Flight to Egypt*

9 Francesco Hayez (1707–76)

Born in Venice, Hayez moved to Rome – where he mixed with Ingres and Canova – then Milan, balancing his painting between the Romantic and Neo-Classical ideals of the age. He eventually became director of the Pinacoteca di Brera.

10 Umberto Boccioni (1882–1916)

This leading Futurist was born in the south but soon moved to Milan. His failed journalism career served him in writing treatises on Futurism, and his paintings and sculptures were among the most admired of his era.

TOP 10 ARTISTIC ERAS IN LOMBARDY

Ancient rock art near Brescia

1 Ancient
From prehistoric rock etchings dating back to the 12th century BC to Roman villas of the 5th century AD.

2 Lombard
Lombard buildings from the 5th to 10th centuries have triangular façades, blind arcades and ribbed vaulting.

3 Romanesque
Architectural style in the 11th and 12th centuries defined by rounded arches and crude, expressive carvings.

4 Gothic
Pointed arches and flying buttresses allowed ceilings to soar in the 13th and 14th centuries. Painting became more expressive and realistic.

5 Renaissance
Classical architecture and elegant painting, with delicate colours and new techniques such as perspective (in the 15th–16th centuries).

6 Baroque
Similar to the Renaissance but with profuse decor; big in the 17th century, but then spiralled into overwrought Rococo in the 18th century.

7 Neo-Classical
Late 18th- to early 19th-century quest for the soul of the ancients; austere.

8 Romantic
A 19th-century return to the Gothic age and overwrought decor.

9 Liberty
The Italian Art Nouveau of the early 20th century delighted in asymmetrical organic curves.

10 Futurist
Italy's Cubism was obsessed with the fast, modern technological world of the early 20th century.

Lombard Experiences

Cruising on Lake Como

1 A Cruise on Lake Como

The loveliest of the Italian lakes *(see pp112–19)* is best enjoyed from the waters. From this vantage point, devoid of traffic jams, you can see the glorious gardens and villas lining its banks (from the road, all you may see is a high wall).

2 Snacking on a Café Crawl

Between about 6pm and 9pm, many Milanese bars and cafés have Happy Hour, when a cocktail costs between €7 and €15 and includes a buffet spread with several courses (meat, fish or pasta). You can easily make a decent early dinner out of it.

3 A Night at the Opera

At Italy's premier opera house, La Scala *(see p82)*, you can enjoy one of the world's best companies in a wondrous 18th-century setting. Inside there is a museum, and guided tours of the theatre are available.

4 A Violin Concert in Cremona

In the city *(see p48)* where Nicolò Amati honed his craft and passed his skills on to Stradivari, they take their violins *(see p45)* seriously. Virtuosos from around the globe come to festivals, concert seasons and trade fairs just for the chance to bow a few sonatas on the city's magnificent collection of original Strads.

5 Sports on Lake Garda

The northern end of Lake Garda is buffeted by strong winds blowing down from the Sarca Valley in the north in the morning (the *sover*) and south up the lake in the afternoon (the *ora*). Together, they make for some of the best windsurfing and sailing conditions *(see p124)* on any lake in Western Europe, and all summer long watersports fans flock from far and wide to Riva and its neighbour Torbole to thrash the waves.

6 A Milanese Shopping Spree

Milan is one of the world capitals of high fashion, home to dozens of top designer names *(see pp72–3)* in its famed Quadrilatero d'Oro – "Golden Rectangle" – of streets *(see p71)*. Add in designer household objects, chic leather goods, Como silk, fine wines and foods, and Milan becomes a shopper's paradise.

Production of Puccini's *Madama Butterfly* at La Scala opera house

7 An Evening on the Navigli

Milan's southern district of canals (see pp28–9) and warehouses has been converted to a vibrant and bustling evening area of restaurants, pizzerias, bars, pubs and funky shops.

8 Exploring the Roof of Milan's Duomo

You can wander freely among the forest of Gothic carving adorning the rooftop of Milan's cathedral (see p14), and onto the peaked roof of the nave for fine views across the city.

Exploring the Duomo's rooftop

9 Hill Walking near the Lakes

Local tourist offices can often supply maps of mountain trails. Pick a point of interest as a goal: a ruined castle (Arco on Garda, Varenna on Como), church (Madonna del Sasso above Locarno on Maggiore, San Pietro above Civate on Como), mountain stream (Fiumelatte by Varenna, Cascata del Varone above Riva del Garda), or prehistoric rock carvings.

10 San Siro Stadium

MAP R2 ■ Piazzale Angelo Moratti ■ Open 9:30am–6pm daily (except match days) ■ Adm ■ www. sansiro.net

Milan's football stadium is Italy's largest and hosts the home games of two of the country's top teams, AC Milan and Inter Milan. Watching a match here is a memorable experience, while the stadium tour and museum offer a fascinating behind-the-scenes glimpse into the clubs.

TOP 10 LAKESIDE ATTRACTIONS

Charming Varenna on Lake Como

1 Varenna, Lake Como
This attractive, authentic village (see p117) has a waterfront promenade, villas, gardens, churches and a half-ruined castle.

2 Isole Borromee, Lake Maggiore
A trio (see pp30–31) of islets off Stresa – two clad in gardens and palaces, the third with a quaint fishing village.

3 Santa Caterina del Sasso, Lake Maggiore
A medieval church (see p108) in a cliff face, just above the water's edge.

4 Rocca di Angera, Lake Maggiore
This 8th-century Lombard fortress (see p107) dominates the headland.

5 Bellagio, Lake Como
Perhaps the loveliest town (see p117) on any of the lakes, with an arcaded harbour, steep alleyways, elegant villas and sumptuous gardens.

6 Como's Duomo, Lake Como
The exterior of the cathedral (see p113) is a feast of statues and bas-reliefs.

7 Villa Carlotta, Lake Como
Visitors can enter this fabulous, art-filled villa (see p114), as well as wander round its botanical gardens.

8 Il Vittoriale, Lake Garda
An over-the-top Art Nouveau villa (see p124) owned by adventurer and poet Gabriele d'Annunzio.

9 Sirmione, Lake Garda
A picture-perfect town (see pp121–122) set on a narrow peninsula, with a dramatic castle and a ruined Roman villa.

10 Heller Garden, Lake Garda
A labour of love by a Swiss dentist, these gardens (see p122) offer visitors a vista of the Alps amid the lakes.

🔟 Small Towns and Villages

Cremona's centre from its Torrazzo

1 Cremona
MAP E6 ■ Visitor info: Piazza del Comune 5 ■ www.turismo cremona.it

Cremona's attractive medieval centre is dominated by the Torrazzo bell tower, the city's symbol; views from the top are stunning. Nearby, the Museo del Violino *(see p45)* tells the story of Cremona's enduring claim to fame, violin making.

2 Borghetto sul Mincio
MAP C5 ■ Visitor info: Piazza Carlo Alberto 44, Valeggio sul Mincio ■ www.valeggio.com

This exquisitely beautiful village, just 20 minutes south of Lake Garda, features a series of watermills and an imposing 14th century bridge.

Pretty Borghetto sul Mincio

3 Lodi
MAP D5 ■ Visitor info: Piazza Broletto 4; 0371-409-238 ■ www.turismolodi.it

Medieval Lodi is celebrated for its Duomo and octagonal church of the Incoronata. The latter is slathered with frescoes, gilded stuccoes and fine paintings by Il Bergognone.

4 Vigevano
MAP B5 ■ Visitor info: Piazza Ducale; 0381-691-636

Lodovico Sforza *(see p39)* was born in the castle that dominates this town of silk and shoe factories. The arcaded Piazza Ducale is by Bramante; the Baroque Duomo was built in 1680.

Arcaded Piazza Ducale in Vigevano

5 Pavia
MAP C6 ■ Visitor info: Via del Comune 18 (Piazza della Vittoria); 0382-39-9790 ■ www.visitpavia.com

The Dark Ages capital of Northern Italy retains its historic centre. As well as the Certosa *(see p41)*, other important churches include the Duomo, of which Leonardo was one architect. There's also a Renaissance bridge and a 14th-century castle with paintings by Bellini and Tiepolo.

6 Brunate
MAP C3 ■ www.funicolare como.it

The funicular from Como leads up to this charming hillside village, which has stunning views over the city and lake, and a mix of Liberty villas and mountain architecture. There are excellent walking trails from here.

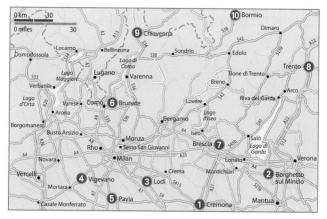

7 Brescia

MAP F4 ■ Visitor info: Viale della Stazione 47; 030-837-8559 ■ www.turismo.brescia.it

Brescia has a fine Renaissance centre, which retains traces of its time as a Roman colony. The San Salvatore e Santa Giulia monastery has historic artifacts, and the art gallery displays works by Raphael and Tintoretto.

8 Trento

MAP H2 ■ Visitor info: Piazza Dante 24; 0461-216-000 ■ www.discovertrento.it

Given its Alpine location and historic centre with sights from from ancient Roman times onwards, Trento is a joy to explore. There's also an innovative science museum.

9 Chiavenna

MAP D1 ■ Visitor info: Piazza Caduti della Libertà; 0343-374-85 ■ www.valchiavenna.com

Set in an Alpine valley, Chiavenna is littered with *crotti* – caverns used to cure meats and cheeses – some of which have been converted into *osterie*. An old stone quarry above town is home to a botanical park, and the Parco Marmitte dei Giganti contains prehistoric carvings.

10 Bormio

Visitor info: Via Roma 131b; 0342-903-300 ■ www.valtellina.it

This year-round skiing village high in the Valtellina is equal parts upmarket resort and medieval village. It's also a gateway to a park full of glaciers, peaks, trails and lovely Alpine vistas.

Trento's medieval cathedral square

🔟 Villas and Gardens

Villa Balbianello, perched above the calm waters of Lake Como

1 Villa Taranto, Lake Maggiore

MAP A2 ▪ Via Vittorio Veneto, Pallanza ▪ 0323-556-667 ▪ Open 8:30am–6:30pm daily (Mar: to 5:30pm; Oct & 1 Nov: 9am–4pm) ▪ Closed 2 Nov–mid-Mar ▪ Adm ▪ www.villataranto.it

The villa in the Verbania district (see p108), built in 1875 by Scotsman Neil MacEacharn, is closed to the public, but you can wander the landscaped gardens filled with exotic plants. Rare species include the world's largest water lily at 2 m (6 ft) across and the towering Metasequoia, which was believed extinct for 200 million years until found in China in 1941.

Gardens of the Villa Taranto

2 Villa Balbianello, Lake Como

Department store mogul and explorer Guido Monzino gave this 1784 villa (see p114) and its gorgeous gardens to FAI (the Italian National Trust) in 1988. A museum within chronicles his adventures from Mount Everest to the North Pole. The property topped Como's famous sights list after appearing in Casino Royale (see p46) and Star Wars: Episode II.

3 Il Vittoriale, Lake Garda

This kitschy Art Nouveau villa (see p124) was created by poet and adventurer Gabriele d'Annunzio, who once flew a biplane over Vienna in 1918 to prove an invasion was possible, and in 1919 used private troops to take over a border town ceded to Yugoslavia, earning acclaim as a national hero and the enmity of those in power. The villa represents his life, loves and philosophy, which are cheerfully explained by guides. The biplane is on show in an outbuilding.

4 Villa Monastero, Lake Como

The original structure (see p113) was not really a monastery, but rather a Cistercian convent founded in 1208. It was disbanded by Charles Borromeo in the 16th century after he heard lascivious stories about its nuns. It is

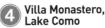

now owned by a science research centre. You can visit the beautiful terrace of palms, cypresses, roses and magnolias, as well as a greenhouse of citrus trees.

5 Villa Melzi, Lake Como

The Vice-President of Napoleon's Cisalpine Republic, Francesco Melzi, had this Neo-Classical villa *(see p115)* built on Bellagio's southern edge. The villa is off limits, but you can wander the gardens to the water's edge, visit a museum of Etruscan, Egyptian and Roman artifacts and see a mock-Moorish temple that inspired a pair of Liszt piano concertos, written during the composer's stay here.

6 Villa Serbelloni, Lake Como

The private gardens of this villa *(see p114)* cover the entire tip of the Bellagio promontory. The guided tours stick mainly to the paths, overlooking the Italianate, English-style and Mediterranean sections. Stendhal described the vista from the top as "sublime and enchanting" – what's more, it is the only spot from which you can see down all three of the arms of Lake Como simultaneously.

7 Villa Cipressi, Lake Como

MAP C2 ■ **Via 4 Novembre, Varenna**
The utterly beautiful Villa Cipressi is now an exclusive hotel, and guests can wander its cypress-shaded gardens, blooming with wisteria.

8 Heller Garden, Lake Garda

Over 30 years, Swiss dentist and naturalist Arturo Hruska transformed his single hectare of lake property into a microcosm of Dolomite and Alpine flora *(see p122)*. Since 1989, Austrian multimedia artist André Heller has kept it open to the public.

Borromeo Palace on the Isola Bella

9 Borromeo Palace, Lake Maggiore

The Borromeo family's 1670 palazzo *(see p30)* on the lush Isola Bella is a glimpse into the lifestyle of the wealthiest of Lombard families.

10 Villa Carlotta, Lake Como

Lake Como is famous for its fabulous villas but, while some gardens are open, few of the buildings themselves can be visited. At Villa Carlotta *(see p114)*, however, you can visit both the Baroque villa, with its Neo-Classical statues and Romantic paintings, and the extensive, lush gardens.

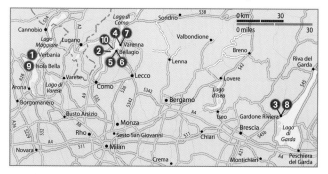

Sports and Activities

① Cycling
AWS, Milan: www.awsbici.com ■ **Xtreme Malcesine, Lake Garda: www.xtrememalcesine.com**
Cycle the canalside paths of Navigli (see p28), hit the mountain-biking trails of Monte Baldo above Lake Garda (see p126) or explore the Franciacorta wine area (see p132) using two-wheeled transport.

② Golf
Golf Club Milano: www. golfclubmilano.com ■ **Menaggio & Cadenabbia Golf Club: www. menaggio.org**
The 27-hole Milan Golf Club is one of the nation's best, and there's a high concentration of clubs at Lake Garda (see p126). The Menaggio & Cadenabbia club at Lake Como is also excellent, as is the Franciacorta club (see p132) near Lake Iseo.

③ Climbing
Arco, Lake Garda: www.mmove. net; www.arcowall.com ■ **Lake Como: www.lakecomoadventures.com**
Milan has several indoor climbing walls, but for the real thing Arco, at the northern end of Lake Garda, has plenty of bolted climbing routes (see p126). Lake Como Adventures runs courses for different abilities at various locations.

Tackling a cliff above Lake Como

Windsurfing on Lake Garda

④ Windsurfing and Kitesurfing
Surf Segnana, Torbole: www.surf segnana.it ■ **Europa Surf & Sail, Malcesine: www.europasurfandsail. com** ■ **La Darsena, Lake Maggiore: www.ladarsenawindsurf.com**
Torbole, at the northern end of Lake Garda (see p126), is one of Europe's premier windsurfing locations and there are good winds at Malcesine too. The northern tips of Lake Como (see p116) and Lake Maggiore are also favourite spots and equipment hire and courses are available at various places around the lakes.

⑤ Swimming
Piscina Solari: Via Montevideo 20, Milan
Milan's Idroscalo (see p61) has beaches and open-air swimming pools, ideal for a refreshing dip on a hot summer's day, while year-round indoor pools include Piscina Solari. And, of course, the cool, clear waters of the lakes are highly inviting.

⑥ Ice-Skating
Agorà: Via dei Ciclamini 23; www.stadioghiaccio.it
The largest indoor ice-rink in Milan, Agorà is southwest of the centre and has regular public sessions. Open-air ice-rinks pop up over Christmas, including one in futuristic Piazza Gae Aulenti (see p94) and another on Como's lakeside Piazza Cavour.

7 Walking

Walking tours *(see p74)* of Milan include free half-day tours, while at the lakes there are classic routes such as the Antica Strada Valeriana at Lake Iseo *(see p132)* and the Via Regina on the west coast of Lake Como.

8 Skiing

Fly Ski Shuttle: www.flyski shuttle.com ■ Cable-car Mottarone: www.stresa-mottarone.it

Thanks to Milan's position near the Alps, a vast range of ski resorts are within easy reach and there's a good shuttle service from the airports. The season starts on 7 December to coincide with the festival of the city's patron, Sant'Ambrogio. Cable-cars take skiers up to to Monte Baldo from Lake Garda *(see p126)* and to Mottarone from Lake Maggiore.

Skiers on Monte Baldo

9 Boats

Kayaking is a fantastic way to explore the lakes; equipment hire is widely available. The lake ferry companies run cruises and there are lots of small-scale private boat tours.

10 Spas

QC Terme Milano: Piazza Medaglie d'Oro; www.qcterme. com ■ Aquaria, Sirmione: www. termedisirmione.it

Time out at one of Milan's many spas is the perfect way to relax. QC Terme, for example, is elegantly luxurious, and includes a bio-spa within a historic tram. Sirmione on Lake Garda is particularly good for spas thanks to the natural thermal water bubbling up at 69° C (156° F).

TOP 10 SPECTATOR SPORTS

Vintage cars in the Mille Miglia

1 Car Racing
www.1000miglia.it
The Mille Miglia vintage car race goes from Brescia to Rome and back.

2 Football
AC Milan and Internazionale, both play at the city's San Siro stadium *(see p51)*.

3 Basketball
www.olimpiamilano.com
Italians love basketball; Olimpia Milano is one of the country's top teams.

4 Motorsports
www.monzanet.it
Events held at the Monza track include the Formula One Italian Grand Prix.

5 Horse racing
www.ippodromisnai.it
Milan's main racecourse is northwest of the city centre, next to San Siro.

6 Ice hockey
www.hockeymilano.it
Hockey Milano Rossoblu is the local team, playing in the top league.

7 Rugby
www.rugbymilano.it
The local top-league club is AS Rugby Milano; Italy is part of the Six Nations.

8 Volleyball
www.powervolleymilano.it ■ www.verovolley.com
Milan's top-league teams are Milano Power and Milano Vero Volley.

9 American Football
www.rhinos.it ■ www.seamen.it
The city's two top teams in Milan are the Rhinos and the Seamen.

10 Cycling
www.giroditalia.it
The first edition of the Giro d'Italia race set off from Milan in 1909 and the city often hosts the final stage.

🔟 Off the Beaten Track

① Parco Agricolo Sud di Milano

MAP C3 ■ www.parcoagricolo sudmilano.it ■ Rice-growing area: www.parcodellerisaie.it

This vast area of agricultural and natural parkland surrounds two-thirds of the city to the south, east and west, and includes the major rice-growing area towards Pavia. Its villages, wildlife reserves and farmsteads (cascine), many with restaurants, are popular among the Milanese for a day out.

② Monza and Brianza

MAP C4 ■ Tourist Board Monza: www.turismo.monza.it ■ Villa Reale: www.reggiadimonza.it ■ Brianza villas: www.villeaperte.info

Monza is at the heart of the Brianza area. The vast parkland surrounding the majestic Villa Reale contains Monza's famous racetrack, Milan Golf Club (see p56), and an open-air swimming pool. Brianza has several grand villas and churches.

Monza's cathedral and bell tower

③ Triangolo Lariano

MAP C3

Lakes Pusiano and Annone are two of a series of peaceful minor lakes in this stretch of land between Como and Lecco. Lake Annone is divided almost in two by a narrow peninsula, and is overlooked by the San Pietro al Monte monastery (see p118).

Abbazia di Chiaravalle's cloisters

④ Abbazia di Chiaravalle

The most striking of the series of working abbeys to the south of Milan, this medieval structure (see p100) has an unusual octagonal bell tower (Ciribiciaccola in the local dialect), an interesting frescoed interior, with some painted by Bernardino Luini, attractive cloisters and a historic 12th-century mill restored to make fit for use. Produce by monks from the on-site farm and from other nearby farms is sold including crafts and beers.

⑤ Foraging in Desio

MAP C4 ■ Wood-ing: www. wood-ing.org

The Wood-ing Wild Food Lab, which is based at Desio, just north of Milan, organizes enjoyable and eye-opening half-day foraging courses in a range of languages. They also run longer trips further afield, intensive profes-sional courses for chefs and tasting evenings with high-quality dishes made from a wide range of natural produce, including tree bark.

⑥ Trezzo sull'Adda

MAP D4 ■ Trezzo sull'Adda Tourist Board: www.prolocotrezzo. com ■ River-boats: www.navigare inlombardia.it

This charming town stands on the banks of the Adda at a double bend in the river – boat trips run on summer weekends. Trezzo can be reached from Milan via the cycle-path from Cascina dei Pomi along the Martesana canal, and is dominated by the ruins of the 14th-century Castello Visconteo.

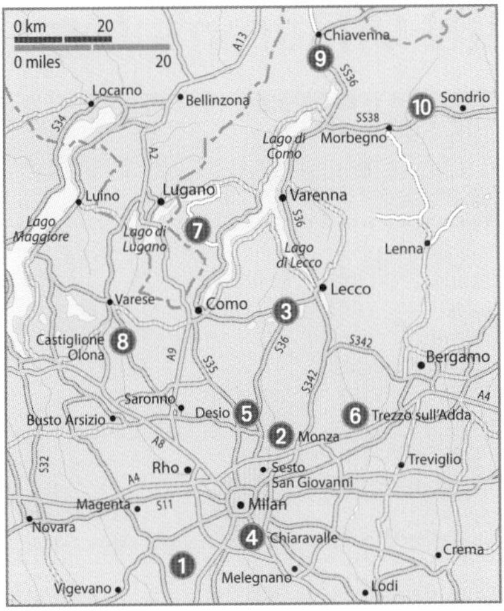

7 Valle Intelvi

This mountain valley (see p118) links Lake Lugano and Lake Como. There are plenty of excellent walking opportunities for all abilities and, at Schignano, an easy woodland footpath, the Sentiero delle Espressioni, passes a series of wooden sculptures. Monte Sighignola, which rises 1,300 m (4,265 ft), has a panoramic terrace just below the summit, known as the Balcony of Italy, with stunning views across the Alps.

8 Castiglione Olona

MAP B3 ▪ Castiglione Olona: www.prolococastiglioneolona.it ▪ Castelseprio: www.castelseprio.net

This medieval village on the banks of the River Olona retains its attractive centre thanks largely to intervention by 14th-century Cardinal Branda Castiglioni. His bedroom within the Palazzo Branda Castiglioni has some exquisite frescoes, as does the chapel. Nearby, the fine monastic complex of Torba was originally a Roman fortress.

9 Valchiavenna

MAP D1 ▪ Valchiavenna Tourist Board: www.valchiavenna.com

Pretty and historic Chiavenna is the main centre of the mountainous Valchiavenna area just north of Lake Como, while nearby Madesimo is a lively ski resort in winter. The footpaths of the Marmitte dei Giganti park near Chiavenna (see p118) take walkers past a series of unusual rock formations, including ice-polished channels, shafts and potholes, and there is a wealth of figurative and geometric ancient rock carvings to be seen.

10 Valtellina

A stunning mountain area, Valtellina (see p118) has excellent sports facilities, charming historic villages such as Bormio, Teglio and Tirano, and a notable food and wine culture. The landscape is scattered with terraces where Nebbiolo grapes for the characterful Valtellina red wines, are grown. Local speciality dishes include *pizzoccheri*, hearty buckwheat ribbons.

The lake at Valchiavenna

TOP 10 Children's Attractions

Gardaland's bright and kid-friendly attractions

① MUBA – Museo dei Bambini

MAP N4 ■ Via Besana 12, Milan
■ 02-4398-0402 ■ Open 9:30am–6pm
Tue–Sun ■ Adm ■ www.muba.it

In the centre of a public park, and designed specifically for children, this museum offers a lively calendar of activities for 1–12-year-olds.

② The Best Science Museum in Italy

Milan's Museo Nazionale della Scienza e della Tecnologia *(see p99)* has the usual impressive, interactive displays of any major science museum – plus Leonardo. Here, full-scale models of his ahead-of-their-time inventions including the paper plans of his helicopter bring his astonishing ideas to life.

Studying a Leonardo machine

③ Gardaland

Italy's top theme park *(see p123)*, on the southeastern banks of Lake Garda, is not quite Disneyland, but it does have roller coasters, a jungle safari, reconstructions of the Pyramids and a thrilling water park. The facilities are good, including a range of refreshments, themed shops and souvenir photos.

④ Lakeside Castles

You can relive the Middle Ages by exploring Lombardy's castles, scrambling up watchtowers and patrolling the ramparts like a soldier of old. At Castello Sforzesco in Milan *(see pp20–21)*, regular tours take you up onto the battlements. Those on the lakes can be more atmospheric. The best fortresses are at Varenna *(see p117)*, Arco *(see p123)*, Malcesine *(see p125)* and Sirmione *(see p122)*.

⑤ Alpyland

MAP A3 ■ Località Mottarone, Stresa ■ Adm ■ www.alpyland.com

Zipping down the 1200-m (3,937-ft) track on the Alpine Coaster, a bobsled rollercoaster at the top of Mount Mottarone (cable-car from Stresa) is an exhilarating experience. The two-seater bobsleds have an individual braking system, and the location guarantees stunning views.

6 Idroscalo

MAP T2 ▪ Open 8am–9pm daily (Nov–Mar: to 5pm) ▪ Adm ▪ www.idroscalo.info

This large artificial lake near Linate airport offers beaches and pools, bicycle hire, a children's play park and watersports, as well as a range of cafés and picnic sites.

7 Prada Accademia dei Bambini

MAP S2 ▪ Largo Isarco 2, Milan ▪ Open 11am–5pm Sat & Sun ▪ www.fondazioneprada.org

At the Prada Children's Academy, top experts from a variety of disciplines, including the arts and sciences, lead fun, free weekly workshops that need to be booked in advance.

8 Gelato Breaks

Italy's gelato puts all other ice creams to shame. There are dozens of classic parlours around Milan – look out for natural colours, as well as for the sign *"produzione propria"*, indicating that it's homemade.

Luscious Italian ice cream

9 Cycling in Mantua

Mantua *(see pp34–5)* is flat, and surrounded by lakes and plains that stretch up and down the Mincio River, perfect to explore with cycling.

10 Puppet Shows

MAP P5 ▪ Teatro Silvestrianum, Via Andrea Maffei 19, Milan ▪ 02-5521-1300 ▪ Open Oct–Apr ▪ www.teatro colla.org

Master puppeteers Cosetta and Gianni Colla keep Italy's rich tradition of puppetry alive and updated.

TOP 10 CITY PARKS IN MILAN

Park Lambro, the city's largest

1 Parco Lambro
MAP C4 ▪ Via Feltre
This large country-park has play areas and a skateboard park.

2 Parco di Porta Nuova
MAP M1 ▪ Via Gaetano de' Castillia
This park has a so-called library of trees made up of mini-forests.

3 Parco Sempione
MAP J1 ▪ Piazza Sempione
This substantial 19th-century park has a children's play area, a lake and cafés.

4 Giardino Indro Montanelli
MAP N1–P1 ▪ Corso Venezia
An 18th-century public park. A plant market/exhibition is held each May.

5 Boscoincittà
MAP C4 ▪ Via Novara
A haven of woodland, streams and lakes, green areas and cycle paths.

6 Giardini della Guastalla
MAP N5 ▪ Via Francesco Sforza
Milan's oldest park, dating from 1555, has a Baroque fish pond with lotuses.

7 Parco Solari
MAP J5 ▪ Via Solari
A pleasant city park with a swimming pool, near the Navigli canal district.

8 Giardini della Villa Belgiojoso Bonaparte
MAP N2 ▪ Via Palestro
A park reserved for children; adults can only enter if accompanied by one.

9 Giardino Perego
MAP M2 ▪ Via dei Giardini
An appealing little park with lots of trees and a children's play area.

10 Parco Papa Giovanni Paolo II
MAP L5 ▪ Via Vetere
This park is set between the San Lorenzo and Sant'Eustorgio basilicas.

🔟 Entertainment Venues in Milan

Teatro degli Arcimboldi dancers

1 Teatro degli Arcimboldi
MAP S1 ▪ Viale dell'Innovazione 20 ▪ www.teatroarcimboldi.it

Opened in 2002 as an alternative to La Scala while the latter was undergoing restoration work, this striking theatre in the redeveloped Bicocca district has a capacity of over 2,300, making it Europe's second largest.

2 La Scala
Housed in an 18th-century theatre, this *(see p82)* is one of the world's top opera companies, where Verdi was house composer, Callas graced the stage and costumes are designed by top fashion names. The season runs from December to May, so book well in advance.

3 Auditorium di Milano
MAP R2 ▪ Via S Gottardo 39 ▪ www.laverdi.org

Since 1999, the "Giuseppe Verdi" Symphony Orchestra of Milan has played in this re-invented 1930s cinema, which stood derelict for decades after World War II. The orchestra, under Conductor Riccardo Chailly and musical director Xian Zhang, has a repertoire ranging from Bach to 19th-century symphonic music and contemporary pieces.

4 Santeria Social Club
Situated in the heart of Milan, this huge multifunctional space *(see p102)* hosts theatre productions, concerts and cultural events. At night, it transforms into one of the city's best live music and club venues. DJs keep the crowds on their feet by spinning the latest dance and electronic beats late into the night.

5 Alcatraz
Located on a street that features a number of hip nightspots, Milan's largest club *(see p96)* is housed in a converted industrial space and hosts live music concerts, events and parties. The action begins around 11pm and goes on until 3am. There is often live music during the

Grand operatic performance taking place on the stage of La Scala

almost 3,000, it attracts well-known stars from the international music scene, from Sting to Rag'n'Bone Man.

8 Blue Note

The first European outpost of the famed New York jazz club serves up dinner and top-line performers from Tuesday to Saturday, and a jazz brunch on Sundays. The line-up is wide-ranging at Blue Note *(see p96)*. Past acts have ranged from Bill Evans and Suzanne Vega to the London Community Gospel Choir. Booking is essential.

9 Hollywood

This stalwart from the 1980s still offers you the best chance in all of Milan to spot a genuine international supermodel, making Corso Como one of the city's most fashionable streets. Though a perfectly standard discotheque from 1986, the glitzy and glamorous Hollywood *(see p96)* continues to draw the most beautiful people in town, so dress to impress.

week and dancing every Saturday and Sunday, with three rooms playing different types of music.

6 Old Fashion Cafe

MAP J2 ■ Viale E. Alemagna 6 ■ 02-805-6231 ■ www.oldfashion.it

This veteran of the Milan nightlife scene remains popular, judging by the crowds hanging around outside waiting to get past the velvet rope. Situated in the Palazzo dell'Arte in Parco Sempione, it has an elegant restaurant and a cosy lounge, both with dance floors. In summer the crowd spills out into the large garden.

7 Fabrique

MAP S2 ■ Via Fantoli 9 ■ 02-5801-8197 ■ www.fabriquemilano.it

Occupying the former premises of a record warehouse, Fabrique is one of Milan's most successful venues, hosting regular live concerts, club evenings and plenty of other events as well, including fashion, art and cultural events. With a capacity of

Live music at Magazzini Generali

10 Magazzini Generali

MAP R2 ■ Via Pietrasanta 14 ■ www.magazzinigenerali.org

Cavernous Magazzini Generali has an auditorium that seats 1,000 for live acts, and it can become a huge disco. It also has a gallery for exhibitions, live poetry readings and more.

TOP 10 Culinary Highlights of Lombardy

Pan-fried Cotoletta alla Milanese

1 Cotoletta alla Milanese

For proof that the Lombards are Germanic at heart, look no further than Milan's archetypal dish, a breaded veal cutlet which is similar to Wiener schnitzel.

2 Ossobuco

Veal chops are cut across the shin bone, lightly fried, then slow-cooked in wine and tomatoes, and served with lemon-parsley-garlic gremolata tossed on top. Proper *ossobuco* is served on the bone (its very name means "bone-hole"). Digging out the rich marrow is considered an integral part of enjoying the dish.

3 Strangolapreti

These little spinach and ricotta balls are called "priest-stranglers" because they are deemed so rich they'd choke a poor prelate's simple palate. Traditionally served simply with butter and grated parmesan.

4 Tortelli di Zucca

Mantua specializes in this slightly sweet first course, stuffing pockets of fresh pasta with a rich pumpkin paste. It's usually topped with a simple butter and sage sauce.

5 Cheeses

Lombardy is the land of Italy's king of blue-veined cheeses, gorgonzola, and its lesser-known cousin taleggio (no mould, just strongly odoured goodness). It is also home to Parmesan cheese: Grana Padano, Parmigiano Reggiano and Grana Lodigiano. On the milder end of the scale are the popular Bel Paese and spreadable, creamy mascarpone.

6 Lake Fish

Several fish favourites are plucked daily from Lombardy's lakes. The best include *persico* (perch), *lavarello* (a whitefish), *trota* (trout), *luccio* (pike), *coregone* (another whitefish) and *tinca* (tench).

7 Panettone

All across Italy at Christmas people snap up boxes of this traditional Lombard cake, though locals enjoy it year-round. It is quite dry, and studded with fruit and candied peel.

Light, fruity panettone

8 Cassoeûla

A way to beat the winter is to indulge in a cassoeûla. Somewhere between a soup and a stew, this throws sausage and chunks of pork into a thick cabbage broth, with polenta on the side.

Cassoeûla

Soft polenta with a savoury topping

⑨ Polenta

Northern Italy's cornmeal side dish can be prepared in a wide range of ways, from a creamy, molten mass rich with butter and cheese to a set paste which is sliced and fried until crisp and golden. Modern cooks also use it as a gluten-free alternative in baking, or in place of breadcrumbs for coating food to be fried.

Saffron-hued risotto alla Milanese

⑩ Risotto alla Milanese

If you order risotto in Italy, you usually have to wait at least 20 minutes, as the cook must constantly stir the rice until it reaches the perfect texture. It is time-consuming to make in small batches, so some restaurants will prepare it only for two or more people. In Milan, they often tinge their risotto bright yellow with saffron, and may throw in some seasonal vegetables. In Mantua, they usually spice it up with sausage.

TOP 10 WINES

1 Bardolino
This wine is a light, balanced red from Lake Garda's Veneto shore.

2 Valtellina
This meaty red from the hills around Lake Como is intensely aromatic and powerful: one type is named "Inferno".

3 Franciacorta
Italy's superior sparkling wine is usually made with Chardonnay, Pinot Noir and Pinot Bianco grapes.

4 Oltrepò Pavese
Also slightly fizzy, lighter and tangier than Lambrusco. The Garda region also produces familiar varietals.

5 Garda Bresciano
A collection of wines from the lower reaches of Lake Garda, including Gropello and the rounder Chiaretto from the Mincio valley.

6 San Martino della Battaglia
A tart white made from Tocai grapes of Friuli; there's also a velvety, fortified dessert liqueur version.

7 Lugana
This balanced white is made from Trebbiano grapes on the southern shores of Lake Garda.

8 San Colombano
Milan's own red wine is primarily significant for achieving the DOC level of status despite being grown on the outskirts of an industrial city.

9 Grappa
Italy's own brand of firewater is a *digestivo* ("digestive" liqueur) which is distilled from the leftovers of the grape-squeezing process.

10 Lambrusco
Thick, dark, fizzy red from Mantua. Cheap but delicious; great with pizza.

Sparkling, sweet Lambrusco

🔟 Cafés and Wine Bars

Cosy, welcoming Bar Magenta

① Bar Magenta, Milan

A lovely corner spot that's a cross between an Irish pub and a Parisian Art Deco café, Bar Magenta *(see p96)* has a zinc bar, high ceilings, and a decent list of dishes along with coffee, cocktails and Guinness on tap. Besides a truly engaging atmosphere, the bar also promotes local artists.

② Cova, Milan

The Faccioli family opened Cova *(see p88)* near La Scala theatre in 1817 and, though it was later moved to Milan's prime shopping street, Via Montenapoleone, it has remained in the family – and continues to be café of choice for the city's elite. Its home-made pastries, chocolates and sandwiches are some of the most exquisite in town, and they brew up a mean cappuccino to boot. There's an elegant little tearoom with refined service, but since this is still Italy you're also welcome to just run in and toss back an espresso.

③ Cremeria Bolla, Como

MAP C3 ▪ Via Boldoni 6
▪ 031-264-256 ▪ www.cremeriabolla.it

Located just behind the Duomo, this long-established café *(see p119)* is open all day serving freshly baked croissants for breakfast, pastries and ice cream. Considered the best in town for hazelnut, pistachio and chocolate flavours, Bolla has a faithful following, from both locals and visitors.

④ Bar Jamaica, Milan

This historic Milanese café *(see p96)* in the Brera district has long been a haunt of artists, writers and intellectuals. It is also where Mussolini used to read (and correct) articles about himself in the daily newspaper, over a cappuccino. It is busy at all hours, serving drinks from coffee to cocktails, as well as hot and cold dishes. The extensive wine list can also be paired with the dishes.

⑤ Il Marchesino alla Scala, Milan

MAP M3 ▪ Piazza della Scala 2
▪ 02-7209-4338 ▪ www.marchesi.it

The brainchild of chef Gualtiero Marchesi, credited for master-minding Italian creative cuisine, this bar-restaurant within La Scala includes a sushi bar from where you can watch the action in the kitchen.

⑥ Zucca (Caffè Miani), Milan

This café *(see p88)* opened inside the Galleria Vittorio Emanuele II *(see p70)* in 1868. Verdi and Toscanini would stop by after La Scala shows and King Umberto I declared that it served the best coffee in Milan. Its location at the galleria entrance gives a great view of the Duomo façade.

Zucca's Art Nouveau interior

7 Pasticceria Marchesi, Milan

A wonderful old-fashioned café (see p96) and pastry shop "discovered" by many a visitor trekking out to see *The Last Supper*. The decor hasn't changed since 1824, the coffee is quite good and the pastries are favoured by Giorgio Armani.

8 Sant'Ambroeus, Milan

Looking every inch the 1936 café from its wood-panelling to its fabulous pink stucco decorations, Sant'Ambroeus (see p88), is counted among the great temples of chocolate in Italy. The speciality here is their *ambrogiotti*: an indulgence of dark chocolate wrapped around a filling of zabaglione cream.

Window display at Sant'Ambroeus

9 Caffè del Tasso, Bergamo

MAP D3 ▪ Piazza Vecchia 3 ▪ 035-237-966 ▪ www.caffedeltasso.it

For over 500 years, the Tasso has been Bergamo's meeting spot for everyone from princes to rebels. Garibaldi and his red shirts met here, and it was once so notorious that a decree (displayed on the wall) was made in 1845 prohibiting rebellious conversations from taking place.

10 Bar Portici del Comune, Cremona

MAP E6 ▪ Piazza del Comune 2 ▪ 0372-027-925

You just can't get a better seat in town than one at an outdoor table set under a lofty medieval arcade with the façade of Cremona's Duomo filling up your panorama.

TOP 10 COCKTAILS AND DRINKS

Fashionable Aperol Spritz

1 Aperol Spritz
This popular bright orange cocktail is everywhere in Italy; it's made with Aperol, Prosecco and soda water.

2 Crodino
A well-known non-alcoholic predinner drink, Crodino also has a distinctive orange hue and tangy flavour.

3 Martini Cocktail
This classic cocktail, made with the famous Italian vermouth, gin and lemon juice, is decorated with an olive.

4 Bellini
A refreshing summer cocktail first created in Venice at Harry's Bar, made with Prosecco and peach juice.

5 Amari
A wide range of this traditional brown herb-based digestive is made in Italy.

6 Grappa
This strong, clear after-dinner drink, made using what is left over from the grapes after they have been pressed, has at least 35 per cent alcohol.

7 Campari
Another classic predinner drink, distinctive red Campari is often served as a Spritz with Prosecco and soda.

8 Bombardino
Ideal as a mountain winter warmer, Bombardino is served hot. It's made with eggnog and brandy and topped with whipped cream.

9 Americano
Despite its name, this cocktail was first conceived in Italy; made with Campari, red vermouth and soda water.

10 Ugo
Light and refreshing, this tasty cocktail hails from northern Italy and combines Prosecco, elderflower syrup and mint.

Restaurants

① Villa Fiordaliso, Lake Garda

Once D'Annunzio house, as well as the place where Mussolini's mistress spent her final days, this historic Liberty-style villa *(see p127)* is now a hotel. It features an excellent restaurant that offers an inventive, if sometimes ultra-minimalist, cuisine.

Villa Fiordaliso's dining room

② Ristorante Cracco, Milan

A bastion of fine Milanese cooking, Ristorante Cracco *(see p89)* was overhauled and reopened under the guidance of Chef Carlo Cracco. With a Michelin star, the menu is adventurous and the wine list exceptional. If the stratospheric prices make you cringe, know that around the corner is Peck, also managed by Cracco, and one of the finest food emporia in Italy, where raw ingredients and prepared dishes can make up a glorious picnic.

③ Trattoria da Pino, Milan

Genuine Milanese home cooking is the order of the day here. You'll be squeezed in with the locals at this simple place *(see p89)*, but it's worth it for the delicious daily specials, combined with bargain prices and great atmosphere.

④ Trattoria al Porto, Lake Iseo

With its appealing rustic-chic interior and welcoming atmosphere, local specialities make up the menu here *(see p133)*. Gabriella cooks up dishes such as lake fish risotto, braised beef with polenta and mushroom gnocchi with a walnut sauce.

⑤ Joia, Milan

Swiss chef-owner Pietro Leeman spent time in the Orient before opening Joia *(see p97)*, Milan's temple of vegetarian cuisine. Many of his dishes have a hint of the exotic that put them in a gourmet category. The wine list is joined by a selection of ciders and organic beers.

⑥ Aimo e Nadia, Milan

It's well worth the longish haul from the city centre to dine here *(see p103)*. Aimo and Nadia Moroni are among the top chefs in all Milan. They are particular about hunting down the best ingredients, and it shows in such delectables as risotto with pumpkin flowers and truffles.

Vibrant, art-bedecked interior of Aimo e Nadia

Stylish Ristorante Berton

 Ristorante Berton, Milan
This *(see p97)* minimalist-chic Michelin-starred restaurant fits in perfectly with its futuristic surroundings at Porta Nuova *(see p43)*. The menu includes lots of seafood.

8 **Il Sole di Ranco, Lake Maggiore**
For more than 150 years, the Brovelli family has run an inn and *osteria (see p111)* in the tiny lakeside village of Ranco, with summertime seating on shaded terraces. The wine list offers more than 1,200 choices, and they'll set up a wine tasting to accompany your *degustazione* (tasting) menu.

9 **Barchetta, Lake Como**
Restaurants in such popular towns as Bellagio rarely rise to the level of quality that Barchetta *(see p119)* has achieved under chef-owner Armando Valli. The signature dish is the *sinfonia degli otto sapori del lago*, a "symphony" of eight lake fishes. For dessert, try the traditional *paradel* – honey ice cream with raisins.

10 **Don Carlos at the Grand Hotel et de Milan**
Named after Verdi's opera, this restaurant *(see p89)* offers a highly memorable experience, serving Italian creative cuisine with oriental touches. The walls feature photos and drawings of La Scala and the discreet background music is operatic. Open for dinner only, the kitchen closes at 11:30pm which is quite late for Milan.

TOP 10 ITALIAN SNACKS

1 Olives
Italy is one of the world's premier olive-growing nations. Enjoy them accompanied by a glass of wine.

2 Panini
Fillings – and a variety of bread – can be chosen when ordering a *panino* sandwich from a bar or delicatessen.

3 Panzerotti
Baked or fried filled dough crescents from southern Italy but now a Milanese delicacy thanks to Luini *(see p89)*.

4 Gelato
Cool and creamy, Italian *gelato* comes in many flavours. Vegan ice-cream is now becoming popular, too.

5 Granita
Ice granules with a (usually natural) flavouring. Lemon and coffee are popular but there may be a selection.

6 Piadina
This Italian flatbread hails from the Adriatic riviera. Classic fillings include soft cheese with ham and rocket.

7 Tramezzini
These white, crust-free sliced-bread sandwiches are surprisingly popular. A "toast" is a toasted sandwich, usually featuring ham and cheese.

8 Bruschetta
A slice of toasted bread topped with garlic and olive oil (*aglio e olio*) or something more substantial.

9 Pasticcini
These mini cakes and biscuits can often be ordered with a coffee or tea for a sweet afternoon snack.

10 Pizzette
Pizzas of every size are everywhere. *Pizzette* are usually small and round, while a *trancio di pizza* is a slice.

Tasty snack-sized *pizzette*

🔟 Shopping Areas in Milan

Typically stylish display at 10 Corso Como

① 10 Corso Como
MAP L2

This *(see p95)* prestige address started out in 1990 as a photography gallery and, over the years a bookshop, a store selling fashion and accessories by innovative designers, a courtyard café-restaurant and a tiny, chic hotel called 3 Rooms have been added.

② Galleria Vittorio Emanuele II

This glorious 19th-century shopping mall *(see p83)*, though small, houses a little of everything. You'll find designer wear such as Prada and

Glass-domed interior of the Galleria

mass-market brands such as La Feltrinelli superstore of CDs and books. For a shopping break, visit the bastion of la dolce vita that is Zucca *(see p88)* in Galleria.

③ Via Manzoni
MAP M2–3

This boulevard became an epicentre of Milanese fashion when Giorgio Armani opened his gargantuan superstore *(see p85)* here in 2000. On Manzoni there's everything from the Roman fashions of Davide Cenci (No. 7) to the check-me-out jewellery of Donatella Pellini (No. 20).

④ Corso di Porta Ticinese
MAP K5

Much more unconventional than Milan's other shopping streets, this vibrant road, which ends up near the Navigli district *(see pp28–9)*, has vintage clothing stores as well as small-scale independent shops stocking niche street-wear labels and one-of-a-kind accessories.

⑤ La Rinascente
MAP M4 ▪ Piazza Duomo
▪ www.rinascente.it

Italy's premier department store was founded in 1865 and has always been influential in the development of local society. Elegant yet approachable, departments include homeware and cosmetics as well as clothing from local new designers and unusual accessories. The top floor dining and food hall has unparalleled views of the cathedral next door.

6 Milan's Markets
MAPS J6; Via Valenza ▪ MAP M1; Via San Marco ▪ MAP J5; Papiniano

The main market is Saturday's Fiera di Sinigaglia on Via Valenza, behind Porta Genova station. Milan's Sunday flea market surrounds the San Donato metro stop in the south. Local markets are on Via San Marco (Mondays and Thursdays), Via Benedetto Marcello (northeast of the Giardini Pubblici) on Tuesdays, and Viale Papiniano near the Navigli (Tuesdays and Saturdays). Markets tend to shut by 1pm, except on Saturdays.

Interior of the food emporium Eataly

7 Quadrilatero d'Oro
MAP L3 ▪ Via Sant'Andrea/Via della Spiga/Via Montenapoleone /Via Manzoni

Milan's aptly-named Golden Quad is a quadrangle of streets containing some of the most exclusive branches of top designer stores. Window-displays may be sensational or simple but they're always extravagant and oozing glamour, while the respectful hush is regularly broken by the low rumble of Ferraris and Lamborghinis. A must-see even for those who aren't big shoppers.

8 Eataly
MAP L1 ▪ Piazza XXV Aprile 10 ▪ www.eataly.net

A foodie's paradise housed in a converted theatre, Eataly sells food-related items alongside a vast selection of the highest-quality food from all over Italy, many products sourced from small-scale producers. There are also a dozen specialist eateries and bars, while themed dinners, tastings, courses and other events are organized too.

9 Corso Vittorio Emanuele II
MAP M4–N3

This pedestrian street at the back of the Duomo is lined with arcades and some of the hippest shops in central Milan, including sophisticated brands like Furla, Pollini and Max Mara.

10 Corso Buenos Aires
MAP P1

This long road is where your average Milanese heads to shop. You'll find everything from hand-made men's dress shirts and Richard Ginori china to bootleg records.

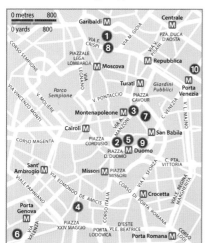

🔟 **Fashion Houses**

Prada, a Milanese company synonymous with high fashion

1 Armani

Italy's top fashion guru is the master of smart clothes that can help anyone look like a model. The first Emporio Armani opened in Milan for casual clothes at low prices and gradually moved towards designing crisp and tailored suits for both men and women.

2 Ermenegildo Zegna

This fourth-generation, environmentally aware firm uses the finest cashmere, merino and mohair in its fabrics. It has become a world leader in fine menswear and accessories for the modern man.

Chic display at Ermenegildo Zegna

3 Prada

With the help of a simple small red stripe, Prada breathed new life into relaxed minimalism. The brand is synonymous with avant-garde style and attention to every detail. You will swoon over their exquisite leather handbags.

4 Mila Schön

A fashion giant, who pioneered the double-face fabric in the 1960s, Mila Schön is a true hub of Milanese and Italian fashion, offering a wide range of accessories and lingerie.

5 Trussardi

Still a family firm, founded by a Bergamasco glove maker in 1910, Trussardi produces classic cuts and leather accessories. Throughout his career, Nicola Trussardi was actively involved in promoting the "Made in Italy" label. Explore leather accessories such as suitcases and bags.

6 Versace

Gianni Versace popularised "violently elegant" designs and costumed many La Scala productions in the 1980s. With an interest in fashion from an early age, he presented his first collection in 1978. Versace is best known for leather accessories and ready-to-wear clothes.

7 Moschino

An enfant terrible of Milan's fashion scene since way back in 1983, Moschino Couture makes way for irreverent and unpredictable looks, classic shapes, perfect cuts and seductive details. Here you will find products with eccentric designs.

8 Missoni

This husband-and-wife team has charmed the fashion world since 1953 with their multi-coloured, zigzag knits. Missoni clothes began to appear in fashion magazines in 1960 and the first Missoni boutique opened in Milan in 1976. The brand is an essential part of the "Made in Italy" label. Here you can pick up colourful designer knitwear.

Fashionable clothes from Krizia

9 Krizia

Ever an eclectic designer, Mariuccia "Krizia" Mandelli flouted trends and won awards since 1954. The brand is rebellious and innovative in its design. In 1971, at a time when midi was the widely accepted length, the fashion house created ripples with very-short shorts.

10 Ferré

The late Gianfranco Ferré was famous for "architectural" fashion, a look that lingers on in clothing and accessories. An Indian experience where he learned about colours and shapes, inspired him to create his first women's pret-à-porter collection in 1974, followed by menswear. Ferré specializes in men's fashion, bags, perfumes and eyewear.

TOP 10 THINGS TO BUY

Designer handbags from Prada

1 Handbags
Swoon over the designs from Prada and Bottega Veneta, or the less pricey label Coccinelle.

2 Designer Clothes
Monumentally important to the world of fashion, Milan is also home to some excellent discount clothing outlets.

3 Shoes
Italian footwear ranges from the practical to the outrageous.

4 Design Objects
Artisinal objects such as kettles, lighting systems and juicers with gorgeous designs are on sale throughout Italy.

5 Linens
Bassetti and Frette offer affordable as well as stylish linens.

6 Art and Antiques
Milan's art dealers offer a rich collection of period works, 19th-century oils and other affordable art.

7 Wine
Lombard wines are excellent *(see p65)*. Try the mighty Barolo, Barbaresco and Barbera red wines at the Piemonte.

8 Silk
Como has long been Italy's chief purveyor of finely spun silk fabrics. The sought-after silks are available to the public in factory warehouses around Como and in shops across Lombardy.

9 Books
A translation of Manzoni's local literary classic *I Promessi Sposi (see p46)* might be a more treasured souvenir than a sheaf of postcards or trinkets.

10 Jewellery
Seek out the bold creations of Donatella Pellini or the cutting-edge minimalism of Xenia.

Milan for Free

① Every First Sunday
www.beniculturali.it

Many of Italy's state-run museums and archaeological sites don't charge admission fees on the first Sunday of the month. Time your visit right and you could be seeing the Pinacoteca di Brera (see pp16–19) or the Castello Sforzesco museums (see pp20–21) absolutely free. At Lake Garda head to Sirmione for the Grotte di Catullo and Rocca Scaligera (see pp121–2).

Grotte di Catullo at Sirmione

② Hangar Bicocca
MAP S1 ■ Via Chiese 2 ■ Open 10am–10pm Thu–Sun ■ www.hangar bicocca.org

This vast converted factory building is now a centre for contemporary art, with exhibitions by artists from all over the world. Free guided tours and bicycle tours of the former industrial area of Bicocca are also available.

Evening visit to Castello Sforzesco

③ Studio Museo Francesco Messina
MAP L4 ■ Via San Sisto 4 ■ Open 10am–6pm Tue–Sun ■ www. fondazionemessina.it

This collection of 80 sculptures and other works by Francesco Messina, one of Italy's most talented 20th-century sculptors, is housed in a deconsecrated church.

④ Free Walking Tours
www.milanfreetour.com

Expert local guides lead half-day walking tours taking in most of central Milan's main sites. Available in English or Italian, they should be booked in advance. The same group offers personalized tours for a fee.

⑤ Street Art
Muri Liberi (free walls) is a city initiative making 100 walls in run-down areas of the city available to street artists. Some of the most intriguing are in an open-air museum called Out, located along Via Pontano.

⑥ Late Entry at Museums
There's free entry from 2pm every first and third Tuesday afternoon of the month and a few hours before closing time on other days at the Museo del Novecento (see p81), Museo di Storia Naturale (see p94), Gallerie d'Arte Moderna (see p92) and at the various museums within Castello Sforzesco (see pp20–21).

7 Casa Museo Boschi Di Stefano

MAP S2 ■ Via Giorgio Jan 15 ■ Open 10am–6pm Tue–Sun ■ www.fondazio neboschidistefano.it

Around 300 (out of of 2,000) works of outstanding 20th-century Italian art collected by Antonio Boschi and his wife, Marieda Di Stefano, are on show in the couple's former apartment.

8 Galleria Vittorio Emanuele II

This elegant arcade (see p42) has lavish frescoes and mosaics, including a bull image famous for the tradition of turning three times with a heel on its genitals for luck. Many of the historic shops and bars are museum pieces in themselves.

Galleria Vittorio Emanuele II mosaic

9 Museo Astronomico-Orto Botanico

MAP M2 ■ Palazzo Brera, Via Brera 28 ■ www.ortibotanici.unimi.it; www. brera.inaf.it

Both the astronomical observatory and the adjacent botanical gardens date from the 18th century and are now owned by the University of Milan. There's a fascinating display of astronomical equipment, whilst the gardens have fun activities for kids.

10 Window-Shopping

It costs absolutely nothing to window-shop the stores of Milan's Golden Quad (see p71) where some displays are like a museum of design. The monthly antiques market at Navigli (see pp28–9) offers a more vintage browsing experience.

TOP 10 BUDGET TIPS

Luscious market produce on sale

1 Low-cost, good quality food can easily be sourced at neighbourhood delis, bakeries and fruit and vegetable market stalls. Milan's leafy parks are great places for a picnic lunch.

2 Bars often charge for table service, and even more for a terrace table; standing at the bar for a coffee is generally a cheaper option.

3 A carafe of a restaurant's own house wine, served by the quarter, half or full litre, is an inexpensive alternative to a traditional bottle, and often as good.

4 Free access to (often quite lavish) buffets is frequently included in the price of a drink at early evening aperitivo time or Happy Hour.

5 Drinks and picnic food can be kept in hotel-room fridges; balconies are ideal for a relaxed meal or snack.

6 Empty plastic bottles can be filled with fresh water at public drinking fountains; potabile means drinkable.

7 British National Trust cardholders are entitled to free or discounted at FAI sites including Villa Necchi Campiglio (see p94) and Lake Como's Villa Balbianello (see p114).

8 The Tourist Museum Card and MilanoCard are among the city's various multi-day discount cards for museums and/or transport.

9 Over-65s and under-18s (or students with an ID card) can generally benefit from ticket reductions at museums, and discounted family tickets are also often available. Be sure to ask.

10 Fares for fast trains are often much cheaper if booked in advance, either online or at the station.

Festivals and Events

1 Carnival
Feb/Mar (ends the first Sat of Lent) ■ Call for information: 02-7740-4343

Carnevale is a combination of religious pomp, fancy-dress parade and Bacchanalian bash in Milan. Carnivals elsewhere end on Martedì Grasso ("Fat Tuesday"), but Archbishop St Ambrose decreed that in Milan it should go on until the Saturday. No wonder they made him a saint.

2 Fashion Week
Jan, Feb, Sep & June

Milan is invaded by models, buyers and media types four times a year who come to the city for fashion week. In mid-January and late June they come for the menswear collections, while February and September are for womenswear.

3 Milan Furniture Fair
Mid-Apr ■ Fieramilano Rho, Milan ■ 02-4997-1 ■ www.fiera milano.it

Hotels are fully booked when the Salone Internazionale del Mobile, or Milan Furniture Fair, takes the stage in mid-April. Be sure to book early if you want to be present for the six days when the entire city comes alive with exhibitions and events related to all the latest trends in furniture and interior design.

Model at Fashion Week

4 Palio di Legnano
Last Sun in May ■ www.paliodilegnano.it

Two years after the Lombard League trounced Barbarossa in 1176 (see p38), the town of Legnano began celebrating. They are still at it today, putting on a display of pageantry that ends with a horse race.

5 Festa dei Navigli
First Sun in Jun

Milan's trendy Navigli canal district (see pp28–9) celebrates the start of summer on the first Sunday in June by bursting into a street fair with artisan stalls and live music.

6 Ferragosto
15–31 Aug

The Feast of the Assumption, held on 15 August, is when most Italians head to the beach or lakes for a two-week holiday, and life in the city slows down. Mantua has a celebration of street artists, but Milan virtually shuts down. Only the restaurants and bars of the Navigli tend to stay open.

Chic seating, Milan Furniture Fair

⑦ Stresa Festival, Stresa
Late Aug–early Sep
■ www.stresafestival.eu

Lake Maggiore's gateway to the Borromean Islands *(see p109)* hosts five musical weeks of concerts in venues throughout the town and along the lake shores.

⑧ Grand Prix, Monza
Grand Prix: 2nd weekend in Sep ■ www.monzanet.it

The biggest Formula One race takes place in mid-September. At other times, you can still watch macho men driving cars at mind-boggling speeds from April through October.

Formula One Grand Prix at Monza

⑨ Stringed Instruments Festivals, Cremona
Late Sep–early Oct ■ Info: Fondazione Antonio Stradivari, Piazza S Omobono 3 ■ 0372-801-801 ■ www.museo delviolino.org

The home *(see p52)* of Amati and Stradivari celebrates luthiers and musicians in a series of festivals, concerts, exhibitions and international competitions.

⑩ Opera Season
Info: 02-7200-3744 ■ tickets: 02-860-775 ■ www.teatroallascala.org

Milan's La Scala *(see p82)* is the most important opera house in the world, and if you ever doubted that opera was high art, an evening at its 18th-century home will convince you beyond all doubt. The season opens on 7 December, the feast day of Milan's patron saint, Ambrose, and is a momentous occasion in the Milanese social calendar.

TOP 10 FOOD FESTIVALS

Bardolino's food and wine festival

1 Festa dell'Oliva, Torri del Benaco, Lake Garda
This annual festival, held in late January, includes visits to olive mills, tastings and live music in the village.

2 Salon du Chocolat, Milan
Europe's largest congress centre, Mi.Co, hosts this fair in February; initiatives include a chocolate fashion show.

3 Venerdì Gnocolar, Verona
Gnocchi are distributed to all in Piazza San Zeno at this colourful historic fair, held on the Friday before Lent.

4 Sagra del Pesce, Riva di Solto
Tasty Lake Iseo fish dishes are served at this festival, held each July on the western shore of the lake.

5 Tortellini e Dintorni, Valeggio sul Mincio
This event in early September focuses on Valeggio's exquisite tortellini.

6 Sagra Nazionale del Gorgonzola
The blue-veined cheese, from the town of the same name near Milan, is the tasty focus of this September fair.

7 Festival Franciacorta
Each September the top wine-making area near Lake Iseo celebrates with numerous wine-themed events.

8 Festa dell'Uva e del Vino Bardolino, Lake Garda
A lively historic festival in early autumn dedicated to the famous local wine, with food stalls, parades and music.

9 Festa del Riso, Carpiano
Fragrant risotto of all varieties is the focus of this October festival held at Carpiano, just south of Milan.

10 Festa del Torrone, Cremona
Cremona's sweet speciality *torrone*, or nougat, is celebrated each November.

Milan and the Lakes Area by Area

Varenna, a typically charming waterside village on Lake Como

🔟 Milan's Historic Centre

The Centro Storico of Milan is home to the cathedral, opera house, the magnificent royal palace, art-filled private mansions and busy pedestrian boulevards. This historic district was once the Roman city of Mediolanum, though its boundary walls vanished long ago. As well as splendid sights, the historic centre contains a grid of shopping streets around Via Montenapoleone known as the Quadrilatero d'Oro, or "Golden Rectangle", home to numerous top-name designer boutiques.

Pocket watch, Museo Pezzoli

MILAN'S HISTORIC CENTRE

- ① **Top 10 Sights**
  see pp81–3
- ① **Places to Eat**
  see p89
- ① **The Best of the Rest**
  see p84
- ① **Milanese Fashion Boutiques** see p85
- ① **Cafés, Bars and Clubs** see p88
- ① **Other Italian Designer Shops** see p86
- ① **Other High-End Shops** see p87

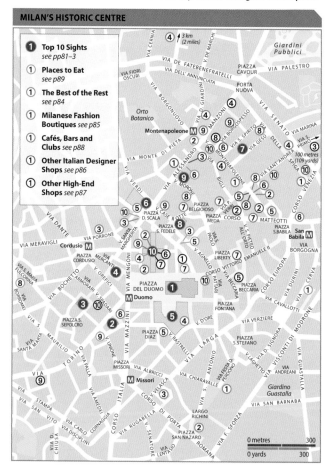

Magnificent interior of Milan's Duomo, with its Great Organ

1 Duomo
MAP M4

The great travel writer H V Morton (see p46) likened Milan's cathedral (see pp14–15) to a forest within the city, its thickets of columns and high vaulted ceilings providing the citizens with a spot of shade.

2 Santa Maria presso San Satiro
MAP L4 ▪ Via Speronari 3 ▪ Open 7:30–11:30am & 3:30–6:30pm Mon–Fri, 9am–noon & 3:30–7pm Sat & Sun

Renaissance architect Donato Bramante knew that the only way to squeeze the impression of a Greek cross into a space that only allowed room for a Latin cross was to concoct a layering of stuccoes, angled niches and frescoes behind the altar to give the illusion of a barrel-vaulted presbytery. Another notable feature here (see p41) is a *Pietà* group by the Lombard sculptor Agostino De' Fondutis.

3 Pinacoteca Ambrosiana
MAP L4

The art-loving Cardinal Federico Borromeo gave the city one of its greatest treasures (see p24) when he bequeathed his private collection of works by Leonardo, Titian, Caravaggio and others, including the original cartoon for Raphael's famed *School of Athens*.

4 Palazzo della Ragione
MAP L4 ▪ Piazza Mercanti ▪ Open for exhibitions ▪ Adm

Milan's 13th-century *broletto* (town hall) is a striking remnant of the Middle Ages (see p42).

5 Palazzo Reale
MAP M4 ▪ Piazza del Duomo 12 ▪ Adm ▪ www.palazzorealemilano.it ▪ Museo del Novecento: Adm; www.museodelnovecento.org

Once home to the Visconti and Sforza families, Milan's Neo-Classical Royal Palace was built under the aegis of Empress Maria Theresa in the 18th century and extended in 1939–56 with the Arengario, a towering pavilion on Piazza Duomo. This houses the Museo del Novecento, an impressive collection of 20th-century paintings and sculpture. Palazzo Reale is also open for exhibitions.

Arengario, Palazzo Reale

Interior of La Scala, viewed from one of its luxurious boxes

6 La Scala
MAP M3 ■ Piazza della Scala
■ www.teatroallascala.org

The world's greatest opera house
(see p62) was built in 1776–8 under
the Austrians. It boasts a sumptuous
interior, excellent acoustics and a
staggering list of premieres (see p47).
Half destroyed in World War II,
La Scala again became the toast
of the town in 1946, when Toscanini
presided over its gala reopening.

7 Museo Bagatti Valsecchi
MAP N3 ■ Via S Spirito 10/
Via Gesù 5 ■ Open 1–5:45pm Tue–
Sun ■ Adm ■ www.museobagatti
valsecchi.org

Two Milanese brothers created this
Neo-Renaissance palazzo in 1883–94.
They acquired as much as they could
in the way of tapestries, furnishings
and paintings from across Italy, and
what they could not obtain in the
original they hired Lombard crafts-
men to imitate. One room is copied

from Urbino's ducal seat, one from
the ducal palace in Mantua, another
is from a palazzo in Sondrio. The entire
effect is a mix of Romantic sensibil-
ities and Renaissance craftsmanship.

8 San Fedele
MAP M3 ■ Piazza S Fedele
■ Open 7am–1:15pm & 4:30–6pm
Mon–Fri

The single nave construction of this
1559 Jesuit temple would become
a blueprint for Lombard churches
built in the Counter-Reformation.
The interior preserves some fine
art, including Il Cerano's Vision of
St Ignatius and Campi's Four Saints
and Transfiguration. The sacristy is
lined by cabinets by Jesuit Daniele
Ferrari, who also carved the pulpit.

The ornate façade of San Fedele

MILANESE LUCK

The central floor mosaic in the Galleria
Vittorio Emanuele II sports the white-
cross-on-red of the House of Savoy
(representing Italy's newly crowned
king who lent the gallery his name
in 1868) and also a bull symbolizing
Milan. According to local tradition,
the Milanese ensure their good luck
by stomping and spinning on the
bull's testicles each time they pass.

⑨ Museo Poldi Pezzoli

MAP M3 ■ Via Manzoni 12
■ Open 10am–6pm Wed–Mon (last
adm 5:30pm) ■ Adm ■ www.museo
poldipezzoli.it

This *(see p45)* splendid private
collection was bequeathed to the
city by Gian Giacomo Poldi Pezzoli
in 1879. The masterpieces all date
from the last half of the 15th century,
including works by Bellini, Botticelli,
Pollaiolo, Piero della Francesca and
Mantegna. There are 18th-century
Venetian cityscapes by Canaletto and
Guardi, and the *Tapestry of the Hunt*
from Tabriz is celebrated. There is
also a collection of arms and armour,
clocks and scientific instruments.

Pollaiolo at Museo Poldi Pezzoli

⑩ Galleria Vittorio Emanuele II

MAP M3

Before modern shopping centres
and malls, there were *gallerie*
(see p42). These late 19th-century
high-class shopping arcades were
roofed by the newest architectural
technology of the age: steel-rein-
forced glass. Milan's Industrial
Age-cum-Neo-Classical example
connected Piazza del Duomo with
La Scala and was so successful it
spawned an Italy-wide trend *(see
pp85–7)*, with copycat *gallerie* popping
up in Naples, Genoa and Rome.

A DAY IN CENTRAL MILAN

▶ MORNING

Start at 10am by exploring
the collections of **Pinacoteca
Ambrosiana** *(see pp24–5)*.

Work your way south to Via Torino
and the jewelbox of a church,
Santa Maria presso San Satiro
(see p81), then walk north up Via
Torino until you reach the Piazza
del Duomo. Continue along the
piazza's western edge and divert
up Via Mercanti to see the raised
porticoes of **Palazzo della
Ragione** *(see p81)*. Now cross
the huge **Duomo** *(see pp14–15)*
square to enjoy the marvels of
Italy's second-largest cathedral.
Don't miss exploring its roof.

Join locals at **Luini** *(see p89)*
for mozzarella-filled doughballs,
then have a drink at **Zucca** *(see
p88)* at the entrance to **Galleria
Vittorio Emanuele II**, the grandest
shopping arcade in Italy.

AFTERNOON

Exit the arcade at Piazza della
Scala, flanked by the opera house
and **Palazzo Marino** *(see p42)*.
San Fedele is located behind the
latter. After seeing this, walk
northeast past the **Casa degli
Omenoni** *(see p84)*.

Turn left to visit the excellent
Museo Poldi Pezzoli, then
continue north on Via Manzoni,
admiring its palazzi until you
come to Milan's shopping street,
Via Montenapoleone *(see p71)*.

Shoppers will spend the rest of
the day here while the museum
hounds can take in the **Museo
Bagatti Valsecchi**. Both should
stop for drinks at **Cova** *(see p88)*.

See map on p80 ←

The Best of the Rest

 Ca' Granda
MAP M4–5 ▪ Via Festa del Perdono 5 ▪ Open 7:30am–7:30pm Mon–Fri ▪ 8am–noon Sat

This massive 15th-century building, originally a hospital, is now part of the University of Milan.

 San Nazaro Maggiore
MAP M5 ▪ Piazza S Nazaro in Brolo 5 ▪ Open 7:30am–noon & 3:30–6:30pm Mon–Fri, 8am–12:20pm & 3:30–7pm Sat & Sun

St Ambrose's fourth basilica grew in the 16th century, when Bramantino added the Cappella Trivulzio.

③ Torre Velasca
MAP M5 ▪ Piazza Velasca 5 ▪ No public access

This skyscraper (see p43) is a 1950s version of medieval tower design.

④ San Gottardo in Corte
MAP M4 ▪ Via Pecorari 2 ▪ Open 8am–noon & 2–6pm Mon–Fri, 2–4pm Sat, 8am–noon Sun

This church was founded in 1336 as a chapel for the Palazzo Reale.

⑤ Museo Teatrale alla Scala
MAP M3 ▪ Largo Ghiringhelli 1 ▪ Open 9am–5pm daily ▪ Adm ▪ www.teatroallascala.org

From scores to costumes, all things related to La Scala (see p82) can be found in this museum (see p44).

⑥ Basilica di San Babila
MAP N3 ▪ Piazza San Babila

The Neo-Romanesque façade provides an unusual contrast to the modern shopping area around it.

⑦ Casa degli Omenoni
MAP M3 ▪ Via Omenoni 3 ▪ No public access

Sculptor Leoni's 16th-century home has a magnificent façade flanked by a Liberty-style tower (see p43).

⑧ Casa del Manzoni
MAP M3 ▪ Via Morone 1 ▪ 02-8646-0403 ▪ Open Tue–Fri 10am–6pm & Sat 2–6pm ▪ Adm ▪ www.casadelmanzoni.it

Italy's greatest 19th-century writer Manzoni lived in this palazzo, which is now his museum (see p46).

⑨ Gallerie d'Italia
MAP M3 ▪ Piazza della Scala 6 ▪ 800-167-619 ▪ Open Tue–Sun ▪ Adm ▪ www.galleriaditalia.com

The Brentani and Anguissola Palaces house the private Gallerie d'Italia, which includes masterpieces from the 19th and 20th centuries.

⑩ Palazzo Morando – Costume Moda Immagine
MAP N3 ▪ Via Sant' Andrea 6 ▪ Open 9am–1pm & 2–5:30pm Tue–Sun ▪ Adm

In an elegant 18th-century town house, Milan's history is documented with art, artifacts and costumes.

Exhibits in the Museo Teatrale alla Scala

Milanese Fashion Boutiques

Versace window display

 Dolce & Gabbana
MAP N3 ■ Via Montenapoleone 4

A three-floor luxury retail boutique, with a fantastic interior in green marble, briar-wood and large mirrors.

6 Missoni
MAP N3 ■ Via Montenapoleone 8 (entrance Via Sant'Andrea)

This shop *(see p73)* is a riot of colourful, iconic patterned knit-wears from Ottavio and Rosita Missoni, who turned the fashion maxims of minimalism and basic black upside down.

7 Tom Ford
MAP M3 ■ Via Verri 3

Synonymous with the resurrection of Gucci in the early 1990s, and later of Yves Saint Laurent, American designer and film director Tom Ford continues to go from strength to strength. This sleek luxury boutique is his first retail outlet in Milan.

1 Gianni Versace
MAP N3 ■ Via Montenapoleone 11 & Versus at Via San Pietro all'Orto

Five floors, with the entire ground level dedicated to accessories. Versace *(see p72)* always manages to surprise.

2 Prada
MAP M3 ■ Galleria Vittorio Emanuele II & Via Montenapoleone 8

Central outlets of the firm *(see p72)* that transformed a handbag business into the high-fashion success story of the 1990s.

Prada handbag

3 Trussardi
MAP N3 ■ Piazza della Scala 5

Founded in 1911, this *(see p72)* glove-making firm is now one of the top designers of supple leather goods and ready-to-wear fashions.

4 Moschino
MAP N3 ■ Via Sant'Andrea 12 & Via V. Capelli 1

Everything from *prêt-à-porter* to jeans from the fashion iconoclast can be found at Moschino *(see p73)*.

8 Krizia
MAP N2 ■ Via della Spiga 23

This *(see p73)* Bergamo native delights in contrary fashions: colourful when black is in, miniskirts when conservative hem-lines are the rage.

9 Giorgio Armani
MAP M2 ■ Via Manzoni 31

The first mega-department store devoted to just one fashion house – that of Milan's very own fashion guru, Armani *(see p72)*. There's a chic café here as well.

10 Ermenegildo Zegna
MAP M2 ■ Via Montenapoleone 27

Detailed perfection in menswear is the watchword in the Ermenegildo Zegna store *(see p72)*, which offers the very best in fabrics and tailoring, plus stylish casual wear.

See map on p80

Other Italian Designer Shops

Frette's showroom, replete with gorgeous linens

1 Frette
MAP M3 ▪ Via Manzoni 11

Among the highest-quality linens in all of Italy: everything from towels to pyjamas to sheets and pillowcases.

2 Ferragamo
MAP N3 ▪ Via Montenapoleone 3 (women's) and 20 (men's)

The Florentine cobbler Salvatore Ferragamo raised footwear to a modern art form when he shod Hollywood stars from Greta Garbo to Sophia Loren. Check out the sales in January and July.

3 Alessi
MAP N3
▪ Via Manzoni 14/16

You'll find kettles, silverware settings and other quirky style items crafted by the top names in international industrial design.

4 Mario Buccellati
MAP N3 ▪ Via Montenapoleone 23

Alessi kitchenware

Since 1919, no two Buccellati jewels have been the same: each gemstone and silver filigree setting is hand-crafted by skilled artisans.

5 Etro
MAP N3 ▪ Via Montenapoleone 5 (fragrances: Via Verri/corner Via Bigli)

Etro's trademark paisley and Pegasus icons abound on silk, cashmere and the finest wools.

6 Valentino
MAP N3 ▪ Via Montenapoleone 20

New York's Metropolitan Museum once mounted a show of Valentino's artistic clothing. Everything is classy, chic and very desirable.

7 Max Mara
MAP N3 ▪ Corso Vittorio Emanuele II

After more than 50 years at the top of their class in womenswear, the Maramotti family's *prêt-à-porter* fashions are more vibrant and wearable than ever.

8 Gucci
MAP N3 ▪ Via Montenapoleone 5 (accessories & café: Galleria Vittorio Emanuele II)

The mating "G"s that once decorated the leather goods of this firm, founded by a Florentine saddlemaker, are a thing of the past, but the quality is still top-notch.

9 Versace Home
MAP M2 ▪ Via Borgospesso 15a

Occupying half the block, this elegant store offers a tempting array of the Versace take on home furnishings.

10 Gio Moretti
MAP N2 ▪ Via della Spiga 4

This boutique offers Giovina Moretti's selection of the best of the season's top fashion and accessories.

Other High-End Shops

DoDo
MAP M4 ■ La Rinascente, Piazza Duomo

This Milanese jeweller specializes in gold charms in the shape of animals and flowers. Part of their profits go to support Italian wildlife.

Cravatterie Nazionali
MAP N3 ■ Via San Pietro all'Orto 17

A vast selection of ties by Italy's top designers can be found here.

Matia's Fashion Outlet
MAP N2 ■ Corso Venezia 37

This store stocks clothing, footwear and accessories from famous brands. Collections from previous seasons can be found in the sale section and discounts are available for the new season's collections.

Dmag
MAP N3 ■ Via Manzoni 44

In the heart of high fashion sits a cut-price designer outlet, with Fendi scarves, Armani slacks, Prada sweaters and Helmut Lang suits among the bargains waiting to be grabbed. Check daily for bargains on the constantly rotating racks.

Excelsior Milano
MAP M4 ■ Galleria del Corso 4

This elegant shopping centre hosts big brands such as Tiffany. Fashion, beauty and accessories are to be found upstairs, while downstairs there is a trendy food store selling quality Italian delicacies.

LaFeltrinelli
MAP M3 ■ Galleria Vittorio Emanuele II

Milan's huge subterranean branch of Italy's premiere chain of books, DVDs, music and a vast catalogue of CDs and vinyls by Ricordi.

Bocca
MAP M3 ■ Galleria Vittorio Emanuele II

This longtime resident of the Galleria Vittorio Emanuele II is the place to find beautifully illustrated Italian exhibition catalogues, past and present as a gift or for your own collection.

Vetrerie di Empoli
MAP M2 ■ Via Montenapoleone 22

A glassware boutique selling elegant, high-quality products within a number of themed rooms.

Città del Sole
MAP L4 ■ Via Torino 57

This is Italy's main chain store for quality educational toys and games. The bright, welcoming store is packed with fun finds.

A board game for kids at Città del Sole

Gastronomia Peck
MAP L4 ■ Via Spadari 9

Superlative Milanese grocers since 1883, with three vast floors of meats, cheeses, vegetables, breads, wines and other delicacies. Its pricey restaurant, Cracco (see p89), is nearby.

Cold counter at Gastronomia Peck

See map on p80

Cafés, Bars and Clubs

Taking a break from shopping at the chic D&G Bar Martini

① D&G Bar Martini
MAP N3 ■ Corso Venezia 15
■ www.dolcegabbana.it

Elegance and style pervade this bar-bistro in the heart of the fashion district, as one would expect from two such glamorous names.

② Zucca (Caffè Miani)
MAP M3 ■ Galleria Vittorio Emanuele II & Piazza Duomo 21
■ www.camparino.it

A gorgeous Liberty-style café, with views of the Duomo, once owned by the Campari family (see p66).

③ Le Banque
MAP L3 ■ Via Porrone 6
■ 02-8699-6565 ■ www.lebanque.it

This business people's lunch spot transforms into a yuppie disco – one of the few in central Milan – with live music after 11pm; dress well.

④ Armani Privé
MAP M3 ■ Via Pisoni
■ 02-7231-8655 ■ Closed Mon, Tue, Sun & Jun–Aug

This classy nightclub has Japanese-inspired interiors and a strict door policy. Obligatory one drink minimum.

⑤ Nepentha
MAP M4 ■ Piazza Diaz 1

Perennial Milan discotheque just one block south of the Duomo, where the chic set come to dine and then dance the night away.

⑥ Princi
MAP L4 ■ Via Speronari 6
■ 02-874-797

The various branches of Milan's best bakery all feature traditional wood-fired ovens and appealing stone and wood decor. Their range of baked goods is mouth watering.

⑦ Sant'Ambroeus
MAP N3 ■ Corso Matteotti 7
■ www.santambroeusmilano.com

This historic café and tearoom is also known for making some of the best chocolates in Italy (see p67).

⑧ Cova
MAP N3 ■ Via Montenapoleone 8 ■ www.pasticceriacova.com

Nestling in the heart of Milan's chic boutique district since 1817, Cova offers excellent coffee and delicious pastries (see p66).

⑨ Savini
MAP M3 ■ Galleria Vittorio Emanuele II ■ 02-7200-3433

This long-established eatery has a café and *pasticceria* as well as an excellent restaurant.

⑩ Signorvino
MAP M3 ■ Piazza Duomo

The Milan branch of this collection of wine bars stands in a prime position on Piazza Duomo, just to the left of the city's iconic cathedral. Come for advice on wines to buy or enjoy here.

Places to Eat

PRICE CATEGORIES

For a three-course meal for one with half a bottle of wine (or equivalent meal), taxes and extra charges.

€ under €35 ■ €€ €35–60 ■ €€€ over €60

1 Trattoria da Pino
MAP N4 ■ Via Cerva 14
■ 02-7600-0532 ■ Closed D & Sun
■ No credit cards ■ €

An *osteria* (see p68) serving simple, traditional dishes in a room behind the street-front bar, using fresh seasonal ingredients.

2 Don Carlos at the Grand Hotel et de Milan
MAP M2 ■ Via Manzoni 29 ■ 02-7231-4640 ■ Closed L & Aug ■ €€€

Open for dinner only, (see p69) and perfect for a post-opera meal.

3 Al Cantinone
MAP M3 ■ Via Agnello 19
■ 02-863-015 ■ Closed 1 week
Aug ■ €€€

This Lombard–Tuscan hybrid is set in two classically elegant rooms.

4 Ristorante Cracco
MAP M3 ■ Corso Vittorio
Emanuele II ■ 02-876-774 ■ Closed
Sun, Aug & Christmas ■ €€€

Minimalist chic modern dining, (see p68) complete with liveried doorman and astronomic prices.

Chefs at work at Ristorante Cracco

5 Luini
MAP M3 ■ Via S Radegonda 16
■ 02-8646-1917 ■ Closed Sun & Mon
■ No credit cards ■ €

Luini may serve only *panzerotti* (pockets of stuffed dough), but locals flock here to eat them.

6 Don Lisander
MAP M2 ■ Via Manzoni 12a
■ 02-7602-0130 ■ €€€

Creative regional, Tuscan and French cuisines in palatial surroundings.

Charmingly elegant Don Lisander

7 Rinascente Food Court
MAP M3 ■ Piazza del Duomo
■ 02-885-2471 ■ €€

Enjoy great views as well as no fewer than seven options to choose from.

8 Hostaria Borromei
MAP L4 ■ Via Borromei 4
■ 02-8645-3760 ■ Closed Sat &
Sun L ■ €€€

Milanese and Italian dishes made using seasonal ingredients are key at Hostaria Borromei.

9 La Vecchia Latteria
MAP L4 ■ Via dell'Unione 6
■ 02-874-401 ■ Closed Sun ■ €€

This welcoming, lunch-only spot serves a range of tasty vegetarian dishes and luscious desserts.

10 Trussardi alla Scala
MAP M3 ■ Piazza della Scala 5
■ 02-8068-8264 ■ Closed Sun ■ €€€

Creative cuisine and a terrific wine list make for a fine dining experience.

See map on p80 ←

🔟 Northern Milan

Etruscan cinerary urn in the Civico Museo Archeologico

Leonardo da Vinci's world-famous fresco, the city's best parks and great museums are the highlights of this area. Three museums trace art from the medieval period (at the Castello Sforzesco) through the golden era of the Renaissance (at the Brera) to Modernism (at the Villa Belgiojoso Bonaparte). Aside from the cultural hightlights, this part of town is also a great place for bargain shoppers, from warehouses lining the street south of the central railway station to the huge shopping boulevard of Corso Buenos Aires.

NORTHERN MILAN

Certosa di Garegnano frescoes

1 Certosa di Garegnano
MAP R2 ▪ Via Garegnano 28
▪ Open 8am–noon & 3:30–5:30pm daily

The 14th-century Carthusian abbey has largely vanished under Milan's suburbs, but its church of Santa Maria Assunta survives. It has a fine late Renaissance façade, and the interior was beautifully frescoed by Daniele Crespi in 1629 with stories of the Carthusian order.

2 San Simpliciano
MAP L2 ▪ Piazza S Simpliciano 7 ▪ Open 9am–noon & 2:15–7pm Mon–Fri, 9:30am–7pm Sat & Sun

One of four great basilicas built by St Ambrose in the 4th century (and finished by its namesake in 401) is popularly dedicated to the Anaunia Martyrs. The external walls are mostly original; the interior was renovated in the 11th and 12th centuries, and frescoed with a rainbow of angels and a *Coronation of the Virgin* by Bergognone in 1515. There are also patches of a late 14th-century fresco still visible in a chapel off the choir.

3 Castello Sforzesco
MAP K2

Milan's vast fortress-castle complex *(see pp20–21)* squats at the north-west corner of the historic centre. It is an intriguing combination of oversized courtyards, lithe towers and medieval nooks and crannies.

Castello Sforzesco

THE ANAUNIA MARTYRS

Byzantine missionaries, Sisino, Martirio and Alessandro, were sent by St Ambrose to Bishop Vigilio of Trent. Vigilio assigned them to convert pagans of the Trentino Alpine valleys, but locals of the Anaunia region refused, and stoned the missionaries to death in 397, making them the region's first church martyrs.

4 Parco Sempione

MAP K2 ■ Piazza Sempione ■ Park: open 6:30am–1 hour past sunset daily; Aquarium: open 9am–5:30pm Tue–Sun ■ www.acquariocivicomilano.eu

Milan's largest park started life as 15th-century ducal gardens, though its layout dates from the late 19th century. An aquarium is housed in a 1906 Liberty-style structure, and the triumphal Arco della Pace *(see p94)* is also located in the park.

5 Pinacoteca di Brera

MAP M2

In Northern Italy, this gallery *(see pp16–19)* is second only to Venice's Accademia (though the Brera has more variety). Since Napoleon inaugurated the collection, it has been housed in the Jesuits' Palazzo di Brera. It includes works by Piero della Francesca, Raphael, Bellini, Mantegna and Caravaggio.

Dome of Santa Maria delle Grazie

6 Santa Maria delle Grazie

MAP J3 ■ Piazza S Maria delle Grazie ■ Church: open 7am–noon & 3–7pm Mon–Sat, 7:30am–12:15pm & 3:30–8:15pm Sun

Leonardo's extraordinary fresco, *The Last Supper (see pp12–13)*, adorns a wall of the convent refectory and is the chief attraction. Other features include a magnificent Renaissance tribune, possibly designed by Bramante, who did the cloister and probably the main portal, as well.

7 Galleria d'Arte Moderna – Villa Belgiojoso Bonaparte

MAP N2 ■ Via Palestro 16 ■ Open 9am–5:30pm Tue–Sun (last adm 4:30pm) ■ Adm ■ www.gam-milano.com

Milan's Neo-Classical (1790) "Royal Villa" housed Napoleon in 1802 and Marshal Radetzky until 1858. It is now an art gallery *(see p44)*, with works by Romantic master Hayez; Neo-Classical sculptor Canova, whose bust of Napoleon sits in the stairwell; Morandi, Corot, Gauguin, van Gogh and Picasso. The villa is set in lovely English-style gardens.

Crivelli triptych in the Pinacoteca di Brera

⑧ Civico Museo Archeologico

MAP K3 ■ Corso Magenta 15 ■ Open 9am–5:30pm Tue–Sun ■ Adm

A few pieces in an otherwise modest collection make this worth a stop. The best are the 4th-century glass Trivulzio Cup and a stunning silver platter from the same period with reliefs of the deities of earth, sky, water and the zodiac. An exhibition is devoted to urban planning and architecture in Milan from the 1st to the 4th century AD. In the 15th-century cloisters, damaged by bombs during World War II, are a pair of brick towers from the Imperial-era city.

Cimitero Monumentale tombs

⑨ Cimitero Monumentale

MAP R2 ■ Piazza Cimitero Monumentale ■ Open 9:30am–5pm Tue–Sun

Milan's vast 19th-century cemetery is filled with Art Nouveau tombs of Milan's top families – a free map shows where such notables as Arturo Toscanini rest. There's a pantheonic monument and a memorial to the Jews deported by the Nazis.

⑩ San Maurizio al Monastero Maggiore

MAP K3 ■ Corso Magenta 15 ■ Open 9:30am–5:30pm Tue–Sun

The sober grey 16th-century façade conceals a magnificent interior with remarkable cycles of Renaissance frescoes. The most striking, by Bernardino Luini, adorn the partition which divides the public area from the section where cloistered nuns once lived. The church's organ, which dates back to 1554, is regularly used for concerts.

TOURING THE GREAT MUSEUMS OF NORTHERN MILAN

▶ MORNING

Start your day off early at the **Santa Maria delle Grazie**. To entirely appreciate the famous painting *The Last Supper (see pp12–13)*, make advance reservations for early admission. Then head to **Castello Sforzesco** *(see p91)* and work your way up to **San Simpliciano** *(see p91)* then make your way southeast to the church of **San Marco** *(see p94)*. Continue up Via San Marco to have lunch at **Latteria San Marco** *(see p97)*, one of Milan's great simple *trattorie*, then head back down the same street, cross Via Pontaccio, and prepare to plunge into the vast art collections of the **Pinacoteca di Brera**.

AFTERNOON

If you're an art fan, you'll probably spend the rest of the afternoon at the Pinacoteca, ready for a *passeggiata* (stroll) and dinner when you emerge near closing time. But if it doesn't grab you, knock off after 90 minutes and you'll have time to continue east along Via Fatebenefratelli to Piazza Cavour. From Piazza Cavour, go down Via Palestro to **Villa Belgiojoso Bonaparte**, then call in at the **Museo di Storia Naturale** *(see p94)* to view dinosaur skeletons and wonderfully outdated 19th-century dioramas. Stroll over to Via Mozart to see how the sophisticated Milanese industrialist class lived at **Villa Necchi Campiglio** *(see p94)*, with its important art collections. Finally, to round off a full and busy day, head to **Panino Giusto** *(Via Marcello Malpighi 3)* for your dinner reservations.

See map on pp90–91

The Best of the Rest

1 Museo del Risorgimento
MAP M2 ▪ Via Borgonuovo 23 ▪ Open 9am–1pm & 2–5:30pm Tue–Sun

Find out about the heroes of Italy's 19th-century *risorgimento* (unification) movement at this museum.

2 San Siro (Stadio Meazza)
MAP R2 ▪ Via Piccolomini 5 ▪ Open for matches ▪ Museum: Gate 14; Mon–Sat ▪ Adm

"The Scala of football", which is shared by rivals Inter and AC Milan.

3 Villa Necchi Campiglio
MAP P3 ▪ Via Mozart 14 ▪ Open 10am–6pm Wed–Sun ▪ Adm

This is an elegant 1930s villa *(see p43)* with important paintings by masters such as Canaletto and Tiepolo.

4 Museo di Storia Naturale
MAP P2 ▪ Corso Venezia 55 ▪ Open 9am–5:30pm Tue–Sun

Dinosaurs and taxidermied creatures are among the exhibits at the natural history museum.

5 Palazzo Litta
MAP K3 ▪ Corso Magenta 24 ▪ Open for exhibitions

Italy's state railway headquarters and a theatre occupy the expansive Rococo palazzo near *The Last Supper*.

6 Trienniale Design Museum
MAP J2 ▪ Viale Alemagna 6 ▪ Open 10:30am–8:30pm Tue–Sun ▪ Adm ▪ www.triennale.org

Design in all its forms, including inventive everyday items, is on display at this museum *(see p42)* on the edge of Parco Sempione. Annual thematic displays begin each spring.

7 Arco della Pace
MAP J1 ▪ Piazza Sempione

Luigi Cagnola built this magnificent triumphal arch in 1807 for Napoleon to pass through when visiting Milan.

It didn't get finished quite in time and was inaugurated instead by a bemused Habsburg emperor.

8 Piazza Gae Aulenti
MAP R2

Named after the architect of the Musée d'Orsay in Paris, this modern piazza offers a range of shops and entertainment venues. It is a great place to grab a bite to eat or wander around the shops.

9 Ippodromo
MAP R2 ▪ Via Piccolomini 2 ▪ Open 9:30am–6pm daily

In 1999, Milan's horse track became home to a bronze horse cast by an American foundation determined to bring to fruition Leonardo da Vinci's oft-sketched equine tribute to Lodovico "Il Moro" Sforza *(see p39)*.

10 San Marco
MAP N2 ▪ Piazza S Marco 2 ▪ Open 7am–noon & 4–7pm daily

Very little is left of the 1254 church, dedicated to St Mark in thanks for Venice's aid in defeating Barbarossa *(see p38)*, but some 13th- and 15th-century frescoes remain on show.

Fragments of fresco in San Marco

Shops

Stylish display of items for the home at Post-Design

1 Post-Design
MAP L1 ■ **Largo Treves 5**

This chic store is a purveyor of the whimsical, stunning design objects produced by Milan's Memphis group, founded in 1981 by Ettore Sottsass and other young designers.

2 10 Corso Como
MAP L2 ■ **Corso Como 10**
■ **www.10corsocomo.com**

While her sister served as editor of Italian *Vogue*, Carla Sozzani opened this boutique *(see p70)* of expensive, eminently fashionable luxury labels on everything from clothes and accessories to books and kitchenware.

3 Surplus
MAP L1 ■ **Corso Garibaldi 7**

If you feel some fashions just never go out of style, visit Milan's top shop for second-hand and reproduction vintage couture since 1979.

4 Cotti
MAP L1 ■ **Via Solferino 42**
■ **www.enotecacotti.it**

Nearly 1,500 Italian wines, *grappas* (grape-based brandies) and other spirits are stuffed into this gourmet foods shop, established in 1952.

5 Emporio Isola
MAP R2 ■ **Via Prina 11**

This is a discount outlet for noted clothing firms. Products are high quality and a wide range of styles, varying from elegant to pure chic, are available. Many bargains are on offer.

6 Dolce & Gabbana
MAP P2 ■ **Corso Venezia 15**

Housed in an old historical mansion, this ultra-chic men's apparel store includes a bar, restaurant, barber's shop and grooming centre.

7 Boggi
MAP P1 ■ **Corso Buenos Aires 1**

Boggi has been dressing the Milanese for years, providing its discerning with classy clothing and footwear at reasonable prices.

8 Furla
MAP P1 ■ **Corso Buenos Aires/ corner Via Omboni**

Located towards the Porta Venezia end of this very long shopping street, Furla provides a constant flow of fashion-forward ideas in handbags.

9 Vestistock
MAP S2 ■ **Via Ramazzini 11**

This historic outlet stocks a vast chic collection of clothing and accessories from famous brands.

10 Rufus
MAP S2 ■ **Via Vitruvio 35**

You'll find great discounts on designer shoes here, with some top names coming in at under €90 a pair.

See map on pp90–91

Cafés, Bars and Clubs

1 Pasticceria Marchesi
MAP K3 ▪ Via Santa Maria alla Porta 11a ▪ 02-862-770

This (see p67) is a delightfully old-world café and chocolatier not far from The Last Supper.

2 Triennale DesignCafé
MAP J2 ▪ Milan Triennale, Viale Alemagna ▪ 02-8754-41 ▪ Closed Mon

Masterminded by chef Carlo Cracco, whose eponymous restaurant (see p68) has two Michelin stars, this (see p94) café-restaurant with splendid views of Parco Sempione is a great place for a light lunch.

3 Just Cavalli Caffè
MAP J2 ▪ Between Via Shakespeare and Via Cameons, Parco Sempione

If Roberto Cavalli's in-your-face approach to fashion appeals to you, you will love this lively café, with its leopard-skin-patterned sofas. There is another Cavalli café in the store in Via della Spiga.

4 Bar Radetzky
MAP L1 ▪ Largo La Foppa 5

This minimalist café has been around for many years, good for a quick espresso in the morning and an aperitivo in the evening.

5 Bar Bianco
MAP K2 ▪ Viale Ibsen, Parco Sempione ▪ 02-8699-2026

A summer-only venue, this bar in the park is open till midnight, with the clientele switching from mothers and children to the city's trendiest out for dinner and cocktails.

6 Alcatraz
MAP L1 ▪ Via Valtellina 25 ▪ 02-6901-6352 ▪ Closed Jun–Sep

Milan's biggest club (see p62), Alcatraz stages top bands visiting Milan.

7 Hollywood
MAP L2 ▪ Corso Como 15 ▪ 338-505-5761 ▪ Closed Mon

Fashion models and designers still claim Hollywood (see p63) as theirs.

8 Bar Jamaica
MAP L2 ▪ Via Brera 32 ▪ 02-876-723

One of the most famous places, Bar Jamaica (see p66) preserves the history of the city. The carbonara is the best you can try in Milan.

9 Bar Magenta, Milan
MAP K3 ▪ Via Carducci 13 at Corso Magenta

This historic café (see p66) is ideal to experience the local scene. Grab a light lunch snack or a beer in the evening. Live music on Thursdays.

10 Blue Note
MAP R2 ▪ Via Borsieri 37 ▪ 02-6901-6888 ▪ Closed Oct–Mar: Mon, Jun–Aug

This famous club (see p63) gives music lovers the chance to listen to some of the greatest jazz talents live.

Live music at Blue Note

Places to Eat

Da Abele's welcoming dining room

1 Da Abele
MAP R2 ■ Via Temperanza 5 ■ 02-261-3855 ■ Closed L & Mon ■ €€

Perfect for dinner if you love risotto, with three choices that change daily. Slightly off the beaten track and popular with locals.

2 Joia
MAP P1 ■ Via P Castaldi 18 ■ 02-204-9244 ■ Closed Sun, Aug & Christmas ■ €€€

Milan's premier vegetarian restaurant serves brilliant meals even a sworn carnivore will love (see p68).

3 Pizzeria Grand'Italia
MAP L1 ■ Via Palermo 5 ■ 02-877-759 ■ €

Enjoy a slice of some of the best pizza in town at this popular pizzeria.

4 Ristorante Berton
MAP N1 ■ Via Mike Bongiorno 13 ■ 02-6707-5801 ■ Closed Sun & Mon L ■ €€€

Run by one of Italy's top chefs, Berton serves amazing food in a refined modern setting. For an even more memorable experience book the special table in the kitchen.

5 Latteria San Marco
MAP M1 ■ Via San Marco 24 ■ 02-659- 7653 ■ Closed Sat & Sun ■ No credit cards ■ €€

This Brera district trattoria has become so famous you must join the queue early to enjoy the simple Milanese fare.

6 Dhaba
MAP N1 ■ Via P Castaldi 22 ■ 02-201-315 ■ €€

Try one of Milan's oldest Indian restaurants for excellent-value tandoori and curries.

7 Tipica Osteria Pugliese
MAP P1 ■ Via Tadino 5 ■ 02-2952-2574 ■ Closed Mon ■ €€

Friendly place with simple, hearty fare from Apulia in southern Italy.

8 Ratanà
MAP S2 ■ Via Gaetano de Castillia 28 ■ 02-8712-8855 ■ €€

Tasting plate, Joia

Set in a former railway building, Ratanà serves a great choice of local dishes, including *Mondeghili* meatballs.

9 Trattoria Alla Cucina delle Langhe
MAP L1 ■ Corso Como 6 ■ 02-6554-279 ■ Closed 3 weeks Aug ■ €€€

This long-established restaurant serves Piedmontese and Lombard classics on its main floor and more informal fare upstairs.

10 Antica Trattoria della Pesa
MAP L1 ■ Viale Pasubio 10 ■ 02-655-5741 ■ Closed Sun ■ €€

A historic restaurant, dating from 1880, serving traditional Milanese fare in a charming period setting.

See map on pp90–91

TOP 10 Southern Milan

The city south of the historic core is dominated by the majority of Milan's most impressive churches: ancient Sant'Ambrogio and majestic San Lorenzo Maggiore; Sant'Eustorgio, with its remarkable carvings and paintings; the Renaissance piles of Santa Maria della Passione and Santa Maria presso San Celso; and the quirky 18th-century cloverleaf of La Besana. There's also the fantastic Science and Technology Museum, housed in a former convent; within its broad scope, the museum pays homage to Leonardo da Vinci's oft-overlooked scientific genius with an excellent display of his technical drawings and models. Further to the south stretch the Navigli canals, once a centre of Milanese commerce and now host to the city's liveliest nightlife and dining scene.

Statue of Constantine at San Lorenzo Maggiore

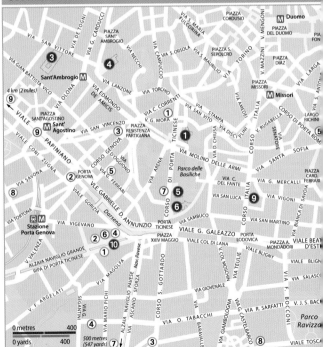

SOUTHERN MILAN

Mosaics in San Lorenzo Maggiore

1 San Lorenzo Maggiore

MAP L5 ■ Corso di Porta Ticinese 39; open 7:30am–6:30pm Mon, Fri & Sat, 12:30–2:30pm Tue–Thu, 9am–7pm Sun ■ Chapel: open 9am–6:30pm daily; adm ■ www.sanlorenzomaggiore.com

A free-standing row of 16 Corinthian columns – once part of a 2nd-century temple – sets San Lorenzo's *(see p40)* frontal piazza off from the road. The vast interior of the church was built on a circular plan, with a ring-shaped ambulatory and raised women's gallery, which often marked such early churches. The chapel has 4th-century mosaics, a 3rd-century sarcophagus and a Roman portal.

2 Santa Maria della Passione

MAP P3 ■ Via Bellini 2 ■ Open 7:30am–noon & 3:30–6:15pm Mon–Fri, 9am–12:30pm & 3:30–6:30pm Sat & Sun

This modest Greek-cross church of 1486–1530 was elongated with a massive nave and deep chapel niches in 1573 to make it the second largest church in Milan. Its interior is dominated by the work of Daniele Crespi: a portrait of San Carlo in the first chapel on the left, most of the Passion series below the cupola at the crossing and the organ doors.

3 Museo Nazionale della Scienza e della Tecnologia – Leonardo da Vinci

MAP J4 ■ Via San Vittore 21 ■ Open 9:30am–4:30pm Tue–Fri, 9:30am–6pm Sat & Sun ■ Adm ■ www.museoscienza.org

The National Science and Technology museum's *(see p44)* subtitle refers to the wooden scale models of Leonardo's inventions, which fill the main hall. Also worth seeing are the telecommunications work of Marconi, plus displays on physics, cinematography and electricity and the Enrico Toti submarine.

Museo Nazionale della Scienza

Sant'Ambrogio's handsome cloistered atrium

4 Sant'Ambrogio
MAP K4

Second only to the Duomo among Milan's great churches (and, to many, more beautiful), this 4th-century basilica (*see pp26–7*), has a cloistered entryway, Paleochristian mosaics, medieval carvings and Renaissance frescoes.

5 Museo Diocesano
MAP K5 ■ Corso di Porta Ticinese 95 ■ Open 10am–6pm Tue–Sun ■ Adm ■ www.museodiocesano.it

This museum houses important works from churches across Milan and Lombardy. In addition to numerous small panels by the 14th- and early 15th-century post-Giotto Gothic schools of central Italy, it holds 17th-century Flemish tapestries and some fine altarpieces. Among these are Hayez's *Crucifixion with Mary Magdalene* and Tintoretto's *Christ and the Adulterer*.

Altarpiece, Museo Diocesano

6 Sant'Eustorgio
MAP K6 ■ Piazza S Eustorgio; open 7:30am–noon & 3:30–6:30pm daily ■ Museum: open 10am–6pm

The chapels (*see p41*) opening off the right side of this ancient church were added between the 11th and 13th centuries, and frescoed in the 1300s and 1400s – Bergognone provided the triptych in the first one. The immense Arc of St Peter Martyr in the magnificent Portinari Chapel was carved by Balduccio.

7 Abbazia di Chiaravalle
MAP S3 ■ Via S Arialdo 102 ■ Open 9am–noon & 2:30–5pm Tue–Sat, 2:30–5pm Sun ■ www.monastero chiaravalle.it

A countryside abbey (*see p58*) now surrounded by suburban Milan, Chiaravalle has survived the centuries since its construction between 1172 and 1221. Its Romanesque architecture is enhanced by 15th- and 16th-century murals and a Luini *Madonna with Child* in the right transept.

8 Rotonda di Via Besana
MAP P5 ■ Via Besana 12 ■ Open 10am–7pm Sat, Sun & hols, 5–6:30pm Tue–Fri ■ Adm ■ www.muba.it

This Greek-cross church, dating from 1713, houses the MUBA children's museum (*see p60*). It is surrounded by a small green park bounded by a lovely rosette-shaped cloister.

⑨ Santa Maria presso San Celso

MAP L6 ■ Corso Italia 37 ■ Open 7am–noon & 4–6:30pm daily

The word *"presso"* reflecting its proximity to the Romanesque San Celso, this Renaissance church shot up with remarkable speed between 1493 and 1506. Its most alluring aspect is the cloister-like court before the entrance, designed by Cesare Cesarino and considered one of the best examples of early 16th-century architecture in Milan.

Canal cruiser in the Navigli district

⑩ Navigli

MAP K6

Milan needed a port, so in the 12th century, the Naviglio Grande – a 50-km (30-mile) canal linking the city to Lake Maggiore – was created. The Naviglio Pavese (that connects Milan to Pavia) was added at the end of the 14th century. Now, the Navigli district *(see pp28–9)* is Milan's liveliest neighbourhood. Its old warehouses contain chic apartments and its towpaths are lined with restaurants, bars and shops. It even stays open during the dog days of August *(see p76)*.

CANAL CRUISES

The tourist office sponsors twice-daily Navigli cruises *(book ahead; check www. naviglilombardi.it)* with an audio guide to tell the story of these canals. On Saturdays this is a Cultural Excursion and on Sundays a Nature Tour, both going further with buses. Tours last about 4 hours.

A DAY IN SOUTHERN MILAN

▶ MORNING

The influence of the Renaissance genius pervades the city of Milan. Begin your day at the Sant'Ambrogio metro stop, then turn down Via GioSué Carducci to Via San Vittore (you'll see across the street the Pusterla di S Ambrogio, a remnant of the medieval city gates). Turn left for the **Museo della Scienza e della Tecnologica** *(see p99)* to explore Leonardo's inventions and wooden scale models.

Make your way to **Sant'Ambrogio** to explore the museum, located above the portico, which has tapestries and paintings related to the church's history. Continue along Via Lanzone Maggiore to visit the basilica of **San Lorenzo Maggiore** *(see p99)*, which houses a vast collection of Roman and early Christian artifacts.

AFTERNOON

Make a detour for lunch at **Orto – Erbe e Cucina** *(see p103)* and then make your way back to **Museo Diocesano** to peruse works such as Tintoretto's Christ and the Adulterer or Ambrosian artworks dating from 4th to 21st centuries.

Nearby, relax with a spot of shopping at **Special Milano** *(see p102)*, in one of the most hip parts of town, where sneakers from all major brands can be found. Head south to **Sant'Eustorgio** for Cappella Portinari to be amid history. The atmospheric **Navigli** district nearby is the perfect setting for a meal at **El Brellin** *(see p103)*, where you can conclude your day with a relaxing evening.

See map on pp98–9 ➤

Shops and Nightspots

Vintage finds at Cavalli & Nastri

1 Cavalli & Nastri
MAP K5 ■ Gian Giacomo Mora 12

Vintage designer clothing for men and women, hand-picked for quality as well as condition. The favourite haunt of stylists and the stylish. There is another branch at Via Brera 2.

2 Coin
MAP J5 ■ Piazza Cantore 12

This large department store near Porta Genova railway station sells all the most popular fashion and home-accessory brands.

3 Biffi
MAP J5 ■ Corso Genova 6

All the major labels for men and women, including whatever's hot this season, selected by Mrs Biffi.

4 Apollo Club
MAP K6 ■ Via Giosuè Borsi 9 ■ 02-8942-0969 ■ Closed Sun

This exciting edition to the Navigli nightlife scene offers cocktails, dining and dancing in a classy retro interior. There are often live bands on Saturdays, while Fridays feature indie-electro sounds.

5 Danese
MAP M5 ■ Piazza San Nazaro in Brolo 5 ■ Closed Mon L, Sun & Aug

Selling furniture icons of Italian industrial design from greats such as Bruno Munari and Enzo Mari, this cool, stylish store is a must-visit for design enthusiasts.

6 Navigli Antiques Market
MAP K6 ■ Naviglio Grande

This vast market (see p29) is held on the last Sunday of the month, stretching along each side of the Naviglio Grande canal as well as down some adjacent side streets.

7 Special Milano
MAP K6 ■ Corso di Porta Ticinese 80 ■ Closed Sun & Mon

In one of the hippest areas in town, this streetwear shop stocks clothes from major international brands. Its sister store Dictionary, aimed at a more fashion-conscious clientele, is at No. 46 on the same street.

8 Santeria Social Club
MAP R2 ■ Viale Toscana 18 ■ 02-2219-9381 ■ €€

The popular Santeria Social Club (see p62) is known for its live shows and DJ sessions.

Shoppers at Viale Papiniano Market

9 Viale Papiniano Market
MAP J5 ■ Viale Papiniano ■ 9am–5pm Tue & Sat

For designer bargains, head for Viale Papiniano, with its many keenly priced stalls offering top brands.

10 Il Salvagente
MAP S2 ■ Via Fratelli Bronzetti 16

The best discount outlet in Milan, with two floors of clothing, shoes and bags at about 50 per cent discount.

→ *See map on pp98–9*

Places to Eat

PRICE CATEGORIES
For a three-course meal for one with half a bottle of wine (or equivalent meal), taxes and extra charges.

€ under €35 €€ €35–€60 €€€ over €60

1 Ponte Rosso

MAP J6 ■ Ripa di Porta Ticinese 23 ■ 02-837-3132 ■ Closed Sun D ■ €€

This cheery Navigli canalside trattoria serves dishes from Milan and Trieste.

2 El Brellin

MAP J6 ■ Alzaia Naviglio Grande 14 ■ 02-5810-1351 ■ €€€

Hearty *cassoeûla* and *ossobuco* with saffron-flavoured Milanese risotto are among the traditional specialities served at this quaint Navigli tavern.

3 Contraste

MAP K6 ■ Via Giuseppe Meda 2 ■ 02-4953-6597 ■ Closed Mon & Wed–Sat L, Sun D, Tue ■ €€€

The young chefs aim to surprise and delight diners with dishes that look amazing and taste even better.

4 Premiata Pizzeria

MAP K6 ■ Via Alzaia Naviglio Grande 2 ■ 02-8940-0648 ■ €

This is Navigli's most popular pizzeria, with semi-industrial decor and a terrace.

5 Orto – Erbe e Cucina

MAP K6 ■ Via Gaudenzio Ferrari 3 ■ 02-8366-0716 ■ Closed Sun, Mon–Fri L, 1 week Aug, Christmas ■ €

Elegant dishes, many vegetarian, incorporate home-grown herbs.

6 Da Giacomo

MAP P3 ■ Via Sottocorno 6 ■ 02-76023313-189 ■ €€€

Superb fresh fish, grilled meats and and traditional Milanese *cotoletta*, in an Art Deco setting. Book ahead.

7 Sadler

MAP R3 ■ Via Ascanio Sforza 77 ■ 02-5810-4451 ■ Closed L, Sun, 1 week Jan, 2 weeks Aug ■ €€€

One of the top chefs in Milan, Claudio Sadler, melds modern techniques sublimely with regional cuisine at the Sadler.

8 Trattoria Aurora

MAP J5 ■ Via Savona 23 ■ 02- 8940-4978 ■ Closed Mon ■ €€

Traditional restaurant with a long-established reputation, the vine-shaded setting is the Trattoria Aurora's pièce de resistance.

9 Aimo e Nadia

MAP R2 ■ Via R Montecuccoli 6 ■ 02-416-886 ■ Closed Sat L, Sun L ■ €€€

Out in the suburbs, Aimo and Nadia (a Tuscan-born husband-and-wife team) run this place *(see p68)* with exquisite taste throughout, and it ranks among Milan's very best.

10 Cantina Piemontese

MAP N4 ■ Via Laghetto 2 ■ 02-7846-18 ■ €€€

This small restaurant serves Piedmontese and Lombard fare. The vegetarian speciality is quiche with bean purée and artichokes.

Charming Cantina Piemontese

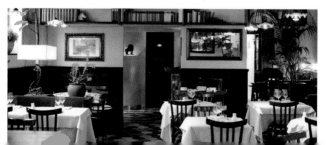

🔟 Lake Maggiore

The westernmost of Italy's great lakes straddles the Lombardy-Piedmont border and pokes its head into Switzerland. The southern half was, from the 15th century, a fiefdom of the powerful Borromeo clan. Maggiore's development as a holiday retreat for Europeans began in 1800 when Napoleon's Simplon highway from Geneva to Milan skirted its shores. Maggiore has fewer resorts than Garda and is not as breathtakingly pretty as Como, although the triplet Borromean Islands are stunning. Still, it avoids the over-development of Garda and the crowds of Como.

**Garibaldi statue,
Verbania**

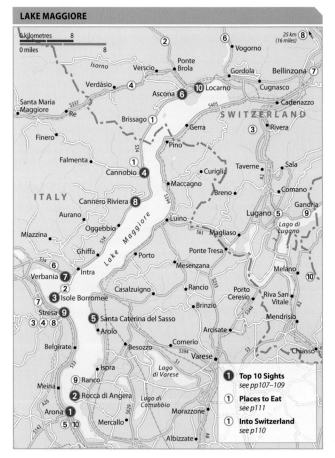

LAKE MAGGIORE

1 Top 10 Sights	*see pp107–109*
1 Places to Eat	*see p111*
1 Into Switzerland	*see p110*

Previous pages *Torri del Benaco, Lake Garda*

① Arona

MAP A3 ■ Visitor info: Piazzale Duca d'Aosta; 0322-243-601

This sprawling modern town was once a stronghold of the Borromeo family, but its fortress was razed by Napoleon. The only lasting monument to the great family is an enormous 17th-century bronze statue of San Carlo Borromeo. Clamber up a ladder-like stair to the head of the 23-m (75-ft) colossus to peek out through his pupils at the 17th-century church below. The road leading to this shrine was meant to be lined with 15 devotional chapels, but only two were finished.

② Rocca di Angera

MAP A3 ■ Angera ■ 0331-931-300 ■ Open end Mar–end Sep: 9:30am–5:30pm daily (Oct: until 5pm) ■ Adm

This medieval castle *(see p51)*, a Borromeo fortress since 1449, preserves a hall of crude frescoes which, dating from 1342–54, count among the oldest surviving Lombard-Gothic works on a non-religious subject. Wooden staircases lead to the tower and lake views. Most of the rooms now house a Doll Museum, with its splendid collection of Japanese figures and 18th- and 19th-century European examples.

③ Isole Borromee

MAP A2–A3

From the 1650s to today, the trio of tiny islands *(see pp30–31)* in the middle of Lake Maggiore has drawn admirers for the gracious palaces and ornate gardens built by the Borromeo family, who still own everything but the fishing village on Isola dei Pescatori. The islands are among Lombardy's top attractions.

Arcaded street typical of Cannobio

④ Cannobio

MAP B2 ■ Visitor info: Via Antonio Giovanola 25; 0323-71-212; www.procannobio.it

By the Swiss border, at the foot of a rushing stream near the Orrido di Santa Anna gorge, Cannobio dates back more than 3,000 years, though its steep, crooked pebble lanes and faded buildings are mainly medieval. Restaurant tables line the harbour.

Borromean Isola Bella

Monastery of Santa Caterina del Sasso, on Maggiore's eastern shore

5 Santa Caterina del Sasso

MAP B3 ■ **Outside Leggiuno** ■ **Open Apr–Oct: 9am–noon & 2–6pm daily (Mar: until 5pm; Nov–Feb: until 5pm Sat & Sun only)**

In gratitude for being saved from a shipwreck, a 13th-century merchant built a chapel into the cliff face above the deepest part of the lake. There are some decaying frescoes, but the main attraction is the setting.

6 Ascona

MAP B2 ■ **Visitor info: Via Papio 5; 0041-848-091-091; www.ascona-locarno.com**

At the Swiss end of the lake, Ascona has been a favourite haunt of such cultural giants as Kandinsky, Freud and Thomas Mann. The town hosts a Harley rally and Jazz festival in July, and a Rolls-Royce gathering and classical music concerts in September. The streets are lined with top-end boutiques and sights such as the 16th-century church Santi Pietro e Paolo. Up on the mountainside is Monte Verità (Hill of Truth), which was established as a progressive colony in the early 20th century.

7 Verbania

MAP A2 ■ **Visitor info: Piazza Ranzoni; 0323-556-669**

In 1939 Mussolini gave the ancient Roman name "Verbania" to a group of villages here that include little Suna, industrialized Intra, and Pallanza, an important town in the Middle Ages. Pallanza's main sight is the landscaped garden of Villa Taranto (see p54), while its Palazzo Viani-Dugnani houses a collection of landscape paintings.

8 Cannero Riviera

MAP B2 ■ **Visitor info: Via Angelo Orsi 1; 0323-788-943**

Despite its northern locale, this sheltered promontory has a truly Mediterranean clime, enabling citrus trees and camellias to flourish. The lake vistas, steep medieval streets and 18th-century houses give it a

---

LAKE MAGGIORE EXPRESS

Spend a day or two seeing what the Lake Maggiore area has to offer. Crossing from Italy to Switzerland, the route consists of a boat trip on the lake and a ride on the Centovalli railway through mountain scenery with many stops along the way (check www.lagomaggioreexpress.eu).

pleasant feel. Most striking are the scraps of islands just offshore, sprouting glowering castles built by lake pirates in the 1400s and later used by the Borromeo clan as a defensive line against the Swiss.

⑨ Stresa
MAP A3 ▪ Visitor info: 0323-301-50; www.parcozoopallavicino.it

The gateway to the Isole Borromee (see pp30–31) is a pretty lakeside town that offers hotels, a grid of trattoria-lined pedestrian streets and a summer music festival (see p77). Just south of the town, the Villa Pallavicino has a botanical garden and a small farm-zoo.

Stresa's lakeside promenade

⑩ Locarno
MAP B1 ▪ Visitor info: in the Casino on Piazza Grande; 0041-917-910-091

Most of this city at the northern end of the lake was rebuilt along modern Swiss lines of concrete, glass and steel. What remains of the medieval city, however, is worth crossing the border for. The 14th-century Castello Visconteo is a highlight, as is the Santuario della Madonna del Sasso (1497), which has paintings by Ciseri and Bramantino (visit by cable-car). Artists Hans and Marguerite Arps donated many works to a modern art gallery in the lovely Casa Rusca.

A DAY ON LAKE MAGGIORE

▶ MORNING

Be at the **Stresa** ferry dock by 10am and buy a day pass for island-hopping as well as your admission tickets for the **Isole Borromee** sights (see pp30–31).

Travel first to Isola Bella to spend a couple of hours exploring the collections of the **Borromeo Palace** (see p107) and the intricate gardens above it. Then catch the 12:25pm ferry for the short hop to the **Isola dei Pescatori** (see p31), where you can settle at a lakeside table on **Verbano's** (see p111) terrace for lunch with a view (book ahead of visit).

MID-AFTERNOON

Wander the tourist/fishing village after lunch before continuing on the boat to **Isola Madre** (see p31).

The **Villa Borromeo** (see p31) on Madre takes only 30 minutes to wander through, but the vast botanical gardens surrounding it are a delight, thick with exotic flora and exotic birds. The multilingual map handed out explains many of the rare specimens and is remarkably informative.

Try to catch a return ferry that stops on the mainland at Lido/Funivia for Mottarone – one stop before Stresa itself. Get off here and stroll along the little-used waterfront promenade for the final 20-minute walk back to downtown Stresa. You will be rewarded with a lovely late afternoon view of the islands on your left, and romantically crumbling, abandoned villas on your right.

See map on p106 ←

Into Switzerland

 Brissago
MAP B2 ▪ www.brissago.ch
Famous for its botanical gardens and two pretty islands, every summer Brissago hosts the JazzAscona festival, where artists perform on stages along the promenade.

 Valle Maggia
MAP B1 ▪ www.vallemaggia.ch
Just outside Locarno, Valle Maggia offers a network of valleys leading up to unspoiled Alpine peaks which are perfect for walks or rides.

 Santa Maria degli Angeli, Monte Tamaro
MAP B2 ▪ www.montetamaro.ch
At the top of the lake, cable-cars rise up to Monte Tamaro, offering great views. Here stands Mario Botta's Santa Maria degli Angeli (1997), an intimate memorial chapel.

Centovalli Railway
www.centovalli.ch
This railway line runs from Locarno (see p109), through narrow valleys and over ancient bridges, to Domodossola in Italy. It's part of the Lago Maggiore Express (see p108).

 Lugano
MAP B2 ▪ www.lugano-tourism.ch
This chic city, the halfway point between Lakes Maggiore and Como, sits on its own lake. It has a historic centre and a lakeside promenade.

 Verzasca Valley
MAP B1 ▪ www.verzasca.net
You can swim in a jade-green lake and explore the tiny hamlets of this pretty valley. Hundreds of trails include high-mountain hikes that cross peaks, passes and pastures.

 Bellinzona
MAP C1 ▪ www.bellinzona turismo.ch
Low-key Bellinzona is home to fine architecture and a stupendous trio of castles granted UNESCO World Heritage Site status in 2000.

 Alto Ticino
MAP C1 ▪ www.ticino.ch
The Alto Ticino, a place of lonesome valleys and soaring skies, has two ancient passes – San Gottardo and San Bernardino – that linked north and south Europe in times past.

Gandria
MAP C2
A romantic hideaway east along the lake from Lugano, Gandria tumbles down the hillside to the water's edge. Terrace cafés offer idyllic views.

Monte Generoso
MAP C2 ▪ www.monte generoso.ch
Capolago is the access point for the rack railway up 1,705 m (5,595 ft) Monte Generoso. The panorama takes in Milan and Turin as well as Lakes Como and Maggiore.

Lake Lugano, viewed from one of its magnificent surrounding peaks

Places to Eat

Dining at dusk at Lo Scalo, Cannobio

PRICE CATEGORIES
For a three-course meal for one with half a bottle of wine (or equivalent meal), taxes and extra charges.

€ under €35 ■ €€ €35–€60 ■ €€€ over €60

1 Lo Scalo, Cannobio
MAP B2 ■ Piazza Vittorio Emanuele II 32 ■ 0323-71-480 ■ Closed Mon, Tue & Nov–mid-Dec ■ €€€

This offers traditional Piedmontese cooking with inventive touches.

2 Verbano, Isola dei Pescatori
MAP A3 ■ 0323-32-534 ■ Closed mid-Oct–Mar ■ €€€

Set on a terrace at the tip of the island, with great views of Isola Bella. The fish is superb.

3 Piemontese, Stresa
MAP A3 ■ Via Mazzini 25 ■ 0323-30-235 ■ Closed Mon & Dec–Jan ■ €€

Enjoy local dishes in the wood-panelled dining room and cobbled courtyard of Stresa's top restaurant.

4 Il Vicoletto, Stresa
MAP A3 ■ Vicolo del Poncivo 3 ■ 0323-932-102 ■ Closed Thu (except Mar–Oct) & mid-Jan–mid-Feb ■ €€

Homemade pasta, tasty risotto and fish from the lake, a good selection of wines and a few veranda tables.

5 La Vecchia Arona, Arona
MAP A3 ■ Via Lungolago Marconi 17 ■ 0322-242-469 ■ Closed Wed ■ €€

Franco Carrera is an enthusiastic and innovative reinterpreter of "traditional" dishes. Book ahead.

6 Milano, Pallanza
MAP A2 ■ Corso Zanitello 2 ■ 0323-556-816 ■ Closed Mon, Tue, Sun D & mid-Nov–mid-Mar (except Dec) ■ €€€

Verbania's best restaurant serves classic Piedmontese dishes and lake fish in lovely grounds.

7 La Rampolina, Campino
MAP A3 ■ Via Someraro 13 ■ 0323-923-415 ■ Closed Mon ■ €€

On a hillside above Stresa, there are lovely lake views from the wisteria-canopied terrace. Local mountain cheeses feature on a tempting menu which also includes several lake-fish specialities.

Appetizer at Verbano

8 Osteria degli Amici, Stresa
MAP A3 ■ Via Bolongaro 31 ■ 0323-30-453 ■ Closed mid-Nov–early Feb ■ €€

This convivial spot has some outdoor tables and a menu ranging from pizza to freshly caught lake fish.

9 Il Sole di Ranco
MAP A3 ■ Piazza Venezia 5 ■ 0331-976-507 ■ Closed Mon, Tue & mid-Dec–mid-Feb ■ €€€

Historic Il Sole (see p69) offers a fresh take on Italian regional cuisine.

10 Enoteca Il Grappolo, Arona
MAP A3 ■ Via Pertossi 7 ■ 0322-477 35 ■ Closed Mon & Wed–Fri L, Tue, 3 weeks Jun ■ €€

This wine bar's menu usually includes platters of local meats and cheeses, polenta and high-quality Piedmont beef, with wine-pairing recommendations for each dish.

See map on p106 ←

🔟 Lake Como

Como is the beauty queen of the Italian lakes, the turquoise and sapphire waters of its three arms – 50 km (30 miles) long, but rarely more than 2 km (1 mile) wide – backed by the snow-capped peaks of the pre-Alps. Its diversity runs from windsurfing and Alpine vistas in the north to the busy towns capping the southern arms, such as Como, a Roman city with a glorious cathedral and silk industry, and Lecco, full of literary associations. For centuries Lake Como has drawn in the wealthy to line its shores with gracious villas and verdant gardens; it has also inspired composers (Liszt, Verdi, Bellini) and writers such as Byron, Shelley and Wordsworth.

Interior of the Basilica in Como

LAKE COMO

1 Top 10 Sights
see pp113–15

1 Places to Eat
see p119

1 Things to Do
see p116

1 Lakeside Towns
see p117

1 Exploring the Area
see p118

Lake Como viewed from the loggia of Villa Monastero, Varenna

1 Villa Monastero, Varenna

MAP C2 ■ Via Polvani 2 ■ Open Mar–Sep: 9am–6:30pm daily; Jan–Feb: 11am–5pm Sun ■ Adm ■ www.villa monastero.eu

This villa (see p54), a former convent, has gardens that stretch right down to the lakeshore, wonderfully shaded throughout by the canopies of cypresses and palms.

2 Basilica di Sant'Abbondio, Como

MAP C3 ■ Via Sant'Abbondio (off Viale Innocenzo XI) ■ Open 8am–6pm daily (until 4:30pm in winter)

In Como's industrial suburbs, this Romanesque church retains a pair of bell towers and an extended choir that links it, architecturally, to the Westwerk style of medieval Germany. The apse is gorgeously frescoed with a series of biblical scenes.

3 Brunate Funicular, Como

MAP C3 ■ Piazza A De Gasperi ■ 031-303-608 ■ Runs every 30 mins 6am–10:30pm daily (until midnight Sat in summer) ■ Adm

The classic journey to this hillside village is to take a short walk from Como's harbour to the funicular station, then ride the funicular up to Brunate. You're rewarded with vistas over Como and the lake, and this is also the starting point of many trails into the surrounding hills.

4 Duomo, Como

MAP C3 ■ Piazza del Duomo ■ 031-265-244 ■ Open 7am–7pm

Como's cathedral was begun in 1396, but not capped with its dome until 1740. The façade's pilasters are lined with saints, and the main door is flanked by the figures of two local ancient scholars, the Plinys, Elder and Younger. Inside there are fine tapestries and an intricately carved and painted altarpiece of 1492.

Vaulted ceilings of Como's Duomo

Statues at Villa Balbianello

5 Villa Balbianello, Lenno

MAP C2 ■ Lenno ■ 0344-56-110
■ Open mid-Mar–early Jan: 10am–
6pm Tue, Thu–Sun (Nov–early Jan:
until 5pm) ■ Adm

The twin turrets and the statue-lined
balustrades that outline the terraced
gardens of this 1784 villa *(see p54)*
have impressed many film directors.
Head to the villa by boat from Lenno
and then proceed on foot. To tour the
villa, it is essential to book ahead.

6 Villa Carlotta, Tremezzo

MAP C2 ■ Tremezzo ■ 0344-40-
405 ■ Open mid-Mar–1 Nov: 9:30am–
5pm (Apr–Oct: until 7:30pm; Jun–Jul:
until 9pm Tue); Nov: 10am– 4:30pm
Sat & Sun ■ Adm ■ www.villacarlotta.it

This *(see p55)* is one of the lake's most
sumptuous villas, with exquisitely
landscaped gardens. Unusually, you
can tour the art-strewn villa here,
as well as its wonderful surrounds.

7 Villa Serbelloni, Bellagio

MAP C2 ■ Piazza della Chiesa,
Bellagio ■ 031-951-555 ■ Tours mid-
Mar–mid-Nov: 11am & 3:30pm Tue–
Sun ■ Adm ■ www.villaserbelloni.com

Bellagio's promontory has been prime
real estate for millennia. Pliny the
Younger had a villa named "Tragedy"
here (it was paired with a "Comedy"
villa on the far shore), which was
replaced by a castle in the Middle
Ages, then a Stagna family villa in
the 15th century. The last Stagna
left it to his best friend Serbelloni in
1788. Serbelloni proceeded to rebuild
the villa *(see p55)* as a summer residence to the main house down in
the village (now Grand Hotel Villa
Serbelloni). In 1959, the summer
home passed to the Rockefeller
Foundation, and now visiting scholars can live and study here for short
periods. It is not open to the public,
but you can tour the gardens.

8 Sacro Monte di Ossuccio

MAP C2 ■ Madonna del
Soccorso: open 7am–7pm daily;
www.sacrimonti.net

This series of 15 chapels standing
in a panoramic position on the
hillside behind Ossuccio is one of
nine such sites in northern Italy,
constructed in the 16th and 17th
centuries to convey the teachings
of the Catholic church with frescoes

Villa Carlotta, Tremezzo

and life-size statues. Here there are 230, made of terracotta and plaster. The final chapel is within the Madonna del Soccorso church.

⑨ Villa Melzi, Bellagio
MAP C2 ■ Lungolario Manzoni ■ 031-950-204 ■ Open end Mar–Oct: 9:30am–6:30pm daily ■ Adm ■ www.giardi nidivillamelzi.it

The manicured gardens surrounding an elegant Neo-Classical home *(see p55)* of Francesco Melzi d'Eril, Napoleon's man in Italy, are now open to the public.

Moorish temple folly at Villa Melzi

⑩ Abbazia di Piona
MAP C2 ■ Signposted off the lake road ■ 0341-940-331 ■ Open 9am–noon & 2:30–6pm daily

At the tip of the Ogliasca peninsula sits this Benedictine abbey, cloaked in silence. The abbey was founded in the 9th century, and the little church has Romanesque carvings decorating the water stoups and the capitals and bases of the columns in the quiet cloister. The monks distill – and sell – some potent liqueurs.

COMO SILK

Como has been Italy's silk capital since 1510. While they now import the spun thread from China, the fabrics Como's artisans weave is still the most sought after by Milan's top designers. There are shops and warehouse stores all around town hawking silk wares. In the city outskirts, there is even a Museum of Silk *(Via Castelnuovo 9; 031-303-180; www.museosetacomo.com).*

COMO LAKE-HOPPING

▶ **MORNING**

To cruise the lake you can buy point-to-point tickets, or consider the single-ticket cruises that visit several towns and may include villa admissions. This itinerary assumes you have checked out Como's sights before spending the night in **Bellagio** *(see p117).* Begin the next day with a cappuccino at Bellagio's **Caffè Rossi** *(Piazza Giuseppe Mazzini 22, Bellagio; 031-950-196)* across from the dock before boarding the 10:30am boat to **Villa Carlotta**, where you have an hour to visit the collection of art and lush gardens of the lake's greatest villa. Afterwards, catch the ferry down to Isola Comacina to dig into a sumptuous feast at the **Locanda** *(see p119).* After a second helping of their "spiked" coffee, you'll have a bit of time to work off the meal by exploring the island's church ruins before grabbing the boat back up the lake to **Varenna** *(see p117).*

MID-AFTERNOON

Continue walking off your lunch by climbing up to the romantic, panoramic Castello di Vezio above the town, then descend and pop into some of Varenna's little churches. Poke around the gardens of **Villa Monastero** *(see p113)*, then finally head down to the lakefront arcade for a short stroll then a meal by the water at **Vecchia Varenna** *(see p119).* Unless you decide to spend a relaxing night in quiet and little-visited Varenna, make sure you finish dinner before 9pm, when the last ferry leaves for Bellagio.

See map on p112

Things to Do

(1) Playing a Round of Golf
Circolo Villa d'Este, Montorfano: 031-200-200 ▪ Golf Club Menaggio & Cadenabbia: 0344-32-103; www. menaggio.org

If you have a handicap of 36 or less, try for a reservation at the Circolo Villa d'Este and check out the course of Golf Club Menaggio & Cadenabbia.

(2) Hiring a Motorboat
Boat hire, Moltrasio: www. nettunonoleggiobarche.it ▪ Boat hire & taxi-boats, Cernobbio: www.taxi boatcernobbio.it

Motorboats are available for hire with or without a licence in many places around the lake, or you can sit back and relax with a private taxi-boat.

(3) Mountain Biking
Bike hire: Comolagobike: www.comolagobike.com

The hills of Bellagio's peninsula are great mountain-bike country.

Mountain biking on a forest trail

(4) Horse Riding
Trekking centre: Maneggio dei Tre Laghi; 392-032-2903

Choose an English- or Western-style saddle and trek mountain valleys off the Menaggio–Porlezza Road.

(5) Climbing
Info at CAI, Via Papa Giovanni XXIII, Lecco; www.cai.lecco.it

You can rock-climb in the mountains ringing the lake's southeastern end.

Windsurfing on the lake

(6) Windsurfing
Windsurfcenter Domaso: 380-700-0010; www.wsc-domaso.com ▪ Fun Surf Centre, Dervio: 338-814-8719; www.funsurfcentre.com

The strong winds of the lake's northern end draw an international crowd of windsurfers.

(7) Flying by Seaplane
Aero Club Como: www. aeroclubcomo.com

Take a bird's-eye view of the lake and alight on water for an unforgettable experience. The pilots at the Aero Club Como are highly professional.

(8) Kayaking
Boat hire: Cavalcalario Club, Gallasco; 3395-308-138 ▪ Società Canottieri, Via Nullo 2, Lecco; 0341-364-273; www.canottieri.lecco.it

Get a deliciously different perspective on Como's fabled coastline, peeking into private lakeside gardens from your own kayak or canoe.

(9) Hiking
There's plenty of choice for walkers around Lake Como including signposted trails from the Brunate funicular (see p113) and the Greenway between Colonno and Cadenabbia.

(10) Lake Cruises
Bellagio: www.bellagioboat service.com ▪ Menaggio: www. menaggiowatertaxi.com

Small-group boat tours from Bellagio can include a visit to Villa Balbianello (see p113) and sunset tours, with Prosecco, run daily from Menaggio.

See map on p112

Lakeside Towns

 Tremezzo
MAP C2 ■ Visitor info: IAT, Via Statale 4; 0344-404-93

A tiny resort whose main claim to fame is the Villa Carlotta *(see p114)*.

 Como
MAP C3 ■ Visitor info: Via Pretorio; 031-304-137; www.lake como.is ■ Local info: near railway station S. Giovanni; 3420-076-403

Italy's silk capital was founded by the Romans and has a spectacular cathedral *(see p113)*, a handful of modest museums, lots of boutiques and two ancient churches.

③ Varenna
MAP C2 ■ Info at Via IV Novembre 7; 0341-830-367

Arguably, Varenna *(see p51)* makes a better base for exploring the lake than busy Bellagio.

④ Menaggio
MAP C2 ■ Visitor info: Piazza Garibaldi 8; 0344-32-924

This is a pleasant little resort on the main ferry lines, with some Baroque churches and a pretty promenade.

⑤ Bellagio
MAP C2 ■ Info at ferry dock on Piazza Mazzini; 031-950-204; www.bellagiolakecomo.com

A popular town, with the gardens of villas Serbelloni and Melzi *(see pp114–15)*, a Romanesque church, a café-lined harbourfront and a pretty warren of medieval alleys.

Bellagio's peninsula viewed from the lake

⑥ Lecco
MAP D3 ■ Info at Piazza XX Settembre 23; 0341-295-720; www.lakecomo.is

The capital of the lake's southeastern arm is famous for sights linked to native writer Alessandro Manzoni, who set parts of his *I Promessi Sposi* *(see p46)* in the suburb of Olate.

 Argegno
MAP C2

Take the cable-car up to Pigra from this picturesque marina and enjoy the wonderful views or follow the road inland to explore the lovely Valle Intelvi *(see p118)*.

⑧ Bellano
MAP C2 ■ Via Vittorio Veneto (in The Town Hall); 0341-821-124

On Piazza S Giorgio sits the black-and-white striped façade of Santi Nazaro e Celso. A steep street leads to the entrance of the dramatic Orrido gorge, which can be explored.

⑨ Lenno
MAP C2 ■ Info at Piazza XI Febbraio; 366-694-7147; open Sat–Mon

Don't miss the 11th-century Santo Stefano and neighbouring baptistry. Just north of town, in Mezzegra, a black cross marks where Mussolini was shot by partisans.

⑩ Torno
MAP C3

This pretty village features a lakeside piazza and a miniscule marina. The medieval church has a narrow bell tower and striking decorated interior.

Exploring the Area

1 Bikesharing
bicincitta.com

There are about a dozen bike-sharing points around Como, including at the main San Giovanni railway station and at Tavernola, near Cernobbio.

2 Civate, Lake Annone
MAP C3 ▪ San Pietro al Monte: www.amicidisanpietro.it

On the shores of Lake Annone, Civate is the starting point for walks up to the attractive monastic complex of San Pietro al Monte which has stunning frescoes.

Fresco at San Pietro al Monte near Civate

3 Valle Intelvi
MAP C2 ▪ Valle Intelvi Tourist Board: www.valleintelviturismo.it

Stretching from Argegno (see p117) up to Lanzo d'Intelvi, this scenic valley (see p59) is flanked by wooded hillsides dotted with ancient villages.

4 Lake Lugano
MAP B2-C2 ▪ Lugano Tourist Board: www.luganoregion.com

It's a 12-km (7-mile) drive from Menaggio (see p117) to attractive Lake Lugano, which spans the Italian-Swiss border, and the pretty town of Lugano itself (see p110).

5 Campione d'Italia
MAP C2 ▪ Campione d'Italia Tourist Board: www.campione italia.com

An Italian enclave, Campione d'Italia has a lovely setting on Lake Lugano. Steps zig-zag from the lake to the Santuario della Madonna dei Ghirli church, with a fine frescoed interior.

6 Pian del Tivano
MAP C2

The panoramic road inland from the lakeside village of Nesso leads to this grassy plateau. It's a popular place for picnics and walking.

7 Lago di Pusiano
MAP C3 ▪ Boat schedules vary: check website www.prolocobosisio.it

This is one of several smaller lakes between the lower branches of Lake Como. Eco-friendly boat tours are organized in summer.

8 Vehicle Hire
Barindelli Tourist Board: www.barindellitaxi.it

As well as providing chauffeured services and private transfers, Barindelli also rents cars and scooters – an ideal way to explore the area.

9 Chiavenna
MAP D1

The charming historic town of Chiavenna is famous for its *crotti* – natural caves used as cellars for storing wine, salami and cheese; many are now restaurants that are wonderful to visit in both summer and winter.

10 Valtellina
MAP D2–F1 ▪ Valtellina Tourist Board: www.valtellina.it

To the northeast of Lake Como, Valtellina (see p59) is famous for its ski resorts. Bormio has a lovely historic centre, as excellent mountain food and robust red wines.

Valtellina ski resort cable-cars

Places to Eat

PRICE CATEGORIES
For a three-course meal for one with half a bottle of wine (or equivalent meal), taxes and extra charges.

€ under €35 ■ €€ €35–€60 ■ €€€ over €60

 La P'Osteria, Argegno
MAP C2 ■ Via Lungo Telo Sinistra 3 ■ 031-447-4072 ■ Closed winter: Tue & Wed ■ €€

Contemporary versions of local dishes, game and quality meats from Piedmont are on the menu. The peaceful position by the river as it flows into the lake is a bonus.

2 Pronobis, Como
MAP C3 ■ Via Lambertenghi 19 ■ 031-261-786 ■ Closed Jan–Nov: Sun ■ €

This country-style deli-restaurant is ideal for lunch in central Como. Try the house meatloaf and homemade pear, walnut and chocolate dessert.

3 Barchetta, Bellagio
MAP C2 ■ Salita Mella 13 ■ 031-951-389 ■ Closed Sep–Jun: Tue & mid-Oct–Easter ■ €€

For such a beloved resort, Bellagio oddly lacks superlative eateries, save perhaps this "little boat" *(see p69)*. Dishes are well-made, the ambience amicable and the prices reasonable.

4 Ittiturismo Da Abate, Lezzeno
MAP C2 ■ Frazione Villa 4 ■ 031-914-986 ■ Closed Mon, Tue–Sat L & Sun D ■ €

Run by a family of fishermen who will show you how the fish is prepared. Try the pasta with lake-fish ragout.

5 Crotto dei Platani, Brienno
MAP C2 ■ Via Regina 73 ■ 031-814-038 ■ €€€

This restaurant is set in a lakeside grotto, with a gorgeous terrace right on the water, and serves regional food with an inventive touch.

6 Vecchia Varenna, Varenna
MAP C2 ■ Contrada Scoscesa 14 ■ 0341-830-793 ■ Closed winter: Mon; Dec & Jan ■ €€

Within a 15th-century building, the most romantic restaurant on the lake serves creative local cuisine.

Locanda dell'Isola's outdoor tables

7 Locanda dell'Isola Comacina, Ossuccio
MAP C2 ■ Isola Comacina ■ 0344-55-083 ■ Closed Nov–mid-Mar, mid-Mar–mid-Jun: Tue ■ €€€

The fixed-price feast has stayed the same since 1947: antipasto, trout, chicken, cheese, fruit, gelato, water, wine and brandy-spiked coffee.

8 Osteria del Gallo, Como
MAP C3 ■ Via Vitani 16 ■ 031-272-591 ■ Closed Sun, Mon D & Aug ■ €

A popular, family-run eatery in Como's historic centre. The menu changes daily but often includes lentil and spelt soup or polenta.

9 Bar Costantin – La Trattoria
MAP C2 ■ Via Camozzi 16, Menaggio ■ 0344-31000 ■ €€

This family-run trattoria offers home cooked lake fish, regional dishes and a good selection of pizzas.

10 La Fagurida, Tremezzina
MAP C2 ■ Via Rogaro 17 ■ 0344-40676 ■ Closed Mon ■ €€

A charming trattoria in the hills, with lake views. Come for tasty homecooking and seasonal dishes.

See map on p112 ←

🔟 Lake Garda

Lake Garda is an area of contrasts. The crosswinds to the north and the dominating slopes of Monte Baldo draw windsurfers and paragliders, while to the south the edges of the lake are gentler, with stony beaches, and lemon and olive groves in the vine-covered hills. Garda also has some of the best Roman-era remains in northern Italy at Sirmione and Desenzano, as well as medieval castles in Torri del Benaco, Malcesine, Valeggio and Sirmione. It is the largest of the main Italian lakes, with a milder, more Mediterranean temperature than might be expected for its latitude. As a result, Lake Garda is the most-visited of the Italian lakes.

Fountain at Il Vittoriale

LAKE GARDA

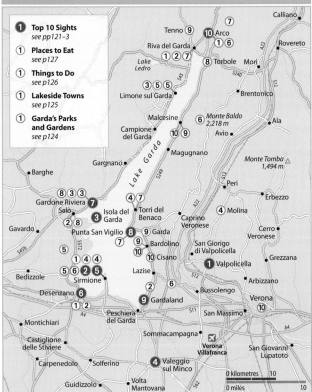

1 Valpolicella

MAP G4 ▪ Visitor info: www.
valpolicellaweb.it; www.stradadelvino
valpolicella.it ▪ Winery tour: www.
seregoalighieri.it

Nestled between Lake Garda and
Verona, Valpolicella has been a
renowned wine-making area since
ancient Roman times. Nowadays it's
particularly famous for its reds – the
complex and heady Amarone, made
using air-dried grapes, as well as
Valpolicella. Among the villages,
hillside San Giorgio is one to see,
while Serego-Alighieri, owned by
descendants of medieval poet Dante,
offers an interesting winery tour.

2 Grotte di Catullo, Sirmione

MAP G4 ▪ Via Catullo ▪ 030-916-157
▪ Open 8:30am–7:30pm Wed–Mon
(until 7pm Sun); winter: 8:30am–5pm
(to 2pm Sun) ▪ Adm

Though the ancient Roman poet
Catullus did take his holidays at
Sirmione, there's no evidence to
suggest that this ancient house at
the very tip of Sirmione's peninsula
was actually his villa – in fact, it was
probably built after Catullus's death,
sometime in the 1st century BC. It is
the best surviving example of a Roman
private home in northern Italy, but
this didn't stop it being misnamed a
"grotto", the result of the romantically
over-grown and cavelike state it had
assumed by the Middle Ages.

3 Isola del Garda

MAP G4 ▪ Boats from
Barbarano and Gardone ▪ 328-612-
6943 ▪ Tours: Apr–Oct: Tue & Thu at
9:30am ▪ Adm (book in advance)
▪ www.isoladelgarda.com

Garda's largest island once housed
a monastery that attracted the great
medieval saints: Francis of Assisi,
Anthony of Padua and Bernardino of
Siena. It was destroyed by Napoleon
and replaced in 1890–1903 with a
Neo-Gothic Venetian-style villa and
luxuriant gardens. Guided tours
include a boat ride and a snack.

Aerial view of lovely Isola del Garda

4 Giardino Sigurtà

MAP G5 ▪ Via Cavour 1, Valeggio
sul Mincio ▪ 045-637-1033 ▪ Open
Mar–Nov: 9am–7pm daily (last adm
6pm); Oct & Nov: until 6pm (last adm
5pm) ▪ Adm ▪ www.sigurta.it

Carlo Sigurtà spent 40 years turning
a barren hillside into one of Italy's
great gardens, with manicured lawns
and pathways amid vibrant flower-
beds and reflecting pools. It's a 20-
minute drive south of the lakeside.

Grotte di Catullo, Sirmione

Dramatic fortress of Rocca Scaligera on Sirmione's peninsula

5 Rocca Scaligera, Sirmione

MAP G4 ▪ Piazza Castello ▪ 030-916-468 ▪ Open 8:30am–7pm Tue–Sat (Apr–Sep: until 5pm Sun; Oct–Mar: until 1pm Sun) ▪ Adm

At the narrowest point of Sirmione's long, thin peninsula, this stone citadel, in use as a fortress until the 19th century, still guards the town – the only way to enter Sirmione is via drawbridge over the moat. It's worth climbing the 30-m (95-ft) tower for the grand panorama.

6 Villa Romana, Desenzano

Mosaic floor at Villa Romana

MAP G4 ▪ Via Crocefisso 22 ▪ 030-914-3547 ▪ Open 8:30am–7pm Tue–Sun (Nov–Feb: until 5pm) ▪ Adm

The most important late Imperial villa remaining in Northern Italy was built in the 1st century BC, but the fine polychrome floor mosaics are mostly of the 4th and 5th centuries. By that time, the local Romans were Christianized, which explains the late 4th-century glass bowl engraved with an image of Christ.

7 Heller Garden

MAP G4 ▪ Gardone Riviera ▪ Visitor info: IAT Gardone; 030-374-8736 ▪ Open Mar–Oct: daily ▪ Adm ▪ www.hellergarden.com

This lovely set of botanical gardens (see p55) in Lake Garda features more than 2,000 Alpine species on its terraced hillside.

8 Punta San Vigilio

MAP G4 ▪ Visitor info: www.punta-sanvigilio.it

This is an idyllic little promontory (see p124) jutting out into Lake Garda, with lemon and olive groves, café tables around an enchanting port, and an exclusive hotel. The Parlo Baia della Sirene (Mermaid's Beach) has an inviting beach club fringed by olive trees, which charges for entry in the daytime but offers activities for children. In the early evenings the beach is free, and it's the perfect place to watch the sun go down.

LAKESIDE BATTLES

In the 13th–15th centuries Venice vied with Milan for control of Lombardy (see p38). The town of Torbole (see p125) was the scene of a historic Milanese victory in 1439. Venice was caught trying to smuggle supplies to the town of Brescia – 26 ships had been sailed up the Adige River and dragged overland via Torbole into the lake.

Gardaland

MAP G4 ■ On the shore road, north of Peschiera ■ 045-644-9777 ■ Closed Nov–Mar (except Christmas–New Year) ■ Adm ■ www.gardaland.it

Under the icon of a green dragon named Prezzemolo ("Parsley"), the park (see p60) boasts roller coasters and carnival rides, a water park, jungle safari, ice shows, dolphin tricks and medieval spectacles. Italy's greatest theme park is a hoot for the kids.

⑩ Castello di Arco, near Riva

MAP H2 ■ 0464-510-156 ■ Open daily Apr–Sep: 10am–7pm; Mar & Oct: 10am–5pm; Nov–Feb:10am–4pm; Jan: 10am–4pm Sat & Sun only (last adm 1 hr before closing) ■ Adm

This 12th-century castle is almost in ruin. Only one wall remains of the central keep, and the sole room in the whole complex to survive intact was filled with debris until 1986. When it was cleared, a number of excellent 14th-century frescoes were found, depicting nobles playing at board games and war.

Magnificent ruins of Castello di Arco

TWO DAYS ON LAKE GARDA

▶ DAY ONE

If you're here to relax and sightsee rather than thrash the waves up near Riva, then spend your days exploring the southern end of the lake. **Sirmione** (see p81) is both a charming and lively base.

On your first day, spend time in **Desenzano** (see p125) to see the **Villa Romana** before driving out to Sirmione itself. Walk out to the far tip of the peninsula to wander the ruins of the **Grotte di Catullo** (see p121). On your way back into town, divert to the right to pop into San Pietro and see its medieval frescoes.

Navigate the throngs of the tiny centre to climb the balustrades of the **Rocca Scaligera** for a sunset panorama.

Stroll through Sirmione's historic centre, ending up at **Trattoria La Fiasca** (see p127) for a delicious lake-fish dinner.

DAY TWO

Set off along the lake's east coast, stopping, soon after pretty Lazise, to visit the free **Olive Oil Museum** (see p126) in Cisano and **Cantina Fratelli Zeni** (see p126) just beyond, for their wine museum and wine-tasting. Make **Punta San Vigilio** your lunchtime break, at a tavern table by the harbour or under the olive trees.

Unless you opt to stay here for an afternoon at the beach, carry on to **Malcesine** (see p125), to see the castle and take the cable-car up **Monte Baldo** (see p126) for some breathtaking panoramic views.

See map on p120 ←

Garda's Parks and Gardens

Abundantly green Arciducale Park

1 Arboreto
MAP H2 ■ Via Lomego, Arco
■ Open Oct–Mar: 9am–4pm; Apr–
Sep: 8am–7pm

The ancient Arciducale Park was built around 1872. The mild climate of the area allows the growth of over 150 species of trees, shrubs and plants such as the holm and the sequoia.

2 Aqua Paradise, Garda
MAP G4 ■ Fossalta 1 ■ 045-696-9900 ■ Adm ■ www.caneva world.it

This extensive water park is a family favourite for its range of waterslides, thrilling rapids and soaking rides.

3 Limonaia
MAP G3 ■ www.comune. limonesulgarda.bs.it

These elaborate, greenhouse-like "lemon houses" have been built since the 1200s to protect Garda's famed lemons from the elements. You can visit the elegant Limonaia del Castèl.

4 Parco delle Cascate di Molina
MAP H4 ■ Località Vaccarole, 37022 Molina, Fumane VR ■ Adm ■ www.parcodellecascate.it

Hiking paths lead to spectacular waterfalls at this little-known park.

See map on p120

5 Olive Groves, Sirmione
Olive groves line the route to the Grotte di Catullo *(see p121)*.

6 Public Garden, Arco
MAP H2 ■ Viale delle Palme

Opposite the casino in the heart of Arco is a beautiful public garden filled with exotic plants and palms.

7 Parco Baia delle Sirene, Punta San Vigilio
Siren's Bay on Punta San Vigilio is a pay beach, but it is a lovely spot set among olive groves *(see p122)*.

8 Il Vittoriale, Gardone Riviera
MAP G4 ■ Il Vittoriale ■ 0365-296-511 ■ Adm ■ www.vittoriale.it

The eccentric, flamboyant Gabriele d'Annunzio *(see p54)* set out the terraced gardens that surround his Art Nouveau residence. There's an amphitheatre, and his mausoleum is at the highest point of the estate.

Villa and gardens of Il Vittoriale

9 Parco Grotta Cascata Varone, North of Riva
MAP H3 ■ Località Le Foci 3, Tenno, Riva del Garda ■ 0464 521 421 ■ Adm ■ www.cascata-varone.com

Make your way over this spectacular gorge via a series of suspended walkways, with white water all around.

10 Giardino Giusti, Verona
MAP H4 ■ Adm ■ www. tourism.verona.it

These formal gardens, with fountains, grottoes and shady bowers, were laid out in the 15th century.

Lakeside Towns

1 Desenzano
MAP G4 ▪ Visitor info: Via Porto Vecchio 34; 030-374-8726

A large and delightful town, settled in the Bronze Age and a retreat since the Roman era. Its top attraction is the Villa Romana *(see p122)*.

2 Salò
MAP G4 ▪ Visitor info: Piazza Sant'Antonio 4; 030-374-8745

This genteelly faded resort became the capital of Mussolini's short-lived Republic of Salò (1943–5) in the closing chapters of World War II.

3 Gardone Riviera
MAP G4 ▪ Visitor info: Corso della Repubblica 1; 030-3748-736

Gardone has many magnificent villas and gardens, including the Giardino Botanico Hruska *(see p122)* and d'Annunzio's Il Vittoriale *(see p124)*.

4 Torri del Benaco
MAP G4 ▪ Visitor info: Viale Gardesana; 045-629-6482

This little town was once the capital of Lake Garda. There's a Scaglieri castle with a modest museum, and a trail leads up from the town to cliffs bearing 8,000-year-old rock etchings.

5 Limone sul Garda
MAP G3 ▪ Visitor info: Via IV Novembre 29; 0365-918-987; www.limonehotels.com

Limone is tucked in a cove, with a long beach, small harbour and dozens of hotels, most of which are closed from November until Easter.

6 Sirmione
MAP G4 ▪ Visitor info: Viale Marconi 8; 030-916-114; www.comune.sirmione.bs.it

The loveliest town on the lake is set at the tip of a long peninsula. It has the ruins of an ancient Roman villa and a medieval castle *(see pp121–2)*.

7 Riva del Garda
MAP H3 ▪ Visitor info: Largo Medaglie d'Oro 5; 0464-554-444; www.gardatrentinonline.it

A bustling town, with the medieval Torre d'Apponale and Rocca Castle. Just inland lies Arco *(see p123)*, home to a ruined castle.

8 Torbole
MAP H3 ▪ Visitor info: Via Lungolago Conca d'Oro 25; 0464-505-177

History put Torbole *(see p122)* on the map in 1439, but it's known chiefly as a good base for windsurfing.

9 Malcesine
MAP H3 ▪ Visitor info: Via Gardesana 238; 0457-400-044

The town's castle contains a room devoted to Goethe, who was briefly suspected of being a spy when he was seen sketching the castle.

10 Bardolino
MAP G4 ▪ Visitor info: Piazzale Aldo Moro 5; 045-721-0078

Bardolino has been famous since Roman times for its light red wine. The town also has two wonderful Romanesque churches.

View over Limone sul Garda

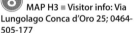

Things to Do

1 Windsurfing
Windsurfers flock to Garda's wind-pounded northern shores, especially Riva and Torbole, for some of Europe's best lake surfing.

2 Diving
While this isn't the tropics, the lake's waters are clearer than you might expect. Sights worth seeing include an underwater Jesus near Riva. Equipment is widely available.

3 Mountain-Biking
Explore the flatlands to the south, tackle mountains rising sheer from the north shores, or simply wend along the lake shore itself.

4 Swimming
Garda's beaches are rocky, but the water is crystal clear. The best are at Sirmione, including Spiaggia Giamaica at the end of the peninsula.

Alpine Climbing near Lake Garda

Lake-swimming near Sirmione

5 Golfing
MAP G4 ■ Gardagolf: Soiano del Lago; www.gardagolf.it ■ Arzanga Golf Club: Calvagese della Riviera; www.arzagagolf.it
Garda is one of Italy's premier golf destinations, with ten clubs on the southern shore including two 27-hole courses, named Gardagolf and Arzaga.

6 Monte Baldo Cable-Car
MAP H3 ■ Cable-car: www.funiviedelbaldo.it
Panoramic revolving pods take 20 minutes to ascend from Malcesine for walking and mountain-biking trails, paragliding and skiing.

7 Climbing and Paragliding
MAP H2-H3 ■ Guide Alpine: www.guidealpinearco.com ■ Climbing Stadium Rockmaster: 334-773-4133 ■ Paragliding Club: www.paragliding malcesine.it
Head to Arco for Guide Alpine and Multi Sport Centre for climbing, or to Malcesine for its Paragliding Club.

8 Kayaking and SUP
SUPs (stand-up-paddleboards) and Kayaks make it possible to explore inlets and bays not always accessible from dry land.

9 Wine-Tasting
MAP G4 ■ Cantina Fratelli Zeni, Bardolino; www.museodelvino.it
Some excellent wines are made on Lake Garda (see p65). Local wineries offer tastings, and Cantina Fratelli Zeni also has a wine museum.

10 Olive Oil Museum
MAP G4 ■ Via Peschiera 54, Cisano di Bardolino ■ Open 9:30am–12:30pm & 2:30–7pm Mon–Sat, 9am–12:30pm Sun (booking required, email: info@museo.com)
This free museum shows the history of olive oil, one of Lake Garda's highlights. There's a waterwheel in action, and huge wooden oil presses.

Places to Eat

 Trattoria La Fiasca, Sirmione

MAP G4 ▪ Via Santa Maria Maggiore 11 ▪ 030-990-6111 ▪ Closed Wed, Jan–early Feb ▪ €€

This local favourite has an inviting atmosphere and a menu featuring dishes such as gnocchi with speck, mushrooms and local Bagòs cheese.

② Antica Hostaria Cavallino, Desenzano

MAP G4 ▪ Via Gherla 30 ▪ 030-912-0217 ▪ Closed Mon, Sun D & mid-Nov–early Dec ▪ €€€

This restaurant offers local dishes and freshly caught lake fish, along with an exceptional wine list.

③ Villa Fiordaliso, Gardone Riviera

MAP G4 ▪ Via Zanardelli 150 ▪ 0365-20-158 ▪ Closed Mon, Tue L, Nov–mid-Mar ▪ €€€

A gorgeous Art Nouveau villa-hotel, *(see p68)* serving local, seasonal produce in dazzling modern dishes.

④ La Rucola, Sirmione

MAP G4 ▪ Via Strentelle 3 ▪ 030-916-326 ▪ Closed Thu, mid-Jan–mid-Feb ▪ €€€

The Bignotti family's genteel restaurant offers a creative menu based on seasonal ingredients and local fish and meats.

⑤ Gemma, Limone

MAP G3 ▪ Piazza Garibaldi 12 ▪ 0365-954-014 ▪ Closed Nov & 1 week Mar ▪ €€

A charming, family-run place with a waterside terrace. Lake fish and organic meats feature on the menu.

⑥ Tenuta Canova, Lazise

MAP G4 ▪ Via Delaini 1 ▪ 045-758-0239 ▪ Closed Tue, Sun D ▪ €€€

Part of the Masi wine-making group, this vineyard hostelry puts the emphasis on the wine, with pairings for each dish on the menu, which includes gnocchi with smoked ricotta.

⑦ Ristorante Gardesana, Torri del Benaco

MAP G4 ▪ Piazza Calderini 5 ▪ 045-722-5411 ▪ Closed Mon & Nov–Mar ▪ €€€

Book ahead for an affordable lunch at the bistro on the ground floor and enjoy a la carte dinner at the restaurant on the first floor.

⑧ Osteria dell'Orologio, Salò

MAP G4 ▪ Via Butturini 26 ▪ 03-6529-0158 ▪ Closed Wed, Feb & last week Jun ▪ €€

This historic hostelry serves dishes such as pasta with Bagòs cheese or duck, and grilled lake fish with polenta, plus excellent local wines.

⑨ Trattoria da Pino Due, Garda

MAP G4 ▪ Via dell'Uva 17 ▪ 045-725-5694 ▪ Closed Mon & Jan–Feb ▪ €

A popular trattoria just outside Garda itself, with a wide shady veranda, serving delicious home cooking.

⑩ Vecchia Malcesine, Malcesine

MAP H3 ▪ Via Pisort 6 ▪ 045-740-0469 ▪ Closed Wed & Nov–Feb ▪ €€€

Enjoy lake specialities and lake views on the panoramic terrace here.

Interior of the Vecchia Malcesine

See map on p120

🔟 Smaller Lakes and Towns

While it is true that the lakes of Maggiore, Como and Garda are the best-developed and most obvious tourist destinations of the region, do not overlook the lesser-known lakes and towns of Lombardy. The museums of Bergamo, Mantua and others may not be as important as Milan's, the villas less grand than Como's, but a few days spent off the beaten path can offer a rewarding break from the crowds that throng Milan's great sights and back up traffic for hours along the big three lakes.

Harbourside, Lake Mergozzo

1 Lake Mergozzo

MAP A2 ■ Granite Museum: Via Roma 4; 0323-670-731; open Jul & Aug: 3–6pm Tue–Sun; Sep, Oct & Mar–Jun: 3–6pm Sat & Sun; www.ecomuseo granitomontorfano.it

Once part of Lake Maggiore and still joined by a 3-km (2-mile) canal, Lake Mergozzo has clear water, idyllic for swimming, while the lack of strong winds makes it a favourite among kayakers. Mergozzo town itself is a delightful place with cobbled lanes colourful buildings and an ancient elm tree which has stood in the main piazza for at least 400 years. The area is famous for its granite, and there's a museum here dedicated to the local quarrying tradition and history.

SMALLER LAKES AND TOWNS

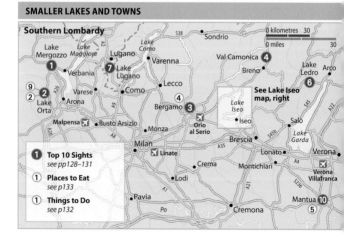

Southern Lombardy

- **1** Top 10 Sights
  see pp128–131
- **1** Places to Eat
  see p133
- **1** Things to Do
  see p132

Sacro Monte di San Francesco, above Lake Orta

2 Lake Orta

MAP A3 ■ Visitor info: Via Panoramica in Orta S Giulio; 0322-905-163; www.lagodorta.piemonte.it ■ Sacro Monte: www.sacrimonti.net

Just west of Lake Maggiore, this delightful little lake amid mountains and woodlands has a smattering of picturesque fishing villages around its shores. The star of the show is the exquisite medieval village of Orta San Giulio and its Piazza Motta. Nearby, Sacro Monte is a series of 20 chapels with statues portraying the life of St Franci. Just offshore is Isola San Giulio, dominated by the Romanesque basilica of San Giulio which has some remarkable frescoes, the earliest from the 14th century.

3 Bergamo

A vibrant city of medieval streets, fashionable boutiques and Renaissance churches, Bergamo is a favourite with Italians and visitors. A cable-car links its upper medieval and lower modern town (see pp32–3).

4 Val Camonica

MAP F2 ■ Visitor info: Via S Briscioli 42, Capo di Ponte; 0364-42-080; www.invallecamonica.it

The villages of Capo di Ponte (Loc Naquane; 0364-421-40) and Nadro di Ceto are the best access points for a visit to see one of the largest groupings of prehistoric rock carvings in the world. It is thought there are 200–300,000 images to be found in this valley north of Lake Iseo. The earliest images are at least 3,000 years old and include hunting scenes with deer and elk.

Val Camonica rock carvings

Fraciacorta vineyards and winery

5 Franciacorta

MAP D3 ■ Franciacorta Visitor Board: www.franciacorta.net

A wine-making area since ancient Roman times, the Franciacorta hills are home to some of Italy's best sparkling wines. Many wineries offer tours and tastings (see p132). Other attractions include the San Pietro monastery, overlooking the Torbiere nature reserve, and Castello Quistini with its fabulous rose garden.

6 Lake Ledro

MAP D3 ■ www.vallediledro. com ■ Museo delle Palafitte: www. palafitteledro.it

This idyllic lake in the mountains just west of Riva del Garda is a relaxing alternative to its larger neighbour. There are four beaches, and canoing,

Ferry port of Pescheria on Monte Isola

walking and mountain-biking are available. The incredible discovery of over 10,000 pillars from Bronze Age stilt-houses was made in the early 20th century; a fascinating reconstruction of such a village sits on the lakeside at the Museo delle Palafitte museum in Molina.

7 Lake Lugano

MAP B2–C2 ■ Visitor info: Campione d'Italia; Via Volta 3; www. campioneitalia.com ■ Swiss Miniatur: adm; www.swissminiatur.ch

Lake Lugano's principal resort, Campione d'Italia, is an Italian enclave within Switzerland's borders. To the south, outside Melide, is the delightfully kitsch Swiss Miniatur, whose "map" of Switzerland, covers all of the country's major monuments at 1/25 of their actual size.

8 Monte Isola

MAP E3 ■ Bicycle hire: Mar–Sep; www.monteisolabici.it

This peaceful, traffic-free island at the centre of Lake Iseo is ideal for a day out. Bicycles can be hired at Peschiera Maraglio, and walks include the path to the Madonna della Ceriola sanctuary at the top of the island, for stunning views over the lake and surrounding mountains. Peschiera is the main ferry stop and Siviano is Monte Isola's charming little capital, while Carzano, on the other side of the island, is a pictur-esque fishing village.

⑨ Lake Iseo

MAP E3–4 ■ Visitor info: IAT Lungolago Marconi 2, Iseo; 030-374-8733; www.visitlakeiseo.info

This is the prettiest of the smaller lakes, and the town of Iseo itself is as touristy as it gets. At Lovere, Galleria Tadini has a small collection of paintings by Bellini, Tintoretto and Tiepolo. The interior of the church of Santa Maria della Neve, at Pisogne, is another delight.

Fresco, Santa Maria della Neve

⑩ Mantua

The palaces, churches and artworks by Mantegna and Giulio Romano help make the town of Mantua (see pp34–5) a must-visit.

TWO DAYS EXPLORING LAKE ISEO AND FRANCIACORTA

▶ DAY ONE

Take an early ferry to Peschiera Maraglio on **Monte Isola** and hire a bike from the Bertelli news-agent's near the ferry stop. Cycle along the waterfront with the lake on your left to reach Siviano. Explore the village and continue to Carzano, stopping for a swim to work up an appetite for a lunch of delicious lake fish specialities at **Locanda al Lago** (see p133). Back on the mainland, head north to **Pisogne** (see p132); climb the tower and see the frescoes in the Santa Maria della Neve church. Return to Iseo in time to explore the centre and stop for a drink in Piazza Garibaldi before dinner at **Trattoria al Porto** (see p133) in Clusane, about 5 miles; stay the night at their sister B&B, **La Casa di Gabri** nearby (see p148).

DAY TWO

Have a leisurely breakfast by the pool then set off to explore the **Franciacorta** wine area. Before hitting the wineries visit the **San Pietro in Lamosa** monastery and walk the trails of the **Torbiere Nature Reserve** (see p132). If it's a Sunday in May or June, pop in to see the roses at Castello Quistini then stop for lunch at the **Solive Agriturismo** (see p133), enjoyed with a bottle of their Curtefranca. Meet your guide from the **Franciacorta Bike Tour** (see p132) and cycle through the vines, stopping for tastings at wineries along the way. Alternatively join a prebooked tour at **Ca' del Bosco** (see p132). Stay in Erbusco for the evening with a tasty meal at **La Smorfia** trattoria (see p133).

See map on pp128–9 ←

Things to Do

(1) Wine-Tasting in Franciacorta

MAP D3 ■ Ca' de Bosco: www. cadelbosco.com

Most of the wineries offer tours and tastings. The prestigious Ca' del Bosco winery combines art and wine; even the entrance gate is a sculpture.

(2) Lovere

MAP D3 ■ Accademia Tadini: Via Tadini 40; 035-962-780; adm; www.accademiatadini.it

Lovere features a waterfront piazza and an intriguing maze of lanes. The Accademia Tadini has a fine collection, with works by Canova and Bellini.

(3) Pisogne

MAP F3

The 13th-century Torre del Vescovo tower dominates this *(see p131)* pretty Lake Iseo village. Santa Maria della Neve has Renaissance frescoes.

(4) Cycle Routes

Franciacorta Bike Tour: www. franciacortabiketour.com ■ Iseo Bike: www.iseobike.com

A bicycle is the perfect vehicle for exploring the Franciacorta wine area. The Vello–Tolino path is popular.

Cycling in Franciacorta

(5) Golf

MAP D3 ■ Franciacorta Golf Club: Via Provinciale 34B, Corte Franca; www.franciacortagolfclub.it

The Franciacorta golf club has an immaculate 36-hole course. For non-golfers there's a wellness area, swimming pool and tennis courts.

(6) Treno dei Sapori

MAP E4 ■ trenodeisapori. area3v.com

Book for a gourmet experience with a difference on this historic train. The trips depart from Iseo and include guided tours, tastings and meals of local foods and wines. On some routes you can make your return by boat.

(7) Antica Strada Valeriana

MAP F3 ■ Lake Iseo: www. iseolake.info

The ancient cobbled Antica Valeriana is a simple footpath with idyllic views linking Pisogne with Pilzone, passing the glacial erosion pyramids at Zone.

(8) Watersports

Experience Lake Iseo from the water, either by kayak, windsurfer, kitesurfer or SUP. Tuition and hire is available at various points around the lake including Iseo and Marone.

(9) Lake Iseo Cruises

MAP E4 ■ www.navigazione lagoiseo.it

Cruises touring the islands of Monte Isola, San Paolo and Loreto offer a memorable viewpoint over the lake and surrounding mountains.

(10) Torbiere Nature Reserve

MAP G3 ■ Visitor Centre: Via Tangenziale Sud, Iseo; www. torbieresebino.it

This evocative expanse of lakes and marshland was once a peat bog, There's now a network of nature trails and a well-placed observation tower. Binoculars can be borrowed for free from the Visitor Centre to spot the diverse range of wildlife here.

Places to Eat

 Trattoria al Porto, Lake Iseo

MAP E4 ▪ Piazza Porto dei Pescatori 12, Clusane sul Lago ▪ 030-989 014 ▪ Closed Wed ▪ €€

Spaghetti with prawns and ravioli with Bagòs cheese are among the highlights at this *(see p68)* rustic-chic trattoria run by the Bosio family since 1862.

Villa Crespi's exotic dining room

 Villa Crespi, Lake Orta

MAP A3 ▪ Via G Fava 18, San Giulio ▪ 0322-911-902 ▪ Closed mid-late Jan, Mon & Tue L ▪ €€€

This stylish restaurant, in a unique Moorish-fantasy hotel *(see pp148–9)*, promises elegant service and top-quality regional cuisine.

3 L'Aragosta

MAP F3 ▪ Piazza Vittorio Emanuele II, 6 ▪ 035-962-600 ▪ Closed Thu ▪ €

Located in the historic centre, this trattoria serves local and regional specialities. Try the homemade pasta with fish sauce and sample the desserts also.

4 Trattoria Sant'Ambroeus

MAP D3 ▪ Piazza Vecchia 2, Bergamo ▪ 035-237-494 ▪ Closed Wed ▪ €€€

An elegant restaurant with a pleasant atmosphere, Trattoria Sant'Ambroeus is located in the main piazza. Excellent local cuisine is served such as *casoncelli alla berhamasca* (pasta).

PRICE CATEGORIES

For a three-course meal for one with half a bottle of wine (or equivalent meal), taxes and extra charges.

€ under €35   €€ €35–€60   €€€ over €60

5 Ochina Bianca, Mantua

MAP H6 ▪ Via Finzi 2 ▪ 0376-323-700 ▪ Closed Mon–Thu L, Sun D, late Jul–mid-Aug ▪ €€

Distinctive variations on local dishes and a judicious use of fresh fish from the nearby Mincio River.

6 La Smorfia, Erbusco

MAP D3 ▪ Via Costa Sotto 9 ▪ 030-726-8434 ▪ Closed Tue ▪ €

Pizzas, gourmet burgers, traditional dishes and a monthly spit roast. Being Franciacorta, the wine list is superb.

7 Solive Agriturismo, Nigoline di Corte Franca

MAP D3 ▪ Via Calvarole 15 ▪ 030-988-4201 ▪ Closed Mon D, Tue ▪ €€

Try this farm's own grilled meats together with a bottle of their full-bodied red Curtefranca.

8 VistaLago Bistrò, Erbusco

MAP D3 ▪ Via Vittorio Emanuele 23 ▪ 030-776-0550 ▪ €€€

Come to L'Albereta hotel *(see p148)* for a hot and cold Sunday brunch and fabulous views over Lake Iseo.

9 Al Boeuc, Lake Orta

MAP A3 ▪ Via Bersani 28, Orta San Giulio ▪ 339-584-0039 ▪ Closed Mar–Dec: Thu; Dec–Mar: open by reservation only, call to check ▪ €

Good wine, regional dishes such as *bagna cauda*, and platters of local meats and cheeses are served here.

10 Locanda al Lago, Lake Iseo

MAP E3 ▪ Località Carzano 38 ▪ 030-988-6472 ▪ Closed mid-Sep–Apr: Tue ▪ €€

Run by a local fishing family, this is the place to enjoy fish-stuffed ravioli.

See map on pp128–9

Streetsmart

Old and new side-by-side in Milan's booming Porta Nuova district

Getting To and Around Milan and the Lakes

Arriving by Air

Milan has two primary airports; **Milan Malpensa**, the main hub, has intercontinental flights plus domestic and European connections. The airport's two terminals are linked by a free 24-hour shuttle; travel time between them is 15 minutes. Malpensa is about 40 km (25 miles) northwest of the city. The railway station is located at Terminal 1 and Terminal 2. Milan Express trains run every 30 minutes to Milan Cadorna station, near Castello Sforzesco to Garibaldi station and Milan Central station. Various bus services connect Malpensa with the city's central station, including **Autostradale, Terravision,** and **Malpensa Express**. **Alibus** runs a shuttle bus between the airport and Lake Maggiore from March to October.

Milan Linate, just 7 km (4 miles) from the city centre, is Milan's second airport. The number 73 **ATM** city bus runs every 10 minutes between the airport and Via Gonzaga, near Piazza Duomo, taking about 30 minutes. Autostradale runs shuttle services to the city centre, and the **Malpensa Shuttle** runs a shuttle between the city's two airports.

Bergamo's **Orio al Serio Airport** is roughly 50 km (30 miles) east of Milan and connected to the city by Terravision, **Orio Shuttle** and Autostradale buses. Orio Shuttle and **ATB** also run bus services into Bergamo; the journey takes about 15 minutes. Milan's airports are the nearest for Lake Maggiore and Lake Como, but **Verona** airport is better for Lake Garda. **ATV** runs buses to Lake Garda that take about an hour.

Arriving by Train

Trenitalia and **Italo** trains run between major cities, with good links throughout Europe. Trenitalia runs the local rail network, and **Trenord** for Lombardy.

Arriving by Road

There are road tunnels through the Alps linking Italy to Switzerland and France, as well as coast roads from France and Slovenia. Northern Italy has a network of motorways and the **Autostrade per l'Italia** website has live traffic updates. Tolls are paid on leaving the motorway; quicker to pay by credit card at one of the dedicated booths (no commission is charged).

Eurolines and **Flixbus** both operate budget longdistance bus services linking cities throughout Europe and Italy, including Milan, Verona, Mantua, Bergamo and Como.

Getting Around by Train

The journey time from Milan to Stresa on Lake Maggiore is around an hour; to Como it is just over 30 minutes. Trains to Desenzano on Lake Garda take 50 minutes from Milan or 20 minutes from Verona, and to reach Iseo you will need to change at Brescia. The journey time from Milan to Verona is just over an hour; from Milan to Mantua it is an hour and 50 minutes.

Tickets for all but the high-speed trains should be stamped at machines near the platform to be validated before boarding.

Getting Around by Bus, Tram or Metro

ATM operates the buses, trams and metro in Milan. The same ticket is valid for all three and should be bought in advance. Stamp the ticket in the machine by the bus or tram doors to validate it. Tickets can also be bought through the ATM Milano mobile app (an English version is available). These are validated via the app on your device when you board. Pay with contactless cards as many times in a day to cap your fare without having to pay more than the daily ticket.

Individual tickets (€2) are valid for 90 minutes and you can change freely between buses and trams within this time and travel more than once with the same ticket on Metro or on Trenord trains within the urban area. Day passes, which cost €7, and threeday passes (€12) are valid for unlimited journeys.

Milan has four metro lines. Ticket information for the Metro is the same as for buses and trams, but tickets bought via the app must be scanned each time you pass through the turnstiles.

There is a useful online journey planner, called **Muoversi in Lombardia**.

Getting Around by Car

Driving in Milan can be difficult, with limited traffic zones (ZTL), tram- or bus-only lanes and pedestrianized areas, but driving is best to explore remote parts of the region. Around the lakes, roads get very busy, and in summer parking is scant; ferries are often the best option.

Blue parking spaces need payment, yellow-lined spaces are reserved for residents and white spaces are for free parking, unless otherwise shown.

Getting Around by Bicycle

Cycle lanes in Milan are on the increase and the city runs a bike-sharing scheme with numerous access points. Both daily (€4.50) and weekly (€9) subscriptions are available, but each journey must have a maximum duration of 2 hours. Subscribe via the **BikeMi** website or mobile app, by calling the info-line or at an ATM info-point.

Smile and Bike rents bicycles at points around the city and runs bicycle tours. Bike hire is widely available at the lakes.

Getting Around on Foot

Central Milan is relatively compact and there are many pedestrianized areas in the centre. At the lakes, towns and villages often have steep, narrow lanes with cobblestones or steps, tricky for people with reduced mobility.

Getting Around the Lakes by Ferry

Travelling by ferry is the best way to get around the lakes. **Gestione Navigazione Laghi** runs regular ferry services on Lakes Maggiore, Como and Garda, including both car and passenger-only ferries, while **Navigazione Lago Iseo** is the operator for Lake Iseo. Both also offer specialist cruises.

Single-journey and all-day tickets are available. Each jetty has its own ticket office which, in quieter periods, opens only about 20 minutes before a ferry is due.

DIRECTORY

ARRIVING BY AIR

Alibus
🔲 safduemila.com

ATB
🔲 atb.bergamo.it

ATM
🔲 atm.it

ATV
🔲 atv.verona.it

Autostradale
🔲 airportbusexpress.it

Malpensa Express
🔲 malpensaexpress.it

Malpensa Shuttle
🔲 malpensashuttle.it

Milan Linate
🔲 milanolinate-airport.com

Milan Malpensa
🔲 milanomalpensa-airport.com

Orio al Serio Airport
🔲 orioaeroporto.it

Orio Shuttle
🔲 orioshuttle.com

Terravision
🔲 terravision.eu

Verona
🔲 aeroportoverona.it

ARRIVING BY TRAIN

Italo
🔲 italotreno.it

Trenitalia
🔲 trenitalia.com

Trenord
🔲 trenord.it

ARRIVING BY ROAD

Autostrade per l'Italia
📞 840 042121
🔲 autostrade.it

Eurolines
🔲 eurolines.eu

Flixbus
🔲 flixbus.com

GETTING AROUND BY BUS, TRAM OR METRO

Muoversi in Lombardia
🔲 muoversi.regione.lombardia.it

GETTING AROUND BY BICYCLE

BikeMi
📞 02-4860-7607
🔲 bikemi.com

Smile and Bike
🔲 smileandbike.com

GETTING AROUND THE LAKES BY FERRY

Gestione Navigazione Laghi (Lakes Maggiore, Como and Garda)
📞 031 579211
🔲 navlaghi.it

Navigazione Lago Iseo
📞 035 971483
🔲 navigazionelagoiseo.it

Practical Information

Passports and Visas

Visas are not required for visitors to Italy from other countries within the European Union (EU), the European Economic Area (EEA) or Switzerland, but a valid identity card or passport is necessary. People travelling from a number of non-European countries such as Canada, the US, Brazil, Australia, New Zealand and Japan can stay for up to 90 days without a visa. For further information on visa regulations consult the **Ministero degli Esteri**.

Customs and Immigration

There are no limits in place on most goods carried between EU countries, including alcohol and tobacco, as long as they are just for personal use. Restrictions apply to firearms and other weapons, animals and some types of food. Arrivals from outside the EU can bring 16 litres of beer and 4 litres of wine, along with 1 litre of spirits or 2 litres of fortified wine; 250g (8.8 oz) of tobacco; and other dutiable goods of up to €430 in value. Amounts of cash over €10,000 taken into or out of the EU must be declared. Non-EU citizens can apply for VAT refunds on goods bought in the EU.

Travel Safety Advice

Visitors can get up-to-date travel safety information from the **UK Foreign and Commonwealth Office**, the **US Department of State** as well as the **Australian Department of Foreign Affairs and Trade**.

Travel Insurance

As with any trip, it is advisable to take out travel insurance to cover healthcare emergencies, transport cancellations, theft and loss. EU citizens carrying an **EHIC** (European Health Insurance Card) are entitled to free emergency healthcare thanks to a reciprocal arrangement with other EU countries. However, prescriptions and non-emergency healthcare must be paid for and can be costly. Australian citizens can also benefit from the **RHCA** (Reciprocal Health Care Agreement) when in Italy.

Health

Vaccinations are not required for visiting Italy and there are no particular health hazards in and around Milan and the lakes. Emergency treatment is provided free of charge at hospitals with a casualty department (pronto soccorso) but there is often a long wait unless it's a serious emergency. Hospitals with casualty departments in Milan include **Ospedale Fatebenefratelli**, **Ospedale Maggiore Policlinico**, and **Ospedale Macedonio Melloni**. On the lakes there are **Ospedale Castelli** (Lake Maggiore), **Ospedale Valduce** (Lake Como), **Ospedale di Lovere** (Lake Iseo) and **Ospedale di Desenzano** (Lake Garda). The **International Health Center** in central Milan has a weekdays-only team of English-speaking doctors and dentists and appointments are usually available at short notice. Free and anonymous testing for sexually transmitted diseases (STDs) is available at the walk-in **CRH-MTS** clinic.

Pharmacies have a green cross sign outside and are the best place to go for minor ailments, as they give well-informed advice and sell over-the-counter medication. When closed they always display the name and address of the nearest out-of-hours pharmacy. The **Boccaccio Pharmacy**, near the Santa Maria delle Grazie church is open 24 hours a day, seven days a week.

Personal Security

Milan is a relatively safe city and doesn't present any particular threats to personal security, although the usual sensible precautions should, of course, be taken with money, credit cards and valuables, especially in crowded areas and on public transport. Don't leave items of value visible in a parked car. Women travelling alone should not encounter particular problems in Milan or around the lakes.

Emergency Services

For most emergencies it's advisable to call the

general **emergency number,** but there are also numbers for the state police, the **fire service** and **ambulance**.

The **Polizia di Stato** (state police) and the **Carabinieri** (military police) have similar roles, and thefts should be reported to one or the other. There are a number of police stations and Carabinieri stations in Milan and on the lakes. A stolen credit or debit card should be blocked immediately by calling the 24-hour Polizia di Stato number. The **Polizia Ferroviaria** (railway police) are present at main stations and can be asked about items lost on trains. Report lost items to the city's **Oggetti Smarriti** (lost property) office.

Travellers with Specific Needs

The excellent **Milano Per Tutti** website has extensive listings of museums, galleries, churches, restaurants and hotels with exhaustive details of accessibility, aimed at travellers with specific needs, and there's also a series of suggested itineraries for visitors to the city as well as advice on transport.

Italian airports and railway stations have very well-organized assistance for travellers with specific needs. Most of the larger, more modern hotels have wheelchair facilities, but bars and restaurants are sometimes lacking. There may be problems due to the age and architecture of the particular building.

At the lakes, the hillside villages can be hard to navigate due to the steep, narrow lanes, cobbles and flights of steps.

Many upmarket hotels now offer gluten-free breakfast options and restaurants occasionally have dedicated menus. Staff are usually sensitive to special dietary requirements regarding allergies.

DIRECTORY

PASSPORTS & VISAS

Ministero degli Esteri
w vistoperitalia.esteri.it/home/en

TRAVEL SAFETY ADVICE

Australian Department of Foreign Affairs and Trade
w dfat.gov.au
w smarttraveller.gov.au

UK Foreign and Commonwealth Office
w gov.uk/foreign-travel-advice

US Department of State
w travel.state.gov

TRAVEL INSURANCE

EHIC
w gov.uk/european-health-insurance-cardl

RHCA
w humanservices.gov.au

HEALTH

Boccaccio Pharmacy
Via Boccaccio 26, Milan

CRH-MTS
Viale Jenner 44, Milan
C 02 8578 9871

International Health Center
Galleria Strasburgo 3, San Babila, MIlan
C 02 7634 0720;
w ihc.it

Ospedale Castelli
Via Crocetta 11, Verbania

Ospedale di Desenzano
Località Montecroce, Desenzano

Ospedale di Lovere
Via Martinoli 9, Lovere

Ospedale Fatebenefratelli
Corso di Porta Nuova 23

Ospedale Macedonio Melloni
Via Macedonio Melloni 52, Milan

Ospedale Maggiore Policlinico
Via San Barnaba 8, Milan

Ospedale Valduce
Via Santo Garovaglio 14, Como

EMERGENCY SERVICES

Ambulance
C 118

Carabinieri
Via Fosse Ardeatine 4, Milan
C 112

Emergency Number
C 112

Fire Service
C 115

Oggetti Smarriti
Via Friuli 30, Milan
C 02 8845 3900

Polizia di Stato
C 113
Piazza San Sepolcro 9, Milan
Piazza Venino 3, Milan
Via Fatebenefratelli 11, Milan
Corso Nazioni Unite 18, Pallanza
Via Roosevelt 7, Como
Via Roma 102, Iseo
Via Dante Alighieri 17, Desenzano del Garda

Polizia Ferroviaria
Stazione Centrale (next to Platform 21), Milan
C 02 6694 535

TRAVELLERS WITH SPECIFIC NEEDS

Milano Per Tutti
w milanopertutti.it

Currency and Banking

Italy's currency is the euro (€). Euro notes come in denominations of 500, 200, 100, 50, 20, 10 and 5 euros, while the coin denominations are 2 and 1 euros, then 50, 20, 10, 5, 2 and 1 cents. The easiest way to get cash is to use a debit or credit card at an ATM (bancomat), and these are easily found in central and suburban Milan. ATMs are also common in all but the smallest villages around the lakes. Commission for exchanging cash is lower at post offices than at banks, while bureaux de change generally have the least favourable rates. Credit cards are becoming more widely accepted in Italy, especially Visa and MasterCard, however some small restaurants will only take cash so check before ordering.

Telephone and Internet

If you are an EU resident, roaming charges for using your mobile phone within Europe were abolished as of 15 June 2017, so costs are now the same as for using it at home. Visitors from other nations will find it cheaper to invest in a pay-as-you-go Italian sim card; Tim, Vodafone, Wind and Tre are the main providers. Payphones are becoming increasingly difficult to find but can be used with a prepaid phone card (scheda telefonica) which can be bought at newsagents.

Area dialling codes (beginning with 0) must be dialled within Italy even for local calls, and Italian mobile phone numbers begin with 3. International country codes should be preceded by 00 (for the UK 44, for Australia 61) followed by the local area code minus the initial zero, and the number. For the USA and Canada you dial 001 followed by the full number.

Free Wi-Fi is widely available in Milan via the **Open WIFI Milano** service; the website has a map of the hotspots. Hotels, cafés and bars often provide free Wi-Fi, and so do both Milan Malpensa and Milan Linate airports and the Autogrill motorway service stations. It's usually available on high-speed trains.

Postal Services

The flat rate for sending letters and cards within Europe is €1, and €2.20 to North America. Stamps (francobolli) are sold at tobacconists (tabacchi) which are recognisable by a large blue or black letter "T" sign; queuing at post offices can be a frustrating experience as service is often very slow. Postboxes are red and can often be found outside tobacconists as well as at post offices. Pre-franked postcards, linked to private postal services, are sometimes available in tourist hot spots, but they should be avoided as they tend to cost more and take longer to be delivered.

TV, Radio and Newspapers

Most hotels in Italy now have satellite TV with international channels. **IsoRadio** is a national radio station (103.3 FM and online) which offers frequent updates on traffic problems, with bulletins in English during the summer. International newspapers and magazines are available at newsagents throughout Milan and, during the high season, in the larger resorts around the lakes.

Opening Hours

In central Milan the majority of shops open at about 9am and close around 7:30–8pm seven days a week. Smaller shops, neighbourhood food stores and banks traditionally open around 8am and close between 12:30–1pm and 3:30–4pm, then stay open until about 7.30pm (though banks close earlier) and are closed on Sundays. Non-stop opening hours (orario continuato) are becoming more widespread, however, opening times should be displayed. Churches observe similar hours to shops, while most museums remain open all day from Tuesday to Sunday but are closed on Mondays and last entry is usually 30 minutes before the official closing time.

Time Difference

Italy operates on Central European Time (CET), which is 1 hour ahead of Greenwich Mean Time and 6 hours ahead of US Eastern Standard Time. The clock moves forward by 1 hour during daylight saving time from the last Sunday in March until the last Sunday in October.

Electrical Appliances

Italy's power supply is 230 volts. Italian plugs have two or three round pins and devices from most other countries will need to have an adaptor.

Weather

Milan has a climate of extremes: very hot and humid in summer (many shops and restaurants close down for much of August) and cold in winter, so late spring and early autumn are the most pleasant times to visit.

The lakes benefit from a much milder micro-climate, as can be seen from the luxuriant and often exotic vegetation, but many of the villas and gardens are closed during winter, as are a lot of hotels and restaurants. During May, June and September the famous gardens are looking their very best and these are, once again, the best times for a visit, particularly since the whole lakes area can get extremely busy in July and August.

Visitor Information

The biggest and busiest office of **Turismo Milano**, the city's tourist department, is in the Galleria Vittorio Emanuele II, on the corner of Piazza della Scala. **Where Milan** is a free magazine and website with a wealth of information on places to stay and things to do, as well as restaurants, clubs, sights, shops and events.

The **Lake Como Tourist Office**, the **Lake Iseo & Franciacorta Tourist Office**, the **Lake Garda Tourist Office**, and the **Lake Maggiore & Lake Orta Tourist Office** can provide information on events, tours, hotels, restaurants, sights and sports facilities.

Trips and Tours

Milano City Sightseeing runs hop-on-hop-off tours around the city by double-decker bus; the price of the ticket includes headphones and there's a registered commentary in a number of languages. Guided walking tours (in English or Italian) of the Historic Centre of Milan are run by **Milan Free Tour**, and are completely free of charge. The local transport company, ATM (see p137) has converted two historic trams into attractive mobile restaurants, called **ATMosfera**, and offer tours of the city with dinner on board every night of the week. Boat trips on Milan's Navigli canals are provided by **Navigli Lombardi** and various itineraries, both long and short, are available.

Many companies offer boat tours of the lakes, and the standard ferry companies also organize various lake cruises. The Gestione Navigazione Laghi ferry services (see p137) cover the lakes of Maggiore, Como and Garda while Lake Iseo is covered by Navigazione Lago Iseo (see p137).

A memorable way to see Lake Como is from the air with a seaplane tour; these are organized by the **Aero Club Como**.

DIRECTORY

TELEPHONE AND INTERNET

Open WIFI Milano
w openwifimilano.it

TV, RADIO, AND NEWSPAPERS

IsoRadio
w isoradio.rai.it

VISITOR INFORMATION

Lake Como Tourist Office
w lakecomo.it

Lake Garda Tourist Office
w visitgarda.com
w gardalombardia.com

Lake Iseo & Franciacorta Tourist Office
w visitlakeiseo.info

Lake Maggiore & Lake Orta Tourist Office
w distrettolaghi.it
w illagomaggiore.com

Turismo Milano
w turismo.milano.it

Where Milan
w wheremilan.com

TRIPS AND TOURS

Aero Club Como
w aeroclubcomo.com

ATMosfera
w atm.it

Milan Free Tour
w milanfreetour.com

Milano City Sightseeing
w milano.city-sightseeing.it

Navigli Lombardi
w naviglilombardi.it

Shopping

Milan is unquestionably Italy's capital of shopping. From the ultra exclusive designer boutiques of the Golden Quad to the independent offbeat stores of Corso di Porta Ticinese, there's something here for everyone. Personal shoppers exist to help those with serious spending in mind to find their way around, and **Exclusive Fashion Tours** runs a good service.

Although fashion is the main focus of the city's retail therapy opportunities, there's much more to Milan than just couture. The city has an excellent range of quality food stores, for example, and delicatessens will usually be able to vacuum pack items on request. The monthly antiques market at Navigli (see pp28–9) is exceptional, while football fans can score souvenirs and official strip of the city's two top teams, AC Milan and Internazionale, at **(AC) MIlano Megastore** and **Inter Store Milano** located in the city centre.

The weekly open-air markets in the villages around the lakes are colourful and popular, and generally sell everything from food to clothing.

Como is well-known for its long silk tradition, and there are a number of stores selling silk items in Como and Bellagio.

Non-EU residents can claim VAT refunds on goods costing a combined total of at least €155 bought from the same store on the same day, by filling in the appropriate forms and having them stamped at customs.

Dining

Milan has a vast and varied choice of eateries of every kind and for every budget. As well as Italian food, there are numerous places serving international cuisine, particularly oriental, and there's a good choice of vegetarian eateries around the city.

Although nowadays the lines dividing the different categories of restaurant have become blurred, a ristorante traditionally offers a more formal dining experience, while a trattoria serves simple home cooking and is often family run. An osteria originally referred to a wine bar with food, whereas nowadays the term is used for a low-key eatery with a relaxed atmosphere – they are now more frequently called enoteca con cucina. Pizzerias are abundant, and usually serve a simple restaurant menu as well as pizzas, which are sometimes available in the evenings only.

Eateries of all kinds tend to open from about noon to 2:30 or 3pm and from about 7 to 10pm, or later in busy areas. Food is served all day in some places at busy holiday times around the lakes.

Cafés often have already prepared hot (tavola calda) or cold (tavola fredda) food and they are increasingly providing freshly cooked dishes too. Brunch is often served at weekends, and most bars and cafés provide a generous buffet of snacks from about 6pm to 8 or 9pm each evening; there's often a set price for drinks at this time, to include the food, which is sometimes substantial and may even include pasta or other hot dishes. Enticing delicatessens (gastronomia) are the best choice for panini (sandwiches), made with top quality ingredients, while markets and food shops are the place to go for putting a picnic together.

Menus are divided into antipasti (starters), primi (pasta or rice), secondi (a main course of fish or meat, sometimes with vegetarian options), contorni (side dishes), formaggi (cheeses) and dolci (dessert). Although a traditional Italian meal would include at least three of these, it's quite acceptable to order just one or two courses from any section of the menu. Side dishes will be served with the main course but the other courses will be served in sequence, unless you specify that you want them at the same time (insieme means together).

Most menus offer a house wine and a choice of wine by the bottle, if not a full, and often extensive, wine list. Tap water, even though it's drinkable, is rarely served, but still (naturale) or sparkling (frizzante) mineral water will always be offered.

Larger eateries often have high-chairs for small children and sometimes there is a special menu; if not, most places will happily serve half portions (mezza porzione) or simple dishes, such as pasta with tomato sauce (pasta al pomodoro) even if these are not on the menu.

Italians rarely leave tips unless the service has been truly exceptional. Watch out for extra service charges added as a percentage, particularly in the tourist resorts.

Accommodation

There's a good choice of hotels at all levels in Milan itself and near the lakes, where there is an exceptional selection of quality hotels located in historic lakeside villas. Direct booking is favoured by many of the smaller hotels but international booking websites such as **Booking.com**, have an excellent range of options. The number of B&Bs in Italy is growing rapidly, and this kind of accommodation option often provides the best deals in terms of comfort, style, price and location and hosts are often keen to help with local advice. **Bed & Breakfast Italia** is a well-arranged website with a wide range of properties, and their BBcard offers a loyalty discount to members. **Homestay** also has a small selection of hosts offering – mostly simple and inexpensive but stylish – private rooms in Milan.

Self-catering offers both flexibility and the chance to shop for and cook local produce. Online booking organizations such as **Home Away** and **Airbnb** have plenty of options in and around Milan. There is also a good choice of self-catering options at the lakes. As well as the online booking agencies there are some good local agencies with lovely properties of all sizes and styles – for Lake Como try **Vacanze Lago**, or **Garda Holidays** and **Lake Maggiore Homes**.

Waterside campsites are a popular option for holidays at the lakes; they often have direct access to the water and sometimes offer watersports on site as well as having other sporting facilities. Accommodation is often available at working farms, called *agriturismo*, where farm experiences, interaction with farmyard animals for children, cookery courses, winetasting and a host of other experiences are sometimes available. Note that the term refers to farms with either a restaurant or accommodation but not necessarily both. The **Parco Agricolo Sud Milano** website lists a good range of *agriturismi* in the Milan area, with details of what they offer, while **Agriturismo Italia** is the official national website and has a full list of recognized *agriturismi*. **Agriturist** is another good website for listings, with information in English.

Hostel World lists budget accommodation in hostels, B&Bs, campsites and apartments.

The local tourist boards *(see p141)* can also provide information and contacts for accommodation.

Prices depend on the kinds of events in the city instead of a specific high season. Better deals can often be obtained by booking direct with a hotel rather than online and some, particularly the smaller hotels, prefer to interact with clients themselves, not always even requiring a deposit for short stay.

Breakfast, parking and use of facilities such as wellness areas and bikes may not be included in the price quoted so it's wise to check before confirming. One extra cost is the *tassa di soggiorno* or tourist tax. This is a municipal tax imposed on the first four nights you stay at any type of accommodation and varies, depending on the local regulations, category and the time of year, from 50 cents to several euros a night per person.

DIRECTORY

SHOPPING

(AC) Milan Megastore
Galleria San Carlo-Corso Vittorio Emanuele II

Exclusive Fashion Tours
w exclusivefashion tours.com

Inter Store Milano
Galleria Passarella 2

ACCOMMODATION

Agriturismo Italia
w agriturismoitalia.gov.it

Agriturist
w agriturist.it

Airbnb
w airbnb.com

Bed & Breakfast Italia
w bed-and-breakfast.it

Booking.com
w booking.com

Garda Holidays
w gardaholidays.co.uk

Home Away
w homeaway.it

Homestay
w homestay.com

Hostel World
w italian.hostel world.com

Lake Maggiore Homes
w lakemaggiore homes.net

Parco Agricolo Sud Milano
w parcoagricolosud milano.it

Vacanze Lago
w vacanzelago.com

Places to Stay

PRICE CATEGORIES
For a double room with breakfast and taxes in high season.

€ under €250 **€€** €250–500 **€€€** over €500

Milan's Luxury Hotels

Antica Locanda dei Mercanti
MAP L3 ▪ Via San Tomaso 6 ▪ 02-805-4080 ▪ www. locanda.it ▪ €€
This 18th-century former apartment building, set between the Duomo and Castello, is a wonderful home-away-from-home. The light-filled rooms offer pale furnishings and wrought-iron bed-steads plus the occasional exposed beam. The more expensive terrazzo rooms have flower-filled rooftop terraces and canopy beds. There is also a small restaurant and bar.

Grand Hotel et de Milan
MAP M3 ▪ Via Manzoni 29 ▪ 02-723-141 ▪ www. grandhoteletdemilan.it ▪ €€
The Grand has been Milan's most intimate luxury hotel since 1863, a darling of inveterate shoppers and La Scala stars (it was Callas's Milan home). Composer Giuseppe Verdi was also a resident for 30 years.

Sheraton Diana Majestic
MAP P2 ▪ Viale Piave 42 ▪ 02-20-581 ▪ www. sheratondianamajestic. com ▪ €€
This Liberty-style hotel is set around a lush court-yard garden. The rooms have a modern elegance and lovely furniture with top-end amenities such as Bose Wave stereos.

Spadari al Duomo
MAP L4 ▪ Via Spadari 11 ▪ 02-7200-2371 ▪ www. spadarihotel.com ▪ €€
This gem of a hotel, filled with original works by contemporary artists, is situated near Piazza Duomo. Stylish rooms include features such as marble sinks and hydro-massage shower stalls.

Armani Hotel
MAP M3 ▪ Via Manzoni 31 ▪ 02-8883-8888 ▪ www.milan.armani hotels.com ▪ €€€
Rooms are decorated with Armani's signature chic and sophisticated style. There's a well-equipped 24-hour gym as well as a soothing spa, and the hotel also features a stylish and gourmet restaurant. The hotel's location in the heart of Milan's shopping area is perfect for retail therapy.

Carlton Hotel Baglioni
MAP N2 ▪ Via Senato 5 ▪ 02-77-077 ▪ www. baglionihotels.com ▪ €€€
This hotel, located on the north side of the shopping district, has 19th-century-style silk brocades and inlaid furnishings. There is also a business centre, a spa and a restaurant.

Four Seasons
MAP N2 ▪ Via Gesù 8 ▪ 02-77-088 ▪ www. fourseasons.com/milan ▪ €€€
Converted from a 15th-century convent in 1993, the Four Seasons retains some fine frescoes. The superior rooms are on the street side, while deluxe rooms open onto the cloisters. Milan's best shops are nearby, and there are two restaurants, one offering a vegetarian menu.

Palazzo Parigi Hotel and Grand Spa
MAP M2 ▪ Corso di Porta Nuova 1 ▪ 02-625-625 ▪ www.palazzoparigi. com ▪ €€€
Located in the lively Brera district, Palazzo Parigi Hotel has elegant rooms and suites with private balconies overlooking the beautiful Duomo of Milan. As a former patrician residence, it is decorated in grand style.

Park Hyatt Milan
MAP L3 ▪ Via Tommaso Grossi 1 ▪ 02-8821-1234 ▪ www.milan.park.hyatt. com ▪ €€€
This luxurious hotel is situated in the heart of the city, just steps from Piazza Duomo and the Scala opera house, and within easy access of Via Montenapoleone's shops. The Ed Tuttle-designed interior features Bang & Olufsen TVs, large marble bathrooms and walk-in closets. There is also a spa with a fitness centre, gold mosaic whirlpool, men's and women's steam rooms and a hammam.

TownHouse Galleria
MAP M4 ■ Via Silvio Pellico 8 ■ 02-3659-690 ■ www.townhouse hotels.com ■ €€€
The exclusive location within the lovely Galleria Vittorio Emanuele II arcade makes any stay here a memorable one. Rooms are equipped with contemporary technology and furnished with stylish design elements. The hotel also has a top floor fitness suite offering wellness treatments.

Milan's Smaller Hotels and B&Bs

Hotel Due Giardini
MAP P1 ■ Via Benedetto Marcello 47 ■ 02-2952-1093 ■ www.hotel duegiardini.it ■ €
Located in a pleasant and convenient neighbourhood which is not too close to the station, but just a short walk away from the shops in Corso Buenos Aires. This hotel offers great value for money. As its name suggests, it really does have two gardens, which are perfect when you want a break from Milan's gritty urban cityscape and relax.

Hotel Metro
MAP R2 ■ Corso Vercelli 61■ 02-4987-897 ■ www. hotelmetro.it ■ €
Near a metro station just outside the city centre, Hotel Metro is well connected for getting around the city. Rooms are functional and come equipped with private, modern bathrooms. A hearty breakfast, which is served in the attic garden, makes for a nice start to the day.

Vecchia Milano
MAP L4 ■ Via Borromei 4 ■ 02-875-042 ■ www. hotelvecchiamilano.it ■ €
This hotel has charming, semi-rustic wooden panelling, good-sized rooms and it is located on a quiet street west of the Duomo. Some of the rooms come with a third bed that folds down from the wall, which is great for families on a budget.

Villa Magnolia
MAP J6 ■ Via Ambrogio Binda 32 ■ 02-8130-200 ■ www.bbvillamagnolia.it ■ €
This attractive early 1900s villa is set in a residential area close to the Navigli district, just south of the city centre, and offers bed-and-breakfast accommodation. It has two double rooms and one suite, sleeping three, and there is satellite TV.

3 Rooms
MAP L2 ■ Corso Como 10, 20154 Milan ■ 02-626163 ■ www.3rooms-10corso como.com ■ €€
Part of the fashionable 10 Corso Como complex (see p70) each of three suites has its own independent entrance. The quirky and colourful decor features iconic design items.

Antica Locanda Leonardo
MAP J3 ■ Corso Magneta 78 ■ 02-4801-4197 ■ www. anticalocandaleonardo. com ■ €€
Situated in a residential building just a couple of minutes' walk from Santa Maria delle Grazie, home to Leonardo's *The Last Supper*, this family-run guesthouse with a

charming little garden offers a peaceful retreat from the bustle of the city.

Antica Locanda Solferino
MAP M1 ■ Via Castelfidardo 2 ■ 02-657-0129 ■ www.antica locandasolferino.it ■ €€
Milan's most eccentric hotel is beloved by celebrities. What it lacks in amenities, it makes up for with its flower-fringed balconies, its homely, mismatched furnishings and breakfast in bed.

Elisabeth Lifestyle Hotel
MAP L5-M5 ■ Corso Italia 11a ■ 02-8909-4270 ■ www. elhmilan.com ■ €€
With bright and modern rooms as well as a gym and sauna, this four-star hotel is located in a lively area. It is only a short walk away from the Piazza Duomo.

Genius Hotel Downtown
MAP L3 ■ Via Porlezza 4 ■ 02-7209-4644 ■ www. hotelgenius.it ■ €€
This cosy modern hotel is on a quiet street beside the Castello. Rooms are compact but modern and clean, with bright, thick carpets, orthopaedic beds and largish baths.

Gran Duca di York
MAP L4 ■ Via Moneta 1a ■ 02-874-863 ■ www. ducadiyork.com ■ €€
In the 19th century this palazzo was used by the nearby cathedral to house visiting cardinals. Today, rooms have comfortable, modern furnishings, and some have terraces. The location in the historic centre is a real bonus.

Hotel Galileo
MAP N4 ■ Corso Europa 9 ■ 02-77-431 ■ www.galileo hotelmilan.com ■ €€
This modern four-star hotel is in the heart of Milan and within easy reach of the Duomo and the trendy shopping district. The 89 spacious rooms have free Wi-Fi.

Hotel Lancaster
MAP J1 ■ Via Abbondio Sangiorgio 16 ■ 02-344-705 ■ www.lancaster hotel.it ■ €€
A lovely Art Nouveau-style town house in a peaceful residential street right by Parco Sempione, this hotel is within easy reach of the centre of the city. A real find, it offers great prices, especially in June and July. Some rooms have terraces. Closed three weeks in August.

Hotel Palladio
MAP P6 ■ Via Palladio 8 ■ 02-5830-6900 ■ www. hotelpalladio.net ■ €€
This is a typical 1920s townhouse, in a quiet residential street very near the lively Porta Romana area with its many bars, shops and restaurants. It offers excellent value, with special rates from June to August. Many rooms have balconies and all have satellite TV. No breakfast is served but there's a café a few minutes' walk away which has warm brioche (sweet croissants) and creamy cappuccinos for a couple of euros.

Hotel S. Biagio
MAP P1 ■ Via Paganini 6 ■ 02-204-7443 ■ www. hotel-san-biagio-it.book. direct ■ €€
Staying at this tiny hotel on a residential street

off Corso Buenos Aires is like moving in with friends. The ten high-ceilinged rooms are large and comfortable, and all have a private bathroom. Rooms are equipped with TV and free Wi-Fi.

Hotel Sempione
MAP M5 ■ Via Finocchiaro Aprile 11 ■ 02-6570-323 ■ www.hotelsempione milan.com ■ €€
Located between the train station and Piazza del Duomo, Hotel Sempione is set in a refurbished historic building. It is also close to the shopping and entertainment hub of Corso Buenos Aires. The simple rooms offer every modern comfort.

Hotel Tiziano
MAP R2 ■ Via Tiziano 6 ■ 02-469-9035 ■ www. hoteltizianomilano.it ■ €€
Set within a 1930s palace designed by architect Piero Portaluppi, this hotel is situated in a pretty area, with rooms overlooking a large, tranquil park. It is also just a short walk to Fieramilano City. Rooms are warmly furnished and come with free Wi-Fi.

London
MAP L3 ■ Via Rovello 3 ■ 02-7202-0166 ■ www. hotellondonmilano.com ■ €€
The most old-fashioned of three hotels on a block near the Castello, London offers friendly service, bright and large rooms with worn but solid furnishings, and 10 per cent off for dining in the restaurant next door. Rooms get smaller as you go up each floor, so try to book one on a lower floor.

San Francisco
MAP P1 ■ Viale Lombardia 55 ■ 02-236-1009 ■ www. hotel-sanfrancisco.it ■ €€
This small, family-run hotel is only six metro stops from the Duomo and three from the main train station. Rooms are sparse but adequate and there is a pretty garden with pergola, lawn and terrace where breakfast is served in the summer.

Santa Marta Suites
MAP L4 ■ Via Santa Marta 4 ■ 02-4537-3369 ■ www. santamartasuites.com ■ €€
A timeless atmosphere is enhanced by historical architectural elements and antique furnishings in the beautifully designed rooms and suites on offer here. The top-floor terrace has views over the rooftops to the city's stunning cathedral.

Westin Palace
MAP N1 ■ Piazza della Repubblica 20 ■ 02-63-361 ■ www.westin palacemilan.com ■ €€
The general decor of the historic Westin Palace is a genteel Empire style, but the "smart rooms" have lots of high-tech facilities, and the plush business centre offers on-staff translators and 13 well-equipped conference rooms. There is also a fully equipped gym.

Ariston
MAP K/L4 ■ Largo Carrobbio 2 ■ 02-7200-0556 ■ www. ariston hotel.com ■ €€€
Offering a novel approach to Italian inn-keeping, the Ariston is an eco-hotel. The electrical devices here are engineered for

low power consumption; the showers conserve water; the tap water and even the air are purified; the breakfast spread is organic. Naturally, the desk rents out Riciclo bicycles for exploring the city.

Capitol
MAP C5 ■ Via Cimarosa 6 ■ 02-438-591 ■ www.hotel capitolmilano.com ■ €€€
This towering modern hotel boasts the latest in business technologies, as well as a fitness centre and rare on-site parking. Free Wi-Fi is available throughout the hotel, but guest rooms also include free fibre-optic broadband and flat-screen HD TV.

Doria Grand Hotel
MAP S2 ■ Viale Andrea Doria 22 ■ 02-6741-1411 ■ www.doriagrandhotel.it ■ €€€
This is a large hotel with modern, comfortable rooms, four conference rooms, and secretarial services. It's ideal for a business trip but, as with many hotels in Milan, special discount rates are available on weekends.

Maison Borella
MAP K6 ■ Alzaia Naviglio Grande 8■ 02 5810 9114 ■ www.hotelmaison borella.com ■ €€€
Overlooking the canal and with an internal courtyard, this attractive hotel has simple rooms and offers a good base among the bars and restaurants of the Navigli district.

Marriott
MAP R2 ■ Via Washington 66 ■ 02-48-521 ■ www. marriott.com ■ €€€
With 20 meeting rooms, a well-equipped business centre and a whole floor of Executive rooms, the Milan Marriott was built for the business traveller. Convenient for the Via Wagner and Piazza De Angeli shopping streets; if only it were nearer the centre for sightseeing when meetings are over.

Mediolanum
MAP P1 ■ Via Mauro Macchi 1 ■ 02-670-5312 ■ www.mediolanum hotel.com ■ €€€
The austerity of this cement-grey hotel is relieved by the personal touch brought by family management. Facilities include a business centre with secretarial services, and there is valet parking.

Starhotel Anderson
MAP S2 ■ Piazza Luigi di Savoia 20 ■ 02-669-0141 ■ www.starhotels.com ■ €€€
This design hotel offers sleek, modern decor. Expect beautiful fabrics, wooden panelling, large, comfortable beds and sumptuous marble bathrooms. It is located next to Stazione Centrale and is just a short walk from Giardini Pubblici. The restaurant, Black, serves first-rate international and local dishes. Guests have access to meeting rooms as well as a fully equipped 24-hour fitness room. There is free Wi-Fi in all the guest rooms.

Tocq Hotel
MAP R2 ■ Via A. De Tocqueville 7/D ■ 02-62-071 ■ www.tocq.it ■ €€€
Situated near the Corso Como and the Porta Nuova district, and close to the Garibaldi metro station, this hotel has well-equipped and modern rooms. Rooms have free Wi-Fi, satellite TV and minibars. Both Italian and American breakfasts are offered.

Una Hotel Century
MAP S2 ■ Via F Filzi 25B ■ 02-675-041 ■ www. unahotels.it ■ €€€
Set near the central station, north of Piazza della Repubblica, this property is made up entirely of sleek, modern business suites, each with a bedroom and separate living room/office. It's an ideal choice for a short business visit.

Places to Stay in the Lakes and in Smaller Towns

Antico Chiostro, Como
MAP C3 ■ Via Lambertenghi 4, 22100 Como, Lake Como ■ 347-0632-137 ■ www.antico chiostro.info ■ €
At this comfortable and welcoming bed-and-breakfast in Como's attractive historic centre. the two suites have beautiful country-style decor, en-suite facilities and a small kitchen area.

Bellavista, Brunate
MAP C3 ■ Piazza Bonacossa 2 ■ 031-221-031 ■ www.bellavista brunate.com ■ €
This Art Nouveau hotel has stunning views over Lake Como from most rooms, as well as from the restaurant and the garden. Located close to the funicular station at Brunate it is easy to reach from Como. The small spa has a colour therapy sauna and a Jacuzzi.

Broletto, Mantua
MAP H6 ▪ Via Accademia
1 ▪ 0376-326-784 ▪ www.
hotelbroletto.com ▪ €
This is a small, family-run
hotel, housed in a 16th-
century palazzo with a
vaguely rustic contem-
porary decor. It is in a
lovely location, just a few
steps from Lake Inferiore.

Hotel Impero, Cremona
MAP E6 ▪ Piazza della
Pace 21 ▪ 0372-413-013
▪ www.hotelimpero.cr.it
▪ €
The 53 rooms of this hotel
are elegantly decorated,
blending period furniture
with modern facilities.
There is a smart wellness
area. Located in the town
centre, the Imperio offers
views over the cathedral
square and the town hall.

Il Sole, Bergamo
MAP D3 ▪ Via Colleoni 1
▪ 035-218-238 ▪ www.
ilsolebergamo.com ▪ €
This family hotel is set
in the historic centre of
Bergamo Alta. It offers
comfortable, homely
rooms with free Wi-Fi.
The in-house restau-
rant offers traditional
cuisine, a fine selection
of wine as well as pizzas
on the menu.

Iseolago, Iseo
MAP E4 ▪ Via Colombera
2 ▪ 030-98-891 ▪ www.
iseolagohotel.it ▪ €
The Iseolago is situated
near the Torbiere nature
reserve and mixes the
best of a resort hotel with
the class of a fine inn. There
is a fitness centre, two
pools, tennis courts, and
watersports at the beach
to keep you occupied. It
is in the suburbs, so you
will need a car.

La Casa di Gabri, Clusane d'Iseo
MAP E4 ▪ Via Risorgimento
Trav. Tredicesima 2 ▪ 349-
291-0479 ▪ www.lacasadi
gabri.com ▪ €
This lovely B&B close to
Lake Iseo has appealing
fresh country-style decor,
a wide and shady veranda
and a large outdoor pool
and garden. Gabriella,
also owner and chef at
the nearby Trattoria del
Porto, provides a varied
and delicious breakfast.

La Veranda, Iseo
MAP F3 ▪ Largo Dante 5
▪ 335-635-2947 ▪ Closed
Jan & Feb ▪ www.bblaver
andaiseo.weebly.com ▪ €
This B&B has a spacious,
vine-covered terrace overlooking one of Iseo's
pretty piazzas, close to
the lake. Owner Flavio
enjoys sharing his local
knowledge and is alwasy
happy to take his guests
on a walk round the town
or out on a tour of the
Franciacorta vineyards.

Le Rêve, Sirmione
MAP G4 ▪ Piazza Carducci
26 ▪ 349-8805-310 ▪ www.
lerevesirmione.it ▪ €
Centrally located in
Sirmione, this friendly
bed-and-breakfast has
four rooms decorated in
a charming country-style
decor. Some have a terrace
overlooking the piazza
and Lake Garda beyond.

Olivi, Sirmione
MAP G4 ▪ Via San Pietro
in Mavino 5 ▪ 030-990-
5365 ▪ www.hotelolivi.
com ▪ €
Just a short stroll from
Sirmione's busy centre,
and on the shore of
Lake Garda, this smart
hotel's facilities include
both indoor and outdoor

thermal-heated pools and
an open-air swimming
pool in summer. Some
rooms have lake views.

Sheraton Lake Como, Cernobbio
MAP C3 ▪ Via per
Cernobbio 41A ▪ 031-
5161 ▪ www.sheraton
lakecomo.com ▪ €€
A contemporary hotel
with comfortable and
stylish interiors, an outdoor pool and pizzeria. It's
a five-minute walk from
the Tavernola ferry stop
so makes an ideal base,
for exploring Lake Como.

Villa della Torre, Fumane
MAP H4 ▪ Via della Torre
25 ▪ 045-683-2070 ▪ www.
villadellatorre.it ▪ €€
Surrounded by vineyards,
this Renaissance villa is
owned by the Allegrini
wine-making dynasty,
The grounds and interior
of the villa, particularly
the statuesque monster
fireplaces downstairs,
are simply breathtaking.

L'Albereta, Erbusco
MAP E4 ▪ Via Vittorio
Emanuele 23 ▪ 030-7760
550 ▪ www.albereta.it
▪ €€€
This gorgeous country-
house hotel is owned by
the prestigious Bellavista
winery and has lovely
views over Lake Iseo.
There are two restau-
rants, a spa and lovely
grounds. Some rooms
have frescoes and are
furnished with antiques.

Villa Crespi, Lake Orta
MAP A3 ▪ Via Fava, 18
▪ 0322-911-902 ▪ www.
villacrespi.it ▪ €€€
Villa Crespi is a fantastical
1879 Moorish-style villa,

complete with minaret, set against a backdrop of mountains. Suites and rooms are sumptuous, with mosaic or parquet flooring, carved wooden furnishings, silk brocaded walls, and bed canopies. The two-Michelin-starred restaurant (see p133) offers two tasting menus and good service.

Self-Catering and Campsites

Campeggio Città di Milano

MAP Q2 ▪ Via G Airaghi 61 ▪ 02-4820-7017 ▪ www.campingmilano.it ▪ €
Milan's only campsite is by the SS22 (take bus 72 from the De Angeli Metro stop) near the San Siro stadium. It has a restaurant and some tents are suspended between the trees.

Campeggio Park Garda, Limone

MAP G3 ▪ Via 4 Novembre 10 ▪ 0365-954-550 ▪ Closed Nov–Mar ▪ www.camping lagodigarda.it ▪ €
Just outside Limone, on its own private Garda beach, Campeggio Park Garda offers a wide range of services: windsurfing and sailing; two pools; a fish restaurant; wood-oven pizzeria; beach grill as well as a shop.

Camping Conca d'Oro, Feriolo di Baveno

MAP A2 ▪ Via 42 Martiri 26 ▪ 0323-281-16 ▪ Closed Oct–Mar ▪ www.concadoro.it ▪ €
This verdant campsite is located outside Baveno, on Lake Maggiore in the Fondo Toce nature reserve.

Amenities here include a restaurant and a mini-market, bikes and kayaks, plus a sandy beach.

Camping del Sole, Lake Iseo

MAP E4 ▪ Via per Rovato 26 ▪ 030-980-288 ▪ www.campingdelsole.it ▪ Closed Oct–Mar ▪ €
This large camping site offers plenty of greenery right on the lake (book ahead for the coveted few lakeside sites). Facilities include a restaurant, a market and a laundry, as well as bike hire, two pools as well as tennis and basketball courts.

Camping Isolino, Verbania

MAP A2 ▪ Via per Feriolo 25 ▪ 0323-496-414 ▪ Closed Oct–Mar ▪ www.campingisolino.com ▪ €
This oasis of tranquillity sits on the promontory of a Lake Maggiore nature reserve along a private sandy beach. It's one of the best equipped camp-sites in the entire region, with a market, pizzeria, restaurant, swimming pool, mountain-bike excursions, windsurfing and entertainment.

Camping Monte Brione, Riva del Garda

MAP H3 ▪ Via Brione 32 ▪ 0464-520-885 ▪ Closed Oct–Mar ▪ www.campingbrione.com ▪ €
Set in greenery near a beach on Lake Garda, this four-star camping and caravan site has minigolf, a swimming pool and table tennis. Small tents can be pitched on terraces of ancient olive trees.

Camping Villaggio Gefara, Domaso

MAP C2 ▪ Via Case Sparse 230 ▪ 0344-96-163 ▪ Closed 6 Oct–20 Mar ▪ www.campinggefara.it ▪ €
This small campsite sits right on the beach on Lake Como, and has a bar and laundry room. There are plenty of shops and watersports nearby.

Residence Aramis Milano, Milan

MAP J6 ▪ Via Mortara 2 ▪ 340-084-8590 ▪ www.residencearamismilano.it ▪ €
Overlooking a canal in the lively Navigli district, this "aparthotel" has accom-modation ranging from rooms to fully equipped apartments sleeping six. All clean and spacious, and come with free Wi-Fi.

Serego Alighieri, Sant'Ambrogio di Valpolicella

MAP H4 ▪ Via Stazione Vecchia, Gargagnago ▪ 045-770-3622 ▪ www.seregoalighieri.it ▪ €
Set in part of the historic wine estate run by the descendants of medieval poet Dante, these lovely apartments have beamed ceilings, wooden floors and their own kitchen. Breakfast is served in the main dining area.

Milanosuites, Milan

MAP L3 ▪ Via San Tomaso 6 ▪ 02-8051-023 ▪ www.milanosuites.it ▪ €€€
A sister operation of, and located next to, the Antica Locanda dei Mercanti (see p144), Milanosuites is set in an 18th-century building with elegant parquet floors and a large living area. There are special rates for weekly rentals.

General Index

Acknowledgments

Author
Reid Bramblett is a travel writer who has authored guides to Italy, Europe and New York, as well as DK's *Top 10 Travel Guide to Tuscany*.

Additional contributor
Sarah Lane

Publishing Director Georgina Dee

Publisher Vivien Antwi

Design Director Phil Ormerod

Editorial Ankita Awasthi Tröger, Rachel Fox, Fay Franklin, Maresa Manera, Alison McGill Sally Schafer, Beverly Smart, Rachel Thompson

Cover Design Maxine Pedliham, Vinita Venugopal

Design Marisa Renzullo, Bharti Karakoti

Picture Research Susie Peachey, Ellen Root, Lucy Sienkowska

Cartography James Anderson, Deshpal Dabas, Casper Morris, Jane Voss

DTP Jason Little

Production Jude Crozier

Factchecker Cristina Dainotto

Proofreader Leena Lane

Indexer Helen Peters

First edition created by BLUE ISLAND PUBLISHING, London

Revisions Dipika Dasgupta, Nayan Keshan, Sumita Khatwani, Shikha Kulkarni, Bandana Paul, Beverly Smart, Priyanka Thakur, Stuti Tiwari, Tanveer Zaidi

Commissioned Photography Helena Smith

Picture Credits

/ Sergio Anelli 20cla, / Fotografo / Agenzia 100c, / Reporters Associati & Archivi / Angelo Novi 46br, / Sergio Anelli 45c; Francesco Prandoni/Redferns 96b; Olaf Protze 30crb; Mats Silvan 2tr, 36–7; Manuel Sulzer 116clb; UIG / AGF / Nardi Alberto 124tl, La Monaca Davide 29tl, / Universal History Archive Portrait of Alessandro Manzoni by Francesco Hayez 46cl.

Hotel Verbano: 111c.

iStockphoto.com: AndreasWeber 108t; bonottomario 129br; rudisill 65tl; Flavio Vallenari 57cl, 104–5.

Joia: A. Mauri 97cb.

Lo Scalo: 111tr.

Locanda dell'Isola Comacina: 119cra.

Museo Poldi Pezzoli, Milan: 45tl.

Museo Teatrale alla Scala: 50b, 62b, 84b.

Pinacoteca di Brera: 16cl, 17tl, 17crb, 17bl, 18tl, 18cr, 19tl, 92bl.

Post-Design: Simone Bacchetti 95t.

Rex Shutterstock: Silver Films / Sotiledip / Nepi 47tl; UIG / Mondadori Electa Electa 10cla, 12–3, 13cr, 13tl, 13bl.

Ristorante Vecchia Malcesine: 127cr.

Robert Harding Picture Library: Riccardo Sala 35tl; Andreas Strauss 114tl.

Photo Scala, Florence: DeAgostini Picture Library / Veneranda Biblioteca Ambrosiana 11tl, 25tl, 44br, 48bl; White Images 39cl.

SuperStock: age fotostock / Yoko Aziz 118ca; Cubo Images 49br; imageBROKER / imageb / gourmet-vision 69br; Marka 64br, 65br, / Jader Alto 61tr; Prisma 126tr.

Villa Crespi: 133cla.

Villa Fiordaliso: Nicolo' Brunelli 68cla.

Zucca (Caffè Miani): 66br.

Cover:
Front and spine: **AWL Images:** Marco Bottigelli.
Back: **AWL Images:** Marco Bottigelli b, Stefano Termanini cla; **iStockphoto.com:** Iryna 1 crb, KavalenkavaVolha tl.

Pull Out Map Cover:
AWL Images: Marco Bottigelli.

All other images © Dorling Kindersley. For further information see:www.dkimages.com

As a guide to abbreviations in visitor information blocks: **Adm** = admission charge; **D** = dinner; **L** = Lunch.

MIX
Paper | Supporting responsible forestry
FSC
www.fsc.org
FSC™ C018179

This book was made with Forest Stewardship Council™ certified paper – one small step in DK's commitment to a sustainable future.
For more information go to www.dk.com/our-green-pledge

DK | Penguin Random House

Printed and bound in Malaysia

First Edition 2003

Published in Great Britain by
Dorling Kindersley Limited
DK, One Embassy Gardens, 8 Viaduct Gardens, London SW11 7BW, UK

The authorised representative in the EEA is Dorling Kindersley Verlag GmbH. Arnulfstr. 124, 80636 Munich, Germany

Published in the United States by
DK Publishing, 1745 Broadway, 20th Floor, New York, NY 10019, USA

Copyright © 2003, 2020
Dorling Kindersley Limited

A Penguin Random House Company

10 9 8 7 6 5 4

Reprinted with revisions 2005, 2007, 2009, 2011, 2013, 2015, 2018, 2020

A CIP catalogue record is available from the British Library.

A catalogue record for this book is available from the Library of Congress.

ISSN 1479-344X

ISBN 978 0 2414 0857 5

SPECIAL EDITIONS OF DK TRAVEL GUIDES

DK Travel Guides can be purchased in bulk quantities at discounted prices for use in promotions or as premiums. We also offer special editions and personalized jackets, corporate imprints, and excerpts from all of our books, tailored specifically to meet your own needs.

To find out more, please contact:

in the US
specialsales@dk.com

in the UK
travelguides@uk.dk.com

in Canada
specialmarkets@dk.com

in Australia
penguincorporatesales@penguinrandomhouse.com.au

Phrase Book

| green | **verde** | *vair-deh* |
| blue | **blu** | *bloo* |

Types of Shop

bakery	**il forno /il panificio**	*eel forn-oh /il /eel pan-ee-fee-choh*
bank	**la banca**	*lah bang-kah*
bookshop	**la libreria**	*lah lee-breh-ree-ah*
cake shop	**la pasticceria**	*lah pas-tee-chair-ee-ah*
chemist	**la farmacia**	*lah far-mah-chee-ah*
delicatessen	**la salumeria**	*lah sah-loo-meh-ree-ah*
department store	**il grande magazzino**	*eel gran-deh mag-gad-zee-noh*
grocery	**alimentari**	*ah-lee-men-tah-ree*
hairdresser	**il parrucchiere**	*eel par-oo-kee-air-eh*
ice cream parlour	**la gelateria**	*lah jel-lah-tair-ree-ah*
market	**il mercato**	*eel mair-kah-toh*
newsstand	**l'edicola**	*leh-dee-koh-lah*
post office	**l'ufficio postale**	*loo-fee-choh pos-tah-leh*
supermarket	**il supermercato**	*eel su-pair-mair-kah-toh*
tobacconist	**il tabaccaio**	*eel tah-bak-eye-oh*
travel agency	**l'agenzia di viaggi**	*lah-jen-tsee-ah dee vee-ad-jee*

In an Emergency

Help!	**Aiuto!**	*eye-yoo-toh*
Stop!	**Ferma!**	*fair-mah*
Call a doctor.	**Chiama un medico.**	*kee-ah-mah oon meh-dee-koh*
Call an ambulance.	**Chiama un' ambulanza.**	*kee-ah-mah oon am-boo-lan-tsa*
Call the police.	**Chiama la polizia.**	*kee-ah-mah lah pol-ee-tsee-ah*
Call the fire brigade.	**Chiama i pompieri.**	*kee-ah-mah ee pom-pee-air-ee*

Communication Essentials

Yes/No	**Si/No**	*see/noh*
Please	**Per favore**	*pair fah-vor-eh*
Thank you	**Grazie**	*grah-tsee-eh*
Excuse me	**Mi scusi**	*mee skoo-zee*
Hello	**Buon giorno**	*bwon jor-noh*
Goodbye	**Arrivederci**	*ah-ree-veh-dair-chee*
Good evening	**Buona sera**	*bwon-ah sair-ah*
What?	**Quale?**	*kwah-leh?*
When?	**Quando?**	*kwan-doh?*
Why?	**Perchè?**	*pair-keh?*
Where?	**Dove?**	*doh-veh?*

Sightseeing

art gallery	**la pinacoteca**	*lah peena-koh-teh-kah*
bus stop	**la fermata dell'autobus**	*lah fair-mah-tah dell ow-toh-booss*
church	**la chiesa/ la basilica**	*lah kee-eh-zah/ lah bah-seel-i-kah*
closed for holidays	**chiuso per le ferie**	*kee-oo-zoh pair leh fair-ee-eh*
garden	**il giardino**	*eel jar-dee-no*
museum	**il museo**	*eel moo-zeh-oh*
railway station	**la stazione**	*lah stah-tsee-oh-neh*
tourist information	**l'ufficio di turismo**	*loo-fee-choh dee too-ree-smoh*

Useful Phrases

How are you?	**Come sta?**	*koh-meh stah?*
Very well, thank you.	**Molto bene, grazie.**	*moll-toh beh-neh grah-tsee-eh*
Pleased to meet you.	**Piacere di conoscerla.**	*pee-ah-chair-eh dee-coh-noh-shair-lah*
That's fine.	**Va bene.**	*va beh-neh*
Where is/are …?	**Dov'è/ Dove sono …?**	*dov-eh/doveh soh-noh...?*
How do I get to …?	**Come faccio per arrivare a …?**	*koh-meh fah-choh pair arri-var-eh ah…?*
Do you speak English?	**Parla inglese?**	*par-lah een-gleh-zeh?*
I don't understand.	**Non capisco.**	*non ka-pee-skoh*
I'm sorry.	**Mi dispiace.**	*mee dee-spee-ah-cheh*

Staying in a Hotel

Do you have any vacant rooms?	**Avete camere libere?**	*ah-veh-teh kah-mair-eh lee-bair-eh?*
double room	**una camera doppia**	*oona kah-mair-ah doh-pee-ah*
with double bed	**con letto matrimoniale**	*kon let-toh-mah tree-moh-nee-ah-leh*
twin room	**una camera con due letti**	*oona kah-mair-ah kon doo-eh let-tee*
single room	**una camera singola**	*oona kah-mair-ah sing-goh-lah*
room with a bath, shower	**una camera con bagno, con doccia**	*oona kah-mair-ah kon ban-yoh, kon dot-chah*
I have a reservation.	**Ho fatto una prenotazione.**	*oh fat-toh oona preh-noh-tah-tsee-oh-neh*

Shopping

How much does this cost?	**Quant'è, per favore?**	*kwan-the pair fah-vor-eh?*
I would like …	**Vorrei …**	*vor-ray*
Do you have …?	**Avete …?**	*ah-veh-teh…?*
Do you take credit cards?	**Accettate carte di credito?**	*ah-chet-tah-the kar-teh dee creh-dee-toh?*
What time do you open/close?	**A che ora apre/ chiude?**	*ah keh or-ah ah-preh/ kee-oo-deh?*
this one	**questo**	*kweh-stoh*
that one	**quello**	*kwell-oh*
expensive	**caro**	*kar-oh*
cheap	**a buon prezzo**	*ah bwon pret-soh*
size, clothes	**la taglia**	*lah tah-lee-ah*
size, shoes	**il numero**	*eel noo-mair-oh*
white	**bianco**	*bee-ang-koh*
black	**nero**	*neh-roh*
red	**rosso**	*ross-oh*
yellow	**giallo**	*jal-loh*

Eating Out

Have you got a table for ...?	Avete un tavolo per ...?	ah-veh-teh oon tah-voh-lah pair ...?
I'd like to reserve a table	Vorrei riservare un tavolo.	vor-ray ree-sair-vah-reh oon tah-voh-lah
breakfast	colazione	koh-lah-tsee-oh-neh
lunch	pranzo	pran-tsoh
dinner	cena	cheh-nah
The bill, please.	Il conto, per favore.	eel kon-toh pair fah-vor-eh
waitress	cameriera	kah-mair-ee-air-ah
waiter	cameriere	kah-mair-ee-aireh
fixed price menu	il menù a prezzo fisso	eel meh-noo ah pret-soh fee-soh
dish of the day	piatto del giorno	pee-ah-toh dell jor-no
starter	antipasto	an-tee-pass-toh
first course	il primo	eel pree-moh
main course	il secondo	eel seh-kon-doh
vegetables	contorni	eel kon-tor-noh
dessert	il dolce	eel doll-cheh
cover charge	il coperto	eel koh-pair-toh
wine list	la lista dei vini	lah lee-stah day vee-nee
glass	il bicchiere	eel bee-kee-air-eh
bottle	la bottiglia	lah bot-teel-yah
knife	il coltello	eel kol-tell-oh
fork	la forchetta	lah for-ket-tah
spoon	il cucchiaio	eel koo-kee-eye-oh

Menu Decoder

l'acqua minerale	lah-kwah mee-nair-ah-leh gah-zah-tah/ nah-too-rah-leh	mineral water
gassata/ naturale		fizzy/still
agnello	ah-niell-oh	lamb
aglio	al-ee-oh	garlic
al forno	al for-noh	baked
alla griglia	ah-lah greel-yah	grilled
arrosto	ar-ross-toh	roast
la birra	lah beer-rah	beer
la bistecca	lah bee-stek-kah	steak
il burro	eel boor-oh	butter
il caffè	eel kah-feh	coffee
la carne	la kar-neh	meat
carne di maiale	kar-neh dee mah-yah-leh	pork
la cipolla	la chip-oh-lah	onion
i fagioli	ee fah-joh-lee	beans
il formaggio	eel for-mad-joh	cheese
le fragole	leh frah-goh-leh	strawberries
il fritto misto	eel free-toh mees-toh	mixed fried dish
la frutta	la froot-tah	fruit
frutti di mare	froo-tee dee mah-reh	seafood
i funghi	ee foon-ghee	mushrooms
i gamberi	ee gam-bair-ee	prawns
il gelato	eel jel-lah-toh	ice cream
l'insalata	leen-sah-lah-tah	salad
il latte	eel laht-teh	milk
lesso	less-oh	boiled
il manzo	eel man-tsoh	beef
l'olio	loh-lee-oh	oil
il pane	eel pah-neh	bread
le patate	leh pah-tah-teh	potatoes

le patatine fritte	leh pah-tah-teen-eh free-teh	chips
il pepe	eel peh-peh	pepper
il pesce	eel pesh-eh	fish
il pollo	eel poll-oh	chicken
il pomodoro	eel poh-moh-dor-oh	tomato
il prosciutto cotto/crudo	eel pro-shoo-toh kot-toh/kroo-doh	ham cooked/cured
il riso	eel ree-zoh	rice
il sale	eel sah-leh	salt
la salsiccia	lah sal-see-chah	sausage
succo d'arancia/ di limone	soo-koh dah-ran-chah/ dee lee-moh-neh	orange/lemon juice
il tè	eel teh	tea
la torta	lah tor-tah	cake/tart
l'uovo	loo-oh-voh	egg
vino bianco	vee-noh bee-ang-koh	white wine
vino rosso	vee-noh ross-oh	red wine
il vitello	eel vee-tell-oh	veal
le vongole	leh von-goh-leh	clams
lo zucchero	loh zoo-kair-oh	sugar
la zuppa	lah tsoo-pah	soup

Numbers

1	uno	oo-noh
2	due	doo-eh
3	tre	treh
4	quattro	kwat-roh
5	cinque	ching-kweh
6	sei	say-ee
7	sette	set-teh
8	otto	ot-toh
9	nove	noh-veh
10	dieci	dee-eh-chee
11	undici	oon-dee-chee
12	dodici	doh-dee-chee
13	tredici	tray-dee-chee
14	quattordici	kwat-tor-dee-chee
15	quindici	kwin-dee-chee
16	sedici	say-dee-chee
17	diciassette	dee-chah-set-the
18	diciotto	dee-chot-toh
19	diciannove	dee-chah-noh-veh
20	venti	ven-tee
30	trenta	tren-tah
40	quaranta	kwah-ran-tah
50	cinquanta	ching-kwan-tah
60	sessanta	sess-an-tah
70	settanta	set-tan-tah
80	ottanta	ot-tan-tah
90	novanta	noh-van-tah
100	cento	chen-toh
1,000	mille	mee-leh
2,000	duemila	doo-eh mee-lah
1,000,000	un milione	oon meel-yoh-neh

Time

one minute	un minuto	oon mee-noo-toh
one hour	un'ora	oon or-ah
a day	un giorno	oon jor-noh
Monday	lunedì	loo-neh-dee
Tuesday	martedì	mar-teh-dee
Wednesday	mercoledì	mair-koh-leh-dee
Thursday	giovedì	joh-veh-dee
Friday	venerdì	ven-air-dee
Saturday	sabato	sah-bah-toh
Sunday	domenica	doh-meh-nee-kah

Information and Records Management

Information and Records Management

DOCUMENT–BASED INFORMATION SYSTEMS

Fourth Edition

Mary F. Robek, CRM
Eastern Michigan University (Retired)

Gerald F. Brown, CRM
Union Pacific Railroad (Retired)

David O. Stephens, CRM, CMC
Zasio Enterprises Incorporated

GLENCOE
McGraw-Hill

New York, New York   Columbus, Ohio   Woodland Hills, California   Peoria, Illinois

Reviewers:

Rosemarie McCauley, Ed.D., Professor
Department of Business Education and Office Systems Information
Montclair State University

Tyrone G. Butler, CRM, CA
TransNational Records and Information Management Services

This program was produced for Glencoe/McGraw-Hill with the
assistance of Chestnut Hill Enterprises, Inc.

Library of Congress Cataloging-in-Publication Data

Robek, Mary F.
       Information and records management : document-based information
systems / Mary F. Robek, Gerald F. Brown, David O. Stephens. — 4th ed.
           p.   cm.
       Includes bibliographical references and index.
       ISBN 0-02-801793-5
       1. Business records—Management.   2. Document imaging systems.
3. Information storage and retrieval systems—Business.   I. Brown,
Gerald F.   II. Stephens. David O.   III. Title.
       HF5736.R53   1996   94-31467
       651.5—dc20   CIP

Imprint 2002

Send all inquiries to:
Glencoe/McGraw-Hill
21600 Oxnard Street, Suite 500
Woodland Hills, CA 91367-4906

ISBN 0-02-801793-5

Printed in the United States of America.

5 6 7 8 9 10 11 12 13 14 15   026   04 03 02

Contents

Part V   *Related Records Management Functions*   *337*

Part VI   *Inactive Records Management*   *461*

Preface

Since the publication of the first edition of *Information and Records Management* in 1974, this book has been generally regarded as the standard reference book in the field of records and information management. This status will be further enhanced by this fourth edition, which has been completely revised to include the many changes that have revolutionized the field of records and information management since the publication of the third edition in 1987. The fourth edition is, largely, a new work.

Major changes and new features of this edition include:

- A new two-chapter section on *electronic records management.* The chapters cover managing electronic records media and automating records management systems and functions. No other records management textbook contains chapter-length material on these topics.

- A new three-chapter section on *image technology for records management.* The chapters include updated information on micrographics systems and new coverage of electronic imaging technology for records management.

- The addition of new automation-related material in all relevant chapters.

- Added focus on new topics and de-emphasis of tangential topics. For example, summarized material on correspondence management and directive management has been moved to appropriate chapters.

- A new co-author, David O. Stephens, CRM, CMC, to replace the late Dr. Wilmer O. Maedke. Mr. Stephens is a leading records management consultant. The authors believe that the resulting combination of educational and practitioner/consultant authors provides the best mix of writing talent.

The problem-solving activities that were introduced in the previous editions continue. At the end of each chapter, the student is given suggested projects, many of which require research in current records management literature, and a case problem for application of the material in the chapters to realistic situations. Teaching suggestions and answers to the case problems and discussion questions are available in the accompanying Instructor's Manual.

The authors wish to thank many member of the Institute of Certified Records Managers and the Association of Records Managers and Administrators, International, who contributed directly or indirectly to the text. Among those individuals are Earnestine Baucham, William Benedon, Fred Boecker, Tyrone Butler, M. Liisa Fagerlund, Jan Graham, Mary Gregoire-Lyons, Rosemarie McCauley, John T. Phillips, William Saffady, Heather Sherman, Donald S. Skupsky, Roderick Wallace, Harriett Welch, and Eileen Weston.

Mary F. Robek
Gerald F. Brown
David O. Stephens

PART I

Records Management
Program Development

Chapter 1

Management of Document-Based Information Systems

Learning Objectives
1. To define *records management* and describe the importance of managing document-based information systems in business and government.
2. To describe the business justification for records management and to list the major components of a formally established records management program.
3. To list the basic principles associated with establishing a records management program.
4. To describe the history and current status of the records management profession.

RECORDS AND INFORMATION: THEIR IMPORTANCE TO BUSINESS AND GOVERNMENT

Throughout the world, all organizations, whether large or small, public or private, have one thing in common: Each produces records and information. Information is one of the world's most important resources. It is needed daily to solve problems and make decisions affecting the future. What people accomplish in organizations depends largely upon the information they possess. Increasingly, the degree of success enjoyed by organizations and the people who work for them depends on how well they manage their information resources. Information is competitive intelligence—a strategic asset of the enterprise. The principal objective of this book is to give its readers the concepts they need to optimize the value of records and information on an enterprise-wide basis.

The Information Society

What is information? A well-known dictionary defines information as "knowledge communicated by others or obtained by study and investigation." What significance does information, as one of the principal sources of knowledge, have in today's world? Peter Drucker, perhaps the foremost management theorist in the United States, offers this observation:

> The productivity of knowledge has already become the key to productivity, competitive strength, and economic achievement. Knowledge has already become the primary industry, the industry that supplies the economy the essential and central resources of production.[1]

One of the first commentators to articulate a theory of the importance of information to society is John Naisbitt. In *Megatrends*, Naisbitt describes the "megashift" which has occurred and continues to occur in the United States—the shift from an industrial to an information society. Although *Megatrends* was written in 1982, it remains of utmost significance for us today as we attempt to understand information, documents, and records, their importance to business and government enterprises, and their larger significance to society as a whole—both now and in the twenty-first century. Consider the following observations from *Megatrends*:

- In an industrial society, the strategic resource is capital. In an information society, the new source of power is not money in the hands of a few but information in the hands of many.
- In an information economy, value is increased not by labor but by knowledge.
- The restructuring of the United States from an industrial to an information society will easily be as profound a change as the shift from an agricultural society to an industrial society.
- The telephone, the computer, and television have merged into an integrated information and communication system that transmits data and permits instantaneous interactions between people.[2]

Business Information: Essential Characteristics

Information is "any intelligence which can be communicated in either graphic form or by alpha-numeric characters." This broad term thus encompasses the entire sphere of records, documents, data, and files created and maintained by organizations. Information is generated and transmitted within every business and governmental organization countless times every minute of every working day. Most of the working time of

office employees is likely to be directly or indirectly involved with information.

Business information takes many forms. *Static* information exists in nonchangeable form; *dynamic* information can be manipulated, updated, changed, or erased easily. Some business information is *recurring*—it is created or generated at regular intervals. *Nonrecurring* information is created on a one-time basis for a specific purpose. Some information requires immediate *action* on the part of the recipient, while other information is *nonaction* in character—it informs the recipient, but no response is required. With respect to source of creation, some information is generated *internally* within the organization that owns it, while other information is received from *external* sources.

Some information is *human-readable*—it can be read by sight. *Machine-readable* information can be read only by means of special equipment. Information is *active* if it is used frequently; it is *inactive* if it is not required for immediate reference but still needs to be kept for some purpose. Information is *record copy* if it consists of *original* documents or otherwise possesses *official status* as a record of the organization's business. Information that does not possess these characteristics is considered to be *duplicative, nonofficial*, or solely of *reference value*. Most information is *documentary* if it has been recorded on some type of durable medium for future reference; *nondocumentary* information is information that has not been recorded and is usually obtained through observation or verbal communication.

Most information is considered to be of *temporary* value: It will lose its value and no longer need to be retained. Some information is considered to be of permanent or *archival* value: It possesses long-term value and is preserved for historical or other research purposes. Finally, it is important to note that information which is not communicated is valueless, and information which cannot be found is similarly worthless. Thus, *the value of information is directly related to its accessibility*.

Business Records, Files, Documents, and Data: Some Definitions

Except for nondocumentary information, business information is transmitted between and disseminated among persons and organizations in the form of *records*. As defined by the Association of Records Managers and Administrators (ARMA International), a record is "recorded information, regardless of medium or characteristics." Records, therefore, include more than traditional paper documents such as correspondence, reports, and forms. The ARMA definition also mentions "any paper, book, microfilm, card, magnetic tape, disk, map, or any copy of a printout that has been generated or received by an organization and has been used by that organization or its successors as evidence of its activities or because of the information contained." Thus, information in the form of drawings, photographs, sound recordings, video recordings, and other material containing information of value to its owner would also be considered records under this definition.

The term *file* and its plural, *files*, can have a variety of meanings in information management. *Files* is a general term which denotes a collection of records or a group of related documents. In its broadest sense, *files* often refers to all or part of the records of an organization. In paper-based recordkeeping systems, *files* usually refers to a collection of file folders containing documents related to each other in some way, while *file* usually refers to documents contained within one file folder. In computer-based information systems, the term *file* and *data files* usually refer to a computer-processable collection of related data stored in some type of electronic device.

The term *document* is narrower in scope than *records*; in paper-based recordkeeping systems *document* usually means "the smallest unit of filing," generally a single letter, form, report, or other item housed in a filing system. This term is important here since the focus of this book is the management and control of documents in organizations: how to control their creation, how to organize them for effective retrieval, whether to convert them to some type of nonpaper medium, how to safeguard them against loss, and whether to store, destroy, or preserve them. This book is subtitled *Document-Based Information Systems* because the management of business documents is what information and records management, a professional management discipline, is all about.

Finally, let's consider the meaning of the term *data* as used in this book. As applied to document-based information systems, *data* means "symbols or representations constituting the smallest unit of document filing in an electronic recordkeeping system." This term is primarily used in conjunction with computer-based information systems and generally refers to any information entered into an electronic storage device or any information processed or generated by such devices.

The Mix of Records Media: Paper, Microfilm, and Electronic

We have stated that records constitute recorded information, regardless of medium or characteristics, and that organizations usually create and maintain records in a variety of forms and formats, or *media*, including paper, microfilm, and various types of electronic recordkeeping devices. A study conducted by the Association for Information and Image Management (AIIM) puts this matter in better perspective. As shown in Figure 1.1, this study indicated that paper is, by far, the dominant information storage form and is expected to remain so for the remainder of this century. Approximately 95 percent of the information in the United States resided on this medium in 1989, and only a 3 percent decline is expected by the year 1999. This study also indicated that the proportion of information held in microfilm format will decrease slightly, from 4 percent to 3 percent over the same period, while electronic media will increase fivefold, from a small base of 1 percent to 5 percent by the close of the century.

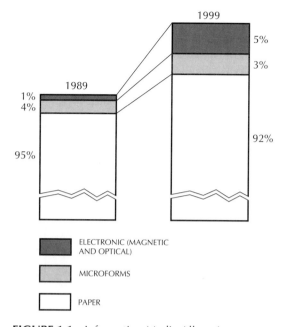

FIGURE 1.1 Information Media Allocation
Source: *Information and Image Management: The State of the Industry—1989.* Association for Information and Image Management, 1989.

The Persistent Growth of Paper Document Filing Systems

Why are paper-based filing systems such a big problem for organizations? We have seen that they constitute over 90 percent of all information resources in the United States, but this statistic alone fails to reveal the essence of the problem. Simply put, the major problem with paper document filing systems is their staggering and unrelenting growth. Despite the explosive growth realized by the U.S. computer industry during the past 15 years, the volume of paper files has grown at an average annual rate of about 7 percent. This rate of growth is about twice as fast as the nation's economy (as measured by the Gross Domestic Product) has grown during the same period.

Perhaps the best evidence we have on the growth of paper document filing systems comes from the American Forest and Paper Association, which keeps statistics on the amount of paper stock used in the manufacture of file folders. Figure 1.2 shows that during the 14-year period from 1979 to 1992, the quantity of paper stock used for file folders increased 91.4 percent, from 127,600 tons to 244,300 tons.

Another study commissioned by AIIM gives the quantity of paper documents created daily by U.S. companies. Figure 1.3 shows an estimate of the quantity of file folder contents, computer printouts, photocopies, letters, and general paper documents created every business day in the United States. Each of these documents must be subject to some level of management control. At a minimum, someone must decide whether and where to file them, and how to organize and index them so that they can be found quickly.

During the early 1980s, when a wide variety of "office automation" technologies appeared on the U.S. market, the terms *paperless office* and *paperless society* became very popular. Some observers predicted the demise of paper document filing systems, as new technology offered the means of replacing paper documents with electronic document images. These predictions have proven false; although the proportionate share of paper-recorded media may decline slightly relative to other media, paper records will continue to grow, and they will continue to create significant management problems for the organizations that own them. The evidence indicates that the management of document-based information systems will remain a "growth industry" for some time to come.

DEFINING INFORMATION AND RECORDS MANAGEMENT

Information management is often defined as the administration of information, its use and transmission, and the application of theories and techniques of information science to create, modify, or improve information handling systems. *Records management* is the application of systematic and scientific controls to recorded infor-

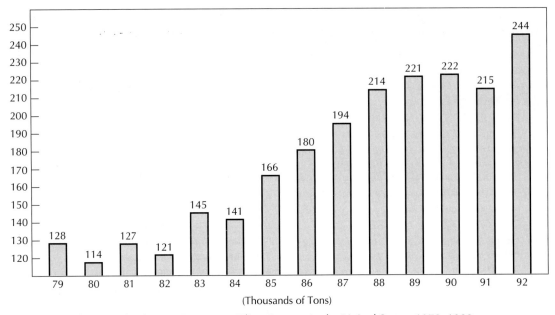

FIGURE 1.2 The Growth of Paper Document Filing Systems in the United States, 1979–1992 (Figures Present Quantity of Raw Paper Stock Used in Manufacturing File Folders) Source: American Forest and Paper Association.

mation required in the operation of an organization's business. These terms are similar in meaning and indeed will often be used interchangeably, or together as a single term—*information and records management*—throughout this book. There are, however, some key distinctions. Records management is a professional management discipline that is primarily concerned with the management of *document-based* information systems, most of which are in paper media format. Information management, on the other hand, is frequently used in reference to *data-based* information systems in computer environments in which the information is stored electronically.

FIGURE 1.3   Paper Documents Created Daily by U.S. Companies Source: "Information and Image Management: The Industry & the Technologies." Association for Information and Image Management.

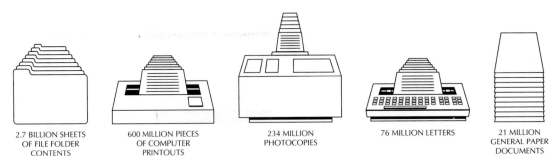

2.7 BILLION SHEETS OF FILE FOLDER CONTENTS

600 MILLION PIECES OF COMPUTER PRINTOUTS

234 MILLION PHOTOCOPIES

76 MILLION LETTERS

21 MILLION GENERAL PAPER DOCUMENTS

Objectives of Information and Records Management

Every professional business endeavor, including information and records management, must address well-defined objectives, and the achievement of these objectives must enhance the value of the business. Most information and records management programs have the following major objectives:

- To furnish accurate, timely, and complete information for efficient decision making in the management and operation of the organization.
- To process recorded information as efficiently as possible.
- To provide information and records at the lowest possible cost.
- To render maximum service to the user of the records.
- To dispose of records no longer needed.

In short, information and records management programs must manage organizational information so that it is timely, accurate, complete, cost-effective, accessible, and usable. This is the basic premise for records management: Better information makes a better business.

Records management objectives are based primarily upon (1) service, (2) profit (or cost avoidance), and (3) social responsibility. Service is of great importance because recorded information is needed by others so that their work is performed most effectively and efficiently. In all organizations, reducing the cost of doing business is important. In private enterprise, profits are essential if the organization is to continue to function. Social responsibility is important because the attainment of organizational goals must be in accordance with the moral, ethical, and legal codes of the society in which the organization operates.

Objectives for records management may be specific or general, written or unwritten, long- or short-term, temporary or permanent, and applicable to the total program or to only segments of the program. Whatever their form or content,

objectives should be established, or there will be no satisfactory basis for determining the program's effectiveness.

Management of the Information Life Cycle

We noted earlier that one of the essential characteristics of information is its value. We mentioned that most records are of temporary value; that is, like most organizational assets, their value for business purposes tends to decline as the time passes and, at some point, they become useless and may be discarded. The proper application of this *life cycle concept* is required in order to achieve the records management objectives mentioned above.

If it is to be effective, a records management program must apply appropriate controls to records during each of the five major stages of the life cycle of information:

1. The *creation* stage, when information and records are produced in a wide variety of forms and formats using different equipment and technologies.
2. The *distribution and use* stage, when information and records are transmitted to those who need them and, upon receipt, are used in the conduct of business.
3. The *storage and maintenance* stage, when information and records are filed or stored according to a logical scheme to permit subsequent retrieval, housed in some type of storage device, and protected and maintained so as to safeguard the integrity of the information. During this stage, the information is active; it is frequently referred to and is thus usually stored close to its users.
4. The *retention and disposition* stage, when information and records decline in value, become inactive, and are then removed from active storage in prime office space, are destroyed immediately if they have no further value, or are transferred to an inactive storage facility for the duration of their retention life.
5. The *archival preservation* stage, when the

few records that never lose their value are preserved permanently in an archive for ongoing historical reference or research purposes.

Figure 1.4 illustrates this concept of records management by the management of the information life cycle.

WHY RECORDS MANAGEMENT?
TEN BUSINESS REASONS

What motivates executives in companies and government agencies to make investments in records management systems and programs? What business problems are they trying to solve? What are the benefits of a records management program, and what are the consequences of its absence? There are ten major reasons why businesses and government organizations need records management.

To Control the Creation and Growth of Records

Without a records management program, an organization has *no effective means of controlling the growth of its records.* As we have seen, despite decades of using various nonpaper information storage media, the volume of paper records maintained by organizations continues to escalate. There are two major reasons: First, if a business expands, so does the quantity of its information. Second, organizations today have a much greater capability to create paper records; office copiers, word processors, computer printers, microfilm reader-printers, facsimile machines, and other office machines all produce large quantities of paper documents. Most studies indicate that organizations generate a net annual growth of about 10 percent in their paper records. However, if the organization's business is particularly paper-

FIGURE 1.4   Five Stages in the Life Cycle of a Record

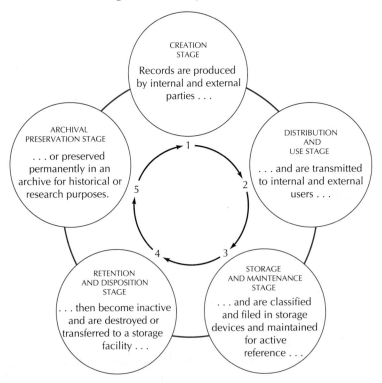

intensive, the annual growth figure is often as high as 20 percent.

To control this growth, organizations must develop and implement a records management program that has two growth-control components: (1) a *creation-control* component that attempts to limit the creation of records not required to operate the business, and (2) a *records retention* component under which useless records are destroyed at about the same rate at which new records are generated, thereby stabilizing the growth of records.

To Reduce Operating Costs

The cost of recordkeeping is a significant component of the administrative overhead costs of running any business. No recent nationwide research study has been conducted to provide credible statistics relative to the cost of storing and maintaining paper records in business offices. However, most figures furnished by filing equipment vendors and other records management specialists indicate that it costs somewhere between $10 and $25 per year to store and maintain one linear inch of records in a business office. When such figures are multiplied by the total quantity of records in the organization, it is apparent that recordkeeping constitutes a major administrative expense. If the organization has no records management program, between 30 percent and 60 percent of its records are either inactive or semiactive and need to be destroyed immediately or transferred from prime office space to a low-cost storage facility. The cost savings resulting from these actions can be substantial. The only way to achieve them is to develop and implement a records retention and inactive records storage program, as a part of a comprehensive records management program.

To Improve Efficiency and Productivity

Today, many office filing systems are not well designed and operated. The files are often poorly organized, and no index exists to facilitate their retrieval. Moreover, many filing systems suffer from a high rate of missing or misfiled records, and the time spent searching for them is nonproductive. Retrieval of information is neither precise nor timely, and the filing systems fall short of the goal of delivering to users exactly the information they need as quickly as they need it. Investments in new computer systems to solve filing problems may prove wasteful unless the manual recordkeeping systems are overhauled before automation is applied. The end result of these problems is that office efficiency and productivity are impaired. A good records management program can help any organization upgrade its recordkeeping systems so that information retrieval is enhanced, with corresponding improvements in office efficiency and productivity. Without such a program, these business goals cannot be achieved.

To Assimilate New Records Management Technologies

As recently as five to ten years ago, most office recordkeeping systems were supported by little or no computer technology. Since the mid-1980s, however, there has been a revolution in computer-related records management systems and technologies. As we shall see, the major ones are optical disk technology, new computer enhancements to microfilm technology, and new records management software for indexing and tracking both active and inactive records throughout an organization. However, organizations cannot take advantage of these technologies without professional records management expertise. A good records management program provides an organization with the capability to assimilate these new technologies and take advantage of their many benefits.

To Ensure Regulatory Compliance

Today there are thousands of laws and regulations enacted by federal and state governments that impose recordkeeping requirements on businesses and even on other government agencies. In terms of recordkeeping requirements, the United States is the most heavily regulated country in the world. These laws and regulations include requirements to maintain certain records, to retain them for specified periods of time, and to report certain information to the government. These laws and regulations can create a major compliance problem for businesses because they are often difficult to locate and even more difficult to interpret and apply. The only way that a business can be reasonably sure that it is in full compliance with these laws and regulations is by operating a good records management program which takes responsibility for regulatory compliance, working closely with the organization's legal department. Failure to comply with the laws and regulations could result in severe fines, penalties, or other legal consequences.

To Minimize Litigation Risks

In the United States, lawsuits are often the means of resolving business disputes. In view of this legal climate, business organizations implement records management programs in order to reduce the risks associated with litigation and potential penalties. Companies which manufacture products that are subject to failure in performance or that may be harmful to the health of consumers, and companies that create environmental hazards, are particularly vulnerable to these types of legal difficulties. Because these types of lawsuits are often decided on the basis of information contained in documents (documents that may extend far back into a company's history as well as current ones), corporations often have strong incentives to be very careful about what documents they retain and for how long. A records management program can reduce the liabilities that can be associated with document disposal by providing for their systematic, routine disposal in the normal course of business.

To Safeguard Vital Information

Every organization, whether public or private, is vulnerable to the loss of vital records and infor-

mation. Such losses can greatly impair the operating capabilities of the organization and may even jeopardize its existence. Thus, every organization needs a comprehensive program for protecting its most vital records and information from loss due to disaster or other causes. These programs are also concerned with maintaining the *integrity* and *confidentiality* of records; thus, protection from intrusion or unauthorized access is often considered. Such programs are usually called *vital records protection programs* and are often operated as a part of an organization's records management program. They are designed to safeguard the organization's vital information assets; they cover all types of storage media and employ a wide variety of protection strategies for vital paper, microfilm, and electronic records. These programs usually include both disaster *prevention* and disaster *recovery* components—the former designed to safeguard vital information before and during a disaster; the latter designed to restore records and information damaged during the disaster. Without these programs, however, organizations are completely exposed to the consequences that would result from the loss of the information required to operate their businesses.

To Support Better Management Decision Making

Although important business decisions must often be made without the availability of all relevant data, a records management program can help to ensure that managers and executives have the right information to make good decisions. For example, a records management program can implement an organization-wide files indexing and retrieval capability so that managers and executives can retrieve and assemble all relevant information for current decisions and future business planning purposes. Such records management systems must inform managers of the existence and location of all files, both active and inactive, as quickly as possible.

To Preserve the Corporate Memory

An organization's historical files constitute its institutional memory, an irreplaceable asset of great value but one often overlooked by managers and executives. The preservation of the corporate memory is perhaps of more immediate concern to organizations having a long history, or to those which have accumulated a considerable quantity of old records over a long period of time. Even newer organizations, however, need to consider this issue, for every business day they are creating the archives of future years. In order to preserve this institutional memory, many organizations establish a company archive, which is often operated as a part of the records management program. Apart from their intrinsic value, business archives—those records which possess permanent value for research or historical purposes—can be very valuable for current business purposes. Such records are often used as background data in making current decisions, in future planning, in marketing programs that emphasize the firm's history and traditions, in employee training programs, or for other business purposes.

To Foster Professionalism in Running the Business

A business office with records and files askew—stacked on the tops of file cabinets and in boxes—creates a poor working environment. When office records and files are poorly maintained, the pride and morale of employees about their place of work are sure to suffer, not to mention the perceptions of customers and the public. Although "image" and "morale" are intangible factors—difficult to quantify in cost-benefit terms—they may be the best reasons to establish a good records management program.

ESTABLISHING A RECORDS MANAGEMENT PROGRAM

In this section, we discuss how to establish a records management program. We first define the scope and content of a comprehensive records management program, and then describe some principles for organizing, staffing, and implementing the program.

Elements and Functions of Records Management Programs

Considerable variation is found among records management programs in business and government. Some large programs are comprehensive and are staffed with a full complement of management, supervisory, technical, and clerical personnel who operate all or most of the program components. Other programs are small—they may be staffed by only one or several records management specialists who perform most or only a few of these functions. The elements and functions of a comprehensive records management program are described briefly below. Each topic is covered in depth in subsequent chapters.

The Records Inventory. A *records inventory* is the first step in the development of a records management program. It is a complete listing of all the records of an organization by records series, together with necessary supporting information. A *records series* is a group of identical or related records that are normally used and filed as a unit and that permit evaluation as a unit for retention scheduling purposes. The inventory identifies the organization's records, where they are located and in what quantity. It provides the facts upon which an analysis of the organization's records is based. Duplication of records can be detected, the duration of the usefulness of files can be assessed, and the legal implications of the records can be appraised. Usually, an inventory reveals that many records can be destroyed immediately or transferred off-site, saving space and releasing equipment from unproductive use.

The Records Retention Schedule. A records retention schedule lists an organization's records and prescribes how long they must be retained. If developed properly through an orderly system of inventory and appraisal, a records retention schedule can substantially reduce recordkeeping costs.

It is one of the principal tools for controlling the growth of the organization's records, and it has many legal benefits as well. The records retention schedule should describe all types of records in terms of origin, physical class, function served, and organizational relationships. Records retention schedules should be followed on a daily basis and be revised to accommodate newly created records series, forms, or reports and changes resulting from the implementation of new records management systems and procedures.

Vital Records Protection and Disaster Recovery Planning. *Vital records* contain information that is essential to reestablishing or continuing an organization in the event of a disaster. When vital records are lost or destroyed by natural or human-caused disasters, an organization's capability to do business is severely diminished. In addition to essential operating records, vital records include records necessary to protect the rights and assets of the organization and its customers, clients, owners, or other groups. Unlike other fixed assets, such as office furniture and equipment, vital records possess qualities of *intrinsic uniqueness*; that is, they either cannot be recreated if lost, or they can be recreated only at a prohibitive cost of money and time. Thus, the organization that owns such records must take steps to safeguard them against loss. A *vital records protection program* identifies these records and ensures their preservation and protection.

Today many organizations are developing *disaster recovery programs,* which are designed to minimize the risk of loss of all vital assets—capital, property, and equipment, as well as records and information. These programs often develop plans for the restoration and recovery of record media—paper records, microfilms, and electronic records—following a disaster.

Active Files Management. Of all the administrative activities of an organization, the storage and retrieval of business records are two of the greatest consumers of space, salaries, and equipment. Time, effort, and money are wasted unless records

can be produced when they are required. Records must be systematically arranged according to a filing plan that will make immediate retrieval possible. We use the term *active files management* in reference to office records that are referred to frequently and therefore require maintenance at departmental or central filing stations—at or near the users.

An effective files management program involves the following elements:

- A sound records classification and filing system.
- The best physical location of active records.
- Designation of official file stations.
- Standards for records equipment.
- Standards for records supplies.
- The best storage medium for the application.

Electronic Records Management. The quantity of business records maintained in electronic formats has increased substantially over the past two decades, and we have noted that significant growth is expected. It is estimated that, in 1993, there was an installed base of approximately 45 million microcomputers in the United States, and this is expected to increase to 65 million units by 1995. Each of these personal computers can be thought of as an electronic filing cabinet; the magnetic and optical storage media used with these devices store a tremendous quantity of business documents and data. Some of this information is unique, some is duplicative of documents that exist elsewhere, but virtually all of it has yet to be subject to proper records management controls. Thus, the creation and maintenance of this information, its protection, preservation, and retention status need to be managed using records management principles and techniques similar in many respects to those employed for records on other media. This is a major challenge and opportunity for records management.

In addition to the management of electronic record media, the term *electronic records management* implies the use of *records management software* to solve a wide variety of records management problems. During the past ten years, many software companies in the United States have developed these software products, most of which are designed to operate on microcomputers. This family of records management software is being used to enhance the management of paper-based filing systems. The indexing, tracking, and monitoring of file folders, records storage cartons, microfilm, and other records media are their major records management applications. These new software products have tremendous significance for records management: When they are used to control an organization's active and inactive records, they provide records managers with new computer capabilities to establish total life cycle control over records and information systems on an enterprise-wide basis.

Image Technology for Document Management. There are two broad categories of image technology for records management applications: *micrographics* and *optical disk filing systems*. Micrographics, a photographic-based medium for document storage and retrieval, is an old technology; microfilm has been used since before World War II. Optical disk filing systems, on the other hand, were introduced into the U.S. market during the mid-1980s.

Micrographics. Microfilm can reduce substantially the clerical labor that is normally required for maintaining information. It also expedites certain office operations by making recorded information more readily accessible for use. Microfilm is also highly important in vital records protection programs. Microfilm copies of irreplaceable records can be deposited in a location other than that housing the original records to prevent loss. Microfilm also conserves space. A reel of microfilm requires only about 2 to 3 percent of the space required by the original records.

We will consider several major categories of micrographics technology: s*ource document microfilm* produced by filming paper documents on cameras; *computer output microfilm* produced by converting data from computer tapes or disks onto

microfilm or microfiche; and *computer-assisted retrieval microfilm systems*, which utilize computer indexing techniques to permit rapid retrieval of document images on microfilm.

Optical Disk Filing Systems. Optical disk filing systems use metal platters as the medium for document storage. Paper documents or microfilm images are electronically scanned, converted to digital format, and then recorded onto the surface of the optical disk by laser. These systems offer a very dense, high-capacity storage medium for large document collections. They also provide very rapid retrieval of the electronic document images on image-capable computer workstations. Since the document images are in electronic format, they can be transmitted via computer networks throughout an organization. Some optical disk systems use artificial intelligence to accomplish content searches efficiently.

Thus, optical disk filing systems represent high-performance solutions to the management of business documents. Some optical disk vendors are developing systems that integrate microfilm and optical storage media into a hybrid image management system. These systems use microfilm scanners to convert the document's photographic image into an electronic image. This is extremely important to the future viability of micrographics technology, since it provides an incentive for users of microfilm systems to continue making investments in this document storage medium.

Inactive Records Management. Office space in most organizations is too expensive for the storage of inactive records, which are those records referred to infrequently—usually less than once a month per file drawer. Inactive records should be transferred to low-cost storage equipment in a low-cost storage facility or be converted to another medium. Centralized buildings or areas established for the storage and servicing of inactive or semiactive records are known as *records centers.*

A properly designed, air-conditioned, and humidity-controlled records center, using inexpensive steel shelving and approved fire-resistant cardboard cartons, can free costly office space, effect savings, and provide efficient reference service. An organization's existing facilities may be modified to fit this type of storage, an entirely new building may be constructed specifically for the purpose, or a more adequate area or building can be leased. Another possibility is employment of the services of a commercial records center. Under this arrangement, an organization's inactive records are stored by the vendor on a fee-for-service basis.

Archives Management.   *Archival records*—are permanent records that document the organization's existence, operations, and functions; they are an organization's institutional memory.

Documents included in an organization's archive include copyrights, deeds, incorporation papers, patents, and trademarks. Annual reports, board minutes, and committee reports possess administrative value over a long period of time. All of these records have historical value both for the organization and for individuals engaged in historical research.

The objectives of an archives management program include the following:

- To identify general appraisal standards for determining the archival value of records.
- To gather the data necessary to determine what is unique about the information in the records under study.
- To apply records appraisal standards in such a way that neither too many nor too few records are retained.
- To determine the most effective and economical means for protecting the organization's records that possess archival value.

Functions Related to Records Management

Several functions related to records management are often operated as a part of a comprehensive program: *forms management, mail/message management, reprographics management,* and *records management procedures manuals.* (Each area is covered by a chapter in the text.)

Forms Management.   Underlying most successful records management programs is a strong forms control unit, with authority to approve or reject all standard business forms reproduced or purchased by the organization. A *form* is a piece of paper on which spaces are systematically arranged for the entry of data. Forms are used to facilitate the handling of recurring, but variable, data. Forms serve as the chief means of communicating information in a standardized, repetitive manner. To manage the organization's forms, records managers usually set up forms control programs that maintain routines for ordering, authorizing, designing, procuring, storing, distributing, reordering, reviewing, and disposing of each type of form used by the organization. Each of these control phases represents an area of specialization in today's records management programs.

Mail/Message Management.   An efficiently run mail/message management program is essential for rapid and economic distribution of information from one department to another within an organization and to and from others outside the organization. The mail/message management program should be designed to provide prompt and accurate collection and distribution, with adequate controls, at minimum costs. E-mail (*electronic mail*), fax (*facsimile transmission*), and bulletin boards are prime distributors of information today. They are often important elements of mail/message management programs, which are sometimes integrated with or otherwise attached to an organization's records management program.

Reprographics Management.   Copying is a rapidly growing component of information. The cost per copy has dropped, but the total expenditure for copying has increased. There are numerous reasons for the accelerating use of copying machines, but of primary importance are the need to have information quickly and to distribute it to many locations or people, the relative inefficiency of manual means, and the availability of high-quality machines providing copies at low unit cost. With the expansion of copying has come the demand for adequate management of copying.

Records Management Procedures Manuals. A records management procedures manual should be designed to inform all personnel of the services that the records management program provides and instruct staff on the proper methods used throughout the records program. The manual should serve as a source of instruction and reference for the personnel responsible for creating, preparing, processing, storing, and disposing of records.

The procedures manual should designate authority for all phases of the records management program. It should clarify organizational structure and the responsibilities of administrators, supervisors, and clerical personnel. It should establish uniform procedures in the creation, processing, retention, maintenance, and destruction of records.

Barriers to Better Records Management

We have noted that this book is based on one central premise: Better records make a better business. And earlier we put forward ten important reasons why businesses and government need records management and why the people who run these organizations are motivated to make investments in these systems and programs. Our case for records management is a persuasive one, but there is another side to the story—a case *against* records management that creates barriers to the development of excellent records management programs in many businesses and government agencies.

The following are three major reasons why

business executives sometimes do not support records management to the extent that they should.

1. *Records management programs do not generate income.* Although every organization needs records management, it is sometimes difficult to justify these programs based on the return on investment they yield, for the simple reason that records management programs do not generate hard cash. In the competition for corporate resources, some executives would rather spend money on income-producing business units than on administrative programs such as records management. While these programs do improve operating efficiency, they generate mostly "soft dollar" savings, and their benefits are often intangible and hard to quantify. Finally, records management programs are often viewed as administrative overhead and are thus highly vulnerable to corporate "downsizing" or cost-containment initiatives, even though one of their main purposes is to help the organization achieve cost-reduction goals.

2. *Records management is not the organization's primary business.* Organizations, and the people who run them, seldom want to achieve excellence in records management. Records management is not their primary business and is, therefore, often relegated to secondary status in the minds of senior decision makers. Further, while top executives often recognize the need for records management, they sometimes tend to see it as an administrative problem that is tangential to the overall success of their business.

3. *Records management programs are usually discretionary.* Except in some government environments where formally organized records management programs are mandated by statute, these programs are always discretionary. Although better records *do* make a better business, organizations can be operated successfully without records management. Too often, senior executives are content with mediocre records management, and they make records management a priority only when it becomes clear that poor records management adversely affects their business in some direct way.

Selling Records Management

These three barriers to better records management create a climate in which records management programs often must be "sold" to the senior executives who have the power to allocate resources to them. The following sales strategies for records management have proved to be successful in many corporate and government environments:

The Strategic Plan.   Every records management program should be initially sold to management and supported on an ongoing basis by the creation of a strategic plan for records management improvement. This strategic plan must articulate a clear vision for records management and its place within the larger organizational culture and environment, and it must contain a clear delineation of short- and long-term goals and strategies for achieving them. The plan should include an executive summary and a section containing a discussion of the organization's current recordkeeping situation and its problems and needs. Finally, the plan should contain a section detailing the recommendations for program improvement. Short-term objectives (to be accomplished during the next one to two years) should be discussed separately from long-term objectives—those to be achieved during the next three to five years and beyond. Every recommendation for program improvement should be accompanied by a clear explanation of the cost and benefits of accomplishing it versus the business risks of failure to accomplish it. This strategic plan should be developed in close concert with appropriate managers and executives throughout the organization (it should never be developed in isolation), presented to these individuals annually, and updated periodically as dictated by changes in business needs and as new technologies create new opportunities.

Value-Added Records Management.   The strategic records improvement plan should emphasize areas that most directly add value to the business. Every short- and long-term objective in the strategic plan should be expressed in terms of how it *adds value* to or enhances the quality of the organization. These expressions should never be communicated in the jargon of records management; rather they must reflect concepts meaningful to the buyer—senior executives. According to James Coulson, head of the Records Improvement Institute, most successful strategic records improvement plans have the following elements:

- A strategy to integrate the management of documents, files, and records of the organization with the management of computer and management information systems.
- A strategy to address the flow of information in the organization, such that productivity gains may be realized through efforts to streamline the transmission of documents and data.
- A strategy to empower all employees to seek "continuous improvement" in the way they create, index, handle, store, and maintain recorded information, such that enhancements in the quality of work and reductions in the cost of doing business may be realized.[3]

Organizational Compatibility.   The strategic records improvement plan should be compatible with larger organizational goals. If the organization is a profit-making enterprise, the plan should emphasize how value-added records management can contribute to net earnings. If the organization is implementing a quality improvement plan, a cost-containment plan, or a productivity improvement plan, the strategic records improvement plan should emphasize how records management can contribute to any or all of these strategies for improving the performance of the business.

Initial Program Development

The first decision the organization management must make is whether to use existing staff to perform some or all of the program start-up tasks, recruit and hire a records manager to perform these tasks, or retain the services of outside consultants to do the job. There are advantages and disadvantages to each of these approaches.

Use of Internal Personnel. If the organization has one or more persons on its staff who possess adequate technical knowledge of records management and they can be temporarily assigned to initiate the program, this alternative may be best. These individuals would already be familiar with the organization, its policies, procedures, and lines of business. Some large companies or government agencies employ records management specialists in one part of the organization, with the intention of using them to establish programs in other areas. However, frequently the organization does not have such persons on staff or they cannot be spared from their duties for any extended period of time.

Employment of a Records Manager. Some organizations elect to employ a records manager to handle the program development and implementation tasks. This approach can work well, but the main disadvantage is that the initial tasks associated with program start-up are usually very time-consuming and labor-intensive. Thus, unless the records manager has been authorized to recruit, hire, and train a staff, program start-up can require from one to three years of dedicated labor, and sometimes much longer if the organization is very large. As a result, many organizations elect to engage outside consultants.

Use of Outside Consultants. There are many advantages to this approach. A good consulting firm should possess a very high level of technical expertise; some of the most knowledgeable records management professionals in the country are consultants. Because they work with a wide variety of clients in business and government, they often possess very broad technical expertise. Because they are outsiders, they are in a position to render objective, unbiased advice. These individuals can sometimes devote their full-time attention to the records management project until it has been completed. Many organizations use outside consultants to perform the one-time tasks associated with program start-up. These often include conducting a records inventory, developing a records retention schedule, developing a uniform files classification system, and developing a wide variety of recommendations in every area of records management. Finally, consultants sometimes prepare strategic plans for records management improvement, present them to senior executives, and assist the client with staff recruitment, training, and the planning and design of specific records management systems.

There are, however, some actual or potential disadvantages to using outside consultants. They can sometimes be more expensive than staff personnel, and if they fail to perform, the organization may be placed in the difficult position of resolving the matter. Organizations contemplating the use of consultants should engage them only if they are highly reputable, if the nature of the assignment has been well defined, if proposals have been solicited from several firms, and if a written agreement containing appropriate terms and conditions has been executed.

Alternatives for Program Placement

Most records management programs today tend to be placed within one of several parts of an organization. The most popular placement option is within the administrative services organization, where records management is often a part of or exercises supervision over office services, facilities management, or other administrative support services. Less frequently, records management is a part of the finance or legal department; still less frequently, it falls within the management information systems, or MIS, organization. This placement is considered by some to be best for the future of records management. The issue of which placement option is best is often the subject of spirited debate in professional circles. There is no "best" place for a records management program within a corporate or governmental structure, except to say, "Wherever it can get the most management attention and support—the higher the better."

There are, however, some advantages and disadvantages to the administrative services versus information systems placement options which are worthy of note. If records management is placed within the administrative services organization, the records manager should report directly to the vice-president for administration, as shown in Figure 1.5. If records management is relegated to the level of the office services or facilities management functions, it is unlikely to enjoy sufficient status to make the kind of organizational impact needed to realize its objectives.

If records management is placed within the information systems, or MIS, organization, again the records manager should report to the vice-president in charge of this organization or, better still, directly to the CIO—the chief information officer. The main advantages to this organizational placement are that records management will be seen as a key component of the organization's total information management program and will enjoy better access to the technical expertise and technology resources which these organizations possess.

The Records Management Policy and Advisory Committee

When a records management program is developed, two important elements will give the program credibility and authority and help make it function more efficiently—a records management policy statement and a records management advisory committee.[4] The records manager should write the policy, and the president of the organization or the board of directors should approve it. It is then published in the records management manual or as a corporate policy. The policy statement should include the following elements:

- Purpose of the program
- A general statement of responsibility
- Program objectives
- Records management responsibilities

The records management advisory committee should be organized and chaired by the records manager. The committee should consist of qualified representatives from the legal department, the internal auditing department, the controller's office, the tax department, and the regulatory agencies function. Both these elements will go a long way towards ensuring the long-term success of the program.

FIGURE 1.5   Records Management in an Organization Chart

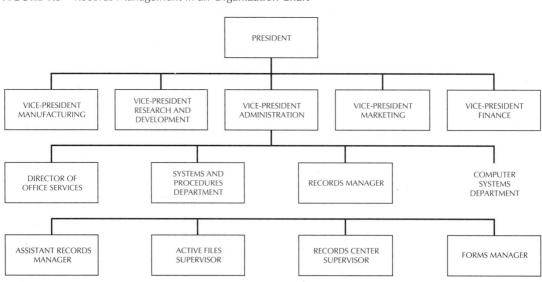

Records Management Program
Staffing and Career Development

There is no magic rule of thumb for how large a records management staff should be. Staff size usually depends on the size of the organization, whether it is particularly paper-intensive (for example, subject to stringent recordkeeping requirements imposed by the government), whether records management is assigned direct responsibility for the operation of central or departmental filing stations, the priority given records management by the organization's management, and other factors. Figure 1.6 shows the full complement of records and information management positions. Note the five levels, or classes, of positions: (1) management and administrative positions, (2) analytical positions, (3) supervisory positions, (4) coordinator positions, and, (5) technical clerical positions. These positions are organized as a career ladder.

FIGURE 1.6   Records and Information Management Career Ladder
Source: *Job Descriptions Guideline*, 1985. Courtesy of ARMA International

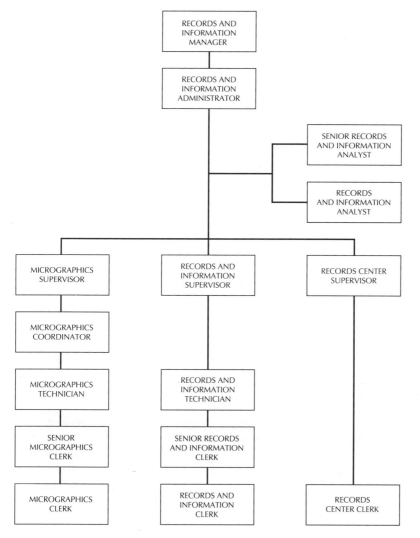

RECORDS MANAGEMENT: HISTORY AND PROSPECTS

This section reviews the historical development and current status of records management, and discusses its future prospects.

History of Records Management

Although government and business organizations have been creating, organizing, and disposing of records since ancient times, records management, as a formal business practice and professional field of endeavor, is a relatively recent phenomenon. Before 1950, formally established records management programs were not known in the business community. These programs had their origins in the U.S. government, later spread to the business sector, and are in wide use today.

The Concept of Vertical Filing. Modern business recordkeeping began about a hundred years ago, with the invention of vertical filing. In 1892, Dr. Nathaniel S. Rosenau first conceived of filing business papers *vertically*, by standing them on their edges in an upright position, housed in file folders constructed of heavy paper stock so that they would stand upright in a drawer.[5] Prior to this time business papers had been filed flat in boxes or pigeonholes; they were usually folded and tied into bundles with string. Retrieval of the records was a cumbersome task.

Early Records Management in the U.S. Government. The federal government can be said to have "invented" records management, conceived of and implemented many of its core concepts, and served as a model for its nationwide emulation by the private sector and by lower levels of government as well. In 1889, the first General Records Disposal Act was passed by the U.S. Congress—the first legal authorization for the routine and systematic disposal of valueless records in our history. In 1912, the U.S. Bureau of Efficiency was created to study government filing practices; it promoted the use of modern office equipment.

Role of the National Archives. The field of records management in the United States is largely an outgrowth of the archival profession; it evolved from federal archival practice. In 1934, the National Archives of the United States was founded, and soon thereafter it conducted the first government-wide records survey. Such an undertaking was essential, owing to the vast quantity of federal records that had accumulated since the formation of the Republic.

In 1943, the National Archives devised the first records disposition schedule, and its use was legally authorized by the Records Disposal Act, which was enacted the same year. This was an extremely significant event in the history of records management, for records retention schedules (as they are more commonly called) remain one of the most important and widely used records management tools today.

In the late 1940s, President Truman established the Commission on the Organization of the Executive Branch of Government—popularly known as the Hoover Commission. The commission authorized the Task Force on Paperwork Management, which was chaired by Emmett J. Leahy, who had been a member of the National Archives staff.

Mr. Leahy is considered a founding father of records management, and his work with the Hoover Commission is of singular importance to the history of this profession. The Hoover Commission sponsored a law that defined the term *records management* for the first time in any federal statute, and required each federal agency to establish an active and ongoing records management program. Thus, the federal government records management program was well under way by the early 1950s. In 1949, the Records Management Division was formally established within the National Archives and Records Service, and in 1950, the regional Records Management Service was established to spread the program to federal government agencies throughout the United States. By 1952, the National Archives and Records Service had established a total of nine federal records centers throughout the country to house the inactive records of federal agencies. The records center concept—another invention of the National Archives—is a central tool of records management that remains widely used by both business and government today.

By the early 1950s, the federal government's records management program could cite numerous significant accomplishments, with savings resulting from its records management actions estimated at $5.5 million.

The Spread of Records Management to the Business Community.

In 1947 the National Records Management Council[6] was founded by Emmett J. Leahy, who served as its first director. During the next ten years, this organization helped more than 40 business corporations to establish comprehensive records management programs.

The council played a critical role in bringing records management to the business sector. Among its many significant achievements, the council sponsored the first conference on records management (1950), helped organize the first accredited records management course offered at the university level (1948) and was instrumental in establishing similar courses in colleges and universities throughout the United States, presented records management seminars to the business community, published the first *Index to Federal Record Keeping Requirements* (1955), and helped to bring records management to the attention of senior executives by getting articles published in business publications. Finally, the commercial records center industry was an outgrowth of the council; today, several hundred firms operate records storage businesses in cities throughout the United States.

Consulting firms also helped develop records management programs for clients in business and government. Manufacturers of filing cabinets were among the first organizations to establish records management consultancies. Remington Rand and the Shaw-Walker Company were among the first to develop this type of business. Finally, the National Records Management Council formed Naremco Services in 1957, and today there

are over a hundred records management consultancies in the United States.

Records Management Professional Associations.

Professional associations have played a key role in the development of the field. A partial list of these organizations can be found in Appendix A.

ARMA International. In 1956, six groups joined together to form the first national records management professional association in the United States—the American Records Management Association, or ARMA, as it is now called. This association began with 500 members but grew rapidly, and became international in 1969 when Canadian records managers from Toronto and Montreal joined it. It is now known as ARMA International; its official name is the Association of Records Managers and Administrators, Inc. This group is the world's leading professional association representing records management interests. It currently has over 11,000 members in approximately 35 countries. The international association is supported by local chapters in any city where the requisite number of members form a local chapter upon approval of a charter. At present, ARMA International has over 140 chapters in four countries—the United States, Canada, Japan, and New Zealand.

At the international, national, and local levels, ARMA International plays a key role in the promotion of records management interests. It holds conferences, seminars, and workshops to provide educational opportunities for its members. It publishes journals, books, newsletters, videos, and other educational materials. Its journal, the *Records Management Quarterly*, is the leading periodical in the field of records management. And it promotes legislative initiatives at the federal and state levels. In short, ARMA International fosters professionalism in records management for the benefit of its members and their employers.

The Institute of Certified Records Managers. Founded in 1975, the Institute of Certified

Records Managers administers a program for professional certification of records management specialists. At present, approximately 600 individuals in some half-dozen countries have been awarded certified records manager, or CRM, status by the institute's board of regents. Candidates for certification must possess the requisite education and experience and must satisfactorily complete a written examination, which is administered by the ICRM. The examination consists of six parts covering the various aspects of records and information management: five parts consist of multiple-choice questions while the sixth part consists of case studies requiring narrative answers. Finally, in order to maintain certification, certified records managers must demonstrate continuing education or other contributions to the field, such as lecturing, and writing.

The Current Status of Records Management

Today records management enjoys perhaps the most prosperous period in its history. It has grown steadily during the past 40 years, and is today a well-established and widely accepted business practice. Many thousands of business firms and government agencies operate records management programs, and the number of programs continues to grow every year. In fact, the growth in ARMA International membership averaged over 6 percent per year throughout the 1980s, so it would be fair to conclude that records management is a "growth industry."

The most significant factors affecting records management during the 1980s and early 1990s were:

1. *Strong growth in the volume and quantity of records.* As we have seen, business filing systems grow at rates often exceeding 7 percent to 10 percent each year. Electronic recordkeeping systems are realizing even stronger growth. This alone generates greater demand for records management solutions to recordkeeping problems.

2. *More complex information needs and increasing difficulties with the performance of recordkeeping systems.* The demands on every

business and government agency are greater today than ever before. Moreover, in this era of corporate restructuring and downsizing, the resources available to deal with these problems often seem to be shrinking. These business trends seem to be reflected in an organization's recordkeeping systems. As these systems continue to grow and new demands are placed on them, new opportunities for records management are created.

3. *New information technologies and the need for specialized expertise in order to apply them successfully.* As we have seen, new optical disk systems, records management software, new computer networks, and other related technologies have developed during the last five to ten years. These technologies create new ways of solving records management problems, and they make records management a dynamic profession.

The Future of Records Management

As shown in Table 1.1, solid growth is forecast for every sector of records management during the 1990s.[7]

Annual growth rates of 20 percent per year would mean that the size of the records management market is expected to double during the next five years. These levels of growth portend a bright future for records management.

What will be the place of records management in the larger spectrum of information systems management in business and government organizations? Two trends are particularly relevant to this issue.

1. *Migration from fragmented to coordinated to integrated information systems.* The Association for Information and Image Management study "Information and Image Management: The State of the Industry—1989" concluded that during the 1990s, organizations will evolve from *fragmented* to *coordinated* to *integrated* information management. The study reported that at the beginning of the 1990s, information management was fragmented in most organizations; that is, the same information was frequently captured onto many

TABLE 1.1   Summary of Growth Projections, 1993–1997

Records Management Program Component	*Five-Year Growth Forecast (% per year)*
Paper document filing systems	7–10
Records centers for inactive records storage	20–25
Vital records protection programs	5-10
Records management software	30-40
Micrographics products and services	5-10
PC-based electronic recordkeeping systems	20-25
Optical disk products and services	25-30

Source: David O. Stephens, CRM, CMC, "The Future of Records Management: A Vendor Perspective," paper presented at the 37th Annual Conference of ARMA International, Detroit, Michigan, 1992.

different media: mechanical (paper), photographic (microfilm), and electronic (computers or optical disks). The AIIM study predicted that by the mid-1990s, organizations will evolve towards coordinated information management, in which duplicate media would be eliminated and there would be greater physical centralization of information systems and storage media. Finally, the study predicted that by the end of the 1990s, organizations will have achieved an even higher plateau: the establishment of a fully integrated, enterprise-wide information system in which the capture and manipulation of text, data, and graphics information will be performed on one interactive system.

2.   *The role of the chief information officer.* If the AIIM predictions are accurate, how can organizations implement them? And what is the place of records management in this new information management environment? A growing number of organizations have created a new position, that of chief information officer (CIO), to coordinate and integrate the many disparate information-related functions. This new "Information Czar" typically assumes responsibility for records management, data processing and MIS, telecommunications, office automation, libraries, archives, microcomputer user support, information and document control centers, executive information systems, and other information-related functions. The goal is to manage the organization's total information resources as a strategic asset of the business.

Both these trends are very positive for the future of records management. Organizations cannot develop coordinated or fully integrated information systems on an enterprise-wide basis without records management expertise. Records managers will continue to be key players in this process as they look towards the twenty-first century.

SUMMARY

Information is one of the world's most important resources; it exists in every organizational enterprise throughout the world. Increasingly, the degree of success enjoyed by organizations and the people who work for them depends on how well information resources are managed.

Business information is created countless times every business day in many different forms and by a wide variety of office machines and technologies. It has many different characteristics, depending chiefly on form, usage, and value. In particular, information has no value unless it is used; in order for it to be used effectively, information must be readily accessible to those who need it.

Business *records* are recorded information, regardless of medium or characteristics. They include information which resides on microfilm, electronic, and other media in addition to paper documents. The management and control of records and documents in organizations—how to control their creation, how to organize them for effective retrieval, whether and how to convert them to a nonpaper medium, how to safeguard them against loss, and whether or when to destroy them—are extremely important issues to business and government because paper document filing systems and other records media have experienced tremendous growth during the past several decades, and continued growth is expected in the future.

Records management is the application of systematic and scientific controls to recorded information required in the operation of an organization's business. Organizations achieve the benefits of records management by establishing formally organized *records management programs*. These programs endeavor to manage organizational information so that it is timely, accurate, complete, cost-effective, accessible, and usable.

One of the core concepts of records management is the *life cycle concept*, in which appropriate records management controls are applied to business records during each of the five major stages in their life cycle: (1) the *creation* stage, (2) the *distribution and use* stage, (3) the *storage and maintenance* stage, (4) the *retention and disposition* stage, and (5) the *archival preservation* stage.

Organizations make investments in records management systems and programs in order to realize their business benefits. The major ones are to control the creation and growth of records, to reduce the costs associated with recordkeeping, to improve the efficiency and productivity of those who must handle and process records, to integrate new records management technologies into the business, to ensure compliance with government-imposed recordkeeping requirements, to minimize the risk of litigation, to safeguard vital information, to support better management decision-making, to preserve records of archival value, and to foster professionalism in running the business.

Records management programs in business and government organizations vary widely in scope and content. Most comprehensive, enterprise-wide programs, however, are comprised of the following basic elements: a records inventory, records retention schedules, a vital records protection and disaster recovery program, a program to enhance the management of active files, an electronic records management program, micrographics and optical disk filing systems, a records center for the management of inactive records, and an archives management program. In addition, comprehensive records management programs often operate several programs closely related to records management: a forms management program, a mail/message management program, a reprographics management program, and a records management procedures manual.

Although good records management will help all organizations achieve their business goals, many do not have good programs. The fact that records management is not the organization's primary business, the fact that these programs are usually discretionary and do not generate revenues are major barriers to the development of excellent programs in many organizations. For these reasons, records management programs often must be "sold" to senior executives. The development of a strategic plan for records management improvement is a proven method of doing this.

Many organizations elect to develop records management programs using their own personnel, while others retain consulting firms to perform many of the one-time, labor-intensive tasks associated with program start-up. Regardless of the method of initial development, the program will usually require a staff for ongoing operation, consisting of a records manager and various analysts, supervisors, technicians, and clerical personnel. These programs are often placed within the administrative services unit of organizations, but placement within the computer services or management information systems unit is increasingly popular.

The profession of records management evolved during the 1940s and 1950s. Many of the early records management concepts were developed by archivists employed by the National Archives of the United States. These concepts were first implemented in the U.S. federal government, and they later spread to the business community. The American Records Management Association was formed in 1956—the first nationwide records management professional association in the United States. Today this association is known as ARMA International; it has over 11,000 members in some 35 countries. The Institute of Certified Records Managers, a certifying body for records management professionals, was started in 1975.

The records management field experienced strong growth during the 1980s, and solid growth is expected to continue during the 1990s. More complex information needs, continuing growth in the volume of records, and new information technologies are major reasons for these positive growth forecasts. Records management is only one professional discipline associated with an organization's total information resources, and the records manager of the 1990s must work effectively with other information disciplines in order to play a prominent role in information systems planning during the years that lie ahead.

QUESTIONS FOR DISCUSSION

1. Explain the importance of business information to society as a whole.

2. List five essential characteristics of business information.

3. Define the word *records* as used in this book.

4. List the major categories of records media. Indicate which one is expected to realize the fastest growth during the 1990s and which the least growth.

5. Define *information and records management*.

6. List and explain the five principal objectives of records management.

7. List and explain the five major stages in the information life cycle.

8. List and explain the ten major reasons justifying the development and implementation of records management programs in business firms and governmental organizations.

9. Most comprehensive records management programs have a dozen or so major components. List ten of them, and include a brief explanation of their main purposes.

10. Many organizations, even some large ones, have not established a formal records management program. List and explain briefly three reasons why these organizations might not have established a program.

11. List and describe three techniques for selling records management to senior executives.

12. Some organizations use the services of an external consulting firm to assist them in establishing a records management program. List several advantages and disadvantages of this approach.

13. Discuss the role of the National Archives of the United States in the early development of records management.

14. What is ARMA and what are some of its main functions in promoting records management?

15. Discuss the major trends affecting records management, both now and in the future.

PROJECTS

1. Contact an executive officer in a business organization in your area who is in charge of administrative services. The organization should not have a formally established records management program. Arrange for an interview to obtain information concerning the organization's system of recordkeeping. List the questions you will need to ask. For your class, prepare a presentation justifying why a comprehensive, formally established records management program is important to the firm.

2. Annotate three articles on the general topic of

records management. Limit your annotations to a maximum of 150 words for each article.

3. Prepare a bibliography of articles written in the past three years on each of the major elements of a records management program.

4. The director of the Management Development and Training Program, Global Export Company, Los Angeles, California, asks you to identify the topics to be discussed in each of the 10 two-hour weekly meetings for the in-service course he is organizing on the basic elements of records management. List the topics you would recommend, in proper sequence, for each of the 10 sessions. Attach a brief account of your rationale for the recommendations you make.

5. Prepare a questionnaire that could be used to conduct a general survey of the recordkeeping or records management practices of a business firm.

CASE PROBLEM

The National Engineering Corporation has been in business since 1958. It has never had an organized records management program. There are 123 office employees under the jurisdiction of the vice-president of Administrative Services. The major problems that exist in regard to the organization's records are the following:

1. Storage and maintenance of records is the duty of every secretary in the organization, and records retrieval time is excessive.

2. Records of the organization have never been inventoried, and no organization-wide effort has been made to dispose of obsolete records.

3. Forms are created and designed by numerous office employees, and there has been no effort to control them.

4. Some very important records relating to the design and manufacturing of some of the firm's products (engineering drawings, design specifications, etc.) were destroyed in a fire last year.

5. Many inactive records that must be retained for legal and business reasons are stored in poorly labeled boxes in closets and hallways, and in a storage shed adjacent to the manufacturing plant.

Identify the actions that should be taken to correct these problems.

NOTES

1. John Naisbitt, Megatrends: *Ten New Directions Transforming Our Lives* (New York: Warner Books, 1982), p. 7.

2. Ibid., pp. 7-8, 16.

3. Jim Coulson, CRM, "How to Market Records Management to Senior Executives," *Proceedings of the 37th Annual Conference, ARMA International,* Association of Records Managers and Administrators, Prairie Village, Kansas, 1992, pp. 413-426.

4. Gail Blount, CRM, "Two Steps Not to Be Overlooked When Organizing Your Records Management Program," *Records Management Quarterly,* October 1984, pp. 17-18, 20.

5. T. R. Schellenberg, *Modern Archives: Principles and Techniques* (Chicago: University of Chicago Press, 1956), pp. 83-84.

6. Naremco Services, Inc., "The National Records Management Council," unpublished paper courtesy of Alan A. Andolsen, Naremco Services, Inc., New York, N.Y., n.d.

7. David O. Stephens, CRM, CMC, "The Future of Records Management." Paper presented at the 37th Annual Conference, ARMA International, Detroit, Michigan, 1992.

Chapter 2

Records Inventory

Learning Objectives
1. To define the term *records inventory.*
2. To list and explain the objectives of a records inventory in a records management program.
3. To identify the distinguishing differences among the major methods used in inventorying the records of an organization.
4. To explain the procedures to be used in taking a records inventory.
5. To describe the structural arrangements of records.
6. To delineate the different methods used in inventorying electronic record media.

WHAT IS A RECORDS INVENTORY?

The *records inventory* is a complete and accurate survey of an organization's file contents. This survey is accomplished by describing, quantifying, and recording information about those records on a standard records inventory form, so that the records can be analyzed for retention, protection, and other purposes. The records inventory is vital to an effective records management program because it both identifies and quantifies all records that are created, referenced, or processed by the organization. Used to assess the functions and activities of a company's records, the records inventory is the first phase in the development and implementation of a records management program. It becomes the working document for preparing the records retention schedule, establishing the vital records protection program, and making other improvements to the records management program.

PLANNING THE INVENTORY

Many of the problems associated with establishing a records management program can be alleviated by careful planning of the records inventory. The inventory, or survey as it is sometimes called, should include the following preparatory steps:

- Commitment from top management.
- Establishment of a work schedule.
- Communication to staff and management.
- Project staffing and training.
- Statement of objectives and strategies.
- Design of an inventory form.

Commitment from Top Management

Before the records inventory begins, the records manager should obtain a written commitment from top management, giving the project director (either an outside consultant, the records manager, or another designated person) the authority to proceed. A directive to middle management should be issued, stating the objectives of the records survey and requesting the cooperation of all concerned.

Establishment of a Work Schedule

The next step in the records inventory planning phase is the establishment of a work schedule that estimates the time required for each department. The schedule should specify:

- The sequence of offices to be visited.
- When each office will be inventoried.
- The name of the person who will act as the coordinator for each office.
- The name of the supervisor who must give clearance and approve the schedule for the inventory.
- Beginning and end dates for the project.

Planning should be flexible and allow for changes in priority. The schedule should provide adequate time for delays and unforeseen events. Figure 2.1 is an example of a time schedule for a records inventory.

For the day-to-day operation, the schedule should show only one or two elements in detail, such as starting dates and review periods, and need not be complex.

Estimating the time requirements for the inventory is not a simple task. These requirements depend on the variety and complexity of records series, the quantity of records, and the amount of collected data. However, experienced inventory specialists have developed methods for preparing estimates of time. Record volume is estimated by means of a *walk-through* survey, which involves counting file drawers or their equivalent and observing the layout and type of records and practices. Inventory specialists have found that at the typical departmental level, approximately 50 to 75 file drawers can be inventoried in one 8-hour day by one analyst, and that there will be approximately one records series for every three file drawers. Stated another way, each inventory form will

Program Element	Staffing	
	Jan. 1 2 3 4 (Weeks)	Feb. 1 2 3 4 (Weeks)
Determining objectives	x x x i	i
Selection of personnel to conduct survey	x x	
Communication	x	
Determining file locations	x	
Specifications of data	x x i i	
Inventory form	x i	
Schedule	x	
Actual inventory	x	x x x x

Developments resulting from
   Records Inventory:
      Retention disposal schedule
      Records center
      Vital records
      Forms management
      Micrographics
      Reports management		

Note: *x* means work time; *i* means review time.

FIGURE 2.1   Inventory Work Schedule

require approximately 30 to 40 minutes to complete, or an average of 16 forms per day. Another guideline for estimating assumes that a fair goal for an inventory analyst with moderate experience in the physical inventory of records is an average of 150 cubic feet of records per day.[1] This of course can vary greatly, however, if the department is not typical.

For example, if most of a department's record volume consists of one records series, the department could be inventoried in a very short time, because there would be only one inventory form for that major series. In a case such as this, most of the time involved in the inventory would consist of measuring, which is the least time-consuming element of the process. Conversely, a highly technical department, such as research or product development, might require a great deal of time, even though volume were relatively low, because of the diversity, complexity, and number of records series that would have to be described.

Communication to Staff and Management

Before the start of any major procedure of a records management program, such as the physical inventory of records, a memorandum should be sent to all supervisors and personnel concerned identifying the nature of the project, why it is being done, how the project might affect normal routine, and when it will begin. If possible, an orientation session should be scheduled for all employees who will be affected by the project.

As part of the overall procedure, the records manager should keep the executive, managerial, and supervisory staff informed of the project's progress. Such briefings, which will help ensure the continued cooperation necessary for success, can be done with regular progress reports, using bar charts to show progress percentages and giving estimated completion dates.

Project Staffing

An early decision that must be made in inventory and retention projects is who will do the work. There are three options, and the choice depends on many factors, including the internal needs and resources of the organization. These options are:

- Use of internal records management staff.
- Use of departmental staff.
- Use of an outside consultant.

Regardless of who conducts the inventory, the techniques used are always very similar. In some organizations, a records retention committee oversees the goals, plan, and purpose of the inventory process.

Use of Internal Records Management Staff.
One approach is for the records management staff to perform the work. This option has the following advantages:

1. The records manager or records analyst can often make an on-the-spot decision about the need for information about certain records, thus reducing the time required to complete the form. The analyst knows how the infor-

mation will be used and will gather data within that framework, thus making the inventory more complete and comprehensive.

2. Although the form itself provides a pattern for interviews, by experience, the trained analyst knows the best interview techniques.

3. The records manager or analyst will eventually have to study the inventory sheets to implement the program. Thus, the first-hand knowledge gained in taking the inventory, coupled with the uniform method of description, will make the analysis and retention schedule development much easier and more effective and practical. Day-to-day program maintenance will also be more efficient.

4. The use of in-house employees eliminates the need to hire outside staff or disrupt the staffs of the departments.

Although highly advantageous, this staff method has some disadvantages that are unacceptable to some organizations. If the organization has no records management staff and plans to use only consultant and general administrative services personnel to implement the program, the internal records management staff approach, obviously, cannot be used. If the organization's records management staff is small, it may take so long to complete the inventory that the information will be outdated by the end of the inventory.

Use of Departmental Staff.
Personnel from each department can be used to conduct their own inventories. The chief advantages of this approach are that the departments know their records and the total organizational inventory can be completed simultaneously, rather than by one or two departments at a time. Reasonably good results can be expected if certain *critical* conditions are met:

- Each department must designate one or more people from its ranks to conduct its own inventory.
- The people must be trained by the records manager in inventory techniques so that the proper information is collected in a *uniform*

way to facilitate uniform interpretation of the data by the records manager.

• A target date for completion must be set and agreed to by all concerned. Without such a date, the borrowed staff may give their attention to other duties and the inventory may bog down.

There are disadvantages to this approach. Some of these are:

1. The departments may not be able to spare the personnel to do the work.
2. There can be a tendency to cover up known deficiencies. Conducting your own inventory is similar to conducting your own audit: There is a danger of bias and loss of perspective in records description.
3. The people who will conduct the retention analysis will not have had the advantage of personally viewing the records and discussing them with departmental personnel, as they would have had if they had performed the inventory.
4. The newly trained will miss deficiencies that the experienced professional would quickly detect.
5. There is the possibility that the departmental personnel may consider the inventory an extra assignment. They may have little interest in it and, as a result, perform a haphazard job.

Use of an Outside Consultant. If there is not sufficient in-house professional staff and if the borrowed-staff approach seems inappropriate, the remaining alternative is to hire a records management consultant. This third approach is more expensive, at least in the short term, but often is the best way. The principal or senior consultant usually has years of experience and normally employs an inventory specialist who may be assisted by the organization's clerical personnel or by personnel from firms specializing in temporary records management help. The analysis, research, and development of the retention schedule is done

by the principal or senior consultant, who supervises the inventory while it is being performed.

Objectives and Strategies

Goals and strategies must also be developed before the inventory commences. The goals of the inventory parallel the goals of the records management program and are actually part of the strategy to achieve those program goals. Inventory goals may be long- or short-range. The short-range goals are usually the goals that parallel the program goals and are the ones that guide the collection in the initial records inventory. These goals are:

• Development of a records retention schedule.
• Development of a records storage and retrieval system for noncurrent records.
• Improvement of active files management systems through micrographics, electronic imaging, or better hard copy systems.
• Development of a vital records protection and security program.
• Judicious use of filing equipment and floor space.

Other goals that may be of less immediate concern, and hence are long-range, are:

• Correspondence management
• Reports control
• Forms control
• Office automation

The strategy to achieve the inventory goals is to obtain sufficient information about the various records so that intelligent decisions can be made in the process.

In selecting items of information to be collected, one must be certain that (1) there is a reason or purpose for gathering the information and (2) the benefit of having the information exceeds the cost of gathering it. For example, it usually is not wise to collect information about a particular record, simply because to do so would make the data inventory complete or because the information may be required at some time in the future. If it were to be required, perhaps to make a micrographics study, the information could be obtained then as easily as at the time of inventory and would be more current. If only essential information is recorded on the inventory form, the project will proceed more expeditiously than if every bit of information is obtained. This does not mean, however, that the inventory form should not provide for this extra information, so that it can be added to the form later, for example, in connection with a feasibility study for microimaging.

Designing the Inventory Form

After determination of the objectives and the information needed to achieve those goals, the design of the inventory form can begin. A form is needed to act as a guide to and checklist of the information required. It provides a uniform method of recording information and ensures that only required information is collected. The preferred size of the form is 8 1/2 by 11 inches, but many different kinds of inventory forms have been designed and used successfully. Although these forms vary considerably, most contain the following basic information:

- *Department or organization name.* To use for identification as inventories are performed departmentally.
- *Name of the records series.* To use for identification; should be concise and descriptive.
- *Purpose or description of the records series.* To provide information necessary to research and determine retention requirements.
- *Time span covered (dates of the records).* To provide growth rate and evidence of current retention practices.
- *Linear measurement of the series* (number of feet that the series occupies in a cabinet or other housing unit and, for magnetic media, a count or an estimate of tapes or disks in addition to the linear measurement). To show total volume on hand, growth rate, equipment utilization; a base factor for calculating sav-

ings and benefits, as well as records center space requirements.
- *Physical description* (size and color for paper records, size of tape or disk for magnetic media). To select correct records housing and to provide a proper mental picture to the analyst.
- *Method of housing* (files, binder, or loose). To determine proper equipment and to use for system evaluation and improvements.
- *Equipment description.* To evaluate equipment utilization, to calculate costs as well as floor space, and to plan efficient use of surplus equipment.
- *Date of inventory, name of contact, name of inventory analyst.* To determine growth and to track information obsolescence. Names are necessary for follow-up information and verification.

Of course, additional data can be added to this collection, or less can be gathered. For example, it may be necessary or valuable to know:

- *Source of information* (used to create record series). This information provides identification of alternate sources of information as a vital records backup.
- *Any records created from information in the records series.* This information gives an alternate source of backup and a factor in retention programming.
- *Original and secondary purposes of record series.* This information is useful in retention and vital protection research and in document flow studies for systems improvements.
- *Original and secondary purposes of component documents that make up the series.* This information is useful in retention schedule development and vital records protection evaluations.
- *Flow of record or component from beginning to end.* This information is useful in a complex systems study such as in image processing and highly active document or image systems.
- *Location of exact duplicate sources of infor-*

mation or alternate sources (different but substantially the same). Few documents are created in only one copy. It is important to know where the other copies are located, as only one copy may be required, at least by law or regulation.

- *Current practice or recommendation of user on retention periods.* This information does not establish the retention period, but is a useful factor in retention analysis and research.

See Figure 2.2*a* and *b* for an example of a records inventory form and the types of information that can be gathered. Usually, not all of Sections I through X are required for all initial inventories. Page 2 of the sample form (Figure 2.2*b*) is normally required for microimaging and file system improvement studies only, together with page 1 (Figure 2.2*a*) of the same form.

The inventory form not only serves as a summary of records function, flow, and description, providing a basis for a records retention schedule, but also gives other statistical data. These data can be used to anticipate records center requirements and to calculate current costs and savings. They can also provide an equipment inventory and may point to other areas that may need further study, such as a forms program, the use of microimaging, or file system improvements.

In those cases, a separate study will be required, although much of the data already gathered may be of value. In studies aimed at file system improvements, knowing the systems currently in use, the file activity, and the equipment use will lead to further improvements. Thus, a comprehensive inventory form, such as is shown in Figure 2.2*a* and *b,* can be used not only for the initial inventory, which may have as its primary objective the development of a retention schedule, but also for specialized studies in microimaging and other systems improvements.

INVENTORY METHODS

The goals of the inventory, the type of information collected, why it is collected, and who will collect it are all important considerations. However, the method used in conducting the inventory is equally important.

Departmental Contact or Liaison

Each department inventoried should have a knowledgeable person assigned as a contact, not only for the inventory but also for other contacts with the records management department. This person may be the office manager or file supervisor or perhaps the department manager or assistant manager. Such an individual must know the various types of records created or maintained and their location, and specifics about their use and value. The inventory specialist cannot conduct the inventory without the assistance of a knowledgeable person in each department. Full-time assistance is by no means necessary, but the inventory should be scheduled to coincide with the contact person's schedule. Alternate schedules or work plans should also be prepared so that the work progresses during those times when the contact person is unavailable.

Initial Interview

The analyst should confirm a day or two ahead of schedule the time of the initial meeting with the departmental contact. As a start, the department's organizational chart should be discussed and the department's primary and secondary functions explained to the analyst. This background will not only be valuable in understanding and describing the records, it will also be valuable in the development of the retention schedule. Sometimes a department may have file manuals or file lists which in effect provide a transcript of all record categories maintained in the department. If available, these should be used as guides in identification. In addition, file drawers should be labeled with the record title, which can assist greatly in identification.

The department contact should also provide a list of stored records, together with their locations. These stored records are usually stashed

FORM 75041 (Rev. 1-87)

RECORD SERIES INVENTORY AND RETENTION APPROVAL

SECTION I

INVENTORIED BY & DATE: *DLB 7/10/95*

FUNCTIONAL CODE: *C-4B* TITLE CODE: *10-101*

DEPARTMENT: *DISBURSEMENTS ACCTG* SECTION: *PAYABLES*

COMPANY NAME: *ACE CORP*

RECORD SERIES TITLE: *DRAFTS ISSUED, VOUCHER COPIES*

CONTACT: *John Doe*

RECORD SERIES ALSO KNOWN AS: *Computer Drafts*

STORAGE CODE: *A* LOCATION & PHONE NUMBER: *STL 1289*

SECTION II — GENERAL DESCRIPTION, PURPOSE AND USE OF RECORD SERIES

Copy of Voucher portion of draft issued for payment of bill or invoice for equipment, supplies or services. File is maintained for reference, proof of payment, audits and as a supporting record for Journal Entries.

SECTION III — FILE EQUIPMENT IN OFFICE

INVENTORY NUMBER	DESCRIPTION	QUANTITY	FLOOR SPACE OCCUPIED (Incl. Aisle)
1 – 8	*7 Shelf Tab SF*	*8*	*50 sq ft.*
9 – 13	*5 dr Ltr File Cab*	*5*	*35 sq ft.*

SECTION IV — VOLUME

INCLUSIVE DATES	RATE OF GROWTH
3/91 – 3/94	*2400 pgs*

MEASUREMENT	GROWTH TIME SPAN
4500 lin in	*per day*

SECTION V — REFERENCES

QUANTITY	TIME SPAN	REFER. TIME
	OFFICE	
30	*day*	*5 min*
	STORAGE	
5	*day*	*5 min*

SECTION VI — FILE SUPPLIES UTILIZED

DESCRIPTION	QUANTITY
File Folders, End Tab ltr size	*30000*
File Folders, 5th Cut ltr size	*1500*

SECTION VII — VITAL RECORDS PROTECTION

☒ REQUIRED ☐ NOT REQUIRED

If required, protected by
☒ Microfilming
☐ Off-Premises Storage/Dispersal
☐ Vital Records Storage Center
☐ Other _____

SECTION VIII — SORTING AND FILING ARRANGEMENT

FILING ARRANGEMENT: *By Year / By Draft #*

PRE-FILE SORTING ROUTINE: *No Pre-file sort. Computer assigned file number*

SORTING MANHOURS: *NA*   SORTING TIME SPAN:

SECTION IX — INPUT/OUTPUT RECORDS

RECORDS USED TO CREATE THIS RECORD (Show R/S No.)	RECORDS CREATED FROM THIS RECORD (Show R/S No.)
Contracts	*Journal Entries*
Leases	*Budget Recaps*
Purchase Orders	*Tax Returns*

SECTION X — DUPLICATE AND ALTERNATE SOURCES

DUPLICATE RECORD SERIES & LOCATION	ALTERNATE RECORD SERIES & LOCATION
Microfilm Copy (10-010)	*Cancelled and Paid Drafts / Purchase Order*

STATUTORY/REGULATORY RETENTION REQUIREMENTS

CFR 49 1220.10 C-4b
MO 143.711 6 yr
AR 84-4711(b) 6 yr.
ICC C-4b 6 yr.

APPROVALS

	INITIALS & DATE	RECORDS MANAGEMENT	PROPRIETARY DEPT.	TAX DEPARTMENT	LAW DEPARTMENT
INITIALS & DATE		*DTG 8/10/95*	*MTK 8/20/95*	*JLA 9/1/95*	*WFK 9/15/95*

RETENTION RECOM.	OFFICE	RECORDS CENTER	TOTAL	OFFICE	RECORDS CENTER	TOTAL	OFFICE	RECORDS CENTER	TOTAL	OFFICE	RECORDS CENTER	TOTAL
	1 yr	*5 yr*	*6*	*1 yr*	*5 y*	*6 yr*	*—*		*6*	*—*		*6 yr.*

REMARKS:

APPROVED-Retention Committee: *D F Godfrey*   DATE: *10/1/95*

OFFICE	RECORDS CENTER	TOTAL
1 yr.	*5 yr.*	*6 yr.*

FIGURE 2.2a Records Inventory Form

FUNCTIONAL INFORMATION

RECORD SERIES TITLE	RECORD SERIES (Retention Sched.) NO.
DRAFTS ISSUED, Voucher Copies	10 – 101

ORIGINATION AND PURPOSE OF COMPONENT DOCUMENTS

DOCUMENT NO. 1

DOCUMENT NAME	
Original Bill or Invoice	
ORIGINATED BY	NO. PARTS
Vendor	3

ORIGINAL PURPOSE OF DOCUMENT
To present charges for materials, equipment or services purchased.

HOW USED IN THIS OFFICE
Proof of Payment, audit, support for General Ledger Entry.

DOCUMENT NO. 2

DOCUMENT NAME	
Payment Authorization	
ORIGINATED BY	NO. PARTS
Dept authorizing Purchase	2

ORIGINAL PURPOSE OF DOCUMENT
Shows departmental authority to pay bill or invoice.

HOW USED IN THIS OFFICE
Initiate payment of bill or invoice and to provide proof of authority.

DOCUMENT NO. 3

DOCUMENT NAME	
Request for Payment	
ORIGINATED BY	NO. PARTS
Payables Section	1

ORIGINAL PURPOSE OF DOCUMENT
Provides auth & info necessary for Data Proc to generate draft and Voucher

HOW USED IN THIS OFFICE
Provides proof of auth granted to D. P. Dept.

DOCUMENT NO. 4

DOCUMENT NAME	
Voucher Copy, Draft Issued	
ORIGINATED BY	NO. PARTS
Data Processing	2

ORIGINAL PURPOSE OF DOCUMENT
Shows purpose of draft and provide acctg info necessary to close & adjust payables accts.

HOW USED IN THIS OFFICE
Proof of payment, audit purpose + support for General Ledger Entry.

FILE CONTENT AND DISTRIBUTION

	DOCUMENT NO. 1	DOCUMENT NO. 2	DOCUMENT NO. 3	DOCUMENT NO. 4
COMPONENT DOCUMENT NAME	Original Invoice	PAYMENT AUTH.	REQUEST FOR PAYMENT	Voucher Copy of Draft.
MEDIA CODE*	F/MS	C/MS	F2 – 4/MS	PO – 3/MS
FORM NUMBER	External	135	23000	35010
JOB NUMBER	NA	N/A	N/A	AT 022
SIZE	Various	Various	$8\frac{1}{2} \times 11$	$8\frac{1}{2} \times 11$
COLOR	Various	White	White	Green
% OF VOLUME	25 %	25 %	25 %	25 %
LOCATION OF DUPLICATE COMPONENT DOCUMENTS (Show Office)	Payables (2) Purchasing (1) Vendor	Payables (2) Auth Dept (1)	Payable (2)	Payables (2) Vendor

*** MEDIA CODE:** C = Corres.; F = Form; PM = Printed Material; PO = Printout; MC = Microfilm-COM; MS = Microfilm-Std.
1 = Typed; 2 = Handwritten; 3 = Horizontal; 4 = Vertical; 5 = Both Sides; 6 = Loose; 7 = Fastened.

FIGURE 2.2b Records Inventory Form

wherever space is available. Usually, stored records are inventoried last. A separate inventory form should be used for stored records, but it need contain only the record title, time span, and number of boxes involved for a records series. If a record series does not have a counterpart active record, it should be described in its entirety.

Cabinet Numbering

Prior to the first interview, at least several sheets of colored *dot labels* should be numbered in sequence beginning with number 1. Each file cabinet or other record housing unit is assigned a sequential number, and that number is noted on the dot label, which is affixed to the piece of equipment. For example, a group of five file cabinets would be numbered consecutively 1 to 5. If these five cabinets were followed by five units of shelving, each unit of shelving would be numbered from 6 to 10. Although only cabinets are given numbers, a particular drawer or shelf can be noted within parentheses following the cabinet number. Thus, 1(5) means "cabinet 1, drawer 5." This notation of the drawer is made only on the inventory form, and not on the cabinet itself. See Figure 2.3 for examples of this subset numbering system.

The analyst asks the contact to identify the cabinets and other housing units, starting at the beginning of a record group or section. As the housing units are identified, the label is affixed to the upper right corner of the file cabinet, and at eye level on shelving in a uniform position. Shelving units may require some deviation from positions described here if they are mobile high-density where the fronts are not always visible. Specialized card files, map tanks, and tub files may also require a little ingenuity. Numbering methods can vary from those described here, as long as uniformity is maintained.

The Anatomy of Document-Based Information

To satisfactorily complete the inventory form, one should understand how records are structured. The progression of information units in records management is as follows: The smallest unit is the *page* or *document*. A document can consist of one or more related pages. For example, a two-page letter is a document, as is a one-page letter. However, when two or more related documents are brought together, they become known as a *file*. Few files are made up of only one type of document, as there are usually several types of documents included in a file. For example, a purchase order file may contain a copy of the purchase order, a price inquiry and quote, a invoice, and a requisition.

When individual purchase order files are brought together, as a group they are known as a *records series* with the record title of *Purchase Order* files. The concept of the record series serves as the basis for how most document-based information systems are organized. Copies of the com-

---

FIGURE 2.3 Subset Numbering System

Cabinet or shelving unit:	Base number in sequence
Drawer or shelf from top:	Number or numbers in parentheses

EXAMPLES:

Cabinet 1, drawer 1	1(1)
Cabinet 1, drawers 1 through 4	1(1–4)
Cabinet 1, drawers 1 through 5	1(1–5)
Cabinets 1 through 5, drawers 1 through 5 each cabinet	1(1–5) through 5(1–5)

ponent documents in the *Purchase Order* files may be, and probably are, also located in other departments and may be part of another file or records series, such as the *Equipment* file or *Authority for Expenditures* records series.

Usually, each records series is assigned a retention schedule number after the inventory is complete. The component files can be assigned subnumbers. By means of the subnumbers, together with form numbers, the documents can be tracked to determine duplicates. This usually requires computer assistance. Again, the amount of effort expended should be cost-effective; that is, the benefits should exceed the costs of tracking the relationships of the different documents and records series.

It is not necessary for the inventory to reflect the exact contents of each file folder, but only the general description of the records series. For example, to inventory a group of general correspondence files, it is not necessary to describe the contents of each file, even though the files have little in common with one another other than that they all consist of correspondence and memoranda. The same applies to subject correspondence files, which also vary greatly in contents.

A record series can also consist of only sequentially arranged documents. For example, a trucking company may have large volumes of documents known as waybills arranged in waybill number order. The documents differ in detail, but are identical in form. The entire series may consist of millions of single-page documents, but all will collectively be considered a record series known as *Waybills.* However, if these were subdivided into types of waybills, such as inbound waybills and outbound waybills, they could be considered two records series, one known as *Outbound Waybills* and the other as *Inbound Waybills.* In summary, the inventory form is used to record information about a records series, not about files.

Guidelines to Completing Inventory Forms

As the cabinets are being numbered (or preferably after), the departmental contact should indicate to the analyst the contents of all drawers and shelves.

This preliminary description should include only the common name for the records series and the section to which they belong. To do this, the analyst at this point simply records, on a clipboard tablet sheet, the dot label number and the title and owner. This is done in ascending dot label number order. It is not unusual for several or perhaps dozens of cabinets or shelves to contain the same records series, so this identification process can proceed rather rapidly. After this preliminary introduction by the departmental contact, the analyst, supplied with clipboard, inventory forms, and pencil, begins the substance of the physical inventory by opening drawer 1 of cabinet 1. At this point, the contact has probably returned to his or her normal duties, and the analyst begins recording information on the inventory form. The form should be self-explanatory, but initially, some guidance in completing it is necessary.

The exact design of the inventory form will vary, but for purposes of this chapter, the form illustrated in Figure 2.2*a* and *b* is used as a training guide. Remember that a separate inventory form is used for each records series. Note that not all information blocks on the form will be completed on the initial inventory, and in fact, some may never be completed. The form, however, provides a single source for all information on a particular records series, including information obtained on subsequent systems studies. Note that the form can be completed in writing or filled in on a computer screen.

Section I of the form has many blocks that are common to all records series, and those portions that are static need not be completed at the file cabinet, but can be done at a more comfortable position at a desk later. Some portions, such as Title Code, *must* be done later, after retention research has been completed. In Section I, only the Records Series Title and Records Series Also Known As blocks need be completed at this time.

Section II of the inventory form is the most important block on the form. It is used to research the legal, operational, and historical values used in retention scheduling and in other areas. If the records series is understood thoroughly, it may be completed at the cabinet. If the records series is not thoroughly understood, the block can be held for the next interview with the departmental contact person. Whenever completed, the block should be concise and accurate and give the purpose, use, and general description of the records series. The purpose should be designed to answer the questions *who, why, where, when, what,* and *how*. Research of legal, regulatory, and internal requirements is based on functions; and the period of retention, as well as the need for protection, must reflect those functions.

Section III not only contains the inventory number of this particular inventory form, but also describes in relative detail the equipment used to house this records series. The sample in Figure 2.2*a* and *b* shows that there is a total of 13 units (8 shelving units and 5 file cabinets). Also the equipment is described in abbreviated form, and the total square feet of floor space (including aisles and access space) the equipment occupies is given.

Section IV of the form shows the volume and time span of the records being inventoried. Time span and the linear measurement must be entered at the cabinet. The rate of growth and growth time span can be calculated at a later time. The measurement is obtained by actually measuring with a tape measure the records contained in the file drawers or shelves. Measurements of paper records should be made with the files loosely compressed. Measurements are still made of microfilm media, such as microfiche, jackets, reels, cassettes, disks, and tapes, to reflect the status of housing utilization, but it is also useful to estimate the number of media units (for example, reels). When estimating rate of growth, keep in mind that one microfilm reel may contain up to several thousand images of paper documents.

Section V, which contains the number of references made to this records series, is estimated at a later time or perhaps during the secondary interview with the department contact. Sometimes, other statistics can provide this information through a logical deduction. For example, if files are requested each time a claim is made, and if the number of claims processed is known, it can be deduced that the number of searches equals the number of claims. If such statistics are not available and if it becomes necessary to know with some degree of precision what the reference rate

is, a simple search tally can be made by those using the files for a period of a week or two. This information is not necessary to the development of a retention period, but it would be of value in deciding if the records could be transferred to a records center and could have an impact on a retention period decision.

Section VI not only reflects the type of file supplies used, but also provides a place to record the quantity used. This quantity, in the case of file folders, is also the number of files. This number is arrived at through estimating and sampling. In other words, one should count the number of files in a typical linear foot of records. The primary value of knowing this type of information is systems improvement. Ordinarily, the quantitative information is not necessary to the establishment of a retention period, but knowing the quantity and type of supplies used is sometimes helpful in making immediate improvements.

Section VII contains information about vital records protection. At the initial stage of the inventory process, not enough is known to enter information on vital records protection. However, the question can be asked of the department contact, and if the information is known, it should be recorded (temporarily until the matter is studied more thoroughly) in this section.

Section VIII shows the sorting and filing arrangement for this records series. This information is not pertinent to the retention schedule, but it is very useful in systems improvement. It is best entered at the time the records are measured.

Section IX shows what records series are used to create the inventoried records series and what records series are created by using the inventoried series. This information is usually obtained by interview with the department contact. The input and output records are indicated by name or record series number.

Section X shows where duplicate copies of the inventoried records series are located and where alternate records are located. This information is obtained through interview with the department contact and by looking at the input and output records. A duplicate is an exact copy of the original; an alternate record is a record in a different format, but one that contains identical information. This is extremely important in determining retention, disposal, and off-site storage.

The *Approvals* section in Figure 2.2*a* is set up for a series of approvals by a retention committee made up of representatives of the proprietary department (the department whose records are being inventoried), the Law Department, and the Tax Department. The records manager serves as the chairperson for the committee. Each committee member enters a recommendation for a retention period for the office and for the records center, and then dates and initials the form. In this same area, the citations for regulatory and statutory requirements may be entered in abbreviated fashion. Approval requirements will vary with organizations, and the form should be adjusted accordingly. Current departmental retention practices can be ascertained from the dates shown in Section IV. These practices, may however, not be a result of departmental policy.

Functional Information (page 2 of the form—see Figure 2.2*b*) contains material that is usually not gathered in an initial records inventory, but may be used as a basis for functional analysis in more complex systems improvement studies and for other elements of a records management program. This form provides a place to record functional information regarding component documents which make up a file in this records series. The lower portion of page 2 describes the characteristics of the documents and the location of duplicate documents.

Variations in Methods

The inventory methods described here are standard practices for implementing an integrated records management program. The methods used for more narrow records management studies are very similar in practice but may be tailored to solve a particular problem. The records manager must always plan the study according to systems principles to ensure that goals are met in the most efficient manner possible. Thus the records manager must be resourceful and imaginative in order

to vary the techniques described in this chapter as circumstances dictate.

For example, some records managers who weigh the costs, benefits, and goals of an inventory decide that a nontraditional inventory substitute is sometimes warranted. This substitute is the *questionnaire method.* In this approach, each department completes a brief questionnaire on the records retained in its office. As a minimum, the department's employees provide the name of the record, a brief functional description, and a recommended retention period. From this list, a records retention schedule is developed. This method is quick and inexpensive and serves a limited purpose. However, it offers no assurance of completeness and little information regarding problem definition, systems improvement, or systematic evaluation for other records management purposes. It is better than nothing, if that is all circumstances and resources allow.

Another common variation occurs with subject correspondence files. As stated previously, these files are treated as one records series, with little detail provided in the initial inventory. However, more information will be required eventually to improve the file system and to establish retention periods. Since making a list of each file is impractical, other methods must be used.

If the goal is to develop a uniform subject file system or to establish retention periods based on subject classifications, the questionnaire method can provide a list of common topics in terms that are familiar to the using department. From this, classifications can be developed; like files can be batched together so that they may be researched as a group, rather than as individual files. A subject file manual, which lists all file classifications, will be even more useful in this case, if it is current and effective.

To carry scientific analysis a step further, statistical sampling can be applied to subjects, if the list of topics is known prior to the sample. Such information as the last date correspondence was added to the file is a useful indicator of file activity. The date of the most recent correspondence will vary greatly between files, but a random sampling of 5 percent will indicate, for example, what percent of the files have had correspondence added in the last 5 or 10 years. The result will not show that all files are obsolete or that particular files should be purged. It will indicate generally, though, the results that can be expected if some of the files are stored or destroyed based on certain cutoff dates. As an example, the sample could reveal that 25 percent of contract-related files have had no activity for the past 20 years. Or that 38 percent of marketing files have had no activity for 3 years. This type of sampling is not a substitute for retention scheduling, but statistics can support a retention recommendation.

Inventory of Electronic Media

The same form used to record information on paper and film media can also be used to inventory records maintained on electronic media, or a special form can be used (see Chapter 8). Electronic records media consist of magnetic tapes, magnetic disks, and optical disks. Sometimes the existence of electronic media is indicated by the presence in the inventory of computer output, such as paper printouts (also known as *hard copy*) or computer output microfiche (also known as *COM*). In these cases, the retention of the computer media may or may not be identical to the retention of the computer output.

Electronic media sometimes have no visible paper or film counterpart and are known to exist only through consultation with the department manager or the MIS manager. Even so, information regarding the electronic record system can be recorded on the inventory form, or a copy of the system documentation, such as a data dictionary which shows the purpose and description of all systems, can be attached. This documentation, usually maintained on electronic digital media, can be printed out or viewed by the records manager using a computer terminal.

The physical measurement of the tapes and disks is usually not required, as the host computer system knows how many tapes or disks are maintained for a particular system or file and how many generations of reports are maintained. This information can be generated by the host computer if needed.

The inventorying of magnetic disks used for word processing and other personal computer applications will have limited value because of the inherent lack of centralized control. However, consultation with the users of these systems may provide a log or other information as to the nature of the information and work performed and how this work interacts with other systems. Frequently, the personal computer user personally controls retention of the electronic records on the magnetic media used in the system but is guided by a department retention policy statement on various categories of records. Chapter 8 contains a more detailed discussion of inventorying electronic records media.

SUMMARY

The records inventory identifies and quantifies the records created and processed by an organization. It becomes the working document for the records retention and disposition schedule, for the vital records protection program, and for systems improvement.

Preparation for the records inventory, which is the first step in developing a records management program, includes commitment from top management, definition of objectives, communication to staff and management, selection of survey personnel, specification of data to be collected, preparation of an inventory form, and establishment of a work schedule. The commitment from top management can take the form of a policy statement that lists the objectives of the entire proposed program and designates who will assume responsibility for the task. The objective of the records program is to assure maximum record availability in minimum retrieval time with a minimum of corporate resources.

The records inventory should be conducted by records analysts who have received special training. The analysts may be consultants, or they may be employees trained by consultants or the records manager. An alternate approach, generally considered less effective, is the questionnaire method, in which departments complete brief questionnaires about the records series maintained in their offices.

A separate form for each records series facilitates the inventory, research, and approval process in records scheduling. The same form used to inventory the paper or film record may also be used to inventory the records maintained on electronic media, although methods will vary.

A work schedule should be established to estimate the total time required for the project and the dates on which the inventory will begin in the various offices. Planning should be flexible and should permit changes in priority when circumstances change.

QUESTIONS FOR DISCUSSION

1. Define the scope of a records inventory and its function.

2. What uses can be made of a records inventory?

3. What records should be included in the records inventory?

4. What areas for further study can be identified through the records inventory?

5. What basic data should be included in the records inventory form?

6. What are three sources from which to recruit personnel to conduct the records inventory?

7. What are some of the advantages and disadvantages of hiring consultants for the records inventory?

8. What are some of the advantages of using in-house personnel in conducting the records inventory?

9. What are some of the disadvantages of the questionnaire method of taking a records inventory?

10. How do inventory methods used for electronic records media differ from those used in inventorying hard-copy records?

PROJECTS

1. Check with a business or governmental agency in your locality to determine where the following records are housed:

   a. Current purchase orders.
   b. Corporate charter.
   c. Duplicate set of corporate minutes.
   d. Copies of early sales promotion pieces.
   e. Specifications for records center.
   f. Extra copies of annual reports.
   g. Correspondence on unemployment compensation.
   h. Blueprints of proposed model change.
   i. Requests for catalogs.
   j. Microfilm of parts inventory.
   k. Tape recordings of minutes of corporate meetings.

2. Select a small- or medium-sized firm in your community where you can talk to the records manager. Find out if a records inventory has ever been made. If so, try to determine how the inventory affected recordkeeping practices. If not, plan the steps to be followed in making a records inventory for this company. Be specific in identifying records by department.

3. Prepare a one-page letter, addressed to all department managers of XYZ Company, explaining what a records inventory is, why it is being conducted, its value, and the role the department manager will play in the process.

CASE PROBLEM

A large school district in a major Midwest city has decided that the district and all schools within it could greatly benefit from a comprehensive records management program that would have as its goals the development of a records retention schedule, a vital records protection program, a central records center for inactive records, and improved retrieval systems, which might involve document imaging.

As the newly hired records manager, you recognize that the first step is to perform a records inventory, and you begin the task of deciding what information must be gathered to meet the goals the school board has established. Using the sample inventory form shown in Figure 2.2*a* and *b*, make a list of which items on the form you will use to collect information and why you will find them useful to meet your program goals.

NOTES

1. Emmett J. Leahy and Christopher A. Cameron, *Modern Records Management* (New York: McGraw-Hill Book Company, 1965) p. 30.

Chapter 3

Records Retention Programs

Learning Objectives
1. To explain the business and legal benefits of establishing a records retention program.
2. To describe the steps involved in planning and developing a records retention program.
3. To discuss the legal issues of records retention program development, including document discovery orders and subpoenas, contempt of court and obstruction of justice issues, antitrust litigation, product liability litigation, and tax liability.
4. To explain how to conduct and document legal research on federal, state, and local records retention requirements.
5. To describe the theory and practice of records retention decision-making, including the concepts of records appraisal and cost–benefit–risk analysis, and the five principles of records retention decision-making.

INTRODUCTION TO RECORDS RETENTION SCHEDULING

Business organizations and government agencies create enormous quantities of records every business day. What ultimately happens to these records? Should they be preserved forever, or should some or all of them be discarded? Who makes these decisions, and how should they be made so that they ensure the best interest of the business? Finally, if a formal program for information retention and document disposal is good for an organization, how can a program be developed that will provide the optimum legal and business benefits?

A records retention program specifies the length of time that business records must be retained. The retention program is based upon the concept that information has a life cycle. Like other organizational resources, the value of most information tends to decline as time passes. An organization needs a program providing for the disposal of useless information in order to control the growth of its records. The records retention schedule constitutes an organization's official policy for information retention and disposal. Without it, records may be unnecessarily maintained for excessive periods of time or hastily disposed of without regard for their value.

A records retention program provides for the identification of records that must be maintained for business purposes, and the systematic destruction of records that no longer serve any useful business purpose. Under this program the process of records retention and disposal is designed to occur regularly—in the normal course of business—rather than on an arbitrary or selective basis. The program should also conserve office space and equipment by using filing cabinets to house only active records. The retention schedules do this by providing for the regular transfer of inactive files to less costly storage areas for subsequent destruction. Finally, the retention scheduling program provides for the permanent preservation of records that have enduring value for research, historical, or other business purposes. The record retention schedule thus specifies four major points:

1. The period of time that records are considered active and, therefore, must be maintained in the primary filing area or office of creation.
2. The point during the life cycle of a record at which the record becomes *semiactive* or *inactive* and thus can be transferred to a secondary storage facility for less expensive maintenance.
3. The total period of time that each type of record—each *records series*—must be retained.
4. Information relating to various aspects of an organization's records management program. For example, the schedule may identify whether a given records series is the official, or record, copy; the method of destruction of each type of record; whether a record is vital and, if so, how it should be protected; whether a record exists on microfilm or other nonpaper media; what the retention of these media should be.

Program Justification: Business and Legal Benefits

The development and implementation of a retention scheduling program can be a relatively time–consuming and costly undertaking. Why, then, are organizations motivated to install these programs? What business objectives are they trying to achieve? There are two major objectives: *economic* and *legal*.

Economic Benefits. Although no credible nationwide study has been conducted to validate the assertion, anecdotal evidence indicates that most organizations retain from 30 to 60 percent more records than are needed to operate the business. The main reason organizations maintain such large surpluses of useless records is, quite simply, that their administrative personnel often feel ill–equipped to and uncomfortable about making record retention or destruction decisions. These decisions are thus often deferred until, after a period of years, the organization has accumulated a large backlog of old records in its offices and storage areas. What is required, then, is a formal program for controlling the growth of the organization's records.

The records retention schedule's function of controlling the growth of an organization's records produces the principal economic justification for the program. It creates a controlled balance between the creation of new records and the disposal of useless ones, thereby stabilizing the growth of the organization's records. This is very significant, because, as was noted in Chapter 1, the average rate of growth of the records of most organizations is between 7 and 10 percent a year. The resulting potential savings include:

- The volume of records in prime floor space can often be reduced by at least 40 percent, if no retention schedule has ever been in effect, or by up to 30 percent if an organization's retention schedule has not been properly maintained.
- The prime floor space required to accommodate records can be substantially reduced, achieving significant annual savings.
- The number of file cabinets and other record housing units can be reduced, also resulting in substantial savings.
- Day–to–day record and information retrieval and handling tasks can be accomplished faster and more easily because unneeded records are discarded and inactive records are transferred to less expensive storage.

Most analyses of the economic benefits of retention scheduling programs are based on computations of the cost of records maintenance in prime office space and the savings resulting from records destruction or removal to less expensive storage areas. Savings result from both immediate and ongoing destruction of given quantities of useless records, plus the lower maintenance costs resulting from the transfer of certain quantities of records to less expensive storage areas. Because records storage and maintenance costs may vary widely, no single cost formula can quantify these benefits. Moreover, separate benefit figures need to be calculated for the first year following program implementation, and for subsequent years. The first–year savings are often based on the rule–of–thumb formula that one–third of the organization's records are active and would thus require maintenance in prime office space, one–third are semiactive or inactive but require continuing retention in a low–cost storage facility, and the remaining one–third are useless and could be destroyed immediately.

Thus, if an organization is maintaining between 30 and 60 percent more records than are required, the savings resulting from a good records retention program could be expected to fall within that range. However, the main point is that the cost of storing records in business offices is extremely expensive; it constitutes one of the biggest administrative overhead expenses of any organization. Any program that can significantly reduce these costs must be taken very seriously by the organization.

Legal Benefits.   Legal benefits can be even more compelling than economic benefits. Indeed, significant fines and penalties can sometimes result from unlawful, risky, or unwise records retention and document disposal practices—risks and liabilities which a properly developed program can help minimize. The schedules do this in three major ways. We will introduce them briefly here and explain them in greater detail later in this chapter.

1.   *Destruction of records in the normal course of business.* The retention schedule can provide evidence that an organization has an official policy for disposing of its records systematically in the normal course of business. This can help the organization avoid certain legal problems associated with arbitrary disposal actions if the disposal of documents should ever become a legal issue.

2.   *Compliance with government retention requirements.* There are literally thousands of statutes and regulations requiring the private sector and government agencies to retain certain records. A properly developed retention schedule can demonstrate to the government that an organization is disposing of its records in compliance with the law. Also, in cases where the legal retention requirements are vague and ambiguous, the schedules can show that the organization is acting in good faith to comply with their intent.

3.   *Protection from the risks of litigation.* Corporations in the United States today must conduct business in a highly litigious climate. Every company that has anything to do with creating a product or that even hires employees is faced with a threat to its assets from litigation. Moreover, success in pursuing or defending a suit often depends on material evidence in the form of business information. A records retention program can help the organization successfully defend itself against lawsuits by providing for the continuing retention of information that would be needed. On the other hand, many attorneys believe that old records rarely contain information either helpful or harmful to the legal defense of an organization. However, such records can sometimes be misinterpreted or can embarrass an organization or result in more serious legal difficulties. Unless litigation or a government investigation is known to have commenced, it is perfectly proper to destroy documents assuming all statutory or regulatory requirements to retain them have been satisfied, and it is usually in the organization's best interest to do so.

STEPS IN PROGRAM PLANNING AND DEVELOPMENT

The development of a records retention scheduling program should be accomplished in a systematic and methodical way. This can be legally important because it may be necessary to demonstrate to legal authorities that the program was developed in the ordinary course of business over a period of time by responsible officials of the organization, and that it is based on professionally sound records management principles. Moreover, the program should be developed as early in the life of the business as possible—before a crisis occurs. These measures can help to avoid the appearance that the program was developed to provide a convenient method of destroying unfavorable evidence prior to litigation or pending government investigation.

Two Basic Principles of Planning a Program

Two basic principles must be considered and adhered to at the time of initial program planning:

Customized Schedule Development. No successful records retention program can simply be dropped in place or copied from another organization. Generic retention schedules or those produced by other companies should be examined as reference materials, but there is no shortcut to a fully customized retention schedule that provides precise policy guidance and comprehensive coverage to each records series maintained by an organization.

Comprehensive Program Coverage. In order to provide comprehensive benefits and full legal protection, a retention scheduling program must include all records maintained by an organization. This includes all paper records *and* information residing on machine–readable media, such as all microfilms, computer–processable data, and records in other formats.

Some records retention schedules are limited in coverage to official, or record, copies of documents and exclude those records series containing duplicate, or reference, copies of records. While these characteristics are indeed relevant in determining the retention values of certain classes of documents, a good records retention schedule will include disposition policy guidance for them. Under the Uniform Photographic Copies of Busi-

ness and Public Records As Evidence Act, which has been enacted by the federal government and by almost all states, duplicates or reproductions of documents have the same legal significance as the original records themselves. In fact, duplicates of documents may be used in place of the originals for any legal purpose, including admission as evidence in courts of law. As we will see, during litigation or government investigation, these copies may be subpoenaed and used against the organization, even though the original records were properly destroyed under the authority of the records retention schedule. Thus, duplicates or reference copies must be included in a comprehensive records retention program in order for it to provide full legal protection.

A still more troublesome issue related to comprehensive program coverage relates to the problem of private files or personal working papers that are typically stored in the desks and credenzas of employees. Should these types of records be scheduled for retention? There is no simple answer to this question. Legally, the private files and personal working papers of employees are clearly subject to subpoenas and discovery orders and thus may be used as evidence against the company during legal proceedings. These records would be very damaging to their owner or the organization if they should contain unfavorable or misleading evidence or information.

In spite of these legal risks, most attorneys and records managers believe that it is simply not practical to extend the coverage of the retention scheduling program to include private files and personal working papers. Many organizations attempt to get around this difficulty by issuing a general policy statement which prohibits employees from maintaining private files or personal working papers at their workstations. Other organizations impose a one–year retention time, or even less, on this material. Of course, human behavior being what it is, the maintenance of such files by employees is a very difficult matter to control, so any policy governing the retention of personal working papers must be strictly enforced. Many attorneys recommend a program of continuing education to advise managers and executives about the risks of maintaining this type of record material. Also, a well–designed and well–operated departmental filing system will eliminate many of the reasons why employees are motivated to retain private files, so records managers should make every effort to address the problem of private files by developing excellent file stations.

Developing Retention Schedules: Initial Planning Steps

Before a program can be pursued, management must endorse the plan, costs must be estimated, and personnel must be assembled. The following program planning steps are recommended:

1. Obtain approval from senior management to develop and operate the program. A directive or policy statement should formally establish the program, require the cooperation and full compliance of all staff members, and assign the responsibility for program development and operation. Usually, the primary responsibility will be delegated to the organization's records manager, but other executives—including the internal auditor, tax manager, controller, general counsel, corporate secretary, or senior administrative officer—may serve on a records retention committee or otherwise be involved.

2. Estimate the resources required for program development. The single largest expense associated with retention schedule program development is conducting the records inventory, which is discussed in Chapter 2. The subsequent tasks can be expected to require about as much time as the inventory itself. Small– to medium–size organizations having 25 to 50 departments or so can expect these tasks to take from one to three months of dedicated labor by an experienced records management specialist. For large organizations with many widely dispersed organiza-

tional units, the project can often require a year or more.

3. Assemble the personnel resources. Records retention schedules may be developed by in–house personnel or by external consultants. Because the task is a one–time, labor–intensive effort, the consultant option is increasingly popular. Whether internal or external personnel are used, they must be trained and experienced records management specialists who are thoroughly familiar with the principles of records appraisal and the other tasks required to develop the program.

Developing Retention Schedules: Major Steps in the Process

Chapter 2 discussed the process of collecting records inventory data. These data constitute the building blocks upon which records retention schedules are developed. At the conclusion of the inventory, the records manager will have dozens, hundreds, or even thousands of forms containing descriptions of every separate type or category of record. These steps are recommended:

1. Consult with the organization's legal counsel about the legal retention research task and other matters essential to developing retention schedules that are legally acceptable.

2. Conduct legal research to determine which records series must be retained to satisfy statutory or regulatory retention requirements imposed by the government.

3. Interview managers, supervisors, and information users in departments throughout the organization about the value of information under their custody for business and archival purposes.

4. Appraise the records to determine their retention values, and determine a retention period for each records series.

5. Select a format for preparing the retention schedules, prepare them in draft form, and

distribute them for review, revision, and final approval.

LEGAL ASPECTS OF RETENTION SCHEDULING PROGRAMS

A records retention program should be considered one element of an organization's larger preventive law strategy, designed to insulate the organization from potential legal problems and risks. Also, the program should be designed to ensure that, in the event legal problems do occur, the organization will have, in a readily retrievable form, the information it needs to defend itself.

Evidence of Systematic Disposal in the Normal Course of Business

A major legal objective and benefit of a retention scheduling program is to serve as evidence that an organization does, in fact, have an official policy for disposing of its business information and that this policy is implemented systematically in the normal course of business. Why is this legally important? Because the law tends to view those activities conducted in the normal course of business as honest or trustworthy. Thus, the trustworthiness or legality of document disposal activities is easier to demonstrate if these activities occur under an established policy and formal records retention program. Without a retention scheduling program the process of disposing of records is inherently selective and arbitrary. From a legal perspective, these arbitrary disposal decisions can be viewed with suspicion and may be negatively construed in judicial proceedings. The intent behind such destruction might be entirely innocent, but there may be what lawyers call "adverse inferences" that need not have arisen had the document disposal occurred under a program of systematic document destruction.

Let's examine this adverse inference point further. Suppose an organization has destroyed certain files without benefit of a records retention program, and suppose these files turn out to contain evidence that has become relevant to a lawsuit instituted against the organization. Under the rules of evidence in legal proceedings, counsel for the opposing party may claim that the documents were deliberately destroyed to prevent their use in litigation. A records retention program can help to protect a company from this type of liability by providing evidence that the destruction of records occurred in the regular course of business and not to conceal unfavorable information or evidence.

Compliance with Document Discovery Orders and Subpoenas

A records retention program can also be very helpful in dealing with document discovery orders or subpoenas. A discovery is a legal procedure where two or more parties in a legal proceeding share information from their own files that is pertinent to the case. This information sharing is usually carried out by a court order referred to as a discovery order. The court will usually issue a document called a *subpoena duces tecum*, which is an order to appear in court or to produce documents. In recent years, the document discovery procedures permitted by the courts have become very liberal. The discovery procedures now require virtually all company documents relevant to a particular legal action to be turned over to the other parties or to the courts during litigation.

How can a records retention schedule be helpful in dealing with discovery orders and subpoenas? The schedule can make it easy to locate and assemble specific categories of documents that may be maintained by many different departments of a large organization, resulting in cost reduction. Moreover, the courts tend to become suspicious when records are missing in response to a subpoena, and they will demand an explanation as to why a subpoena cannot be fully complied with. If the requested records have been properly destroyed in accordance with the organization's official records retention policy, this fact may provide a satisfactory explanation to the court as to why the subpoenaed records are unavailable.

Contempt of Court and Obstruction of Justice Issues

Records management specialists should be aware that they or other employees of their organization may be held in contempt of court if they disobey a court order, including a subpoena to produce records. Contempt of court is committed whenever a court or an administrative tribunal orders documents to be produced and the party defies the order by failing to deliver the documents or by deliberately destroying requested documents. The result can be severe legal penalties, which may consist of fines or even imprisonment.

Obstruction of justice statutes must also be considered whenever a company wishes to destroy records:

- Upon learning of any investigation or proceeding in which the documents might be relevant.
- Upon learning of a government inquiry but before being contacted by authorities.
- In the course of voluntary cooperation with government authorities.
- After a court orders documents to be produced.

To avoid these potential criminal penalties, the records retention program should have a mechanism or procedure for advising company officials of these criminal provisions. In–house counsel should advise all affected persons to stop disposing of relevant information based on the foregoing principles.

Antitrust Litigation

The U.S. antitrust laws are designed to promote free trade and competition and to inhibit monopolistic business practices that constrain competition or otherwise act in restraint of free trade. Companies that enjoy a very large market share of a particular industry or that engage in marketing practices that could be construed as price–fixing may be susceptible to antitrust litigation actions brought against them by the U.S. Department of Justice.

Antitrust cases are often decided on the basis of documents that may extend far back into a company's history. A records retention program that requires the disposal of certain classes of documents after expiration of their value for business purposes can be very helpful in insulating the company from discovery problems and other legal difficulties related to the antitrust litigation process.[1] Such documents as sales contracts, marketing plans, agreements with wholesalers and distributors, and records documenting contacts with customers and competitors all have a high probability of being requested. Many attorneys specializing in antitrust law believe that these and other documents can be more harmful than helpful to a company's case. Therefore, they recommend short retention periods; that is, retention periods that are sufficient to meet minimum business needs.

The following summary of an actual litigation case illustrates these principles. In the spring of 1987, a large manufacturer of garage doors lost the liability phase of an antitrust lawsuit by default after it was disclosed that the company had engaged in "flagrant and willful destruction of records," in the words of the judge who heard the case. The judge ruled that the company's corporate counsel ordered key sales documents destroyed *after commencement of the lawsuit*. The damage award was reported to be approximately $69 million.[2]

Product Liability Litigation

Companies that manufacture products or provide services which may fail to perform and thus be harmful to the health of users or consumers face exposure to product liability lawsuits.[3] By law the manufacturer of a product or the provider of a service is answerable for the performance of that product or service. The legal system thus expects manufacturing companies to act as "responsible citizens" and take appropriate measures to ensure the safety of the public where the use of their products is concerned. Thus, a manufacturer must perform sufficient product testing and maintain adequate records to convince the court that it is acting as a responsible citizen. When a manufacturer "knew or should have known" of the danger to consumers and failed to alert the public or stop manufacturing the product, the legal system can impose high damages for this "reckless" conduct, including punitive damages.

The result of product liability lawsuits can be very high insurance premiums, liberal settlements to the injured parties, or other adverse financial consequences.

A properly developed records retention program can help to ensure that companies which may be susceptible to this type of legal exposure will preserve those records that would be needed to organize a successful defense in lawsuits to refute unwarranted product liability claims. Some examples of records that often become significant in product liability lawsuits include research and product development records, design and engineering records, quality control and product inspection records, warranty records, customer service records, and records showing the quality of raw materials. In many cases, records retention policies will need to be established for these classes of records that extend through the period of warranty and sometimes through the period of product usage by the customer. Such lengthy retention periods are based on the assumption that the manufacturer has acted legally and responsibly in all product management activities.

Two actual cases emphasize the gravity of these matters.

> *In a 1988 product liability case against a manufacturer of firearms, a U.S. circuit court of appeals ruled that if the manufacturer knew or should have known that the documents would become material at some point in the future, then such documents should have been preserved. Thus a corporation cannot blindly destroy documents and expect to be shielded by a seemingly innocuous document retention policy.[4]*

The significance of this ruling is that, in this case, the company's records retention policies came under judicial review with respect to their reasonableness. The manufacturer argued that its failure to produce certain customer complaints and product examination reports resulted from the fact that the records had been properly destroyed after three years pursuant to its records retention schedule. The court held that this three–year policy may have been insufficient for these types of documents and remanded the case back to the trial court to hear additional evidence on the issue.

In a 1984 product liability case against an aircraft manufacturer, the judge of a U.S. district court who heard the case found that

> *the defendant engaged in a practice of destroying engineering documents with the intention of preventing them from being produced in law suits. Furthermore, I find that this practice continued after the commencement of this law suit and that documents relevant to this law suit were intentionally destroyed. I am not holding that the good faith disposal of documents pursuant to a bona fide, consistent and reasonable document retention policy cannot be a valid justification for failure to produce documents in discovery. That issue never crystallized in this case because [the defendant] has utterly failed to provide credible evidence that such a policy or practice existed. The policy of resolving law suits under merit must yield when a party has intentionally prevented fair adjudication of the case. By deliberately destroying documents, the defendant has eliminated plaintiffs' right to have their case decided on its merits. Accordingly, the entry of a default is the only means of effectively sanctioning the defendant and remedying the wrong. . . .[5]*

The judge entered a default judgment against the defendant in the amount of $10 million because of the selective destruction of documents, without even considering the merits of the case.

CONDUCTING LEGAL RETENTION RESEARCH

According to a widely respected sourcebook on legal recordkeeping requirements, there are over

4,700 federal statutes and tens of thousands of state statutes and regulations containing requirements to retain certain records for varying periods of time.[6] Some of these requirements are applicable to businesses or government agencies in general, but most of them apply to specific classes of records maintained by certain types of businesses engaged in producing specific products or services. How does an organization know which of these thousands of requirements apply to its own business? Which of the organization's many records are governed by these requirements? Although it is generally true that a relatively small percentage of all records of most organizations must be retained in compliance with these laws, the task of locating and interpreting the laws to ensure that the records retention policies fully comply with them is a daunting one!

Planning the Legal Research

We mentioned earlier that the records manager should consult with the organization's legal counsel to define the scope of the retention research task and should then devise a plan for executing it. Such consultation should result in a legal research plan[7] addressing the following issues:

1. What general business activities may be subject to recordkeeping statutes or regulations? Examples would include the nature of business incorporation, labor and employment practices, and tax administration, each of which is subject to legal recordkeeping requirements.
2. What products or services does the business provide that may be subject to legal recordkeeping requirements? Does the organization own any property that may be subject to environmental or other regulations?
3. What geographic areas (countries, states or provinces, localities) do these business activities occur in?
4. Which of the organization's industries or business activities are or may be regulated by the government and thus may be subject to recordkeeping laws and regulations? Which federal, state, or other agencies of government regulate these activities?
5. What is the organization's litigation history, and what does this history suggest in terms of developing records retention policies that would be in the organization's best interest?
6. What future role does the legal counsel wish to have in the development and operation of the organization's records retention program?

In planning the legal research, the records manager should consider the types of situations that will be encountered as the review of laws and regulations progresses.[8] There are seven possible scenarios:

1. No statutory or regulatory requirement can be found which requires the retention of a given records series. This will be the most frequent occurrence since the government imposes no retention requirements for the majority of business records.
2. A statute or regulation is found containing a requirement to retain a particular record or defined class of information for a specified period of time.
3. A statute or regulation is found containing a requirement to maintain the record, but no definite time period is specified.
4. A statute of limitation is found which appears to indicate that a particular record should be retained for some period of time.
5. A limitation of assessment period is found in a tax law or regulation, which indicates that certain finance and accounting records should be retained for a period of time.
6. A statute or regulation is found that limits or defines a certain action, which would necessarily result in a certain retention period.
7. A ruling from case law is found that provides a legal precedent or other guidance relative to the retention of certain records.

Each of these legal circumstances is discussed later in the context of its significance in making records retention decisions respecting individual classes of records.

Researching Federal Requirements [9]

United States laws and regulations are contained in the *United States Code*, the *United States Code Annotated*, or the *United States Code Service, Lawyer's Edition*, any or all of which can be found in a law library. The latter two sources are best because they are more current with annual supplements and because their indexes are more detailed and easier to use. Records retention statutes should be referenced by consulting index headings such as "Records," "Reporting," and "Limitations of Actions." Relatively few records retention requirements are contained in the U.S. federal statutes; those applicable to the records of most organizations are found in federal *regulations*.

Federal regulations are rules adopted by agencies of the U.S. government that implement laws enacted by Congress. These requirements are legally binding on all parties affected by them; they carry the full force and effect of law. For most organizations, regulations will be the primary source for determining the legal requirements for retaining records.

Federal recordkeeping regulations are contained in two publications: the *Code of Federal Regulations* and the *Federal Register,* both of which can be found in any law library and in many corporate libraries as well. The *Federal Register* is a daily issuance that contains both pending and final rules that are promulgated each business day, while the *Code of Federal Regulations* contains an annual codification of all rules in force at the time of its publication. Thus, it will be necessary to consult both these sources to ensure that the records retention research is complete and addresses the latest requirements. However, the indexes to these publications are often difficult to use for records retention research purposes.

The U.S. government does publish another book which provides partial assistance in locating federal recordkeeping regulations: the *Guide to Retention Requirements*, which is issued by the Office of the Federal Register and is available for purchase from the Superintendent of Documents, U.S. Government Printing Office, and from commercial sources. This book is quite useful in records retention research, as it contains a digest of many records retention laws and regulations. However, the book is incomplete with respect to coverage; moreover, the brief abstracts of the requirements are often insufficient to permit proper interpretation.

Researching State Requirements

The legal research should include a search of the laws for every state in which the organization has offices or does a substantial volume of business. This research is particularly important for insurance companies, banks, and other organizations that are regulated at the state level. These laws are contained in state statute books, which will not be available except in the largest corporate libraries. Statute books from all 50 states plus the District of Columbia and U.S. territories will usually be available in law school libraries, large public libraries, or law libraries serving the court system in state capitals. Again, the researcher will need to locate recordkeeping requirements by consulting index headings such as "Records," "Recordkeeping," and "Limitations of Action."

Like their federal counterparts, agencies of state governments do sometimes promulgate regulations affecting recordkeeping. However, these regulations are often difficult to obtain, particularly from one central source if the research includes many or all states. Some 40 states publish their regulations; it will often be necessary to request these regulations directly from the agencies.

Local and International Requirements

Although the federal and state laws and regulations will constitute the great majority of recordkeeping requirements for most organizations, it may be necessary to address local and international laws as well. Both jurisdictions will pose difficulties for the researcher. Apart from property and other tax assessments, official financial disclosure statements, business licensure, and occasionally environmental matters, local governments rarely enact ordinances stipulating record retention requirements. Any such requirements would need to be obtained directly from officials of the local government.

If the organization is a multinational corporation or otherwise does business outside the United States, its international units would generally be subject to the laws of the various countries involved. Unlike the United States, most other countries have enacted only a few laws relative to records retention. These laws generally apply to books of account and other accounting and general business records kept by merchants and traders. Such laws are known to exist in approximately 20 countries; ten years is the most common statutory retention requirement for these types of records. Multinational firms engaged in businesses such as petroleum exploration and production would need to do more definitive research to ensure compliance. In most cases, it will be necessary for the records manager to consult with legal counsel to proceed with this task, which may involve extensive communications with ministries of government or attorneys in the countries involved.

Other Records Retention Research Sources

Figure 3.1 indicates a number of published records retention sourcebooks that will be helpful to the researcher. One is worthy of special mention: *Legal Requirements for Business Records* is a three–volume sourcebook containing the full text of approximately 7,000 federal and state laws and regulations applicable to records retention and recordkeeping. An annual supplement is available from the publisher via subscription. The publisher of this service also offers a software product to facilitate the legal research and schedule development processes. The researcher can search the laws and regulations on a computer for relevant retention requirements. Other features of the software also assist in schedule preparation.

Two commercial computerized legal research services can also be used to conduct legal research in recordkeeping statutes and regulations. One is LEXIS (a service of Mead Data Central Company) and the other is Westlaw, which is owned by West Publishing Company. With both of these full–text legal databases, the researcher can access legal requirements by searching for very complex but precise terms to retrieve relevant information. For example, the researcher would search for words such as *records* or *recordkeeping* used with a specific number of other words such as *retained* or *retention* or *keep* or *maintain*. Such search techniques will sometimes retrieve laws not relevant to the research objective, but these commercial databases can be very useful in accomplishing records retention research.

Statutes of Limitation

We have referred to *statutes of limitation* or *limitations of actions* as being relevant to records retention. In the records management field many misconceptions have resulted from these laws and what their significance is for developing records retention schedules. The most important thing to understand is that statutes of limitation *do not prescribe a records retention period*; they are not requirements to keep any records for any length of time. Instead, the statutes of limitation prescribe a time period during which an organization can sue or be sued on a matter, or they prescribe a time period during which a government agency can conduct an investigation or audit of a company. For example, if an organization is harmed because another party breaches a contract, in most states the business will have six years from the time of the breach to bring a lawsuit. After the six–year period, the business loses any legal right to sue for the breach of contract. Although the organization may want to keep some records related to the contract during the period specified by the statute of limitation, there is no legal requirement to retain these records.

Guide to Information Retention for Financial Institutions
    1982, with annual updates through 1994. Approx. 250 pp.
    Southern Vital Record Center (Dataplex Corporation)
    P.O. Box 14975
    Jackson, MS 39236–4975

Guide to Record Retention Requirements
    1992, 6th ed. 485 pp.
    Commerce Clearing House, Inc.
    4025 West Peterson Avenue
    Chicago, IL 60646

Guide to Records Retention
    1992, 2 vols. Approx 250 pp.
    William A. Hancock, Editor
    Business Laws, Inc.
    11630 Chillicothe Road
    Chesterland, OH 44026

Insurance Record Keeping Requirements
    1991, with annual updates through 1994. 4 vols. Approx. 2,000 pp.
    Roderick C. Wallace, Editor
    Insurance Record Services, Inc.
    9932 Parkway Drive
    St. Louis, MO 63137

Legal Requirements for Business Records
    1988, with annual updates. 4 vols. 2,100 pp.
    Donald S. Skupsky, JD, CRM, Editor
    Information Requirements Clearinghouse
    5600 South Quebec Street, Suite 250–C
    Englewood, CO 80111

Legal Requirements for Microfilm, Computer and Optical Disk Records
    1991. 389 pp.
    Donald S. Skupsky, JD, CRM
    Information Requirements Clearinghouse
    5600 South Quebec Street, Suite 250–C
    Englewood, CO 80111

National and International Records Retention Standards
    1991, 2d ed. 726 pp.
    Fred E. Guymon
    Eastwood Publishing Company
    130 South Eastwood Drive
    Orem, UT 84058

Recordkeeping Requirements
    1988. 344 pp.
    Donald S. Skupsky, JD, CRM
    Information Requirements Clearinghouse
    5600 South Quebec Street, Suite 250–C
    Englewood, CO 80111

Records Retention Guidelines for U.S. Based Telephone Companies
    1990. 148 pp.
    Compiled by Communications Industry Action Committee
    ARMA International
    4200 Somerset Drive, Suite 215
    Prairie Village, KS 66208

Records Retention Procedures
    1990. 192 pp.
    Donald S. Skupsky, JD, CRM
    Information Requirements Clearinghouse
    5600 South Quebec Street, Suite 250–C
    Englewood, CO 80111

FIGURE 3.1   List of Records Retention Sourcebooks

Each organization should develop its own strategy for dealing with statute of limitation issues as they relate to records retention. In the past, many attorneys advised their clients to keep all relevant records for the longest period specified in these statutes in case of litigation. However, with the increasing use of discovery by opposing parties, some attorneys now recommend destroying records much earlier under an approved records retention program. The following guidance may prove helpful: Keep records for the entire statute of limitation period *if your organization is likely to be the plaintiff*; that is, it will be likely to sue another party. Conversely, your organization may wish to destroy records at an earlier date *if it is likely to be the defendant*; that is, your organization is likely to be sued by another party and the other party may have little proof in its possession.[10]

In summary, each organization should make records retention decisions based on the perceived benefits or risks of retaining certain information for the maximum statute of limitation period in all relevant jurisdictions, or destroying it at some earlier point in time. In any case, both federal and state statutes must be researched, since limitations of action relevant to records retention issues are enacted by both levels of government. Table 3.1 includes a chart showing state statutes of limitation in five legal areas relevant to records retention: general contracts, sales contracts, product liability, improvements to real property, and personal injury. Of course, the opinion of the organization's legal counsel should be solicited on these questions.

Interpreting and Applying the Statutes and Regulations

If records retention laws and regulations are sometimes difficult to locate, they may be even more difficult to interpret and apply to specific records series. Many of these requirements tend to be somewhat vague and ambiguous—they are often expressed in general language designed to make them applicable to generic classes of information

that are retained by an entire industry or type of business. On the other hand, the wording may be so specific that it applies to one particular type of information that is widely dispersed throughout the filing systems of the regulated parties. The result is that it is often extremely difficult to match the language of the requirements with the records series maintained by the organization.

The researcher should exercise his or her best judgment to ensure that the decisions resulting from this analysis are reasonable and were made in good faith. The researcher should not be overzealous and apply these requirements to a certain group of records unless the case is fairly clear that compliance compels such a decision. It is very important to remember that these regulations were developed by the government to give it the capability to accomplish its own regulatory objectives. An organization is under no obligation to comply with ambiguous regulations to its disadvantage, unless there is persuasive justification. When two or more legal requirements pertain to the same record type, the longest legal requirement should be considered the operative one for retention decision–making purposes.

Another troublesome issue is that many of these requirements are not expressed as definite time periods. In these cases, the regulated parties are required to "keep" or "maintain" or "retain" certain records or information, but no time period is specified. What should the records manager do in these cases? Unfortunately, some persons interpret these records maintenance requirements to mean that the organization should preserve all related records permanently or indefinitely. There may indeed be cases in which this interpretation will be justified, but such a decision is generally unnecessary. If the government imposes records maintenance requirements but offers no guidance as to their duration, it would seem reasonable to conclude that regulatory officials could probably not enforce these regulations by imposing penalties for noncompliance. However, the organization's retention policy for such records should be a conservative and reasonable one. In these cases, it may be advisable to communicate

TABLE 3.1 State Statutes of Limitation Relevant to Records Retention

(NUMBER OF YEARS FOR COMMENCING LEGAL ACTIONS)

State	General Contracts	Sales Contracts	Product Liability	Improvements to Real Property	Personal Injury
Alabama	6	4	10	—	2
Alaska	6	4	—	6	2
Arizona	6	4	12	8	2
Arkansas	5	4	3	5	3
California	4	4	—	10	3
Colorado	6	3	2	8	2
Connecticut	6	4	10	8	3
Delaware	3	4	—	6	2
Dist. of Columbia	3	4	—	10	—
Florida	3	4	—	15	4
Georgia	6	4	10	10	2
Hawaii	6	4	—	6	2
Idaho	5	4	10	6	2
Illinois	10	4	12	4	2
Indiana	20	4	10	12	2
Iowa	10	4	—	15	2
Kansas	5	4	—	10	2
Kentucky	15	4	—	7	5
Louisiana	10	3	—	10	10
Maine	6	4	—	10	6
Maryland	3	4	—	20	3
Massachusetts	6	4	—	6	2
Michigan	6	4	—	10	3
Minnesota	6	4	—	12	2
Mississippi	6	6	—	6	6
Missouri	10	4	—	10	5
Montana	8	4	—	10	3
Nebraska	5	4	10	10	4
Nevada	6	4	—	12	2
New Hampshire	6	4	12	—	3
New Jersey	6	4	—	10	2
New Mexico	6	4	—	10	4
New York	6	4	—	—	3
North Carolina	3	4	6	6	3
North Dakota	6	4	10	10	6
Ohio	15	4	—	10	2
Oklahoma	5	5	—	10	2
Oregon	6	4	8	10	2
Pennsylvania	4	4	—	12	2
Rhode Island	10	4	10	10	3
South Carolina	6	6	—	13	6
South Dakota	6	4	3	10	3
Tennessee	6	4	—	4	1
Texas	4	4	—	10	2
Utah	6	4	2	7	3
Vermont	6	4	—	—	3
Virginia	5	4	—	5	2
Washington	6	4	—	6	3
West Virginia	10	4	—	10	2
Wisconsin	6	4	—	6	3
Wyoming	10	4	—	10	4

Source: Compiled from *Legal Requirements for Business Records: State Requirements,* vols. 1-2. Information Requirements Clearinghouse, 1993.

with the government agencies involved and request clarification of these matters. Of course, the advice of counsel can also be solicited.

Documenting the Legal Research

At the conclusion of the legal retention research, the records manager will have located all laws and regulations imposing records maintenance or retention requirements on the organization's records. The records manager now knows which of the organization's records must be retained in satisfaction of these requirements, and for how long. However, before proceeding with the remaining retention schedule preparation tasks, it is important to properly document the results of the legal research. The reasons are twofold: (1) the organization's attorneys should be provided with complete legal research documentation to enable them to determine whether the law has been reasonably applied, and (2) it may be necessary at some future time to provide evidence to regulatory officials or to courts that the organization has done its best to comply fully with all applicable legal requirements.

Three methods are commonly employed to document legal retention research. Any or all may be done:

1. Post the proper statutory or regulatory citation of all legal requirements on all records inventory worksheets.
2. Make copies of relevant laws and regulations and file them as supporting papers with the inventory worksheets or in a separate file.
3. Post a summary of the legal requirements on the retention schedules themselves or on a separate supporting document.

RECORDS RETENTION DECISION MAKING: THEORY AND PRACTICE

Once the government–imposed retention requirements applicable to each records series have been determined, the next step in developing the records retention schedules is to analyze the records to determine their retention values. This task consists of conducting interviews with numerous persons throughout the organization who are knowledgeable about the value of the information, followed by a careful appraisal of the records and, finally, the formulation of retention decisions for each series of records. The records manager must have a solid knowledge of the theoretical concepts associated with information retention and should follow some practical guidelines to enable these theories to be put into practice. A detailed discussion of records retention theory and practice follows.[11]

Two Theories of Information Retention

Different types of records have value for differing time periods, and the process of deciding which records should be retained for how long is fraught with a good deal of guesswork and uncertainty. Predictive judgments or forecasts must be made concerning the probable future use of information.

If this decision–making process is inherently judgmental, how can the process be refined so that the decision maker can have a high level of confidence in the validity of his or her judgments? The answer lies in two theories that serve as the conceptual framework for making records retention decisions: records appraisal and cost–risk–benefit analysis.

The Concept of Records Appraisal.   The first efforts to articulate a formal theory of information retention were not made by records managers but by archivists. During the first half of the twentieth century, archivists in both the state and federal governments first addressed the question of which records should be kept and which should be thrown away. What evolved from these deliberations became known as the concept of records appraisal.

Primary and Secondary Values of Information.   The records appraisal concept is based on the principle of information value determination. The theory may be summarized as follows: All records possess either temporary or permanent value, in the sense that the information contained in them should either be kept forever or destroyed at the conclusion of the record's life cycle. All records possess *primary value*, which is defined as the value of the information in support of the purpose for which it was created. Most records possess one or more *secondary values*, that is, the actual or potential uses of information for purposes other than the purpose for which the information was created.

Primary value is further defined to mean the *administrative* or *operational* value of the information in support of the purpose for which it was created. Secondary values are usually defined to mean *research* or *historical* uses to which information might be put. Records are said to possess these values if they have been or might be useful to historians or other researchers for purposes having nothing to do with the reason the records came into being. Under the records appraisal concept, some records are also considered to possess *fiscal* or *legal* values, which can be either primary or secondary values depending on the specific uses of the information.

As a general rule, the expiration of primary value occurs when the records make their life cycle transition from an active to a s*emiactive* or an inactive state. Records usually need to be maintained at or near the point of use while they possess primary value, but they may be transferred to remote storage for the duration of their value for secondary purposes. It should be noted, however, that many records series possess primary and secondary values which *run simultaneously* during all or a portion of their life cycle. These nuances must be examined before a good retention decision can be made.

Inadequacies in the Records Appraisal Concept.
Although the records appraisal concept is certainly a valid approach to formulating records retention decisions, it is not without its deficiencies. The major shortcoming in the concept is that it does not adequately consider the costs, risks, and liabilities of information retention as compared to the benefits. In other words, the records appraisal concept fails to consider information retention decisions in *a business context*.

In making any business decision, managers and executives must consider the benefits of a course of action as compared to various alternatives, and whether these rewards justify the assumption of certain costs and varying degrees of risk. These decisions must frequently be made in an atmosphere of uncertainty. Decision makers are not in possession of all the relevant obtainable facts, and they may encounter difficulties analyzing those facts they have in terms of their significance to the issue at hand. So it is with many, perhaps most, records retention decisions.

How, then, can the records appraisal concept be refined or augmented so that these issues will be addressed? The answer lies in our second theory of information retention—cost–risk–benefit analysis.

The Concept of Cost–Risk–Benefit Analysis.
Cost–risk–benefit analysis holds that after the expiration of a record's primary value for administrative or operational purposes, any decision to retain information for secondary purposes should be based on a careful assessment of the projected costs, risks, and benefits of retention for various time periods.

This analysis is not needed to justify information retention for the duration of its primary value, since the costs, risks, and benefits are part of the costs, risks, and benefits of doing business. Nor is this type of analysis needed to justify retaining certain records because of statutory or regulatory requirements. Such retention of records is nondiscretionary if the organization wishes to comply with the law.

However, let us assume that an operating manager or corporate attorney indicates that a particular group of records is no longer needed to satisfy administrative or operating requirements after, say, two years, but that he or she wants to keep the records for another 20 years. In this instance, the principles of cost–risk–benefit analysis should be applied.

An Example of Risk–Benefit Determination.   An example from product liability litigation will illustrate these principles. A retention interview with a product liability attorney might elicit the opinion that certain quality control and product design records relative to product manufacturing and testing should be retained permanently or for the life of the product.

In support of this retention judgment the attorney might state that the particular product is subject to failure in performance, which might result in death or injury to persons using it. This could, in turn, result in claims against the manufacturer or, worse, a product liability lawsuit. Further, the attorney might state that, if the case were to be decided against the manufacturer, liberal settlements to the injured parties might result. Finally, the attorney might base his or her justification for permanent retention of the records on the assumption that if the records were to be produced as evidence during the proceedings, they would be more helpful than harmful to the manufacturer.

Information Retention: A Double–Edged Sword. Let us examine the assumption on which the attorney's recommendation for permanent or long–term retention is based. If it is true that the records are likely to be more helpful than harmful to the manufacturer's legal defense, it is also true that the opposite conclusion (one justifying short retention with disposal immediately after expiration of the term of the product warranty) might be equally valid. If a product liability action is groundless, the information contained in quality control and product testing records may be quite helpful.

On the other hand, if the product manufacturer in our example has not designed the product in accordance with professionally acceptable standards, the existence of records documenting this could be quite harmful to the company in its defense. In short, from a legal perspective, information can be either helpful or harmful to an organization depending on specific legal or business contingencies that may arise at any time during the life of the business. In other words, "the sword can cut both ways."

In the above scenario, it is not the records manager's responsibility to challenge or refute the assumptions offered by corporate counsel. Moreover, the records manager certainly must never attempt to establish records retention policies to protect the wrongdoer by concealing wrongful acts. Rather, it is the records manager's job to ask whether these quality control records have ever contributed to the successful or unsuccessful legal defense of the company, how often this has occurred, how old the records were, and what the financial aspects of the settlement were. These questions are designed to bring the risks and benefits of information retention more sharply into focus. The ultimate objective is to develop a program to provide legal protection to honest, properly managed organizations by ensuring that extraneous materials have been destroyed so that the organization's legal counsel can present its defense in the best light.

Conducting User Interviews to Determine Operational Values

Once the legal considerations applicable to each records series have been determined, the next step is to determine how long the records are needed to satisfy business needs. This task requires the records manager to conduct interviews with managers, supervisors, or other persons using or having charge of the records in each department. These persons can offer the best opinions as to when the usage of information is sufficiently low to make it feasible to transfer the records to a low–cost storage facility or to destroy them outright.

Because these opinions are subjective judgments and because many users tend to exaggerate their own operational needs for information, the records manager must conduct these interviews very carefully. The following are guidelines[12] to ensure successful user interviews:

1. Never conduct user retention interviews until the legal research has been completed. Users generally have superficial knowledge of legal requirements, and often try to overstate their significance unless the requirements have been precisely defined beforehand.

2. Prior to the interviews, review all records series and assign a preliminary retention period to each. These proposed retention periods should be as short as possible; they serve as a point of departure for discussion during the interview. In many cases, these preliminary retention periods will turn out to be valid. In other cases, they may be too long, in which case the interviewee will indicate that the records are not needed for such a long period of time. On the other hand, if a proposed retention period turns out to be too short, the interviewee will have to justify why the record requires a longer retention period.

3. During the interviews, identify and discuss every actual or potential use of the information in each records series, including operational, financial, legal, and research uses. These discussions should isolate the value of the information over time, and the benefits, cost, and risk of retaining it or disposing of it after various time periods.

4. Never ask a user "How long do you need these records?" Managers often overstate their records retention needs because they do not want to make a mistake and not keep records long enough. Rather, ask the following types of interview questions:

   • Why is this information beneficial to your department, and what would be the *specific consequences* of its absence?
   • When does the information become inactive, and how often is it referred to after it becomes inactive?
   • How old is the information that is needed in response to the majority of queries?
   • How old was the oldest information in response to any query?

Determining Fiscal and Tax Retention Values

Records with financial or tax value are those that relate to the financial transactions of an organization, especially those required for audit or tax purposes. These records may include ledgers, budgets, invoices, canceled checks, payrolls, vouchers, and so on. For a relatively short period of time, these records also have operational value; for example, financial records are created to ensure the timely payment of obligations and the proper receipt and crediting of receivables. Many of these records may also be maintained for their legal value under contract law, tax law, or other statutes and regulations. These records often possess tax value because they support the organization's financial audits and tax returns.

The records retention program can be vital in ensuring that a company preserves those records needed to compute and substantiate the organization's tax liability. In most tax audits, the burden of proof resides with the taxpayer and not with the government.

The following guidelines are useful in determining the fiscal and tax retention value of the organization's records:

1. The limitation of assessment laws should always be identified since they serve as an important basis for retaining financial records subject to audit. These statutes prohibit government revenue authorities from conducting tax audits or assessing or collecting taxes after termination of the limitation on assessment period.

2. U.S. federal tax regulations state that "any person required to file a return of information with respect to income shall keep such permanent books of account or records, including inventories, as are sufficient to establish the amount of gross income, deduction, credits, or other matters required to be shown by such person in any return of such tax or infor-

mation." Here, the term *permanent* refers to the ability of the records to last for long periods of time rather than a required permanent retention time.

3. Most companies retain tax returns and work papers, general and subsidiary ledgers, and other summary financial records for long periods of time (at least ten years and sometimes for the life of the corporation), while bulky detail records (source documents for financial transactions) are usually retained no longer than six to seven years, or until the completion of all tax audits, whichever is later.

4. The U.S. federal tax regulations contain special provisions relative to the maintenance and preservation of computer and microfilm records for tax purposes. These requirements must also be determined in developing the records retention program.

5. State requirements for tax records generally follow the federal limitation of assessment period.

The records manager should determine the fiscal and tax value of the organization's records by consultation with the chief financial officer, the controller, the tax manager, or other corporate finance or accounting personnel.

Determining Historical Value: The Retention Schedule's Archival Function

Since records disposal actions are irrevocable, the records retention scheduling program should identify those records that have value for illuminating the history of the organization and preserve them as archival records. These might include records related to the organization's founding, major events, or growth and development, and records documenting its performance and contribution to the community, state, or nation. These efforts at historical preservation can also have important business benefits: Archival materials are often used in marketing programs, in public relations, in management education and training, and for

legal purposes. It is very important that the value of records as historical documents not be overlooked in developing the records retention scheduling program. In most cases, the archives of an organization containing its permanent records will represent an extremely small percentage of the total records volume of the organization, usually not over 1 to 2 percent. In government agencies, this figure is usually higher because such organizations may maintain more historical records for use by the general public.

It is often difficult to project which records currently in use will be valuable for historical purposes. If the organization has an archivist on its staff, this person should definitely participate in the retention decision–making process, since the archivist will be in the best position to determine the historical needs and objectives of the organization and can identify those records that will satisfy these needs. Chapter 19 contains further guidance on this very important element of the organization's records management program.

Making the Final Records Retention Decisions

At the conclusion of the records appraisal process and when all cost–risk–benefit analysis has been completed, the records manager is ready to make the final decisions concerning the retention of each records series. A retention period must be established to govern the disposition of each series throughout its life cycle. The following principles should be used to formulate *valid* records retention decisions—decisions that will be in the best interest of the organization:

*   *Principle 1.* Avoid the "every conceivable contingency" syndrome. A records retention program cannot and should not be designed to accommodate every conceivable need for information at any future time, however remote the probability of the need might be.
*   *Principle 2.* Information should be retained if there is a reasonable probability that it will be needed at some future time to support some legitimate legal or business objective

and the consequences of its absence would be substantial.

- *Principle 3.* Records retention policies should generally be conservative in the sense that they should not expose the organization to an inordinate degree of risk. If the only benefit of a short retention period is saving in space, a substantial degree of risk is usually not justified.

- *Principle 4.* Retention decision makers must be mindful that the presence or absence of information can be either helpful or harmful to an organization, depending on specific legal or business contingencies that may arise at any time during the life of the business. It is difficult to predict the occurrence of these contingencies with any certainty. Therefore, the best way to minimize the risks associated with document retention is to provide for systematic disposal immediately after the expiration of a document's value for legal and business purposes.

- *Principle 5.* A retention period is most likely to be valid if it is based on a professional consensus of the opinions of persons most knowledgeable about the value of the information and the costs, risks, and benefits of its disposal.

It will be observed that the foregoing principles are in conflict with each other. Some of them indicate shorter retention periods, while others support longer, more conservative ones. How can the retention decision maker reconcile these principles? The best advice is this: Records retention policies are most likely to be in the organization's best interest if they reflect a middle–of–the–road perspective—not too long, not too short. Such an approach will usually produce the best results in controlling the growth of records and achieving the other legal and business benefits of the retention scheduling program.

Optimum Distribution of Retention Periods

Table 3.2 provides guidance relative to the optimum distribution of retention time periods. This distribution of retention time periods reflects average time periods needed in order to effectively control the growth of records.

Although Table 3.2 can only provide, at best, imprecise guidance as to how long an organization should keep most of its records, the significant point is that the average retention period for most organization records would fall in the four– to seven–year range. Moreover, the chart indicates that approximately 50 to 80 percent of an organization's records should be retained for seven years or less. Many studies have shown that 90 percent of all references to files are to

TABLE 3.2   Optimum Distribution of Retention Time Periods: A Suggested Guide

RETENTION RANGE	PERCENTAGE OF TOTAL RECORDS SERIES
Less than 1 year	2–5
1 to 3 years	10–20
4 to 5 years	20–30
6 to 7 years	20–30
8 to 10 years	10–20
11 to 20 years	5–10
Permanent	2–5

Source: Based on an analysis of the records retention schedules developed by David O. Stephens, CRM, during the period 1979–1993.

records that are three years old or less. Older records are used very rarely in the conduct of business. The organization should endeavor to retain very few records longer than ten years; still fewer should be scheduled for permanent retention.

SCHEDULE ISSUANCE, APPROVAL, AND IMPLEMENTATION

After a retention period is assigned to all records series, the next step in retention schedule development is to prepare the schedules in final form. This requires that a retention schedule format be selected for organizing the records series and their retention periods. The following schedule format options are most popular:

1. *Department records series format.* Here, one retention schedule is prepared for each department, division, or other organizational entity, and each records series maintained by the entity appears on the schedule. This format is perhaps the most popular one. Its principal advantage is that it provides precise retention guidelines that are specific to the department's records; thus, the retention policies are easy to apply and implement.

2. *The functional format.* Some retention schedules are formatted either by functional type or class of records or by major business functions of the organization. Under this format option, the organization would issue separate schedules for legal records, human resources records, and so on. This option is increasingly popular, particularly for the general administrative records that are commonly maintained by most or all departments. The main advantage is that it can be easier and quicker to produce retention schedules in this format. The main disadvantage is that these types of schedules are harder to apply; the retention guidance will sometimes be imprecise and the coverage will not comprehensively include all records maintained by an organization.

3. *Integrated retention schedule and file plan format.* Retention schedules are often integrated with an organization's file plan or filing index; the retention policy appears on the same document with the file plan specifying how the records must be organized, indexed, and filed. This is an increasingly popular format option, as the users are furnished with guidance as to how to organize and index their records as well as how long to retain them. If the file plan is a uniform files classification scheme in which subject categories of records are hierarchically arranged, the retention periods typically appear at the secondary category level of the hierarchy since this level most often equates to the records series.

It is also necessary to select a form and format on which to print and issue the retention schedules. Again, several options are widely used:

1. *Standard retention schedule form.* Figure 3.2 shows a standard form for printing and issuing records retention schedules. Here the records series are listed, together with their retention periods, which are displayed in columnar format. The "in dept." column prescribes the time the record must be retained by its creating department, while the "in storage" column displays its retention in an off–site storage location. Finally, the "total period" column indicates the total authorized life of the records series. Although it is not shown on the sample, this type of schedule form often contains approval blocks for the signatures of various corporate officials. These approval blocks are not mandatory, but they may make it easier to demonstrate to legal authorities that the schedules are, in fact, the official policy of the organization. This type of standard form is widely used in corporate environments.

2. *Narrative retention schedule format.* The retention schedules can be formatted in narrative fashion and typed on plain paper for issuance as a policy directive in the organization's administrative or records management manual. In this case, each page is not signed by authorizing officials, but such approval is usually shown by signatures on a cover page for the entire issuance. Frequently, the records series will be accompanied by a narrative description of the series and its con-

Description of Record (including Form Number, if any)	Department	Retention of Original Record			Original Record Micro-filmed	Retent of Micro-film
		Total Period	In Dept.	In Storage		
Accounts Payable Distribution Ledger – All Div.	Accts. Pay.	7 Yrs. Min. or to I.T.R.	1 Yr.	6 Yrs.	No	
Accounts Receivable Individual Records	B.F.C.	7 Yrs.	–	7 Yrs.	No	
Accounts Receivable Ledger Cards – Form 820	Accts. Rec.	6 Mos.	6 Mos.	–	Yes	5 Yrs.
Accounts Receivable (& Related Reserves) Doubtful – Closed A/C 1328 & 1329	Corp. Gen. Acct.	7 Yrs.	2 Yrs.	5 Yrs.	No	
Accounts Receivable Ledger:						
Employees – Acct. 1341 – Form 1610 – All Div.	Corp. Gen. Acct.	7 Yrs.	7 Yrs.	–	Yes	7 Yrs.
Misc. – Acct. 1343 – Form 1610 & 2709 – All Div.	Various	3 Yrs.	3 Yrs.	–	Yes	7 Yrs.
Accounts Receivable Posting Control – Form 1321	BMG Gen. Acct.	6 yrs.	6 Yrs.	–	No	
Advertising Artwork	BMG Adv.	Indef.**	Indef.	Indef.	No	
Advertising Artwork	Intl. Adv.	Indef.	Indef.	–	No	
Advertising Releases	BMG Adv.	2 Yrs.	2 Yrs.	–	No	
Advertising Releases	Intl. Adv.	2 Yrs.	1 Yr.	1 Yr.	No	
*Agreements as to Patents & Inventions – Form 3601 & 1785	Patents	20 Yrs.	–	20 Yrs.	No	
American Society of Insurance Management, Inc.	Insurance	Perm.	–	Perm.	No	
*Ann Arbor Laboratory (Accounting & Payroll Records)		–	–	–	Yes	Perm.
Application File:						
Approved, not joined	Mkt. Pers.	1 Yr.	1 Yr.	–	No	
Not Approved	Mkt. Pers.	6 Mos.	6 Mos.	–	No	
Assembly Master Operation Sheet	Plt. Acct.	I.T.R.	I.T.R.	–	No	
Attendance Record – Vacation & Sick Leave Credits & Absences Without Pay – Various Form Nos.	Payroll	7 Yrs.	2 Yrs.	5 Yrs.	No	

*	– Revised Since Last Issue
**	– Specific Authority Required before Destroying
I.T.R.	– Income Tax Release

FIGURE 3.2 Master Records Retention Schedule

tents in order to facilitate proper identification. Finally, the retention periods are sometimes expressed in sentence format so as to clarify the disposition instructions. This schedule format is especially popular among government agencies. Figure 3.3 shows a sample.

3. *Computerized records management database.* During the past several years, a large number of commercial software products have been devel-

oped to automate various aspects of an organization's records management program. Some of these products provide records retention modules such that the retention periods for each records series can be entered into a designated field in the computer's database. This capability can greatly enhance the organization's ability to manage its records. Chapter 9 contains a discussion of records retention automation.

General Records Schedule 10
June 19—

GENERAL RECORDS SCHEDULE 10

Motor Vehicle Maintenance and Operation Records

These records pertain to the management, maintenance, and operation of motor vehicles used by agencies.

41 CFR 101–38 prescribes policies and procedures. Standard Form 82, which is an annual motor vehicle report required by the Office of Federal Supply Services, General Services Administration, is the only standardized record. Certain cost and inventory control forms have been developed, but they are not mandatory. This schedule covers agency records pertaining to the daily use and operation of the vehicles.

In general, records pertaining to motor vehicles reflect a threefold responsibility: (a) the accumulation of cost and operating data for internal accounting and management purposes and for reports submitted to the Office of Federal Supply and Services (Standard Form 82, Annual Motor Vehicle Report); (b) the maintenance of the vehicles themselves; and (c) protecting the interest of the Government in accident claims against it. The records themselves consist of chauffeur service logs and reports, vehicle repair and maintenance check–off sheets, cost ledgers, and claims correspondence and forms.

All records described in this schedule are authorized for disposal in both hard copy and electronic forms, as provided in GRS 20, Electronic Records, and GRS 23, Records Common to Most Offices Within Agencies.

ITEM NO.	DESCRIPTION OF RECORDS	AUTHORIZED DISPOSITION
1.	*Motor Vehicle Correspondence Files.* Correspondence in the operating unit responsible for maintenance and operation of motor vehicles not otherwise covered in this schedule.	Destroy when 2 years old.
2.	*Motor Vehicle Operating and Maintenance Files.*	
	a. Operating records including those relating to gas and oil consumption, dispatching, and scheduling.	Destroy when 3 months old.
	b. Maintenance records, including those relating to service and repair.	Destroy when 1 year old.
3.	*Motor Vehicle Cost Files.* Motor vehicle ledger and work sheets providing cost and expense data.	Destroy 3 years after discontinuance of ledger or date of work sheet.

FIGURE 3.3   Records Retention Schedule—Narrative Format
Source: Courtesy National Archives and Records Administration

Approval of the Retention Schedules

The final draft of the records retention schedules should be approved in writing by those managers and executives within the organization who have an interest in or authority for the preservation and disposal of the organization's records. These will usually include operating managers from each department, the organization's legal counsel, and its chief financial officer, controller, or tax manager. Schedule approval may also be obtained from the organization's corporate secretary if this executive is officially responsible for the organization's books and records, from the internal auditor, or from the chief administrative officer if this executive is responsible for the operation of the records retention program. By approving the schedules, each of these officials is certifying that the retention periods contained in the schedules are sufficient to meet the needs of the business within their respective areas. This approval process is designed to make it easier to demonstrate to the courts or to regulatory agencies that the schedules are the organization's official records retention policy, and that the policy has been developed in a proper and responsible manner. Complete and accurate records of the schedule approval process should be maintained; no individual in the organization should be empowered to modify the schedules without following the designated procedure.

These approvals can be secured by concurrent review by the responsible individuals or by the committee method of schedule approval. Some organizations find it expeditious to organize a records retention committee consisting of these officials or their designees, so that the retention schedules can be discussed by the group and approved or revised as necessary.

SUMMARY

The records retention schedule is an essential basic component of every comprehensive records management program. It specifies the length of time that records must be maintained by the organization and when they may be destroyed. The retention scheduling program is designed to control the growth of the organization's records, reduce the cost of recordkeeping, minimize the organization's exposure to the legal risks that may be associated with document retention and disposal, and ensure compliance with records retention laws and regulations.

A records retention program must specify a retention period for every records series maintained by the organization. A retention period must comply with any applicable statutes or regulations imposed by the government, and it must address the organization's business needs for information retention. Finally, the retention periods must be devised with a view towards minimizing the risk of liability lawsuits, and they must also result in the permanent preservation of information of historical value. These objectives can be achieved if every records series is properly appraised to establish its retention values for operational, legal, fiscal, and historical purposes. An analysis to determine the costs, benefits, and risks of retaining the records or disposing of them after various periods of time is also required to satisfy legal and business policies. If they are to successfully control the growth of records, these retention periods should be as short as possible; the majority of them should fall in the four– to seven–year range.

In order to develop an excellent retention scheduling program, the records manager must have quality records inventory data describing every records series, conduct legal research to determine which records series must be retained to satisfy federal, state, and other statutory or regulatory retention requirements, consult with legal counsel to obtain advice relative to the organization's legal needs for information retention, interview department managers to solicit input concerning the business value of records, and interview various financial officers and other corporate staff members who have authority for the preservation and disposal of the organization's records. After the schedules have been prepared in draft form, many or all of these officials should review them to ensure that the retention periods are in the organization's best interest.

QUESTIONS FOR DISCUSSION

1. Discuss the four major functions of the records retention schedule in providing for the disposition of the organization's records.

2. Describe the administrative and economic benefits of operating a quality records retention program.

3. Describe the legal objectives and benefits of the retention scheduling program.

4. What are the major steps in developing a records retention program? List five of them and explain them briefly.

5. What should the records manager do to help ensure compliance with the obstruction of justice statutes? Indicate the circumstances under which records disposal actions must be halted in compliance with these laws.

6. Describe the records retention implications of product liability lawsuits. How can the records retention program be designed to mitigate the risks of this type of litigation?

7. Explain five principles for planning the task of conducting legal retention research so as to ensure that all relevant statutes and regulations are located.

8. How do statutes of limitations affect records retention?

9. Explain the concept of records appraisal and its use in determining the retention values of an organization's records.

10. List and describe briefly four principles designed to ensure successful retention interviews with departmental personnel.

11. How can the retention scheduling program support the tax audit needs of an organization? List and describe several ways.

12. This chapter defined five principles of making valid records retention decisions. List and describe three of them.

13. Describe two formats for issuing records retention schedules and distinguish between them.

14. Which corporate officials should review and approve the organization's records retention schedules and why?

PROJECTS

1. Assume that you are a records consultant and have been asked to submit a plan for establishing a records retention schedule at the Seth Jones Corporation, manufacturer of small appliances. Prepare an outline showing the steps you would include, and give the rationale for each step.

2. Assume that you are the records manager of the Great Lakes National Bank. Visit a local library or a legal library and determine which title and parts of the *Code of Federal Regulations* govern records retention for your employer.

3. Determine the first–year dollar savings from implementation of the records retention schedule. Assume that all records destroyed were contained in five–drawer file cabinets in office space that cost $20 a square foot a year and that the file cabinets cost $500 each. Your retention schedule resulted in the disposal of 10,000 cubic feet of letter–size documents.

4. The administrative vice–president, who is in charge of records management, has asked you to select the best means of appraising records prior to the development of a records retention schedule. Write a memo stating your position.

CASE PROBLEM

You have just been appointed records manager of a large, highly diversified multinational corporation having business interests in some 35 states and 20 foreign countries. The company is engaged in four major lines of business: petroleum exploration and production, shipbuilding, farm equipment manufacturing, and food processing. In some of these businesses the company enjoys a large market share, and in one line of business its market share is dominant. Altogether, these four lines of business consist of 50 departments at corporate headquarters, manufacturing plants in 10 states and 5 foreign countries, and sales offices in all 35 states and 20 foreign countries. In total, the company has approximately 500 departmental entities. The company has never had a records retention scheduling program, and a preliminary survey reveals that approximately 200,000 cubic feet of old records (some dating from the 1920s) are being housed in over 100 storage facilities throughout the company. The corporation's legal counsel has recently met with the senior vice–president for administration; the result of this meeting is that you have been asked to do the following:

1. Develop a plan for records retention schedule development, estimating the resource requirements and the details of how to complete the project.

2. Prepare a presentation to senior management justifying the retention scheduling program. The presentation must present a summary of the benefits to be realized, including details of why this program will be legally important to the company.

3. Develop a plan for conducting the legal research required to support this project, and present this plan to the corporation's legal staff.

NOTES

1. See Howard Adler, Jr., and Sharon J. Devine, "How to Avoid Antitrust Death by Document: Some Thoughts on Document Management," *ACCA Docket*, Spring 1992, pp. 30–38.

2. See Michael Allen, "Cleaning House: U.S. Companies Pay Increasing Attention to Destroying Files," *Wall Street Journal*, Sept. 2, 1987.

3. Preston W. Shimer, "Product Liability Issues for Records Managers," *Proceedings of the 35th Annual Conference, ARMA International* (Prairie Village, KS: ARMA International, 1990), pp. 526–535.

4. Lori Block, "Record Retention on Trial: Which Documents Can Be Safely Destroyed?" *Business Insurance*, March 9, 1992, p. 75.

5. Carlucci et al. vs Piper Aircraft Corporation. Nos. 78–8370–Civ–JCP to 78–8372–Civ–JCP. United States District Court. *102 Federal Rules Decisions*. 1984. pp. 472–489.

6. Donald S. Skupsky, JD, CRM, *Legal Requirements for Business Records* (Englewood, CO: Information Requirements Clearinghouse, 1993), Vols. 1–4.

7. Donald S. Skupsky, JD, CRM, *Records Retention Procedures* (Englewood, CO: Information Requirements Clearinghouse, 1990), pp. 19–20.

8. Donald S. Skupsky, JD, CRM, *Recordkeeping Requirements* (Englewood, CO: Information Requirements Clearinghouse, 1988), p. 46.

9. For a comprehensive discussion of researching federal, state, and other legal records retention requirements, see Skupsky, *Records Retention Procedures*, Chap. 4.

10. Skupsky, *Recordkeeping Requirements*, p. 63.

11. David O. Stephens, CRM, "Making Records Retention Decisions: Practical and Theoretical Considerations," *Records Management Quarterly*, January 1988, pp. 3–7.

12. See also Skupsky, *Records Retention Procedures*, pp. 69–74.

Chapter 4

Vital Records Protection and
Disaster Recovery Planning

Learning Objectives

1. To explain the need for vital records protection and disaster recovery planning in a records management program.
2. To describe how vital records are identified, and how they differ from important and useful records.
3. To list criteria for selecting the appropriate methods of protecting vital records.
4. To explain the concepts and techniques of protecting vital electronic records in microcomputer and larger computing environments.
5. To describe the methods of recovering damaged vital paper, microfilm, and electronic record media after a disaster.
6. To identify guidelines for developing vital records operating procedures.

THE BUSINESS IMPORTANCE OF VITAL RECORDS PROTECTION

Records managers typically spend most of their time planning and designing new information retrieval systems, improving existing ones, planning and implementing records retention programs, or managing records centers and the inactive records they contain. Although these activities are essential in accomplishing organizational goals, another records management task transcends these in importance: *vital records protection and disaster recovery planning*. This activity ensures the continued viability of the organization and the businesses it operates. Indeed, the very survival of the organization may depend on whether vital business information has been protected and is available for use immediately following a disaster.

In its *Standard for the Protection of Records*, the National Fire Protection Association states that "businesses have been discontinued because of the insurmountable task of replacing organizational and operational records."[1] An organization can simply lack the informational capability to get back into business following a major disaster. Without critical operating records, the business may not be able to service existing customers, secure new ones, manufacture products, borrow money, collect its debts from its creditors, justify its tax liability to the government, enforce its contracts, defend itself against liability lawsuits, or even substantiate the losses it has sustained in the disaster on insurance claims. Moreover, if an organization's management is found to have been negligent by not performing proper disaster recovery planning, the organization and individual

68

officers and directors may face more lawsuits. If the lack of a disaster recovery plan results in personal injury or death, financial loss, or inability to deliver products or services under contractual obligation, the organization's officers and directors can be held liable. According to Gerald Stephens, president of the Society of Chartered Property and Casualty Underwriters,

> *Once it has been established that a business or public entity has failed to make a reasonable effort to prevent loss, breach of duty creates the basis for claims of negligence. The issue then becomes not whether the company is liable, but the extent of the damage and the amount of compensation to the injured parties.*[2]

Although the consequences of a disaster can be severe, few organizations have minimized these risks by developing good disaster recovery programs. Still fewer protect their vital records, particularly those on paper and other nonelectronic media formats. Perhaps the major reason is that expenditures for disaster recovery and vital records protection purposes *produce no return-on-investment unless a disaster actually occurs.* Then, of course, such investments pay for themselves many times over. However, this attitude is changing. Largely as a result of a recent spate of natural disasters in the early 1990s, the disaster recovery field is growing rapidly. It has evolved into its own professional discipline, with its own association, conferences, and certification program. It is supported by a large and rapidly growing community of vendors, consisting of vital records protection companies, computer backup and data protection companies, software vendors, and many others.

Vital Records: Their Essential Characteristics

Vital records contain information needed to reestablish or continue an organization in the event of a disaster. They are needed to recreate the

company's legal and financial position and to preserve the rights of the company and its employees, customers, and stockholders.

To be defined as *vital*, business records must be *irreplaceable* and *required to operate the business* (the business could not operate without them) either during the disaster or immediately thereafter. Business records are vital mainly because of their *intrinsic uniqueness*. An organization has four categories of assets: *people; property* (inventory and other physical assets such as land, buildings, and equipment); *capital*, whether in cash or investments; and, finally, *records* and the information they contain. Records and information, because of their uniqueness, are difficult or impossible to replace if lost or destroyed. Information is a vital asset to an organization because it:

- Establishes the legal status of the organization as a business entity.
- Documents the assets and liabilities of the organization from a financial perspective.
- Documents the operations of the organization, which enable production processes or other work to be accomplished.

Records not defined as *vital* may be classified as *important* or simply *useful,* as described later in this chapter.

Disaster Recovery Planning and Its Relationship to Records Management

A *disaster* is a sudden, unplanned calamitous event—for example, a fire, theft, or flood—that makes it impossible for an organization to perform critical business functions for some period of time. *Disaster recovery planning,* sometimes called *contingency* or *emergency preparedness planning,* is the advance planning and preparations necessary to minimize loss and ensure continuity of critical business functions.

Disaster recovery planning is broad-based; it attempts to mitigate all types of business risks that may result from a disaster. Information protection is, therefore, one key element of a comprehensive disaster recovery planning program. A comprehensive discussion of disaster recovery planning, often undertaken by senior management committees or computer specialists, is beyond the scope of this chapter. Rather, our focus here will be on *records-related* disaster recovery planning, which is of immediate concern to the records manager.

The Basic Elements of Vital Records Protection

Safeguarding vital records includes protecting them against the ordinary hazards of fire, water, mildew, light, dust, insects, rodents, acids and their fumes, and excessive humidity. These records must also be protected against human hazards such as theft, misplacement, and unauthorized access. Disasters such as earthquakes, windstorms, explosions, bombings, nuclear fallout, and radiation must also be considered. The records must be protected not only from actual destruction, but also from loss of legibility to the extent that the records' legality may be questioned. Although these hazards cannot all be eliminated, the objective is to reduce them to an acceptable minimum.

Vital records may consist of active records or inactive records (although many vital records lose their vital quality when they become inactive). Active vital records, such as accounts receivable, certain personnel records, and current marketing records, must be available for frequent reference. The protection program may include duplication of vital records by means of micrographics or direct copying. It may also include the preservation of an extra copy, created in the normal work flow, in an off-site or vaulted area. The program is often expanded beyond the protection of vital records to include all records of high value or importance to the organization.

In deciding whether these "important" records should be safeguarded, the records manager must compare the cost of protecting records to the cost of reconstructing them and to other direct monetary losses, if the records are destroyed

prematurely. First selecting vital records and then protecting them are calculated risks, because there is no absolutely certain method of protection. The main purpose of the vital records protection plan is to protect the *essential information* contained in the records rather than the records themselves, although the evidential value of the record must also be considered and protected if necessary.

Initiating the Program. An organization-wide vital records protection program needs endorsement by senior management. A senior executive should issue a written directive which formally establishes a program for the systematic protection of all vital records, assigns the responsibility for program development and implementation to the records management department, and solicits the cooperation of all personnel.

Although the program can be operated as an independent effort, it is usually best to develop and operate it as a component of the organization's larger disaster recovery and contingency planning efforts. For example, if a company-wide vital records and disaster recovery committee is established, it may recommend the creation of essential documents for postdisaster reconstruction, such as powers of attorney and legal authorization to reconstitute the board of directors and committees.

Vital Records Protection: A Form of Business Interruption Insurance

Insurance is the normal means of protecting ourselves against loss from disaster. Records cannot be insured for the value of their content, so in a sense, vital records protection programs become a type of insurance. The "premiums paid" are the costs of the protective measures taken, such as microfilming. But just as in other insurance matters it is not wise to overinsure or underinsure; the cost of protection should never exceed the potential loss. Thus, as part of the *risk analysis* the records manager must consider the nature of potential disasters that an organization might be subject to, the likelihood of these disasters, and the consequences should they occur. This preliminary evaluation helps to decide if protection is needed and to what degree by identifying organizational objectives and types of disasters that would pose a reasonable threat to them.

The Seven Classes of Disasters

To facilitate this type of evaluation, potential disasters and losses have been classified into seven groups, as shown in Table 4.1. Note that the frequency of occurrence diminishes as the severity of the disaster increases. The greater likelihood of loss occurs with the Class 1 disaster and the least with the Class 7. It does not follow, though, that a Class 7 loss would necessarily be the least costly. Thus, the records manager must examine the categories of potential loss and determine the implications for protection consistent with his or her situation.

A *Class 1* disaster is the most severe and would have national or international consequences across all businesses. Although less probable in the post-Cold War era, a Class 1 disaster should not be ignored in records managers' planning efforts. For example, a general nuclear attack would put many industries out of business. Nonessential businesses, such as the cosmetic industry, would probably lose their entire market; vital industries could be nationalized immediately so

that they could resume operations as quickly as possible. Providing communications, transportation, fuel, construction, health care, sanitation, food, and clothing for millions would be essential functions of the government at such a time. Many, if not all, of these vital functions would be carried out through existing private institutions. Cost, reimbursement, and revenues would be secondary, if not entirely suspended, functions.

The national, state, and local governments must consider disaster contingencies that include the records and information necessary to carry out their vital functions. Thus, in preparing for a Class 1 emergency, each organization should determine what role it is likely to play in reconstructing and reestablishing its function in society. Only after that role has been determined can the organization decide which, if any, of its functions would be vital to that role and which records and information and other resources would be needed to carry it out.

A *Class 2* disaster would be a local or regional catastrophe, such as a major hurricane affecting an entire city, state, or region. In this type of disaster, local government must continue essential municipal services. Vital records for a city, for instance, might be the roster of all city employees, a list of temporary places of housing with appropriate legal documentation, and blueprints and plans of all the major buildings in the

TABLE 4.1   The Seven Classes of Disasters

CLASS	DEFINITION	EXAMPLE
1	Most severe conceivable; national in scope	Nuclear attack
2	Severe natural disaster affecting local area	Earthquake, flood, tornado
3	Destruction of major building of an organization during working hours	Fire in manufacturing plant
4	Destruction of major building of an organization during nonworking hours	Fire in Federal Record Center, St. Louis
5	One or two functions of an organization affected	Bomb thrown into tape library or computer center
6	Subfunction affected	Research notes of chemist destroyed
7	Lost document	Letter of commendation lost

city, as well as of the city's sewage, water, and underground power sources. Procedures for performing essential services should also be available.

For businesses, the need for records protection in a Class 2 situation is quite different from the need in a Class 1 situation. In Class 2, some of the services and products needed to protect employees or citizens—police, medical personnel, food supply, etc.—may still be available and the remainder can be brought in. Economic considerations would not be suspended; and in all likelihood, each company or institution would expect to resume operations and to protect the legal and financial interests of its employees, customers, and stockholders.

A *Class 3* disaster is similar to a Class 2 disaster but differs in one major respect. A Class 3 disaster is one that destroys the major building of an organization during working hours, but that is the only destruction in the area. Thus, much more assistance is readily available in this single-site disaster. Backup computer systems may be put into operation, and adjacent facilities may be rented or bought. Many other remedies are possible when there is only *one* victim of disaster in a large metropolis.

To the organization, however, a Class 3 disaster is still major. Employees may possibly be killed or disabled, so emergency procedures must be safeguarded and readily available.

A *Class 4* disaster is identical to a Class 3 except that it occurs during nonworking hours, when most of the personnel are not on the premises.

A C*lass 5* disaster affects only one or two functions of an organization. For example, a bomb is thrown into the tape library of the computer services department or a tornado strikes the corporate headquarters and destroys the office of the corporate secretary. A Class 5 disaster may not put the company out of business but may cost it millions of dollars if the records destroyed are not readily available elsewhere. In this type of disaster, the destroyed records may be vital to a particular business component, such as a tape li-

brary, *but the component itself, while extremely important to the organization, is not vital.*

A *Class 6* disaster affects one subfunction. For example, in a chemical company, research notes are usually documented in laboratory notebooks and are usually considered to be extremely valuable. These notebooks are safeguarded to provide continuity in the event that the researcher is disabled or dies and also to protect them against accidental loss or theft. A duplicate set of these records, maintained at another site on a daily basis, would provide appropriate protection for these vital records.

In other business situations, the most valuable and important document in the organization may happen to be the one lying on the manager's, engineer's, or designer's desk at the moment of the disaster. To protect such documents, on-site secure storage and duplication for off-site dispersal are sometimes warranted, as will be discussed later. Again, this is a security decision that can be made only on an individual basis.

A *Class 7* disaster is a lost or stolen document. While not usually considered a disaster, this is a very common security problem and must not be overlooked in vital records protection planning. One lost file can be very expensive; making micrographic copies of vital documents and maintaining good records management methods can eliminate or greatly reduce this problem.

IDENTIFYING VITAL RECORDS

Most medium-size to large organizations have hundreds or thousands of records series. Even smaller organizations have dozens of different types of records. How does the records manager determine which ones are vital? This is, arguably, the most important (and certainly the most conceptually difficult) aspect of developing a vital records protection program. This two-step process requires the records manager to identify the *functions* that are essential to the primary mission of the organization. Then, the records manager must identify the *records* whose informational value to the organization is so great, and the consequences of loss so severe, that special protection is justified to reduce these risks.

This process must be *very selective* and protect only that information that is *absolutely essential* to the resumption of normal business operations. Published literature on vital records protection indicates that only about 2 to 7 percent of the total records of an organization are vital, depending on the type of organization, the nature of its business, and the degree of risk that management is willing to accept.

Records Protection Priorities

All records are *relatively* important. Thus, the selection of vital records should be considered from a priority perspective.

Vital Records—Highest Protection Priority. This category includes records essential to protect the critical financial, legal, and operational functions of the organization and its customers, employees, shareholders, or other client groups— information without which the business could not operate. *Uniqueness* and *irreplaceability* must also be considered. This category includes information that either could not be replaced at any cost or that, if lost or destroyed, would result in grave business consequences, such as loss of customer base or production capability. The loss of the information would subject the organization to an unacceptable level of risk; thus, these vital records must be protected immediately as a matter of highest priority.

Important Records—Secondary Protection Priority. These records are also essential to protect organizational assets, but they could be replaced or recreated. For records in this category, a cost analysis should usually be performed to determine whether the cost of reconstructing or regenerating the information would exceed the cost of protecting it. The records manager should also consider the time and difficulties that would be involved in recreating the information and how soon after a disaster the organization would need it to resume business. In many cases, it will be evident that special protection is justified for these important records. For example, if the records would be needed to resume business one day or one week after the disaster, and it would require several weeks or months to recreate them, special protection would obviously be the correct business decision.

Useful Records—Lowest Protection Priority. This category includes those records that would be inconvenient to lose and that would be useful, but not essential, to the organization in resuming normal business operations. Some of this information may warrant special protection, but the information having higher priorities for protection purposes should be protected first.

Using Records Inventory Data and Conducting Management Interviews

Chapter 2 described the process of collecting records inventory data. These data are invaluable in developing a vital records protection program; the records manager cannot identify vital records without knowing what records exist. With these inventory data in hand, it is necessary to interview the organization's management staff to solicit their opinions concerning the value of the information under their jurisdiction and the consequences of its loss. These qualitative judgments are an essential first step in the risk analysis process.

The records manager should interview the managers of each major department; sometimes interviews with managers, supervisors, or technical specialists in subdepartments will also be required. The following are guidelines to ensure the success of these interviews:

1. Never begin an interview by asking "What records do you have that are vital?" Managers first need a basic understanding of the distinctions between *vital*, *important*, and

useful records. Thus, the records manager should acquaint them with these concepts.

2. Ask managers to envision a scenario in which all the records in their departments were destroyed, and then ask them to consider, in specific terms rather than generalities, how this would affect the entire organization's ability to conduct business.

3. More specifically, ask managers:

- Whether the absence of any records series under their jurisdiction would prevent the organization from conducting business.
- What the specific operational, financial, or legal consequences would be if each records series did not exist.
- Which records series could not be replaced at any cost.
- Which records series have been dispersed to remote locations in the normal course of business, and whether the number of dispersal points would make reassembly of the records series practical.
- Which records series could be recreated by internal resources, which ones could be reassembled from external sources, and what the cost of records series replacement would be.
- How soon after the disaster the records series would be needed to resume business operations.
- Whether it is practical to duplicate the documents in the records series to create an extra security copy for off-site storage, and if so, how often such duplication should be performed.
- When, in the life cycle of each vital records series, the information loses its vital quality.
- Whether any departmental resources are available for expenditures for information protection.

Next, it is generally advisable to interview the organization's senior executives. These individuals usually have a broader perspective on the nature of the entire business. The records manager should review the departmental recommendations with these individuals, solicit their judgments concerning the protection status of the organization's information, and enlist their support for the investments that will be required to reduce these risks.

Vital Records Analysis and Summary Work Sheets

During this process, it is a good idea to use vital records work sheets, so that findings and analyses can be recorded in a methodical manner. Figure 4.1 presents an example of a vital records analysis sheet. In the top line, Vital Records Classification: (1), the name of the record appears. Under Vital Records Documents: (2), supporting documents or documents necessary to aid in reconstruction of vital records are listed. Under Retention and Disposition Schedule: (3), cross-references should be made to coordinate the instructions of this schedule. In Distribution of Copies: (4), the sources of copies of records are listed.

A brief statement of the purpose and value of the records is given under Reason for Protection: (5). The type of protection (e.g., dispersal, evacuation, microfilm, vault storage) is specified under Protection Method: (6). The manner in which the records will be filed is specified under Filing: (7). The length of time the record is to be retained is recorded under Retention: (8). The cost of maintaining the vital record may be estimated for the year under Cost: (9). This may include the cost of an additional copy or the cost of reducing the size of the copy.

From the vital records analysis sheets, spreadsheets summarizing the information may be prepared for each function. These spreadsheets should be approved prior to implementation of the program. Figure 4.2 is an example of a vital records summary sheet.

Defining an Acceptable Level of Risk

If an organization does nothing about planning for recovery from a disaster, it will face maximum

VITAL RECORDS ANALYSIS	
Vital Records Classification: (1)	Minutes of Directors Meetings
Vital Records Documents: (2)	None
Retention and Disposition Schedule: (3)	Minutes of Directors Meetings
Distribution of Copies: (4)	Board of Directors, Vice Presidents
Reason for Protection: (5)	To provide policies and history of enterprise
Protection Method: (6)	Vaulting
Filing: (7)	Chronological
Retention: (8)	Permanent
Cost: (9)	$12 annual maintenance

FIGURE 4.1 Vital Records Analysis Sheet

exposure to the risks of a disaster. Conversely, if an organization develops such an elaborate program that the consequences of a disaster are practically nil, the cost would be very great. In order to manage risks so they are reduced to an acceptable level, the organization should develop a program based on reasonable judgments and on a careful cost-risk-benefit analysis. Making reasonable judgments concerning the business consequences resulting from the loss of vital information constitutes a *qualitative* approach to risk analysis. If the organization wishes to adopt a

FIGURE 4.2 Vital Records Summary Sheet

VITAL RECORDS SUMMARY SHEET *Administrative Records for Off-Site Storage*							
					Cost		
Code	Description	Recommended Protector	Routing to Records Center	Records Center Retention	Initial	Annual Maintenance	Total
001	Articles of Incorporation	RC	Initial	Permanent	$10	$10	$20
002	Constitution and Bylaws	Forward to RC	As Issued	Permanent	10	15	25
003	Copyrights	Copy to RC	As Issued	Permanent	12	12	24

more *quantitative* approach, the following formula[3] may be used:

$$R = P \times C$$

where

    R = *risk*, sometimes referred to as the annualized loss expectancy (ALE)

    P = *probability* that such a loss will be sustained in any given year; the likelihood of such an occurrence based on available historical or other data

    C = *cost* of the loss, usually the cost to replace the information so that it can be used to resume normal business operations.

The result of these calculations is the probable annual dollar loss that the organization would experience should it lose the information contained in a particular records series. This type of quantitative risk analysis is particularly useful in making decisions as to whether to protect important records of secondary protection priority. On the other hand, this analysis would not usually be performed on irreplaceable vital records of highest protection priority, since replacement is not possible and the risk of loss is unacceptable.

An example will illustrate this method of quantitative risk analysis: If the cost (C) of losing and replacing an important record is estimated at $30,000 and the probability of loss (P) is 1.0 (the loss is expected to occur an average of one time each year), the cost of the loss or replacement—the annualized risk (R)—would be $30,000. The records manager must then compare this figure to the cost of protecting the records. If the protection cost is somewhat or substantially less than the cost of loss or replacement (R), the investment in protection is justified.

The records manager can apply this formula to quantify the cost and risks associated with every records series classified as Important—Sec-

ondary Protection Priority. Sum totals can then be computed for all the records series so classified. As noted earlier, it will be evident that expenditures for special protection will be the correct business decision for many of these types of records.

SELECTING METHODS OF PROTECTING VITAL RECORDS

Having identified the approximately 2 to 7 percent of the organization's records that are worthy of protection, the records manager must decide how to protect them. There are two basic methods of protecting vital records, although there are variants of each, and a combination of methods is often used to enhance the degree of protection and further reduce the risk of loss. The two methods are *on-site* protection and *off-site* protection.

On-site protection involves protecting vital records *on the organization's premises* at or near the point of creation or use of the information. Off-site protection involves storing the original records (or more frequently a copy of the records) *in a facility remote from the organization's place of business. Duplication and dispersal*, often considered a third method of protection, is actually a variant of the off-site method, since the duplicate copies are (or should be) dispersed to an off-site location.

On-Site Protection

On-site protection of vital records consists of a variety of facilities and equipment designed to safeguard vital records housed in office buildings, plants, or other production facilities. Included are vital records buildings, standard records vaults, file rooms, and fire-resistant filing cabinets and safes. Each of these has its own protective capabilities and proper and improper uses in protecting various classes of vital records from various types of disasters.

Vital Records Buildings. A vital records or document building may be feasible for a large volume of vital records if on-site space is available. However, this type of facility may afford more protection to records if it is located off-site or in a remote area. The vital records building, whether located within a company complex or at a remote site, should be *detached* and *inconspicuous* as well as fire-resistant, and constructed of noncombustible material throughout, including floors and roof. The building should be able to withstand, without collapsing, a fire that might completely consume floor coverings and all other combustible contents. The building should have noncombustible interior equipment and adequate controls for humidity, temperature, ventilation, lighting, etc. Suitable fire extinguishing equipment and burglar alarm systems should also be installed. Its location should be carefully considered; a vital records building should never be located in an area subject to flooding, near a rail line, or in other areas subject to hazards of any kind.

Standard Records Vaults. The standard records vault is a fire-resistive enclosure constructed within an office building or other workplace and generally used for the protection of large quantities of vital records that need to be maintained on-site—as close to the users of the information as possible. Vaults are often the only practical method of fire protection in non-fire-resistant buildings. If they are located in a fire-resistive building with a sprinkler system and/or a smoke or heat detection system electronically connected to the local fire department, their protective capacity is even greater.

The purpose of the vault is to maintain an interior temperature level such that the paper records or other media housed within will not be subject to combustion or data loss for a period of time consistent with its rating in the event of a fire in the immediate vicinity of the vault. Standard records vaults may be designed to provide two, four, or six hours of protection. This means that the paper documents should remain undamaged for these periods of time; however, microfilm or computer media would deteriorate sooner. Of course, a safe or a fire-resistant file cabinet con-

taining these media could always be placed in the vault, thereby enhancing the duration of protection. The National Fire Protection Association (NFPA), which issues design and construction standards for records vaults, does not use the term *fireproof* vault, but records managers often use this term in reference to vaults having the higher four- or six-hour ratings, particularly if they are located in good buildings. These vaults should be capable of offering outstanding on-site protection against fire for the vital records housed in them.

To provide effective fire protection, the records vault must be designed and constructed in accordance with NFPA standards. These are contained in Chapter 2 of the NFPA's S*tandard for the Protection of Records.*[4] These standards prescribe characteristics of the structural components of the vault—its walls, ceiling, floor, door, and the penetrations of the enclosure required for utilities and security and protective systems. Vault doors bearing Underwriters Laboratories rating labels for two, four, and six hours are available, and it is very important that the structural components of the vault be designed to be consistent with the door rating, so that the vault can provide protection for the prescribed period of time. If the vault is to be used to house permanent archival records as well as vital ones, its heating and air conditioning systems should be capable of maintaining constant temperatures of 60°F ± 3° and a relative humidity of 50 percent ± 5 percent. For vault storage of microfilms, even dryer humidity conditions are recommended—20 to 30 percent is the optimum range specified in standards issued by the American National Standards Institute.

The National Fire Protection Association's vault standard indicates that the use of an automatic sprinkler system is optional. A decision not to install sprinklers would be based on the small probability of a fire originating within the enclosure and the considerable problems associated with water damage to the records. Of course, installation of a fire detection system should always be considered. Halon-type fire suppression systems are sometimes used in lieu of sprinkler systems in vaults, but the U.S. Environmental

Protection Agency has identified Halon as an "ozone depleter," and has called for a complete phaseout of this chemical by the year 2000.

The records manager should always ensure that every vault in his or her organization is being used properly for the purpose for which it was designed. Frequently, vaults are misused as a place to store inactive, nonvital records, office supplies, holiday decorations, etc. Vault space is expensive, and its use should be restricted to housing vital records that require on-site protection.

File Rooms for the Storage of Important Records.   File rooms are generally much larger than vaults and are significantly less fire-resistant. Standards for their design, operation, and use are contained in Chapter 3 of the NFPA's *Standard for the Protection of Records.*[5] The standard states that file rooms should not be used for protecting irreplaceable vital records; if this class of records is housed in this type of facility, the degree of protection should always be enhanced by duplication, dispersal, or other appropriate off-site protection strategies. Thus, the use of these rooms should be restricted to the organization's *important* or *useful but nonessential* records.

The NFPA standard requires the file room to be a fire-resistant enclosure with insulated openings in a fire-resistant building. The enclosure must be used exclusively for the storage of records. No combustible material is permitted in the file room, other than the records themselves. The standard requires sprinkler protection, a file room door (which should be rated by Underwriters Laboratories, Inc.), and various other design and construction details that reduce the threat of fire.

Fire-Resistant File Cabinets and Safes.   For small quantities of highly active vital records that must be maintained at or near the point of use, fire-resistant file cabinets or safes can provide good protection against fire hazards. Unfortunately, these devices are often utilized by persons who have not properly evaluated their benefits and risks in protecting vital records. Following are guidance on their use:

1. Using these devices is always better than leaving vital records unprotected and completely exposed to the hazards of fire. However, their protective capabilities are relatively low in certain situations, particularly when compared to off-site protection options, and their use may entail some degree of risk.

2. The level of risk associated with these devices depends chiefly on the environment in which they are placed. If they are used as on-site protection devices in fire-resistive buildings having excellent fire protection systems (fully sprinklered, with an early-warning smoke and/or heat detection system electronically connected to the local fire department), the level of risk may be relatively small.

3. Reliance on these devices as the *sole means* of vital records protection in non-fire-resistive buildings would expose the organization to a much higher degree of risk and may thus be considered an unwise protection strategy, particularly for the most vital and irreplaceable records. In these situations, a fire may rage out of control for time periods exceeding the protective capacities of the equipment.

4. These devices are best used for small quantities of very active vital records that need to be kept close to the users for immediate reference. Whenever possible, these devices should be used in concert with other vital records protection strategies (e.g., off-site dispersal of security copies of vital records), thereby augmenting the degree of protection and reducing the risk of loss.

Chapter 7 contains a discussion of the protective capabilities of fire-resistant file cabinets and safes, as defined by the National Fire Protection Association, Underwriters Laboratories, Inc., and other organizations which test and rate these devices.

Off-Site Security Storage of Vital Records

Off-site records protection involves storing the original vital records (or a duplicate security copy) in an off-site facility situated sufficiently remote

FIGURE 4.3 Granite Mountain Records Vault
Source: Courtesy of Church of Jesus Christ of Latter–Day Saints

FIGURE 4.4 Interior of the National Storage Company, Master Microfilm Vault
Source: Courtesy of Underground Vaults and Storage, Inc.

from the original records such that the facility would not be subject to the same disaster. Generally, this method is more reliable than on-site protection. Although a disaster could occur at either site, if the records have been duplicated and dispersed to an alternate location, the possibility of a full recovery is much greater.

Some remote facilities are owned and operated by the organization whose records are stored there. Others are owned and operated by vital records protection companies. These facilities may be detached, free-standing, above-ground structures, or they may be underground facilities converted from caves, mines, or tunnels. One well-known commercial facility was converted from ammunition bunkers that were used to store explosives during World War II. An example of a privately owned and operated vital records protection facility is shown in Figure 4.3. This facility was excavated in a granite mountain, and is used to store the vital records of the Church of

Jesus Christ of Latter-Day Saints. A commercial facility is shown in Figure 4.4.

Commercial vital records facilities are growing in popularity and are available in all parts of the United States. These facilities provide services such as private vaults built to specifications of the client, special storage in microfilm vaults, small-item storage in private vaults, special storage in magnetic tape vaults, safe deposit drawers fitted with locks in private vaults, bulk and general storage, privately operated records storage rooms, sophisticated electronic document transmission capabilities, and emergency relocation centers.

The advantages of using commercial vital records protection facilities include:

1. Greater protection and security through specialization in protecting records.
2. Easy accommodation of expanding records volume, thus eliminating long-range storage space planning.
3. A professional staff to provide fast, accurate, low-cost retrieval.
4. Availability of specialists to consult with on problems of equipment, methods, and procedures.

Considerations for selecting and operating a remote storage site, either organization-owned or commercial, include the following:

1. The records should be at a safe distance from the home office but as accessible as possible.
2. The records should be in a location controlled by the organization and available for use in an emergency as well as for regular audit.
3. The location should provide a site where company officials can establish emergency operations with survival rations and shelter for personnel.
4. The facility should be designed to minimize the risks of damage from any and all hazards to which it might be exposed: fire, flood, earthquakes, winds, etc.

5. Operating personnel should have received maximum security clearance.
6. The operating personnel should be able to provide all necessary records services.
7. In addition to regular communication channels, there should be emergency communications to connect the remote facility and the home office directly.

Duplication and Dispersal of Vital Records

There are basically two types of duplicating, each of which may involve dispersal. The first type involves *preparing extra copies when the record is created.* These copies may serve purposes other than protection. The second type of duplication is *scheduled reproduction of existing records* by any process, such as microfilming, magnetic tape or disks, or photocopy. To maximize the cost benefit, it is normally desirable to use the reproduction for a purpose other than just protection. This is often possible with microfilm.

Dispersal consists of creating duplicate hard or microform copies of records (where this is legally acceptable) and placing them in a second location for normal business needs. The dispersal method can be *built-in* or *improvised.* Built-in or existing dispersal means that copies of records are created in the normal course of business and routinely dispersed to remote locations. For example, copies of vital records produced and stored at a branch office of an organization may also be stored and used in the home office, thereby reducing the risk of loss. Also, copies may be held in a statutory office of record such as the courthouse for land titles. To have direct access to records held by such a statutory custodian, it is necessary to maintain inventory lists of these vital records.

The federal government serves as a depository of duplicate records such as defense contracts, income tax records, social security records, etc. State governments have copies of motor vehicle registrations, income tax returns, and other records. Banks, insurance companies, law firms, and accounting firms may also be sources of duplicate records.

To be effective, built-in dispersal must be regular and ongoing. There must also be some assurance that copies of the records can be obtained promptly when needed in postdisaster activities. Routine, or built-in, dispersal should be given careful consideration because it usually involves little additional cost for the organization.

Improvised or *designed dispersal* may take the form of creating an extra copy specifically for dispersal to a remote location for vital records protection purposes. The extra-copy method is more economical than duplicating after creation, because it employs existing office procedures and requires little additional expense.

At the outset of the vital records protection program, it is always necessary to reproduce a number of existing documents of which there are no extra copies. If, during the normal use of records, multiple copies are not and cannot be created, provision must be made for reproduction on an on-going basis. Photocopy reproduction of limited numbers of documents at scattered locations is satisfactory; but microfilming is usually preferred for large volumes. Microfilm is used when the nature or volume of the records is such that filming is the most feasible means of duplication.

The process of microfilming is fast, and microfilm requires little storage space. The use of microfilm and computer tape for storing information can reduce storage space requirements by as much as 98 percent. Where micrographics production capabilities are available, they may offer the safest and most economical method of vital records protection. Microfilm does require special storage considerations, however, for it is subject to damage or destruction at temperatures exceeding 200°F. There is potential danger in storing microfilm in insulated file cabinets, safes, or vaults constructed with a crystalline insulating material. This material generates interior steam when heated by fire, and the steam raises the interior temperature. If microfilm is stored in such equipment, steam may enter the microfilm containers and destroy the records.

If the microfilm is packed in airtight storage containers before it is placed in a safe or vault where there is danger of steam damage, greater protection is provided because the airtight container retards the passage of steam to the microfilm.

PROTECTING VITAL ELECTRONIC RECORDS

Computers and the information in them constitute a critically important asset of any business. The protection and security of this asset must be a top priority of every vital records protection and disaster recovery program. Thus, we will consider the protection and security of personal computers (PCs) since these types of computers are of immediate concern to the records manager. We will also take a brief look at vital records protection in larger computing environments such as mainframe systems.

Protection and Security of PC-Based Records

As was noted in Chapter 1, it is estimated that, in 1993, there was an installed base of approximately 45 million microcomputers in the United States. This is expected to increase to 65 million units by 1995; the growth rate of these devices is estimated at somewhere between 12 and 20 million new units installed each year. The magnetic and optical storage media utilized with these devices store an unknown but tremendous quantity of business documents and data, some of which would be considered vital. Almost every business is extremely dependent on these electronic recordkeeping systems, but very few such systems have been subject to proper vital records protection and disaster recovery measures. Traditional and new approaches for the protection, security, and recovery of PC-based records are discussed below. Records managers are often called upon to develop PC-records protection programs, so an understanding of these measures is a must.

Importance of PC-Data Backup. The single most important action any business can take to provide for the protection and security of PC-based records is to perform regular and frequent backups. These backups are necessary to protect the records from hard-disk "crashes" (the disk self-destructs), resulting in the instant destruction of all documents and data residing on the disk. It has been said that there are only two kinds of microcomputer users—those who have lost data from a crash or from other causes, and those who are going to lose some or all their data. Thus, these backups should be considered a mandatory component of all microcomputer system operations.

A good backup capability enables backup to any logical drive—another hard disk, a network drive, or removable media—and of multiple drives in a single operation. Backing up to tape is much faster and easier than backing up to diskettes; it permits any type of backup to be performed in a single operation. Tape cartridges are also easier to transport and keep track of.

Types and Frequency of PC-Data Backups.

With respect to method and frequency, there are three basic options[6] for backing up PC-based records: *full system, incremental,* and *differential.*

1. *Full-system backup.* A full-system backup produces a duplicate security copy of all hard-disk files (or all files selected by the user), including all data files and software resident on the system each time the backup is performed. In the event of a system crash, the user can restore all data files and software to get the system back on-line. This backup routine, while essential, can be very time consuming and require many diskettes. Most users consider one full system backup per week or even per month to be adequate. However, if large quantities of very vital data reside on the system, the highest degree of protection can be afforded by making two or even three complete backup sets daily or as frequently as possible, alternating them between on-site and off-site locations.

2. *Differential backups.* This back-up routine involves making backup copies of all files that have been changed or updated since the last full backup, e.g., every day or every week. In this case, the differential backup can be used to restore the entire system, using only the full system backup plus the differential backup. Thus, the old and updated files would be contained on these two sets of backup media.

3. *Incremental backups.* This PC backup routine is used to copy only the files that have changed since the last incremental backup. This procedure greatly reduces the time and media requirements. Full system restoration thus requires restoring the most recent full system backup copy, and then successively restoring each incremental backup copy containing the changed records.

Backups of PC-Data on Local Area Networks.

Local Area Networks (LANs) are a popular computing strategy. The installed base of LANs was estimated at 600,000 sites in 1993, and at least 16 million microcomputers are connected to them in American business. A tremendous quantity of vital electronic records reside on these PC networks; thus, every PC-LAN must have a viable data protection strategy. For a centralized network-wide backup strategy, tape cartridge media provide sufficient storage capacities for large quantities of vital LAN-based data. Optical-disk-based systems can also be used for network-wide backup.[7] Or, individual LAN users can be responsible for performing their own data backups, using the methods discussed for PC-based records.

Regardless of the particular backup strategy selected, the records manager must prepare a policy clearly delineating responsibilities to perform these backups, including a way to assure compliance.

Software Backup Options for Vital PC Records.

There are a variety of software backup options from which to choose,[8] described below.

1. *Use of operating software's backup utilities.* The simplest option to PC data backups is to utilize the backup commands provided with the PC's operating software and back up all or selected documents and data resident on the hard drive to removable floppy diskettes, which would then be stored on-site or off-site. In single-user installations with small amounts of vital PC records, this approach can work well. However, this is the slowest method of PC data backup, and it is prone to errors. Moreover, the operating software may provide little flexibility in allowing the user to select which files are vital and require backup.

2. *Use of special backup software.* A much better option is to use special PC backup software which can be purchased from software vendors. These relatively inexpensive programs are generally easier and faster to use, and offer features such as error detection and the ability to control tape backup units. They are designed to automate the backup process from hard disk to removable diskettes (or tape cartridges or cassettes), and they support restoration of data to the hard disk. The best programs can restore information from a damaged disk, back up data from multiple or logical drives (including tape drives), and provide good error detection and recovery.

3. *Use of automatic, on-line backup software.* The most advanced PC backup software is designed to operate on-line, with a minimum of user intervention. The user preselects the vital PC data to be backed up and specifies the backup frequency. At the designated backup intervals, the software automatically scans the hard disks of all PC's protected by the system, and recognizes any new or updated files. The vital data is then compressed and encrypted, and is transmitted via standard telephone lines to a remote protection site. The software vendor charges the user or subscriber a fee that includes the software license fee and a specified amount of backup time, with surcharges for additional time. The subscribers are provided with on-line access to their stored files, and upon request, the vendor can deliver the backup files to the customer on various forms of duplicate media: floppy disks, tapes, optical disk, or hard-disk drives. Future options to this PC data protection technology are likely to include high-speed mo-

dem transmission (satellite or fiber optic modems) and the capability of backing up scanned images of documents and data resident on PC-based optical disk systems.[9]

On-Site Storage of Removable Media

Of all the record storage media used today, diskettes are the most vulnerable to loss of data if they are exposed to strong magnetic fields or elevated temperature and humidity conditions. For diskettes, specially designed fire-resistive storage cabinets can be used as an on-site protection method. An example of a fire-resistant safe for magnetic media is shown in Figure 4.5.

Records managers should give careful consideration to the risks that may be associated with reliance on these devices. If the building in which the cabinets are placed has excellent fire protection, the risk of loss of data on the media in the cabinets may be minimal. On the other hand, if the building has no sprinkler system or smoke and heat detectors, the records manager may not wish to rely upon these cabinets as the sole protection strategy for the vital PC diskettes containing irreplaceable data. In these situations, off-site storage of vital diskettes should be considered to augment the degree of protection, since the severity

FIGURE 4.5 Fire–Resistant Safe
Source: Courtesy of Diebold, Incorporated

and duration of a fire may well exceed the protective capability afforded by these devices.

PC Security Against Human and Technical Threats

Human and technical threats, such as malicious tampering and computer viruses, can also destroy PC-based records or make them irretrievable.

Password Protection. This procedure is perhaps the most common means of protecting PC data against access by unauthorized persons. It is used to make PC data files irretrievable by persons who do not know the proper password character code, which is required to access designated data resident on the system. PC software can be programmed so that data files are compressed or encrypted with a password key assigned to a designated individual. Where PC hardware is concerned, passwords can also be used to make the operation of the computer itself impossible.[10] Passwords are generally used to assign privileges of system access and operation to employees who have a need to perform designated functions. Generally, the system administrator and other technical personnel who are responsible for the entire system may have unrestricted password access to the system, while data entry personnel are authorized only to enter data and users are authorized only to retrieve and view data.

Records managers should take appropriate measures to protect the integrity of passwords for all electronic recordkeeping systems under their jurisdiction. Passwords should never be displayed on the computer screen. No printed list of passwords should ever be posted or displayed in the office near the PC workstations. If a master list of passwords is maintained in a text file on the system, it should be encrypted. Passwords should be changed at regular intervals, and they must be invalidated whenever an employee's status changes.[11]

Computer Viruses. A computer "virus"—a computer program that can insert a copy of itself

into another program—can cause the corruption of vital electronic records, and appropriate safeguards should be in place to prevent the introduction of a virus into the organization's electronic recordkeeping systems. Most viruses are believed to originate in corrupted software procured from external sources and installed on an organization's computers. The virus's ability to replicate itself can result in its spread throughout an entire computer system or network. Some viruses are designed to modify or delete all or selected data files resident on hard disks or other storage media; others can cause software failures, damage hardware components, or prevent the recording of data. A virus can also be time-sensitive and not cause damage until sometime in the future.

Special security procedures should be implemented to prevent the contamination of vital electronic records by computer viruses. Because corrupted software is the source of most viruses, proper controls should be in place to manage software acquisition and use. No software of unknown origin should ever be used by an organization, and newly purchased software should be tested by antiviral programs if there is any reason to suspect infection. Infected computers and copies of potentially infected software programs should be removed from service, and infected workstations should be disconnected from workstations.[12]

Vital Records Protection in Large Computing Environments

Information protection in large mainframe or minicomputer computing environments is seldom a records management responsibility. This duty typically rests with data processing personnel assigned to the computer services or MIS department. However, records management personnel need to have a working knowledge of this aspect of information protection.

Traditional Magnetic Tape Backup Systems. For several decades, magnetic tape backup with off-site rotation of updated files has been the primary method of safeguarding vital mainframe-based computer records. More recently, write-once and rewritable optical disks have been used for backup of vital data recorded on fixed magnetic disk drives. The very high storage capacities of optical disks make these media particularly suitable for backing up large tape libraries, thereby reducing the number of backup media required and increasing the efficiency of the backup process.[13]

As in PC-computing environments, backup routines are performed for selected vital data, or full-system backups may be performed for all data files and system documentation. Again, the backup routines vary in frequency: daily, weekly, or three times a week are most common.

Electronic Vaulting. The traditional off-line approaches described above make the organization vulnerable to the loss of critical data between backups. Regardless of how frequently tape backups are generated and shipped off-site, if the organization's data center is destroyed or is otherwise inoperable, all on-line transactions entered since the last backup may be lost. This risk is particularly great in businesses that are *transaction-processing intensive.* Examples are large financial institutions, brokerage houses, credit card firms, and airlines, which are heavily dependent on on-line transaction processing systems that are critical to the survival of the business. The nature of worldwide financial systems in the global economy, with trading markets in London, New York, and Tokyo, allows no practical window of time to bring on-line transaction processing systems down to generate tape backups. Moreover, the loss of only a few hours transactions between daily backups can mean millions of dollars of lost revenue in these situations. The only good answer to minimizing these risks lies in the newest technology for mainframe data protection: on-line electronic vaulting.

This method of protecting mainframe-based computer data provides for the on-line, real-time duplication and transfer of critical data to a remote CPU, tape drive, or other device. Thus, the risk of data loss between backups is eliminated

(or greatly minimized) since the critical data are transferred to a remote site on a near real-time basis. The basic technology to accomplish on-line electronic vaulting has been available for some years, but because of the slow speed and high cost of transmitting large volumes of backup data via standard telecommunications links, the practice was not an economically viable backup strategy for many organizations. However, two recent developments are bringing electronic vaulting within reach of a much larger body of mainframe users: a decline in the cost of high-speed digital communications links and the parallel development of new electronic vaulting software, which has been greatly improved in both price and performance.[14]

AFTER THE DISASTER: RECOVERY OF DAMAGED RECORDS

In order to be complete, an organization's disaster recovery plan must include a section on the recovery of vital records and other damaged records media. The organization's disaster recovery teams should have comprehensive guidance on what to do "when the smoke clears and the waters recede"; as soon as the office building is declared safe to enter, they must know how to prevent further damage to any records that have not been completely destroyed, and how to salvage and recover damaged records media so that they can be restored to their original business use. The records manager will play a key role in this process because recovery of the paper records, microfilms, and diskettes that may have been damaged will usually fall under his or her area of responsibility.

The Records Recovery Plan

The atmosphere during and immediately following any business disaster is generally one of controlled chaos. Managers and executives often intermingle with police, firefighters, medical personnel, and journalists at the disaster site. This chaos can be minimized if the records recovery plan contains the organization's master list of vital records, the precise floor, room, and cabinet location of these records, and the location of keys to open locked rooms, cabinets, safes, and vaults so that the recovery teams can access these records. The vital records master list should also show which vital records have been backed up, the off-site location of these records, and instructions for obtaining the records so that they can be used to conduct business as soon as the situation demands.

The records recovery plan must also include detailed recovery measures for wet record media. Water damage to records is a factor in at least 90 percent of all records-related disasters, and most wet paper records and microfilm and some wet computer media can be successfully restored. Finally, the plan must indicate which vital records have top priority for recovery purposes, how to stabilize the environment to prevent further damage to the records, and how to salvage the damaged media.

A records recovery checklist in the disaster recovery plan usually contains the following information:

- The names and phone numbers of disaster recovery team members and their backups.
- The names and phone numbers of document restoration experts and companies with vacuum chambers, freezing facilities, or fumigation capabilities.
- The names and phone numbers of companies having large portable fans and dehumidifiers for rent.
- A designation of locations to which damaged records can be relocated for air drying and other restoration measures.

With a good records disaster recovery plan, the records manager and other members of the records recovery team will be prepared to begin the recovery process as soon as they are given access to the damaged facilities.

The First Priority: Prevent Further Damage to Records

The first 48 to 72 hours following the disaster are the most critical in terms of whether the recovery efforts will be successful. Thus, restoration efforts must be executable within these time frames if they are to be successful.[15] The prime objective during this initial recovery period is to remove the records from the disaster site and relocate them to an environment where further damage will be minimized and restoration can begin. An ideal relocation environment is a cool and dry one, with temperatures of less than 60°F and a relative humidity of about 45 percent. This will retard the growth of mold and mildew and provide a longer period of time for restoration. During the planning process, the records manager must identify an appropriate relocation site and make provisions to enable the emergency transfer of all damaged records to it. The recovery site should usually be in close proximity to the organization's offices, but it must not be vulnerable to the same disaster affecting the prime site.

Records Removal from the Disaster Site

Records removal is often a very time-consuming and difficult task. Dry office records weigh approximately 30 pounds per cubic foot, but water-soaked, their weight can increase to 60 or more pounds. Removing hundreds of cubic feet of wet records down stairwells when no elevator service is available can be a tremendous task. The records recovery plan must contain a detailed plan for accomplishing this. The following steps should be considered:

1. Remove irreplaceable vital records of highest recovery priority first, including any indexes or inventories required to access these records.
2. Remove all active records currently being used by office personnel for in-process work, even though these records might not have been damaged or classified as vital on the

vital records master list. A list of these records must often be developed at the disaster site.

3. Next, remove all other vital records appearing on the vital records master list, beginning with the wettest records, which will often be found in the basement or on the lowest floors.

4. Lastly, remove nonvital records on a priority basis, beginning with the wettest first.

5. Do not open file cabinets still hot to the touch. Delayed ignition (spontaneous combustion) can occur when drawers of hot cabinets are suddenly opened.

6. If possible, transport entire file cabinets intact, or remove file drawers without disturbing their contents.

Initial Restoration Steps at the Recovery Site

Once the records have been transported to the recovery site, restoration can begin. The initial restoration strategy will depend on whether there is sufficient time and resources to work with a given quantity of damaged records. If the temperature and humidity are high, the quantity of water-soaked records is large, and resources are limited, it may be necessary to freeze some or all the wet records in order to buy time for a full recovery.

Wet records can be placed in a freezing compartment to prevent further deterioration and provide more time to arrange for permanent restoration. The records can be frozen indefinitely, but they must be restored immediately upon removal. The records disaster recovery plan should include provisions for freezing facilities if temperature and humidity conditions in the area warrant this measure.

If the wet records are threatened by mold and mildew, fungicides such as thymol, Formalin, or o-phenyl can be used to retard their growth, but these chemicals can pose health hazards and must be handled with care; their use is best left to professional document conservators.

If the records have been damaged by fire, full recovery is much less probable than damage by water. Although some restoration is possible, the technical assistance of a professional document conservator will usually be required.

Air-Drying Paper Records

Water-damaged paper records can be successfully restored and returned to business use by means of air-drying. This restoration method is most effective if the records are damp but not completely soaked, when the records are not threatened by mold or mildew, when the quantity of records is relatively small, and a full recovery can be completed within 72 hours.

Air-drying is a very simple process: The records should be placed in a cool, dry room and removed from file cabinets or other containers so as to provide maximum exposure to the flow of air. Large fans are used to circulate air over the records. Heated fans can be used in cold temperature conditions.

Vacuum Drying Water-Soaked Records

In cases where air-drying is not feasible, vacuum drying may provide the best means of restoring water-damaged paper records, particularly if a large quantity of very wet records must be restored. There are three methods of vacuum drying for paper records: *vacuum freeze drying, thermal vacuum freeze drying,* and *vacuum drying.* Each of these methods uses airless chambers to remove the water from the records, and although the methods vary, the basic principle is the same: The wet records are placed in the chamber, the air is then removed from the chamber, and a negative air pressure is created. The water on the records is vaporized—it is converted from a liquid to a vapor—and is then expelled from the chamber as steam, leaving the records dry.[16]

A number of commercial companies provide this type of document restoration service; the records disaster recovery plan must include their names and phone numbers so that they can be contacted quickly.

Recovery of Water-Damaged Microfilms

Microfilm, microfiche, and other photographic-based records media can often be successfully restored if they have been water-soaked but not exposed to elevated temperatures. These media are imperiled at temperatures in excess of 150°F. Duplicate copies of microfilms of vital records (or the original master films) should *always* be stored in a secure, off-site location for security purposes. However, if water-soaked microfilms require restoration, recovery operations can be mobilized at a film processing lab or microfilm service bureau. Wet silver halide or emulsion films should be kept in clean cold water. Care should be taken to preserve the integrity of carton labels containing index data, without which the document images cannot be accessed. The wet films must then be reprocessed and duplicated onto new silver film if archival quality is required.   Wet vesicular and diazo copy films can also be successfully recovered if they have not been exposed to high temperatures. These can be washed in cool water and dried with paper towels. These microfilms may, of course, require no recovery if their masters exist in undamaged condition.

Recovery of Magnetic Media

Removable magnetic media can also be salvaged if they are water-soaked but have not been exposed to high temperatures. There are, in fact, instances in which magnetic tapes have been fully recovered and returned to service after having been fully immersed in unclean river water for a period of two weeks. The integrity of the data on magnetic tapes is imperiled at temperatures in excess of 150°F, and diskettes (the most vulnerable of all record media) are threatened with loss of data at 125°F or a relative humidity exceeding 80 percent. The recovery of fixed magnetic disks is, of course, much more problematic if they have been exposed to either water or high temperatures. Such media are generally unrestorable.

Assuming no backup media are available, the restoration of water-damaged magnetic tapes is accomplished by hand-drying the tapes with lint-free cloths; then running them through a tape cleaner or winder (but not on a regular tape drive); then running them over cleaning tissues. When the tapes are reasonably dry, they should be run over the tissues *and* the blades, and then read and copied onto new media.

Water-soaked diskettes should be kept in cool distilled water, dried with lint-free towels, and then copied onto new diskettes, if they have not been warped or magnetically damaged.

VITAL RECORDS PROGRAM IMPLEMENTATION

Once the vital records protection program has been approved and the methods of protection have been selected, procedures must be established covering the use of records in daily activities, in emergencies, and after disasters. These procedures assume that ordinary common-sense precautions for the protection of records will be observed, as well as special procedures for vital records.

Secret or confidential records can be secured by storing them in containers or areas with key or combination locks different from those in general use. Only authorized personnel should have access to these records. The transmittal of confidential records, whether by messenger, mail, or facsimile, should be safeguarded by such precautions as locked pouches, sealed containers, and the use of bonded personnel. Drills to train employees in what to do with records in emergencies are recommended.

To ensure the completeness of preparations for postdisaster activity, some companies test the procedures established for the vital records program by simulating the effects of a disaster. Key personnel are sent to the dispersal site (vital records storage location) where they participate in the reconstruction of records and continuance of operations. This type of exercise has frequently pointed out the need for additional records to be classified as vital, as well as the need for changes in facilities or equipment.

VITAL RECORDS MASTER LIST

Page _____ of _____ (1)

Department (2) _____ Section (3) _____ Effective Date (4) _____

Department No, (5) _____ Schedule No. (6) _____ Revision No. (7) _____

(8) Item No.	(9) VR Code	(10) Record Title	(11) Form or Rpt.No.	(12) Size Inches Hor.	Vert.	(13) Protection Instructions	(14) Method	(15) Class	(16) Freq.	(17) RC Re-tention

FIGURE 4.6   Vital Records Master List

Vital Records Master List

In implementing the vital records program, a *vital records master list* is recommended. This master list provides each department with a complete list of all vital records for which it is responsible. The records management department should maintain a complete set of master lists, stored in the vital records center. The complete list describes those records that would be needed to maintain essential operations following a disaster, to recreate the company's legal and financial positions, and to meet obligations to stockholders, employees, and outside interests. Figure 4.6 is an example of a vital records master list.

Transfer of Vital Records

Most records are transferred to vital records centers on a weekly or monthly basis, although some companies, notably banks, find it desirable to transfer certain vital records daily. Collection points within the company should be established.

Vital records are destroyed regularly as specified on the vital records master list. Those vital records that are to serve later as retention copies are transferred to inactive records. No records should be destroyed without notifying the originating department of the intent to destroy them. This is necessary because status of the records may change while they are in storage.

FIGURE 4.8   Records Maintenance Program Card Envelope

FIGURE 4.7   Vital Records Control Card

VITAL RECORDS CONTROL CARD

Dates of Receipts (1)	Box Control (2)	Remarks (3)
	Retention (4)	Scheduled/ Item No. (5)
	Code (6)	Title (7)
	Division (8)	Form Report No. (9) Frequency (10)

Vital Records Control Card
FORM 5982-2

RECORDS MAINTENANCE PROGRAM CARD ENVELOPE

From:

Department _____   Record Title _____

Division _____   _____

Name _____   Inclusive Dates of Contents

Title _____   _____

Business Month _____

Package Serial No. _____

To: VITAL RECORDS CENTER

RMPCE
FORM NO. 5982-7

FIGURE 4.9   Records Maintenance Program Card

An audit of vital records to determine compliance with the vital records protection program should be made periodically. The audit consists of reviewing the dates on the records maintenance program cards or the vital records control cards and comparing the date of receipt of documents with the frequency noted on the vital records master list. Figures 4.7, 4.8, and 4.9 illustrate types of transfer forms.

The Vital Records Manual

Establishing procedures for the operations of the vital records protection program is useless if these procedures are not understood and followed by all concerned. Maintaining communications about the program is one of the prime responsibilities of the records manager.

Communication may take the form of written procedures, informal memorandums about new developments, seminars for department heads or persons responsible for the vital records in departments, or visits to the vital records center. A vital records manual, published separately or as part of the records management manual, is perhaps the best tool of communication.

The manual may be divided into three parts. The first part should describe the procedures of the vital records protection program and list its objectives. In the second part, the vital records master list should be explained. The third part should be devoted to instructions for reconstructing vital records in the event of a disaster and the use of equipment that would be available. Chapter 16 contains a detailed discussion of this type of records management manual.

SUMMARY

Vital records protection and disaster recovery planning are, it can be argued, the most important tasks that records managers accomplish on behalf of their organizations. This is because the very survival of the organization—its continued viability as a business entity—may depend upon whether critical business records have been protected and are available for use immediately following a disaster. Without vital operating records, the business may not be able to service existing customers, secure new ones, manufacture products, borrow money, collect debts from its creditors, enforce its contracts, defend itself against liability lawsuits, or even recover the losses it has sustained in the disaster on insurance claims.

Vital records contain information needed to reestablish or continue an organization in the event of a disaster. They are necessary to recreate the company's legal and financial position and preserve the rights of the company and its employees, customers, shareholders, or other client groups. Vital records are irreplaceable, and they are required to operate the business; the organization could not operate without them. *Disaster recovery planning* consists of the advance planning and preparations which are necessary to minimize loss and ensure continuity of the critical business functions of an organization in the event of a disaster. Both functions involve the security of the vital information assets of an organization, and the records manager must possess extensive knowledge of both in order to discharge his or her duties responsibly.

Safeguarding vital records involves protecting them against natural and human-caused disasters to which an organization may be exposed. The objective is not to completely eliminate these hazards and their resultant business risk, but to reduce them to a level considered to be acceptable to the organization's management. Although a vital records protection program can be developed as an independent effort, it is usually best to develop the program as one component of the organization's larger disaster recovery planning program. Such an approach will often require the records manager to lead or serve on an organization-wide disaster recovery committee.

In identifying an organization's vital records, the records manager must distinguish between those that are truly vital to operate the business, as compared to those that are important or merely useful. Generally, only a small percentage of an organization's records are vital—2 to 7 percent is average for most types of organizations. Some important but replaceable records will, however, be found to be worthy of special protection against loss, based on an analysis of the cost of protection as compared to the cost of replacement.

Vital business records are protected by a combination of on-site protection strategies (e.g., storage in safes, vaults, or fire-resistant file cabinets) and off-site methods of protection (e.g., dispersal of security copies, with storage in company-owned or commercial records protection facilities). Frequently, a combination of these approaches is employed to enhance the degree of protection. Microfilming is often used as a vital records protection medium because large volumes of vital documents can be filmed and stored off-site easily.

Records managers must often devise strategies for protecting vital records on electronic media, particularly those residing on microcomputers and PC networks. A variety of backup routines and special software are available to safeguard vital PC-based records.

The records manager must also develop programs for PC security against human and technical threats. Password protection and security procedures against computer viruses are common strategies. On-line electronic vaulting is an increasingly popular data protection strategy in mainframe computing environments.

The records manager must develop a records disaster recovery plan for the recovery of paper records, microfilm, and electronic records media that may be damaged during a disaster. These records media can often be successfully restored and returned to their normal business use, particularly if they have not been damaged by fire or otherwise exposed to intense heat. Common recovery methods include air-drying and various vacuum drying techniques for water-damaged paper records, reprocessing for microfilm, and various cleaning and reprocessing procedures for removable magnetic media.

Implementation of the vital records protection program requires the development of a variety of written operating procedures, tests, and audits, all designed to evaluate the ability of the program to perform successfully under simulated postdisaster scenarios.

QUESTIONS FOR DISCUSSION

1. What hazards do vital records protection programs safeguard against?

2. Describe the basic legal principle that is relevant to corporate liability resulting from a disaster.

3. What use can the records manager make of the classification of potential disasters?

4. How does the National Fire Protection Association differentiate *vital* and *important* records?

5. What information does the vital records analysis sheet provide?

6. Describe some questions the records manager should pose to a department manager during a vital records interview.

7. What are the two commonly used methods of records protection?

8. What is the difference between *built-in* dispersal and *improvised* dispersal?

9. How can microfilm be used to safeguard vital records?

10. In what ways are hazards to microfilm records different from the hazards to paper records?

11. What are some criteria for selecting and using insulated records storage equipment in protecting vital records?

12. Describe the conditions under which remote storage of records would be chosen to safeguard vital records.

13. What factors are considered in the selection of a remote storage site?

14. List and describe several characteristics of electronic records that pose special problems in terms of their protection as vital records.

15. What are some of the advantages of using a commercial vital records protection company?

16. List and describe three commonly used backup procedures for PC records.

17. List and describe the three major categories of PC backup software.

18. What is the principal advantage of on-line electronic vaulting in comparison to traditional tape backup methods of data protection?

19. What is the purpose of the vital records master list?

20. What information should the vital records manual contain?

PROJECTS

1. Select a prominent industry in your area. Interview several records managers who work for these companies to determine what types of vital records protection programs are implemented. Write a brief report of your study. State some generalizations that will answer these questions: Is a particular type of vital records protection program more common than others? Do the records protection programs vary with the size of the organizations? If dispersal is used, are records dispersed within or outside the organization? Do the protection programs include electronic records media? Do the programs have a plan for the postdisaster recovery of damaged records media?

2. Determine which companies in your area use the following protection methods:

   a. Vital records building
      (1) On-site
      (2) Off-site
   b. Commercial vital records protection company
   c. Standard records vault
   d. Safe
   e. Fire-resistant file cabinets

   Present your findings through the use of a table or chart.

3. Review the literature for descriptions and pictures of underground records storage facilities. Prepare a table showing the advantages of each *or* the differences between company-owned and commercial facilities.

4. Review the product literature and trade publications for commercial software programs designed to back up vital PC data. Prepare a table showing the advantages and disadvantages of each product.

5. Prepare a checklist of the resources in your community for the recovery of damaged records media.

CASE PROBLEM

You are the new records manager of the American Export Corporation. You have submitted a proposal to your senior management to develop a vital records protection and disaster recovery plan, but the proposal and its associated expenditures have not yet been approved. Early one hot July morning, fire breaks out in the corporate headquarters building. The damage assessment reveals the following:

1. The fire started in the basement and spread to the first two floors before it was contained.

2. The basement was flooded and many old, archival-type records stored there were destroyed; others are completely water-soaked.

3. The Overseas Export Orders and the Export Customs History files on the first and second floors were largely destroyed, although some are slightly charred but water-soaked.

4. The PC network on each of the affected floors was destroyed; officials have not yet determined the backup status of the electronic records on this LAN.

5. Several standalone PCs on the third and fourth floors have their backup diskettes stored on-site, are unprotected, and have been water-soaked.

6. The Accounting Department's microfilm room on the fourth floor contains large quantities of water-soaked microfilm, some original master microfilms, others copy films.

The fire officials have declared the building safe to enter.

1. Describe your actions during the next three to four days. You must provide the details of your disaster recovery actions and explain why they are required to deal with this disaster.

2. Describe how a vital records protection program and disaster recovery plan could have minimized the damage resulting from this fire.

NOTES

1. *Standard for the Protection of Records* (Quincy, Mass. National Fire Protection Association, NFPA 232, 1991), p. 13.

2. See Randall C. Miller, "Your Legal Liability in a Corporate Disaster," *Contingency Journal,* Jan.–Mar. 1990; Michael H. Agranoff, "Personal Liability for IS Disasters," *Contingency Journal,* Oct.–Dec. 1990; and Eileen S. Wesselingh, "Regulatory Standards: Their Impact on Information Systems and Your Potential Liability," *Contingency Journal,* July–Sept. 1990.

3. William Saffady, *Managing Electronic Records* (Prairie Village, Kansas: ARMA International, 1992), pp. 119–120.

4. *Standard for the Protection of Records*, pp. 6–9.

5. Ibid., pp. 9–11.

6. John T. Phillips, CRM, *Organizing and Archiving Files and Records on Microcomputers* (Prairie Village, Kansas: ARMA International, 1992), pp. 34–35.

7. Saffady, pp. 127–128.

8. David Fogle, "No Sweat Backup Software," *PC World,* July 1991, pp. 181–194.

9. Richard Newman, "PC Backup Technology Arrives," *Disaster Recovery Journal,* Jan./Feb./Mar. 1990, pp. 53, 64.

10. Phillips, p. 34.

11. Saffady, pp. 124–125.

12. Ibid., p. 125.

13. Ibid., pp. 127–128.

14. Tom Flesher, "Electronic Vaulting Alternatives," *Disaster Recovery Journal,* Apr./May/June 1990, pp. 32–34.

15. Julia Niebuhr Eulenberg, *Handbook for the Recovery of Water Damaged Business Records* (Prairie Village, Kansas: ARMA International, 1986), p. 12.

16. Eric G. Lundquist, *Salvage of Water Damaged Books, Documents, Micrographics and Magnetic Media* (San Francisco: Document Reprocessors Publications, 1986), pp. 31–38. See also William Spawn, "After the Water Comes," *Bulletin of the Pennsylvania Library Association,* Vol. 28, No. 6, Nov. 1973, pp. 242–251 and Peter Waters, *Procedures for Salvage of Water-Damaged Library Materials* (Washington, D.C.: Library of Congress, 2d ed, 1979).

Xerox Corporation

**Establishment of a Records
Management Program**

Xerox Corporation is a manufacturing company doing business in a global market. Known as the "Document Company," Xerox is involved in every step of document processing. The company has more than 100,000 employees worldwide.

Xerox Records Management has been in existence since 1964 and is headquartered in Rochester, New York. The activity is responsible for consulting, design and development of the corporate retention schedule, file management (hard copy and electronic), vital records, archives and museum, and Records Centers. There are two Records Centers. The larger is in Rochester, and a satellite Records Center is located in El Segundo, California. The Rochester facility contains 111,000 cubic feet of hard-copy storage, 12 million disk pages of optical-disk storage, and 9,000 nine-inch tape cartridges. The latter are used for disaster recovery.

William Olsten Award Winner for 1992

Xerox Corporation was selected as the 1992 winner of the William Olsten Award in the Major Corporation category, based on its total records management operations and its advancements in information technology. Xerox has one of the largest and most sophisticated networks in the United States. The network spans 40,000 workstations, all capable of storing electronic records on optical disk. Xerox was cited as an example of a company on the cutting edge of records-management progress.

**Xerox Corporate Records
Management Policy**

Records are to be retained and protected as long as needed for normal business operations and as long as required to fulfill Xerox Corporation's obligations to its shareholders, customers, employees, governmental agencies, and the general public.

It is Records Management's responsibility to ensure proper retention and protection of all necessary records, provide for safe and economical storage, and ensure prompt disposition of records which have outlived their usefulness.

Records Management Program

All records management services for Xerox are provided by its Corporate Records Management section. In addition, Xerox Records Management offers consulting services to companies outside Xerox in establishing and implementing effective records-management programs.

Xerox Records Management is responsible for the following specific functions:

- Development and maintenance of the Corporate Records Retention Schedule
- Customer training
- Customized retention schedules for individual departments
- Consultation on international records-management policies
- Records inventory analysis
- Records storage-equipment analysis
- Establishment and maintenance of standard filing procedures (Uniform Filing Classification System)
- Records disposition
- Management summary reporting
- Consultation for external customers
- Secure and economical records storage in all formats (hard copy/electronic/lmicrofilm/magnetic tapes/etc.)
- Electronic records retention on and retrieval from optical disk
- Vital records protection
- Records retrieval service
- Records destruction
- Archives/Xerox historical collection

Records Management has increased its visibility and recognition within Xerox by demonstrating the synergy between Records Management's goals and corporate goals. The integration of electronics in scanning, digitizing, faxing, ordering, transmitting, storage, archiving, design, and on-line fulfillment attests to the corporate commitment of emphasizing continuous improvement in Xerox's records management.

Xerox is currently changing its Records Management operation from a totally centralized organization to a combination of centralized and decentralized operations. It is continuing to maintain a central staff that is responsible for policy development, retention-schedule maintenance, consulting, training, and advanced technological studies. The decentralized operations will consist of a team of over 1,000 records coordinators throughout the corporation, who will be responsible and accountable for compliance with the Xerox Records Management Policy.

PART II

Active Records Management

Chapter 5

Uniform File Classification
Systems

OVERVIEW OF UNIFORM FILE CLASSIFICATION SYSTEMS

File systems consist of documents, file folders, and files dispersed throughout the organization. These systems usually take into account incoming and outgoing correspondence, internal and external supporting materials, working papers, and other related records. Locating even one document from as few as a hundred can be time-consuming unless the documents are arranged in some systematic order. Finding a document or file from groups containing thousands of documents absolutely demands a disciplined method of filing, storage, and retrieval. This chapter discusses how to determine when and to what degree uniform file classifications systems are warranted, how to select or design the best system for a series of records, and what rules and practices must be used uniformly throughout an organization to make the system work efficiently. To establish the best possible plan for an organization, one must consider the objectives of filing systems, file system development, classification, coding, indexing systems, and various alphabetic, alphanumeric, and numeric filing systems.

Filing System Objectives

Most people tend to see filing from their own perspective. To the administrative assistant, the

98

most important documents are probably pieces of correspondence; to the accounting clerk, they are forms; to the engineer, they may be project or case files, plans, maps, or other drawings; to the school registrar and to the personnel officer, person- or case-oriented files would come to mind. Efficient filing depends on uniform files classification systems that make sense to the users. This includes all users organization-wide.

1. *The principal objective of filing is for users to be able to retrieve information when needed.* Personnel and organizations may change, but a well-designed filing system remains constant. Anyone using the files arrangement documentation should be able to retrieve a desired record. As changes occur in departments, and files concerning research and development become manufacturing files or operations files, uniform files classifications simplify the transfer process since the files classifications fit all departments.

2. *A good filing system identifies and preserves the set order of records.* Certain records belong with other records, and their meaning would be destroyed if the records were separated.

3. *A good filing system establishes uniform files classification.* Uniform files classification preserves the set order of records and establishes common titles. Records classification imposes order and logic upon records. Classification also recognizes differences in the value of records. A well-designed system recognizes all elements in an organization's collection. The most important feature in deciding how to file a record is to consider the title under which a record may be requested.

File Systems Development

The role of file system development in records management is to establish classification systems and to help formulate plans, provide training, assess effectiveness, provide services, and adjust policies and procedures to changing needs.

Organizational assets, such as people, equipment, money, and space, influence file systems development, and similar organizations may allocate resources differently to produce different systems. A well-designed system will recognize the goals and priorities of the organization. It will also recognize that priorities are different at different levels of management and in different parts of the organization.

The records inventory, discussed in Chapter 2, describes, identifies, locates, and quantifies all the records of an organization. The information provided in each records series tells why each department exists, how it functions, and how its activities result in records. The records inventory can provide a structure on which all elements of the records management program can be built, including the file plan.

File Plan

The records management team, consisting of the records manager, owners of the records involved, and professional staff, is responsible for developing the *file plan*—selecting the file arrangement, deciding on access to the files, choosing the classification system, deciding on the index, monitoring the project, and presenting the plan to management.

The file plan specifies the logical order of documents or files, the arrangement or scheme by which all documents may be identified, stored, and retrieved.

As with the records retention and disposition schedule, a records inventory is necessary in order to develop the file plan for organizing records.

File Arrangement

Filing and retrieval in its most simple form requires arranging the documents or file folders in either numerical order, ascending from the numeral 1, or arranging them in the order of the alphabet. A straight numeric arrangement is 1, 2, 3; and an alphabetic arrangement is A, B, C. Arrangements can and do become more complex, but all are variations of these. Numerical file arrangement is generally considered easier to learn, although not necessarily better than alphabetic, for one simple reason: There are only 10 digits to consider (0 through 9) in numeric filing, while there are 26 letters to arrange in alphabetic file arrangements. Most of us can recall that in our childhood we learned to count to ten before we learned the alphabet. However, the ease factor can be overcome through training, and trained persons can become as comfortable with the alphabet as they are with numbers. Although the learning curve for alpha filing must be considered in designing or selecting a system, it should not be a deciding factor. It may be possible that an alphanumeric filing arrangement is best suited to the file group. The ultimate decision must be based on the peculiarities of each record series, information needs, and most importantly, productivity. When studying standard filing arrangements, keep in mind that the file arrangements discussed in this chapter can be applied to any of the basic types of records and systems discussed in Chapter 6.

Accessing Records

Whether a *direct access* or an *indirect access* system would be better is determined by the type of records being filed. The volume of records may also be a factor in determining whether the file will be organized as a direct or indirect access system.

Direct Access. When the volume is small and files are arranged alphabetically or when files consist of documents referred to by preprinted numbers, no file code or index is necessary. The information in the system can be retrieved by *direct access*. A direct access system based on subjects written out as complete words must be alphabetic. The captions on the file folders act as an index. Increased volume may be facilitated by file codes and by the use of a file manual which, in essence, is an index.

Example. An example of a direct access file is shown in the following collection of information on records management software:

> AIS (ASSURED INFORMATION SYSTEMS, INC)
> ARC   (ACTIVE RECORDS CONTROL)
> ARMS (AUTOMATED RECORDS MANAGEMENT SYSTEMS)
> BETA DATA
> CASS
> CIMS (CAPITAL INFORMATION MANAGEMENT SYSTEMS)
> STAR
> STORMS
> TRIMS   (TOTAL RECORDS AND INFORMATION MANAGEMENT SYSTEM)

A decision had to be made as to whether to label these files by acronym or by company name or software name. In this case, acronyms were selected because of their frequency of use and the small size of the file. However, in a larger file, it might be more appropriate to label the file folders by company name or software name or both.

Advantages of Direct Access Systems. The advantages of a direct access system are as follows:

1. The need for an auxiliary index is eliminated.
2. Browsing is possile.
3. Time is saved in filing and searching.
4. The parameters of the file are delineated because the parameters of the contents are spelled out.
5. No automated or mechanical assistance is required.

Disadvantages of Direct Access Systems. The direct access system has these disadvantages:

1. File captions on documents are longer than codes, although it is not always necessary to type the caption on the document.
2. Each person working in the files must have knowledge of the system.

3. The system can be cumbersome to use when large volumes of records are stored.
4. Selecting appropriate terminology is difficult, particularly in subject files.
5. Confusion and congestion may exist if many files have similar names.
6. The creation of multiple folders for a topic (*Automobile, Car, Dodge*) may be a problem if there is no index or file manual to show whether a file already exists under a particular name.
7. It may be difficult to automate larger direct access systems.

Indirect Access. Many sophisticated filing systems use a *hierarchical* structure. The hierarchical filing system requires the user to refer to an index to determine the location of a record. These systems, therefore, are indirect access systems.

Example. An example of an indirect access system is the numerical coding system used by the Friend of the Court. As each new case comes in, it is coded by two digits of the current year (94), followed by its *accession* (acquisition) number.

94-1052   LeMieux, Elizabeth Mary
94-1053   Ptacek, Joseph
94-1054   Masero, Margaret
94-1055   Marik, Vladimir

Notice that the numbers are assigned in sequential order as the cases are received. However, an alphabetic index is necessary for retrieval of cases by name and would appear as follows:

LeMieux, Elizabeth Mary   94-1052
Marik, Vladimir   94-1055
Masero, Margaret   94-1054
Ptacek, Joseph   94-1053

Advantages of Indirect Access Systems. Advantages of indirect access filing systems include the following:

1. Coding of documents can aid filing and searching because reference to the index may only be required once for an intermittent series of documents, provided the correct number is carried forward from each to the next.
2. A code is easier to note and to refer to on a document than a word caption or subject, and consistency is easier to control.
3. Codes are easier to handle in publishing an index manual.
4. Less skill may be required of file personnel because only one person may be required to do the coding.
5. Security is provided for all records; individuals unfamiliar with the coding system have more difficulty locating specific records readily than in alphabetic systems.
6. Duplication of filing captions is avoided because each code can be used only once.
7. Sorting is easier.
8. Greater accuracy in filing and retrieving is generally provided; out-of-sequence color-coded files are easier to spot than non-color-coded files.

Disadvantages of Indirect Access Systems. An indirect access system has the following disadvantages:

1. An index is necessary to use the system. An index must be consulted before one can locate a record.
2. The maintenance of indexes and coding operations is quite often time-consuming and can create bottlenecks.
3. In-file browsing (reading the file captions) such as is possible in an alpha subject file is not feasible.
4. When the file number is not known, retrieval is much slower than with the direct access system.
5. Misfiled records are difficult to locate.
6. Mistakes in the code can cause serious misfiling, unless a check is made against the previously filed material.
7. It is often difficult to determine the correct coding from an index without reviewing the file itself. This often involves selecting sev-

eral file-number possibilities or making several trips from the index to the files.

CLASSIFICATION

Classification is the process of putting like things—records of a similar subject or category—together. A classification, then, is a group of records related by common characteristics. Classification systems are often considered when the present system is inefficient in filing and storing information; when there are excessive misfiles; and when there are variations in the subjects by which the users request the same file. However, a classification system may not be the panacea or cure-all that may be anticipated unless it is carefully planned and developed. Because volume is the real reason for classifying, it should be the main determinant in deciding whether subject classification is required. Generally, if the volume of a file system is more than two file drawers, the file should be classified. In order to classify a record, one must understand records, how they derive value, the life cycle of records, and the mix of records media and their environment as discussed in Chapter 1.

Records classification systems are part of records control. Word processing, forms management, reports control, and distribution programs can be integrated with records classification systems to identify records early in their life cycle. A difficulty in designing a classification system is in deciding which characteristics should be used to form groups and how the groups are related. Some file groups fall into a natural order, for example, a customer file where customers are filed by company name or a client file where names of clients are filed alphabetically. Records may also be classified by function. For example, all marketing records may be grouped together. Classification of subjects narrows searching; it can reduce 50,000 possibilities to relatively few.

Objectives of Classification

The primary reason for a classification system is to provide an overall view of how a company's information resources fit together. The system recognizes differences in records, allows for growth, and provides day-to-day guidance to users. Terms familiar to the organization ought to be used. The objectives of organizing a uniform files classification system are to provide:

- A listing or data bank of all created information.
- A critical path for locating information for retrieval maintenance, retention, and disposition.
- Uniformity of efficient file usage by users who are transferred from one department to another.
- A method of flagging one records series for retention that at the same time permits duplicate copies to be flagged for destruction.
- A listing of information by type, which aids in the development of a records retention schedule, as well as the identification of vital records.
- Continuity because only trained records personnel modify the file plan.

Steps in Classifying

Classification systems are not only difficult to develop and administer but, compared to other systems, are also costly and time-consuming, and are often a source of constant criticism. Organizing these systems into a smooth, efficient information network requires a thorough knowledge of record systems concepts, techniques used in analyzing the subject matter, file arrangement characteristics, and classification principles. In addition, it requires a thorough understanding of the functions of the organization, the functions of records, and how the information is used. It also requires a strong sense of logic and good reading comprehension. Above all, it requires a developed talent for organizing, simplifying, and communicating with the user. Figure 5.1 shows the basic steps in building a uniform file classification system.

Development of a file system begins with reviewing the current status, using the records

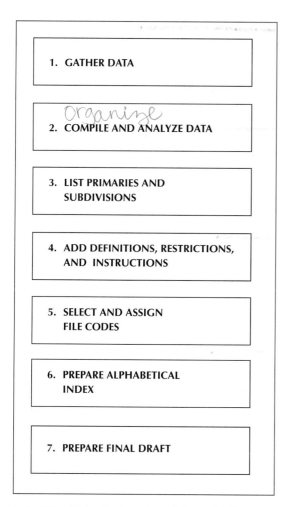

1. GATHER DATA

2. COMPILE AND ANALYZE DATA *Organize*

3. LIST PRIMARIES AND SUBDIVISIONS

4. ADD DEFINITIONS, RESTRICTIONS, AND INSTRUCTIONS

5. SELECT AND ASSIGN FILE CODES

6. PREPARE ALPHABETICAL INDEX

7. PREPARE FINAL DRAFT

FIGURE 5.1 Basic Steps in Building a Uniform Files Classification System

inventory and records retention schedule. The retention schedule serves as a link to each records series and file folder. It can also serve as a major positioning step toward a parallel index for both paper and electronic records which will be developed as the classification system is developed.

It is also necessary to review the systems that are currently in effect. User requirements play a very important role in evaluating current systems. When the user is involved in system design, a better final product is achieved, and the new system is more readily accepted.

As current systems are analyzed, several al-

ternatives for classification may become evident. For example, *Bankrupt Accounts* may be a subdivision of *Accounts Receivable*. However, since not all of the file users may know which particular receivable accounts are bankrupt accounts, it may be necessary to cross reference these accounts under *Credit*. Another example is that some employees may refer to *stationery* as *bond paper* and others may refer to it simply as *paper*. It is necessary to find a simple term, a logical classification, and one that most users would identify.

Each alternative for classification must be reviewed, and the strengths and weaknesses of each should be identified. Expectations of using a new system include more effective and efficient filing of records, more timely retrieval of information, and saving in floor space.

However, cost and benefits must be determined to justify the new system. The expected outcomes must be quantified in dollar savings for comparison with actual costs and other resources required to implement the new filing system. The decision of which alternative to implement should be based upon benefits, costs, and implementation resources.

Although this process represents a major task, analysis of the documents to be filed and careful classification makes it quite manageable.

Principles of Classification

Several important principles should be understood before classifying subjects is attempted.

Logic. Logic is the track on which a good classification system runs smoothly. Logic speeds learning tremendously and makes memory a secondary consideration. Logic demands that classifications proceed from the major to the minor. The major heading is an all-inclusive caption, such as *Canada*. The *provinces* of Canada would be the next division. The next minor division would be *districts,* followed by *cities* and *towns.*

Standardization. The terms in the general classification plan should be standardized because many different terms can describe the same record or subject. This is particularly true when an organization has been subjected to many mergers, and employers bring their old company's terminology to the new company.

Practicality. As an example, an academic way of classifying metals would be *Ferrous* and *Nonferrous*. This classification might be necessary in a file system under certain circumstances. Usually, though, a simple classification of *Metals: Steel, Aluminum, Copper* and so forth would do the job just as well; and the classifier would not have to be concerned about whether a metal was ferrous.

Simplicity. Two classifying terms should not be used together if it can be avoided. For example, rather than using *Office Supplies: Stationery: Bond Paper,* it would be simpler and better to use *Office Supplies: Paper: Bond* since *Stationery* is unnecessary. Also, names of clients, companies, and locations are a simple method of classification. For example, unless it is absolutely necessary to group all warehouses together, it is better to classify them as *Buildings: Superior: Warehouse* rather than as *Buildings: Warehouse: Superior,* where *Superior* is the location of the warehouse.

Some people call a warehouse a storeroom or a storehouse, or if it happens to be part of another facility, they may think of it under the facility's name. In any case, they will almost always know its location, so the simplest way to classify it is under its location. Subject filing can be facilitated if the captions are kept as short as possible, just long enough to get the idea across.

Functionality. Important categories under major divisions should be selected to reflect permanent functions. Even though the Accounts Payable Department may issue purchase orders, the subject *Purchase Orders* should not be classified under *Accounts Payable*. Sooner or later, the function will be moved to the Purchasing Department and the classification will then be obviously wrong.

Retention Consciousness. Classification terms should be selected that will keep together similar records with similar retention periods. But file efficiency should not be sacrificed for this feature.

Mutual Exclusivity. If classifications are not mutually exclusive, ambiguity and confusion may result. For example, if there is a classification *Petroleum Products* and also a *Motor Fuels,* where would *Gasoline* be classified? This type of ambiguity causes a great many problems.

Flexiblity. Even if all of the previous principles are followed, the possibility that different or additional classifications might be required in the system in the future must not be overlooked. The classification system should be flexible enough to permit easy expansion.

Perspective. When developing a uniform file system for use by more than one department, the perspective of a particular subject will be different for each department. The accountant may see a truck as a capital asset while the engineer may see it as equipment. This difference in perspective of the users must be considered and provided for.

Determining Classes of Records

In planning a uniform files classification system, consideration must be given to determining classes of records and selecting subject headings and subdivisions of the system. The selection of subject terms and headings is essential to filing and retrieving information. The subject heading must be concise, accurately descriptive, technically correct, and capable of only one interpretation.

Through these examples we can see some of the problems that are greatly magnified when large subject file systems are used. For example: Is a health insurance policy filed under *Insurance* or *Health*? Are purchases for the repair of the home filed under *Home Maintenance* or *Pur-*

chases and Warranties? A close examination of these seemingly clear topics will reveal other ambiguities. From this microcosm we can see the magnitude and the complexity of problems in designing, selecting, evaluating, and using the subject file system in large organizations. A subject is a noun. The noun must have a very broad meaning, allowing intricate breakdowns through subheadings. *Headings* (file folder *captions* or *titles*, or file manual outlines in a coded system) are developed by studying and analyzing functions and outlining them in a hierarchical fashion.

Major Headings. For most systems, the entire scope of subject matter is divided into about 7 to 10 major divisions. These divisions are called *majors* and usually represent the main functional areas of the organization the system serves. Describing the records series by the function they perform is called *functional filing*. The number of major groupings (functional areas) will vary with the size and complexity of the organization. There may be as few as 5 primary groupings and as many as 30 subdivisions for each functional area. Secondary classifications are then arranged within each primary classification. The number of secondary classifications will also depend on the size of the organization and may vary from 5 to 30. The tertiary classifications can then be determined; these usually are fewer than secondary classifications. If there are too many subdivisions, the classification scheme is probably too detailed to be practical.

Almost all organizations share the same functions. Some of these functions or subject areas are shown in Figure 5.2.

Other major areas can be added to the list, depending on needs and the type of organizations:

> Legal
> Management Information System
> Quality Circles

Any other category that matches major departmental functions may be included. These catego-

```
Administration
Finance and Accounting
Human Resources
Marketing
Operations
Purchasing
```

FIGURE 5.2   Functional Areas of an Organization

ries may not be familiar terms to some organizations so a more appropriate term is chosen. For example, in a religious organization the marketing function might be called *Evangelization* or some suitable similar term. *Operations* can refer to patient care in a health care organization, to transportation for a railroad, or to production for a manufacturing firm. Useful techniques to determine subject headings include looking at the subject heading at the beginning of the document, looking for references to past communication in the document, and consulting with the receiver of the document.

Primary-Level Headings. After the majors are established, each is subdivided into the most important categories within that major. These are called *primaries* (primary-level headings). Figure 5.3 shows the functions presented in Figure 5.2 expanded with possible subdivisions.

Secondary- and Tertiary-Level Headings. In turn, each primary can then be subdivided into *secondaries* as shown in Figure 5.4.

Each secondary can then be subdivided into *tertiary*, or third, *breaks*. (The subdivisions are also referred to as *breaks*.) Ideally, a total file caption should not consist of more than six breaks. Most often, the name of the major is not placed on the folder label, but instead is represented by a color stripe, thus reducing the number of breaks required.

Captions. Notice that in Figures 5.3 and 5.4 the breaks are kept in alphabetic order, just as they are

Administration
    Administrative Services
    Consultants
Finance and Accounting
    Accounting
    Banking
    Credit
    Economics
    Funding
    Investment
Human Resources
    Employees
    Fringe Benefits
    Job Descriptions
    Training
Property
    Buildings
    Equipment
    Land
    Patents
Marketing
    Advertising
    Pricing Policies
    Service Policies
Operations

FIGURE 5.3 Functional–Area Headings with Primary Subdivisions

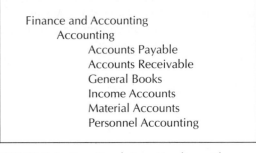

Finance and Accounting
    Accounting
        Accounts Payable
        Accounts Receivable
        General Books
        Income Accounts
        Material Accounts
        Personnel Accounting

FIGURE 5.4 Functional–Area Heading with Primary Subdivision and Secondaries

when filed in a file drawer. These outlines are translated into file captions. For example, a caption for *Personnel Accounting* would be as follows:

Finance & Accounting: Accounting:
    Personnel Accounting: Payroll Deductions:
        Social Security: 1993-

If the major *Finance & Accounting* was represented by a color code or another code, the caption would appear as:

    Accounting: Personnel Accounting:
        Payroll Deductions: Social Security:
        1993-

Note that the classification terms are rather brief and commonly used terms. There is no punctuation except for the colons that separate the breaks. There are no sentences and no unnecessary words. Yet, the caption contains enough information to identify the general contents of the file and to distinguish it from other files in the system. That is all that is required. Filing these captions is rather simple, if they are filed in a manner similar to filing proper names. Treat the first break as you would the surname, the second break as you would the first name, the third break as you would the middle name, and so on.

In this example all *Finance & Accounting* files are brought together physically in the file drawers by the color code. Within that color code grouping, all accounting files are arranged together alphabetically, and all *Personal Accounting* files will be adjacent to one another. Finally, the third break will distinguish the divisions of subject matter within *Personnel Accounting*. Instead of searching accounting subjects, which under a topical system could be captioned under any one of the breaks from *A* to *Z* over hundreds of file drawers, we have confined the search area to a very narrow corridor, which makes alphabetic subject filing feasible. With this system, each subject area becomes its own small subsystem, almost like a separate records series.

In any existing classification system there is the problem of deciding at what point a classification should be subdivided. If a totally new subject develops out of the correspondence, a cross-reference is established and ultimately the file is split into separate headings (not subdivided).

Implementing a Files Classification System

Implementing a files classification system can change records management from reactive to proactive. Reactive managers solve problems as they occur. Proactive managers anticipate problems and build systems that lead the organization to desired goals. One way to develop a uniform files classification system is to start by reviewing the records inventory and the retention schedule. The retention schedule may require some adjustment in the classification scheme since all records in a series should have the same retention period. The records inventory may have been taken using the computer to input data about the various records series that are being inventoried. It is therefore possible to sort these records series alphabetically by records series or department. It may be found that the same records series exist in several departments. Regardless of location or duplication, the same records series will be assigned the same classification. However, in developing the classification scheme, duplicates are eliminated unless the retention periods vary, and the records series titles are arranged and rearranged to establish primary classifications based on function. The focus is on function and not on the originator of the record.

Some record series, such as policies, procedures and regulations, and reference materials, may pertain to all primary classifications. For example, both the Human Resources and the Accounting and Finance Departments may have policies, procedures and regulations, and reference materials. In these cases, it may be more efficient to set up standard secondary categories that are repeated for each primary. The location may always be the same so that these records are easy to find, and they are stored with the other files that they pertain to.

In a uniform files classification system, an alphanumeric code is established for each records series. These codes are discussed later in this chapter.

Using and maintaining a files classification system requires qualifications in the records personnel similar to that of records analysts, but to a much lesser degree than is required for the analysts who design the system.

Documenting a Files Classification System

As the files classification system develops, the headings are recorded in a listing or database which can become the index. The location of each file is listed on the index. Extensive cross-referencing may be necessary in order to cover all the headings by which various users may request a file. A *cross-reference* is a notation showing that the record may be filed elsewhere. The notation may be made on the document being filed, on a cross-reference form, or in the index. A *cross-index* to the files classification system lists the records series in alphabetic order, cross-referenced to their alphanumeric codes.

Where multiple names for the same records series were eliminated from the classification system, these names should be cross-referenced to assist users of the files in recognizing currently-used titles. The cross-indexed listing showing the coding under which the records will be found is the first step in developing the index and a users' manual to the filing system. Documentation will be discussed in more detail in Chapter 16.

CODING SYSTEMS

File coding systems facilitate filing, retrieval, and refiling of records. Codes of subject headings are placed on the labels of file folders, on storage equipment, and on records. However, like all file systems, the files of the subject system can be arranged numerically, alphabetically, or alphanumerically. In addition, color can be used as a code, and more recently, bar codes. Each type of coding system has many advocates who can provide convincing reasons why their choice is the best. However, at this time there has been no definite study to determine which is indeed the best, if there is *one* best way. The records manager must study the administrative environment, practices, and particular needs to reach a decision as to which type of coding system is best and the degree of uniformity required.

Using coded labels on folders may reduce the number of misfiles. Indirect access systems or numeric subject classifications are based on a code. The code may be a number, an alpha abbreviation that is easily remembered, or a nonsignificant letter or letters. In any case, an outside index of some sort is almost always necessary. Coding systems used with subject filing are: variation of alphanumeric, decimal-numeric, duplex-numeric, and block-numeric.

When attempting to classify a document, it is often difficult to determine the correct coding from an index without reviewing the file itself. This often involves selecting several file number possibilities or making several trips from the index to the files.

Alphanumeric Codes

An *alphanumeric coding system* consists of a combination of capital letters and numbers, or a combination of capital letters and lowercase letters in addition to numbers, such as *A-1*. One such code is a phonetic arrangement. Since it differs significantly from other alphanumeric codes, it will be discussed separately at the end of this section.

In most cases of alphanumeric codes, the primary break is alphabetic and secondary breaks are numeric. For example, in the case of *HUMAN RELATIONS,* the primary break may be *HR*. Secondary breaks would have a numeric designation, and tertiary breaks would also have numeric designations.

HR	HUMAN RELATIONS	
HR-01	Employee Policy	
HR-01-01		Compensatory Time
HR-01-02		Maternity Leave
HR-01-03		Paternity Leave
HR-02	Seniority	
HR-02-01		Rights
HR-02-02		Rosters

This same file could be set up in an outline form using both lowercase letters and numbers, as follows:

HR	HUMAN RELATIONS	
HR 1	Employee Policy	
HR 1.a		Compensatory Time
HR 1.b		Maternity Leave
HR 1.c		Paternity Leave
HR 1.c.1		Applications
HR 1.c.2		Benefits

This is an example of the functional filing system with alphanumeric outline codes that can be used in a subject filing system in addition to the file name. This coded filing system is used by the U.S. Army. Each alpha element is an indicator of the function served by that portion of the file.

As an alternative, functions may be coded in two or three letters. Each function may be further identified by a colored strip on each file folder tab. Within each broad function, the expanded function areas—*subsets*—may be coded numerically as shown below.

ADM	ADMINISTRATION	
	ADM 01	Administrative Services
	ADM 02	Consultants
	ADM 03	Litigation
FIN	FINANCE	
	FIN 01	Accounts Payable
	FIN 02	Accounts Receivable
	FIN 03	Debentures
HR	HUMAN RESOURCES	
	HR 01	Employees
	HR 02	Fringe Benefits
	HR 03	Job Descriptions
	HR 04	Training

Conventions usually followed in developing codes are that if the heading consists of several words, the code is made up of the first letter of each word. If the heading consists of only one word, then a short code is made up by using the first letter and subsequent consonants only (leaving out the vowels). For example, if the spelled-out heading is *MAINTENANCE*, the abbreviated code could be *MNTNC*, although a long-accepted abbreviation for *maintenance* is *MTCE*. Using codes made up only of consonants does require an index as the code itself could stand for many things. A good guideline to follow in developing codes is to use common abbreviations as codes, such as *MTCE* (*maintenance*) or *MFG* (*manufacturing*). The alphabetic coding system will normally have between two and six letters. Notice how *RECORDS RETENTION* can be coded in from two to six letters.

RR	**RECORDS RETENTION**
RTN	**RECORDS RETENTION**
RCRT	**RECORDS RETENTION**
RCDRT	**RECORDS RETENTION**
RCDRTN	**RECORDS RETENTION**

Phonetic Systems. Systems for arranging records phonetically have been developed for organizations that maintain large volumes of records filed by name. Because many names sound alike but are spelled differently, records are sometimes difficult to find. To overcome this difficulty, a phonetic classification system brings all such names into one location in the files. Numbers on driver's licenses in some states are examples of the use of phonetic systems.

Several phonetic file arrangements are based on a numerical code that represents certain key letter sounds in the alphabet. The key letters are consonant sounds. The vowel sounds are eliminated. One such system is Soundex, developed by the Remington Rand Office Systems Division of Sperry Rand Corporation.

When filed alphabetically, names are arranged in sequence according to exact spelling and are therefore dependent upon the accurate interpretation of the spoken or handwritten name. Conversely, when filed the Soundex way, varied spellings of the same name or misinterpretations of the handwriting of a name are brought together in one file location. The Soundex coding system reduces name filing to the use of one alphabetic letter and a three-digit code number. The first letter of a surname or company name is not coded. The names are arranged alphabetically in 26 letter sections, i.e., *B* for *Bayer*, *H* for *Harrison*, *S* for *Schneider*. Within each of the 26 letter sections, only six groups of consonant letters are used. Each of the six groups has a code number used for filing. The code number applies to each letter in its group.

Rules for Soundex Coding. Rules for Soundex coding can be summarized as follows.

1. To code a name, use three digits. When no consonants or insufficient code consonants appear in a surname or organization name, add one, two or three zeros to give a three-digit code. For example, Goodyear is coded G360; Levy, L100.

2. Two letters together (double letters) are considered as one letter. For example, *Abbott* is coded *A130*; *Farrell*, *F640*; *Kelly*, *K400*.

3. Consider any combinations of two or more equivalent letters *together* as having the same number as a single letter. For example, *Biggs* is coded *B200*; *Jackson*, *J250*; *McCarthy*, *M263*; *Opffer*, *O160*.

4. When the first (initial) letter is immediately followed by the same letter or one more of its

FIGURE 5.5 Soundex Code

Group Letters and Equivalents*	Code Numbers†
BFPV	1
CGJKQSXZ	2
DT	3
L	4
MN	5
R	6

*The vowels—*a, e, i, o, u*—and three consonants—*w, h, y*—have no number equivalent and are not coded.

†Zero (0) is used to express no consonants following the first letter; for example, *Day* would be coded *D000* and *Shaw* would be coded *S000*.

equivalent letters (no separators) with the same code number, all the letters are considered as one first letter and are not coded. For example, *Czerny* is coded *C650*; *Scott, S300*; *Sczsatkal, S324*.

5. Vowels and the consonant *y* are separators. Consonants having a code number when separated by vowels or *y* are coded individually. *H* and *w* (not separators) are not coded, and are considered as nonexistent in the name when coding. For example, *Ferrara* is coded *F660*; *Kozsasick, K222*; *Lyles, L420*; *McClelland, M244*.

The records are sorted and filed by the alphanumeric code, according to rules previously stated. Since the code takes the place of the surname, it is considered the first filing unit in the arrangement. The balance of the name (first name, middle initial, etc.) is filed as the second and succeeding file units. For example,

First	Second	Third
B650	Gerald	F.
B650	Harold	M.
B651	Alice	O.

Color Codes

Color coding is used frequently with both alpha and numeric file arrangements. The term *color coding* is not always used correctly, however. When a particular visual mark is used to represent a number, a word, or a group of words, it is in the true sense a code. For example, a color stripe on a file folder label can be used to represent—that is, take the place of—a subject classification, such as a major category. The name of the category never appears on the label, but the meaning of the color code is understood. As a fundamental rule, identical colors are filed together. If a file plan uses nine different-color stripes on its file labels and each stripe represents a different classification, all files of the same color would be filed together.

The stripes are normally arranged in the alpha order of the words that they represent. Thus the green labels representing the classification *Administration* would be filed before the blue labels representing the words *Finance and Accounting*. The same principle applies if the colors represent numerals. The use of color codes is usually limited to ten or less because of the limited number of clearly differentiated colors available and because the codes must normally be memorized. Color blindness must be considered in color selection.

Another use of color with filing is recognition enhancement. In this case, color does not represent a number, a word, or a letter, but rather highlights it. Thus, preprinted labels, usually bordered in color or made of colored paper stock, also contain the letter or digit that they highlight. Sometimes all letters or digits are color-enhanced, but usually only key labels have color. Although the color can aid in sorting and in spotting or preventing misfiles, it actually does not enter into the alpha or numeric file arrangement. This type of file labeling is frequently used with open-shelf file arrangement, where file folder tabs are visible. Colors can be well worth the added effort and expense of the label because the color pattern established by the series of identically colored labels will be broken by the foreign color of the misfiled record. See Chapter 7 for further information on the use of color.

Bar Codes

The bar code technology developed for labeling products now has been incorporated into file folder labels and records management software to provide tracking systems with various levels of information and control. Everyone is familiar with the universal product code (UPC) that is used to scan products purchased in the supermarket. Similar codes are found in retail stores and in luggage check-in counters at airports. Mail delivered by the United States Postal Service frequently carries a bar code.

Bar codes are a form of automatic identification system. A bar code symbol is a pattern of variable-width bars and spaces which represent numeric or alphanumeric data in machine-readable form. The general format of a bar code symbol consists of a leading margin, start character, data or message characters, check character (if any), stop character, and trailing margin.

Bar codes can appear on file folders, file boxes, forms, individual pieces of correspondence, and charge-out or retrieval tracking forms. Bar codes also appear on employee badges and charge cards. When it is scanned by a wand, the bar code can be used for input into the computer system. This saves time, saves work, and decreases chances for error.

Documents with bar codes—file folders or boxes—can be tracked by means of the bar code system. Reports can be generated showing which file folders were accessed during the month, which file folders were returned during the month, and which file folders are out of the file. In the records center, the bar code system can be used to keep track of all boxes in the center, date accessioned, number of times accessed, and current location. The United Parcel Service uses bar codes to keep track of parcels in the delivery pipeline. As documents or folders are charged out, they can be tracked using the bar code system.

Chapter 9 contains further discussion of the use of bar code technology in records management systems.

Numeric Codes

In numeric filing, numerals are used as codes. The codes replace fully worded captions. The format and structure of the subject file codes vary widely from company to company. Some code symbols consist of unsegmented numbers, such as 1207; others of segmented numbers, such as 14-3-4 or 14.3.4; and still others of combinations of words or letters and numbers, such as A-12-1-2. The filing manual usually will specify the approved file code format. Although it is a simple and fast method, numeric sequencing is not actually an autonomous system of filing. Behind every numeric system there is an alphabetical index, classification record, or listing that controls the numbers. The time needed to maintain the auxiliary index or listing must be considered as part of the total filing time for this system.

A control device used in numeric filing is the *accession book*. When a new file is created, it is entered in the accession book. If bar codes are used on the new files, the files can be entered into the computerized accession book by scanning the caption on the new file. Use of the accession book eliminates the issuance of several code numbers for the same file or the same code number to several different titles. Three common forms of numeric subject filing systems are decimal-numeric, duplex-numeric, and block-numeric.

Decimal-Numeric Codes. *Decimal-numeric* systems have been developed for use by libraries, railroads, engineering firms, pharmaceutical houses, and governmental agencies. The best-known decimal-numeric system was developed by Dr. Melvil Dewey in 1873, for library use. This system was almost universally used until the 1970s when libraries began to automate their listings of holdings. The Library of Congress, among the first to automate, developed the Library of Congress classification system.

Today, smaller libraries and public libraries continue to use the Dewey decimal system for classification, but colleges and universities have changed to the Library of Congress classification system in order to use the same computer codes and system. With the advent of microcomputers, the use of the Library of Congress classification system is not as important as it was in the era of mainframes.

One other consideration may have been that the Library of Congress classification system is based on the alphabet. For example, the letter *K* indicates the broad category of *LAW*, and *P* indicates the broad category of *LITERATURE*. The letter *R* could be added to the code to identify *BRITISH LITERATURE* (*PR*), or the letter *Q* to indicate *SPANISH LITERATURE* (*PQ*). The Dewey decimal system is limited to ten general divisions, each of which is divided into ten parts. Figure 5.6 illustrates the main categories and subdivisions of categories of the Dewey decimal system. While the Dewey decimal system is a good example of a coded-classified system, it is not recommended for subject filing.

The Dewey decimal system makes use of standard codes; for example, 03 is the code for dictionaries. Thus, 103 would be the classification for dictionaries in philosophy; 203, religious dictionaries; 303, social sciences dictionaries; 403, language dictionaries, and so forth.

If the material can be classified into ten headings or less, the Dewey decimal system can be modified to serve as the classification system. The success of any decimal system depends upon the original categories selected. If the main categories are too specific, if they overlap, or if the categories fail to cover the entire subject, the system will break down. Establishing a decimal system of classification requires the ability to analyze and classify clearly and accurately, as well as knowledge of the subject matter. The users should be able to use the system easily.

The advantages of a decimal system are as follows.

FIGURE 5.6   Example of a Dewey Decimal Index

```
000   General works
100   Philosophy and related disciplines
200   Religion
300   Social sciences
400   Languages
500   Pure sciences
600   Technology (applied sciences)
700   The arts
      710   Civic and landscape art
      720   Architecture
      730   Sculpture and plastic arts
            731   Processes of sculpture
            731.1   Composition and design in sculpture
            731.2   Materials
            731.3   Equipment
            731.4   Methods and techniques of sculpting
                  731.41   Modeling
                  731.42   Molding
                  731.43   Stamping
                  731.44   Casting
                        731.441   Plaster and cement casting
                        731.442   Casting and synthetic plastic
      740   Drawing and decorative arts
      750   Painting and paintings
      760   Graphic arts
      770   Photography and photographs
      780   Music
      790   Recreation
800   Literature and rhetoric
900   General geography, history, etc.
```

Employee Policy	77.0
Fringe Benefits	77.1
Compensatory Time	77.1.1
Maternity Leave	77.1.2
Paternity Leave	77.1.3
Personal Business	77.1.4
Sick Leave	77.1.5
Time Off	77.1.6
Vacations	77.1.7
Labor Agreements	78.0
Grievances	78.1
Seniority	78.2
Rights	78.2.1
Rosters	78.2.2
Strikes	78.3

FIGURE 5.7 Decimal–Numeric Subject Filing System

Employee Policy	77-0
Fringe Benefits	77-1
Compensatory Time	77-1-1
Maternity Leave	77-1-2
Paternity Leave	77-1-3
Personal Business	77-1-4
Sick Leave	77-1-5
Time Off	77-1-6
Vacations	77-1-7
Labor Agreements	78-0
Grievances	78-1
Seniority	78-2
Rights	78-2-1
Rosters	78-2-2
Strikes	78-3

FIGURE 5.8 Duplex–Numeric Subject Filing System

1. The system allows unlimited expansion.
2. Retrieval of a document by number is quicker and easier than by name.
3. Materials are grouped by subject in the same section of the file.

The disadvantages of a decimal system are as follows.

1. The primary categories are limited to ten.
2. Carelessness in the use of numbers can result in the loss of papers for indefinite periods of time.
3. There is no flexibility in the system.

Figure 5.7 shows the decimal-numeric subject filing system utilizing decimal points to distinguish between primary, secondary, and tertiary headings.

Duplex-Numeric Codes. The *duplex-numeric* subject filing system is a variation of numeric codes and uses numbers and hyphens to achieve codes, as shown in Figure 5.8.

The name *duplex-numeric* is used because the code has two parts: A subject heading is included in the caption with the numeric code. As subject headings are added to the file, the codes are expanded to accommodate the new material.

Maternity Leave Bonus	77-1-2-1

Block-Numeric Codes. The *block-numeric* subject filing system consists of assigning a block of numbers to each of the major functions of the organization. Figure 5.9 shows how, for example, the functions of an organization might be assigned block numbers.

Within each functional unit, the codes are further identified by secondary and tertiary numbers similar to the assignment of these numbers to the decimal-numeric and duplex numeric systems as shown below.

ACCOUNTING	000
Policy	000 00
Accounts Payable	000 01
Accounts Receivable	000 02

An important consideration in assigning numbers for block subject filing is that some block numbers should be skipped initially between secondary headings in order to allow for growth.

Functional Unit	Block Numbers
Accounting	000–299
Administrative Management	300–599
Finance	600–899
Human Resources	900–1199
Management	1200–1499
Management Information Systems	1500–1799
Marketing	1800-2099

FIGURE 5.9 Block–Numeric Coding for a Subject Filing System

INFORMATION INDEXING SYSTEMS

Information searching systems are based on an index. The word *index* comes from the Latin word *indicare* ("indicate") and is the source of the term *index finger*, as well as the pointer to information in a storage and retrieval system. Thus, for our purposes, an *index* is an arrangement of names or topics in either alphabetic or numeric order that provides the searcher with the key needed to locate an item filed within a system. Suppose, for example, personnel records are arranged in Social Security number order. A file arranged in alpha order by name and giving the Social Security number for each employee will serve as an index to the numerically arranged file system. Indexes often are computer-generated. Thus an index may be retrieved in alphabetical order even though the data may have been entered in random order. Manual or computer indexes are used in all types of records media, including microfilm.

Generally, an index consists of an alphabetically ordered set of words or phrases called headings. Subheadings may be included under main headings and cross-references from one heading to another may be present. A *relative index*, sometimes just called an *index*, is a dictionary-like listing of all possible words and combinations by which material may be requested. Without a relative index, it is difficult, if not impossible, for employees to operate a subject file.

An index to information may also be called a *relative index*. An example of a relative index is the index found in the Yellow Pages of the telephone directory. The relative index is also a cross-reference system because it contains all titles under which material may be filed.

The items in an index are arranged in a searchable order—alphabetical, numerical, chronological, hierarchical, or arbitrarily systematic. Examples of each type include a file index (alphabetical); a report-number index (numerical); an index to historical events (chronological); a taxonomy (hierarchical); and an index to a coded collection (arbitrarily systematic). The index may also be a combination of these arrangements. An index is known by many other names, depending on the body of knowledge that it covers. It may be called a dictionary, a data dictionary, a thesaurus, a catalog, an authority list, or an access guide. The subject headings contained in the index may also be known as *keywords*, *topics*, *items*, *concepts*, or *descriptors*. This is not to imply that the words can be used interchangeably, but rather that the concept is basic to a searching system. Many indexes are computerized, but whether limited to manual systems or computerized, the functions of the index are similar.

Examples of indexes which have become databases are those developed by H. W. Wilson, who started indexing articles in magazines under their authors and specific subjects. Cross-references were provided to link related subjects. The very high standards of consistency and accuracy that were evident at the beginning have continued to make the Wilson company's on-line databases among the best in the world. Two of these indexes are *Readers' Guide to Periodical Literature* and *Business Periodicals Index.*

Whether the index is kept on cards or in the computer, additional information such as the status of the file or when it began may be accumulated about the file itself. An example of a computer listing of a primary file classification definition is shown below. Entries for each of the associations listed in the 300 series would follow.

ASSOCIATIONS/ORGANIZATIONS—300

For matters dealing with trade and other associations, Chamber of Commerce, clubs, committees, civic groups, professional associations, and similar organizations.

A card file may include a short paragraph describing the contents of the file folder. This information may assist new employees in determining the contents of the file, as well as remind more experienced employees. The short paragraph may also be used in a subject heading listing to remind users of the contents of the file. An example of such a paragraph on an index card or subject heading listing appears below:

CREDITS & COLLECTIONS

Includes documents pertaining to the impending or actual attachment of wages or assets in payment of an outstanding debt.

Functions of an Index

Indexes vary in organization, format, vocabulary, breadth of selection, and depth of analysis. The type of index used depends on the kind of material contained in the collection, the range of questions posed by the user, and the mechanical or electronic devices available to search the collection.

Indexes must respond to search objectives, and they therefore vary in methods of arrangement, types of headings, and structure. Search objectives may be synthetical, analytical, or hierarchical.

A *synthetical* index brings together like items or concepts, as in a coordinate indexing system or a keyword subject index. Each significant word in a title becomes an entry point and appears in place. The keywords searched for may be highlighted or the entries can be printed out so that keywords may be compared easily. For example, the title *Animal Protection* can be retrieved by looking under the keyword *Animal* or the keyword *Protection.*

An *analytical* index isolates single items or concepts, as in an index of specific topics of information included under broader headings. For example, in an index to a subject file of a railroad, *Safety Appliances* may include specific topics, such as *Brake Step, Crossover Steps, End Platforms, Footboards, Handhold, Handrails, Running Boards,* and *Sill Step Guards.*

A *hierarchical* index is based on an orderly arrangement of items, or concepts, such as in a classified index. An example of hierarchical structure is provided in Figure 5.10. Although this is in reality a file plan, it is an example of a hierarchical classification system. It provides the file number under which the topic is filed, and thus it can also be considered an index.

General Guidlines for Developing an Index

The quality of an index depends on a compromise between user requirements and production capabilities, such as cost, time limits on preparation and publication, overall size, and the skill of the indexers and other personnel. The problem of indexing is compounded by the variety of language which can be used to express concepts and by the impossibility of anticipating all conceivable points of view that a user might have at some future time. However, some general guidelines may be followed.

```
1.0   Human Resources
      1.1   Recruitment
      1.2   Personnel Administration
      1.3   Employee Benefits
            1.3.1   Health Insurance
                    1.3.1.1   Blue Cross/Blue Shield
                    1.3.1.2   HMO—Health/Hospitalization Maintenance
                              Organizations
                    1.3.1.3   Executive Health Plan
            1.3.2   Dental Insurance
            1.3.3   Life Insurance
            1.3.4   Pension Program
            1.3.5   Stock Investment Plan
            1.3.6   College Tuition Assistance
            1.3.7   Workers' Compensation
      1.4   Labor Negotiations
      1.5   Affirmative Action
      1.6   Employee Assistance Program
      1.7   Professional Development and Training
      1.8   Planning and Budgeting
      1.9   Accounting
            1.9.1   Payroll Administration
```

FIGURE 5.10   Hierarchical Structure

The index should encompass the entire collection, and exceptions should be noted. (Exceptions would include limited use of generic names, limited cross-referencing of synonyms, and name changes restricted to the last few years.)

An index should supply information not actually found in the collection when that information facilitates the use of the index, for example, full names, names recently adapted or changed, general names, and so forth.

The users' vocabulary should be considered in selecting headings for the index. The development of the classification system may have led the records manager to obtain such a detailed understanding of a particular function that the knowledge level of the user is neglected.

Headings should be used consistently so that users can develop a frame of reference. The form of multiple-word headings depends upon the kind of material indexed and the search habits of the prospective users. Technical headings should be used as the main headings, but jargon headings need to be cross-referenced to the technical headings. Synonyms or near synonyms are useful in the index to help point to the main heading. Typical factors to be considered are whether the full legal names of companies or organizations should be used, whether the users of the file are familiar with them, and whether some cross-referencing would be helpful.

The success of an index depends on the degree of similarity of approach reached by the indexer and the user of the index, on the proper choice of index terms, on controlled or natural language, and on appropriate format.

Indexes Maintained on Computers

Many companies today are using computerized indexing systems for both active records and inactive records. The index can be devised to give a summary of the complete file that is maintained in electronic format, on paper, or on microform. Keyword cross-referencing can be included, as well as a history of the file, such as the date it was opened and the last day it was accessed. In cases where files are periodically transferred to inactive storage, the computerized index can also be used to print labels for new file folders. These same computerized systems can be used for checkout notations, inventory control, follow-up, and calculation of reference ratios.

TYPES OF INDEXES

Indexes vary from simple listings of words or phrases in alphabetic order to complex computerized systems. Indexes are used to assist users in locating information in the form of list index, chain index, coordinate index, and phonetic index. Formats of indexes vary from 3- x 5-inch cards (index cards) to on-line computer systems, such as KWIC, KWOC, and SPINDEX.

List Index

The simplest kind of index to compile is an alphabetic *list index* of words or phrases. This list may be a table of contents, a telephone list, or an office location list. A popular type of index associated with many small filing systems is an alphabetic list of the file headings—subjects, concepts, and names.

Chain Index

In a *chain index*, a subject is linked in a hierarchy to its direct relations. The Dewey decimal system described earlier shows the subdivision classifications which could be developed into a subject indexing system. This is also true of the Library of Congress classification system.

   The chain indexing concept originated with the Indian librarian Ranganathan and has been adopted and expanded by Western librarians and information scientists.

Coordinated Index (Uniterm System)

Developed in the early 1950s by Dr. Mortimor Taube and his associates, the uniterm system of *coordinate indexes* has as its hypothesis that a document can be indexed with a set of individual, brief terms. Each document or item is numbered as it is received. Words are extracted directly from the text and are used without change for index terms (*uniterms*). In manual systems, a separate card must be created for each uniterm. In automated systems, programs specify specific fields for the uniterms. In order to retrieve related documents, each must contain some identical index term.

   The technique of coordinate indexing has been employed by records managers in logging documents received. Descriptors are extracted from the wording of the text and often include the name of the sender and receiver.

   Disadvantages of this system are that since the author's terminology is used, it may not be universal or even accurate; the system is based on words, not concepts; and related documents may remain unconnected by index terms.

Phonetic Index

The Soundex system described earlier is an alphanumeric filing system. An innovative use of Soundex was developed in the records management program in the Rapid Transit Project in Vancouver, British Columbia. Keywords (subject- and name-type data) are converted by the computer into a phonetic code to minimize both computer storage requirements and the occurrence of sorting errors due to spelling and terminology ambiguities. Airline reservation systems use this same method of converting passenger names to a Soundex code to conserve computer storage. One such format is the computerized index created in database indexing.

Database Index

In relational database systems, the term *index* is used differently from in manual systems. In the database environment, an index is a file that relates key values to records that contain those key values. Within relational model systems on both mainframes and microcomputers, the main mechanism for increasing the efficiency with which data are retrieved from the database is the use of indexes.

An index can be created and maintained for any column or combination of columns in any table. A table, in a database environment, is another name for a relation. A *relation* is a two-dimensional table in which all entries are single-valued; each column has a distinct field name; all of the values in a column are values of the attribute that is identified by the column name; the order of the columns is immaterial; each row is distinct; and the order of rows is immaterial.

Once the index has been created, it can be used to facilitate retrieval. In powerful mainframe relational systems, the decision concerning which index or indexes to use (if any) during a particular type of retrieval is one function of a part of the database management system (DBMS) called an *optimizer*. The function of the optimizer is to select the best way to satisfy a query. No reference is made to any index by the user since the system makes the decision in the background. In less powerful systems, the user may have to specify that a given index should be used. Several indexes may be linked to the database and each index is updated as new data are entered. Direct data entry, therefore, has a rippling effect on all the indexes that are in use.

As filing systems become larger and more sophisticated, computerized indexes show a trend toward the creation of a database of information about corporate records. The indexes vary with the type of filing system selected and are usually set up in an alphabetic arrangement.

ALPHABETIC ARRANGEMENT

Alphabetic arrangements are used because they are natural and correspond to our language; thus, they are self-identifying. These arrangements normally do not require an external index, because

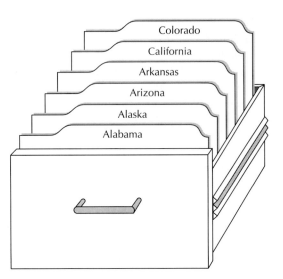

FIGURE 5.11   Alphabetic Arrangement

the file is arranged alphabetically by name of subject as shown in Figure 5.11.

Alphabetic filing, of course, requires a good, almost instinctive, knowledge of the alphabet. But it also requires a knowledge of alphabetic rules for filing. For example, the clerk must know if *MacDonald* is filed before or after *McDonald*. Although each organization can develop its own rules for alpha filing, it is recommended that standard rules be followed. The Association of Records Managers and Administrators, Inc. (ARMA International) has developed standard rules for alphabetic and numeric filing. ARMA's *Alphabetic Filing Rules* appear as Appendix D.

Rules for Alphabetic Arrangement

Three questions arise in arranging items in alphabetic order: (1) What is alphabetic sequence? (2) What is alphabetic order? (3) What is the order of entry?

Alphabetic sequence can be used for the arrangement of names, locations, subjects, titles, or any common characteristic. For example, all accounts receivable have a customer's name. Sales territories are divided into regions, and sales analyses can be made on the basis of alphabetically arranged regions.

Alphabetic order can be achieved by three different conventions: (1) letter by letter, (2) word by word, or (3) unit by unit. In the letter-by-letter arrangement, the letters in the title are simply strung together, for example, *HarryBaxterBrown.*

In the word-by-word convention, "The first basic rule is that cards (documents) are filed word by word, and the words are filed letter by letter, according to the order of the English alphabet."[1]

In the unit-by-unit arrangement, the basic rule established by ARMA is that "each word, abbreviation, and initial is a separate filing unit, unless otherwise defined in a specific rule. Alphabetizing of each unit is completed before proceeding to the next unit."[2]

The unit-by-unit convention establishes the foundation for making decisions regarding prefixes, combinations, and compound words.

Order of entry is finding the first unit to be considered in filing. Because there is a wide range of interpretation concerning the selection of the first unit in filing, standard rules have been developed through the years. As early as 1876, librarians were developing alphabetical filing rules. Two librarian publications on filing rules are *Filing Rules for Dictionary Catalogs of the Library of Congress* and *ALA Rules for Filing Catalog Cards.*

The standard rules for filing along with the conventions for alphabetic arrangement are followed in subject filing.

SUBJECT FILING SYSTEMS

More sophisticated subject filing systems have been developed as materials to be filed became more numerous and complex. These systems all use classification schemes of the hierarchical variety, and either assign numeric or alphanumeric file codes to the file or require the typing of alphabetic subject classification captions on the file tab. The folders are then filed in alphabetic sequence. Since the arrangement is alphabetical, no external index is required. The system, therefore,

is considered to be a direct access system. All subject systems have their roots by nature in words, which require an alphabetic arrangement. This alphabetic arrangement may appear only in the index depending on the system used. Even when the index is contained on the magnetic disk of a computerized index, it is usually accessed by word, not number. Codes are added, if desired, after the overall classification patterns have been established.

There are really only two basic methods used to organize subject files. Subject files are organized alphabetically by subject, with or without the use of codes. Subject files without the use of codes are called *alpha-classified.* Subject files with the use of codes are called *coded-classified.*

Alpha-Classified Systems

Alpha-classified subject files simply arrange captions (headings) in alphabetic order. Alpha-classified systems are typically thought of as either topical (dictionary) or hierarchical (encyclopedic). Geographic filing is a type of topical filing, since each country or each city can be considered a topic. While the encyclopedic filing system is a type of hierarchical filing system, a distinction may be made, because the files of a small organization could be arranged in an encyclopedic fashion without coding, but the file system of a large organization would have to be expanded to include coding.

Topical Filing Systems. A *topical*, or *dictionary*, arrangement consists of topics arranged according to subject headings behind guides ranging from *A* to *Z*. In this simple system, there are no numbers used and there is no attempt to group or classify, because the small volume does not warrant these added steps. Alphabetic arrangement of subject files is quite natural and direct because the files are arranged by the words that describe their content.

The topical system is also called a dictionary system because the captions on the file folders are arranged in alphabetic order similar to the way words in a dictionary are arranged. This system is practical for only one or two file drawers and is usually not practical for business records. As the volume of records increases, the retrieval of information from a topical system becomes more difficult. No index is necessary since the subjects are filed alphabetically, but many users prefer to keep an index in order to verify captions and eliminate duplication. The use of an index eliminates the need to browse through the file to see if a folder already exists for a particular subject.

Most of us are already familiar with the most elementary form of subject file, which is the personal file that we maintain in our homes. A typical home subject file consists of a dozen or so file folders, usually contained in a file box. Each file folder has a topic printed on the file folder tab to serve our own particular needs. Typical file captions for these types of files are shown in Figure 5.12(a).

Encyclopedic Filing Systems.   The *encyclopedic* filing system is an example of small-scale hierarchical classification. The encyclopedic arrangement differs from the topical, or dictionary, arrangement in that topics are subdivided so that several folders may contain information which pertains to the main topic. Figure 5.12 (*b*) shows a personal file structured in an encyclopedic arrangement. Compare the entries with those in Figure 5.12 (*a*), which identify the same information.

The Yellow Pages section of the telephone book is a good example of the encyclopedic filing system. An index showing all published main headings precedes or follows the classified directory. The user can refer to the index for cross-references to appropriate headings.

Another example of an encyclopedic file is the vertical file maintained in some libraries. It consists of folders arranged alphabetically and cross-referenced. This is a direct access file since

FIGURE 5.12   Two Variations on a Personal Subject File. (a) Topical (Dictionary) Arrangement; (b) Encyclopedic Arrangement

Automobile Maintenance	Automobiles
Certificates, Licenses, and Titles	Insurance
Checking Account	Loans
Education	Maintenance
Employment	Titles
Health	Banking
Home Maintenance	Checking
Loans and Mortgages	Savings
Insurance	Education
Purchases and Warranties	Employment
Savings Account	Health
Tax Receipts (Deductions)	Home
Tax Returns	Insurance
	Maintenance
	Mortgage
	Purchases and Warranties
	Taxes
	Federal
	State

        (a)   *(b)*

Czechoslovakia	5.0	Country
(Ceskoslovensko)		(Local spelling)
Bohemia	5.1	Province
(Cechy)		(Local name)
Karlovy Vary	5.1.1	City
Prague	5.1.2.1	City—store 1
(Praha)		(Local name)
Prague	5.1.2.2	City—store 2
(Praha)		(Local name)
Moravia	5.2	Province
(Morava)		(Local name)
Brno	5.2.1	City
Olomouc	5.2.2	City
Slovakia	3	Province
(Slovensko)		(Local name)
Bratislava	3.1	City
Prezov	3.2	City

FIGURE 5.13 Geographic File for Czechoslovakia

no index is necessary to find the desired heading. An example of the cross-referencing used in this file is that *Soviet Union* may be cross-referenced several times—under *The Union of Soviet Socialist Republics, USSR,* and *Russia,* for example. The physical file for cross-referenced material would be located in only one place, in this case under *Soviet Union.* Now, however, since many of the republics of the former Soviet Union have become independent countries, material for each country would be filed in its appropriate place, such as under *Azerbaijan* or *Ukraine,* with a possible cross-reference to *Soviet Union* for older material.

Geographic Filing Systems. Records which are arranged by the locations of the clients may be filed alphabetically. It is necessary to decide whether the records are to be filed geographically by country, state (or province), county (or parish), or city, or by some other geographical unit, such as under *Northwest, Southwest,* etc., or by street name. The location of the client is the first unit of consideration, followed by the name. As trade

becomes increasingly global and multinational, it is necessary to translate foreign names to their English equivalents for the maintenance of the files in the United States. A cross-reference to other languages is a necessity. If the files are extensive, it is possible to establish an alphabetic index for the countries and cities involved, and to assign alphanumeric codes. For example, suppose a company is establishing a file for its branches in Czechoslovakia. The file might appear as shown in Figure 5.13.

For a small number of stores, an alphabetic listing of provinces and cities might be adequate. The coding might be added if users were having difficulty in locating desired records. In addition, as geographic and political boundaries change, the files must be updated to identify changes and geopolitical circumstances.

Coded-Classified Systems

Coded-classified systems can be hierarchic systems or random systems. As the volume expands, the distance between *A* and *Z* can become considerable, and the distance between related topics also expands. This expansion is further aggravated when different terms are used to describe identical or closely related subjects. Even so, an alphabetic arrangement provides the flexibility of language that is desirable to meet the unforeseen direction subject matter may take as time progresses. Thus, a means had to be developed to bring related subject matter together in the file so that we could enjoy the benefits of the one-drawer search, even though the entire system may consist of hundreds of file drawers. This is achieved through hierarchical classification with codes.

Hierarchical Filing Systems.   The *hierarchical* subject filing system uses classification of one type or another to bring related material together. This divides and thus reduces the search area. For example, instead of having subjects pertaining to personnel interspersed over a hundred or even a thousand file drawers, they are brought together in five or ten adjacent file drawers.

Each major subject category in a hierarchical filing system is organized from the most general to the most specific. A collection of records is first divided into broad groups and then subdivided by successive levels of subordinate and more specific topics. The hierarchical system is the principle upon which computerized database systems operate.

Random Filing Systems.   The oldest type of subject arrangement is *random*, where file folders are numbered sequentially as they are created. A subject index is therefore necessary to retrieve them. The index is controlled from a card file or from a computerized index. The file is assigned a sequential number so that the files are in sequential numeric order, but the subjects in the files are in random order. This system is generally not recommended because all file activity becomes concentrated at the end of the numeric series causing congestion. It also does not permit systematic disposal, review, or browsing. The assignment of file folders may be as follows:

1	Hiring Practices
2	Authorizations
3	Insurance Registers
. . . .
37500	Employee Terminations

A numerically sequential listing is thus maintained as file folder numbers are assigned to new material as it is received. If the system has any merit, it is in minimizing the expansion of files, because most expansion is at the end. The random subject filing system is simple to use. An example of an alphabetic index to the random file would be as follows:

Authorizations	2
Employee Terminations	37500
Hiring Practices	1
Insurance Registers	3

An aid to the random filing system that may make it more popular today is the bar code. A label with the bar code symbol can be affixed to the tab of the folder thus eliminating the need to key in the number. Since the index can be updated as the bar codes are added to new material and input (scanned) into the system, the index can be kept current more easily. With bar codes on the folders, it is possible to scan in the charge-outs and keep a computer listing of who has what file, as well as generate various user reports.

NUMERIC FILING SYSTEMS

Filing systems which use numbers exclusively are straight numeric arrangement, middle-digit arrangement, terminal-digit arrangement, and chronological arrangement.

Straight Numeric Systems

Straight numeric filing is a system in which consecutively numbered folders are placed in a file in exact sequential order. The straight numeric arrangement of records is usually used for records that are prenumbered, such as checks, invoices, vouchers, licenses, purchase orders, warranties, and insurance policies. The system is easily established in law firms, insurance firms, and hospitals. When the system is used for records that are not prenumbered, numbers are assigned to records in consecutive order from an accession book. Numbers may be assigned by using the next available bar code to facilitate computer tracking.

Because it is based on counting, the straight numeric system offers the file clerk definite advantages:

1. It is not necessary for the clerk to become familiar with any radically new filing method.
2. The system is easy to expand; as new items appear, they are simply assigned the next number in sequence, either in the accession book or from the bar codes available.
3. It is simpler to pull a block or group of consecutively numbered folders or documents from a straight numeric system because related material can be kept together.
4. The guiding arrangement is normally very stable because the numbers are consistent and predictable.
5. Items are easily sorted for filing once they have been assigned a bar code or coded with the file number.

The disadvantages of the straight numeric system are the following:

1. The most active folders (those in and out most often) tend to be at the end of the number series, unless the series is made up of randomly assigned numbers, such as Social Security numbers. Frequent referral to these folders produces time-consuming congestion, which slows down the entire filing-and-finding process.
2. It is impossible to make one file clerk responsible for a single unit and, therefore, impossible to fix responsibility for a specific section of files.
3. If old records are removed selectively, rather than by batch such as by year, and new ones

added, the guides must be changed correspondingly.
4. In a straight numeric system, the clerk must be concerned with the entire folder number to find or file accurately. The possibility of human error increases in direct proportion to the length of a series of digits that must be recalled.
5. The possibility of transpositions of digits in a number is limited only by the length of the number. If a clerk is expected to remember the sequence of digits in a number such as 273684, it is easy to understand how he or she might change the position of one or more of the digits, causing a misfile. Color coding is recommended.
6. There is no satisfactory way to handle miscellaneous items. Either a separate alphabetic section may be established for them, or the relative index must provide for miscellaneous folders.

The main numeric divisions would be used as the tab captions for the guides. Individual folders, when required, are used for each consecutive number and are placed in back of each main numeric

FIGURE 5.14 Straight Numeric File Arrangement

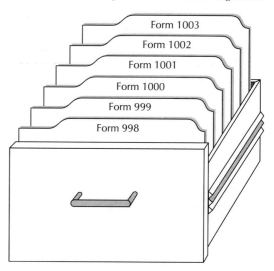

division. (See Figure 5.14.) The volume of records will determine the number of numeric divisions. Divisions are usually made at even numbers, such as 100, 200, etc.

Middle-Digit Filing

Middle-digit indexing is the basis for a *middle-digit filing* arrangement. Middle-digit indexing is a system in which predetermined or consecutively assigned numbers of units (or documents) are divided into groups of two digits, with placement made into the major section of the file according to the middle digits of the identifying number. Since the indexing sequence is predetermined, the indexing system becomes a filing system. Assume that a clerk is working with a folder numbered 273684. This folder would be divided into two-digit groups and read 27-36-84 in middle-digit filing.

Working with this system, the clerk files, first, according to the middle digits (36), the *primary* digits; next, according to the digits on the extreme left side (27), the *secondary* digits; and last, according to the two digits on the extreme right side of the number (84), the *tertiary*, or *final*, digits.

Figure 5.15 illustrates a file using middle-digit indexing. The file drawer number would be the primary digit, 36; the guides would provide the secondary digits, 27, 28, 29, etc. The tertiary

FIGURE 5.15 Middle–Digit File Arrangement

29–36–99
29–35–00
29–36
28–36–99
28–36–00
28–36
27–36–99
27–36–84
27–36–00
27–36

Drawer 36

digits, from 00 to 99, would be filed behind each guide.

Advantages of Middle-Digit Indexing. The advantages of the middle-digit indexing system are as follows:

1. It is simpler to convert from a straight numeric system to middle-digit filing than from a straight numeric system to terminal-digit filing, because files can be regrouped in batches of 100.

2. Sorting operations are equally simple because the clerk uses a sorter with a hundred divisions, speeding the sorting operation and reducing the errors in sorting and filing. Usually only two sorts are required.

3. The important advantage of middle-digit filing in comparison to straight numeric filing is its almost perfect distribution of folders or documents throughout the entire system. This makes it possible to place responsibility for accuracy in filing on the clerk assigned to a specific section. It also eliminates the queuing or congestion that occurs with straight numeric arrangements, which tend to concentrate file activity in the most recent or higher sequential order.

4. Filing speed and accuracy increase over straight numeric filing. Misfiles are fewer, because each file clerk can be held responsible for work in a section of the file. The clerk's efficiency grows as she or he becomes more familiar with a particular section.

Disadvantages of Middle-Digit Indexing. The disadvantages of the middle-digit indexing system are as follows:

1. While distribution of records is relatively good, it is necessary to rearrange the files when large blocks of files are pulled.

2. Tab arrangements remain constant, but it is always necessary to *improvise* each guiding system.

3. Middle-digit filing works most effectively with numbers *not exceeding six digits*. If more

than six digits are used, the secondary digits expand from two digits to three. Then a thousand-division sorter would be needed, usually out of the question because of the space required by the equipment. The only remaining solution would be a third sorting operation. While it eliminates the space problem of the thousand-division sorter, the extra operation slows down the filing function and frustrates the purpose of the entire system.

4. Middle-digit filing requires the file clerk to be trained to read folder or document numbers in an unusual manner. The clerk must start reading in the middle of the number, move next to the left, and finally to the right. This method is contrary to normal reading and is difficult to learn; it requires retraining of file clerks.

Compared to straight numeric filing, middle-digit filing provides more practical, effective distribution of active and inactive records or documents throughout the system. This broader distribution is accomplished by filing according to primary and secondary digits. While numbers in all numerical systems are used in consecutive sequence, in a middle-digit filing system it is impossible to have more than 100 consecutively numbered folders or documents filed together in any one section. For example, the folders filed after guide number 27-36 would be 27-36-00 through 27-36-99. The next guide in the system would be 28-36.

Blocks of 100 consecutively numbered folders can be pulled from a specific section in a middle-digit system. Among the users of this system are some insurance companies, which find this a distinct advantage because they often issue policy numbers to agents or agencies in blocks of 100, or multiples thereof.

While relatively good distribution of active and inactive records is accomplished with middle-digit systems, the problem of file rearrangement is not eliminated. For example, assume that an insurance agent leaves one firm and transfers his policies to his new affiliate. Assume further, that, while with the first firm, he had used one complete block of numbers for his policies. All these policies would have to be pulled and canceled, leaving a gap in the files.

Terminal-Digit Filing

Like the middle-digit system, *terminal-digit* filing was developed to overcome concentrations of active records in one area, which occurs when records are added in consecutive order. It can be used readily where a large volume of records is filed numerically, such as insurance policy numbers, vehicle serial numbers, or Xrays.

The numbers are read from right to left in groups of two, three, or four digits, or in a combination of two and three digits. These groups, from right to left, are known as primary, secondary, and tertiary, as shown in Figure 5.16

In the first example, the primary digits are 21; the secondary digits, 43; and the tertiary dig-

FIGURE 5.16 Terminal–Digit Groupings

Arrangement	Tertiary	Secondary	Primary	File Caption
Two-digit groups	65	43	21	65-43-21
Three-digit groups	987	654	321	987-654-321
Four-digit groups	2109	8765	4321	2109-8765-4321
2-3-3-digit groups	876	543	21	876-543-21
3-2-2-digit groups	76	54	321	76-54-321

its, 65. As a general rule, the number of digits used in the primary, secondary, and tertiary groups are determined by the potential range of the series of numbers the system is designed to accommodate. If the range is great enough, three- or four-digit groups may be used. As with consecutive numeric filing, there is usually an alphabetic index to the numerically sequenced material. While numbers are organized consecutively, the method of filing on the shelf or in the drawer differs from straight numeric filing. Terminal-digit indexing is shown in Figure 5.17.

The primary digits (84) are usually indicated on the file drawers. One set of primary digits may occupy several drawers, particularly if numbers are grouped by three or four digits. All folders in each drawer should end in the primary digit (84). The guides in the drawer are the same as the secondary digits (36, 37, 38). The folders are filed

after the guides according to the tertiary digit. As a file expands, guides may be placed at the left, showing tertiary number divisions for approximately every 20 folders.

Advantages of Terminal-Digit Filing. The advantages of the terminal-digit indexing system include the following:

1. Records numbered sequentially are separated, thus distributing the activity of the files.
2. One clerk can be assigned to a particular section, thus placing responsibility.
3. Sorting is faster, easier, and more accurate, usually requiring only two sortings before filing.
4. The size of the numbers will not affect the system because filing is done according to the primary and secondary digits.

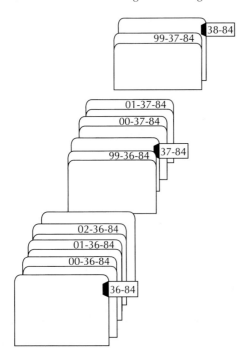

FIGURE 5.17 Terminal–Digit File Arrangement

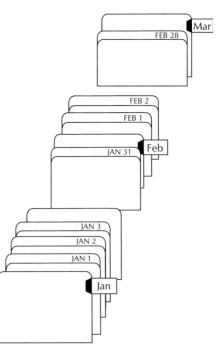

FIGURE 5.18 Chronological File Arrangement

Disadvantages of Terminal-Digit Filing. The disadvantages of the terminal-digit indexing system are the following:

1. The clerk must go to each of the many locations in the file to pull a block of consecutively numbered folders.
2. The changeover to terminal-digit indexing may be both time-consuming and cumbersome because it requires a file-by-file resorting.
3. File clerks have to be trained to read folder or document numbers in an unusual manner.

Chronological Filing

Chronological files arrange documents in order of date, usually for follow-up of activities or information. The captions on the folders are usually numerical dates, with the month digitized; but they can also be alphanumeric, such as *January 1, 1995.* Alphanumeric captions are the exception. Folders are usually arranged in numeric order, regardless of the alpha arrangement of the actual name of the month. See Figure 5.18.

SUMMARY

A uniform file classification system encompasses a file plan, classification, coding, information indexing systems, alphabetic, subject, and numeric filing arrangements. The principal objectives of filing are to be able to retrieve information when needed; to identify and preserve the set order of records; and to establish uniform file classification. File arrangement may be either in alphabetic order or numeric order in ascending or descending order. The filing system may also be set up as a direct access system or an indirect access (coded subject) system.

The classification process includes determining the classes of records and the subdivisions. Classification should be logical, standardized, practical, simple, functional, retention conscious, mutually exclusive, flexible, and conscious of perspective. An essential part of any classification system is its documentation. File coding systems facilitate filing, retrieval, and refiling of records. Coding for various file plans may be alphanumeric, numeric, decimal-numeric, duplex-numeric, block-numeric, or phonetic. Codes may also be established by color or with bar codes to facilitate finding and tracking of documents and files. Phonetic codes have also been developed to bring together all names that sound alike.

An index is a dictionary-type listing that shows all possible words and word combinations by which material may be requested. A relative index is also a cross-reference system because it contains all titles under which material may be filed. Indexes may be synthetical, analytical, or hierarchical. Indexes vary from simple listings of words or phrases in alphabetical order to complex computerized systems.

Filing systems include alphabetic, alphanumeric, and numerical systems. Subject files are used when the record is requested by subject matter rather than by a person's name, a project or a case name or numbers, a transaction document number, or some other numerical identifier used for specialty records. Subject files range from the simple, small-volume topical subjects to the classified topical or hierarchical system. Subject files may be arranged by numbers or alphabetically using whole words that have been arranged into units. Subject files arranged by whole words alphabetically do not require an external index. Numeric or coded subject files require an index to translate the subject to code.

Classifying records for efficient retrieval and filing requires a good knowledge of the organization's functions, a logical mind, good reading and verbal skills, and a firm grasp of the principles of classification.

Organization assets such as people, equipment, money, and space influence file systems development. Similar organizations may allocate resources differently to produce different systems.

QUESTIONS FOR DISCUSSION

1. What factors must be considered in establishing the best possible file plan for an organization?
2. What are the objectives of filing systems?
3. What are three basic types of file arrangement?
4. Differentiate between a direct access filing system and an indirect access filing system.
5. What is classification?
6. When are classification systems considered?
7. What criteria are used in determining subject headings?
8. What are the functions of coding systems?
9. How are file coding systems for subject headings used?
10. What is the basis for phonetic file arrangement?
11. What classification system was developed in order to facilitate the automation of library holdings?
12. What are the advantages of a decimal filing system? What are the disadvantages?
13. Describe the duplex-numeric filing system.
14. Describe the block-numeric subject filing system.
15. What are some examples of the different indexing systems?
16. What are the differences between the three search objectives of an index?
17. What organization has developed standard rules for filing?
18. What are the three conventions for determining alphabetic order? Explain how they differ.
19. What is order of entry?

20. What are the two ways subject files may be organized?
21. How does the encyclopedic filing system differ from a dictionary arrangement?
22. What are the advantages of a hierarchical filing system?
23. What is a random filing system?
24. Compare the middle-digit filing system to straight numeric filing.
25. Identify the advantages and disadvantages of the terminal-digit indexing system.

PROJECTS

1. Put the following list in alphabetic order. First do this manually. Note the difficulties caused by spelling. If you were verbally asked to find some of these names in the files, what problems might you encounter? If you have database software available, create a database consisting of two fields. Enter your name and the following list of names into the database. Sort the names. Print out the results.

John Wozniak
Gene R. Wrigglesworth
Joseph R. Weber
Denby Tao-Yuan Wu
Wu Shijuei
Violet Wuerfel
Anna Belle Werth
Mary Worth
Letty Wunglueck
Mike Jaeger
M. Yager
Edward Zarafonetis
Roger Zauel
Jung Suk Youn
Robert Young
Peter Yates
Toshihisa Yotsuyanagi
V. J. Wrobleski
Ching-Juan Wu

Elfreda Wrathell
Sharon Wroblewski
Wong Tony Young
Gregory Yeatts
Judy Jong
Artee Younge

2. Take the alphabetic list completed in Project 1 and assign Soundex codes to each last name.

3. Arrange the Soundex codes into correct file-drawer order. If you have database software available, print out four fields of data: the Soundex code, the last name, the first name, and the middle name. Be sure that the Soundex codes and first names are either sorted or indexed.

4. What advantages are apparent in a Soundex coding system? Is the Soundex coding system better than alphabetic filing for this particular list of names? Why? Are there any disadvantages?

5. Following is a list of 12 subject headings and 26 company names and addresses. Alphabetize the list of services, and classify the companies alphabetically according to the type of service they provide. Use your database software to do this. Create a database with a field for services, name of company, address, city, state, and ZIP Code. Create a report form to group on *services* and print out the report.

Services

Janitor Service
Insurance
Foam Rubber *see* Rubber—Foam and Sponge
Facsimile
Fabrics
Audiovisual Equipment—Dealers
Automobile Renting and Leasing
Laundries—Industrial *see* Overall Supply
  Service; *see also* Uniform Supply Service
Gutters *see* Eavestroughs and Downspouts

Banks
Furniture Repairing and Refinishing
Automobile Body Repairing and Painting

Company Names

Youngs Refinishing, 113 Elm, Wyandotte, MI 48192

Frankenmuth Mutual Insurance Co., 1167 Eureka, Wyandotte, MI 48192

Lease Care of America Inc., 22725 Greater Mack, St. Clair Shores, MI 48011

Wilson's Bumping & Painting, 12931 Northline, Southgate, MI 48195

Ricoh Diversified Business Products, Inc., 37655 Interchange, Farmington Hills, 48018

Classic Copy Service, Inc., 3981 Varsity Drive, Ann Arbor, MI 48106

State Farm Insurance, 28747 Church, Flat Rock, MI 48134

Taylor Janitorial Service, 2110 Fourth, Wyandotte, MI 48192

Security Bank and Trust, 14753 Northwestern Highway, Southfield, MI 48037

Society Bank, 2121 Washtenaw, Ypsilanti, MI 48197

Xerox Fascimile Equipment, 23999 Northwestern Highway, Southfield, MI 48037

Riverside Insurance Company, 2341 W. Jefferson, Trenton, MI 48183

Karate Maintenance, 28742 Detroit, Flat Rock, MI 48134

A V Sales Center, 55 Oakland Avenue, Pontiac, MI 48056

Downriver Collision, 2323 Dix, Lincoln Park, MI 48146

Thrifty Rent-a-Wreck, 29111 Wick Road, Romulus, MI 48174

Security Bank & Trust, 14951 Dix-Toledo Road, Southfield, MI 48037

Todd Audio-Visual Service Inc., 134 Manchester, Highland Park, MI 48203

Pondarose Collision, 4168 Biddle, Wyandotte, MI 48192

Detroit Bank & Trust, Fort at Washington Blvd, Detroit, MI 48226

Canon Fax, 41180 Bridge Street, Novi, MI 48375

Payette Insurance Agency, 1420 Ford Avenue, Wyandotte, MI 48192

American Building Maintenance Company, 4400 12th Street, Detroit, MI 48229

Ann Arbor Bedding Co., 5060 Jackson Road, Ann Arbor, MI 48108

Super Suds Laundry, 14401 Ford, Dearborn, MI 48201

Commerical Gutter Systems, 5621 East DE Avenue, Kalamazoo, MI 49001

6. Use the Yellow Pages of your telephone book. Add at least two additional services to the database created for Problem 6 and at least two company names for each of the services that you add.

7. Sort or index on ZIP Code field. Print out the name in ZIP Code order, followed by the company name, street address, city, and state.

CASE PROBLEM

Dr. Edward Smith, who chairs the Special Education Department of your school, has asked for assistance in reorganizing the department's files. The files consist of six drawers full of correspondence from vendors of furniture, equipment, and supplies and from students, alumni, and applicants for admission. Faculty information for 20 faculty members and approximately a hundred applications for faculty positions are also included in the files. Course syllabi for each of the 50 courses taught in the department are also kept there. All of the material is arranged in alphabetic order in one continuous file.

Present procedures are as follows:

1. The administrative assistant files each piece of correspondence according to the name of the addressee.

2. Correspondence is filed behind each of 26 guides for the letters of the alphabet.

3. Inquiries about admissions are filed in the general file according to the addressee's name, although another faculty member whose office is located elsewhere in the building is designated as admissions advisor.

4. Correspondence is placed behind the guides in chronological order with no attempt made to group letters from one person or company.

Dr. Smith recognizes problems in retrieval when the administrative assistant is on vacation and asks you to make some recommendations on how to better organize:

1. Faculty personnel files

2. Course syllabi

3. Applications and alumni files

4. Vendors

Write your report in a memo format outlining recommendations for organizing each of the file groups listed.

NOTES

1. *Filing Rules for Dictionary Catalogs of the Library of Congress* (Washington, D.C.: Government Printing Office, 1969), p. 187.

2. *Alphabetical Filing Rules* (Prairie Village, Kansas: Association of Records Managers and Administrators, Inc., 1986).

Chapter 6

Filing System Maintenance

Learning Objectives
1. To identify factors which help reduce the area and time of a records search.
2. To identify basic record types.
3. To explain the primary tools used for identifying records.
4. To explain the use of color in records management.
5. To describe files maintenance procedures.
6. To describe the records identification systems used in records management.
7. To list standards for filing.
8. To recommend solutions for common filing problems.
9. To make recommendations for safeguarding the security and confidentiality of records.
10. To describe the process for file reorganization.
11. To make recommendations for small business filing systems.

ISOLATING THE BASIC TYPES OF RECORDS

File systems consist of documents, file folders, and files dispersed throughout an organization. These systems usually incorporate incoming and outgoing correspondence, internal and external supporting materials, working papers, and office-related records. Records managers long ago discovered breaking, or subdividing, to be the secret of finding the needle of information in an office's haystack of papers. Subdividing within file groups was discussed in the previous chapter, but the first consideration of organizing records is consideration of the basic types of records.

Reducing the Area and Time of a Records Search

Separating papers into basic types aids the finding of material by immediately reducing the area of search. Other factors which will aid in reducing the area and time of search are disposal, identification, volume, and completeness.

Disposal. Separation into basic groups keeps essential documents apart from short-lived papers, which may be disposed of earlier than essential documents. For example, case working papers are kept separate from essential case papers to facilitate disposal of the working papers. Transitory and convenience files also have a shorter life span than the general correspondence records. Differing retention periods are therefore a good reason for filing these types of records separately.

Identification. The inability to readily recognize the papers of each type may affect the file-type decision. If it is difficult to distinguish technical reference and transitory materials from general correspondence, it may be better to keep them together to avoid filing errors.

Volume. The quantity of papers involved is important. If less than a file drawer of case records or technical reference material is involved, separating the material from the general correspondence will be of little value. On the other hand, it does not take many transitory, working, or convenience papers to justify separation. While no set volume figure can apply to separating file types in every office, this chapter attempts to give some guidance for common file types.

Completeness. The needs of files users for complete information (telling the whole story of transactions) should not be overlooked in organizing files. If photographs and correspondence are separated, either both files may have to be searched when records are requested, or the user runs the risk of taking action without the complete facts. Usually, it is the physical characteristics of papers, such as the size of engineering drawings, which require materials to be filed separately, even though filing materials together would be preferable.

Basic Record Types

Basic record types include general correspondence; transitory correspondence; case records; case working papers; technical reference materials; extra convenience copies; film, tape, and disk records; cartographic materials and drawings, and cards. Other types of records which may be maintained are ledger books, suspense files, and perhaps other categories.

General Correspondence. The general correspondence file consists of letters, memorandums, telegrams, enclosures, reports, and miscellaneous materials, arranged by subject. This file may also be known as the *central file*, the *subject file*, or the *correspondence file*. Almost every office requires a file of this type for those papers that are most often requested by subject. The general correspondence file often includes papers belonging to other basic types for ready access or if the volume of such papers is small.

Transitory Correspondence. Transitory correspondence consists of easily used routine materials, e.g., short-lived papers involved in answering routine requests for information or publications, in requesting or transmitting routine data to other offices, in making hotel reservations or arranging for conferences, and the like. Transitory correspondence often may be authorized for disposal within six months or less. Every office has such papers and needs to segregate them. They should be kept in folders separate from general correspondence if they amount to 5 percent or more of the papers.

Case Records. A case file relates to a specific person, company, client, project, event, geographic area, or other unique entity. Case files commonly refer to purchase orders, contracts, investigations, requisitions, loans, research projects, construction projects, or personnel transactions. The papers may cover one or many subjects concerning a case or project and will always be filed by a name or a number. Another distinguishing feature of case records is the similarity in the nature of the papers within each case folder which make up the total file. This procedure aids in distinguishing case records from the general correspondence, which is filed by subject. Since a case file is first identified by its functional classification, case files may be integrated into the filing system either alphabetically by the name of the case or numerically by its number.

It is possible to have many files classifications in a single case file. For example, if several major projects are underway, the decision needs to be made as to whether accounts payable and accounts receivable should both be included in each case file, or whether they should be maintained as separate files. If they are separated by project and filed with other records about the project, the result is the project case file incorporating multiple files classifications. Accounts payable and accounts receivable use the same files classifications regardless of whether they are arranged in a case file or not. A rule of thumb for case files is that they should be arranged by function in order to avoid obsolescence of the classification scheme.

Case Working Papers. Reference materials and other data collected for the project, materials involved in summarizing or analyzing the data, and drafts or other preliminary papers leading to a finding can be classified as working papers. If working papers can be easily distinguished from important case papers, they should always be segregated. These papers should be viewed as a segment of a case history file segregated to aid disposition of short-lived specific classes of material. To avoid screening for disposal, such papers are placed in separate folders, side by side, distinguished one from the other by the color of the label or the position of the folder tab. Case working papers are usually disposed of after a period dating from the close of the case.

Technical Reference Materials. Offices involved in research, product development, statistical reports, and information gathering and dissemination typically have duplicate materials of publications already available in library facilities. This reference material may be received from government agencies, colleges and universities, private research organizations, trade associations, and other sources. As a broad rule of thumb, if more than one drawer of the general file consists of reference materials, separate filing is warranted.

Extra Convenience Copies. Extra copies of documents created or received that are retained solely for ease of use make up the convenience file group. The day file of letters written by an office, arranged in date order, is a typical example of a convenience file.

Film, Tape, and Disk Records. Electronic or other mechanical reproductions of sound or coded information are usually kept separate because of their physical characteristics. Still pictures are used in many instances to record individuals, activities, or progress and must be treated as records. Still picture negatives, as well as motion pictures and videotapes, demand separate housing and special care for preservation.

Sound recordings from some office dictating machines may be transcribed to paper records so that the recording media can be discarded or reused. Other recordings are not transcribed and must be preserved, as in some grievance hearings. Even a small volume of cassette tapes, disks, or off-size recordings requires a separate file.

Word processing storage media have also added to the diversity of records storage. While many organizations use hard disks for the storage media, many others are faced with storing hundreds of full floppy disks that are maintained for periods of time.

Long-time storage of electronic media for audio, text, and graphics leads to the problem of having equipment to read the media as technology progresses.

Other items in this basic type are magnetic and paper tapes, Xray films, and micrographics.

Cartographic Materials and Drawings. Maps, charts, aerial photographs, physiographic diagrams, and engineering drawings have a variety of formats and sizes. This variety normally separates them from other records. Field survey notes, geodetic surveys, astronomic readings, and similar computations usually are considered cartographic in nature. The term *charts* (hydrographic, nautical, weather, aeronautical, etc.) includes graphic presentations (bar, pie, tabular, line, etc.). Aerial photographs include the negative and positive (print) film and other items such as flight line indexes, mosaics, and graphic indexes. Engineering drawings may be blueprints, diazo prints, pencil sketches, or tracings on vellum. These drawings require special reproduction equipment and special storage systems. Some oversize maps and drawings can be folded and interfiled among related subject or case files. However, if more than

10 percent of the maps, charts, or drawings are oversize, separate filing is necessary. Too many bulky, folded papers will seriously handicap filing and searching in standard-size records.

Cards. The variety of card files is almost as great as the variety of case files. However, their size and format make them a logically separate file group. Common sizes used as indexes, catalogs, or summaries are 3 by 5 or 5 by 8 inches. The Hollerith punched card and the microfilm aperture card are variations of card files.

Once records have been separated into types, it is possible to select a system for arranging the records of each separate file type.

PRIMARY TOOLS FOR LOCATING RECORDS

Personnel and organizations may change, but a well-designed and well-maintained filing system remains constant, and anyone using the file arrangement documentation should be able to retrieve the desired record. As changes occur in departments, and files concerning research and development become manufacturing files or operations files, standard filing systems simplify the transfer process. The primary tools for locating records are arrangement of documents, labeling, indexing, use of color, and automation.

Arrangement of Documents

The basic file arrangement is either alphabetic or numeric, and one or a combination of these arrangements is used in the design of a file system. For a full discussion of filing arrangements, see Chapter 5.

Table 6.1 is a summary of file arrangements for documents having a variety of filing features. Filing features of documents are used to assist in indexing.

Indexing

Indexes facilitate the locating of files. In some offices, records can be found more rapidly by maintenance of a separate name index to the subject file. The index is arranged alphabetically by the name of the person or organization referred to in the correspondence or document. If a large file is organized by developing a uniform files classification system, the UFCS provides a listing, or database, of all created information and can be used as an index. It is then also possible to flag a records series for retention and at the same time flag duplicate copies for destruction. The listing of records also aids in the development of a retention schedule and permits identification of vital records. The UFCS also provides continuity since only trained records personnel can modify the file plan.

The index is used as a finding tool for indirect access files and in refreshing the memory of possible locations in a large alphabetic subject file. The index is usually not required for small subject files. The index can be maintained in a card file or in a computer listing.

Preparing Cards for Indexing. A uniform style should be followed for all cards in a card index file. A typical style is to type the name in index form at the top of the card, about three spaces from the left margin and three lines from the top. Parentheses are used to show nonindexing units, for example, *(the)*. The Association of Records Managers and Administrators suggests that the diagonal [/] be used to show indexing units. Other methods are to type the first indexing unit in all capital letters with other units in upper- and lowercase; to type all indexing units in capital letters; and to type all indexing units in upper- and lowercase without the diagonals.

A cross-reference card lists another title or name by which material may be requested and notes the name under which the material will be found. Three lines below the indexed name, the cross-reference name is typed in the usual envelope style, in all caps. If the cards are to be used in a numerical system, a code number is usually typed in the upper right-hand corner. See Figure 6.1.

TABLE 6.1 File Arrangement for Different Filing Features

Filing Feature of Document	Usual Filing Sequence	Most Suitable File Groups	Need for Index File (by Second Filing Feature)	Need for Cross-Referencing a Document within the File	Likelihood That Document Description Used in Request Will Pinpoint File Location	Likelihood of File Designation Being Shown on Document When Originated	Likelihood of File Designation Being Expressed the Same on Documents to Be Filed Together	Ease and Accuracy in Marking a Document for Filing	Ease and Accuracy in Sorting and Filing
Names of people, organizations, or firms.	Alphabetic by name.	Case. Case working. Technical reference.	Normally not needed, except for precedent cases.	If more than one name involved.	Usually. Foreign, organization, and unusual names may be troublesome. The larger the file, the greater the problem.	Nearly always.	Usually, except for misspellings. Exchanging personal and organization names causes inconsistency.	Fast and easy, if names can be underlined. Fairly slow if names must be written. Spelling errors may occur in unfamiliar names. Adherence to filing rules required.	Slow and difficult. Eye must scan each letter of each word to determine sequence: words and titles vary widely in length. The larger the file, the greater the problem, and the greater the need for rigid adherence to filing rules.
Names or titles of projects, publications, products, or things.	Alphabetic by name.	Case. Case working. Technical reference.	Normally not needed, except for precedent cases.	If more than one name or title involved.	Sometimes. Project titles may be troublesome. The longer the name or title, the less chance of agreement. The larger the file, the greater the problem.	Usually.	Usually. Difficulties may occur with project and other long titles.	Fairly slow. Key words to be underlined may be buried in long titles. Incomplete titles may have to be completed by handwriting. Adherence to filing rules required.	Slow and difficult. Eye must scan each letter of each word to determine sequence: words and titles vary widely in length. The larger the file, the greater the problem, and the greater the need for rigid adherence to filing rules.
Geographic areas or location.	Alphabetic by name (often sub-arranged by people, things, etc.)	Case. Case working. Technical reference.	Frequently needed as location is not always known.	If more than one location involved.	Sometimes. Record may be requested by city but filed by state, or may be requested by people, organizations, or things without the location given. The larger the file, the greater the problem.	Usually. Location is shown, but not sub-arrangement file designation.	Depends on consistent choice of locational level for each paper.	Fast, if location can be underlined. Sub-arrangements often require handwritten designations.	Fairly difficult, depending on number of breakdowns and subarrangements. Precise filing required. The larger the file, the greater the problem.
Numbers or symbols.	By number or symbol.	Case. Case working. Technical reference.	Name index needed to obtain number or symbol, not known or incorrectly shown.	If more than one number or symbol involved.	Depends upon widespread use of the numbers or symbols within the office and extent of use on documents received from the outside.	Nearly always— but sometimes omitted.	Nearly always.	Fast, if numbers or symbols are short or segmented. Numbers or symbols susceptible to transposition and other errors.	Easy, if numbers or symbols are short or segmented. Transposition and other errors likely.
Dates.	By date prepared or used.	Convenience. Transitory. Suspense.	Not needed unless large volume filed only by date.	Not needed.	Usually for suspense. For convenience or transitory files, exact date often not known.	Always.	Always.	Fast and accurate. Marking rarely needed.	Easy and accurate.
Subject topics.	Alphabetic by subject topic, or by numeric or alphanumeric file code.	General correspondence (may include cases sub-arranged by names or numbers). Technical reference.	Occasionally an index by names of people, firms, and organizations needed.	If more than one subject involved, or document is brought forward.	Unlikely. Request may be vague, and differing terms may be used to describe same document. Relative index may be needed to determine proper subject topic.	Unlikely, since subject, if shown, rarely matches subject outline topics.	Unlikely.	Slow, as content must be read. Use of file code speeds writing, but may require reference to subject outline or relative index. Faulty decisions and errors in writing may occur.	Difficult, if alphabetically filed by word topics. Easier if filed by short file codes. The more complex the code the more difficult the accuracy.

Source: NARS Files Operations.

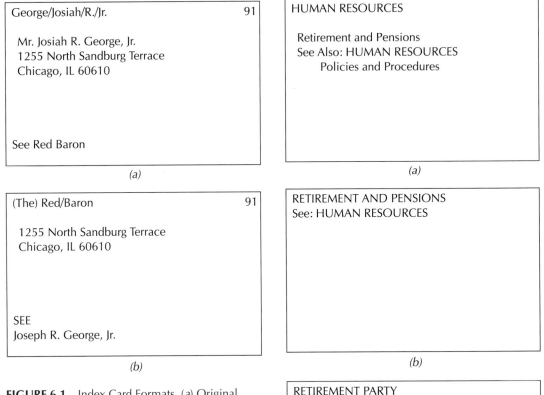

George/Josiah/R./Jr.   91

Mr. Josiah R. George, Jr.
1255 North Sandburg Terrace
Chicago, IL 60610

See Red Baron

(a)

(The) Red/Baron   91

1255 North Sandburg Terrace
Chicago, IL 60610

SEE
Joseph R. George, Jr.

(b)

FIGURE 6.1   Index Card Formats. (*a*) Original
Card; (*b*) Cross–Reference Card

HUMAN RESOURCES

Retirement and Pensions
See Also: HUMAN RESOURCES
      Policies and Procedures

(a)

RETIREMENT AND PENSIONS
See: HUMAN RESOURCES

(b)

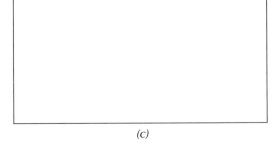

RETIREMENT PARTY
See: HUMAN RESOURCES

(c)

FIGURE 6.2   Sample Index Cards. (*a*) White
Card—Major Classification; (*b*) Blue Card—
Subdivision; (*c*) Pink Card—Cross–Reference

After the proper caption is chosen, all synonymous terms should be cross-referenced, as
should all subheadings of the main classification.
Figure 6.2 illustrates the use of cards in showing
subdivisions and cross-referencing in a card index. All major headings are typed in all caps.
Different-colored cards are used for major classification cards (white), subdivisions cards (blue),
and cross-reference cards (pink).

All three colored cards should be interfiled to
form the index. The white cards represent the
captions to be found in the file drawers. In revising files, a cross-reference to the old subject heading that will not be used will help users become
accustomed to the new terms. An example appears in Figure 6.3. Card files other than index
card files can be maintained using the same procedures.

Labeling

Once the filing arrangement has been determined,
it is possible to plan the labeling of the drawers,
folders, guides, and shelves. Labels are used to
identify the contents of drawers, shelves, trays,
bins, binders, boxes, and folders. They come in
strips, rolls, fanfolds, pads, and in various colors

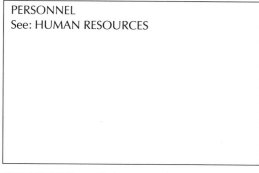

PERSONNEL
See: HUMAN RESOURCES

FIGURE 6.3 Cross–Reference to New Caption—
Pink Card

or with color stripes. Labels reinforce and strengthen, as well as accent, the area to which they are applied. *Labeling* is marking records or containers with identification information. Labels may also be identified with a bar code that can be scanned into the computer.

Folder Labels. File folder labels identify the contents of the folder. The information on the label is used to find the file's place in the arrangement. The more dependent one is on arrangement for locating records, the more important labeling

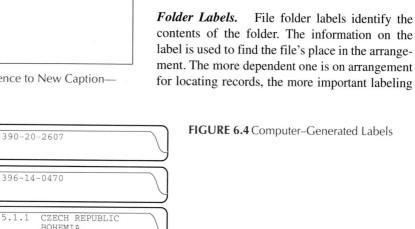

FIGURE 6.4 Computer–Generated Labels

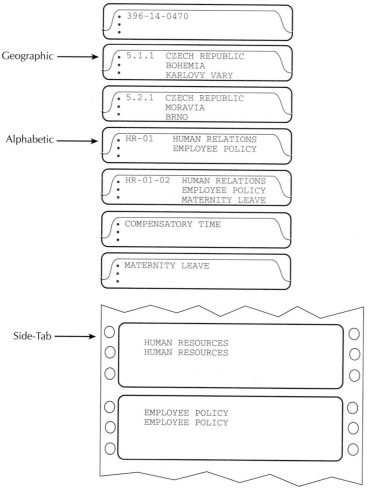

becomes. Labeling is particularly critical in direct access files. Figure 6.4 is an illustration of computer-generated labels for top-tab folders.

The folder labels may be gummed or self-adhesive and are affixed to the tab at the back of the folders. Since the tabs may be either at the top or at the side, it is necessary to prepare labels accordingly. Folder labels may have color strips or may be one color only. For preparation on the typewriter, folder labels come in rolls, fanfolds, or pads. Continuous-form labels are available for computer preparation. Hanging folder labels are inserted into plastic tabs which are inserted into the slots of the front flap of the folder. This is a variation from the regular file folder where the label is attached to the tab at the back of the folder.

When files are transferred to inactive status on a regular basis, it is common practice to generate a complete set of labels for the new time period.

Typing Labels. To keep labels neat and uniform, the following rules should be observed:

1. Start typing labels two spaces from the left edge, directly below scoring.
2. Capitalize the headings. The major heading may be typed in all caps. The label caption should be complete. Invert the name where necessary.
3. Omit punctuation. Use two spaces where a period or comma normally would be.
4. Position the year and month on the label so as not to interfere with the main caption.
5. Spell out subject names and titles in full. Use cuts of tabs to fit headings.
6. Avoid misspellings, erasures, and strikeovers.

Labels should be applied in a uniform position on the folders. To do this, a handful of folders can be spread out on the desk with the edges even. A pencil mark can be drawn along a ruler placed vertically against the folders at the extreme left edge of the tabs. This pencil mark at the upper left corner of each folder is the guide for placement of the label. The labels should not overhang the curved corners of the folder tabs.

Labels on folder tabs and guide tabs may also be of the insert type and used with plastic or metal label protectors.

Drawer Labels. Label information identifies the contents of a drawer and corresponds with the coding system. Drawer label information is inclusive and concise. The labels are usually available in card stock paper, in perforated sheets, and in a variety of colors, and can be slipped into the holders of the file drawers.

Numeric labels simply list the first and last folder in the drawer, such as *1-99*. The alphabetic range of the drawer may be indicated by single, double, or multiple notations. Single or open notation simply shows the first letter of the contents of the drawer, such as *A*. Double notation shows the range; that is, the first and last letter of the alphabet for the material contained in the drawer, such as *A-As*. Multiple notation is similar to double notation, but it lists combinations within the range, such as *A-As* and *Al-An*. Labels for file drawers should correspond in color with the labels used in the file unit. The information is usually centered and printed (by typewriter or computer printer) in capital letters without punctuation. An example of a label for a file drawer appears in Figure 6.5.

Guide Labels. Guide labels may be affixed to guide tabs or inserted into plastic or metal holders to identify a section of records and information. Guide labels are prepared similarly to folder labels.

FIGURE 6.5 File Drawer Label

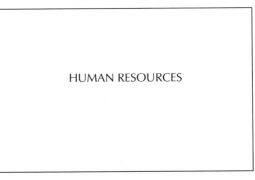

HUMAN RESOURCES

Shelf Labels. Shelf labels may appear at the end or front edge of a shelf unit to identify the contents of the entire shelf unit or an entire range of shelf units. The labels may be affixed to the shelf unit itself or inserted into metal holders on the ends or front edges of the shelf units. Color and printing formats are similar to those used for folder and guide labels.

Use of Color

In records management, color is used in coding equipment; in supplies such as folders, labels, tabs, signals, guides; in stripping for microfiche, film, and storage media; and in commercially prepared systems.

Color in Supplies. Color is used to identify records and to make filing and retrieval easier and faster. Bars of color can be imprinted, or they can be added to file folders in a uniform location for identification. The numbers appear on backgrounds of different colors on blocks of labels that may be attached to the folder tab. Twelve colors can identify a year's cycle, and in alphabetic filing, groups of letters are assigned specific colors. Major divisions of a company's file can also be assigned different colors. Both conventional file folders and hanging file folders are available in a variety of colors.

Color may show the hierarchical structure of the file. Main headings may appear on colored guide tabs, for example, yellow. All subheadings, in the second position, may appear in the same color, for example, on green guide tabs. Further breakdowns may continue with blue or violet. It has been recommended that color selection for tabs should follow the colors of the rainbow— red, orange, yellow, green, blue, indigo, violet— to further assist in a predictable plan.

In shelf filing, color permits misfiles to be spotted with a minimum of effort. Color and bar codes are also used on labels of magnetic tape, on cartridges and reels of microforms, and on the boxes in which they are stored. Thus, identification, filing, and referencing are made easier.

Color is used, too, in visible files to identify different functions, time periods, and departments. For example, computer disks can be color-coded by department, project, type of work, or any other special feature.

Color can be used in the form of ink highlighters to mark text that should be called to someone's attention, or to ease recall. Color can assist in decision making. For example, a person reading a report that requires a decision can underline positive points in green and negative points in red. The predominant color probably points to the correct decision.

Trays for paper now come in a variety of colors. Paperwork that is passed on to other employees can be sorted into different color trays; for example, red, for reading; black for filing; and almond for out-going mail. Other supplies, like colored dots or colored pushpins, can flag paper for the attention of individual employees or actions.

Security. To enhance security, reports in a particular color can be cycled so that the previous copy of that color must be turned in when the new one is delivered. Color can also be used to limit access to a particular record, such as payroll reports. For example, if red covers are used only for payroll reports, unauthorized use of the reports can more easily be identified.

Equipment. There is a growing trend toward using color for storage equipment and furniture. Different-colored filing cabinets can be used for different records. Color-coordinated workstations in the open office can be used to identify different work groups.

Commercially Prepared Systems. Commercially prepared filing systems are available from a variety of vendors. A small filing system may require only a set of alphabetical tabs, subdivided through the alphabet. A set of tabs for the months of the year and days of the month are also available. It is possible to buy color-coded labels for the various letters of the alphabet and affix colored codes for

FIGURE 6.6 AlphaCode Filing System
(Courtesy of TAB Products Co.)

FIGURE 6.7 Colored Folders
(Courtesy of Atapco Office Products Group)

the first three letters of the filing unit to the tab of the folder. For example, the AlphaCode system of the Tab Products Company shows the same color for the first letter, a second color for the second letter, and a third color for the third letter. This system is very popular in open-shelf filing since misfiles stand out. See Figure 6.6.

Some vendors offer folders in 25 different colors, providing arrangement opportunities either alphabetically, chronologically, or by client. See Figure 6.7.

Automation

Many companies today are using computerized indexing systems for both active records and inactive records. The index can be devised to give a summary of the complete file that is maintained in electronic format, in paper, or on microform. Keyword cross-referencing can be included, as well

as a history of the file, such as the date it was opened. In cases where files are periodically transferred to inactive storage, the computerized index can also be used to print labels for new file folders. These same computerized systems can be used for checkout notations, follow-up, and calculating reference ratios.

Bar-Coding. If the file folders are bar-coded, scanning of the user's bar code facilitates checkout. It is possible to check the computer monitor to learn whether a folder is in the file or checked out to a particular user. It is also possible to keep an audit trail of all users. Figure 6.8 is a sample of a file folder with a bar code.

Information Management. Files management may be contrasted to information management in that information systems are usually large collec-

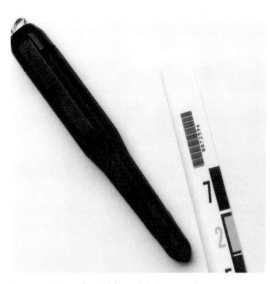

FIGURE 6.8 File Folder with Bar Code
(Courtesy of TAB Products Co.)

tions of data, typically stored in a corporate database or other computer system. On-line information systems usually deal with discrete units of data or information. Information systems have no set order to the information contained and are intended to be extracted, sorted, or compared.

RECORDS MAINTENANCE PROCEDURES

The file system consists of an alphabetic or numeric arrangement, a file plan, file controls, and records maintenance procedures. Records maintenance procedures are developed to preserve, secure, and distribute document information. Ineffective filing classification systems make it difficult to find information when it is needed for operations and decision making. Ineffective systems may cause unnecessary duplicates to be retained, make it difficult to purge files of obsolete records, and make it hard to know where to file. The filing procedure consists of receiving the document, inspection, preparation for filing, indexing, coding, cross-referencing, preparing file folders, and filing.

The day-to-day activities of filing consist of collecting, inspecting, and preparing materials for filing; indexing; coding; cross-referencing; alphabetic or numeric sorting; charging out materials; following up; finding lost records; filing; refiling; maintaining the files; and developing standards for filing work.

Collection of Material

Where active files are centralized, file material should be collected from all section file boxes at least once each day. The volume of work to be filed will determine the frequency of collection trips, and a definite collection schedule should be adhered to. The collection holder should be designed to keep separate material from each collection point.

Upon receipt of records in the files section, the distribution clerk will sort them into file groups and deliver each group to the file clerk assigned to that file. Sometimes a count is made at this point to keep track of volume. Where filing is decentralized, the importance of filing material on a regular basis cannot be overemphasized. Someone in each department should have the responsibility of maintaining the files—to file new materials received, to refile materials which have been removed from the file and returned, and to track materials which have been out of the file for an extended period of time.

Inspection

When records are ready for filing, they should be checked to be sure they are officially released for filing action. In records maintenance procedures, this is called *inspection.* A release mark such as an initial, a signature, or a stamp shows that a record has been released. Before sending a letter to the file, the letter writer or his or her secretary should indicate where cross-referencing is necessary. By agreement, the request for cross-reference may be indicated by drawing a line beneath the name or subject.

Useless material such as working papers, extra copies, preliminary drafts, or informational material that has served its purpose should be removed to prevent overburdening the files. The file manual should indicate which material should be excluded from the files.

Preparation for Filing

When papers are checked in by the file clerk, all pins and paper clips should be removed from the material. Related papers should be stapled together, and small papers should be mounted on a standard-sized sheet. Torn or work papers may be reinforced with mending tape. Oversize documents may have to be folded to the dimensions of the folder.

Indexing

If the record has been officially released for filing, it is then indexed, or classified, by an index clerk who scans the record to decide its proper filing classification. Selecting the correct category under which to file each document is indispensable to location and retrieval.

In order to design a filing system that will meet the needs of the users, it is necessary to know how users will most often request the particular records, that is, which filing feature will they most frequently request. Most people tend to see filing from their own perspective.

Correspondence.   To the secretary, the most important type of document is probably correspondence. Users may request letters or memorandums by one or more of the following eight filing features, shown in Figure 6.9.

- Name of organization.
- Date prepared or used.
- Surname of individual.
- Title of individual.
- Name (title) of project, product, or transaction.
- Location (geographic or political division).
- Number (symbol) assigned to transaction, commodity, location, project, individual, or organizational unit.
- Subject topic describing the content.

For personal letters, the name of the writer may be used. Not every piece of correspondence has all eight filing features, but most have more than one.

Forms.   To the accounting clerk, the most important type of document may be forms. The most common filing features of forms are shown in Figure 6.10 and include:

- Title of form.
- Surnames (names or titles) of individuals or organizations.
- Names of organizations.
- Numbers (symbols) assigned for transaction control or other identification.
- Subject.
- Dates.

Because forms are used often in case files, they are usually filed by name or number.

Reports.   The manager may perceive the most important type of document to be a report. Figure 6.11 shows the principal filing features of reports as:

- Assigned control numer.
- Subject.
- Surname of author.
- Number of project or contract with which identified.
- Name of originating organization.
- Date.

Some file systems classify recurring or periodic reports under *Reports.* Subdivisions are arranged by report title or by form title if the report is a form.

In some offices, the person releasing the material marks the index reference or code. Consulting the relative index for the files may give some clue as to selecting a category for an item that is difficult to index.

Coding

At the time of indexing, the file code should be indicated on the record by colored pencil: This is

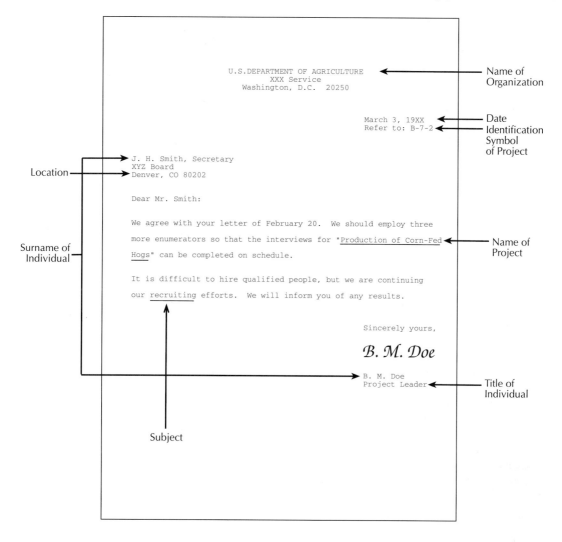

U.S.DEPARTMENT OF AGRICULTURE ←————— Name of
XXX Service   Organization
Washington, D.C.   20250

March 3, 19XX ←———— Date
Refer to: B-7-2 ←———— Identification
                                    Symbol
                                    of Project

Location ————→ J. H. Smith, Secretary
XYZ Board
Denver, CO 80202

Dear Mr. Smith:

We agree with your letter of February 20. We should employ three

more enumerators so that the interviews for "Production of Corn-Fed ←——— Name of
                                                                           Project
Hogs" can be completed on schedule.

Surname of
Individual

It is difficult to hire qualified people, but we are continuing

our recruiting efforts. We will inform you of any results.

Sincerely yours,

B. M. Doe

B. M. Doe ←————
Project Leader ←——— Title of
                                    Individual

Subject

FIGURE 6.9 Filing Features of Correspondence (Courtesy NARS Files Operations)

called *coding.* If the firm name has several words, underline only the keyword and place numbers above the remaining words in the order in which they are to be considered in filing. If a subject heading is selected, it should be circled or written at the top of the page. Only the most important subject heading is circled. If a numeric system is used, the code number is determined from the index and written at the top or at the right-hand corner of the material. Some file operators prefer to write both the subject heading and the code number on the material to be filed. This speeds identification for future refiling.

Cross-Referencing

If a record could be called for under more than one name or classification, a cross-reference notation is made on the record when it is coded. This is usually done by underlining any secondary classifications and placing an X before the underlined item. A cross-reference sheet (Figure 6.12), card,

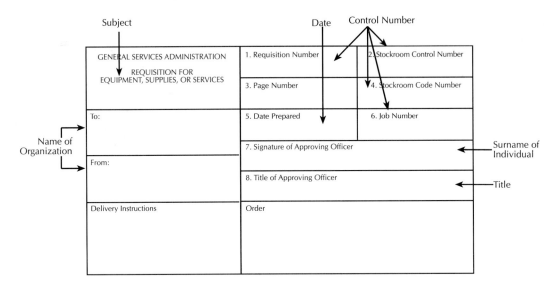

FIGURE 6.10 Filing Features of Forms (Courtesy NARS Files Operations)

or folder is then completed. In some cases, however, an extra copy, such as a photocopy, is made at the source. The latter copy must be clearly marked as cross-reference material or the two copies may end in the same file. While cross-refer-

encing is safer than risking the loss of an important paper, it is expensive because additional filing time and materials are involved and the amount of records in the file is doubled. It should be used with care and prudence.

FIGURE 6.11 Filing Features of Reports (Courtesy NARS Files Operations)

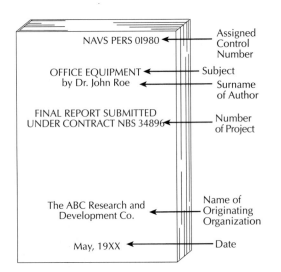

FIGURE 6.12 Cross–Reference Sheet

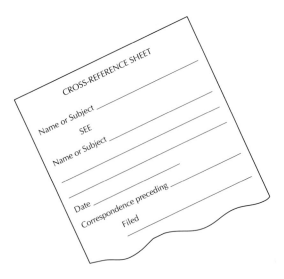

Sorting

Sorting is the process of arranging records in the order in which they will eventually be filed; it is the preparatory step to actual filing. The sorting process is divided into various stages, depending on the volume of records to be filed. The use of sorting devices increases the speed of handling quantities of records because it reduces travel motion and drawer opening during the filing process. A cost-benefit analysis should be made to decide how fine the sort should be. Use of terminal- and middle-digit filing can greatly reduce the need for pre-file sorting in numeric file arrangements. Standard sorters are available with 25 divisions, 50 divisions, or multiples of 50, with fused or insertable tabs. In alphabetic and numeric files, the number of guides or compartments necessary for file sorting should be approximately 10 percent of the number of guides for the system in use. In large files one guide for each drawer is needed. For numeric sorting, guides should be provided in multiples of 10 or 20, whether 100s, 1000s, or 10,000s. For geographic sorting, guides should be labeled with state or country names, followed by cities sorted alphabetically.

There are three general tools for sorting records: (1) horizontal sorters for fine sorting (Figure 6.13), (2) vertical sorters for rough sorting

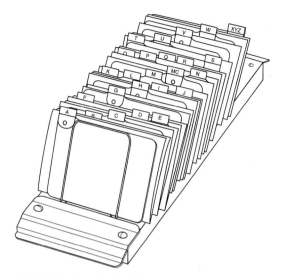

FIGURE 6.14 Vertical Sorter

(Figure 6.14), and (3) circular sorters also used for fine sorting (Figure 6.15).

Sorter divider labels should conform to the filing system. In most cases, numerical sorting is the quickest method, for there are only ten primary divisions used. After fine sorting is completed, the clerk should count the number of pieces to be filed and record the amount on a daily tally sheet. When records are placed in file drawers, the clerk should work from the front to the back of the file drawer to minimize work.

Alphabetic Sorting Procedure. As a quick aid in presorting, records may be divided into alphabetic divisions, such as the following:

A B C	3
D E F G	4
H I J K L	5
M N O P Q R	6
S T U V W X Y Z	8

These divisions are merely suggestions and should be modified to particular needs. Each group of records can then be sorted for individual letters. The documents for each letter can then be

FIGURE 6.13 Horizontal Sorter

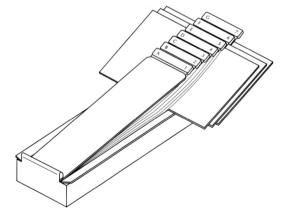

FIGURE 6.15 Circular Sorter
(Courtesy of TAB Products Co.)

arranged in alphabetic order. If there is more than one record for a particular name and location, the record with the most recent date should be placed on top.

Numeric Sorting Procedure. When a numeric classification system is used, the records are sorted by digits, starting with the extreme right and moving a column at a time to the left. The units column is sorted into ten piles (0–9). The piles are stacked into one pile in numeric order with the highest number on top. This process is repeated for the next column to the left until all the columns have been sorted. After the last column has been sorted, the pickup of the group is reversed so that the highest number is on the bottom and the complete pile is in strict numeric order.

Filing

After records have been coded and cross-referenced, they are ready for filing or storing. *Filing* is the process of inserting the item into its proper folder in the file. If a filing shelf is available (see

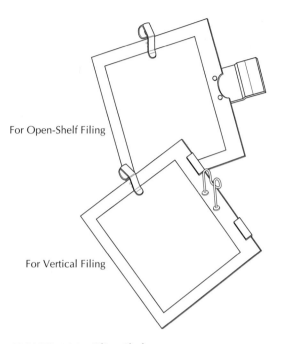

For Open-Shelf Filing

For Vertical Filing

FIGURE 6.16 Filing Shelves

Figure 6.16), it should be hooked onto the drawer handle or the side of the opened drawer.

In searching for the correct folder, find the correct guide and then continue to the correct folder. When placing the record in the folder, double-check the accuracy of the drop. The same caption should appear on the records already in the file. The folder should be placed in the file with the tab side to the rear of the file. The headings of the records to be filed are placed to the left. The documents are arranged in chronological order within the file with the latest on the top because it is assumed that the most recent will be referred to most frequently.

An individual folder, or special-name folder, is prepared for each subject when four or more pieces of correspondence accumulate concerning it. Otherwise, a miscellaneous folder is used for relatively inactive subjects. These are kept in alphabetical order, with the latest piece of correspondence on top if there are several.

Files in folders may be subdivided for two reasons: volume and subject content. When volume becomes too great for the designed capacity of the file folder and the subject content has not changed, the file is simply divided by date. A common rule of thumb is that when the last *score* (indented or raised line near the bottom edge of a folder) is folded, and the folder reaches its capacity ($^3/_4$ inch), the file is subdivided. For efficiency, the file should not be allowed to expand beyond $^1/_2$ inch in depth.

The second occasion for subdividing occurs when the subject content of the folder develops subset subjects. Then, subdivision is made regardless of volume. For example, a file may be set up on the general subject of *Motor Oils*. As time progresses, it may be necessary to subdivide the general file into various tests and evaluations. The documents should be subdivided, either by type of information or chronologically. These divisions are made not only after files have been established, but also during the conversion progress, if the files are being reorganized. In some instances, the files may be organized into case files.

Charge-Out

The charge-out system helps the file clerk to keep track of materials removed from the file and to locate them quickly. It is a reminder that the material is temporarily out of the file and that the material might be needed in research or decision making. Only those persons responsible for the files should remove materials from them.

Because of the availability of photocopying equipment, the clerk can make a photocopy of the requested material, record the name of the recipient, and thus keep the files intact.

If the record copy is to be removed from the files, a *charge-out guide* is inserted into the file to show that the folder or document has been removed. It is actually a substitution card. The tab of the charge-out guide extends above the folder to signal a withdrawal. The face of the guide provides space for the name of the borrower and the date of the charge-out, or in colored plastic *out guides*, a pocket holds a copy of the charge-out request. A duplicate copy can be maintained in the

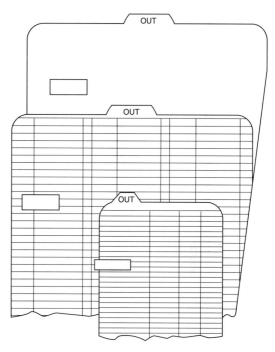

FIGURE 6.17 Out Guides

tickler file for follow-up. When the material is returned, the name of the borrower is removed or crossed out and the guide is used again. A container should be available for placing returned documents for refile.

Several variations of the charge-out guide are the *out card*, *out sheet*, and *out folder* shown in Figure 6.17. When the charge-out requisition calls for one document or a few related documents, an out card or out sheets may be substituted in the folder. The requisition card is attached to the out card to save rewriting. When the requisition calls for an entire folder, the operator may replace the original material with either an out guide or out folder. The out folder method allows additional filing to be made while the original folder is out of the file.

Follow-Up

Records that have been released for filing may require follow-up action. To ensure the action will be taken at the appropriate time, provision for follow-up can be made by using such manual devices as a pending folder, a card tickler, a desk calendar tickler, or a charge-out card. Follow-up records include papers on prospective customers, delinquent customers, expiring subscriptions, expiring life insurance, orders, and so on. Where bar-coding is used on documents, forms, or boxes, the item can be scanned and the name of the recipient can be scanned to maintain a computer listing of all charge-outs. In addition, some systems allow for scanning each time a document moves to a new location so that the document may be tracked at all times. This permits computer reports at any time showing the location of the charge-out documents or documents in transit. A report may also be printed daily to show documents which have exceeded their check-out time, or any other action which should be taken on that specific date.

Any of the manual follow-up devices mentioned previously can be used in conjunction with a set of month guides and one or more sets of day guides for each day in a month. In the follow-up file the guide for the current month is at the front of the card-file holder, and the other months follow in sequence. When a follow-up action is necessary, the information is written on a 3- by 5-inch card and filed in the correct day guide of the follow-up file.

Reliable follow-up, whether done on the computer or manually, is one of the important services of the active records center. If a good follow-up method is not devised, documents awaiting future action will accumulate, preventing referral to information and also risking the loss of the documents.

IDENTIFICATION SYSTEMS

Identification schemes identify each class of records and group-related classes of records. The identification scheme reflects the structure of the classification system. Most classification schemes have three levels of organization—a broad division, such as *accounting*, subdivisions for major activities within the group, and a third level of breakdown.

Identifiers that are consistent help users find and use information and make training easier. The same system should be followed in all departments enabling users to understand the overall system.

The capacity of an identification system varies with the scheme selected. For example, in a numeric system, if the primary division consists of 99 divisions (1–99), and the secondary, 100 (0-99), and the tertiary, 100 (0–99), a total of 990,000 combinations is possible.

All systems should be devised to make computerization easy. A decision needs to be made as to whether fields will be sorted on text fields (character-by-character) or as numeric fields. In the case of numeric fields, each group of numbers should be the same size consistently.

Identification systems are an important segment of any records systems; they encompass guides, binders, folders, tabs, labels, signals, and the use of color.

Guides

Guides are to the file clerk what signposts are to the tourist. Without file guides, the file clerk would have to look at every paper in the file until he or she came across the right one. Many different types of guides are available for cards filed in trays or drawers as well as for letter-size documents.

In addition to supporting folders, guides show the exact location of records and folders and speed up the accuracy of filing and retrieving. Guides show the major subdivisions and minor subdivisions by position. Guides on tabs in the first position (extreme left) may show the major headings or, if the file is very large, may show the subdivisions of the main topic. Guides in the second position may be used for a chronological or alphabetic breakdown.

In most card or suspension guiding systems,

only the guide tabs are visible. Cards are usually of the same size and lower than the tops of the guides.

The major requisite of a guide is durability. Durability is determined by the type and weight of paper used and the construction of the tab and rod projection. The weight of the guide can be determined from its thickness, which is measured in terms of points, one point being equivalent to $1/1000$ inch. Guides are available in fiber, pressboard, manila, bristol board, plastic, and light metal.

Fiber guides are made of hard, tough, flexible, long-fiber paper, usually black. Fiber guides are also available in various thicknesses.

Pressboard guides are the most commonly used for general purpose filing. They are stiff enough to support the contents of the drawer in upright position and flexible enough to ensure serviceability. The standard weight is 25 points.

Manila guides are popular as card file guides or in transfer files. They are less expensive than pressboard guides and also less durable.

Bristol board is similar to pressboard and is used primarily for temporary card indexing. It has great tear resistance and combines the features of stiffness with strength and flexibility.

Binders

Binders for computer output are designed in two basic styles, depending on whether they are to take burst or unburst forms. Continuous forms can be bound in one long accordion piece (unburst), or they can be run through a special machine called a burster that pulls them apart at the perforations to make burst forms before binding. The trend is toward unburst forms. Burst forms can be handled like any other records. Binders are available to fit any printed form. The dimension of the form at the bind edge is specified first: for example, 8 1/2 by 11 inches, if unburst; 11 by 8 1/2 inches, if burst. The quality of the binder varies with its ultimate use. Heavy-duty binders are available for frequent reference. Lightweight binders are so inexpensive that they can be thrown away with the form to save the cost of disassembly.

Folders

Folders segregate papers into related groups behind the guides. If guides are signposts, folders could be likened to house numbers that follow street signs. Folders are justified when related correspondence or other documents are to be retained either for future reference or to avoid summarizing and transferring data to cards or computer media. Folders are available in a wide variety of styles and materials.

Two common styles of folders are top-tab and side-tab folders. Side-tab folders, shown in Figure 6.18, are used in lateral and open-shelf filing. Top-tab folders are used in drawers.

Important characteristics for folders are stiffness and a minimum of thickness. If the folder is not stiff enough, the contents cause it to bend and buckle, resulting in jumbled and torn papers. A hard, smooth surface will resist soil and allow the folder to slide easily between the other folders. Other desirable characteristics are resistance to tearing and a high folding endurance.

Because there are many variations in the quality of raw materials, processes, and skills in manufacturing, the general use of the folder should be kept in mind in choosing between comparative grades and qualities. The more common folder

FIGURE 6.18 Side–Tab Folders (Courtesy of VRE, Inc.)

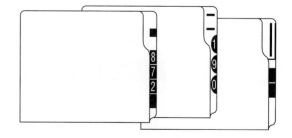

materials are pressboard, manila, kraft, and red rope or fiber, as well as the recently introduced colored plastic.

Pressboard is the same material that is used in making guides. It is used where large or bulky papers must be filed and where handling or use outside the file drawer is frequent. This type of folder usually comes with a metal, plastic, or celluloid tab. It requires a cloth expansion hinge on the bottom. The usual weight for pressboard is 25 points.

Manila is the most popular type of folder material.

Kraft is darker in color than manila, so it does not show the soil readily. It is comparable to manila in quality, price, and common weight.

Red rope, or *fiber,* is a heavier material, made from sulphite with a tough jute and hemp fiber. It is usually given a trade name by manufacturers and is especially popular for file pockets and envelopes.

Folders may be scored ro permit expansion, or they may come in a bellows-folded style, which flattens out and makes a more solid base for papers as the file contents increases. Special purpose folders, called pocket folders, are made with bellows folds on the ends and bottom.

Folders are used for a variety of data-processing applications. They are available in various sizes with built-in pockets to house disks or diskettes, with or without related papers or interpreted copy.

Suspension or hanging folders differ from conventional folders in that they are technically equipment rather than a supply item, and they do not have the same uses. Instead of stiffness, the hanging folder needs tough, flexible material that will hold the papers while hanging from metal rails (see Figure 6.19).

Suspension folders may house several conventional folders, each containing correspondence, orders, or invoices for the same project,

FIGURE 6.19   Hanging Folders for Computer Printouts (Courtesy of Robert P. Gillotte Co.)

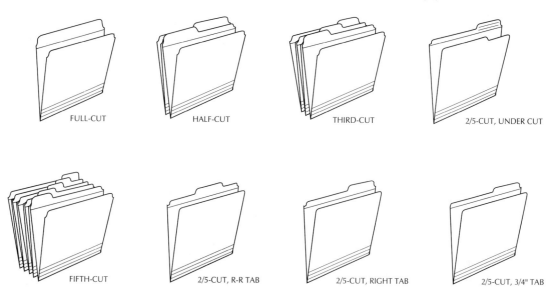

FIGURE 6.20 Various Types of Folder Tabs (Courtesy of Shaw–Walker Co.)

person, or firm. Special folders, which are 9 inches from the fold to top edges, are available for this purpose. These interior folders may also be used as liners to the suspension folders and to simplify transfer of records.

Folders are sometimes known as individual, special, or miscellaneous. *Individual* folders are created when at least four pieces of correspondence have accumulated for a particular topic and the folder is so labeled. *Special* folders are designed to collect data of a certain type, such as application blanks or letters of congratulations. A *miscellaneous* folder contains a variety of correspondence without any topic warranting an individual folder.

Tabs

A tab is a projection on the top or side edge of the guide or folder. Tabs on guide systems or folders may be either flat or angular. When encased in plastic or metal, the tabs are available with a 45-degree slant backwards for increased visibility.

Folder tabs range in width from a one-fifth to full-cut length, as shown in Figure 6.20. One-third cut is the most popular, with half-cut tabs used for longer titles. Special systems use special widths, such as two-fifths cut. Folders are usually undercut just below the tab to allow more reading space for the label.

In a file drawer, tabs are arranged in either a staggered or straight-line method. In the straight-line position, the tabs are in the same position, one behind the other. Printed tabs are available. One popular style is the miscellaneous folder with alphabetical division.

Signals

The use of signals to denote placement of information on a filed card is one of the outstanding features of visible filing equipment. The various positions and colors of signals mean specific actions. Dates and quantities, for example, are brought to the attention of the reader. By such signals, a whole tray of cards can be scanned and the items requiring immediate attention quickly spotted. See Figure 6.21.

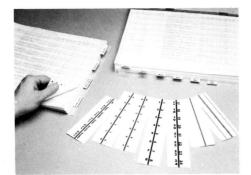

FIGURE 6.21   Signals
(Courtesy of Tabbies)

File Fasteners

To insure against loss of small documents or
where a file consists of multiple-size documents,
each document may be fastened to the back of a
file folder by means of an Acco fastener as shown
in Figure 6.22. Two holes are punched in the top
of the document, and the document is threaded
over the prongs of the fastener, which is attached
to the back of the folder. This method to safeguard
documents is particularly useful where files are
transported over long distances or where files are
taken out in the field.

PRESERVING AND SAFEGUARDING FILES

Finding lost records, maintaining files in good
condition, developing standards for filing tasks,
and safeguarding information are all important to
the task of keeping an organization's files in good
working order.

Finding Lost Records

It is said that experience is the best teacher. Accordingly, the following suggestions for finding
missing records have been collected from experienced file clerks:

FIGURE 6.22   Folder with File Fasteners
(Courtesy of Esselte Pendaflex Corporation)

1. Check the folders before and after the one
   where the record belongs; check between the
   folders and at the bottom of the drawer.
2. Look for a similar name or number (*Roberti*
   for *Roberts*). Look under other vowels following the initial letter (*Ra, Re, Ri, Ro, Ru*).
3. See if the name or number was transposed
   (*George Richard Co.* for *Richard, George,
   Co.* and *10750* for *10570*).
4. Check alternative letters and spellings (*h* for
   k, *a* for *o*.
5. Try a similar sounding name (*Braun, Brown,
   Browne*).
6. Look in the sorter.
7. Look in the messenger's transfer bag, or
   check to see if the record could be en route.
8. Check the miscellaneous folder to see if a
   special name folder should have been used.
9. Look in the charge-out tickler for the name of
   the last person to check out the material:
   Check his or her pending tray.
10. Look in the relative index for titles under
    which the material might have been misfiled.

Maintaining Files in Good Condition

Folders should be reviewed regularly and new folders made up when necessary. With day-to-day use, folders and tabs do get worn and should be replaced when the condition is first noticed.

Records can get lost if everyone has access to the files. The National Office Products Association has identified 22 common filing problems; they are listed in Table 6.2.

Developing Standards for Filing Tasks

Productivity standards for filing should be developed and followed for active records control. The records manager should periodically determine if the standards are realistic and whether accuracy suffers when employees are aware that production is being measured. For this reason, it may be well to have an evaluation committee that can give its appraisal of filing accuracy and the standards developed. A committee approach has the advantage of generating more interest in the filing problems and of getting suggestions for improvements from the file operators.

Standards vary because of the variances in types of records and working conditions. Suggested standards for filing tasks are shown in Table 6.3.

Safeguarding Information

The need for policies to safeguard information has become apparent by increases in thefts of files, tapped data transmissions, information disclosures, modification of data, and destruction of information. The use of computers and time-sharing facilities has added to the problem. This usurping of valuable personal information, both by insiders violating confidentiality rules and by outsiders breaching system security, is going to increase in coming years.

More comprehensive information about people is being collected in large-scale record systems that are evolving, such as charge-card systems and national information systems. As more organizations make use of the low-cost and flexible services of both local area networks (LANs) and wide-area networks, they become more high-payoff targets of computer theft. Thus, security in multiple-user facilities is even more important than it used to be. The need for administrative, technical, procedural, and physical safeguards to information is also reflected in recent federal and state legislation.

In government, as in the private sector, the cost, economy, and technological feasibility of protecting records must be weighed against privacy, the public's right to know, and other civil liberties.

Administrative measures needed to implement records protection policy may include establishing and enforcing rules of access; adding computer software that appropriately screens requests for access and also keeps accurate and complete records of access and disclosure; and installing locks and similar security devices. Each computer network user has an access password, and the network administrator is able to maintain information security by giving access to different levels of information. In cases where individual computer workstations are used, it may be necessary to have removable media to safeguard information. Where hard disks are used—and information is not downloaded to removable disks and the hard disk file erased—access to the computer workstation should be limited to those persons who are cleared to use the information. In all cases of computer use, backup copies are essential.

In some cases all employees who are allowed direct access to the systems of records and information will have identical authorization, and thus the use of physical safeguards, such as a guard at the computer facilities or a card key to some doors, will be sufficient protection. In some small manual systems, requests for information may be handled by the records staff, who have full authority, as

TABLE 6.2 Common Filing Problems

TROUBLE	SOLUTION
There are too many filing places.	Centralize filing of records of common interest in one location under one supervisor. File specialized records in departments where handled, but follow established handling procedures.
Everybody is a file clerk.	Centralize authority with responsibility. Allow only designated persons to use files except in emergencies.
Files do not keep pace with firm's progress.	Check size of alphabetic breakdown to see if it is adequate. Check type of alphabetic breakdown to see if it fits customer name patterns.
Files are disordered; they show no particular plan or arrangement.	Pick a ready-made, engineered system that best fits your needs. Adjust it, if necessary, as time goes on. Your office products dealer carries several systems and can suggest one to suit your needs.
System does not fit the way material is requested.	Study the possibilities of using subject, geographic, or numeric filing, as well as alphabetic filing, for certain specialized materials.
Filing decisions are erratic.	Start a filing procedure manual and then *use* it! Do not depend on snap judgment or the opinions of others. When a problem arises, make a ruling; then write it down.
It takes too long to find a folder.	Have an index guide for each inch of active drawer space or each six to eight folders. Twenty-five guides per drawer provide the best efficiency.
It takes too long to find a card in the card files.	Have no more than 30 cards to a guide in an average reference file, no more than 20 in an active or growing one, and definitely no more than 10 to 15 to a guide in a posted record file, such as a ledger.
Drawers are jammed too tight.	Allow 3 to 4 inches of working space in letter files, 1 to 2 inches in card files.
Bulging folders slow down filing speed.	Have no more than 25 sheets per folder for best efficiency; do not exceed 50.
Papers pile up in the Miscellaneous folder.	Create a file for a firm or individual after the sixth letter to your firm. If that does not work, a larger number of divisions is needed in the index.
Individual folders are too full.	Make a special name guide for the individual; then put a set of period or chronological folders in back of the guide.
Guides are in bad condition.	Replace broken guides. Use reinforced tabs in the active file. Use angular tabs for easier reading. Use tab inserts for greater versatility and less expansion.
Folder tabs are difficult to read.	Use gummed labels; they strengthen and add legibility. Use reinforced tabs when reference is frequent. Use a good grade of material for active files.
Folders are out of sight.	Use stiffer folders. Use scored or bellows folders for better expansion. Investigate use of suspended folders.
Folders wear out too soon.	Use at least an 11-point folder for frequent use out of the file; 14-point or pressboard for heavy use. Save space yet add strength with double-tabbed folders.
Old correspondence is slowing up filing of current papers.	Transfer old material at least once a year. See if some types of correspondence need to be filed at all.
File storage is using up valuable floor space.	Check use of five-drawer cabinets. Check shelf filing for certain records. Establish a definite destruction plan for all types of papers you file. Consolidation of files might help.
Finding material requested *before* it is filed is difficult.	Hold the material arranged for filing in a sorting device.
Getting papers into the folders takes too long.	Use sorting devices to completely arrange the papers.
Filing work is tiring.	Use filing shelf to free both hands for filing. The stool is another handy device to ease fatigue.
Finding checked out papers or cards is difficult.	Keep track of removed papers and cards with out guides or folders.

Source: National Office Products Association

TABLE 6.3   Standards for Filing Tasks

Task	Units per Hour
Type 3- by 5-inch cards, labels, or tags.	100
Code one-page letters.	200
Sort 3- by 5-inch cards.	300
Sort indexed or coded correspondence.	250
File 3- by 5-inch cards.	180
File correspondence.	250
File vouchers numerically.	700
Retrieve 3- by 5-inch cards.	180
Retrieve correspondence and prepare charge-out forms.	70

well as the ability, to decide that an employee's use is legitimate.

FILE REORGANIZATION

Reorganizing existing subject file systems is a major undertaking in records management and normally is not recommended unless the existing system is beyond repair. Records analysts who do this type of work are usually specialists because it requires unique skills and talents. Working as an apprentice with an experienced analyst is an excellent way to enter the professional ranks of records management because the principles learned here are useful in almost all other areas of the field.

A file reorganization may involve only a few file cabinets or it may involve hundreds, but the principles of conducting the project are the same for either. A distinction must be made, however, between reorganizing and organizing. The term *reorganizing* means that most of the files in the system will be retained (except for needed purging) and changed over to a new system. *Organizing* means that existing files will be left as is, destroyed, or stored, but they will not be integrated into a new system. The latter uses the same techniques for developing the file plan, but the actual conversion process is not involved.

Uninterrupted Operations

A basic principle in a file reorganization project is that the file department must not be hindered in its operation during the conversion. In addition, the file department personnel should not only be trained in the new system as it is being developed, but should also be consulted for their knowledge and experience before the change decision.

Analysis of Data

The project begins by interviewing the department manager or representative to determine the functions of the department. Organizational charts should be studied, and any other information about the department's activities should be obtained from the various section chiefs. Complaints regarding the existing system should be noted, but no action taken at this time. This is done so that particular attention is given to correcting past mistakes and ensuring they do not recur in the new system.

Tentative File Plan

After activities are analyzed and understood in general terms, a tentative file plan is developed in outline form, such as was seen in Chapter 5, Figure 5.2. This plan is discussed again with the management and section chiefs, as well as the file department; deletions, additions, and changes are made until everyone is satisfied that all of the known subject matter is included and organized in a logical and correct manner. Particular attention must be given to the terminology of the users and file room staff.

Conversion

As the conversion progresses, subjects overlooked or previously unknown will develop, and they must be studied, discussed, and properly integrated into the system. If the system is to be classified numerically, a coding system must be devised. It is made part of the file manual used by the analyst during the conversion process and must be continually changed as required during conversion. The same applies to an alpha-classified system.

To prevent disruption in the conversion process, actual conversion begins with drawer 1 and proceeds in sequence, so that at any time everyone knows at what point the new system begins and the old system ends. Each file must be scanned, not read, to avoid wasting time. Scanning involves looking for key phrases to determine the subject matter and to decide if subject matter changes within the file. If it changes, the file must be divided.

In an alpha system, the exact file captions are written on 3- by 5-inch cards, with the old file number written in the upper right-hand corner. The card is attached to the file and turned over to the conversion assistant, who types the new label from the card, places the documents in a new folder, and affixes the label. The card is then filed by the old file number to give a quick reference to the new caption. These index cards are retained for about a year after the conversion is complete, because correspondence will be received that makes reference only to the old number.

In a numerical system, the new number is entered in the upper left corner, with the old number entered on the right. In this case the card is prepared in duplicate, and one serves as the new index, which will be used to prepare the final file manual. With alpha systems, the label is prepared in triplicate. One label is affixed to the folder, the second and third to 3- by 5-inch cards. One card is filed in the same alpha sequence as the files. This gives the analyst a quick and convenient method of checking to see if a file has already been prepared on the subject or if inconsistencies exist. The other card is placed in a pocket inside the cover of the file folder to be used as a charge-out to eliminate the need to write a long caption at the time a file is charged out.

As the files are completed, they are placed in the file cabinets emptied during the process. Thus, on a day-by-day basis, the new file system grows and is used as it is being established. When unforeseen subjects occur, entire file patterns must be changed to fit the subject into the system if the system design is not flexible enough to accommodate it. In this case, the analyst and assistant must backtrack and change cards, captions, and folder arrangement.

Time Estimate

The file conversion process is slow. A team of two analysts and a conversion assistant may be expected to complete one file drawer per working day, if the documents are placed into new folders in date order and the duplicates purged. This is important in estimating completion times and in measuring productivity. The task can be even more challenging if the new system must be integrated into an organization-wide uniform filing system because many additional problems will be encountered in designing file patterns that serve the needs of the department while maintaining organizational uniformity.

File Manual

When the system is complete, a final file manual is prepared for everyone who uses the system. Follow-up audits must be made frequently at first to determine if the system is being used properly and to detect and correct any problems. Details of preparing the file manual are discussed in Chapter 16.

SMALL-BUSINESS FILING SYSTEMS

Although the concepts presented in this book are applicable to all sizes of business organizations, it might be well to point out that frequently records management expands with the growth of the organization. In some instances, a secretary has been charged with developing a subject file. As time progresses, the need for storing records outside the office becomes evident, and the need to segregate vital records becomes apparent. If these three functions can be implemented, this small company then has three elements of a total records management program: files management; records storage; and a vital records program. Depending on the size of the firm and the personnel involved, other aspects of records management will possibly need to be added.

One true story illustrates the possibilities of growth in a small business. A secretary developed her filing program to include all of the functions of a total records management program. The development entailed adding more personnel with the growth of the company and identifying records management functions into separate positions. She ultimately became the corporate records manager and also eventually served as president of ARMA International.

Vendors of filing supplies are often an excellent source of information on implementing a files management program in a small firm. Vendors offer alphabetic, numeric, and geographic preprinted guides and tabs. Vendors also offer general advice for files management. In some cases, where equipment is involved, vendors also offer to do feasibility studies.

If the person responsible for maintaining the records of a small company does not have the time to devote to the project and does not have the capability of adding staff, several options are available: outsourcing and the hiring of temporary services.

Outsourcing

If the individual responsible for managing the company's records is not totally knowledgeable in records management, the services of a consultant may help the individual plan the program. The program may be implemented by doing whatever

is possible in house. However, firms that provide needed services include off-site records centers, microfilming service bureaus, and accounting and bookkeeping service agencies. Many of these firms have consultants available to recommend implementation of needed services. It is important to remember that regardless of who provides the service, the person responsible for managing the company's records maintains the responsibility.

Temporary Services

Several of the leading temporary help agencies offer assistance with various aspects of records management, from consulting to the actual work performance. If the continuous use of a temporary service is not feasible, it would be necessary to have a designated employee trained to maintain the records management program that has been established.

Regardless of who is responsible for managing the records in a small firm, that person must have the cooperation of all staff members. All staff members must understand the importance of records management to provide the right information at the right time at the least possible cost. Their cooperation in using and maintaining an efficient records systems is essential. The person responsible for the records management program can assist in its success by providing a manual of procedures. That person must also be cognizant of how technology can be used to the fullest (within the constraints of budget) in carrying out the necessary program.

SUMMARY

In order to maintain an efficient and effective filing system, it is necessary to separate records into basic types and to consider factors such as disposal, identification, volume, and completeness. Basic types of records include general correspondence; transitory correspondence; case records; case working papers; technical reference

material; extra convenience copies; film, tape, or disk records; cartographic materials and drawings; and cards.

The primary tools for locating records are arrangement of documents, indexing, labeling, use of color, and automation. File arrangement may be alphabetic or numeric, or a combination. Indexing assists with finding records by arranging items in a searchable order. Labeling identifies the contents of drawers, shelves, trays, bins, binders, boxes, and folders. Color is used in supplies, in assisting to provide security, in designating equipment, and in commercially prepared systems. Automation is used to maintain an index and to track records.

File maintenance procedures include collection, inspection, preparation for filing, indexing, coding, cross-referencing, sorting, filing, charge-out, and follow-up.

Identification systems identify each class of records and group-related classes of records. They include guide systems, binders, convention folders, suspension folders, tabs, and signals.

Lost records may be found by checking before and after the folder where the record belongs, looking for a similar name or number, and looking in the sorter, transfer bag, and charge-out tickler. Productivity standards for filing should be developed and followed for active records control. The need for policies to safeguard information is becoming increasingly apparent. File reorganization means that most of the files in the system will be retained and changed over to a new system.

Suggestions for how small business can implement a records management program include the use of outsourcing and temporary services.

QUESTIONS FOR DISCUSSION

1. What kind of records are included in file systems?

2. What are the factors which will aid in reducing the area and time of search for records?

3. What are some other names for files of general correspondence?

4. When are case working papers usually disposed of?

5. When is separate filing of technical reference materials warranted?

6. What is a common problem with long-time storage of electronic media for audio, text, and graphics?

7. What factors make cards a logically separate file group?

8. What are the primary tools for locating records?

9. How is color used in records management?

10. How is the computer used in records management?

11. How does information management differ from files management?

12. What are the day-to-day activities of filing?

13. What are some procedures which should be followed in preparing papers for filing?

14. What are the eight features of correspondence by which it may be indexed?

15. What are the common features of forms by which they may be indexed?

16. What are the common features of reports by which they may be classified?

17. What are three general tools used for sorting records?

18. When are files in folders subdivided?

19. What are the variations in charge-out forms?

20. What are some manual devices which can be used for follow-up of records?

21. What are some devices used as identification systems in filing?

22. What are some possible solutions to common filing problems?

23. What problems point to the need for policies to safeguard information?

24. What are some administrative measures that could be taken to safeguard information?

25. How does reorganizing files differ from organizing files?

26. What are two options for records management available to companies which do not have the capability of adding staff?

PROJECTS

1. Visit a small professional services office such as a lawyer's, a dentist's, or a doctor's office in your area. Ask to see how basic types of records are filed, such as (*a*) general correspondence; (*b*) case files; (*c*) working case papers; (*d*) technical reference materials; (*e*) film, tape, or disk records; (*f*) cartographic materials and drawings; and (*g*) cards. Prepare a written report on the file folders (if any) and housing used for these records.

2. In the office visited for Project 1, ask the following questions: (*a*) What arrangement (alphabetic, numeric, or alphanumeric) is used for the records stored? (*b*) What labeling is used on folders, drawers, guides, or shelves? (*c*) What use of color is made in supplies or equipment? (*d*) Are bar codes used? Prepare a written report on your findings.

3. Visit an organization in your community that has a records manager. Ask to review the file maintenance procedures, such as: (*a*) collection of materials to be filed; (*b*) inspection; (*c*) preparation for filing; (*d*) indexing; (*e*) coding; (*f*) cross-referencing; (*g*) sorting; (*h*) filing; (*i*) charge-out; and (*j*) follow-up. Prepare a report describing these procedures.

4. Visit local office supply stores, and collect samples of materials for identification systems, such as guides, binders, folders, signals, and labels. Also collect samples of out guides, binders, and fasteners. Prepare a bulletin board for the records management class showing these supplies.

5. Call the temporary help agencies in your area. Ask what services they offer in records management. Apply for a position as a temporary in records management. Prepare a written report.

6. Indicate the indexing order for the following names. Show cross-referencing where required. Use Appendix D to get the "ARMA Rules for Alphabetic Filing."

As Written

1. W. Oscar Collins
2. John McHale
3. Ronald MacDonald
4. Sander VanOcker
5. Pope John Paul II
6. Mother Theresa
7. Buffalo Bill
8. Anne Jirgal Estate
9. KDAL Radio
10. YMCA, 901 North 21 Street, Superior, WI 54880
11. Fannie Farmer Candies, Inc.
12. J. C. Penney Co., Inc.
13. NBC, Washington, DC
14. Anheuser-Busch Co.
15. U-Haul Co.
16. Los Alamos Fencing Station
17. 4 Hour Dry Cleaners
18. 400 Club
19. Anthony Yano, Owner, Yano Brothers
20. Industrial and Electric Utilities Division, Allis-Chalmers Corp.
21. Ann Arbor News
22. Nakladatelstvi Universam vPraze
23. Taxpayers Information, Internal Revenue Service, United States Government.
24. Colorado Department of Education
25. Fort McCoy
26. Quebec
27. Principat d'Andorra
28. Suomen Tasavalta (Finland)
29. Republik Oesterreich (Austria)
30. Household Finance, 2662 East Hennepin Avenue, Minneapolis, MN 55534
31. Local 395, AFT
32. Department of Business and Industrial Edu-

cation, College of Technology, Eastern Michigan University

33. Walter Reuther Labor Relations Library, Wayne State University, Detroit, Michigan

34. Karlovy Vary, Bohemia, Czech Republic

35. Washtenaw County Department of Public Assistance

CASE PROBLEM

The Fruit Tree Experimental Station maintains a large volume of records containing experimental data, research reports, and publications used by 30 scientists. In addition to research information, the office retains ordinary business records, such as correspondence, payroll records, and personnel records.

The director, Janine Perez, believes that the research scientists are wasting valuable time looking for information. In addition, there are other problems. The majority of the research data are kept in notebooks that are difficult to handle or stored in the personal directories of each scientist on the local area network (or personal computers). Some of this research has been downloaded to either 5 1/4-inch or 3 1/2-inch disks.

The scientists' offices are becoming overcrowded with filled filing cabinets. On the average, each scientist has four 4-drawer cabinets. At least one of the drawers is used to house computer disks. Stacks of unfiled material are everywhere. The costs for filing equipment and supplies have increased about 25 percent each year for the past two years. In addition, many of the scientists are asking for additional space in their computer directories.

The director has decided to centralize all hard copy records in an area adjacent to that of the local area network administrator. She has also delegated the responsibility of establishing a centralized records control program to a records manager. She estimates that, initially, one clerk and the records manager can operate the central records center. She has given the records manager the authority to choose the equipment and supplies to be used in the central records center. The records manager is thinking about the use of open-shelf filing equipment for a large portion of the hard copy records. The director, whose brother-in-law is the sales representative for a manufacturer of lateral filing systems, has suggested that the records administrator look into the use of lateral files and color coding.

The scientists are fighting the reorganization of the records program because, in their opinion, the records should be located in the offices of the personnel who create and use them. They object to the proposed use of open-shelf filing equipment because they believe it will not protect the records from unauthorized access. They would also like to have appropriate housing for the disks they are storing.

Assume that you are the records manager. Write a memo to the director indicating:

1. How you propose to do a needs analysis in this hostile environment.

2. The kinds of equipment that you suggest be used.

3. The space requirements (assume the volume of records reported is correct and project future needs).

4. Personnel requirements.

5. Floor plan for the proposed space, equipment, and personnel.

6. How color could be used in the proposed records area.

7. How a records management manual would help both the scientists and the persons responsible for records maintenance.

Chapter 7

Facilities and Equipment
for Filing

Learning Objectives

1. To identify the reasons for careful selection of records housing equipment.
2. To describe the criteria and considerations in selecting equipment.
3. To explain how the ratios of (*a*) retrieval, (*b*) activity or reference, and (*c*) accuracy can assist in the selection of equipment.
4. To explain the difference between *cost avoidance* and *expense reduction* in cost justification of equipment.
5. To explain manual, card, and automated filing equipment.
6. To describe the advantages of vertical file cabinets, lateral filing equipment, open-shelf filing, and mobile aisle systems.
7. To explain the procedures and considerations in space planning.
8. To describe the need for the systems approach to space planning.
9. To discuss facilities management in terms of the many components that have an impact on records management.
10. To discuss ergonomic principles.

THE EVOLUTION OF FILING EQUIPMENT

Because paper was the traditional records medium, traditional filing equipment was designed to hold paper documents, such as correspondence and cards. However, the media that a records management program must handle have evolved to include CD-ROM and optical disks. Other types of media such as microfilm and, with the greater use of computers, magnetic tapes and disks enclosed in a variety of containers require housing of various sizes and shapes. As media have evolved, so has the equipment required to hold them. The records manager is confronted with a wide array of file housing, from manual to mechanical to electronic types. The records manager must be able to make informed decisions not only about which equipment is best suited to the types of records an organization has, but also about how that equipment can best be arranged in the work area to assure productivity.

FUNCTIONS OF HOUSING

Records housing is a vital consideration in the storage and retrieval function of the records management program. Records are housed for safety and preservation and are retrieved for reference and updating. Regardless of the medium, the function of the housing is to store records for quick retrieval when they are needed for reference. A well-designed system makes retrieval easier and more efficient.

Analyzing filing equipment needs is a means of reducing costs and, at the same time, improving the efficiency of recordkeeping. In this chapter, *filing* means storing and retrieving of documents, rather than simply placing documents in the appropriate folders. The role of the records manager in equipment selection is to procure only the filing equipment that will provide the most efficient information retrieval at the lowest cost and that will use the least amount of office space. Figure 7.1 shows the variety of shapes and sizes from which the manager can choose.

Control of Files

One of the factors that will affect selection of equipment is where control of the files is placed, whether the files are centralized, decentralized, or decentralized with centralized control. If control

is centralized, all housing for filing is procured through a central point and thus may be standardized. If control is decentralized, housing for files is obtained at the point of storage, and thus each location may procure different housing. No organization should permit its records to be scattered randomly wherever they happen to be created or to have accumulated. Neither should an organization arbitrarily force the centralization of records without regard to the practical needs of the offices that must use the records.

Unless the organization is extremely small, with a file area exceptionally well located for central access, a completely centralized file system is not desirable. On the other hand, a completely decentralized system encourages duplicate filing and usually results in poor use of equipment. With the file function distributed over the entire secretarial and clerical staff, time may be lost because file operations and maintenance are imposed on people who may be unskilled in the intricacies of proper filing.

Centralized Files.   *Centralized files* are records of common interest or value to many employees that are placed in one location under the control of

FIGURE 7.1   Variety of Sizes and Shapes in Filing Equipment (Courtesy of Russ Bassett Company)

one supervisor. These records may include general correspondence, orders, invoices, estimates, quotations, credit memos, shipping information, and so forth. Central location and control has the following advantages:

- Responsibility is easily placed.
- There is less duplication of personnel, equipment, supplies, and space.
- Better quality of work results because of the full-time work of specialists.
- There is greater use of filing facilities.
- All related data are kept together.
- Uniform service is provided to all departments.

Fully centralized filing can work reasonably well for the smaller firm where each organizational unit has convenient access to the files. As the size increases, however, certain records are better filed in the department where they originate and where they get frequent reference. In some cases, in large firms, records may be both centralized and decentralized, depending on the records series.

Decentralized Files. *Decentralized files* are records that are made and used by a single organizational unit and that are maintained and controlled at the point of origin. Decentralization of records should be considered when the following conditions exist:

- Only one organizational unit is concerned with records.
- The centralized filing unit location is too distant for adequate service.
- Information from the files must be immediately available.
- Constant reference is made to the records by only one organizational unit.

Decentralized Files with Centralized Control.
Many organizations use a modified filing system in which the filing control is centralized but certain records are located at the point of use to facilitate administrative operations. Typical decentralized records include those of the personnel, credit, sales, payroll, engineering, and financial departments. For control, all sections are unified under one responsible records manager, whose job is to establish and maintain uniform file systems throughout the organization and also to provide the necessary supervision over the program.

Such a program offers the following advantages over decentralized files:

- A uniform system is established.
- Duplication is cut down.
- Untrained personnel are freed from recordkeeping operations.
- File equipment and file supply purchases are reduced.
- "Can't find" ratios are reduced.
- Better controls on the accession and destruction of records are established.
- Information retrieval is facilitated by providing a single source.
- Responsibility is assigned.

Safety and Preservation

Selecting appropriate housing is the first step in the safeguarding and preserving of records. The choice concerns size of housing, type of housing, and construction. While discarded boxes from paper supplies are sometimes used to store paper records, the choice of commercially available housing varies from cardboard to wood to metal.

Records protection equipment is classified by the National Fire Protection Association (NFPA) in terms of two elements: (1) an interior temperature limit and (2) a time in hours. The rating system includes three temperatures:

350°F (177°C)	Suitable limit for paper records.
150°F (66°C)	Limiting temperature for photographic records.
125°F (52°C)	Suitable for most magnetic media

The time limits range from 1/2 hour to 4 hours. The four categories of records storage equipment that the NFPA identifies are: insulated records containers, fire resistant safes, insulated filing devices, and insulated file drawers.

Insulated records containers and *fire-resistant safes* are available with a time limit ranging from 1 to 4 hours. *Insulated filing devices* have a time limit of from 1/2 hour to 1 hour. *Insulated file drawers* have a 1-hour limit. This means that the equipment must sustain sudden exposure to high temperatures to the extent described in the requirements without exploding as a result of such exposure.

The NFPA indicates that ordinary, uninsulated steel files and cabinets provide only a limited measure of protection from an exposure to fire, as heat is usually sufficient to char file contents if it is quickly transmitted to the cabinet interior. However, these cabinets can be very useful where the major fire exposure is from the records themselves. Ordinary cabinets are commonly used for records of no extraordinary value. They are also used for the organized storage of valuable records in protected facilities, including vaults, file rooms, and document buildings. A records vault or file room in which all records are kept in metal file cabinets is much safer than one in which the records are kept in cardboard boxes or on open shelves.

An ignition in open-shelf files can be beyond manual control within a few minutes. Files and cabinets made of wood, fiberboard, or other combustible materials can release their contents in a fire, adding to the fire hazard. They should not be used for valuable-records storage.

Another consideration is that storing records in housing not designed for that purpose may result in damaged records, as well as prove inefficient for retrieval.

Records not secured in the vital records protection area but requiring similar protection should be housed in equipment that offers both fire protection and security protection. Locks, insulation, and restriction of access to file areas may be required to safeguard records in everyday use. Se-

curity is discussed in greater detail later in this chapter.

Quick Retrieval

The efficiency of a filing system can be determined by the number of manual operations required to locate a specific item. Since roughly 70 percent of the cost of maintaining a filing system involves labor costs, equipment that facilitates filing and retrieval reduces per unit costs of these activities. Overall costs are decreased if retrieval speed is enhanced through reduced operation time.

The type of filing system is usually selected after considering the following:

- Cost of maintenance.
- Degree of readability.
- Accuracy of input.
- Quality of service required by the people who need the information contained in the records.

In most cases, the object of efficient filing is to make the retrieval and the refiling operations take less time than the actual reference operations. *Reference time* is the length of time the document or file is examined. An evaluation of the equipment is essential. Evaluation can reassure management that the system in use is the most efficient, or the evaluation can assist in selecting a better system.

Retrieval Ratio. A *retrieval ratio* may be useful for auditing the filing system. The retrieval ratio is obtained by dividing the time spent retrieving documents by the total number of records retrieved for one month.

$$\frac{\text{Retrieval time}}{\text{Total number of records retrieved}}$$

A comparison from month to month will help determine the efficiency of the staff and may serve to identify problems associated with retrieving records in that environment. A work standard of finding a document in less than 3 minutes is a common guideline.

In some cases, the *turnaround ratio* may be of more interest—the average time it takes to retrieve a document *and get it to the requester* divided by the total number of requests. A turnaround ratio that is considerably higher than the retrieval ratio may indicate that there is a serious time lag in getting the documents to the requester and that these procedures may need to be improved.

Activity, or Reference, Ratio. An *activity ratio* measures file activity and is calculated by dividing the number of records requested each month by the total number of records in the system.

$$\frac{\text{Records requested each month}}{\text{Total number of records in the system}}$$

Documents are retrieved for information that can help with decisions—either day-to-day or long-range. Reference to documents will show the status of the company—profit, overhead, costs, and projected income. Customers may require answers to their questions. Records may be referenced for evidence concerning legal questions, for historical information, and for decision making.

The activity (reference) ratio may assist management in determining the number of people required to retrieve records for reference. A low activity ratio, such as 5 percent, may signal that the records are inactive and should be transferred to inactive storage.

Accuracy Ratio. The *accuracy ratio* measures how many of the requested documents were actually found. It may be an indication of the efficiency of the personnel retrieving the records, or it may be an indication that the records have not been stored in an organized manner. The accuracy ratio is calculated by dividing the number of records found by the number requested on a periodic basis. Suppose, for example, in June:

$$\frac{999 \text{ records found}}{1,000 \text{ records requested}}$$

This ratio, 99.9 percent, indicates a well-organized system in which staff is efficient in retrieving records. When the ratio is calculated at 97 percent or below, the system needs attention.

Updating. New requirements in the department are frequently identified by employees through suggestions for improving the system or through identification of problem areas. Thus, productivity of human resources may be improved by considering employee suggestions and needs and implementing change as necessary. *Updating* may apply to reorganizing documents already in the files, to adapting the filing system to meet records needs, to upgrading equipment, or to providing information to employees.

Procedures for adding to or changing information in existing records are required to maintain the integrity of the information. Procedures are discussed further in Chapter 16.

Proposed upgrade of equipment may be required because of the volume of records, the age of the present equipment, or changes in records media, or to save space, reduce labor, or improve efficiency. The proposed upgrade of equipment should be evaluated using the same criteria used for original purchases.

EQUIPMENT SELECTION CRITERIA

In selecting filing equipment, the manager uses criteria that focus on compatibility with filing systems, ease of access, room for growth, cost, space requirements, simultaneous use, security, and long-range planning.

Compatibility

Housing should be compatible with the size of the documents that are stored in it. For example, a file of 4- by 6-inch cards should be stored in 4- by 6-inch drawers, not in a correspondence-size filing cabinet. Supplies should also be compatible with the equipment. Selection of tabs for file folders, for instance, is determined by whether the folders are placed on open shelves or in filing cabinets.

Ease of Access

Conditions affecting the use of files should be analyzed. The equipment should be adjustable if it is to be used from both a sitting and a standing position. If reference can be done in the file, the equipment should be different from that used if records have to be removed for notations. The need for accessibility to copying machines, conveyor belts, pneumatic tubes, video display terminals, computers, bar code scanners, or other reading devices may affect the type of equipment that is selected.

Room for Growth

Equipment may need to be multipurpose—adaptable to more than one function and perhaps even adaptable to more than one location, initially. In allowing room for growth, one must anticipate annual growth of the records series to be housed in the equipment, as well as the planned transfer to inactive storage. The organization of the records and access to them require that equipment, security, and space all be considered simultaneously in planning for growth of the records series to be housed.

Cost

The initial cost of filing equipment is only one of the factors to be considered in determining the expense of equipment. Maintenance, operating costs, repair, and floor space costs may exceed the original price of equipment very quickly.

Costs involved in buying equipment are of two types: recurring costs and nonrecurring costs. *Recurring costs* are items such as supplies, power, insurance, taxes, and direct labor. *Nonrecurring costs* are one-time costs, such as purchase price, transportation costs, and installation charges.

The decision to buy new equipment is usually made on the best estimate that the capital investment will be recovered and that a cost savings will result. The capital recovery period may be anywhere from one year to twenty or more, depending on the item purchased and its rate of obsolescence. A payoff period beyond ten years is difficult to estimate in light of inability to predict economic conditions and future technological innovation. If it can be shown that a new piece of equipment will save money and pay for itself in a reasonable amount of time, the venture usually will have management support.

Two approaches to cost justification are cost avoidance and expense reduction. *Cost-avoidance justification* is a recommendation to purchase equipment to avoid another cost. For example, increased workload may be offset by the addition of power files. The proposed costs of additional personnel can be balanced against the costs of purchasing the power files.

Expense-reduction justification attempts to reduce or eliminate costs. The simplification of a procedure or the combination of activities may result in an expense reduction. Obviously, the elimination of a procedure should eliminate the costs associated with it. If the manager can show that the purchase of equipment will provide additional benefits and can be paid for by staff reduction, he or she may be able to persuade management to go along with the equipment purchase. A decrease in staff can be achieved through attrition, that is, not filling vacant positions. The equipment costs will be recovered in employee wages. Another common way to reduce staff is to transfer personnel replaced by automation to other departments.

The dollars saved by installing new equipment can be measured in hard dollars or soft dollars. *Hard dollars* are moneys that are spent for measurable expenses and that have been budgeted for in future years. *Soft dollars* are moneys the company can recapture from automation through increased productivity. Identifying soft dollars is not always easy. If an employee is made more productive through automation, the additional productivity that is realized is the soft-dollar benefit. This benefit may take the form of time saved, and it is assumed that the time will be put to other use. This savings allows for job enrichment of employees and permits employees to take on more diversified duties. It may provide employees with meaningful, satisfying work at as high a level of responsibility as they can handle.

Guides in Cost Expenditures. Robert N. Allerding, CRM, Chief of Records Management, Ohio Department of Commerce, has prepared selected guides and standards for information management as shown in Table 7.1. Allerding's calculations are based on information provided by 21 records managers from the United States and Canada. Allerding calculates that the annual cost of owning and operating a standard four-drawer filing cabinet is $1,839.47. Since the contents of a

four-drawer filing cabinet is usually calculated at 100 linear inches, the cost per linear inch would be $18.39. From his experiences, Allerding has also calculated the average cost of a misfile as $147.94. This cost is based on the number of documents not found and the time involved in looking for the lost documents. In addition to the equipment and personnel costs to file and retrieve records, the costs of space, supplies, and overhead are also included in Allerding's calculations.

Space Requirements

Space requirements are sometimes measured in footprints. The footprint of any item is the space that is required for the item to stand on. The footprint for a letter-size filing cabinet measuring approximately 14 7/8 inches by 28 9/16 inches is approximately 3 square feet. Allowing for aisle

TABLE 7.1 Information Records Management

SELECTED MANAGEMENT GUIDES AND STANDARDS IN COST EXPENDITURES*

ROBERT N. ALLERDING, CRM
Revised June 12, 1992

		Annual Cost of Owning and Operating a Standard Four-Drawer File Cabinet	
Current cost of creating a business letter (Dartnell)	$ 10.67	Space (6 sq. ft.)	108.42
Cost of records stored in active files, per file drawer	12,048.95	Supplies (per drawer)	823.60
Cost of records stored in a four-drawer cabinet	48,195.80	Cost of cabinet (based on depreciation over 10 years)	40.41
Estimated cost of filing, per inch	18.39	File Clerks pay for handling 12 cabinets based on 22 working days per month ($295.13	
Based on one operator for 12 cabinets, the annual cost to maintain 100 inches of records (a standard four-drawer file cabinet)	1,588.27	per week)	1,180.54
		Overhead (25% of labor)	304.10
Average cost of a misfiled record	147.94	Total	1,839.47

*Based on a survey of 21 records managers in United States and Canada.

space or pull-out space, the requirement for space is doubled to 6 square feet.

The footprint of a legal-size file measuring approximately 18 inches wide and 30 inches deep is approximately 3.75 square feet. Again, allowing for work space, the requirement is doubled to 7.5 square feet.

In cases where housing is of various sizes, the footprint may be determined by multiplying the length by the width of the housing.

The requirement for space can be affected by use of the housing for more than one purpose, for example, as a space divider as well as for housing records. The amount of floor space required also varies with the height of the files, since the higher the file, the less footprint space is required to store the same amount of records.

Simultaneous Use

Frequently, filing equipment must be accessed by many different users simultaneously. If this is the case, additional floor space around the files may be required. In addition, the procedure for charging out files must be strictly adhered to. Simultaneous use of files may be facilitated through the use of rotary files described later in this chapter.

Security

Security of records is discussed many times in this book. However, because of its significance, security must be listed here as one of the very important selection criteria for equipment.

Long-Range Planning

Because many offices move an average of once every three years, the cost of moving the files is an important consideration in the selection process. The site of filing operations must be evaluated to be sure that it is structurally strong enough to hold the records and filing equipment. In addition, the growth of the files must be considered.

REPLACING EQUIPMENT

The criteria for selection of equipment discussed above are also valid in replacing equipment. In addition, the following specific considerations are also noteworthy.

Reasons for Replacing Equipment

Equipment may need to be replaced because of inadequacy, obsolescence, deterioration, or effect on morale. Changes in procedures may require different equipment. New products may make old ones obsolete. Deterioration of equipment, file cabinets for example, may lead to safety hazards and unsatisfactory working conditions. The hazardous nature of a process or the age of equipment may lead to employee dissatisfaction and low morale.

Records Considerations

In deciding whether to replace equipment, the manager has three main concerns regarding records: the present filing system, the use of the file, and conversion problems.

Present Filing System. Present filing system considerations include:

- Characteristics of the records to be filed.
- File system used.
- Media used to maintain the records.
- Volume of records.
- Current method of cross-referencing.
- Current method of housing.

Use of the File. Reference analysis is useful in developing the points to consider in the use of the file, such as:

- Average number of inquiries.
- Average number of documents retrieved to answer one query.
- Average time required to retrieve and refile one record.
- Time required to get the desired information from the records.
- Number of people who must access the equipment at any given time.

Conversion Problems. Conversion considerations include:

- Need to recopy current records into a different format.
- Average refiling and retrieval time of the proposed system.
- Overall cost, including conversion costs.
- Improvements in services resulting from the new system.
- Advantages of the proposed system in terms of the annual savings in time and money.
- Length of time needed to amortize the new system based on projected savings.

Employee Comfort

Employee comfort is another important factor in ensuring the efficiency of the system. Employee comfort will be discussed in more detail in the section on ergonomics in this chapter. The manager must consider:

- The average height of the equipment.
- The average reach necessary to retrieve a record.
- Whether the employee needs to stand or may sit in the operation of the equipment.
- Whether the new units will be accessible to more than one person at a time.
- Whether the peak level of activity can be adequately managed by the number of units that are proposed.

Technical Aspects of Automated Equipment

In looking at automated equipment, the manager must consider technical aspects of the proposed system. These include:

- The capacity of the files within the limitations of space (cubic or linear measurement ratios to square feet).
- The units required to house current and projected material.
- Power requirements of the system, including the number of new electrical lines that will be needed.
- Emergency power supplies.
- Safety devices that are built into the system.
- Whether motion can be reversed in the middle of a cycle.
- The method of identifying the records.
- Service aspects, such as the service contract, the nearest service available, convenience of the parts supplier, and installation by the vendor.

HOUSING FOR MANUAL FILING SYSTEMS

Manual filing systems include records housed in vertical file cabinets, open-shelf files, lateral filing equipment, mobile aisle systems, slant files, rotating shelves, and specialized filing equipment. Considerations for purchase of filing systems include advantages and disadvantages, suitability, and grades of filing cabinets.

Vertical File Cabinets

File cabinets are available in many different sizes and types, but those for index cards and letter-size papers are most popular. Drawer files, or *vertical file cabinets,* are also called *standard* filing cabinets. Letter-size cabinets have from one to five drawers. The one- and two-drawer models may be used on a desk or table. The two- or three-drawer cabinet is desk height and is usually used at the side of a desk to increase the work area and provide ready access to active papers. The traditional counter file cabinet contains only three drawers. Compact files are also available in counter style. Compact files reduce the height of each drawer and fit four drawers into the height of the normal three. They are also available in a five-drawer size that fits into the traditional four-drawer height.

The four-drawer correspondence cabinet is the most popular office style. The five-drawer cabinet is gaining in popularity because it provides 25 percent more filing area than the conventional four-drawer unit in the same floor space.

Cost of housing active records is usually calculated in linear inches. A *linear measure* is a measurement of length, such as is achieved using a ruler or yardstick. Inactive records are measured in cubic feet. A *cubic foot* is an area measuring one foot long, one foot wide, and one foot high. A typical file cabinet drawer contains 1 1/2 cubic feet of records.

A full 28-inch file drawer should contain no more than approximately 25 linear inches of records. The remaining 3 inches of space is for accessing records for retrieval or for adding records to the file. While estimates vary, a linear inch, including folders and guides, contains approximately 200 documents. Using these estimates, a typical file drawer would hold 5,000 documents. File cabinets for cards may house sizes of 3 by 5, 4 by 6, or 5 by 8. The number of drawers is determined by the height and width of the cabinet. Drawers designed to house slides and computer disks and diskettes are also available.

Most files drawers have a compressor built into them to hold the folders upright. The compressor can be adjusted to secure all records tightly in the file or to leave 3 or 4 inches of working space in the file drawer. The mechanical details of file cabinets differ with each manufacturer.

Advantages and Disadvantages.   Since drawers must be opened on standard file cabinets to gain access, more time is required in the filing process than with open-shelf equipment. If equipment is moved frequently, standard file cabinets have the advantage over larger open-shelf equipment or equipment that is fastened to the floor with a track system, because they are relatively easy to move.

Suitability.   File cabinets are suited to records that permit drop-in filing using suspension folders, for records requiring extra protection and security, for alpha-captioned file folders, and particularly for alpha classified subject file systems.

Grades of File Cabinets.   File cabinets are graded standard, commercial, utility, and nonsuspension. The grades are used to distinguish several lines of one manufacturer rather than to compare two file cabinets made by any two manufacturers. Therefore, the commercial-grade file cabinet of one manufacturer could be superior in quality to the standard-grade file cabinet of another. The only certainty is that for all manufacturers the standard-grade file cabinet is the highest quality. This grade, as well as the commercial-grade file cabinet, is 28 inches deep. Commercial-grade cabinets are substantially the same as standard but without the luxury fittings.

Utility grades are definitely inferior in mechanism and appointment and are not over 26 1/2 inches deep. Nonsuspension cabinets, as the name implies, have drawers without suspension channels to support them while open. They are just a step above storage drawers.

Special-Purpose Cabinets.   Business has brought about the standardization of forms to the point where office products dealers can supply special-purpose cabinets as a standard item. These include cabinets for correspondence (8 1/2- by 11-inch records), legal-size, legal blanks, invoices, ledgers, checks, fingerprints, catalogs, maps, blueprints, charts, Xrays, computer disks and diskettes, microfiche, and various sizes of index cards. Jumbo, storage, and general purpose cabinets are

FIGURE 7.2 Multipurpose File with Hanging Magnetic Tapes
(Courtesy of Wright Line Inc., a unit of Barry Wright Corp.)

also available. A cabinet for magnetic tapes is shown in Figure 7.2.

Open-Shelf Files

Open-shelf filing is just what the name suggests, storage of records on open shelves rather than in closed drawers. Folders are placed vertically on fixed or adjustable shelves and arranged in rows with tabs to the outside for easy reading.

Because employees do not have to open drawers to file or retrieve records, open-shelf equipment is considered by some to save labor and time. Other advantages claimed over drawer-type equipment are economy of space and less cost.

Economy of Space. Savings of up to 50 percent of floor space are common because there are no drawers to open into the work space and because shelves can be stacked higher than cabinets and still be accessible.

Cost. *Labor costs* can be reduced by as much as 25 percent because retrieval can be easier and faster and because more than one person can file or retrieve at the same time at different places along the open shelf.

The equipment is also the least expensive to purchase. However, because of its size and structure, open shelving is generally more difficult to move than are file cabinets. Records in open-shelf files are not as secure as in enclosed cabinets. In the event of a fire in an open-shelf file, the documents could be enveloped in flame within a few minutes.

Records that are well suited to open shelving include life insurance applications, bank mortgage files, hospital medical records, blueprints, and engineering records. If blueprints and engineering records are rolled, the storage unit is generally very deep and specially designed. Any similar record that can be filed numerically and that is referred to infrequently is a candidate for open-shelf filing.

Lateral Filing Equipment

Lateral filing equipment, also known as *side-open* file cabinets, is a form of open-shelf filing units. The conventional drawer is replaced by a rocking compartment that drops forward. The important feature of the side-open file is that it projects only about 6 inches into the working aisle, instead of approximately 28 inches for the vertical file drawer. Laterals usually have roll-out doors that recede into the top of the shelf. They may be equipped with locks. Laterals are used most frequently for purposes of office layout or special use in private offices rather than in large central file areas.

Lateral filing equipment can be designed to have drawers, boxes, roll-out cradles or shelves, and doors. The *drawer-type* equipment is similar to a regular filing cabinet, but in the side-file, the drawer opens from the side. Side-read index guides are used in the roll-out files. These units can be equipped to handle either suspension or regular folders. Shelf partitioning supports folders or divides other stored materials. All material can be reached easily. See Figure 7.3

The *box-type* lateral file cabinet consists of top- and side-open-edged metal boxes or trays as shown in Figure 7.4. Top- or side-tab folders can be used in it. The boxes are hooked onto the rails of a freestanding metal frame. The boxes, into which the material is placed, hang at a slight angle, creating a step effect to expedite the filing work. A tilt-down front and shelf arrangement are also available.

The *roll-out cradle file* is more like a shelf

FIGURE 7.3   Side–open Lateral Filing Cabinet
(Courtesy of TAB Products Co.)

FIGURE 7.4 Lateral file
(Courtesy of Shaw-Walker Co.)

file in some respects, with the added convenience of permitting access to the filed material in the same way that the side-open cabinet does. In fact, the same cabinets used for some roll-out units are available as stationary shelves without the cradle. An optional retractable door is available on some models for either the roll-out or stationary shelf units.

Mobile Aisle Systems

The mobile-aisle system, shown in Figure 7-5, conserves filing space. Sets of file shelves are moved, either manually or by motor, on a carriage that is either imbedded in the floor or contained within a special platform. The additional sets of cradle files move horizontally in front of the first set and have one less file unit in each row so that the operator can move the front set in either direction to get to the desired section of the rear unit. Stationary shelf units can be used for the rear unit, but they are not as accessible for operation as cradle units.

The mobile aisle system is also known as a high-density system, a vertical mechanized file, or an *automated* or *motorized* file. Three types of systems are available: manual, mechanical, and

electrical. The manually operated system is used for lightweight storage. The mechanical system is a medium-size unit and is suitable for medium-weight capacities, up to 30,000 pounds per module. The electrical movable shelving system is suitable for large systems with higher weight requirements than the other systems. All electrical systems should be approved by Underwriters Laboratories (UL). Safety features are built into the system to stop the movement of the file if the sensing device encounters an object. Safety features include toe-level sweeps and manual reset buttons. Safety floors are available as are more than 200 other control combinations.

Important considerations in evaluating mobile aisle systems include:

1. Is the rail attached permanently to the floor? Can it be adjusted, moved, or removed easily?
2. What size wheels are used? Are wheels used to guide the system?
3. What type of wheel bearings are used? (Wheel bearings determine the weight capacity of the carriage.)

FIGURE 7.5 Mobile Aisle Filing Units
(Courtesy of White Office Systems, Inc.)

4. How many wheels are driven? (If not all wheels are driven, the front part of the carriage will move before the rear. This is known as *racking.*)

5. How much weight will each carriage hold? (The industry standard is that a welded-steel carriage for structural strength is recommended to maintain 1,000 pounds per carriage-foot capacity.)

6. Can existing shelving be used? Are panels available to match decor?

7. Which of the three available handles (single crank, three-prong, fold-away) is best for this application?

Slant Files

Slant files also come with a rolling base. A row of several stacked units may be anchored to a wall, with two other rows on heavy-duty ball-bearing wheel carriages. Since the other rows have one less stack, the units are rolled apart creating access to the row against the wall. The result is one aisle and six rows of files. This type of file is a variation of the traditional mobile aisle shelving system.

A space saver in open-shelf filing (that is not motorized) is the slant file shown in Figure 7.6. The file module is shaped like a parallelogram. The slant files are available 10 or 15 inches deep. The 10-inch size is designed to hold standard documents and the 15-inch is designed to hold Xrays. The floor space required for a slant file varies with the length of the file.

Advantages of this style of open shelving are increased visibility and flexibility. This file may fit where other styles would not. When arranged as a mobile-shelf system, the file may hold up to 25 percent more rows in the same floor space.

Rotating Shelves

Rotating shelves contain two file units back to back, with the shelves inside a closed container as shown in Figure 7.7. To gain access to stored material, a unit is turned around. Units may be purchased with locks. Optional features include racks for data binders and reels, slanted library display, roll-out reference shelf or trays, and security drawer. The files can be placed against the wall, used as a room divider, or installed within a wall with access from two separate rooms. Rotating files provide fast access and also save up to two-thirds of the floor space of conventional files.

FIGURE 7.6 Slant Files
(Courtesy of Jeter Systems Corp.)

FIGURE 7.7 Twinfile Rotating File Cabinet (Courtesy of TAB Products Co.)

FIGURE 7.8 Hanging Tape Storage Cabinet (Courtesy of Wright Line Inc., a unit of Barry Wright Corp.)

Specialized Filing Equipment

In addition to housing for standard records of traditional sizes, other units have been designed or adapted for special types of records and media, such as magnetic media, tape, microforms, CD-ROMs, and optical disks.

Magnetic Media Filing. Magnetic media are housed in equipment similar to that used for paper records. The basic forms of magnetic media used in information processing are floppy disks, computer tape reels, and hard disks. Magnetic tape cassettes used to store dictation come in at least three sizes—the standard cassette for tape recorders, the microcassette, and the minicassette.

Magnetic tape cassettes and cartridges used in dictation are also stored in conventional file cabinets, using special drawer partitions or trays. Specially designed rotary files are available in either desktop or freestanding versions.

Diskettes may be stored in tub or tray, suspension, binder, box, or rotary files. The diskette itself comes with a protective envelope to prevent

damage to the magnetic surface. The envelope is also used for labeling and sequencing the file.

Computer tapes and disks have protective packaging and are usually stored in lateral or open-shelf files specially partitioned or equipped with hanging racks. Security and sturdiness are important criteria in evaluating this equipment.

Tape Storage. Tapes should be stored vertically. Two types of enclosures are available for storing tapes. The first is the *plastic canister* that completely encloses the reel, protecting it from dust. The second is the *wraparound plastic band* that encircles the reel's flanges. Tapes enclosed with the plastic band are shown stored in a hanging tape cabinet in Figure 7.8.

Techniques for handling magnetic tape are very important. Tape edges are vulnerable to damage, which will result in reading and recording problems. Carelessly grasping the flanges damages protruding tape edges. The tape must be mounted properly on the tape drive; otherwise the tape will rub against the flanges as it unwinds,

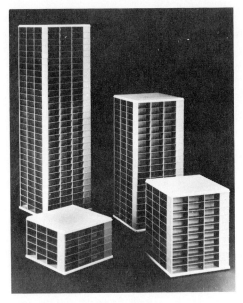

FIGURE 7.9   Carousel File for Microfilm (Courtesy of Information Design Inc.)

causing edge damage. Damaged tape may fail completely on the computer, and dirty tapes may cause lost computer time. When a tape is removed from a canister, the canister should be closed immediately to prevent dust from accumulating in it.

Microforms. Housing for microfilm varies with the medium—roll, cartridge, microfiche, jacket, or aperture card. The desired housing holds the microform records neatly in place. If the microforms are housed in drawers, a plastic compressor is often used to help maintain the file. Roll and cartridge film may be housed in a desktop rotary unit, in a carousel adjacent to the desk, or in a microfilm cabinet along the wall. See Figure 7.9. Desktop storage is ideal for a small but select group of films.

Microfiche may also be housed in a tray or rotary unit or in panel storage on the desk. See Figure 7.10. In addition, microfiche may be housed in a panel attached to the reader-printer or, for large-volume housing, a cabinet along the wall.

Depending on volume, microforms may also be housed in a vertical file, a mechanical automated file, a movable aisle file, or a cabinet.

CD-ROM and Optical Disk Storage. Any of the housing identified for use with microforms is suitable for housing CD-ROM and optical disks. A popular type is the jukebox shown in Figure 7.11. As the volume of these media increases, the styles of housing units available will increase.

FIGURE 7.10   Microfiche Desktop Storage Systems. (*a*) Tray Storage; (*b*) Rotating Panel Stand (Courtesy of ACCO USA, Inc.)

(*a*)

(*b*)

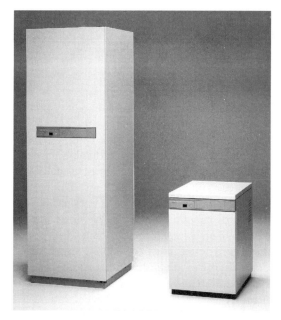

FIGURE 7.11 Jukebox and Drive (Courtesy of Hitachi America, Ltd.)

Suspension Folder Equipment. Hanging folders and frames come in a number of sizes to fit most drawer and lateral filing equipment. The frames are adjustable to the drawer length. Some file drawers are made to take hanging folders without inserting rails. This equipment can be placed at the side of the desk for individual reference or located centrally where several persons can work the equipment simultaneously.

Hanging folders are suspended from rods by means of metal extensions at the top of each folder. Index guides, used to hold regular folders upright, are not necessary since the folders are suspended.

Noncorrespondence Equipment. Large and cumbersome sheets of blueprints, plan drawings, tracings, maps, charts, negatives, sepias, and similar noncorrespondence materials call for a different type of housing than do standard records. Housing for these records follows three basic forms: flat filing, hanging filing, and rolled-plan filing.

In *flat filing*, counter-high units of wide, shallow shelves or drawers provide a working surface. Shelving units can go as high as the ceiling. If flat filing is used, however, the documents are usually numbered, and an index is kept at a place convenient for reference. Documents are sometimes attached to the bottom of shallow drawers. The drawer, with the document attached, is removed completely for use.

In hanging files, plans and other large sheets are suspended vertically to increase their accessibility and to give them added protection. If documents are hung vertically, an identifying clip is usually affixed to the rod.

Pigeonhole units in single cabinets or built-up sections accommodate *rolled plans* and similar papers. The units can be horizontal or vertical, and the holes can be round or square. Some experts, however, say reference to rolled papers is extremely difficult and should be avoided. One solution is the sectionalization of the rolled paper. However, this is not desirable either.

Figure 7.12 shows a vertical filing unit that permits filing of drawings of various sizes. This is

FIGURE 7.12 Vertical File for Drawings of Various Sizes (Courtesy of Planhold)

called *tank-type* equipment because of the lid top, which lifts up to permit access to the file.

CARD STORAGE AND RETRIEVAL SYSTEMS

Card filing systems serve three primary functions:

- The are a quick reference to information.
- They are used as an index to information stored elsewhere.
- They serve as a record of activities.

Some examples of the first function would include cards with telephone numbers, names and addresses, or account numbers. The second type would include a relative index maintained on cards for subject filing of indexes to numeric or geographic filing. A card used in such a way may contain a single line of information, such as *George Richard 1255*. The third type is sometimes called a *posted* record. It may also be called a *secondary* record because the information has been posted from a source document or primary record. Posted records include customer ledger cards, inventory data, pricing information, and purchase records. These documents can be used for reference, to reproduce information, or to activate a communications device or computer.

Card records vary in size from small tickets to large, complex ledger cards. They range in volume from little desk trays of a few hundred cards to large mechanical files with a capacity of more than a million cards. Card files can range in complexity from a little box to a highly sophisticated random-access retrieval system. The variety of equipment available to house card systems is extensive. However, much information formerly held on cards is now being stored in databases within the computer. The use of cards, and the housing for them, is therefore decreasing.

Cards may be filed *vertically*—in an upright position—or *horizontally,* in which case records are usually found in an overlapped arrangement. Cards filed horizontally with just the margin showing are called *visible card files.* The cards filed in this system can be referenced or updated without removal from the tray housing them. Vertical files of cards may be housed in boxes, drawers, trays, tubs, visible files, wheel files, rotary files, or in conveyor files. See Figure 7.13.

Boxes

Box files range from the 3 by 5 index card to correspondence size. Diskettes can be stored in

FIGURE 7.13 Visible Card Files (*a*) Aristocrat Kardex, (*b*) Linedex (Courtesy of Kardex Storage and Retrieval Systems)

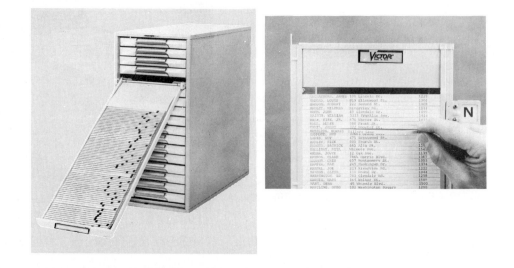

plastic boxes, which may have hinged lids or removable covers. While box files may be typical in the small office or for personal use, box files are also useful for protection, transportation, and storage of records.

Drawers

Perhaps the most widely used equipment for cards is the cabinet with drawers sized to fit the cards, or with dividers in large drawers. Cabinets come in various sizes and heights to accommodate a variety of records. The drawer front may display a small label with indexing information on it.

Trays

Card trays or microfiche trays may be of the individual type or part of a complex sliding file. Small card trays are made of wood, metal, or plastic. Their major advantage is portability. They can easily be stored in a desk drawer. A variety of trays is available that can increase the utility of any desk drawer. These may be cross-file letter trays or cross-file card trays. Experience has shown that at least one-third of the card body should be exposed above the sides of the tray. Full-sided trays are not as efficient as trays with lower sides.

Shelf tray files, resembling large lateral files, are also available. Rows of trays may have locking covers that roll out of the way into recessed tracks when the trays are in use.

Tubs

Multiple-tray tub files come in single-level or multiple-level styles for card records in a wide range of sizes and capacities. There are files where the trays slide from side to side and others where the tub itself is movable. Files with trays that slide from side to side are sometimes called *reciprocating*. (See Figure 7.14) Files with sliding trays are available in adjustable heights for sitting or standing. Because the tub file provides open access to the records stored in the unit when it is in use, it is sometimes called an *open-access* file. These files are available in two widths and will accommodate

FIGURE 7.14 Rolling Tray Multiaccess Tub File (Courtesy of Afro–Lecon, Inc., Watson Industries Division)

up to three levels of any size cards, microfiche, aperture cards, tab cards, or checks. Units can be joined in rows, and upper trays and carriages will roll from one unit to another. Trays and carriages can be mixed and matched to provide a variety of storage. Also available for the top part of a tub file is a writing surface, which converts the file to a tub desk.

The card systems described thus far have been for systems that serve as a record of activities. Card systems that may serve as both quick reference to information and a record of activities are the visible files.

Visible Files

Records used in visible files vary from one-line strips to large charts that range several feet in both dimensions. Therefore, visible filing systems are housed in a variety of cabinets, including horizontal visible, vertical visible, pocket visible drawers, hanger visible cards, and visible book units.

Cards are filed either horizontally or vertically in a shallow frame or tray so that the bottom margin of each card is exposed, providing for quick visibility. The bottom margin contains pertinent data summarizing the information on the major area of the card. Standard horizontal visible equipment provides 3/16- to 5/16- inch margin visibility. Card capacity per tray depends on the card size and the margin exposure used, but 80 cards per tray is an average figure. Cards are usually fastened so that they can be raised and flipped by pivoting about the top edge. Thus, computer information on any card can be viewed in full, or additional data can be written on the card without removing it.

In some instances the files rotate or revolve and are either fixed or mobile. They range from desktop models to floor models. The type of equipment selected depends on the form and nature of the record to be filed; the frequency of use; the proximity of the file to its users; its portability; and whether the cards are used for reference only, as a hand-posted visible file, or to house barcoded employee cards.

Wheel Files

Wheel files hold cards in the shape of an upright wheel and rotate like a Ferris wheel. They differ from carousel files, which rotate horizontally like a lazy Susan, although the terms *wheel file* and *carousel* are sometimes used interchangeably. Wheel files come in several styles. A single desktop wheel file is shown in Figure 7.15. It can be used for account numbers, telephone numbers, names, and calling or business cards. Automatic wheel files can even be built into desktops so that any card can be found in three seconds at the press of a button.

FIGURE 7.15 Wheel File
(Courtesy of Business Efficiency Aids, Inc.)

FIGURE 7.16 Rotary Stand and Turntable
(Courtesy of Ring King Visibles, Inc.)

Wheel files are generally limited to standard card sizes, 5 by 8 inches and smaller. Large, cabinet-size wheels are usually limited to no more than 5,000 cards per wheel and cards no higher than 5 inches. One operator can usually handle up to 50,000 larger cards, and up to twice that many smaller cards.

Rotary Files

Rotary files are designed to hold cards, documents, microfiche, and diskettes. Figure 7.16 shows a rotary stand and turntable. As files were mechanized to house documents larger than cards, carousel-type rotary files that could be rotated among many workers became popular. These units permitted an operator, seated at a push-button console, to activate the mechanism that brought the desired tray or shelf to the access point.

AUTOMATED FILING SYSTEMS

Manual filing systems require the employee to go to the records. In large records systems, it is more expedient to bring the record to the employee through the use of automated filing systems.

Automated filing equipment began with rotary card files. These rotary files were then enlarged to house correspondence. Files were then automated so that a single drawer, shelf, or bin could be selected. The retrieval of a single card or folder was the next step in automation. Today's automated document filing systems include electronic retrieval of bar-coded items or digitized documents.

Advantages of Automated Systems

Automated systems have the following advantages:

- Documents can be filed randomly.
- Retrieval is quicker or, in electronic systems, instantaneous.
- The need for cross-referencing is reduced or eliminated.

Automated systems can be either mechanical, electromechanical, or electronic.

Conveyers

Electromechanical and electronic selection of individual drawers, shelves, or bins is also known as using vertical conveyers, vertical carousels, or power files. Conveyers are one type of electromechanical filing system. Conveyers are used in a retrieval system to bring carriers or folders to the point of reference. They can also be used to move

FIGURE 7.17 Electronic Reciprocating File (Courtesy of White Office Systems, Inc.)

individual documents either horizontally or vertically. The carriers are designed for all card sizes, microfilm jackets, aperture cards, and letter- and legal-size records. A reciprocating file is a power file where the whole file remains in tact as in a Ferris wheel. One shelf takes the place of another in front of the worker as shown in Figure 7.17. The trays fit into shelves, which can be raised or lowered.

Electronic Retrieval

Random-access filing systems offer automated or mechanical retrieval of files by means of an identifier in a particular field. A file can be selected no matter where it is located in the system. Remstar's File-Pic 2000 file manager is shown in Figure 7.18. It is a vertical power file carousel in which files rotate as in a Ferris wheel. It is compatible with many software and computer systems. The system has programmable data fields which allow access to frequently used data without physically accessing paper files. It lets you create, manage, and track up to eight file databases. The system permits bar-code reading and printing. It supports alphanumeric or terminal-digit filing. The system can house CD-ROMs, optical disks, magnetic tapes, disk packs, small parcels and parts, as well as folders, cards, or trays.

Another power file vertical carousel is the White Power File 6600 shown in Figure 7.19. This system is ideal for storing cards, microfiche, roll film, cassettes, small parts, or small media. It is also used for redeemed coupons, canceled checks, time cards, returned business reply cards, and sales expense slips. This system brings the file to the operator. Operator control panels provide single push-button shelf selection with the shelf index immediately adjacent to the push button. A variety of computer control and file tracking methods are available, including check-out file and item management programs, which can use and create bar code labels. A microprocessor chooses the shortest filing route for fast productivity. Many other vendors have similar equipment.

In bar-coded tracking systems, the electronic

FIGURE 7.18 Vertical Carousel with Automated Storage and Retrieval System
(Courtesy of Remstar International, Inc.)

FIGURE 7.19 Power Files
(Courtesy of White Storage and Retrieval Systems, Inc.)

memory units that can be hooked into optical scanning systems indicate the name of the person who has a record and the date the record was withdrawn from the files.

Even more sophisticated retrieval systems have been designed to house records such as microimage documents and documents on optical disk or CD-ROM. Retrieval is automatic, and a view of the record occurs in three seconds after the keyboard entry. Information that was previously in hard copy may now be retrieved from the computer monitor.

SPACE PLANNING

Space planning is the coordination of physical components within the available floor space to provide maximum efficiency in the most attractive arrangement.

Need for Space Planning

Planning may be required for new, remodeled, or currently used areas. It may occur when:

- A new or modified system or procedure is adopted.
- A change in work procedures or personnel occurs.
- A change in organizational structure occurs.
- Complaints from employees about their work stations are justified.

Space planning involves a review of objectives, a systems approach, study of the work flow, and design of workstations.

Objectives. The objectives of space planning are to ensure the comfort of the records management staff, maintain an efficient flow of work, facilitate supervision, establish the location of furniture and equipment, and provide for future needs. Space planning involves more than just putting file housing in a given amount of empty space. Movement in the work area, human anatomy, environmental factors, such as light, color, sound, and heat—all must be considered to avoid stress and other factors that affect productivity. This has led to the systems approach in planning for work flow and workstations to meet objectives.

Systems Approach. An emerging trend is that of looking at buildings as systems and using the systems approach to forecast space needs. The total office systems approach is an integration of ergonomics, electronics, and business systems with company goals and policies for purposes of improving company motivation and productivity. One of the considerations is growth space. *Growth space* is of particular concern to records managers. It is the space contiguous to the operational unit that allows for its planned growth. In some cases, growth space is released to the records manager, but in others, the facility manager controls the space and releases it periodically.

Once an efficient, well-organized records system has been housed in suitable equipment, the facility will be complete if the equipment is positioned to attain maximum efficiency. The important concern to records managers in the systems approach is the flow of work.

Work Flow. Work flow is the path or steps that work takes from origination to completion. The work flow of a department or entire organization should be analyzed regularly. A work flow chart is frequently used for analysis. It is a pictorial representation of how the job done in a particular office integrates with jobs done in other departments. For example, the flow of records from active status to the records center can be diagrammed to show all of the work steps and personnel involved. The objective of work flow analysis is to complete the task in the fewest number of steps and least amount of distance between steps with the fewest number of people involved. At each step a workstation must be provided that will facilitate the flow of work.

Workstations. The workstation must be considered a system in which each component harmonizes with the others; it may be adjusted to meet the particular needs of the operator. Ergonomic considerations in the workstation (discussed later in the chapter) are illustrated in Figure 7.20. The workstation should be designed for the particular tasks which will be completed at that point. The workstation should contain only those features which are necessary to complete the tasks. This will avoid clutter and simplify the work flow.

The latest trend in office furniture is toward *system furniture.* System furniture is a combination of freestanding desk-storage units, work surfaces, panels, panel-hung components, files, storage units, and other ancillary equipment that creates a workstation in what is known as the open office. The workstation is designed with comfort and efficiency as key priorities, with the hope that this will lead to maximum productivity. Figure 7-21 shows workstations designed for both electronic and nonelectronic tasks.

Approaches to Space Planning

Ineffective use of space is a continuous liability. The individual daily loss in efficiency may be small, but the aggregate loss may be significant. Two basic approaches to space planning are the symmetrical-technical approach and the flexible-personnel approach.

The *symmetrical-technical* approach is the traditional approach, in which efficiency, work, and cost expenditures are emphasized. It stresses function of equipment and is based on symmetry and uniformity. An appearance of order prevails through the arrangement of furniture and equipment.

The *flexible-personnel* approach strives to avoid monotony. It is based on variation in the office to create a pleasant work atmosphere. The concept is known as office landscaping. Walls may be of different colors, and furniture is not necessarily uniform in color, texture, or style. Real or artificial plants, rather than traditional partitions, are used as room dividers. Communication and the interaction of people are given high priority. The goals of landscaping are privacy without isolation, visual control of personnel, and instantaneous communication. The workstations are ar-

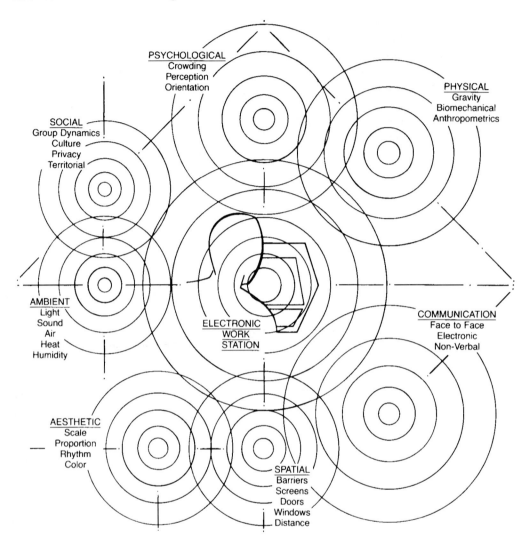

PSYCHOLOGICAL
Crowding
Perception
Orientation

PHYSICAL
Gravity
Biomechanical
Anthropometrics

SOCIAL
Group Dynamics
Culture
Privacy
Territorial

AMBIENT
Light
Sound
Air
Heat
Humidity

ELECTRONIC
WORK
STATION

COMMUNICATION
Face to Face
Electronic
Non-Verbal

AESTHETIC
Scale
Proportion
Rhythm
Color

SPATIAL
Barriers
Screens
Doors
Windows
Distance

FIGURE 7.20   Ergonomic Considerations in the Workstation
(Reprinted from the May issue of *Modern Office Procedures* and copyrighted 1982 by Penton/IPC
subsidiary of Pittway Corp.)

ranged irregularly, based on the work flow and traffic patterns of the organization. The purpose is to give personal identity to each group, and thus to each individual within the group.

Space Estimates

The space requirements for the filing area are difficult to generalize, particularly when the trend

seems to be toward office landscaping and larger workstations. In the past, however, studies have shown that 60 square feet for each clerical employee is an adequate standard. This provides for a 54-inch desk, a chair, a file cabinet, and aisle space. Many of the modern cubicles are 8 by 8, or 64 square feet.

These space estimates are upgraded through the levels of management. For example, a supervisor would have 100 or 125 square feet; a depart-

FIGURE 7.21 Ergonomic Workstations
(Courtesy of Data–Mate by the Maine Manufacturing Corp.)

ment manager, 250 to 300 square feet; and an executive, 400 to 450 square feet.

Figure 7.22 shows a traditional compartmentalized file room. The use of space is determined by the nature of the work; the available total area; the extent of service areas; the need for privacy; the type of equipment; the number of machines; and the shape, exposures, and obstructions of the total space.

The spacing of filing equipment depends upon the frequency of use and the function of the material filed. Figure 7.23 shows the different space requirements for both shelf and drawer files. Space requirements for the various automated filing equipment vary with the volume of the records and the number of modules in use.

Layout Guidelines

Over the years, guidelines for office layout have been developed to increase efficiency. These guidelines include the following:

1. *The layout should be kept flexible.* Plans for any major procedural changes, such as the automation of manual routines, should be provided in the layout.

FIGURE 7.22 Compartmentalized File Room

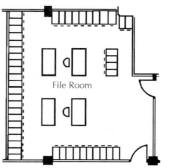

File Room

2. *One large area is preferable to an equivalent area of small rooms.* The single area permits better lighting, ventilation, supervision, and communication.

3. *The workstation of the supervisor should be positioned to permit total observation of the work area.*

4. *Dominant work flow and communication needs should be given highest priority.* Unnecessary circulation of records should be avoided. Work should come to the workers, and where practical, mechanical or electronic systems should be used to move the work.

5. *Central service work, such as central files, should be conveniently located near the work units and the personnel whom they service most.*

6. *In allocating work space, provisions should be made for the peak-load rather than for the bare-minimum requirements.* Past annual volume of work should be used as the basis for planning and allocating space. Where maximum and minimum standards have been set, it should be remembered that maximum standards provide for expansion and usually increase efficiency.

7. *Standard space guides should be adhered to in planning and allocating space.* Where maximum and minimum standards have been set, it should be remembered that maximum offers an easy opportunity for social contact. Enclosure offers employees an opportunity to have their own territory. *Territory* is the perception of one's own space.

FIGURE 7.23 Space Requirements for Shelf and Drawer Files

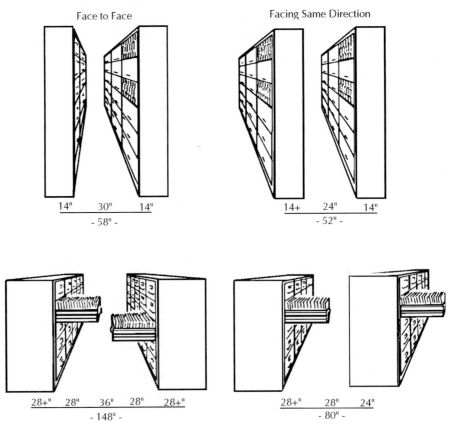

Building Security

Identification can be checked by a security officer at the entrance of the building, or employees may secure access to the building through physical or electronic access devices.

Physical Devices.   Physical devices extend the ability of records and security staffs by providing a delay to an intrusion, alerting the security staff to a problem, and allowing response time. Security functions which the records manager may need to monitor in cooperation with the facility manager include locksmithing and key control, and testing, maintenance, and repair of fire- and life-safety systems.

Many organizations are subscribing to *integrated security systems (ISS)* to control access to buildings and offices. The ISS monitors the exits and hallways of the areas through television cameras. Ultrasonic detectors, microwave sensors, and infrared invisible light beams can detect movement and variations in heat and can indicate these variations on the master console. ISS is a combination of security and disaster protection. ISS also monitors smoke and fire detectors, heating, air conditioning, and lighting. Any change beyond acceptable parameters is indicated on the master console, and the appropriate staff can be alerted.

Electronic Access.   Electronic access control to secure areas consists of card systems and biometrics. *Electronic security cards* resemble credit cards. The identification card is placed in a card reader next to the door and the door automatically unlocks, if access is permitted. The card system records the date and time of entry, the employee's name, the door number, and whether or not entry is granted. Some systems can sound alarms if unauthorized entry is attempted.

Biometrics access control devices measure unique personal characteristics. Common biometrics devices include fingerprint scanners, voice determiners, and recognizers of retinal eye patterns. The *fingerprint scanner* works similarly to the electronic security card. The finger is placed against an electro-optical plate. The fingerprint is compared by a laser scan to the fingerprint that has earlier been programmed into the security system. A match permits entry. *Voice-activated access systems* require the prerecording of the employee's voice pattern into the computer system. As the employee speaks into the access system, verification is made by comparing the voice patterns. Access is granted to matches. *The retinal eye pattern recognizers* operate similarly to both fingerprint scanners and voice-activated access systems.

Electronic Records.   With so much information being in electronic form today, an information protection program becomes imperative. Factors to consider include:

*   Source of critical information and possible means of degeneration or exploitation.
*   Unacceptable risks to sensitive or critical information that should be ranked in priority for safekeeping.
*   Weaknesses in present protection program.
*   Cost of protecting information versus cost of losing it.

Policies and Procedures.   Policies and procedures regarding security control concern access to the facility. They also regulate movement within the facility. Policies also require the report of hazardous conditions. Education of the staff concerning good safety and security is an ongoing activity.

Facilities Management

The records manager and filing personnel should be responsible for planning the proper use of space in the active records area, but space planning is seldom done by the records management staff alone. Options include a facility manager from within the firm, a facilities management consultant, or a planning committee composed of records personnel. Since 1980, a professional organization, the National (later International) Facilities Management Association, is available to facility managers. *Facility management (FM)* is the practice of coordinating the physical workplace with the people and work of the organization. It seeks to integrate the principles of business administration, architecture, and the behavioral and engineering sciences. The skills required today for managing a plant operation go beyond traditional steam-fitting, sheet metal, and plumbing skills. Today's facility manager needs knowledge of electronics and computer skills. The intelligent building is an example of information services that make the facility manager's task easier today. The concept of facilities management is often simplified to focus on purpose, place, and people. Facilities management has the responsibility for HVAC (heat, ventilation, air conditioning) systems, humidity, acoustics, vertical and horizontal transport, energy management, emergency power, and telecommunications. All of these responsibilities are combined in managing an intelligent building.

Intelligent Buildings. The concept of an *intelligent building,* or a *smart building,* has existed for over 20 years. With the deregulation of the telecommunications industry, the number of intelligent buildings is expected to increase dramatically. An intelligent building incorporates one or more of three basic information services. The first of these services concerns automation systems for building controls, such as HVAC operation, elevators, and control of lighting and life-safety systems, maintenance, and operation. These were the first services that were automated in facility management.

The second intelligence feature is advanced telecommunications, which had its impetus after deregulation. This service may include systems for voice communications only or systems that allow simultaneous text, sound, image, and data transmission. Dish receivers for both microwaves and satellite reception can be part of this feature. With the widening use of multimedia, records managers will be faced with the problem of storing multimedia consisting of CD-ROMs, optical disks, and computer memory.

Office automation is the third information service that can be made available in an intelligent building. Networks can be made available throughout the building for greater efficiency.

If more than one tenant is occupying the same building and these three information services are made available to all tenants, this service is known as *shared tenant services (STS).* Where STS is permitted by local utility regulation, considerable savings have been effected.

Floor Load. One of the basic considerations in the construction of a building for a records manager is the floor load. *Floor load* capacity is the weight of records and equipment that a floor can safely accommodate. Floor load is the sum of dead weight and live load. *Dead weight* is the weight of the inanimate objects, such as furniture, equipment, and records. *Live load* is the allowance for the weight of the personnel working in the area.

HVAC Systems. Heating, ventilating, and air conditioning systems are often considered together. In planning the heating of a building, the temperature cannot be considered separately from humidity.

Temperature. An uncomfortable office, either too hot or too cold, can cause workers to be unproductive, to make errors, to have reduced concentration, or to be absent. Temperature is affected by the location, size, and shape of the work area; the number of people working in the area; and the kind and amount of equipment. Both people and equipment tend to generate heat. The accepted temperature for the office is from 68°F to 72°F. Temperature and humidity must be considered together in determining the comfort level of workers.

Humidity.   Relative humidity is the amount of moisture in the air as compared with the greatest amount that the air could contain at the same temperature, expressed as a percentage. The relative humidity for safety of records is between 40 and 60 percent. If the relative humidity falls below 25 percent, static buildup may occur.

Ventilation.   Ventilation is the circulation of air in the building. In some cases, the outside air may be brought into the building and circulated. In other cases, the inside air may be filtered and then recirculated. The outside temperature may be a factor in the decision to recirculate air. Some buildings may be sealed and ventilation controlled by air pressure. The air pressure prevents outside air from coming into the building. Gases may be emitted from new furniture or carpeting, such as in a new car smell. Some people may be allergic to these fumes. One case of the ill effects of poor ventilation, reported as the "sick building" syndrome, occurred in Detroit.

Air Conditioning.   With the advent of the computer, many people have come to believe that air conditioning is a necessity in an environment that houses the computer. This was the case for the vacuum-tube computers, but microcomputers do not generate that kind of heat. Air conditioning is now utilized for the benefit of the worker as well as for the equipment. However, air conditioning is susceptible to mold and creates an ideal environment for encouraging the growth of bacteria. Controls must be provided to ensure that diseases such as Legionnaires' disease, which resulted from mold in the ventilating system, do not occur.

Computer-controlled building systems came on the market in the early 1970s. They provide individualized environments and substantial savings in both cost and size of the plant. HVAC systems of large complexes can be controlled by personal computers that can troubleshoot the systems and provide a historical record of their operations. These systems can work with fully integrated fire and life-safety or security systems.

Managing HVAC systems has come to be known as *energy management*. Some energy-saving measures are easy to implement, such as reducing the size and number of electric lights or installing storm windows; others involve an extensive program of replacing or upgrading heating and air-conditioning equipment (called *retrofitting*).

Acoustics.   *Acoustics* is defined as the characteristics of an area that have to do with how sounds and noises can be heard or transmitted within it. Sound may be desirable or undesirable. While some offices may pipe in music, others are concerned with noise reduction. Noise can be controlled by engineering and by architecture. A useful tool to measure the noise level and assist in engineered control is the noise reduction coefficient.

The *noise reduction coefficient* (NRC) is the average of sound absorption coefficients tested at 250, 500, 1,000, and 2,000 cycles per second. This average gives the general effectiveness of a material as a sound absorber and is expressed as a decimal. For example, *.95NRC* indicates that about 95 percent of the average sound energy striking a tested material is absorbed.

Vertical and Horizontal Transportation.   While vertical transportation brings to mind elevators for transporting workers to their appropriate floors, vertical transportation must also be considered in records management. Elevators may be needed to transport inactive records down to the loading dock or to transport new equipment to the appropriate floor. In some cases, the size of the equipment to be purchased is limited by the size of the vertical transport.

Horizontal transport in records management may mean conveyers, hand trolleys, or electrical carts for the transport of records from one area to another.

Energy Management.   One of the highest cost items using energy is lighting. A sufficient quantity of light is important for the accurate performance of a task. Poor light can cause visual problems and a decrease in employee morale. To provide adequate lighting for individual work and to conserve energy, the use of task and ambient lighting has emerged. *Task lighting* is lighting that is provided for an employee to perform a specific task. Very often the light fixture is built into the furniture. *Ambient lighting* is the background lighting. It is used to supplement task lighting. A checklist for the design of a centralized file room appears in Figure 7.24.

Emergency Power.   In the event of loss of electrical power from the primary source, provisions for backup emergency power must be provided. This may take the form of another generator. In the event of a major disaster, the operation of the firm, including that of the records management program, would be in serious jeopardy without alternate sources of power.

Fire-Safety Systems.   *Sprinkler systems* can minimize damage to records from fire in large records areas. In some cases the damage done by the water may be greater than the damage done by the fire, but the use of zoned sprinklers with time delays does offer protection.

Telecommunications.   In addition to telephones, the records manager, has the additional concern of increased computerization of business functions, and the interconnections of computers through hard-wiring of the telephone system. Communications is where the records manager and the facilities manager must work closely together. To the records manager, the communications system is like an electronic highway over which information flows. To the facilities manager, the communications system is a major user of space (anten-

FIGURE 7.24   Centralized File Room Design Checklist

I.   Existing Facilities
   A.   Current space utilization
   B.   Additional space availability

II.   Work Flow
   A.   Users
   B.   Communication flow
   C.   File room personnel

III.   Building Security
   A.   Physical devices
   B.   Electronic access
   C.   Electronic records
   D.   Policies and procedures

IV.   Facilities Management
   A.   HVAC
      1. Temperature
      2. Humidity
      3. Ventilation
      4. Air conditioning
   B.   Acoustic
   C.   Vertical and horizontal transport
   D.   Energy management
      1. Lighting
      2. Emergency power
   E.   Fire-Safety Systems
   F.   Telecommunications
   G.   Plumbing

V.   Ergonomics
   A.   Space requirements
   B.   Color
   C.   Furniture
   D.   Aesthetics
   E.   Equipment
   F.   Carpet and drapes
   G.   Plants and pictures

VI.   Federal Legislation
   A.   Occupational Safety and Health Act of 1970
   B.   Americans with Disabilities Act of 1990

VII.   Other
   A.   Budget
   B.   Specifications
   C.   Evaluation

nae, risers, file servers, modems, closets, and wire trays).

ERGONOMICS

Facilities management incorporates the principles of ergonomics in coordinating the workplace with people and their work. *Ergonomics* is the science concerned with the design of an effective work space for people working with machines. Maximum efficiency can be attained when ergonomic factors, such as anatomical, physiological, and psychological factors, are considered in the design of workstations. These ergonomic definitions are shown in Figure 7.25.

Anatomical Factors

Anatomical considerations include analysis of body structure and size and movement in the work area. Designers are concerned with *anthropometry*, which is the study of human body measurements, for the correct scaling of sizes, heights, and shapes of furniture and equipment to the dimensions of the workers. *Biomechanics* is the study of the body forces of human beings. Biomechanical factors help a designer to plan work spaces and layouts that will minimize the strain of physical work. Designing the proper *seating* is a function of biomechanics. Good seating may be achieved by proper dimensions, construction, and flexibility in the chair. Chairs should be designed for comfort, freedom of movement, and minimum of fatigue. An adjustable chair provides for individual differences.

Psychological Factors

Psychological factors affect both the behavior and the attitude of workers. Workstations should be designed to minimize the causes of stress and disruption. The environment should contribute to productivity. The perception of the firm's good-

will is affected by how the worker feels about management's concern for his or her well-being.

Social Factors

Sufficient privacy and quiet should be planned into the workstation. While people need to feel a part of a social group, they also have a need for privacy and territory and for boundaries for their work space and personal use. The use of modular paneling instead of open landscaping is an attempt to meet both open and closed needs, called *enclosure* and *access.* This design separates workers, but also offers them an easy opportunity for social contact.

Spatial Factors

Spatial factors should include consideration of the needs of all people for a barrier-free environment, which promotes access to full employment for all. Other spatial factors that may be used positively are screens, which may serve to provide privacy for workers, doors wide enough for the handicapped as well as for movement of records, windows protected from glare, and the confining of the work flow to within a reasonable distance.

Communication Factors

Social needs, as well as business needs, are met by facilitating communication. Communication at the workstation may be face to face, nonverbal, or electronic. Face-to-face communication is clarified by body language (nonverbal communication). Electronic communication not only includes the telephone for worldwide access, but also the computer. The merger of these two technologies is called *telematics.* Communication may include dictation, electronic mail (E mail), voice-mail systems, and teleconferencing. In today's world, use of the telephone makes possible telecommunications of facsimile transmission (fax), micrographics to fax communication, and computer-to-computer communication. Work space for these devices must be provided. Sufficient footprint space

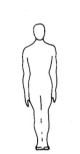

THE INDIVIDUAL

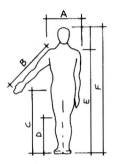

ANTHROPOMETRICS
(Body Dimensions)

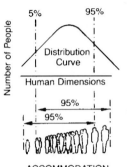

ACCOMMODATION
Designed to Suit Approx. 95% of Users.

BIOMECHANICS
Application of Body Forces.

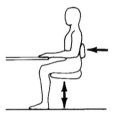

SEATING
Support of Body in Work Position;
Against Forces of Gravity.

CONTROL & DISPLAY
Interface with Equipment.

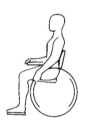

BARRIER FREE
Accommodation of Handicapped
in the Work Environment.

SOCIAL
Arrangement for Privacy
and/or Interaction.

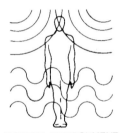

GENERAL ENVIRONMENT
Light, Noise and Interior Climate.

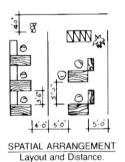

SPATIAL ARRANGEMENT
Layout and Distance.

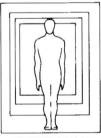

PSYCHOLOGICAL
Attitudinal Mental Image and Behavioral
Response to the Structure
of the Environment.

TOTAL OFFICE
SYSTEMS APPROACH
An Integration of Ergonomics,
Electronics and Business
Systems with Company Goals
and Policies for Purposes of
Improving Company Motivation
and Productivity.

FIGURE 7.25   Ergonomic Definitions
(Reprinted from the May issue of *Modern Office Procedures* and copyrighted 1982 by Penton/IPC
subsidiary of Pittway Corp.)

for the equipment, space for easy access, and space for input and output are important considerations.

Aesthetic Factors

The working environment can be made more pleasant through the use of color, carpeting, drapes, plants, pictures, furniture, and the like.

Color theory is built around color contrast, the relation of one color to another, and the relationship of color to the work environment. Earth tones have increased in popularity. Light colors brighten up an area and make it appear larger. Dark colors can make an area appear smaller. The choice of color should be based on the space involved, the amount of time spent in the area, the type of work performed, the furnishings, and the equipment.

Carpet and drapes, if appropriate to the work area, contribute to the decor and perception of the firm. Plants can be real or artificial. Live plants may be provided and maintained throughout the organization by professional horticulturists.

Although some managers prohibit personal additions to the work area, such as pictures, other managers subscribe to a service which changes pictures in selected areas on a regular basis. Furniture should be appropriate to the area and meet anthropometric needs.

Ambient Factors

Ambient factors affect security, safety, and self-worth. They include environmental factors such as light, color, acoustics, air, heat, and humidity. Color is also considered an aesthetic factor.

SUMMARY

Records managers are faced with maintaining filing systems for records on a variety of media besides paper. Managers must select the records housing that will provide the most efficient information retrieval at the lowest possible cost and that will use the least amount of office space.

Equipment is selected on the basis of compatibility with records, ease of access, room for growth, cost, space requirements, simultaneous use, security, and long-range planning. Specific considerations in replacing equipment include the present filing system, the use of the file, conversion problems, employee comfort, and the technical aspects of automated equipment.

Housing for manual filing systems includes vertical file cabinets, open-shelf filing, lateral filing equipment, mobile aisle systems, slant files, rotating shelves, and specialized filing equipment.

Card storage and retrieval systems include boxes, drawers, trays, tubs, visible files, wheel files, and rotary files. Automated filing equipment brings the record to the employee. It includes conveyers and electronic retrieval of files.

Two basic approaches to space planning are the symmetrical-technical approach and the flexible-personnel approach. The symmetrical-technical approach is the traditional approach to space planning, based on efficiency, work, and cost expenditures. The flexible-personnel approach strives to avoid monotony. It is based on variation in the office to create a pleasant work atmosphere.

Devices used for building security may include physical devices such as ultrasonic devices, microwave sensors, infrared invisible light beams, and electronic access devices.

Engineering factors to consider are floor load, temperature, humidity, ventilation, air conditioning, acoustics, vertical and horizontal transport, energy management, emergency power, fire-safety systems, plumbing, and telecommunications. Three basic information services may be utilized in the management of an "intelligent building." The first concerns automation systems for building controls, the second is for advanced communications, and the third is for office automation.

Ergonomics, the science that fits the work place to the person, is being used more and more in office design to increase both productivity and job satisfaction. Ergonomics considers anatomical, psychological, social, spatial, communication, aesthetic, and ambient factors in the selection of facilities for records management.

QUESTIONS FOR DISCUSSION

1. What are some records media that records managers must provide for in addition to paper records?

2. Discuss equipment selection criteria for a records management program.

3. What are two approaches to cost justification?

4. What are some reasons for replacing equipment?

5. How does magnetic media storage differ from paper storage?

6. What are some of the advantages of lateral filing equipment?

7. What are the advantages of open-shelf files?

8. What types of records are usually housed in open-shelf files?

9. What are three advantages of automated equipment over manual devices?

10. Describe the guidelines for selection of card storage and retrieval systems equipment.

11. What equipment is available for card files?

12. Describe the housing available for visible index file systems.

13. What types of reference material are kept in visible files?

14. What is the difference between a *carousel* and a *wheel* file?

15. What are some ways of filing maps and charts?

16. What are the objectives of space planning?

17. What is the difference between the two basic approaches to space planning?

18. How is the amount of space for filing work determined?

19. What are some of the systems that are managed by facilities management?

20. What is ergonomics?

PROJECTS

1. Prepare a layout for a file room, 20 by 24 feet. The equipment in this room includes 50 four-drawer cabinets, two desks, two tables, five chairs, and one copying machine. The desks are 36 by 54 inches, the copying machine, 54 by 54 inches. The personnel using the room are one supervisor, one receptionist-file clerk, and one other file clerk.

2. Describe the layout of a file room with which you are familiar. Point out some ways in which it could be improved. Give reasons for your suggestions.

3. Visit a records installation of your choice. List your recommendations for any changes in the equipment used by the organization for records management. On what evidence do you base your recommendations?

4. Visit a records installation. Prepare a report that follows the records through their creation, use, maintenance, and destruction, by describing the equipment used at each step.

5. Locate an establishment in the community where visible indexing systems are used. Prepare a chart that describes the types of visible records and the uses made of them. Describe the media and the equipment used to house the records.

6. Prepare a chart that describes the advantages and disadvantages of the following manual card systems.

   a. Box
   b. Drawer
   c. Tray
   d. Rotary
   e. Wheel

List some card storage applications that you think are best adaptable to each type of equipment.

7. Prepare a report on mechanical and automated filing equipment not described in the text. (A good source is advertisements in current periodicals.) Show comparisons of the equipment. Make recommendations for their use.

CASE PROBLEM

Records of retired faculty are housed in the basement of the Administration Building in letter-size, 4-drawer file cabinets. The records, although letter-size, are housed in legal-size folders and consequently must be stored length-wise in the drawer, rather than crosswise. The records take up about 30 cabinets. The drawers are not labeled as to their contents. The personnel clerk who is responsible for retired faculty records has just joined ARMA and is writing a proposal for how best to reorganize these records for safety and ease of access. You have just completed a records management course and have been assigned to assist the personnel clerk in this project.

The personnel clerk asks you to consider the three options below and write up the procedure necessary to get the information on which to base the decision. She asks that you include as much cost information as possible and recommendations for which vendors in the area to contact for further information. The options are:

a. To box the records in records center boxes and have shelving installed in the area.

    (1) Should the legal-size folders be changed to letter-size folders?

    (2) Should the Maintenance Department be asked to install wooden shelves, or should the shelving be steel?

    (3) Should lateral files with color-coding be purchased?

b. To have the records microfilmed and a microfilm reader-printer installed at the workstation of the personnel clerk.

c. To have the records filmed onto optical disk and retrieved from the computer unit at the personnel clerk's desk.

Tenneco Inc.

Active Records Management

Tenneco is a multi-industry corporation with major interests in manufacturing, natural gas pipelines, packaging, and real estate. With corporate headquarters in Houston, Texas, Tenneco employs over 75,000 people worldwide. Fred Boecker is Records Manager at Tenneco. Supervisors include Harriett Welch of Records Administration and Earnestine Baucham of Records Control.

Records Management provides complete records management services for all Tenneco Gas companies and Tenneco Inc. Houston-based offices, establishes and maintains records retention schedules, and is responsible for ensuring that those programs comply with Tenneco standards. For non-Houston-based companies, Records Management provides advice and assistance in establishing and implementing effective records management programs; it is also responsible for ensuring that these programs comply with established Tenneco standards.

Corporate records are defined as any information, regardless of media (hard copy, microfilm, electronic), that has been created or received in the transaction of the company's business or the business of its subsidiaries. Each department and field office is responsible for the maintenance, retrieval, transfer, and destruction of its records according to established filing procedures and retention schedules. Guidelines for subject filing and classification are included in Tenneco's *Records Management Reference Guide.* The *Guide* also contains alphabetic filing rules which employees are expected to follow, thus ensuring uniformity throughout the company .

Records Control maintains more than 125,000 cubic feet of records in storage. Records Administration is responsible for assisting with the design and implementation of effective records systems for departments; establishing standard filing procedures; assisting with the selection of file personnel upon request; training file room personnel; establishing standards for supplies and equipment used in filing; assisting with the design, layout, and equipment requirements for the file rooms; and assisting departments with file relocation. In addition Records Administration identifies micrographics applications; determines disposition of records obtained through acquisitions; and establishes and maintains a vital records program for the company and its divisions and subsidiaries.

In assisting with the design and implementation of effective records systems, the user's needs are determined through meetings which include the specialist, management, and departmental personnel. The specialist examines and evaluates the department's current recordkeeping methods, and a recommendation for an improved records system is presented to management based on the evaluation, user needs, conformity to standards, and retention requirements. The system design includes manual and/or automated information retrieval, micrographics applications, vital records protection programs, equipment and space needs, and retention schedules.

Upon approval by management, implementation of the new system is directed by the specialist. This includes training personnel in system implementation procedures and maintenance of the records system; consulting with the department on a regular basis during systems implementation; writing records management procedures for the department; and conducting periodic reviews of the records systems to monitor efficiency and compliance with retention guidelines.

A variety of folders are used within any given file. Kraft folders are used if the volume of material is small. Pressboard folders are used for large volumes or for housing records with long retention periods. Redrope pockets are used to house material such as catalogs, booklets, or anything which cannot be perforated for fastener folders.

Each department is asked to maintain a classification list which lists folder titles in the files. This provides an inventory of all the files, helps identify missing files, orients new users to the system, and maintains consistency in the filing system. Departments are also asked annually to select material from their files that can be destroyed or transferred to Records Control.

Active records management at Tenneco is an example of a comprehensive, corporate-wide endeavor.

PART *III*

Electronic Records Management

Chapter 8

Electronic Records

Learning Objectives

1. To define electronic records, their importance to government and business, the problems associated with their management, and the challenges and opportunities these problems will create for records managers during the future.
2. To list various types of electronic records and the media used to store them.
3. To explain principles for inventorying electronic records.
4. To describe the various methods and techniques for managing active electronic records which reside on nonremovable electronic records media.
5. To elucidate the proper methods of labeling and identifying electronic files on removable media.
6. To describe special software for managing documents and files in PC computing environments.
7. To list guidelines for the selection, handling, and storage of removable electronic records media.
8. To describe principles and techniques for managing inactive electronic records including the development of records retention schedules for electronic records.

THE IMPACT OF THE COMPUTER ON RECORDS MANAGEMENT

According to an article in *Fortune* magazine, electronic computing is not yet the largest industry in the world—at less than $400 billion in annual sales, it is smaller than either the petroleum or the automobile industry—but "it has become the most important because of its power to transform the way people work."[1] According to the *Fortune* article, worldwide annual shipments in 1993 included some 12,000 mainframe computers, just

under a million minicomputers, about 6 million high-performance workstations, and a staggering total of 31 million microcomputers (PCs). The article estimates the total worldwide installed base of mainframes at 70,000 and the installed base of PCs at 135 million.

Few people would dispute the notion that the widespread use of electronic computers has been, by far, the single most significant occurrence to affect records management during the past ten to twenty years. Such an assertion is justified for the following three main reasons.

1. *Computers generate enormous quantities of records.* The many millions of computers are huge records-creation devices; they store an unknown but tremendous quantity of business information on the several types of storage devices and media that accompany them. This tremendous quantity of electronic records is growing rapidly, and continual growth is sure to occur. In addition to the electronic records they produce, computers and their peripheral devices produce huge quantities of paper and microfilm records. Thus, records managers have many more records to manage than would be the case if computers were not so ubiquitous in virtually every business office.

2. *There are numerous problems associated with the management of electronic records—problems that require records management solutions.* Computers are relatively sophisticated machines, but their use still causes many records management problems not unlike those encountered in noncomputerized recordkeeping environments: Electronic files can still be poorly identified, mislabeled, "lost," or otherwise difficult to retrieve; electronic information loses its value and needs to be systematically destroyed just as paper records do; electronic records are just as vulnerable as any other record to the risk of disaster (indeed, the risks are often greater) and require special protection; and removable electronic media need to be stored and managed properly just as noncomputer media do. These problems and many others are analogous to traditional records management problems, and each of them can be solved by properly applying traditional records management principles to electronic recordkeeping environments.

3. *Computers provide new ways of solving records management problems.* Prior to the advent of computer technology, records managers had no software to index, track, and monitor file folders or records storage cartons; no bar codes to enhance record media circulation control; no software for computer–assisted microfilm retrieval; no optical disk systems; no electronic forms management; and none of a dozen more computer–related techniques for solving the problems associated with document–based information systems. This book presents records managers with guidance to enable them to apply these electronic records management technologies successfully so that the value of document–based recordkeeping systems can be enhanced in business and governmental organizations.

This chapter is about managing electronic records. More precisely, it is about ways to improve the management of computer–based information through better management of the media on which electronic records are stored. Records managers are most often required to solve the problems associated with managing microcomputer-based electronic records. Records managers are generally not as directly involved in managing the electronic records that reside on the larger mainframe and minicomputers, as this task is usually the primary responsibility of computer specialists who work in data centers and MIS departments. On the other hand, records managers are frequently involved in developing and implementing records retention schedules for records that reside on large computers. They are often responsible for storing security copies of magnetic media generated by the computers in vaults, records centers, or other facilities over which they have jurisdiction, and for accomplishing various other records management tasks involving large computers.

MAJOR TYPES OF ELECTRONIC RECORDS

Electronic records may be defined as records containing *machine–readable*, as opposed to *human–readable,* information. A collection of electronic records is often generally referred to as a file; the term *file* is often used together with other terms denoting the physical storage medium on which the information is recorded. Examples include the terms *disk files*, *tape files*, and *image files*.

The machine–readable information recorded on electronic records takes the form of *character–coded electronic signals* and exists in three primary forms: text, data, or electronic images.

Text Files

Text files are usually produced by word processing programs or by other software. The records consist of character–coded letters, digits, or other symbols appearing in typewritten documents, such as correspondence and reports. Text files are most often created by keyboard entry of the data, but optical character recognition (OCR) programs, electronic messaging software, and various other types of computer programs may also be used to create them.

Each individual character in a text file document is represented by a predetermined number and sequence of *bits*; this sequence is determined by the type of digital coding scheme utilized by the computer system. Most text files are created using either the ASCII or the EBCDIC coding scheme. ASCII—the American Standard Code for Information Interchange — is used in virtually all minicomputers and microcomputers, and in many non–IBM mainframe computer systems. The EBCDIC scheme—the Extended Binary Coded Decimal Interchange Code—is used for text files created on IBM mainframes and other IBM-compatible mainframe computers.

The particular type of coding scheme employed in creating text files can sometimes have important records management ramifications. Because the ASCII file format is the broadest compatibility for file interchange, it is the best option for insuring that text files can be read and processed over a period of years on a variety of computer devices. Thus, text files having long retention requirements should generally be preserved in ASCII format whenever possible.

Data Files

Data files are computer–processable files that store numeric data (and frequently some textual information as well) as *quantitive values*, so that the numbers can be manipulated utilizing arithmetic computations. Text files also store numeric digits, but the digits are stored simply as characters, without regard to their quantitive significance. Another distinction between data and text files is that data files are stored in a more structured manner. These electronic records are normally subdivided into one or more *data elements*, also referred to as *fields*, which store designated categories of computer data. Data fields are sometimes further subdivided into *subfields*. For example, in accounting or general ledger files, separate fields and subfields would be dedicated for credits, debits, etc.

Image Files

Image files are electronic records which contain computer–processable images of documents that generally existed in hard copy format prior to having been converted to image files. These files consist of digitally coded document images; they are created by electronically scanning the hard copy documents or by various other methods, including computer–aided design programs, fax modems, and business graphics software programs. Image files may be stored on magnetic or optical media. Optical media are an increasingly popular storage option for very large quantities of documents because these media have such high recording densities.

STORAGE MEDIA FOR ELECTRONIC RECORDS

Text files, data files, and image files can be stored on a wide variety of storage devices, or media. However, two broad classes are most common:

magnetic media and optical media. *Magnetic media* are the much older of the two and have been used to store electronic records since the advent of electronic computers in the early 1950s. *Optical media*, on the other hand, are comparatively new devices for electronic records storage, having been introduced commercially in the mid–1980s.

Magnetic Media

Magnetic storage media come in a wide variety of types and sizes, each having its own uses in storing electronic records. As a generic class, however, all types of magnetic media share a common physical attribute: They are ferromagnetic, that is, they are coated with a recording material which is capable of being magnetized when placed in a magnetic field, and of retaining magnetization when the field is removed. The most common magnetic media are magnetic disks, diskettes, and magnetic tapes.

Magnetic Disks.   *Magnetic disks* are platter–shaped storage devices on which data are recorded and retrieved. Magnetic disk drives may contain one or more platters with highly polished aluminum substrates, on which the information is recorded by magnetizing small areas of the platter's surface in a manner corresponding to the bit patterns associated with the text, data, or image files. The disks are divided into tracks, and successive bits are recorded in a linear fashion within each track. The actual recording is performed by an electromagnetic read-write head, which aligns the material in the proper direction. The recording material itself may be gamma ferric oxide, in which small iron particles are dispersed in a binder compound that binds the particles to the disk substrate. Alternatively, a thin metallic film, which provides more durable properties, may be used as the recording material.

Magnetic disk drives are the preferred storage medium in high-performance computing environments requiring very rapid, on–line access to electronic records. These disks may be *fixed* (per-manently installed within the computer itself) or *removable* from the computer when not in use for near–line or off–line storage. Fixed disk drives with high-storage-capacity platters are generally used in the larger mainframe and minicomputer installations; these disks usually vary in storage capacity from about 500 megabytes to 5 gigabytes or more. The lower capacity fixed disks used in microcomputers typically have storage capacities ranging from 40 to 200 or more megabytes. The removable hard disk cartridges are intended for desktop installations and typically offer about 44 megabytes of storage capacity. In terms of physical size, the larger, high-capacity magnetic disks range from 9 to 12 inches in diameter, while the low-capacity disks range from 2 to 5.25 inches in diameter. See Figure 8.1 for an illustration of a 5.25-inch magnetic disk drive with fixed media.

Magnetic Tape.   A removable magnetic storage medium for electronic records, *magnetic tape* is a ribbon or strip of plastic film coated with a magnetic recording material. In mainframe and minicomputer installations, the most widely used magnetic tapes are half an inch in width, 10.5 inches in diameter, and 2,400 feet in length, and are mounted on open reels. As shown in Figure 8.2, these nine-track tapes utilize gamma ferric oxide as the recording material and have a storage ca-

FIGURE 8.1   A 5.25–Inch Magnetic Disk Drive with Fixed Media
(Courtesy of Western Digital Corporation)

FIGURE 8.2   Nine–Track Magnetic Tape and an IBM 3480 Tape Cartridge
(Courtesy of International Business Machines Corporation)

pacity of 6,260 bits per linear inch of tape, or 160 megabytes. Because access to the data recorded on them is serial, this medium is unsuitable for rapid, on–line access; thus, magnetic tapes are used mainly for batch processing applications, data archiving for off–line storage, and duplication of on–line files for disaster backup protection.

A newer type of magnetic tape is the IBM 3480 magnetic tape cartridge, or "3480 cartridge". These smaller and easier-to-handle tapes measure 4 inches by 5 inches by 1 inch. The standard cartridge contains 550 feet of magnetic tape and stores 200 megabytes of data. The recording material is chromium dioxide. Like their nine–track counterparts, they are used primarily for data archiving and off–line storage purposes.

Diskettes.   *Diskettes*—flexible, or *floppy*, removable magnetic media—are encountered in virtually every business office that has a PC. They are of polyester construction; the recording surface is usually gamma ferric oxide. As shown in Figure 8.3, the surface of a diskette consists of an inner track and an outer sector for data recording, and a cover opening for the read-write head. The most common sizes are 5.25 inches and 3.5 inches. The

smaller size has steadily replaced the 5.25-inch disk since its introduction in the mid–1980s. The most common usage for these media is near- and off-line file storage, data archiving, and backup. In IBM–compatible PC installations, the 3.5-inch floppy disks, or diskettes, typically provide 720 kilobytes or 1.44 megabytes of storage capacity, the former being double–sided/dual density and the latter double–sided/high density.

Optical Media

Like magnetic disks, optical disks are platter–shaped storage devices, but they utilize an entirely different, nonmagnetic recording technology to write the data on the disks. Optical disk systems use high concentrations of laser light to record information on the disk platters. During recording operations, the laser light alters the light reflectance characteristics of the recording surface of the disk. Depending on the particular recording method utilized, the laser may form holes or pits in the recording surface, or bumps or bubbles. Optical disks are typically used in conjunction with magnetic storage in many records management system configurations, as any information that can be stored on magnetic disk or tapes can also be stored on optical disks.

In a records management context, the most significant and attractive feature of optical disks is their very high recording densities, densities much higher than those of magnetic media of comparable size. Depending on the size and type of disk, optical disks can accommodate storage capacities of up to 10 gigabytes, making them the highest-capacity storage medium for business information in existence. For business documents and data, the two main types of optical disks are the WORM (*write once read many* times) disk, and the rewritable optical disk. As the acronym indicates, write–once disks are not erasable; once information has been recorded in a given area of the disk, that area cannot be reused. These disks are manufactured in sizes ranging from 5.25 to 14 inches in diameter. The rewritable optical disks are manufactured in sizes ranging from 3.5 to

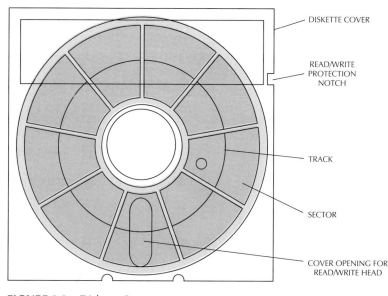

DISKETTE COVER

READ/WRITE
PROTECTION
NOTCH

TRACK

SECTOR

COVER OPENING FOR
READ/WRITE HEAD

FIGURE 8.3 Diskette Structure
(Courtesy of ARMA International)

5.25 inches; these are used primarily in computer installations, while the WORM disks are used primarily in large electronic recordkeeping systems. Both types of optical disks are used mainly to provide on–line access to documents and data, as well as for off–line data archiving and disaster backup purposes. See Figure 8.4 for an illustration of write–once and rewritable optical media.

ELECTRONIC RECORDS MANAGEMENT: PROBLEMS AND ISSUES

Electronic records and the systems that support them suffer from many of the same records management problems that beset their paper and microfilm counterparts These major problems are:

1. *Inadequate consideration is often devoted to the creation of records.* Because computers are such powerful information–processing devices, people at times create records on them that have little utility, are seldom if ever read and used, and perhaps should have never been created in the first place. This is particularly true with many management reports that are printed in hard copy or microfiche format. The report writer capabilities programmed into many software packages often generate lengthy reports, sorted in innumerable ways, that are of questionable utility. Once printed, however, they require considerable labor and expense to classify, file, and maintain. Records managers should provide guidelines to departmental personnel encouraging them to create and maintain only those computer–generated records that are needed to accomplish some valid business purpose.

2. *Inadequate attention is often devoted to the organization and identification of electronic records resident on–line on nonremovable media.* Because electronic records are machine–readable (they cannot be read by sight), it can be difficult to retrieve them unless adequate attention is devoted to how the files are named and identified, what tools are developed to facilitate their efficient retrieval (e.g., data dictionaries, thesauri, and other index devices), how they are organized into directories, subdirectories, and other structures designed to enhance retrieval, and what other software-related tools are available to enhance the file search capabilities of the users.

(a)

(b)

FIGURE 8.4   (a) Write–Once and (b) Multifunction Rewritable Optical Disk Cartridges
(Courtesy Panasonic Communications and Systems Company)

3.   *Inadequate attention is often devoted to the organization and identification of electronic records resident off–line on removable media.* Particularly in the case of PC–based electronic records on removable media, the creators of re- movable media often identify and label them in a very arbitrary and haphazard manner. The labels on diskettes often consist of brief and very cryptic terms which are insufficient for effective use of the records. As they grow in volume, these media are often poorly organized, and frequently no inventory exists to indicate their specific contents, date ranges, or other data needed to manage them.

4. *The protection and security of electronic records is often overlooked.* Even though electronic records often contain mission–critical information which is never printed and is thus unique and irreplaceable, many vital electronic records are unprotected and their owners are fully exposed to the risks of their loss from disasters or other causes. Again, this is particularly true in PC computing environments. Similarly, despite passwords and other options for protecting electronic records against unauthorized intrusion, theft and other threats to their integrity remain a major problem in many organizations which maintain sensitive data.

5. *The retention and disposition of electronic records is often overlooked.* Because electronic records consume so little space and are not a visible problem in many offices, their retention status is often not considered. Even many records managers often do not include these records within the scope of their retention scheduling programs. Electronic records, however, are subject to regulatory retention requirements as well as the risks associated with litigation, just as much as their paper and microfilm counterparts. Moreover, there is usually no business justification for retaining useless electronic information, however small its size.

6. *The relatively short usable life of many electronic records may be insufficient to meet the organization's retention and archival needs.* Because the proven longevity of some electronic records media is relatively short and because these records cannot be read or used without the proper hardware and software, electronic records may not be a suitable format for long–term retention or permanent archival preservation. The useful life of these records is significantly shorter than that of paper and microfilm records. Thus, records managers must often work with data processing personnel to develop and implement suitable options for those electronic records that must be retained for many years.

7. *The ownership status and management responsibility for many electronic records is unclear.* Although the users of electronic records have the strongest proprietary or ownership interest in them, it is often unclear who has primary management responsibility for these records. This is particularly true in the case of PC–based electronic records. The creators of these records often regard the records as their own private files or personal working papers, and they sometimes feel free to manage them as they please, remove them from official custody, or even dispose of them without regard to their status as official records, their retention, or other considerations. Many organizations have issued neither policies prescribing the management responsibilities for electronic records, nor guidelines for their use. Thus the roles of the data processing or MIS department, the records management department, or other units of the organization in managing electronic records may be undefined. In these situations, records managers should adopt a very proactive posture in defining an appropriate role for themselves in the management of electronic records.

INVENTORYING ELECTRONIC RECORDS

The first step records managers should take in developing a program for managing electronic records is to conduct an inventory of them. As described in Chapter 2, this is required in order to determine the problems posed by electronic records and to formulate strategies for solving them. An inventory of the organization's electronic records will disclose the types and quantities of records on hand, their condition, the equipment used to process and house them, and many other details essential to establishing appropriate records management controls over these records.

Inventories of hard copy and microfilm files are typically conducted on a department–by–department basis and consist of collecting descriptive data concerning each records series. This approach is also workable for electronic records, but some variations are required to ensure that the inventory of electronic records is comprehensive.

1. *The records series concept should be applied to electronic records.* The term in data processing parlance that equates most closely to the term *records series* is *data set.* For our purposes here, a data set is defined as a separate body of computer data (text files, data files, or image files) that is logically related, serves a common purpose or function, and can thus be considered as a discrete unit for records management purposes.

2. *All electronic records series in each computer or electronic imaging system should be inventoried.* For those computer and imaging systems installed in and operated by a particular department, it is appropriate to conduct the inventory of electronic records on a department–by–department basis. However, for those systems operated by a centralized data processing unit or by an outside service bureau, it will be necessary to collect certain inventory data from the persons who operate the system, while other data must be collected from the end users—persons in the various program units who actually use the records to conduct business.

Electronic Records Inventory Data

Most of the basic records inventory principles discussed in Chapter 2 are applicable to inventorying electronic records. In addition there are special inventory data that must be collected for each electronic records series in order for the inventory to be complete and of maximum utility in developing programs for the management of electronic records media. Figure 8.5 shows a sample of a records inventory form specially designed for inventorying electronic records.

Name of Electronic Series. As is the case with nonelectronic media, the series name must be reflective of its nature and contents. Names such as "Computer Printouts," "Floppy Diskettes," or "Magnetic Tape," which describe the type of storage media on which the records reside, are inappropriate names for electronic records series.

Rather, terms that reflect the type and nature of the records themselves should be chosen. These terms should be both generic and specific as to record content. Examples might include "New Drug Development Reports: Monthly and Year–End Summaries" or "Electric Power Usage Reports—By Municipality."

Series Description. As with nonelectronic records series, a brief description of the series purpose, use, and detailed contents will be sufficient. However, with electronic records series, it is important to note any details relevant to the series status as an electronic record; i.e., the name of the automated information system on which the electronic record resides, the type of files (e.g., text, data, or image), or the copy type for removable media (e.g., working copies, storage copies, backup or security copies).

Medium Description. The inventory analyst must note the type of storage medium on which the electronic records series resides (e.g., fixed, hard disk, magnetic tape, diskettes, compact disks, optical media) and the physical size and recording format or capacity of the medium (e.g., 5.25-inch diskettes/360 kilobytes).

Date of Records and Medium. The inclusive (beginning and ending) dates covered by the series should be shown on the inventory. In some cases, it may also be useful to note the medium manufacturing and recording dates, as this may be relevant in projecting the useful life of the records.

Hardware and Software Environments. The type of computing equipment used to record and process the electronic records must be shown, together with the operating system software, the applications software, and specific brand names and versions of each of these components of the computing system. An example might be "Standalone word processor IBM–compatible microcomputer with 4 megabytes of random–access memory and a 120-megabyte hard disk drive uti-

RECORDS INVENTORY WORKSHEET—ELECTRONIC RECORDS

Instructions: Complete this form for each electronic records series or data set in your organization. Complete one form for each separate body of computer data (text files, data files, or image files) that is logically related, serves a common purpose or function, and can thus be considered as a discrete unit for records management purposes.

NAME OF COMPUTER SYSTEM/SUBSYSTEM/APPLICATION _____

NAME OF RECORDS SERIES _____

SERIES DESCRIPTION _____

_____

_____

MEDIA DESCRIPTION _____

DATE OF RECORDS/MEDIA _____

HARDWARE/SOFTWARE DESCRIPTION _____

_____

NETWORK ENVIRONMENT _____

VOLUME OF RECORDS _____

FREQUENCY OF UPDATES _____

RATE OF ACCUMULATION/FUTURE GROWTH _____

REFERENCE/RETRIEVAL ACTIVITY _____

_____

RETENTION STATUS _____

PROTECTION STATUS _____

RELATIONSHIP TO OTHER RECORDS _____

_____

REMARKS/NOTES FROM INTERVIEWS WITH END USERS/COMPUTER

SPECIALISTS _____

_____

_____

INVENTORY ANALYST _____ DATE _____

FIGURE 8.5   Records Inventory Worksheet for Electronic Records

lizing MS–DOS 6.0 and Windows 3.1 operating software and WordPerfect 6.0 for DOS and 6.0 for Windows word processing software."

Network Environment.   If the computing system is connected to a local or wide area network (LAN or WAN), the type and characteristics of the net-work should be noted, for example, "Novell LAN supported by file server with 2.0 gigabytes of capacity."

Volume of Records.   The size and quantity of records consumed by the electronic records series should be noted, expressed in any manner appropriate for the type of records being inventoried. For series resident on fixed disks, the volume of records is normally expressed in bytes; for removable media, an item count should be recorded. If the electronic records series does not fill a given medium, it is often useful to note the percentage occupied and available for future growth.

Rate of Accumulation or Future Growth. The anticipated annual growth of the electronic records series should be shown; it can be expressed in bytes per year or disks per year.

Reference Activity. The inventory should include the method and frequency of references to the files, the nature and speed of the queries, who performs the references, and other relevant details respecting the access and usage of the electronic records series. Distinctions must be made between on–line, near–line, off–line/on–site, and off–line/off–site retrieval activity. On–line retrieval of documents data resident on fixed magnetic disk drives or other high performance, direct–access devices generally support near instantaneous retrieval requirements of between a few seconds down to a fraction of a second. Near–line retrieval of documents or data is generally accomplished by the use of storage devices such as optical disk jukeboxes, which support very rapid retrieval requirements of 15 seconds or less. Off–line/on–site retrieval situations generally involve the use of removable media stored near the computer, which must be manually mounted in drives; retrieval times are usually measured in minutes. Off–line/off–site retrieval situations involve the storage of removable media in records centers, data vaults, or other remote facilities. Retrieval time is usually measured in hours or even days.

Retention Status. Any written policies or operating practices (whether formal or informally executed) that govern the disposition of the electronic records series should be detailed on the inventory. The inventory analyst should determine the period of time that the electronic records series is deemed to be active (accessed and used for quick reference purposes and updated) or the time period or events that cause the series to become inactive (e.g., the data are superseded; the project is completed; the fiscal year expires, etc.). Finally, the inventory analyst should note any ongoing need to retain the electronic records after they become inactive, as expressed by the persons using or managing them. Examples might include audit requirements, long–term research needs, or litigation potential. Chapter 3 contains a detailed discussion of these issues.

Protection Status. The inventory should include a summary of the protection status of any electronic records series which is vital—the information is required to operate the business and the consequences of its absence would be unacceptable. The inventory analyst should note whether the series is currently being protected in any manner. Examples of protection strategies for vital electronic records include the creation of security copies of magnetic tapes, diskettes, and other removable media for on–site or off–site storage in a data vault or other secure facility and the use of special software programs for on–line electronic vaulting.

Relationship to Other Records. The inventory of each electronic records series must include the relationship of the series to other related records. Examples would include any indexes (whether integral to the series being described or maintained separately) or other related records maintained in electronic, hard copy, or microfilm formats. If the series exists solely in electronic format and is never printed in any form, this should be noted. If the series is duplicated, in whole or in part, in hard copy, microfilm, or other format, this should also be noted.

MANAGING ACTIVE ELECTRONIC RECORDS

With traditional paper and microfilm record media, records managers employ specific methods and techniques for managing active records. Many of these concepts are directly applicable to the management of electronic records. Active electronic records are those resident on nonremovable (fixed disks) media within the computer itself and those residing on near–line removable media kept near the computer for quick access, as well as off–line removable media kept on-site for slower but still convenient reference.

Active electronic records maintained in PC computing environments are of more immediate concern to records managers than those maintained in the larger computing environments. This chapter focuses on PC–based records maintained in IBM PC–compatible environments utilizing the MS–DOS operating system supplied by Microsoft Corporation. This operating software is installed in approximately 75 percent of the world's PCs; it manages the electronic signals and records between the computer and popular applications software programs such as word processors and spreadsheets, which constitute the majority of electronic records that records managers are called upon to manage.

PC–Based Nonremovable Media

Twenty years after its invention, the microprocessor, a thumbnail-size computer chip composed of a tiny sliver of silicon, has suddenly made possible PCs as powerful as mainframe computers. The microprocessor has always been a more affordable source of computer processing power than the mainframe, but during the early 1990s, these small devices finally caught up with mainframes in speed. The Pentium microprocessor, manufactured by Intel Corporation, successor to this company's 486 chip, is rated at a processing speed of 100 MIPS (millions of instructions per second), the same as a typical mainframe. Yet this small microprocessor carried a sale price of less than $1,000 when it was introduced. As a result, PCs are currently making obsolete the technology used in many earlier mainframe and minicomputer environments. Moreover, PC hard disk drives can now store 50 times the amount of data that more costly computers could store just a few years ago.[2] What this means is nothing less than a revolution in electronic recordkeeping in the "office of the 1990s." It has equally significant implications for the future of records management because records managers are, or at some point should be, responsible for many of the electronic records that are created and stored in PC computing environments.

Fixed Disks, Directories, and Subdirectories – *Folders & Subfolders*

PC–based electronic records are organized in the computer system into *directories* and *subdirectories,* which are created and managed by the operating system that controls the computer's basic functions. This method of organizing PC–based files is analogous to organizing paper documents into file folders and then storing them in separate drawers of a file cabinet. A computer's fixed hard disk (which may be thought of as an electronic file cabinet) can store hundreds, thousands, or even tens of thousands of files. However, as is true with paper records, the greater the volume of computer files, the more difficult the files are to manage and retrieve effectively. Thus, it is critical that records managers and PC users work closely together to organize PC–based records in a manner which will permit their precise and timely retrieval.

Under the MS–DOS operating system, the software's instructions can be used to group related files into directories. When the directories become too large, they can be further subdivided into subdirectories in which subordinate groups of files are stored within a larger directory. The organization of PC–based records into directories, subdirectories, and files creates a kind of filing hierarchy referred to under the DOS operating system as a *directory tree.* DOS considers the *root directory* to be the starting point for all subordinate subdirectories established under it. In managing PC–based records, a directory serves as a kind of table of contents to indicate to the user the index address of the files stored on the disk.

Electronic records are further organized and identified under DOS by *filename* and *filename extension.* Disks may also be identified by separate *volume names*, or divided into separate *partitions*, particularly if they are high–capacity fixed disks. The computer actually stores files on cylinders, tracks, and sectors of the disk. It locates them for retrieval by using a *file allocation table* to keep track of clusters of occupied disk sectors that contain the data in various files.[3]

Applying Traditional Files Management Concepts to PC–Based Records

In order for retrieval of documents to work efficiently in paper document filing systems, files must be organized into logical categories and subcategories, and they must be identified using a controlled vocabulary which establishes consistency in identifying and labeling the files. These classic records management principles have been used successfully for decades. Notwithstanding the computer's powerful capability to search a database using keywords or other retrieval techniques, these traditional file management principles can be applied to electronic records. If they are not, the users will experience some level of difficulty in precise and timely retrieval, particularly if the quantity of electronic records is great. To do this, careful consideration must be given as to how to organize directory structures, how to name documents and files, and how to label removable media.

Organizing Directories and Subdirectories. Large electronic filing installations will generally require a custom–designed hierarchy of directories and subdirectories reflecting a logical organization of the records. This can be accomplished in a variety of ways. A separate directory can be set up for each major software program (e.g., WordPerfect, Lotus), with subdirectories established for each department, project, or individual user. Alternately, entire directories can be established for each major project, with subdirectories for each individual user for the text and data files they create. Regardless of the directory-subdirectory hierarchy that is selected, it must reflect the specific retrieval needs of the users.

Naming Individual Files and Documents. If dozens, hundreds, or even thousands of documents and files are created and are arbitrarily assigned different file names, names that are too cryptically abbreviated to be understood, or names that are too broad or too narrow to accurately reflect the content of the records, retrieval can be a very difficult task, especially if an entire collection of electronic records needs to be searched and assembled from different directories and subdirectories, or worse, from the PCs of different departments or different network servers.

Under the DOS operating system, this problem is exacerbated by the filename limitations imposed by the software: A DOS filename may be no more than eight characters in length, with an optional extension of no more than three characters. The situation is considerably better under some other operating systems: The Apple Macintosh system allows filenames of up to 31 characters, and the system allows individual documents to be filed in "folders" that can be "nestled" within larger folders, which can contain combinations of programs, data files, or text files, an electronic filing methodology which is analogous to the directories and subdirectories established under the DOS operating system.

Establishing Filename Conventions. Regardless of the constraints imposed by the computer's operating system, records managers should provide guidance to all system users for naming files in a manner that reflects a given file's origin, content, and purpose, such that the file can be identified and retrieved by persons other than the person who created it and assigned the filename to it. Two approaches are commonly employed to do this.

1. *Develop a data dictionary or a thesaurus.* These data retrieval tools are designed to provide consistency in naming files so that numerous computer users in multiple departments utilize the same indexing terms to identify documents in a computer database. The purpose and structure of these tools are very similar to the uniform files classification schemes employed for paper records. Data dictionaries and thesauri vary in format, but they all contain a listing of document indexing terms, both general and specific, and cross–references to related terms, to provide a controlled and standardized indexing vocabulary with filename conventions for electronic records.

2. *Relate the organization's file indexes for paper records to its electronic records.* If the organization has a well–developed uniform files classification system consisting of standard primary, secondary, tertiary, and other subordinate subcategories, together with a numeric or alphanumeric coding scheme, the system can be applied to the indexing of electronic records. The same terms and numbers (or abbreviated versions of them) can be used for filenames of computer records. Primary and secondary categories can be directories and subdirectories, while subordinate categories can be used to name "folders" or individual files or documents.

Labeling and Identifying Removable Media

Thus far, our discussion has focused on identifying PC–based electronic records on fixed, nonremovable hard disks. It is equally important that the documents which reside on diskettes be labeled and identified properly. These removable media have a kind of character limitation of their own: The small labels on 3.5- and 5.25-inch diskettes often do not permit complete index data to be recorded on them. Moreover, these media are often poorly organized in storage trays or cartons, and they are frequently uninventoried. The following are guidelines for identifying electronic records stored on diskettes, hard disk cartridges, optical disk cartridges, computer tapes, or other removable media. A master inventory should be created for these media which shows:

- The name of the department or organization which created the disk, tape, or diskette, or the organization which is responsible for the medium.
- The names of the files by records series, in-cluding a listing or description of the files which the medium contains.
- The name or type of computer on which the medium was created and can be processed.
- The name and version number of the software used to process the data.
- The type and capacity or recording density of the medium.
- A serial number or other unique identifier of the medium (e.g., tape or disk numbers).
- The date or range of dates on which the data were recorded and/or the inclusive dates of the records.
- Any special security requirements or access restrictions applicable to the medium.
- Whether the medium is a working copy for use on the computer, a backup copy, or a storage copy.

As in the case of electronic records on fixed disks, records on diskettes should be designated for specific applications. Users should never intermix records of different projects or departments on the same medium. This is especially important with low-capacity diskettes; high-capacity magnetic tapes and optical disks, in particular, do sometimes contain multiapplication data.[4]

SOFTWARE FOR MANAGING ELECTRONIC RECORDS

Documents in electronic format can sometimes be electronically "misfiled" or can be otherwise difficult to locate. To find these documents by scanning directory listings and viewing documents on the screen can be just as time-consuming as thumbing through file folders stored in a cabinet. Fortunately, the computer industry has developed a number of software–based solutions to this problem. These software products may be grouped into three categories as follows.

Search Capabilities in Previously Installed Software

Many of the most popular PC software packages in use have some special document search and retrieval features that the users may not be aware of. A good example is the document summary capability supplied with the newer versions of WordPerfect. Because the filename conventions in this software are so limited with respect to number of characters, a document summary capability is provided in order to facilitate file retrieval. This feature permits the user to enter the document name (up to 68 characters in WordPerfect), the document type (up to 20 characters), and the document creation and revision dates, the author, the subject, account field, keywords, and an abstract at the time of the document creation. With this detailed index data, subsequent searches will obviously be facilitated.

Files Management Software for Standalone PCs

There are software products that provide a wide range of files management functions designed to enhance the user's ability to retrieve and manage electronic records on a standalone PC. Some products provide special *shells* to enhance the capabilities of the standard DOS shell by enabling the user to obtain a better view of the files listed on the directories and subdirectories of the hard disk, and to scroll and view selected files. Some products provide a *string search* capability, which enables the user to search an entire disk by entering a string of text reflecting the contents of a particular file. Some products also provide a wide variety of special file management functions, including the ability to transfer entire directories and their contents from one directory to another, change drives, rename volumes, etc. Finally, some software programs are programmed with diagnostic utilities designed to detect and repair many common disk problems. These utilities may protect media from viruses or other defects, optimize the performance of the hard disk by reallocating space on it, and so forth.

Document Management Software for LANs and WANs

In large local or wide area network PC environments in which very large quantities of documents are maintained, the need for better file man-

agement can require special software. A family of document management software products is available for this type of PC computing environment. Some of the functions of this type of software include the ability to execute searches from any point on a local or wide area network regardless of the number of network file servers, the ability to transmit documents and their associated index data within and among any server on the network, the ability to retain the documents of individual users on both the network servers and the users' workstation disks, and various other network management functions.

Most of these types of software products also provide a variety of sophisticated document search and retrieval features, including indexing the full text of documents and maintaining an abstract description of each document in the database of the user's home file server, the ability to conduct network–wide full–text searches by any word, phrase, or combination of words in a document, and a computer–assisted indexing capability, by means of which the system automatically assigns the directory structure. Alternately, the network administrator or the user may assign the directory structure by selecting the appropriate data for fields such as document type, subject, author, and descriptive keywords.

STORAGE AND HANDLING OF REMOVABLE MEDIA

It is important that records managers provide a proper storage environment for electronic records and that the personnel observe proper procedures in handling the media. Improper environmental conditions can adversely affect the stability and longevity of these media. High temperature and humidity levels can accelerate their deterioration. In general, a cool and dry environment is best for electronic record media; hot and humid conditions promote the degradation of the binder materials used in the construction of these media.

Storage Conditions for Magnetic Media

The optimum environmental conditions for magnetic media is an air-conditioned facility capable of maintaining a constant temperature of 63° F to

68° F, and a relative humidity of 35 to 45 percent. Temperature and humidity levels should be constant—free of fluctuations—as this can exacerbate damage to the binder materials of these media.

In addition to temperature and humidity conditions, an ideal environment for the storage of magnetic media should provide protection from fire, water damage, and theft or other human–caused threats. As described in Chapter 4, a data vault for long–term magnetic media storage should be designed and constructed in accordance with standards issued by the National Fire Protection Association.

It is important to note that storage copies of magnetic tapes must be properly maintained, especially if they must be stored for long periods of time. Otherwise, they may be subject to loss of the data recorded on them. Such tapes must be wound and rewound at regular intervals and at normal speeds with constant tension. If the tapes are stored under the optimum environmental conditions, rewind intervals as long as 3 $1/2$ years may be acceptable. If the storage conditions are less than ideal, rewinding should be performed annually or more frequently.

Storage Conditions for Optical Media

Ideal temperature and humidity conditions for long-term storage of optical media have not yet been established. Records managers must, therefore, rely on guidance provided by optical media manufacturers in their product literature. However, such guidance is problematic because the composition of these media varies, and because the temperature and humidity limits may be applicable for the extreme ranges beyond which deterioration will occur, rather than the constant optimum levels for long–term storage. In the absence of reliable technical standards for optical media storage, records managers may wish to adopt the guidelines provided for magnetic media and await further developments.

Guidelines for Handling Removable Media

Improper handling of removable magnetic and optical media by users is a common cause of physical damage to the information recorded on these media. This is particularly true in the case of working copies of such media that are handled frequently by users. Records managers should issue the following guidelines to alleviate this problem:

- Magnetic and optical storage media should always be handled by touching their protective housing.
- Reels of magnetic tape should be handled and carried by their hubs.
- Magnetic and optical media should never be placed under heavy objects or squeezed, as this can damage the data recorded on them. These media should always be stored vertically; they should never be stacked horizontally on shelves or left unprotected on window sills, desktops, or storage cabinets, where they may be exposed to direct sunlight or other sources of heat.
- Magnets should be prohibited from all areas where magnetic media are stored or utilized.
- Smoking should be prohibited in areas where media are stored, as smoke particles can be potentially destructive to such media.
- Food and drink should also be prohibited.

RECORDS RETENTION IN COMPUTING ENVIRONMENTS

It seems safe to speculate that the growth of electronic records must be at least double that of paper records—somewhere between 20 and 40 percent per year. What happens to these computer data and text files? Can the principles of records retention be applied to govern their disposition?[5]

Although retention scheduling of paper and microfilm files is widely practiced by organizations throughout the United States, these programs often do not include electronic records. Perhaps the major reasons are that the retention of electronic records does not pose a visible problem in business offices, and that these records do not consume significant quantities of office space. Moreover, data processing and information systems specialists have not often put the matter of electronic records retention high on their agendas, nor have they frequently requested the assistance of records managers in addressing the issue.

Nevertheless, the principles of records retention scheduling can and should be applied to electronic records. These records should be stored, retained, and scheduled for disposition just as their hard copy or microfilm counterparts. Electronic records which should be scheduled for retention include data and text files produced by computer software (e.g., word processing, spreadsheets, database programs, graphics, etc.), and stored on various types of electronic media (e.g., hard disks, floppy disks, magnetic tapes, or optical disks).

Some Principles for Scheduling Electronic Records for Retention

The following discussion relates the traditional principles of records retention scheduling to electronic records maintained in computing environments.

1. *The records series concept must be properly applied to records in electronic format.* In order for an electronic records retention program to be workable, a retention period must be established for each *electronic records series*—defined here as a discrete body of computer data that can be considered as a single unit, or series, for purposes of establishing a retention policy to govern its disposition. It will usually not be necessary for a separate retention period to be established for each individual report, just as it is not necessary to establish one for each individual document in a records series of hard copy records. In electronic recordkeeping systems, the records series concept will usually equate to each data set—each major class or subclass of reports, data files, or text files maintained in each system, subsystem, or database.

2. *The end users (owners of the records) must usually be consulted in formulating valid retention periods for electronic records.* This is particularly true in mainframe computing environments, where a retention period should be estab-

lished for every major class (and many subclasses) of computer data. Because they use the data to conduct business, the end users of the computer records should usually be consulted and asked to render a judgment as to the retention value of this information to meet the operational requirements of the business.

3. *The principles of records appraisal and cost-risk-benefit analysis can be applied to electronic records.* The principles of determining retention values outlined in Chapter 3 should be applied to electronic or any other record medium. The concepts of primary and secondary values and the benefits or risks of retaining or disposing of records are just as valid for computer–processable records as for any other business record.

4. *Government retention requirements may apply to but do not usually specify electronic records as an authorized or required retention medium.* With rare exceptions, statutes and regulations do not address the retention of electronic records per se. Almost all the federal and state laws and regulations that require records to be retained are silent on the issue of which record medium must be used to satisfy the government's retention requirements. Thus, the presumption is that unless a particular medium is specified, users may retain the required records in any form or format they desire. A notable exception is the Internal Revenue Service's Revenue Procedure 91–59, which specifies that taxpayers retaining tax records on computer systems must maintain the electronic records and the related hardware and software required to process them for the period of time they are subject to a tax audit.

5. *Computer files are just as vulnerable to the risks of litigation as other business records.* Electronic records are subject to subpoenas and document discovery orders by adverse parties in legal proceedings just as information on hard copy or microfilm is. For purposes of evidence, the law makes no distinction as to the physical format or medium on which requested information resides. Full legal protection is possible only if the organization's records retention program includes computer records.

6. *Computer media used to retain electronic records are generally not considered to possess qualities of archival permanence in the same sense as paper and microfilm media.* If an organization must retain computer records for many years, it must usually rely on paper or microfilm output to meet its long–term archival needs. Even though computer tapes, disks, and other storage media are constantly being improved with respect to their ability to maintain the stability and integrity of the data they contain for long periods of time, these media cannot be read and used without the proper hardware and software. Because the hardware, software, and other components of a computer system become obsolete relatively quickly (the components often have a service life of less than five years), it may be impractical to retain electronic records for long periods of time.

7. *The principles of official and nonofficial records are relevant to retention determinations respecting computer records.* Unless information exists solely in electronic form, computer data and text files are often considered to be nonofficial in character; thus, a shorter retention period may be justified for them as compared to the hard copy or microfiche output. This output is often considered to be the record copy that reflects the organization's official position on a matter. Under this principle, most word processing text files, most or all computer *processing files* (data files generated and processed before the production of a *master file*) and perhaps all electronic mail and voice mail may be considered nonofficial and thus subject to relatively short retention policies—a few days, weeks, or months; seldom longer than a year or two.[6]

8. *The concepts of active, semiactive, and inactive hard copy records equate to on–line, near–line and off–line computer data for purposes of establishing retention periods for electronic records.* Active electronic records should remain on–line if they must be processed and retrieved in

"real time" to meet heavy user reference needs. The term *near–line* refers to semiactive computer files resident on removable media kept on–site—near the computer for quick processing. Inactive electronic records would include those archived or copied from internal memory onto external, removable media for storage in a secure, off–site location. Retention periods for electronic records series should be established to provide for the on–site and off–site phases in the life cycle of each series.

9. *The total retention period for an electronic records series depends on how long the information needs to be retained in a computer–processable format.* If computer data or text files no longer need to remain in a manipulatable state, there is no justification for retaining them in a computer–processable format. Thus, the total retention period for an electronic records series would be determined on this basis. Of course, business or legal needs may justify further retention, but these retention needs can usually be satisfied by transferring or archiving the data onto alternative storage media.

10. *For computer records having permanent or long–term retention requirements, COM or COLD systems often provide the best retention media.* At the point in their life cycle when computer records no longer need to remain in a computer–processable format but still require long–term or permanent retention, the records can often be dumped to computer-output-generated microfilm. COM provides a relatively inexpensive data storage medium which can offer excellent archival properties for the long–term preservation of computer records. A newer technology, COLD (*com*puter-*o*utput-to-*l*aser-*d*isk), is also being used for this purpose. In COLD system applications, data from the host computer are downloaded to a microcomputer equipped with an optical disk drive. The data are then archived onto an optical disk for subsequent retrieval on the PC. Again, the high storage capacity of these disks coupled with the relatively low cost of this form of optical disk technology make the COLD system an excellent archival medium for many types of semiactive and inactive computer data.

11. *Retention periods for electronic records will usually (but not always) be shorter than those for records in hard copy or microfilm formats.* By its very nature, computer information is valuable because it is highly dynamic—it is processed and manipulated each day in response to the organization's current business operations. This characteristic usually has a relatively short life span; computer files rarely need to be retained longer than three to five years, and are frequently disposed of in a matter of days, weeks, or months in the data processing cycle. By contrast, the static information contained in hard copy or microfilm files is immutable or frozen in time and format. Thus it tends to possess operational or research value for longer periods of time and will often require longer retention than electronically based records.

[handwritten margin note: not true]

12. *The small quantity of physical space consumed by electronic records does not, by itself, justify long retention.* The retention value of any business information should be determined by an assessment of the costs, risks, and benefits of its presence or absence after varying time periods. The mere fact that computer records do not constitute a space problem does not justify retaining them indefinitely. Storage on disk drives can be very expensive and thus should be limited to records needed to operate the organization's business or to comply with legal retention requirements.

13. *Detailed transactional data versus cumulative summary data will often be the basis for short- or long-term retention decisions.* Many detailed transactional computer data files can be disposed of routinely in the data processing cycle—after the data are updated or superseded—or they may be destroyed after relatively short periods of time; e.g., at the end of the month, quarter, or year. On the other hand, summary data containing cumulative information (e.g., annual reports) will often require longer retention.

Records Retention in Mainframe Computing Environments

The manager of the computer operations department usually implements a tape or disk management system to provide for the disposition and reuse of electronic record media which reside on the host or mainframe computer. Under these systems, the computer keeps track of all tapes and disks under its control. The system's operations utilities can be programmed to indicate the number of generations of reports that should be maintained, and the disposition process is applied when the system erases, or scraps, tapes containing obsolete data and makes them available for reuse.

None of these steps, however, should be accomplished in the absence of records retention analysis provided by the organization's records manager. The records manager should establish retention periods for the mainframe's electronic records by interviewing the end users of the record in each department, and by applying the concepts and principles of records retention.

Records Retention in PC Computing Environments

PC computer systems present special records retention challenges for records managers because PC users often consider these electronic records to be nonofficial personal files to be used and disposed of at their discretion. Also, because of the nature of PC data, the records series concept can be harder to apply to these types of electronic records.

Most PC–based computer systems contain considerable information in both operations and applications software concerning the type, size, age, and other characteristics of the records that enable the retention period of electronic records to be established and the disposition of the records to be effected. For example, directory and subdirectory names, volume indicators, filenames and extensions, file dates, and file sizes expressed in bytes can all be obtained easily by the records manager.

In order to apply the required disposition instructions in the records retention schedule, the organization's PC users must scan directory listings for files that match the records series in the schedules. Because of filename character limitations, this can be a very time-consuming and laborious process, particularly if the users have not adopted systematic naming conventions that are consistent with the records series in the retention schedules.[7]

Many organizations have adopted a records retention policy for records residing on PCs that requires the end user to retain PC–based records no longer than the retention period for the official hard copy output, as specified in the retention schedules. Often, the PC records retention policy indicates that users may, at their discretion, destroy the electronic version of the record sooner, since it would not be considered the record copy.

If the organization's PCs are linked by a local area network (LAN), the LAN administrator (as well as the end users) should be consulted in performing retention analyses on PC–based records and devising retention policies for them.

Applying Retention to PC–Based Electronic Records

In traditional hard copy or microfilm environments, records retention periods are typically implemented by effecting the disposal of all documents comprising an entire records series within a certain date range. Assuming the records are well organized, a detailed review and purging of selected documents is seldom practiced, as this is very time-consuming and may result in adverse legal consequences if it can be demonstrated that the selective weeding of documents is contrary to the established retention policy.

How are these retention practices applied to PC–based electronic records? Under the MS–DOS operating system, the user can delete single files, selected groups of files, or all files on a directory or on a disk, including the directory itself, just as operators of manual filing systems can destroy single documents, folders, groups of folders, or the contents of entire cabinets or shelves.

Unless the electronic records have been logically organized by directory and subdirectory on the hard disk into categories corresponding to their retention status, unless a retention field has been programmed into the database, and unless disposal dates have been properly entered, the process of applying retention to PC–based electronic records can be as time-consuming as it is in manual recordkeeping environments, or even more so. The user must scan directory listings to determine the files that are eligible for disposal as provided by the retention schedule. For these reasons, it is essential that records managers work with end users to organize PC–based records in a manner that will facilitate the implementation of retention policies.

In applying retention to PC–based records, records managers and users should be aware of the capabilities of the *Undelete* function. Under MS–DOS and certain popular word processing programs such as WordPerfect, it is possible in some cases to undelete a file using optional DOS utility programs. This is possible because DOS does not actually erase a file that has been deleted; rather, it simply makes the disk space occupied by the file available for new files, and it deletes the index data that provide access to the file, so that the file will no longer be shown in a directory listing of files.

In some cases, the Undelete capabilities of the DOS utility programs may prove useful in correcting file deletion errors which may be made during the process of applying retention to these PC–based records. Records managers should be aware, however, that the restoration of deleted records could expose the organization to some degree of legal risk: If records exist and are subpoenaed, they must be produced, regardless of the difficulties that may be associated with retrieving them.

The Archival Status of Electronic Records

Records managers are often called upon to provide guidance relative to retention and archival needs to both end users and data processing and MIS personnel. Because the useful life of electronic records is significantly shorter than that of paper and microfilm records and because these records cannot be read or used without the proper hardware and software, records in electronic format may not be suitable for long–term retention or permanent archival preservation.

- *Archival standards for electronic record media.* With respect to their properties of stability and longevity, national and international standards have been issued for various types of paper and photographic record media. However, these standards have not been published for magnetic or optical record media.

  Records managers must rely on technical guidelines and various studies conducted by media manufacturers, governmental agencies, and other interested parties. While some of these studies may be of questionable validity, they do provide some degree of guidance to records managers in arriving at logical and informed decisions concerning the length of time that information recorded on electronic media may be usable.

  The U.S. National Institute of Standards and Technology (formerly the National Bureau of Standards) conducted studies during the 1980s which suggest that magnetic tapes composed of gamma ferric oxide recording material will be processable or readable for a period of 10 to 20 years. However, this period assumes that the tapes will be stored and maintained properly. Optical storage media have no known archival properties; manufacturers of these media assert that they will retain playback utility for periods ranging from 10 to 100 years, depending on the type of medium and the particular recording technology employed. However, because optical media are such new storage devices, the manufacturer's stability claims are necessarily based on accelerated aging tests rather than actual operational experience.

- *Media hardware and software dependence.* Magnetic and optical media have no utility unless appropriate hardware and software are available to process and read the information recorded on them. In this regard, the archival situation is highly problematic: The hardware would need to be supported by its manufacturer over a multigenerational period and new versions of software would need to be managed over a period of years. The dynamic nature of the computer industry, with its short system life cycles and rapid product obsolescence, would suggest that lengthy or permanent retention requirements for electronic media would be difficult to meet.

Records managers have three main options for dealing with this issue:

1. *Preserve the electronic records in ASCII format.* As noted earlier, this data format provides the most flexible option for future processing on a variety of computer platforms.

2. *Rely on micrographic media for long–term and archival retention purposes.* Several options exist here: As noted earlier, the electronic records can often be dumped to COM microfiche or COLD optical media; the records can be microfilmed at the time they are converted to electronic format for long–term storage purposes; or a micrographics subsystem can be sometimes designed into an optical imaging system, in which the film is scanned and digitized for subsequent display at the user workstations.

3. *Retain the paper records.* While this may not appear to be an attractive option, it often proves to be the simplest and best method of dealing with the risks that may be associated with the nonarchival properties of electronic record media.

SUMMARY

The widespread use of computers has been the single most significant occurrence to affect the field of records management during the past two decades. This is true because computers generate enormous quantities of records for records managers to manage, because there are numerous problems associated with the management of electronic records—problems that require records management solutions—and because computers provide many new tools for solving records management problems.

Electronic records consist of machine–readable information in the form of character–coded electronic signals, and they exist in three primary forms: text files, data files, and image files. These files reside on two major classes of electronic storage media: magnetic media and optical media. Magnetic media, in turn, consist of magnetic disks, tapes, and diskettes, each of which is coated with a recording material that is properly magnetized during data recording operations. Magnetic disks are used primarily for rapid, on–line access to electronic records, while magnetic tapes and diskettes are used mainly for off–line data storage and archiving and to provide security and disaster backup for mission–critical electronic records.

Optical storage media, the newest major class of storage media for electronic records, were commercially introduced during the mid–1980s. These devices provide much greater storage capacities than their magnetic counterparts, and their principal records management application is for the storage and rapid retrieval of large collections of documents. Optical media are available in erasable and nonerasable formats.

Electronic records pose the following major records management problems: Many electronic records are unused and unneeded; they are often poorly organized and identified on both removable and nonremovable media; their security and protection status as vital records is often overlooked; inadequate provisions are made for their retention and disposal; they have a relatively short usable life which may be insufficient to meet their organization's retention requirements; and their ownership status and the responsibility for their management is often unclear.

To be properly managed, electronic records must be inventoried. The inventory should be conducted at the records series, or data set, level, and it should describe the content, use, purpose, and other characteristics of all electronic records maintained by the organization.

Records managers should provide extensive guidance to their organizations on the management of both active and inactive electronic records, particularly those that are filed in PC-computing environments. The basis for much of this guidance can be found in traditional records management concepts applicable to hard copy and microfilm records media, as these concepts are largely transferable to electronic records.

Active electronic records should be properly organized into a logically related hierarchy of directories, subdirectories, and files, and they must be identified and labeled using terms specific to their purpose and content. The filename conventions established by a data dictionary or a thesaurus, both of which provide a controlled vocabulary for filing the electronic records, are proven tools to ensure accurate and consistent retrieval of electronic data. These records management techniques are still necessary even though the computer has relatively powerful and sophisticated search capabilities.

Records managers should ensure that all electronic records maintained on removable media are labeled, identified, and inventoried in a manner that permits their effective management.

A wide variety of software is available to enhance the management of electronic records that reside on standalone PCs, as well as those connected to networks. This software is generally designed to assist the user in locating files appearing on directory listings, to retrieve files, to manage directories and disks, and to manage electronic records residing on network servers of local or wide area networks.

Records retention schedules should be developed to provide for the disposition of all electronic records, including those residing in both mainframe and smaller computing environments. Most of the principles associated with developing records retention schedules for hard copy and microfilm media are relevant to developing schedules for electronic media.

QUESTIONS FOR DISCUSSION

1. The widespread use of computers has been called the single most significant occurrence to affect records management during the past two decades. Why is this assertion justified? List and briefly discuss two primary reasons.

2. Define and discuss the principal types and characteristics of electronic records.

3. There are three major types of magnetic storage media. What are they?

4. From a records management perspective, what is the principal advantage of utilizing optical storage media?

5. List and briefly discuss four records management issues and problems affecting electronic records.

6. Define the term *data set* and discuss its significance in inventorying electronic records.

7. File cabinets, file drawers, and file folders are common storage devices for paper documents. What are their counterparts in electronic filing systems?

8. Explain why filename conventions are so important in managing electronic records efficiently, and describe some common tools and methodologies for this technique.

9. Special shell software can be purchased to enhance the files management capabilities of PC–based records controlled under the MS–DOS operating system. Briefly discuss these enhanced capabilities.

10. Special document management software can be acquired to enhance the management of electronic records maintained in local or wide area networks. Discuss the major functions of this software.

11. List and discuss ten principles of developing records retention schedules for electronic records.

12. The archival status of electronic records media is an often debated (and frequently misunderstood) issue in data processing and records management circles. Discuss this issue in the context of its records management significance, and describe some approaches to dealing with it.

13. List the optimum temperatures and humidity ranges for the storage of magnetic media.

14. List three do's and don'ts for the handling of electronic record media.

PROJECTS

1. You are the records manager of the Global Electronics Corporation. Your records management program has been mostly directed towards managing records on paper and microfilm formats, but you want to extend its scope to include computer–based electronic records as well. Prepare a presentation to your firm's senior management detailing the specific records management problems encountered by Global's electronic records, and how you propose to solve them.

2. You are the records manager of the Global Electronics Corporation. You have just been given a mandate to extend the company's records retention program to include all electronic records in the firm. Develop a detailed action plan for how you propose to proceed with this project. The plan must include inventorying and retention decision–making

steps applicable to electronic records in both mainframe and PC computer environments.

3. Electronic records management problems are very similar to those encountered in traditional recordkeeping environments. Prepare an outline for a research paper entitled "Traditional versus Electronic Records Management: Common Problems, Common Solutions."

4. You are the records manager of the North Slope Petroleum Company. Your supervisor, the vice-president for Administration, has asked you to work with a team of computer specialists from the MIS Department on a project to select one or more software packages to improve the management of North Slope's standalone and networked PCs. Prepare a report for the vice-president for Administration indicating the functional capabilities such software is to have, and how it could improve the retrieval of PC–based data and enhance the overall performance of the firm's PCs.

5. Review three of the leading PC magazines, locate articles and vendor advertisements on software products for PC documents and files management, obtain vendor literature from the software houses, and prepare a report of your findings, indicating what products you believe to possess superior features and why.

CASE PROBLEM

You are the new records manager for the Life Insurance Company of North America (LICNA). This medium–size but rapidly growing insurance company has not had a records management program—one has just been authorized by the firm's Executive Management Committee—and there is much to do in order to establish control over the firm's approximately 20,000 linear feet of active and inactive paper records. Moreover, the management of electronic records appears to be a real problem. You are asked to meet with LICNA's chief information officer, the vice-president of

Management Information Systems, and the manager of the Data Center. These individuals request your assistance on a special ad hoc study team to review the status of the firm's electronic records management, determine its problems, and propose appropriate solutions.

At this initial meeting, you learn that:

- No formal policies or procedures exist to govern the retention of LICNA's electronic records, regardless of whether they reside on the mainframe computer, on a file server that supports one of the firm's 20 local networks, or on a standalone PC.

- The storage copies of the magnetic tapes are stored in an off–site vault. However, upon inspecting the facility, you learn that it is not really a data vault, but a storage room in an unsprinklered office building. The room has a window–unit type air conditioner and a Halon–type fire suppression system, but the gas cylinder is located outside the room where the tapes are stored. There is an inventory of the tapes to control their rotation cycle, but no other descriptive data appear on the inventory.

- LICNA's approximately 2,000 PC users were recently surveyed to determine their level of satisfaction with these machines. The users of standalone units expressed frequent complaints with hard–to–locate documents, particularly if the quantity of files on their hard drives is great. The users were furnished with no guidance as to proper organization of filing structures on their PCs, nor any guidance as to naming files, developing thesauri, or using other PC files management techniques. Moreover, these matters were not covered in the basic courses taught on how to use word processing or spreadsheet software. No special files management software had been acquired or installed on any standalone or networked PCs.

- The users of PCs on LICNA's large wide area network expressed frequent complaints about their inability to retrieve and share certain files across the network.

- No written guidance or procedures had been furnished to PC users relative to the handling or storing of removable computer storage media.

- The LICNA executives indicated that they have been investigating converting the firm's insurance policy files to an optical disk system, but they are concerned about the archival status of this storage medium, in light of the fact that the firm's policy files often have a very long active life and an inactive life of 15 years.

You must work with LICNA's Electronic Records Management Project Team to conduct a detailed study of these matters and develop an action plan for problem resolution. Prepare a report containing three sections:

1. A section entitled "Current Situation of LICNA's Electronic Records Management," detailing the problems you identify.

2. A section entitled "Action Plan," recommending how to address the problems identified in the current situation section.

3. A section entitled "Executive Summary," outlining the benefits of your major recommendations, as well as the consequences of failure to adopt the proposed recommendations.

NOTES

1. Stratford Sherman, "The New Computer Revolution," *Fortune*, June 14, 1993, p. 58.
2. Ibid., pp. 56,66.
3. John T. Phillips, CRM, *Organizing and Archiving Files and Records on Microcomputers* (Prairie Village, Kansas: ARMA International, 1992), p. 20.
4. William Saffady, *Managing Electronic Records* (Prairie Village, Kansas: ARMA International, 1992), pp. 138–139.
5. For a general discussion of electronic records retention, see William Saffady, "Retention Schedules for Electronic Records," in *Managing Electronic Records* (Prairie Village, Kansas: ARMA International, 1992), pp. 87–109.
6. Donald S. Skupsky, JD, CRM, "Establishing Retention Periods for Electronic Records," *Records Management Quarterly*, April 1993, p. 40.
7. John T. Phillips, CRM, *Organizing and Archiving Files and Records on Microcomputers* (Prairie Village, Kansas: ARMA International, 1992), p. 13.

Chapter 9

Automation of Records Management Systems and Functions

Learning Objectives

1. To present an overview of records management automation, its benefits, the preconditions for its successful implementation, and its place within the larger framework of an organization's enterprise-wide computer automation strategy.

2. To describe records management software, its major types and functions, and how it is used to solve records management problems.

3. To explain the technical and business criteria for evaluating commercially available records management software products.

4. To describe bar code technology and its uses in solving a variety of problems associated with the management of document-based information systems.

5. To list the several steps in planning and implementing automated records management systems.

AUTOMATION OF PAPER-BASED SYSTEMS

No one knows how many separate paper-based recordkeeping systems there are in the offices of business and governmental organizations throughout the United States. The total number must surely be in the millions, since each department or office usually maintains from several to a dozen or more separate records series. We do, however, have some idea about the number of paper-based recordkeeping systems that have been enhanced by some form of computer technology, and the number is very small relative to the total number of recordkeeping systems—probably no more than 1 percent.

The major tool for automating paper-based recordkeeping systems is *records management software*, during the approximately ten years since this software has been available from commercial sources as packaged off-the-shelf products, only about 5,000 systems have been installed.[1] Because the benefits of implementing automated records management systems are often very significant, it seems reasonable to conclude that the future will bear witness to the computerization of these systems on a scale previously unseen.

Using computer technology to enhance the quality and performance of paper-based document information systems will surely be at the top of the agenda of virtually every records manager in the United States. These information specialists must therefore know when, how, and why to computerize the many active and inactive recordkeeping systems that are maintained in offices and departments throughout their organizations. Those that succeed in this most important endeavor will take their places among the highest-ranking information executives within any enterprise.

As recently as the mid-1980s, records managers who desired to establish some degree of computer control over their organization's recordkeeping systems were faced with the difficult task of in-house development of applications software to run on large mainframe computers. These endeavors were frequently frustrating; records management applications seldom enjoyed priority among the dozens of business functions that in-house data processing specialists were called upon to computerize, so delays of months or even years were not uncommon before an automated records management system was up and running. Once implemented, the system had to compete for machine time with many mission-critical applications, and the records manager often remained at the mercy of MIS personnel to maintain or enhance the systems.

Today, all this has changed. Records managers now have a whole new array of tools at their disposal with which to establish computer control over their organization's records. This chapter discusses two of the main ones—records management software and bar code technology—which are often combined into a single system having the power to truly revolutionize the way both active and inactive records are managed in any organization. We will review these new records management technologies—their features and functions, their sources of supply, and strategies for their implementation—as the chapter progresses. Other major tools for records management automation, including micrographics, electronic imaging, and new forms management technologies, are discussed in subsequent chapters of this book.

Benefits of Automation

How can records management software and bar code technology be applied to help organizations solve their records management problems? The proper application of records management software and bar code technology produces five major benefits.

1. *It provides a computer capability to establish total life cycle control over records on an enterprise-wide basis.* This is, arguably, the central underlying goal of records management, and these new tools give records managers, for the first time ever, a relatively affordable computer capability to achieve it. Records management software and bar code technology can be applied to active records in single filing stations, throughout a department or division, or throughout the entire enterprise. Further, these tools can be applied to inactive records in records center environments. Finally, if the database of active records is successfully integrated with the database for inactive records and is combined with the records retention program, the system is capable of providing the organization with something it has never had before: a computer capability to know of the existence and location of all its files; in other words, it has established computerized life cycle control over them.

2. *It greatly improves the performance of the recordkeeping system, enhancing the accessibility of the information contained in the records, so that the goal of precise and timely retrieval can be achieved.* The main criterion for evaluating the performance of a recordkeeping system is whether it consistently delivers precise and timely retrieval. This level of system performance means that, in response to every user request for information, the recordkeeping system delivers exactly the documents requested as quickly as they are needed so that business can be conducted in an efficient manner. In order to be judged successful, a recordkeeping system should be capable of performing at this level at least 95 percent of the time. Records management software and bar code technology can contribute greatly to this goal.

3. *It provides multiple pathways by which the information contained in recordkeeping systems* *can be accessed, which significantly optimizes the value of these systems to their users.* Today, the great majority of the records and files maintained in business offices are unindexed. The records are sequenced in a manner which permits them to be accessed in a walk-up mode, without first consulting an index to verify their existence or determine their location. While the simplicity of this approach is not without merit, it often limits the value of the records because the information can only be located by the manner in which it has been identified and filed. When an organization's records are indexed on the database of a good records management software program, they are accessible by any number of keywords and other record identifiers in the database. Thus, multiple pathways into the system are possible, and the records are more valuable to their users than ever before.

4. *It provides significant benefits in work measurement, cost reduction, productivity improvement, and better services to customers and clients.* Any time users of records are provided with new tools to access information faster, their productivity increases because they can handle a greater volume of work for the same or less expenditure of time. Moreover, the organization's operating costs are contained, since the same or fewer staff are needed to handle the work. In addition, the technology provides new capabilities for analyzing and measuring the work associated with maintaining records and information. The work can be tracked and monitored, which enables it to be planned and scheduled more efficiently. Of even greater significance, however, are those applications of records management automation that result in better service to customers and clients—the persons for whom the organization exists. Such applications are nearly always justified by cost; indeed, their introduction is compelling if the organization is to grow and prosper in an intensively competitive business climate.

5. *It provides a means of upgrading the status of the records management function and those who work in it.* When automated records management

systems are introduced on an enterprise-wide basis, the records management function is no longer perceived as one of maintaining physical custody over records and files. Rather, the records management function is enhanced because it is now responsible for managing an on-line, instantly accessible corporate information database about the largest information store in the entire enterprise—its document-based information systems.

RECORDS MANAGEMENT SOFTWARE: AN OVERVIEW

The term *records management software* refers to a family of software products mostly developed to operate on PC computer platforms and designed to provide various types and levels of computer control over a wide variety of records management functions. The term can also be properly used in reference to any records management software program designed by an organization's internal computer personnel.

The development of this software was made possible by the parallel development of the MS-DOS operating system and database management technologies during the early 1980s, and the subsequent explosion of microcomputers as major tools for business office computing. This type of computing environment provided a practical platform on which to run specially designed applications software to index, track, and monitor the movement of file folders in active paper-based recordkeeping systems, as well as the storage cartons containing inactive records stored in records centers. These are, in fact, the major functions performed by records management software. By the early 1990s, there were at least 50 commercially available records management software packages sold by some 40 software vendors in the United States and Canada—all designed to perform these records management functions.[2]

Records management software is designed to operate on almost all major types and sizes of PC hardware, and because of increasing competition and product maturity, some of the newest products offer excellent functionality at an increasingly affordable price. The end result: Increased market acceptance and an excellent opportunity for records managers to take advantage of this situation to improve the quality of recordkeeping in their organizations. The development of these products was one of the two most significant occurrences to affect records management during the decade of 1980s, the other being the development of optical disk technology.

Software for Active Recordkeeping Systems

Many records management software programs are designed to index, track, and monitor the status and movement of active files maintained in office filing systems. Most of these software programs can:

- Permit entry of descriptive data relative to the contents of individual file folders in the database, for subsequent retrieval by filename, number, keywords, or a variety of other search parameters.
- Store standard subject filing categories from a files classification scheme in the database for subsequent manipulation and retrieval.
- Manage the file folder charge-out and return function.
- Print bar code labels and monitor the movement of files by point-to-point tracking as they are passed from workstation to workstation in the processing cycle.
- Print new file folder labels (on demand or by batch) and a variety of reports showing the status of the organization's records.

This type of software can be installed in one or several departments, in a central file room, or throughout the organization. Normally, these types of automated records management systems are oriented towards file folders as the unit of record control. Some systems, however, are geared towards extending control at a lower level—to individual documents. In these cases, descriptive data concerning the nature and content of each form, letter, report, or other item must be entered in the database. Of course, this level of record indexing usually results in much greater computer storage requirements, but if users require rapid access to records at the individual document level in order to work productively, such a system would need to be implemented.

Software for Inactive Recordkeeping Systems

Other records management software programs are designed to manage an organization's inactive records stored in a records center, as described in Chapters 17 and 18. The major functions of these systems are to:

- Maintain the index or inventory of all records stored in the facility by showing the contents of each carton or other storage container and sometimes each file folder stored in each box.
- Store other data required to effectively manage the records, such as the inclusive dates of the records in each carton, retention schedule data, and disposal dates.
- Reserve shelf space for incoming cartons and report on free shelf space available to house them.
- Monitor and track the movement of all records withdrawn from and returned to the center.
- Print *pick lists* showing those cartons eligible for destruction, print destruction notification forms to obtain authority to dispose of records, and print certificates of destruction to show evidence of the actual destruction.
- Print reports of user statistics and manage the charge-back function in cases where users are assessed fees for their stored records.

Bar code technology is particularly useful when it is integrated with software for records center management. This application of bar code technology is discussed later in this chapter.

Software for Records Retention and Total Life Cycle Records Management

Fully functional software systems provide an enhanced records retention capability; they may also integrate the active file folder management function with the inactive records center management function to provide a greater degree of total life cycle control over the organization's records. In these systems, the objective is to establish computer control over both active and inactive records—from creation to destruction. These products may provide some or all the following features:

- They may support the on-line development of records retention schedules, including the entry of records inventory data, the inclusion of citations for statutory and regulatory retention requirements, and the maintenance of the approved retention schedules in the database, such that a proper records series title and retention period can be established for every record in the system.
- They may support the calculation of file folder "pull" dates and generate a list of the records eligible to be destroyed or transferred from departments or file rooms to the records center.
- They may support the full or partial integration of the index of file folders with the inventory of storage cartons, such that the system knows the location of all active and inactive records under its control.

Other Software Functions

While the functions described above are the ones offered most frequently in records management software products, others are worthy of mention. Some programs provide various vital records protection and disaster recovery functions, either as a module of a larger records management software program or as a standalone product. These may include:

- Maintaining a listing of vital records in the database, together with instructions as to how to protect them against loss.
- Managing the rotation schedule for the regular or periodic transfer of vital records to a vault or other secure off-site facility.
- Maintaining the inventory of the records protection facility and performing various other tasks associated with managing the facility.

Some software programs are specially designed to perform archives management functions. These products usually maintain archival accession records and finding aids in their databases. The more sophisticated programs enable the archival facility to share data describing their holdings electronically with other institutions. These and other matters concerning archival automation are discussed in Chapter 19.

Finally, some software products are designed for managing specific types of files. The major ones are legal records, patient medical records, engineering records, and accounting records.

SOFTWARE ACQUISITION

When should records managers consider automating records management functions through the use of records management software? Should the software be acquired from commercial sources, or should it be developed in-house by the organization's computer systems specialists? What are the preconditions for implementing an automated records management system? How should this application be sized in terms of the computer power that will be required to run it, and does the organization have sufficient hardware in place, or must hardware also be acquired along with the software? The records manager must address each of these issues during the early planning stages.

Planning for Automation

If the records manager believes his or her organization could benefit from automation, when and how should system development proceed? Today, the application of computer technology to automate business functions such as recordkeeping is widely accepted, particularly if recordkeeping systems are performing poorly and the benefits of automation are easy to identify and quantify.

The question, then, is not *whether* to apply technology to any sizable records management problem, but *when* and *how*. However, records managers need to understand that, like most technologies, records management software cannot simply be dropped in place. The most important precursor to applying this technology is that the organization must have good manual records management systems and programs in place *before* attempting to install records management software. Otherwise, the new system is likely to be so riddled with errors that user confidence in its performance will soon deteriorate, and the integrity of the system may be virtually impossible to restore. Assuming high-quality manual systems exist, the records managers should then conduct a requirements analysis to determine the organization's precise needs for records management software.

The Requirements Analysis

The purpose of the *requirements analysis* is to determine whether and where records management automation is needed. This analysis is performed by conducting a survey of recordkeeping systems in one or more areas of the organization (including the records management department) to identify problems and business objectives and to determine how records management automation might help the organization achieve these objectives.

The following general guidelines are of critical importance to any effort to determine whether and where records management automation is needed.

Identify Poorly Performing Recordkeeping Systems.
The users of selected or all document-based information systems in the organization should be surveyed to determine their level of satisfaction or dissatisfaction with the recordkeeping systems they use. A questionnaire can be used initially, but it should be supplemented by personal interviews with users. The survey questions should be designed to identify, in both quantitative and qualitative terms, the performance of the systems in consistently delivering precisely the information desired by the users, as quickly as they need it in order to do their to work productively.

The source of any problem must then be identified. Very often the problem will be that the manual, paper-based recordkeeping system has been poorly designed or is being poorly executed by those responsible for operating it. Frequently, the introduction of a new filing scheme, new procedures, and better training for the system operators and users will go a long way towards enhancing system performance. After these measures have been implemented, the system might very well benefit from software automation.

Identify Functions and Recordkeeping Systems Requiring Automation.
Even if the organization's recordkeeping systems are performing well, this does not, by itself, suggest that they do not need to be enhanced by automation. Organizations *must* automate their recordkeeping systems at some point if they are to remain competitive. Thus, records managers should identify the mission-critical business functions of their organization, determine the level of computer automation that has already been applied to their recordkeeping systems, and then determine whether new enhancements to these systems would contribute to the success of the business as a whole. What can not now be done with manual systems that employees would be able to do if the recordkeeping systems were technology-enhanced?

Records managers should always remember that any effort to apply computer automation to records management systems must begin by defining the *business objectives* of the potential application. Never permit objectives to be obscured by technology. Computer hardware and software

are merely tools; it is the use of these tools to achieve business objectives that is always of prime importance.[3]

Conduct a Physical Survey of the Recordkeeping Systems.

Once the best candidates for automation have been identified, a detailed physical survey of those systems should be conducted. The records manager should determine, at a minimum, the following details concerning each recordkeeping system surveyed:

- The type of records, how they are organized and arranged in the filing system, and the individual types of documents contained in the files.
- The sources of creation of the documents, how they are received and filed into the system, the quantity of files, and their rate of growth.
- Who uses the files, how often, for what purpose, how this usage declines over time, when and why files become inactive, and what happens to them when they do become inactive.
- How the files are accessed and used (i.e., by name, number, keyword), the existence and quality of any indexes, whether the retrievals are for single document or item lookup or whether the entire file must be reviewed, and whether usage of the information in the files could be facilitated if the files could be accessed by other search parameters now unavailable with the manual system.
- The level of indexing required to facilitate access to the files, e.g., inclusive carton contents, file folder label data, or individual documents.

Identify Internal Resources to Support Automation.

The records manager must next identify the organization's internal resources for implementing an automated records management system. These resources include:

- A description of the existing computing environment, including the mainframe, PC, and LAN hardware, the computer operating environment, and major classes of software supporting the organization's computer applications.
- An analysis of the availability of in-house or consultant personnel to install the new records management application and to maintain the system over its service life. This would include performing any custom programming or other technical support that may be required.
- An analysis of whether the department which will operate the system has or can obtain sufficient staff and budgeting support to acquire and maintain the system.

Prepare the Requirements Analysis.

Sometimes called a *needs analysis*, the requirements analysis is a written report containing a comprehensive analysis of the organization's needs for automated records management systems. The requirements analysis is a preliminary planning document; its primary purposes are to advise the organization's senior management of the need for automated records management systems and to obtain approval to proceed with the subsequent system acquisition tasks. Sometimes, the scope of analysis is limited to the automation requirements of a single department or even a single recordkeeping system, but the needs analysis always contains a definition of the problem posed by the current system and the business objectives of the unit as related to the recordkeeping system. The requirements analysis may also include what are often called *functional systems specifications*, which are detailed specifications for how the proposed system is to perform in delivering information to the users. The requirements analysis may also include a cost-benefit analysis, proposed hardware and software, or other details of system acquisition and development.

The requirements analysis should conclude with a statement of priorities for records management automation; potential applications should be ranked in priority order as to where the needs for and benefits of automation are likely to be greatest. The report should also contain a request for authorization to proceed with further systems analysis for those high-priority applications that must be implemented immediately or during the current or ensuing budget year.

Selecting Appropriate Hardware

In selecting appropriate hardware for an automated records management system, the best general guidance is to first try to fit the application on a PC because this will usually be the least expensive platform and it will provide the records manager with the highest degree of control over the system. Because the computing power of these machines has increased so dramatically in recent years, PCs can usually process and store the data required in all but the largest automated records management systems. Finally, the PC platform provides, by far, the largest selection of packaged software programs from records management software vendors. As shown in Figure 9.1, Sections V and VI, at least 45 out of the 50 records management software programs surveyed in 1993 were written for IBM PCs or compatibles and the MS-DOS operating system. Thus, the PC option is usually the easiest to acquire and implement.

A decision to run the records management application on a higher-capacity platform (e.g., mainframe, minicomputer, or a LAN/file server) would be based on the following factors:

- The size of the application (the number of records to be stored and processed) and the database required to support it are projected to be larger than can be handled on a PC.
- The user community is large, and the users are located in disparate, remote sites and are already supported by mainframe-based or wide area network computing resources.[4]

Finally, records managers are often confronted with the question of whether a non-IBM platform should be selected to run the application. Records managers should discuss this (and many other) issues with computer services personnel, who may have the authority to review and approve the acquisition of any hardware and software proposed for use by the organization. As shown in Figure 9.1, Sections V and VI, non-IBM hardware platforms for records management applications include DEC/VAX, Sun, and Apple/Macintosh, while non-DOS operating systems include UNIX, OS/2, VMS, MVS, and System 7 (Apple/Macintosh) among others. If the organization has most or all IBM or compatible hardware or a PC network to which these devices have been connected, the records manager will probably want to remain in this type of computing environment. On the other hand, if the organization has made a corporate commitment to DEC/VAX, Apple/Macintosh, or some other type of hardware environment, this situation may drive the hardware and software decision for the records management system.[5]

In-House Software Development Versus Purchased Software

The best general guidance concerning whether to buy an off-the-shelf records management software package or develop it internally is to first try to locate packaged software that meets all or most of the important functional requirements of the application, even if some custom programming is required to make the package a perfect fit. Generally, in-house software development should only be considered in cases where the needs of the application are unique or very specialized and packaged software is simply not available. Because of increasing product maturity, better functionality, and more competitive pricing, purchased packages are generally a better option for the buyer than in-house development. The buyer benefits from the experience of the entire user community in purchasing a product with a proven record of success.

EVALUATING SOFTWARE PRODUCTS

Where can records managers purchase packaged records management software? What criteria

FIGURE 9.1   Records Management Software Market Analysis, 1993

The following data were compiled from information published in *Software Directory for Automated Records Management Systems,* edited by John T. Phillips, CRM, and Paul M. Tarrant, MSLS (Prairie Village, Kansas: ARMA International, 1993).

I.   Total Records Management System Population

50 systems sold by 39 vendors

II.   Age of Records Management Software Products

Date Introduced to Market	No. of RM Systems
1985 or Prior	14
1986	6
1987	4
1988	5
1989	6
1990	5
1991	2
1992	4
1993	1
Not reported	3

III.   Number of Installations per Records Management System

Installations	No. of RM Systems
Fewer than 10	8
10 to 49	12
50 to 99	6
100 to 199	7
200 to 499	5
More than 500	4
Sales not reported	8

IV.   Base-Price Analysis*

SINGLE-USER RM SYSTEMS		MULTI-USER RM SYSTEMS	
Cost	No. of RM Systems	Cost	No. of RM Systems
Less than $1,000	13	$1,000 to $2,999	5
$1,000 to $2,999	10	$3,000 to $4,999	5
$3,000 to $4,999	2	$5,000 to $9,999	11
$5,000 to $9,999	11	$10,000 to $14,999	11
Above $10,000	2	$15,000 to $24,999	0
		$25,000 to $49,999	5
		Above $50,000	3

*Base software price not reported for 4 systems.

(continued)

FIGURE 9.1   Records Management Software Market Analysis, 1993 (continued)

V.   Hardware-Software Compatibility

Hardware	No. of RM Systems
IBM PCs or compatibles	47
IBM, other than PCs	17
DEC/VAX	15
Sun	7
Apple/Macintosh	5

VI.   Operating System-Software Compatibility

Operating System	No. of RM Systems
DOS	45
UNIX	24
OS/2	14
VMS	13
MVS (or other IBM)	6
System 7 (Apple/Macintosh)	4
AIX	2
PICK	1
WANG VS	1

VII.   Graphical Interface

Windows-based products: 16 systems
X-Windows (DEC windows, MOTIF,
    etc.): 6 systems

VIII.   LAN Compatibility*

LAN	No. of RM Systems
Novell	37
Banyan Vines	30
3COM	28
Token Ring	28
Lantastic	7
Any supporting NetBios	6

*Multi-user version of product available for 41 systems.

IX.   Application Programming Languages

Language	No. of RM Systems
C	19
Clipper	9
FoxPro	5
Foxbase	3
Assembler	3
C++	3
Focus	3
Cobol	2
DataFlex	2

X.   Interface to Other Systems

Interface Systems*	No. of RM Systems
Optical disk systems	20
Image scanners	20
FAX import/export	12
CAR systems	8
MARC:amc	7

*Systems with which RM system can interface.

should be used to assess product quality? As to the first question, the best place to start is the shopper's catalog of the records management software industry: the *Software Directory for Automated Records Management Systems*, which is published annually by ARMA International.[6] The 1993 edition contains data concerning a total of 50 records management software programs offered by 39 vendors.

An evaluation of these products[7] involves an analysis of two broad areas:

- *Technical evaluation of product quality.* The records manager must evaluate the technical aspects of the software—its features and functions—in order to make a judgment as to its performance and how well it can be expected to meet the needs of the users.
- *Business evaluation of product and supplier.* The records manager must evaluate the *value* of the software in terms of its price-performance characteristics and how they compare to competitive products, as well as the quality, reputation, and stability of the software company and its ability to provide good after-the-sale product support.

Technical Evaluation of Features and Functions

The major criteria relative to the technical capabilities—features and functions—of records management software products are as follows.

Ease-of-Use Features. Does the software come with a comprehensive, easy-to-understand user manual that is well indexed? Does it provide good, illustrated examples of system operations? Does it have a dictionary of terms? Does the system provide *on-line help screens*—a list of operating procedures that can be accessed while using the system so that the user does not have to refer to the user manual. Are these screens really helpful and easy to access? Is a help screen index provided? Does the software provide a *tutorial disk*—an on-line, step-by-step set of instructions in op-

eration of the system? If the software is *menu-driven*, are these menus logical and easy to access and navigate through? Can the user *toggle between files*—shift back and forth between sections of the database easily?

Data Retrieval and Search Capabilities. Does the software have very powerful and flexible search capabilities? The best products provide search capabilities for any and all fields in the database. Does the product provide *keyword searching*—the ability to search any single word within a field? *Phrase searching*—the ability to search two or more consecutive words in a field? *Boolean logic*—the use of *and*, *or*, or *not* to combine search statements to expand or limit the scope of the search? *Wild card searching*—the ability to use wild card symbols to represent multiple prefixes or suffixes of words (e.g., *automate*, *automation*) or alternate word spellings (e.g., *labor*, *labour*).

Data Field Characteristics. What is the maximum length of character fields and text fields, and can each of these types of fields be searched? Can the numeric and date fields be *range searched*—can the search be defined by using range symbols, such as symbols for *greater than* or *less than*?

Data Entry Features. Does the software provide for *full-screen editing*—the ability to move through the data entry fields to add and edit records? *Code tables*—the use of tables to store authorized field values which can be accessed during data entry?

Security Features. Does the software provide *user password access* to limit access to the levels of the database to users with proper passwords? Does it provide *multilevel security* at the menu, record, or field levels to restrict access to specified menus, record types, and fields?

Reporting Features. How many standard reports have been programmed into the system, and are they useful for the proposed application? Does the software provide *user-defined reports* to enable the user to customize the search and sort parameters and the output format of reports? Does the system print file folder labels, bar codes, billing invoices, or statistical graphs and charts?

Business Evaluation

Even if a particular records management product has excellent functionality in meeting the needs of the buyer, is easy to use, and provides other good technical features, it can still be a poor choice that may cause significant problems during the service life of the system. Thus, the records manager should perform a *business evaluation* of the product as compared to competing products (if any) and attempt to assess the quality of the software vendor. This evaluation is essential to ensure that a particular product is a good value for the money and that the supplier will stand behind his or her product with good after-the-sale support. The following criteria should be addressed in this business evaluation.

1. *Product price evaluation.* Figure 9.1, Section IV, contains an analysis of records management software pricing data based on 1993 reported base prices. The term *base price* refers to the price of the software only, exclusive of add-ons such as customization, maintenance, installation, and training. Note that the base price of single-user systems ranges from less than $1,000 to around $10,000, with most systems priced below $3,000 at the low end, and from $5,000 to $10,000 at the high end. As would be expected, the multi-user systems are more expensive; they range from less than $3,000 to more than $50,000, but the majority of products are priced at about $10,000. The important thing to note here is that the best products for a given application from a technical perspective should be compared with the prices of other products of equal or similar quality to arrive at a judgment as to which one offers the most value for the money.

2. *After-the-sale support.* It is usually not enough for a records management software vendor to send a customer diskettes, manuals, and other shrink-wrapped product components; the company should be capable of providing a number of post-sale services that are usually required for a successful installation. These include customizing the software, providing on-site installation services, providing ongoing maintenance support, and training system operators and users. These services are usually priced as extras on top of the base software licensing fee, so the records manager needs to determine what they will cost and exactly what is provided.

Vendor-supplied post-installation maintenance, which is usually provided under an annual maintenance contract, is most often priced at 12 to 15 percent of the software license fee. Software maintenance usually takes the form of telephone support, on-site technical assistance, or mirror-image modem support, under which remote support is provided by linking the screens of the customer and supplier via modem and phone lines. This enables the screens of the system to appear at both locations simultaneously for problem diagnosis and resolution.

3. *Vendor quality and stability.* Finally, records managers should rigorously evaluate the quality and reputation of the software vendor before making any purchasing decision. Vendor integrity and professional reputation are of supreme importance—an intangible factor that should *always* be considered in making any procurement decision. The records manager should consider whether the vendor is so small that business failure may be likely. In recent years the records management software vendor community has had an attrition rate of up to 20 percent each year. If the vendor has a high level of sales, this would be an indication of product acceptance and may also indicate a degree of stability and financial strength. Records managers should always check user references, ask for information relative to the vendor's financial condition, and visit installations for live product demonstrations if possible.

In cases where the buyer is considering several competing software programs, the records manager may wish to adopt a quantitative methodology for arriving at the product that offers the best value for the price. Figure 9.2 shows a records management software product analysis worksheet. This form can be used to assign weighted numerical ratings to the technical and business criteria for evaluating competing software products. Although the weighted ratings assigned to each criterion will sometimes require making arbitrary judgments, this approach should prove useful in arriving at a good software acquisition decision.

Justifying the Cost of the New System

Pay Back Period

The final step in the software acquisition process is to perform a cost justification in order to determine whether the new automated recordkeeping system will yield sufficient benefits as compared to the existing manual system so as to justify the organization's investment in it. Financial executives and other managers frequently want to know whether this investment can be expected to generate a return on investment and, if so, how soon the investment will yield a payback.

In order to answer these questions, it is necessary to calculate the actual cost of the existing system during the current year and for several ensuing years, based on reasonable growth projections. These costs must then be compared to the projected cost of the new system. The one-time costs of the hardware and the software and of converting from the existing to the new system must be differentiated from the recurring costs of operating the system on an ongoing basis.

The benefits of the new system must then be calculated. These fall into two main categories: quantifiable hard-dollar saving in personnel or other resources (including productivity benefits resulting from more efficient work flow and enhanced access to information) and nonquantifiable, or intangible, benefits such as improved staff morale. As noted earlier, some hard-to-quantify benefits such as providing better service to customers and staying ahead of the competition can provide the most compelling reasons to invest in automated records management systems. Such benefits nearly always justify investments in a new automated recordkeeping system.

The cost-justification analysis is completed by comparing costs and benefits. As a generalization, good automated records management applications should be able to generate a return-on-investment within two years.

SYSTEM CONVERSION AND IMPLEMENTATION

Having now acquired the requisite hardware and software, the records manager is ready to install them and begin the process of initial system implementation. This requires the conversion of records into the new system. The term *system conversion* refers to the tasks associated with making the transition from the manual procedures supporting the recordkeeping system to the computerized procedures for the new system.[8] System conversion includes planning, installing, testing, and debugging the software; converting any existing computerized data that needs to be imported into the new database; entering new index data into the database from manual indexes; performing data validation and error corrections; and training all personnel in the use of the new systems.

Conversion Planning. The records manager should prepare a detailed conversion plan, outlining how each of the conversion tasks will be performed and the time, resources, and responsibilities required to accomplish them. Figure 9.3, the Conversion Timetable Chart, is a useful tool to facilitate conversion planning.

Software Installation. The relatively straightforward operation of software installation consists of actually installing the records management soft-

FIGURE 9.2   Records Management Software Programs: Product Quality Analysis Worksheet

FEATURE (A)	IMPORTANCE (B)	WEIGHTED TOTAL SCORE (C)
0 = Missing 1 = Poor 5 = Average 10 = Outstanding	1 = Low 5 = Average 8 = High 10 = Vital	C = A X B

	A	B	C

Technical Features

Ease of use _____ × _____ = _____

Data retrieval and search capabilities _____ × _____ = _____

Data field characteristics _____ × _____ = _____

Data entry features _____ × _____ = _____

Security features _____ × _____ = _____

Reporting features _____ × _____ = _____

Business Evaluation

Product pricing

   Base price _____ × _____ = _____

   Add-ons _____ × _____ = _____

Post-sale support

   Installation and Training _____ × _____ = _____

   Maintenance _____ × _____ = _____

Vendor quality and stability _____ × _____ = _____

Total Score _____

Name of vendor _____ Product _____ Date _____

ware on the computer on which it is to operate. Some software is advertised as self-installable, but most programs must be installed by the vendor, usually for an extra fee.

System Testing and Debugging. Data must be entered for this purpose, and the person testing the system must go through all steps and perform all functions to ensure that the system performs properly. In multi-user systems operating on a network, testing should also include the communications components of the system, to determine whether the interfaces that communicate with other system components are performing properly. All nonfunctioning parts of the programs must be debugged, or corrected.

Conversion and Import of Existing Data. In many cases, record index data resident in existing computer databases may be transferred, or *imported*, into the new records management database. This process, known as *data conversion*, often requires extensive programming and must usually be handled by the software vendor's technical staff working in conjunction with the customer's computer systems personnel. Figure 9.4 shows a data conversion form that is useful in executing this process.

Entry of New Index Data. A very important system conversion task, the entry of new data involves keyboard entry of existing index data into the new database. This task can be very labor-intensive and expensive—it can easily exceed the base price of the software and take weeks or months to complete. Decisions must be made concerning what data must be entered initially (during system conversion) and on an ongoing basis. Perhaps the biggest decision is whether to enter some, all, or none of the *backfile* index data or whether to simply begin entering new index data from *day one forward*. Like most business decisions, data entry decisions should be made on the basis of costs and benefits—the cost of entering the data versus its expected use and value to the system users. As a generalization, most if not all index data on active records should be entered, since they will be used most heavily. On the other hand, index data on inactive records can be entered as time permits, if at all, or they can be entered at a basic rather than at a detailed level. The index data usually exist on index cards, log books, or file folder tabs for the active records, and on records transfer sheets and carton labels for the inactive ones. If the index data exist at a remote site away from the computer, they can sometimes be captured by entry into portable *laptop* or *notebook* computers and subsequently transferred into the main index database.

Data Validation and Error Correction. Because the accuracy of the index database is of utmost importance, the data should be validated and errors must be corrected. Incorrect data will, of course, result in *electronic misfiles*—unsuccessful searches or irretrievable records. The goal should be an error rate not exceeding 1 percent; a .5 percent goal is preferable. While temporary personnel are often used to perform the data entry, only experienced internal staff should perform data validation. Validation can be accomplished on a field-by-field, line-by-line basis, or a sampling methodology can sometimes be employed.

System Training. Separate, specialized training is usually required for the records manager, the system administrator (if this responsibility is assigned to someone other than the records manager), the records management staff, data entry personnel and other system operators, departmental users, and finally, senior managers and executives. The training should range in scope from an introductory overview of the system to more in-depth, hands-on work directly with the database, to include data entry, search and retrieval functions, report generation, etc.

Ongoing System Maintenance

Most automated records management systems require upgrades and enhancements over their service life. The records manager or system adminis-

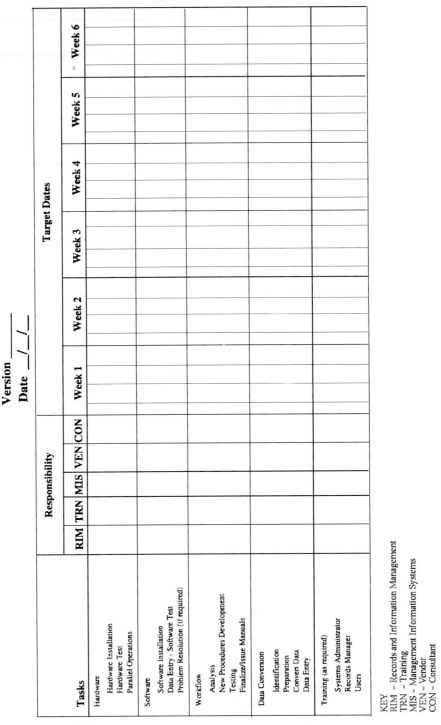

Conversion Timetable Chart

Version _____

Date ___/___/___

Tasks	Responsibility					Target Dates					
	RIM	TRN	MIS	VEN	CON	Week 1	Week 2	Week 3	Week 4	Week 5	Week 6
Hardware Hardware Installation Hardware Test Parallel Operations											
Software Software Installation Data Entry - Software Test Problem Resolution (if required)											
Workflow Analysis New Procedures Development Testing Finalize/Issue Manuals											
Data Conversion Identification Preparation Convert Data Data Entry											
Training (as required) Systems Administrator Records Manager Users											

KEY
RIM = Records and Information Management
TRN = Training
MIS = Management Information Systems
VEN = Vendor
CON = Consultant

FIGURE 9.3 Conversion Timetable Chart (Courtesy of ARMA International)

Records Management Software
Data Conversion

System _____

Contact _____ Title _____

Dept. _____ Ext. _____ Date _____

| Data/Field | Source | Need | | | | Field Description |
| | | R/C | | ADMIN | | |
		P	S	P	S	

Needs Key
R/C = Records Center/Data Input
ADMIN = Records Administration
P = Primary
S = Secondary

FIGURE 9.4 Records Management Software Data Conversion Form
(Courtesy of ARMA International)

trator should continually monitor the performance of the system and the level of satisfaction of the users. When system changes are needed, a system change or enhancement request form (see Figure 9.5) can be used to document the required modifications or upgrades.

BAR CODE TECHNOLOGY FOR RECORDS MANAGEMENT

Bar code technology is frequently offered as an optional enhancement to packaged records management software to create a more powerful automated records management solution to recordkeeping problems. This technology can be applied in many formats: loose paper documents, file folders, records in storage cartons, microfilm and microfiche, and optically stored records. Bar code technology is relatively inexpensive, and because its benefits are often substantial, it frequently provides an excellent, cost-effective solution to many types of records management problems.

History and Description of the Technology

Bar codes were first used in the railroad industry during the 1960s as a means of facilitating the location of railroad cars. The railroads needed a better method of tracking and monitoring the location of their inventory of rolling stock, and inventory management remains the primary use of bar code technology today. Bar codes are applied to products in supermarkets and department stores, to stock items in warehouses, to books in libraries, to mail and parcels—to virtually anything that needs better location tracking and inventory control—including record media in recordkeeping systems.

A bar code consists of lines and spaces of varying widths; the lines are positioned in a vertical format to create an optical code field. The codes are scanned and read by a device utilizing laser light to sense the light and dark areas in the code field. Each vertical line or section of lines in the bar code field represents a single numerical digit or letter. Most printed bar codes also include printed characters to permit sight recognition of the code. See Figure 9.6 for an illustration of bar codes used for mortgage loan files.

There are several types, or *symbologies,* of bar codes, each of which is based on ASCII character data sets. Code 39 is the most common symbology used for records management applications; it incorporates the full 128-character ASCII data set. This class of bar code offers greater compatibility, and a large body of supportive software is written for it.[9]

Benefits of Bar Code Technology

The application of bar codes to record media in conjunction with records management software offers several important benefits.

1. *Keyless data entry provides faster, more accurate circulation control.* Manual techniques for tracking and monitoring the movement, or *circulation,* of records include the use of outcards, index cards, log books, etc. These techniques are all subject to significantly high error rates; their effectiveness in maintaining the integrity of the recordkeeping systems depends on whether files operators and users fill out these record control devices accurately and consistently. With the use of bar codes, the keying of data is eliminated. The bar code is simply scanned whenever a record is withdrawn from the system. Thus the error rates are greatly reduced. The data entry process is also significantly faster than with keyboard entry.

2. *There is greater accuracy in record location monitoring.* Once records have their unique bar code identification, recording their movement into and out of the file room or storage facility becomes a simple matter of scanning the bar code and indicating with a key stroke or two that the records are being sent to a particular department or individual. When the record is returned, another scan indicates to the computer that the record has been returned for refiling. Under most systems, all transactions are automatically date- and time-stamped and the operator performing the action is identified. Identifying the current location of any record becomes a simple matter of an inquiry to the computerized system.

3. *Misfiles are reduced.* As each record is placed in its proper shelf location for storage, employees can scan both the record's bar code and a separate bar code affixed to the shelf location. This verifies the record's accurate placement, discloses any misfiles, and enables them to be corrected.[10]

4. *The records disposition process is facilitated.* Records management software can be programmed to generate a pull (or pick) list, sorted in location order, to facilitate the removal of records

FIGURE 9.5   System Change or Enhancement Request (Courtesy of ARMA International)

Change ☐
Enhancement ☐
Other ☐

System Change/Enhancement Request
Request # _____

System _____

Initiated By _____   Title _____

Dept. _____   Ext. _____   Date _____

Explanation of Request (Use attachments to further explain/illustrate request)

_____

_____

_____

_____

_____

_____

_____

Requirements

_____

_____

_____

_____

_____

_____

_____

Other Contacts

Name/Ext. _____

Name/Ext. _____

Departmental Signoff — *Testing Accepted and Implementation Authorized*

Signature/Date _____

Departmental Approval

Signature/Date _____

FORM TYPE CODE

5-character code that identifies the
form type (HUD-1, Deed of Trust, etc)

LOAN ID CODE

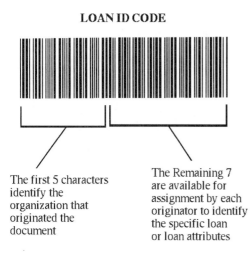

The first 5 characters
identify the
organization that
originated the
document

The Remaining 7
are available for
assignment by each
originator to identify
the specific loan
or loan attributes

FIGURE 9.6   Bar Codes for Mortgage Loan Files
(Courtesy of Intelus)

from cabinets or shelves for transfer to the records center. Likewise, a similar list can be generated in the records center indicating those records eligible for destruction. In both cases, the bar codes affixed to the records can be scanned to create a record of these actions, and no time is wasted searching for them since the list is sorted in location order.

5. *Records "lost in transit" can be tracked.* The automated records management system can be programmed to generate a daily report of records withdrawn from storage but not yet received at their destination. This is possible in systems where the recipient is required to scan the records at the user point upon receipt. This permits a search for these records to occur immediately instead of days or weeks later when someone discovers the problem.

6. *Productivity benefits are possible through work flow analysis.* The system can be programmed to generate reports showing the quantity of records processed by individuals or units. This facilitates an analysis of work patterns and provides volume trend data for more efficient production of the work.

While these are the primary records management benefits of bar code technology, there are other benefits which are specific to various applications.

Specific Applications for Bar Code Technology

Bar-coding permits an enhanced level of record control across all media formats: single, loose paper documents; collections of documents housed in file folders; records in storage cartons; and micrographic media, computer tape, and optical media.

Single Forms or Loose Paper Documents.   In some recordkeeping systems, single paper documents or forms are processed in an unfoldered manner by persons at one, several, or many workstations. After processing, the loose documents are usually transferred to a single storage location for continued maintenance. Medical claims are a good example of this type of records processing. If hundreds or even thousands of these documents are in the processing cycle at any given time, the rapid location of a single document can be difficult, particularly if a customer is waiting on the telephone and wants to know the status of his or her file.

Although such applications often make good candidates for microfilm or electronic imaging, bar code technology can greatly improve the degree of control an organization has over these types of records. Bar codes can be affixed to each form or single document upon creation or receipt, workstations with hand-held scanners can be placed at the key processing points (see Figure 9.7), and the documents can be scanned each time they arrive at or leave a workstation in the records processing cycle. This point-to-point tracking can show the exact location of any given document at any point in time, as well as enhancing the efficiency of the work flow.

Documents Housed in File Folders.   In the file folder application, bar codes are used to replace the card indexes and manual log books commonly used in many file rooms. The bar codes are affixed to the file folders (or they may be preprinted on them) and are scanned when the folders are withdrawn from and subsequently replaced in the file room. Portable scanners may be placed at the remote user points, increasing the folder tracking capability. See Figure 9.8.

Records Housed in Storage Cartons in Records Centers.   Each carton is assigned a bar code, a separate bar code may also be assigned to the particular shelf where the carton is housed, and the bar codes can be affixed to both the cartons and the shelves. In addition to circulation control and disposition benefits, this application of bar codes also maximizes the efficient use of a records center's shelf space and makes it easy to move cartons from one shelf location in the center to another. See Figure 9.9.

CAR Microfilm Systems.   The microfilm cameras used to film documents in a computer-assisted retrieval (CAR) system are equipped with bar code scanning and encoding capabilities. A bar code is affixed to the paper documents prior to filming and is read by the scanner as it is being filmed. The roll and frame numbers are simultaneously assigned, and the bar code number and microfilm image identifier are stored in the database of the CAR system's computer. The computer (usually a PC) interfaces with the camera as the CAR software stores the bar code number and

FIGURE 9.7   Bar Code Workstation for User Document Processing Station (Courtesy of Intelus)

FIGURE 9.8   Hand–Held Bar Code Workstation
(Courtesy of Intelus)

FIGURE 9.9   Bar Coding System Used for Tracking Storage Cartons
(Courtesy of O'Neil Product Development Inc.)

roll and frame number at the time of filming. Thus, the documents are automatically indexed by linking the roll and frame number with the database of index data previously loaded with the bar code identifiers. The major benefits of this application of bar code technology are that it greatly increases index  production and decreases the data entry error rates that occur during manual, keyboard indexing.

Bar Code Equipment

Bar code equipment consists of printers to generate the bar code labels, recognition hardware to read them, and the previously described records management software, which manages the database. See Figure 9.10 for an illustration of this equipment.

FIGURE 9.10 Bar Code Equipment (Courtesy of Intelus)

Printers. If the bar code labels are not preprinted and purchased from commercial sources, a printer must be available on which to generate them. Ink jet, dot matrix, or laser printers may be used, but the good-quality laser printers are usually recommended for clear, sharp labels that can be easily read. A special font cartridge is required to print the labels.

Recognition Hardware. *Readers, scanners,* or *wands* read the bar codes for transfer of the data to the database for processing and storage. Platform-type scanners are stationary and are connected to the document management hardware at the central processing station, while the portable units are used away from the computer. Scanners may be *contact* units in which the device must be brought into contact with the label as it is read. The noncontact *laser gun* units can effectively read labels held several inches away from them. The portable units are used to perform tasks away from the central processing station (e.g., at user points). The data recorded in them are periodically uploaded into the software's database.

SUMMARY

Among the millions of paper-based recordkeeping systems in the United States, only a very small percentage are supported by some form of computer technology. However, during the 1980s, a new records management tool became available which enhanced the management of these recordkeeping systems—records management software. This type of computer software is designed to index, track, and monitor active records maintained in file rooms and departmental filing stations, as well as inactive records maintained in records centers. It is a major tool for developing an automated records management system and for automating records management functions. The principal benefits of this software are as follows: (1) It provides a computer capability to establish total life cycle control over records; (2) it can significantly improve the performance of recordkeeping systems by improving the accessibility of the information contained in them; (3) it provides multiple pathways by which information in recordkeeping systems can be acessed; (4) it can improve productivity, reduce costs, facilitate work management, and provide better services to customers, all through enhancements in recordkeeping; and (5) it can upgrade the status and quality of the organization's records management program.

Although records management software can be developed in-house by an organization's own computer specialists, procurement of this software from commercial sources is an increasingly attractive option. However, in order to implement a successful automated records management system, the records manager must perform careful automation planning and conduct a requirements analysis to determine whether and where records management automation is needed.

This type of analysis is conducted by identifying recordkeeping systems that are performing poorly, by identifying business functions and recordkeeping systems which could benefit from automation, and by conducting a physical survey of the records and the organization's existing computer resources on which an automated records management system could operate. Finally, the records manager must size the potential automation application, select an appropriate hardware platform for it, and determine whether in-house software development or the purchase of software from commercial sources would be in the organization's best interest.

If the records management software is to be acquired from commercial sources, the records manager must identify products that match the organization's needs and evaluate them to determine their quality and value. A technical evaluation of product quality consists of assessing the performance characteristics of the products—their features and functions. The main ones are ease of use, data retrieval and search capabilities, data field characteristics, data entry features, security features, and reporting features. A business evaluation of product value and vendor quality should also be performed. This would include a product price evaluation, the capability of the vendor to provide good after-the-sale support, and an assessment of the vendor's integrity, professional reputation, and stability. Finally, the records manager should prepare a cost justification to determine whether investment in the automated records management system is a sound business decision.

After the software is acquired it must be installed, and the existing manual system must be converted to the new computerized one. This process requires proper conversion planning, software testing, and the entry of existing and new index data into the software's database. Finally, proper training must be conducted for all system users.

Bar code technology is often combined with records management software and is offered as an optional enhancement with many packaged software products. This technology can enhance the management of records in single-form or loose-document format, file folder or storage carton format, microfilm, or optically stored media. Bar codes improve the management of the record media by enhancing the system's ability to control the inventory and track and monitor the location of the records. They also provide faster, more accurate record circulation control, reduce misfiles, facilitate the records disposition process, and improve productivity. When applied to CAR microfilm systems, bar codes can greatly increase the production and accuracy of the computerized index supporting the system. Bar code equipment, which is relatively inexpensive, consists of printers to generate the bar code labels, recognition hardware to read them, and software to manage and index the database.

QUESTIONS FOR DISCUSSION

1. The proper application of records management software and bar code technology can produce at least five major benefits in upgrading the quality of records management in organizations. Discuss each of these five benefits briefly.

2. Discuss the historical development of records management software, including the factors that made it a feasible and relatively affordable solution for records management problems.

3. Discuss the major functional capabilities of records management software in managing active recordkeeping systems.

4. Discuss the major functional capabilities of records management software in managing inactive recordkeeping systems.

5. What functional capabilities must records management software have if it is to provide total life cycle management over an organization's records?

6. There are five major components of a requirements analysis. List and briefly discuss three of them.

7. Although most automated records management systems can be implemented on a PC computing platform, there are several factors that would necessitate implementing the system on a large platform. Discuss these briefly.

8. List and discuss three criteria for evaluating the technical merits of the features and functions of records management software programs.

9. A business evaluation of packaged records management software products consists of a price evaluation and an assessment of the vendors' quality and capability to deliver good post-installation support. Discuss these criteria briefly, indicating why they are important.

10. One of the most important decisions concerning the conversion and initial implementation of a new automated records management system concerns entering new index data into the software's database. Discuss this issue, addressing the question of whether to enter backfile index data and how to prioritize data entry decisions.

11. There are at least six major benefits of applying bar code technology to enhance records management systems. Discuss three of them briefly.

12. Discuss the benefits of applying bar codes to single forms or loose paper documents.

13. Describe how bar code technology can be applied to CAR microfilm systems, indicating its major benefit in this application.

14. There are two major classes of bar code readers or scanners used in records management applications. Describe them briefly.

15. Discuss how bar code technology can be applied to establish point-to-point tracking of documents or file folders which are processed at numerous workstations. What are the benefits of this type of application?

PROJECTS

1. Obtain a copy of the latest *Software Directory for Automated Records Management Systems,* which is published by ARMA International. Use it to acquire product literature on five records management software programs. Review this literature and prepare a report on the features and functions of the products, indicating relevant comparisons among them.

2. Use the *Software Directory for Automated Records Management* to determine whether a records management software vendor is located near you. If so, phone the company,

schedule a visit with the company, and ask to see a demonstration of the product. Prepare a report of your observations.

3. Determine whether any company or agency of government in your area has implemented an automated records management system utilizing records management software or bar code technology. Visit the installation, see a real-life demonstration of the system, get some hands-on experience with it, and prepare a report describing the system, its features, and its benefits to the organization.

4. You are the records manager of Global Agricultural Products Corporation. You have placed automation and the acquisition of new records management software on your agenda for the coming year. Prepare a requirements analysis, indicating how you would proceed to assimilate this technology into the company.

5. You are the records manager of Mountain Pacific Electric Power Company. You are in charge of the company's records center, which currently stores some 120,000 cartons of records. The records are indexed on the computer, but no bar code technology is used. Prepare a report to your company's senior management as to the benefits of applying bar code technology to your records center.

CASE PROBLEM

You are the new records manager of the Mid-Atlantic Manufacturing Company. You and your supervisor have agreed that records management automation will be your top priority for the upcoming fiscal year and that much careful planning will be required in order to develop and implement a comprehensive program of records management automation on an enterprise-wide basis. You have not yet performed a requirements analysis to determine what Mid-Atlantic's records management automation priorities should be, but you have conducted a brief, walk-through survey of the recordkeeping situation in the company, in which you made the following observations:

- Except for basic listings of records and files on word processors, no computer capability exists to index, track, and monitor any of the company's paper-based recordkeeping systems.

- The company has an inactive records storage facility, but it is not computer-enhanced in any way.

- The company has an off-site vault for the storage of its vital records, but better inventory control is needed over the rotation of the microfilms, magnetic tapes, and paper records that are stored there.

- The company has a CAR microfilm system for its accounts payable files, but much time is expended in indexing these documents on the computer, and the indexing suffers from a high rate of errors.

- The company has a set of well-developed records retention schedules, but no aspect of the records retention and disposition program has been computerized.

- The company has a collection of old, historically valuable archives, but these are unindexed; no archival accession records or finding aids have been prepared for them.

- The company's largest file room houses its customer files. These files are sequenced in customer-number order, and the users complain that the records would be more valuable to them if they could be accessed in numerous other ways: by product installation, by account size, and by other access pathways that would be very useful for customer management and marketing purposes.

- The customer files are used frequently by the marketing and customer services departments. Folders are frequently withdrawn from the system and are passed from desk to desk in these units before being returned to the central file room. The rate of "missing" files is high, and these departments cannot respond to customer queries very effectively.

Prepare a paper entitled "Strategic Plan for Records Management Automation" for the Mid-Atlantic Manufacturing Company. The plan must consist of the following components:

1. A summary of the major benefits to be derived from the installation of automated records management systems.

2. A discussion of the current situation concerning records automation at the company, including the consequences of failure to automate the recordkeeping systems.

3. A requirements analysis detailing the priorities for records management automation.

4. A plan for the acquisition and implementation of commercial records management software.

5. A plan for applying bar code technology to help solve the company's records management problems.

NOTES

1. This figure was tabulated from statistics appearing in the 1993 edition of *Software Directory for Automated Records Management Systems*, in which records management software vendors throughout North America report the total number of systems installed to date. Although some sales figures are of questionable reliability, the aggregate numbers can be taken as a valid indication of the degree of market penetration the commercial records management software industry has made to date. See John T. Phillips, CRM, and Paul M. Tarrant, MSLS, *Software Directory for Automated Records Management Systems* (Prairie Village, Kansas: ARMA International, 1993).

2. Ibid.

3. Frank McKenna, *Records Management in the 1990s: A Survival Guide* (Crows Nest, NSW, Australia: GMB Research and Development Pty. Limited, 1993), pp. 2, 54.

4. James V. Davis, "Choosing Records Management Software," *Records Management Quarterly*, July 1988, p. 4.

5. Ibid., p. 3.

6. *Software Directory*, p. 3.

7. See *Criteria for Developing/Evaluating Records Management Software* (Prairie Village, Kansas: ARMA International, 1990).

8. See *Converting from a Manual System to an Automated System* (Prairie Village, Kansas: ARMA International, 1992).

9. Virginia A. Jones, "How Bar Coding Can Be Used in Records Management," *Office Systems*, October 1992, p. 47.

10. James F. Minihan, "Combining Bar Coding and Imaging for Comprehensive Records Management," *Proceedings of the 35th Annual Conference, ARMA International* (Prairie Village, Kansas: ARMA International, 1990), pp. 134–148.

The City of Ottawa

Automated Records Management System

The City of Ottawa, Ontario, is Canada's national capital. A total of approximately 3,000 municipal employees serve a population of some 630,000 citizens. Like every large municipality, the City of Ottawa generates very large quantities of records, records which require good management in order for city services to be delivered efficiently and in a cost-effective manner. To achieve these objectives, the City of Ottawa has, over a period of years, implemented a comprehensive high-quality records management program. Its main features serve as an excellent model for any municipal government—or indeed for any corporate enterprise—not only in Canada, but anywhere records and information need to be managed to the highest standards of professionalism.

The Keys to Success in Records Management

The City of Ottawa has found the formula for achieving success in records management: good leadership and a close relationship with the city's information systems unit. Under the leadership of Corporate Records Manager Claire Lee, the city has implemented a full-scope records management program consisting of all the major components required for efficient management: citywide management of all active and inactive files, microfilm production, the development of records management policies and procedures, and training and auditing to assure program compliance.

Ottawa's program is large scale: the city has 40 full-time records management positions: it provides technical assistance to 432 decentralized file stations; it implements a citywide uniform files classification system covering some 2.5 million records, and it oversees a large records center operation which manages approximately 26,000 cubic feet of inactive records in commercial storage.

The centerpiece of the program, however, is the type and degree of computer automation which has been applied to it. This would not have been possible without a close relationship between records management and the city's Informatics Services Branch—the computer services arm of city government. The city is currently in the process of developing a *Corporate Information Management Strategy* which will cement this relationship by officially and formally bringing Corporate Information Systems and Corporate Records together. This fusion of technical talent will enable the city to develop the kind of automated records management systems that will be needed to manage the complex enterprise of city government in the coming years.

The Underlying Strategy: Total Life Cycle Management of Records

The City of Ottawa has designed its records management program in such a way that the *life cycle concept* of records management can be translated from philosophy to reality. The city's records management systems are developed to manage records from their creation to their final disposition, from custodian to custodian, and from one storage medium to another. Under the life cycle concept, both active and inactive records are managed in an integrated records management system. The *Corporate Records Classification System* (CRCS) serves as the basis for indexing and classifying the city's active records at the file station level, while the *Corporate Records Scheduling System* manages records as they move from active to inactive status in the disposition process.

The Corporate Records Classification System

The CRCS is the corporate standard filing system for the city's municipal records. The system is designed in a hierarchical format and is built around the city's business functions and activities, which serve as the basis for the subject categories comprising the six-tiered classification scheme. The system includes standard record codes, titles, keywords, scope notes, alpha-numeric indices and naming conventions, all designed to provide a standard, citywide filing vocabulary and to assist departmental personnel in accurately indexing their records. Both subject and case files are handled under the same template. Mary Gregoire-Lyons, Corporate Records Systems Analyst, joined the city in 1985 and has since played a key role in developing the system.

Automation of the Records Management System

Ottawa's records management system is automated by an on-line mainframe computer database system designed in-house by Corporate Records Management in conjunction with the Informatics Services Branch and with substantial input from representatives of the user departments. Astrid Graham, Manager of Systems Development, and David J. Kent, Senior Computer Systems Analyst, played key roles in the technical aspects of the system's design. The system is designed so that it can be shared with other municipalities. The system module for the management of active records supports the operations of the Corporate Records Classification System and provides control over the inventory of records at the departmental file stations. The module providing management over inactive records contains "individual record life histories," and includes disposition data from creation of the records to their final disposition.

The automated records management system contains 225 separate programs. Users can access the system through dumb terminals or networked PC's. The category scope notes can be accessed through the local area network. The system is currently being upgraded to include enhancements for the records retention module.

The City of Ottawa is proud of its Corporate Records Management Program; the proper management of public records is one of the most important responsibilities of any government, and city officials support this program because they believe it serves the public interest for Ottawa and its citizens.

PART IV

Image Technology for Document Management

Chapter 10

Microfilm Imaging Systems and Technology

Learning Objectives

1. To explain the fundamentals of a microfilm system.
2. To identify the various photographic films used in microfilm systems.
3. To describe the effects of reduction ratios, magnification ratios, image orientation, image density, contrast, and resolution on image capture and display.
4. To explain the operation, components, and benefits of the rotary microfilm camera.
5. To describe the operation, components, and benefits of planetary and other flatbed cameras used to photograph small documents and engineering drawings.
6. To list design use and benefits of the various microforms used in microfilm systems.
7. To discuss the operation and purpose of various peripheral equipment such as processors, duplicators, and jacket and aperture card loaders used to produce the final imaged film medium and its carrier.
8. To describe the hardware and software used in film imaging and display, including computer-assisted retrieval systems (CAR) and computer-output microfilm (COM).
9. To explain the design, purpose, and operation of microfilm readers and reader-printers.

MICROFILM: AN OVERVIEW

Microfilm has been used to store and retrieve document-based information for well over a half century. Initially used by banks to capture and display images of processed checks, it is now used in virtually all industries, institutions, and government agencies as a substitute for paper documents.

Although microfilm can reduce records storage space requirements by 98 percent, this is not the primary reason for its enthusiastic acceptance. Through improved film, cameras, processing techniques, versatile microforms, and high-quality viewers, fast retrieval of high-quality document images is possible, with great savings in labor and distribution costs. It is, therefore, essential that the records manager have a thorough knowledge of microfilm technology and techniques so that its full potential can be realized in the management of records.

Microfilm technology for source documents is very similar to the technology used in ordinary photography. Both make use of a camera, a lens, film, and a subject. In each technology the subject is captured on film as a much smaller image than the actual subject. In both instances the film is developed so that a latent image becomes visible, and that image is normally "negative" in character. The differences, though, are quite distinct. Microfilm is used to capture images of documents that contain relatively small characters or words; ordinary photography is usually used to capture the image of a much larger, three-dimensional object. Hence, microfilm requires specialized cameras, specially formulated film, film duplicating machines, different techniques, and printing, viewing, and enlarging methods that enable the small characters to be read easily. The film containing the micrographic images is captured and retained on some type of carrier, often a reel or cartridge, referred to generally as a microform, and is displayed on optical projection devices called readers or viewers. A reel or cartridge of microfilm may contain thousands of images, so an effective indexing system is also needed to quickly locate a particular document. If required, a paper print can be produced using the copier system built into a viewing device called a reader-printer.

FILM TECHNOLOGY

Maintaining the quality of microfilm involves an understanding of film technology.

Camera Film

The film most commonly used in source document microfilm cameras is *silver halide film*, or more simply *black and white silver microfilm*. A type of this film is also used as a copy film to make contact prints or duplicates. The film consists of a polyester base on which a silver halide emulsion is coated. It is the emulsion that bears the photographic image. This image is created when light is reflected from the surface of the document through the camera lens to the film. The emulsion captures the image of the document as though the emulsion were a mirror.

In the development process, that portion of the emulsion struck by light (white background) hardens and remains fixed to the base of the film. The portion of the emulsion that is not affected by light is removed, thus creating a visible image. The developed emulsion has a blackness or density that is proportional to the amount of light it received. Thus the portion of the document that is white will be shown on the film as black, and the portion that is black will be clear or, when light passes through, white. This is called a *negative image*.

The emulsion side of camera film is easily recognized. On undeveloped film, the emulsion has a grayish color and is wound toward the core of the reel. When the film is developed, the emulsion side will have a dull black finish, and if the image is viewed from the emulsion side, it will appear as a mirror image, that is, in reverse. The base side of the raw film is black, and when the film is developed it has a glossy finish. It is necessary to recognize the base and emulsion sides in order to properly load film for display and for contact printing.

The most common film widths used today in microfilming are 16 millimeters (16 mm), 35 mm, and 105 mm. Film thickness varies from a minimum of 2.5 mils (.0025 inch) to 7 mils, with 5 mils (.005 inch) being the most common. However, thin film, which is 2.5 mils, is becoming very popular because of its high packing density. Film is packaged in rolls of 100- and 200-foot lengths for conventional cameras, and the standard reel for processed microfilm will hold 100 feet of 5-mil film or approximately 200 feet of 2.5-mil film.

The 16-mm film is mainly used for small documents. The size usually used for engineering drawings, large maps, newspapers, and the like is 35-mm microfilm; 105-mm film is sometimes used for extremely large engineering drawings or when the high reductions required of 35-mm film are not possible. Film of 105-mm width is also used for microfiche created for small source documents and for computer-output microfilm (COM) to be discussed later. Systems requirements generally dictate the size of film to be used.

Another type of camera film is called *dry silver film* because no wet chemistry is used in its processing (development). The chemical properties needed for development are contained in the emulsion and are activated by a heat process. This type of film can be used only with source document cameras and COM recorders specifically designed for this film. Its advantages are convenience, elimination of a separate development machine, and immediate processing of the image.

Copy Film

Copy films, which are sometimes referred to as *print films,* are used to make duplicates of the processed camera films. Copy film can be *sign-maintaining* (the background is the same as that of the original) or *sign-reversing* (the background is the reverse of that of the original). Films with these characteristics are also referred to as *nonreversal* and *reversal* films. This duplication is done through *contact printing* utilizing various specialized duplicating machines, some highly automated and high-speed and others almost entirely manual. These *duplicators* are designed to duplicate one particular microform exclusively. In general, the emulsions of the copy film and the camera film are placed in contact and exposed to a light source. The copy film is then developed according to its peculiar specifications. The most common types of copy film used are *diazo, vesicular,* and *silver.*

Diazo Film. *Diazo film* is a nonsilver film used exclusively for contact printing. When processed, it has a blue, blue-black, or black appearance,

depending on the color of the dye incorporated into the coating. It derives its name from the diazonium salts which, together with a dye, make up the light-sensitive coating on the triacetate or polyester base. During exposure, ultraviolet light passes through the clear lines of the original negative image and strikes the diazo coating forming a negative image on the diazo film, thus maintaining the same sign (nonreversal) as the original film. The latent image is developed by exposing the diazo film to ammonia vapors in a development chamber of the duplicating machine. There are aperture card duplicators, sheet film duplicators for microfiche, and roll-to-roll duplicators.

Some diazo duplicators using anhydrous ammonia require outside venting for ammonia fumes and others are designed with an ammonia absorber system, which does not require outside venting. Even so, according to Xidex Corporation, a leading manufacturer of diazo film, the room used to duplicate should be well vented. With proper installation, vented or nonvented duplicators should exhibit very low ammonia levels—below 10 PPM (10 parts per million). Individuals with a normal sense of smell can detect ammonia levels of less than 10 PPM. Levels higher than 20 PPM not only are easily detected but will cause some level of discomfort. The OSHA (Occupational Safety and Health Act) limit for ammonia in the workplace is 50 PPM, well over the early warning threshold of less than 10 PPM. So when diazo film is treated with proper respect, there should be no fear of its use.[1]

For ecological and health reasons, diazo film that can be processed without ammonia gas or liquids has been developed and is available. The properties needed for development are incorporated in the film and are released through heat application, thus eliminating the problem of ammonia fumes. Processing of this type of diazo film is slower than the standard ammonia type, and a specially designed duplicator must be used.

Vesicular Film. Sometimes called *thermal film, vesicular film* is developed by a heat process. Like diazo film, it is available in the same widths as camera film. In appearance, when exposed and developed, it does not look like other microfilm because it usually has a green, beige, or light blue color. It is a reversal film: A positive original produces a negative vesicular copy.

Vesicular film is used extensively with COM because of its reversal capabilities and its simplicity. Though vesicular film can be used with source document film, it is generally not considered as effective as diazo or silver print film for these two reasons: Many find that vesicular film does not have the range needed to duplicate the wide variety of contrast found in source document film, and it reverses the normal negative image of source document film. Vesicular film, like diazo film, is a slow film and is most sensitive to ultraviolet light. Thus, it can be subjected to ordinary room light during development without adverse effects.

Silver Print Film. *Silver print film* is available in the same widths as original camera film. There are two types of direct silver print film. One is a reversal film, which produces positive copy from a negative original or vice versa. The other type is a nonreversal, or sign-maintaining, film.

The duplication process must be done under darkroom conditions. The printer is a simple exposing device around which the original and the print film wind, make contact, are exposed, and rewind onto take-up reels. The exposure setting, which is determined by a series of exposures at various settings called a *step test*, must be made prior to using the machine. A step test is normally required only once and is valid for all film having the same background density. However, exposure may be adjusted by the operator to reproduce film that does not meet the established standards for density. After exposure, the film is developed in the same manner as camera film. Silver print film costs more than other duplicating film and requires liquid chemical processing and darkroom work, so it is not widely used. Its chief advantage is a slight margin of improved quality in duplicating low-contrast images.

Image Quality

Image quality is extremely important in micrographic systems because the user of the microfilm image rightly expects to be able to read the microfilm with the same ease that can be enjoyed with the original document. The high ratios of image-size reduction to magnification on paper or projection screen cause any flaw in a film image to be magnified perhaps as much as 40 times its film size. These flaws can result from an aberration in the camera lens, vibrations in the camera, damaged or spotted film, overdevelopment or underdevelopment of the film, overexposure or underexposure, slippage, and other problems. If these flaws are discovered in time, some corrective action, such as refilming, can be taken. Early discovery also permits early correction, which can avoid future flaws. Two major quality checks should be made routinely as a part of the filming process: resolution test and lighting and density test.

Resolution. *Resolution* is the measure of the sharpness of the characters of the image on the film. The test to determine the quality of resolution is partially subjective. It involves photographing a test chart that consists of various patterns to which numeric values have been assigned. The most common test chart is the National Bureau of Standards (now known as the U.S. National Institute of Standards and Technology) Resolution Test Chart 1010 (see Figure 10.1). This chart consists of 26 patterns of decreasing size. The numeric value assigned to the largest size is 1.0, with a higher value assigned to each successively smaller pattern. Each pattern consists of five parallel horizontal and five parallel vertical lines that form 90° angles. The pattern on the film is viewed under a 50× or 60× high-quality microscope to determine the smallest pattern that can be recognized.

Recognition is the subjective part of the test. One method is to count the lines in both the horizontal and vertical portions of the pattern. If all lines in a pattern are clear enough to be counted, the image is recognizable. Beginning with a pat-

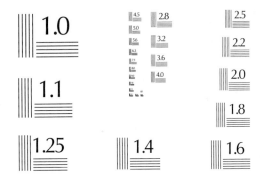

FIGURE 10.1 Resolution Test Chart 1010 (Courtesy of U.S. National Institute of Standards and Technology)

tern that can be recognized, smaller patterns should be viewed in sequence until the smallest recognizable pattern is determined. The numeric value assigned to that pattern is said to be the resolution of the film.

Standards of resolution are usually stated in terms of lines per millimeter. The lines per millimeter can be determined by multiplying the resolution pattern number by the reduction ratio used in filming. Thus, if an image is reduced 30 times from its original size (reduction ratio) and the resolution pattern number is 4.5, the lines per millimeter measure is 135. If the standard is 120 lines per millimeter, then numbers above that—e.g.,135—indicate a better resolution than the standard. It is not satisfactory to simply state the standard as 4.5 unless the reduction ratio is always the same. By incorporating the reduction ratio into the formula, the lines per millimeter standard is valid regardless of the reduction ratio used in filming.

Lighting and Density. On negative-appearing film, the blackness of the film background depends on the amount of light reflected from the document (see Figure 10.2). The black background is measured by a *densitometer*, which mea-

FIGURE 10.2 Film Density

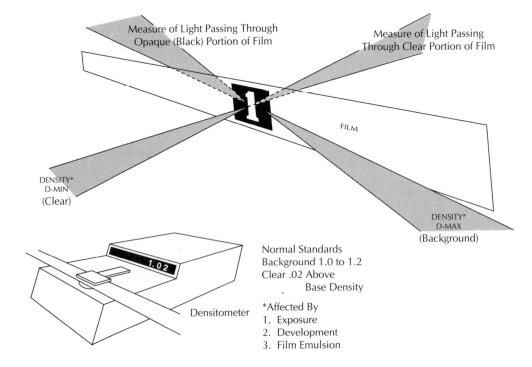

sures the amount of light transmitted through the background. The measurement, which is stated in numbers, is called *background density*. This density forms the contrast between the background and the clear lines of the image. If the film is underexposed, the density reading will fall below the set standard, which is usually 1.0 to 1.2. If it is overexposed, the density reading will be numerically higher than the standard. Different textures and colors of the document require different lighting because their reflective capabilities vary. Hence, lighting must be adjusted either manually or automatically during the filming process to provide optimum density.

The density of the clear portion of the film is referred to as D-Min, and the density of the black portion of the film is called D-Max. The D-Min density is measured most often in checking the contrast of positive-appearing COM film, which normally has a clear rather than a black background. Contrast usually describes a quality of the subject of the film image, such as the document. If the subject has high contrast, the film can have a density higher than the standard of 1.2 and have very good readability. On the other hand, a low-contrast subject, such as a carbon copy of a letter on pink paper, would be more readable on film with a density of less than the standard of 1.0. Thus the standard density that is considered optimum is not always the best density for every image.

The type of reader-printer can also be a factor in determining the proper density of the film, and this should be considered both in reader-printer selection and in establishing in-house specifications for a particular application. This type of specification should be determined by a step test prior to implementation.

Reduction and Magnification Ratios

A *reduction ratio* is the size of the film image compared to the original document (see Figure 10.3). A reduction of 24:1 (spoken as "twenty-four to one" or simply "24"), for example, means that the image on the film is 1/24 the size of the original document. It follows then that more document images can be captured on a reel of film when a high reduction ratio is used than when a low reduction ratio is used. The size of the document, the size and clarity of the characters on the document, and the screen size and magnification of the reader often influence if not dictate the reduction ratio used. For example, if the character sizes are 1/8 inch and the document is filmed at 30×, but magnified back on the reader at 15×, the size of the character on the reader screen will only be 1/16 inch, perhaps too small to be read. Table 10.1 shows common document sizes and the reductions frequently used.

Most small-document cameras have fixed reduction ratios or perhaps a selection of two, while large-document flatbed (*planetary*) cameras have variable reductions from 16× to 36×. The magnification lens on a reader can be either fixed or variable. (These cameras and readers and their operation are discussed later in this chapter.) Reduction ratios from 150× to 400× or more have been used for catalogs and books. These ultrahigh reductions are used with the microfiche format and are referred to as *ultrafiche*. One 4- by 6-inch ultrafiche can contain more than 4,000 pages of data. Ultrafiche can only be produced under laboratory conditions and will probably be replaced with electronic imaging, discussed in Chapter 11.

Figure 10.4 provides formulas for calculating reduction and magnification ratios based on certain known and unknown factors. These formulas are helpful in specifying camera reduction and reader magnification or print-size output.

Document Image Orientation

Document image orientation, or *mode*, is the manner in which the document image is positioned on the film. Modes are described as being either *cine* or *comic* and either *duplex* or *duo*. (See Figure 10.5.)

The *cine mode* takes it's name from cinema film. In this mode the horizontal lines of the film

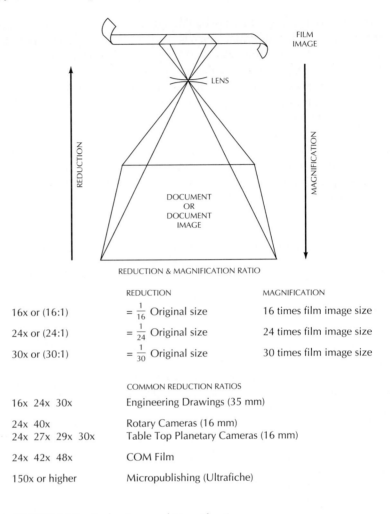

FILM IMAGE

LENS

REDUCTION

MAGNIFICATION

DOCUMENT OR DOCUMENT IMAGE

REDUCTION & MAGNIFICATION RATIO

	REDUCTION	MAGNIFICATION
16x or (16:1)	$= \frac{1}{16}$ Original size	16 times film image size
24x or (24:1)	$= \frac{1}{24}$ Original size	24 times film image size
30x or (30:1)	$= \frac{1}{30}$ Original size	30 times film image size

COMMON REDUCTION RATIOS

16x 24x 30x	Engineering Drawings (35 mm)
24x 40x	Rotary Cameras (16 mm)
24x 27x 29x 30x	Table Top Planetary Cameras (16 mm)
24x 42x 48x	COM Film
150x or higher	Micropublishing (Ultrafiche)

FIGURE 10.3 Reductions and Magnifications

run across the width of the film. This mode is also frequently called the *portrait mode.*

The *comic mode* takes its name from the manner in which the frames of comic strips are placed. In this method, the horizontal lines of the image run the length of the film. This mode is also frequently called the *landscape mode.*

The *duplex mode* images both sides of the document simultaneously, side by side. This type of imaging method is performed using a rotary type microfilm camera. The 16-mm film is wide enough to accommodate the images of two 8 1/2-inch wide cine documents when a 32 × or higher reduction is used. This method is commonly used to image checks, because the endorsements as well as the face of the check can be displayed.

The *duo mode* also places the front-side images of cine documents side by side on the film. This method masks one side of the film while imaging the other. When the entire length of the

TABLE 10.1   Common Document Sizes and Reductions

16-MM NONPERFORATED FILM	
Size	*Reduction*
8 ¹/₂ × 11 in. (A size)	24×
8 ¹/₂ × 15 in.	27×
11 × 17 in. (B size)	29×

35-MM NONPERFORATED FILM	
Size	*Reduction*
18 × 24 in. (C size)	16×
24 × 36 in. (D size)	24×
36 × 48 in. (E size)	30×

film has been exposed on one side, the reels are reversed in the camera unit and the other side is exposed from the opposite end. Stated simply, the images run up one half of the film and back down the other half. As in the case of duplex, the reduction ratio must be increased to place two images side by side on the film. The purpose of this method is to allow the use of high reduction ratios while fully utilizing the film to increase the number of documents that can be imaged on one standard reel or cartridge. As with duplex images, a rotary camera equipped with this feature is required.

MICROFORMS

Microform is a generic term for any form, either film or paper, that contains microimages.[2] The major microforms used today are of two types: roll film, consisting of open reels, cassettes, and cartridges, and unitized microforms, consisting of aperture cards, microfilm jackets, and microfiche (see Figure 10.6).

Roll Film

Roll film is the most economical and most frequently used microform. Roll film is suitable for low-reference, long-term-retention, sequentially ordered documents, as well as high-reference, randomly arranged documents that are retrieved by automated systems. Variations of the roll microform are the open reel, the cassette, and the cartridge, or magazine.

The *open reel* of 100 feet of 5-mil film or 200 feet of 2.5-mil film is widely used. It is usually stored in a cardboard or plastic carton that is labeled and filed. A full reel of 16-mm film (100 feet) can contain approximately 2,800 images of 8 1/2- by 11-inch documents filmed in the comic mode at a reduction of 24:1. A full reel of 35-mm film (100 feet) filmed with a fixed standard aperture of 1.75 inches will contain approximately 600 images or frames.

The *cassette* has the same film capacity as the open reel, but the supply reel containing the images and the take-up reel are contained in the same unit, just as in audiocassettes and videocassettes. Cassettes have never been widely used.

A. Original Size of Document
B. Desired Size of Reproduced Document
C. Reduction Ratio
M. Magnification
V. Viewer Image (Width by Height)

FORMULA TO DETERMINE M:

$$\frac{B}{A} \times \frac{C}{1} = M$$

(Example)

$$\frac{11}{22} \times \frac{10}{1} = \frac{110}{22} = 5$$

FORMULA TO DETERMINE B:

$$\frac{M}{C} \times \frac{A}{1} = B$$

(Example)

$$\frac{5}{10} \times \frac{22}{1} = \frac{110}{10} = 11$$

FORMULA TO DETERMINE C:

$$\frac{A}{B} \times \frac{M}{1} = C$$

(Example)

$$\frac{22}{11} \times \frac{5}{1} = \frac{110}{11} = 10$$

FORMULA TO DETERMINE A:

$$C \times \left(\frac{Vw(x)Vh}{M} \right) = A$$

(Example)

$$10 \times \left(\frac{5.5(x)11}{5} \right) =$$

$$10(1.1w(x)2.2h) = 11w\ (x)\ 22h$$

FIGURE 10.4 Magnification and Reduction Ratio Formulas

The *cartridge*, or *magazine*, contains only the imaged reel because the take-up reel or device is in the reader. Both cassettes and cartridges are used to facilitate threading the film in a viewer and also to protect the film.

Unitized Microforms

Unitization uses a single frame of microfilm or a series of related microfilm frames with the same independence and flexibility found with paper documents. This approach includes aperture cards, jackets, and card jackets.

Aperture Cards. *Aperture cards* combine the advantages of the tab card with the advantages of microfilm. Even though the tab card was eliminated over two decades ago in data processing operations, it is still used today as a convenient carrier for microfilm, particularly 35-mm images of engineering drawings and maps. *Aperture* is the name of the card because it has a rectangular opening (aperture) in which a strip or frame of microfilm is mounted. These cards can be keypunched and sorted on standard unit-record equipment; however, filing and retrieval are usually performed manually from the data specified at the top of the card.

FIGURE 10.5 Microfilm Image Orientations

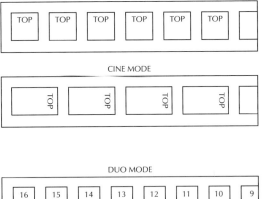

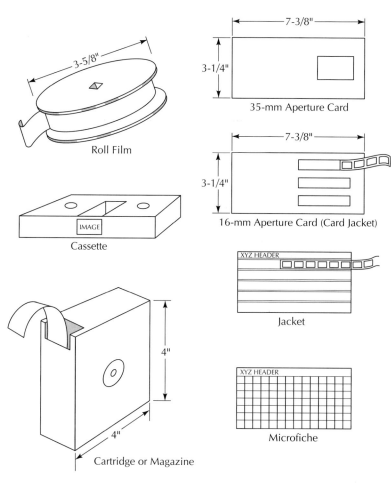

REEL MICROFORMS

UNITIZED MICROFORMS

Roll Film

Cassette

Cartridge or Magazine

35-mm Aperture Card

16-mm Aperture Card (Card Jacket)

Jacket

Microfiche

FIGURE 10.6 Microforms

The microfilm image of an engineering drawing mounted in an aperture card not only is much smaller than the original document, but also can be filed as a separate unit with an ease and uniformity not possible with the original drawing.

Although the aperture card is used most frequently for engineering drawings, it is also used for small-document filming. Therefore, aperture cards are designed not only for 35-mm microfilm but for 16-mm microfilm and a combination of these sizes. The 35-mm aperture card is used primarily for engineering drawings, and the 16-mm card for office-type documents.

The 35-mm aperture card has been standardized through U.S. Department of Defense requirements, and all cards are manufactured to meet exacting specifications. This standard card is known as the Military D (Mil D) aperture card.

A single frame of 35-mm microfilm is mounted in the aperture of the card, thus providing an inexpensive and efficient method of handling and using a single, separate frame of microfilm. The method of mounting 35-mm microfilm in an aperture card varies with the type of card used. There are four basic types of Mil D aperture cards, each having a distinct mounting system.

1. The *cold seal card* has a pressure-sensitive transparent tape that overlaps the edge of the aperture to which the frame of film is mounted. A temporary, factory-installed protective sheet of glazed paper is placed over the adhesive until the film is mounted.

2. The *suspension-type card* has extremely thin sheets of optically clear polyester material mounted over the front and back of the aperture. The sheets are sealed on three sides of the rectangle. The microfilm is slipped into the pocket formed by the clear sheets from the unsealed end.

3. Another aperture card uses a heat-sensitive adhesive around the edges of the aperture to hold the frame of film in place. The edges of the aperture are recessed so that the frame of film may be mounted without adding significant thickness to the card.

4. The *diazo and vesicular copy cards* are identical in design to the type 1 or type 3 aperture card. The only difference is that the cards are furnished by the manufacturer with unexposed diazo or vesicular film mounted in them. The copy card is used to duplicate the microfilm mounted in another card or imaged on a roll.

The mounting of the microfilm in the 35-mm aperture card is performed by a mounter designed to cut and mount the film with precision and speed. The film is mounted so that when the card is viewed from the printed side, the top of the image is to the top or the left of the aperture and the data are right reading (nonmirror image). With a hand mounter, 200 to 400 cards can be mounted per hour, depending on the skill of the operator. Automatic mounters will provide much higher rates.

Identification data are usually first keypunched on a master data card rather than directly on the aperture card. The reason for this is that the aperture card is much more expensive than the standard punch card, and mistakes on the punch card are therefore less costly. The data are then transferred from the master data card to the aperture card by means of a reproducer or keypunch machine.

Card Jackets.   The 16-mm aperture card is referred to as a card jacket. While similar to the 35-mm aperture card, it is different in the size and number of apertures. It is designed to hold strips or a single frame of 16-mm microfilm. It can also hold a combination of 16-mm and 35-mm microfilm, and the apertures can be arranged to conform to the size of the Mil D aperture.

Film mounting is done by the suspension method used in the type 2 Mil D aperture card previously described. Although the width of the aperture corresponds to the width of the film, the length, number, and positions of the apertures will vary. The apertures are always parallel to one another but may run in either a horizontal or vertical direction. By means of a specially designed mounter (inserter), strips of 16-mm film are inserted into the pockets of the apertures (channels) and cut.

The purpose of the jacket is to group related microfilm frames, such as images of a student record, into one microform that can be used in the same fashion as a file folder. Frames of microfilm can be added as required, without damaging or replacing the card. A specially designed mounter is used to insert the frames into the card. The image of the frame about to be inserted can be viewed on a projection screen that is part of the mounter. Hand mounters equipped with an eyepiece magnifier are also available for in-file updating.

Microfilm Jackets.   Microfilm jackets are another unitized microform. The jacket consists of two very thin pieces of rectangular, optically clear polyester material sealed together on two sides to form a jacket or envelope. The jacket is subdivided into horizontal channels, either 16-mm or 35-mm wide, into which strips of microfilm are slipped from an open end. A file title can be typed or written on a tape strip across the top of the jacket. The jacket, which is available in various card sizes, is filed in the same manner as an index card. The most common size is 4 by 6 inches. Individual frames or strips of film can be added at any time. A machine similar to the one used for 16-mm aperture cards inserts the film into the jackets. These microforms are very popular because they allow the film to be handled in a manner similar to paper files. Most frequently, they are used for case files and project-type applications.

Microfiche.   *Microfiche* is very similar to the microfilm jacket in appearance and function. It is a piece of sheet film that contains as many as several hundred exposures, depending on the reduction used. The sizes of microfiche vary, but the most common are 4 by 6 inches and tab card size. Microfiche is used frequently for catalogs and large computer reports with wide distribution, pro-

viding savings in distribution costs, paper, and space.

Microfiche can be created in several ways. One way is to make a contact print of a microfilm jacket, using sheet diazo or vesicular film cut to the same size as the jacket. A second way is to use a step-and-repeat camera, which exposes each image successively on a sheet of silver film, perhaps in an updatable process, providing exact horizontal and vertical image alignment. A third way to create microfiche is to use a COM recorder, which generates microfiche directly from computer tape or disk. COM recorders and step-and-repeat cameras are discussed later in this chapter.

The microfiche has uniform rows and columns of images to aid in indexing. Rows are identified by letters of the alphabet and columns by number. For example, a particular frame can be identified by the grid coordinates F-12, meaning row F, column 12. When a microfiche is created by a COM recorder, the entire microfiche is often indexed automatically in a corner frame of the microfiche.

FIGURE 10.7   Rotary Camera
(Courtesy of Eastman Kodak Company)

ROTARY CAMERAS

High-volume records, particularly those that have a relatively short retention period, require a fast, efficient, and economical method of microfilming. The *rotary camera* is designed to serve this purpose, and it is used primarily to film the ordinary variety of office documents, such as checks, invoices, and sales slips.

Design Principle

The rotary camera consists of a film unit (camera) and a machine that transports and illuminates the documents during the filming process. The first type of rotary camera, still current on the market, is shown in Figure 10.7. The documents are fed into the machine and rotated (hence the name) out of the machine into a receiving tray. As the document is transported through the machine by means of belts, its image is reflected by several mirrors to the lens of the film unit (camera) within the machine. The film in the camera advances in the same direction and at the same relative rate of speed as the documents, creating the effect of a stationary image. As the end of the document passes through the photographic field, the camera shutter is tripped. Thus, documents may be of any practical length, although their width is restricted by the width of the input channel (frequently 12 inches). Lighting is provided by a bank of small lamps within the machine, which uniformly illuminates the document as it passes through the photographic field. Because the focal length of the lens and the distance from the document to the lens are fixed, the reduction ratio cannot be varied without changing the film unit.

A second type of rotary camera, recently introduced, operates very similarly to the first type, except that the document passes through the photographic field on a straight path rather than rotating. Thus it feeds from one side of the unit to the receiving tray on the opposite side of the machine. The straight path is said to reduce the jamming of documents as the documents do not have to rotate, causing the documents to bend in the process. (See Figure 10.8.)

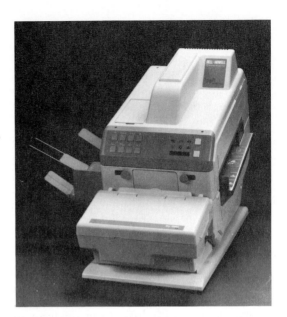

FIGURE 10.8   Microfilm Rotary Camera with Straight Path
(Courtesy of Bell & Howell Co.)

Filming Speeds

Although the paper passes through the machine at a rate of 9,000 feet or more per hour, the actual filming rate is determined by the skill of the operator and the condition of the documents. Ordinary letter-size documents of average condition and uniform thickness can be filmed at an effective rate of approximately 3,000 pages per hour by an experienced operator using an automatic feed. Hand feeding the same documents would reduce the filming rate to about 1,000 to 1,500 pages per hour, depending on the skill of the operator. The condition of the paper, including such elements as frayed edges, staples, nonuniform thickness, and a mixture of sizes, may make automatic feeding less productive and therefore not feasible.

Film Unit

The film unit contains the film, shutter, and lens, which determines the reduction ratio used. Common reduction ratios for rotary cameras are 24×, 32×, and 40×, but the most frequently used ratio is 24×. These reductions may vary a diameter or two between different manufacturers. The rotary camera generally uses 16-mm microfilm in reel lengths of 100 feet for 5-mil film and 215 feet for 2.5-mil film. Some older models can use 200-foot rolls of 5-mil film as well.

As with all microfilm cameras, the film unit is equipped with end-of-film warning devices and film footage indicators. When the camera is loaded or unloaded, the film is advanced to avoid fogging of the images, so that daylight loading (subdued light) is possible. Some models provide for cassette-type loading and unloading. This not only provides light protection and simplifies loading but also allows for the assignment of a cassette to a particular department or project, providing for add-on filming for multiple departments using the same camera.

Lighting Controls

To achieve optimum background density, the amount of light should vary with both the reflective property of the document and with the relative speed of the film. It is quite common for office documents to have a wide range of colors, each having different reflective properties, thus requiring lighting controls on the rotary camera. These controls may be automatic or manual, the latter being set by the operator or service technician.

Automatic exposure controls are without question the most efficient and are on most modern microfilm cameras. Just before the document enters the photographic field a light meter scans the document and automatically adjusts the voltage so that the light intensity is best for that document as it is being photographed.

Automatic Feed Mechanisms

The automatic feed mechanism inserts one sheet of paper at a time into the intake opening of the camera by means of a friction wheel. This feeding

is done very rapidly and with minimal operator assistance compared to hand feeding. Hand feeding, while sometimes necessary because of the condition of the documents, requires the operator to place each document into the intake opening of the machine, where it is fed through by wheel and belt traction. The automatic feed mechanism works well with documents of uniform thickness and size, such as checks. But photographing less uniform documents requires operator skill and attention and results in a slower filming rate. With automatic feed and high-speed rotary cameras, 500 or more check-size documents can be filmed per minute.

Receiving Trays and Stackers

As the documents emerge from the rotary camera, they fall into a receiving tray. This tray is usually located directly above the input opening of the machine, or opposite the input opening if the camera is the straight-path type, as shown in Figure 10.8.

Heavier documents, and particularly those in good condition, will stack nicely in the order in which they were filmed. But flimsy documents or those of small or varying sizes may have a tendency to tumble, and stacking will not be entirely satisfactory. To prevent this, a stacking device is available for some cameras that ensures that the records will be stacked uniformly and in order. Having this stacking device or else a camera that does not tumble the documents is extremely important when the documents are not to be destroyed, such as bank checks.

Check Endorser

A check endorser is an optional accessory; it endorses checks as they are being filmed. This economy feature combines the endorsing procedure with the filming procedure.

Sequential Numbering Device

Another accessory available on some rotary cameras is a device that imprints a sequential number on the document as it enters the camera. After the documents are filmed, the document description (usually a number), the sequential number, and the roll number can be keyed into a computer database to provide a ready index to any document filmed. The advantage of this system is that the documents can be filmed in random order. If the data keyed to the database is *part of* other data input, required by normal processing, this indexing involves no extra data entry, except the sequential number, and even this *could be* automated. The image search is then made of the film by sequential number. A blip system, or image-count device, would enhance retrieval even more.

Image-Count Device

An image-count device (often referred to as a *blip system*) places a square mark below each frame of microfilm. When the film is used on an image-count roll-film reader, the image number is keyed into the reader, and the blips, or square marks, are counted as the film traverses. This system, coupled with the sequential numbering device, provides random input and access through an external index showing the roll and image number. Some cameras image three different sizes of blips, or squares, under the document images, which provides a three-level search of the book-chapter-verse variety. Automatic retrieval of document microfilm images begins with the filming and usually the rotary camera.

THE ENGINEERING PLANETARY CAMERA

Although the term *planetary* can be correctly applied to any overhead flatbed camera, it is usually understood to refer to a large camera used primarily to microfilm engineering drawings and other large documents. Because of the exacting standards required of engineering drawings, the camera is designed with the best precision optics and focusing arrangements possible.

The camera machine consists of a large rectangular table, a column that supports the film unit

(camera) overhead, overhead lights, and an exposure and control panel.

General Principle

Unlike the rotary camera, both the microfilm and the document must remain perfectly stationary during the planetary camera exposure. These cameras have variable reductions, which are increased by elevating the film unit and decreased by lowering it. As the reduction increases, the photographic field increases; and as the reduction decreases, so does the size of the photographic field. The *photographic field* is that area of the camera table (and the document on it) that will be captured on the film.

The document to be filmed is laid flat on the camera table (known as the *copy board)* and is illuminated by a set of flood lamps mounted on each end of the table. The amount of light required is registered through a light meter, and the light intensity is adjusted accordingly.

This type of camera usually uses 35-mm microfilm, but a few are designed for 70-mm and 105-mm microfilm. The film image, as a part of a 35-mm roll, is approximately 1.25 by 1.75 inches. The standard, or traditional, planetary camera provides a roll of latent images on 35-mm film that is processed separately and mounted into aperture cards. However, a processor planetary camera (see Figure 10.9) produces an imaged frame of 35-mm microfilm, mounted in an aperture card, *completely processed and ready to use.*

Film Unit

The film unit of the ordinary planetary camera is sometimes referred to as the camera or camera head. This component is mounted on a rigid column and is centered directly over the copy board. The basic components of the film unit are the lens, the film transport system, the film aperture, the platen, and the shutter. Of course, like any photographic camera, the film unit also contains the film.

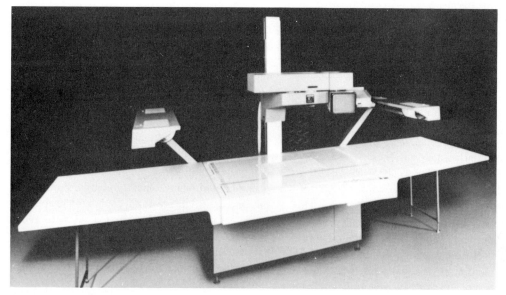

FIGURE 10.9 Processor Camera
(Courtesy of 3M Company)

Copy Board and Lighting

The *copy board* is a rectangular table measuring a little over 5 feet in length and 4 feet in width. Because large documents measuring up to 45 by 63 inches are laid on the copy board for microfilming, securing devices are needed to prevent rolling or curling. Some cameras are equipped with a vacuum system that holds the copy tightly to the board, removing wrinkles and curls. If a built-in hold-down device is not used, hold-down bars of some type are necessary to hold the rolled or large documents flat on the copy board.

On occasion, it is necessary or desirable to illuminate the document from underneath as well as from above. This type of lighting is called *backlighting*. When backlighting is used, the surface of the copy board must be made of a translucent opal glass or plastic, together with subsurface illumination. Normally, backlighting is used in combination with toplighting, when data are printed on the reverse side of a drawing, which is the practice of some companies. Backlighting is also used to improve line-image quality.

The toplighting is provided by a bank of incandescent or fluorescent lights mounted on each end of the camera above the copy board. It is essential that the copy board be evenly lighted to provide uniform image density. There should be no overhead lights that could cast shadows or cause other unevenness. In the more recent models, the light intensity is automatically controlled by a light meter and voltage control system.

Reduction Ratios

The reduction ratio is achieved by raising or lowering the film unit. As the film unit is moved, the lens is automatically adjusted to the reduction. The range of reductions varies from model to model, but a range of 12× to 36× is common. The most frequently used reduction ratios in engineering drawing work are 16×, 24×, and 30×.

The selection of the reduction ratio will depend on the size of the document and the size of the letters on the document. Table 10.2 shows maximum document size for reduction ratios.

Camera Operation

The document should not only be flat but also be centered on the copy board, with the edge of the

TABLE 10.2 Maximum Document Size for Reduction Ratios

Reduction	Document Size*
16 ×	19 × 26 in.
24 ×	28 × 39 in.
30 ×	36 × 48 in.

*Many standards call for maximum sizes of 18 by 24 inches, 24 by 36 inches, and 34 by 44 inches, respectively, to allow tolerances for printout equipment and paper.

document parallel to the edge of the table. This can be accomplished by centering devices provided with the camera or by using a centering rule system laid out on the copy board. A centering rule is divided into two equal parts, with zero at the center mark. The rule is scaled in inches from the center. For example, a 20-inch document would be centered if both the left and right ends rested on the 10-inch marks to the left and right of the center mark. The same system can be applied to the ends of the copy board for centering by depth. Proper alignment of the document on the copy board is important so that the image can be mounted parallel to the edges of the aperture in the aperture card, and for uniform display and print.

The document should be placed on the copy board so that its long dimension parallels the long dimension of the copy board and the top of the document is to the rear of the camera. An exception to this is letter-size documents, which may be placed in the opposite (vertical) position.

When documents are too long or too wide for the copy board, they are filmed in sections, with about a 2-inch overlap. This is called *sectionalizing*. Sectionalizing is used frequently in microfilming engineering drawings. With this method, each frame or section is identified with a code, such as F-1 or F-2. To be readable, the code should be half an inch high. Most standards also require the drawing number to be on each frame. (See Figure 10.10.)

The aperture card is the carrier of the processed image. The drawing number and frame number, or card number at least, must be printed on the top edge of the card in a uniform fashion, so that it can be manually filed. The index to this system can be computer-generated using either a mainframe system or a PC, to provide access by selected parameters. However, if the system is already designed for manual filing of the card without a computer index, it may be desirable to retain that system, which arranges the cards in drawing number order. In this case, the index data can be keyed directly from the film before it is cut and mounted, using blank tab cards. From these tab cards, the data are duplicated onto the aperture cards before the film is mounted, so as to avoid possible damage to or miskeying of the film-mounted aperture cards. After mounting is complete, the image can then be displayed on an aperture card or microfiche reader and may be printed on paper using an aperture card printer.

Processor Engineering Camera

Processor camera technology is well suited to the microfilming of engineering drawings. The camera differs primarily from the standard planetary engineering camera in that a completely developed, archival quality, ready-to-use microfilm image, mounted in a 35-mm Mil D aperture card, is filmed and processed at a rated speed of 150 cards per hour. This processing is accomplished by an internal chemical processing system, located in the camera module, consisting of development, fixing, and washing. The aperture cards containing unexposed, premounted film come packaged in a daylight load cartridge of 250 cards. The camera also has an optional roll-film attachment for systems that require that microform rather than the aperture card.

The processor camera is particularly suitable when almost instant turnaround is required or desirable. It eliminates separate processing and card mounting, and interfaces well with electronic imaging, which is discussed in Chapter 11. The camera has most of the features found on the standard planetary camera. The indexing system[3] previ-

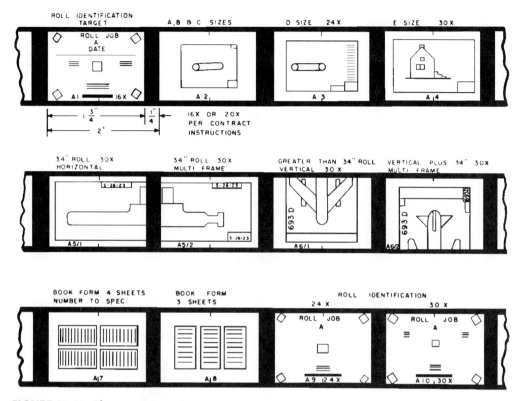

FIGURE 10.10 Planetary Image Orientation. (Top) Average–Size Documents; (Center) Sectionalizing Method Used for Oversize Documents; (Bottom) Placement of Multiple Sheets (Courtesy of U.S. Department of Defense)

ously alluded to allows indexing to be performed at the camera, turning processor cameras into *titling* cameras.

OTHER FLATBED CAMERAS

The engineering planetary camera is only one of several types of cameras that operate on the same principle. Other cameras are the small-document planetary camera, the step-and-repeat microfiche camera, and the updatable microfiche camera.

Small-Document Planetary Camera

The *small-document planetary camera,* also called a *table model planetary,* is often a miniaturized model of the large engineering planetary camera.

Using 16-mm film, it is designed with various features such as variable reductions, automatic exposure controls, blip marks, bar code readers, and with some models, automatic document feed. Figure 10.11 shows a typical modern small document planetary camera.

The photographic field is commensurate with its reduction capability. Those cameras having a reduction of 29× are capable of filming documents up to 11 by 17 inches, using 16-mm film. Lower reductions result in smaller photographic fields.

The small planetary is used to film documents that cannot be satisfactorily microfilmed on rotary cameras, such as files that are fastened by a brad, bound books, or booklets. It is also used for microfilm jacket work and microfiche work

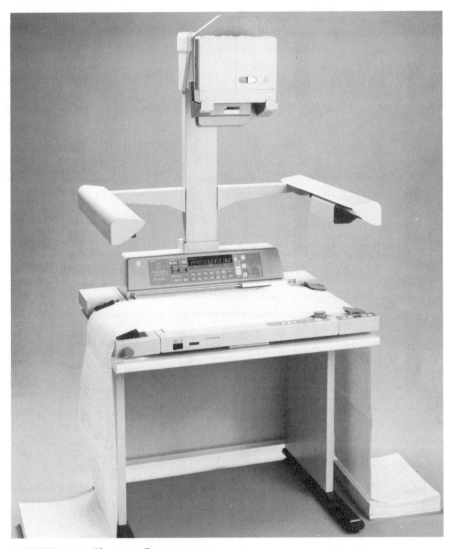

FIGURE 10.11 Planetary Camera
(Courtesy of Minolta Corporation)

because the comic, or portrait, mode cannot be obtained on the rotary camera if the document is over 11 inches long. Filming rates of 600 to 1,000 documents per hour are not unusual with manually positioned documents, and rates of as much as 2,700 documents an hour can be obtained with automatic feeders, which are available on some models. With an automatic feeder, it is possible to automatically film both sides of a document without manual intervention. Most table model planetary cameras have the ability to encode document marks (blips) and may be interfaced with a PC to permit efficient image capture and indexing for CAR (computer-assisted retrieval) systems, which will be discussed later in this chapter. The Minolta DAR 2800 camera not only automatically feeds documents, it has a bar code reader to read bar codes printed on letter-size targets. The bar codes control camera functions such as *space, double-sided filming*, and *blip mark*. These targets are interleaved with the documents prior to filming.

Step-and-Repeat Microfiche Camera

Microfiche can be created by filming the source document on 16-mm or 35-mm film and inserting the film in a jacket or stripping it in parallel rows to make a master microfiche from which sheet film copies can be made. A more precise and simple method, however, is to use a *step-and-repeat camera* (see Figure 10.12).

This camera is basically a flatbed camera with the film unit overhead and the document held stationary as it is imaged. But the similarity to other planetary cameras ends there. The camera is designed so that the images are exposed in uniform rows and columns on a sheet of 105-mm film. Usually, each camera has a set reduction ratio, but multiple reduction ratios are available.

The film units are programmed to provide precise alignment of the images according to established standards of rows and columns. The placement of the images on the microfiche is accomplished by a programmed movement of the film over a stationary aperture as a platen holds the film in place during exposure.

Some step-and-repeat microfiche cameras develop the film internally using either the same technology as the processor camera or a dry-process thermal (heat) development. In these processes, the entire microfiche is developed and can no longer be changed, modified, updated, or deleted.

Updatable Microfiche Camera

Another type of step-and-repeat camera uses a nontraditional imaging process to create an updatable microfiche. This process permits an image to be added to the microfiche at any time, and also allows for changing or deleting images previ-

FIGURE 10.12 Step-and-Repeat Dry Process Camera (Courtesy of 3M Company)

ously recorded. This camera, called a *record processor* by the manufacturers, uses a process called *transparent electrophotography (TEP)*. The process uses a clear proprietary polyester-type material with a photoconductive layer coating as its film. The microimages are created by a toner and are electrostatically fused to the clear base material, which is photosensitized in the record processor.

The master fiche, which has a positive polarity, is filed near the camera in a protective envelope. When additions or changes must be made, the master fiche is removed from the envelope and inserted in the camera. After the imaging operation, it is refiled in the protective envelope.

Personnel who use the fiche receive diazo or vesicular duplicates and discard them after use, rather than refiling them. Primarily, the copy procedure is followed to protect the original, but labor savings and file integrity and controls are side benefits. In evaluating this system, the total process speed should be considered because it affects the number of cameras and operations needed and may be the source of potential bottlenecks. Archival quality and the legal acceptance of this form of micrographics should be investigated for each proposed use.

FILM PROCESSING

When an organization does considerable microfilm work or when there are short turnaround requirements, it is sometimes advisable to develop or process the microfilm in-plant. Although gross savings of $1 to $2 per roll can be realized, the cost of the equipment, the cost of labor, the cost of chemicals, and the availability of trained personnel must be weighed against the added cost of commercial processing.

Processor

The machine used to develop microfilm is called a *processor*. There are several types of noncom-

mercial processors on the market, and all of them process film to archival quality standards. These processors are relatively simple to operate and generally do not require a darkroom. They develop 16-mm or 35-mm microfilm at a rate of 5 to 10 feet or more per minute. Some models will also accept 70-mm and 105-mm microfilm.

There are three types of processors (see Figure 10.13). In a *deep tank processor*, the film is supported by bottom and top rollers and is pulled through the chemicals by a lead in a serpentine path. A *roller transport processor* also moves the film in a serpentine path, but the film is transported by many rollers. The third type moves the film in a *straight path* through the solutions and wash by means of rollers. The type of processor will dictate the length of film lead required, if any, processing speed, and wash time.

Most processors are operated in daylight, but the exposed film is protected either by a canister

FIGURE 10.13 Types of Processors

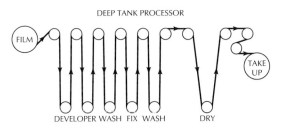

DEEP TANK PROCESSOR

FILM · TAKE UP

DEVELOPER   WASH   FIX   WASH   DRY

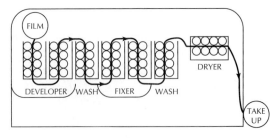

ROLLER TRANSPORT (EK PROSTAR TYPE)

FILM · DRYER · TAKE UP

DEVELOPER   WASH   FIXER   WASH

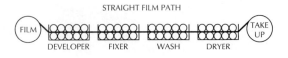

STRAIGHT FILM PATH

FILM · TAKE UP

DEVELOPER   FIXER   WASH   DRYER

outside the processor or by a processor cover or lid, if the film reel is placed inside the processor. (See Figure 10.14.) After the film is threaded into the processor, it passes through a developer solution, a stop bath, a fixing solution, a washing process, and a dryer, and finally emerges from the machine and winds onto another reel. Some processors also have additional bleaching tanks for full or partial reversal processing. Reversal processing changes what would normally be a negative image to a positive image and is used primarily when copies will be created by using sign-maintaining diazo film.

The processor must also have a temperature-controlled water supply and drain. Water flows constantly into the machine, circulates, and drains out through a standpipe or overflow system.

Development

The factors affecting development of the film are the temperature of the developer, the length of time the film is in the solution (called *dwell time*),

FIGURE 10.14 Kodak Prostar I Processor (Courtesy of Eastman Kodak Co.)

the condition of the developer, and the agitation of the film. The higher the temperature of the developer, the less time the film is required to be in the solution. Either higher-than-required temperatures of the developer or a slower transport speed will increase development and may overdevelop the film. Overdevelopment is generally characterized by a higher-than-standard background density.

When the film is transported through the developer at a fixed rate of speed, there is little that can be done about controlling the length of time the film is in the developer. Therefore, if the rate of speed is fixed, the only other way of controlling the development is to control the temperature of the developer so as to prevent overdevelopment or underdevelopment.

With use, the developer becomes less effective; therefore, it must be replaced as recommended by the manufacturer and replenished as necessary. Agitation of the film is provided automatically as the film is transported through the machine. As soon as the film leaves the developer, it is submerged in a fixing (or hypo) solution, which stops the development action and hardens the emulsion. The hypo dissolves the unused silver bromine that was not reduced to metallic silver during processing. This silver can be reclaimed from the used hypo and sold. After fixing, the film is washed and dried.

READERS

Ultimately, the acceptance of microfilm depends on the design and quality of the *reader* used to view the film. A reader must have an excellent illumination system and good optics and provide fast access to the image required. If it lacks any of these, the user will not be completely satisfied. Microfilm readers come in many different sizes, designs, and shapes. Outwardly, they most resemble a video display terminal or monitor used with personal computers or perhaps a television screen. However, they are designed to display only still images previously captured on film.

General Design Principles

A microfilm reader is in a way similar to a slide projector used in regular photography. An essential part of the microfilm system, readers are the equipment that enlarges the microimage on the film with great clarity so that the tiny characters can be easily read. The reader, or *viewer* as it is sometimes called, has an optical system similar to that of most projectors. It includes a lamp, a reflector, a condenser, a lens, and usually a mirror or two to direct and invert the projected image. But unlike the photographic projector, the microfilm reader has a self-contained screen in the unit.

Readers project the image from either the rear of the screen or the front of the screen (see Figure 10.15), with the rear-projection system being the most common. The front-projection readers have an opaque screen, whereas the rear-projection readers have a translucent, frosted screen. Within these two categories, there are many specific types or designs. The earliest type—and one that is still very common—is the roll-film reader. Other types of readers are microfiche, aperture card, and portable (so-called briefcase) readers. Also, there is another class that could be called hand-held readers, which ranges in size from very small to book-size.

Projection of the microfilm image is accomplished by a light beam that is directed through condensers to the film and through the lens (which magnifies and projects the image) to a mirror. The mirror in turn reflects the image back to the viewing screen. Some readers can rotate the image on the screen as much as 360 degrees, usually by use of an optical prism but sometimes just with a rotating microform carrier. This feature, known as *image rotation,* is useful for precise print alignment or for ease of reading if the image is skewed on the film.

The size of the reader screen and the size of the image depend on the magnification powers of the lens and the length of the optical path. The magnification of the reader should correspond to the reduction of the image on the film, if an original-size image is required. An image filmed at

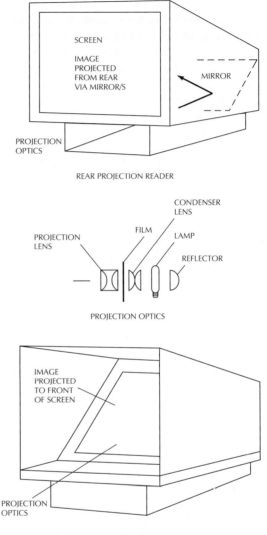

FIGURE 10.15 Reader Projection Systems

24× reduction will be shown in its original dimensions on the reader screen if it is magnified at 24×. If, on the other hand, it was filmed at 30× reduction and magnified on the reader screen at 15×, the image will be half size, and so on. Some readers have a zoom lens; the user can change the magnification of the lens by adjusting it with a dial. Others have a dual-lens system; they contain more than one lens, each having a different magnification. If the viewing screen is not large enough for the magnification, the entire image cannot be seen at one time, unless it is scanned by moving the film carriage. Magnification and reduction ratios take on an added importance when paper prints are made from the projected image, as the printed image may be larger than the paper if the correct ratio is not selected.

Types of Readers

The reader must be selected on the basis of the microform that is to be used. Some readers will accept more than one microform, but generally there are separate types of readers for microfiche or microjackets, aperture cards, and roll film. All operate on the same basic optical system but differ in the microform carriage mechanism.

Roll-Film Readers. Open-reel readers have spindles for the supply reel and the take-up reel. The film is wound from the supply reel and is threaded through glass flats over the lens and onto the take-up reel. The reels are rotated by motor or crank to move the images across the lens and the screen. Motorized readers are common and greatly facilitate retrieval. The speed of film movements with motorized readers is variable and can be adjusted by the operator from a very high speed to a very slow, page-by-page movement (see Figure 10.16).

Cartridge Readers. Cartridge-loaded readers automatically thread the film; they are always motorized and are generally considered the most efficient. However, the cost of the reader and the cartridges probably would not be justified if the reader is used on a low-reference basis.

Cassette Readers. The cassette-loaded roll-film reader is similar to the cartridge type. The cassette has both the supply reel and take-up reel encased in a plastic container with an aperture through which the film image is projected. The spindles on the reader connect with the reels in the cas-

FIGURE 10.16 Roll Form Reader–Printer (Courtesy of Eastman Kodak Co.)

sette, which move the film. One major advantage of the cassette is that the film need not be rewound to remove it from the reader. Cassette-loaded readers are not widely used.

Roll-film-type readers are best suited for CAR systems to be discussed later in this chapter.

Microfiche Readers. Microfiche readers are distinguishable from other microform readers by the film carriage. The carriage consists of two glass flats between which the microfiche or microjacket is placed. The carriage moves on a plane in all directions over the light source. An XY-grid coordinate pattern identical to the page format of the fiche or jacket is placed adjacent to the film carriage. A pointer on the film carriage is moved to a chosen frame or page on the grid pattern. The counterpart frame or page on the fiche is then displayed on the screen. Microfiche viewers have many designs and sizes and are generally the least expensive of all readers. Microfiche readers are used most commonly with COM and also with all jacket systems. They can also be used with aperture cards if the carriage is large enough. (See Figure 10.17.)

FIGURE 10.17 Microfiche Reader–Printer (Courtesy of Eastman Kodak Co.)

Aperture Card Readers. The aperture card reader is similar to the microfiche reader, except that the glass flats into which the aperture card is placed are stationary, or nearly so, and the screen is generally larger with a lower magnification lens.

Most aperture card readers have magnifications of 15×, and the screen is most frequently 18 by 24 inches. However, some are equipped with a dual or zoom lens. The optical system is designed to project the entire film area of a Mil D aperture card, regardless of the film reduction. But in the case of desk model aperture card readers, the screen is usually much smaller and only a portion of the aperture card image can be seen. For viewing, the film carriage can be moved and the image scanned on the screen. The image can be rotated by changing the position of the aperture card.

Multiformat Readers. Since the basic difference between types of readers is in the film carrier system, it can be seen that interchangeable film carriers would make a reader serve all microformats. Interchangeable film carrier readers work reasonably well, but there is an inconvenience of changing carriers, if done very often.

The reader does provide the ability to upgrade and adapt, if the changing is done infrequently.

READER-PRINTERS

Essentially, the designs of the reader-printer and reader are about the same, except that the reader-printer can provide, at the press of a button, electrostatic plain paper prints of the image displayed on the viewing screen. These plain paper prints are made using the same technology employed in electrostatic copiers that are commonplace in today's office. Although the sizes of the reader and reader-printer are about the same for all types of microform readers, the units designed for aperture cards are somewhat larger and produce paper prints up to 18 by 24 inches and larger. (See Figure 10.18.) There are also machines that are just printers and are designed for high-volume printing of engineering drawings from aperture cards. These normally do not have a viewing screen. Older types of reader-printers use coated-paper electrostatic prints or dry silver paper prints, a photographic paper developed instantly by application of heat.

FIGURE 10.18 Aperture Card Reader–Printer (Courtesy of Minolta Corp.)

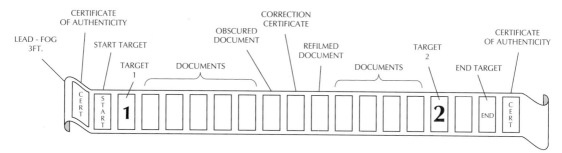

FIGURE 10.19 Certifications and Targets on a Strip of Microfilm

CERTIFICATIONS AND TARGETS

Generally, roll-film microfilming involves inserting certifications and guides, called *targets*, within each roll for identification and for legal and retrieval purposes (see Figure 10.19).

Certifications

Microfilm is normally accepted as evidence in a court of law, providing it is properly certified. In substance, a *certification* states that the records were imaged in the normal course of business. The exact wording of the certificate should be prepared or approved by legal counsel. This signed certificate should be the first and last document photographed on the roll of film. If documents are added to the roll of film, another certificate should be imaged at the end of the additions, certifying the authenticity of the documents and the reason for the addition. If, during the course of filming, the operator notices that a document was photographed folded or in such a manner that a portion or all of it was obscured, the document should be reimaged immediately. A certification of correction should follow the obscured image and precede the refilmed image. The certification should be personally signed and dated by someone with knowledge of what has occurred, such as the operator, even though the form is preprinted.

Targets

Targets are visual guides to roll film. They are usually letter-size sheets of paper with large words, letters, numerals, or signs printed on them. They may contain such words as *START*, *END*, *CORRECTION*, *REFILM*, and *INDEX*, which relate to the certification, and numerals such as 1, 2, 3, etc. to denote segments of the roll relating to an external index. Other targets, such as bar codes, provide function commands to the camera.

The number target is used for retrieval purposes and is usually an 8 1/2- by 11-inch sheet of paper with 4- to 6-inch numerals printed on it. These number targets are used as points of reference to an external index, usually typed on the carton or film cartridge, showing the contents of each segment. Number targets are normally filmed at the beginning of each segment, starting with numeral 1. With a line-code retrieval system, the segments correspond to the number legend on the vertical side of the reader screen. When the microfilm is to be subsequently cut and put into microjackets, a target is normally used to indicate a change of jacket. This target may simply read *INDEX*, or it may be of any design, provided it is very large and distinguishable as a separating target, even to the naked eye. Alphanumeric targets and separating targets, other than bar-coded targets, are often filmed repetitively to assist recognition as the film is being traversed.

COMPUTER-ASSISTED RETRIEVAL (CAR)

Prior to the use of computer technology to retrieve micrographic images, all documents had to be arranged in sequential order or in some other organized grouping before filming. This preparatory sorting was required for filming or for filing in hard-copy systems, so it did not add a significant cost burden to the filming process. However, it often did not offer any significant savings either.

When roll film was used in the early systems, retrieval required spinning through the reel in much the same manner as one would thumb through the pages of a book, stopping on or about the desired page. To expedite this process, various techniques were developed, including the odometer, or film measurement, method and line coding or blip (page) count.

With these methods, a manual index is created by the operator as the documents are filmed, relating a group of documents to their place on the roll of film, either by measuring the distance the reel has traveled, as shown by the odometer, or by counting the number of pages or blips, shown by the page counter. (See Figure 10.20.)

Although these semiautomated methods are still used and may still be justified for any number of reasons, they fail to provide precision retrieval at maximum speed and do not address the very labor-intensive process of pre-film sorting or complex retrieval.

The microfilm industry recognized these limitations and designed equipment that uses the full potential of the computer to allow filming of documents in random order and to permit fast, precise retrieval. Systems and equipment designed to use the computer to index the documents imaged on the film are generally called *CAR (computer-assisted-retrieval) systems.*

Single-Level Blip Systems

The basic element of CAR reel microfilm systems is the use of the blip, a rectangular mark about 1/8 inch in size, positioned below each document image as it is filmed. There is one blip per image, and the document image address corresponds to its sequence on the reel of film. Thus the film address of the first image on roll 101, for example document A, would be 101-0001; the address of the second image, document B, would be 101-

0002; and so forth. After the address is keyed into the search keyboard, the reader used with these systems optically counts the blips as the film traverses. It stops when the exact address is reached and the desired image is displayed on the reader screen.

By the early 1990s, the industry was in the third generation of CAR microfilm equipment. Each generation of systems and equipment has reached a higher level of computer interaction. This has resulted in the elimination of problem areas in filming, encoding, data entry, and retrieval, and it has minimized human intervention in the process.

In first-generation systems, all blips were uniform in size. Counting a blip equaled counting a page, and if all pages were part of the same file, there was no problem. Such would be the case if each page were independent of the others within the file. For example, 4,000 random-ordered freight bills might be imaged on one cartridge of film, with each one-page freight bill having a separate bill number. With this arrangement, a single-level blip system worked well.

However, sometimes, the cartridge needed to be regularly divided into batches, with each batch representing perhaps a separate date. Or in other cases, the cartridge might need to be divided by files, which meant that only the cover sheet of each file need be blipped and indexed, leaving its contents to be displayed and read in the original ordered sequence. This need to divide the cartridge into logical segments generated the concept of multilevel blip systems.

Multilevel Blips

To alleviate the segmenting problem, a multiple-level search system was devised, using blips of three different sizes. No more than one blip is used for each document image. The sizes are referred to as *maxi, midi,* and *mini* or, just as often, *primary, secondary,* and *tertiary.*

To illustrate how this system works, assume that a paper records series is arranged as follows: first, by date; second, within the date grouping by

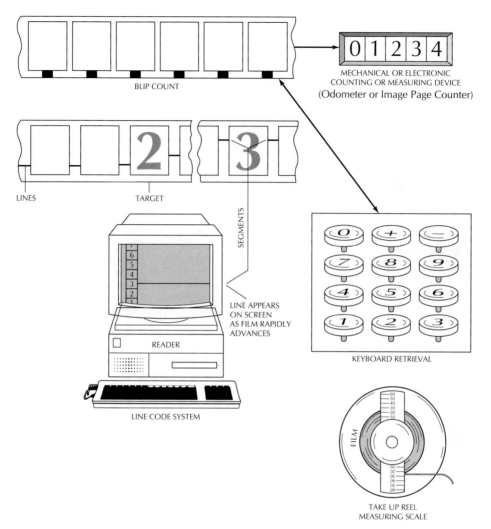

FIGURE 10.20 Semiautomated Retrieval Systems

invoice number; and third, by an indefinite number of supporting documents for the invoice. The primary break is assigned the largest blip, the secondary break is assigned the middle size, and the tertiary break is assigned the smallest blip. In making a search, the computer prompts the operator, after a request for a document is entered, to select a particular cartridge and insert it into the microimage terminal. It then directs the CAR reader, sometimes called a *microimage terminal*

(see Figure 10.21), to count a specific number of primary blips to locate the appropriate date segment of the reel. Next, without hesitation, it directs the retrieval unit to count a specific number of secondary blips to arrive at the proper invoice. It will then move blip by blip through the supporting documents until the entire file has been viewed or printed. At any level of the search, a browsing scan can be directed by the operator if exact index information is unknown. With a microimage ter-

Figure 10.21 Microimage Terminal (Courtesy of Eastman Kodak Co.)

minal, equipped with logic and proper computer interface, this entire search would have only minimal operator intervention. This search method is often referred to as the *book-chapter-verse* or *block-batch-item* method.

Although most CAR systems have three-level-search capability, usually only two of the levels are used. For example, the first level might be the file number and the second level the items or pages in the file. Usually, the item level is not indexed as such, but the blips are used for automatic printing, with the blip aligning the image for proper printing.

Data Entry Approaches

Of course, to make retrieval of any specific document possible, the document identification first must be keyed or scanned into the computer, to-gether with its access address, including the reel number. Data entry was a major problem in CAR systems until the early 1990s for two reasons. The first is that manual keying of data into the computer is labor-intensive, and the second reason is the probability of occasional errors.

The approach to data entry depends on the type of software and hardware utilized for the system. Three approaches are possible.

1. The *standalone* approach utilizes dedicated software and a PC or a minicomputer to drive both the microfilm camera and the microimage terminal equipped with an RS 232 C interface. The main advantage of the standalone approach is ease of installation and a well tailored applications program. Its disadvantages are that it might duplicate data capture done in the mainframe and that it requires a dedicated computer.

2. The *in-stream* approach utilizes mainframe hardware and software. Its advantages are that it can utilize data already captured on the mainframe, thus reducing the amount of data entry, by adding a field for the microimage address. It also eliminates the need for dedicated PCs, as the mainframe monitors can be used. The disadvantages are the programming resources and time required to modify the existing applications program.

3. The *distributed* approach is a combination of in-stream and standalone approaches. It utilizes a PC but permits the PC to communicate with the mainframe, thus eliminating the need to rekey common information required for the CAR system.

While each of these approaches has merit under the right conditions, we concentrate here on describing how the standalone system operates for data entry and retrieval in conjunction with the bar code.

Data Entry and the Bar Code. Data entry begins with the PC-driven camera, which images the page and the proper-size blip under each image. As the operator feeds the documents into the camera, a scanner reads a bar code on the document showing a file number or other identifier. As the document is filmed, the computer automatically assigns the microfilm address to the index.

If the bar codes are generated with the file number printed on them, the file number can, as stated above, be scanned and entered automatically; however, this process still requires that the labels be affixed manually to the documents, before filming. Manual intervention can be avoided almost completely if it is feasible to preprint bar codes on the documents signifying an identifier such as an invoice number, thus eliminating the tape process.

When the file numbers are predictable, such as sequential numbers from 1,000 to 10,000, the PC can generate the bar code labels in order, printing them on self-adhesive tape using a bar code printer. The bar code tapes are affixed to the documents prior to filming. Another shortcut to bar coding downloads a file from the mainframe, such as a list of social security numbers or employee names or some other data that match the documents to be microimaged, and prints that data through the PC to a bar code printer.

COMPUTER-OUTPUT MICROFILM (COM)

Another powerful combination of micrographic and computer technology produced computer-output microfilm, commonly known as COM. COM captures the electronic data output from the computer, on microfilm without a paper intermediary, usually in the form of microfiche. The unit that records the alphanumeric data on film is the COM recorder, or COM unit. It is a substitute for the impact line printer or laser page printer that creates paper printouts.

COM recorders can microfilm the equivalent of 160 or more pages measuring 11 by 14 inches per minute, with minimum manual intervention. A full microfiche at 42× reduction contains 224 frames, or 207 pages, of data. Thus, COM can generate vast amounts of information readable by eye, without paper, at very fast speeds, with a minimal labor and distribution cost, and with all the space-saving advantages of microfilm. It is, therefore, a prime tool in information and records management.

It is important to understand that while the COM recorder may be a substitute for the line or page printer, it is not a substitute for the computer. The data supplied to the COM recorder are the output of the computer; the COM recorder merely captures that output on microfilm. The basic system must still be designed and the computer programmed to manipulate and produce the desired information in a usable and efficient format. In addition, not all paper computer output is suitable for COM. Evaluation of COM systems is discussed in Chapter 12.

General Equipment Characteristics

There are several models, makes, and designs of COM recorders available. It is important to thoroughly research the current market for desired models and features.

Cathode-Ray Tube Recorder.   Initially, the COM recorder used a very small internal cathode-ray tube to display computer-output data one character at a time at incredibly high speeds while imaging them through a camera lens onto silver film. This type of technology is giving way to a newer laser technology, which is more compatible with electronic laser imaging.

Laser Technology.   Depending on whether the COM recorder is on-line or off-line, it receives its data stream directly from the computer mainframe or indirectly from a tape generated by the mainframe computer. COM recorders can be either on-line or off-line at the stroke of a key on a PC keyboard.

On-Line Systems. With an on-line system, the host computer sees the COM recorder just as it would a page printer, sending data to the recorder through a thin fiber-optic cable. When the recorder receives its data, it in turn sends out commands to its subsystems, which record the data stream into an eye-readable report on microfiche. The COM recorder need not be adjacent to the computer or even in the same room or on the same floor. However, it is necessary to have some human supervision of the recorder to make certain that it is ready to receive data and output film, and to make quality spot checks. This is by no means a full-time activity, so that person may have other responsibilities, such as source document microfilming, scanning, performing other computer room duties, or even programming the format, duplication, and distribution for each of the reports.

Knowledge of COBOL or other mainframe languages is not necessary. The COM system is programmed for each report using a PC and a PC language such as C. For example, it needs to know number of lines per frame, number of copies to be made, who is to receive the copies, titling, reduction, bar-coding, report number as-

signment and control, indexing, and other technical data. All of these operating instructions for the COM system are stored in the RAM (random-access memory) of the PC, which drives the COM system. The unique report number is the key to job identification and run. A report is defined as computer output of data in visual format, whether it be on monitor screen, paper, or film.

Before the computer operations supervisor sends a report, the COM unit is checked via a phone call to determine if it is ready to run. This may be a quick phone call or a personal check. If for some reason, the COM recorder is not able or ready to run, the computer operator's console will show "No Path Available" and the data stream will have to wait until the COM unit is readied, which should be as quickly as possible, as that channel is shut down until it can receive.

Once the report is sent to the COM unit, the PC takes over and no further personal attention is normally required, other than quality checks.

Off-Line Systems.   When one considers the simplicity of the on-line systems, it is a wonder that an off-line system is used at all. Primarily, off-line is used when the COM recorder is not hard-wired to the host computer. This occurs most frequently when an organization does not have its own recorder and uses a commercial service bureau. In order to COM-record data off-line, a computer tape is required. The tape, a 3480 cartridge with up to a 32724 bpi capacity, is placed into the tape drive of the recorder. The tape may be blocked at a different density; however, older 1600 or 6250 bpi 10-inch tapes must first be converted to the newer densities and cartridges before they can be run on the COM tape drive. Overall, direct on-line systems are more trouble-free, more simple, and easier to operate than off-line systems.

Dry and Wet Silver Systems.   Although most laser COM systems use dry silver film which is processed (developed) by a heat drum, it is possible to have both dry silver film and wet (chemically developed) silver film in the same system. The processing box, or component, of the system is modular and can be changed by an operator without technician assistance. Wet silver film is more stable than dry, but dry is far more convenient.

Equipment Configurations

Earlier COM configurations provided for a recorder, which in some models produced a role of undeveloped film or a cut microfiche completely developed with a dry silver process. Subsequent steps, each having its own equipment, included a separate processor and a high-speed or medium-high-speed vesicular or diazo duplicator, which usually included a collator. There was much human intervention in what would otherwise be a highly automated process. So the manufacturers designed a system that interlinked all processes in a *train* configuration. This meant that all steps in the process would be operated without human intervention, except for spot quality checks and possibly film and tape loading, from the very start of the data stream to the distribution of the last microfiche.

The *train system* consists of four interlinked *boxes,* or units. The following is a rather generalized description of these units.

The *first box* is the tape drive into which a 3480 cartridge (which is slightly larger than a microfilm cartridge) is inserted if the system is run off-line, and to which the fiber optics cable is connected if the system is run on-line. The PC that drives the system is also connected to the tape drive.

The *second box* is the COM recorder itself, which contains the laser tube. In this box the laser beam, controlled by the recorder, writes directly on the film, after having been directed by several mirrors through one of two lenses, depending on whether the 42× or 48× reduction is chosen. In addition to the unexposed film supply, this unit also contains the heat drum to develop the dry silver film or a chemical and water supply if it is a wet silver unit.

The *third box* is the interlink to the duplicator. After the recorder processes the film and cuts the fiche from the roll of supply film, the micro-

fiche is transported to the interlink where the bar code is read to determine how many copies should be made and who should receive them.

When this is done, the fiche moves on to the *fourth box*, where the duplicates are made from either vesicular or diazo film, and sorted and collated for distribution.

Copy Film Selection

Normal polarity for COM output is positive, showing a clear background. The background of the dry silver–processed film is basically clear, with a light blue tint. A duplicate made from vesicular film has a reversed polarity, or sign, from the original; hence the duplicate vesicular fiche will be negative, a desirable condition. If diazo is used, the opposite will be true, as diazo is sign-maintaining. A positive diazo fiche will result from a positive original. The type of copy film to be used must be decided at the time of equipment acquisition.

Imaging Forms

Sometimes it is desirable to have a form "overlay" for the data, even if the form is just a box with horizontal lines. In the past, the form had to be etched in glass and precisely aligned so that the data would fit precisely within the form lines. With the advent of the laser, optically created form slides are no longer necessary. Instead, with special software, an *on-line soft form overlay* can be programmed and stored in the PC, to be called out automatically as needed. These forms can be quite complex. They are usually required when the image captured is supposed to match a computer-generated paper document used elsewhere, such as a W-2 income tax form. A complex form may require a day or two of programming time, so some organizations contract out this task to companies who specialize in this type of work.

Feasibility of COM

Generally, where there is wide distribution of computer printouts, COM is feasible. The use of

COM often results in an increase in the frequency and number of copies distributed simply because a wider or more frequent distribution of hard copy would have been too expensive. Caution, however, should be exercised to ensure that unneeded copies are not produced through COM. Given that all savings are somewhat relative, it is nevertheless not unusual for a single COM application to save thousands of dollars per year.

Normally, the advantages of COM include a substantial reduction in paper costs. As an example, a 4-by-6 microfiche at a 42× reduction contains the equivalent of 207 pages of 11- by 14-inch computer print. This represents an approximate cost of about $1.25 in paper. The material cost for the original microfiche is about 20 cents, and for the copy, about 5 cents. Thus COM microfiche represents only 5 to 20 percent of the cost of paper, depending on the number of copies per original required.

The cost of mailing COM-generated microfiche as opposed to mailing the equivalent amount of paper is extremely low. The equivalent of 75,000 pages of printout can be mailed first class in microfiche form for around $3. This same amount of paper would fill 15 standard record center cartons and cost considerably more to ship in any transportation mode. In addition to these factors, microfilm saves space and is very easy to use. Although the monetary savings calculated here as an example can be real and valid, they are only so if there is a real and valid reason for creating the fiche in the first place.

Indexing systems vary for microfiche; however, most are so simple that the eye-readable header permits using it with practically no instruction or experience.

The cost of producing COM computer reports is much less than that of producing paper printouts on the page printer. The COM recorder can record on film 10 to 20 times faster than a page printer can print on paper, and in addition, the decollating and bursting functions associated with computer printouts are eliminated. Although the cost of on-line disk storage for computer systems is being drastically reduced, much of this data must still be placed on microfilm via COM for record purposes because unlimited storage on-line would be too expensive.

SUMMARY

The records manager must understand microfilm technology to use its capabilities fully, to explain them to prospective users, to evaluate systems, and to select appropriate equipment.

Camera microfilm is a specially prepared silver halide film, designed specifically to photograph documents. Most frequently, microfilm is processed with chemicals as is ordinary photographic film. Some silver film, however, is developed with heat, rather than wet chemistry, and is called dry silver film. Dry silver film is less stable than wet silver and tends to fade when exposed for a long period of time to strong ultraviolet light such as is used in a microfilm reader. Diazo, vesicular, and silver print film are used to make contact prints of original camera film. Diazo maintains the same sign as the original, and vesicular reverses the sign.

The most common camera used for office document filming is the rotary camera. There are several types of flatbed cameras, such as the engineering planetary camera, the small-document planetary (table model) camera, the processor camera, and the step-and-repeat camera. Various indexing systems are used during the filming process, including image blip count systems, odometer, segmenting, target, and line code as well as computer-assisted indexing. Reels, cartridges, microfiche, jackets, and aperture cards are all known as microforms.

Microfilm is developed in a processor. The densitometer is used to measure density of the image after processing, and the microscope is used to measure resolution, as a part of quality control.

Readers and reader-printers magnify the microimages so that the data may be read. A reader-printer will provide an enlarged or full-size paper reproduction of any microfilm image. There are motorized and manual roll film readers and reader-printers. Readers are designed primarily for a specific type of microform.

Computer-assisted retrieval (CAR) systems use the computer to index records and to provide an access address for each image on film. The most common CAR system uses a multilevel blip count system as an access locator device. The PC, by means of bar coding, drives the camera and serves as a retrieval device. CAR systems permit the filming and fast retrieval of randomly arranged documents imaged on a reel or cartridge of microfilm.

Computer-output microfilm (COM) techniques convert the digital output data from a computer to microfilm, using laser beam technology, thereby avoiding the use of paper printouts. Off-line systems require a computer tape for input to the COM recorder, and on-line systems accept a data stream directly from the host computer just like a page printer. The COM equipment configuration, often called a train, consists of at least four boxes or units that completely record, process, duplicate, and distribute the microfiche output without human intervention. Most COM recorders use dry silver film, can operate either on- or off-line, and are driven by a personal computer.

QUESTIONS FOR DISCUSSION

1. Why has microfilm become so widely accepted as a records management tool?

2. What basic elements of micrographic principles and technology should be understood by the records manager?

3. Explain the term reduction ratio.

4. Identify the physical characteristics of each of the following categories of microforms:

   a. Roll film

   b. Aperture card

   c. Microfilm jacket

   d. Microfiche

5. What is a rotary camera?

6. Describe how the document flow differs in the two types of rotary cameras discussed in the text.

7. What is the rated filming speed of a rotary camera? What determines the actual filming rate?

8. What are the more commonly used rotary camera reduction ratios?

9. What are the various image positioning techniques or modes that can be used when operating a rotary camera? Explain the difference between the various techniques.

10. Describe the purpose and benefits of the following features available on most rotary cameras:

   a. Lighting controls

   b. Automatic document feed

   c. Receiving trays and stackers

   d. Image blips

   e. Sequential numbering device

   f. Blip or image counter

11. What are the two types of planetary cameras? How do they differ in size and purpose?

12. What likenesses and differences exist in the operation of rotary and planetary cameras?

13. Explain the major differences between the following types of flat bed cameras:

   a. Microfiche processor camera and updatable microfiche camera

   b. Small-document planetary camera, engineering planetary camera, and engineering processor planetary camera

14. What factors should be considered by the records manager when deciding whether to

process microfilm in-house or whether to have it processed commercially?

15. What are the differences between the following types of print (copy) film:

    a.   Silver print film

    b.   Diazo film

    c.   Vesicular film

16. What features should the records manager look for when selecting a microfilm reader?

17. Identify the differences between the following types of microfilm readers: roll film reader, microfiche reader, and aperture card reader.

18. What is a microfilm reader-printer, and what is the most common type of print process used today?

19. Explain how bar codes are used in computer-assisted retrieval.

20. Explain how the multilevel blip systems are used in CAR.

21. Explain how the PC can control microimaging as well as image retrieval.

22. What is a COM train system?

23. What is the difference between on-line and off-line COM systems? What are the advantages and disadvantages of each?

24. What is the advantage of using dry silver film in COM recording?

25. Explain three major advantages of using COM.

PROJECTS

1. As the records center supervisor of an international oil company, you are asked to make recommendations to the organization's records manager concerning the installation of an in-house microfilm program. Until now, all microfilming of your organization's records has been done commercially.

    a.   Prepare an annotated bibliography of at least five magazine articles that will provide you with the essential information for your report.

    b.   Write the report.

2. Obtain literature describing the features of two different small-document (table model) planetary cameras, and write a report evaluating the significant differences in features, design, and technology.

3. Call a local COM service bureau or an in-house COM department to determine the cost to produce or buy one original 42× microfiche containing the equivalent to 207 pages of 11- by 14-inch computer printout and the cost per vesicular copy. Also contact a purchasing department or a data processing department of a local organization to determine the approximate cost of 11- by 14-inch computer paper used on a high-speed laser page printer. Based on the purchase price of 2 million sheets of paper and the comparable cost of COM microfiche, what would be the net effect on costs?

4. Visit a local organization that uses a CAR system to film and retrieve document images. A vendor of CAR equipment or the local ARMA or AIIM chapter can offer advice and assistance on this visit. Write a report describing this system and the chief benefits obtained.

CASE PROBLEM

You have been asked by the manager of your real estate department to recommend an effective microfilm system for all of your organization's worldwide real estate titles, leases, and licenses, which will be centralized next year. At this stage of the study, costs are not considered because the real estate manager just wants to know if it can be done, how it would be done, and if a workable system can be created. The system will be limited to the approximate 20,000 real estate files now located in two offices. Approximately 5 percent of the files will be closed and replaced with a 5 percent addition each year. Each file contains 5 to

50 documents with an average of 25 pages per file. The documents are no larger than 8 1/2 by 11 inches and are of varying condition and color. It is estimated that 150,000 documents are added annually. The files must be retained for one year after completion of the contract or sale of the property. The records are most often referred to in the real estate office by any one of ten land agents working there. On the average of three times per week, a file must be sent to one of the ten field offices of the Law Department. The real estate manager does not want to retain the original documents.

For the following aspects of the program, make recommendations and explain your reasons:

1. Type of microform to be used.

2. Type and number of cameras, readers or readers-printers, and other required equipment.

3. Method of initial conversion (in-house or commercial).

4. Length of time required to complete.

5. Interruption factor.

NOTES

1. Xidex Corp., *Innovator*, "Ammonia and Photo Imaging, Health Issues," April 1983.
2. *Glossary of Micrographics* (National Micrographics Association, 1973; now AIIM.)
3. Richard R. Bordas, "Aperture Cards: Still an Excellent Communications Tool," *Inform* (Association of Information and Image Management (AIIM), 1989.

Chapter 11

Electronic Imaging Systems

Learning Objectives

1. To describe the capabilities and advantages of optical disk–based electronic systems.
2. To list the major components of electronic imaging systems and their purposes.
3. To explain the various types of optical disks and their characteristics.
4. To discuss the benefits and design of networks.
5. To list the benefits and economics of computer-output-to-laser-disk (COLD) imaging systems.
6. To discuss how the electronic imaging systems can interact with departmental and enterprise-wide computer systems.
7. To discuss how hybrid micrographic systems are complementing electronic imaging systems.

AN ALTERNATIVE TO MICROFILM

In the early 1960s there was some experimentation by the Ampex Corporation and some user corporations with the use of magnetic videotape to record document images, but the process proved to be economically and technically unfeasible. In more recent years, however, the use of laser videodiscs prompted a new interest and successful application of electronic imaging of documents.

A newer technology, sometimes known as an optical disk system, but more often as an *electronic imaging system (EIS)*, or as *electronic image management (EIM),* has made great inroads into document-based information systems during the last 10 years, and at times is providing a viable alternative to microfilm systems. Like microfilm systems, EIS stores document images, retrieves them, displays them, and transmits them in a highly automated electronic fashion. Through television and the computer monitor, society has become very accustomed to the electronic image, and perhaps this may account for the ready acceptance of this technology.

As we saw in the last chapter, microfilm technology is essentially a photographic approach to document management, utilizing silver halide film to record microimages of business documents. The electronic imaging system achieves practically the same results by using laser beam technology to digitize an image and to record that image digitally on an optical digital data disk, commonly known as an *optical disk*.

The microfilm image is an analog image which can be seen with the naked eye, although more clearly under magnification. Conversely, the electronic image is created by a binary digital representation of an image, which is called a *bit map* and is transparent to the user, just as the data on a magnetic disk are transparent until read and displayed on a computer monitor. However, in either case the image is viewed on a display device—the electronic image being displayed on a high-resolution computer monitor and the micrographic image, on an optical projection screen known as a reader.

There are many similarities between microfilm systems and electronic imaging systems. Table 11.1, which compares the two systems functionally, shows that there is no great reduction in the amount of hardware or imaging labor. However, there are potentially significant technological and operational advantages to justify the change.

ADVANTAGES OF ELECTRONIC IMAGING

Since the system is electronic, there is nearly instant access to the image, which is very valuable for active records. In addition, the image may be transmitted over a network so as to be a valuable part of a work flow program and a readily available shared resource. With the same monitor, the image can be integrated with data and word processing systems, enabling the office worker to match an incoming electronic image with an existing (in-file) document image. The office worker can also call up relative data from a mainframe database, respond to the incoming document through word processing utilizing windowing techniques, and finally refile the electronic documents to complete the transaction.

The electronic imaging system, while it can be used simply to file, refile, and retrieve document images, can also be a vital part of transaction processing. As such, justification for such a system may have different criteria than a simple comparison of clerical and equipment costs to those of another system. Sometimes, the electronic image can be a vital part in a strategic plan that can be the lifeblood of the organization. If the function is vital, such as customer service, introduction of the system can be easily justified, but on different grounds.

The exact components of the system may vary slightly, depending on the configuration, but generally a system, whether standalone or distributed on a network, will have at least the following components:

- Scanner (digitizer)
- Disk drive and disks
- Monitor
- Printer
- Control computers and software

Larger network or distributed systems may also have a device called a *jukebox*, to automatically load disks, and many workstations, each consisting of a personal computer (PC), monitor, and printer. Smaller standalone systems may have all of the components and software in one package, sold and installed just as would be done with

TABLE 11.1   Functional Comparison of Microfilm and Electronic Systems

Similarities	Microfilm Systems	Electronic Systems
Records Imaging	Camera	Scanner
Media	Film	Optical disk
Display	Reader	Monitor
Paper print	Reader-printer	Laser printer
Retrieval	Computer index	Computer index
Indexing	Data entry	Data entry
Manual Actions	Document prep	Document prep

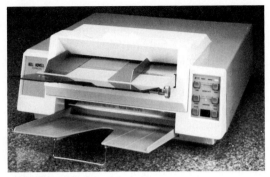

FIGURE 11.1 Scanner
(Courtesy of Bell and Howell)

a microfilm computer-assisted retrieval (CAR) system. Such standalone systems are basically used as a simple file-retrieve-refile system, utilizing the PC to index the system and to control imaging, retrieval, and display.

SCANNERS

To record a document image on an optical disk using an EIS, the paper document is manually fed into a *scanner*, or *digitizer*, in a manner similar to that used for microfilming (see Figure 11.1). The document is indexed so that it can be displayed on an electronic screen at some later time. This operation is quite simple; however, the bit-map technology behind it is not only fascinating, but con-

FIGURE 11.2 Bit–mapped Image
(Courtesy of Association for Information and Image Management)

siderably more complicated than the scan process appears.

Overview of Bit-Mapping

An array of charge-coupled devices in the scanner make a scan of the document. This scanning is called *bit-mapping*. A document page is electronically divided into an imaginary grid of millions of bit locations on which black and white dots, or bits, called *pixels* (*pic*ture *el*ements) are recorded.

When the page is scanned, the scanner does not, for example, recognize the letter *A* and record the binary EBCDIC/ASCII code for *A*. Rather it just recognizes the white and black pixels that make up that character (see Figure 11.2) and records the grid box where a portion of the image is located.

A black bit (part of the total image) is recorded as a 1, and a white bit (clear background or white space) is recorded as a 0. These bits are recorded in digital raster format from left to right, top to bottom as a series of 1's and 0's on an optical disk mounted on a disk drive.

The disk drive uses a powerful laser light to create extremely small pits or bubbles on the surface of the disk. Each pit or bubble represents a 1, and the absence of the pit or bubble represents a 0. These pits can then be read by a less powerful laser light recreating the scanned image on the screen or on paper.

All of this extremely intricate yet simple recordkeeping and processing is controlled by a computer, which could be as small as a PC or as large as a mid-size computer. In actual practice, the bit-map coding is first recorded on a magnetic disk in the processor for reviewing, quality check, and compression, and then transferred to the high-density optical disk in the disk drive for permanent storage or automated random retrieval.

Compression

One of the elements of the bit-map technology that is virtually transparent to the user is the *compression ratio*. The compression ratio is controlled by software. Computer scientists, finding that they did not need to record all of the white spaces, that is, the 0's, reduced the coding from a ratio of 7:1 to a ratio of 30:1. For example, an average 400-word page bit-mapped at 200 dpi (dots per inch) requires 467 kilobytes. Compressed at 28:1, the document image requires 17 kilobytes. The exact amount depends on other factors such as the amount of line work, the amount of contiguous white space on the document, the amount of text on the document, and the compression method.[1]

Compression is accomplished in the control computer, prior to sending the binary codes to the disk drive and optical disk for recording. The significance of compression is that it increases the disk capacity. The exact ratio obtained is determined by the factors previously mentioned, rather than a turn of the dial by an operator, and can vary from document to document. So, as a result, a scan sample is necessary to make accurate estimates of job volume and disk capacities.

The same software that compresses the image must also decompress it. This limits the use of the compressed image to computers that have the same compression software.

Resolution

Another factor related to scanning is *resolution.* Resolution in electronic imaging is somewhat different from resolution as applied to micrographics. In micrographics, resolution relates primarily to a quality standard, and in electronic imaging, it relates to a planned readability factor. Resolution is expressed in dots per inch (dpi). A dot is a pixel

or a bit, the smallest element of a bit map, and as stated earlier, it may be either a 1 or a 0. The dots are in effect square. The fewer dots per inch, the more ragged will the edges of a visual character appear on anything but vertical or horizontal images. The effect of this is that a higher number of dots per inch results in sharper images. (See Figure 11.3.)

Generally, 200 dpi is entirely satisfactory for all office document images and is almost considered a standard, except for engineering drawings. A resolution of 200 dpi means that one square inch of the document will have 200 pixels horizontally and 200 pixels vertically, or 40,000 dots.

Selection of a higher resolution results in increased scan time and added disk storage space, since more bits must be scanned. Proportionately, an increase from 200 dpi to 300 dpi is an increase of 50 percent. That translates to an approximate 50 percent increase in scanning time as well as disk storage space. Generally, many scanners will have controls permitting the selection by the operator of either 100, 200, 300, or 400 dpi, but less expensive scanners may have a fixed 200-dpi resolution.

Scanner Types

Scanners range in size from that of a table top copier to the approximate size and appearance of a microfilm rotary camera. There are two basic types of scanners used for office-size documents—the flatbed and the sheetfed type. Flatbed and sheetfed scanners can be *monochrome* (black and white), *gray-scale*, or *color.*

The *flatbed* type is similar to many office copiers in that a bound book, for example, can be placed face down on the transparent glass top and scanned from below. Of course, it is also suitable for single-page documents, but this type of scanning is very slow, so the volume must be low.

The *sheetfed* digitizer, utilized to scan high-volume documents, is used most frequently for office systems. Sheetfed scanners have belt- or roller-driven feeders that automatically transport documents from a stack tray at a rate ranging from

FIGURE 11.3 Effect of Resolution on Readability (Courtesy of Association for Information and Image Management)

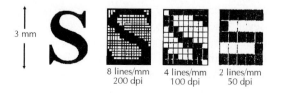

3 mm

| 8 lines/mm | 4 lines/mm | 2 lines/mm |
| 200 dpi | 100 dpi | 50 dpi |

one to four pages per second per 8 1/2- by 11-inch page, at 200 dpi. At the high end, the throughput rate per hour, depending on scanner model, is approximately 1,000 to 7,000 pages.

It is important, though, to realize that rated or transport speed is not necessarily the same as real-life speed. Paper hoppers for automatic feeding may hold as few as 50 sheets or as many as 500 at one time, which means that frequent operator attention will be required. Even if all goes well, with no jamming, skewing, or other mishap, operator loading of the paper hopper alone would actually reduce scanning output per hour and should be factored in when making estimates. Sampling tests provide the best estimators before beginning a major application. Generally, when we discuss black and white scanners, we are speaking of office-size paper document scanners. In addition to this type of scanner there are also microfilm scanners.

The *micrographic* scanner is used to scan microfilm images in various microformats, such as aperture card, jacket, microfiche, and roll film. Sometimes film is scanned to convert to an all-electronic system, sometimes to create a hybrid image transmission network system, and sometimes to facilitate scanning speed, such as with engineering drawings. *Large-size document scanners* are used to digitize engineering drawings varying from C to E size.

The *facsimile transceiver* is still another type of scanner that can be used for input. The fax machine can and is used as an image scanner, as part of a work flow system.

Gray-scale or *color scanning* usually requires a special scanner for imaging gray-scale documents, halftones, or color documents. Gray-scale scanning may require more than eight times as much disk space as simple black and white office-document scanning. Even more space will be needed for color. Some scanners are equipped to automatically sense the need to enhance an image, to recognize gray-scale images and photographic halftones, and to adjust. Others just provide for manual adjustment to enhance (improve) an image. In the feasibility and systems design process, it is necessary to know what type of documents will be scanned into the system so that appropriate equipment is acquired.

Other selection factors must be considered in addition to the type of scanner. Very likely your scanner will also require an interface kit, such as a *SCSI* (meaning *small-computer system interface*, pronounced "Scuzzy"), which may also be required for all of the major components of the system.

Some scanners are designed for single-sided scanning, and others allow for duplex scanning, which means scanning both sides, often simultaneously. If there are many documents in the proposed system that contain information on both sides, it could be critical that a duplex scanner be selected.

Another consideration is the paper-size limitation. Normally, sheetfed scanners handle documents up to approximately 8 1/2 by 17 inches, although some have a limit of 8 1/2 by 14 inches. There are also minimum lengths and widths for documents, such as 2 inches, which must be considered because of a need to match the paper transport system in the scanner. Again, it is important to know the nature and condition of the documents that the system will encounter in actual day-to-day operation.

DISKS AND DISK DRIVES

The system will have one or more optical disk drives and at least one magnetic disk hard drive and floppy drive, as the magnetic disk is also used in electronic imaging systems.

Magnetic Disks

The magnetic disk is used for software and indexing. It also stores images temporarily until they are checked for quality, indexed, and transferred to the optical disk for permanent storage and retrieval. The magnetic disk is not used to store images permanently because it does not have the high packing density or the permanency of the optical disk. The optical disk has an areal density

FIGURE 11.4 Optical Disks and Cartridges
(Courtesy of Maxell Corporation of America)

of 15 to 50 times that of a magnetic disk and has
an estimated postrecorded life span of 100 years.
In addition, the optical disk does not wear from
daily use.

Optical Disks

In appearance, the optical disk is platterlike, resembling closely the audio compact disk used for
recording music. The disk is actually enclosed in
a rectangular plastic cartridge, which is usually
provided by the manufacturer of the disk drive or
by the disk vendor (see Figure 11.4). There are
four types of recording technology used in disk
manufacture, and all seem to work with about the
same degree of reliability and stability.

Optical disks are not entirely interchangeable. Even though they may use the same write
technology and may be the same size, they are

still proprietary. A Brand X disk drive requires a
Brand X optical disk. This may seem to put the
buyer into a one-source purchasing situation,
which would have its disadvantages. The manufacturers, however, have licensed other vendors to
also sell their disks, so that disks are available
from several sources.

Not all of the disk space is usable for image
storage, as some of it contains formatting data.
The disk is formatted before images are recorded
so that it is evenly divided with pie-shaped segments, called *sectors*, which make up part of the
image address. Disk byte capacity varies between
manufacturers.

The life span of an optical disk is estimated to
be 100 years after it has been recorded, but only
about five years before it is recorded. This means
that a partially filled disk may not be suitable for
additional recording after it is five years old, even
though it may still be read. The life span is not of
great importance since the disk can be duplicated

to a new disk at any time to restart the life cycle; however, cost and time factors must be considered. What is more important than disk quality in long-term retention is the ability to display the image as years go by and current technology makes the old obsolete.

Types of Optical Disks. There are three basic types of optical disks: the write-once disk, known as *WORM,* meaning *write once read many times* disk; the *rewritable,* (sometimes called the erasable or magneto-optic (MO), disk; and the *CD-ROM.* WORM disks are used most often in document imaging systems because documents provide evidence and should not be altered. With a WORM system, the laser beam permanently encodes the image using pits or bubbles to write the image.

However, if the document images are not used for evidentiary purposes, rewritable disks could be used and reused. The rewritable disk uses *magneto-optics technology.* A laser light *and* a magnetic field change the polarity of the bits (0's to 1's and 1's to 0's), which alters or deletes the previously recorded image. In addition to document images, the rewritable disk is also used as a substitute for computer magnetic data storage. Rewritable disks require a drive designed specifically for rewritable disks.

The third type of disk, CD-ROM, was until recently only created in a lab outside the using office. This disk is used as a publishing medium for catalogs, directories, and similar reference books. It is mastered and reproduced in large quantities and is a *read-only memory* (ROM) disk. The disk is "read only" because it is not suitable for recording, since it is already permanently written on. The CD-ROM cannot use a WORM disk drive. It must have a separate disk drive, especially designed for the CD-ROM. CD-ROM is usually not part of the document imaging system and normally is not used for images, but rather for computer databases. When the ROM disk is created in-house, using a mastering recorder, a disk referred to as *CD-recordable (CD-R)* is used. The CD-ROM and CD-R can share the same disk drive. This in-house method is generally consid-

---

Bytes per Page (*B*)

$$B = \frac{(H \times R) \times (W \times R)}{8 \text{ (bits)}} \times \frac{1}{C}$$

$$= \frac{(11 \times 200) \times (8.5 \times 200)}{8} \times \frac{1}{10}$$

$$= \frac{2200 \times 1700}{80}$$

$$= 46{,}750 \text{ bytes (46.7 kilobytes)}$$

Pages per Disk (*T*)

$$T = \frac{D}{B}$$

$$= \frac{10{,}200{,}000{,}000}{46{,}750}$$

$$= 218{,}000 \text{ pages}$$

Symbols

B = Bytes per page
H = Height of document
R = Resolution
W = Width of document
C = Compression ratio
T = Total pages
D = Disk capacity

Factors

Disk size	12 in., 10.2 gigabytes
Page size	$8\frac{1}{2}$ x 11 in.
Compression ratio	10:1
Resolution	200 dpi

FIGURE 11.5 Calculation of Bytes per Page and Pages per Disk

---

ered economically feasible when the total distribution per disk is less than 40. Even without distribution, however, it can be convenient and economical for such procedures as tape backup and archiving.

Sizes of Optical Disks. Optical disks come in various sizes. The WORM disks are available in single- or double-sided 3.5-inch, 5.25-inch, 12-inch, and 14-inch sizes. The rewritable disks come in 3.5 inches and 5.25 inches, and CD-ROM and CD-R disks have a diameter of 4.75 inches. Although areal densities are usually expressed in bits per inch, records managers are usually interested in pages per disk. Expressed in average 400-word, 8 1/2- by 11-inch, black and white pages, with 200 dpi resolution and a 10:1 compression ratio, a 12-inch WORM disk, double-sided, will have a capacity of approximately 200,000 pages. This can vary depending on the compression and other factors. See Figure 11.5 to understand how to make these calculations.

Disk Drives

An optical disk system may contain one or more disk drives, which contain the read-write laser head and the laser beam used to record or read digitized images on the disk. The drive or drives are interfaced with a SCSI to the control processor, and data are transferred from the scanner through the processor to the controller for the disk drive. The disk is inserted into the drive, either manually or robotically if a jukebox (autochanger) is used. The disk rotates at various speeds, around 3,000 rpm, depending on the design of the drive, as the laser beam reads or writes on the disk from above. A head crash, which in magnetic technology can destroy all data, is not likely with an optical disk system, since the laser beam permits the laser head to be located at a relatively far distance from the medium. WORM drives, CD-ROM drives, and rewritable disk drives all require separate, specially designed drives, and a separate drive is required for each size disk. Multiple drives may be used with a system. Also, there are multifunctional drives which accept either MO or WORM disks.

The specification sheets for WORM (or, for that matter, all) disk drives are very technical and generally are used to compare the features of various manufacturers when purchasing. They include such speed items as *data transfer rate*, *disk access*

time, and *seek time*. Other specifications are *media tolerance*, which affects data reliability with older previously recorded disks, *error corrections* affecting data loss due to dust or static electricity, and finally *estimated drive life*. However useful these specifications are in deciding between various drives, the main consideration is compatibility with disks in use.

MONITORS

Monitors are an important part of the equipment configuration in a document imaging system. It is possible to use a VGA monitor such as is used in the typical PC system, but the screen will probably not be large enough, clear enough, and fast enough to *optimize* the benefits of the imaging system. After all, the end product of the imaging system is the image of the document that appears on the monitor, and so it may be a false economy to compromise the quality and size of that image. The monitor is an important tool, and it is only good business to provide workers with the best tools available at a cost consistent with their productivity. One can estimate that the five-year cost of a knowledge worker who will be using the monitor is approximately $150,000. If we increase the productivity of the worker by only 1 percent, we have gained more than is needed to pay for the difference between a marginally and a fully satisfactory monitor.

Size

Image monitors need to be larger than the typical PC monitor. A minimum size for the full-time worker is 19 inches measured diagonally across the screen. This size screen will display side by side (full page) 8 1/2- by 14-inch images at about a *25 percent reduction* in size, thus eliminating the need to scroll or zoom. The ability to scroll or zoom at times is an asset, but the price in productivity is a degree of distraction and speed every time it is done. However, it should be kept in mind that while the overall page images fit on a 19-inch screen, they are reduced in size, including the characters. Thus, an 8-point character may be just large enough to be viewed without eye strain at the reduced size. If the characters on the original are so small that reducing them 25 percent would make them difficult to read, it may be necessary to display full-size images, side by side. In this case, a monitor would have to measure 24 inches diagonally, but a 21-inch screen might provide a satisfactory compromise. Thus, in quality monitors, we see that there are basically three sizes for imaging—19, 21, and 24 inches. It follows then, that it is necessary to know the physical characteristics of the documents that will be scanned and displayed in the system before selecting a monitor.

Resolution

Just as resolution was involved in scanners, it is also involved in the display devices. Remember that the typical resolution for an imaged document is 200 dpi. Most imaging monitors have a screen resolution of 1,600 dots (pixels) across and 1,200 dots vertically (1,600 × 1,200). On a 19-inch screen, this is equivalent to a density of 120 dpi.

If the bit-mapped document image is also 120 dpi, there is a perfect fit, enough room on the screen for all of the dots being displayed. If the scanned image is 200 dpi, some of the dots for the display will have to be eliminated. This takes time and degrades the image to some degree. So it can be seen that the resolution of the monitor screen should be compatible with that of the scanned image, for the fastest and best image. If that 19-inch monitor had a resolution of 2,048 by 1,538 (screen size of 13.65 by 10.25 inches), the dot density (image resolution) would be raised to 150 dots per inch.

One might ask, Why bother scanning at a 200 dpi resolution when the monitor will only display (actually, this is a high-resolution screen) 150 dpi. The answer is that a 200-dpi image scan matches many printers that have the capability of printing at the 200-dpi resolution.

Refresh Rate

Another factor in high resolution monitors is the *refresh rate*. According to *Imaging* magazine,[2] "*Refresh rate* is how often the monitor redraws the screen. It is measured in cycles per second (Hz). You need 75 Hz. Anything lower than 75 hz has noticeable flicker—The image seems to waver—which causes eye fatigue." This factor should be shown on equipment specifications.

Color Monitors

Color monitors should only be used in imaging if there is a true need for them. For example, if an insurance company were required to maintain a color photo in the claim file, it would be necessary to have not only a color scanner, but also a color monitor. For imaging, a monochrome monitor is preferable because of clarity and faster refresh rates.[3]

Image Display Controllers

The image display controller, located in the computer, is an internal electronic board that controls all of the display functions, but primarily screen image display, clarity, and speed. In regard to clarity it should have as a minimum the ability to generate a resolution of 1,600 by 1,200. The controller may also do other things, but not all controllers do all of the potential functions, as they vary in design and costs. Some of the monitor functions controlled are compression and decompression, image rotation, refresh rates, gray scale, and windows acceleration. Some monitors are priced to include the controller, but a specific controller can be purchased to meet individual needs.

PRINTERS

Printing the electronic images back onto paper may seem to be paradoxical, but it really is not, if used properly. For example, a customer has asked for a copy of the warranty on the machine that

FIGURE 11.6 Laser Printer
(Courtesy of Fujitsu Computer Products)

seems to be decreasing. In selecting a printer, one should consider the system's needs.

Paper size: What size paper prints will the system require?

Scale: Will the image need to be reduced or enlarged?

Speed: How fast will it print?

Resolution: What is the required clarity (300 dpi or more)?

Paper load: What is the required capacity of the input hopper?

Quantity: Will the printer be centralized or desktop?

Compatibility: How will the printer interface with the computer?

Users of the electronic imaging system should be encouraged to make paper prints judiciously and to avoid the re-creation of another paper convenience file. However, there are times when a print will have to be made just so that the document can be changed or annotated, rescanned, and indexed back into the system.

JUKEBOXES

Jukeboxes are also known, more formally, as *autochangers, automated disk libraries,* or *optical disk changers*. The jukebox gets its name from the coin-operated record players of the 1940s and 1950s. The musical jukebox would robotically pick a record selected by the listener and place it in position for the recording needle head to begin playing. When the music was finished, the jukebox would put the record back on the shelf. A customer could select one record or several, depending upon how many coins were inserted into the machine. Mechanically, the optical disk changer does almost the same thing with the optical disk.

The jukebox is used with a single user who has many disks or on a network of users of the same library. In contrast with a standalone disk drive, where the user is prompted by the monitor to select a numbered disk, and insert it into the

was just purchased. The warranty file has been imaged on optical disk, so it is necessary to make a copy of the electronic image on paper to provide the customer with the document requested. To do this, the document is recalled on the screen and the Print command on the PC is pressed, causing the printer to produce a paper copy. The clarity and print speed achieved depends to a great extent on the type and model of printer used and the resolution of the scanned image. There are two basic types of printers in use today for imaging—the laser printer and the inkjet printer—both of which are also used for data output printing from the PC and word processor (see Figure 11.6).

Of the two types of printers, the laser printer produces the highest-quality output but is also the most expensive, even though the price differential drive slot, the jukebox selects the disk robotically and places it in the drive, positioned so as to rotate under the laser head, where the controller will direct it to be read or to record. One or more disk drives are located inside the jukebox, where the disk is protected from dust or other particles that may interfere with reading or writing the disks.

Jukeboxes are configured in many ways. Basically, WORM-type units accept 5.25-inch or 12-inch double-sided optical disks with a disk capacity from 5 to 100 cartridges. Other types and models are made for rewritable disks, and at least one, the Eastman Kodak Automated Disk Library, has a 60-disk capacity, handles both write-once and rewritable 5.25-inch disks simultaneously, and it is compact. Another manufacturer advertises that it will configure a jukebox in any size up to 1,020 disks and several drives. In addition, Hitachi, a leading manufacturer, has an expansion unit that will increase the capacity of its unit from 64 to 144 disks. So it is apparent that if there is not a suitable off-the-shelf unit, one can be custom-fitted for a special need. The LMS LF 4500 Rapid Changer holds 5 cartridges in a magazine and reads both sides of a disk simultaneously, giving a remarkably fast search. This compact drive has a total capacity of 28 gigabytes (see Figure 11.7). The jukebox, through its controller, knows what

FIGURE 11.7 Rapid Changer
(Courtesy of Phillips LMS)

disk to select and place in a drive, but also files the disk in the most convenient rack, so as to optimize travel time to and from the laser head.

Without jukebox capabilities, the electronic imaging system remains semiautomatic despite its sophistication, in that the manual insertion of a disk restricts its usefulness in work flow techniques, in networking, and in speed of retrievals. So it follows that the jukebox enhances the efficiency of electronic imaging systems tremendously, but it also adds substantial costs which must be justified.

A jukebox with a capacity of 64 twelve-inch cartridges will hold up to 448 gigabytes of near-line storage, or approximately 12 million pages of document images. This is the equivalent of 750 full letter-size four-drawer file cabinets. This kind of compacted storage is amazing in itself, but it should be kept in mind that every one of the images stored in the jukebox has to be scanned and indexed in some way. This quantity of material would require over 2,300 personhours of scanning at a relatively high-rated speed of 72 pages per minute, which in real world time would probably double. (See Figure 11.8 for calculations.) So justification of a system design must look not only at the costs and benefits of retrieval but also at the costs of image capture and storage so as to achieve the optimum balance between costs and benefits.

WORKSTATIONS, SYSTEMS, AND SOFTWARE

The computer drives the imaging system. It not only processes the binary bit stream used to record and retrieve the image, it controls the functions of the scanner, the disk drive, the jukebox, the monitor, magnetic storage, and the printer, as well as performs indexing retrieval and other software functions. In the earlier years of electronic imaging, the mainframe computer was sometimes used as the central processing unit in an enterprise-wide system, but today the trend is to process the data with the PC, which is now much more powerful than it was even five years ago, or with a mid-range computer. Depending on the configu-

---

Jukebox Capacity in Pages

Pages per jukebox = pages per disk × jukebox disk capacity
$$= 218,000 \quad \times 50$$
$$= 10,900,000 \text{ pages}$$

Disk Requirements per Project

Total Disks Required = $\frac{\text{total pages in project}}{\text{pages per disk}}$

$$= \frac{10,900,000}{218,000}$$

$$= 50 \text{ disks}$$

FIGURE 11.8   Calculation of Jukebox Capacity

ration used, the PC may act as a separate external server, or it may act as the central control computer for the entire system. As a central control computer, it manages all of the actions of the various components. Software, such as IBM ImagePlus, is also required.

Each workstation, whether standalone or on a network, will have a PC, with keyboard and monitor, that will enable the user to retrieve and to view images and data. Other functions may also be performed.

There are basically two types of electronic document imaging systems, as stated previously. One type is an electronic file system, and the other type is a distributed image processing system.

The *electronic file system* is a counterpart to the microfilm-based computer-assisted retrieval (CAR) system. With this type of electronic system, paper documents are scanned in random order, indexed and recorded on an optical disk in binary format, and retrieved and displayed on a computer monitor, utilizing a computerized database. The basic function of the system is to index a document, file a document, retrieve a document, and complete the cycle by re-filing it, all electronically.

The hardware for this type of system is relatively uncomplicated and may be purchased as a turnkey system, ready to plug in (see Figure 11.9). The major components of this type of system would be a PC with a magnetic hard drive, a high-resolution monitor, a keyboard, a scanner, a printer, and a 5.25-inch WORM disk drive. In addition, applications and operating software programs are required and would be provided by the vendor of a complete standalone turnkey system.

This type of system could also be purchased with off-the-shelf components, even with some components already in the office of the new user, such as a PC, keyboard, and monitor, upgraded by the installation of additional boards. Software could also be purchased or developed. However, all of this integration requires considerable technical knowledge, as all of the components and software must be fully compatible. Even so, using computers and monitors that are already available in the office is an avenue of cost reduction that can be discussed with the integrator or vendor of the new system.

The Single-Station System

The *single-station electronic file system* is most often used when the operator is the prime user of the system rather than a facilitator or information provider to another user. This does not mean that the operator is the only user or that there is only

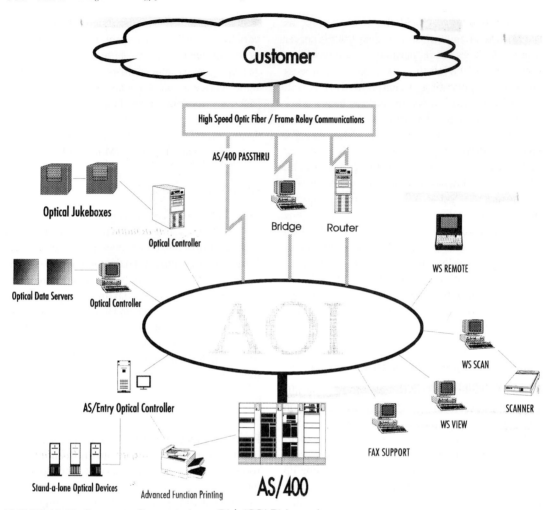

FIGURE 11.10 Computer-Output-to-Laser-Disk (COLD) Laser Access (Courtesy of Advanced Optical Imaging, Inc.)

images may be enhanced, and significant data, such as the purchase order number, invoice number, and vendor code, may be keyed into the system. These are put into an electronic file folder so that related documents are kept together. It should be noted that there is no duplication of data entry. From this point on, any one of the documents can be retrieved electronically at any of the workstations.

Once the document image has been recorded on the optical disk and its disk address entered into the index, the image is sent to the check-

writing station, where it is held in an electronic inbasket (a buffer) until one of ten clerks is ready to process it. This routing is done automatically, but there can be a manual override, should there be a need to send a document to another workstation, for perhaps some exception work. Our invoice is displayed on the screen as soon as the previous invoice is finished. The check-writing station's PC is interfaced with the mainframe computer's accounts payable system, and all data are entered into the system using the high-resolution imaging monitor with windows.

The mainframe computer generates the check, which is attached to a voucher that explains the payment to the payee while providing a record of payment on optical disk for the paying company. The check is mailed.

If there is some exception to the invoice as it is being processed, the invoice is routed to the exception clerk. The exception clerk reviews the electronic file folder. If there is a correction to be made or if payment is not in order, the clerk will either telephone the supplier or, using an imaging screen, windows, and word processing software, write a letter to the supplier or to the purchasing department. If the letter is mailed out, it is printed on a laser printer, which is part of the workstation. If the letter is addressed to the purchasing department, which is a part of the LAN, it is sent electronically. If the letter must be retained after being read, it is scanned into the system as part of the file folder.

In this system, the two exception clerks also respond to telephone requests and letters from vendors or other parties who might have some question or complaint about correct or prompt payment. The electronic file system is particularly useful on these occasions, as the clerk can easily call up on the screen the appropriate file with no delay, answer the question, or even enter the invoice into the system for payment if required.

HYBRID SYSTEMS

Hybrid systems, as used here, refers to a sharing of technology between micrographic systems and electronic imaging systems. In almost all instances it involves an inroad by EIM into micrographic imaging systems and often a complementary micrographic response.

Most hybrid technology is possible because microfilm images in almost any format can be scanned and digitized to create a bit-map image from the analog microfilm image just as paper documents are scanned. Hence it is practical with existing technology to read paper to optical or magnetic disk, creating a bit-map image, and to read the disk to display an image on film just as it

would be on a monitor screen or on paper through a printer.

Some of the applications of hybrid systems which will be discussed here are scan-on-demand micrographic to EIM conversions, aperture card and CAD applications, COM image output, and image transmission systems.

Scan-on-Demand Conversions

Hybrid systems are used in backlog conversions of micrographic systems to EIM systems. To avoid the expense of converting all micrographic records in a system, *scan-on-demand* techniques are used, that is, the backlog is scanned only as needed. Specifically designed multimedia micrographic scanners make it feasible to scan microfilm records into the EIM system quickly and easily. This may require the scanning of almost any micrographic microform such as roll film, jackets, and aperture cards, so multimedia capability is required. (See Figure 11.11.)

Aperture Card Applications

Aperture cards remain a viable part of engineering documentation in conjunction with electronic scanners and *CAD (computer-aided design)* systems. Today not only can the film image in the aperture card be scanned in order to be electronically displayed, but the aperture card can also be the recipient of a CAD-created image written directly on the dry silver film in the card which is instantly processed for viewing or printing using a thermal technology. In addition it is easier and faster to scan the image of a large drawing mounted in an aperture card, than it is to scan the original document with a large-document scanner; thus the aperture card becomes an intermediary in the imaging process.

COM Image Output

Ordinarily, COM recorders record only digital ASCII data and do not bit-map analog images. However, recognizing a need to record both ana-

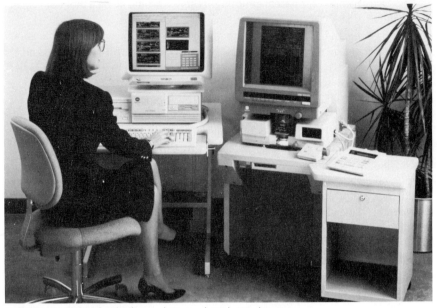

FIGURE 11.11 Hybrid Film and Optical Disk Workstation
(Courtesy of Minolta Corporation)

log and digital information and the need to move information to and from film, Anacomp, the leading manufacturer of COM recorders, has added a bit-map function to its top-of-the-line Datagraphix XFP 2000 COM Recorder (see Figure 11.12).

This technology is being used at the Army Personnel Center in St. Louis, Missouri, where personnel records previously recorded as analog images on updatable microfiche are being scanned and bit-mapped from the updatable film into the existing optical disk–based electronic image system. With this system, the COM recorder can output, on microfiche, bit-mapped images of the updatable film in addition to images scanned currently onto disk from paper documents. As the need arises, the microfiche copies of service records are provided to former service members or other government agencies.

Microfilm Image Transmission

Hybrid systems may utilize microfilm and magnetic *and* optical disks in the same imaging system, such as with image transmission systems. Image transmission systems have been marketed for almost ten years and are still used successfully as a hybrid system. Bell and Howell displayed such a system at the 1993 AIIM equipment show. This demonstration illustrated how the Ministry of Revenue in Quebec, Canada, successfully uses a combination optical disk and CAR microfilm system. One of the largest imaging systems in North America, this organization had been using 16-mm cartridge-loaded microfilm CAR systems for some time. The microfilm cartridges are loaded into any one of eight microfilm jukeboxes, each containing 1.8 million microfilm images. The jukebox robotically selects a cartridge of microfilm, locates the correct image, scans (bit-maps) it, and in less than 10 seconds, transmits the electronic bit-mapped image to the requestor at one of the workstations on the LAN. This same network, however, is shared with other files of the Ministry, which are recorded on optical disk using an optical disk jukebox. Both the optical disk image and the microfilm image are displayed utilizing the

FIGURE 11.12   Computer Output to Microfilm (COM) Recorder
(Courtesy of Anacomp)

same electronic image display monitors on the network. The system is effective and fast and provides random access for both optical disk and microfilm-based electronic images.

Other Hybrid Uses

Another method of marrying film to a bit-mapped electronic image uses a microfilm rotary camera to simultaneously image on film and disks. This provides an analog image on microfilm, and an exact duplicate bit-mapped image on optical or magnetic disk (see Figure 11.13). This type of hybrid operation is done for one or more possible reasons, such as using the microfilm image as a backup or protection copy, using the optical disk

image during the high-activity, short-retention period of a record, and using the film for the long-retention, low-reference period to save on media cost or for legal reasons.

THE FUTURE OF MICROFILM

The new electronic imaging technology is an exciting and challenging tool for the records manager. It provides the records manager with the ability to manage documents in ways that were not possible or feasible ten years ago. Some have thought that the optical disk would render micrographics obsolete, just as it was thought that television would make the radio obsolete. Yet we know, the radio is stronger than ever, judging by

FIGURE 11.13 Film and Scan Hybrid Rotary Camera (Courtesy of Eastman Kodak Co.)

the number of licensed stations. What happened in the radio broadcast field is that new segments of the market were carved out and formats became more flexible. Such will probably be the case in the micrographics industry, but only time will tell. For right now, micrographic products and services are still being purchased at a healthy rate, although market share of the micrographics imaging industry appears to be somewhat flat. According to AIIM's 1992 annual report,[4] based on revenues, micrographics captured 47 percent of the imaging market and electronic imaging captured 53 percent. This reflected a 4 percent drop in micrographics and a 4 percent gain in electronic imaging. This report also reflected a steady gain of electronic imaging, similar to that gained in the year reported, over the previous three years. So the trend is to electronic imaging, but continued and slower growth for micrographics is also predicted in this same report.

From a technological and practical viewpoint, the hybrid systems, which are largely transitional, already show signs of permanency: a case of finding a niche. Also, film in itself has a permanence which appeals to many on the basis of legal and archival needs as well as backup for disaster planning. Film is an information medium that can be read with the human eye, and its usefulness is not dependent on the availability of specific hardware and software 10 or 15 years down the road. Joan Mariani Andrew, of Bell and Howell, said in a recent article, "Industry analysts are quick to dismiss microfilm technology as low tech and out of date in the '90s, but the very fact that it is low tech is what makes it the only storage medium other than paper that is immune to obsolescence. Today and in the foreseeable future, microfilm remains the best alternative for long-term record retention, inexpensive storage and digital backup."[5]

Finally, there are many organizations that have high-volume microfilm systems with considerable hardware investment and which are quite satisfied with that level of technology. After all, it is entirely reasonable to ask why one needs 2-second retrieval, if 2-minute or 2-hour retrieval would suffice. It is a case of designing a system that meets current and foreseeable needs at a reasonable cost consistent with those needs.

SUMMARY

Optical disk systems are descendants of other electronic imaging systems, such as videotape and videodiscs. Although technologies of micrographics and electronic imaging are quite different, they have similarities.

A workstation for an electronic imaging system is made up of the following components: scanner, disk drive, display monitor, personal computer, printer, and jukebox. A single-station standalone system is usually purchased as a turnkey system but could be configured from off-the-shelf products.

A group of workstations linked together is called a network. The three types of networks are the local area network (LAN), metropolitan area network (MAN), and wide area network (WAN). Most networks are LANs serving a limited geographical area, such as an office or group of office buildings. Networks are also known as distributed networks and central networks. All workstations on a distributed network have the same controls as their peer workstations. A central network is controlled primarily by a central processor. A process to record computer output on an optical disk is called COLD (computer-output-to-laser-disk). This is an alternative to microfilm-based COM.

Workflow is a network system designed to process electronic images of documents from entry into the office to final disposition or output. It interfaces with mainframe hardware and software and applications systems, including word processing.

Hybrid systems are imaging systems that interact with both micrographic technology and optical disk technology. This includes the scanning of micrographic images for COM microfiche output; scanning for input to optical disk systems; simultaneous filming and scanning of documents; image transmission of micrographic images; scanning of microfilm images for conversion purposes; scanning of microfilm in aperture cards; and creation of film images directly from CAD vector systems. While electronic imaging will probably dominate the document imaging field in the future, micrographics will continue to play an important, but more limited, role.

QUESTIONS FOR DISCUSSION

1. Explain how electronic imaging systems and micrographic systems are similar.

2. Explain why instant access after imaging is valuable.

3. Explain the major difference in sheetfed and flatbed scanners. When would each most likely be used?

4. What is bit-mapping?

5. Explain what is meant by compression and why the operator does not select the compression ratio.

6. What factors are involved in selecting a scanner for purchase?

7. Why are magnetic disks used in optical disk systems?

8. Describe the types and sizes of optical disks.

9. What is the purpose of a disk drive and a disk drive controller?

10. In a typical document imaging system, should a monochrome or a color monitor be selected? Why?

11. What size monitor screen is required to view two letter-size documents side by side at full size?

12. Describe the function of a jukebox.

13. What is meant by *turnkey* and *standalone* systems?

14. What is the purpose of networks?

15. What is a LAN?

16. If a COLD system is installed, what system might it replace?

17. Describe a work flow system.

18. What is a hybrid system?

19. What are some of the reasons that some organizations simultaneously microfilm and scan documents?

20. Name some reasons microfilm will probably continue to be used in addition to electronic imaging systems

PROJECTS

1. Read three magazine articles that deal with electronic imaging systems in specific organizations. Summarize each article in approximately 200 words.

2. Read an article or opinion on the legality of optical disk systems, and summarize it in 500 to 700 words.

3. Prepare a chart of manufacturers and sellers of optical disks and disk drives, arranged by product description.

CASE PROBLEM

You work for a large chemical company that has 350,000 technical reports on product development. Each report consists of an average of 15 pages. These files are complete with no additions or changes made to them after a report number is assigned. As products are discontinued, the reports are removed from the active files and stored in a records center for a period of 50 years to protect against product liability lawsuits. The reports are indexed by the product report number, the product group number, generic product name, and ingredient data. The indexes are all computerized and are accessed by an on-line display monitor in the file area and in the using offices.

The files are accessed daily by some 30 engineers, chemists, and customer service representatives. All of these personnel are located in the same building—one group on the tenth floor, the others on the eighth floor—and the files are on the tenth floor. Approximately 350 searches are made daily. To protect the record, only photocopies are sent to the requestor; the actual report never leaves the file area. The central file area consists of 400 letter-size file drawers in 80 five-drawer file cabinets. The area uses 640 square feet to house the records and employs one supervisor, three reference clerks, and six librarians who extract and index. Data entry is done in the data processing department from the index sheets prepared by the librarians.

The company wants to reduce space, save the time and cost of making copies, and reduce the wait time for service. From an economic and technical viewpoint, would you recommend a CAR microfilm transmission system or an optical disk system? Explain your reasons.

NOTES

1. Don M. Avendon, *Introduction to Electronic Imaging*, (Silver Spring, Maryland: Association for Information and Image Management, 1992), p. 23.
2. Marta Neilson, "Imaging's Biggest Myth: We Can Skimp on the Monitors," *Imaging*, Vol. 2, No. 8, August 1993.
3. Ibid.
4. *Information and Image Management: The State of the Industry 1992* (Silver Spring, Maryland: Association for Information and Image Management), pp. 5–6.
5. Joan Mariani Andrew, "Counterpoint," *Imaging World*, Vol. 2, June-July 1993, p. 21.

Chapter 12

Imaging Systems Evaluation and Systems Design

Learning Objectives

1. To identify the advantages and limitations of using micrographic or electronic imaging in the management of an organization's records.
2. To learn what information should be gathered in a fact-finding survey and why such a survey is necessary.
3. To learn how to determine the economic and technical feasibility of using an imaging system in the management of records.
4. To analyze information gathered in an imaging system feasibility study in order to enable the effective design of an appropriate system.
5. To make plans to implement an effective and cost-justified imaging system.

THE VALUE OF A SYSTEMS DESIGN STUDY

If microfilm or optical disk were the definitive answer to every records management problem, the records manager would be concerned with only one question—"Can our documents be imaged?"—in his or her effort to devise better systems. However, imaging is not the answer to every problem, so the manager must ask two questions—"Can our documents be imaged, and should they be imaged?" The answer to the first question is "yes" in almost all cases. The answer to the second question is more complicated. To answer the second question, an intimate knowledge of micrographics and electronic imaging is required, in addition to a general knowledge of computer science. This means that one must understand the advantages, capabilities, limitations, costs, and savings potential of imaging.

The old adage *If it's not broke, don't fix it* generally applies to document-based information

systems as it does to many areas. However, this does not imply that we cannot look for more effective ways of accomplishing our tasks. The systems design study improves the chances that imaging will be used judiciously. "Judicious use" simply means that the imaging system employed is used wisely to improve information systems at costs that are equal to or less than any other system *that will achieve satisfactory levels of efficiency*. In a study of the existing file system, all aspects of filing, interfiling, refiling, sorting, as well as quantities and volumes of documents and related clerical activity, must be examined, with an eye to improvement.

REASONS FOR THE STUDY

The systems design study can be triggered by various events. It can be part of a systematic

313

planned records analysis, perhaps emanating from the original records inventory. For example, the analysis may point to a problem, and the study can be made to determine if imaging will solve that problem. More frequently, however, systems design studies are prompted by obvious records problems, such as the volume and storage of records, which have resulted in increased labor costs and a backlog of work.

Sometimes the systems design study is used to evaluate an existing document imaging system to determine if it is performing as planned and to see if the predicted cost factors materialized. The development of new technologies may warrant taking a second look at existing systems to see if they can be improved. Previous studies which may have found imaging systems not to be feasible may be re-evaluated, especially when new technologies appear on the market. Occasionally, an organization will unwisely decide on a universal imaging program and order studies to "substantiate" the economic benefits. Studies performed under such circumstances are never impartial.

When department managers are confronted with this situation, they frequently turn to the records manager for assistance. The astute records manager will consider all alternatives, including microfilm, optical disk, and other media as well as improved hard copy systems.

Generally, the imaging systems study consists of four phases:

1. Data collection and analysis
2. Problem definition and system design
3. Cost justification and approval
4. Implementation

Although the records manager attempts to approach the study in a rather structured manner, some aspects of the study will from time to time have to be modified because of the circumstances of the project. In these situations, one needs to keep the objectives of the study in mind and let common sense and reason reign. The following descriptions of the various phases should be understood as guides and considerations in the process.

DATA COLLECTION AND ANALYSIS

The records manager will most often begin the study with a fact-finding survey. The data collected in the fact-finding survey is almost identical to the data collected in any records analysis, including the initial records inventory, and hence a records management approach to an imaging study is not only logical but avoids duplication of effort. Frequently, a specially designed form is used to collect the data, but that is not always necessary. If the records inventory form is still fairly current, most of the information for the imaging systems fact-finding form can be obtained from it. The fact-finding form provides a simple guide in conducting the imaging study and cost analysis. The method of data collection used for the imaging system is the same as that used in the inventory, as was discussed in Chapter 2. The reasons certain information is collected and the impact that information may have on an imaging system are discussed in this chapter. Like the records inventory form, a separate form is prepared for each records series being studied. Using the inventory form shown in Figure 12.1*a* and *b* as a guide in this discussion, we can learn how and why certain information is collected in phase one of the study. We will also learn to appreciate the value of the information obtained in the initial records inventory. We will begin the analysis with Section II.

Section II: General Description, Purpose, and Use of Record Series

A thorough understanding of the purpose of the organization's records and records series is necessary so that, in solving one problem, others are not created. This knowledge provides the basic foundation for the study.

Understanding the function, purpose, and

flow of a record means knowing why a record came into existence, who created it, when it was created, as well as how it is used in a particular office. Furthermore, it means knowing what records or sources of information are used to create this record and also the information provided or records created from this record. Every records series serves a particular function in an organization, and if that function happens to be vital, the supporting records may also be vital. If so, imaging should be considered as a method of vital records protection.

Procedural Considerations. First of all, it is very important to determine the *point of stability* in the flow of the document. Stability is the point at which no more annotations or additions are made to the document or file. This is important because conventional microfilm cannot be annotated and WORM optical disk imaging systems can only be annotated by making a copy, annotating the copy, and re-scanning the new document into the system. If the point of stability is established early, microfilming can simply be postponed until the file is closed. A flowchart may be helpful in this analysis, such as is provided in Section XIII of the form in Figure 12.1*b*.

In microfilm systems, *additions* to the file may require splicing or using jackets or other insertable or updatable microforms. However, in electronic imaging there is the advantage of adding documents easily at any time and bringing them together into a file for display without splicing or special microforms.

If the document or file is subject to annotation *throughout its normal life,* such as is the case with some engineering drawings and other types of records, the analyst must consider alternate methods of annotation, perhaps using a microform that has a paper area for annotating, such as an aperture card, or by reimaging. When this type of problem is discovered in the study, it should prompt the analyst to investigate the technical possibilities of the potential systems or microforms before proceeding further.

User Considerations. In studying the flow of the document, user considerations are also important to a successful system. For example, if the record is an architectural plan, viewed at the construction site as well as at the office, paper prints will be required, and equipment will be required to make the print. At the construction site, the lack of electrical power, the weather, the bright sun, and normal convenience would probably make a portable viewer and screen image impractical for the engineer. On the other hand, the construction site office might be equipped to use aperture cards and perhaps produce prints on site if needed.

In some operations, telephone inquiries are answered using microfilm or optical disk as the information source. In this type of use, speed is normally an important factor. A few moments waiting on the telephone can seem interminable to a caller, so even a slight delay can have an adverse effect on customer relations. In such a situation it is important not only to know how fast the current system is, but more importantly, to provide adequate service if the speed is satisfactory. It should be noted that the "satisfactory levels of efficiency" discussed earlier in this chapter may require a much higher level of technology and thus may have a cost that far exceeds the present cost. When this occurs, the required level of efficiency should be closely examined to determine if it is really necessary. Usually, the retrieval speed requirement is established by the person responsible for providing the service, usually the manager or the manager's manager. Ultimately, it is a matter of managerial judgment tempered by costs.

User considerations also include ergonomics, that is, those aspects that deal with the physical problems people experience with the machine. At the simplest level, the analyst needs to be concerned with employee comfort and physical welfare. An uncomfortable position, eye strain, long reaches, and insufficient work surface can all impede efficiency.

The number of people who use these records and where they are located is very important. We need to know, for example, if ten employees each

FORM 75041
REV. 9-81

INVENTORY AND RECORD SERIES SUMMARY

SECTION I				
1 INVENTORIED BY AND DATE: DLD 4-30-79			6 SCHEDULE NO. 10-101	7 RETENTION PERIOD 6 Years
2 RECORD TITLE: Drafts Issued, Voucher Copies			8 STORAGE CODE A	9 ICC CODE C-4b
3 RECORD ALSO KNOWN AS: Computer Drafts			10 CONTACT W. A. Proov	
4 DEPARTMENT: Disbursements Accounting		5 SECTION: Payables	11 APPROVED BY	

GENERAL DESCRIPTION, PURPOSE AND USE OF RECORD SERIES

SECTION II

Copy of voucher portion of draft issued for payment of bill or invoice for equipment, supplies or services. File is maintained for reference, proof of payment, audits and as a supporting record for journal entries.

RETENTION REQUIREMENTS / VOLUME

SECTION III

COMPANY		REGULATORY	
OFFICE 1 year		ICC/FRA RETENTION 6 years	
RECORD STORAGE 5 years			
TOTAL 6 years			

SECTION IV

OFFICE		VOLUME STORAGE	
1 LINEAR MEASUREMENT 4500 lin inch	3 RATE OF GROWTH 2400 pages	1 CUBIC FEET 2700	3 RATE OF GROWTH 500 cu ft
2 INCLUSIVE DATES 3/77 - 3/78	4 GROWTH TIME SPAN per day	2 INCLUSIVE DATES 1/74 - 12/78	4 GROWTH TIME SPAN per year

REFERENCES / SORTING AND FILING ARRANGEMENT

SECTION V

QUANTITY	TIME SPAN	INDEX TIME	SEARCH TIME	REFER. TIME
		OFFICE		
30	day	.5 min	1 min	5 min
		STORAGE		
5	day	.5 min	6 min	5 min

SECTION VI

a FILING ARRANGEMENT	b PRE-FILE SORTING ROUTINE
by year	No pre-file sort
by draft #	computer asg file #
	SORTING MANHOURS / SORTING TIME SPAN N/A

EQUIPMENT IN OFFICE / FILE SUPPLIES UTILIZED

SECTION VII

a DESCRIPTION	b QUANTITY	c FLOOR SPACE	d INVENTORY NUMBER
7 Shelf TSF	8	50 sq ft	1-8
5 dr ltr File Cabinet	5	35 sq ft	9-13

SECTION VIII

a DESCRIPTION	b QUANTITY
File folders, end tab ltr size	30,000
File folders, 5th cut ltr size	1,500

INPUT/OUTPUT RECORDS / DUPLICATE AND ALTERNATE SOURCES

SECTION IX

a RECORDS USED TO CREATE THIS RECORD (Show R S No.)	b RECORDS CREATED FROM THIS RECORD (Show R S No.)
Contracts	Journal Entry
Leases	Budget Recaps
Purchase Orders	Tax Returns

SECTION X

a DUPLICATE SERIES	b ALTERNATE SERIES
(10-010) Microfilm copy	Canc & Pd Drafts
	Purchase Orders

FILE CONTENT AND DISTRIBUTION

SECTION XI

COMPONENT DOCUMENT NAME	DOCUMENT # 1 Original Receipt or invoice	DOCUMENT # 2 Payment authoriza.	DOCUMENT # 3 Request For Payment	DOCUMENT # 4 Voucher Copy of Draft
MEDIA CODE	F/MS	C/MS	F2-4/MS	PO-3/MS
FORM NUMBER	External	N/A	23000	35010
JOB NUMBER	N/A	N/A	N/A	AT022
SIZE	Various	Various	8½ x 11	8½ x 8
COLOR	Various	White	White	Green
% OF VOLUME	25%	25%	25%	25%
LOCATION OF DUPLICATE COMPONENT DOCUMENTS (Show Office)	Payables (2) / Purchasing / Vendor	Payables (2) / Auth Dept (1)	Payables (2)	Payables / Vendor

* MEDIA CODE: C - Corres; F = Form; PM - Printed Material; PO - Printout; MC - Microfilm-COM; MS - Microfilm-Std.
1 - Typed; 2 - Handwritten; 3 - Horizontal; 4 - Vertical; 5 - Both Sides; 6 - Loose; 7 - Fastened

FIGURE 12.1 (*a*) Inventory and Record Series Summary—Page 1; (*b*) Inventory and Record Series Summary—Page 2

FUNCTIONAL INFORMATION

Drafts Issued, Voucher Copies

ORIGINATION AND PURPOSE OF COMPONENT DOCUMENTS

SECTION XII

DOCUMENT # 1

A DOCUMENT NAME
Original Bill or Invoice

B ORIGINATED BY
Vendor

C. NO. PARTS
3

D ORIGINAL PURPOSE OF DOCUMENT
To present charges for materials, equipment or services purchased.

E HOW USED IN THIS OFFICE
Proof of payment, audit
Support for Gen Ledger Entry

DOCUMENT # 2

A DOCUMENT NAME
Payment Authorization

B ORIGINATED BY
Dept Authorizing Purchase

C. NO. PARTS
2

D ORIGINAL PURPOSE OF DOCUMENT
Shows departmental authority to pay bill or invoice.

E HOW USED IN THIS OFFICE
Initiate payment of bill or invoice and provide proof of authority.

DOCUMENT # 3

A DOCUMENT NAME
Request for Payment

B ORIGINATED BY
Payables Section

C. NO. PARTS
1

D ORIGINAL PURPOSE OF DOCUMENT
Provides authority and information necessary for Data Processing to generate draft and voucher.

E HOW USED IN THIS OFFICE
Provides proof of authority granted DP

DOCUMENT # 4

A DOCUMENT NAME
Voucher Copy, Draft Issued

B ORIGINATED BY
Data Processing

C. NO. PARTS
2

D ORIGINAL PURPOSE OF DOCUMENT
Shows purpose of draft and provides accounting information necessary to close and adjust payables.

E HOW USED IN THIS OFFICE
Proof of payment, audit purposes and support for Gen Ledger Entry.

PROCESSING AND TRANSMITTING OF COMPONENT DOCUMENTS

SECTION XIII

INTERVIEW QUESTIONS	DOCUMENT # 1	DOCUMENT # 2	DOCUMENT # 3	DOCUMENT # 4
Triggered By	PO or Del Receipt	Receipt of Service or Material	Receipt of Payment Auth	Request for Payment
Received From (Office)	Vendor	Using Dept	Using Dept	Data Processing
Parts Received (Quantity)	2	1	1	2
Process Begins (When)	within 24 hours	within 24 hours	within 24 hours	within 24 hours
Records Referenced In Processing	PO & Agreements	PO & Del Ticket	Original Bill Payment Auth	Request for Payment
Additions & Deletions Made (Period of Time)	30 days	None	None	6 months
Additions/Deletions Consist Of	Adj for O/C	---	None	Adj for O/C
Sent From This Office To	Purchasing		Data Processing	Draft and voucher to vendor
Returned To This Office	After verification		After Draft Issued	
Copy/Original Retained In Office	Original	Original	Original	Copy & Film
Processing Period This Office	10 days	10 days	10 days	2 days
Reference Period This Office	1 year	1 year	1 year	3 years

REMARKS

Note - Component 4 Process - Comp 1-2-3 are sent to DP and are returned from DP with voucher as complete file.

make three searches per day or if one employee makes thirty searches per day. So the narrative should tell us how the work is distributed. Distribution of work will be discussed further in Section V.

Section III: Retention and Legality

Managers sometimes expect imaging systems to solve paper-volume problems when they should first take a close look at retention schedules. If, for example, records are being retained five years when one year would suffice, paper volume will be five times greater than it should be; the documents should be destroyed rather than imaged. In analyzing costs of paper systems and imaging systems, always keep in mind the retention factor because that time frame governs the whole costing procedure. If records are retained for five years, the cost attributed to their maintenance covers a five-year period also. Retention periods have a direct bearing on feasibility. Very short retention periods (days, weeks, or months) seldom warrant imaging. Long retention periods, such as those for archival records, often justify micrographic imaging. And high labor costs for imaging can be more easily justified for long-term records than for short-lived ones.

In a study of the legal aspects of retention, the possible legal restrictions on microfilm imaging and electronic imaging should also be considered. Today most, if not all, courts will admit microfilm as evidence, and common opinion today is that optical disk–based document images will be accepted on the same basis as microfilm. Most, if not all, states have a Uniform Photographic Copies of Business and Public Records as Evidence act, or rules of evidence, and many have at this time modified some of those acts to specifically allow electronic images. A recent study and report indicated that the specific term *optical disk* or similar terms have appeared in at least 80 statutes of 19 states within the last five years, indicating a trend.[1] An AIIM task force[2] recommended among other things:

If you change your laws at this time, avoid listing specific technologies. Instead permit the use of any technology that accurately reproduces the original *or the equivalent.*

But these legal factors do not in themselves preclude the obligation to retain the original document for a period of time. Some states still require keeping hard copy records, even though they are already imaged on film or other media. Some documents by their very nature require that the original be maintained, such as titles and deeds, negotiable instruments, and anything else that denotes ownership rights that can be transferred. Research will reveal if a dual set of records is required, and if it is, the cost can be anticipated. Nevertheless, even in these cases the original hard copies can be stored, and the document image used to full advantage in the office. The legal discussion here is meant to alert the analyst to investigate these matters and is not in any sense a comprehensive basis for legal or retention analysis.

At this point, we can add the distinction between office retention and records center storage. This is important because the cost for retrieval and refile vary greatly between the two. This will be studied more when *references* are analyzed.

Section IV: Volume

Accurate estimates of volume are extremely important. By sampling, measuring, and counting we can obtain fairly accurate estimates of the total pages received daily and yearly and the total records on hand both in the office and in storage. A 10 percent underestimate on large volumes can cause serious budget and timetable crises, so it is best to include a reasonable margin for error. In either micrographic applications or in EIM applications, volume relates to imaging and imaging involves a manual operation which translates into time frames and labor costs. Also, if a microimage transmission system is contemplated, or an EIM system is anticipated, volume relates to on-line or near-line storage capacity requirements. For example, for relatively low volumes and moderate retrieval rates, an off-line storage rack for film cartridges will suffice, as the cartridge can be manually selected and inserted into the reader. In the same manner, an off-line optical disk can be selected and placed into the drive for display in the monitor. Such is the case with many standalone systems.

However, higher volumes and retrieval rates may indicate the need for on-line or near-line retrieval. This requires the use of a jukebox to robotically select a disk or cartridge for scanning and display on a monitor. Furthermore, the volume of records that must be stored near-line will also dictate the size of the jukebox required. All of this adds to cost estimates and server power.

Backfile. One of the most important decisions that must be made before the feasibility report can be finalized is what to do with the backfile, if there is one. In many systems, the backfile consists of those records that are retained beyond their peak access period. For example, Section XIII of the data collection form may indicate that the records reach a stability point within 30 days of creation or receipt, and reference activity may decline after about 60 days in the life cycle. Total retention, however, may be six years. If we calculate the total number of records in this series, we realize that we have almost 3,000 cubic feet of records that will not be part of our new system, unless these old records are also imaged. This group of records is called *backlog* or *backfile.* In the instance cited here, the 3000 cubic feet of records would be phased out over a period of perhaps five years, at a rate of about 500 cubic feet per year. It probably would not be cost-justified to image this series. Indeed, their disposal date might arrive before the backlog imaging was completed.

If the backfile records had a long retention period, perhaps 50 or 100 years, we might consider imaging those records, if the reference rate justified it. Here again, it is necessary to base this judgment on costs or other intangible needs. Quite often, the backfile records are not imaged, but rather are stored in a well-organized records center and retrieved as needed. As a compromise to this, sometimes a *scan-on-demand conversion* or *film-on-demand conversion* is performed. This means that the backfile is not imaged unless the record is retrieved for some reason and it is anticipated that there will be future retrievals. If, however, the records are, for example, real estate records and if one is retrieved from storage because the property is sold, it would appear likely that the record would not be retrieved again. Hence, there would be no need to image it after the life cycle ended, other than for historical purposes.

The backfile on permanent records is usually imaged because the records are archival and hence imaging is economically justified. Film- or scan-on-demand is not ordinarily a viable option in this case, unless current records are more active. Often, in this situation, the records have completely stabilized when they are received in the central file area. Indeed, it is not too unusual to say that the older records are more likely to have reference activity than the new.

Section V: References

Often the uninformed think of microfilm or optical disk as a dead storage medium, whereas the opposite is true. Imaging systems, although perhaps suitable for archival storage, are most beneficial when used frequently. A well-designed imaging system saves retrieval and filing time. Since the amount of time saved is proportionate to the time spent searching for or filing information, the highly active system offers greater *opportunities* for saving than the infrequently used system. The word *opportunities* is emphasized, because the right system, equipment, and medium must be coordinated and used to realize the inherent potential of the system.

In analyzing reference activity, it is important to distinguish among reference time, retrieval (search) time, and index time. In this study, reference time is the length of time that the document is in use once it is retrieved. It is important to determine if screen-viewing is sufficient or if paper prints are necessary, in the event of long reference times. Retrieval time is the length of time that is required to move to the file location, withdraw the file, and provide it to the user. Sometimes retrieval is self-service and information is obtained in the file area, thus eliminating the travel time associated with a refile operation. Refiling is essentially the reverse of the filing process. Index time is the time normally spent in locating the name or number under which the document is filed. Filing and interfiling are rather similar and usually require about the same time when done in an office environment, where expansion of the files is not involved. Hence they can be treated as a group. Refiling can be somewhat faster than filing because often the place in the file is marked by a charge-out card, which facilitates the refile.

A stopwatch timing is generally not necessary to determine current file activity time. Ordinarily, a file activity time sample can be made of groups of documents, perhaps numbering 50 each. These can be timed to determine the average time, if this batch size is typical of the batches of the current process. However, if the current method has a travel-to-retrieve time ratio of 5 to 1, or even 1 to 1, travel time to and from the file is probably excessive, and the paper system should be reexamined to improve that ratio by improved batching systems.

The purpose of knowing current retrieval time requirements is to be able to show, in a mathematical cost analysis, potential savings or increased costs comparing a new system to an existing one. This information will also indicate if the present system meets the time norms of the units it serves.

The distribution of the searches among the workers in the office must also be noted and considered. For example, if 30 searches per hour are divided equally among three workers, we may require three workstations, or we may have one centrally located, depending on various demands put upon the system. Perhaps the searches are divided equally among three people, but the searches are made centrally by one person, again, providing another alternative to consider. Document traffic could have an impact on the speed of the server, the jukebox, and cache. Peak load times should be noted so that proper EIM components are selected and the peaks provided for.

Section VI: Sorting and Filing Arrangement

In the sample, the records are first arranged by the year—that is, all 1994 drafts are filed together—and secondly, within that year, they are filed by draft number. Also, in this case the index from vendor name to draft number is created automatically on the computer as the drafts are generated. Obtaining this information from observation and from the present users is very helpful, as the information will very likely provide the index parameters that will be used on any new system, or it may point out a weakness that could be improved.

In this section also is a place to record the number of personhours spent in pre-file sorting, that is, preliminary sorting to facilitate final filing. In the sample, there is no pre-file sorting. However, sometimes considerable personhours are expended in this type of sort, and if so, this information alerts the analyst to a great potential for labor reduction. This can be accomplished by random filing using a computer-generated index, bar code, or OCR scanning.

Section VII: Equipment in Office

This section lists all the filing equipment used in the office to house the current records which are being proposed and evaluated for imaging. This information is used to determine the value of the equipment if it is released and used elsewhere, sold, or scrapped. It also provides us with the amount of floor space that would be freed if an imaging system were justified and installed.

The value of space is low compared to the value of labor. Although a good imaging system will save more money in labor than in space, space is still a prominent factor. Rental on office space can range from an extremely low $10 per square foot per year to $50 per square foot per year, and even more in specialized circumstances. Records maintained in file cabinets require about one square foot of space for each cubic foot of records. If, for example, an office area rented for $20 per year per square foot and it cost $20 per cubic foot to image those records, the cost of imaging would be recovered in one year, if the records have a retention period that long or longer.

There are instances, though, when using the square-foot value is not entirely realistic. If the records must be retained in the office for reference and no space is available, the only alternatives, after proper retention considerations, are to move to larger quarters or to install an imaging system. In such a case, imaging is almost always far less costly, regardless of the current cost of floor space.

In calculating the amount of floor space saved through imaging, in addition to the equipment footprint, all necessary aisle space should also be included, unless it is a general purpose aisle that will be retained in any event. The value of space saved is figured by calculating the square footage and multiplying that by the rental factor established or estimated by the corporate financial officer.

The value of freed file equipment varies greatly and ultimately depends on a figure considered reasonable and real to management. Most often, the cost-avoidance approach is used. This approach assigns a value that represents an expenditure avoided by future purchases of equipment. In other words, it assigns the current used-equipment retail price. It is unrealistic to assign a wholesale used-equipment value, unless the equipment will actually be sold to a dealer. New equipment values can be used, if the equipment takes the place of new equipment purchases.

Section VIII: File Supplies Utilized

File folders cost money, and this section will tell us how much is spent annually for file folders. It will also tell us something about the system and will enable us to perhaps determine if the current system is operating efficiently. File folders are normally not used if all files contain only one document. This system, however, contains at least four documents per folder. When one considers the relatively low search rate, it appears that perhaps file folders, with their attendant annual set-up expense and folder cost, are not warranted. Even so, computer-assisted retrieval (CAR) techniques could provide electronic file folders. If microfilm was being considered as an alternative system, the number of file folders may be an indicator of the number of jackets or aperture cards that might be required.

Section IX: Input/Output Records

In this section are listed those records or documents that are used to create this record or the records or documents that emanate from this record. Few records are an island unto themselves, and related records must be considered in designing a new system. These records may indeed become a part of the proposed system and may require a detailed study on each record involved.

Section X: Duplicate and Alternate Sources

Duplicate records are "carbon copies," so to speak, of the original. Duplicates that have been made unique by the addition of annotations are not actually duplicates, but often can be considered such since one copy at least provides duplicate information. Alternate sources of information are records that contain duplicate information, but not necessarily in duplicate format. Like those records listed in Section IX, these records are related to the main record studied and must be considered in their entirety in designing any new system.

Section XI: File Content and Distribution

This section not only describes the file, but also describes the documents that make up this file. This particular sample in Figure 12.1 shows that the record consists of four single-page documents and describes how those pages are distributed and their characteristics. If the record consists of only one page each, only one column in Section XI need be completed. These data help us to evaluate the technical feasibility of imaging and allow us to calculate imaging estimates and time frames. Not all of the lines of Section XI are pertinent to imaging, so if a line is not applicable it should be ignored. Size and color of the documents are almost always pertinent to imaging. The percent of volume for a particular column means that the information shown applies to the percent of the total documents in the system. For example, we can estimate that documents No. 3 and 4 combined represent 50 percent of the total documents in the system.

Section XII: Origination and Purpose of Component Documents

This section allows us to describe in narrative fashion who originates the documents, why they were created, and how they are used now. The document numbers shown in Section XII correspond to those document numbers shown in the previous section. This information permits us first to establish a retention period if that is not already done. Secondly, it helps the analyst to make an intelligent judgment in designing a new system and in communicating with the proprietary office personnel. By understanding the records thoroughly, it is possible to look at all related records and their processing and to design a comprehensive image flow system. For example, one may find that duplicate files that are presently retained could be eliminated by a network imaging system. Other systems improvements may be possible; however, present system elements must be understood first.

Section XIII: Processing and Transmitting of Component Documents

This section is a type of flowchart describing the life cycle of each of the four documents that make up the file; it is used in conjunction with Section XII. A large or more standard flowchart can also be used, if preferred. Indeed, an entirely different form can be used for this survey, if it seems more convenient. One important factor that can be ascertained from this flowchart is the point of stability, previously mentioned. Other facts in the chart suggest other questions, such as why does it take up to 24 hours to begin processing? Is this desirable? Would a shorter time be preferable? Would a shorter processing time provide tangible benefit? These questions are pursued because we have the technology to answer them, if it is economically feasible.

In tracing the flow of the record from beginning to end, one needs to take note of facts such as are illustrated in this text. We make notes of potential shortcuts, problems identified, and tentative solutions, all of which must be evaluated or tested before the study is complete. Thus, completion of the data collection gives the analyst a full picture of the present system and permits an imaging design from the bottom up.

PROBLEM DEFINITION AND SYSTEMS DESIGN

The process of analyzing the data actually begins as the data are collected. The experienced analyst sees problem areas and visualizes potential solutions as the problems are encountered. Problems will generally fall into one or more common areas. These areas are as follows:

- Loss of records
- Slow retrieval
- Excessive volume of records
- Lack of space
- Excessive waiting for access to records
- Excessive personhours spent in filing and retrieval
- Delays in processing
- Loss of records in process

The analyst talks and listens to the user who may not know the solution, but generally has a fair idea of the problem. These suggestions deserve first attention, and analysis of the data collected will not only confirm the problem but indicate where it occurs.

If the present system is complex, a flowchart of the activities associated with the records should be made. The flowchart is then studied to see if any actions can be eliminated through an imaging system. For example, a separate stamping action could be combined with an automatic endorsing devise on a rotary camera or scanner. Or perhaps a sorting or index reference could be eliminated by using a random imaging and retrieval system of either the microfilm or optical disk variety.

The size and form of the record, the reference data, indexing methods, volume, and turnaround requirements will all give some indication of the type of system needed and will provide the initial direction for the balance of the study.

At this point, a knowledge of micrographic and electronic imaging technology becomes necessary. In reviewing the present system, the analyst calls upon available technology to simplify, increase speed, or otherwise improve operations and to solve problems. Certain situations are key indicators for using a particular type of system. For example, a series of sequentially numbered but independent documents lends itself to roll film applications. Files or groups of related documents indicate the possible need to use a unitized microform, such as a jacket or microfiche, or a standalone imaging system. Maps or plans which are larger than B size are usually well suited to microfilm 35-mm aperture cards, although they could be scanned and digitized and viewed on a display monitor also.

Random input and computer-assisted retrieval can be used to eliminate labor costs in systems that require extensive sorting. CAR may also be indicated for systems that require complex indexing. In summary, after zeroing in on a potential system, the analyst should feel that the proposed system is both technically and economically feasible, that it will solve the problems, and that it will be acceptable to the user. The acceptability factor is dependent on establishing a close relationship with the user in the development phase.

Sometimes a particular indicator may appear to be suitable to more than one type of system, and both will need to be evaluated. Very likely, there are other factors involved that will also contribute to the selection criteria. This is particularly so in situations where electronic imaging systems are being considered or preferred.

THE FLOWCHART

Once a tentative system is selected and all the previously mentioned factors in the survey are carefully considered, a flowchart for the *proposed system* should be developed to aid in understanding and to ensure that all facets have been covered. The flowchart can be of any style, and symbols can be adapted to imaging requirements. See Figure 12.2 as a simple example of a flowchart. Usually, there is a master chart in which a number is given to each major function. A chart is then developed for each of the major functions and possible subfunctions. A brief narrative explaining the chart can accompany it.

TESTING AND EVALUATION

Once a tentative system is decided upon, a sample of the records should be imaged as a test to determine costs and to work out procedures in detail. The first test should include a large enough sample to be representative of all documents that will be encountered in the normal course of work. The main purpose of the preliminary test is to evaluate the system chosen and the image quality and to obtain cost estimates. If the proposed system is a micrographic system, it is important to evaluate the microform chosen. The microform must meet the requirements in every way. For example, a system may be technically suitable, but if the microform chosen bottlenecks the flow, it is most likely not the proper medium to use. If it appears that the system is acceptable, a final test should be performed. If the system requires computer assistance, the program software and the applications program should be put in place.

In those situations where an EIM network

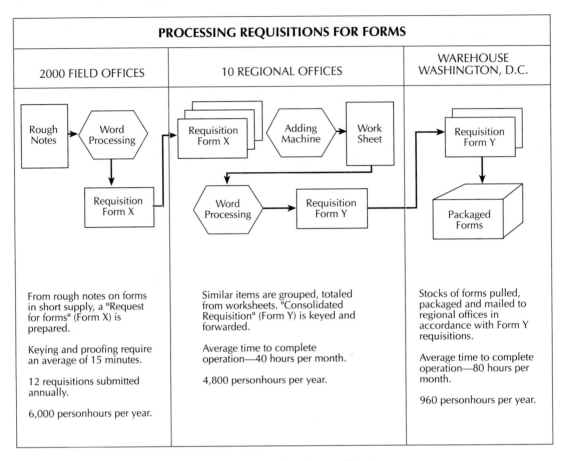

The flowchart content:

PROCESSING REQUISITIONS FOR FORMS

2000 FIELD OFFICES	10 REGIONAL OFFICES	WAREHOUSE WASHINGTON, D.C.

From rough notes on forms in short supply, a "Request for forms" (Form X) is prepared.

Keying and proofing require an average of 15 minutes.

12 requisitions submitted annually.

6,000 personhours per year.

Similar items are grouped, totaled from worksheets. "Consolidated Requisition" (Form Y) is keyed and forwarded.

Average time to complete operation—40 hours per month.

4,800 personhours per year.

Stocks of forms pulled, packaged and mailed to regional offices in accordance with Form Y requisitions.

Average time to complete operation—80 hours per month.

960 personhours per year.

- The flowchart shows what jobs are being performed, where, how, and by whom.
- It identifies all documents, forms, and reports in a procedure.
- It identifies the equipment used and the output of the equipment.
- It records every action required to produce the final product.
- It provides statistical data such as volumes, personhour costs, and numbers of offices involved.

FIGURE 12.2 Sample Flowchart
(*Simplified Flowcharting*, p. 1, General Services Administration, National Archives and Records Administration, Office of Record Managment)

system is proposed and the configuration and software are contracted for through a systems integrator, this phase is performed by those specialists. If the mainframe computer is used as the host server or interfaces with a system server, the in-house computer and systems personnel will also play a major role in planning and implementation.

The final test should be comprehensive enough to predict the full-scale effect. Actual use of the system chosen in the office under normal working conditions parallel to the existing system is very helpful before investing in equipment. If that is not possible, visiting off-premise installations similar to the proposed installation would also be suggested. Micrographic equipment is usually available on a trial basis, and standalone electronic imaging systems may also be available on a demonstration basis. The records manager should play a major role in any EIM system development. EIM deals with document-based imaging systems, and document-based information systems are the responsibility of records management.

COST JUSTIFICATION AND APPROVAL

Almost every organization has a need to justify capital expenditures, and imaging systems can involve capital costs that are quite significant. All imaging systems have some common costs such as the cost of labor and image capture, the cost of image retrieval and display, and the costs of equipment, maintenance, and space. In any paper-based information system, we also have these comparable costs including space, equipment, supplies, and labor. Assigning costs to these factors is one task, but determining how to justify these costs is another matter.

What Is Cost Justification?

Cost justification, in its simplest form, consists of comparing the total costs of an existing system to the total costs of a proposed system. If the proposed method costs less than the existing, we could declare that the new system was justified and that there would be a *savings* of *x* number of dollars per year. For example, if the existing system is considered satisfactory, there is no reason to change it *unless* there is a monetary savings that would justify the expense and effort. Even if the existing system is not entirely satisfactory, this method of cost justification is still legitimate, as it

can show a savings while solving some problems or at the very least show that it will cost very little to solve these problems.

Sometimes, the problem that an office is experiencing is quite significant, and a major overhaul in the system *appears* to be necessary. Really serious problems must be addressed through either improving a hard copy system or through computerization or through improved imaging systems. In all of these cases it would still be beneficial to perform the imaging fact-finding survey. However, in place of just comparing the costs of one new system against an existing system, it is necessary not only to compare the costs of all potential systems but also to compare the effectiveness of the systems.

Early in this chapter, it was stated that the optimum system should provide information at costs that are equal to or less than any other system that will achieve satisfactory levels of efficiency. A proposed systems remedy might cost millions of dollars, simply because the *satisfactory levels of efficiency* are set very high, and perhaps even too high. Sometimes a high premium is paid to achieve a small percentage of the overall benefit. For example, in at least one instance, 80 percent of the benefits were achieved for only 20 percent of the total cost. To evaluate this, one needs to be able to identify the benefits, the source of the benefits, and the related costs and to decide if the costs are justified. How is this done? The records manager needs to compare the costs and the benefits. Sometimes the benefits, however, are soft or intangible benefits. In this case, we have at least identified the cost, so that a manager can make a decision as to whether the intangible benefit is worth the cost.

Establishing *satisfactory levels of efficiency* should be done with some degree of caution or with a caveat to require that all the system features be necessary or justified if costs are a concern. Occasionally, a system is a part of a larger corporate strategy, and the cost is de-emphasized in favor of appearance, speed, image, and timeliness, which are some of the intangibles discussed previously.

Developing Cost Estimates

Developing cost estimates involves careful attention to small details as well as to large ones. A fraction of a cent may seem immaterial, but if multiplied by thousands or millions of times for each action, the total amount can become significant.

Labor.   To accurately assess labor costs to record the images on either microfilm or optical disk, one must know actual production speed capabilities. For most accurate results there should be an on-site test under actual or simulated conditions.

Moreover, normal lost production time should not be ignored. If the test indicates an imaging rate of 3,000 documents per hour, the analyst would be wrong to assume that the operator will perform at this rate every minute of every hour of the workday. More than likely, a conscientious operator will perform work functions no more than 75 percent of the workday. The other 25 percent will be valid work time such as answering the phone, placing imaged paper documents on the shelf, attending meetings, fixing paper jams, dealing with machine failures, and so forth. Although work-measurement techniques can be used to improve the efficiency of the productive time, it is best to base the study costs upon factors that can normally be expected. If an organization has had experience with imaging productivity and has historical production statistics which include "non-productive time," these statistics may be used in lieu of a test.

One important facet of any imaging operation, microfilm or optical disk, is document preparation. The documents may be in folders, and the folder may or may not be properly indexed and indexing time as a result may go way over the budget. Pages may be fastened with staples, and staple removal alone may take as much time as the filming or scanning. Pages that are ragged, crumbled, or folded will have to be straightened. All of this contributes to increased labor costs and longer completion times. If *day-forward conversion* or *scan-on-demand conversion* can be used,

these problems can be eliminated by procedural changes.

Material.   The cost of material is easier to estimate but should still be calculated cautiously. In microfilming, the most frequent factor overlooked is film waste. Film lead and trailer can account for 10 percent of a full reel of film. When less than full reels are used at one time, the percentage of waste could be much higher. Next, the amount of film needed should be estimated according to reduction ratios, document volume and size, and camera type. For example, 2,400 feet of paper documents carefully aligned in a long row and adjacent to one another would require 100 feet of microfilm if filmed at 24 × reduction. This is so since a 24 × reduction means that the film would be 1/24 the length of the documents being filmed. Of course, we need not lay out a hundred feet of documents to estimate film requirements. It can be done mathematically and easily. A simple nonmathematical method is to film a batch of documents and count the number of document images contained on a foot of film. This method includes the spacing between images and is very reliable for estimating total film footage required, based on page volume. Of course, camera spacings vary and can be adjusted. Tables and charts are available for general estimates. As a rule of thumb, a 100-foot roll of 16-mm film will contain about 2,800 images of letter-size documents filmed at 24 × in comic mode. A 100-foot roll of 35-mm film will contain approximately 500 fixed-size frames if filmed on a large-size engineering planetary camera. On a planetary camera the same amount of film is used for each frame, regardless of the reduction. Other items such as reels, cartridges, labels, jackets, print paper, toner, splicing tape, clips, cards, and processing chemicals or service costs should be included in the estimate. Some of these items are costly, and others can be included as miscellaneous and simply added in bulk to each roll or batch.

In an electronic imaging system, the major supply items are the optical disks and cartridges, magnetic disks, and ink-jet cartridges or toner for laser printers. The number of optical disks required depends on the number of images that will be stored on them. One should refer to the previous chapter to determine how to calculate the number of document images that can be stored on a particular size disk. One should also recall that the number of images that can be stored per inch is also determined by the resolution required and by the compression ratio. This requires, as in the case of microfilm, actual on-site tests, not only for imaging speed but also for image quality, compression, and image storage density. The number of disks not only relates directly to cost per disk, but is directly affected by a decision or requirement to image backfile documents. Fewer disks will be required initially if noncurrent records are stored in hard copy form. However, this decision is based on the number of searches made once current processing is complete.

Equipment. The third factor, the cost of equipment, can be assessed in various ways. Some organizations show it as a one-time cost; others ignore it, if this type of equipment is already on premises; and others prorate it over the equipment's expected lifetime. One needs to consult the organization's accountant as to how the equipment cost will be handled and do so accordingly in the costs summary. Because of the expense, equipment maintenance must not be overlooked. Annual service contracts give an accurate budget figure for this expense, including both labor and material. Service contracts frequently cost an annual 10 percent of the purchase price of the equipment. Equipment costs pertain to software and to all hardware, such as cameras, scanners, monitors, readers, printers, computers, jukeboxes, and storage racks. Sales taxes should also be included, and in some areas, there may also be a property tax of some sort, which should be included in annual costs.

Supervision and facilities costs may or may not be considered, depending on the circumstances. For example, if the project does not require incremental supervision expense, such expense is not included in the operations cost.

Service Bureaus. Service bureaus are often used when backfile conversions are deemed necessary for either optical disk systems or micrographic systems. However, backfile conversion is generally a costly approach and should be done only after careful study. The alternative is to retain the noncurrent records (backfile) in a manual access system, if the reference rate permits it. Service bureaus are also contracted to do day-to-day work, when turnaround and costs permit. Service bureaus are used for such reasons as lack of equipment, limited staff or limited space to perform the work, and a lack of experience. When service bureaus contract to do the work, they usually quote a price on a document basis rather than as a total job. So, it is still necessary to know exact volumes and other details obtained from the study, and it is also necessary to write job specifications. Materials, however, are usually included in the price quoted by the service bureau.

THE FEASIBILITY REPORT

The *feasibility report*, or needs assessment report, is often submitted at the same time as the final office test. In order to obtain an approval from upper management to install a multithousand-dollar or even multimillion-dollar system, a detailed report of feasibility should be prepared and submitted to management.

The report, in simple terms, is a before-and-after picture of the system. It should show the cost of the old system in terms of labor, space, materials, and equipment, and the cost of the proposed imaging system in the same terms. The cost of the proposed system should be appreciably less than the cost of the old system, if the level of system efficiency is the same. If the level of efficiency of the new system is much greater than that of the old system (and that new level is required), there may be an added cost.

The exact format of the report is largely a matter of the particular circumstances and company policy, but a suggested format follows:

I.   Executive summary
     A. Purpose of study
     B. Source of data
     C. Recommendation and reasons
     D. Brief description of proposed system
II.   Cost-comparison summary
     A. Cost of old system
        1. Labor
        2. Space
        3. Materials
        4. Equipment
     B. Cost of new system
        1. Labor
        2. Space
        3. Materials
        4. Equipment
     C. Savings or cost on annual basis
III.   Details of cost
     A. Old system
        1. Labor
        2. Space
        3. Materials
        4. Equipment
     B. New System
        1. Labor
        2. Space
        3. Materials
        4. Equipment
IV.   Appendix and Charts

Figure 12.3 is a form that can be used both in writing the feasibility report and in developing and comparing costs. If it is used in the feasibility report, the Explanation or Reference columns are used to indicate an item number which refers to a detailed explanation in the appendix. In addition, this form can serve as a checklist to determine if all factors have been included.

THE REQUEST FOR PROPOSAL (RFP)

The *request for proposal* (RFP) is a document usually prepared by the purchasing department of an organization in cooperation with the using department and the systems analysts involved. The RFP is sometimes referred to as a *bid request* or as a *request for quotation (RFQ)*. A feasibility report is usually prepared as a preliminary estimate prior to the preparation of a *request for proposal*, so that at least ballpark costs and equipment requirements are known before the proposal is requested.

However, the RFP does more than just ask for a price quotation. It describes for the prospective vendors and all of those in the approval chain the overall objectives of the system, that is, precisely *what* the system is supposed to do. It may also specify the type of system desired. The vendor is requested to respond by stating *how* it will be done, what is required to do it, and the cost. However, the vendor may need more specific information to respond to the request.

The type of information that is normally required is a description of the using organization, the current staff and location of operation, and a brief overview of the current methods. It should also provide an overview of how the proposed system is expected to work in the generic plan, while at the same time accepting alternate suggestions from the vendor.

Specific tasks that are anticipated and specifications of systems requirements, such as equipment, data entry, document entry, document description, imaging speed, retrieval speed, number of workstations, workflow requirements, location of network if applicable, and software and hardware integration if desired, should be described. If the system desired is turnkey, it should be so stated, or if the vendor is to provide backfile conversions, details should be furnished. All invited vendors should have equal opportunity for pre-award on-site visits and meetings.

In addition, timetables for submission of proposals and awarding of contracts and implementation, as well as the basis for award, should be clearly stated. Usually, the RFP will provide a tentative system, with an estimated cost, if one has been developed in-house, but alternate hardware, systems, and approaches are often invited. Vendor information should also be requested. This includes a recent financial statement, vendor history, client reference lists, and specific experience or product lines.

SYSTEM COMPARATIVE COST SUMMARY
☐ Initial   ☐ Annual

System A: _____

System B: _____

Cost Factors	System A	System B	Ref
LABOR Sorting, Pre-file,Pre-film			
Staple Removal and Prep			
Coding,Indexing,Data Entry			
Filing/Refiling			
Retrievals and Look Up			
Filming/Scanning			
Jacket/Aperture Card Loading			
Programming/Training			
MATERIALS Folders and Labels			
Film,Processing & Cartridges			
Optical Disks and Cartridges			
Jackets/Aperture Cards			
Print film			
EQUIPMENT & SPACE Maintenance			
Cameras/Scanners			
Readers/Monitors			
Computers/Drives/Software			
File Cabilnets/Shelving			
Jukeboxes & Controllers			
Telecommunications			
Floor Space			
TOTAL SYSTEMS COSTS			

FIGURE 12.3 Cost Comparison Summary
(Insurance Records Services, Inc., 9932 Parkway Drive, St. Louis, MO 63137, 800-882-3753)

IMPLEMENTATION PLANNING

After the vendor selection has been made, all approvals acquired, the system design confirmed, and tests made, there is usually some lead time prior to delivery of hardware. This time can be used for planning for a smooth implementation. This implementation process consists of three phases: training, backfile conversions, and facility modifications and plans.

Training

The first step in training is to prepare a detailed procedures manual for the specific project involved. This serves two purposes. It codifies the procedures so that there will be complete uniform understanding of how the work should be accomplished. It describes equipment and supplies to be used, as well as all steps in the operation. The second step is to train the personnel who will actually be doing the work. Often, employees can be somewhat apprehensive about a new project and welcome an early introduction to the new equipment and procedures. If demonstration equipment is available, the employee can exercise hands-on practice in dry runs.

Backfile Conversions

Backfile conversion, if required, must be planned for in an organized way. If the analysis indicates that the records to be imaged should be retained, it is necessary to plan a method of storing the records in an inexpensive area, where they can be economically retrieved if necessary. Sometimes, it is less expensive to store the originals for a period of time than it is to check each document for clarity. In most cases, however, the originals may just be retained until a spot check is made, and in the case of microfilm, until processed.

Our analysis may have informed us that we have many documents fastened together with staples. These staples normally must be removed, and the removal may take as long as the imaging. Rather than have the imaging device tied up while staples are removed and tears taped, it makes much better use of equipment to have preparation and imaging done simultaneously.

At this time, it is important to finalize just how indexing will be done and by whom. It may be done simultaneouly by the automatic reading of a bar code or in other ways discussed in Chapter 11.

Facility Modification and Plans

When the imaging is done in work-flow processing, a special area is generally not required. In most backfile operations, however, a separate office area should be set aside that is comfortable and well lighted and away from distractions. It is important that the vendor provide exact electrical requirements, so that the electrical requirements can be installed prior to delivery of the equipment. There must be shelving for the records prior to filming or scanning and for temporary storage afterwards. Very likely, the documents will require security during nonwork hours, and so it is best to place the temporary storage in that secured area.

EVALUATING COMPUTER OUTPUT SYSTEMS

Computer-output microfilm (COM) and computer-output-to-laser-disk (COLD) are the two methods used today to eliminate computer output to paper. COM and COLD technologies have been discussed in previous chapters. However, in this chapter the feasibility, or economic evaluation, of these methods is compared.

COM Systems

Although technological marvels, COM systems actually output ordinary microfilm. Therefore, the decision to use COM can be based on data similar to those gathered for a conventional microfilm study. But in addition, it is also necessary to know the cost of producing the identical information on paper using on-line or off-line high-speed laser printers. Ultimately, the cost of paper output versus film output, with attendant expenses, will be compared and be a major factor in the evaluation process. Such costs may include:

1. Computer costs (allocated)
2. Print costs (allocated)
3. Number of copies needed
4. Paper and forms costs
5. Postage and distribution costs
6 Paper-handling costs

When the current computer and peripheral costs are known, they must be compared to producing and distributing the same number of copies using COM and microfilm readers or reader-printers. The cost of producing COM microfilm depends on several factors such as volume, type of microform, and whether the work is done on in-plant equipment or by an external service company. Estimated COM equipment and supply costs can be obtained from equipment manufacturers, or turnkey service costs may be obtained from service bureaus that may do the work on a contract basis. Organizations that produce high volumes of COM reports may find it advantageous to own and operate their own equipment, whereas lower-volume shops may find it advantageous to use service bureaus. Such a decision is generally based on an economic comparison and security and turnaround requirements.

In addition to costs previously mentioned, the COM recorder has the added advantage of recording a page of output on film, 10 to 20 times faster than a laser printer can print on paper. This speed can have strategic advantage. The use of COM complements normal data storage methods. Although, it is usually desirable to maintain data on disks on-line, it is a reasonable option to store that data on microfiche, rather than tape or disk, after its reference activity peaks.

Generally, where there is wide distribution of computer printouts, COM is feasible. The use of COM often results in an increase in the frequency and number of copies distributed simply because a wider or more frequent distribution of hard copy would have been too expensive. Caution, however, should be exercised to ensure that *unneeded* copies are not produced through COM. This in-creased distribution can often improve customer service at a minimal cost, even though its use cannot realistically be classified as a savings. All savings are relative, but it is not unusual for a single COM application to save thousands of dollars per year.

Normally, the advantages of COM include a substantial reduction in paper costs. As an example, 4 by 6 microfiche at 42× contains the equivalent of 207 pages of 11- by 14-inch computer-printed paper. This represents an approximate cost, based on 1994 prices, of about $1.25 in paper. The material cost for the original microfiche is about 20 cents and the copy about 5 cents. Thus COM microfiche represent only 5 to 20 percent of the cost of the paper that would have been used. The cost of mailing COM-generated microfiche as opposed to mailing the equivalent amount of paper is extremely low. In addition, microfiche saves space and is very easy to use.

COLD Systems

COLD systems, however, do not use film, and hence do not require microfiche readers. Nor do they require any distribution time or costs, other than the network costs, which may already be available. A jukebox, with controller and server, may be required, as are optical disks. These items are not low-cost items by any means, and unless the networks and optical disk imaging systems are already in place, it may be difficult to justify the costs. However, COLD like COM can be produced through an outside service bureau. In such a case, no equipment other than ordinary computer display monitors is required. The service bureau has compatible jukeboxes, disk drives, controllers, and servers. Tapes or disks are delivered via telecommunications to the service bureau, and all retrievals are made on-line without human intervention. In any event, either COM or COLD is justified by the elimination of the costs, computer time, space, and paper associated with standard computer hard copy output. And so, the comparison is narrowed to actually comparing the costs and advantages of COLD and COM systems. In summary, a comparison of the costs of COLD and COM, both in-house and through service bureaus, appears to show that within a few years COLD technology will replace microfiche, except for specialized or unique situations, or where an adequate network is not available.

SUMMARY

An imaging system evaluation study has as its objective determining if documents should be imaged. Problems with an existing system, re-evaluation of existing systems, new technology, or even managerial edict may prompt a system evaluation.

Much of the information gathered to evaluate systems has already been collected in the records inventory form. Such a form can serve dual purposes and be used as a guide to analysis. Retention, protection, and volume; labor, equipment, and material costs; and document flow are all significant, in addition to color and condition of the documents themselves.

In defining problems, it is necessary to speak with users of the records. Typical problems are lack or cost of space, lack of speed, delays, lost records, and excessive labor costs in handling records. A simplified flowchart can also be useful in defining a problem and in understanding document flow. After a tentative decision is made on the type of system desired, test runs should be conducted, using time and motion methods. In some instances a pilot system may be installed on a smaller scale.

Cost justification normally involves comparing labor, equipment, space, and materials costs of the present system to those of a proposed system. Sometimes, the new system may cost more than the old and still be justified because the newer system specifies a higher level of efficiency. Feasibility studies indicate comparative costs and identify needs. A request for proposal is prepared by the purchasing department and is sent out to vendors with tentative system specifications, requesting prices and proposed methodology.

After the system has been approved, planning for implementation is finalized. This normally includes specific plans for training and for facility modifications. Training may include hands-on training on- or off-site for operators and others using the system. It also may involve writing job specifications for operators to ensure that consistency is maintained and that the work methods are universally understood. If a backfile conversion is required, specifics on staffing, staging, and tracking, as well as document preparation, must be finalized and specified in the project manual. If the new system is to run concurrently with the old for a period of time, provisions for maintaining order must be coordinated with all users.

Both COM and COLD are electronic methods to eliminate paper reports. The systems are normally justified by comparing their costs with the cost of printing, distributing, and storing paper output. COLD systems differ from COM systems in that COLD also eliminates the microfilm output and the related distribution costs. Most COLD systems use existing networks and computer display terminals. Unless service bureaus are used, COLD systems normally require a jukebox with drives, which can be relatively expensive. COM utilizes relatively inexpensive microfiche readers, and for this reason can sometimes be less expensive than an all-electronic process.

Service bureaus should be considered as an alternative to in-house imaging, whenever this is feasible, especially where equipment is expensive and volume relatively low.

QUESTIONS FOR DISCUSSION

1. Explain what is meant by a *satisfactory level of efficiency*.

2. Name at least four events that might *trigger* an imaging systems study.

3. Why would it be unwise to presume that imaging is a cure-all solution?

4. List the four phases of the imaging study.

5. How is a fact-finding survey similar to the records inventory studied in Chapter 2?

6. Why would original documents such as titles, deeds, and negotiable instruments be retained in hard copy form?

7. Why is it important to understand the purpose and use of the record being studied?

8. How are additions to the file accomplished by electronic imaging, and how are they accomplished by micrographic systems?

9. How are annotations handled in a micrographic system and how are they handled in EIM?

10. Why is distribution of work important to consider in a document imaging study?

11. Why is it important to know the retention period early in the study?

12. How does the number of documents impact on the imaging study?

13. What is a backfile conversion, and what are alternate ways to handle it to reduce cost and save time?

14. Why are imaging systems best used in a highly active environment?

15. In an imaging system, is space conservation or labor conversation most important? Why?

16. What is the difference between a duplicate information source and an alternate information source?

17. What is meant by a *point of stability* in document flow, and what is the significance?

18. What problems are frequently found in analyzing document systems?

19. List at least four key indicators that often suggest what type of imaging system to use.

20. Why is a request for proposal prepared?

21. What is a cost justification in simple terms?

22. What is the difference between the request for proposal and the feasibility report?

23. What are the three phases of system implementation?

24. What is the essential difference between COM and COLD systems? In what ways are they similar?

PROJECTS

1. Review the form illustrated in Figure 12.1*a* and *b* and indicate for each block if the information is applicable to no imaging system (N), to an electronic imaging system (E), to a micrographic imaging system (M), or to both micrographic and electronic (ME) systems.

2. Read three magazine articles that deal with micrographic or electronic imaging systems in specific organizations. Summarize each article in approximately 200 words.

3. Write a 500- to 750-word report on electronic imaging systems. Base your report on at least three magazine articles, which you are to identify in a bibliography at the end of your report.

4. Write a 500-word article on the topic "How a Small Company Can Profit From Applying Imaging Technology to Its Records." The article should be suitable for publication in the monthly newsletter of a local chapter of the Association of Records Managers and Administrators or the Association for Information and Image Management.

CASE PROBLEM

The Andress Manufacturing Company has decided to make an imaging feasibility study. As the records manager for the organization, you have been given the responsibility. Identify in outline form, the step-by-step procedures you would follow in developing a feasibility study.

NOTES

1. Insurance Records Services, Inc., 9932 Parkway Drive, St. Louis, Missouri 63137, 800-882-3753.

2. Association for Information and Image Management, *Task Force Report*, AIIM/92-114, Annex C. American National Standards Institute, *Technical Report for Information and Image Management: Performance Guideline for the Acceptance of Records Produced by Information Technology Systems, Part II*, ANSI/AIIM TR31-1993.

Hewitt Associates

Hewitt Associates LLC is an international firm of consultants and actuaries special-izing in the design, financing, communication, and administration of employee benefit and compensation programs. Hewitt Associates was founded in 1940 to render an impartial and unbiased consulting service to its clients.

In rendering outsourcing administrative services, Hewitt Associates offers participant services through the Benefits Center. A caller (participant) interacts with a Hewitt Associates representative who is trained in providing the information necessary to make informed decisions. Many of these inquiries revolve around forms sent in by the participants.

In managing participant information through a Benefits Center, it is necessary to provide a balance between enhanced service and reduced operational costs. Imaging technology enables the electronic routing, distribution, storage and retrieval of participant information from the desk top. In addition, it improves client and participant service by enabling representatives to answer participant inquiries without necessitating a return call. However, imaging technology alone does not address all the requirements of a complex records management system.

Hewitt Associates chose to implement a hybrid solution because it not only addresses the needs of the users, but also meets the long–term records management requirements of the firm. The benefits of the hybrid solution are threefold: auto-mated records management, a single user interface, and flexible archive media. The hybrid solution provides the users with the necessary pieces of information to do their job, regardless of the format or location of the information. Through the hybrid solution, the user can access digitized images, voice, word processing documents, spreadsheet data, or video.

As part of the implementation of the Hybrid solution, a Records Management Model was developed to define the following characteristics for each record:

- Legal requirements
- Record ownership
- Unique user requirements
- Retention characteristics
- Record classification
- Storage media
- Cost structure

This model provides the foundation for managing all records used by the firm's business process. The hybrid solution implements the model through an architec-ture that utilizes a central catalog. Users will retrieve all information from the same

Chapter 13

Forms Management

Learning Objectives
1. To explain the need for an effective forms management program.
2. To enumerate the objectives of a forms management program.
3. To identify the program elements of a forms management program.
4. To identify various types of paper–based forms.
5. To enumerate various types of electronic forms.
6. To identify options of machine–readable formats.
7. To explain how to establish an effective forms analysis program.
8. To list guidelines for forms design.
9. To identify parts of a form.
10. To identify tools used in forms inventory and appraisal.
11. To identify organizational relationships of the forms management program professional staff.

WHAT IS FORMS MANAGEMENT?

Forms management may take place through a forms control program within the records management function, or a forms management program which incorporates many of the records management functions. In either case, a forms control or management program provides administrative control, increases productivity, minimizes errors in data capture, and uses the best media, design, systems, and procedures available for providing the organization with the required information.

Correspondence and reports may outnumber the business form in executive offices, but in all other offices, three out of every four records are business forms. Business forms serve as the primary means of communicating information in a methodical, standardized, and repetitive way. A well–designed form constitutes the equivalent of a flowchart which describes and standardizes a process. The form serves as a catalyst in providing information in an organized fashion so that it is possible to determine if a task has been completed or to reach a decision about a course of action.

By their very design, forms often guide the flow of work through an office or a number of offices within an organization. They are popular as business records because they improve efficiency. Forms facilitate the rapid collection and transmittal of information in a compact manner. If they did not exist, administrative costs would rise dramatically.

Goals of Forms Management

The primary purpose of a forms management program is to reduce labor, material, and storage costs as well as to increase efficiency. A secondary objective is to produce attractive, efficient forms that will enhance the image of the organization. Forms management is achieved through the use of work flow analysis and graphic design techniques and by weighing the work implications of each form before it is created. The result should be improved operating efficiency and better service to the entire organization. An experienced staff, working in cooperation with all the other departments of the organization, can provide the following services:

- Ascertain that each form fulfills a basic requirement of an approved operating procedure.
- Eliminate unnecessary forms and combine forms where possible.
- Determine the best medium for a form—preprinted paper, form template on computer screen, or electronic form.
- Design each form so that it will perform its purpose efficiently and effectively as well as enhance the image of the firm.
- Implement forms design uniformity and standardization.
- Conform to legal requirements for using logos and fulfilling contract obligations.
- Coordinate forms management with other information management functions, such as MIS and accounting.
- Establish a system of stock control and replenishment that will make forms available, when needed, in economical quantities.
- Automate forms applications and systems, if feasible.
- Specify the most economical method of manufacture.
- Reduce the cost of gathering and disseminating information.
- Meet International Organization for Standardization (ISO) standards.

Forms Control

To provide administrative control of forms, records managers should be given authority to establish forms control programs within their total records management system. Forms control programs involve routines for designing, procuring, storing, distributing, reviewing, and disposing of all of the organization's forms. Before forms are created, the need for their existence should be determined. The total life of the form should be charted before its creation. The person creating the form should be charged with the following responsibilities:

- Proving the need for the form.
- Identifying the purpose or purposes for which the form will be used.
- Specifying how the form will be used.
- Determining the medium to be used.
- Determining the number of copies that will be prepared.
- Listing the titles of the personnel who will receive copies.
- Stating how the copies will be prepared.
- Specifying how the copies will be distributed.
- Determining where the copies will be retained.
- Determining how long the copies will be retained.

Control also ensures the adequacy of all historical records, in terms of both business needs and legal requirements. Standardization of routines increases efficiency and reduces costs.

Need for Efficiency. Despite an efficient forms program, individual forms may lack efficiency. Virtually every office has to use many forms, a situation which results in significant use of staff time. It is essential, therefore, that office forms be well designed so that they are easy to use.

Imperfections in forms are usually the result of improper design because of a failure to understand what information is needed on the form. Other deficiencies are usually due to one or more of the following factors:

- The form is the wrong one for the procedure it is supposed to serve.

- The form is more difficult to fill in than it should be.
- The form requests unnecessary information.
- The information requested duplicates or overlaps information supplied on another form.
- The instructions prescribing the form's use are incomplete or vague.
- The form is obsolete.
- Design standards are not followed.
- Too many copies are made and kept.

Cost of Forms.   Paper–based forms are easier to prepare than reports, letters, and most other media for the transfer of information. Indeed, the ease with which forms can be prepared sometimes leads to the creation and distribution of many unnecessary forms. Even though a small amount of time is required to complete one form, large amounts of time are wasted when many people fill in many superfluous forms.

In a typical office, there are too many forms. Many forms request an excessive amount of information; many seem to be designed to confuse and slow down the user and increase the likelihood of error, Too many are reproduced in the office, and too many are stored for longer periods than necessary. The net result is high costs and low efficiency.

The cost of printing forms is only a small portion of the total cost of using forms. Clerical expense in processing forms is the most significant factor. The costs of printing, file maintenance, and clerical processing are shown in Figure 13.1.

Program Elements

There are nine major elements in a well–organized forms management program.

1.   *Planning and training*. A forms management program must sell its services. This calls for such activities as establishing goals for executive approval, building acceptance of the program by related staff officials, and developing understand-

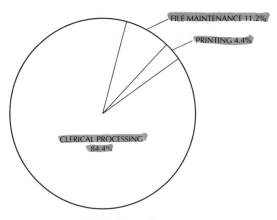

FIGURE 13.1 Cost of Forms

ing by operating personnel. Included in such planning is training that sponsors and permits broader participation in the goals of forms management and that provides technical guidance for forms originators. Technical guidance includes not only information about design principles, but also instruction on the use of software to create electronic forms and instruction on electronic data interchange.

2.   *Coordination and liaison*. Many parts of an organization have an interest in forms management, and this requires teamwork. Program leadership to provide coordination with such other service facilities as reproduction, supply, and distribution is necessary. If there is to be a well–coordinated program, there must be an effective tie–in with the management of directives, reports, and electronic media. The program also needs well–selected and thoroughly oriented forms liaison representatives in each department.

3.   *Procedural analysis*. Most proposals for a new, revised, or reprinted form should be analyzed from the point of view of the procedure that gives the form meaning. The content of the form is evaluated; its effect upon work methods and procedures is studied; and the best medium (preprinted paper, template electronic, full electronic form, or electronic data interchange) is selected. Every item and every copy request gets careful scrutiny. The greater the usage of the form and its cost, the more intense should be the analysis. Some organizations may adopt a cost threshold and thereby spend little time reviewing forms defined as "low cost."

4. *Design standardization.* Standards for layout and construction are required for good forms design. Standardization is closely intertwined with the fact–finding and challenging stages of forms analysis. Content is translated into a format that will ensure easy reading. It is spaced and arranged to accommodate desired entries and to meet the needs of the writing, transmitting, and filing methods. Form medium, size, typography, and construction, including color and kinds of paper and carbons, are determined accordingly.

5. *Registration and identification.* Each request for a new, revised, or reprinted form should be channeled to a central point to be recorded and assigned for analysis. Essential data on numbering and identification, previous or proposed form revisions, volume, use, production, and distribution should be available at this control point. Title, number, and approval or edition date are assigned as positive identification. The title links the form to its function. The form number and edition date show that the form has been authorized for use.

6. *Procurement and reproduction.* Specifications for efficient and economical procurement and printing should be developed and coordinated with the units performing these functions. Appropriate justification should be required for specialty forms and special bindery operations such as punching, stapling, perforating, folding, and padding.

7. *Distribution and storage.* Specifications for effective storage and distribution should be developed and coordinated with both originating offices and supply facilities. Methods should be provided for determining current supplies, establishing initial minimum and maximum stock levels, designating minimum order packages, purging obsolete forms, and setting distribution patterns and controls.

8. *Follow–up.* After a time the more complex forms must be followed up. The forms may be obsolete because of changes in procedures or law. They may be difficult to use, may contain redundant information, or may not provide space for required information. Spot checks should be made with users and originators. This process is also useful in promoting the program, maintaining proper liaison, and obtaining provable data on benefits and savings for reporting purposes.

9. *Program reporting.* A continuous record of results should be accumulated as the program progresses. Before–and–after data can be gathered (showing clerical, printing, and other savings) as changes in forms and procedures are made. These facts, with recommendations, should be reported to top management for use in appraising the forms management program and in shaping policy.

PAPER–BASED FORMS

Forms may be paper–based or electronic. Paper–based forms provide records of both constant and variable data. On the printed form, constant information is preprinted with the variable information keyed in and printed on the form by the user. On a computer form, a blank form with the constant information appears on the visual display terminal (VDT) ready for entry of variable information. Then the complete form, with both constant and variable information, is printed in one operation.

Paper–based forms are also known as hardcopy forms. These are printed on paper, cardboard, or plastic. Electronic forms are form templates created with a computer and stored on electronic media.

Paper forms are usually classified by the method of construction used in the manufacturing process: cut sheets, unit sets, or continuous forms. Specialty forms may include pegboard forms, checks, and office supplies such as tags, labels, mailers, and envelopes.

Cut Sheets

Cut sheet forms are single–copy forms. They may also be referred to as flat forms, flat sheets, or single sheets. See Figure 13.2. Cut sheet forms are the most popular type of form because they are sufficient for many business applications and are relatively easy and economical to produce. Cut sheets may be glued at one edge to form a pad. Padding makes cut sheets easier to distribute, store, and use. Cut sheet forms may be produced in–house using any combination of word processing, desktop publishing, or forms design software, and laser printers or copiers. Various forms manufacturers and printing companies specialize in producing cut sheet forms.

Unit Sets

Unit–set forms are multipart forms that are preassembled into a form set. See Figure 13.3. Unit–set forms can be interleaved with one–time carbons, may be constructed using carbonless papers, or may contain spot carbons. One–time carbon sets permit easy removal of the inexpensive carbon paper. Carbonless paper is more expensive

FIGURE 13.3 Unit Sets

than one–time–use carbon paper. Spot carbon forms have carbon coating on the back of the form for the parts of the form that are to be reproduced on subsequent copies. Thus, confidential or unneeded information is not duplicated.

A form layer is also called a ply. A three–part form is considered to be three–ply—the original and two copies. Unit sets are also referred to as snapouts, snapsets, and snap–aparts.

Continuous Forms

Continuous forms are also called fan–fold forms. See Figure 13.4. They consist of strips of connected forms that can be separated by perforations. They may be single or multipart forms. Continuous forms contain line–hole punching for fastening to an alignment device such as the pins of a printer or another pin–feed business machine. One such form is the register form. Register forms were developed for use in an autographic register. The autographic register is widely used in small stores to make a duplicate of the sales record in one writing. The original is given to the customer, and the duplicate is automatically stored in a compartment of the register. Register forms are relatively inexpensive and convenient to use.

FIGURE 13.2 Cut Sheets

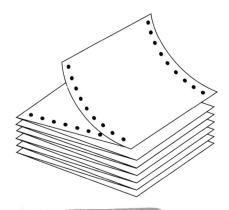

FIGURE 13.4 Continuous Forms

Specialty Forms

Specialty forms may include pegboard forms, bank checks, or office supplies such as tags, labels, mailers, and envelopes.

Pegboard forms are also called one–write systems and are used for cash receipts, check writing, accounts receivable, and accounts payable. The pegboard has a row of pegs (pins) affixed down the side of the board. The objective is to hold two or more forms in alignment (registration) in order to provide duplicate copies in one writing operation.

Bank checks can be constructed as cut sheets, unit sets, or continuous forms. Bank checks are printed with magnetic ink so that they can be read by high–speed sorting machines.

Tags are manufactured from a variety of materials such as tag stock, cloth, and plastic. They are used for many applications such as inventory control, production control, and shipping.

Labels are one of the oldest types of forms and are commonly used to ship packages and boxes. Labels are also used to identify items, to list contents, to communicate instructions, or to warn of danger. The most convenient kind of label is pressure–sensitive. Pressure–sensitive adhesive can be permanent or removable. Labels used on file folders may have a band of color to facilitate filing and retrieving.

Mailers are a combination of continuous envelope and form set filled in by computer printers.

The printer performs a one–write operation which simultaneously addresses the outer envelope and fills in the form on the inside of the envelope through the use of carbon spots, pattern carbons, full carbons, or carbonless paper. The mailers are then separated and ready for mailing.

Envelopes are not always considered business forms. However, envelopes are preprinted in a standard format in a variety of sizes and uses. Today envelope design must conform to U.S. Postal Service specifications.

ELECTRONIC FORMS

Electronic forms may take the form of electronic forms composition, template electronic forms, full electronic forms, machine–readable forms, electronic data interchange, and electronic funds transfer.

Electronic Forms Composition

The design of camera–ready copy for paper–based forms is called *electronic forms composition.* The designing of forms on the computer using forms design software is replacing the manual creation of forms using paper, pen, forms rulers, and guides. Forms can be designed using popular desktop publishing software, presentation graphics, and even spreadsheet software. Unfortunately, use of this software does not allow for alignment of line spacing with fill–in equipment. Use of this kind of software does not permit direct conversion to electronic forms.

Electronic Forms Software

Inexpensive software to design electronic forms is widely available. More sophisticated software capable of filling in forms from various databases, as well as creating the forms, is more expensive. One such package from Delrina Technology, Inc., of Toronto was used in Desert Storm, the U.S. military operation in the Middle East. The U.S. government purchased 500,000 copies for use in designing and completing forms.

Electronic forms are desirable because they contain a mapping process. *Mapping* is programming each data field to control the efficient fill–in of variable data. Mapping assigns space to data fields for input. It also assigns definitions, formulas, and restrictions to these data fields. For example, data entry errors can be detected if the data do not meet the parameters identified for that field. If the name of a private first–class was entered for a position designated as "General," the system would reject the entry.

Each data field in an electronic form must be mapped. The forms designer determines the easiest and most efficient method for the end user to fill in the form. Filling in the form may be done by use of the computer keyboard; automatic fill–in from a database, data blocks, or other related forms; formula calculations done by the computer; automatic date and time fill–ins; and selection from a multiple–choice list.

The space where the data element is to be filled in has a variety of names: fill–in space, field, data block, data entry block, and cell (taken from the spreadsheet).

Evaluating Software. In evaluating forms design software, one needs to assess the availability of forms rules and forms grids and the ease with which the software can be used for:

- Drawing accurately.
- Drawing ballot boxes and columns.
- Positioning rules, captions, or text accurately.
- Handling text adequately.
- Adding screens and reverses.
- Importing graphics files.

Other considerations for selecting software for designing forms include:

- Graphic interface for viewing the form easily.
- Availability of form templates.
- Printing options.
- Compatible graphics files.
- Bar code generation and use.
- Network version.

- Amount of disk space needed to hold the program.

Considerations for filling in the form include:

- Lock forms designs, which can be changed only by authorized personnel.
- Electronic signatures to authorize and protect transactions.
- Field security to protect data.
- Database look–up.
- Automatic calculations.
- Data entry validation.
- Programmable automatic fill–ins for date, time, name, address, and so on.
- On–line help.

Template Electronic Forms

The electronic form can be one that is created on the computer and then printed, or one by which the entire transaction is processed electronically on the computer. On a computer form, a blank form with the constant information appears on the screen ready for entry of variable data. The blank form is also known as a *form slide* or a *form template*. In either case, preprinted form or computer form, only the variables are written or keyed. In most cases, a hard copy is made.

True Electronic Forms

A *true electronic form* is designed, filled in, and processed from the computer workstation. There is no need for a hard copy. The use of electronic forms reduces capital outlay for printing, storage costs, distribution costs, cost of wasted inventory of obsolete forms, and cost of repetitive entry of data.

Machine–Readable Forms

In addition to the true electronic form, other technologies are used in various formats to enhance data entry. *Machine–readable forms* include those created for bar code scanning, optical mark scanning, optical character recognition, magnetic ink character recognition, and intelligent character recognition.

Bar Codes. Bar codes are popular on forms, file folders, and office supplies such as tags, labels, and envelopes because bar codes can be scanned to provide a fast and accurate way to get data into the computer. Retail and food items, books, return–mail envelopes, magazine covers, and many other items use bar codes.

The U.S. Postal Service uses *POSTNET* bar codes (see Figure 13.5) to scan ZIP Codes and route mail more efficiently. The bar code is sprayed on as the address is read by an optical reader. The Postal Service offers a reduced rate to bulk mailers who apply their own bar codes. In addition, the Postal Service uses FIM (facing iden-

tification mark) bar codes for business–reply envelopes.

Commonly used bar codes in addition to POSTNET include the universal product code (UPC), Code 39, and Code 2 of 5. Libraries also have their own industry–specific bar codes for inventory and charge–out applications. Bar codes can be printed on laser printers using desktop publishing programs. However, it is much easier and more reliable to use specific bar code software.

The *UPC* (see Figure 13.6) is used by the retail and food industry for pricing and inventory. All packages carry a UPC that is scanned at the checkout counter. The UPC is a combination of a five–digit manufacturer or distributor number and a five–digit product number. The numbers are issued to manufacturers by the Uniform Product Code Council, Inc.

FIGURE 13.5 POSTNET Bar Code

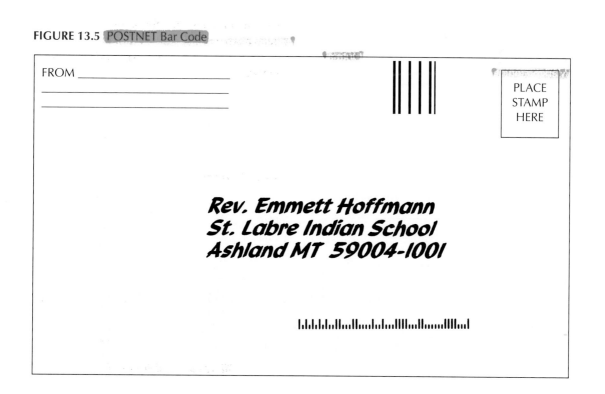

FIGURE 13.6 United Product Code (UPC) Label

Code 39 is used in shipping and warehouse applications. Code 39 can have a variable length and can contain both alphabetic and numeric data.

Code 2 of 5 is used for warehouse applications as well as airline tickets and baggage handling.

Optical Mark Scanning. Scan sheets are forms on which pencil marks can be added to serve as computer input. Major applications for scan sheets are scoring multiple–choice tests, performing market research, reading meters, and recording inventory. See Figure 13.7

FIGURE 13.7 Example of Scan Sheet for Optical Mark Scanning

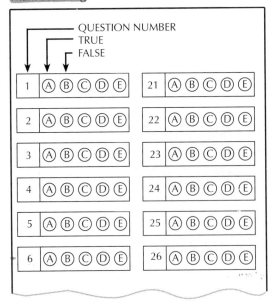

Optical Character Recognition. Optical character recognition (OCR) scanners scan printed information. While some type fonts have been designed specifically for OCR, today's scanners read entire typed pages including graphics. Scanners can also read handwriting if the writing conforms to the manufacturer's instructions. See Figure 13.8.

Magnetic Ink Character Recognition. Magnetic ink character recognition (MICR) was developed by the banking industry specifically to help solve the problem of processing millions of documents. Specially shaped numbers are printed in horizontal bands on the check with magnetic ink containing iron oxide. See Figure 13.9. At the left are bank identification numbers. At the right is account number information. When received at the bank for payment, these checks are processed through a reader–sorter. The numbers are magnetized and read into the computer. The checks are also sorted into bins for further processing and distribution. MICR can also be used on other business papers, in addition to checks.

Intelligent Character Recognition. Intelligent character recognition (ICR) engines can capture data from practically any size, shape, or type of paper, without the restrictions typically associated with other data capture processes, such as timing marks, special inks, or registration marks. ICR may be used to interpret handwritten numerical data on a form. ICR engines can automatically read scanned or faxed handwritten and machine–printed characters, and then convert them into computer–usable ASCII data. The data are presented in a standardized format that provides for generating, receiving, and processing information with no human intervention. The extracted data can be used with any software product for any type of data analysis. The data captured can thus be matched with data in any database. ICR can be integrated with other technologies to make use of interactive, shared information structures, relational segmentation, and classification techniques.

Applications for the use of ICR are being

FIGURE 13.8 Optical Character Recognition Scanner
(Courtesy of Xerox Corporation)

developed for toll plaza monitoring and collection, law enforcement, asset control, and border control. ICR is currently being used for automatic license plate reading by Canadian customs.

Electronic Data Interchange. Also making its impact on records management, electronic data interchange (EDI) is a standardized method of electronically transmitting and processing data from one computer to another. An EDI message is a collection of data logically grouped into segments that are exchanged to convey information. Messages are composed of specific segments that represent a business transaction. EDI requires standard means for information elements called data elements. The transaction set of an EDI message consists of segments of data elements, headers and trailers, delimiters, and syntax. The *transaction set* is the grouping of data elements needed to provide information in the document. The seg-

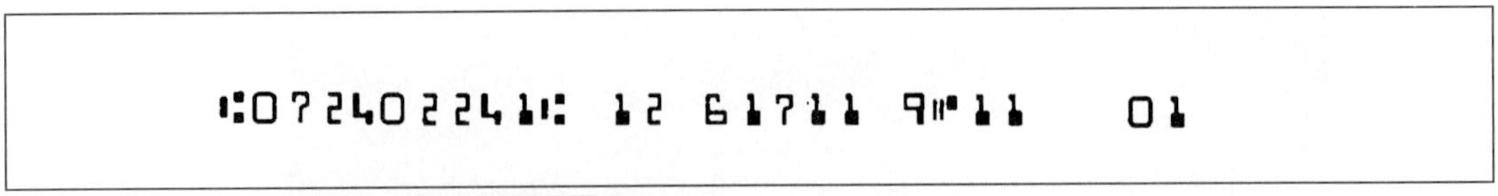

FIGURE 13.9 Magnetic Ink Character Recognition (MICR) Copy from a Check

ments of data elements group them into a logical relationship. The headers and trailers indicate the beginning and end of the message. The delimiters are the separators between segments. Syntax is the order of the information (headers, segments, and trailers).

Documents, such as purchase orders, invoices, shipping notices, or requests for quotes, can be transmitted electronically around the world. Since these messages are in a nonproprietary, noncopyrightable, publicly accepted format, the data contained can be used to automatically update inventory, issue material releases against open purchase orders, invoice a customer, pay a supplier, and advise a party of a shipment or discrepancy. The grocery industry estimates an overall savings of $300 million per year using EDI for purchasing and direct store delivery.

The benefits of EDI include improved service, cost reductions, and more effective organizations. Improved service provides for faster and more accurate flow of information and new ways of working together. Cost reductions are achieved through less paper, reduced inventories, less time spent "expediting," and implementation of just–in–time manufacturing methods and warehouse replenishment. EDI reduces the time before goods are shipped by 30 to 50 percent. EDI reduces the inventory on hand and reduces temporary storage. More effective organizations are achieved through reduced overhead functions and the realignment of functions and resources to meet business goals.

Electronic Funds Transfer.   Electronic funds transfer (EFT) is a subset of EDI and permits the transfer of funds from one account to another and the verification of account balances around the world. EFT is of interest to chief executive and finance officers because of the impact that can be

made on costs, accounts receivable, accounts payable, corporate cash management strategies, and quality and service improvements. In addition, EFT can influence a corporation's ability to reduce overhead, manage the creation and maintenance of the audit trail, enhance materials management, improve inventory controls and forecasts, and maximize the effective use of logistical resources.

Automatic Teller Machines.   A subset of EFT is the automated teller machine (ATM). ATMs are bank terminals, found at locations throughout the city, that enable depositors to deposit and withdraw funds and to transfer funds from one account to another.

FORMS ANALYSIS

To assure maximum efficiency in the use of forms, whether preprinted or electronic, periodic reviews should be made of the forms currently in use. Their relationships to other forms, procedures, machines, and new technology should be considered. Improvements indicated by the studies should be initiated immediately.

Forms analysis involves intensive questioning of the plans, ideas, and work of others. Forms analysis attempts to reduce production costs by challenging the need for every form, every item on the form, and every copy of the form. Forms analysis should result in reducing forms fill–in and processing costs. Forms analysis should result in improving the efficiency of information processing.

Forms analysis is a multielement investigation and evaluation of the nature of and reason for each form, its relation to other forms already in existence, the utility and effectiveness of the form

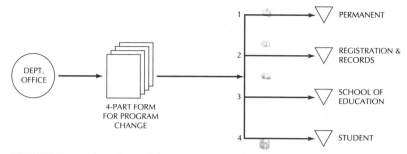

FIGURE 13.10 Flowchart of the Disposition of Copies of a Four–Part Form

as an information–processing device, and the manner in which copies will be reproduced.

In this preliminary stage of forms management, it is necessary to estimate closely the potential cost of designing, printing, processing, and retaining the form. An important factor in this process is to determine the procedure that will be used in the distribution of the copy or copies of the form. A flowchart is sometimes helpful in providing a graphic picture of the life of the form. Figure 13.10 illustrates the use of a flowchart to show the disposition of copies of a four–part form.

Forms Control Files

Forms analysts must rely heavily on the control files, a basic part of a forms management program. Forms control files are inventories and may consist of two types: the numeric history file and the functional classification file.

Numeric History File. The numeric history file provides a complete picture of each form from its inception through its development to its current status. Figure 13.11 shows the folders arranged by form number.

The control number assigned to each form indicates that it has been approved. The numbering system should be as simple as possible. The numeric history file consists of copies of each form used by the organization placed in a visible file in numeric order so that the form numbers are easily visible and the forms can be easily located.

A numeric history forms file can be set up by establishing a folder for each form and filing it by form number. Each numeric folder should eventually contain the following items:

- A copy of the current edition of the form, and any previous editions, marked "Permanent Copy."
- Drafts showing significant stages of development and pertinent correspondence.
- A copy of the directive authorizing use of the form.
- The original request for approval of the form and any requests for revisions, indicating the names of all units using the form and the rate of use.

FIGURE 13.11  Numeric History File

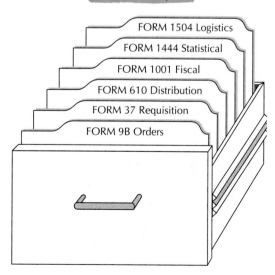

- Evidence relating to the official final approval for the printing or reproduction and issuance of the form.
- The form history record, with a record of all actions taken on the form, including a cross–reference to the functional file.

The numeric history file must be constantly reviewed and updated. Folders on discontinued or obsolete forms must be promptly withdrawn, appropriately annotated, and placed in a separate discontinued numeric history file for disposition at such time as required by the organization's records retention schedule.

Functional Classification File.   The functional classification file provides the means by which forms dealing with related subject matter are brought together. One copy of each form is classified by purpose and placed in a subject–title folder, as shown in Figure 13.12.

The main purposes of the functional classification file are to accomplish the following:

- Avoid the creation of a new form that is very similar to an existing form. The existing form should be revised to serve the need.

FIGURE 13.12 Functional Classification File

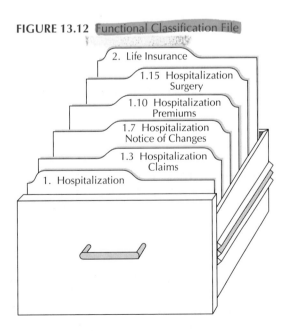

- Detect those forms that could be eliminated or consolidated with similar forms.
- Single out those forms that should be standardized for organizationwide use.
- Identify forms that should be analyzed and redesigned for simplification and uniformity of format, nomenclature, item sequence, spacing, sizing, and so forth.
- Generate studies of forms in relation to their governing systems and procedures or organizational areas that will result in improvements beyond the form itself.

The functional classification control file used in any organization depends on the size of the organization, the number of forms involved, and the number of functions within the organization. Such classification brings together forms that serve similar operational purposes: payroll, sales, personnel, purchasing, and so forth. Each of these classifications might in turn be subdivided.

The functional classification file is not an easy type of file to develop. It is, however, the best type of control file to use when making an analysis of the organization's forms. A forms management office that is unable to keep its numeric and functional files up to date will gradually weaken its position until it finally loses control over the forms of the organization.

Forms Catalog

A forms catalog should be custom–built to fit the conditions of the organization and its forms management program. The following conditions should be considered in determining the nature of the catalog:

- Whether the catalog is needed primarily by originators or by a decentralized forms management program staff.
- The degree to which directives prescribing the use of forms are on a well–organized and coded basis and also contain illustrations of the forms involved.
- The cost of preparing and maintaining the

catalog as measured against its value in promoting standardization and efficiency.

Executives should not be hasty in insisting upon a comprehensive forms catalog, particularly under a new program. A simple forms listing might be issued during the implementation phase, and plans might be developed for a more elaborate listing. Not until the development stage of a new program has been completed can the forms staff make a sound management judgment on the question of whether to issue a descriptive catalog or only a numeric listing. See Figure 13.13.

Forms catalogs may range from a simple listing of forms by number only (serving principally for identification and supply requisitioning) to comprehensive catalogs. Such detailed catalogs may include edition date, title of the form, coded references to manuals or regulations prescribing their use, functional classification, special safeguards, using organizations, unit of issue, stock points, and accountable forms.

Forms Inventory and Appraisal

The first step in the analysis of forms already in use is the taking of an inventory. A forms inventory permits the analysis of forms by function. This type of inventory aids in the elimination,

simplification, and combination of forms. It can also help to extend the usage of well–conceived and proven forms throughout the organization.

When an inventory of forms is made, a copy of each form should be collected. A form, such as the one in Figure 13.14, can be used in collecting data for the forms inventory and appraisal.

Forms Distribution Charts. There are several ways to chart the progress of a form from origination to final disposition. For this purpose forms distribution charts may be devised (see Figure 13.15).

Forms distribution charts are not intended to take the place of analysis or substitute for the preparation of work process charts. They can give clues to the existence of extra copies and the backtracking of copies. Forms distribution charts are a starting point for study and effective improvement work. They can be prepared rapidly. The facts do not need to be charted unless they are complex and a graphic presentation is desirable to make them easily understood.

Recurring Data Charts. In charting the contents of forms, the simplest way to compare items is to make a spreadsheet containing a brief description of each item and the form involved. A recurring data chart, such as the one shown in Figure 13.16,

FIGURE 13.13 Forms Catalog

```
                                                                                      PAGE:
     CATALOG OF PUBLIC FORMS                               DEPARTMENT:   EDU

       4041        APPLICATION FOR RENEWAL OF A BOARDING SCHOOL LICENSE                 31001
        _X_ BUSINESS: Educational Services
        ___ LOCAL GOV'T
        ___ INDIVIDUAL            ___ OTHER USERS
       PURPOSE OF FORM:   APPROVE BOARDING SCHOOLS
       AUTHORITY:  State Statute          CITATION:  ACT 451 OF 1976
       REPORTING FREQUENCY: Annually        PAGES:  3      ANNUAL VOLUME:  OUT, 16      ; IN, 16
       ACT 133 OF 1982 COMPLIANCE: (Y/N) __

       4110        BILLING FOR SERVICES (REHABILITATION                                 31002
        _X_ BUSINESS: Services (Non-Financial)
        ___ LOCAL GOV'T
        ___ INDIVIDUAL            ___ OTHER USERS
       PURPOSE OF FORM:   REIMBURSE VENDOR
       AUTHORITY:  State Administrative Rule
       REPORTING FREQUENCY: As Needed--One Time   PAGES:  1   ANNUAL VOLUME:  OUT, 26000   ; IN, 26000
       ACT 133 OF 1982 COMPLIANCE: (Y/N) __

       4124        PRIVATE SCHOOL APPLICATION FOR DRIVER EDUCATION CERTIFICATE          31003
        _X_ BUSINESS: Educational Services
        ___ LOCAL GOV'T
        ___ INDIVIDUAL            ___ OTHER USERS
       PURPOSE OF FORM:   REQUEST CERTIFICATE STOCK
       AUTHORITY:  State Administrative Rule
       REPORTING FREQUENCY: As Needed--One Time   PAGES:  1   ANNUAL VOLUME:  OUT, 85   ; IN, 85
       ACT 133 OF 1982 COMPLIANCE: (Y/N) __
```

FORMS INVENTORY AND APPRAISAL

Date of Inventory _____ Prepared by _____ Approved by _____

Department _____ Division _____ Section _____ Location _____

Form Title	Form Number	Function	No. of Copies	Retention Period		
				First Copy	Second Copy	Third Copy

FIGURE 13.14 Data Collection Form

is frequently helpful in this connection. The recurring data chart will give the forms analyst a clear picture of those items that are:

- Common to all forms in the group.
- Common to some, but not to all, forms.
- Found only on one form in the group.

Reductions in the number of forms are usually based on data of this kind because these data help identify forms that can be combined or eliminated.

Procedural Questions.   Often the forms originator will not have assembled the data or made the examination for new and revised forms. When this is the case, or if the originator has overlooked something significant, he or she should expect a challenge from the forms staff.

The questions to be asked will vary according to circumstances, but the following are those asked most frequently:

1. What are the purposes of the form, the operation, and the procedure? What are the essential needs or unalterable limitations?

2. How is the work done (the processes, operations, and documents involved)?
3. Why is the work done in the manner prescribed?
4. Who does the work and to what extent?
5. Where is the work done, and what limitations does this impose?
6. When is the work done, and what limitations does this impose?
7. Which related activities elsewhere need consideration in relation to the form or work being studied?

A record of the procedures involved in the use of the form, setting forth in sequence all operations concerned, will aid analysis. Usually, a simple flowchart is adequate, but sometimes other types of charts are necessary. Where a series of forms has to be studied, it may be advantageous, as an alternative, to mount specimens on a large spreadsheet and record the associated action.

Quantitative Information.   Quantitative information can be collected simultaneously with the procedural information. Whenever practicable,

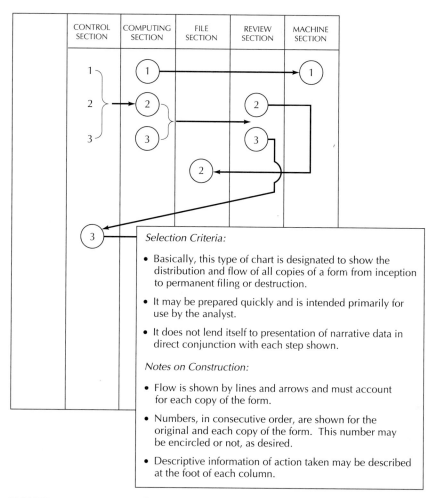

FIGURE 13.15 Form Distribution Chart
Source: *Records Management Handbooks,* General Services Administration

statistics should be obtained that are indicative of the following:

- Number of operations undertaken and forms completed.
- Incidence of work over a selected period.
- Volume of arrears of work at selected points in time.
- Time taken to do work or complete forms.
- Costs of the various stages of work.
- Number and nature of errors, queries, or other indications of ineffectiveness or inadequacy.

Clearly, so much review work will not be done for every form. Rather, it will be limited to those with a large usage, those which are basic to significant procedures, and those which are costly in terms of printing. The forms inventory and analysis should provide a complete history of the form. It will also provide the information needed to determine if the form pertains to an authorized responsibility of the originator, if the information needed to complete the form is available at some other source, and if the information will serve a useful purpose to the organization.

RECURRING DATA ANALYSIS CHART											PAGE OF PAGES

ACTIVITY	TITLE											
DATE OF ANALYSIS	*Voucher for Returned Check*	*Returned Check*	*Returned Check*									
ANALYZED BY												
ITEMIZED DATA	NO. 1	NO. 2	NO. 3	NO.	NO.	NO.	NO.	NO.	NO.	NO.		TOTAL
1	Name	√	√	√									3
2	address	√	√	√									3
3	Reason for return	√		√									2
4	Classification	√											1
5	Date	√	√	√									3
6	Amount	√	√	√									3
7	Class of tax	√	√	√									3
8	Original No.	√	√	√									3
9	Deposited	√	√	√									3
10	Period	√											1
11	Unclassified No.		√	√									2
12	Check signed by		√										1
13	17		√										1
14	21		√										1
15	69		√										1
16	List No.		√	√									2
17													
18													

FIGURE 13.16 Recurring Data Chart

Improving Procedures

Every form is involved with a procedure. A procedure consists of all of the steps that are taken to record, analyze, transmit, and store information needed to serve a single, specific purpose. A form frequently is an instrument that puts a procedure in motion. But the form is generally subordinate to the procedure, not the procedure to the form.

Checking all the forms in a system would be an involved and very lengthy undertaking. A more logical approach would consist of an analysis of all of the forms involved in a procedure. One procedure may consist of relatively few forms. Because they have a common matrix, all the forms in a procedure tend to dovetail and interlock. They are appropriate for analysis because of their similarity of purpose.

Forms analysis at the procedural level, therefore, is an ideal way to analyze related forms. Because so many forms are related, and because studying them individually denies the analyst the whole picture of a procedure, it is important that the analyst understand the procedure so that his or her analysis can be thorough and complete. Each procedure and its related forms should be examined periodically.

To study a procedure and the role forms play in it, the analyst first needs facts. The facts enable the analyst to discover the answers to the what, when, where, who, how, and why questions for each step of a procedure involving a form (see Figure 13.17).

In addition to identifying necessary facts when studying a procedure, the forms analyst learns the reasons for a procedure. Such a study will reveal any source documents required for the completion of a form. The analyst also learns how many copies of the form are distributed.

The better informed the analyst is about any procedure and its related forms, the easier it will be for the analyst to convince others of the need for forms analysis. By becoming familiar with background data before discussing the role of all forms in a procedure with the people who prepare and use them, the analyst will be able to:

- Ask more pertinent questions and more intelligently interpret the answers.
- Obtain better cooperation because of the analyst's demonstrated interest in the work and the willingness to help.
- Shorten the time of interviews because the facts are known.
- Obtain all of the information needed in one visit without interrupting people several times.

Sources of Data. Usually, several sources are available for obtaining background data important to a procedural study. These are the main sources to check:

1. Manuals, regulations, or directives describing functional responsibilities and procedures bearing on the forms under study.
2. Organizational charts showing relationships of the units responsible for the forms to other units.

3. Reports of previous studies and correspondence concerning problems encountered in preparing or using the forms.
4. Functional and historical forms management files to review the history of the development of the form, identify any forms that are similar or related to the ones under study, and determine how often and in what quantities additional copies of the form were reproduced.
5. Completed forms on file, showing types of errors made in completing the forms, revisions, or additions.
6. People who participated in previous studies of the forms.

An analyst may find that even an operating official, working on his or her own forms, has incomplete background facts about the procedures controlling the use of those forms elsewhere in the organization. Others with whom the analyst is working may likewise be unfamiliar with various parts of the paperwork background. The analyst may need to prepare an outline to follow before interviewing the people concerned with the procedure and its forms.

Collecting Data through Interviews. Interviewing people in any procedural study should never be done without adequate preparation. Most analysts have found it desirable to do the following:

- Explain the purpose of the study to the supervisor of the person to be interviewed and have the supervisor make the initial contact. At times, this explanation should be in writing before meeting with the supervisor.
- Plan for short interviews—no longer than one hour. Consider the workload of the person, and select a time that least interferes with his or her other activities.
- Prearrange the questions and discussion points of the interview in logical sequence.

Initiating Forms Analysis Projects. Some forms management offices put the internal organization of forms on a project basis. The elements involved in project analysis are the following:

Initiating Forms	Why?	Reevaluating Forms

NEED
 	
What do the forms in the procedure accomplish which justify their existence?
 	
What other forms are related, or duplicate in whole or in part the information requested?
 	
What inadequacies are there in the forms in the procedure?
	WHY this need?	**NEED**
		
		Is the information needed?
		
		Does the cost exceed the worth?
		
		Is there a better source or a better way?
		
		Can the forms or items on the forms be –
		    Combined?
		    Eliminated?
		    Simplified or resequenced?
		    Added?

PEOPLE Who requires the data? Who enters the information? Who extracts the information?	WHY by these people?	**PEOPLE** Can the work be assigned to other units or clerks to simplify the work or combine its handling? Can the forms in the procedure be resequenced to simplify the entering or extracting of the information?
PLACE Where are the forms in the procedure written and processed? Where are the forms sent? Where are the forms filed?	WHY here?	**PLACE** Can the writing of the forms and their processing be combined with similar work done in another unit? Can the forms be completed in the field without the need of feeder forms, or having to copy the information on another form in the office? Does the design of the forms aid in their filing, finding, storage and disposition?
TIME When are the forms in the procedure written? When are these forms processed? When are the forms filed?	WHY at this time?	**TIME** Are the various processing steps taken in their proper order? Can the peakloads be leveled off by better scheduling of the forms flow? Can information be requested so it can be processed during a slack period?
METHOD How are the forms in the procedure written? How is the information on these forms processed? How are these forms transmitted? How are the forms filed?	WHY this method?	**METHOD** Can the writing method be changed for the better? Can the routing or mailing method be changed? Have the forms been geared to the most efficient office equipment?

FIGURE 13.17 Guide for Basic Analysis of Forms

- Title, purpose, and scope of project.
- Organizational component concerned.
- Plan for arriving at a possible solution.
- Estimated work–hour savings or other benefits to be derived.
- Estimated work–hours budgeted to the project.
- Estimated beginning date.

This type of analysis can formalize the work, highlight its nature, keep tab on the progress made, and aid in reporting what has been done. Projects furnish a basis from which an analyst can initiate broad studies of functions or systems.

Generally, there are at least two groups of people to be interviewed in a procedural study: those concerned with entering data on forms and those concerned with extracting or summarizing data from them. In addition, there may be people who are involved in other phases of handling or processing the forms, such as those who review, audit, transmit, or file them. When more than one copy of any form is prepared, different groups of people may be involved in the data extraction and processing performed for each copy.

The forms analyst should first determine the responsibilities of the person being interviewed in relation to the form. Does the form exist solely or partly for his or her use? Which items are entered on the form, and which copies are prepared to satisfy his or her requirements? For what purposes does this person need forms, items, or copies?

The analyst discusses each step with each person processing the form. He or she also makes a note of the supplies and equipment used; notes how often a person processes the form and the average amount of time spent on one process; examines any forms from which, or to which, information is copied as part of preparing or using the form under study; and collects filled–in copies of all forms and copies of any related documents pertinent to the study.

The analyst ensures a comprehensive interview. The analyst does not rely entirely on what was said, but also goes to the point of use and observes the complete process.

Areas for Study. Clues to areas for possible analysis are obtained from several sources:

- Suggestions made by the operating personnel.
- Areas suggested by top management for potential savings and improvement.
- Operational areas in which problems are known to exist, such as backlogs, bottlenecks, unusual time lags, excessive volume, repetition, or numerous errors.
- Review of forms and information collected for the forms management files.

A well–balanced project schedule should include short–term projects that can be completed quickly and that will yield results to show immediately the benefits of forms management. It should likewise include long–term projects on more complicated or well–entrenched operations, which will involve considerable expenditure of time but pay substantial dividends in work hours and improved operations.

Task Force. A variation of project work is to set up special task forces to study specific segments of an organization's forms. Under this plan, members of the forms management staff join with members of a particular activity to review all of the forms used by that activity. For example, the data processing division studies all forms that are later keyed or scanned into the computer. When the two groups are studying payroll forms, for instance, the accounting division will assign personnel to work with the task force.

The task force method has the benefit of assuring that a whole group of related forms will be considered at one time rather than piecemeal. Another advantage is getting wider support for forms management and changes. A disadvantage is that the task force is not a continuing entity. Its members have full–time jobs in their own divisions and usually give these jobs first priority.

Developing and Presenting Improvements

For all the forms used in the procedure under study, the forms analyst determines the following:

- Are all items needed?
- Should new ones be added?
- Is information available at another source?
- Can forms be eliminated, combined, resequenced, or simplified?
- Are all copies needed?
- Does the cost exceed the worth?

In this way, the forms analyst knows how far he or she can go in questioning the necessity of the procedure. The analyst is now ready to develop any proposed form or forms and to recommend changes in the related procedures or equipment. He or she uses the best part of what exists—making changes only when they will provide real advantages. There is no point in change for the sake of change. Unless a real advantage is revealed, no change should be made.

If a visual presentation will help, the analyst makes the necessary charts showing the "before" and "after" work flow. He or she makes a pencil layout of the form or forms. These, included with the "before" charts developed in the fact–finding stage, are all the pictorial presentations these improvements will need to afford easy comprehension by the viewers. It is advisable to present any detailed cost, potential improvements, and work–hour savings in written form.

PARTS OF A FORM

There are five parts to almost every form: heading, introduction, instructions, body, and close. The *heading* is the facilitative part of the form and includes a title and a form number. The identification of the form may also be part of the heading and includes edition date, page identification, and supersession notices. The *introduction* explains the purpose of the form. Sometimes the purpose is identified in the title. *Instructions* include items that explain how to fill in the form and what to do with the form. The *body* consists of the grouped or sequenced items calling for the information desired. The *close* provides space for approving signatures.

In designing the body of a form it is necessary to identify all of the data elements needed to obtain the information required for a transaction. The data elements are also known as data fields in electronic records. The data fields used constitute the record. A group of related records constitutes a file, and a group of related files constitutes a database. A database can represent the corporation since its file organization may include files of all of its divisions.

The file organization is also known as the file structure or data hierarchy. The data hierarchy is a four–level organizational structure of information that ranges from the most basic level—the data element—to the broadest level of the database. It is important to note that the data element or field consists of one or more characters. These may be alphanumeric characters or symbols. The data hierarchy gives a total picture of the information system of the organization and the relationship of its parts. The corporate database may include hundreds of data elements which can be arranged to provide a variety of information. Data elements are selected to respond to a specific query, such as a telephone listing. The data elements in the telephone listing may show the following: name, position, department, address, and extension or number.

Some of the data elements used in the telephone listing may be used in calculating the payroll: name, department, and so on. Other data elements that need to be added are social security number, employee number, rate of pay, hours worked, and deductions.

The data elements identify all the bits of data that can be collected. The data elements also show how large the field must be to hold the characters necessary to provide the data. As data elements are identified to constitute information, only those data elements are used in the form. Thus, duplication of data is eliminated.

The Facilitative Area

Every form has two jobs to do. The main one is collecting information. The subsidiary one, which internally assists it to do its main job of providing information, may be referred to as facilitative. A portion of every form should be set aside for accomplishing the facilitative task. There should be space for such items as organization name; form title; identification of form including number and edition date; instructions for filling in; and routing instructions on how to handle the form after it is filled in. The area of the form devoted to the facilitative task is peripheral to providing information. This is evident in Figure 13.18.

Organization Name. Some company forms are filled in by the organization's customers. If this is the case, the name of the organization should be included with the title.

Form Title and Subtitle. The title of a form can appear in any one of several positions, as shown in Figure 13.19. Top left can be used when the upper right corner is reserved for filing data. Otherwise, the title can be centered at the top. In a vertical file card where the top is reserved for filing data, the title can be placed at the bottom of the card in the margin, the area that is used as gripper space to hold the card in the typewriter.

A subtitle may be desirable from the reader's point of view to explain or qualify the main title. If, for example, there is more than one form called "Daily Warehouse Record," each form should be distinguished by a subtitle, such as "Shipments and Receipts," centered under the main title.

Form Number. Organizations have found the assignment of numbers to forms to be a necessary control device. Straight numeric order is the simplest and most flexible pattern. Elaborate numbering patterns, with alphabetic or numeric prefixes or suffixes to identify using offices, should be avoided. Reorganizations, transfers of functions, and other changes within the company break up

such patterns and invariably lead to a troublesome wholesale renumbering of large groups of forms. It may be desirable in some cases to print the old form number in parentheses after the new number, such as "Form 192 (formerly Form 102)," and then discontinue use of the old number.

The lower right or lower left margin is the most advantageous location for the form number and edition date for the following reasons:

- It prevents the tearing or obliterating of the number when a form is stapled in the upper left corner.
- It permits the form number to be seen readily when forms are bound at the top.
- It serves as an aid in stocking, particularly when forms are stocked in small quantities in supply cabinets.

There is an additional advantage in placing the form number in the lower right corner. The number can be seen readily when forms are filed in folders in upright filing cabinets.

On certificates, the number should be printed in a small typeface so as not to detract from the appearance. Also, the number should be placed so it will not interfere with the limited working area.

When a form consists of separate sheets, the form number should appear on each sheet. Thus, if one sheet is separated from the others, it is quickly identified. When a form is printed on front and back, the form number should also appear on the back.

Instructions. Brief general instructions are placed at the top of the form below or near the title to tell the reader immediately how many copies are required; who should submit the form; and where, when, and to whom copies should be sent.

If detailed instructions appear elsewhere, such as on the reverse side of the form, reference should be included in the brief general instructions. Instructions to amplify items of information or column heads should be placed in parentheses after the item or head. Short instructions that relate to a specific section should be placed with the

THE PRINTED FORM

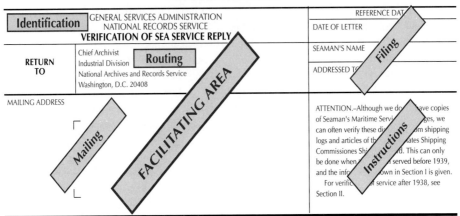

Section I.–INFORMATION NEEDED FOR VERIFICATION OF SEAMAN'S SERVICE PRIOR TO 1939

Columns A and B.–Always filled in.
Column C or D.–Complete whichever is checked.
You can get some of this information from former employers, or from alphabetical lists of owners and vehicles in the annual volumes of the "List of Merchant Vessels of the United States," "Lloyd's Register," and the "Records of the American Bureau of Shipping." The larger public libraries have these volumes.

☒ A	☒ B	☐ C			☐ D
NAMES OF VESSELS	RATINGS HELD (Each voyage of vessel)	DATES OF EACH VOYAGE	SIGN-ON PORT FOR EACH VOYAGE	DISCHARGE PORT FOR EACH VOYAGE	DATES OF SERVICE ON EACH U.S. SHIPPING BOARD VESSEL

(If more space is needed, use reverse)

Section II.–FOR VERIFICATION OF SERVICE AFTER 1938 (Write to one "X" ed)

☐ UNITED STATES COAST GUARD
MERCHANT VESSEL PERSONNEL RECORDS AND WELFARE SECTION
WASHINGTON, D.C. 20408

☐ MARITIME ADMINISTRATION
PERSONNEL OFFICER
WASHINGTON, D.C. 20408

SIGNATURE OF CHIEF ARCHIVIST   DATE

FIGURE 13.18 Working and Facilitating Areas of the Form
Source: *Records Management Handbooks,* General Services Administration

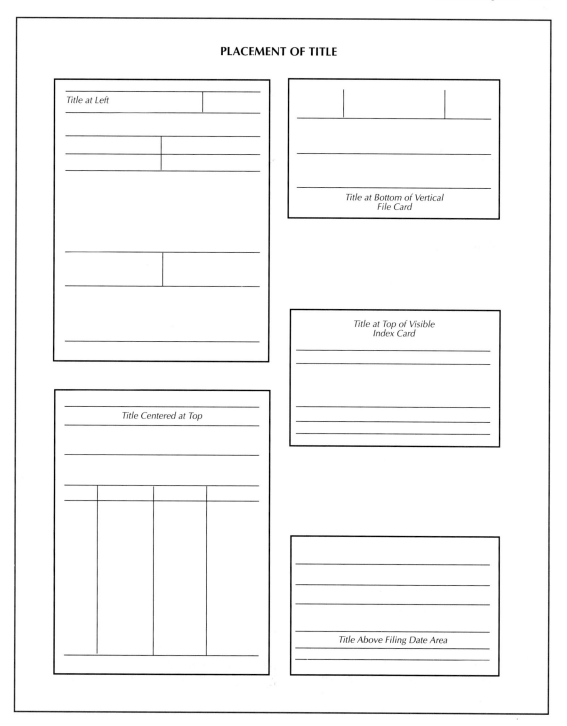

FIGURE 13.19 Placement of Form Title
Source: *Records Management Handbooks,* General Services Administration

section head. These points are depicted in Figure 13.20.

Lengthy instructions are placed:

- On the front of the form if there is sufficient space for both instruction and fill–in data.
- On the back of the form if there is not enough space on the front.
- On a separate sheet or in a booklet.
- In an administrative directive prescribed by the organization.

Instructions should not be placed among entry spaces because that gives the form a cluttered appearance and impedes completion. If the form is printed front and back, all entry spaces should be located, if possible, on the front of the form. This eliminates turning the form over to complete fill–ins.

Routing.   Effective routing and mailing design techniques simplify handling of papers. In addition, they reduce the chance of error and speed delivery of mail.

Whenever possible, a form should allow space in which to identify the addressor and the addressee. In this way, it becomes self–routing; the need for a transmittal letter or routing slip is eliminated. Some ways of placing the routing information are shown in Figure 13.21.

"To" and "From" boxes may be placed:

- On one line across the form.
- One under the other.
- One at the top and the other below in the space customarily used for a signature.

Identification of a Form

When a form is used for the first time, the first thing a person reads is the title, to get a quick idea of what the form is about. The title also facilitates the requisitioning, stocking, and issuing of forms. In addition to the title, identification includes agency name, form number, date of edition, appropriate supersession notice, and any control symbols.

Different readers are, of course, interested in different parts of the identification. A member of the public is most interested in the organization name and title; a stock clerk is interested in the form number, edition date, and supersession notice; a file clerk is most interested in the form number. Yet, where the identification data are placed on the form is important to all readers.

Edition Date.   Forms practice requires each form to show an edition date (the month and year sent to print). The original number assigned is usually retained on any revision of the form, but the edition date should be changed to reflect each successive revision in content or design.

Edition dates are valuable for reference purposes in writing procedures, in ascertaining whether the current edition of a form is being used, in advising users that old editions of a form may not be used, and in the disposition of obsolete stocks. Edition dates are generally placed after the form numbers in parentheses.

Page Identification.   When a form consists of multiple pages, folded or stapled, page numbers help to:

- Aid the printer in the assembling of material for printing and in the collating of material after printing.
- Key instructions to the form.
- Identify the form, particularly when pages of the form are separated to fill in or process.

The page number is usually placed in the upper right corner. When continuation sheets are used for the completion of a form and the number of such pages to be used is unknown at the onset (as in requisition and purchase order forms), each page should be numbered in this way: "Page _____ of _____ pages." The page number and total number of pages are entered in the blank spaces by the person completing the form.

Supersession Notice.   Supersession notices adjacent to the new form number can be helpful, for example, "Replaces Form 103, June 1988, which

BRIEF INSTRUCTIONS

Brief general instructions placed at top of form

> Submit in duplicate, to the Records
> Administration Division by the
> 15th of each month.

Reference to detailed instructions

> CONSTRUCTION CONTRACT
> (See instructions on reverse)

Instructions to amplify items of information

> 3. NAME UNDER WHICH FORMERLY
> EMPLOYED FEDERALLY (if other than
> item 2).

Short instruction relating to specific section

> PART B—MEDICAL RECORD
> (To be completed by physician)

LENGTHY INSTRUCTIONS

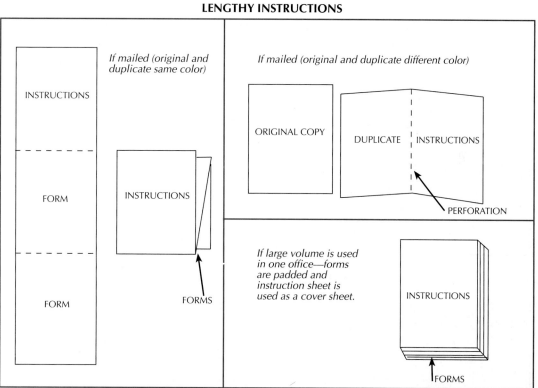

INSTRUCTIONS

FORM

FORM

If mailed (original and duplicate same color)

INSTRUCTIONS

FORMS

If mailed (original and duplicate different color)

ORIGINAL COPY

DUPLICATE · INSTRUCTIONS

PERFORATION

If large volume is used in one office—forms are padded and instruction sheet is used as a cover sheet.

INSTRUCTIONS

FORMS

FIGURE 13.20 Placement of Form Instructions
Source: *Records Management Handbooks*, General Services Administration

TO/FROM ARRANGEMENT

ONE AND TWO LINE VARIABLE FILL-INS

TO

Place at Top Under the Title

TO

FROM

Place at Top Left Under Title

TO

Place at Top of Form

FROM

Place at Bottom of Form

ONE LINE PREPRINTED CONSTANT ROUTING

TO
PUBLICATIONS DIVISION
ATTN: PUBLICATIONS CONTROL OFFICER

FROM

Note Preprinted Titles Instead of Names

TO

FROM
DIRECTOR, OPERATING FACILITIES

Place at Top Under Title

FROM/TO ARRANGEMENT

*Placed at Top
Left Under
Title*

2. FROM

3. ROUTING
☐ TO ADMIN.
  DIVISION
☐ THROUGH ADMIN. DIV. TO
  ADJUDICATION DIV.
☐ TO ADJUDICATION
  DIVISION

PREPRINTED MULTIPLE ROUTING

TO:	1.	EASTERN PUBLICATIONS DEPOT
(Route	2.	PUBLICATIONS CONTROL OFFICER
in	3.	FORMS CONTROL STAFF
Order)	4.	WESTERN PUBLICATIONS DEPOT

Same Routing in All Cases

TO: ("X" Proper Box)
☐ REPRODUCTION BRANCH
☐ GRAPHICS BRANCH
☐ FISCAL DIVISION

Routing Not Constant in All Cases

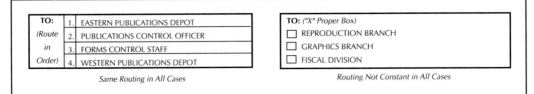

FIGURE 13.21 Placement of Form—Routing Information
Source: *Records Management Handbooks,* General Services Administration

will not be used." Supersession notices have proven particularly advantageous during the first three or four years of a new or revitalized program, when a large quantity of forms are revised, consolidated, and eliminated. Such notices also serve as guides to users and stockroom clerks in eliminating obsolete stocks and requisitioning current forms. The supersession notice may be printed in the bottom margin of the form near the form number.

The notice should specify whether existing stocks of the replaced form may be used. If the existing stocks cannot be used and if the new form has a different number, the number and date of the replaced form should be included in the notice. If a sizable number of forms are superseded by one form, a separate notice may be more appropriate to inform interested personnel of the change and to avoid giving the form a cluttered look. There also may be space limitations that would not permit a lengthy supersession notice.

Some ways of wording a supersession notice follow:

1. When revising an existing form, use:
   a. *Previous editions are obsolete.*
   b. *Previous editions may be used until supply is exhausted.*
   c. *Existing stocks of* [form number and edition date] *will be used.*
   d. *Existing stocks of* [form number and edition date] *will not be used.*

2. When replacing an existing form with a different number, use:
   a. *Replaces* [form number and edition date], *which is obsolete.*
   b. *Replaces* [form number and edition date], *which may be used until supply is exhausted.*

3. For a combination of the above supersession notices, use:
   a. *Existing stocks of* [form number and edition date] *will be used.*
   b. *Replaces* [form number and edition date], *which is obsolete.*

The Working Area

The part of the form that is devoted to the substantive work of the form is its reason for being; this part is usually called the working area. (See Figure 13.18).

The working area of the form must be just as carefully designed as the facilitative area. Careful consideration must be given to the arrangement of the information requested (proper grouping, sequencing, and aligning of data), margins, spacing, and methods by which the respondent will supply the information.

FORMS DESIGN

Forms design is the outgrowth of forms analysis. Only after the need for the form has been established and the effect of the methods and procedures controlling its use have been ascertained can design of a form begin. The design of a form evolves as one integrates the various needs of the people filling it in, of the processors of the information it contains, of the printer who manufactures it, and of the personnel staffing the mailing and filing stations.

Forms analysis resolves what goes on the form, while forms design continues the analysis until it resolves how best to arrange and present the information. In resolving the how, the designer must weigh the often conflicting needs of the people mentioned previously. This how is important because the design of a form is one reflection of the degree of efficiency with which a system functions. Design helps to determine whether it will take 30 minutes to fill in a form, or whether the task can be done in 12 minutes.

A form should be designed to meet the requirements of the system for which it is to be used. It should also be designed to reduce the amount of clerical labor required for completing the form, to reduce clerical errors in form completion, to reduce printing and paper costs, and to increase managerial efficiency.

Principles of Forms Design

The design of an efficient form requires ability in paperwork simplification and a knowledge of the purpose and use of each form. Good design will result in a form that is easier to (1) read and understand, (2) fill in, and (3) file.

Design Rules.   The application of the following design rules for simple forms will usually result in a form that is efficient to use.

1. Study the purpose and use of the form, and design the form with the user in mind.
2. Keep the design simple, eliminating unnecessary information and lines.
3. Include a form number and name on each form.
4. Use standardized card or paper size where practicable.
5. Use standardized terminology in wording instructions.
6. Arrange items on the form in proper sequence.
7. Preprint constant data to keep variable (fill–in) data to a minimum.
8. Allow sufficient spacing for the method of fill–in (manual or machine).

Design rules include attention to arrangement (grouping of data, item sequence, and alignment), size, margins, space, box design, horizontal rules, printed captions, columnar (tabular) format, two–sided format, computer forms design, and standards.

Arrangement

To make the completion of a form easier, its arrangement should be conducive to continuous execution. Any other arrangement invites mistakes and lowers the quality and quantity of output. To introduce continuous execution into the design, three basic arrangement factors are involved:

Grouping of data
Item sequence
Alignment

Grouping of Data.   If different persons are to enter data on the same form, the data to be filled in by each person should be grouped according to the sequence of the processing steps involved. This eliminates any need for searching or backtracking. If a form is used as a source document to collect data on different types of material, related items or related kinds of material should be grouped.

Sometimes it is helpful to identify the groupings. The main grouping may be numbered; if there are subgroupings, they may be lettered. These various ways of grouping are shown in Figure 13.22.

Item Sequence.   After related items have been put together, they should be placed in a sequence that will eliminate any unnecessary writing motions and make it easy to transcribe information from the form. The value of the same–item sequence is shown in Figure 13.23.

Numbering the items on a form makes reference easier and faster. If an item has several component parts, they may be identified by following the traditional number–letter outline system.

Alignment.   The data on a form are arranged so that the flow of writing is continuous from left to right and from top to bottom. When this straight–line flow concept is observed, data are entered on the form without any wasted motion. Items on a form can be aligned vertically for a minimum of tabular and marginal stops.

Size

The sizes of the paper stock on which forms are printed have been standardized. The full sheet is cut into equal divisions that, when printed, provide finished forms in standard sizes.

The argument for standard size does not rest

CORRELATE ITEMS WITH SEQUENCE OF PROCESSING STEPS

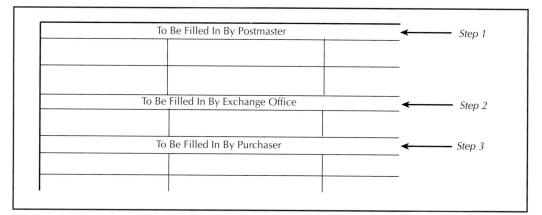

GROUP ITEMS

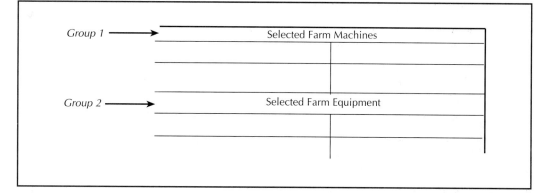

IDENTIFY GROUPS FOR REFERENCE

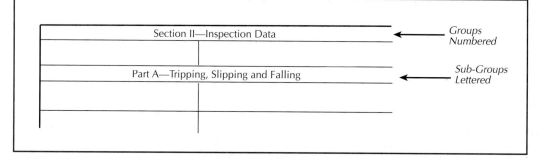

FIGURE 13.22 Various Methods of Grouping Data on Forms
Source: *Records Management Handbooks,* General Services Administration

VALUE OF SAME ITEM SEQUENCE

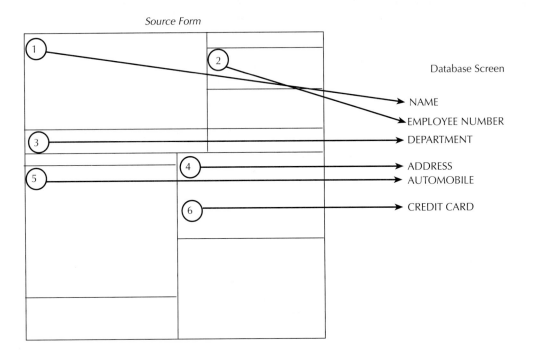

FIGURE 13.23 Same–Item Sequence of Forms

on reduced paper costs alone. The best economics of scale are in the areas of machines, equipment, and supplies, all of which have also been standardized in size. Any time a nonstandard-size form forces use of other nonstandard items, the costs mount rapidly. Nonstandard–size filing cabinets, for example, cost about 40 percent more than standard–size filing cabinets.

Margins

Reproduction facilities require margins as working space for sprocket holes that permit the mechanical gripping of paper during the printing process and for trimming the paper when several copies of a form are printed on large sheets. It is essential to allow minimum margins of 1/3 inch at the top, 1/2 inch at the bottom, and 3/10 inch at the sides. If card stock is used, at least 1/8 inch should be allowed as margin on all sides.

On some types of forms the image must extend to the edge of the paper; for example, a card form with limited space, or a group of forms that are put together in overlapping positions to indicate comparative and cumulative figures. Extending the image to the edge of the paper requires printing on a sheet of paper larger than the trimmed–and–finished form size and then trimming to finish to the desired size. This is called bleeding, which means to print the ink off the edge of the trimmed sheet.

If a form requiring bleeding is designed for offset printing, lines should be drawn beyond the image size. When the sheet is trimmed, the lines will bleed off the edge of the paper, leaving a clean edge. When possible, bleeding should be avoided because it can increase handling costs.

Spacing

Horizontal and vertical space requirements are determined by the number of fill–ins to be entered and the nature of the printed matter, such as box captions, column and section headings, and text. The writing method (hand, typewriter, or a special office machine) determines the amount of space that should be allowed for fill–in data, while the number of characters per inch of typeface used determines the amount of space to be allowed for the printed matter.

Horizontal spacing is based on the number of characters written per inch, which is controlled by the writing method used to enter the data. Vertical spacing is based on the number of writing lines that can be written per inch. Although most forms are typewritten, some are handwritten, and a small percentage combine these methods.

Box Design

The box design is sometimes called the upper left corner (ULC) arrangement because of the location of the printed captions (see Figure 13.24). The box design presents a pleasing appearance, because the alignment of vertical rules and a common left margin eliminate the cluttered appear-

ance common to unplanned forms. Horizontal rules and printed captions are a very important part of box design.

Horizontal Rules. Horizontal rules extend from the left to the right margin. Boxes are made by the insertion of vertical rules, which are aligned wherever possible to keep the number of typewriter tabular stops to a minimum. The typing position of each line should begin from a common left margin.

Printed Captions. Printed captions—items of information requested—are placed in the upper left corner of the boxes. Therefore, the captions are always visible when the form is in a writing machine and the entire width of the boxes below the captions is available for the fill–in data. Box design frequently increases available space by as much as 25 percent over the caption and line arrangement.

Each caption should be complete in itself but can be simplified, defined, or qualified by means of brief, amplifying statements in italic typeface

FIGURE 13.24 Box or Upper Left Corner Arrangement
Source: *Records Management Handbooks,* General Services Administration

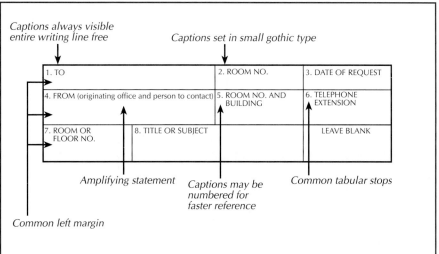

in parentheses. A blank space reserved for future use by someone other than the person filling in the form should be so marked. A box head such as "Do not write in this space" or "Leave blank" may be used. If the space is to be reserved for a rubber stamp, the number of characters to go in the space should be computed in the same way as for a written entry. Because each space is clearly defined and each box is limited to one entry, there is never any doubt concerning the box to which a caption applies.

Columnar (Tabular) Format

Columnar (tabular) format is used when several entries of the same type are to be used under one heading. This eliminates the repetition of descriptive items for each type of information, thus saving space. (See Figure 13.25.)

Two–Sided Format

Printing a form on both sides of a sheet of paper is sometimes advantageous. For example, a non-standard–size form may be reduced to standard size or additional sheets of a form may be eliminated by two–sided printing. When a form is to be printed on both sides, the printer needs to know how the reverse side is to be printed in relation to the front. This decision should be based on the use of the form and the method of filing or binding.

The usual methods of two–sided printing are shown in Figure 13.26. Two–sided printing has also become extremely important in recycling and in supporting environmental standards.

Computer Forms Design

Computer–printed forms share many of the characteristics of other office forms; however, there are some specifications that apply only to computer forms. Line and tab spacing requirements and form sizes are different from those for hand-written or typed forms. Computer forms are pin-fed by sprocket holes in their edges, rather than roller–fed as typewriter forms are. Computer forms are usually designed so that several documents can be printed simultaneously by the computer. This permits maximum use of the computer system's printers. For example, checking account statements for banks are usually printed two at a time on a computer printer. This cuts print time in half for the computer, because it prints one line at a time regardless of the characters involved.

Computer forms are continuous, which means they are printed on long uncut rolls of paper that are perforated between each page. After forms have been run through the computer printers, they are often run through two machines: one, called a decollator, separates the copy and removes the carbon paper; the other, called a burster, tears the individual pages free from each other along the

FIGURE 13.25 Columnar Arrangement
Source: *Records Management Handbooks,* General Services Administration

From Stock Issue and Historical Record Cards			
		Amount	
Quantity On Hand	Total Value (Omit cents)	Over Inventory	Under Inventory

HEAD TO HEAD

Head (top) of front to head (top) of back

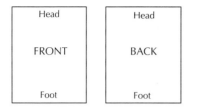

HEAD TO SIDE

Head (top) of front to right of back

HEAD TO FOOT

Head (top) of front to foot (bottom) of back

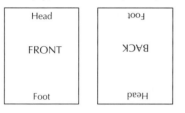

Head (top) of front to left of back

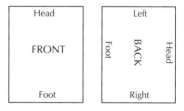

FIGURE 13.26 Two–Sided Printing
Source: *Records Management Handbooks,* General Services Administration

perforation lines. These processes are usually done with computer–printed information such as invoices, billing notices, and bank statements. Computer reports containing many pages that will all be used in the same place are usually not burst; instead, they are bound at the top to form a book.

Establishing Standards

Over the years a well–defined set of forms design standards has been developed and used by the federal government to speed and facilitate the reading, writing, transmitting, and filing of forms. This set of standards was developed to serve as an aid to federal government agencies in the development of their own standards. They include 17 characteristics found adaptable to standardization. A large organization may wish to develop more explicit criteria in the light of its own circumstances and to expand on the number of different items covered. Specific criteria for the design of specialized classes of forms can be developed. The standards developed by the federal government are located in Appendix B. Forms Management Program Checklists are shown in Appendix C.

Global Standards. As the world moved to a global economy, leaders in business and government realized that the lack of a uniform standard of quality was inhibiting the flow of free trade. In 1987, the International Organization for Standards

(ISO) published a series of guidelines for quality. These guidelines became known as ISO 9000. Compliance with ISO 9000 requires an on–site review by an impartial, accredited auditor, who verifies that the manufacturing processes meet the international standard and that the appropriate documentation is in place.

As ISO 9000 gains international acceptance, registration (also known as certification) is becoming an important marketing advantage. ISO registration can help companies compete for business as a quality supplier. In addition, by bringing manufacturing processes up to ISO 9000 standards, many companies are gaining the rewards of reduced costs and increased efficiency.

All five standards, ISO 9000–9004, deal with the need for an effective quality system: ensuring measurements are valid with regular calibration of measuring and testing equipment; providing product identification and traceability; maintaining an adequate recordkeeping system; and having adequate product handling, storage, packaging, and delivery systems.

The adequate recordkeeping system is concerned with the forms and other records in the organization's quality system documentation. Examples include the forms (or computer disks) upon which tests are recorded, or photometer calibration records, or copies of purchase orders for materials to specific standards and the vendor's certification thereof, or notation of product weights. Forms may need to be modified or new forms created to meet the requirements of the ISO standards.

FORMS MANAGEMENT PERSONNEL

The improvement of forms should be a cooperative effort of all those who create, fill in, use, or otherwise handle forms. In practice, however, most improvements come either from the office of the official who originates the form, a forms management analyst, or a systems and procedures analyst.

Operating Officials

Forms originate in the office of an operating official, because he or she is the one who knows how the form is used and how its use affects other operations in the office. It is usually at this location that the decision to go to electronic forms or electronic data interchange is made. If a form is to be revised, the official must decide which changes are best and approve the final revision. Operating officials, therefore, should know about useful methods of forms analysis and improvement.

It is natural for the operating supervisor or administrator to feel that his or her everyday operating responsibilities are enough without worrying about the analysis and improvement of forms. A common reason given for delaying action on forms improvement is that operating problems take up all available time.

What many officials fail to notice, however, is that unsuitable forms or the need for more forms actually cause many of those operating problems. For example, in some offices much of the correspondence results from unclear instructions on forms concerning entries to be filled in or actions to be taken. The official frequently spends time correcting and clarifying misunderstandings caused by unsuitable forms. If the official realized the time that could be saved with improved forms, that alone would be sufficient incentive to improve them.

Some officials are already studying forms just to keep them current with changing operations and conditions. With just a little more study, many changes could be developed into substantial improvements. This is not to imply that the operating official should attempt to be a forms management analyst. Supervisors should, however, be aware of the time they and their subordinates spend both in studying forms for possible changes and in handling problems caused by unsuitable forms.

Forms Analysts

The magnitude of the forms problem has warranted the establishment of a forms management staff in many organizations. This staff assists operating officials in the analysis of the more complex forms used in the organization.

In many instances, the forms management staff is able to suggest improvements that the originator did not think of. Many forms travel beyond the originating office to other departments for their preparation or use. Even in large organizations, most of the forms are of the administrative type, and there are many similarities in departmental operations.

The skilled forms analyst has a knowledge of standard forms and electronic forms as well as of organization–wide practices. The forms analyst is sufficiently detached from the operating task to see procedural aspects that those closer to the operation may not see. He or she is in the best position to be an intermediary between the originator and the users. The forms analyst will usually also be the forms designer, bringing the viewpoint of that technical specialty to bear on the matter.

Professional Staff

The heart of any forms management program is the professional staff. They possess the necessary procedural analysis capabilities, the knowledge of forms design and construction standards, and the information about paper, carbons, and the processing equipment. No form should ever be sent to the printer without staff approval. The most frequently used way to secure that approval is to fill in a form data sheet. Such a form is shown in Figure 13.27.

To manage forms, records administrators establish programs involving routines for ordering, designing, procuring, storing, distributing, reordering, reviewing, and disposing of each type of form used by the organization. Each of these control phases represents an area of specialization in today's forms management program.

Control of forms within an organization is best accomplished by centralizing the responsibility for planning, coordinating, simplifying, and policing them. The forms management staff must

have the authority to operate freely across organizational lines. Experience shows that a successful forms management program is as dependent on all interested employees in the organization as on the professional staff and the liaison representatives.

Forms Liaison Representative. In large organizations, each department should assign one person to serve as a forms liaison representative with responsibility for coordination with the forms management professional staff. This person should have a thorough knowledge of the paperwork within his or her unit.

A forms liaison representative in each department becomes even more valuable in studies of methods and procedures. These studies must encompass the details of each office's routine. The operational knowledge provided by the forms liaison representatives accelerates the process of analysis and helps assure departmental acceptance of improvements.

Top Management

No matter how well conceived the forms management program may be in other respects, the program will not achieve its objectives without top management's guidance. The direction taken by the program, like that of any other managerial program cutting across all segments of an organization, should reflect the view of top management.

To keep informed, top management should require reports of the benefits produced. It must evaluate the reports and intervene as the facts warrant. There are several matters in which top management should be particularly interested.

1. *User reaction.* The forms program should devote some time to interviewing users of forms about the shortcomings of forms. Users should not, however, be pressured to prove their criticisms.

2. *High–usage forms.* Top management should

FORM DATA SHEET

1. PLEASE PREPARE AND SUBMIT THIS FORM IN DUPLICATE WHEN REQUESTING A NEW FORM OR REVISION OF AN EXISTING FORM.
2. ATTACH LAYOUT OF PROPOSED FORM

FORM IDENTIFICATION

FORM TITLE (BRIEF AND DESCRIPTIVE)		FORM NUMBER
REQUESTED BY	DEPARTMENT OR LOCATION	☐ REVISED ☐ NEW
WHO PREPARES FORM	OTHER DEPARTMENTS USING OR HANDLING FORM (To be consulted for suggestions or approvals)	

PURPOSE AND USE DATA

METHOD OF MAKING ENTRIES
☐ PEN   ☐ PENCIL   ☐ ELITE TYPEWRITER   ☐ PICA TYPEWRITER   OTHER (MAKE AND MODEL NO.)

COPIES TO BE PRODUCED BY (DITTO, MIMEOGRAPH, ETC.)	NUMBER OF COPIES	CAN WINDOW ENVELOPE BE USED ☐ NO ☐ YES
DATA TO BE COPIED FROM (FORM NUMBERS)	DATA TO BE COPIED TO (FORM NUMBERS)	FORMS WITH WHICH COMPARED, ATTACHED, ETC.
REQUIRES REDESIGN OF WHAT OTHER FORMS	OBSOLETES WHAT OTHER FORMS	DISPOSITION OF OBSOLETE STOCK ☐ USE UP BEFORE USING NEW FORM ☐ DESTROY

RECOMMENDED USE
☐ REGIONAL   ☐ AREA   ☐ CORPORATION WIDE   ☐ OTHER (SPECIFY)   IS FORM SENT OUTSIDE CO. ☐ NO   ☐ YES

EXPLAIN BRIEFLY THE BASIC PURPOSE AND WHY THE CHANGE OR NEW FORM IS DESIRABLE

WILL REVISION IN PROCEDURE BE REQUIRED ☐ NO ☐ YES	NEW EQUIPMENT NEEDED IN USING THIS FORM (TYPEWRITERS, FILES, ETC.) ☐ NO ☐ YES (LIST)
ESTIMATED CLERICAL HOURS PER MONTH TO PROCESS FORM	ANTICIPATED SAVINGS OR BENEFITS (IN DOLLARS OR CLER. HOURS)

FORMS SPECIFICATIONS

COPIES	PAPER WEIGHT AND GRADE	COLOR	COLOR OF INK	DEPARTMENT WHERE FILED	HOW WILL EACH PART BE FILED BY TEL. NO., DATE, ETC.	BINDER, FILE, JACKET, ETC.	HOW OFTEN REFERRED TO AFTER FILING	HOW LONG RETAINED (MOS.-YRS.)
1. (ORIG.)								
2.								
3.								
4.								

FINISHING

TO BE PRINTED
☐ ONE SIDE ONLY   ☐ TWO SIDES   ☐ HEAD TO HEAD   ☐ TUMBLE STYLE (HEAD TO FOOT)   SIZE (WIDE X HIGH) X   TO BE USED ☐ SINGLY   ☐ IN SETS

NO. OF HOLES	DIAMETER	CENTER TO CENTER	KIND	SHEETS PER PAD	SHEETS PER SET

USAGE

QUANTITY ORDERED (CIRCLE ONE) SHEETS SETS PADS BOOKS	INITIAL DELIVERY	TO LAST (NO. OF MONTHS)	DATE REQUIRED	APPROX. COST PER M
HOW OFTEN PREPARED (DAILY, WEEKLY, ETC.)	ANNUAL USAGE	PEAKS (MONTHS AND QUANTITIES)		CHARGE COST TO ACCT. NO.

APPROVAL SIGNATURES	DEPARTMENT SUPERVISOR	DATE	SYSTEMS DEPARTMENT	DATE
	DEPARTMENT MANAGER	DATE		

FIGURE 13.27 Form Data Sheet

know which forms have a high annual usage. Benefits from improving or eliminating them will be far greater than those from tinkering with low–usage forms.

3. *Forms wastage.* Millions of unused forms become obsolete every year. The tendency to overorder can only be thwarted by taking note of how current the form is. Personnel often hesitate to order 100 copies, so the order is made out for 1,000.

4. *Relationships.* Coordination is paramount in providing suitable forms. Top management should be watchful for poor teamwork—the originator not giving the forms analyst time to review a form, the forms analyst moving too slowly in the review work, or the originator not notifying the forms management program of changed usage requirements.

The Originator

If more than 10,000 copies of a new form are to be used in a year or if the form will require more than 30 minutes to fill in, the originator should study the whole procedure for which the form is required. The input and output of the work should be considered as well as the main processes. It is particularly important to review the complete picture when subordinate processes such as copying or recording are to be undertaken separately, before or after the main process.

The originator should be sure to gather up–to–date facts and information about the procedure; the purposes for which the form is required; and the circumstances in which it will be completed, dispatched, filed, sorted, and handled. Where relevant, such information as the cost and effectiveness of arrangements and operations, the incidence of errors in completion, queries and difficulties, and the scope for possible change and improvements should be obtained. Direct, on–the–spot investigation and observation are vitally important.

The Consumer

The consumer is the person who initially fills in the form. The consumer should be provided with sufficient writing space for the entry of data, captions that are easy to understand, instructions that are correctly placed and clearly written, and a logical sequence of items. The forms improvement role of the consumer is to inform the forms management office of problems encountered in filling in a form.

By reviewing filled–in forms in the files, the forms management staff can determine whether it has provided the consumer with sufficient space. Spaces repeatedly left blank by the consumer may be an indication that such items are unnecessary. On the other hand, information written on the form for which no space is provided may indicate the need for a remarks section or the need for a new or additional section.

The Processing User

After a form has been filled in, the next step usually consists of someone reading the information that has been entered. Usually, this reader is expected to take action. The reader may be a supply clerk or an accountant. The effectiveness of the information supplied on the form is the final measure of its worth.

If the information supplied presents processing problems, the form cannot be considered a good one, regardless of how easy it was to enter information on it. The processing user is, therefore, especially interested in orderly organization of the information and in uniform design of related forms. The forms improvement role of the processor is to tell the forms management staff promptly of any processing difficulties caused by any form.

The Reports Management Staff

Because so many reports are forms, there may be conflict about who does the analysis on report forms. But once the information requirements are approved by the reports staff, the forms staff should not duplicate the effort. The forms clearance document may often be used as the reports clearance document for those forms that are also reports.

When the reports management office undertakes procedural study, it should always inform the forms management office. The two offices should compare notes on whether there is overlap in gathering the data. There is, of course, no conflict between reports management and forms management on the design of forms. Forms design personnel should plan and design all of an organization's forms.

The Directives Specialist

Most forms should be prescribed in an appropriate directive. Such directives provide the best medium for supplying guidance that cannot be fully placed on the face of the form. The following are examples of information to be included in directives:

- Specified instruction on who prepares the form, number of copies prepared, and where and when copies are submitted.
- A specimen of the form with sample entries, when this would help ensure accurate completion of the form.
- A description of the filing system to be used, but only if the records are to be maintained in a specific way.
- Any unusual information about the source and date of supply.

The clearance of directives with the forms management office will often prevent erroneous references to titles or obsolete editions of forms. Clearance also serves to correct instructions calling for the use of an electronic format when printed forms would be more appropriate.

It is important that users of forms be notified of the discontinuance of a form by means of the same directives that required the original use of the forms. It is axiomatic that the office originating a form (or the office responsible for its continuing use) should also be the office discontinuing the form.

Procurement Personnel

The stocking of paper–based forms includes procurement, reproduction, storage, and distribution. These are tasks normally assigned to publication and supply or similar departments. By preparing accurate specifications, forms management personnel can be very helpful to those performing these tasks.

An important part of the relationship between forms management personnel and the supply department is the method for handling stock replacement orders. A stock replenishment notice is usually prepared by supply operations personnel when the stock level of any form reaches the established minimum.

Alternatives to In–House Staff

In small organizations or organizations which do not have a forms manager, several alternatives are available to provide good forms management: outsourcing and vendors.

Outsourcing is using an outside contractor to provide forms management services such as forms design, production, inventory control, and storage of forms. All functions of forms management may not be readily available through this service.

Vendors can provide forms design and printing technology, as well as a selection of preprinted forms which can be customized to meet individual firm requirements at considerably less cost than original design. In most cases, it is essential for the records manager or his designee to work closely with the vendor.

SUMMARY

Forms serve as the chief means of communicating information in a standardized, repetitive manner. By their very design, forms often guide the flow of work through an office. Forms provide data for policy formulation, operational control and improvement, and performance evaluation.

The goals of a sound forms management program include the following:

- Control the design, issuance, and use of forms.
- Establish standards for uniformity and simplicity of forms.
- Improve the appearance and functional efficiency of forms.
- Eliminate unnecessary forms and unnecessary items on forms.
- Consolidate forms serving similar purposes to prevent overlapping and duplication.
- Analyze the cost of forms in relation to the value of the information provided.
- Determine appropriate forms media, reproduction, stocking, and distribution methods.

Paper–based forms include cut sheets, unit sets, continuous forms, and specialty forms. Electronic forms include template electronic forms, full electronic forms, machine–readable forms, electronic data interchange, and electronic funds transfer.

Forms analysis seeks to improve procedures through collecting data, initiating forms analysis projects, maintaining forms control files, and inventorying and appraising forms.

Parts of a form include the facilitative area of name, title, form number, instructions, and routing. The identification area includes edition number, page identification, and supersession notice. The working area is the area where data elements are arranged for collection of the desired information.

Forms design includes suggestions for arrangement (grouping of data, item sequence, alignment), size, margins, spacing, box design, horizontal rules, printed captions, two–sided format, columnar (tabular) format, computer forms, design, and standards.

Personnel involved with forms management are the forms analyst, top management, the originator, the consumer, the processing user, the reports management staff, the directives specialist, and procurement personnel. Alternatives to in–house forms management staff include outsourcing and vendors.

QUESTIONS FOR DISCUSSION

1. Why are forms the most widely used of all business records?

2. What are the goals of forms management?

3. What are some of the factors that contribute to the inefficient use of forms?

4. Identify the comparative costs of printing, filing, and processing forms.

5. Explain the need for each of the following forms management program elements:
   a. Planning and training
   b. Coordination and liaison
   c. Procedural analysis
   d. Design standardization
   e. Registration and identification
   f. Procurement and reproduction
   g. Distribution and storage
   h. Follow–up
   i. Program reporting

6. How does electronic forms composition differ from full electronic forms?

7. What are some factors to consider in evaluating the ease with which software can be used?

8. Describe the features of each of the following media in machine–readable forms:

a.   Bar codes

b.   Optical mark scanning

c.   Optical character recognition

d.   Magnetic ink character recognition

e.   Intelligent character reading

9. What cost–reduction benefits can be achieved through electronic data interchange?

10. What is forms analysis?

11. What information should be available in each numeric forms file folder?

12. What are the main purposes of the functional classification file?

13. What is the purpose of each of the following?

a.   Forms inventory and appraisal sheet

b.   Forms distribution chart

c.   Recurring data analysis chart

d.   Forms catalog

14. What facts are needed by a forms analyst in studying a procedure?

15. Almost every form contains five parts. What are they and what does each part usually include?

16. What are the expected results of good forms design?

17. What specifications are unique to computer forms?

18. What organizational personnel should be involved in the forms management program?

19. Explain the role of each of the following in the forms management program:

a.   Top management

b.   The originator

c.   The consumer

d.   The processing user

e.   The reports management staff

f.   The directives specialist

g.   Supply personnel

20. What are some alternatives to using in–house forms management?

PROJECTS

1. Analyze and improve the job reclassification form shown on page 379.

a.   Make a written analysis of the form by listing (1) all omissions of necessary information, (2) all unnecessary information requests, and (3) evidence of poor form design.

b.   Redesign the form.

2. Obtain an employment application form used by a business organization, government agency, educational institution, or employment bureau.

a.   Write a critical analysis of the form.

b.   Redesign the form to reflect the improvements suggested by your analysis.

3. Arrange for an interview with the forms manager, records manager, office manager, or some other officer of a company in your area who is responsible for the management of the organization's forms.

a.   Develop a forms management program checklist for your interview that will assist you in gathering information concerning the company's policies regarding forms creation, analysis, design, and procurement.

b.   Collect a copy of each form used by the company.

c.   Write an analysis of the company's forms program.

4. Arrange for an interview with the owner of a small business in your area—one employing five or fewer persons.

UNIVERSAL ELECTRONIC COMPANY
Job Reclassification Form

Requested by _____ Approved by _____

Employee Name _____ Address _____

Name of Department _____ Date Hired _____

Marital Status _____ Sex _____

Reason for Reclassification _____

Employee Social Security Number _____ Age _____

Present Job Title _____

Present Salary _____ Hour _____ Day _____ Week _____ Month _____ Year _____

Proposed Job Title _____

Proposed Salary _____ Hour _____ Day _____ Week _____ Month _____ Year _____

a. Collect a copy of each of the forms used in operating the business.

b. Prepare a forms management manual for the company.

CASE PROBLEM

The Delage Jewelry Manufacturing Corporation has been using three separately prepared forms to complete and ship an order. About 200 orders are shipped each day. Each of the three forms used for shipping, billing, and customer notification of shipment is typed in a separate department. The shipping label, invoice, and packing slip (shipping memorandum) contain a great deal of duplicate information. The following data are commonly required by each of the three departments (the figure in parentheses indicates the number of digits or letters required for recording a typical item):

Order number (6)
Date (14)
Customer order number (5)
Sales representative name (15)
Customer name and address (48)
How shipped (10)
Terms (16)
Quantity ordered (3)
Quantity shipped (3)
Back–ordered (3)
Description (32)
Unit price (6)
Total amount (8)
Sales tax (5)
Invoice total (9).

Prepare a suitable form for use in the order–processing procedure of the company, with suggestions for efficient preparation of the form.

Chapter 14

Mail Management

Learning Objectives

1. Identify the functions of mail management programs.
2. Define the responsibilities of mail supervision.
3. List the basic precautions for mail center security.
4. Identify the scope of mail operations.
5. Describe requirements for preparing addresses for scanning by OCR equipment.
6. List the advantages of using nine-digit ZIP Codes.
7. Identify mail services provided by the U.S. Postal Service.
8. Describe international mail services available.
9. Identify basic automated equipment needed for mail handling.
10. Enumerate the process of planning a mail center.
11. List the types of electronic message transmission systems that are used in today's modern office.

WHAT CONSTITUTES A MAIL MANAGEMENT PROGRAM

Mail includes letters, postcards, electronically transmitted messages, documents, publications, directives, forms, packages, or any other written communication received for distribution or dispatch. Mail handling involves that part of the communications process that gets the written word from one point to another. The challenge for today's records manager is that communication is electronic as well as by the traditional hard copy. Mail handling includes not only the receipt and transmission of written materials coming into an organization or leaving it (external mail), but also the movement of received or internally generated documents from point to point within the organization (internal mail). The heart of the mail management program, however, involves effectively organizing mail stations and establishing work-able standards and procedures to govern the detailed processing of the mail throughout the organization. The mail management program encompasses both *mail supervision* and *mail operations,* which together constitute a total program for handling mail.

GOALS OF A MAIL MANAGEMENT PROGRAM

The goals of all management programs are to motivate the staff, control costs, generate revenue, market effectively, and project a good public image. Few, if any, executives will dispute the contention that there is a close correlation between effectiveness in transmitting written communication and effectiveness in carrying on an organization's objectives. The promptness of replies to incoming mail is often considered a reasonable yardstick by which to measure the efficiency of an organization's operations. The elimination of duplicate mail and correction of addresses also reflect the company's efficiency. Such standards of efficiency are frequently applied by management as well as by the organization's customers. In order to meet the goals of the program, it is necessary to identify the functions that should be included in a mail management program, such as the following:

- Identifying the objectives of the program. Keeping all affected personnel informed of policies, standards, and procedures for prompt, accurate, and economical mail operations.
- Planning and installing efficiently organized mail stations.
- Ensuring that all incoming mail is promptly moved from the point of receipt to the action office.
- Ensuring that outgoing mail meets established mail preparation standards and is economically and expeditiously dispatched.
- Providing for the continuous monitoring of mail operations throughout the organization in order to implement improvements when they are needed.
- Ensuring correct, speedy, and economical movement of the organization's mail in the postal system.
- Providing essential information to executives concerning the volume and types of mail processed, postage costs, and time needed to move mail within the organization, as well as cost-saving techniques.

MAIL SUPERVISION

Mail supervision consists of those activities that are necessary to ensure that the written word is moved from the point of origin to its destination in a manner that meets stated organizational goals. These activities include assigning program responsibilities, developing an organizational plan, establishing realistic objectives, developing and implementing standard procedures and practices, monitoring day-to-day operations, and evaluating and reporting results.

Program Responsibilities

Mail management may be the responsibility of the records manager. The assignment for the mail program should be formally spelled out because of the need for the mail manager to monitor scattered mail operations performed by the different types of personnel, as shown in Figure 14.1. One of the main responsibilities of the mail manager is planning the program objectives.

Program Objectives

The overall objective of a mail management program is to provide rapid handling and accurate delivery of mail throughout the organization at minimum cost. To do this, processing steps are kept to a necessary minimum; sound principles of work flow are applied; modern equipment, supplies, and devices are used; and, in general, operations are kept as simple as possible.

Organizational Characteristics

There is no one solution to the organizational problem of determining which of the mail operations should be centralized at a mail station and which should be decentralized to the many offices that prepare mail. Various characteristics of an organization and its mail will affect the decisions. These include the size and complexity of the organization, the volume of mail handled, the physical housing of the organization, and the nature of the organization's functions.

Typically, the first three of these organizational characteristics tend to be interrelated. For example, the fewer the number of employees in the organization, the more likely it will be to have a simple structure, a low volume of pieces of mail, and a compact office layout in only one building.

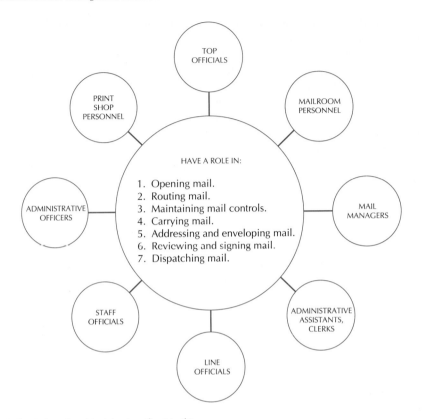

HAVE A ROLE IN:

1. Opening mail.
2. Routing mail.
3. Maintaining mail controls.
4. Carrying mail.
5. Addressing and enveloping mail.
6. Reviewing and signing mail.
7. Dispatching mail.

FIGURE 14.1 Who Is Involved in Moving the Mail?
(Courtesy of *Managing the Mail,* p. 2)

Operating Standards

The success of a mail manager's program can be measured in terms of how well the people involved in mail handling perform in accordance with approved operating standards. Whether the manager is dealing with full-time mailroom personnel or the other personnel engaged in part-time mail operations, the manager must make certain that the personnel have mastered and applied the standard procedures. Several managerial tools are available to the mail manager to ensure that the program is operating efficiently: survey techniques, controls, manuals, training, and promotion.

Survey Techniques. Survey techniques include periodic samplings of mail, full-scale reconnaissance surveys of mail performance, and more detailed surveys of mail problem areas. Survey techniques can provide data on the average time lapsed in replying to important classes of mail, determining causes of bottlenecks and delays, implementing the proper techniques to improve mail performance, or determining if the most appropriate types of postal services or rapid communications methods are being used to meet delivery time requirements. Problem-solving surveys can result in improvements such as smoother mail-flow patterns, revised and simplified mail-handling procedures, reduced mail-processing costs, and installation of automated or mechanized equipment if speed, frequency, and volume requirements justify it. Analysis survey techniques are also useful in planning the best possible mail stations for the existing space or for a new building.

Controls.   Controls include directives and manuals identifying the mail systems; the recording of the receipt of important mail, its location, and the time lapse in replying to it; and periodic audits of mail operations.

Production measurements should be discussed with the staff to ensure that the reports accurately reflect the volume of work being handled. The records manager should look for opportunities to demonstrate that reports are being used to improve operations, not done just for the sake of doing a report.

Directives and Manuals.   Communication with the staff is necessary and can be done by reviewing procedures, service levels, and quality standards. Special meetings can be held with the staff to ensure that they know the importance of their functions. Mail center employees should be fully informed in the use of their equipment, mail delivery schedules, processing standards, and quality controls. Directives are normally issued to provide broad policy guidelines, assignment of duties, and instructions for carrying out policies and procedures. These procedures should be outlined in the mail procedures manual and a copy made available to all persons involved with the handling of the mail. The mail manual should include all key contacts, managers' names, locations, and phone numbers. The staff must be well informed regarding company policies, postal rates, regulations, and any special needs or mailing problems that may occur. Postal rates should be published separately since they are subject to change more frequently than other parts of the manual. See Chapter 16 on Records Management Manuals.

Training.   It may be necessary to provide training for all operating personnel. A well-conceived training program is a most useful tool in assuring that mail personnel have the knowledge and skills needed to carry out the standard operating procedures. The mail procedures manual can be used in the training process. Very important parts of training are regular staff meetings and one-to-one sessions with subordinates. Open communication of ideas and concerns is vital to excellence in the mail-handling program.

Promotion.   Promotion campaigns can be undertaken to convince employees that improving mail handling not only benefits the company, but also helps them in doing their own jobs. A promotion campaign can be undertaken to speed replies to mail, to reduce internal mail processing costs, to reduce postage costs, and to speed up properly prepared mail.

Posters, bulletins, articles in newsletters, and exhortations by top management have all been successful in mail improvement campaigns. Videos that can be used in training are available on various aspects of mail management.

Computer Software

The computer is a useful tool in the mailroom and provides a wide variety of cost-cutting options. Computer software is available to update ZIP Codes, to correct spelling of streets and cities, to provide postal discount information, to facilitate express mail service, and to generate reports of mailing operations. Mailing-list enhancement software that contains the U.S. Postal Service national database of all addresses in the country is available on CD-ROM. A mailing list can be compared with the Postal Service national database and corrected. Nine-digit ZIP Codes are provided, and the program will correct spelling, punctuation, and street suffixes. This software, available on compact disk, requires a CD-ROM drive, which can be attached to the computer. The CD-ROM drive is relatively inexpensive and easy to attach. The software not only updates addresses that have been changed, but it also tags "nonaddresses." Duplicate-recognition software is also available.

Also available is mail management software that will scan the mailing list and determine which presort discounts are applicable. The software will determine whether the mailing qualifies for the discount available to five-digit presort and how many letters go into each bundle or tray. The software will print the postal bar code as well as labels for the address. The software also checks for duplicate addresses and near duplicates. Reports generated by the software indicate what was spent sending to each ZIP Code and the amount of money that was saved by presorting. In addition, tray and bag tags can be generated.

The Postal Service also has for loan a software program that explains the steps a letter takes as it travels through the post office. It suggests the steps that can be taken to reduce processing costs and shows postal discount programs. It also has a spreadsheet module that shows postal discount programs.

Mail Center Security

Mail is sometimes lost or stolen from company mail centers, or while en route to or from the post office. Since much of this mail is quite valuable, such losses can be costly. Although the vulnerability of a mail center may vary depending on the nature of the business, basic precautions can be taken to improve overall mail center security:

1. Know your employees. Do not hire anyone to work in your mail center without first determining his or her background.

2. Secure your mail room against access by unauthorized persons. Keep it locked whenever possible, especially when no one is on duty. Consider having a sign-in sheet for persons entering and leaving the mail center, including times of arrival and departure.

3. Keep valuable mail separate from other mail. Document each transfer of registered mail by requiring the receiving party to sign for custody.

4. If company funds are handled as a part of the mail center operation, establish adequate controls to fix individual responsibility for any losses that may occur. Do not keep postage stamps in unlocked drawers. These stamps are as good as cash to a dishonest employee.

5. Keep your postage meter locked when it is not in use. Check outgoing metered mail periodically to determine if employees are using metered postage for their own personal mail. Establish adequate controls to ensure all refunds for unused or spoiled postage meters are made to your company.

6. Establish procedures to account for valuable items that were mailed but for some reason were returned to your company.

7. Postal regulations suggest that postage meter stamps be placed in the upper right corner of the address label or tag. This procedure acts as a deterrent to theft by "overlabeling," a technique to divert the parcel to a name and address controlled by the thief.

8. Vary times and lines of travel between post office and plant if currency or other valuable mail is regularly sent or received. Check periodically to determine if mail messengers are making unauthorized stops or are leaving mail unattended in unlocked vehicles.

9. Employees caught stealing should be prosecuted. There is no greater deterrent to a potential thief than the knowledge that prosecution will follow. The Postal Inspection Service will extend full cooperation in the investigation of any mail theft case.

10. Consider whether your organization could be a possible target for receiving a bomb in the mail. Motives for mail bombs often are revenge, extortion, terrorism, or business disputes. While the likelihood of your company ever receiving a bomb in the mail is remote, if you have any reason to believe that a letter or parcel is suspicious, contact your local police department and postal inspector for professional assistance. In a high-risk type of industry, a security check of all incoming mail may occur before any mail is delivered to the mailroom.

MAIL OPERATIONS

The term *mail operations* identifies the series of tasks performed by action officers, mail room personnel, secretaries, clerks, and others in moving an organization's written communications. Mail operations include:

- Sorting and opening incoming mail.
- Determining and indicating the routing of incoming mail.
- Recording the receipt and referral of selected types of mail.
- Maintaining control records on the location of response to selected types of mail.
- Picking up and delivering written communications in accordance with established messenger schedules and routes.
- Addressing and enveloping mail.
- Clearing, reviewing, and signing outgoing communications.
- Determining the required method of delivery.
- Dispatching outgoing communications and distributing record and information copies.

Processing Incoming Mail

The mail manager must plan a series of detailed procedures covering the processing of incoming mail within the central mail room. Resposibilities for effective processing of incoming mail are presented in Figure 14.2.

Scope of Outgoing Mail Management

Outgoing mail management is concerned with speeding the flow of mail from the preparing offices to the final destination. Centralized outgoing mail operations at mail stations will not provide the natural solution that it does for processing much of the incoming mail. Today the trend is toward placing much of the responsibility for outgoing mail operations on the offices that prepare, review, or sign mail. The mail manager must spell out clearly in directives, for example, which offices shall be responsible for checking outgoing mail for accuracy and completeness; for dating the mail; and for addressing envelopes, inserting letters in them, and sealing them.

FIGURE 14.2 Incoming Mail Processing Responsibilities

1. Schedule some mailroom employees to process incoming mail before regular office hours if deliveries and volume justify it.
2. Limit the receipt of personal mail in the organization's regular mail channels.
3. Provide facilities for receiving mail that is of varying size or requires special protection.
4. Provide written routing guides to mail stations to instruct clerks in approved routing patterns for all types of mail if volume warrants.
5. Process the great bulk of incoming mail with no more than three sorting operations.
6. Send routine mail to the action office without opening or formal routing whenever possible.
7. Route mail by direct sorting into the compartments of a sorting device, if the designation is ascertainable from the piece.
8. Write the approved office identification symbol directly on the face of a piece of opened mail if necessary.
9. Use extra copies, as needed, to route mail to be delivered to more than one office having a direct interest in the piece.
10. Use routing slips for single copies of any mail that must be sent to several offices in rotation.
11. Time-stamp selected types of mail only when it serves a critical purpose or need.

Outgoing mail involves the mail manager in many of the following matters:

- The traditional dispatching operations performed by mail rooms.
- Reply time limits for various types of mail.
- Reply clearance, review, and rewrite policies.
- Mail signature authority.
- Policies on use of various postal services other than message transmission methods.
- Payment of postage costs to the U.S. Postal Service.
- Postal regulations concerning the addressing, sequencing, and physical format of mail pieces.
- Quantity mailings addressed and prepared, using mechanized or computerized mailing list techniques.

Processing Outgoing Mail

A series of repetitive tasks is involved in processing an organization's individual pieces of outgoing mail. By their very nature, certain of these tasks must be performed by central mail rooms, while others can be performed at action offices. Outgoing mail processing responsibilities are presented in Figure 14.3.

SORTING AT THE POST OFFICE

Computerized mail-processing machines at the post office include optical character recognition (OCR) equipment and bar code sorters (BCSs). Readable mail is quickly and accurately read, coded, and sorted by the equipment. Use of this equipment provides increased speed, efficiency, and accuracy in the processing of mail as well as reduced costs. Some restrictions as to size of the mail are required in order to make use of this equipment.

Optical Character Readers (OCRs)

Mail to be sorted at the post office passes by a computer scanner for a quick read of the delivery address. If the address is within the readable space of the mail piece, it can be read through the OCR. From the scanner, the mail goes past the OCR's printer, which sprays on a bar code representing the ZIP Code or the nine-digit ZIP Code for that address. Once the bar code is applied, the mail piece is channeled into one of the OCR's delivery areas. From the OCR delivery area, the mail is processed on the bar code sorters. The BCS scans the bar code, and the mail is sorted into the appropriate channel for delivery to the appropriate letter carrier. This equipment is programmed to read and sort at the rate of up to 36,000 pieces of mail per hour.

In order to take advantage of the automated equipment, the mail piece must conform to restrictions of size, address location, address characters, lines of the address, print quality, and spacing.

Address Location. The OCR read area is an imaginary rectangle as shown in Figure 14.4. The sides of the rectangle are 1/2 inch from the right and left edges. The bottom of the rectangle is 5/8 inch from the bottom edge, and the top of the rectangle is 2 3/4 inches from the bottom edge.

Address Characters. The OCR will read most typewritten and other machine-printed addresses. However, handwriting and print styles such as script, italic, artistic, and other highly stylized characters may require human intervention. The OCR also has difficulty in reading dot matrix print if the dots that form each character are not touching each other.

Print Quality and Color. When characters are faded, broken, or smudged, the OCR has difficulty in reading them. Good contrast between the paper and the ink facilitates OCR reading.

Spacing. Spacing between characters, words, and address lines is important. There must be a clear vertical space between characters and between words, or the OCR will not register where one element ends and the next one begins. For

1. Receiving mail from messengers returning from delivery routes.
2. Sorting incoming mail into that which is ready for delivery and mail for which further processing is required before it is transmitted outside the organization.
3. Mechanically reviewing outgoing mail for completeness, accuracy, and conformance with mail preparation standards.
4. Dating mail and conforming file copies to reflect the name and title of high-level signers as required.
5. Preparing and addressing mail in accordance with postal requirements, including use of ZIP Codes.
6. Selecting appropriate envelopes to fit mail pieces, and properly folding and sealing self-mailers in accordance with postal requirements.
7. Stripping mail to separate file material, information copies, mail control forms, and the like from the outgoing letters, and dispatching file or information copies to appropriate destinations.
8. Packing, wrapping, and labeling parcels to protect contents adequately during transmission.
9. Placing mail that is sent by bulk rates into envelopes and sealing the envelopes.
10. Identifying the class or type of mail service required on mail pieces.
11. Preparing required receipts for registered, certified, or insured mail and customs declarations for certain foreign mailings.
12. Sequencing, generating labels, facing, and packaging third class bulk mailings to meet postal requirements.
13. Presorting outgoing mail to facilitate postal processing by separating airmail and special delivery, registered mail, parcels, local mail, first class letter mail, etc.
14. Sacking and otherwise physically facilitating the pickup of outgoing mail dispatched via the postal system.

FIGURE 14.3   Outgoing Mail Processing Responsibilities

similar reasons, the OCR also needs a clear horizontal space between each two lines of the address.

Minimum Size Standards

Pieces 1/4 inch or less in thickness are mailable provided they are rectangular in shape, at least 3 1/2 inches high, at least 5 inches long (items sent to foreign countries must be at least 5 1/2 inches in length), and at least .007 inch thick (about the thickness of a postal card). Mail not meeting these standards will be returned to the sender.

Nonstandard-Size Mail.   First-class mail or single-piece third-class mail weighing 1 ounce or less is nonstandard if it exceeds *any* of the following size limits:

- Its height exceeds 6 1/8 inches.
- Its length exceeds ll 1/2 inches.
- Its thickness exceeds 1/4 inch.
- Its length divided by its height is less than 1.3 inches or more than 2.5 inches.

The same criteria apply to international letters and regular printed items weighing 1 ounce or less. A surcharge, in addition to the applicable postage and fees, is assessed on each piece of nonstandard-size mail.

ADDRESSING MAIL

All mail needs a complete delivery address and should also have a return address. In addition, there may be special service requirements. The format prescribed by the Postal Service for use with automated sorting equipment should be fol-

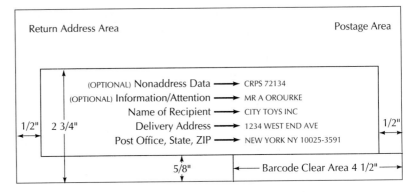

FIGURE 14.4 Optical Character Recognition (OCR) Read Area

lowed. This involves using the nine-digit ZIP Code. Labeling, direct addressing, and tabbing must also be considered in preparing the mail. The following guidelines are recommended.

Return Address

The return address should include:

- Sender's name.
- Sender's street address, post office box number, or rural route number and box number.
- Sender's city, state, and ZIP Code or nine-digit ZIP Code.
- Country (if mail is going to a foreign country).

Destination Address

The destination address should include:

- Recipient's name (or company name if applicable).
- Recipient's street address, post office box number, rural route number, or highway contract route number.
- Recipient's city, state, and ZIP Code or nine-digit ZIP Code.

- Country name, preferably in capital letters, as the last line of the address.

For international mail, include the city or town, provincial or state name, and applicable foreign postal code, if known.

In the address line, the following abbreviations should be used: *N* (North), *S* (South), *E* (East), *W* (West), *NE, NW, SE, SW*; *AVE* (Avenue), *ST* (Street), *DR* (Drive), *RD* (Road), *PL* (Place), *CIR* (Circle); *RM* (Room), *STE* (Suite), *APT* (Apartment).

Special Service Endorsements

All markings for special services should be placed above the delivery address and to the right of the return address on all articles. This requirement applies to endorsements for registered, insured, certified, collect-on-delivery (COD), and return receipt for merchandise services, as well as for endorsements for special delivery, restricted delivery, and return receipt requested.

Format. For the best service, the Postal Service recommends the following guidelines:

1. Capitalize everything in the address.
2. Leave out all punctuation in the address, except the hyphen in the nine-digit ZIP Code.

3. Use common abbreviations found in the *National Five-Digit ZIP Code and Post Office Directory.*
4. Use the two-letter state abbreviations.
5. Use complete and correct ZIP Codes or nine-digit ZIP Codes.

When both a post office box number and a street address are used, the mail will be delivered to what appears on the line immediately above the city, state, and ZIP Code line.

GRAND PRODUCTS INC
475 L'ENFANT PLAZA WEST SW
PO BOX 320 *(Mail will be delivered here.)*
WASHINGTON DC 20260-6320 *(ZIP + 4 corresponds to P.O. box.)*

Nine-Digit ZIP Code

In 1983, the Postal Service began use of an expanded, nine-digit ZIP Code, called ZIP+4 Code. It is composed of the original five-digit code plus a four-digit add-on. Use of the four-digit add-on number is voluntary. However, it helps the Postal Service direct mail efficiently and accurately. The four-digit add-on number identifies a geographic segment within the five-digit delivery area, such as a city block, an office building, an individual high-volume mailer, or any other unit that would aid efficient mail sorting and delivery. This reduces the amount of handling and significantly decreases the potential for human error and the possibility of misdelivery. Use of the nine-digit ZIP Code can lead to better control over postal costs and possibly to postage rate stability.

The nine-digit ZIP Code is intended for use primarily by business mailers who prepare their mail with typewritten, machine-printed or computerized addressing formats that can be read by the Postal Service's automated scanners during processing. Mailers who qualify receive a rate discount on first-class nonpresorted nine-digit ZIP Code mailings of at least 250 pieces and on pre-sorted nine-digit ZIP Code mailings of at least

500 pieces. There are also discounts for bulk business mail.

Packaging and Addressing Parcels

Proper packaging and addressing of parcels is the best way to prevent parcel damage and loss. A container strong enough to protect the contents during handling should be used, and the contents should be cushioned to make sure they do not move within the container. The address should be printed on one side of the parcel only. In addition to the address on the container, address information should be placed inside the container, on the contents, or loose inside the container. Pressure-sensitive filament or reinforced tape is recommended for closing and reinforcing the flaps and seams. Wrapping paper and string should be avoided because string can cause damage in processing. If the package is valuable, it should be insured for replacement. The post office cannot insure the informational value of a document.

CLASSES OF MAIL

Mail service provided by the U.S. Postal Service includes express mail, first-class mail, second-class mail, third-class mail, fourth-class mail (parcel post), Mailgram service, and priority mail.

Express Mail

Express mail is the Postal Service's overnight mail service. At the time of this writing, up to 70 pounds can be delivered overnight. All packages mailed by 5 p.m. (or other local acceptance times) will be available for pickup at the destination post office by 10 a.m. the next day or delivery will be made (or attempted) by 3 p.m. the next day, including weekends and holidays. With computerized tracking and tracing, it is possible to determine the status of the mail in 20 seconds or less by calling 1-800-222-1811.

Mailing sites include the local post office, collection boxes, company offices, and airport mail facilities. In addition to being dropped off at an express mail post office, express mail can also be deposited in collection boxes located in convenient locations. It is possible to call for on-demand pickup or hand the mail to your letter carrier. Your local post office can provide specific express mail acceptance times for your area. Airport mail facilities (AMF) are available in 65 airports nationwide.

Additional express mail services include express mail custom designed service, express mail international service, and express mail military service. Custom designed service allows the customer to select the time and place for both acceptance of mail and needed delivery of the shipment. The rates for express mail custom designed service are determined by the weight of the packages and the express mail service options used. International express mail service is available in either on-demand service or in international custom designed service. Delivery is available to over 150 countries and is assured in one to three days. On-demand service permits shipping to different addresses at various times. International custom designed service is for regular shipping schedules that can benefit from individualized processing and transportation prearrangements. Express military mail service provides shipment to APO/FPO addresses at domestic prices.

Paying for Charges.   Express mail services may be paid for using the express mail corporate account, postage meter, stamps, cash, or credit card. The corporate account may be opened at any express mail post office by completing the application and by depositing an amount of money equal to an estimated two weeks' express mail postage charges or $100, whichever is higher.

Competition from the private sector in next-day delivery services exceeds the volume of deliveries handled by the U.S. Postal Service. Companies that started with large-package service are now combining that service with overnight delivery, as well as increasing the weight of packages that they will handle.

Rates for overnight service are high, but the service is often essential. In many cases, first-class letters to a single destination can be consolidated and shipped as a single overnight package, making the cost per piece less than first-class mail.

Fast-mail abuse is caused by employees sending packages and correspondence through delivery services that could have been routed through regular mail. In other cases, employees seek one-day delivery when three-day service would have been adequate. To curb this abuse, companies can require their personnel to make a decision about the timeliness of the material and then support that decision. This can be done through the use a form that commits them to a time limit in which the material must be delivered.

Codes for overnight mail can also be assigned to track which division spends the most money on fast-mail service. Other firms designate one person to sign off on all express mailings and allow that employee to make all decisions regarding which delivery method to use.

First-Class Mail

First-class mail is used for letters, postcards, postal cards, greeting cards, and personal notes weighing less than 11 ounces. It is used for sending checks and money orders. For mail weighing 11 ounces or more, priority mail is used. First-class mail mailed within the customs territory of the United States generally may not be opened without a federal search warrant.

Priority Mail

Priority mail is first-class mail weighing 11 ounces or more. When the speed of express mail is not required, but preferential handling is desired, priority mail offers a two-day expedited delivery at the least expensive rate. Maximum weight for priority mail is 70 pounds, and the maximum size is 108 inches in length and circumference combined. The local post office has priority mail stickers, labels, envelopes, and boxes available at no extra change. A presort discount is available for large mailings and a flat-rate 2-pound envelope is also available.

Business Reply Mail

Business reply envelopes are provided to customers to facilitate orders, payments, and subscriptions. The Postal Service has made available its business reply mail accounting system (BRMAS). This computerized system starts to count and calculate at the bar code sorter. The system is triggered by a preprinted bar code on the mail that identifies the company name, type of piece, and corresponding rate charged per piece.

To use BRMAS, the envelope must include the assigned nine-digit ZIP Code, the corresponding preprinted bar code, and the appropriate facing identification mark (FIM C), and the card paper stock must meet computerized equipment processing standards.

Second-Class Mail

Second-class mail is only available to publishers and registered news agents who have been approved for this privilege. The applicable single-piece third- or fourth-class rate must be paid for magazines and newspapers mailed by the general public. Additional details are available from your local post office.

Third-Class Mail

Third-class mail, also referred to as bulk business mail or advertising mail, may be sent by anyone, but is used most often by large mailers. This class includes printed material and merchandise weighing less than 16 ounces. There are two rate structures for this class: single-piece rate and bulk rate. Many community organizations and businesses find it economical to use the bulk rates. Also, individuals may use third-class mail for mailing lightweight parcels.

Fourth-Class Mail (Parcel Post)

This service is used for packages weighing 1 pound or more. If first-class mail is enclosed or attached, first-class postage must be paid for the enclosure or attachment. Packages mailed within the continental United States can weight up to 70 pounds and measure up to 108 inches in length and girth combined. The delivery goal for parcel post is seven days or less to most areas, depending on distance.

Mailgram Service

Mailgram is a registered trademark of Western Union Corporation. The Mailgram service provided by the Postal Service is an electronic message service which provides next-day delivery for messages sent to any address in the United States. The messages are transmitted for delivery with the mail for the next business day. Mailgram service is also available for Canadian addresses. Mailgram messages can be sent by calling Western Union and dictating the message to the operator. The message can also be sent by your office Telex or TWX. In Alaska, call Alascom, Inc., for Mailgram service, and in Hawaii, call the local post office for information on how to send a message.

INTELPOST

INTELPOST (*inter*national *el*ectronic *post*) service is an international facsimile message service available between the United States and more than 40 foreign countries. A black-and-white image of the document (text as well as graphic) is printed and delivered in the destination country. Depending on the chosen delivery option, the facsimile message will be delivered either the same day or the next day.

International Mail

Airmail and surface mail can be sent to virtually all international destinations in a variety of ways:

1. Letters, postcards, and letter packages—items of mail containing personal handwritten or typewritten communications.
2. Aerogrammes—air letter sheets which can be folded into the form of an envelope and sealed.
3. Printed matter—regular printed matter, books and sheet music, publishers' periodicals, catalogues, directories.
4. Small packets—items of merchandise, commercial samples, or documents which do not have the character of current and personal correspondence.
5. Parcel post—packages of merchandise or any other articles that are not required to be mailed at letter postage rates.
6. Express mail international service—high priority or other urgently needed items, including merchandise in many instances, that can be sent to more than 150 countries.

All categories of international mail, other than express mail, may be sent either airmail or surface mail. However, all letters and postcards originating in the United States and intended for delivery in either Canada or Mexico receive first-class mail treatment in the United States and airmail treatment in those two countries.

Special Services of U.S. Mail

Cash receipts provide proof of payment of postage and other services. The cash receipt is provided at no cost upon request.

The *certificate of mailing* proves an item was mailed. It does not provide insurance coverage for loss or damage or provide proof of delivery.

Certified mail provides a mailing receipt, and a record of delivery is maintained at the recipient's post office. A return receipt to provide the sender with proof of delivery can also be purchased for an additional fee. For valuables and irreplaceable items, insured or registered mail is recommended. Certified mail service is available only for first-class mail. Certified mail service is not available for international mail.

Collect-on-delivery (COD) service is used when the sender wants to collect for merchandise and postage at the time a parcel is delivered. COD service may be used for merchandise sent by first-class mail, express mail, priority mail, third-class mail, or fourth-class mail. The merchandise must have been ordered by the addressee. Fees charged for this service include insurance protection against loss or damage. COD items also may be sent as registered mail. COD service is limited to items valued at a maximum of $600. This service is not available for international mail.

Insurance coverage of up to $600 can be purchased for third- and fourth-class mail, as well as for third- and fourth-class matter that is mailed at the priority mail or first-class rate. Insurance coverage up to $25,000 can be purchased on registered mail. For articles insured for more than $50, a receipt of delivery is signed by the recipient and filed at the delivery post office. The amount of insurance coverage for loss will be the actual value, less depreciation, and no payments are made for sentimental losses or for any expenses incurred as a result of the loss.

Recorded delivery (international mail) is similar to certified mail service in that it is intended for letters, documents, and items of little or no value. It is for the customer who wants a record of mailing on international mail, and who wants to know that a record of delivery exists, if an inquiry is necessary. For an added fee, the customer can purchase a return receipt at the time of mailing.

Registered mail is designed to provide added protection for valuable and important mail. Insurance may be purchased on domestic registered mail up to $25,000 at the option of the mailer. Return receipt and restricted delivery services are available for additional fees. Registered mail to Canada is subject to a $1,000 indemnity limit. For all other foreign countries, the indemnity limit is currently $32.35. Registered articles are placed under tight security from the point of mailing to the delivery office. First-class or priority mail postage is required on domestic registered mail.

Restricted delivery means that the sender's mail is delivered only to the addressee or to someone authorized in writing to receive mail for the addressee. Restricted delivery is offered in connection with return receipt service and is available only for registered mail, certified mail, COD mail, and mail insured for more than $50.

Restricted delivery mail addressed to officials of government agencies, members of the legislative and judicial branches of federal and state governments, members of the diplomatic corps, minors, and individuals under guardianship can be delivered to an agent without written authorization from the addressee.

Return receipts are the sender's proof of delivery. A return receipt can be purchased for mail which is sent COD or express mail, is insured for more than $50, or is registered or certified. The return receipt shows who signed for the item and the date it was delivered. For an additional fee, the sender can get the addressee's correct address of delivery or request restricted delivery service.

Special delivery service is available on all classes of mail except bulk third-class. It provides for delivery even on Sundays and holidays, and beyond normal delivery hours. This delivery service is available to all customers served by city carriers and to other customers within a 1-mile radius of the delivery post office. The mailing should be endorsed *SPECIAL DELIVERY.*

Special handling service is available for third- and fourth-class mail only, including insured and COD mail. It provides for preferential handling to the extent practical in dispatch and transportation, but does not provide special delivery. Special handling does not mean special care of fragile items. Anything breakable should be packed with adequate cushioning and marked *FRAGILE.*

Private Delivery Systems

While the above information applies to the Postal Service, the information is useful even when using private delivery services. Many alternate mail services compete with the Postal Service for mail

and parcel delivery business. While United Parcel Service (UPS) and Federal Express seem well known, a check through the Yellow Pages of the telephone book will provide the names of other delivery or courier services in your area.

Most of these companies specialize in the delivery of shipments, but other organizations, such as bus lines, airlines, and messenger services, also provide package delivery as an additional service.

MAIL CENTER EQUIPMENT

Automated equipment for all aspects of mail processing is governed by four objectives: (1) Eliminate manual tasks; (2) take advantage of all postal discounts; (3) reduce labor costs; and (4) produce marketing mail that elicits a response. The amount of throughput per hour can be increased significantly and labor costs can be decreased through the use of automated equipment. Automated equipment can help keep mailing lists up to date and provide nine-digit ZIP Codes so that discount plans can be used. Direct-mail marketing is on the rise, and modern equipment permits some companies to prepare advertising in-house. Other organizations are able to outsource the task of creating and mailing advertising pieces. Equipment is available for labeling, direct address, folding and inserting, tabbing, applying postage, sealing envelopes, and sorting. A word of caution, however. You must know your mail usage before purchasing automated equipment. There are machines that can be overpriced when compared to mail volume.

Labeling

Labels in volumes of more than 3,000 per month should be applied via an automatic labeler. The equipment can apply up to 25,000 labels per hour compared to the average of 300 per hour done manually. Labelers in this class are quiet, inexpensive, small, and easy to use. Equipment for automatic pressure-sensitive labels is being replaced by equipment that will apply clear labels and also tab open-ended mail pieces with clear or opaque tabs.

Direct Addressing

A goal of aesthetically minded mailers is to print the address directly on the envelope. Specialized printers are available that print the address and postal bar code directly on the envelope more efficiently than standard computer printers. These printers are available in dot matrix, ink jet, laser, and letter-quality daisy wheel. Printing directly on the envelope eliminates the label costs as well as the two-step process of printing and then applying the label. The daisy-wheel printer uses a film ribbon and costs about one fourth the cost of a laser cartridge (per thousand printed). The daisy-wheel printer is also more flexible than other printers and can print on sizes up to and including 10-by 13-inch flats. Laser-type envelope printers print at speeds of up to 900 pieces per hour, while the daisy-wheel printer can print up to 2,500 addresses per hour.

Folding and Inserting

The average worker can fold and stuff approximately 120 envelopes per hour. The standard tabletop folder-inserter can accomplish the same task at speeds of up to 3,600 completed envelopes per hour. For smaller organizations, an automatic tabletop folder-inserter that processes 900 envelopes per hour is available. A tabletop folder-inserter may eliminate the need for a separate stand-alone paper folder because many units can act in a fold-only mode, as well as fold and insert.

Tabbing

Mail pieces that are folded and sent without an envelope must now be tabbed shut in order to receive the automation discount. The tab is a small adhesive piece of paper that is applied to keep the open ends together. Self-mailers are used by direct marketers because they save the cost of the envelope and they eliminate the barrier of envelopes, possibly increasing the probability of being read. Desktop equipment for tabbing self-mailers shut operates at from 10,000 to 22,000 per hour and is available from leading hardware providers.

Applying Postage

The basic method of applying postage with a postage meter is to draw the envelope under the meter head where the postage is applied by ink imprint. Oversized envelopes and packages are weighed on a separate scale, and meter tapes are applied for the postage. The use of pressure-sensitive tape instead of glue-and-water paper tape has eliminated some of the paper jams associated with paper tape postage meters.

Electronic Postage Meters. The most basic mailing system incorporates a lightweight scale and a postage meter. The scale can measure letters and packages weighing up to 3 pounds and calculate the postage using computer software. Advantages of electronic postage meters include accuracy, speed, savings, the ability to be replenished by telephone, and accountability.

The software incorporated into the weighing system not only weighs the piece, but also calculates the proper discounts for larger volume mailings. A special telephone hookup with the post office can replenish the postage meter. Older models require that the meter be carried to the post office to get the postage replenished. Mailing experts estimate that businesses using mechanical mailing scales waste 15 to 20 percent of their total postal expenditures by applying too much postage. Accountability is another feature available on electronic meters. The meter can produce reports showing the postage used by each department for charge-back purposes.

A variation of the postage meter is an automatic stamp-affixing machine. High-speed automated equipment can apply actual postage stamps rather than use ink imprinting. Many direct-mail experts agree that the more personalized the communication (such as using postage stamps), the more likelihood that the recipient will read it.

Small-volume postage meters are priced at less than $200 for a 5-pound scale. This size mailing system is appropriate for a volume of 50 pieces or less each day. The entire mailing system can be contained on a countertop or small table.

Sealing Envelopes

The sponge on the secretary's desk has been replaced by automated equipment. As the volume of mail increases, the postage scale is generally upgraded to handle more weight and is linked to a combined meter–envelope sealer.

Burster and Inserter.   Large volume mailers have a need for a burster and inserter to automatically separate continuous fan-fold printings and stuff envelopes. A postage meter can be interfaced with a folder-inserter for in-line processing. Figure 14.5 shows the Pitney Bowes Spectrum Tabletop Inserting System, which can feed and collate five sheets, fold and insert them into an envelope, and seal the flap at the rate of 4,000 No. 10 envelopes per hour. Other machines are available that can also apply the postage.

Sorting

The advantages of using a sorter are that it reduces the need for manual labor, speeds up the processing, and makes it possible to organize mailings to take advantage of postal discounts. For a high-volume operation, a Bell & Howell Jetstar 850, shown in Figure 14.6, is typical of a unit that can sort 36,000 envelopes an hour. This is made possible by a wide-area bar code reader that scans all printed information within a four-inch band across the front of an envelope. As it scans, it sorts the envelopes. The Postal Service discount depends on what level mail is sorted. The closer the sort to the mail's final destination, the greater the discount.

Remote Encoder.   Remote encoding machines will allow any and all mail to be bar-coded and processed mechanically. These machines will record an image of each mail piece, encode a temporary identifier on each piece, and deposit the mail in a temporary holding bay. The address images will then be communicated via satellite to

FIGURE 14.5   Tabletop Inserting System (Courtesy of Pitney Bowes)

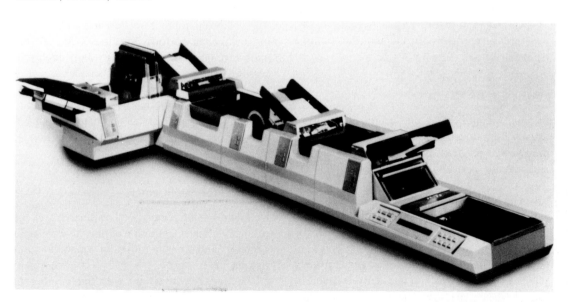

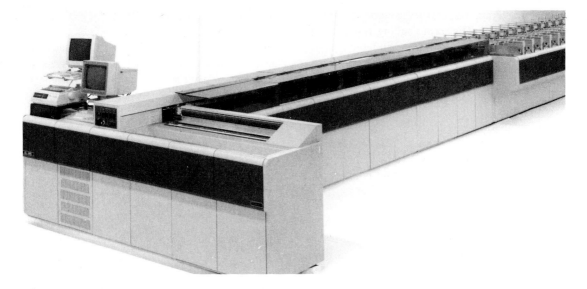

FIGURE 14.6   Mail Sorter
(Courtesy of Bell & Howell)

remote contractor sites and displayed to human operators. The operators will read the monitor screen and key in sufficient information at their workstations to retrieve the proper nine-digit ZIP Code. The information will be communicated back to the site where the mail piece will be routed once more through the machinery to have the bar code applied. Remote encoding machines are expected to be in use by 1995. Needless to say, they are very expensive and require attentive maintenance.

MAIL CENTER LAYOUT

In small organizations, one central mail center usually can perform most of the necessary mail-processing operations and provide direct pickup and delivery service to action offices.

Conversely, the larger the number of employees in an organization, the more likely the organization is to have a complex structure, a high volume of mail, and a dispersed office layout possibly involving locations in several buildings. In large organizations the central mail center usually serves as a central pickup and delivery point of the Postal Service. It routes incoming mail to intermediate mail stations, which perform most of the mail-processing steps other than those decentralized to the action offices. With this type of organization, no one mail center will have an overload of mail pieces to process or too many action offices for which to provide pickup and delivery service.

Today, microprocessors used to control mailing equipment perform functions ranging from mail sorting to remote encoding. Many microprocessors combine the features of smaller units and add the power of computer controls. They provide a level of automation that frees staff to attend to other tasks and are making automated equipment increasingly attractive to small and medium-size businesses.

Planning the Mail Center

Planning a mail center involves analysis of the company's needs, definition of objectives, plan of strategy, and consideration of financial constraints.

A *needs analysis* reviews the number of

pieces going out, the cost, the number of pieces of undeliverable mail, customer complaints, and postal discounts.

Objectives may include goals to be accomplished, such as same level of service with fewer employees, lower costs per unit, taking advantage of greater discounts, reduction of undeliverables, and faster delivery.

Strategy involves review of objectives, plan of equipment and software to reach those objectives, review of procedures in mail handling, and review of the mail center to determine if it should be restructured.

Financial constraints involve the original investment costs, whether to buy or lease, and determination of the payback period for the equipment to be added.

Gathering Information.   In order to aid the decision-making process, several sources of information are available. National and local postal forums and seminars provide information on mail processing and equipment. A national Mail-Com is held annually with over 100 vendors participating and over 100 seminars available. Vendors of mail-processing hardware and software demonstrate their equipment and present a wide variety of options for handling mail. Seminars are presented frequently by postal officials and industry leaders. Mailing-equipment representatives are willing to meet with individuals in their current mail center to observe the operation and to offer suggestions for automated methods. Automated mail technology is so diverse that specialists for each function of the operation may be required.

The local Postal Service customer-service representative and readability specialist can provide insight into postal regulations and recommendations.

Low-Volume Mail

In most low-volume mailings, all that is necessary to send out the mail is a lightweight scale and a postage meter. This system is appropriate for a volume of 50 pieces or less a day and is small enough to be contained on a countertop. Figure 14.7 shows a Pitney Bowes mailing system suitable for a small office. With such low volume, the mail is handled as ancillary duty by a clerk or an administrative assistant.

It is possible for smaller mailers to participate in the postal automation program using a standard personal computer and printer. With the appropriate software, automation envelopes and labels can be created, bar codes can be printed, and nine-digit ZIP Code information can be current.

Mid-Volume Mail

Mid-volume mailers sending from 100 to 1,000 pieces of mail a day usually require a slightly larger system. The scale is generally upgraded to handle more weight, and it is linked to a combined meter-envelope sealer. Depending on the kind of organization and its mailing needs, other equipment may be added.

Large-Volume Mail

Companies sending 1,000 or more pieces of mail a day generally have a full-time employee handling the mail. Mailing professionals estimate that automated and semiautomated equipment can increase an employee's efficiency at least twofold. Equipment necessary at this level includes a burster and inserter to automatically stuff envelopes, and an automated weighing system to seal and stamp the mail. Figure 14.8 is an illustration of a modular mail center for a large-volume operation. It consists of sorting pockets, mail sort and dump table for incoming mail, sort and wrap table for outgoing mail, and a utility table. The postage scale and meter can be placed at the end of the sort and wrap table. Less equipment would be necessary in low-volume and medium-volume mailing operations.

Modern electronic mailing systems integrate all of the processing which can be accomplished by the push of a button. Mailing systems have become smaller as integrated circuits have re-

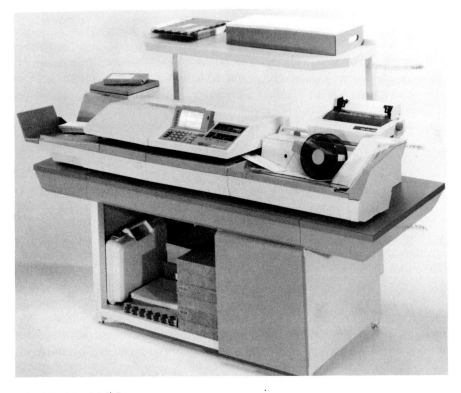

FIGURE 14.7 Mail Processor
(Courtesy of Pitney Bowes)

placed vacuum tubes and mechanical systems. For handling mail internally in large organizations, mechanical mail delivery systems are available.

Mechanical Mail Delivery Systems

Mail can be delivered internally by manual or mechanical services. The choice depends on factors such as the volume of the correspondence, the frequency of delivery, the number and location of delivery sites, and the cost. Messenger service can be replaced by mechanical means when the volume of documents to be distributed is large and the locations are fixed. Mechanical mail delivery systems include the pneumatic tube, conveyor belt, and mail robot.

Pneumatic Tube. One mechanical distribution system is the pneumatic tube, which carries material quickly and accurately to its destination. The initial installation cost is high, but maintenance cost is low. They are easy to use and do not require mechanical skill to operate. The pneumatic tube is used in hospitals to transport records from one area to another. It is particularly useful to transport mail pieces between floors.

Conveyor Belt. In high-volume areas, belt conveyors, such as the one shown in Figure 14.9, can be used. This conveyor provides continuous bidirectional and vertical service. For vertical delivery (from one floor to another), automated chain conveyors and cart-lift systems are available.

Mail Robot. A more visible mechanical system is the mail robot, or mailmobile. The mailmobile is an unmanned, self-propelled vehicle that follows an invisible guidepath made of harmless chemicals to move from office to office. The guidance

FIGURE 14.8 Modular Mail Center
(Courtesy of Delco Associates)

system can be changed as the needs of users change. The mailmobile automatically stops at designated workstations for pickup and delivery.

ELECTRONIC MAIL SYSTEMS

Electronic mail can take the form of communicating via telephone lines from computer, terminal, or fax machine to other electronic equipment. Types of electronic mail that must be considered by the records manager include E-mail, public data networks, teletypewriter networks, facsimile, service bureaus, teleconferencing, commercial communications systems, voice mail, and bulletin board systems.

Electronic Mail (E-Mail)

E-mail is a system of communication in which the message is transmitted electronically from one computer terminal to one or more locations via telephone lines. E-mail can be available on the local area network (LAN) or it can be connected to other LANs in the organization. E-mail can also be used through public data networks and from computer to computer (with the required software). Messages are sent over LANs or satellite networks, or by other means. Messages can be sent as data or nondata. *Data messages* are numerical symbols. *Nondata messages* can be text, graphics, images, or voice. It is cheaper to send a document of up to ten pages by E-mail than by overnight courier or by express mail.

E-mail is fast replacing the typed memo systems for internal communication. The messages can be read as soon as they are sent if the user is on-line, since the user may be notified when a message is received. The messages can be deleted immediately after the information has been received or action is taken. A copy of the message can be printed out if it is necessary to save the hard copy. Messages can be stored by subject in various folders of the receiver's mailbox. Messages are sometimes classified according to access by others, and internal E-mail and E-mail sent on public data networks is usually considered "private," as opposed to messages sent to a bulletin board system, which are available for all to read.

Passwords are commonly used as a security measure in E-mail. It is important to remember that even when messages are deleted, they remain in the memory of the computer until the space where the original message was located has been overwritten. E-mail software programs are available with a variety of features such as password security, deferred delivery, message-waiting indicators, and concurrent operations with other functions such as word processing.

E-mail services are expected to grow 50 percent annually. AT&T is a recent entry into the E-mail market with an additional option. Users can retrieve messages without a computer by dialing a toll-free number, keying in a mailbox code on the telephone, and activating a computer-generated voice-read message.

Public Data Networks. Public data networks, such as MCI, offer third-party access to large databases. This service acts as a clearinghouse for

FIGURE 14.9   Document Conveyer System
(Courtesy of Acme Visible Records)

the electronic messages of subscribers. The subscriber can access the network through a telephone number and then reach another computer that is part of the network. These services usually offer hard copy mail as well as other miscellaneous services.

Teleconferencing

Technology can bring people and ideas together despite geographic barriers through *teleconferencing*. The purpose of teleconferencing is to permit people at different locations to conduct meetings together. Teleconferencing includes computer conferencing and videoconferencing. The simplest method of teleconferencing is computer conferencing.

Computer conferencing is a method of sending, receiving, and storing typed messages within a network of users. This requires communication software that runs on a network's host and terminals for each of the participants. Messages may be sent to specific individuals or to a set of individu-

als, or they may be "broadcast" to all receivers. One advantage is that users can use the system at their convenience. Recipients are automatically notified of incoming messages.

Videoconferencing is a variation of computer conferencing with camera. The technology varies, but what is needed is a large screen, cameras that send three-dimensional pictures, and an on-line computer system to record communication among participants.

Information Utilities

Commercial communication services, also known as *information utilities*, can be accessed by users from their personal computers via telephone lines. Two major information utilities are CompuServe and Prodigy. These commercial services charge an initiation fee and a monthly fee. If local-line access to information utilities is available, users do not pay any long-distance telephone charge. Specialized services are also available on-line, such as Westlaw (law), Lexis (law), Grassroots (agriculture), Official Airlines Guide (travel), and Skrupsky's Legal Requirements for Records Management.

CompuServe. CompuServe services include weather reports, UPI (United Press International) news, a travel reservations system, home shopping, banking, and medical and legal advice, as well as E-mail and stock quotations. Other services include program packages, text editors, encyclopedia reference, games, a software exchange, and programming languages. Some of these services have an additional charge to the basic connect fee.

Prodigy. Prodigy was introduced jointly by IBM and Sears and is aimed at the home user. However, it has found its way into some offices. Services include news and financial services, product reviews, home shopping, and games. Users can also interact through bulletin boards and personal messages.

Bulletin Boards

A bulletin board system (BBS) is in many ways like the main street of a small town. Multiple conversations take place at the same time; you can choose in which conversation to participate. If you need a service, you can run into the shop that provides that service. Where a small town might have a bank and a post office, a BBS might have an archive of public domain software and an E-mail center so that you can send messages to other people on the bulletin board (or elsewhere around the world).

Specialized BBSs can be set up. For example, Internet allows you to connect to Spacelink, which is sponsored by NASA's Marshall Space Flight Center in Huntsville, Alabama, and contains information about shuttle launches, astronauts' biographies, and NASA publications. Another Internet BBS is ISCABBS, which contains public

domain software. Users of Hewlett Packard calculators may wish to use Internet's NEW.

Bulletin boards are also established by many enterprising individuals who charge a small fee for participation.

Facsimile

Facsimile (fax) is a remote photocopying system. To some users, fax is a simple form of E-mail. A facsimile machine scans a document and electronically transmits an actual image to a receiving printer via telephone lines or satellite. Facsimile can transmit printed or handwritten material, as well as graphics. Businesses that require fast and accurate exchange of written information frequently use facsimile. Another advantage is that facsimile signatures are legally binding.

Facsimile machines are classified into groups, according to international standards for the equipment. The Group IV international standard was established in 1984. The Group IV machines are designed to work with value-added networks and offer higher image quality than Group II machines. Such machines permit storage of facsimile transmission on computers, multiparty delivery, retrieval at subsequent times, and display on computer terminals. Other popular convenience features include multipage transmission, automatic and turnaround polling, automatic dialing, time and date stamp, security access, and receipt confirmation. The store-and-forward feature allows documents to be sorted electronically and sent at the time the user chooses, such as when transmission costs are lowest. Automatic polling permits multiple copies to be automatically transmitted to a number of points at the same time.

Group III machines can transmit a page in less than a minute. Many Group III machines have polling and automatic delivery options. They also have higher resolution output than Group I and Group II. Resolution, or image quality, is measured in terms of pixels, the number of dots per square inch. Group III machines usually have twice as many pixels as earlier machines, making text more readable.

Where fax is used constantly, a dedicated telephone line is required. Where fax is used only occasionally, the regular telephone line can be used for either voice or fax. The fax machine looks like a copying machine, and multipurpose equipment is available where the same machine can be used as a printer, a photocopier, or a fax. The volume of use determines whether separate machines are warranted.

Courier Facsimile Service.   Courier facsimile services can be used when next-day delivery services are not fast enough, when the facsimile equipment of communicating organizations is not compatible for E-mail, or when either of the organizations does not have facsimile equipment. With these services, documents are given, either physically or electronically, to the service, which transmits them from one of the service's offices to another. The receiving office delivers the documents or message to the intended recipient. One commercial service promises door-to-door service in two hours and one-hour service if documents are dropped off at one of its offices.

Fax Service Bureaus.   Facsimile machines can be found in copy centers, hotels, drugstores, supermarkets, and even yarn shops. A fax can be sent through a coin-operated, self-service machine or it can be handled for the customer for a very reasonable service charge.

Teletypewriter Networks

In a teletypewriter network, users use a keyboard machine known as a teleprinter or teletypewriter to transmit messages. The material sent is thus limited to text. Western Union Telegraphic Co. (WUTCO) offers three services: Telex I, Telex II, and Teletex.

Telex.   Telex I is a Western Union worldwide teletypewriter exchange service that uses the public telegraph network. Telex I uses a five-bit

Baudot code and transmits about 67 words a minute. Telex II was formerly called Teletypewriter Exchange Service (TWX). Telex II uses ASCII (American Standard Code for Information Interchange), which is a standard computer code, and transmits about 100 words a minute. Telex I and Telex II are standard worldwide. All telex terminals are compatible, and the same machine that is used to type the message prints out a hard copy of a message that is received.

Subscriber services to telex are available. Subscribers can dial in to a network from terminals directly connected to the service, as a leased-line subscriber, from any communications carrier, and from other data terminals that communicate over telephone lines. Since the industry has been deregulated, Western Union can connect with overseas numbers.

Teletex.   In 1980 an international standard was established for a new service called Teletex. Teletex is thirty times faster in sending messages than Telex. Teletex also can send and receive messages simultaneously. Teletex terminals are intelligent, offering both word processing and data communications features.

Voice Mail

A voice mail system (VMS) makes possible the use of the most efficient and most natural form of communication—human speech. Voice mail is similar to the recording of messages on a home message recorder. The difference is that the message is digitized and can be reconstructed in audio or visual format. Voice mail is the system that turns spoken words into digital "mail." Voice mail exchange was invented by Gordon Matthews, president of VMX, Inc. (originally ECS Communications), who is the patent holder of the VMX system.

To get on the voice mail system, the user dials the number and dictates the message into the phone. The system attempts to deliver the message immediately, but if the recipient is not in, the message is filed in memory. Later, when the recipient dials his or her voice mailbox, the system

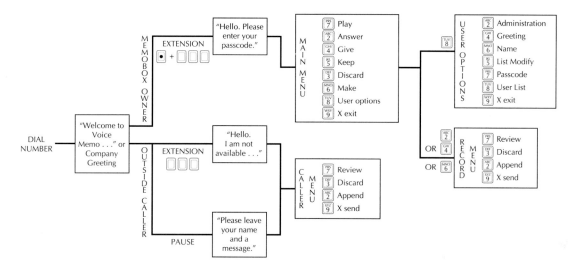

FIGURE 14.10 How a Voice Mail System Operates (Courtesy of Centigram Corp.)

tells the recipient that a message is waiting, and then it reconstitutes the digital data back into the voice of the sender and delivers the message. Figure 14.10 shows how a voice mail system operates.

Voice mail offers an opportunity for increasing office productivity. The typical manager spends 75 percent of his or her day talking to people, much of the time on the telephone. However, nearly three out of every four phone calls do not get through to the right person, and half the calls that are completed are inconsequential—notice of meetings, requests for documents, and so on. VMS presents the opportunity to alleviate disruptions caused by trivial calls. It is predicted that VMS will replace memo writing because it is quicker and actually less expensive to pick up a phone and dictate a call than it is to spend time writing a memo. Super-PBXs (private branch exchanges) are being developed by VMX, Bell, and Datapoint to provide full voice mail services.

Voice mail systems can be handled just as if the information had been generated on a computer keyboard, once the caller's voice has been converted into digital data. The same voice message can be sent to groups of people, or it can be transmitted during the night to someone at a remote location with another voice mail system for next-day delivery. Voice mail is on-line 24 hours a day, seven days a week, and can be accessed from any telephone.

SUMMARY

The challenge to records management today is that communication is electronic as well as by hard copy. The heart of the mail management program becomes one of organizing communications stations as well as mail stations and establishing workable standards and procedures to govern the detailed processing throughout the organization. The objectives of the mail management program are to motivate the staff, control costs, generate revenues more effectively, and project a good public image.

Mail supervision consists of those activities

that are necessary to ensure that the written word is moved from the point of origin to its destination in a manner that meets stated organizational goals. These activities include assigning program responsibilities, developing an organizational plan, establishing realistic objectives, developing and implementing standard procedures and practices, monitoring day-to-day operations, and evaluating and reporting results.

Mail operations include sorting and opening incoming mail, determining and indicating the routing of incoming mail, recording the receipt and referral of selected types of mail, maintaining control records on the location of response to selected types of mail, picking up and delivering written communications in accordance with established messenger schedules and routes, addressing and enveloping mail, clearing, reviewing, and signing outgoing communications, determining the required method of delivery, and dispatching outgoing communications and distributing record and information copies.

Computerized mail processing machines at the post office include optical character readers (OCRs) and bar code sorters.

All mail needs a complete delivery address and should also have a return address. In addition, there may be special service requirements. The format prescribed by the U.S. Postal Service for use with automated sorting equipment should be followed. This involves using the nine-digit ZIP Code. Labeling, direct addressing, and tabbing must also be considered in preparing the mail.

Automated equipment for all aspects of mail processing is governed by four objectives: (1) Remove manual tasks; (2) take advantage of all postal discounts; (3) reduce labor costs; and (4) produce marketing mail that elicits a response. Modern electronic mailing systems integrate all of the processing, which can be accomplished by the push of a button. Mailing systems have become smaller as integrated circuits have replaced vacuum tubes and mechanical systems. For handling mail internally in large organizations, mechanical mail delivery systems are available.

Equipment is available for labeling, direct address, folding and inserting, tabbing, applying postage, sealing envelopes, and sorting.

Planning a mail center involves analysis of the company's needs, definition of objectives, plan of strategy, and consideration of financial constraints.

Electronic mail can take the form of communicating via telephone lines from computer, terminal, or fax machine to other electronic equipment. Types of electronic mail that must be considered by the records manager include E-mail, public data networks, teletypewriter networks, facsimile, service bureaus, teleconferencing, commercial communications systems, voice mail, and bulletin board systems.

QUESTIONS FOR DISCUSSION

1. What are the goals of a mail management program?

2. Explain the difference between the terms *mail supervision* and *mail management.*

3. List the basic precautions for mail center security.

4. What is the difference between *internal mail* and *external mail*?

5. What is the scope of *outgoing mail management*?

6. Describe the requirements for preparing addresses for scanning by OCR equipment.

7. What are the advantages of using nine-digit ZIP Codes?

8. What is the difference between first-class mail and priority mail?

9. What is Mailgram service?

10. Describe six different ways to send international mail.

11. What is the difference between *certified mail* and *registered mail*?

12. What are the advantages of an electronic postage meter?

13. What is the basic automated equipment needed for mail handling?

14. Describe the process of planning a mail center.

15. What benefits can accrue from redesigning a mail center.

16. What automated equipment is usually found in a high-volume mail operation?

17. What characteristics of an organization determine whether mail operations are centralized at the organization's mail center or decentralized to preparing offices?

18. What are three different types of mechanical mail delivery systems?

19. When would a mechanical mail delivery system be selected?

20. Describe types of electronic mail.

21. How does voice mail differ from making regular telephone calls?

PROJECTS

1. Outline a 40-minute speech, which you are to present at the national MailCom Conference, on the topic "Improving Mail Operations in the Small Business Office."

2. Do a run-through of the speech for your class.

3. Identify the local companies that provide mail-handling services by checking the Yellow Pages of the telephone book. Ask one of the vendors to come and speak to the class about the services the company provides.

4. Call your local post office and ask to borrow any available videos on how mail is handled automatically.

5. Research and write a report on the remote encoder.

6. Write the step-by-step procedures you would follow in creating a mail center in a large company that has decided to reorganize its mail operations.

7. Prepare a scrapbook of advertising of automated equipment that could be used in a mail

center. Photocopy advertisements in current periodicals.

8. Attend a program on mail-handling improvement that is sponsored by a local chapter of a professional organization such as ARMA.

9. Visit a mail center of your choice. Ask about the mail security measures that are being taken. If time permits, ask about the automated mail-handling equipment that is being used. Report to the class either by preparing a written report or by presenting the report orally.

10. Visit a mail center of your choice. Ask if you can videotape the automated equipment that is being used to show it to the class. Videotape the mail center manager telling you about improvements she or he would make in the mail center if money were no object.

CASE PROBLEM

The records manager of the Superior Excavating Company, realizing that the company's mail program has serious problems, decided to establish a mail-handling improvement program. The manager began by conducting a survey of the organization's 150 office employees and its 5,000 customers. The chief complaints were as follows:

1. Mail takes at least 5 days to be delivered to the department concerned.

2. Much of the mail is returned because of insufficient address.

3. Mailings are labor-intensive, and a choice has to be made between getting regular work done or getting the mailing out.

4. The postage meter is frequently out of postage causing a trip to the post office and other delays.

Identify the actions that should be taken by this records manager to improve the organization's mail management program.

Chapter 15

Reprographics and Copy
Management and Control

Learning Objectives

1. To identify the scope of reprographics and copy control in a records management program.
2. To state the basic principles of an effective copy management program.
3. To identify the reproduction processes and equipment that should be considered in establishing and maintaining a reprographics and copy management program.
4. To determine the criteria for the selection and use of reprographics and copy equipment.
5. To establish effective methods of reprographics and copy program control.
6. To explain how to conduct a reprographics management program evaluation.

WHAT IS REPROGRAPHICS AND COPY MANAGEMENT?

The major purpose of a reprographics and copy management and control program should be to provide the organization with an efficient operation at the lowest possible cost. A reprographics and copy management program should determine how reprographics equipment is used, identify the requirements for duplicate records, and provide control over copier purchasing and production costs. Market analysts estimate that the acquisition of a new copier results in an immediate increase in the volume of copying of as much as 25 to 30 percent. Industry studies note that the average business document gets reproduced as many as 19 times and that American business produces as many as 400 billion copies annually. As much as 35 percent of the copies produced are unnecessary.

Reprography is the facsimile reproduction of graphic material. In the field of records management, reprographics takes on a much broader meaning and function. It involves the management of copying practices, procedures, equipment, and supplies to provide the most effective and economical copies of information. *Copying* refers to the process of making copies either with an office copier, offset, or other type of duplicator. It is also possible to make copies using the printers of various computer systems.

406

The most commonly used machines for copying are electrostatic copiers and offset duplicators. The primary difference between copiers and duplicators is that copiers make copies directly from an original, while duplicators require the preparation of an intermediate master from which copies are made. *Duplicating* then refers to the process of making duplicate copies. In the past, large-scale duplicating was done primarily with duplicators using masters, but today much duplicating is done as copying, and the terms are frequently used interchangeably. Usually, duplicators are used for jobs requiring large numbers of copies per original and copiers are used for jobs requiring relatively small numbers of copies per original. In many cases the term *copy management* is used interchangeably with the term *reprographics management.*

GOALS OF A REPROGRAPHICS AND COPY MANAGEMENT PROGRAM

Management of reproduction equipment begins with identifying objectives and establishing guidelines for the acquisition of equipment. The required features of copiers must be selected based on need. Other reproduction methods must also be evaluated. Multifunction devices need to be explored. A reprographics management program review needs to be in place based on the overall objectives of the program.

A reprographics and copy management program should provide for the following:

- Testing and evaluation of equipment.
- Selection of the best equipment for the application.
- Establishment of operation guidelines.
- Procurement and placement of equipment.
- Replacement of equipment based on usage, need, reliability, and technological innovation.
- Efficient and economical method of supply reorder.
- Ongoing monitoring of usage and problems.

- Timely resolution of problems.
- Accurate, timely records of usage, cost, and service.
- Testing and evaluation of supplies: paper, toner, developer.

The array of copiers, duplicators, and printers now available to business and government organizations has been both beneficial and detrimental to effective communications. Copying is essential to the organizations; it is a convenient aid in the distribution of information necessary to carry out an organization's mission. However, the proliferation of unnecessary copies of records continues to be one of the major barriers to successful management of information. Organizations whose total reproduction costs were negligible, in only a few years, have found their annual copying costs approaching six figures or more.

As a result of these increasing costs, managers have begun to study copying practices to determine whether these costs were justified and whether they could be reduced. The records manager also became concerned, not only because of the direct costs incurred, but also because of the effects these copies had on the management of records. It was apparent that many of the copies being produced daily in large quantities were being filed away, thus adding to records management problems by increasing volume and filing activity.

In the years since these problems were recognized, many advances in copier technology have been made, pricing methods have been improved, and the causes of the problems arising from copier use have become known. Although much has been done to control copying costs, volume control remains a continuing problem.

ACQUISITION, CONTROL, AND EVALUATION OF EQUIPMENT

Evaluating the many variables involved in copier selection is not easy. The type and design of the copier, the number of copies required, turnaround requirements, and the availability of other types of reproduction equipment are all factors to be considered. Because all of these factors vary from one organization to another, no one formula can be uniformly applied to all offices. Before copying equipment is acquired or replaced, it is necessary to consider:

1. Types of documents currently being copied.
2. Projected copying needs.
3. Grade level of equipment used.
4. Time spent copying.
5. Alternatives of (*a*) sharing existing equipment, (*b*) acquiring separate equipment, and (*c*) upgrading existing equipment.
6. Alternate reproduction methods.
7. Features of equipment that are required and those that are just "nice to have."
8. Length of time equipment is to be used—(*a*) extent of usage (e.g., three shifts for two years) and (*b*) potential use by other departments.
9. Electrical and ventilation requirements.
10. Information on supplies.
11. Installation and removal charges.
12. Maintenance and servicing arrangements.
13. Training provided.
14. Financial and other advantages of all types and makes available.
15. Cost-benefit analysis of leasing costs and purchase options.
16. Rental cancellation information.
17. Imminent technological improvements.
18. New techniques.
19. Industry or market trends.
20. Best location for the equipment.

The process involved in deciding the proper reproduction method for a particular situation involves determining copying requirements, copier justification, equipment evaluation, and equipment selection.

Copying Requirements

Analyzing the copying currently being done throughout the organization usually results in the elimination of inefficient practices. The copying work that is actually required is then documented. Such documentation should take the form of a profile of the organization's copying activities. This profile should include the following information.

1. *The intended use of the copier.* Specialized uses may indicate a need for specialized equipment. On the other hand, a request based on convenience use may mean that there is no actual need at all.

2. *The intended operators of the copier.* Some copy machines are difficult for the casual user to operate and therefore are not suitable for self-service operation.

3. *Equipment now being used.* If a centralized facility is now being used, some reasons should be identified as to why it is no longer adequate.

4. *Volume anticipated.* An estimate of the total number of copies per month should be made, as well as an estimate of:

   a. The number of copies per original.
   b. The kind of documents.
   c. The size and composition of the jobs being done.
   d. The urgency of the various copying requirements.
   e. The amount of copying that requires special handling.

This information will assist in determining the type of copier required. Figure 15.1, Copying Workload Survey Record, is an example of a form that can be modified to meet any organization's needs. The form can be completed as the copies are made. The data can then be analyzed to determine copier needs.

Copier Justification

An analysis of the need for a copier begins with copier justification. The most direct way to control copy costs is to make certain that (1) a copier is required and (2) the proper machine is selected.

					Number of			
Date	Your grade/ rank	Office symbol	Room no.	Document copied (name, number, type, etc.)	Pages in document	Copies per page	Total copies	Minutes elapsed (waiting and copying)

Please use a separate line for each document copied.

Copier (make and model) _____

Location (room number) _____

FIGURE 15.1 Copying Workload Survey Record
(*Copy Management Handbook*, General Services Administration (GSA), Washington, D.C.:
Government Printing Office, p. 13)

Every request for a copier should be evaluated and economically justified before it is approved. A cost justification requirement, if it is strictly enforced, will do much to prevent escalating copier costs. Costs can be analyzed by reviewing cost per copy, looking at total cost factors, and determining cost savings.

Cost per Copy. First, the cost per copy should be considered. To determine the copy costs, it is necessary to know the material cost or the meter charge for the copier. The purpose of this analysis is to determine how much, in terms of specific quantities, the copier is used for multiple-copy reproduction. On the basis of the data, a high-speed copier with special pricing for multiple copies may be considered, or other reproduction methods may be used. If the number of copies required per original is relatively large, perhaps 50 or more, it may be less expensive to use another reproduction process than the copier. However, to determine at what point the other process would be more economical requires a cost analysis of alternative processes and consideration of the number of originals. A comparison of costs per copy can then be made.

A cost-per-copy figure may create the false impression that copies are inexpensive. Also, there are certain situations where the cost-per-copy can be dropping at the same time that the total cost is rising, for example, when copying volume is rising at a greater rate than costs. When copies are produced by commercial printing services, the cost per copy decreases as the number of copies increases. Cost per copy is only part of the total cost factors that must be considered in comparing copy equipment.

Total Cost Factors. To control the total copying costs of the organization, it is essential to seek economy in the procurement, maintenance, and use of reproduction equipment. This involves consideration of both the tangible and intangible costs of the copying operations as well as making cost comparisons between one machine and another or between one year and another.

For purchase of equipment, supplies, and maintenance contracts, the cost per unit is usually based on the total quantity purchased: the bigger the quantity, the lower the price. For organizations that must purchase copier paper from the vendor of the equipment, it is possible to negotiate copy credit allowances for sheets of paper that are not usable.

Cost Savings.   Additional savings can be accomplished by implementing the following procedures:

- Replacing equipment with less-expensive makes and models.
- Negotiating for more favorable rental plans and purchase prices.
- Using more efficient rental plans.
- Consolidating equipment and supplies.
- Simplifying invoice procedures.
- Reducing copying requirements.
- Effectively using purchased equipment in lieu of rentals.

In addition to verification of the need for the copier, equipment requests must be reviewed centrally because not all factors may be known by a single department. An obvious and simple solution to the copying problem at the local level may be viewed differently from a broader point of view for many reasons:

1. Budget considerations may limit spending.
2. Plans to make major changes in the whole system may affect individual equipment decisions.
3. An upcoming reorganization may make it desirable to postpone or eliminate equipment acquisition plans.
4. Relocation of various offices may change the office configuration and require a different need for copiers.

Equipment Evaluation

Once a need for equipment has been established, appropriate machines should be evaluated. The cost of the machine or the rental rate, in addition to the cost of the materials or meter charges, should be considered. Generally, cost is evaluated on a per-copy basis for a specific department The reliability and reputation of the equipment manufacturer, the copy quality, and the availability and cost of maintenance are also important factors.

A cost-analysis worksheet for copying equipment developed by the General Services Administration of the U.S. government is shown in Figure 15.2. Every reprographics and copy management and control program should use an evaluation form that includes both the purchase and rental cost (including options) for each copier being acquired. A comparison of purchase and rental costs for the same time period may be shown. A three-year period is frequently used as a base line. On the basis of this comparison, the most cost-effective machine available to meet the requirements of each application should be selected. During this selection process, it should be kept in mind that the least expensive machine may not be the most cost effective if its manufacturer has a record of providing poor service or if the machine cannot meet the needs of the user.

Equipment Selection

The goal of equipment selection is to match equipment to copying needs. The profile of the organization's copying activities provides the raw data needed to properly match equipment to the organization's copying needs. The manager can then decide whether a reprographics center should be established to handle the special and high-volume copying jobs, where in the organization the sharing of equipment is feasible, and which units of the organization will require their own equipment. The profile will also assist in determining just what capabilities each item of equipment must have in terms of production speed and special features or accessories.

Options.   After the guidelines for the acquisition of equipment are reviewed, it is still necessary to review the options to purchase, rent, lease, or pay per copy. Studies of copying equipment emphasize the need for making cost comparisons prior to determining the method of acquisition. In many cases, savings can be realized through the purchase of equipment rather than through leasing equipment.

Choosing the Vendor.   After selecting the features and size of the copier, choosing the right

Acquisition factor	1st year	2d year	3d year	4th year	5th year	6th year
Cost of purchase (excluding installation and maintenance)	$3,000					
Installation and maintenance (cumulative)	400	$700	$1,000	$1,300	$1,600	$1,900
Total costs (cumulative)	3,400	3,700	4,000	4,300	4,600	4,900
Cost of lease—cumulative (includes installation and maintenance)	1,200	2,400	3,600	4,800	6,000	7,200
Cost of purchase exceeds lease by	2,200	1,300	400			
Cost of lease exceeds purchase by				500	1,400	2,300

FIGURE 15.2 Cost Analysis Worksheet for Copying Equipment (*Copy Management Handbook*, GSA, p. 35)

vendor is vital to good copy management. The criteria should include (1) reliability, (2) copy quality, (3) service, (4) price, and (5) ease of use. There are certain efficiencies to be gained by working with one vendor who provides manufacturing, sales, service, supplies, administrative support, and financing options. Single-source responsibility for all copying needs can save time and energy.

Some vendors offer discounts, service contracts, and the use of a demonstration model for a trial period. A standard guideline is to purchase in bulk to obtain discounts whenever possible.

Although *reliability* is a critical factor in the selection of equipment, it may be difficult to measure. Two measurements that may help in the decision-making process are the number of copies between service calls (CBSCs) and service-call frequency (SCF). The *CBSC* measures the average number of copies that are made before a service call is required. *SCF* is the number of calls in a year.

Service is an important consideration because a copy machine requires more service than any other piece of office equipment. Most machines

are sold directly by manufacturers and their dealers. The exception is personal copiers, which can be purchased at office supply stores. In lease agreements, the cost of service is often incorporated into the lease price.

User Support

The success of a copy management program depends very heavily upon the support of everyone who uses the reproduction services. All personnel should be informed of their responsibilities for good copy management. Managers at all levels should be held accountable for the copying done by their units.

Record Copy. Today it is increasingly difficult to determine which of the black and white pages is the original. The record copy is the official file copy and is usually maintained by the originator of the document, except in cases where the record copy holder is specified by law. Such cases include the corporate secretary or city clerk for minutes, the finance director for budget information, and the corporate or city attorney for lawsuits.

One way to reduce filing of duplicate materials is to stamp the record copy with the word *ORIGINAL* in color (blue, green, or red) so that the record copy is easily identifiable. For documents that are signed, such as contracts or correspondence, the signature may be signed in a color other than black. Recipients of pages with *ORIGINAL* stamped in black or with black signatures will immediately know that their pages are duplicate copies and need not be maintained if no longer useful.

Legal Restrictions.   Everyone should be aware of the restrictions included in the copyright law regarding what can be copied and the purposes for which authorized copies may be reproduced. Many people who would never consider breaking a law do so quite frequently by reproducing certain materials on office copiers.

Federal copyright law prohibits reproduction of copyrighted material without permission. The copyright law that became effective January 1, 1978, is more definite and inclusive than previous copyright laws.

In addition to the copyright law, there are federal and state laws that prohibit the reproduction of certain government-originated documents. A list of these documents is shown in Figure 15.3.

Unnecessary Copies.   So much emphasis is placed on the cost of reprographics equipment that, as a result, their value is often overlooked. This is because the costs are crystallized in terms of a payable item and the savings are hidden in many clerical operations. If there were not so many valid uses of the office copier, management would dispense with it rather than attempt to control it. However, there are many abuses and misuses of the office copier that add to its cost and detract from its overall value. Good copy management reduces unnecessary copying by educating users of copying equipment and making them responsible for their copying practices.

The modern office copier has become so popular because of its simplicity and convenience. Two types of copier abuse are making the extra copy and making the information copy. The extra-copy habit can add a considerable sum to reprographics costs. Many people make an extra copy "just in case" or to see if a better copy can be obtained on the second try. These practices are expensive and unnecessary. Users must be instructed to order only the number of copies required and to be satisfied with readable reproductions.

The making of an information copy is an abuse that should not occur under most circumstances. Magazine articles are frequently copied, filed, and never referred to. Usually, the article could just as easily be cut from the magazine. Likewise, some cautious managers make a copy of everything that passes over their desk. Education is the best method of controlling unnecessary duplication. This includes suggestions for distribution and routing. Reducing the *distribution* list cuts the time spent in copying the materials, lowers copy costs, and saves time for the recipients in screening their mail. A single copy may be sent to a department or division for *routing* to its staff members. For very large reports, a limited number of copies may be produced; then only the title page and index need be circulated in order to inform people of the availability of the report. Those persons who actually need the information can request it. This procedure reduces copying and distribution costs, and saves time for many employees.

Copy Management Guidelines.   Basic copy management guidelines that need to be called to the attention of all users include the following:

1. Be sure the copies are needed before producing them.
2. Make only the number of copies required.
3. Order blank forms and publications through regular supply channels. Use the copier only in extenuating circumstances for copying of this type.
4. Copy no personal or other unauthorized documents.
5. Use the print shop or copy center for large

1. Congress, by statute, has forbidden the copying of the following subjects under certain circumstances. There are penalties of fine or imprisonment imposed on those guilty of making such copies.
   a. Obligations or securities of the United States Government, such as—
      (1) Certificates of Indebtedness.
      (2) National Bank Currency.
      (3) Coupons from Bonds.
      (4) United States Bonds.
      (5) Federal Reserve Bank Notes.
      (6) Federal Reserve Notes.
      (7) Treasury Notes.
      (8) Silver Certificates.
      (9) Gold Certificates.
      (10) Fractional Notes.
      (11) Certificates of Deposit.
      (12) Paper Money.
      (13) Bonds and obligations of certain agencies of the Government such as FHA, etc.
      (14) U.S. Savings Bonds.
      (15) War Savings Stamps if in albums filled or partially filled. (They may be photographed only if the reproduction is either 25 percent smaller in each dimension or 50 percent larger in each dimension.)
      (16) Internal Revenue Stamps. (If it is necessary to copy a legal document on which there is a cancelled revenue stamp, this may be done provided it is for lawful purposes.)
      (17) Postage Stamps Cancelled or Uncancelled.
      (18) Postal Money Orders.
      (19) Bills, Checks, or Drafts for Money drawn by or upon authorized officers of the United States.
   b. Adjusted Compensation Certificates for Veterans of the World Wars.
   c. Obligations or Securities of any Foreign Government, Bank or Corporation.
   d. Copyrighted material of any manner or kind without permission of the copyright owner.
   e. Certificates of Citizenship of Naturalization. (Foreign Naturalization Certificates may be photographed.)
   f. Passports. (Foreign passports may be photographed.)
   g. Immigration Papers.
   h. Draft Registration Cards.
   i. Selective Service Induction Papers which bear any of the following information: Registrant's earnings or income; dependency status; court records; previous military service; physical or mental condition.
   j. Badges, Identification Cards, Passes, or Insignia carried by Armed Forces personnel or employees of the Federal Government.

2. Copying the following is also prohibited in certain states:
   a. Automobile licenses.
   b. Driver's permits.
   c. Automobile Certificates of Title.

FIGURE 15.3 Material That May Not Be Copied (*Copying Equipment*, GSA)

copying jobs when these facilities can produce the jobs more efficiently.

6. Use contracting for copying when this option is more effective than using in-house facilities.

7. When time allows, make one copy for circulation rather than distributing a copy to everyone concerned.

8. Make two-sided copies. One-sided copies should be the exception.

9. Retain unusable single-side copies for scratch paper.

10. Recycle unusable copies or retain them for credit.

11. In case of machine malfunction, notify the proper person that service is required and

leave a note on the machine to keep others from trying to use it.

12. Keep the copying area free of staples, paper clips, and other foreign objects.

13. Set the copier for proper quantity and paper size before beginning a run.

14. Before starting a large job, run a test copy to ensure that the copier is functioning properly.

15. Accept copies that are legible rather than attempting to secure "perfect" copies.

16. Use a work surface other than the top of the copier for the disassembly or assembly of documents.

Program Evaluation

To help identify areas for improvement of the copy management program, detailed records should be kept on all copying and duplicating equipment and their use. A folder for each copier should contain all contracts, update sheets, written correspondence, maintenance reports, service calls, and reports of oral communication concerning the equipment. Copies of requests for service due to equipment malfunction will assist in evaluating the equipment for replacement. Meter records can show usage by department, as shown in Figure 15.4. In addition, the equipment history card will provide data for various reports, such as billing reports, locator reports, budget expenditure reports, service reports, and productivity analysis reports.

A *billing report* may be calculated each month for all machines. The statement may include rent, maintenance, taxes, installation and removal charges, prompt payment discounts, and copy credits.

The *locator report* provides a monthly inventory of equipment, including make, model, serial number, location, monthly volume, volume by user, and other pertinent information. The volume by user may be used for charge-back purposes.

A *budget expenditure report* provides current and year-to-date computations on all expenses. The report can be formatted to show the expenditures by department. A separate report can be compiled to show expenditures by vendor.

The *service report* provides a service history of all equipment. The report includes the date of request, type of problem, date of repair, and nature of repair. The service report may be prepared by department and by vendor.

The *productivity analysis report* may list the monthly volume of all machines, or it may be printed as an exception report—listing only those machines performing out of their recommended volume range. If machines are producing at volumes considerably below their capabilities, there is a good chance that there are too many machines available. Conversely, excessively high volumes might be an indication that more copying equipment is needed or that inappropriate use is being made of existing equipment.

In addition to monthly volume, the production analysis reports may contain a six-month history, current costs, exception information, and replacement recommendations. The production analysis report is usually organized by vendor, make, and model.

These reports are useful in selecting equipment, in allocating equipment to departments, in determining charge-back costs, and in replacing equipment. Because of constant changes in equipment, there is always some area where program improvements can be made. After possible improvements are identified, plans can be formulated for implementation.

EQUIPMENT FEATURES

Copiers and duplicators come with a variety of special features and attachments designed to meet special requirements. Along with the evolution of copiers have come greater reliability, greater sophistication of design and electronic construction, better supplies, enhanced service, generous warranties, and performance promises. The trend to-

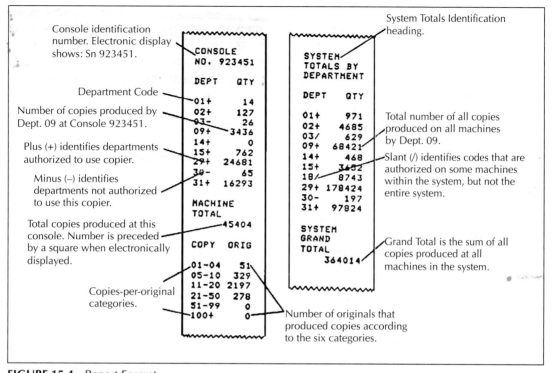

FIGURE 15.4 Report Format
(*Copy Management Handbook,* GSA, p. 10)

ward modularity permits users to have a choice of features tailored to their needs. Most copiers today are microprocessor-controlled, so they can monitor themselves and perform self-adjustments internally as they operate. This decreases downtime and increases productivity. The change from coated paper to plain paper was the beginning of many other significant changes in copiers. The following are some of the major options that are available today, with remote diagnostics being a promising new feature: copy controls, automatic document feeder, recirculating document handlers, sorters, collators, and duplexing.

Remote Diagnostics

There are three levels of remote diagnostics. The first is a meter-reading capability. This feature programs the copier to call a host computer with periodic meter readings. The second level of remote diagnostics is designed to automate service and customer support. Each manufacturer has its own definition of this level, but the consensus seems to be that of informing a host computer that some sort of part or supply failure will occur in the copier. On the drawing board is a device that will interface directly with the copier: When a problem occurs, the device will call the dealer location to alert him or her of the problem. The device will also be capable of monitoring jam counts. A data bus is also being developed that will perform a total computer diagnostic check. The data are then loaded into a mainframe so that a complete file of the copier's internal processing is available for analysis. The third phase of remote diagnostics allows a host computer to make service corrections on copiers within its network.

This requires built-in sensors, and at the present time, the cost is almost prohibitive.

Control Panel

The control panel and message display should be clearly visible and easy to understand. Some copiers have a message display that gives step-by-step instructions on how to complete a copy job.

Copy Control

Copy controls are designed to encourage employees to be more aware of their patterns of use of the copy machine. Several variations of copier controls are available. The most popular is a small keypad on which the designated user keys in his or her number. This command "unlocks" the copier and allows access to only authorized personnel. The control can identify the individual user, the specific department involved, and the job and client. On smaller machines, the access code can be contained in a key box which the user inserts into the machine. Other variations include card access. In this system a card worth a certain number of copies is issued to the user. As copies are made, the cost of each is deducted from the card until the account is used. The card must be recharged to permit future use. A variation of the card system is to use the proprietary card already issued to the employee, such as the company ID card, which the employee may be required to wear.

The most obvious benefit of a copy control system is the ability to keep a running total of copies produced for every job and purpose. This facilitates charge-back billing to clients for clerical work done by the piece, such as in legal offices, advertising agencies, and engineering firms. Charge-back billing makes it easy for employees to realize that each copy represents money.

Document Feeders

Three basic types of document feeders are in general use: (1) single-sheet feeders, which accept originals fed in by hand; (2) stack feeders, which can accommodate and feed automatically an entire stack of originals; and (3) recirculating stack feeders, which make multiple copies of a stack of originals by repeatedly recycling an original document page by page over the exposure platen. The stack of originals is recirculated in this manner for the number of copies required. The recirculating feeder eliminates the need for a sorter or collator because multiple sets can be produced one at a time.

On smaller machines, paper is available in a single tray for letter-size paper or in a dual tray, with trays for both letter- and legal-size paper. An additional paper source, where single sheets of letterhead, colored paper, or transparencies can be fed in, is also available. Dual-input trays and dual-output stacks allow loading and unloading of paper while the system continues printing.

Automatic Document Feeder (ADF)

The ADF takes originals, automatically positions each one on a platen, makes the selected number of copies, and then transports the original in proper sequence to a receiving tray. Semiautomatic document feeders are also available: The originals must be fed in by hand, one at a time; they are then positioned automatically on the platen for copying. Another type of feeder is the *computer-forms feeder*. This is usually part of the automatic document feeder. Individual pages of unburst fanfold are copied and moved along. The fanfold is then automatically restacked.

Reduction and Enlargement

Degrees of reduction vary. Legal-size documents and computer printouts may be reduced to letter size. Another reduction mode can put two letter-size pages onto one sheet. The *zoom* reduction and enlargement feature allows enlargement or reduction to occur in 1 percent increases (from 50 percent to as much as 400 percent).

Sorting and Collating

A *sorter* is an on-line device that places copies in predetermined bins one at a time as they are produced, thus assembling all the pages of a given document into each bin. Sorters are used with both copiers and duplicators. This option relieves the operator of this finishing task.

A *collator* is an off-line device that has separate feeding bins for separate page stacks. All first pages are loaded into one bin; all second pages are loaded into another bin. After all the page stacks are loaded into the collator, the machine is turned on and feeder arms push the top sheets from each bin into position so that they can be gathered into sets by the operator or automatically by the machine. Collators are usually used with offset duplicators, where a large number of copies are made from each original.

Duplexing

The capability of automatically copying on both sides of the paper is called *duplexing*. Two-sided copies are made simply by placing the machine into the duplex mode and copying two originals or both sides of the same original. Advantages of two-sided copying over one-sided copying are that the copies look more professional, are more easily handled, and are less costly to produce, mail, and store.

Original-Size Sensing

The copier is capable of copying originals of various sizes automatically. Automatic reduction and enlargement will permit the copier to automatically adjust the image size to make it fill the size of the copy stock selected.

Job Recovery, Interrupt, and Programming

Job recovery comes into play after a misfeed or jam has been cleared. The copier's memory tells the operator how to restack the originals so the copy job can be completed without missing any pages. *Job interrupt* permits the operator to stop a job in progress to allow another job to be completed. Then the copier remembers how to finish the first job. *Job programming* permits the selection of all the features and number of copies of a frequently repeated copying task to be programmed into the copier's memory. The job can be recalled and run as often as needed without resetting each particular feature.

Book Copy Mode

The book copy mode permits facing pages of a bound volume to be copied a page at a time without the need to move the book on the platen.

Finishing

High-volume equipment can come equipped with jogging and stapling devices called finishers. Other finishers include a hole-punching device.

Binding

Binding equipment provides high-quality documents with a professional look. Several types of equipment are available from a variety of vendors. These include hot- and cold-glue binders, thermal-tape binders, and devices that bind documents together using punched holes and plastic inserts. Binding equipment is most frequently used in conjunction with offset duplicators.

Clamshell Access

The copier opens like a clamshell at the touch of a button. This provides easy access for clearing jams and misfeeds and for performing routine maintenance. This feature is usually available on smaller copiers.

Repeating

With the repeating feature, images of a graphic element can be repeated, almost like a wallpaper design.

Deletion

With the deletion feature, copy may be improved by editing out marginal notes, stray markings, and staple lines. Proprietary information can be selectively deleted for different audiences.

Other Features

Electronic copiers have several other features that are designed to provide maximum production with continuous operation. Several nonstop operating features maximize productivity. Production can continue even while forms are changed, new jobs entered, paper loaded, or finished output removed for distribution. Input disk buffering eliminates the need for the equipment to stop printing while accepting additional jobs or mounting a new tape.

COPIERS

Copiers have become indispensable to office operations. From carbon paper for making copies, the technology has progressed to thermal, photo, and digital copiers. Today, almost 80 percent of the copy machines sold are meeting the needs of small and medium-size businesses. These copiers generally fall into the personal copier or convenience copier size. Convenience copiers include low-range copiers and mid-range copiers. Larger organizations may utilize larger equipment in copying or duplicating centers or xerographic duplicating environments. While photocopiers utilize analog technology, digital technology facilitates the use of color and integration with other digital devices for processing activities of the office.

Personal Copiers

The desktop-model personal copiers produce up to 10 copies per minute (cpm) and offer limited capabilities. The features are usually limited to the ability to lighten or darken copies and the option to use legal-size paper. Their appeal is their small footprint and fairly aggressive pricing. This size copier is typically found in home offices and the executive suite and usually is used to produce fewer than 400 copies in a month. As a result, maintenance costs are minimal and downtime is negligible. However, toner needs to be replenished periodically and is considered to be expensive.

The future of personal copiers is directly related to the emergence of low-cost fax machines and multifunctional devices. Fax machines have already been linked to small-volume copying machines. This linkage is strengthened by the capability of using similar paper.

Convenience Copiers

Convenience copiers usually operate at speeds ranging from 10 to 45 cpm and are used in installations generating between 1,500 and 20,000 copies per month. According to BIS Strategic Decisions, convenience copiers represent nearly 70 percent of the copiers in the United States. Convenience copiers are easy to use and are usually found in various satellite centers of departments of medium-size companies, as well as in a dedicated copy center. Convenience copiers include low-range and mid-range copies:

- *Low-range copiers.* Low-range copies produce about 12 to 15 copies per minute. They are used where volume falls into the range of 1,500 to 10,000 copies per month.
- *Mid-range copiers.* Mid-range copiers operate at about 30 copies per minute. Mid-range copiers are usually used where production of copies falls between 7,000 and 20,000 copies per month.

Convenience copies are made by employees who require a few copies for their own use immediately. There is a possibility that professional and other highly paid staff members may be doing a disproportionately large amount of the copying.

Responsibility for the maintenance of the convenience copier must be assigned. One employee may be designated as the contact person for each copier with responsibility to replenish the paper supply and to call for maintenance. The convenience copier may be located in the center of the work area or in a small area set aside as the local copy center. A fax machine to service this work group may also be located in this area or be part of a multifunction piece of equipment.

Reprographics and Copy Center

It is possible that an organization served exclusively by user-operated convenience copiers may benefit from establishing a centralized reprographics and copy center. Copy centers are usually dedicated areas or remote operations designed for reproduction. They are usually found in businesses with more than 50 employees. The equipment

operates at speeds ranging from 50 to 90 cpm with monthly outputs of up to 100,000 pages. Figure 15.5 is an illustration of a leading copier, the Lanier 7100. These copiers can perform a variety of tasks, such as enlarging, reducing, printing both sides at once, printing in various colors, collating, binding, punching holes, and stapling. An employee with specialized training in using all of the functions of the equipment performs the service for other employees on a priority basis.

Central Reproduction

Central reproduction departments (CRDs) are geared to volumes of from 100,00 to 450,000 copies per month at speeds exceeding 90 cpm.

FIGURE 15.5 Copier
(Courtesy of Lanier Worldwide, Inc.)

The CRD may contain sophisticated copiers or printing equipment or both. Printing and graphics have developed from letterpress to offset printing and phototypesetting to digital multifunction systems.

Phototypesetting equipment, compatible with word processing or desktop publishing (DTP) software and copiers, is found in organizations where in-house composition and printing of documents is justified by costs. In organizations where oversized documents, such as maps or blueprints, are in common use, the reprographic equipment may duplicate these documents size for size, or enlarge or reduce them. Graphics departments are currently the biggest users of digital copiers. Digital copiers and duplicators fit best in central reproduction departments (CRDs).

In-house printing and graphics operations tend to be the center of imaging and graphics communications in organizations and are known as in-plants. The broad definition of an in-plant is "a printing facility set up inside an organization whose primary business is not printing." There are an estimated 100,000 in-plant printing operations in North America today. The reasons for the popularity of in-plant operations are cost, confidentiality, and control. Graphics is assuming more of a service-bureau role. However, it is necessary to understand the distinction between the high-end users of DTP applications for corporate publications in large-volume publishing applications and the average users, who use DTP for occasional or low-volume routine applications.

The equipment and staff of the CRD are contingent upon the volume and complexity of documents to be reproduced. Some organizations have a policy to contract out jobs that need design services or require quantities beyond the capacity of their normal requirements and equipment.

Digital Technology.   Analog technology is being supplanted by digital technology in the production of copiers. The photocopy cartridge device in analog copiers transfers the image from the original to the copy using the same general principle as a camera. In digital technology, instead of taking a picture of the original, the copier scans the original and transfers digital impulses to paper. The limiting factors of switching from analog to digital copiers are the need to set costs and the need to speed up production. At this time, analog copiers have the advantage. Digital technology allows for more versatility with multifunction products, however, and offers network capabilities. The microprocessors found in digital equipment provide the electronic space where the machines load and run their programs. Figure 15.6 is an illustration of digital technology in a multifunction system, Docutech, Xerox's high-volume reproduction system.

Color Copiers

Color digital copiers are outselling monochrome digital units by five to one. It is estimated that by 1995, some 100,000 color placements will nearly all be digital. Color copiers are available that can reproduce exact colored copies. Other color copiers offer a choice of printing in solid colors other than black. A full-color machine, such as the Minolta CF 80 shown in Figure 15.7, may be found in a CRD. In addition to the optional features offered by analog copiers, digital color copiers offer the following features:

- *Stretching, squeezing, and slanting.* This feature permits the stretching of a headline across the width of the document; uses a one-directional zoom to compress copy; and slants copy left or right in italicized fashion.
- *Overlaying.* A special background pattern for material on the original which is selected from a menu of built-in or imported designs.
- *Inlaying.* By placing an area of one original into a space on a second, both spaces can be copied as one composite document.
- *Screening.* A gray tone is placed behind an area.
- *Mirror imaging.* The image is turned over.
- *Reverse imaging.* Blacks are made white and whites black.
- *Color converting.* Any color may be changed

FIGURE 15.6 High–Speed, High–Resolution Reproduction System (Courtesy of Xerox Corporation)

to any other color. Color is determined by selecting percentages of four primary colors—yellow, magenta, cyan (blue), and black—to achieve the desired hue.

REPRODUCTION EQUIPMENT

Because modern electronic copiers are amazingly fast and versatile, they have become an important element in the convergence of technologically oriented office systems. Multifunction systems utilizing microprocessors are the wave of the future. However, nonelectronic equipment is very functional and economical. Nonelectronic reproduc-tion equipment includes offset duplicators, spirit duplicators, and stencil duplicators.

Multifunction Systems

Multifunction devices (MFDs) combine laser printing, facsimile, digital scanning, and photo-copying. The multifunction device eliminates re-dundancies that exist when you have separate ma-chines. Copiers and printers both print; digital copiers, fax machines, and scanners all scan; and each machine has its own control panel, housing unit, and power supply. A multifunction device can combine the duplicate features.

A multifunction system will allow one device to serve as a fax, a file service, a printer, and a copier. The copier can function as a convenience copier or a text processor and communicate with other office equipment. These copies can receive coded data, translate them, and form a line of characters that is scanned. The data are then transmitted to a photosensitive device, where an image is created and transferred to paper or through fax to various locations.

The electronic printing system can also store forms, type sizes and styles, page formats, logos, and signatures and create them electronically upon demand, concurrently with the variable data. The copier can also be used when it is necessary to alter some portion of a form, such as blocking out confidential information. In this case an overlay would mask the confidential portion. Electronic masking or windowing is available on some copier models. Additionally, electronic forms can be changed automatically without interrupting the operation of the printer. In the copier marketplace, multifunction products are available as high-end console systems and as mid-range desktop systems.

Isolated standalone equipment is also being replaced with multifunction devices. However, the cost of a separate copier, fax, and printer is often less than a multifunction device. User access to these three processes is more limited in a multifunction device than with three separate machines. A multifunction device that aids in this process is the intelligent processing unit.

The *intelligent processing unit* (IPU) is a computer interface for image editing, printing, and scanning functions. It permits a copier to be

FIGURE 15.7   Full–Color Copier with Computer Connectivity
(Courtesy of Minolta Corporation)

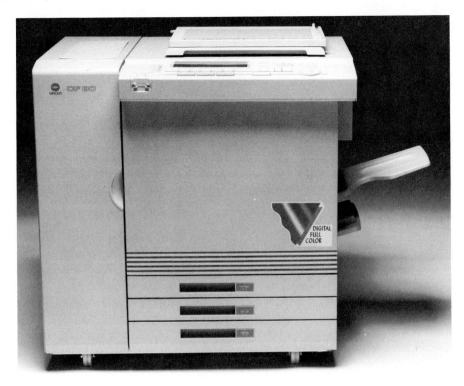

used as both a printer and a scanner. The IPU contains a power supply and a logic board. The IPU permits a file to be sent to the computer from the printer. Images, which are scanned in, can be viewed and edited on the computer. An optional film projector for 35-mm slides or negative film can be connected to the copier-printer to produce color copies. An optional video adapter can be used for printing input from a still video player, VCR, or TV tuner. A counterfeit protection system can be built into color laser copier printers. The system will not print a copy of any bank note currency which has been registered in memory, but instead prints a blank page. The system also imprints every color photocopy made from the machine with its serial number in an invisible format. The IPU makes printing on demand possible.

Printing on Demand. Today, technologies such as high-tech facsimile devices, scanners, desktop publishing equipment, and high-speed duplicators have made printing on demand (POD) possible. Information that previously existed on computer printouts or offset-printing negatives is available in computer files that can be shared by any number of users.

Systems Applications

Systems applications combine a network of subsystems to develop new and improved procedures to carry out a major activity. The cost of the new resource is balanced by the benefits associated with the change. The copier is one resource which offers much in systems integration. Systems applications for copiers vary from using the copier to alter existing documents to transforming information from media such as computer memory to hard copy or distributing information directly from computer memory to other locations via fax. Transmitting information from microfilm via fax is also possible.

Computer to Copier. Where many high-quality copies of a document are needed, it is possible to

format the copy directly from the computer to the copier. The page printing on the copier is usually more efficient than page printing on laser printers.

Microfilm to Copier. It may be necessary to distribute hard copies of a document which resides on microfilm. If this requirement occurs on a regular basis, it may be cost effective to adopt the technology of reading microfilm directly into the copier in order to make the required number of hard copies.

Shared-Output Technologies

The output of document copy from information systems, office automation, and printing and graphics can now be combined with a variety of reprographic processes. All three of these output processes include ever-increasing automation and computerization, and result in shared technologies, such as information systems, office automation, and graphics and printing.

Information Systems (IS). Information systems originated with the mainframe computer, moved on to personal computers, and are now available on local area networks (LANs). IS output continues to be highly textual, but desktop publishing, presentation graphics, and spreadsheet and database applications are used increasingly and integrated with text. Where LANs are available, use of electronic mail and maintenance of calendars is increasingly popular. Problems of slower speeds and memory shortages in LANs and limited vendor selections have made other document-producing entities, such as multifunction devices, increase in popularity. Multifunction devices are defining a new and expanding niche in the office automation marketplace.

Office Automation. Office automation is the integration of technologies such as improved telecommunciations, high-tech photocopiers, sophisticated word processing, spreadsheets, databases, and enhanced facsimile technology to produce both text and graphics. Office automation has been evolving in a piecemeal fashion in many organizations and has sometimes been an elusive goal rather than a stable entity. Desktop publishing is an example of an office automation application.

Desktop Publishing. Desktop publishing (DTP) has hastened the obsolescence of old methods and job descriptions. DTP has streamlined the production tasks of typesetting, designing pages, generating galleys, proofreading, and correcting and preparing pages for the printer. Text and graphics software, scanners, and printers are part of the office automation environment. The nature of the hardware and software required by professional publishers is not substantially different from what is sold for DTP. Some basic DTP work can be done on a standard VDT screen, but to get the most out of the software, many DTP systems require a graphic display terminal (GDT). *Scanners* (machines that scan text or illustrations from hard copy and convert the images to digital data for the computer) expand what a DTP system can do, but they also add to the cost. The text and graphics software and the printer should be purchased at the same time since each depends on the other in minute detail and they should fully support each other. Printers to be considered for publishing include laser printers, ink-jet printers, and pen plotters.

Laser printers produce printed matter with a professional look that was once attainable only through typesetting and photocomposition processes. A laser printer is a combination of a computer and printing device in one system. Light from a laser beam exposes images onto photosensitive material, and images are then transferred to the printed page through contact with toner. The resolution of printouts from laser printers is high and comes close to looking like typeset text. A major advantage of laser units is that each page is entered into the machine's memory before the page is printed. The unit uses random-access memory (RAM) for collection and composition of data received from the computer. Photos and graphics can be scanned into the computer system. This means that with laser printers, images such as charts and graphics can be printed just as easily as words. One weakness of laser printers is that they cannot be used to print multipart forms. Impact printers are necessary for this process. However, multiple copies of each original sheet can be printed and grouped to produce the multipart form. In the selection of a laser printer, the following factors should be considered:

- *Cost.* The more expensive models offer additional features and may be desirable for special applications. The selection should be based on the features that are required.
- *Compatibility.* Many laser printers are designed to be used with a variety of computers. However, it is necessary that the printer that is selected be compatible with the computers in place.
- *Size.* The footprint of a printer may be very small. The printer may even be designed to be portable for use when traveling.
- *Service.* The warranties and availability of service need to be considered and are important enough to be the determining factors if all other factors are equal.
- *Upgrading potential.* Some models are built to allow the easy addition of greater memory or the capacity to handle advanced desktop-publishing software. If the range of future applications is uncertain, upgrading potential may be an important consideration.

Ink-jet printing is used for high-quality printing with diverse character patterns. It produces very brilliantly colored (as well as black) text, charts, graphics, and other illustrations. Tiny drops of ink are sprayed onto the paper. These can be mixed to print bright colors and hues. Ink-jet printing requires paper with special absorption qualities that will keep the ink from smudging, cracking, or bleeding. This specially coated paper needs surfaces on which the inks dry rapidly. Paper of this quality will allow halftones to print without spreading and will insure clear, intense characters. The paper must also feed reliably.

Pen plotters may be fiber-tip, felt-tip, or ballpoint. The plotters move rapidly along the surface of the paper. Pen plotters, which were used almost exclusively in engineering and drafting applications just a few years ago, have found their way into thousands of offices because of graphics technology.

Nonelectronic Duplicators

Nonelectronic duplicators can be divided into three major categories: offset, stencil, and spirit. While large organizations may not consider stencil or spirit processes, improvements in the ease of operation of the equipment and the quality of the copies, as well as the lower cost of equipment and supplies compared to copy machines, continue to make these processes viable options for many organizations.

Offset Duplicators. Offset duplicators are most often found in a print shop or a reprographics and copy service center. Offset duplicators are usually not suitable for a walk-up convenience copying environment. They are best operated by specifically trained persons. Offset duplicators are more efficient and economical when the number of copies to be produced from each original is relatively high. Offset duplicators come in a variety of sizes—from small table models that require additional off-line equipment such as platemakers to integrated copy production systems that produce complete copy sets as a finished product.

Offset masters can be made by several methods. One of the most common methods employs an electrostatic copier. In this process, the original is copied onto special, treated paper, which is then used as a duplicating master. Special equipment can be used to produce masters in the form of aluminum plates. Aluminum plates will make

from 10,000 to 50,000 copies; electrostatic masters will make up to 5,000 copies; and direct impression (those done on a typewriter) will produce up to 2,500 copies.

Offset presses that use either inexpensive electrostatic paper masters or metal plates to create a printed page are frequently less expensive and just as quick as copiers.

Stencil Duplicators. The stencil master is a fibrous wax-coated sheet that is impervious to ink. The master is "cut" by direct pressure, such as typing or drawing, so that ink can flow through it during the duplicating process. Stencils can also be prepared on electronic stencil makers, which employ the principle of optical scanning. Photographs and illustrations, as well as text, can be electronically cut into the stencil. The master, or stencil, is attached to a drum or cylinder which rotates during the printing operation. Between the master and the drum is an ink-saturated pad. When the operation starts, the paper upon which the copy is to be made is carried to the master and forced against it by the impression roller. This causes ink to flow through the openings in the stencil to the paper, and thus make the copy.

Hand-prepared stencils are usually used to produce several hundred copies, but electronically produced stencils will make from 5,000 to 10,000 copies and provide a relatively high-quality image.

Spirit Duplicators. The spirit duplicator is also called a "liquid" or "fluid" duplicator because alcohol is used as a solvent for the image-transfer process. A common term is *ditto machine*. This process uses a carbon master that may be prepared on a typewriter or by hand. The carbon master contains a special dye. The master is attached to a revolving drum and as the master comes in contact with copy paper that has been lightly coated with the spirit fluid, the fluid dissolves some of the dye in the image area of the master and transfers it to the copy paper. Each carbon master can produce up to 500 copies.

EQUIPMENT PLACEMENT

Placement of equipment should not occur by chance. Poorly planned equipment placement may result in some parts of an organization being over-supplied with copying capability while others may not have enough to meet their needs. Understanding the valid uses of the copier and pinpointing its misuses through analysis are not enough. Solutions to the problems of using the copier must also be found and implemented. Two major methods of reprographics and copy control are centralization and decentralization. Utilization of both centralized and decentralized systems is also commonly found in large organizations.

Centralization

Centralization is almost always considered as a means of controlling costs. However, the merits of centralization must be evaluated on an individual office basis. When determining the need for a centralized copier service, there are some general criteria that can be applied to specific situations:

1. *Needs of the offices using the service.* Different offices have different needs, and not all needs are compatible with a centralized service. These needs will manifest themselves in the way the copier is to be used. Factors such as security, systems use, and urgency must be kept in mind.

2. *Locations of offices using the service.* If the offices using the service are widely dispersed, centralization may not be feasible because of time loss and distance.

3. *Volume of use.* The aggregate volume should be high enough to warrant centralization. In addition, the volume produced by each office must be considered. If an individual office has an unusually high volume, it may require its own copier.

A centralized copier service has several advantages:

1. It provides a service to offices that do not need a copier of their own.

2. It reduces costs because some machines can be eliminated and requirements consolidated. Also, increasing the number of copies made on each machine through centralization can reduce the cost per copy through volume-pricing arrangements.

3. It provides a reserve facility for peak demand or periods when another copier is broken down.

4. Maintenance is more consistent and more easily provided.

5. It can provide a more diversified service by having several copying machines of different capabilities. Moreover, such a copying center might also include other types of multiple-reproduction machines.

Decentralization

Decentralization of reprographic services should be considered only when there is a substantial amount of duplication. Decentralization of copier services has advantages that should be considered:

1. It allows better control of what is being copied because the person responsible for control is the manager of the immediate office. As a general rule, the smaller the office is, the better the control will be.

2. Transit time is reduced and, in many cases, eliminated. This results in reducing labor costs and delays in obtaining the copy.

3. Additional personnel are not needed to operate the copier because decentralization policy is almost always self-service. However, one or two persons should oversee copier operations.

REPROGRAPHICS MANAGEMENT PROGRAM REVIEW

Once a reprographics management program is established and operating efficiently, the manger should evaluate it periodically. A periodic review schedule should be developed to determine the effectiveness of the program.

The General Services Administration of the federal government has developed a self-inspection guide for government agencies to assist them in evaluating copy management. The guide includes compliance checklists to determine the availability of common centralized service, match equipment to copying needs, maintain records, review equipment requests, review supply procurement policy, and review copy management efforts. The self-inspection guide provides effectiveness checklists for program management, managers, key operators, convenience copier users, copy center supervisors, and supply operations. Similar reprographics management program checklists can be of great value in enhancing the effectiveness of reprographics management programs in business organizations.

Program Management

This checklist contains questions relating to overall program effectiveness. The questions should be answered by the individual who is responsible for the copy management program.

1. Is the responsibility for the copy management program assigned to one office or official?
2. Is that office in the reporting chain to the organization's records manager?
3. Is the assignment of a responsible office or official spelled out in a formal directive?
4. If copy management responsibilities have been delegated to various levels of the organization, are delegations understood by each of the responsible individuals?
5. Is justification required before an office can acquire or upgrade a copier?
6. If a request for new or upgraded equipment is submitted, does a manager other than the originator of the request assess the need for it?
7. Have users been instructed in the correct operation of equipment?

8. Are personnel generally satisfied with the copying service?
9. Are inventory and copy production records maintained for copying equipment in regional and area office locations?
10. Are supplies for agency copiers ordered in bulk?
11. Has a key operator, a person responsible for routine preventive maintenance and replenishing supplies, been assigned for each convenience (unattended) copier?
12. Does each key operator have an alternate?
13. Do users know who have been designated key operator and alternate?
14. Have you received any significant complaints concerning the copy management program?
15. Is there a published list of documents that are not authorized to be copied posted near the copiers?

Manager's Checklist

These questions are intended for managers who are likely to be knowledgeable about copy management practices and in whose office space copying equipment may be located.

1. Is the copying service adequate?
2. Is the equipment operable most of the time?
3. Are inoperable or malfunctioning copiers repaired promptly?
4. Has action been taken to minimize unauthorized copying?
5. Are supplies for copiers obtained from a central source?
6. Is copying equipment conveniently located?
7. Has a key operator been assigned for each convenience copier or copiers? If "yes,"
   a. Have key operators been properly trained?
   b. Have trained alternates been assigned to act in the absence of key operators?
8. Have employees been instructed to:
   a. Batch work to minimize trips to the copier?

b. Check the quantity dial and paper-size control on the copier before using the machine?

c. Copy on both sides of the paper whenever practicable?

d. Obtain blank forms from stock, rather than copying them?

e. Send materials to printing facilities when quantities are large enough to make it more economical than using copiers?

f. Accept copies that are legible, rather than seeking the "perfect" copy?

9. Is a single copy circulated or posted when it will suffice, rather than making separate copies for all concerned?

10. Are lower-graded employees routinely assigned copying tasks when feasible?

11. Are adequate supplies of blank forms obtained and maintained through normal supply channels, thus eliminating the necessity for copying them?

12. Is the time lost by secretaries and other personnel due to travelling to a copier facility, waiting for machine availability, or redoing poor quality copying within reasonable limits?

Key Operator's Checklist

These questions are for operators assigned to convenience copiers only. All key operators should be queried.

1. Have you received training for each copier that you maintain?

2. Did the training include:
    a. Loading paper?
    b. Clearing jams?
    c. Replenishing toner?
    d. Making minor adjustments?

3. Are the copiers operable most of the time?

4. When the copiers are inoperable, are they repaired promptly?

5. Are the copiers located at a convenient distance from where you normally work?

6. Do you order supplies from a central supply point?

7. Is the area around the copiers kept neat and clean?

8. Do you have an alternate?

9. Has your alternate been trained?

10. Have names and phone numbers of you and your alternate been posted near your copier(s)?

Convenience Copier User's Checklist

User opinions should be assessed by sampling the total population. Responses from a 10 percent sample of users for each convenience copier will usually suffice.

1. Is the copier that you use conveniently located?

2. Is the copier usually functioning when you need to use it?

3. Does the copier usually make acceptable copies?

4. Is the copier usually available when needed?

5. Are waiting lines common?

6. Are there always enough supplies on hand for the copier (such as paper and toner)?

7. Do you consider copying services adequate?

8. Do you batch your copying work when you can to make fewer trips to the copier?

9. Do you make two-sided copies whenever you can if the copier has this capability?

10. Do you obtain blank forms from stock rather than copy them?

11. Do you check the quantity dial on the copier before using the machine?

12. Do you know whom to contact if you experience any difficulties with the copier?

13. Do you try to make only the number of copies requested or required?

14. Do you examine the first copy for acceptability before continuing with multiple-copy jobs to avoid making unusable copies?

15. Do you know the maximum number of copies per page allowable on the copier?

16. Do you know the procedure for getting jobs done that are too large for the copier you use?

Copy Center Supervisor's Checklist

The questions on this checklist should be directed to those persons primarily responsible for the operation of copy centers.

1. Is preventive maintenance performed on copying equipment daily?
2. Have the operators been trained by the equipment vendors?
3. Are records maintained that indicate:
    a. The number of jobs accepted?
    b. The number of pages in each job?
    c. The number of copies per page?
    d. The name of the requester?
    e. Special processing required, such as collating, stitching (stapling), and reduction?
4. Are production records on rented equipment monitored to ensure that the correct rental plan is in effect?
5. Are most copying requests handled on a first-come, first-served basis?
6. Is the center's work usually accomplished without scheduling overtime?
7. Are equipment users and operators aware of the types of documents that may not be copied?
8. Are copying supplies requisitioned from a central source?
9. Is the center kept clean and neat?
10. Are monthly production volume figures maintained?

Supply Operations Checklist

The primary purpose of this checklist is to help the evaluator determine whether copier supplies are purchased economically. Obtaining supplies from a central supply point, such as a store that orders supplies in bulk from manufacturers, is generally the best arrangement because these stores receive appreciable discounts. Additional information concerning the ordering of copier supplies can be obtained by examining vendor invoices or other purchasing documentation. The evaluator should interview the manager of the store or supply point, if there is one. Otherwise, the persons doing the ordering should be interviewed.

1. Store or supply point managers only:
    a. Do you usually have adequate (but not excessive) supplies on hand for the agency's copiers?
    b. Do you have records that indicate the organization's rate of consumption of supplies? (If "yes," supply copies of records going back at least six months.)
    c. To the best of your knowledge, are all of the organization's copying supplies ordered from you?
    d. Is there any program in the organization to inform personnel ordering copying supplies of savings to be gained by ordering from the store?
    e. Have you weighed all options in buying supplies that may yield lower costs, such as blanket purchase agreements or bulk purchasing?
    f. Has the organization issued formal procedures for evaluating the efficiency and effectiveness of current procurement methods and sources?
    g. Are procurement methods and sources reviewed annually?

2. Individual or operating unit ordering supplies:
    a. Is there a central point from which you order supplies?
    b. Do you maintain adequate (but not excessive) supplies of paper and toner for your copiers?
    c. Do you usually have enough supplies on hand?
    d. Do you feel that your system of ordering supplies is adequate?

SUMMARY

Copy and reprographics involves the management of copying practices, procedures, and devices to provide the most effective and economical creation of copies of information. The terms *reprographics* and *copy* are often used interchangeably. An effective copy management program should identify the basic copying requirements of each organizational element, provide cost justification, evaluate equipment, select equipment, define user support, identify copy management guidelines, and provide for program evaluation.

The technical processes of duplication differ in type, cost, and results. Not all equipment features are necessary for every copier. Equipment features include remote diagnostics, control panels, copy controls, automatic document feeders, reduction and enlargement, sorters and collators, duplexing, job recovery, interrupt, and programming, book-copy mode, finishing, binding, clamshell access, repeating, and deletion.

Personal computers are found in executive suites and home offices. Convenience copiers range from desk-top models to sophisticated floor models that perform multiple tasks in distributed locations. A copy and reprographics center makes the copier accessible to groups of users who may not need a separate machine. A central reproduction department is a centralized system of in-house copying and printing for large volume. Use of printing is recommended when large volume is needed or when the copy requires reproduction of a number of photographs, illustrations, or colors.

Criteria for the purchase of equipment should be based on the proposed use of the reprographic equipment. To properly determine the need for a copier, it is necessary to know the intended use of the copier, the intended operators of the copier, the equipment now being used, and the volume anticipated. A reprographics and copy management and control program should use an evaluation form that identifies the type of equipment requested, current equipment now in use, proposed use of machine, volume of use, and required features.

Two major methods of reprographics control are centralization and decentralization. Centralization is almost always considered as a means of controlling costs and may include a copy center. Decentralization should be considered only when there is a substantial amount of duplication or distance suggests a convenience copier.

A periodic review schedule should be established to determine the effectiveness of the reprographics management program. Evaluation checklists should be developed for program management, key operators, convenience copy users, copy center supervisor, and supply operations.

QUESTIONS FOR DISCUSSION

1. What is the function of a reprographics and copy management and control program?

2. Identify some ways by which a reprographics and copy management and control program can provide an organization with efficient operations at low cost.

3. What are some basic principles around which an effective copy management program should be structured?

4. Describe the two main ways of arranging copying equipment.

5. Describe when a reprographics and copy center might be more cost effective than convenience copiers located throughout the organization.

6. Describe when convenience copiers located throughout the organization might be more cost effective than a reprographics and copy center.

7. What factors should be considered when determining the need for a copier?

8. What is the purpose of a reprographic equipment evaluation form?

9. What should be included in a reprographics management program review?

10. When should a key operator's checklist be used?

PROJECTS

1. Assume that you are the manager of a reprographics and copy control program for a company that uses the following reproduction services:

  a. Convenience copiers.

  b. Reprographics center.

  Write a directive, which is to be sent to all employees of the company, informing them of the organization's policy regarding the use of reproduction equipment. The purpose of the directive is to control reproduction costs.

2. Write the step-by-step procedures you would follow in creating a centralized reproduction service in a large company that has just decided to establish such control.

3. Write the instructions to be followed by employees in a company using a decentralized reproduction and copy services program.

4. Prepare a checklist that can be used by a reprographics program control manager when copy reproduction equipment is being considered for purchase.

5. Review the current periodicals for advertisements of color copiers. Make a list of all of the features of the equipment.

CASE PROBLEM

You are the employee responsible for maintaining the copying machines dispersed throughout the Kilgore Manufacturing Corporation. The organization employs 12,560 production workers and

762 office employees in nine departments. A sampling of the copying requirements of each of the nine departments is as follows:

  a. Executive offices

    Copies of letters for file

    Copies of memos for distribution

    Reports (1) internal

        (2) external—stockholders

  b. Human resources

    Applications

    Personnel actions

  c. Purchasing

    Bids

    Specifications

  d. Accounting

    Fiscal reports

  e. Payroll

    Notices of changes and corrections

  f. Engineering

    Blueprints

    Engineering drawings

  g. Sales

    Specifications

    Advertising copy

    Promotional brochures

    Sales letters

  h. Manufacturing

    Production reports

    Forecasts

  i. Shipping

    Extra copies

Muriel Robertson, records manager, tells you that the vice president for Administrative Services thinks the organization may be ready for a centralized reprographics and copy center. She also indicates that if you can build a case for the need for such a center, she thinks you will have a good chance to become its manager. She asks you to write a report addressing:

1. The objectives of a reprographics management program.

2. Which of the listed copying requirements could be done using a convenience copier, the reprographics and copy center, or outside services.

3. The minimum features that a convenience copier should provide for the applications listed.

4. The services that a centralized reprographics and copy center could provide.

Chapter 16

Records Management
Manuals

Learning Objectives
1. To state the purposes and advantages of records management manuals.
2. To explain the different types of records management manuals.
3. To explain how to plan and sequence the procedures for preparing records management manuals.
4. To list effective guidelines for writing records management manuals.
5. To identify guidelines for publishing, distributing, and maintaining records management manuals.

INTRODUCTION

A records management manual is an essential part of the program of records control. The manual is the official handbook of approved policies and procedures. The manual may deal with policies and procedures separately, or in a small organization the procedure may immediately follow the policy it is to implement. A *policy* is a broad guideline for operating the organization. There is usually at least one policy for each of the objectives of the records management program. A *procedure* provides detailed instructions on how the policy is to be carried out.

Because procedures may change more rapidly than policies, some records managers prefer to separate procedures from policies in the records management manual. Since procedures may involve several departments, it may be necessary to assure concerned department heads that the pro-

cedure has been properly coordinated through the use of a procedures clearance and approval sheet as shown in Figure 16.1. The procedure for approving procedures should be described in detail in the manual. A policy tells what is to be done, and the procedure tells how it is to be done.

Standard Policy

Items and situations that arise repeatedly may be handled by a standard policy. For example, a study of adjustment letters over a period of time will reveal sentences, paragraphs, and complete letters that may be suitable for each kind of adjustment. Once these patterns are recognized, a decision can be made as to how each should be handled and the procedure can be outlined in the manual. In this case, a good correspondence secretary can then

U.S. DEPARTMENT OF AGRICULTURE Agricultural Stabilization and Conservation Service **PROCEDURE CLEARANCE AND APPROVAL SHEET** *See instructions below*	TITLE AND NUMBER OF ISSUANCE

PROGRAM EFFECT OF ISSUANCE (brief statement of significance)

EFFECT THIS ISSUANCE WILL HAVE ON BUDGETED OPERATING COSTS

DECREASE ☐   INCREASE ☐   NO CHANGE ☐

1. INITIATNG OFFICE CLEARANCE

PREPARED BY		CLEARED BY (SIGNATURES)	
WRITER	EXT.	UNIT HEAD	DATE
DIVISION		DIVISION DIRECTOR	DATE

2. DIRECTIVES MANAGEMENT BRANCH, AS DIVISION

REMARKS	SIGNATURE	DATE

3. OTHER CLEARANCES

ORGANIZATION	SIGNATURES	DATE

4. FINAL APPROVAL

The document described above is hereby approved and should be facsimiled as follows:

TITLE	SIGNATURE	DATE
AFTER APPROVAL RETURN TO:	ROOM	EXT.

INSTRUCTIONS FOR THIS FORM

1. Prepare in original and one copy.
2. Attach original to outside front cover of Procedure Jacket (Form CSS-416) containing copy of procedure being cleared.
3. Retain copy with original of procedure.
4. After final approval send original of this form to DM Branch with:
   A. Edited and approved copy of procedure
   B. Original of procedure
   C. Reproduction Order
5. Original of this form with approved copy of procedure will be filed in DM Branch.

FIGURE 16.1   Procedures Clearance and Approval Sheet

process most letters without reference to higher authority or without the need for personally dictated letters.

The manual should specify in detail the scope of the entire records management program of the organization and also provide instructions for carrying out all aspects of the program. Large organizations that establish extensive records management programs should have a comprehensive manual. In some cases, each function of records management, such as records retention, filing, microfilming, and records center operations, may have its own manual. Small organizations should have at least some written record of recommended procedures for their clerical personnel. As organizations mature, manuals may be expanded not only to describe day-to-day operations, but also to consider policies and procedures for emergency, disaster, and postdisaster operations. Policies for disasters, such as fires, floods, tornadoes, hurricanes, or earthquakes, need to be in place in areas where such disasters are possible.

Communication

Once a procedure is developed and expressed in written form, its primary purpose is to communicate information to the appropriate people. Management must decide not only who is to prepare and authorize the procedure, but also who is to receive and use it, the most effective manner of presentation, and what efforts are necessary to maintain and enforce it.

Advantages. The advantages of using written procedures manuals include the following:

- All operations of the organization can be standardized.
- Communication is facilitated throughout the organization.
- Manuals can be used as a training and job orientation medium.
- Established policies are clarified.
- Coordination of effort is ensured.
- Reference sources are established.

- Authority and responsibility are defined.
- Policies are preserved even though personnel changes occur.
- Supervision is strengthened.
- Employee relations are strengthened.
- Control points are established for cost analyses.
- Control of forms throughout the organization is established.
- The tendency of employees to be secretive about a job is eliminated.
- A written procedure serves as an invitation for others to improve or clarify it.

Considerations. If the records management manual is to do the job expected, the following aspects require careful consideration:

- Purposes to be served by the manual.
- Objectives to be achieved.
- Type of manual to be developed.
- Processes to be followed in developing the manual.
- Procedures to be followed in writing the manual.
- Policies for manual usage.

PURPOSES OF RECORDS MANAGEMENT MANUALS

Use of a records management manual establishes responsibility for the various phases of the records management program, assists with training of employees, saves money, reduces errors, standardizes procedures, increases productivity, and makes provisions for changes.

Establishing Responsibility for the Records Management Program

In a large organization a records manager will work in close cooperation with other executives and departments. If there are hundreds of employees in an office, they will devise and use many different, and often conflicting, policies and procedures unless uniform guidelines have been developed in written form.

The misconception prevails that in a small office a manual is not essential because there are so few workers and they usually work together much of the time. But in a small office a manual may be needed even more than it is in a large office. The manager or supervisor in charge of a small office usually has many diverse duties and is not always available for consultation about organization policies and procedures. A records management manual that presents all pertinent information will, therefore, help employees in small offices to use records more efficiently.

Records management manuals should be designed not only to fix responsibility for performing assigned duties, but also to identify procedures for discharging such responsibilities. When an employee is provided with a manual, that individual can be held responsible for the manner in which assigned duties are performed.

TRAINING EMPLOYEES

The records management manual can be used to train new employees because it presents the established systems and procedures that have been adopted by the organization. The manual can also be used in conjunction with on-the-job training programs for experienced employees. If the manual is to be of the greatest value possible, it must provide information about the responsibilities of those whom it is intended to serve.

Saving Money

The major advantage of using a records management manual is the saving of money in the handling and use of records. Savings will result from the reduction of time required to give directions to new employees. Money will also be saved in reduced errors and in increased productivity.

Reducing Errors

Another advantage of using a manual is the reduction of time wasted by employees because of errors in their work. Oral instructions are more likely to result in improper performance of work than are written instructions.

Standardizing Procedures

Using a records management manual promotes the standardization of procedures. Standardization of records management procedures benefits an organization in the following ways:

- Overlapping functions and needless duplication of work are eliminated.
- Smoother work flow is achieved throughout the entire organization.
- Greater harmony and cooperation will result within and among the various departments.
- Written directions and instructions can be tested, revised, and improved.

The degree of standardization required must be presented carefully in the manual. Some methods and procedures from which no deviation is permitted can be identified. But inflexible methods and procedures will restrain individual initiative if all regulations are strictly interpreted and improved procedures cannot be implemented.

Increasing Productivity

Written procedures, in a records management manual or handbook, can increase productivity. When employees can read exactly what work is to be completed and how it is to be completed, productivity will be increased. Productivity will also be increased if needless duplication of work is eliminated. Overlapping functions among various departments can also be eliminated, resulting in a smoother work flow and increased productivity for all concerned.

Making Provisions for Change

Most office employees are content to be told how to do their work and are not concerned about improvements. Provision should be made, however, for those who wish to suggest changes that will result in benefits to the organization. Consequently, even where permanent records management manuals are in use, there should be periodic review and change. Beneficial suggestions and new methods should be adopted and inserted in the records management manual.

OBJECTIVES OF RECORDS MANAGEMENT MANUALS

A records management manual should be designed to inform all personnel of the services that are provided by the records management program. It should also establish an understanding of the benefits to be derived from an integrated and centralized system. The primary purpose of the manual, however, is to provide a source of instruction and guidance for personnel who are responsible for creating, preparing, processing, storing, and disposing of records. To achieve these desired objectives, records management manuals should generally include the following:

1. Designate authority for the centralized control of all records management activities.
2. Define the relationships between records management personnel and the other departments of the organization.
3. Establish uniform procedures in the creation, processing, retention, and destruction of records throughout the organization.
4. Provide a source of instruction and guidance for all personnel who create, use, and maintain an organization's records.
5. Create an understanding among all employees of the basic principles of good records management and a recognition of the advantages that will result.

6. Encourage constructive suggestions about the program from employees.
7. Communicate changes in records management policies and procedures.
8. Coordinate or combine similar records management functions and activities throughout the organization.
9. Serve as a training device for new employees.

TYPES OF RECORDS MANAGEMENT MANUALS

Records management manuals may be written to cover a variety of subjects, and they may be classified under a variety of headings. Most records management manuals can be classified as one of four types:

> Policy manual
> Organizational manual
> Administrative procedures manual
> Operating procedures manual

Since each records management manual has its own special needs, the type of manual adopted for a particular program should be based upon the purpose to be served. For some programs, a single purpose is to be served by the manual, whereas in other programs several purposes need to be served.

In some organizations, information is selected from one or more of the basic types of manuals and brought together in the form of a handbook that is distributed to all new employees. In other organizations, specialized information may be selected from a basic organization manual for use by employees performing specialized tasks. Handbooks might be developed to cover such specialized areas as filing, analysis, forms design, and so on. The use of handbooks helps both management and employees to reduce the misunderstandings that arise when policies and procedures are not written.

Policy Manual

A policy is a basic guide to action that prescribes the boundaries within which activities are to take place. It reveals broad managerial intentions or forecasts broad courses of managerial action likely to take place under certain conditions. The policies of an organization, or a unit within an organization, provide the framework around which all actions are based. A *policy manual* contains decisions, resolutions, and pronouncements of the issuing organization or unit.

Most organizational units establish general principles to govern the conduct of their affairs. Such policies should be somewhat elastic and take into account possible future conditions. A functional policy does not really exist unless it is in writing.

Advantages.   The advantages of using policy manuals are the following:

- Written policies require managers to think through their courses of action and to predetermine what actions will be taken under various circumstances.
- A plan of action is provided for most problems requiring attention; only unusual decisions remain to be made by top executives.
- More equitable treatment of all employees is provided.
- Employees can function freely within the framework of stated policy.

Disadvantages.   The disadvantages of using policy manuals include the following:

- Written policies are not always interpreted in the way intended by the writer.
- Changing conditions require more flexibility than is usually found in written policies.
- Written policies will often discourage innovation among employees.

Organizational Manual

The organizational manual provides a detailed description of the relationships of the various departments and their respective divisions. Such relationships are illustrated by organizational charts, accompanied by descriptions of the various positions charted. A common breakdown of headings in organizational manuals can be made by general function, responsibilities and authority, or relationships with others. Each section of the manual might consist of a description of the duties and responsibilities of the office or department covered in that section, an organizational chart, and a listing of the administrative officers and supervisors of the office or department.

Advantages.   Some of the principal advantages of organizational manuals are the following:

- The lines of authority and responsibility are clearly drawn.
- Continued handling of basic responsibilities is assured when turnover occurs.
- Constructive and critical thought is exercised in preparation of the manual, usually resulting in the best choice of alternatives.
- Emphasis can be properly placed on line and staff relationships.
- Overlaps and gaps in responsibilities can be reduced.

Disadvantages.   Some of the principal disadvantages of organizational manuals include the following:

- The many informal relationships that take place daily are not shown.
- Style of leadership (democratic or authoritarian) in discharging responsibilities cannot be shown.
- A status quo may be established that resists change.
- "Compartmentalized" thinking of various specialists may discourage informal coopera-

tion among personnel in different departments and units.

Authorization. Authorization for organizational manuals is the direct responsibility of top management, but the actual work of preparation is ordinarily delegated. Staff specialists who are familiar with organizational principles may be called upon for technical help, and each department head may be asked to prepare a preliminary draft of the section of the manual covering his or her own department.

Administrative Procedures Manual

The administrative procedures manual contains principles of operation that affect all departments of the organization. The manual identifies standard methods that explain how various aspects of the organization's work are to be carried out. This type of manual gives an overview of general procedures that are to be used in the various departments and divisions of the organization. Much of the material included in an administrative procedures manual can be used as the content of departmental operating procedures manuals as well as for specialized handbooks.

Operating Procedures Manual

The operating procedures manual deals with the internal policies, organization, and processes of one department or function of an organization. The contents of this type of manual can be focused in any one of several directions. The manual can emphasize the performance of individual tasks and jobs, departmental practices, or general practices in a special field. Several examples of operating procedures manuals as they relate to records management are given in the following paragraphs.

Records Management Program Manual. A records management program manual defines the scope of the program, its authority, the services it

provides, and an introduction to the concepts to enhance its understanding and acceptance. It will also outline, briefly, common procedures required to use the services and the responsibilities of all concerned. Procedures manuals that may be included in the records management program manual or developed separately are the correspondence, filing, or mailing manuals.

Filing Manual. A filing manual should identify the requirements and procedures for proper filing and list those rules, regulations, and systems that are deemed necessary to make the files of the organization an effective service instrument. Many organizations discover that a filing manual is an invaluable aid in facilitating supervision, training new personnel, improving filing, and standardizing filing work. If this work is decentralized, the manual has the advantage of making filing uniform in all departments. ARMA's *Alphabetic Filing Rules* (see Appendix D) are frequently included in filing manuals.

Records Retention and Disposition Manual. The records retention and disposition manual includes a copy of the records retention and disposition schedule (RIDS) and describes all types of records in terms of origin, physical class, function served, and organizational relationships. It should be revised to accommodate newly created forms or reports and changes resulting from the implementation of new records management systems and procedures. The records retention and disposition schedule is a document that authorizes and provides for the transfer and disposition of all records of the organization. (See Chapter 3.)

The RIDS manual should include information about controlling designated records and information so that the organization will be in compliance with mandated federal, state, and local government requirements for retaining records and information, thus reducing an organization's legal exposure.

In addition, policies and procedures for discarding unneeded or duplicate records and transferring inactive records to less expensive storage are included in the manual. The RIDS manual also provides control mechanisms and procedures necessary to preserve the vital and important records of an organization.

Vital Records Manual. A vital records manual, published separately or as part of the records management manual, is perhaps the best tool of communication for fostering understanding of and compliance with the vital records program. The manual should be divided into three parts. The first part should describe the procedures of the vital records protection program and list its objectives. Policies and procedures for security control of access to the facility and regulation of movement within the facility must be addressed, as well as the physical security of records. In the second part, the vital records master list should be explained. The third part should be devoted to instructions for reconstructing vital records in the event of a disaster and to the use of equipment that would be available.

Procedures for maintaining vital records must be made routine. Vital records are the records necessary to the continuity of an organization's activities under emergency conditions. To determine which records are vital to the organization, an organizationwide functional chart must be developed and analyzed. Analysis includes looking at data concerning the identification of records to be protected, justification for protection, methods of protection, cost of protection, and retention needs. An example of a vital records analysis sheet is seen in Chapter 4, Figure 4.1.

Procedures for transferring vital records to the vital records center are an important part of the vital records protection manual. Vital records include substantive and procedural records required for emergency operations. They are the records that would be needed immediately and that should normally be kept at alternate or relocation sites for emergencies. Records are transferred to vital records centers on a daily, weekly, or monthly basis. Collection points within the company are established. At these points, one of two methods of transferring records may be utilized: (1) the vital records transmittal label or (2) the records maintenance program card envelope. In either case, these procedures are explained in the vital records protection manual.

Other procedures to be included in the vital records manual are those that cover the use of records in daily activities, in emergencies, and after disasters. These procedures assume that ordinary commonsense precautions for the protection of records will be observed, as well as special procedures for vital records.

Common control devices for all records include the control of keys and the use of request forms to prevent unauthorized persons from gaining access to records. Responsibility for the safe return of records can be pinpointed through the use of a computerized tracking system or through a card system. An ordinary precaution against wear, loss, unauthorized destruction, or removal of loose pages is the permanent binding of records.

Procedures for the protection of both paper and electronic records should be part of the vital records protection manual. Vital records should normally be in the form of paper copies so that they can be used directly without reliance on electronic equipment. However, the risk of losing records maintained in electronic form can be determined to be minimal.

The *vital records master list* is frequently included as part of the vital records protection manual. It indicates which records are vital, how and when records are to be prepared and shipped to the storage location, and the time period covered. Figure 4.6, in Chapter 4, is an example of a vital records master list. The vital records master list also provides each department with a complete list of all vital records for which it is responsible.

Disaster Protection Manual. The disaster protection manual may consist of a disaster protection plan, information about disaster preparedness, procedures for a disaster in progress, and plans for disaster recovery. The *disaster protec-*

tion plan may consist of information about structures, occupants, and hazardous materials with corresponding drawings and floor plans, as well as procedures to safeguard records. The records manager and the facilities manager need to cooperate in establishing guidelines for the safety of employees, as well as records.

The disaster protection manual may indicate type of construction, percentage of combustible construction, year of construction, type of structure, stairways, floor openings, roof coverings, alarm systems, obstacles, number of occupants, furnishings, number of and placement of extinguishers, types of materials used, type of hazard and precautions, property name and address, responsible party, emergency contacts, and telephone numbers. Arrangements may be made in advance to use similar electronic equipment of other organizations in the reconstruction of records. Identification of suppliers of services for the drying of records can also be done as part of the planning process.

A separate plan for disaster protection would have to be devised for each department, depending on its records and its physical location.

A section on disaster preparedness is part of the total disaster protection planning manual. *Disaster preparedness* consists of policies and procedures to make sure employees are aware of potential disasters, as well as the actual implementation. To ensure the completeness of preparations for postdisaster recovery of information, some companies test the procedures established for the vital records programs by simulating the effects of a disaster. Key personnel are sent to the dispersal site (vital records storage location) where they participate in the reconstruction of records and continuance of operations. This type of exercise has frequently pointed out the need for additional records to be classified as vital, as well as the need for changes in facilities or equipment. The basic plan for postdisaster recovery of information must address not only equipment and supplies to reconstruct the information, but also provisions for living accommodations for the individuals involved. Possible sites for the reconstruc-

tion activities must be identified and supplied, as must housing accommodations.

The *disaster-in-progress* section of the disaster protection planning manual is difficult to anticipate. This section may deal with expectations based on local conditions. While it is possible to plan for many eventualities, general principles of safety and security for personnel and records are the basis upon which most decisions can be made in emergency circumstances.

Disaster recovery of information may be facilitated by policies adapted earlier for the duplication and dispersal of records. If arrangements for use of another organization's electronic equipment have been made and service bureaus identified to assist with the drying of records, the time for disaster recovery can be considerably limited.

Safety Education Program. Education of the staff concerning good safety and security is an ongoing activity. Security is a 24-hour, 365-day responsibility. Policies and procedures should address emergencies, such as power failures, water line breaks, explosions, bomb threats, fire, and natural disasters. Health concerns of employees, including serious injuries or heart attacks, need to be addressed, both in policy and in emergency procedures for meeting such eventualities. Policies regarding the need to report hazardous conditions need to be emphasized.

Correspondence Manual. A correspondence manual is a means of standardizing the methods and products of a correspondence department in a large organization. The manual might cover such topics as the handling of correspondence, the supervision of correspondence, intracompany correspondence, and the structure and tone of letters. A correspondence manual is particularly helpful in large organizations having several branches or many departments, in each of which some correspondence is prepared. It develops a uniform policy, fixes responsibility, and promotes public goodwill. Although much of this information is available in business English textbooks, it is better to prepare a correspondence manual that will

EXECUTIVES' CONSULTANTS, INC.
International Building/190 North Michigan Avenue/Chicago, IL 60601

Date   January 2, 19--

Inside address   Mr. Richard L. Rhodes
                  Executive Editor
                  Firestone Press
                  1801 Fairburn Avenue
                  Chicago, IL 60632

Salutation   Dear Mr. Rhodes:

Body of letter   This letter is typed in the Modified-Block Style
                  with mixed punctuation. When mixed punctuation
                  is used, a colon is placed after the salutation
                  and a comma is placed after the complimentary
                  close.

                  The basic difference between this style of letter
                  and the Full-Block Style is that the date and the
                  closing lines begin at the center. The closing
                  lines may be indented to the center of the paper
                  or five spaces to the left of the center and
                  blocked in that position.

                  The Modified-Block Style of letter is one of the
                  most popular styles because it is easy to set up,
                  yet it is not extreme in format.

Complimentary   Sincerely yours,
close indented to
center of page
                                        Vivian B. Johnson

Writer's name   Vivian B. Johnson
Official title   Business Consultant

Typist's initials   s1

FIGURE 16.2 Modified–Block Letter Style

establish company standards and help solve the particular letter-writing problems of the organization. For example, the company may wish to standardize on a letter style to be used through the organization and include that style in the procedures manual. Since the modified-block style is easy to set up and not considered extreme, the style may be selected for use throughout the organization. See Figure 16.2.

Report Manual. Raising consciousness about the necessity of reports and the quality of the reports can be achieved through a reports manual. Reports serve two major functions: (1) They convey information to management for problem solving and decision making; and (2) they furnish employees in other offices within the organization with information that is essential for them to perform their work. A well-planned system should result in each employee receiving only the information needed to make the decisions or monitor the activities for which that employee is responsible. Adherence to the reports manual can prevent the creation of nonessential and unauthorized reports and new reports that cannot be justified, can provide clear and complete instructions for report preparation, and can assist in the analysis of reports for the purpose of eliminating those that are not paying for themselves.

A good reports manual will provide all report writers or producers with standard practices and instructions in a form that is convenient and easy to use. Such manuals should further help employees to help themselves in improving the quality of the reports they produce. The manual should contain practical guides for effective report writing as shown in Figure 16.3.

The reports manual can contain a reports index which lists all reports issued within the organization. The report titles should be arranged alphabetically by subject matter. The reports index is useful for reference and research purposes.

Mail Manual. A mail manual is usually prepared by the mail supervisor and gives specific instruc-

tions in all phases of handling both incoming and outgoing mail. The mail manual would include procedures for all of the responsibilities outlined in Chapter 14 on mail management for both incoming and outgoing mail. Some large organizations use a mail manual as one means of training mailroom personnel in their work. If the mail supervisor has authority over the organization's messenger service, instructions regarding pickup of mail from each department are also included.

ISO (International Organization for Standardization) Requirements. A part of ISO 9000 is quality system documentation. This includes what the employee needs to know (1) to do his or her job; (2) to understand the policy; and (3) to follow a procedure. This is done through three levels of documentation: the quality manual, operating procedures, and work instructions.

The *quality manual* records the policies and objectives of the organization regarding quality and the means used in meeting the ISO standards.

Operating procedures apply to individual departments and are a statement of what is done in each of the departments.

Work instructions specify the how-to of each task or individual activity. The work instructions describe the forms used for recording the measurements, amounts, and the other records. The ISO 9000 standards may require new records series, new retention periods, and some writing or editing, as well as redesign of forms.

The writing of ISO 9000 standards requires that both the subject matter experts involved in each task and activity and the professional writers who will assure a consistent use of language, style, and format work together.

PLANNING THE MANUAL

The records management manual should be planned in accordance with the size of the organization, its field of operation, and the degree to

- Keep the background and need of the reader in mind.
- Make the report as brief and as simple as possible.
- Include only the information that directly applies to the subject.
- Verify the accuracy and reliability of all facts used.
- Use a writing style that is clear and easy to read.
- Use illustrations and visual displays whenever possible (charts, diagrams, graphs, and pictures).
- Organize the report carefully, dividing the report into parts that are logically arranged.
- Make the report attractive in appearance, and make every effort to avoid crowding.
- Conclude the report with a brief summary of important points covered.
- Draw conclusions that are soundly based on facts.
- Make recommendations that are supported by reported evidence.
- Use a report title that gives a concise description of the information presented.
- Place the report control number and code on the title page or the first page of the report.
- Include the date of submission of the report.
- Include a table of contents in long reports.
- State the objectives or purpose of the report.
- For long reports, present a summary at the beginning. This summary should include the writer's main recommendations.
- Include lengthy exhibits in an appendix at the end of the report. Such exhibits are statistical tabulations, charts, graphs, lists of references, regulations, and instructions. Exhibits such as these should be included only if they are essential.
- Include complete information.

FIGURE 16.3 Principles of Good Report Writing

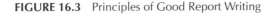

which the organization's activities are centralized or decentralized. Planning a multiple-purpose records management manual that includes organization policies, procedures, and instructions involves the following activities:

- Determining the subjects to be included.
- Organizing a committee on manual preparation.
- Identifying sources for manual material.
- Setting up a schedule.
- Collecting and analyzing the data.

Before any of the activities are initiated, however, the project of establishing a records manage-

ment manual should be authorized by top management. Once approval is given, authority for the preparation of the manual should be delegated to, or assumed by, the records manager.

Subjects to Be Included

Only the information that is needed to accomplish the objectives of the records management program should be included in the manual. The manual content can usually be accurately determined from an identification of the elements of records management that have been implemented in the structure of the organization. Logical topics to include are the following.

- Introduction
- Active files management
- Forms control
- Reports control
- Correspondence control
- Directives management
- Disaster recovery
- Mail management
- Micrographics and imaging system management
- Inactive records control
- Records management and the law
- Records retention and disposition
- Vital records management
- Copy reproduction control
- Archives management
- Computer use in records management
- Glossary
- Index
- Appendix

Manual Preparation Committee

All members of the organization should be informed of the plan to prepare a records management manual. Their suggestions and ideas about what to include should be solicited. Appointment of a committee of employees often provides encouragement to all organization employees to participate in the preparation of the manual. Better understanding of records management policies and procedures, as well as greater acceptance and use of the completed manual, usually results from such participation. Special attention should be directed to supervisors because they are usually excellent sources for appropriate manual content.

Committee Membership. The manual preparation committee should ordinarily be composed of an individual representing each specialty reflected

in the records management program. Subcommittees should consist of a representative from every department that is in any way affected by records management policies and procedures.

Responsibilities. The chairperson bears responsibility for success of the project. This individual must be acquainted with all major aspects of the records management program as well as be familiar with the entire organization for which the manual is to be prepared. He or she should also possess some familiarity with the special records management requirements of the various departments of the organization. Thus, the records manager should serve as the chairperson.

The manual committee should determine how many manuals are to be prepared (one multiple-purpose manual or separate departmental or staff manuals) and the content of each manual.

Sources for Manual Material

Many procedures manuals are not effectively used, if they are used at all. Some typical flaws of manuals are poorly expressed instructions and directions; poorly arranged content; unattractive format; difficulty in locating specific subject matter; too high a level of abstraction to be useful; faulty or indistinct illustrations; insufficient use of blank space; insufficient headings and subheadings; obsolete material; complex and verbose wording; lack of step-by-step sequence for job procedures; too large, bulky, or heavy for daily use; inaccessibility to employees who need it; and irrelevant content.

Most of the faults are the result of hasty or inadequate planning. Some problems occur because the manual writers did not familiarize themselves with the work of the employees for whom the manual was written. Many writers neglect to put themselves in the position of the user; consequently, they fail to comprehend the employee's lack of understanding. Sources of manual material include manuals of other organizations, vendors, and professional organizations, as well as internal sources.

Manuals from Other Organizations.

Manuals from Other Organizations. In spite of their faults, manuals used by other organizations probably are the best source of material for preparing a manual. These manuals will be helpful in determining topics to be included in the manual under consideration.

Vendors of records management equipment and supplies can supply information about what other organizations are including in their records management manuals, as well as topics that vendors can develop as a service to their clients.

Professional organizations also have helpful information for developing manuals and, in some cases, actual handbooks on specific topics. These organizations include the Association of Records Managers and Administrators, International, the American Management Association, the Administrative Management Society, and the National Association of Educational Office Personnel.

Internal Sources. Internal sources include employees, executives, and reports. The employees who will be using the manual are excellent sources of what it should contain. Interviews with executives, especially the personnel manager, training director, and supervisors should provide additional insight into the needs for the manual. Speeches and published articles of executives of the organization can also provide clues for topics to be covered, as can grievance records, minutes of meetings of the organization's board of directors, and reports of executive conferences. Other sources are bulletins, company circulars, and organization magazines.

Collecting and Analyzing the Data

After the committee has been appointed, one of the first steps the committee should take is the "selling" of supervisors and department heads on the need for involving their employees. Supervisors should check with their employees to determine what may be wrong with work procedures currently in use.

Checklist. To expedite and simplify a checkup of this nature, a checklist containing questions about the job should be prepared. The supervisor should go over this list with all employees working on similar jobs. The checklist might include such items as the following:

- Step-by-step procedures used on the job.
- Equipment and materials used.
- Records filed and maintained.
- Filing procedures followed.
- Storage facilities used, if applicable.

Questions. Questions that supervisors will ask employees depend on the job specifications and operations. As jobs are analyzed, more questions will present themselves. Securing the cooperation of employees will be the major task facing the supervisor. The supervisor may find it necessary, in some instances, to convince employees that they, too, will benefit from the implementation of new procedures. The process of analyzing job operations and procedures is an essential element in the data-collecting phase of preparing a records management manual, and perhaps the most important of all.

Writing Procedures. Although the supervisor may not write the final draft of procedures to be incorporated into the manual, he or she will be in a position to list the steps from which the final form can be prepared. A supervisor who is thus involved in the manual preparation process will be more likely to use the published manual.

Classifying Information. After all of the information has been gathered, the records management manual committee must classify it into appropriate categories. The type and number of *categories* will be determined by the scope of the organization's records management program. Ordinarily, one or more categories should be established for each element of the program.

Scope of the Manual. After the data have been properly sorted and categorized under the desired headings, the information should be studied and analyzed on the basis of its appropriateness and the need for its inclusion in the manual. A subcommittee can be appointed for each area of records management to be included in the content of the manual. Each subcommittee should consist of an appropriate member of the records management staff, the departmental supervisor, and one or more employees. Each subcommittee should prepare a preliminary draft of the material to present to the committee in charge of writing the final draft of the proposed manual.

WRITING THE MANUAL

The actual writing of the records management manual should be done by the records manager and the supervisors of the various phases of the records management program. Both the qualifications of the writing team and the format and content of the manual are major considerations.

Qualifications of the Writing Team

Qualifications needed by the members of the writing team include the following:

- Writing ability.
- Knowledge of the organization's structure, policies, and operations.
- Experience in working in a records management program, preferably in a supervisory or coordinating capacity.

In addition, members of the writing team should be provided with the proper amount of time needed to do a good job.

Format and Content of the Manual

Since much of the information in a records management manual is subject to frequent revision, the manual should be bound in a looseleaf binder so that pages can be deleted and inserted easily. It is possible to have the manual on-line so that it can be referred to from the computer terminal, thus eliminating the need to store a hard copy. A good manual should provide for updating, to include changes in organizational policies, improvement of operating procedures, and the correction of errors.

Only those facts that are needed to achieve the objectives of the records management program should be included in the manual. Quality, rather than quantity, is the prime consideration. The organization of the content should be in logical order and usable sequence. Following is a recommended sequence for the contents of a multiple-purpose records management manual.

1. Cover
2. Authorship and date of publication
3. Authorization
4. Preface
5. Table of Contents
6. Organizational charts
7. Procedures section
   a. Job descriptions
   b. Flowcharts
   c. Step-by-step instructions
   d. Illustrations
8. Glossary
9. Index

Cover. The manual title and company name should appear on the cover of the manual. The cover should be distinctive so that it is readily distinguishable from other publications of the organization. An appealing title should be selected, and the lettering should be simple, readable, and attractive; it might be embossed in a color that contrasts with the color of the binder. A line drawing, a cartoon, or an appropriate verse will help to make the appearance of the manual attractive to the reader.

Authorship and Date of Publication. All personnel who assist in the preparation of the manual should be given recognition. The date on which the manual is issued should also be mentioned on the same page.

Authorization.   To secure acceptance by the organization's employees, the manual should be introduced with a page showing the authorization for it, including the signatures of the members of top management who approve its contents.

Preface.   The preface should be kept as brief as possible. It should include the organization's definition of records management, the purposes of the manual, the purposes of the organization's records management program, the advantages to be derived from proper use of the manual, and a statement soliciting suggestions for improvement of the manual. Acknowledgments of assistance in manual preparation may be included, but such a list should be brief. The main purpose of the preface is to tell the organization's employees the reason for the preparation of the manual and acquaint them with its coverage.

Table of Contents.   The table of contents lists subject headings and identifies their location in the manual by page numbers. Very often, page numbers are carelessly omitted from the contents by manual writers. This is inexcusable. The manual should be designed to be easy to use in locating information. Readability is enhanced through the use of lots of white space, bulleted lists, illustrations, and desktop publishing. Tabs, in staggered positions and attached to a divider page, are also frequently used by manual writers to indicate each section of the manual.

Organizational Charts.   A chart showing the structure of the entire organization should be included in the records management manual. This chart should show the relationship of the records management department to other departments in the organization and the lines of authority and responsibility. A records management organization chart that provides a graphic picture of the structure of the program and the positions of au-

thority and responsibility for each phase of the program should be provided.

Procedures Section.   Information concerning organizational procedures can be transmitted in numerous ways, including by means of job descriptions, flowcharts, step-by-step instructions, and illustrations. A job description gives a word picture of each job in relation to the work of the entire department. Flowcharts can be used to show the movement of records within the organization, from the time of their creation to their destruction.

The major part of the records management manual should be devoted to standard instructions for performing a task. They may be written in a variety of forms and illustrated in a number of ways. Illustrations of correct methods of performing a specific task are helpful when they appear at the top of a page and the step-by-step instructions are presented below the illustrations on the same page.

Glossary.   Definitions for all technical terms should be provided to assist the user in interpreting the instructions and directions as well as to help him or her to understand the philosophy of the writer. A records management manual should, for example, include definitions of the following terms: *record*, *active record*, *inactive record*, *obsolete record*, *vital record*, *important record*, *records series*, and *records schedule*.

Index.   The accessibility of the needed information depends on the index as well as the table of contents. An index should be a helpful guide for the rapid location of any information contained in the manual. The index should list the contents of the manual in alphabetical order. After the manual is written, the indexer should search each page for keywords that should be indexed, noting the page on which they occur. If computer software is not used to index the keywords, the keywords should be written on separate cards and then alphabetized. It is advisable for a second indexer to prepare an index to be checked against the first one, to avoid omission of keywords.

ACHIEVING READABILITY

The language and style of the information presented in a manual should be made as interesting and readable as possible. Three elements are essential for readability: *clarity, brevity, and simplicity*. Because the manual must be understood by all who will use it, the level of writing should be aimed at those employees who possess the lowest level of reading comprehension.

Basic Principles

Most writers seem to find it hard to achieve a simple, direct style of writing. Although it is impossible to reduce writing to a simple set of rules, there are basic principles that should be followed to make the records management manual a useful employee tool. Among them are the following:

1. Express ideas in a positive way.
2. Use terminology that can be understood by all users of the manual.
3. Use the command style of writing, which prescribes the action to be taken by the reader: "Remove the disk" rather than "The disk should be removed."
4. Be concise in stating procedures and directions.
5. Use short sentences.
6. Build each paragraph around a single point.
7. Underline or capitalize statements or words that are to be emphasized.
8. Use standard spelling, grammar, and punctuation.

To make the information well organized and easy to follow, use major and minor headings. Source data should be checked to ensure that all of the writing is accurately presented. It is a good idea to identify source material by a system of superscript numbers in the text and numbered notes at the ends of chapters or sections.

Format for Writing Manuals

The narrative style is the most commonly used form of writing in manuals. The playscript format, however, is sometimes more effective. This technique identifies, in step-by-step sequence, each worker responsible for each particular part of a job. It can be used for a one-person procedure, but it is more effective for interaction procedures. A common form of playscript writing uses two columns. The column at the left identifies the person whose job it is to perform the required action. The column at the right identifies the action to be taken. The playscript technique is shown in Figure 16.4.

Greater clarity in presentation of material in the manual can be obtained through the use of charts, cartoons, diagrams, and examples. It is relatively easy to communicate proper style of letters, forms, and reports by showing examples in illustrations. All material should be in the normal work flow sequence. The amount of detail necessary depends upon the complexity of the procedure being presented.

Reading Level. It is imperative that only those words that are familiar to the reader be used. Highly technical words should be defined for the reader because the purpose of the manual is to transmit information. In recent years, communication specialists have made numerous studies of readability. These studies show conclusively that different levels of readability exist. The level of writing that is easy reading for the college graduate may be difficult for those below that educational level. A level that is easy reading for the high school graduate may be difficult for those with less education. Readability levels exist for each general level of education.

Robert Gunning, an authority on the measurement of readability, found from his surveys that more than one third of business writing is above college level in reading comprehension.[1] Other authors, such as Flesch, Chall, Conard, Harris, and McLaughlin, have attempted to establish criteria for readability.[2]

Gunning also found that, except for highly technical writing, readability can be kept at or below the eleventh grade (high school junior) level. Gunning has developed a simple measure

Procedures Manual 39

SUBJECT: Requesting Photocopies

RESPONSIBILITY	ACTION
Requesting Employee	1. Prepares master; proofreads master and makes any necessary changes.
	2. Completes requisition form, making certain to state number of copies needed.
	3. Sends requisition with master attached to duplicating service.
Duplicating Supervisor	4. Approves requisition and assigns job to duplicating clerk.
Duplicating Clerk	5. Makes requested number of copies.
	6. Inserts completed copies and master into mailing envelope.
	7. Places envelope in outgoing mail box.
Requesting Employee	8. Checks completed work for clarity and correct number of copies.
	9. Files master if no additional copies are needed.

FIGURE 16.4   Procedures Written in Playscript Style

of readability, which he calls *the fog index.* The method of calculating the fog index, based on Gunning's index formula, is shown in Figure 16.5.

Gunning's table for interpreting the difficulty of written or printed material is shown in Figure 16.6. It is as applicable to all other forms of written communication as it is to narrative manuals.

Graphics

In addition to the illustrations, flowcharts, organizational charts, and pictures used in the records management manual, the writer may want to include a common symbol or logo. Where the manual is a collection of standard operating procedures, the format of the procedure usually contains the company logo in a prominent place on each procedure. Where creative talent is available, a drawing of a cartoon figure or a symbol can be used throughout the manual to draw attention to various topics. Cartoons can also be used to illustrate various foibles that the policies and procedures are designed to correct.

To find the Fog Index of a piece of writing, follow these steps.
1. Choose a sample of 100 words or more. Samples should be free from quotes from other writers.
2. Divide the number of words in the sample by the number of sentences. This gives you the AVERAGE NUMBER OF WORDS IN A SENTENCE.

EXAMPLE

Number of words in the sample 118
Number of sentences 8
AVERAGE NUMBER OF WORDS IN A SENTENCE 14.7
(or 15)

3. Divide the number of words of three or more syllables by the number of words in the sample. This gives you the PERCENT OF DIFFICULT WORDS.

EXAMPLE

Number of words of three or more syllables 15
Number of words in the sample 118
PERCENT OF DIFFICULT WORDS 12.7
(or 13)

4. Add AVERAGE NUMBER OF WORDS IN A SENTENCE to PERCENT OF DIFFICULT WORDS.

EXAMPLE

AVERAGE NUMBER OF WORDS IN A SENTENCE 15
PERCENT OF DIFFICULT WORDS 13
   TOTAL 28

5. Multiply this total by 0.4 to give you the Fog Index of the sample.

EXAMPLE

28 times 0.4 equals a Fog Index of 11.2
(or 11)

The general public can easily understand a Fog Index of 12 or less. A higher Fog Index means you are in danger of being ignored or misunderstood.

FIGURE 16.5   A Method of Measuring Reading Ease (Based on Robert Gunning's Fog Index Formula)
(*The Directives Improvement Workshop*, GSA, National Archives and Records Service, Office of Records Management)

PUBLICATION

Publication of the manual can occur after review of the draft and approval of the final copy. There are many factors to consider for the first product including the selection of the reproduction process, the size and weight of paper, the design of headings, the use of color, the organization of the material, and the binding.

Review of the Draft

After a complete draft of the manual has been written, a limited number of copies should be presented to key executives, supervisors, and employees for criticisms and suggestions. This action frequently results in improvements. Sometimes suggestions made by reviewing personnel will result in combining subjects, revising ma-

	FOG INDEX	READING LEVEL
	17	College graduate
	16	College senior
	15	College junior
	14	College sophomore
Danger Line	13	College freshman
	12	High school senior
	11	High school junior
	10	High school sophomore
	9	High school freshman
Easy Reading Range	8	Eighth grade
	7	Seventh grade
	6	Sixth grade

FIGURE 16.6   Gunning Fog Index Interpretation Table
(Robert Gunning, *How to Take the Fog Out of Writing,* Chicago: The Dartnell Corp.,
1959)

terials, or adding major items previously over-looked.

Approval of the Final Copy. After the incorporation of corrections and suggestions made by reviewing personnel, the manual should be presented to the appropriate executives for approval.

Reproduction Process

The records management manual can be published by any one of several processes, including xerography, desktop publishing, and typesetting. Factors that will probably determine the method of publication are unit cost, quantity, and appearance. Before production can begin, decisions must be made about manual size, paper quality, type of binding, dividers, and pagination. It is usually wise to seek competent advice from the reprographics manager or a commercial printer.

Size. If the records management manual is intended to be used as a reference book, an 8 1/2- by 11-inch size is most satisfactory. A convenient size for pocket-size manuals is 4 1/2 by 6 1/4 inches. Other popular sizes include 6 by 9 1/8

inches, 5 1/2 by 8 1/2 inches, and 3 3/4 by 5 1/8 inches. These page sizes can be cut from sheet sizes usually carried by printers. If the manual is printed, the 6- by 9-inch page size, typical of books, is appropriate. If the manual is prepared in typed form, the 8 1/2- by 11-inch size is preferable.

Weight of Paper. The weight of the paper used is generally determined by the number and size of the pages in the manual. When the number of pages is less than 25, a thick paper can be used. For manuals consisting of larger number of pages, a thinner paper stock should be used to eliminate unnecessary bulk.

Headings. Headings can be made to stand out on the page by the use of sufficient white space around them. The use of subheadings also improves readability.

Color. The use of color helps to make headings stand out. Color will increase the cost, however.

Organization. Arrangement of the material to be included in the manual will contribute to its usefulness or disuse. Suggestions for the arrangement of materials for effective manuals include:

1. Sections used most frequently should be placed at the front of the manual.
2. Related sections should be placed close together.
3. Related sections should be cross-referenced.
4. Sections should be set apart by stiff divider pages, preferably of a color different from the other pages of the manual.
5. Sections should be tabbed for quick reference.

Binding. Manuals consisting of fewer that 50 pages can be enclosed in printed covers of heavier paper and just stapled together. However, where manuals consist of a large number of pages and many sections, a three-hole binder is frequently suggested. The advantages are that the manual can be revised easily and select pages can be duplicated as needed. However, the disadvantages are that pages may be lost or simply not updated. The alternative for large manuals is to bind the pages permanently. Factors to be considered in selecting the binding are cost and ease of use.

DISTRIBUTION

The records management manual should be governed by a policy for its distribution, as well as a selected distribution list.

Policy

The policy to be followed in distributing records management manuals should be determined before the manuals are prepared. Every employee who needs the information contained in the manual should receive one. At least one copy of the manual should be available for ready reference in each department or division that has use for it. Copies of manuals that pertain to specific

jobs should be immediately available to every employee performing such work.

Distribution List

A file that identifies the location of every manual issued should be kept by the records management office. A master set of unbound pages should be kept in the records management office for demand copies or new printings. Some organizations print and attach the name of the recipient of the manual to the cover. This is done in the belief that the employee will become more interested in the contents of the manual if it is personalized.

MAINTENANCE OF MANUALS

Unless some provision is made at the time of its original publication for future revision of the records management manual, much of the manual's potential usefulness is lost. Employees who use the manual and find the contents obsolete soon ignore it entirely. Therefore, an audit or manual update is essential to ensure that revisions of procedures are noted and adhered to.

Revision

All changes in the records management manual should be cleared through the records management office so that proper authorization and conformity in format are obtained. Revised sheets should follow the established format of the manual. New material will probably have to be added every three to six months. Old material will probably need modification just as frequently.

Audit

Experience has shown that management should not expect all employees to make changes or insertions in manuals even though revised pages or supplements have been delivered to them in person. Employees frequently put off making the changes or insertions until the items become lost or mislaid. The only way to make certain that manuals will always be kept up to date is to put someone in charge of inserting or changing the material. Even then, further checking is often necessary. The following suggestions may assist in solving the revision-control problem.

- Keep a record of all employees who receive a copy of the material.
- Assign responsibility to one person for updating the manual.
- Inform each manual holder by written memorandum to remove obsolete sheets and destroy them.
- Send each manual holder, every six months, a checklist of the procedures that have been added to or deleted from the manual.
- Assign a clerk to audit all manuals, checking several each week so that all manuals are inspected once every six months.

MAINTENANCE OF COMMUNICATION

Manuals are an important part of administrative communication. Administrative communication in business is a costlier process than most people seem to realize. It consumes a large part of the time of management. Frequently, staff exists for the sole purpose of meeting administrative communication needs. Many other employees also spend much of their time performing communication tasks. These activities result in huge monetary costs, to say nothing of expenditures of energy. As costly as the preparation of manuals and handbooks is, their absence would be many times more costly.

In achieving its goals, the organization has an established plan of operation. For the plan to be completely effective, there must be a great deal of communication between and among organization employees. Communication may take the form of written procedures, informal memorandums, directives, seminars for department heads or responsible persons, and visits to various offices where records are generated or stored.

Written Procedures

Without written procedures, organizations could not maintain coordinated group efforts. Management cannot function in a decision-making capacity except by receiving information needed for decisions and then communicating these decisions to the proper persons. Written procedures are effective in recording all the steps taken to record, analyze, transmit, and store information needed to serve a single, specific purpose. These steps may be incorporated into a *procedures manual* which is a source of instruction and reference for personnel responsible for creating, preparing, processing, storing, and disposing of records.

Informal Memorandums

Informal memorandums can be used to guide, instruct, or inform employees in their work. Informal memorandums may take the form of administrative letters or notices. A more formal communication is the directive.

Directives

The term *directive* is applied to any written communication that guides, instructs, or informs employees in their work. Included among directives are formalized statements of policy and procedure, administrative letters, bulletins, notices, and regulations. Directives may be permanent or temporary. *Permanent* directives establish policies and procedures that continue in effect indefinitely. *Temporary* directives should be complied with and then the copy should be destroyed.

Seminars

Communication can be improved by providing seminars for department heads and other responsible persons. The seminar may cover topics to be included in the manual and offer workshops in analyzing procedures or writing effective procedures. Improving written communication is always a welcome seminar topic.

Visits to Offices

For those concerned with writing effective manuals and analyzing procedures throughout the organization, a visit to the departments concerned is indispensable to writing correct procedures.

SUMMARY

A records management manual should specify in detail the scope of the organization's records management program and provide instructions for carrying out all aspects of the program. Large organizations with elaborate programs should have a comprehensive manual or a number of specific operating procedures manuals; small organizations should have at least some written record of recommended procedures for clerical personnel.

Because each records management program has its own special needs, the type of manual adopted for a particular program should be based upon the purpose to be served. Most records management manuals in existence can be classified as one of these four types: (1) policy, (2) organizational, (3) administrative procedures, or (4) operating procedures.

Planning a multiple-purpose records management manual involves the following activities: (1) determining the topics or areas of activity to be included; (2) organizing a committee on manual preparation; (3) identifying sources for manual information; and (4) collecting and analyzing the data. The actual writing of the manual should be done by the records management staff. Three elements are essential for readability: clarity, brevity, and simplicity. The level of writing should be aimed at those users who possess the lowest level of reading comprehension.

Publication of the manual includes a review of the draft, approval of the final copy, selection of the reproduction process, binding, size, paper,

and organization. The records management manual should be governed by a policy for its distribution.

Maintenance of the records management manual is an ongoing project. Maintenance involves the audit of its use to ensure that policies and procedures are followed and revision of the manual to incorporate suggestions of the users as well as of the policy makers.

Communication may take the form of written procedures, informal memorandums, directives, seminars for department heads or responsible persons, and visits to various offices where records are generated or stored.

A copy of the manual should be provided for every employee who needs the information contained in the manual. Provision for revision of the manual should be made at the time of its original publication.

QUESTIONS FOR DISCUSSION

1. Why is a records management manual an essential tool in both large and small organizations?

2. Identify the purposes served by each of the following:

   a. Policy manual

   b. Organizational manual

c.   Administrative procedures manual

d.   Operating procedures manual

3. What is a multiple-purpose records management manual? What activities are involved in planning a multiple-purpose manual?

4. How should the topics to be included in a records management manual be determined?

5. Who should serve on a manual preparation committee?

6. What are some typical flaws in records management manuals?

7. What are some good sources of information for the content of a records management manual?

8. How should data for the manual be collected?

9. How should the data collected for the manual be analyzed?

10. Who should prepare the first draft of material to be included in the manual? Who should prepare the final draft?

11. Why is it desirable to use the looseleaf method of binding a records management manual?

12. Identify the need for, and recommended content of, each of the following parts of a records management manual.

a.   Cover

b.   Authorship and date of publication

c.   Authorization

d.   Preface

e.   Table of Contents

f.   Organizational charts

g.   Procedures section

h.   Glossary

i.   Index

13. What are some principles to follow in achieving readability in a manual?

14. What are some important factors to consider regarding the mechanical process of publishing a manual?

15. What controls are important in distribution of a manual?

16. What controls should be exercised over manual maintenance?

PROJECTS

1. Locate a procedures manual and evaluate it. You may select a records management manual, secretarial manual, general office procedures manual, or one of a similar nature. Prepare a written report of your evaluation. Your report should include a consideration of the following evaluative criteria:

a.   Structural organization.

b.   Presentation of content.

c.   Use (and helpfulness) of illustrations.

d.   Accessibility of information.

2. Select a records management task involving more than one person, and write appropriate step-by-step procedures to be followed by the persons involved in performing the task.

a.   Identify the task and the persons involved in performing it.

b.   Write the step-by-step procedures required in narrative style.

c.   Write the step-by-step procedures required in playscript style.

3. Prepare a questionnaire that can be used by a local chapter of the Association of Records Managers and Administrators to survey its membership on the topic "The Format and Content of Records Management Manuals in Current Use."

4. Interview the person in charge of maintaining the records of a small organization (employing from one to five office workers) to determine the step-by-step procedures required in performing a task involving the records. Write the step-by-step procedures for the task in either narrative style or playscript style.

CASE PROBLEM

The vice-president of administrative services of the Jackson Publishing Company has requested that you, the organization's records manager, prepare an administrative procedures manual for the entire organization's use. Prepare the general instructions for all records management personnel to be used in performing their duties. These instructions will also serve as a model for all records management employees.

NOTES

1. Robert Gunning, *The Technique of Clear Writing* (New York: McGraw-Hill, 1968).
2. Beverley L. Zakaluk and S. Jay Samuels (eds.), *Readability: Its Past, Present, and Future* (Newark, Delaware: International Reading Association, 1988).

Corporate Model

Inter-American Development Bank

The Inter-American Development Bank (IDB) was created in 1959 to help acceler-ate the economic and social development of its member countries in Latin America and the Caribbean. It is owned by the 44 member countries and employs approxi-mately 1,800 people worldwide. Based in Washington D.C., it is the principal source of external public financing for most Latin American countries. Its cumula-tive lending and technical cooperation for development projects and programs amounted to nearly $56.8 billion in 1992.

Statement of Problem

Over 470 forms were in use at IDB in 1992. They recognized the need to automate paper-bound business processes in order to improve productivity in their organiza-tion. IDB's goal was to streamline the complicated and expensive process of producing, buying, storing, modifying, and disposing of paper forms.

The bank initiated a general forms management project to examine pertinent issues surrounding the use of electronic forms, forms routing, data encryption and validation, electronic signatures, and various security items such as access to forms, data confidentiality, and administration of security.

Current Process

Under the existing system forms were filled in on a typewriter and then routed via internal company mail to gather additional information and authorization. For example, a purchase request for a new desk would be filled in by an employee. The form would then be sent to a central hub where it is stamped and then distrib-uted to the manager for approval. The form was then returned to the central hub and then sent to the purchasing department. Under this system, it took as long as four to five days for a form to arrive at the service provider's desk. IDB wanted to shorten the time frame between form origination and the provision of service.

Selection Criteria

The evaluation methodology was largely based on comparative technical and functional assessments of the vendors' responses to questions regarding their product's capability and the bank's "hands-on" assessment of features and functionality. As part of the evaluation, particular emphasis was placed on forms development, form filling features, forms routing and performance, ease of use, and system requirements.

The following aspects were seen as critical for the successful solution:

- *Electronic signatures* must be used to provide validation in the same manner as handwritten signatures on printed forms.
- *E–mail connectivity* should allow for the electronic transfer of information (IDB uses a proprietary mail system—a sophisticated communication system).
- The *forms* must be simple to access and easy to learn and use on a day–to–day basis.
- *Database connectivity* is necessary—IDB has a large DB2 data infrastructure that the forms software must be able to access.
- *Data protection*—the forms software must ensure data integrity of existing data structures.

Solution

Of the vendors who responded to the bank's request, two possible solutions were considered. The first provided for the simple creation of forms and then printing and routing the form through the bank's internal mail system. The second solution, Delrina FormFlow ™, provided a total integrated solution involving the creation of electronic forms, routing of forms through e–mail, a tracking facility, and electronic signatures. The steering committee felt that while the first solution would be very easy to implement, it fell far short of its goal of using electronic forms to improve business efficiencies.

Delrina FormFlow was chosen for its ability to integrate with a wide variety of standard applications including database (such as the company's DB2 database) and e–mail systems and for the ability to create custom applications which guide the user via menus organized by service areas.

How FormFlow Has Been Implemented

The first application to be developed is a purchase requisition application which integrates with the bank's mail system to allow for the routing of a form to the correct service provider following proper authorization at the appropriate management levels. The application also has complete audit–trail functionality and review–status functionality so that both job initiators and service providers can check the current status of requests.

In addition, the project management team has designed the core application so that it can be re–used as a template for automating other forms, thus allowing rapid development and deployment of the organization's over 400 forms. Ultimately, this flexibility will allow the bank to escalate the use of electronic forms organization–wide in a short period of time.

Return on Investment

Using electronic forms provides IDB with a more cost–effective method of creating and modifying forms. The use of electronic forms eliminates the significant time costs associated with maintaining paper forms, as it can take four to five weeks to get new forms through the bank's existing procurement process.

Although it is too early in the implementation of electronic forms to measure exact cost savings, the bank has identified four key areas in which it will both improve efficiencies and save money:

- Time compression—more efficient business processes
- Reduction of personnel
- Printing of forms—since forms are printed only when required, the need for large quantities of preprinted forms will be eliminated
- Storage—warehousing of preprinted forms will be eliminated

The bank anticipates that the project will have fully paid for itself within the first 18 months of implementation. Finally, the project has accrued some unanticipated benefits, the most significant of which is an improved receptivity to technology within the organization as users receive better service internally and upper management sees real cost savings as the need for paper forms diminishes.

Future

Subsequent to the development and full deployment of the initial purchase requisitions application, the bank plans to implement all of its over 400 forms in the next two years. Deployment will be done first within the administrative department and then bank–wide. In addition, because Form Flow allows for rapid application development, the bank views the solution as a dynamic process that will be enhanced as feedback is received from users.

PART VI

Inactive Records Management

Chapter 17

Records Center Planning
and Design

Learning Objectives
1. To explain the purposes and functions of a records center in a records management program.
2. To establish criteria for planning the requirements for a records center facility.
3. To establish criteria for the selection of records center equipment.
4. To identify criteria for planning the layout of a records center facility.
5. To identify the different types of records storage space-numbering systems and explain the advantages of each.
6. To explain the advantages and disadvantages of a commercial records center as compared to an in-house facility.

THE NEED FOR A RECORDS CENTER

Storing records is not new; organizations were storing records long before the advent of records management. The difference is that in the past, organizations simply stored their records in a spare room, unused basement, or a warehouse. They stored their inactive records but seldom exercised control over them until something was needed from the storeroom or until the storeroom became full or until it became apparent that their old records were in an unmistakable mess.

The result of such haphazard storage methods was that retrieval of documents from storage was not only more costly and time-consuming, but also that more and more inactive records remained in the office, because of a loss of confidence in the system, thus adding to the problem.

Records management solved the problems by doing just what its name implies—it managed records by introducing controls into the age-old practice of storage, using techniques that had been successfully used by archivists for years.

What Is a Records Center?

The terms *records center* and *archives* are often confused and used synonymously. This is not correct. An archives (the term is short for *archives repository*) is dedicated to the preservation of records for historical purposes. Its records are primarily permanent records of a government, institution, or other organization, retained for the benefit of the scholar and posterity. A records center, however, is used to store and control inactive records that are maintained for operating or administrative purposes and for a relatively short time. Although the term *records center* may sometimes be used to describe an active central file area and *archives* to describe inactive records storage areas, this is not the generally accepted terminology.

The Value of a Records Center

A well-run records center can save an organization thousands of dollars per year, chiefly by economies in space and equipment. It provides a viable and economical alternative to archival micrographics storage, expensive office retention, or premature destruction of records. For example, when records are housed in a typical modern office in standard four-drawer file cabinets, they require 1 square foot of floor space for each cubic foot of records. In comparison, when they are stored on shelves in a record center, that ratio can be increased to up to 5 cubic feet of records to each square foot of floor space. In addition, the cost of the office space is much greater than that of the records center, which compounds the cost differential. Thus, if office space costs $20 per square foot per year and records center space costs $5 per square foot per year, there would be an annual savings of approximately $19,000 for every 1,000 cubic feet stored in the records center, plus a one-time savings of $71,000 based on the replacement value of the 185 file cabinets released.

Also by contrast, the cost to microfilm a cubic foot of records could range from $50 to $200 depending on methods, equipment, type of record, and labor costs. Thus it could cost $50,000 or more to microfilm 1,000 cubic feet of records as compared to approximately $3,000, including related labor, to store the same volume of documents in a records center.

These related labor costs depend on the total number of employees and total volume stored. Figure 17.1 demonstrates the computations used to arrive at these conclusions. The reader may refer to the chapters on micrographics to arrive at a cost estimate for that process.

SELECTING THE FACILITY

The selection of a records center facility requires, among other concerns, consideration of space requirements, security, and location. The primary challenge is to determine how much space will be required.

An understanding of the techniques used in the modern records center is required. Generally, the architectural principle of the skyscraper is used to conserve floor space. Records are generally maintained in standardized cardboard cartons, which are placed on standardized steel shelving. Figure 17.2 shows a photo of a typical stack area of a records center.

Estimating the Volume of Records

The initial inventory, after analysis, will provide a relatively sound basis for determining immediate volume or quantity of records on hand, thus enabling an estimate of space requirements. The records retention schedule can be used to estimate future volumes to be stored and the future space needs. If inactive records are currently stored in a storage facility, the volume stored is a fair indicator of minimum space needs. If there appear to be no organized storage or disposal plan and no prior formal disposal efforts, a somewhat empirical but often used estimating rule is that one-third of the total inventory will be active (retained in the office), one-third inactive (stored in a records center), and one-third destroyed.

Applying this formula to the total cubic feet in the inventory as a starting point, plan space sufficient to house one-third of the total. To this is added approximately one-third of that amount for expansion. Expansion requirements are difficult to estimate. Certainly, a careful analysis of the retention schedule will help to decide if more

---

OFFICE COST FACTORS

4-drawer file cabinet capacity at 20 linear inches per drawer $\frac{80}{15}$ = 5.3 cubic feet

4-drawer file cabinet floor space (including aisle space) 15 inches x 54 inches = $\frac{810}{144}$ square inches =

   5.6 square feet

Ratio of cubic feet to square feet (5.3:5.6) 1:1 approximately

Floor space cost, annual = $20 per square foot

Cost per cubic foot of records, annual = $20

RECORDS CENTER COST FACTORS

Ratio of cubic feet to square feet   5:1 (optimum)

   Cost per square foot of floor space $5

   Cost per cubic foot of records $\frac{\$5}{5}$ = $1.

COMPARISON OF SPACE COSTS

Office: 1,000 cubic feet at $20.	=	$20,000
Record Center: 1,000 cubic feet at $1.	=	$ 1,000
Annual Savings		$19,000

COMPARISON OF EQUIPMENT COSTS

Office: 185 4-drawer, letter-size cabinets at $400	$74,000
Records Center: Shelving and cartons at $3 per cubic foot	$ 3,000
Equipment Savings	$71,000

FIGURE 17.1   Cost Comparison—Office Space Versus Records Center Space

records will come into the records center than will be destroyed. There are few records centers that have an accession rate lower than or even equal to their disposal rate, and so a growth factor should be considered. This factor is difficult to determine, because one cannot easily foresee new regulations that might lengthen retention periods or lawsuits and mergers, delayed audits, or increased volume of business that could increase record holdings.

Some records centers operate at near capac-ity, which provides a very economical low annual storage cost per cubic foot of records. However, a safe margin in planning a records center would be a 75 percent occupancy rate, leaving a space vacancy of 25 percent after all records found suitable for storage are accessioned. A high vacancy rate, however, is an indication of wasted floor space and, hence, increases the annual cost to store a cubic foot of records. Trends in microimaging or computer technology may equal-ize the accession-disposal ratio by reducing vol-

FIGURE 17.2 Typical Records Center Stack Area (Courtesy of Allied Signal)

ume intake in the future. The retention schedule may also be refined as time progresses, thereby reducing retention periods and records center holdings.

Estimating Space Requirements

After the volume of records has been estimated, the process of selecting a facility with sufficient space may begin. Because the records are measured in cubic feet, the height of the ceiling as well as the floor space must be considered. Experience has shown that in a well-designed records center, the ratio of 1 cubic foot of records to 1 foot of rise to 1 square foot of floor space is approximately .333 cubic feet. Applying this factor to the known elements, such as cubic-foot measurement of records, square-foot measurement of floor space, and the height of the shelving stack, we can determine unknown factors of space requirements. The following formulas are useful in estimating space requirements for the stack area of the records center.

$$\frac{\text{Volume of records}}{\text{Stack height} \times .333} = \text{floor area required}$$

$$\frac{\text{Volume of records}}{\text{Floor area} \times .333} = \text{stack height required}$$

$$\text{Floor area} \times \text{stack height} \times .333 = \text{volume capacity}$$

The formulas include aisle space but do not include administrative, processing, or staging areas. An illustration of how to use these formulas appears later in this chapter when shelving and layouts are discussed. For the optimum square-foot to cubic-foot ratio, the building or room selected should have a ceiling height that would allow 14-foot shelving, thus providing an approximate ratio of 4 to 1 or more.

Other Architectural Considerations

Determining the size of the building or room is only one of several considerations that must be taken into account. Elements such as floor strength, temperature and humidity, security, and location of the facility must be evaluated in depth. There are certain standards upon which a judgment can be based in evaluating these factors, but it should be recognized that these are really recommended standards. Therefore, guided by local regulations and laws, and the advice of engineering professionals, records managers must decide for themselves what is acceptable.

Floor Strength. Floor strength is of prime importance and should be appraised by competent engineering personnel. If the floor is not strong enough to support the weight of records, it could sag or collapse. The engineer's appraisal will depend on the weight of the records and the height of the records stacks. The standard (1-cubic-foot) records center carton weighs approximately 30 pounds when filled, but can weigh as much as 50 pounds, and stack heights may rise to within 2 feet of the ceiling, if floor strength permits. On the average, 50,000 cubic feet of records will weigh 1,500,000 pounds (30 pounds per cubic foot), and will probably be contained in a 10,700-square-foot area. This produces an average per-square-foot floor load of 140 pounds. The engineer's appraisal may limit the height and placement of the stacks. If such is the case, the selection must be reevaluated, because more floor space will be required. Although this is basically an engineering problem, it is one that a records manager must be well aware of in the planning process.

Temperature and Humidity. Heating, ventilation, and air conditioning (HVAC) are necessary considerations. If cost were not a factor, we would desire the same climate conditions as are provided to the office areas. Ideally, for the protection of the paper, film, and other media, and for the comfort of the employees, temperatures in the general stack area should be 72°F, plus or minus 10 degrees, depending on the season. Temperatures in the vault or archives areas should be 70°F, plus or minus 5 degrees, with humidity held at 50 percent, plus or minus 5 percent.[1]

In addition to costs, the decision to install HVAC equipment depends on two factors: the climate of the area where the center is located and the retention period of the records. High-quality paper records have survived 100 years or more without temperature and humidity controls in moderate climates. However, in a warm, humid climate, such as the Gulf Coast of the United States, air conditioning would be highly desirable if not required. In any case, good ventilation is necessary. If the center will hold a large collection of permanent records, more stringent temperature and humidity standards will be required than if the majority of the records are to be held for a short period of time. If the center's collection of permanent records is relatively small, that collection can be segregated into a small, controlled area of the center. This would avoid the higher cost of regulating temperature and humidity throughout the facility. One should first determine HVAC needs and wants and then consult a HVAC contractor or specialist to determine the best method consistent with economic restraints.

Security of the Building

Because records have value, the security of the building is important. Hazards from fire, water, vermin, vandals, sabotage, and rioters should be anticipated and guarded against.

Fire Protection. Fire is probably the most serious hazard. The local fire marshal should be consulted before consummating any building plans because fire regulations will dictate minimum standards for fire protection. Fire regulations vary from community to community and could affect elements of the floor plan, such as the width of the aisles, the height of the stacks, sprinkler requirements, and placement and specifications of portable fire extinguishers, interior fire hoses, fire alarms, fire walls, and exits. (See Figure 17.3 for a list of design standards and regulations.)

Sprinkler systems are necessary for the records center. Prior to July 1973, many managers of records centers and archives thought that sprinklers would do more harm to the records than the fire itself. But the disastrous fire at the National Personnel Records Center in St. Louis, Missouri, put the debate to rest forever. The sixth floor of the 1.2 million-square-foot records center was completely destroyed by a three-day fire. The entire building was threatened, along with the military records of practically all former U.S. service personnel. The National Archives and Records Service, manager of the federal records centers, had long recognized the dangers of not having sprinklers in the center, and for some years had requested funds to install sprinklers. Unfortunately, appropriation of the funds had not come in time. The investigation revealed that if the center had had sprinklers, the fire would not have spread beyond the aisle of origin.[2]

Water-soaked records can be restored, but fire usually damages records beyond restoration. In addition, the safety factor must be considered, because the intensity of a records center fire is enormous and the danger to property and persons in the immediate area is great. The damage from sprinkler water can be minimized by the installation of an early-warning smoke-detector alarm system, in addition to the sprinkler system. The purpose of the smoke detector when used in conjunction with sprinklers is to detect the fire before the heat becomes great enough to activate the sprinklers. Many jurisdictions require that all sprinkler systems be designed by professional engineers, who will follow local codes and submit plans before installation. In the absence of this requirement, most sprinkler contractors would probably fill that function.

The federal government, in its standards for federal records centers, has specified that sprinkler heads should be spaced a maximum of 10 feet apart and placed at least 18 inches above the top combustible stored records container. Because of sprinklers and fire protection needs, the top shelf should not be used for storage of records. However, it is important that the local fire code be reviewed before plans are finalized for the records center facility. Needless to say, the building should be of permanent construction to protect against fire as well as other hazards.

Water Protection. Water is almost as deadly an enemy to paper records as fire. The roof of the building must be in good condition so that there are no damaging water leaks. If there are floors above the records center, a simple and common accident, such as a toilet overflow, could cause damage to the records. If the area has overhead pipes, a leak in these pipes could transform the

FIGURE 17.3 Resources for Design Specifications

- NFPA 232-1991, *Standard for the Protection of Records*
- NFPA 232AM-1991, *Manual for Fire Protection for Archives and Records Centers*
- NFPA 70, *National Electric Code (ULI, IEEE)*
- NFPA 10, *Standard for Portable Fire Extinguishers*
- NFPA 101, *Life Safety Code*
- NFPA 13, *Standard for Installation of Sprinkler Systems*
- NFPA 90A, *Standard for Installation of Air Conditioning and Ventilating Systems (ASHREA)*
- BOCA 1990
- OSHA Part 1910
- Local and state codes and regulations

records center into a veritable shower bath, with the situation made worse if the water is very hot. If a basement area is selected, there is not only the problem of dampness, but also the additional danger of flooding from storm water or underground springs. A sump pump can sometimes alleviate this threat, but pumps have been known to fail during electrical storms when the danger is greatest. Basement areas, although convenient and inexpensive, are not generally desirable because of this water hazard, unless they have been designed to guard against it.

Vermin.   Vermin can usually be controlled by chemical means. If the records center shares the building with another tenant, the other party's area might be a breeding ground for such creatures. A discreet investigation will reveal if the other areas are a potential source of infestation.

Vandalism.   The possibility of damage from riots, sabotage, vandalism, and the like is ever-present. Therefore, the building should have limited access and, preferably, no windows. If the building is shared with other occupants, access to their area should not require entry into the records center. The records center should be as secure as possible from unauthorized entry to preclude the necessity for a watchman or guard.

Location

Ideally, the location of the proposed center would be in the same building as the office it serves. But this is often not possible or practical because of the space cost factor and because the offices may be decentralized. Most modern office buildings are designed so that even the basement areas are fully utilized for office or service space. Some older office buildings do have basement areas that are otherwise unproductive and which can be used as a records center, but the danger of water damage should be carefully considered.

   If the records center must be separate from the offices, there is the question as to how far it should be removed. The distance depends to a great extent on the activity of the records stored. Theoretically, no record should be required in less than 24 hours. In practice, however, quicker turnaround time may be the norm, and distance becomes a more important factor. It is sometimes possible to obtain an adequate building for records storage within a few blocks of the organization's offices at a fraction of the cost of office space, and a messenger can make deliveries three or four times a day or make special runs, if necessary. If the record requested consists of only a few pages, it may be feasible to deliver the record via fax.

   But, usually, buildings that meet all the other standards are not available at such close proximity without a high rental. The facility should be within commuting distance and have good highway access. Thus, if deliveries to and from the records center are properly scheduled, the transportation cost becomes a minor expense. It is also important that there be economical telephone service available, as most records will be requested by phone or fax, and toll or long-distance calls could add considerably to the operating expense.

Other Building Features

The building should be constructed of noncombustible or fire-resistant material and designed to meet seismic and hurricane standards. Adequate loading dock facilities are necessary, as records will be accessioned and destroyed in truckload or near-truckload quantities. Also a freight elevator is required if the records center occupies areas above ground level. In addition, doors and halls must be wide enough to allow passage of freight-handling equipment. Parking space for records center employees and customers and adequate rest rooms are also a necessity.

Space Requirements for Nonstack Areas

In addition to space for stacks, other space requirements must be determined and planned. These include areas for administration, processing, staging, disposal, reference, and special archival or security needs. The exact space requirements for these areas will vary, although some generalizations can be made.

Administrative Area. The administrative area is the office space set aside for records center personnel to perform the many desk tasks involved in ensuring proper controls. The amount of space required depends largely upon the size of the operating staff. *As a guide*, there should be 100 square feet per person, but office layout techniques can be used to determine exact requirements. The administrative area, at least, should be air-conditioned and equipped with typical office equipment as well as appropriate computer stations. Adequate fluorescent lighting rated at 50 foot-candles at 3 feet above floor level is necessary. This area should be close to the stack area for quick access and convenience.

Processing Area. The processing area should be near the loading dock, the stack area, and the office, if possible. It may be desirable to combine the administrative and processing areas if space permits. The processing area is a make-ready room and is used in sorting operations for refiles and interfiles and for marking containers and other preparatory work. This room should be equipped with sorting racks and shelving as determined by the system used. The doorways and aisles should be wide enough for material-handling equipment to pass through easily.

Reference Area. Most records centers have a reference area that is used by customers and, at times, by records center personnel who extract information from the records. This area should be furnished with desks, proper light, and air conditioning. A microfilm reader or reader-printer should be available in addition to copying and fax machines. The reference area can be a part of the office area because the physical requirements are about the same. The amount of space required depends entirely upon the needs of the organization.

Staging Area. A staging area is essential to almost any efficient records center operation. Since records cannot always be shelved immediately upon receipt, there must be an open area that is secure for intermediate storage. Shelving could be used, but an open area will facilitate the handling of records. Because this area would be used for temporary holding, space sufficient for two or three days' accessions should be adequate.

Ideally, the room should be adjacent to the dock area to expedite unloading time. Like the processing area, it should have a doorway wide enough to accommodate forklift and pallet. Although this temporary storage space need not meet the high standards of the stack area, it should be reasonably secure to protect the records. If a staging area is not provided, the records manager will be severely hampered in scheduling accession operations and in economically using personnel.

Disposal Area. For similar reasons, a disposal area is also advantageous. Conceivably, the staging and disposal areas could be combined. It is better, however, if they are separate to avoid confusion and the possibility that records for accession could inadvertently be destroyed. When records are removed from the shelves for disposal, there is normally a time lag before a scrap paper dealer can pick them up for burning, shredding, or recycling. The disposal area permits small-quantity disposals to be accumulated for sale to a dealer. It also allows large-quantity disposals to be removed from the shelves on a time-available basis without the need for immediate destruction action. This area should also be located near the loading dock because the value of the scrap paper can be lessened by an inconvenient disposal area. Depending on the volume of and market for scrap paper, it may be beneficial to own a commercial shredder and bailer; however, this is usually not necessary. Most scrap paper dealers will give a certificate of cremation or shredding, if required. Some will bring disposal equipment to the site and perform the destruction there. But for small-quantity destructions of classified or confidential records, it is quite likely that some type of shredder device would be required.

Building a New Facility

When a records management program is first organized, an existing building, either owned or leased, will usually be used as a records center. After the program has proven its worth, however, the organization may decide to build a records center designed specifically for its needs. Before undertaking such a task and making such an investment, extensive study of current operating costs and the organization's requirements should be made to justify the facility and also to assure proper design. Although the design must be tailored to the organization's own needs, the various federal records centers and many private records centers provide excellent patterns and should be visited. In addition, the General Services Administration of the U.S. government has established and published standards for federal records centers,[4] that should be studied and considered by anyone planning a new records center.

RECORDS CENTER EQUIPMENT

A thorough understanding of shelving and other equipment used in the records center is essential to proper design. Records centers are designed and equipped to meet the specific requirements of the organization they serve, so equipment requirements may vary.

The most common types of equipment used in the records center are the open steel shelf and cardboard container. The shelf-carton method has been used extensively by the vast majority of private and commercial records centers. It is considered efficient and economical for the following reasons:

1. It is relatively inexpensive.
2. It affords excellent use of space.
3. It does not ordinarily require the unpacking of records before they are accessioned.
4. It simplifies disposal.

The system works well when the following conditions prevail:

1. The standard records center carton can be used for most records.
2. The shelving is standardized.
3. The retrieval rate is low.
4. Interfiling is minimal.

The Records Center Carton

The records center carton has been standardized so that it holds letter-size documents placed in one direction and legal-size documents in the other. This carton measures on the inside 15 inches deep, 12 inches wide, and 10 inches high. It occupies 12.5 inches by 16.5 inches of shelf space because of its cap lid. It is constructed of heavy corrugated cardboard, rated at a minimum at 200 pounds per square inch bursting test. It normally has handholds cut into the ends. In addition to the cap (shoe-box type) lid, a flap top (cracker-box type) lid is also used. In approximate measurement, one carton is considered 1 cubic foot of records. Two of these cartons will hold the entire contents of one legal-size file drawer, and three cartons will hold the contents of two letter-size file drawers. When the carton is filled, it weighs from 30 to 50 pounds, so it must be durable enough to withstand stress during shipment or in normal handling.

Exact specifications for the carton will depend on the individual organization. Some cartons are designed so that they are assembled automatically with one pull motion; other less expensive types are assembled by interlocking the flaps and require no tape or staples. All are purchased flat or unassembled. The shoe-box lid affords good protection from overhead water damage but requires slightly more shelf space. Sometimes, one end of the carton has a form printed on it to give uniformity in labeling. In other cases a typed label is pasted on the carton to serve the same purpose. There are many small details to consider when a carton is designed, such as placement of the handholds or the printing. For example, the printed form could be obscured by the handhold or the cap lid, or the handhold may be placed too low so that the thumbs cannot rest on top of the lid as the carton is carried. Finally, failure to print assembly instructions on the carton may cause box failure.

Special and Nonstandard Containers

Other sizes and styles of cartons are used for varying reasons (see Figure 17.4). Some records managers find that a carton designed to hold the entire contents of one file drawer simplifies indexing and expedites transfers of records to the records center. The fault with this type of container is that when it is full, it weighs too much for one person to handle safely. There may also be many instances when the carton will be only partially full, thereby wasting space. On the other hand, some organizations use a carton smaller than the standard carton. A smaller carton is much easier to handle, and in some cases, it better suits transfer methods. Remember, though, that nonstandard or specialized cartons may add considerably to the cost, and may waste valuable space in the records center.

Nearly every records center, however, will use some special cartons in addition to the standard one. As an example, engineering roll drawings are usually stored in long, squared cartons measuring 4 by 4 by 40 inches, with the length varying according to the drafting standards of the organization. The standard records center carton is sometimes cut down to a height of 5 inches to store reels of microfilm or index cards. These are then stacked two high in place of one standard container.

Shelving Types

The type of shelving that is most commonly used is a fairly standard industrial-type steel shelving. We will refer to it here as *standard records center shelving*. Basically, each shelving unit consists of four 13-gage round-edge angle-upright posts, drilled with holes every inch so that they can be fastened to the shelves at selective intervals. The 18-gage steel shelves also have holes drilled on each corner; they are fastened to the uprights with

1/2 inch stove bolts and nuts. To this are added various braces. (See Figure 17-5.) There are other types of shelving than the standard that may also achieve good results in cost, space economy, and safety.

The height of the shelving unit can rise to approximately 14 feet without the need for catwalks, because this height can be safely reached with ladders. Catwalks involve considerable expense, and their use is difficult to justify under normal circumstances because the cost of the equipment must be weighed against the cost of space. When catwalks are used, the units may rise to heights of 25 feet or more. (See Figure 17.6.)

Shelving Sizes

The shelving, which is normally steel, is constructed so that it will accommodate the standard records center carton with economy and fully use the available floor space. The shelves of a unit normally measure 30 inches in depth and 42 inches in length, and they will accommodate six standard-size cartons, stacked in a single layer. The 30- by 42-inch shelf is a standard manufactured size and is satisfactory.

However, a 32- by 42-inch size is preferred by some because it eliminates the overhang created when two cartons with cap lids are placed end to end on it (front and back), measuring about 32 inches. The 32-inch size costs slightly more, and it does not save any more space than the standard size. Elimination of the box overhang, however, does make the shelf edge more visible for shelf labels. Some records managers eliminate the front overhang by shifting it to the rear of the shelving unit, which will be explained more fully later on.

Many organizations stack cartons two layers to a shelf to conserve shelving material. The saving in material, however, must be weighed against the additional time and motion required for retrievals, refiles, interfiles, accessions, and disposals.

Standard shelf sizes vary in length in 6-inch increments—for example, 24, 30, 36, 42, and 48

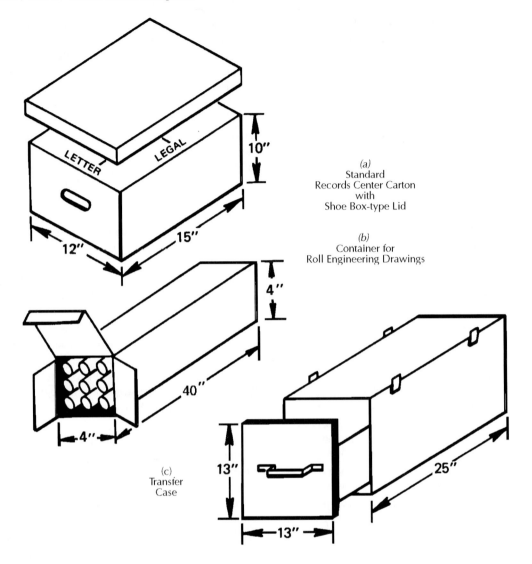

FIGURE 17.4 Records Center Containers

inches. In width, they vary in 3-inch increments, up to 18 inches, and in 6-inch increments, from 24 to 36 inches, such as 9, 12, 15, 18, 24, 30, and 36.

Sizes other than the 30- by 42-inch shelving are used, but on an exception basis. They are normally limited to the 15- by 30-inch size, used when the unit is placed against a wall with insufficient space for a 30- by 42-inch unit, or the 30- by 30-inch unit, used when there is insufficient space for the 30- by 42-inch unit.

Shelving Assembly

Standard shelving units are normally assembled on the floor and then raised to an upright position.

PARTS
1. Upright or "Angle Post"
2. Shelf
3. End Panel or "Partition"
4. Back Panel
5. End Sway Braces
6. Back Sway Braces
7. Angle Gusset

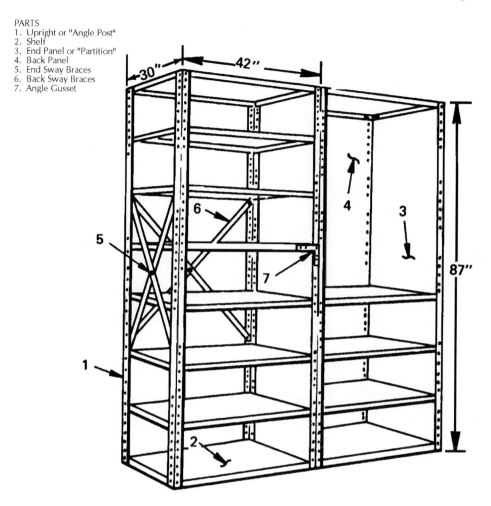

FIGURE 17.5 Shelving and Component Parts
(Courtesy of Do–Mor Manufacturing Company, Inc.)

Generally, the maximum length of an angle iron upright is 10 feet 3 inches. If longer lengths are required, it will be necessary to weld additional upright material to the post or to splice onto it. The manufacturer can advise on this or provide the modification before delivery. Many organizations will opt to have the shelving installed according to their own specifications, in which case the manufacturer or vendor can provide a ready-to-use installation. The top of the top shelf (e.g.,

Shelf 15) should be bolted even with the top of the 14-foot 3-inch uprights. Shelves should be bolted on both the front and the side flanges of the upright on all corners of the shelf.

Upright angle posts are made of 13-gage steel and have holes drilled at 1-inch intervals for the entire length on both the front and side flanges. The front flange of the angle is 1 inch wide, and the side flange is 1 3/4 inches wide. It is important that the front flange of the upright be facing the

FIGURE 17.6 Catwalk Shelving
(Courtesy of Union Pacific Railroad)

clipped to the pre-bored angle posts. The bottom shelf is spaced about 3 inches above the floor, primarily as a safeguard against water damage. End panels are generally used for the ends of a row and back panels when the shelving is placed against a wall or used as a partition. Clips may be used for all shelves, in lieu of bolts, except for the top and the bottom. They do not provide the strength of the nut and bolt, but do simplify assembly and shelf adjustments.

After assembly, each unit, consisting of four uprights and shelves, is then raised and bolted to other units, forming rows in accordance with a floor plan. The rows are then anchored across the top with slotted angle irons to the walls and other rows to provide maximum stability.

Shelving units are arranged in rows in several ways. If the units are attached only on the sides, it is a single unit arrangement. This can be a 15-inch shelf against the wall, or a 30-inch shelf that provides access from both sides. The second way is to arrange them in a row, side to side and back to back with other units. This is called a double-unit arrangement and is most common with 30-inch-deep shelves. With this, only the front carton is visible from the aisle, but both the front and rear cartons are accessed from the same aisle, and the same holds true for the companion unit in the next aisle. A third type of arrangement is called a triple-unit arrangement. This arrangement fastens three rows of units back to back, with access to the third unit, which is sandwiched between the other two, made rather difficult. It is suitable for only the most inactive records and is not commonly used.

Double-unit arrangements are used to conserve aisle space, and, therefore, their use in the records center is quite common. The less-active records are placed to the rear of the shelf. Mobile storage units, discussed in Chapter 7, are not used very often in the records center because of their relatively high cost.

long side of the shelf. This provides the maximum shelf opening. Thus, a 42-inch shelf has a 40-inch opening.

Shelves should be bolted to the upright holes every 12 inches, center to center from the top, leaving fourteen openings of 11 inches each in the unit. The top of the bottom shelf (Shelf 1) will be 3 inches from the floor. Thus, a 14-foot 3-inch unit actually has fifteen shelves. Shelf 15 is normally not used for records storage. Cross braces are added to the sides and back of the units.

Figure 17.5 shows two single units fully assembled with their component parts. Not all components in this illustration will be required for every unit of shelving. Shelves are placed 12 or 25 inches apart (depending on whether boxes are single- or double-stacked) and are bolted or

Transfer Cases

As an alternative to the shelf-carton method, the interlocking, drawer-type transfer case is sometimes used (see Figure 17.4c). This case approximates the size of a standard letter-size file drawer and is, in fact, a metal or fiber box with a sliding drawer. These containers interlock so that they can be stacked almost as high as shelving, without the need for additional equipment.

The chief advantage of the transfer case is that it can be used in much the same manner as a file cabinet, while its modular design gives it flexibility and mobility. In addition, drawer for drawer transfers can be used, which simplifies indexing.

The chief disadvantages are the difficulties in accessions and disposal in the records center. The cases are heavy when full, and the removal of one module may require moving many. The use of drawer-type cases in a records center may be justified in those instances where reference or interfile activity is sufficiently high to offset its disadvantages. However, they should only contain a small percentage of the total records housed. Overall, handling problems and personal injury possibilities tend to greatly reduce the use of this type of container.

Peripheral Equipment

In addition to shelving units and transfer cases, the records center requires other types of equipment, such as ladders, hydraulic lifts, three-sided stock trucks, carts, sort racks, and a motor truck vehicle.

Ladders. Because height is the key to space economy, safe mobile ladders will be required. The most suitable ladder for the records center is the platform ladder (see Figure 17.7). It is designed like a movable stairway, with handrails, a platform at the top for placing cartons, and spring wheels that make the ladder stationary when in use. The front wheels swivel and the rear wheels are rigid. The number of ladders that will be required varies, but as a rule of thumb, at least one per records center clerk. The ladders need not all be the same height. Ladders are manufactured to OSHA regulations, so one should not assume that any design or size is available. A ladder high

enough to safely access the fourteenth shelf has an overall height of a little over 11 feet from the floor to the top platform rail, and about 8 1/2 feet from the floor to the top step. The top step can be as deep as 30 inches.

The important things to remember about these ladders when making a layout of the stack area of a records center are the width and length of the base and the end-of-aisle shelf access. The width of the base directly affects the width of the access aisles, and the length of the base affects the width of the main aisle. End-of-aisle shelf access is best explained through illustration, (see Figure 17.8), but as we will see in discussing layout, there are solutions to this particular problem.

FIGURE 17.7 Platform Ladder

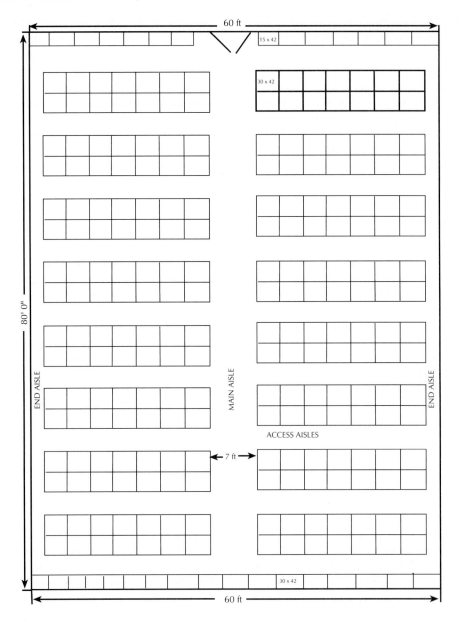

FIGURE 17.9   Records Center Layout

end of the shelving row. This permits access to all of the shelves, some of which would have otherwise been blocked by the ladder. (See Figure 17.8.) If the side emergency aisle is not available, access to the portion of shelves blocked can be accomplished by using a lower ladder, or by backing the higher ladder into the aisle, steps first, which is rather cumbersome and somewhat unsafe.

Shelving heights are limited by the height of the ceiling. Space must be provided for overhead sprinklers and fluorescent lighting. The shelving height can rise to within 2 feet of the ceiling; however, local fire codes should be checked first. Economy of space comes primarily from height, so the highest level consistent with safety should be utilized if possible.

Because an architect's floor plans cannot always be trusted for complete detail, particularly if the structure is old, the manager should visit the area personally, make a few spot measurements, and note any physical differences not shown on the floor plan, before commencing the layout.

Lighting

Once the row layout is determined, the lighting scheme can be devised. Fluorescent lights are preferable because they reduce glare, do not cast shadows, and are more economical than incandescent lights. Lights should be placed over aisles, in a continuous strip, with convenient wall switches. The federal records centers provide a reasonable standard[6] to follow in lighting stack areas. The standard provides for continuous-strip, 8-foot, single-strand, 215-watt fluorescent lighting giving 40 foot-candles of light at the level 3 feet above floor level. No lighting fixture should be placed lower than 1 foot above the top shelf. Poor lighting, needless to say, can be detrimental to the efficiency of the operation. Lighting, like other building matters, is an engineering problem that is best solved by consulting the professional.

Space Utilization

As noted earlier, there is approximately a 0.333-cubic-foot capacity per foot of rise to every square foot of floor space in the well-designed records center. This was expressed in several formulas, which can be used to approximate cubic-foot capacity and floor space requirements. The validity of these formulas can be best understood by applying them to the hypothetical records center layout shown in Figure 17.9. The area of this records center measures 60 feet by 80 feet, or a total of 4,800 square feet. There are two hundred forty-one 30- by 42-inch units, 14 feet high, each containing 84 cubic-foot cartons. There are also fourteen 15- by 42-inch units, 14 feet high, each containing 42 cubic feet. The total is 20,832 cubic feet. To determine the actual cubic-foot-to-square-foot ratio, divide the total cubic feet by the square feet as follows:

$$\frac{20{,}832 \text{ cu. ft.}}{4{,}800 \text{ sq. ft.}} = 4.34$$

To test the formula against the actual ratio of 4.34 to 1, multiply 0.333 by the height of the stacks.

$$0.333 \times 14 = 4.66 \text{ cu. ft. per sq. ft. ratio}$$

Because this formula is used merely as an estimating tool, complete mathematical accuracy cannot be expected. Obstructions such as doorways, pipes, and columns, as well as the shape and size of the room, must be considered in estimating space and in achieving optimum cubic-foot ratios. However, these formulas are helpful in space estimation and as guidelines in testing the efficiency of the layout.

A study of the floor plan in Figure 17.9 will show that there is a good use of space and adequate aisle widths. Maximum use of space does not necessarily result in optimum efficiency, for all factors must be considered. For instance, although a four-wheel cart may fit in the main aisles, it may not be possible for a human being to pass through while the cart is there. Even the double-unit arrangement of shelving is not efficient in every records center, although it is in general use. The efficiency of operations must have priority over full utilization of space.

SPACE-NUMBERING SYSTEMS

In a well-run records center, an effective numbering system for storage space is absolutely essential. Every cubic foot of shelf space must have a unique address, just as every dwelling has an address, so that it can be located. The system will vary from organization to organization, but it should be adopted only after very serious consideration. It is extremely difficult to change the system once installed. The system should be simple, consistent, functional, and flexible.

Row/Space-Number Method

Although there are many variations in space-numbering systems, one common method in use incorporates the row number with a box (space) number. In this method, each row of shelving units is assigned a sequential number, which is posted on the main aisle end of the row. Each unit in the row is evenly subdivided into box spaces, also numbered sequentially, beginning with 01 in the first unit and proceeding through the last space in the row (see Figure 17.10). The combination of the row number with the space (box) number makes up the entire address. For example, the entire address for space 48 in row 101 would be 101048. Since each row is numbered in identical fashion—that is, each row begins with space 01 and proceeds in sequence—space 48 in row 102 has the complete address 102048. The entire address is commonly referred to as a space number or sometimes as a locator number.

In single-depth units, the subdivision of the shelves within the row usually follows this pattern: Space 001 is placed on the left side of the bottom shelf of the first unit in the row; space 002 is placed to the right of 001; and 003 is placed to

the right of 002. Space 004 would be just above 001. Numbering continues until the top of the first unit is reached. Then the numbering continues in the same manner, beginning at the left bottom of the next unit. It continues until it reaches the end of the row. The numbering pattern is repeated in the next row, and so on. (If the row runs right to left, the numbers read right to left, rather than left to right as described here.)

In a double-depth shelf, box 001 is placed to the left rear of the bottom shelf and box 002 is placed in front of 001. Box 003, placed at the rear, is to the right of 001, and 004 is placed in front of 003. Box 005 is placed to the right of 003 in the rear, and 006 is placed in the front and to the right of 004. The numbering pattern continues from bottom to top through the first unit. The sequence is continued in the same manner, from the bottom shelf of the second unit until the end of the row is reached. It should be noted that the even numbers are to the front and the odd numbers are to the rear, so that front or rear positions can be readily determined by the number.

Row-Unit Method

A variation of this method is to divide the row into shelving units (numbered from the main aisle side), and the unit into spaces in the same fashion as previously described, except that the subdivisions (spaces) of each unit begin with 01 (see Figure 17.11). Thus each unit in a row has an identical box space number sequence, assuming each unit has the same box capacity. This method can further be refined to a row-unit-shelf-space arrangement.

Row-Unit-Shelf-Space Method

This method subdivides the shelf into a 1 through 6 or 12 box arrangement (see Figure 17.12). This is a flexible system, but it adds to the complexity

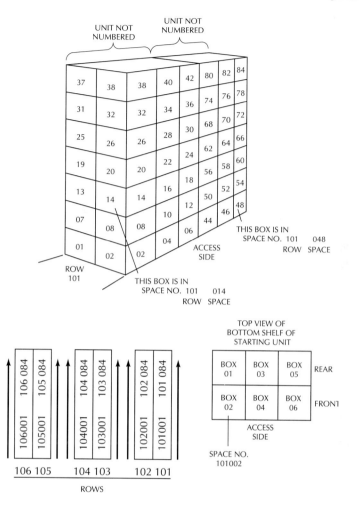

FIGURE 17.10 Row/Space–Number Method

and the length of the address number. As an example, what could be a seven-digit space number, becomes a nine-digit space number. Note the significance of the numbers.

101	02	10	12
Row	Unit	Shelf	Space

In either of these two variations, one of the advantages is that from the address, the searcher can determine if a ladder will be required, because sixth and seventh digits will always indicate how high the shelf is from the floor level. Also, the searcher can quickly determine if the space is toward the end, middle, or beginning of the aisle through observing the unit number, and the last two digits will indicate if the box is in a front or a rear space.

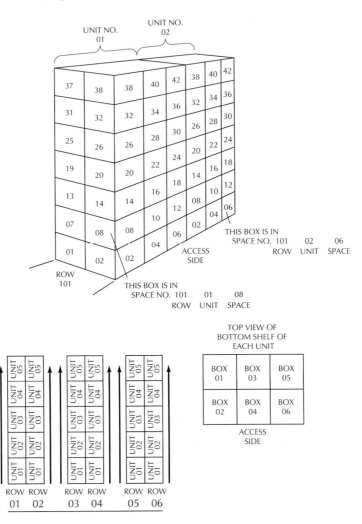

FIGURE 17.11 Row–Unit Method

Sequential Zigzag Method

For small records centers, a nonsignificant sequential numbering system can be used (see Figure 17.13). In this system the numbers are usually arranged unit by unit, from the bottom to the top and from the top to the bottom, from left to right, down one aisle and back up the next. This zigzag arrangement is used so that the number before and the number after are never more than a step or two away. However, it does have disadvantages: It fails to give the approximate location of the space since its numbers have no significance other than sequencing. Also, it hinders search efficiency because it lacks the repetitive pattern of numbering with the rows.

Oversized Material

One problem that is common to all systems is the occasional need to store oversized cartons or volumes that do not lend themselves to a uniform numbering system. This problem is solved rather simply if a row-unit-shelf-space arrangement is used. A code can be assigned in lieu of the box number to indicate the entire shelf. Another way to handle the situation is to assign to the package the first number of the space it occupies and to blank out the rest. Many records managers simply reserve a certain area for nonstandard material and use a separate system that is compatible with their main stack area.

STAFF REQUIREMENTS

It is not easy to estimate the staff needs of a records center before it is operational because the requirements will depend largely on the activity of the records. The generally accepted norm for inactive records is one search or less per month per file drawer (1 1/2 cubic feet). The emphasis should be placed on the word *less* because the rate of one search per 1 1/2 cubic feet of records per month is actually much too high if it prevails throughout the records center.

Although no conclusive and comprehensive production studies have been made, it is the experience of at least some records managers that one clerk can produce approximately 20,000 actions per year in addition to accession and disposal duties. Thus, hypothetically, a 50,000-cubic-foot records center could be staffed by two clerks and a supervisor. Although this rule of thumb cannot be applied to every organization, it is reliable enough for initial staffing purposes if the records in the center are truly inactive. There are exceptions to the norm for inactive records. For example, some types of businesses and organizations have an exceptionally high volume of records with a low reference rate. In this case, the search rate per cubic foot will be less, possibly requiring fewer clerks.

Another factor that relates directly to staff requirements is the physical arrangement of the records center. Sometimes there is a tendency to be preoccupied with economizing in equipment and space at the expense of added labor. Actually labor is far more expensive than equipment or space in a records center, and this fact should be considered when high-rise shelving, double units, triple units, or multiple-layer carton stacking is contemplated. These methods, while economizing in space and equipment, add time and motion to records center actions. They should be considered in light of increased labor costs. If increased time and motion result in the need for an additional employee, it may be better to use lower shelving or single units or to have one shelf for each layer of cartons. The question of space and equipment costs versus labor costs is left to the judgment of the records manager.

Still another factor that must be considered is the union agreement. If the clerks are members of a labor union, certain restrictions may be placed on their duties, thereby creating a need for additional personnel. Union agreements should be discussed with the labor relations officer before making final plans for personnel requirements. It is desirable to diversify the duties and work assignments of clerks as much as possible to gain maximum use. The supervisor, too, should have productive as well as supervisory duties, if union agreements permit it.

COMMERCIAL RECORDS CENTERS

Early in the planning process, one should investigate the feasibility of using a commercial records center, regardless of the size of the organization. A commercial records center can be a substitute for, or annex to, an in-house operation. Most large cities have at least one commercial records center. A commercial records center is professionally supervised and staffed, and therefore can provide service tailored to the organization without the immediate supervision of the records manager. Of

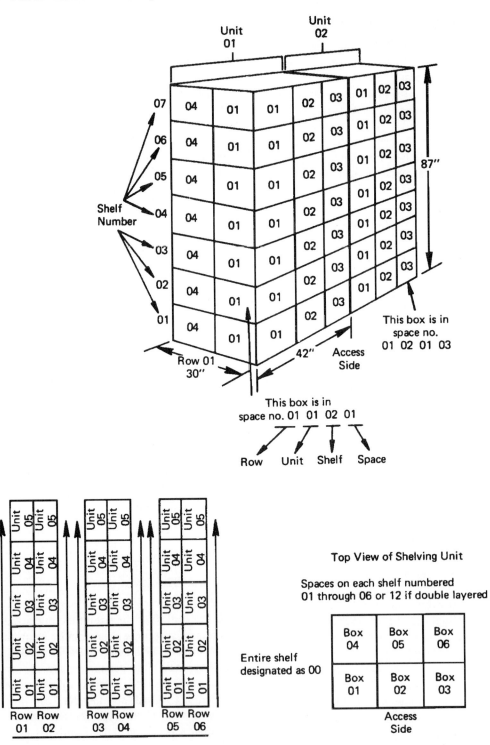

FIGURE 17.12 Row–Unit–Shelf–Space Method

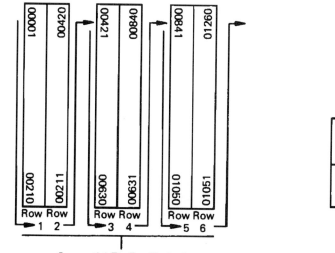

Sequential Zig Zag Method

Top View of Bottom Shelf of First Unit		
Box 01	Box 03	Box 05
Box 02	Box 04	Box 06

Access Side

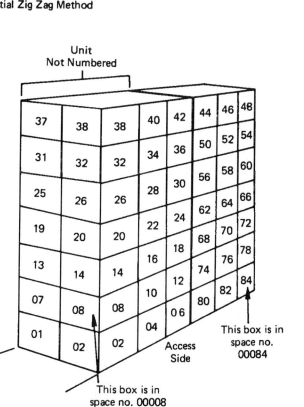

FIGURE 17.13 Sequential Zigzag Method

course, coordinating efforts are still required, but the records manager need not be present at the facility.

Choosing a Commercial Records Center

Factors that should be considered in selecting a commercial records center are:

- The quality, reliability, efficiency, and integrity of management and staff.
- The charges for space and service.
- Adaptability to your organization's needs.
- Accessibility and security.

Quality of Staff and Management. The first consideration is probably the most important, because even an in-house operation would fail unless its staff was competent and dedicated. Several references from the records center's clients should be obtained. In addition, the records manager should speak with colleagues and other users of commercial records centers.

Charges for Space and Service. Prices for space and services are competitive among most commercial records centers within a given geographical area. But a commercial records center that is far from large metropolitan areas may have an edge on space and labor prices. Labor may be charged on a flat-fee-per-action basis, on a contract basis (which provides for a determined number of actions), or on a time-spent basis at so much per hour. The last method is economical and equitable, provided the integrity of the center is beyond question. Space prices can be quoted on either a per-cubic-foot basis or on a per-square-foot basis if a private area is required. In order to avoid budget overruns, it is wise to investigate closely all transaction fees and other possible hidden costs.

Adaptability. Most commercial records centers are highly adaptable to the client's needs. The commercial records center should provide the following: 24-hour service, reproduction capabilities, teletype service, facsimile transmission, and bar code facilities as well as temperature and humidity controls.

Accessibility and Security. The center must be accessible by public carrier, for records must be shipped to it and retrievals made from it. In addition, it should provide good security. Most professionally managed commercial record centers provide as much security as possible for their locale. Some facilities are underground and are impervious, for the most part, to natural disaster and damage. This type of installation provides excellent protection for valuable and vital records.

Transportation Costs

Most frequently, transportation of the records is either provided by the organization's own vehicles or by the commercial records center. However, if an out-of-town commercial records center is contemplated, the distance factor must be considered. Distance involves two major considerations: the cost of transportation and the time element for retrieval. The cost of transportation is bidirectional in that there are costs involved in shipping the records to the out-of-town records center and costs in retrieval and possibly return of the records. The most economical method of transporting the records to the center is to ship in trailer loads, if the volume warrants this type of shipment. A 40-foot trailer will hold about 1,000 cubic feet of records, and when the trailer is shipped via a railroad flat car, the cost per cubic foot, even for distances as far as 500 miles or more, can be very reasonable. Rail and trucking rates can be obtained from corporate transportation specialists. To ship in trailer-load volumes, it is normally necessary to accumulate records and to ship on an annual or semi-annual basis.

Regardless of the quantity of the records that are regularly shipped, the transportation costs must be considered as part of the storage costs. Transportation charges can be offset if the storage space costs are lower out of town than they are locally and if the retention period is of sufficient length. As an example, if local storage costs are $3 per cubic foot per year, out-of-town storage costs per year are $1.50 per cubic foot, and transportation costs $1.50 per cubic foot, the records must be retained for a period of one year to pay for the cost of the transportation. Each year thereafter would show a savings of $1.50 per cubic foot for records stored at the out-of-town facility. Conversely, a lesser differential in storage space costs or a shorter retention period could make out-of-town storage unfeasible.

There are also transportation costs involved in making retrievals, but these costs are so variable that it is difficult to anticipate them with accuracy. If the records reference rate is very low, retrieval transportation costs would probably be of little significance. At the same time, a very high reference rate may not necessarily present inordinate transportation costs. For example, if a re-

quest for 100 paid vouchers was made on a given day, the entire 100 vouchers could very likely be shipped in a single carton for as little as $5, or 5 cents per record. If a single retrieval happened to be a 10-pound ledger, however, shipping might cost from $4 to $5. So the nature of the records and the patterns of retrieval must be taken into account.

It should be understood also that distance and rates are not always in direct proportion to one another; beyond a certain point, distance is no longer an economic factor. Distance does become a major factor if retrievals must be made in less than 24 hours. Most express services can normally deliver a package within 24 hours, if the distance does not exceed 800 miles.

Whether the commercial records center is local or out of town, there is always the additional expense of preparing records for shipment and the

FIGURE 17.14 Commercial Records Center Schedule of Charges

1. Monthly storage charge per cubic foot.

    Main center

Under 1,000 cubic feet:	25 cents
1,000 to 5,000 cubic feet:	20 cents
Over 5,000 cubic feet:	Price on request

    Special vault

Under 1,000 cubic feet:	50 cents
1,000 to 5,000 cubic feet:	40 cents
Over 5,000 cubic feet:	Price on request

2. Receiving, indexing, and handling: One time cost at $1 per cubic foot

3. Regular reference: $2 per file or cubic foot up to $15, then hourly rate ($15)

4. Refile, returns, and interfile: $2 per file or cubic foot up to $15, then the hourly rate ($15)

5. Destruction or removal charge: $1 per cubic foot

6. Pickup and delivery (small quantities): $15 per work hour, plus 25 cents per mile

7. Additional services (repacking, cataloging, and other special assignments): $15 per hour

8. Minimum charges: $20 per month for billing under $100 quarterly

expense of accessioning them at the commercial facility. Figure 17.14 shows a schedule of charges of a commercial records center in a large metropolitan area.

The commercial records center, whether it is blocks away or miles away, provides a valuable service; but the needs and recordkeeping costs of each organization must be analyzed to determine the economic and operational feasibility of using one.

SUMMARY

A records center is a facility used for organized storage and retrieval of inactive records. It is an effective method for retaining records and reduces expenses for office space and equipment. Inactive records are generally housed in standard-size cardboard cartons, which are placed on shelving 10 feet or more in height.

Planning for a records center requires an estimate of the volume of records to be stored; the estimate is obtained from the records inventory. In addition, a long-range estimate of space needs must be made.

The facility selected for the records center must have suitable temperature and humidity conditions; must be adequately protected from fire, water, and vermin damage; and must be secure from vandalism, sabotage, and other dangers. The company-owned records center should be at least within commuting distance of the offices it serves. It should have adequate office space in addition to space for processing, referencing, staging, disposing, and loading of records for shipment. A detailed and scaled layout should be made before shelving is purchased or installed.

A very common space-numbering method is known as a row/space-number system, but other systems have also been used successfully. Staff requirements vary, depending on the activity of the records. As a rule of thumb, one clerk can handle 20,000 records center actions per year.

Commercial records centers may be considered in lieu of, or as an adjunct to, a company-owned records center. If the commercial records center is properly managed, distance may not be a major factor.

QUESTIONS FOR DISCUSSION

1. Why is it less costly to store records in a records center than it is to file them in cabinets?

2. What is the difference between storing records and filing records?

3. How does an archive differ from a records center?

4. How are space requirements for a records center determined?

5. What are ideal temperature and humidity ranges for a records center? Under what circumstances must the temperature and humidity in a records center be controlled?

6. What security precautions should be taken when planning a records center?

7. What factors should be considered when deciding on the location for a records center?

8. Why should an administration area be provided in a records center?

9. In planning a records center, why is it necessary to provide each of the following:

   a. A processing area

   b. A reference area

   c. A staging area

   d. A disposal area

10. What is the size of the standard records center storage carton? Why is this a desirable size?

11. When should nonstandard or special records center storage containers be considered for use?

12. Why is it desirable to use 32- by 42-inch steel shelving in a records center?

13. What is a transfer case? What are the disadvantages of using transfer cases?

14. When planning the layout of a records center, what factors must be taken into consideration for each of the following?

    a. Aisle clearance
    b. Shelf arrangement
    c. Lighting
    d. Space utilization

15. Explain the differences between the following space-numbering systems:

    a. Row/space-number method
    b. Row-unit method
    c. Sequential zigzag method

16. What factors should be considered when determining staff requirements for a records center?

17. What is a commercial records center? Under what circumstances is it wise to consider the use of commercial records centers?

PROJECTS

1. You are the assistant records manager in a large organization that is considering the construction of a new records center. The records manager has instructed you to gather information that will help to prepare a report on existing records center facilities in the United States. Prepare an annotated bibliography of the five best periodical articles you can find on this subject.

2. You have recently been placed in charge of the records in a small company with a total of 14 employees. The company has been in business for 37 years. All the records over five years old are packed in cardboard boxes and stored in various places throughout the building—some in the basement, some in the attic, and some in closets. A 20- by 20-foot windowless room near the main office has just been made available for inactive records storage. Draw a plan of the proposed layout for the new records center.

3. Prepare a questionnaire to be sent to all members of your industry-specific group in the Association of Records Managers and Administrators (ARMA International) for the purpose of gathering information on records center physical facilities.

4. You have been asked to address the Twin Cities chapter of Professional Secretaries International on the topic "Planning an Inactive Records Storage Room for Small Companies." Prepare an outline for your 30-minute speech.

CASE PROBLEM

Your organization has decided to outsource as much of its administrative services work as possible. The vice-president of administrative services has asked you to obtain a cost estimate from a local commercial records center for accession, storage, retrieval, and disposition of all records currently held in the in-house records center. If this proposal is acceptable, the records manager will be responsible only for coordination, contract administration, and policy. You review your annual production statistics and find the following:

records, but for files such as subject correspondence files, claims files, and personnel files the span of time on each file will probably vary greatly within a carton. In this case, usually the oldest date in a carton and the most recent date are shown to give some indication of the age of the files. This, however, *cannot* be used for disposal purposes, but the batch grouping can.

A temporary transfer number is assigned to and written on the carton by the transmitting office. It is used only for identification purposes until the carton is assigned a permanent records center space number. The temporary number on the carton is matched with that number shown on the transfer list when it is accessioned.

Transfer Approval

When the transfer list is received in the records management office or the records center, the staff reviews it for completeness, continuity, and eligibility. The completeness check involves making sure that all records on the transfer list are physically accounted for, that the correct name of the record is shown, and that the subdetail is sufficient for retrieval. The continuity check entails reviewing past accessions of that records series to verify that all prior records have been received (i.e., the oldest records should be accessioned first). The eligibility check involves checking the record items on the transfer list against the retention schedule to determine if they are eligible for records center storage. It is for this reason that many organizations require the retention schedule number to be shown on the transfer list. Listing this number not only facilitates checking in the records center, but it also serves as a reminder to the sending office that only authorized records may be stored.

Pickups

When the transfer list has been approved, the shipment is scheduled for pickup. Pickup procedures will vary for each organization; they depend on the location of the records center, union agree-

ments, and organizational structure. Frequently, the mail or messenger department will handle the pickup, but sometimes it is done by records center personnel. The frequency of pickups will depend on the volume and distance. If the records center is located in the same building as the offices, it can be done on a daily basis. If it is some distance away, a truck will be required, and pickup will probably be scheduled on a weekly or semi-monthly basis. The transmitting office should be notified of the pickup date and any changes that are made in the schedule.

Space Assignments

When the records are received in the records center, they are normally placed in a staging or processing area where they are checked against the transfer lists. If all cartons shown on the transfer list are accounted for, the shipment is ready for space assignment.

Space numbers are normally assigned to, and written on, the carton in the processing area. To accomplish this, the records center must have a complete and current register of space vacancies. Without such a register, space assignment would be practically impossible. Even if all vacancies were visible, a physical inventory of available space would be very time-consuming and inefficient.

A manual register of available spaces can be maintained in several ways, all of them similar. The manual systems described here can also be computerized. The principle of all of these systems is the perpetual inventory. With this system, as spaces become vacant they are added to the register, and as they are filled they are removed. The system varies according to the format of the register. Some registers consist of a page of plain paper for each row in the records center. As a space becomes vacant, the space number is written on the sheet; as the space is filled, the number is scratched off. This is perhaps the most basic method and can be used with success when the vacancy rate is relatively low. However, if there are a large number of open spaces, searching for a

Dept	Accounting	RECORDS CENTER INDEX and TRANSFER LIST	Control Number 950
Sect	Payables		
Page	1 of 1		

Box No.	Description of Rercord(s)	Date From	Date To	Record Center Space Number	Title Code	Function Code	Retention Period
	PAID DRAFTS	Jan	Jun		179	55b	6 yrs
1	00001 - 01578			10014			
2	01579 - 02852			10015			
3	02853 - 04215			10016			
4	04216 - 07514			10017			
5	07515 - 08950			10018			
6	08951 - 10450			10019			
7	10451 - 11917			10020			
8	11918 - 14329			10021			
9	14330 - 16744			10022			
10	16745 - 18009			10023			
11	18010 - 21710			10030			
12	21711 - 23002			10031			
13	23003 - 25119			10032			
14	25120 - 27900			10033			
15	27901 - 30005			10034			
16	30006 - 31074			10035			
17	31075 - 32224			10036			
18	32225 - 34015			10037			
19	34016 - 36310			10038			
20	36311 - 37450			10039			
21	REPORTS OF DRAFTS ISSUED A to L	Jan	Dec	10040	210	55d	2 yrs
22	M to Z			10041			

For Storage in:	☒ General Record Center	☐ Security Record Center

Name of Person Transmitting Records *John Doe*	Phone No. 3353	Room No. 2010	Location Fall Winds	Date 1-3-1994

FIGURE 18.1   Records Center Index and Transfer List

					DEPT.	052 Accounting

RECORDS CENTER CONTROL CARD

SECT.	Payables
RECORD TITLE CODE	052-179

Function Code	55b	Record Title	PAID DRAFTS	COMPANY NAME XYZ Company
Company Retention	6 yrs	Also Known As	Cash Vouchers	

Dates	Transfer Control Number	Sub Detail	Space Number	Dates	Transfer Control Number	Sub Detail	Space Number
JAN–JUN 94	950	00001–01578	10014	JUL–DEC X4	954	65075–68921	40402
		01579–02852	10015			68922–74011	40401
		02853–04215	10016			74012–77981	40401
		04216–07514	10017				
		07515–08950	10018				
		08951–10450	10019				
		10451–11917	10020				
		11918–14329	10021				
		14330–16744	10022				
		16745–18009	10023				
		18010–21710	10030				
		21711–23002	10031				
		23003–25119	10032				
		25120–27900	10033				
		27901–30005	10034				
		30006–31074	10035				
		31075–32224	10036				
		32225–34015	10037				
		34016–36310	10038				
		36311–37450	10039				
JUL–DEC 94	954	37451–38319	40221				
		38320–39441	40222				
		39442–40317	40223				
		40318–42211	40224				
		42212–44016	40225				
		44017–45098	40226				
		45099–46980	40227				
		46981–47889	40228				
		47890–48942	40229				
		48943–49820	40230				
		49821–59052	40400				
		59053–65074	40401				

FIGURE 18.2 Records Center Control Card

particular number could be very time-consuming. A more efficient method is to list all space numbers for a row in sequence on a page. These space listings can be computer-generated using a personal computer and printout. As the space becomes vacant, the number is checked with pencil. As it is filled, the check is erased. This method has the added advantages of placing the numbers in serial order and of showing vacancies in serial order. If all rows contain the same number of spaces, the preparation of the basic form is quite simple, for one form will serve for all rows. However, if the rows vary in the number of spaces, the form must be altered to suit the capacity of each row.

Another method of maintaining a space inventory is to write a vacancy number on a 3- by 5-inch card and to file the card in numeric order. Cards are not maintained for filled spaces. When assignments are made, the cards are simply removed and no search is required. The cards are then taken to the processing area and fastened to the carton. When the cartons are destroyed, the cards are removed and refiled as a space vacancy. Other variations of these methods, including the use of computer databases, can be devised to meet the needs of specific organizations.

Sections of a records center should not be reserved for the exclusive use of a particular department or office. Allocation should be random, and assignment made on the basis of availability. By assigning space on an availability basis, every single cubic foot can be used. However, some discretion should be used in making space assignments. Records that appear likely to be more inactive than average are assigned to less accessible spaces, such as the higher shelves and rear spaces. Records that have more valuable information may be assigned to certain areas where proper protection is afforded. In addition, when possible, the records of the same series should be kept together, because this simplifies disposals and references.

After the space assignments have been completed, the records are placed on the shelf whose number corresponds to the number on the carton.

If the records are not contained in cartons, perhaps because of irregular size, the space number is written on the records as they are placed on the shelves. Finally, the space number is written on the transfer list adjacent to the appropriate item as the records are placed on the shelves.

MANUAL INDEXING METHODS

Because a records center may serve more than a hundred different offices and contain more than a thousand separate series of records, a good indexing system is essential. The most common manual systems are the *control card system* and the *transfer list system*. There is a third system that combines elements of these two; we will call it the *control card–transfer list system*.

Control Card System

The control card system consists of a ledger sheet or card for *each records series* held in the records center (see Figure 18.2). These cards are kept in departmental (retention schedule) order in either alphabetic order by records series title, or numeric order by title code. Each transaction (box or space number) shown on the transfer list is posted to these cards. If the transfer list contains 22 boxes, there will be 22 entries on the control card. This operation involves a complete transcription. The transfer list (see Figure 18.1) should include all data necessary for retrieval, such as the date span, the space numbers for each carton, and the subdetail description of the record. Although this system requires the additional task of transcribing, it is still highly efficient, provided transcription errors are minimal. As a precaution against such errors, the transfer lists are usually retained in departmental order. With this system, the burden of locating the space numbers is placed on the records center staff.

A search of the index is conducted by (1) locating the control card for the records series requested, (2) searching subdetail for the proper space number, and (3) retrieving the records.

Transfer List System

With the transfer list system, both the department and the records center maintain copies of the transfer list. These lists are searched to secure the space number assigned to a given record. This system works reasonably well if the transfer list is limited to one series per sheet. If more than one series is listed on the same transfer list, searching becomes progressively more difficult as the lists accumulate. The system's chief advantage is that no transcription from the list to the control card is involved (see Figure 18.1).

A search of the index is conducted by (1) scanning copies of all transfer lists submitted to the records center for prior accessions, (2) locating the correct space number by cursory review, and (3) retrieving the record.

Control Card–Transfer List System

The control card–transfer list system is a marriage of the first two systems. Basically, this system involves maintaining an index to transfer lists that contain one or more series of records. The steps in this procedure are as follows:

1. Maintain a control card or ledger sheet for each series of records, as is done in the control card system.
2. Assign each transfer list an identifying number as it is received.
3. Post to the control card from the transfer list only the date range of that series and the *transfer list* number. This eliminates posting all subdetail and space numbers. (See Figure 18.3.)

Search of the index is done as follows:

1. Scan the record series control card to find the date range and corresponding transfer list number.
2. Retrieve the appropriate transfer list, which is in numeric order by department.
3. Scan the appropriate transfer list for specific record identification and space number.

The advantages of this system are that it reduces transcribing to one entry per record series for any one transfer list and still provides a systematic method for locating the proper transfer list when retrieval is required. Because all retention requirements may be shown on the control cards, they can be used to determine specific destruction eligibility.

SEARCH AND CHARGE-OUT PROCEDURES

Stack areas should be closed to everyone except authorized records center personnel. Without this restriction, controls and security would be impossible in many areas. If the records center is located within the same building as the offices it serves, it is possible that some work-in-file activity may be allowed for a limited number of outside personnel. If proper instruction and a watchful eye are provided, there may be no serious problems; however, it is best to discourage permitting unauthorized personnel into the stack area.

Record Requests

Users of the records center may be required or encouraged to request records in writing on a prescribed form and to provide space numbers through an index search previously described in order to reduce work for the records center staff.

RECORDS CENTER RELATIVE INDEX			DEPT.	052 Accounting	
			SECT.	Payables	
			RECORD TITLE CODE	*052-179*	

Function Code	55b	Record Title	PAID DRAFTS		
Company Retention	6 yrs	Also Known As	Cash Vouchers		

Dates	Company	Sub Detail	Transfer Control Number	Dates	Company	Sub Detail	Transfer Control Number
JUL-DEC 90	*XYZ*	*50152-95000*	*650*	*JAN-DEC 94*	*AOK*	*0002-8914*	*952*
JAN-JUN 91	*XYZ*	*00001-48150*	*704*	*JAN-JUN 94*	*UOP*	*0501-0982*	*953*
JUL-DEC 91	*XYZ*	*48151-97072*	*744*				
JAN-JUN 92	*XYZ*	*00001-54010*	*801*				
JUL-DEC 92	*XYZ*	*55011-92017*	*892*				
JAN-JUN 93	*XYZ*	*00001-42110*	*907*				
JUL-DEC 93	*XYZ*	*42111-78529*	*925*				
JAN-JUN 94	*XYZ*	*00001-37450*	*950*				
JUL-DEC 94	*XYZ*	*37451-79080*	*954*				

FIGURE 18.3 Control Card–Transfer List System

If the requests or charge-out forms are prepared in the requesting office, the time spent will not be significant and can be absorbed without overtime or added personnel. But if all form preparation and space-number lookup is performed in the records center, the workload may require hiring additional personnel. While clerical time required to complete the form is not significant, lookup of the space number in the indexes, can usually be accomplished more easily by the department owning and requesting the record. Other managers will argue that the records center exists essentially to provide reference service and should therefore have a large enough staff to perform that service. The system used is a matter of management policy, which each records manager will have to decide. In many records centers, telephone requests or electronic mail are encouraged, particularly if there is significant distance involved. Fast service is good service, and anything that will expedite information retrieval should be used, including facsimile transmission, on-line computer systems, teletype, or telephone, as long as it is economically feasible. The charge-out form is frequently used to make a request for a record. If the request is received by telephone, the form is prepared by the person taking the request. Otherwise, it is prepared by the requestor. In a large records center, it often becomes necessary to have requestors furnish a personal identification number to ensure that records are not charged out to the wrong individual.

Charge-Out System

A fundamental control in records management is the *charge-out system.* In essence, it is simply making a record of a loaned record. The principle of this system is commonly used in many occupational areas other than records management. For example, it is used in lending libraries, equipment rental firms, and banks. In the case of records management, a document is being loaned and the charge-out form is the record of that loan.

The charge-out system is used (1) to keep track of a record while it is outside the records center, (2) to ensure its return, and (3) to provide follow-up analysis. A simple charge-out method is to record the name of the requestor, the record identification, and the date on a cardboard form. The form is then filed in the container in place of the record withdrawn.

Usually, however, the charge-out is a snap-out form, completed in triplicate. The form must contain at least the name, telephone number, and location of the requestor; the name and full description of the record; the space number; and the date. The first copy replaces the record in file, the second copy is attached to the record as a routing slip, and the third is placed in a suspense file for follow-up, if required. Additional copies may be used for reference analysis of various sorts and for other purposes (see Figure 18.4).

Considerable search time can be saved if, instead of making special trips to the stack area for each request, the requests are accumulated and put in space-number order, thus reducing travel time to and from the stack area. However, turnaround time and frequency of requests may not permit this batching.

When the records are located, the routing copy of the charge-out form is attached to the record, transmitting it to the requestor, and the charge-out portion is placed in the carton in lieu of the record being removed; it should be visible from the top of the box. Because the form is often quite small, it should be attached to a sheet of cardboard, 8 1/2 by 11 inches in size, so that it can be seen in the carton. If the record cannot be located, a "Not in File" notation, the date, and the initials of the searcher are written on the request form, which is returned to the requestor.

If the record is charged out when the search is made, the name of the party to whom the record is charged, the date of the charge, the date of the search, and the searcher's initials or number are written on the request form and returned to the sender. It is a matter of policy whether records center personnel or the requestor contacts the party who has the record. Generally, it is better for the requestor to make the contact, because he or she knows how long the file will be needed or what information is needed. In any event, the charge-out in the file should be flagged so that the second requestor will receive it when it is returned. If the original holder of the record gives it to a second party, the records center should be notified, and a new charge-out should be made to the second party.

In the case of a charge-out or a "Not in File" search, the reference analysis portion of the search request form should be retained in the records center file for future analysis of reference activity, just as though the record had been retrieved. Also, it is usually advisable to notify the requestor immediately by telephone or fax if the records cannot be located or if they are charged out.

Deliveries

Frequency of deliveries depends on the distance and turnaround time requirements. Because deliveries are smaller in volume than pickups, interoffice messenger service may normally be used on a daily basis. Sometimes, requestors will state "Call when record is ready." In this case, the requestor will pick the record up personally.

Follow-Up Procedures

Most records are returned to the records center within a week or two after they are charged out. However, there are always a few that are not returned until the holder is reminded that he or she should do so. Usually, the reminder is a form

RECORD CENTER CHARGE OUT					
FORWARD RECORD TO	NAME *JOHN DOE*		ROOM *200*	TELEPHONE *2236*	
	DEPARTMENT/SECTION *ACCTG, PAYABLES*		DATE *2-1-93*		TO ROUTE

DESCRIPTION OF RECORD

RECORD TITLE	*Paid Draft*
SUB-DESCRIPTION	*12141*
COMPANY NAME	*XYZ Co*
DATE OF RECORD	*MAY 3 1993*
SPACE NUMBER	*10021* ☐ PERMANENT WITHDRAWAL

BELOW FOR RECORD CENTER USE ONLY

☑ RECORD ATTACHED	☐ NOT IN FILE			
☐ NOT IN FILE-CHARGED TO	NAME	ROOM	DATE	
DATE SEARCHED	*2-1-93*		SEARCHER #	*W200*
DATE REFILED			SEARCHER #	

TO ROUTE

TO RECORD CENTER

Room 10, Basement

CHECK THIS BOX

☐

(LEAVE FORM ATTACHED)

FIGURE 18.4 Record Request and Charge-Out Form

letter to which the suspense copy of the charge-out is attached.

The suspense copy is filed in a tickler file in the records center office, at time of charge-out, usually to be called 30 to 60 days from the charge-out date. As records are returned, the follow-up or suspense copy is removed from the suspense file. On the final due date, the remaining cards are removed and attached to overdue notifications, which are sent to the holder of the record or the holder's immediate supervisor, depending upon policy. A photocopy of the notification form and attachment is often made so that a second follow-up can be done if the first one brings no results. If all else fails, a telephone call or personal visit may result in a return of the record.

If the holder of the record indicates that the record will be needed for an extended period of time, the suspense copy of the charge-out form should be refiled, and the whole process should be repeated. If the holder claims that the record has been returned, then a thorough search of the processing areas and the office areas should be made

as well as a second search in the stacks. If all these efforts fail to locate the record, a notation explaining the events should be made on the charge-out form in the stack file and the form should remain there until the record is returned. The suspense date for return of charge-outs should be realistic; a time period that is too short will simply mean that more notifications are required than necessary. If a record is reactivated and remains in the office, a permanent withdrawal charge-out should remain in the file for as long as the series is retained in the records center.

REFILES AND INTERFILES

Although refiles and interfiles are quite similar, some differences should be noted. *Refiling* is the process of filing records that have been charged out. *Interfiling* is the placing of documents into containers that were previous accessioned in the records center.

The refiling process is somewhat faster and easier than the interfiling process because there is a charge-out form that directs the clerk to the proper place in the carton. When a record is refiled, the charge-out form should be removed from the carton and the routing slip should be detached from the record and matched with the charge-out to ensure correct refiling. This matching is very important: A misfile in the records center is extremely difficult to find because of its random space arrangement.

An interfile, on the other hand, poses several problems. First of all, an index search may be required to determine the correct space number, if that is not known. Secondly, the records center clerk must not only find the proper place in the carton to file the record, but must also be certain that space is available for the record. This latter point is not always easy to judge if some records are currently charged out of the carton. Because of the space problem, files sent to the records center should be complete when accessioned and interfiles should be discouraged.

If a carton is filled and records still remain to be filed, the records are placed in an overflow carton, which has its own space number. A cross-reference that refers the searcher to the overflow carton should be placed in the original carton. One overflow carton will usually serve the overflow of more than one records center carton. Thus documents in the overflow carton should be filed by the space number of the original carton, and the carton should be subdivided by guides indicating row numbers.

DISPOSALS FROM THE RECORDS CENTER

The records manager is the custodian of the records in the records center and not the owner. Therefore, the records may not be destroyed without the concurrence of the owner and those authorized to approve destruction. Although the records retention schedule indicates when a record will be eligible for destruction, there are many events, such as pending lawsuits, merger negotiations, hearings, and new laws and regulations, that might cause a hold order to be placed on the records. The final approval of the record owner limits pos-

sible premature destructions and also strengthens the confidence of the user in the records center. This procedure does not weaken the purpose or effectiveness of the retention schedule, but rather complements it. Without such approval, longer retention periods would probably be required because of uncertainty and the "just in case the record is needed" attitude that so often prevails.

Suspensions of the retention schedule should only be made when authorized by the law department or some corporate official. Technically, the owner of the document may for valid reasons recommend that the record be retained beyond the prescribed period. Although only a recommendation, this request is in most cases a valid reason to suspend the retention schedule.

DISPOSAL SYSTEM

Even though final approval is required of the owner, the records center initiates the destruction process. To do this effectively and efficiently, a system is needed.

The disposal process actually begins when the records are originally accessioned into the records center. As a part of this process, the future date of destruction is noted on the transfer list and one copy of the list is filed in a suspense file by the earliest destruction date shown. When that date arrives, the descriptive information on the records is transferred to a destruction authorization form either by attachment, transcription, computer, or photocopy. After the form is prepared, it is sent to the originator of the records transfer for approval to destroy. Figure 18.5 is a sample disposition authorization form.

If there is more than one destruction date shown on the transfer list filed in the suspense file, the records destroyed are crossed off that list after disposal and the transfer list is refiled by the next upcoming destruction date shown. In lieu of retyping the description on a destruction form, the transfer list can be converted to a destruction form by using a form overlay and an office copier.

Another system, which is based on the same principle, uses 5- by-8-inch cards that are filed by

---

RECORDS DISPOSITION AUTHORIZATION   NO. <u>80001</u>

Page <u>1</u> of <u>1</u>

☒ XYZ COMPANY   ☐ OTHER COMPANY _____

NAME & TITLE: <u>John Jones, Supv, Records Center</u>   DATE: ___<u>January 4,</u>_____ 19 <u>9-</u>

LOCATION: <u>Fall Winds Campus</u>   APPROVED: <u>*John Doe, Mgr Acctg*</u>
              (Signature of person responsible for records)

APPROVED: <u>*Gery Bishop, RM*</u>

The above individual is authorized and directed to destroy the following records:

APPROVED: <u>*SS P Kennedy*</u>
              Controller

FORM #	NO.	PERIOD FROM	TO	RETENTION SCHEDULE ITEM #
	Paid Drafts #50152 - 95000 //////NOTHING FOLLOWS/////	Jul 1 199-	Dec 31 199-	052-179

I disposed of records listed on this form by   ☐ Burning,   ☐ Shredding,   ☒ Salvage

Signature <u>*John Jones*</u>   Date <u>*Jan 10*</u>   19 <u>9-</u>

RETURN ORIGINAL FORM TO RECORDS MANAGEMENT OFFICE-ST. LOUIS AFTER DISPOSAL

FIGURE 18.5 Records Disposition Authorization Form

year and month. When a transfer list is received, the number assigned to the list (or its date and source) is transcribed onto the card. When the due date arrives, the card is pulled; it refers the records manager to the proper transfer list. The advantage of this system is that it eliminates filing the transfer list in the suspense file. A personal computer may serve the same purpose as the card file, using fairly common packaged software such as a calendar or date file. The file need contain only the transfer list number, so that it can be retrieved and converted to a disposition authorization form on a given date.

Authorization Form

When the destruction authorization is prepared, it is sent for approval to the office where the records originated. If some records are to be held for a longer period, the reason should be stated in writing, a new destruction date should be assigned, and these items should then be deleted from the authorization. When the authorization is returned to the records center, the space numbers covering those records approved for destruction should be listed separately on 3- by 5-inch cards and the cards should be arranged in numeric sequence. With these cards used as a pull list, the records are removed from the shelves and the appropriate card is attached to the carton with tape. The attached card can be used as a check to ensure that the proper carton has been removed.

After the accuracy check, the cards should be removed from the carton and filed in a space-availability file, if such is the system, or used to post entries on a space-availability register. Also, the appropriate entries on the records control card should be noted to indicate destruction, and deletions should be made in the indexing system used. Finally, the number of cubic feet destroyed should be recorded for future analysis and reporting, and a signed copy of the destruction authorization should be returned to the owner of the records.

Destruction Practices

When the records are removed from the shelves, they should be taken to a disposal staging area where they can be held until picked up for recycling, shredding, or incineration. It is important that the dealer furnish certificates of disposal and be bonded for performance. Some records managers have their own commercial-size shredders, but usually it is more economical to outsource this work.

It is usually the practice to dispose of the records cartons along with the records, as the value of the cartons does not warrant the expense of disassembly and they are frequently battered or marked by use and time. However, the use of high-quality cartons especially designed for easy assembly and disassembly and extended use may make reuse more economical than disposal. This factor, like so many in records management, requires individual evaluation and cost analysis.

STATISTICAL ANALYSIS

Statistical analysis is used frequently in records management and particularly in the management of records centers. It is primarily used in the records center for the analysis of reference activity and to project future space requirements so as to avoid unexpected out-of-space conditions.

Reference Analysis

Reference analysis, a valuable procedure in managing a records center, should be made at least annually. It should be made at other times when there is an obvious change in work flow patterns. This analysis will enable the records manager to know the following:

- How many references are made for any given records series.
- The age of the records that are being referenced.
- The number of records that cannot be located or charged out.
- Who uses the records center.
- When the records are used.
- How old records are when they cease to be used.
- Where high-activity records are located in the records center.

To make this analysis, statistics are accumulated on a per-action basis by filing a copy of the charge-out form in a reference analysis file or through computer data entry. This file is designed to accumulate data in a functional manner and may be arranged or sorted in one or more of the following ways.

1.   *By record series.* To determine the number of searches, the time span of the records searched, the number of "cannot finds" and charge-outs, and the source of the request for this records series.

2.   *By user or owner of the record.* To determine the types of records used, the age of the records used, the number and frequency of requests, and the number of follow-ups required by this user.

3.   *By date.* To determine the source of the requests and periods of high or low activity on a particular records series.

4.   *By space number.* To determine the high and low activity areas in the records center.

In addition to this reference analysis file, a work sheet can be prepared directly from the charge-out slips that are in the file. On a daily basis the clerks who conduct the searches can tally the number of searches per day, per month, and per year. This can produce an aggregate total or be analyzed by department, division, or unit. Figure 18.6 shows an annual and monthly breakdown of the number of searches by departmental user.

Projections of Space Needs

Most records centers show at least a gradual growth in volume due to hold orders, mergers, and increased business. As the demographer projects the population of the world, so must the records manager project the records "population"

FIGURE 18.6 Reference Analysis Report

Department	JAN	FEB	MAR	APR	MAY	JUN	JUL	AUG	SEP	OCT	NOV	DEC	TOT
Secretary - 01	0	0	0	0	0	1	0	2	0	0	3	0	6
Treasurer - 02	0	0	0	0	0	1	0	0	0	0	0	0	1
Executive -10-11-12-13	42	5	6	3	4	7	4	1	4	9	41	15	141
Profit Planning 07-08-09	1	3	16	10	4	1	1	16	1	6	2	0	61
Info & Con Sys 15-16-17	0	0	0	1	2	4	3	1	0	0	3	2	16
Law - 20-21-22-23-24	10	22	13	10	11	4	6	7	8	15	6	6	118
Operating - 30 - 43	27	33	23	9	12	26	12	8	13	20	19	11	213
Traffic Analysis - 44	2	1	0	0	0	1	3	0	0	3	0	0	10
Traffic Commerce - 45	14	18	17	10	4	7	10	3	10	5	3	4	105
Traffic Corresp - 46	0	0	0	0	0	0	0	0	1	0	26	0	27
Traffic Divisions - 47	40	28	23	31	12	8	17	21	37	30	21	15	285
Traffic Rates - 48	136	185	254	154	238	224	150	153	170	148	196	129	2137
Traffic - Sales - 49	0	0	0	0	0	0	0	0	0	0	0	0	0
Pur & Matls - 55	47	24	39	19	12	21	19	30	8	9	347	15	590
Truck Lines - 59	21	6	6	4	14	4	2	26	7	59	3	2	154
Missouri Imp Co - 60	0	0	0	0	1	0	0	0	0	0	0	0	1
APT Co - 61	8	2	0	1	197	1	2	0	3	9	19	3	245
C&EI Sec & Treas 03 - 04	11	0	0	0	0	0	0	0	0	0	0	0	11
Auditing - 65	788	1877	1590	421	1441	340	893	2724	1072	947	1768	1645	15506
Budget - 66	37	94	2	13	0	1	9	72	0	1	0	0	229
Fin Acctg - 67	0	0	0	3	0	0	0	0	0	3	0	0	6
General Accts - 68	0	1	1	1	7	3	1	0	0	1	0	0	15
Statistics - 69	0	0	0	0	8	3	0	24	0	0	0	0	35
Taxes - 70	416	517	8	379	1512	7	10	135	5	0	26	115	3130
Disb - Bills - 74	27	14	14	12	15	13	9	17	26	13	13	8	181
Disb - Matl - 75	0	2	5	0	0	0	0	0	0	1	0	0	8
Disb Payables - 76	995	20	26	169	49	65	314	583	56	242	55	43	3617
Dist Payroll - 77	1	1	19	4	2	4	1	2	11	4	1	0	50
Frt Rev Acctg - 80	67	71	54	91	87	85	91	79	110	67	77	52	931
Regional Station - 85	17	38	39	29	37	78	50	66	44	36	34	33	561
Passenger - 88	0	0	0	0	0	0	0	0	0	0	0	0	0
Mail Acctg - 89	0	0	0	0	0	0	0	0	1	0	0	0	1
ECE - 90	110	60	133	187	118	187	113	120	159	155	143	79	564
Car Accounting	17	4	8	18	0	1	1	10	0	0	1	2	62
TOTAL FOR MONTH	2834	3026	2296	1579	3788	1098	2721	4100	1746	1783	2807	2179	29957

of the records center. Waiting until there is no more space indicates a failure in advanced planning. At that point, the records center cannot accept any new accessions, and consequently, records transfers back up in the offices and create chaos in the office records systems.

Statistical analysis for this situation is primarily concerned with accession and disposal ratios. If the volume of records taken into the records center exceeds disposals from the records center, sooner or later, if nothing changes, the records center will be filled to capacity. The challenge is to determine when this is likely to happen and to prevent it. To estimate the full date, it is necessary to look at typical accession and disposal volumes from the past few years and apply those historical numbers to the future. If the full date appears to be a year or more in the future, plans should be made immediately to provide a remedy. If it is less than that, you are in an emergency situation and action should be initiated as soon as possible to eliminate or reduce the problem. Possible solutions to the problem include:

1. Review the retention schedule to try to reduce retention periods to provide for additional disposals.
2. Review the hold-order file to see if some of the records being held beyond normal retention periods can be destroyed.
3. Perform a reference analysis to determine high-volume, low-reference records that may be considered for a reduced retention period or off-site storage.
4. Contract with a commercial records center to provide a quick and inexpensive solution, particularly for hold-order records or other high-volume, low-reference records.
5. Look into additional in-house space through expansion or a larger records center. This is the least desirable alternative, but it may be necessary.

INTRACENTER TRANSFERS

Once records are accessioned into the records center, it is generally best to leave their space assignment number unchanged. Changes sometimes become necessary, however, because of unexpected reference activity, the threat of water damage, facility modification, transfers to a commercial records center, or some other reason. When this occurs, all indexes, such as control cards, transfer lists, the space registry, and the cartons themselves, must be altered to reflect the new space numbers. This pebble-in-the-pond effect can create a stifling work load, so changes should be made only under the most urgent circumstances. Changing the space numbers on the various indexes is not only time-consuming, but is often difficult unless assisted by other indexes.

If the system is computerized, a listing of the records being moved can easily be provided in space-number order together with descriptions of the records. With this listing, the new space number can be written adjacent to the old on the listing as the carton is placed on the shelf. At the same time, the space number written on the carton should be changed to the new space number. Later, the new space number can be entered into the computer database to update the system. In the meantime, the temporary listing in old space-number order can be used as an index from the old number to the new for search purposes.

If the transferred carton has the department name, record title, transfer number, and space number written on the outside of the box, as required by many organizations, that information together with the new space number can be entered onto a transfer list as the records are being accessioned into the new space. The old number should also be noted on the list so that other indexes can be updated later.

If neither of the above situations exists—completely labeled cartons or a computerized system—then it is necessary to identify the records and their owners. From this information, the transfer list used to transmit the records to the records center can be located and used to accession the cartons to the new space. At this point, the reaccessioning procedures are the same.

To avoid duplication, the emptied spaces should not be reused until all indexes containing the old space-number listings are changed to the new.

MOVING A RECORDS CENTER

Moving a records center involves not only transfering the records from one place to another but also reassigning space numbers. When an entire records center is relocated, the changing space-number assignments is much more critical and time-consuming than with intracenter transfers. This is so because the volume of records is greater and also because *all* search, refile, and interfile activities are affected.

If a straight sequential numbering system is used in the old records center and will be used in the new, there is no space assignment problem because the cartons are simply moved to their like-numbered space in the new center.

Space-Number Conversion Table

If new space numbers are to be assigned in the new center, a table should be developed that will serve as an index to convert the old number to the new. In addition, this table must be completed as the records are moved so that the new records center can be completely operational upon occupancy. The table should list the old carton number in numeric sequence and, adjacent to it, the new number. This is done as the cartons are placed on the new shelves, with the result that the conversion table index is created at the exact time the change of space actually occurs. From this table, indexes can be changed and new locations determined quickly by referring to the old number to determine the new.

If new shelves are to be installed and numbered, this should be done prior to the transfer of the records to minimize interruption. If the old shelves are to be moved with the records and reinstalled, it will be necessary to have a temporary staging area until the records can be moved to the new shelves. This can be done in phases, so that only a portion of the records are in the staging process at one time. For example, the contents of ten rows of shelves can be staged on pallets as the shelving housing them is partially disassembled, moved to the new records center, placed in its proper place, and numbered according to the new plan. When the shelving is ready, the staged records can be moved and accessioned. The process repeats the procedure until all records have been transferred.

ACTIVITY REPORTS

Specific work quotas for records center personnel are usually not recommended because employee pressure has been known to cause misfiling and inaccurate reports. In addition, time requirements for records center actions are so variable that equitable quotas are not feasible. Although quotas cannot be applied to an individual's output, statistical projections, based on production reports, can be used to justify staffing needs; to compute the backlog of personnel work hours; to estimate time requirements for accessions, disposals, and indexing; and to estimate cost savings through use of the records center.

In addition, a weekly or monthly report of overall records center activity will provide valuable statistical information to the records manager as previously described. The report, prepared by the records center supervisor, should contain the number of references, refiles, and interfiles; the number of cubic feet accessioned and destroyed; and the amount of vacant space available. These data are accumulated from the daily reports of the records center clerks and from the accession and disposal activities.

It is important that the calculation method be standardized for the various records center actions. Usually, each record or file requested is counted as a search. If the record is not in the file because of a previous charge-out or cannot be located, it is still counted as a search. If different records requested happen to be in the same carton,

description of the records in the carton. A control-card system, a transfer-list system, or a combination of these is used as an index to the stored records. The latter provides the simplest and least costly method in terms of indexing and retrieval.

All records retrieved from the records center should be charged out to the user, and follow-up controls should be used to ensure the return of records. Disposal of records from the records center must be authorized, and indexing and inventory controls changed when the records are removed.

Space-need projections are made regularly to ensure adequate space. Intracenter transfer of records should be avoided, if possible, because of the indexing changes involved. Moving a records center can be greatly facilitated by creating a space-number conversion table as the records are being moved.

The computer is often used for indexing records center holdings and for providing other inventory and statistical reports. A cost analysis of computer versus manual systems should be made before a computer program is inaugurated. Regular activity reports, made to provide statistical data, are essential for staffing and space planning. Emergency planning is required for the safety of personnel and the protection of records.

QUESTIONS FOR DISCUSSION

1. Why is a dedicated and well-trained staff of importance in the operation of a records center?

2. Who are the "customers" of a records center?

3. What responsibility does the records center staff have to the user?

4. Why is it necessary for the staff of a records center to provide its users with the published operating policies and procedures of the records center? How much flexibility can there be in carrying out established policies concerning use of the records kept in the center?

5. Explain the origin and content of the transfer list that accompanies records transferred to the records center.

6. Why is it necessary for the records management office or the records center staff to review the transfer list before records are actually sent to the records center?

7. How are space locations determined for records received by the records center?

8. Identify and distinguish between the indexing methods commonly used by records centers.

9. What factors must be taken into consideration when establishing records center search and charge-out procedures?

10. Why is it necessary to establish a follow-up policy? Explain the various procedures that can be used when follow-ups must be made.

11. Explain the procedural differences between refiling and interfiling.

12. Why and how often should the records center staff make a reference analysis?

13. What are some common arrangements for establishing and maintaining a reference analysis file?

14. How are disposals of records handled by the records center staff?

15. How can future space needs be adequately and accurately projected?

16. Why is it desirable to establish policies and procedures for intracenter transfers of records?

17. What basic clerical operations should be reviewed when determining whether to computerize records center indexing procedures or not?

18. What records center reports can be processed by a computer?

19. What records center activity reports should be made to management on a regular or periodic basis?

20. What plans should be established for con-

ducting records center operations in the event of unforeseen emergencies?

PROJECTS

1. The Houston chapter of the Association of Records Managers and Administrators is sponsoring a two-day seminar, "Improving Records Center Operations." As the program chairperson of the Houston chapter, you are in charge of preparing a tentative 16-hour seminar program featuring a variety of activities—speakers, panel debates, discussion groups, and so on. The Houston chapter anticipates attendance of from 150 to 175 people. A committee will assist you in securing program participants. Your job is to decide on the topics that will be addressed at the seminar.

2. Construct a questionnaire that could be used to gather data concerning all aspects of records center operations. Assume that the questionnaire will be sent to all members of the Association of Records Managers and Administrators.

3. Prepare an outline for a speech entitled "The Disposition of Obsolete Records from a Records Center" that is to be delivered at the regular monthly meeting of the St. Louis chapter of the Association of Records Managers and Administrators.

4. Prepare an annotated bibliography of five periodical articles on the topic "Records Center Operations."

CASE PROBLEM

You have just completed your first year as records center supervisor of the Griffen Manufacturing Corporation, which was established 20 years ago. The records center was planned by your immediate superior, the organization's records manager, just before you were employed by the company. The first annual report of the records center's operations must now be prepared for submission to the records manager. Prepare an outline of the report, which shall include cost savings. Use the following data in preparing your report:

Records on Hand: 38,550 cubic feet
Accessions:5,210 cubic feet
Disposals: 5,350 cubic feet
Reference requests (searches):   15,958
Refiles and Interfiles: 29,750
Available space at end of year: 2,005 cubic feet
Floor space used—stack area: 10,690 Sq. Ft.
Floor space—nonstack area: 1500 square feet
Cost of floor space (and utilities): $5.00 square foot (stack area)
Cost of office space: $20.00 square foot (nonstack area)
Number of records center clerks: 2
Total annual payroll and fringe: $88,400
Cartons and other expenses: $12,800

Chapter 19

Archives
Management

Learning Objectives
1. To define archives management and explain its goals, its objectives, and its relationship to records management.
2. To explain the types and functions of archives.
3. To identify the criteria for appraising the value of archival records.
4. To explain the basic principles for the arrangement of, access to, and use of archival records.
5. To describe the principles of conservation of archival materials to ensure their permanent preservation.
6. To explain the justification for establishing an archives and to explain its operation and use.
7. To explain the various methods of archival automation to facilitate the retrieval of archival records and enhance their use and value.

INTRODUCTION

Archives management programs are often operated as a part of records management programs, and the records retention schedule is frequently used as the means of identifying records possessing permanent archival or historical value, and scheduling them for transfer to the organization's archive at a point in their life cycle when they have no further value for operational, legal, or other business purposes.

The U.S. National Archives and Records Administration defines archives as "the noncurrent records of an organization preserved because of their continuing, or enduring, value," while *permanent records* are defined as those having "sufficient historical or other value to warrant continued preservation beyond the time they are needed for administrative, legal, or fiscal purposes."[1]

Goals and Functions of Archives Management Programs

Archives management programs play a very important role in the life of an organization. Unless the organization's archival records are properly preserved and accessible, the organization's history and culture will ultimately be lost. An understanding of this history and culture is important to a business enterprise and is perhaps even more important to agencies of government, which are legally or otherwise obliged to preserve archival records for their value to posterity in elucidating the history of communities, states, and the entire nation.

Although different types of archival repositories serve different groups and thus may vary in their specific mission and character, all share a common purpose: to acquire, preserve, and make available for use records having permanent business, research, or historical value. More specifically, a formal program for the management of archives usually includes the following six basic functions:

1. *Appraisal*—The process of determining the value and thus the final disposition of records and designating records as either temporary or permanent, which may be accomplished as a part of the process of developing records retention schedules or as a separate act.

2. *Accessioning*—The transfer of the legal and physical custody of archival records from their offices of origin to the archival facility; also the creation of records documenting receipt and acceptance of the records into the archives.

3. *Preservation*—The specific steps undertaken to maintain, repair, restore, or otherwise conserve archival records in appropriate facilities and equipment.

4. *Arrangement and description*—The process of determining an appropriate method of organizing archival records and of developing *finding aids* (indexes or other lists, whether manual or automated) to describe the records and to facilitate their retrieval and use.

5. *Access and use*—The implementation of policies and procedures governing the access and use

of archival records by employees of the organization which owns them or by the general public.

6. *Reference and staff services*—The provision of facilities and a staff of *archivists* having professional training in archival administration to assist researchers or other persons in the use of archival records. In some particularly proactive archival programs, these services may include outreach activities to market the use of the program to persons or professional groups throughout the community, the state, or the entire nation.

Each of these six basic functions of an archives management program will be discussed in greater detail later in this chapter.[2]

Relationship Between Archives and Records Management

The relationship between archives and records management has been the subject of much discussion and debate in professional circles for many years.[3] The records management field evolved from the archival profession during the 1950s and in subsequent years achieved a separate professional identity with its own community of vendors, educational courses of study, professional association, and certifying body. Nevertheless, the two professions still share much in common, and records managers need a good understanding of archival principles and practices in order to develop a comprehensive records management program. We shall begin this discussion with some observations concerning the similarities and differences between archives and records management principles and practices.

1. *Primary objectives.* Archivists are primarily concerned with the permanent preservation of historically valuable records in order to serve the ends of researchers or other users of original source materials. The principal objectives of records managers are more directly related to the core objectives of their organization's business: improving administrative efficiencies, reducing costs, and improving the productivity of information users.

2. *Media management.* Archives management and records management are both concerned with managing the same types of record media: information in all forms and formats. Archivists, however, usually begin their hands-on management of these media at the last stage of their life cycle — after they have been judged worthy of archival preservation and are transferred to the archival repository. Records managers, on the other hand, are concerned with the management of all record media from the earliest phases of their life cycle.

3. *Condition and value of records.* Archivists and records managers share a common interest in the quality of recordkeeping systems and the value of the information they contain. Records managers work to improve the quality of both active and inactive recordkeeping systems, while archivists have a strong interest in receiving archival records in good order when they are accessioned into the archives. Moreover, the interests of both groups directly intersect during the records appraisal process, when decisions are made about which records series possess archival value and thus will be transferred to the archives.

4. *Indexing and retrieval systems and techniques.* The systems and techniques used to organize, index, and retrieve common office records are quite similar to those used for collections of archival material. The major differences are that most archival records will not be retrieved and used nearly as frequently as active office records or even as frequently as most inactive records stored in a records center. Both archival and nonarchival records require indexing capabilities that support *precise* retrieval, but archival retrieval does not usually need to be as rapid or *timely.*

The records manager is responsible for managing the "archives of the future." Hence, the records manager must understand the functions and basic techniques of the archivist so that he or she can recognize and preserve archival material in usable form.

The Archivist

The professional archivist usually has a background in history and social or library science. (As used here, the term *professional* means that the archivist has completed academic work and has experience in the management of archives and the appraisal of archival material.) A business archivist's background may be in history, economics, or business administration. It is not unusual for an archivist to hold advanced degrees and to have had specialized training in archival theory and techniques. An archivist may also pass examinations and become a Certified Archivist, as designated by the Institute of Certified Archivists.

The Society of American Archivists is the professional association through which archivists exchange information about developments and techniques. This organization has contributed significantly to the progress being made in standardizing terminology, methods, and techniques, and in improved training programs. It has provided the incentive to research and to publish information about technical developments in the preservation and use of records. The society's flagship publication is the *American Archivist,* but it also publishes a variety of books and other types of archival reference materials.

TYPES AND FUNCTIONS OF ARCHIVES

Archival repositories (or *depositories,* as they are sometimes called) are of three general types: public archives, private archives, and manuscript repositories.

Public Archives

Federal, state, and local governments create many records in the ordinary course of business. Some of these records are of the average business variety and are treated like any other business record. Other records that have served their primary purpose have permanent value and are retained in the archives. These records document the history of the government, its agencies, and the citizens it serves. Among the many types of records maintained in public archives are census records, tax assessments, land records, and mortgages. Some of these records are maintained for administrative and legal as well as historical purposes.

Private Archives

Private archives are established to preserve the history of an institution, a corporation, or a family. Many churches, businesses, and associations maintain a private archive to provide evidence and information of their organization's functions, policies, procedures, and operations. This chapter is concerned, for the most part, with private business archives.

Manuscript Repositories

In addition to their own private archives, many universities maintain archives of other records. These manuscript repositories often contain collections of unpublished manuscripts or records of a particular activity or function not related to the university. For example, Wayne State University in Michigan maintains the archives of labor history and urban affairs. In its collection are the records of several labor organizations, including the United Auto Workers. There are also personal papers of individuals associated with the labor movement and with urban affairs.

The difference between a private archives and a manuscript collection is that, in the case of the former, the scope of the holdings is limited to an organization and its affiliates, whereas the latter is devoted to the records of an outside organization or individual that has a common function or was involved in a common activity.

BASIC ARCHIVAL TECHNIQUES

Basic archival techniques include records appraisal, archival arrangement, preparation of finding aids, and development of policies governing access and use.

Archival Appraisal

Archivists, like records managers, do not want to preserve useless records. They are selective in choosing material for permanent retention in the archives, and the material they choose must serve the purpose for which the archives was created. This selection process, referred to as *archival appraisal*, is the process of determining the value and thus the disposition of records based upon their current or future administrative, legal, and fiscal value; their evidential and informational research value; or their relationship to other records.

The archival appraisal of records is perhaps the most difficult and important task any archivist must accomplish. This task determines what will be preserved for posterity and what will be discarded. These decisions must be made on the basis of predictive judgments relative to the probable future use and value of record material. These judgments are irrevocable: Once destroyed, archival records cannot be re-created; they are gone forever.

A detailed discussion of administrative, legal, and fiscal values of records appears in Chapter 3. However, the archival appraisal process must also consider other characteristics of records: their evidential and informational values.

Evidential Value. Records have evidential value when they document how an organization came into being, how it developed, how it was organized, what its function has been, and the results of its activities. Thus, archivists must be concerned with the relative importance of each department or agency within the organization, the function it performs, and the activities it is engaged in.

The amount of documentation generated by any office or department depends upon the relative importance of the organizational unit. Offices that make policy or important decisions will usually produce more documentation of archival value because their functions are more significant than those of other offices or operational units.

The activities of an organization are of two types: substantive and facilitative. *Substantive* activities contribute directly to the functions of the organization. For example, if the function of an organization is to produce automobile electronic parts, engineering activities would be substantive. Substantive activities usually produce at least some documentation that would be appraised as possessing archival value. *Facilitative* activities, on the other hand, contribute indirectly to the function of an organization and are common to many organizations having different functions. For example, an in-plant printing department, while very necessary, is a supportive operation and does not contribute directly to the mission of the parent organization. Because this type of activity is not unique, it may be expected to produce very little in the way of archival documentation.

In documenting both the substantive and facilitative activities of an organization, it is necessary to consider the transactions that constitute those activities. Transactions are of two types: policy making and operational. Policy-making transactions will usually generate more documentation of archival value than will operational transactions because they have a greater overall effect on the organization and because operational transactions are generally routine in nature.

Informational Value.   While records with evidential value document the life span of an organization, records with *informational value* simply, as the name implies, provide information. Informational value is often called research value. Because the value of a record is intrinsic, the record should be evaluated on its own merits. An appraisal of records with informational value requires a knowledge of research needs and methods. It also requires a knowledge of the discipline to which the records pertain. If the archive contains documents covering a wide scope of interests, professional assistance will be needed because archivists cannot be expected to be knowledgeable in all fields. But if the records are retained primarily for historical research or if their scope is narrow, most archivists, by virtue of their training, can do the appraisal without outside assistance.

There are no absolute standards by which informational value appraisals can be made. In appraising records, archivists normally use their own professional judgment. However, what one archivist may consider important, another may consider worthless. T.R. Schellenberg, perhaps this century's leading archival theorist, said regarding this diversity of judgment: "Diverse judgments, in a word, may well assure a more adequate social documentation."[4] Still, there are some standards upon which the judgment can be made. For example, age alone can be a factor in appraising records for historical use. Records 100 years or older are usually retained regardless of content. Also, the uniqueness of the information is a factor considered in appraisal process. Regardless of the particular approach to appraisal decision making that the archivist may employ, it is critically important that the archivist preserve documentation showing the appraisal criteria utilized and the reasons or justification for the preservation or disposal decisions that are made.

Records pertaining to a noted or historical person usually have informational value, especially if the individual originated the records. Records pertaining to significant historical events, such as wars, disasters, and political innovations, will frequently have historical or research value.

Business archives normally consist of papers of company presidents and other policy-making officers and generally offer valuable insight into the reasons for corporate actions. These records have informational value.

Appraisal Guidelines

The records appraised as possessing archival value and accepted for permanent retention in the archives should have at least some of the following attributes:

1. The records document the creation and organization of the company or its subsidiaries.
2. The records document or provide evidence of the company's activities and the consequences of those activities.
3. The records are noncurrent, that is to say, all references pertaining to the subject activities have ceased.
4. The records provide information relative to significant technical questions regarding the company's operations.
5. The records meet possible scholarly needs for the information that is incidentally or accidentally contained in them.
6. The records contains marginally written notes of significance by company officials.
7. The records contain original signatures of officers of the company or other prominent persons.
8. The records have continuing legal or operational value to the company.

The National Archives and Records Administration maintains vast quantities of personnel records of both military and civilian personnel of the federal government, chiefly to substantiate the rights of individuals or their heirs, should such information be needed. In the case of local and state government archives, records pertaining to vital statistics, property rights, and corporate activities are preserved for the benefit of the local community and also for use by researchers for, say, sociological studies.

Archivists cannot retain all material that comes into their possession. They must be selec-

tive and preserve only the material that has evidential or informational value. In many instances, it would be sufficient to retain only a sample of the series rather than the whole series. Further, in some instances an overabundance of records only serves to make the entire collection more difficult to use effectively. In cases where the sheer volume is a problem, the originals can be microfilmed and then, if they have no value, they can be discarded. In these cases, it is the information that is valuable, not the documents themselves.

ARRANGEMENT OF ARCHIVAL RECORDS

An archives exists to be used. Efficient use of an archives requires that the records be arranged according to the principles of provenance and original order. In addition, storage techniques, locating systems, and finding aids must be developed so that the records can be easily retrieved when needed.

Levels of Arrangement

Archival arrangement is the process of organizing archives, records, and manuscripts in accordance with accepted archival principles. These principles serve as guidelines for indicating the best method of physically arranging archival records into logical groupings. Normally, archival records are organized into one or several levels in a hierarchical fashion, from broad to more specific groups or categories, so that the information can be retrieved efficiently. The following levels of archival arrangement are commonly recognized and used.

1. *Record group level.* This highest level of archival arrangement usually refers to the records of an entire institution, agency, or company. Sometimes referred to as a *fond*, particularly in European archival practice.

2. *Subgroup level.* A body of related records

within a record group, usually consisting of the records of a primary subordinate unit of a major organization, such as a subsidiary company. A division, or other primary subordinate unit, a subgroup of archival records may, in turn, be divided into as many groupings as are necessary to reflect the successive organizational units of the organization's hierarchy.

3. *Collection level.* In archival practice, this term is similar in meaning to the terms *record group* and *subgroup*, although it is most often used in reference to the private papers created by individuals or families rather than those of organizations and institutions. The term *collection* also refers to artificial accumulations of manuscripts assembled by a person, organization, or archival repository and devoted to a single theme, event, or type of record. In the plural, *collections* refers to the total holdings—accessions and deposits—of an archival repository.

4. *Records series level.* As defined in Chapter 2 and applied here, the records series consists of separate file units of documents arranged in accordance with a filing system established by the office which created the records. The records in the series are maintained as a unit because they relate to a particular subject or function, result from the same activity, or have a particular form, or because of some other relationship arising out of their creation or use.

5. *File unit level.* A group of related documents or other items of information usually maintained in file folders organized in some logical sequence within a records series is a file unit.

6. *Document* or *item level.* The smallest unit of record material which accumulates to form file units within a records series, the document or item usually consists of a single record, letter, memorandum, report, form, or manuscript sheet.

This hierarchical concept of archival arrangement and the various levels that constitute the hierarchy are the basis for the manner in which archival records are organized. However, to complete our understanding of archival arrangement, it is necessary to explain two other basic concepts—provenance and original order.

Provenance and Original Order

Provenance means that archival records should be maintained in an archival repository in groups that correspond to their source of creation. Therefore, records that are received from an agency or a department should remain as a distinctive group and should not be intermingled with those of other offices or arbitrarily rearranged under other groups. The reasons for this principle are as follows.

1. The records provide better evidence of the activities of an organization when they remain intact.
2. The records of one organization constitute an integrated whole. If the records are arranged in another order, such as by subject, research becomes more difficult, if not impossible.
3. Records arranged by unit of organization make description and location easier.

The principle of *original order* is nearly synonymous with that of provenance. It means that the records are left in the order that existed when they were in current use, provided there is enough semblance of order to assure easy retrieval. Rearranging records in good order would be time-consuming and probably fruitless because the new arrangement would serve an undefined need. If the records are entirely without order, however, a simple plan of arrangement should be devised. Because archival records are created in the normal routines of an office, the best way to preserve them is to retain their original order. The original order of the records can often tell the researcher the importance of the records, the importance inherent in certain topics, and the intrinsic value of the records.

The principles of provenance and original order apply most often to records that have evidential value. Records that are retained for informational value are usually arranged by subject or other category that will assist the researcher.

Indexing and Retrieval Techniques

Archival indexing and retrieval techniques consist of creating various types of *finding aids* to index, list, or otherwise describe the holdings of the archival repository in order to facilitate their use. Finding aids consist of descriptive media—published and unpublished—created by the repository to establish physical and intellectual control over the records. Common types of archival finding aids include inventories, guides, and registers, described as follows:

1. *Archival inventory.* The basic archival finding aid, an inventory generally includes a brief history of the organization or person whose records are being described and a descriptive list of each records series within the record group or subgroup. The inventory may also include such detailed descriptive data as file titles, inclusive dates, quantity, arrangement of each records series, relationship to other series, and a description of the significant subject content of the records.

2. *Register.* Similar to the inventory, the register is an archival finding aid which was developed by the Manuscript Division of the Library of Congress to describe groups of manuscripts, collections, and records by indicating their provenance, scope, and content, including inclusive dates, biographical notes about the person, family, or organization reflected in the records; their arrangement; and other descriptive data. Sometimes registers are general in nature; other times their coverage is detailed to include a list of events, letters sent and received, and so forth.

3. *Guide.* This archival finding aid is a more general description of the holdings of an archival repository; it usually describes and indicates relationships between holdings, with record groups, papers, collections, or comparable bodies of materials as the units of entry.

Other common types of archival finding aids include shelf lists, catalogs, index cards, accession folders, and various types of record indexes and listings. Technologies and systems for automating these basic, manual archival finding aids are discussed later in this chapter.

The archivist must make very important decisions relative to the level of detail that should be employed in preparing finding aids to describe each record group, subgroup, or collection. These decisions are so important because the process of preparing finding aids is usually very time-consuming and thus expensive. Finding aids can be prepared to any level in the hierarchy of records: from a general narrative description of the records of an entire record group or collection to a detailed description of each individual document or item in the collection. Decisions concerning the depth of finding aid descriptions are usually made on the basis of factors such as the size and value of the collection, its probable future use, and the resources available to prepare the finding aids. Of course, very detailed finding aids will certainly facilitate the use of a collection, but item-level descriptions are not always essential (indeed, they are seldom justified), especially for very voluminous collections.

In addition to finding aids, archival storage and retrieval systems include shelf-numbering systems and box or container labeling and numbering techniques. Many of these systems share certain common features with the numbering systems used in records centers.

Typically, archival storage cartons are labeled with, at least, the record group name, records series, and other levels in the hierarchy of arrangement, and the box number. Also, the description on the finding aid will show the address of the container. Finally, the finding aids are usually filed by record group, such as the department agency or number.

The following plan is illustrative of a common scheme for arranging various types of archival material in an archival repository:

1. Corporate and financial records
   By name and company
      By name of record
         By date
2. Biographical records
   By name of individual
      By date
3. Biographical photos
   By name
      By title
         By date
4. Facility photos
   By location
      By name
         By date
5. Maps and prints
   By company
      By type
         By date
6. Movies and film clips
   By title
      By subject
         By date
7. Publications
   By title
      By date
8. Organizational records
   By name of organization
      By date
9. Administrative and operational records
   By type of technology or discipline
10. Equipment and product data
    By type of equipment
       By date
11. Advertisements and marketing
    By product name
       By date
12. Sampling of selected records
    By name of record
       By date

Storage Techniques

Archival records are usually maintained on stationary or movable steel shelves, using acid-free (not under a pH of 5.6) containers that are usually constructed of 40- to 60-pound pressboard. The type of carton used in an archives is quite different from that used in a records center. The archives container is of either the horizontal or vertical variety (see Figure 19.1). That is, the records are either laid flat or placed on end. These containers are designed with hinged lids that protect the records from dust and help to reduce moisture or fire damage, and they are usually much smaller than standard records center cartons.

Access Restrictions

Every archive should have a statement of policy that establishes general rules for access to the records. This protects the records from damage and prevents pilferage and disruption; also, the owners or creators of the records have certain rights of privacy, which must be respected. Sometimes the depositor may impose additional restrictions on use. It is extremely important that the archivist respect and enforce these restrictions with the highest professional ethics because a breach of trust would destroy the confidence of future depositors and possibly do great harm.

Conservation of Archives

The preservation of records from deterioration is not an exclusive function of the archivist. But because archival records always demand the greatest possible care to prevent their deterioration, this subject is worth discussing.

Nature of Paper. The longevity of a paper document depends upon the quality of the paper. Paper consists primarily of cellulose fibers which are held together by sizing agents such as glue, rosin, and starch. The two types of fibers commonly used in the manufacture of paper are rags and wood. Of these, rag provides the highest-quality

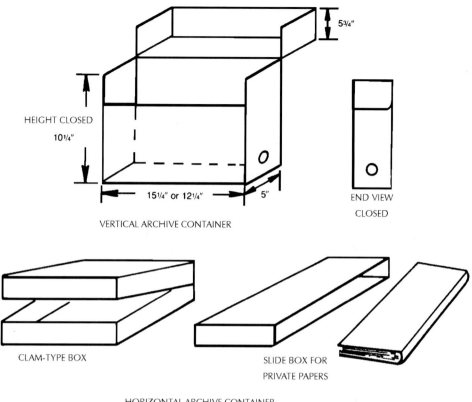

5¾"

HEIGHT CLOSED
10¼"

15¼" or 12¼" — 5"

VERTICAL ARCHIVE CONTAINER

END VIEW
CLOSED

CLAM-TYPE BOX

SLIDE BOX FOR
PRIVATE PAPERS

HORIZONTAL ARCHIVE CONTAINER

FIGURE 19.1   Archive Containers

paper; however, the amount of acid material or rosin used in the process decreases its permanency.

Nature of Writing Medium.   India inks, typewriter inks, and printing inks are considered permanent and will not fade over the years. Iron gallotannate inks are the black and blue-black record inks used today; they have relative permanence. Pencil graphite and carbon paper are permanent unless erased or smudged. However, so-called washable inks and the modern-day dye inks, which are available in many colors, do not have the permanence of the iron gallotannate inks and will completely fade in time. Nutgall ink, which

was used on many old records after 1830, was a forerunner of the present-day iron gallotannate inks and exhibits many of its properties. Nutgall ink fades with time but leaves an iron-salt residue that can be read with ultraviolet light or when photographed with infrared techniques, even though it is not legible to the naked eye.

Environmental Dangers.   The deterioration of paper records can be caused by many factors other than physical abuse. Both natural sunlight and artificial light high in ultraviolet rays will cause low-grade paper to yellow and become brittle and high-grade paper to bleach and become brittle. Yellowing and brittleness are also caused by exposure to high temperatures, even for a short period of time.

For the best preservation of all types of paper, temperatures should be kept at a constant 65°F to 70°F. Humidity should remain at about 50 percent because readings below 30 percent can cause drying and brittleness, while readings above 75 percent can cause molding, discoloration, and weakening of the paper. Air conditioning, with proper air filtration, is the best protection against deterioration from fungi, acid, and other agents harmful to paper.

Insects and rodents are also a source of danger to paper because many varieties will eat the paper. Fumigation and pest-control devices should be used to deal with this type of danger. Some archives have fumigation tanks, which they regularly use when accessioning new material to prevent infestation and spread of the vermin.

Handling of Archival Records. Unless records are given reasonable care when handled and stored, they can be damaged. Large volumes should be laid flat on the shelves, but smaller volumes can be set on end properly braced with book-end-type equipment. Cartons should have covers to protect the records from dust and moisture. The records should not be packed so tightly in the carton that they are damaged when inserted or removed, nor so loosely that they fold or bend. Loose documents should be placed unfolded in an envelope before being placed in a carton. Folded documents should be flattened and placed in acid-free folders. Rubber bands should not be used and should be removed because the rubber deteriorates and adheres to the paper. Twine is recommended as a substitute. Paper clips will rust with time and mar the surface of the paper; they should be removed before storage. Plastic paper clips can be used if it is absolutely necessary to clip documents together.

Lamination, Encapsulation, and Microfilming. Because archival repositories often contain large quantities of old records in a deteriorating condition, archivists are confronted with the problem of how to prevent further deterioration and provide for the permanent preservation of valuable documents. Three methods are commonly used: lamination, encapsulation, and microfilming.[5]

Lamination involves using a chemical process to deacidify documents by soaking them in chemical solutions to neutralize the acid content of the paper. Then, the document is sealed between two sheets of plastic. This document conservation technique originated in the National Archives during the 1930s, was later refined by William J. Barrow, a professional manuscript conservator, and was for many years widely used in archival repositories. However, the technique is seldom practiced today because it is expensive and it irreversibly alters the original state of the documents.

Encapsulation is a document conservation technique developed by the Library of Congress. The process involves encapsulating a document in a sandwich of two sheets of polyester film. Encapsulation is generally less expensive than microfilm and preserves the documents in their original condition.

Microfilming is frequently used to capture a photographic image of archival records on a permanent photographic medium. In addition to its value as a preservation and conservation medium, microfilm has several other significant advantages to the archival repository: savings in space, enhancements in the accessibility of the document, better security, and ease of distribution. Microfilm requires a fraction of the space needed to store paper records. If the microfilms are well indexed, the retrieval of archival records can be significantly enhanced, and duplicate copies of the microfilms can easily be made and distributed to other repositories or to an offsite location for security purposes. Archivists who wish to use microfilm as a document preservation medium must, however, take care to produce and store the film so that it retains its properties of archival permanence.

ESTABLISHING AND OPERATING THE ARCHIVES

Most of the principles and methods of maintaining an archives discussed earlier in this chapter can be applied to a business archives. The records manager will often require the assistance of an archivist in making appraisals. Assuming that the program would be operated as an adjunct of the records management office rather than as a separate entity, the archives will often be located in the records center. A specific and suitable section of the records center should be allocated to archival material. The space-numbering system and control systems can be the same as for the records center. However, an additional index and set of finding aids should be established as though the archives was a separate facility. The index should be in addition to the regular index, because some of the records in the archives section may still have business value.

If some archival material is to be retained in offices, such as public relations or engineering offices, notations of the location of this material should also be included in the finding aids so that the researcher will have one central source to retrieve the records. Although it is desirable that all archival material be retained in the archives, this may not always be the practice.

Although there is nothing to prevent the records manager from simply setting aside archival material and following archival practices, it is best to have formal recognition of an archival program from top-level management. This recognition is absolutely essential if the program is to be funded separately and is beneficial if the archives is to be used fully.

When the program is established, a statement of policy and procedures should be drawn up and approved by top management. First, the policy should outline the scope of the archives, thereby limiting the material accessioned to those records that serve the needs of the company and the purpose of the archives. Second, it must prescribe access policies and the authority of the archivist.

This statement must be tailored to the organization, recognizing the practices and needs peculiar to the company. Figure 19.2 shows a sample statement of policy and procedures for a company archives.

BUSINESS ARCHIVES

There are two types of business archives.[6] The first consists of records maintained as part of a research collection of a university; the second is a private archives, maintained by a company to provide historical documentation of its organization and activities. This section deals primarily with the latter type, but the factors involved in appraisal may be identical in both cases.

Because a primary function of any business is to make a reasonable profit for its owners, it is often difficult to justify expenditures for nonprofit activities such as the establishment of a formal archives, particularly because a full- or part-time archivist would have to be employed. For this reason the function of the archivist is often performed by the records manager. Some organizations have recognized the public relations, research, and legal values of a well-managed archives and have employed a full-time, professional archivist to perform this activity. Whether the archivist performs the added duties of a records manager or the records manager performs the added duties of an archivist depends for the most part on the emphasis desired by the organization.

The Value of Business Archives

Though company officials may not recognize it, a certain amount of archival material is preserved through the records retention schedule. This material can include the records that have been assigned a permanent retention period, such as the minutes of board and stockholder meetings, general ledgers and journals, articles of incorporation, annual reports to stockholders and regulatory agencies, records of capital investment, au-

---

STATEMENT OF POLICY AND PROCEDURES
THE ARCHIVES
OF
XYZ COMPANY, INC.

1. *General Purpose:* The purpose of the archives of the XYZ Company is to preserve the documented history of the company, its subsidiaries, and predecessor companies for the benefit of advertising, public relations, the scholar, and posterity, as well as for operational use.

2. *Funding:* The archives program is to be funded separately and is under the jurisdiction of the archivist.

3. *Location of Archives:* Archival records may, depending on the rate of reference, the need for special security, or other factors, be housed in any one of the following three locations:

    a. Archives room of the records center
    b. Private vault
    c. Public relations office

4. *Scope of Collection:* The collection will include items such as the following.

    a. Corporate and financial records
        (1) Minute books and charters
        (2) Annual reports
        (3) General ledgers and journals
        (4) Records of significant litigation and legislation
        (5) Records of mergers and acquisitions
        (6) Records of bankruptcy proceedings
    b. Biographical records
        (1) Papers of former company presidents
        (2) Papers of any policy-making officer
        (3) Oral history tape recordings
    c. Photographic and cartographic records
        (1) Still and movie photographic material
        (2) Maps and plans
    d. Publications
        (1) House organs
        (2) Histories
        (3) Others (selective basis)
    e. Organizational records (selected)
        (1) Professional and trade associations
        (2) Employee organizations
        (3) Regulatory agencies
    f. Administrative and operational records
        (1) Computers
        (2) Management information systems
        (3) Major improvements

FIGURE 19.2   Statement of Policy and Procedures for a Company Archives

g. Product and equipment data

h. Samplings of other significant records and document-type memorabilia

5. *Access and Restriction Policies:*

   a. Access to any archives, manuscripts, or private papers will not be allowed until twenty-five (25) years have elapsed, without special approval of the president, vice-president(s), secretary, treasurer, director of public relations, or the archivist.

   b. Certain records or papers, designated as restricted, will not be available for access, even though twenty-five (25) years have elapsed, without express approval of the officers named in paragraph 5a.

   c. Special considerations will be given by the officers (named in 5a above) when the researcher is especially qualified to examine these records or when the best interest of the company demands it. To be properly qualified, the nonemployee researcher shall:
   (1) Be a college or university professor and supply a statement of research objectives.
   (2) Be a student in good standing at a college or university and submit proper attestation of qualification by his or her instructor.
   (3) Be a nonacademic researcher and supply a statement of objectives and references.

   d. The director of public relations will have access at any time, and other company employees may research those archival records that still have operational value when they are properly authorized.

   e. Photographic reproductions may be made only with the express approval of the director of public relations or the archivist, and the researcher is not authorized to deposit these reproductions with another organization or person without permission.

6. *Accessions and Appraisal:*

   a. Accessions—Accessions will normally be from the following sources.
   (1) Records center transfers and disposals
   (2) Persons or officers within the company
   (3) Persons outside the company

   b. Appraisals—All records will be appraised by the archivist, upon receipt or transfer to the records center and before destructions are authorized, to determine suitability for retention. Regardless of sources, accessions will be limited to the scope of the collection.

FIGURE 19.2   Continued

thority to issue stocks and other securities, deeds, franchises, and many engineering records. These records are preserved principally for legal, operating, or fiscal purposes and for possible scholarly research. They may not be archival when created, but eventually they will be, because they provide the best evidence of an organization's function and activities.

When a corporation is dissolved and loses its corporate identity through a merger, many of these records cease to have business value, but their archival value remains. Such records may include correspondence files of corporate executives; photographs of facilities, products, or equipment; records of corporate involvement in community affairs; records of employees and pay schedules; noteworthy litigation; or marketing plans and product development. The preservation of such archival materials by a business may be based on a sense of responsibility to posterity or on a desire to encourage business history and research. There is a very fine line between appraising records for retention scheduling purposes and appraising for archival purposes; many highly respected records managers, who serve dual roles, maintain that there is no significant difference.

George David Smith and Laurence E. Steadman[7] have pointed out the practical value of a corporate archives:

> *A history of the company is an important though generally unexploited corporate resource. It has many values extending well beyond the celebratory function of the conventional "company history," in either its publicity brochure or anniversary-book form. . . . Once managers recognize the value of the corporate past, they can enhance their ability to diagnose problems, reassess policy, measure performance, and even direct change.*

All of these benefits that accrue from an appreciation of an organization's history ultimately can translate into better management and increased profits.

Convincing management to invest a small portion of its resources in a formal archival program is not an easy task, but a visionary management that appreciates the Smith-Steadman concept of business archives would very likely direct that the program be implemented. The first such visionary was Harvey S. Firestone, Jr., in 1943. Since then, many companies in the United States have established archives. Even so, the number represents only a small percentage of corporations that have recognized the value of business archives. The litigious environment in which corporations operate today makes the selling job more difficult because many executives believe that the information in the archives could be more harmful than helpful to the company in the event of litigation.

Records managers should remember that even in the most receptive business environment, the development and continued existence of corporate archives will depend on a program justification based on costs, benefits, and risks. Such a justification should be based on the uses to which the corporate archives can be put in the ongoing life and operations of the firm. It will usually not be enough to justify the existence of the archives

based on the intrinsic historical value of old records.[8]

ARCHIVAL AUTOMATION

Archivists have been engaged in efforts to automate the finding aids of the holdings in their repositories since the early days of electronic computing.[9] Basically, these efforts have focused in three areas:

1. The development of national standards for archival automation so that the finding aid data of individual repositories can be electronically shared with other archival repositories throughout the country.
2. The automation of the finding aids of individual archival repositories, so as to facilitate access and use of the holdings.
3. The preservation and use of electronic archives—records of historical value which reside on various types of computer-processable storage media.

National Standards for Archival Automation

During the mid-1960s, the Society of American Archivists established the Committee on Automated Techniques for Archival Agencies. During the same period, the National Archives initiated its first major automation project called Spindex II, a continuation of an earlier project sponsored by the Library of Congress. Both of these efforts were concerned with creating a computer system that could be used by archival repositories throughout the country. This required the standardization of finding aid structures, terms, data fields, and other format elements used to describe collections of records. This was a difficult undertaking since archival repositories maintain unique collections that are described in various levels and depths and that utilize finding aids of widely diverse types and formats. Nevertheless, these efforts continue even today; their ultimate objective is to establish uniform format standards for finding aids that can be used with any computer and its software programs, and permit the electronic exchange of finding aid data between repositories.

More recent efforts at developing national standards for archival automation resulted in the RLIN and MARC-AMC projects. The RLIN (Research Library Information Network) is a service of the Research Library Group, which operates an on-line catalog for rare books and other research materials. Archivists and manuscript curators realized that this on-line service could be utilized as a national database for archival holdings, so they began to contribute descriptions of their holdings to it.

Another effort at establishing a national database of archival holdings was co-sponsored by the Library of Congress, the Committee on Archival Information Exchange of the Society of American Archivists, and a similar group within the American Library Association. These organizations developed the *m*achine *r*eadable *c*ataloging format for *a*rchival and *m*anuscript *c*ontrol—MARC-AMC. Once data from finding aids is entered into this database, it can be transmitted electronically to national networks such as RLIN, OCLC, and others.[10] These systems greatly enhance researchers' ability to determine whether remote archival institutions contain holdings that are relevant to their research interests.

Automation of Finding Aids for Internal Repository Use

Just as librarians were eager to use computers to automate their card catalogs, archivists were also eager to use these machines to automate their finding aids. From the earliest days of computing, it was obvious that computer automation of finding aids could offer greatly enhanced search capabilities to the use of archival materials. Paper-based finding aids are frequently bulky and cumbersome to use, and they have very limited cross-referencing capabilities to enable the researcher to locate relevant information which may exist in many record groups or collections, or in many records series of a large record group or collection. With the ability to perform keyword searches in all data fields, computerized finding aids can greatly facilitate the use of the holdings of virtually any archival repository.

Mainframe-Based Systems

Prior to the advent of microcomputers, the first efforts to automate archival finding aids utilized mainframe computers. Since they are usually located within universities, government agencies, or large businesses, most archival repositories have access to mainframe-based computing resources.

A well-known example of an early mainframe-based archival automation system uses the Paradigm system installed at the University Archives of the University of Illinois at Urbana-Champaign. As originally designed, this system contained the automated finding aids of the approximately 2,700 collections in the archives, of which over 400 were private manuscripts (personal papers of faculty members). For each collection, the following data were entered into the university's mainframe computer: collection name, accession number, inclusive dates, dates of accessioning, type and quantity of documents, access restrictions, several name and subject descriptors indicating the nature of the collection, and shelf location data. It should be noted that this level of finding aid automation is relatively general; as originally configured, the Paradigm system did not include file folder or item and document level data.[11]

Although this mainframe-based approach to

archival automation has its advantages, it suffers from many of the disadvantages of many mainframe computing applications: custom programming is required to produce the software to run the applications, long lead times are usually required to develop the applications, and the archival repository is dependent on the computer department's staff for all system development and support functions. This situation began to change during the 1980s with the advent of the microcomputer, the development of the DOS operating system and database management technology, and the creation of thousands of applications software programs to run on these small computers, including some programs specially designed to automate the finding aids of archival repositories.

PC-Based Software for Archival Automation

Beginning in the mid-l980s, archival automation software products were developed for operation on microcomputers. During the ensuing years, the prices of both the PC hardware and the archival automation software have become much more favorable, to the extent that the tools for archival automation are affordable for virtually any repository. This software is easy to install and use, and it provides a convenient method of computerizing many basic types of archival finding aids in most small to medium-size and some larger repositories.

Archivists who want to install this type of computer system should define their requirements carefully, evaluate a number of competing products, and select the product that comes closest to satisfying their requirements. The best products have a substantial base of successful installations, provide flexibility for customization, have powerful data retrieval capabilities, and are sold by reputable software companies which can provide good after-the-sale product support. Chapter 9 contains a more detailed discussion concerning evaluating software products.

Electronic Archives

Businesses and government organizations have been creating significant quantities of records in electronic (machine-readable) format for many years, and some of these records possess archival value. The archivist is therefore faced with the responsibility of how to preserve and manage these electronic archival materials.

The following are some guidelines which should prove helpful to both records managers and archivists in planning and implementing policies and programs for machine-readable archives:

1. *Computer media containing machine-readable records are generally not considered to possess qualities of archival permanence in the same sense as paper and microfilm media.* As noted in Chapter 8, if an organization wishes to retain computer records for many years and be assured of being able to read them, it must usually rely on paper or microfilm output to meet its archival needs. High-quality paper records and archival microfilm can be expected to have a readable life span of several hundred years if these media are stored properly, but the guaranteed readability of computer media is much more problematic. Even if the data on the computer media retain their integrity for, say, a hundred years, the archival repository must maintain the proper hardware and software to read the records. Such maintenance is very problematic because these system components have a relatively short service life. Many organizations address these problems by preserving the electronic records in ASCII format, which provides the best and most flexible option for processing the records on a variety of computer platforms.

2. *Unless computer-based archival records need to remain in a computer-processable format in order to support ongoing research requirements, it may be difficult to justify the cost of preserving them in this format.* Most historical research is accomplished using static rather than dynamic

data. Only very specialized computer databases would need to be preserved in computer-processable format in order to support sophisticated research requirements. Some examples might include census data, medical research data, and space exploration data.

3. *Electronic archival records can often be transferred to COM or COLD media, both of which are better and more practical for permanent archival storage.* Computer-output microfilm (COM) often provides a better medium for archival retention than magnetic media. If it is properly produced and stored, COM can offer excellent archival properties for the permanent preservation of computer data. The microfilm (or microfiche) can be produced at a point in the life cycle of the records when they no longer need to remain in a computer-processable format but require archival retention. At a more sophisticated level of technology, computer-based archival records can sometimes be preserved on COLD (computer-output-to-laser-disk) media, which would provide better archival properties than magnetic media, but still may not be sufficient to ensure the same degree of permanent usability as hard copy or microfilm media.

The archives of most organizations constitute a very small percentage of the records holdings, usually not over 1 to 2 percent and seldom more than 5 percent. However, this small quantity of records is extremely important to the life and culture of the organization, and the records manager must be both intellectually and technically equipped to manage these archival records. Otherwise, the corporate memory will be lost to history.

SUMMARY

Archives are defined as "the noncurrent records of an organization preserved because of their continuing, or enduring, value." These are records that never lose their value and thus require permanent preservation in an archival repository. Formal programs for the preservation and use of archival records are called archives management programs. These programs are often run by one or more archivists, although records managers frequently play the primary or a secondary role in selecting the records that will be preserved in the organization's archival repository, or in managing the facility itself.

Archives management programs consist of a number of basic archival functions; the most important are appraisal, accessioning, preservation or conservation, arrangement and description, and reference services for archival records.

The records management profession evolved from the archival profession in the United States during the 1950s, and today the two professions have separate and distinct identities. In the government arena, however, the relationship between archives and records management is still quite close. The two professions share much in common: they manage the same records media; both are concerned with the quality and condition of records; and both use similar systems and techniques to facilitate their access and use.

There are three types of archival repositories: public archives, private archives, and manuscript collections. An archival record is one that has evidential value or informational value. *Evidential value* means that the record documents the function and activities of an organization. *Informational value* means that the record provides unique or valuable information for research and is not necessarily associated with the function or activity of an organization. These record values constitute the essence of the archival appraisal function—making the critically important decisions about which records to retain for posterity and which ones to destroy.

Activities of an organization are either substantive or facilitative. They are substantive when they contribute directly to the organization's functions and facilitative when they are supportive in nature and are common to many organizations that have different functions. Substantive activities usually produce a larger quantity of archival documentation than facilitative activities. These factors must be considered in the archival appraisal process.

Archival records are arranged according to the principles of provenance and original order. These principles mean that the records should be grouped according to their origin and that the order which was used during their active life should be retained. Under these principles, the records of an organization will usually be preserved in hierarchical groupings that correspond to their provenance and original order. These groupings are the record group level, the subgroup level, the records series level, the file unit level, and the document or item level.

Archival indexes, or finding aids, consist of inventories, registers, guides, catalogs, shelf lists, and other types of indexes used to describe the records of individual record groups or collections of manuscripts, so as to facilitate access and use of the records.

Archival records should be preserved in facilities and equipment designed to ensure their permanent life, to arrest further deterioration, and to ensure that the records will remain in a usable condition. Encapsulation and archival microfilming are common preservation techniques; lamination is seldom used as an archival preservation method today.

The business archives is established to preserve the history of corporate organizations and to serve the needs of scholarly research, public rela-

tions, and posterity. The records manager frequently serves as the archivist and must make appraisal decisions as part of the retention program. The business archives is frequently a part of the records center.

Archival automation programs are used to computerize the finding aids of a repository, so as to facilitate access and use of its holdings. In a larger context, these programs are also concerned with developing national standards for archival automation, so that the finding aid data of individual repositories can be electronically shared with other repositories throughout the country. Finally, archival automation is concerned with the preservation and use of electronic archives—records of historical value which reside on various types of computer-processable storage media. In recent years the development of PC hardware and applications software specially designed to automate archival finding aids has provided new opportunities for archival repositories to take advantage of computer technology to improve access and use of their holdings.

QUESTIONS FOR DISCUSSION

1. Why is it important for the records manager to have an understanding of archives management?

2. List and describe briefly four basic archival functions.

3. At what time in the life of records are they usually appraised for their archival value?

4. What are the three general types of archives? What are the purposes or functions of each?

5. What is the difference between the substantive activities and the facilitative activities of an organization?

6. What are the distinguishing differences between the evidential value and the informational value of records?

7. Explain the difference between provenance and original order.

8. Why must restrictions be placed on the use of, or access to, archival materials?

9. Identify the archival values possessed by business records.

10. Identify the steps involved in establishing and operating a business archives. Why is each step essential?

11. What factors must be considered in the preservation and care of material stored in an archives? Explain the importance of each.

12. Describe one of the several major projects undertaken at the national level to develop national standards for archival finding aids.

13. Electronic archives will often be impractical for all but the largest and most specialized archival repositories having sophisticated research requirements. Explain why.

14. Describe the principal advantages of PC-based archival automation programs over their mainframe-based counterparts.

PROJECTS

1. The Association of Records Managers and Administrators' board of directors has asked you to make a survey of its membership to determine the status of business archives. Prepare a questionnaire, which is to be sent to all members of the association, to gather the appropriate data.

2. Write an article on the topic "The Influence of Automation on Archives Management" for publication in American Archivist magazine. Your article should be between 1,000 and 1,200 words. It should include a bibliography consisting of at least five periodical references.

3. As the records manager in a large organization, you have decided to seek permission to establish an archives management program.

   a. Read at least three periodical articles that will provide you with background information for justification of your request.

   b. Write a report to the vice-president of administrative services

      (1) explaining the need for an archives management program within your organization and (2) requesting authority to establish the program.

   c. Attach an annotated bibliography (approximately 60 words per article) to support your request.

4. Outline a 40-minute speech, to be presented at the annual convention of the Society of American Archivists, on the topic "Appraisal Criteria for Archival Records."

5. Prepare a plan for archival automation of your organization's archival repository. Indicate the objectives and benefits of the program and the basic approach for computer technology to be employed.

CASE PROBLEM

The Life Insurance Company of North America (LICNA) has just completed an inventory of all of its records. Many of the records found in an old warehouse date from 1910, when the company was founded. LICNA's management feels that many of the records may have historical value, but it does not want to retain all to preserve a relative few. About one half of the records pertain to LICNA, and the other half pertain to several smaller insurance companies that have been merged into LICNA over the years. The archivist is asked to make a tentative appraisal of the records for historical value from a skeletal list provided. If the tentative appraisal warrants, a detailed appraisal will be commissioned. You have been assigned to assist the archivist. From the following list, which represents records from all companies, indicate which records would most likely *not have* historical value and explain why. Of those records that are to be preserved, which do you think would be essential to reconstruct a basic history of the company?

Register of canceled bonds, 1910-1925

Minute books of directors meetings, 1910-1946

General ledgers, 1945-1946

Journal entries, 1910-1946

Annual reports to policyholders, 1910-1946

Salary schedules for officers, 1910-1935

Personnel files (incomplete series): clerks and operating personnel, 1919-1934

Reorganization proceedings (bankruptcy), 1932

Bills of lading, 1941-1945

Trial balances (accounting records), 1927-1940

Canceled stock certificates, 1951-1956

Correspondence files of corporate secretary regarding legal matters, 1920-1955

Canceled property leases, 1960-1975

Album of advertising clippings, 1923-1935

Box of photos, unidentified, dates unknown but obviously old

Miscellaneous correspondence files of the president's office dealing with various financial matters, 1945-1955

Payroll records, 1923-1937

Reports of state insurance examinations, 1910-1927; 1975 to present

Acquisitions of other companies, 1965 to present

News releases, 1985 to present

Videotapes, 1988 to present

Purchase orders, 1985 to present

Accounts payable files, 1985 to present

NOTES

1. National Archives and Records Administration, *A Federal Records Management Glossary* (Washington, D.C.: U.S. Government Printing Office, 1989).

2. For further readings on each of these basic archival topics, see the books published in the "Archival Fundamentals Series," published by the Society of American Archivists, Chicago, Illinois. See particularly: James M. O'Toole, *Understanding Archives and Manuscripts,* 1990; Frederic M. Miller, *Arranging and Describing Archives and Manuscripts,* 1990; Thomas Wilsted and William Nolte, *Managing Archival and Manuscript Repositories,* 1991; F. Gerald Ham, *Selecting and Appraising Archives and Manuscripts,* 1993; and Mary Jo Pugh, *Providing Reference Services for Archives and Manuscripts,* 1992.

3. See T. R. Schellenberg, "Archival Interests in Records Management," in *Modern Archives: Principles and Techniques* (Chicago: University of Chicago Press, 1956), pp. 26-43; Frank B. Evans, "Archivists and Records Managers: Variations on a Theme," *American Archivist,* Vol. 30, 1967, pp. 45-58; Richard H. Lytle, "The Relationship Between Archives and Records Management: An Archivist's View," *Records Management Quarterly,* April 1968, pp. 5-8; Bill Walker, "Records Managers and Archivists: A Survey of Roles," *Records Management Quarterly,* January 1989, pp. 18-20; Robert L. Sanders, "Archivists and Records Managers: Another Marriage in Trouble," *Records Management Quarterly,* April 1989.

4. Schellenberg, p. 149.

5. Kenneth W. Duckett, *Modern Manuscripts* (Nashville: American Association for State and Local History, 1975), pp. 101-107.

6. See Edie Hedlin, *Business Archives:* An Introduction (Chicago: Society of American Archivists, 1978); "Business Archives: A Special Issue," *American Archivist,* Vol. 45, No. 3, Summer 1982.

7. George David Smith and Laurence E. Steadman, "Present Value of Corporate History," *Harvard Business Review,* November-December 1981, pp. 164-173.

8. David O. Stephens, "The Records Manager's Role in Archives Management." Paper presented to the Diamond State Chapter, ARMA International, Wilmington, Delaware, November 15, 1983.

9. See Charles Dollar, *Archival Theory and Information Technologies: The Impact of Information Technologies on Archival Principles and Methods* (Macerata, Italy: University of Macerata Press, 1992). Available from the Society of American Archivists, Chicago, Illinois.

10. Duckett, p. 161.

Lockheed Corporation

The Corporate Records Center

The Lockheed Corporation, Calabasas, California, recognized the value of a records center as one of the most important components of an effective records management program and built its own corporate records center in 1965.

Lockheed ranks among the top 45 industrial companies in the United States and the second largest defense prime contractor. It employs 70,300 people around the world, of whom more than 20 percent are scientists and engineers. Lockheed is preeminent in the fields of spacecraft, space systems, fleet ballistic missiles, and aircraft for airlift, reconnaissance, antisubmarine warfare, and other special missions. The corporation is a major producer of tactical weapon systems, electronics and communications systems, marine systems, and ships, and is a major provider of scientific, engineering, and technical support services.

As Corporate Director, Management Support Services, for Lockheed, William Benedon is responsible for corporate administrative services, including word processing, graphic arts, and office layouts, and for coordinating and directing the records management efforts of the multidivision company operation involving all aspects of records administration and office automation applications. He is a Certified Records Manager and holds a master's degree from New York University Graduate School of Business Administration. Before joining the Lockheed staff in 1954, he was Records Administrator for the state of New Jersey. In 1980, Mr. Benedon received the Silver Anniversary Special Services Award from the Association of Records Managers and Administrators (ARMA) for 25 years of outstanding service and contributions to the association and to the records management profession. He is also editor emeritus of the association's magazine, the *Records Management Quarterly*. The "William Benedon Professional Achievement Award" was established in his honor in 1994 by the Greater Los Angeles Chapter/ARMA.

The Lockheed records center was planned as part of the total corporate records management program under the leadership of Mr. Benedon. He believes "when scientifically designing for housing records, a records center provides maximum capability for economy, rapid processing and retrieval, and security."

Located in Lockheed's Kelly Johnson Research Center Facility in Saugus, California, the center was designed to provide the optimum in the maintenance of inactive, archival, and vital records.

Basic Structure

The center is a single-level, square building with a loading dock area. The exterior walls are 6-inch, tilt–up concrete slab, and the interior walls are 8-inch concrete block. The building is 17 feet of clear height in storage and service areas, and there are no windows. It is a class B vault with two 2-hour doors. A vital records vault is located underground below the office area. This is a class A vault with a 4-hour door and 12-inch reinforced concrete walls.

Size and Capacity

The building has a total of 57,127 square feet. It consists of the main area, 49,478 square feet; the vital records area, 3,434 square feet; the processing area, 1,372 square feet; and the office area, 2,743 square feet. Administrative space is provided for the supervisor and other personnel, for a conference room, for a reference room, and for a lobby. The building can house 244,769 cubic feet of records. It has built-in expansion capacity. Since it was first occupied in November of 1965, two additions have been completed in 1970 and 1981. The present holdings of the center are 235,000 cubic feet.

Shelving and Containers

All steel, 30- by 42-inch and 32- by 42-inch bolt-assembly shelves on 23-inch centers are used. They are placed back-to-back with 4-inch space on the 30- by 42-inch units to prevent overhang. A combination of T- and L- shaped uprights are used for support. Standard corrugated containers are used—12- by 10- by 15-inch double wall, 125 lb., hand holes, shoe lid cover. X-ray and magnetic tape containers are 6 by 16 by 15 inches. Engineering drawing containers are 4 by 4 by 45 inches with tuck-in ends. Aisles between shelving are 32 inches. In the engineering area, however, they are 45 inches. The main aisles are 6 feet, 7 inches, wide.

Servicing and Handling Equipment

Equipment used in the Lockheed records center includes steel 9-step pulpit ladders, a hydraulic lift platform with 500-pound capacity, a forklift to handle 2,000 pounds, conveyers, jacks, library trucks, a pickup van for special delivery of records, a dumbwaiter that operates between the main floor and the underground vault, and a laser copier and fax for reference needs. There are also 5 area telephone reference stations in the main area with direct dialing to all Lockheed facilities and a two-way, on-spot communication system.

Air Conditioning and Humidity Control

Because appropriate atmospheric conditions are critical in effective maintenance of records, the Lockheed center has air conditioning throughout the entire building with 16 units on the roof. This design prevents the entire system from ever going out at one time. The vault, as well as the two additions, are humidity controlled at a 60 percent maximum level to protect microform and magnetic records.

Fire Prevention and Security

Because fire is always a major threat to records, the center has a sprinkler system throughout. A fire hose as well as extinguisher stations are also provided. Because the main area is a class B vault and the underground section is a class A, maximum security is provided. There is also 24-hour guard service at the facility. Security clearance is also a requirement. Emergency lighting is available at the center in the event of a disaster.

Microfilm and Magnetic Tape Storage

Microfilmed vital records are maintained in the underground vault. Motion picture film is stored in the vault and also in the main storage area. Data processing tapes for vital record rotation and retention are kept in the vault as well as in the main storage area.

Records Destruction

A majority of Lockheed's records are recycled. The bulk of the classified records are destroyed by a commercial disintegration company. Small volumes are destroyed by a pulping machine.

Automated Control System

The center uses a fully automated on-line system for control. It is the LARCS (Lockheed Automated Records Control System), which was designed and developed in-house. It operates on NOMAD 2 database on the MDAL 1400A mainframe computer. The system covers all aspects of records center operations as well as company-wide retention scheduling, vital records, and other areas of records management. It operates via PROF terminals, which also provide electronic mail and word processing capability.

Personnel

The efficiency of the center is reflected in the minimal number of employees required to operate it. There is a center supervisor, one records center control clerk, and three records center clerks.

All aspects of the Lockheed Corporate Records Center show that the goals of a facility of this type are being met: economy, efficiency in processing and retrieval, and security.

Appendixes

Records Management Professional Organizations

A number of associations devote their professional activities exclusively or partially to the field of records management and information control. The names and addresses of the best known of these associations have been selected from various sources, especially the *Encyclopedia of Associations*, Twenty–Eighth Edition, edited by Peggy Kneffel Daniels and Carol A. Schwartz, (Detroit, Michigan: Gale Research, Inc., 1993).

Administrative Management Society   AMS
    1101 l4th Street NW
    No. 1100
    Washington, DC 20005-560l
      Members: 4,000

American Management Association   AMA
    135 West 50th Street
    New York, NY 10020-1201
      Members: 70,000

American Video Association   AVA
    2885 N. Nevada Street No. 140
    Chandler, AZ 85225
      Members: 2,000

Association of Commercial Records Centers   ACRC
    P. O. Box 20518
    Raleigh, NC 27619
      Members: 400

Association for Computing Machinery   ACM
    l5l5 Broadway, 17th Floor
    New York, NY 10036
      Members: 75,000

Association of Independent Information Professionals
    c/o Law Library Management   AIIP
    38 Bunkerhill Drive
    Huntington, NY 11743
      Members: 500

Association for Information and Image Managers
    1100 Wayne Road   AIIM
    Silver Springs, MD 20910
      Members: 8,500

Association for Information Management   AIM
    6348 Munhall Ct.
    P. O. Box 374
    McLean, VA 22101
      Members; 1,000

Association for Systems Management   ASM
    1433 West Bagley Road
    P. O. Box 38370
    Cleveland, OH 44138-0370
      Members: 7,000

Association of Records Managers and
Administrators, Inc.   ARMA Intl
    4200 Somerset   Suite 215
    Prairie Village, KS 66208
      Members: 11,356

Automatic Identification Manufacturers   AIM
    634 Alpha Drive
    Pittsburgh, PA 15238-2802
      Members: 178

Business Forms Management Association   BFMA
    519 SW 3rd Street
    No. 712
    Portland, OR 97204
      Members: 1,800

Data Processing Management Association   DPMA
    505 Busse Highway
    Park Ridge, IL 60068
      Members: 24,000

DEMA, The Association for Input Technology and Management
    101 Merritt 7, 5th Floor   DEMA
    Norwalk, CT 0685l
      Members: 1,600

Electronic Funds Transfer Association   EFTA
    950 Herndon Pkwy
    Suite 390
    Herndon, VA 22073
      Members: 175

Financial Executives Institute   FEI
    Ten Madison Avenue
    P. O. Box 1938
    Morristown, NJ 07962-1938

Information Technology Association of America
    1616 N. Fort Meyer Drive   ITAA

Suite 1300
Arlington, VA 22209
   Members: 700
Institute of Certified Records Managers   ICRM
P.O. Box 8188
Prairie Village, KS 66208
   Members: 600
International Information Management Congress
1650 30th Street No. 205 W   IMC
Boulder, CO 80301
   Members: 800
ISDA—The Office Systems Cooperative
37 W. Yokuts
Suite A-4
Stockton, CA 95207
   Members: 125
Midwest Archives Conference   MAC
c/o Kraft General Foods Archives
6350 Kirk Street
Morton Grove, IL 60053
   Members: 1,100
National Archives and Records Administration
Volunteer Association   NAVA
Room G-8
National Archives
8th at Pennsylvania NW
Washington, DC 20408
   Members; 170
National Association for Check Safekeeping   NACS
c/o National Automated Clearing House Association
607 Herndon Pkway
Suite 200
Herndon, VA 22070
   Members: 77
National Association of Government
Archives and Records Administrators   NAGARA
New York State Archives
Cultural Education Center
Room 10446
Albany, NY 12230
   Members: 345
National Association of Small Business
Investment Companies   NASBIC
1199 N. Fairfax Street
Suite 200
Alexandria, VA 22314
   Members: 375

National Business Association   NBA
5025 Arapaho
Suite 515
Dallas, TX 45248
   Members: 60,000
National Business Forms Association   NBFA
433 East Monroe Avenue
Alexandria, VA 22301-1693
   Members: 2,300
National Office Products Association   NOPA
301 N. Fairfax Street
Alexandria, VA 22314
   Members; 7,000
National Records Management Council
60 East 42nd Street   NAREMCO
New York, NY 10165
   Non-membership
Nuclear Information and Records
Management Association   NIRMA
210 5th Avenue
New York, NY 10010
Office Automation Society, International   OASI
6348 Munhall Ct.
P. O. Box 374
McLean, VA 22101
   Members: 500
Society for the Advancement of Management
126 Lee Avenue   SAM
Suite 11
Box 889
Vinton, VA 24179
   Members: 11,000
Society of American Archivists   SAA
600 S. Federal
Suite 504
Chicago, IL 60605
   Members: 4,500
Society for Information Management   SIM
401 North Michigan Avenue
Chicago, IL 60611-4267
   Members: 2,500

APPENDIX B

Forms Design Standards

The following standards should be applied by the initiating department when drawing a rough sketch of the form to be submitted with the forms requisition. The forms management staff in reviewing the request will make any necessary adjustment of specifications before forwarding the requisition for duplicating or printing.

1. **Cut-Form Sizes**
   - Any size that can be cut from 32 x 42 inches without waste, particularly sizes 3 $1/2$" x 8", 4" x 5 $1/4$", 8" x 10 $1/2$" and 16" x 10 $1/2$".
   - Normal file card sizes: 3" x 5", 4" x 6", 5" x 8".
   - Post card sizes: 3 $1/4$" x 5 $1/2$".

Considerations:

   a. Avoid crowding content.
   b. Conform to dimensions of storage and filing facilities (i.e., legal size, letter size, etc.).
   c. Fit to standard office machines for filing (i.e., typewriter, bookkeeping machine, etc.).
   d. Fit to standard-size envelopes.

2. **Paper Weight and Grade**
   Operating unit ordinarily should specify one of the following four:

   - Mimeograph—36 lb. (basis 17" x 22")
   - Card—180 lb. (basis 25 $1/2$" x 30 $1/2$")
   - Sulphite—32 lb. (basis 17" x 22")
   - Bond (25% rag)—32 lb. (basis 17" x 22")

Selection should be based upon:

   a. Handling requirements
   b. Writing method
   c. Number of copies to be made at one writing
   d. Length of time the form will be retained

   e. Printing requirements (i.e., printing on two sides, by a given process, etc.)
   f. Filing and storage space requirements (affected by thickness of paper)

3. **Color of Paper**
   Specify color only when needed for emphasis or for more efficient filing, routing, or sorting. Reduce the need for colored paper by use of sorting symbols, bold headings, heavy ruled lines, or other devices when possible. Exceptions permissible for specific organization or operating requirements.

4. **Color of Ink**
   Specify other than black ink only when fully justified by volume and increased efficiency in use of the form and when the more economical possibilities of colored paper are inadequate. Two colors should be avoided except under extreme justification.

5. **Identification and Heading**
   Heading may be centered across entire top of form or centered in the space to the left of any entry boxes placed in the upper right. (Upper right should be designed for file or other ready-reference entries if needed.) Within space decided upon, arrange information generally as follows:

   - Form number and issuance or revision date— upper left corner.
   - Agency name and location (if needed)— upper left (under form number) or top center (depending on its importance in use of form).
   - Form title—center of top (under agency name and location, if that item is centered). Use conspicuous type.
   - Bureau of the Budget number and expiration date, for federal report forms— upper right corner.

Exception: Run identification across bottom of vertical-file-card forms unless needed for file-reference purposes.

6. Instructions

Well-designed forms require few instructions other than captions and item headings. When required, instructions usually should:

a. Be set in two or more narrow columns rather than full-width lines
b. Be listed as numbered items rather than in paragraph style
c. Be placed as near to the items to which they apply as possible (unless their length would detract from an effective layout)

When instructions are segregated on a form, they should be placed:

a. At top right or top center, if concise and applicable to the whole form
b. At bottom, if that will make possible more economical use of space
c. On reverse side, if no space available on the face

7. Address

If name and address are inserted on form by agency prior to mailing, position of name and address should be suitable for window-envelope use. Forms requiring return to an agency should be identified as provided under Standard No. 5.

Forms intended for use in window envelopes must conform to postal regulations, which in general provide that nothing other than name and address, and possibly mailing symbol, shall appear in the window. The form must fit the envelope to avoid shifting of the address. Standard-size envelopes only should be used. *Post Office Department Schedule of Award of Contracts for Envelopes is* the guide to standard envelope sizes.

8. Preprinted Names or Facsimile Signatures

If form is to be stocked for continuing use, personal name or signature of official may be preprinted only on special justification or by legal requirement (to avoid having large numbers of forms made obsolete by change of official. Preprinting of titles only or the use of rubber stamps or automatic signature inscribers are alternatives to be considered.

9. Form Arrangement

a. Align the beginning of each writing space on the form vertically for minimum number of tabular stops.
b. If box design is used:
   (1) Serially number each box in its upper left-hand corner
   (2) Start caption in upper left corner; to right of number, leaving fill-in space below caption
   (3) Draw box size to provide sufficient space for fill-in

c. Place essential information where it will not be obscured by stamps, punches, or staples, or be torn off with detachable stubs.
d. Group related items together
e. Include "to" and "from" spaces for any necessary routing.
f. Provide for use of window envelopes, when appropriate, to save additional addressing.
g. To the extent practicable, provide the same sequence of items as on other forms from which or to which information is to be transferred.
h. Arrange information for ease in tabulating or transferring to machine punched cards, if those are involved.

10. Check Boxes

Use check boxes when practicable.

a. Place check boxes either before or after items, but all in the corresponding positions within any line series.
b. Avoid columnar grouping of check boxes if possible, because of poor registration when carbon copies are required. Place check boxes before first column and after the second column when there are two adjacent columns of questions.

11. Margins

Printing Margin.
Printed all-around borders usually should not be used since they tend to increase production problems and costs. In any event an extra margin of 3/8 inch or not less than 3/10 inch from

edge of paper should be allowed on all four sides for gripping requirements in printing and as a safety margin for cutting. No printing, neither border nor text, should be permitted in that space.

Binding Margin.

For press-type holder, side or top, 1 inch; for ring binder, 1 inch (printing permitted but no fill-in within these margins).

Fill-in Margin.

Top typewriting line, at least $1^1/_3$ inch from top of paper if possible. Bottom typewriting line, not less than $^3/_4$ inch from bottom. Hand fill-in permissible above or below these lines.

12. **Space Requirements for Fill-in**
    - Typewritten—10 characters to the horizontal inch to accommodate both elite and pica typewriters; 3 fill-in spaces to the vertical inch, each space being double typewriter space.
    - Handwritten—one third more space horizontally than for typewritten fill-in; 3 spaces to the vertical inch, space double that of typewriter space.

13. **Rulings**
    a. Use heavy $1^1/_2$-point or parallel $^1/_2$-point rulings as first and last horizontal lines, between major divisions, and across column headings.
    b. Use $^3/_4$-point rulings across bottom of column headings, and above a total or balance at the foot of a column.
    c. Use hairline rulings for regular lines and box lines when no emphasis is required.
    d. Use $^1/_4$-point rulings for vertical subdivision of major sections or columns.
    e. Use leaders as needed to guide the eye in tabular or semitabular items.

14. **Signature and Approval Date**
    - Single handwritten signatures usually go at bottom/right of last page. Allow $^1/_2$ inch (three single typewriter spaces) vertically and 3 inches horizontally.
    - Two handwritten signatures, normally left and right at bottom of last page.
    - Space below the $^3/_4$-inch bottom typewriter margin generally reserved for handwritten signatures and dates.

15. **Two-sided Forms**
    a. Two-sided forms ordinarily should be printed head to foot (top to bottom of back), especially if top-punched for binder use.
    b. If punched in left margin for binder use, two-sided forms should be head to head.
    c. Three- or four-page forms (one sheet folded once) should be head to head throughout if open-side style, and head to foot if open-end (so that when opened for use, head of third page follows foot of second page).
    d. Head-to-foot open-end forms are preferable for machine fill-in.
    e. For multi-page forms, separate sheets of proper page size should be used instead of larger sheets folded to page size, unless the larger sheets can be cut economically from standard paper sizes and run on standard printing or duplicating equipment.

16. **Pre-numbering**
    Use pre-numbered forms only if accounting or control is required for each form or document. Place numbers in extreme upper right corner.

17. **Punching**
    For standard press-type and three-hole ring binders:

    - Distance from edge of paper to center of hole should measure $^3/_8$ inch;
    - If two holes are punched, for press-type fastener, the distance between centers should be $2^1/_4$ inches;
    - If three holes are punched, distance from center to center of adjacent holes should be $4^1/_4$ inches.

APPENDIX C

Forms Management Program Checklists

Control over a forms management program can be established through the use of forms management program checklists. Such checklists should cover forms management responsibilities, operating procedures, staff, and forms review.

Forms Management Responsibilities

1. Is forms management part of an overall records management program?
2. Is there a current directive or other authority that outlines the policy, objectives, and responsibilities for forms management?
3. Is the responsibility for the overall planning, developing, and coordinating of forms management standards and procedures assigned to a specific office at the executive level?
4. Are the aforementioned responsibilities assigned to a specific official at the executive level?
5. Are forms management responsibilities delegated to lower organizational levels?
6. Is there a requirement to periodically evaluate the effectiveness of forms management activities and compliance with established standards and procedures?
7. Is there a requirement to implement recommendations that result from evaluations?
8. Is there a requirement for developing standards and procedures to establish and improve the flow of information between forms management, reproduction, procurement, and supply?

Forms Management Operating Procedures

1. Is there a current directive that outlines the duties, procedures, and standards for forms management tasks?
2. Is there a directive that describes clearance and coordination procedures for originators of forms, public-use reports, and forms management?
3. Is there a directive that describes clearance and coordination procedures between forms management personnel and the offices responsible for the printing, procuring, and stocking of forms?
4. Is there a directive that states the lead times for forms analysis, clearance, design, composition, in-house printing, and outside printing?
5. Does the aforementioned directive include the requirement that all forms must be cleared by forms management before printing or procuring?
6. Do reproduction and procurement directives also include the requirement that all forms must be cleared by forms management before printing or procuring?
7. Have the directives been distributed to those who need the information at all organizational levels?
8. Are written instructions or implementing directives available to prescribe the use of every form?
9. Is there a requirement to review all implementing directives and to ensure that all references to forms and edition dates are correct before they are published?
10. Is a forms catalog or index issued on a periodic basis?
11. Is there a schedule for reviewing, updating, and cancelling forms listed in a catalog or inventory?
12. Is analysis a regular function in the forms management program?

Forms Management Staff

1. Is there a staff assigned to forms management duties?
2. Is the staff proficient in its handling of the workload and its assigned responsibilities?
3. Is the staff well trained in selling new ideas for efficient, effective systems or procedures?
4. Is the staff well trained in methods, procedures, and techniques for forms analysis, forms design, forms composition, and writing of specifications?
5. Does the staff participate in and initiate management studies to analyze forms and procedures and to recommend improvements?

6. Does the staff provide technical assistance to forms liaison representatives and to forms users and originators?

Forms Review

1. Do forms provide sufficient space for data entry and to accommodate the needs of the method used to enter the data?
2. Is extensive research needed to complete the forms?

3. Are blank forms conveniently available to individuals?
4. Do form sizes permit easy handling, reading, and use?
5. Are form sizes compatible with the filing and processing equipment?
6. Do forms contain clear, concise, and legible instructions?
7. Are computer forms compatible with the equipment for which they are designed?

APPENDIX D

ARMA Alphabetic Filing Rules

INTRODUCTION

This edition of ARMA's Alphabetic Filing Rules is designed to be a working tool, not a textbook. The basic premise used is that **filing is done for ease of retrieval.** For this to happen, it is absolutely necessary that filing rules be standardized and **documented** for the use of all personnel who file or retrieve the documents. **Documenting** filing decisions will ensure the **consistency** which is necessary for easy retrieval. These Rules are designed with space to check or annotate each rule used. This format allows the standard to be the **documentation** source.

The approach taken in compiling this publication gives simplified standard rules to follow. These rules will be applied to all general alphabetic filing. There is a section of specific rules which is designed for filing needs which may be found in specialized businesses. An appendix of those indexing practices which may already be in use in some offices is included. These other indexing practices are not recommended by ARMA. The index will lead to all entries.

The **Simplified Filing Standard Rules** set standards which ensure **consistency** in filing. These Simplified Rules are designed to be the first step toward automated filing and retrieval. Included are some major changes from accepted alphabetic filing rules which need to be considered. These changes affect the filing of some compound words, numbers which are not spelled out, abbreviations, acronyms, governmental designations, etc.

- The **Specific Filing Guidelines** should be used by those offices which have large files for one type of business; i.e., hotel suppliers, law offices, or when identical names appear more than once.
- The **Automated Conversion Guidelines** give points to consider when in the planning stage preceding conversion of an alphabetic file to an automated system for sorting and/or retrieval.
- The **Appendix** contains common indexing practices that violate the principles of consistency. It is recommended that these practices not be used when a new filing system is set up.
- A bibliography and index are included. Use of these tools will lead to the information needed when making filing decisions. For definitions of terms, see ARMA's *Glossary of Records Management Terms.*

Different offices have different needs for information retrieval. Those offices which have large files of one type of record may want to use one of the rules in Section II. The choice, or present use, of a standard rule, a specific guideline, or another practice should be checked and any deviation noted. There are also offices which have unique filing problems which may not be included. Document the solutions to these problems. Creativity in designing filing systems which aid in the retrieval of information is acceptable. It is imperative to have **documentation** available which will ensure **consistency** in filing and retrieval.

These Rules are written to be used. Use them well, and to assure consistency, place a check mark by, or annotate the rules which apply, listen for different ways requests are stated to help modify the system to improve retrieval; be creative. Enjoy participating in the information management profession.

GENERAL GUIDELINES

Alphabetic filing rules are written for one purpose—to make retrieval easy through **consistency** in filing .

Each organization may either accept the ARMA standard or establish its own alphabetic filing rules from a combination of the standard rules, specific guidelines or the other indexing practices. The choice should be determined by the organization's particular record retrieval needs. The rules used must then be **documented** and **communicated** as standard procedures to all personnel responsible for filing and retrieving information and records.

ARMA has chosen to define the filing method as *unit by unit.* The definition of a unit is as follows:

A filing unit may be a number, a letter, a word or any combination of these as stated in the simplified, specific, or appendix sections.

Refer to the individual rule being used to determine the correct interpretation of a filing unit.

One or more filing units are a filing segment, i.e., the total name, subject or number which is being used for filing purposes.

It is imperative that the users of the files be thoroughly instructed on the design of the system. Both filing personnel and others who may retrieve documents from the files should receive periodic refresher instruction on the system. This will ensure **consistency** in filing and retrieval of information.

Computers may be used to enhance filing and retrieval. When computer use is anticipated, alphabetic filing rules should be compatible with the capabilities of the computer. This compatibility will ease the change to, and utilization of, new technologies. Many of the following rules are written with this in mind.

Remember, **consistency** and **documentation** are the key elements in making alphabetic filing rules effective.

SECTION I

SIMPLIFIED FILING STANDARD RULES

The following seven rules provide consistency in simplified filing.

1. Alphabetize by arranging files in **unit-by-unit order and letter-by-letter within each unit.**
2. Each filing unit in a filing segment is to be considered. This includes prepositions, conjunctions and articles. The only exception is when the word *the* is the first filing unit in a filing segment. In this case, *the* is the last filing unit. Spell out all symbols, e.g., &, $, #, and file alphabetically.
3. File "nothing before something." File single unit filing segments before multiple unit filing segments.
4. Ignore all punctuation when alphabetizing. This includes periods, commas, dashes, hyphens, apostrophes, etc. Hyphenated words are considered one unit.
5. Arabic and Roman numbers are filed sequentially before alphabetic characters. All Arabic numerals precede all Roman numerals.
6. Acronyms, abbreviations and radio and television station call letters are filed as one unit.
7. File under the most commonly used name or title. Cross-reference under other names or titles which might be used in an information request.

EXAMPLES FOR APPLYING THE SIMPLIFIED FILING STANDARD RULES

Personal Names

1. **Simple Personal Names** Use the last (surname) as the first filing unit. The first name or initial is the second filing unit. Subsequent names or initials are filed as successive units.

As Written	Unit 1	Unit 2	Unit 3	Unit 4
O. Betty Greene	Greene	O	Betty	
Wm. David Michael Kelly	Kelly	Wm	David	Michael
Julie Tregaskis	Tregaskis	Julie		

2. **Personal Names with Prefixes** Surnames which include a prefix are filed as one unit whether the prefix is followed by a space or not. Examples of prefixes are: D', Da, De, Del, De la, Della, Den, Des, Di, Du, El, Fitz, L', La, Las, Le, Les, Lo, Los, M', Mac, Mc, O', Saint, St., Ste., Te, Ten, Ter, Van, Van de, Van der, Von, Von der.

As Written	Unit 1	Unit 2	Unit 3
Dan P. DeLeon	DeLeon	Dan	P
Peter J. Leuck	Leuck	Peter	J
Winifred A. LeVan	LeVan	Winifred	A
Warren C. Mace	Mace	Warren	C
S. John MacGregor	MacGregor	S	John
Thomas R. Macy	Macy	Thomas	R
Donna Mc Allister	McAllister	Donna	
John R. Mc Manville	McManville	John	R
Verna Morrison	Morrison	Verna	
Helen Grace M'Peters	MPeters	Helen	Grace
Mary J. Saint Thomas	Saint Thomas	Mary	J
Joseph H. St. John	StJohn	Joseph	H
F. P. Van der Linden	VanderLinden	F	P

3. **Personal Names with Personal and Professional Titles and Suffixes** Suffixes are not used as filing units except when needed to distinguish between two or more identical names. When **needed,** a suffix is the last filing unit and is filed as written, ignoring punctuation

As Written	Unit 1	Unit 2	Unit 3	Unit 4
John J. Johnson, 3d	Johnson	John	J	3
John J. Johnson, II	Johnson	John	J	II
John J. Johnson, C.P.A..	Johnson	John	J	CPA
John J. Johnson, Jr	Johnson	John	J	Jr
Maj. John J. Johnson	Johnson	John	J	Maj
Mayor John J. Johnson	Johnson	John	J	Mayor

John J. Johnson, M.D.	Johnson	John	J	MD
Mr John J. Johnson	Johnson	John	J	Mr
John J. Johnson Ph.D.	Johnson	John	J	PhD

4.   Personal Names Which Are Hyphenated Ignore the hyphen and file the two words as one unit.

As Written	As Filed	
	Unit 1	Unit 2
Mary-Kay deWinter	deWinter	MaryKay
Don Miller	Miller	Don
Peter Winter	Winter	Peter
Kathy Winter-Smith	WinterSmith	Kathy

5.   **Pseudonyms and Royal and Religious Titles** Pseudonyms are filed as written. Personal names which start with a royal or religious title and are followed by **only** a given name(s) are filed as written.

As Written	As Filed		
	Unit 1	Unit 2	Unit 3
Dr Seuss	Dr	Seuss	
Grandma Moses	Grandma	Moses	
Pope John Paul	Pope	John	Paul
Queen Elizabeth II	Queen	Elizabeth	II
Sister Teresa	Sister	Teresa	

6.   **Foreign Personal Names** If the surname is identifiable, file the name as any other personal name is filed. If there is a question about the surname, use the last name as the first filing unit and make a cross-reference from the first name.

As Written	As Filed		
	Unit 1	Unit 2	Unit 3
Camillo Benso Cavour	Cavour	Camillo	Benso
Gerard De Geer	DeGeer	Gerard	
	Lim	Yauw	Tjin
	(See Tjin Lim Yauw)		
Sri Muljono	Muljono	Sri	
	Sri	Muljono	
	(See Muljono Sri)		
Lim Yauw Tjin	Tjin	Lim	Yauw

Note: When corresponding with many people from other countries, refer to *ANGLO-AMERICAN CATALOGUING RULES,* Second Edition, for the correct filing procedure.

7.   **Nicknames** When a person commonly uses a nickname as a first name, file using the nickname. Cross-reference from the given name only if necessary.

As Written	As Filed		
	Unit 1	**Unit 2**	**Unit 3**
	Carter	James	Earl
	(See Carter Jimmy)		
Jimmy Carter	Carter	Jimmy	
Dizzy Dean	Dean	Dizzy	
	Dean	Jay	Hanna
	(See Dean Dizzy)		
Betty Hersey	Hersey	Betty	

BUSINESS AND ORGANIZATION NAMES

1. Business and organization names are filed as written according to the Simplified Standard Rules and using the business letterhead or trademark as a guide. Names with prefixes follow the example for Personal Names with Prefixes on page 546.

As Written	As Filed			
	Unit 1	**Unit 2**	**Unit 3**	**Unit 4**
1 -A Photo Service	1 A	Photo	Service	
3M	3M			
XXI Club	XXI	Club		
A-1 Printing Company	A1	Printing	Company	
AAA Travel Agency	AAA	Travel	Agency	
Able Action Plan	Able	Action	Plan	
AFL-CIO	AFLCIO			
American Insurance Co.	American	Insurance	Co	
Amoco	Amoco			
Angleton's of Boise	Angletons	of	Boise	
The Book Shop	Book	Shop	The	
Century 21	Century	21		
Century Cleaners	Century	Cleaners		
CH$_2$M Hill	CH$_2$M	Hill		
Child's Play	Childs	Play		
Dr. Spock'sClinic	Dr	Spocks	Clinic	
Ft. Ord Taxi	Ft	Ord	Taxi	
l.B.M.	IBM			
	(Use for International Business Machines Corp)			
	International	Business	Machines	Corp
	(See IBM)			
Mrs. Peter's Computers	Mrs	Peters	Computers	
Mt. Blanc Sound Shop	Mt	Blanc	Sound	Shop
St. Lukes Hospital	StLukes	Hospital		
There's Always Flowers	Theres	Always	Flowers	
Tom Wikon Painting	Tom	Wikon	Painting	
Wagon Works	Wagon	Works		
WGKM Radio Station	WGKM	Radio	Station	

Note: When necessary to ensure information retrieval, cross-reference between acronyms and the complete name.

2. Subsidiaries of businesses will be filed under their own name with a cross-reference to the parent company if needed.

As Written	As Filed			
	Unit 1	Unit 2	Unit 3	Unit 4
Ore-lda Foods, Inc. (See also H. J. Heinz Co.)	H (for subsidicries see Ore Ida Foods Inc Star Kist Foods Inc Weight Watchers I nternational)	J	Heinz	Co
	Ore Ida	Foods	Inc	

3. Place names in business names will follow the *Simplified Filing Standard Rule* that each word filing unit is treated as a separate filing unit.

As Written	As Filed			
	Unit 1	Unit 2	Unit 3	Unit 4
Alabama Power and Light	Alabama	Power	and	Light
New Jersey Coliseum	New	Jersey	Coliseum	
SeValle Publications, Inc.	SeValle	Publications	Inc	
St. Louis Power Company	StLouis	Power	Company	

4. **Compass Terms in Business Names** Each word/unit in a filing segment containing compass terms is considered a separate filing unit. If the term includes more than one compass point, treat it as it is written. Establish cross-references as needed.

As Written	As Filed			
	Unit 1	Unit 2	Unit 3	Unit 4
North East Forms Co.	North	East	Forms	Co
North Eastern Microfilm	North	Eastern	Microfilm	
North-East Data Co.	NorthEast	Data	Co	
Northeast Systems	Northeast	Systems		
Northeastern Equipment Co.	Northeastern	Equipment	Co	

GOVERNMENTAL/POLITICAL DESIGNATIONS

When filing governmental/political material, the name of the major entity is filed first, followed by the distinctive name of the department, bureau, etc.

This rule covers all governmental and political divisions, agencies, departments, committees, etc., from the federal to the county/parish, city, district and ward level.

Federal

Prefix with the name of the government and eliminate the department, i.e., Department of the Interior, Department of the Treasury, etc. File titles of the office, service, bureau, etc., by their distinctive names.

United States Government
    Coast Guard

United States Government
    Environmental Protection Agency

United States Government
    Forest Service

United States Government
    Interstate Commerce Commission

State and Local

State, county, parish, city, town, township and village governments/political divisions are filed by their distinctive names. The words "county of," "city of," "department of," etc., if needed and as appropriate, are added for clarity and are considered filing units.

Note: If "of" is not part of the official name as written, it is not added.

As Written	As Filed			
	Unit 1	Unit 2	Unit 3	Unit 4
Kane County Department of PublicWorks	Kane	County	Public	Works
City of Lovelock	Lovelock	City	of	
Nevada Departmentof Highways	Nevada	Highways	Department	
Washoe County	Washoe	County		

Foreign Governments

The distinctive English name is the first filing unit. If needed, the balance of the formal name of the government forms the next filing unit(s). Divisions, departments and branches follow in sequential order, reversing the written order where necessary to give the distinctive name precedence in the filing arrangement.

States, colonies, provinces, cities and other divisions of foreign governments are filed by their distinctive or official names as spelled in English. Cross-reference written name to official native name where necessary.

As Written	As Filed			
	Unit 1	Unit 2	Unit 3	Unit 4
Commonwealth of Australia	Australia			
Bermuda	Bermuda			
East Germany	East	Germany		
London, England	London	England		

Note: A current copy of *The World Almanac and Book of Facts* is an excellent reference for the translation of foreign names into English and for clarification of relations between governments. Another source is the book *Countries, Dependencies and Areas of Special Sovereignty* published by U.S. Dept. of Commerce, National Bureau of Standards, Institute for Computer Sciences & Technology, Gaithersburg, MD 20899.

SECTION II

SPECIFIC FILING GUIDELINES

Often, certain organizations correspond with, invoice, etc., specific groups of people or businesses. When this is the case, special filing systems may be developed to aid in the filing and retrieval of records. The following guidelines may be applied. Remember to **document** the decision to ensure **consistency.**

PERSONAL NAMES

Legal offices only, may need to relate the files of both partners of a marriage. If a married woman chooses to maintain her maiden name or connects her maiden name to her husband's surname with a hyphen, file using one spouse's surname and cross-reference from the other spouse's name.

As Written	As Filed			
	Unit 1	Unit 2	Unit 3	Unit 4
Rhonda J. Bluer-Acker	Acker (See Acker Wm Mrs)	Rhonda	J	Bluer
	Acker	Wm	Mrs	
Becki Blake	Blake (See PetersJohn J Mrs)	Becki		
	Bluer Acker (See Acker Wm Mrs)	Rhonda	J	
	Peters	John	J	Mrs

BUSINESS NAMES

When the same filing segment is applicable to more than one location, filing order is determined by an identifying location. In the case of banks, unions, etc., this location may be a branch, local number, post, etc. For most businesses, it will be an address. When using an address, cities are considered first, followed by states or provinces, street names, house number or building number in that order.

Address Arrangement

When the first units of street names are written as figures, the names are considered in ascending numeric order and placed together before alphabetic street names.

Street names with compass directions are considered as written. Numbers after compass directions are considered before alphabetic names (East 8th, East Main, Franklin, SE Eighth, Southeast Eighth, etc.).

If a filing unit within an address is not necessary for identification, it does not have to be used.

BUSINESS NAMES (CONTINUED)

As Written	As Filed					
	Unit 1	Unit 2	Unit 3	Unit 4	Unit 5	Unit 6
Assoc. of Hotel Employees, Portland, ME [2]*	Assoc	of	Hotel	Employees	Portland	ME
Assoc. of Hotel Employees, Portland, OR [2]	Assoc	of	Hotel	Employees	Portland	OR
The Baltimore Sun	Baltimore	Sun	The			
	Benevolent (See Elks Club	and	Protective	Order	of	Elks [7]
Chamber of Commerce, Phila, PA	Chamber	of	Commerce	Phila	PA	
Springfield Chamberof Commerce, IL	Chamber	of	Commerce	Springfield	IL	
Springfield Chamber of Commerce, MA	Chamber	of	Commerce	Springfield	MA	
Chicago First National Bank Aspin Branch	Chicago	First	National	Bank	Aspin	Branch
Chicago First National Bank Oaks Branch	Chicago	First	National	Bank	Oaks	Branch
College of Idaho	College	of	Idaho			
	College (See Notre Darne)	of	Notre	Dame [7]		
College of Ste Catherine, Library School	College	of	SteCatherine	Library	School	
Columbia Public Library, Columbia, AL	Columbia	Public	Library	Columbia	AL	
Columbia Pubic Library, Columbia, MD	Columbia	Public	Library	Columbia	MD	
Elks Club [7]	Elks	Club				
Grinnell College	Grinnell	College				
Insurance Library, Chicago	Insurance	Library				
Library of Congress	Library	of	Congress			
Lincoln School, St Paul. MN	Lincoln	School	StPaul	MN		
Lincoln School, Wllmar MN	Lincoln	School	Willmar	MN		
	Local (See UAW)	125	UAW			
Mary Carter Paints, 3404 3d St., Waco. TX	Mary	Carter	Paints	Waco	3	
Mary Carter Paints, 415 East Main St.,Waco,TX	Mary	Carter	Paints	Waco	East	Main
Mary Carter Paints, 210 Main St., Waco, TX	Mary	Carter	Paints	Waco	Main	
Mary L Carter, Inc., Austin, TX	Mary	L	Carter	Inc	Austin	
Mary L Carter, Inc., 414 3d St., Waco, TX	Mary	L	Carter	Inc	Waco	

BUSINESS NAMES (CONTINUED)

As Written	Unit 1	Unit 2	Unit 3	Unit 4	Unit 5	Unit 6
			As Filed			

As Written	Unit 1	Unit 2	Unit 3	Unit 4	Unit 5	Unit 6
Motel 6, Reno East [5]	Motel	6	Reno	East		
Motel 6, RenoSouth	Motel	6	Reno	South		
Motel 6, RenoWest	Motel	6	Reno	West		
Motel Idanha	Motel	Idanha				
College of Notre Dame [7]	Notre	Dame				
Readers Digest (CH) [2]	Readers	Digest	CH			
Readers Digest (NY)	Readers	Digest	NY			
The Southwind Motel	Southwind	Motel	The			
St Joseph's Hospital, Chicago, IL	StJosephs	Hospital	Chicago			
St. Joseph's Hospital, Milwaukee, Wl	StJosephs	Hospital	Milwaukee			
UAW Local 52 [7]	UAW	Local	52			
UAW Local 85	UAW	Local	85			
Local 125, UAW	UAW	Local	125			
University of California, Berkeley	University	of	California	Berkeley		
University of California, Riverside	University	of	California	Riverside		
University of lowa	University	of	lowa			
VFW Post 45	VFW	Post	45			
VFW Post 121	VFW	Post	121			
The Wall Street Journal	Wall	Street	Journal	The		
YMCA, 1515 1st Miami, FL	YMCA	Miami	FL			
YMCA, 2101 Ohio, Miami, FL	YMCA	Miami	FL	Ohio		
YMCA, 801 S W 1st Ave., Miami, FL	YMCA	Miami	FL	SW		

Note. Bracketed *numbers refer to the appropriate Simplified rule* on page 545.

SPECIAL SECTION

1. **Compass Terms in Scientific Document Filing**

    Compass terms are frequently applied to technical studies conducted by geographers, geologists, geophysicists, and other scientists studying the earth's surface. To maintain a geographically organized file, the compass term is treated as an adjective and is filed after the name only in scientific *document filing.*

As Written	As Filed		
	Unit 1	**Unit 2**	**Unit 3**
Northwest Castle Rock	Castle	Rock	Northwest
South Padre Island	Padre	Island	South
Texas	Texas		
East Texas	Texas	East	
WestTexas	Texas	West	
Eastern Williston Basin	Williston	Basin	Eastern

2. **Guardians, Receivers, Trustees in Legal Files**

    Guardians, trustees, receivers, or agents act for another person or organization and their names are not indexed. Such guardians, receivers, trustees, and agents may be persons, financial institutions, or companies. *Records are filed by the name of the person or organization for whom the guardian, trustee, receiver, or agent is acting.* For instance, if the Pacific Security National Bank is the trustee for Angela Dixon, a minor, the original records are filed by the name of Angela Dixon. A cross-reference is made in the name of the guardian, receiver, trustee, or agent to refer the filer to the name of the individual or organization for whom the agent is acting.

As Written	As Filed			
	Unit 1	**Unit 2**	**Unit 3**	**Unit 4**
Brockman & Clapp, Agents	Brockman	and	Clapp	Agents
		(See Rytex trucking)		
Colfax Webb, Receivers	Colfax	Webb	Receivers	
		(See Samuelson Instrument Co)		
Angela Dixon	Dixon	Angela		
William E. Nadeau	Nadeau	William	E	
Pacific Security National Bank	Pacific	Security	National	Bank
		(See Dixon Angela)		
Rytex Trucking	Rytex	Trucking		
Samuelson Instrument Co.	Samuelson	Instrument	Co	
Forrest W. Work, Guardian	Work	Forrest	W	Guardian
		(See Nadeau William E)		

3. **Religious Titles**

With numerous files using religious titles, the title may become the last filing unit.

As Written	As Filed		
	Unit 1	Unit 2	Unit 3
Sister Bernadette	Bernadette	Sister	
Father William Buechner	Buechner	William	Father
Sister Mary Elizabeth	Mary	Elizabeth	Sister
Sister Teresa	Teresa	Sister	

SECTION III

AUTOMATED* CONVERSION GUIDELINES

This section covers some of the considerations which must be understood to ease the transition from a manual to an automated or electronic, alphabetic filing system. Each automated system has its own peculiarities, so the most important step is to identify a person in the organization who understands both the software and the hardware that will be used. It is important to establish a good communication base with this person. This person who should be able to provide the following information:

1. What the hardware/software combination can do now;
2. How much time and cost will be involved if programming is needed for changes in the sort capability; and
3. Are the program changes going to be cost-effective or does the present sort format need to be reassessed?

Once there is a liaison person to work with, communicate how the alphabetic file is designed and how items should be sorted. Some of the questions which need answering are listed below.

1. When inverting personal names, should prefixes be included with the surname?
2. If prefixes are included with the surname, will the computer read/sort those with spaces between the prefix and the following name differently than those without spaces?
3. What happens with name suffixes? Will the output read: Kearns, Jr. Glenn E. or Kearns, Glenn E. Jr?
4. Does the computer have a table which converts abbreviations to the full name; i.e., Wm. to William?
5. What happens when the computer sorts punctuation (hyphens, apostrophes, spaces, periods, etc.) and diacritical marks? Wi!l the result throw the alphabetic sequence out of order?
6. Does the computer sort all Arabic numbers first? How does it sort capital and lower case letters? How are symbols sorted?
7. Should numbers be right justified? If so, how many characters should be planned for and do zeros need to be used to the left of the number itself?
8. If prepositions, articles and conjunctions are not to be used as filing units, does the system have a "stop list" which allows the words to be ignored?
9. Is there a limited field size? If so, is it satisfactory to abbreviate government names, i.e., U.S. Gov., or use a truncation/wild card option?

*Automated implies hardware from mainframes through personal computers and word processors

10. Is it advisable to provide two separate name fields for each record: (1) a field for the indexed name to be used primarily for alphabetic sorting and (2) a field for the name as written to be used for printouts on correspondence, directories, labels, etc.?

Before the complete alphabetic file (database) is entered into the automated system, carefully choose a sample of typical filing segments including items which may present filing problems. Have this input sorted and checked to see that the output is as planned. There will probably be more questions at this time. As these problems are solved, **document** the solutions. When the first phase of research is completed, reassess the alphabetic filing needs.

Some inconsistencies can be resolved at the time of data entry. If the information is to be placed on coding sheets to be used by data entry personnel, the coding must be set up in advance to reflect the filing order as it will appear in the database. The coding must be **consistent.** When the information is being input directly from file folders, data entry personnel must be instructed to input the data the way it is to be sorted and printed; e.g., St. for Saint is always entered "Saint," or St. for Street is always entered "Street."

The time and effort put into preparing the information to be input will pay off in ease of retrieval and usable output.

Automating files can be fun, challenging, frustrating and rewarding. Think about the fun and rewards when the frustrations are no longer overwhelming.

APPENDIX

OTHER INDEXING PRACTICES

The indexing practices in the Appendix are a collection of some of the more common, inconsistent practices which have been in use over a long period of years. These practices are included in this publication only to aid in proper documentation of the rule actually being used. It is important to note that most practices violate the rule of consistency and thus may interfere with the effective filing and retrieval of documents. For ease of reference, these practices are arranged in the same order as the examples for the Simplified Filing Standard Rules. Remember to note and cross-reference which Standard Rule, Specific Rule, or Other Indexing Practice is used in the filing system.

PERSONAL NAMES

1. **Personal Names with Prefixes**
   a
   Where there are a significant number of names starting with a particular prefix, such as Mc or Van, the prefixes are filed as a separate letter group preceding the other names.

As Written	As Filed		
	Unit 1	**Unit 2**	**Unit 3**
David L. De Chambeau	DeChambeau	David	L
Bill R. De La Rosa	De La Rosa	Bill	R
Sally Deaton	Deaton	Sally	
Robert MacCaw	MacCaw	Robert	
John McGiff	McGiff	John	
Peter McGill	McGill	Peter	
Dana Maas	Maas	Dana	
F. P Van der Linden	Van der Linden	F	P
John Van Hook	Van Hook	John	
Mary Vance	Vance	Mary	

b

When the' prefix is separated by a space from the rest of the surname, file each part of the surname separately with the first prefix as the first unit.

As Written	As Filed			
	Unit 1	**Unit 2**	**Unit 3**	**Unit 4**
Dan P. De Leon	De	Leon	Dan	P
Peter J. Leuck	Leuck	Peter	J	
Winifred A. LeVan	LeVan	Winifred	A	
Peter Mac Bride	Mac	Bride	Peter	
Warren C. Mace	Mace	Warren	C	
S. John MacGregor	MacGregor	S	John	
Frank Van der Linden	Van	der	Linden	Frank

c

All M', Mac and Mc' surnames which are pronounced "mac" are filed as if they were spelled "mac."

As Written	As Filed		
	Unit 1	**Unit 2**	**Unit 3**
Robert M'Caw	M'Caw	Robert	
Warren C. Mace	Mace	Warren	C
John McGiff	McGiff	John	
PeterMacGill	MacGill	Peter	

2. **Personal Names with Suffixes**

a

Seniority designations, as Sr., Junior, Jr., 2d, etc., are considered separate filing units and filed in abbreviated form in numeric sequence when needed for identification. (Sr. equals 1st, Jr. 2d.)

As Written	As Filed			
	Unit 1	Unit 2	Unit 3	Unit 4
John J. Johnson Sr.	Johnson	John	J	Sr
John J. Johnson II	Johnson	John	J	II*
John J. Johnson Jr.	Johnson	John	J	Jr
John J. Johnson 3d	Johnson	John	J	3d

*Numbers precede alphabetic equivalent.

b

Degrees, military ranks, and professional titles which are commonly abbreviated are left in abbreviated form with each segment of the abbreviation filed as a separate unit.

As Written	As Filed				
	Unit 1	Unit 2	Unit 3	Unit 4	Unit 5
John Johnson, C.P.A.	Johnson	John	C	P	A
Dr. John Johnson	Johnson	John	Dr		
Maj. Gen'l John Johnson	Johnson	John		Maj	Genl
Mayor John Johnson	Johnson	John	Mayor		
John Johnson, PhD	Johnson	John	Ph	D	

c

(1) A personal title (Miss, Mr., Mrs., and Ms.) is spelled out and used as the last indexing unit when needed for identification.

(2) College and university degrees, professional certifications, and military ranks are spelled out and used as the last indexing unit when needed for identification.

As Written	As Filed			
	Unit 1	Unit 2	Unit 3	Unit 4
Miss Marion Brown	Brown	Marion	Miss	
Mr. Marion Brown	Brown	Marion	Mister	
Mrs. Marion Brown	Brown	Marion	Mistress	
Ms. Marion Brown	Brown	Marion	Ms	
Marion Walter Brown	Brown	Marion	Walter	
Captain Marion Walter Brown	Brown	Marion	Walter	Captain
Prof. Marion Walter Brown	Brown	Marion	Walter	Professor

4. **Personal Names which are Hyphenated**

   When the surname of an individual is hyphenated, use the last segment of the surname as the first filing unit. The first name or initial is the second filing unit. The first segment of the hyphenated name is the last filing unit.

As Written	As Filed		
	Unit 1	Unit 2	Unit 3
Helen Canizales-Diego	Diego	Helen	Canizales
Patsy Hopper-Ragan	Ragan	Patsy	Hopper
Wm. B. Ragan	Ragan	Wm	B

5. **Nicknames**

   When a person commonly uses a nickname for the first name, find out if the nickname is truly the given name. If a given name is available, file under that name and cross-reference from the nickname.

As Written	As Filed		
	Unit 1	Unit 2	Unit 3
Dizzy Dean	Dean	Jay	Hanna
	Dean	Dizzy	
	(See Dean Jay Hanna)		
Jimmy Carter	Carter	James	Earl
	Carter	Jimmy	
	(See Carter James Earl)		
Betty Hersey	Hersey	Betty	

6. **Abbreviated Given Names**

When a given name is written in an abbreviated form, file it as if it were spelled out.

As Written	As Filed	
	Unit 1	Unit 2
Chas. Peterson	Peterson	Charles
Rbt. Peterson	Peterson	Robert
Wm. Peterson	Peterson	William

BUSINESS NAMES

1. **Articles, Prepositions, &, AND**

   A, an, the, prepositions, &, and conjunctions are disregarded in filing. These words are placed in parentheses to indicate that they are not used in filing.

As Written	As Filed		
	Unit 1	**Unit 2**	**Unit 3**
Garfield for President Club	Garfield (for)	President	Club
Gatzka & Sons, Inc.	Gatzka(&)	Sons	Incorporated
Rain or Shine Apparel	Rain (or)	Shine	Apparel
Top of the Mark	Top (of the)	Mark	
The Watson Plumbing Co.	Watson	Plumbing	Company(The)

2. **Individual Names in Company Names**

   a

   When a company name begins with the full name of an individual, file the surname first, then the given name, initials and the balance of the name. Cross-reference as necessary.

As Written	As Filed			
	Unit 1	**Unit 2**	**Unit 3**	**Unit 4**
Geo. Banta Company, Inc.	Banta	George	Company	Incorporated
F. G. Olendorf Co.	Olendorf	F	G	Company

   b

   When a company named for an individual(s) becomes so well known that to reverse the names would cause confusion, file as written; cross-reference as necessary.

As Written	As Filed		
	Unit 1	**Unit 2**	**Unit 3**
J.C. Penney	J	C	Penney
Marshall Field & Co.	Marshall	Field (&)	Company
Montgomery Ward Co.	Montgomery Ward		Company

3. **Hyphenated Business Names**

   a.   When two or more initials, words, names, word substitutes, or coined words in a business name are joined by a hyphen, the hyphen is disregarded and each part of the name is considered to be a separate unit. (If a surname and a coined name are used to form a business name, a cross-reference should be prepared.)

   b.   Articles, prepositions, and conjunctions that are joined to other words by hyphens also follow this rule: Each is a separate unit.

   c.   When a hyphen joins two parts of a single word, both parts are considered together as one unit. Words of this type often begin with anti-, bi-, co-, inter-, intra-, mid-, non-, pan-, pre-, re-, self-, trans-, tri-, un-, and the like.

As Written	As Filed			
	Unit 1	Unit 2	Unit 3	Unit 4
A-C Supply Corp.	A	C	Supply	Corporation
A-Jay-Zee Co.	A	Jay	Zee	Company
Anti-Defamation League	Anti-Defamation	League		
Beef-N-Boards Restaurant	Beef	N	Boards	Restaurant
Cams-Smith Drug Store	Cams	Smith	Drug	Store
Co-operative Marketing Co.	Co-operative	Marketing	Company	
Gaslight Drive-ln Theater	Gaslight	Drive	In	Theater
Inter-Ocean Insurance Co.	Inter-Ocean	Insurance	Company	
Stedman Serv-Ur-Self	Stedman	Serv	Ur	Self
Trans-Canada Railroad Line	Trans-	Canada	Railroad	Line
Tri-City Transport Co.	Tri-City	Transport	Company	
U-and-I Laundry	U	and	I	Laundry

4. **Abbreviated Business Names**

   a

   A business which is known by an abbreviation of its name is filed under the full name of the company. Cross-references are made from the abbreviation if necessary.

As Written	As Filed			
	Unit 1	Unit 2	Unit 3	Unit 4
IBM	International	Business	Machines	Corporation
3M	Minnesota	Mining (and)	Manufacturing	Company
	Three	M		
	(See Minnesota Mining and Manufacturing Company)			

   b

   When a business name contains an abbreviated word, file the abbreviated word as spoken.

As Written	As Filed		
	Unit 1	Unit 2	Unit 3
Peter's of St. Louis	Peter's(of)	Saint	Louis
Ste. Joan Winery	Sainte	Joan	Winery
W. State Foodland	West	State	Foodland

5. **Contractions and Possessives**

   Alphabetize and file to the apostrophe, and then stop. File as if any letters in the unit which follow the apostrophe do not exist.

As Written	Unit 1	Unit 2	Unit 3	Unit 4
	As Filed			
Johnson's Appliance Shop	Johnson ('s)	Appliance	Shop	
Johnsons Apparel Shop	Johnsons	Apparel	Shop	
Johnstons' Service Station	Johnstons'	Service	Station	
What's Cookin Restaurant	What('s)	Cookin	Restaurant	
Who's Who in America	Who ('s)	Who (in)	America	

6. **Single Letters in Names**

   Single letters appearing in company names, including radio and television call letters, are treated as separate units, even though they may be written together without spaces.

As Written	Unit 1	Unit 2	Unit 3	Unit 4	Unit 5
	As Filed				
ABC Cartage Company	A	B	C	Cartage	Company
K & E Supply Company	K (&)	E	Supply	Company	
KFGT Radio	K	F	G	T	Radio
Triple T Beverage Service	Triple	T	Beverage	Service	
WGNB Television	W	G	N	B	Television

7. **Numeric Names**

   Names containing numbers are filed alphabetically as if the numbers were spoken.

As Written	Unit 1	Unit 2	Unit 3	Unit 4
	As Filed			
1st Ave. Drug Store	First	Avenue	Drug	Store
Four Ply Wood Products	Four	Ply	Wood	Products
Hank's Pewter Shop	Hank's	Pewter	Shop	
Marty's Finger Steaks	Marty's	Finger	Steaks	
Marty's 400 Dolls	Marty's	Four	Hundred	Dolls
914 Club	Nine	Fourteen	Club	
1010 Downing St.	Ten	Ten	Downing	Street

8. **Business Names** sometimes contain compound place words. These compound place words are filed as one unit.

As Written	Unit 1	Unit 2	Unit 3	Unit 4
	As Filed			
Los Angeles Coliseum	Los Angeles	Coliseum		
The New York Times Company	New York	Times	Company	The
St. Louis Power Company	Saint Louis	Power	Company	

9. **Business Names with Compass Terms**

   Each word in a name containing compass terms is considered a separate filing unit. If the term includes more than one compass point, treat each compass point as a separate word even if written together. Establish permanent cross-references for compass points written as one word (Northeast, see North East).

As Written	As Filed			
	Unit 1	**Unit 2**	**Unit 3**	**Unit 4**
North East Dairy Co.	North	East	Dairy	Company
Northeast Farms	North	east	Farms	
Northeastern Gage Co.	North	eastern	Gage	Company
North Eastern Zinc	North	Eastern	Zinc	

10. **Subsidiaries and Divisions**

    Subsidiary companies, divisions and affiliates are filed after the parent company's name. The parent or holding company name is the first filing unit.

    Insert a cross-reference from the subsidiary, etc., when needed for retrieval.

    A complete listing of the organizations under the parent or holding company can be inserted in the file for convenience.

As Written	As Filed				
	Unit 1	**Unit 2**	**Unit 3**	**Unit 4**	**Unit 5**	**Unit 6**
Crosley Division, Avco Corp.	Avco	Corporation	Crosley	Division		
Stromberg Carlson, a Div. of General Dynamics Corporation	General	Dynamics	Corporation	Stromberg	Carlson	(a) Division (of)
Electronics Laboratory, General Electric Company	General	Electric	Company	Electronics	Laboratory	
Delco-Remy Division of General Motors Corporation	General	Motors	Corporation	Delco-Remy	Division (of)	
The Procurement Division, Martin Company	Martin	Company	Procurement	Division (The)		
Remington Rand Division Sperry Rand Corporation	Sperry	Rand	Corporation	Remington	Rand	Division
Vickers Inc. Division of Sperry Rand Corporation	Sperry	Rand	Corporation	Vickers	Incorporated	Division (of)

Federal

a

Departments and agencies of the federal government are indexed under United States Government, first by the department title, and then sequentially by order of authority. Alphabetic sequencing begins at the secondary level (the department, bureau or office).

> United States Government
> > Commerce, Dept. (of)
> > > Economic Development Administration

> United States Government
> > Treasury, Dept. (of the)
> > > Internal Revenue Service
> > > > Taxpayer Information

> United States Government
> > Labor Department (of)
> > > Labor Standards Bureau (of)
> > > > Occupational Safety Office (of)

b

Omit government name and file by the principal words in the name of the department and then by bureau or other units necessary for filing purposes.

> Agriculture, Forest Service
> Interior, Mines (Bureau of)

> Commerce, International Trade Administration
> Consumer Affairs (Office of)

Notes:

(1) Use the *United States Government Manual* as a guide for names of branches, executive departments, committees, commissions, etc., of the United States Government.

(2) When a great deal of correspondence is carried on with one branch of the government, set aside a special section of the files for these records. File the agencies and offices alphabetically within the special section.

Military

File camps, forts, arsenals, bases, stations, depots, etc., after the prefix "United States Government."

> United States Government
> > Camp Edwards
> United States Government
> > Caven Point Terminal
> United States Government
> > Fort Sam Houston
> United States Government
> > Hawthorne Ammunition Depot

APPENDIX E

Records Management Publications

Sources for this information include *Ulrich's International Periodicals Directory, 1993–94,* 32nd edition (New Providence, New Jersey: R. R. Bowker, 1993)

Administative Management (New York)
Dalaton Communications, Inc.
1123 Broadway
Suite 1100
New York, NY 10010
also available online.
Vendors: DIALOG
Information Services, Inc.

Administrative Management/Jimu Kanri
(text in Japanese)
Industrial Daily News, Ltd.
Nikkan Kogyo Shinbun Ltd.
1-8-10 Kudan Kita
Chiyoda-ku, Tokyo 102, Japan

Advanced Imaging
P T N Publishing Corp.
445 Broad Hallow Road
Suite 21
Melville, NY 10747-4722
FAX: 516-845-2797

American Archivist
Society of American Archivists
600 S. Federal
Suite 504
Chicago, IL 60605
FAX: 312-347-1452

Business Computer Digest
Association of Computer Users
Box 2189
Berkeley, CA 94702-0189
also availabe online.
Vendor: NewsNet.

Business Computer News
Moorhead Publications Ltd.
797 Don Mills Road
Toronto, Ont.

M3C 3S5 Canada
FAX: 416-696-7395

Computer Data Storage Newsletter
(text in English)
Micro-Journal S.a.r.l
11 rue de Provence
75009 Paris, France
FAX: 1-48-24-22-76

Computer Decisions (1969–1990)
F M Computer Publications
25 W. 43rd Street
Suite 707
New York, NY 10036

Computers and Information Systems Abstract Journal
Cambridge Scientific Abstracts
7200 Wisconsin Avenue
6th Floor
Bethesda, MD 20814
FAX: 301-961-6720

ComputerWorld
(available in English, Spanish, Japanese, Norwegian, and Danish)
Computerworld, Inc.
375 Cochituate Road
Box 9171
Framington, MA 01701-9171
also available online.
Vendors: DIALOG
Information Services, Inc. (File No. 674)
Mead Data Central, Inc.

Corporate Computing
Ziff–Davis Publishing Co.
950 Tower Ln. 19th Floor
Foster City, CA 94404

Data Communications
McGraw-Hill, Inc.
1221 Avenue of the Americas
New York, NY 10020

subscriptions: Box 473
                  Hightstown, NJ 08520
also available online.
Vendors: DIALOG
          Information Services, Inc. (File No. 624)
          McGraw-Hill Publications Online
          Dow Jones News Retrieval
          Mead Data Central, Inc.
          NewsNet (TE37)

Data Entry Management Association Newsletter
(short title: DEMA)
          Data Entry Management Association
          101 Merritt 7 Corporate Park, 5th Floor
          Norwalk, CT 06856-5131
              FAX: 203-846-0883

Data Management (1951–198?)
          Data Processing Management Association
          505 Busse Highway
          Park Ridge, IL 60068-3191

Data Management Review
          Technical Enterprises, Inc.
          4811 S. 76th Street
          Suite 210
          Milwaukee, WI 53220
              FAX: 414-423-2433

Data Management Update
          Database Research Group, Inc.
          31 State Street
          Suite 800
          Boston, MA 02109-9834
              FAX 617-227-2396

Data News Weekly
          Data Enterprises
          Box 51933
          New Orleans, LA 70151
              FAX: 504-523-7364

Data Training
          Waingarten Publications, Inc.
          25 First Street
          Cambridge, MA 02141-1810

DataBase Management
          Auerbach Publishers
          One Penna Plaza

          New York, NY 10017
              FAX: 617-423-2026
subscriptions: 210 South Street
                  Boston, MA 02111-9990

Database and Network Journal (UK)
          A. P. Publications, Ltd.
          377 St. John Street
          London EC1V 4LD England
              FAX: 071-837-1197

Database Programming and Design
          Miller Freeman, Inc.
          600 Harrison Street
          San Francisco, CA 94107
              FAX: 415-905-2232

Datamation
          Cahners Publishing Co.
          Division of Reed Publishing Co., Inc.
          275 Washington Street
          Newton, MA 02158-1630
              FAX: 617-558-4506

EDI Forum
          EDI Group, Ltd.
          Box 710
          Oak Park, IL 60302
              FAX: 708-848-0270

EDI News
          Phillips Publishing, Inc.
          7811 Montrose Road
          Potomoc, MD 20854
              FAX: 301-309-3847
also available online.
Vendor: NewsNet (TE80)

Electronic Imaging Report
          Phillips Publishing Inc.
          7811 Montrose Road
          Potomoc, MD 20854
              FAX: 301-309-3847
also available online:
Vendor: NewsNet (EC02)

Form
          National Business Forms Association
          433 East Monroe Avenue
          Arlington, VA 22301
              FAX: 703-836-2241

G C A Bar Code Reporter
Graphics Communication Association
100 Dangerfield Road
Alexandria, VA 22314
FAX 703-548-2867

Government Computing Digest
Synergistic Enterprises
132 Adrian Cres.
Markham
Ontario L3P 7B3 Canada
FAX: 416-472-3091

Government Computer News
Cahners Publishing Co.
Division of Reed Publishing (USA) Inc.
8601 Georgia Avenue, Suite 300
Silver Springs, MD 20910
FAX: 301-650-2111
subscriptions: 44 Cook Street
Denver, CO 80206-5800
also available online.
Vendors: DIALOG
Information Services, Inc.
also available on CD-ROM.

Government Executive
National Journal, Inc.
1730 M Street NW
Suite 1100
Washington, DC 20036
FAX: 202-833-8069

Government Technology
G T Publications, Inc.
9719 Lincoln Village Dr.
No. 500
Sacramento, CA 95827-3303
FAX: 916-363-5197

Graphics Arts Monthly
Cahners Publishing Co.
Division of Reed Publishing Inc.
249 West 17 Street
New York, NY 10011
FAX: 212-463-6733

Imaging Service Bureau News
Image Publishing, Inc.
105 Valley Road

Box 3149
Westport, CT 06880-5133
FAX: 203-222-7871

IMC Journal
International Information Management Congress
1650 38th Street
Boulder, CO 80301-2623
FAX: 716-383-8442

Infocus
Business Forms Management Association
519 SW 3rd St. No. 712
Portland, OR 97204

INFODB
Data Base Associates
Box 215
Morgan Hill, CA 95038-0215
FAX: 408-779-3274

Inform
Association for Information and Image
Management
1100 Wayne Avenue
Suite 1100
Silver Springs, MD 20910

Information Management
Center for Management Systems
Box 208
Sioux City, IA 51102

Information Management Bulletin
(Information Resource Management Association)
Idea Group Publishing
4811 Jonestown Road
Suite 230
Harrisburg, PA 17109-1751
FAX: 717-541-9159

Information Management and Technology
CIMTECH
University of Herfordshire
College Lane
Hatfield, Herts.
AL10 9AB England
FAX: 0107-272121

Information Processing and Management
  (text in English, French, German, Italian)
  Pergamon Press, Inc.
  Journals Division
  660 White Plains Road
  Tarrytown, NY 10591-5153
    FAX: 914-333-2444
and Headington Hill Hall
  Oxford OX3 0BW England

Information Processing Society of Japan Transactions
  (text in Japanese, English)
  I P S of Japan
  Joho Shori Gakkai
  27th floor
  STEC Joho Building
  1-21-1 Nishi–Shinjuku,
  Sjinjuku-ku, Tokyo 160 Japan
    FAX: 03-5322-3534

Information Resources Management Journal
  (Information Resource Management
  Association)
  Idea Group Publishing
  4811 Jonestown Road
  Suite 230
  Harrisburg, PA 17109-1751
    FAX: 717-541-9159

Information Systems (Tarrytown)
  Pergamon Press, Inc.
  Journals Division
  660 White Plains Road
  Tarrytown, NY 10591-5153
    FAX: 914-333-2444
and: Headington Hill Hall
  Oxford OX3 0BW England

Information Systems Management
  Warren Gorham Lamont
  One Penn Plaza
  New york, NY 10019
    FAX: 617-423-2026

Information Technology Notes
  London and South Eastern Library Region
  (LASER)
  33-34 Alfred Place
  London XW1E 7DP England

Information Today
  Learned Information, Inc.
  143 Old Marlton Pike
  Medford, NJ 08055
    FAX: 609-654-4309

Information Week
  C M P Publications, Inc.
  600 Community Drive
  Manhasset, NY 11030
    FAX: 516-365-4601
also available online.
Vemdor: NewsNet (TE34)

InfoWorld
  InfoWorld Publishing
  (subsidiary of IDG Communications)
  155 Bovet Road
  Suite 800
  San Mateo, CA 94402
    FAX: 415-358-1269
also available online.
Vendor: Mead Data Central, Inc.

Journal of Imaging Science & Technology
  Society for Imaging Science & Technology
  7003 Kilworth Ln
  Springfield, VA 22151
    FAX: 703-642-9094

Journal of Information Recording Materials
  (text in English and German)
  (summaries in English, German, and Russian)
  Gordon & Breach Science Publishers
  270 Eighth Avenue
  New York, NY 10011
    FAX: 212-645-2459

Journal of Information Technology JIT
  (Association for Information Technology)
  Chapman and Hall
  2-6 Boundary Row
  London SE1 8HN England

Journal of Micrographics/MAIKURO SHASHIN
  (text in Japanese)
  Japan Microphotography Association—
  Nihnon Maikuro
  Shashin Kyokui
  2nd Ohkouchi Bldg.

1-9-15 aji-Machi, Chiyodi-ku
Tokyo 101, Japan

Journal of Systems Management
Association for Systems Management
Box 38370
Cleveland, OH 44138

LAN Technology
M & T Publishing Inc.
(subsidiary of Markt & Technik)
411 Borel Avenue
Suite 100
San Mateo, CA 4402
FAX: 415-366-1685

Link–Up
Learned Information, Inc.
143 Old Marlton Pike
Medford, NJ 08055
FAX: 609-654-4309

Management World (1960–1990)
Administrative Management Society
1101 14th Street NW
Suite 1100
Washington, DC 20005

MIS Week
Fairchild Publications Inc.
7 East 12 Street
New York, NY 10003

Modern Office Technology
Penton Publishing Inc.
1100 Superior Avenue
Cleveland, OH 44114-2543
FAX: 609-696-8765

Multimedia and Videodisc Technology
Future Systems, Inc.
Box 26
Falls Church, VA 22040
FAX: 703-532-0529
also available on line.
Vendors: DIALOG
Information Services, Inc.
NewsNet (EC70)
Network Magazine
155 E 4905 S.

Salt Lake City, UT 84107
FAX: 801-261-5623

The Office
Office Publications, Inc.
1200 Summer Street
Box 120031
Stamford, CT 06912-0031
FAX: 203-359-0943

Office News
Thomson Publications Australia
47 Chippen Street
Chippendale NSW
2008 Australia
FAX: 02-698-3920

Office Productivity
Maclean-Hunter, Ltd.
Business Publications Division
Maclean-Hunter Bldg.
777 Bay Street
Toronto, Ont.
M5W 1A7 Canada
Office Products Analyst
Industry Analysts, Inc.
50 Chestnut Street
Rochester, NY 14601
FAX: 716-454-5760

Office Products Industry Report
National Office Products Association
301 North Fairfied Street
Alexandria, VA 22314
FAX: 703-683-7552

Office Systems (year)
Office Systems
941 Danbury Road
Box 150
Georgetown, CT 06829
FAX: 203-544-8465

Office Systems Research Journal
Office Systems Research Association
Washington University Campus
Box 1141
1 Brookings Drive
St. Louis, MO 63130
FAX: 314-935-4479

Office Technology Management (1966–1992)
Business Technology Management, Inc.
1225 Franklin Avenue
Suite 210
Garden City, NY 11530

PC Computing
Ziff-Davis Publishing Co.
Computer Publications Division
950 Tower Lane
Foster City, CA 94404
FAX: 415-578-7059

PC Magazine
Ziff-Davis Publishing Co.
One Park Avenue
New York, NY 10016

PC Today
Peed Corporation
120 W. Harvest Drive
Box 85380
Lincoln, NE 68501-5380
FAX: 402-477-9252

PC Week
Ziff-Davis Publishing Co.
10 Presidents Landing
Medford, MA 02155-5446
also available online: Vendors: DIALOG
Information Services, Inc.

PC World
PC World Communications, Inc.
501 Second Street
Suite 600
San Francisco, CA 94107
FAX: 415-442-1891

Subscriptions:
P. O. Box 55029
Boulder, CO 80322-5029

Prologue: The Journal of the National Archives
US NARA Trust Fund Board
Seventh Street & Pennsylvania Avenue, NW
Washington, DC 20408
FAX: 202-501-5239

Records Management Quarterly
ARMA International
4200 Somerset Drive
Suite 215
Box 8540
Prairie Village, KS 66208

Software Magazine
Sentry Publishing Co., Inc.
1900 West Park Drive
Westborough, MA 01581

Software World
A. P. Publications, Ltd
377 St. John Street
London EC1V 4L England

Xinxi Shijie/Information World
(text in Chinese)
China New Technology Pioneering Enterprise
Building No. 6
State Science Commission
Guojia Kexue Weiyuanhui
Weingongcun, Beijing 100081
Peoples Republic of China

Glossary

Accession A shipment of records received into the Records Center or archives for storage and retrieval.

Accession book A control device used in numeric filing to keep track of new files as they are created.

Accessioning The conveyance or transfer of the legal and physical custody of archival records from their offices of creation to an archival repository; also, the creation of records documenting receipt and acceptance of the records into the archives.

Access restrictions In archives management, the policies imposed by an archival repository to limit or restrict open access to and use of some or all the holdings of the repository to certain persons and/or for certain periods of time.

Access time The interval between the time records are called for or requested and when delivery to the requesting party is completed.

Accuracy ratio A measure of how many of the requested documents were actually found.

Acid A chemical substance capable of forming hydrogen ions when dissolved in water. Acids can weaken cellulose in paper, board, and cloth.

Acid–free In chemistry, any material with a pH of 7.0 or higher. Acid–free paper refers to paper that is free of active acid during its manufacture. However, over time, acid may form in some papers and boards.

Acid migration The transfer of acid from an acidic material to a less acidic or neutral one. This can happen when an acidic material and a less acidic material come into contact with each other, such as the cover of a book or pamphlet to the less acidic paper of the inside text.

Activity (reference) ratio A measure of file activity. It is calculated by dividing the number of records requested each month by the total number of records in the system.

Administrative value In records appraisal, the usefulness of a record in the conduct of an organization's business; the value of a record for the purpose for which it was created. Also referred to as *operational value*.

Adverse inference A finding by a court that information contained in records that were inappropriately destroyed by a person or party is incriminating or unfavorable to that party, even though the information is not available to the court.

Air drying A method of drying damp (but not completely soaked) paper records by placing the records in a cool, dry room, and exposing them to maximum air flow, frequently aided by the use of fans.

Alkaline Having a pH greater than 7.0. Alkaline substances may be added to materials to neutralize any acids present. They may also be added during manufacturing (as of paper) to form a buffer against the later formation of harmful acids. Some common buffers are magnesium carbonate and calcium carbonate.

Alphabetical filing Arrangement of records in accordance with the alphabet. The records may be arranged by subject, name, organization, or place.

Alpha classified Subject files without the use of codes.

Alphanumeric A filing system combining alphabetic and numeric symbols to develop codes for classifying information.

American Standard Code for Information Interchange (ASCII) A widely utilized coding scheme which specifies bit patterns for computer-processable information. The ASCII coding scheme is utilized in virtually all minicomputers and microcomputers and in many non-IBM mainframe computer systems.

Analog copier A copier that can transfer the image from the original to the copy using the same general principle as a camera

Analog image A non-electronic image; non-digitized.

Analytical index An index that isolates single items or concepts, as in an index of specific topics of information included under broader headings.

Aperture card A tab–size card with a rectangular hole cut into it which is designed to hold a frame of microfilm.

Appraisal, records The process of determining the value and thus the disposition of records, and designating them as either temporary or permanent, which may be accomplished as a part of the process of developing records retention schedules or as a separate act. The evaluation of a document's worth or value for retention or archival purposes, based upon its current or predicted future use(s) for administrative, legal, fiscal research or historical purposes.

Archival, archivally sound Durable, permanent, and suitable for preservation in archives. Although no specific standards exist for labeling a material archivally sound, it is understood to suggest that the material is very durable.

Archival value In records appraisal, the determination that records possess current or future value in elucidating the history or an organization and are thus worthy of permanent preservation. Also referred to as *historical value.*

Archives The noncurrent records of an organization preserved or appropriate for preservation because of their continuing, or enduring value. A place in which archival records or other important historical documentation are permanently maintained.

Archivist A person responsible for or engaged in one or more of the following activities in an archives: records appraisal and disposition, accessioning, preservation, arrangement, description, reference service, and exhibition or publication of archival materials.

Areal density The number of bits of data that can be recorded in a given space on a particular medium.

Arrangement, archival The process and results of organizing archives, records and manuscripts in accordance with accepted archival principles, particularly the principle of *provenance*, at as many as necessary of the following levels: record group, subgroup, collection, records series, file unit, and individual document or item. Arrangement of archival materials into logical groupings based on these general to specific levels of arrangement is designed to establish physical and intellectual control over the records and facilitate their access and use.

Association of Records Managers and Administrators, Inc. (ARMA International) A professional association representing records managers and records management interests throughout North America and in other countries. Membership is approximately 11,000.

Authority list Relative index showing key words by which subjects are classified, also known as a thesaurus.

Authorization Signatures of top management who approve a particular project.

Automatic teller machines (ATM) Terminals that enable depositors to deposit and withdraw funds and transfer funds from one account to another without human assistance.

Automation, records A general term referring to the application of a wide variety of computer-based systems and technologies to improve the management and performance of recordkeeping systems.

Auxiliary file A synonym for random file or a file of supporting documents.

Backup In vital records protection and disaster recovery planning, the act of creating an extra copy of vital data resident on the internal storage device of a computer and placing that copy in a secure location remote from the site where the computer is located.

Bar code A type of coding used in automatic identification systems consisting of lines or bars and spaces of varying widths positioned in a vertical format to create an optical code field which, when read by an optical reader, can be converted into computer-processable data. In records management applications, bar codes can be affixed to loose paper documents, file folders, records storage cartons, microfilm, or other record media to provide an enhanced level of item tracking and inventory control over a collection of stored records.

Bar code sorters A machine reader that sorts readable mail quickly and accurately by bar codes printed on the mail.

Baud A unit of transmission speed in electronic communications; generally, a baud equals a bit of data per second.

Billing report A report that includes rent, maintenance, taxes, installation and removal charges, prompt payment discounts, and copy credits.

Bit Abbreviation for binary digit; the smallest unit of information recognized by a computer. Also used as a unit of measurement of a computer chip's memory capacity.

Bit mapping A process of scanning a document to convert it to binary codes, representing either black or white pixels, which are recorded on an optical disk or magnetic media for electronic display of the document image. Also called *raster scanning, digitizing,* or simply *scanning.*

Bits Per Inch (BPI) A measure of the density of data on magnetic tape.

Bleed To run off the edge of the trimmed printed sheet.

Block numeric Consists of assigning a block of numbers to each of the major functions of the organization.

Body of the form A part of a standard business form consisting of grouped or sequenced items calling for the information desired.

Boolean logic In electronic recordkeeping systems, a search technique in which the terms *and*, *or*, or *not* are used in a search statement for the purpose of expanding or limiting the scope of the search, thereby providing more precise retrieval of required data.

Box design A set-up that includes printed captions located in the upper left corner of the form.

Break Subdivision in a file classification system.

Bulletin boards Multiple conversations take place on the computer at the same time and the user can choose in which conversation to participate.

Business archives The historically valuable records of a private business corporation.

Business form A document with a fixed arrangement of captioned spaces designed for entering and extracting prescribed information. The most widely used type of business record.

Business reply mail Envelopes provided to customers to facilitate orders, payments, and subscriptions.

Byte A sequence of adjacent binary digits that are operated upon as a unit and constitute the smallest addressable unit of data in a computer system.

Calcium carbonate A commonly used buffer. See *alkaline*.

Caption Information that appears on the label of a guide, folder, or file drawer.

Carousel file. A file which rotates horizontally like a lazy Susan and may house letter-size documents or cards.

Cartridge, film The container that facilitates loading and unloading a reel of microfilm.

Cathode ray tube (CRT) Device similar to a television tube, used to display text in computer systems.

Centralized files Records of common interest to many employees that are placed in one location under the control of one supervisor.

Central processing unit (CPU) The part of the computer that contains the main storage, arithmetic unit, and special register groups; Performs arithmetic operations, controls instruction processing and other basic computer operations.

Central reproduction A location housing sophisticated copiers and/or printing equipment geared to volumes of from 100,000 to 450,000 copies per month at speeds exceeding 90 cpm.

Certified mail Mail for which the Postal Service provides a mailing receipt. A record of delivery is maintained at the recipient's post office.

Chain index An index that links subjects in a hierarchy to their direct relations.

Charge-back A system of charging whereby total costs of the copier are divided by total number of copies produced to determine cost per page. This cost per page is then charged to each department for the number of copies it produced.

Charge-out A record made of papers removed from the file; the act of removing papers from a file for loan purposes.

Checklist A list contains step-by-step procedures on the job, lists of equipment and materials used, and/or questions to be asked in completing tasks.

Chemical stability The characteristic of a material that indicates its resistance to degradation and decomposition. A necessary characteristic of materials used in preservation. See also *archivally sound*.

Chief information officer A senior executive position established in many organizations whose primary responsibility is to coordinate, manage and integrate the many disparate information-related functions of the organization.

Chips Microprocessors that are complete computers on a single chip of silicon.

Chronological filing Arrangement of documents in order of date, usually for follow-up of activities or information.

Cine mode A manner of positioning an image on microfilm when the data line run the width of the film. This is also referred to as *portrait mode*.

Classification A process of putting like things together. Also, a group of records related by common characteristics.

Classified filing A system in which related material is filed under a major subject heading. Also known as the *encyclopedia system*.

Client/server architecture A term used to describe how the user (client) works with and uses the various servers (PCs) on a telecommunications network. Other network servers are: File Servers, Database Servers, Image or Optical servers, OCR, FAX and Print Servers, and Scan/Work Station Servers.

Close of the form A space on a standard business form for approving signatures.

Code A piece of information such as a number, an alpha abbreviation that is easily remembered, or nonsignificant alpha letter or letters.

Coded classified Subject files classified with the use of codes.

Coding Marking the indexing units on the document to be filed.

Color coding A system in which a color is used to represent a number, a word, or a group of words.

Comic mode A manner of positioning the image on microfilm when the data lines run the length of the film. This is also called *landscape mode*.

Commercial records center A business that provides off-premises records service to various businesses through storage, retrieval, and disposition of inactive business records, and other related tasks for an established fee, or contractual arrangement.

Compact disk, read-only memory (CD–ROM) A compact laser disk with read-only memory, designed for recording document images and information for mass distribution.

Compression A process of eliminating the zero codes (white spots) on the disk in order to increase storage capacity of the optical disk. A compression ratio is a relative indication of the amount of compression used.

Computer-assisted retrieval (CAR) System that uses on-line digital data to locate microfilm images arranged in random order, usually on a reel format.

Computer conferencing A method of sending, receiving, and storing typed messages within a network of computer users

Computer output microfilm (COM) Process of recording computer digital output directly onto microfilm.

Computer output to laser disk (COLD) Process of transferring computer output to and optical disk (See also *COM*).

Conservation In archives management, the specific steps undertaken to maintain, repair, restore or otherwise conserve archival records. Basic archival conservation techniques include encapsulation, fumigation, and microfilming. Also called *archival preservation*.

Contact printing, microfilm A process of film image duplication requiring the emulsion of the original film to be placed in contact with the emulsion of the copy film while exposed to a light source, followed by development.

Contempt of court A finding by a court or administrative tribunal where the court or tribunal orders documents to be produced by a person or party for use in legal proceedings and the party defies the order by failure to deliver the requested documents to the court.

Continuous forms A group of forms consisting of strips of connected forms that can be separated by perforations. Also known as *fanfold*.

Control card An index card used to locate and retrieve a record stored in the records center.

Convenience files Files located near the point of usage.

Convenient copier A copier that usually operates at speeds ranging from 10 to 45 copies per minute and is used in installations generating between 1,500 and 20,000 copies per month.

Conveyers A type of electromechanical filing system that can bring carriers or folders to the point of reference or can be used to move documents either horizontally or vertically.

Coordinated index An index in which each document or item is numbered as it is received and words are extracted directly from the text and are used without change for index terms (uniterms).

Copy center A dedicated area or remote operation designed for reproduction.

Copy film The film used to duplicate an original film through contact printing.

Copy management The system of supervision that determines how reprographics equipment is used, identifies the requirements for duplicate records, and provides control over copier purchase and production costs.

Copying Process of making copies either with an office copier, offset, or other type of duplicator.

Correspondence Interoffice letters, letters, memorandums, postal cards, printed information slips, and so on.

Correspondence manual A manual used as a means of standardizing the methods and products of a correspondence department in a large organization.

Cost-avoidance justification A method of proving the value of new equipment or procedures by demonstrating that other costs can be avoided.

Cost/risk/benefit analysis In records retention decision-making, the concept that records should be retained based on the cost, risks, and benefits of retaining or destroying the records and how these factors decline, expire or increase during their life cycle.

Cross index An index that lists the records series in alphabetical order, cross-referenced to their alphanumeric codes.

Cross reference A notation showing that the records may be filed elsewhere.

Customer A user of records center services.

"Cut" sheets Single-copy form which may also be referred to as a *flat form, flat sheet,* or *single sheet.*

Data A general term used to denote raw facts and figures from which conclusions may be inferred.

Database In electronic recordkeeping systems, a set of computer data, consisting of as least one file or group of related files, usually stored in one system or subsystem and made available to one or more users for various applications.

Database management system Software that integrates data files into a database and then integrates it with application programs and computer hardware.

Database server, optical disk system A server that controls and processes the indexes to the optical disks on a telecommunications network.

Data dictionary Broadly, a compilation of significant data elements in a database, the standards for them, and the procedures for processing them. In records management, a listing of document indexing terms which are designed to provide consistency in identifying documents and files in an electronic recordkeeping system so that the records may be effectively retrieved.

Data element In electronic recordkeeping systems, a combination of characters or bytes referring to one separate item of information, such as a name, address or age, in a database. Also referred to as a *data item.* Standard means for information defined in EDI.

Data files Computer-processible files which store numeric data (and sometimes data in text format) as quantitative values, which permits the numbers to be manipulated using arithmetic computations.

Data range The period of time covered by records in the file.

Data set A separate, discrete body of computer data (text files, data files, or image files) that is maintained within a computer system, subsystem or database and is logically related, serves a common purpose or function, and can thus be considered as a separate unit for records management purposes. Also referred to as an *electronic records series.*

Data validation The process of verifying the accuracy of all data entered into an electronic recordkeeping system, so as to ensure the integrity of the system.

Decentralized files Records that are made and used by a single organizational unit and that are maintained and controlled at the point of origin.

Decimal-numeric coding A numeric coding system for subject filing systems.

Decollator A machine that separates copies of computer printouts and removes the carbon paper.

Deleting In electronic recordkeeping systems, the process of removing or erasing recorded information from a medium, especially from a magnetic disk, diskette or tape. Sometimes called *scratching* or *erasing.*

Descriptor A broad subject heading that stands for an idea or concept.

Desktop publishing The use of a personal computer to format documents to appear as if they are typeset.

Destruction authority A formal authority to destroy records.

Destruction, records The process of obliterating or otherwise rendering illegible, irretrievable, or unusable information contained in a record.

Destruction suspension The procedure to cease the routine destruction of records when it is determined that those records may be relevant to foreseeable or pending litigation, a government investigation, or a regulatory audit.

Diazo film A contact print film with a diazonium coated emulsion used to duplicate microfilm images.

Digital copier A type of copier that scans and transfers digital impulses to paper.

Digitize The process of electronically converting an analog image or document to a bit map image by electronic scanning.

Digitizer An alternate name for an electronic image scanner which "digitizes" or " raster scans " a document image.

Direct-access filing A system that permits access to files without reference to an index.

Directive A written instruction communicating policy and/or procedures in the form of orders, regulations, bulletins, circulars, handbooks, manuals, notices, numbered memorandums, and similar issuances.

Directory A method of organizing and managing PC-based electronic records into logical groups, with an index or table of contents listing all files contained within the directory to facilitate their access and use.

Disaster A sudden, unplanned calamitous event that creates an inability on the part of an organization to perform critical business functions for some period of time.

Disaster preparedness A set of policies and procedures to make sure employees are aware of how to handle potential disasters, as well as actual implementation of such procedures.

Disaster recovery manual A manual consisting of a disaster recovery plan, information about disaster preparedness, procedures for disaster-in-progress, and plans for disaster recovery.

Disaster recovery plan A plan consisting of information about structures, occupants, and hazardous materials, as well as procedures to safeguard records.

Disaster recovery planning The advance planning and preparations necessary to minimize loss and ensure continuity of the critical business functions of an organization in the event of a disaster.

Discovery The legal process that permits parties involved in a legal proceeding to obtain records and information relevant to the proceeding that are in the possession of another party.

Disk drives, optical Devices used to drive, record, and read optical disks.

Diskettes Platter-shaped devices used for the storage of electronic records in computer systems. Also termed *floppy disks*; these magnetic storage devices are commonly used for off-line storage of electronic records in PC computing environments.

Dispersal In vital records protection, the act of placing copies of vital records in locations other than those housing the originals. Dispersal may be "built in" as a part of existing procedures, or "improvised" by creating an extra copy of the vital records for storage in a secure location, usually remote from the organization's primary place of business.

Disposal In records retention programs, the process of destroying obsolete records.

Distribution list A file that identifies the location of every recipient of the document.

Document A record which constitutes the smallest unit of filing, generally a single letter, report, form, or other item contained within a recordkeeping system. Also, the smallest unit of filing. Sometimes called a *page*.

Document production The process of retrieving and producing a record for use in a legal proceeding.

Drawer file cabinet Vertical file cabinet, also called standard filing cabinet which usually houses correspondence.

Duplex numeric filing A system in which numbering consists of two or more parts separated by a dash, a space, a period, or a comma, such as 85-1.

Duplicating The process of making duplicate copies

Electronic archives Historically valuable records that exist in machine-readable or computer-processible form.

Electronic data interchange (EDI) A standardized method of electronically transmitting and processing data from one computer to another.

Electronic filing The storage and retrieval of information in digital, computer-processible form.

Electronic form Any form designed for use with electronic equipment. May take the form of electronic forms composition, template electronic forms, full electronic forms, machine-readable forms, electronic data interchange, and electronic funds transfer.

Electronic forms composition The design of camera-ready copy for paper-based forms.

Electronic funds transfer EFT) A subset of EDI which permits the transfer of funds from one account to another and to verify account balances around the world.

Eletronic mail (E–mail) A message that is transmitted electronically from one computer terminal to one or more locations via telephone lines

Electronic records Records containing machine-readable, as opposed to human-readable information and consisting of character-coded electronic signals that can be processed and read by means of computers.

Electronic records series A separate, discrete body of computer data (text files, data files or image files) that is maintained within a computer system subsystem or database and is logically related, serves a common purpose or function, and can thus be considered as a separate unit for records management purposes. In data processing terminology, referred to as a *data set.*

Emulsion, microfilm The silver halide coating on one side of the microfilm that retains the image photographed.

Encapsulation An archival conservation technique designed to assure the permanent preservation of valuable documents by "encapsulating" them between two sheets of polyester film, thereby arresting further deterioration.

Encapsulation, polyester Encapsulation using polyester film.

Encyclopedic filing system Topics are subdivided so that several folders may contain information pertaining to the main topic.

Ergonomics Science concerned with the design of an effective work space for people working with machines.

Evidential value The usefulness of records in documenting the functions and activities of an organization or institution; how it came into being, how it developed, how it was organized and the results of its activities. A primary criterion used in appraising records to determine their archival value.

Exception report Listing of those machines performing out of their recommended volume range.

Expense-reduction justification A method of proving the value of new equipment or procedures by demonstrating that current costs will be less.

Express mail Overnight mail service of the United States Postal Service.

Extended binary coded decimal interchange code (EBCDIC) A coding scheme which specifies bit patterns for computer- processible information for electronic records created on IBM mainframe and other large computers.

External communication The structured communication that is conducted with people and groups outside the organization.

Facility management Practice of coordinating the physical work place with the people and work of the organization.

Facsimile (FAX) A remote photocopying system which scans and transmits images to a receiving printer via telephone lines or satellite.

FAX server, optical disk system A server that controls all FAX Functions in the imaging system.

Federal Records Act of 1950 A law enacted by the United States Congress that defined the term *records management* for the first time in any federal statute. This law also required all agencies of the federal government to establish a records management program.

Fiberboard A kind of paper board consisting of laminated sheets of pressed fiber.

Field A category of information that contains data items in a database. Also referred to as an *attribute.*

File or files A group of related documents. In paper-based recordkeeping systems, the singular form often refers to one or more documents contained within one file folder. The plural form is a general term which denotes a collection of records, or a group of related documents or file folders which have been arranged in a predetermined manner in order to facilitate their retrieval and use. In electronic recordkeeping systems, refers to a single or group of related computer-processible data resident on some type of electronic records storage device.

File integrity Accuracy and completeness of the records.

Filename In PC-based electronic recordkeeping systems, the name assigned to an individual document filed within the system, which serves as the means of retrieving it. May be combined with a "filename extension" to provide a more descriptive document identifier.

File plan A logical order of documents or files; an arrangement or scheme by which all documents may be stored.

File server A computer dedicated to processing and storing data in a network computing environment. Sometimes called a *network server.*

File server, optical disk system A server that controls information traffic on the network and provides necessary files and software.

Filing The process of arranging and sorting records so that they may be retrieved rapidly when needed.

Filing manual A manual that identifies the requirements and procedures for proper filing.

Filing unit Each word, abbreviation, or initial used to file information.

Finding aids In archives management, refers to a wide variety of archival indexing and retrieval systems and techniques to describe the holdings in an archival repository in order to facilitate their use.

Fire–resistant file cabinet A file cabinet or other

record container constructed with special insulation for the purpose of reducing the risk of loss of its contents from elevated heat conditions usually produced by fire.

First–class mail A service of the United States Postal Service used for letters, postcards, postal cards, and for sending checks and money orders weighing less than 11 ounces

Fiscal value In records appraisal, the usefulness of a record in serving as documentation of the financial transactions of an organization, or as evidence of the organization's tax liability.

Fixed magnetic disk drive A magnetic disk drive with non-removable, rigid platters; the most common type of hard disk drive. A direct access storage device.

Flat filing Wide, shallow shelves or drawers are housed in counter high units that provide a working surface.

Floor load The capacity of a floor area to support a given weight expressed in terms of pounds per square foot.

Flowchart A graphic illustration of the procedural steps in an operation.

Fog index A measure of readability based on length of words and length of sentences.

Footprint Space that is required for the item to stand on.

Format See **Layout.**

Forms analysis The process of determining what information should be provided on specific forms.

Forms analyst Person who determines the need for each type of form used by an organization and makes recommendations concerning cost reduction and efficiency improvements.

Forms catalog May range from a simple listing of forms by number only to comprehensive catalogs with detailed information.

Forms control Routines for designing, procuring, storing, distributing, reviewing and disposing of all of the organization's forms.

Forms design The process of assembling the required data into a logical format that satisfies recommendations made as a result of the analysis of forms.

Forms distribution chart A chart showing the existence of copies and the backtracking of copies.

Forms inventory A survey of all forms used to identify problems such as duplication or improper application of technology.

Forms management The function that establishes standards for the creation, design, analysis, and revision of all forms within an organization and assures that they are designed, produced, and distributed economically and efficiently.

Fourth-class mail A service of the United States Postal Service used for packages weighing one pound or more; parcel post.

Freeze drying A method of drying wet paper records by quick-freezing and subsequently drying the records in a vacuum chamber.

Fumigation A method of conserving valuable documents by exposing them to a poisonous gas or vapor, usually in a vacuum or other airtight chamber, to destroy insects, mildew, or other hazards that may endanger them.

Functional classification file A forms control file that brings together forms serving a similar purpose so that they may be studied for possible combination.

Functional filing A method of filing that describes the records series by the functions they perform.

Geographic file A file in which records are arranged alphabetically according to location.

Guide In archives management, a type of finding aid that includes a general description of the holdings of an archival repository. Also, a divider used in files to identify sections of the file and to provide physical support for records.

Guide tab A projecting portion of a guide that shows the filing caption.

Handbook A publication consisting of established rules to be followed by employees in performing their individual tasks.

Hard disk crash The failure of a microcomputer's internal storage device, resulting in the instant destruction of all documents and data residing on the disk.

Heading The facilitative part of the form that includes a title and a form number.

Hierarchical index An orderly arrangement or items, or concepts, such as in a classified index.

Hierarchical filing system A filing system that uses a classification system to bring related material together.

Historical value In records appraisal, the determination that records possess value in elucidating the history of an organization and are thus worthy of permanent preservation as archival materials. Also referred to as *archival value.*

HVAC Heating, Ventilation, Air Conditioning.

Image count A method of retrieval of a microfilm

image, that optically counts the images on a roll of microfilm, using an external computer index to determine the image number.

Image files Electronic files that contain computer–processible images of documents for storage on magnetic or optical media.

Imaging A term used to describe the process of recording an image of a document on either microfilm or optical disk.

Imaging, document The process of creating an exact image of a document utilizing either electronic or photographic technology.

Important records Records containing information that is essential to operate an organization and protect its assets, but which could be re-created or replaced if destroyed. Decisions to take special measures to protect these records from loss should usually be based on a determination as to whether the cost of replacement exceeds the cost of protection.

Improved dispersal The creation of additional copies especially for dispersal.

Inactive records A series of records with a reference rate of less than one search per file drawer per month.

Index An arrangement of names or topics in either alphabetic or numeric order. A listing of the headings (titles, captions) of the files showing their locations.

Indexing In manual filing, determining the name or number under which a document is to be filed. In electronic filing, identifying the keyword under which a document may be retrieved.

Indirect access filing Reference to the code under which the material is filed must be made before the file can be referenced.

Information Generally, knowledge communicated by others or obtained by study and investigation. Intelligence which can be communicated in either graphic form or by alphanumeric characters. Facts or data communicated or received. Data placed into a meaningful context for users.

Informational value The usefulness of records in documenting the persons, things, or other matters dealt with by an organization, in contrast to documenting the organization's functions and activities. A primary criterion used in appraising records to determine their archival value.

Information management The administration of information, its use and transmission, and the appli-

cation of theories and techniques of information science to create, modify, or improve information handing systems.

In-House Performing a function within the organizational structure, rather than through an outside source. Opposite of **Out-sourcing.**

Ink-jet printing A printing method using tiny drops of ink that are sprayed onto specially coated paper.

In-plant Refers to a printing facility set up inside an organization whose primary business is not printing

Input Data entered into a computer system, usually for future retrieval and manipulation.

Inspection The process of checking records to be sure that they are released for filing.

Institute of Certified Records Managers An organization which administers a program for professional certification of records management specialists. Certification is awarded based on satisfactory completion of a written examination, as well as review of professional credentials.

Instructions A list that explains how to fill in the form and what to do with the form.

Intelligent character recognition (ICR) A data capturing process that can capture data from any size, shape, or type of paper, without the restrictions typically associated with other such processes.

Intelligent processing unit Computer interface that permits a copier to be used as both a printer and a scanner.

Interfile The process of putting documents in their proper sequence and place in a file when they have not previously been withdrawn.

INTERPOST International facsimile message service available between the United States and more than 40 foreign countries

Inventory, archival In archives management, a type of finding aid used to describe collections or groups of records in a manner that facilitates their retrieval and use.

Inventory, records An identification, description, and qualification of all of the records possessed by an organization.

Job interrupt A device that permits the operator to stop a job in progress to allow another job to be completed.

Job recovery A device in the copier's memory that tells the operator how to restack the originals so that the copy job can be completed without missing any pages.

Jukebox A multi-disk computer-controlled device used to store and robotically retrieve the optical disk and to mount the disk on a drive with rapid on-line response.

Keyword searching In electronic recordkeeping systems, the ability to search for any single word within certain or all fields of a computer database, thereby providing more precise retrieval of required data.

Lamination An archival conservation technique involving the deacidification of paper documents, which are then sealed between two sheets of plastic. The technique is not widely practiced today because it alters the original state of the documents.

LASER An acronym from its descriptive name, meaning Light Amplification by Simulated Emission of Radiation. It is an extremely narrow and coherent beam in the visible light spectrum. Among other uses, it records and reads bit-maps on optical disks.

Latent image, microfilm An undeveloped image on the emulsion of exposed microfilm.

Lateral file Side-open file cabinet; may also mean shelf filing.

Layout The shape, size, style, and general makeup of a particular form. Also called format.

Legal retention considerations A term that refers to a number of legal issues that may indicate how long an organization should retain certain of its records so that it can successfully defend itself against litigation actions, enforce its legal rights, or meet its other legal obligations and needs.

Legal retention research The process of identifying and interpreting the laws and regulations promulgated by all jurisdictions which contain records retention requirements applicable to an organization.

Legal value In records appraisal, the usefulness of a record in complying with statutes and regulations, as evidence in legal proceedings, or as legal proof of business transactions.

Life cycle The life span or time period from the creation or receipt of a record through its useful life to its final disposition. The five stages in the life cycle of a record include the creation stage, the distribution and use stage, the storage and maintenance stage, the retention and disposition stage, and the archival preservation stage.

Lignin A plant substance generally responsible for the strength and rigidity of plants but considered a detriment to the stability of manufactured paper and board. The term *lignin-free* indicates that the majority of lignin has been removed during the manufacture of paper.

Limitation of assessment The period of time, after a tax return is filed or the tax becomes due, during which the taxing agency can determine or modify the tax owed. This time period is often considered to be a relevant factor in making records retention decisions concerning various types of financial records which may be subject to audit.

List index The simplest kind of index to compile—an alphabetical list of words or phrases.

Local area network (LAN) The interconnection of computing devices within a defined and relatively limited geographical area, thus permitting the sharing of electronic records and other computing resources by all users having access to the network.

Locator report A monthly inventory of copier equipment, including make, model, serial number, location, monthly volume, volume by user.

Magnetic disk A platter-shaped device used for the storage of electronic records in computer systems; generally used in high performance computing environments requiring very rapid, on-line access to electronic records. A direct access storage device.

Magnetic ink character recognition (MICR) Specially shaped numbers are printed in horizontal bands on checks with magnetic ink containing iron oxide. MICR can be used as computer input or to facilitate sorting.

Magnetic media A general term which refers to a variety of devices on which computer-based records are stored. These media are constructed with a ferromagnetic recording material on which the electronic records reside. The most common electronic media are magnetic disks, diskettes, and magnetic tapes.

Magnetic tape A strip of plastic film coated with a magnetic recording material and wound onto reels of various sizes; used for the off-line storage of electronic records in computer systems.

Magneto optical disk A re-writable optical disk (MO)

Mail Letters, postcards, electronically transmitted messages, documents, publications directives, forms, packages, or any other written communication received for distribution or dispatch.

Mail center Location where mail operations take place

Mailgram Electronic message service of Western

Union which provides next-day delivery in the United States.

Mail handling The process of getting the written word from one point to another.

Mail manual A manual that gives specific instructions in all phases of handling both incoming and outgoing mail.

Mail operations A series of tasks performed by action officers, mail room personnel, secretaries, clerks, and others in moving an organization's written communications.

Mail robot An unmanned, self-propelled vehicle that follows an invisible guidepath to move from office to office.

Mail supervision Activities that ensure that the written word is moved from the point of origin to its destination in a manner that meets stated organizational goals.

Mainframe The central processing unit of the largest size computer system or a large centralized host computer used on a corporate-wide basis.

Majors Divisions that represent the major functional areas of an organization.

Manual A published control device under which an organization or a group within an organization functions.

Manuscript repository An archival facility established for the purpose of preserving collections of historically valuable records, usually from sources other than the organization which operates the repository. University archives that preserve archival records covering many fields of study and which were created by many disparate organizations and individuals are a prime example of manuscript repositories.

Mapping The process of programming each data field of an electronic form to control the efficient fill-in of variable data by assigning definitions, formulas, and restrictions to these data fields.

Microcomputer The smallest computer size; usually synonymous with *personal computer*, or PC. This class of computers includes desktop and portable units, referred to as *notebook* and *subnotebook* microcomputers.

Microfiche A sheet of microfilm containing multiple microimages in a grid pattern, usually 4 x 6 inches in size.

Microfilm Photographic film, with specially designed emulsion. used primarily to photograph documents and other information material. The term is also used as a verb to describe the process of microfilming.

Microfilm image transmission An automated system that robotically retrieves cartridges of microfilm, locates requested image or images, raster scans the image, and transmits it over the telecommunications system to the requestor who reads the documents on a display monitor.

Microfilm jacket A unitized microform similar to the microfiche in appearance and function, constructed of two clear sheets of polyester acetate material, a header strip, and sealed on the edges and at 16mm intervals forming channels for strips of microfilm.

Microform A term describing the format in which microfilm may be utilized, such as a reel, cartridge, microfiche, film jacket, or aperture card. A generic term for any form, either film, paper, or plastic, that contains microimages.

Micrographics The art of producing or reproducing information in miniature form.

Microimaging The process of imaging documents onto microfilm. A synonym for microfilming.

Microprocessor A term for the central processing unit of a computer, particularly those installed in microcomputers or PC's.

MicroSoft disk-operating system (MS–DOS) An operating software system developed and marketed by Microsoft Corporation which controls the basic operating functions of IBM and compatible microcomputers or PC's. These basic functions include the electronic signals between the computer and various applications software programs, such as word processors and spreadsheets.

Middle-digit filing A system in which predetermined or consecutively assigned numbers of units (or documents) are divided into groups of two digits, with placement made into the major section of the file according to the middle digits of the identifying numbers.

Minicomputer A computer of medium size and capacity.

Mobile aisle file Movable sets of file shelves. They are moved, either manually or by motor on a carriage that is either imbedded in the floor or contained within a special platform.

Model A representation of a subject of inquiry, used frequently in systems analysis to evaluate alternatives.

Monitor An electronic image display device, consisting of a cathode ray tube (CRT) and various internal electronic boards and controllers.

Multifunction device A device that combines laser printing, facsimile, digital scanning and photocopying.

Narrative style A detailing of events in prose form.

Near-line storage The storage of optical disks or other computer media in a jukebox or other retrieval device which provides rapid, unattended access to the electronic records resident on the media.

Neutral Having a pH of 7.0. Neither an acid nor an alkaline substance.

Non-perforated microfilm Microfilm that does not have sprocket holes on each edge.

Nonrecords Extra copies of documents kept solely for convenience of reference. In government usage, records not usually included within the scope of the official records of an agency or governmental organization.

Non-recurring costs One–time costs, such as purchase price, transportation costs, and installation charges.

Non-removable media Magnetic or optical disk storage devices which are "fixed" within the disk drives which are used to record the information residing on them. These media provide very rapid, on–line processing and retrieval of electronic records.

Numeric filing Arrangement of records in ascending order or sequence (i.e., 1, 2, 3, 4, 5, and so forth).

Numeric history file A form control file consisting of copies of each form used by the organization, placed in a visible file in numerical order.

Obstruction of justice A deliberate and malicious act to interfere with a government investigation or judicial proceeding.

Office landscaping The arrangement of production units within an open area separated by equipment or other dividers, based on the needs of work flows, traffic patterns, and communication networks.

Off-line information Information stored on media located apart from the computer device on which it will be retrieved and processed.

Offset A process or the equipment used for high–volume duplication of copies from a specially prepared master.

Off-site protection The protection of vital records by storage of the original or a copy of the records in a facility remote from the organization's place of business.

On-line help screens In electronic recordkeeping systems, operating procedures that can be accessed on–line while using the system, so that the user does not have to refer to a user manual.

On-line information Information stored on media housed on magnetic or optical disk drives within a computer system, thus permitting very rapid access and continuous processing.

On-site protection The protection of vital records which are maintained in facilities and equipment located on the organization's premises, at or near the point of creation or use of the records.

Open shelf filing Storage of records on open shelves rather than in closed drawers.

Operating procedures manual A manual that deals with the internal policies, organization, and processes of one department or function of an organization. Such a manual can emphasize the performance of individual tasks and jobs, departmental practices, or general practices in a specific field.

Operational value In records appraisal, the usefulness of a record in the conduct of an organization's business; the value of a record for the purpose for which it was created. Also referred to as *administrative value*.

Optical character reader (OCR) A machine for reading a bar code that is displayed on the mail representing the zip code for that address.

Optical character recognition (OCR) A method of entering data into a computer by using an optical scanning device to read the contents of documents.

Optical character recognition server (OCR) A server that processes all OCR (Optical Character Recognition) functions on an Electronic Imaging Network.

Optical disk A platter-shaped device for the storage of very large quantities of electronic documents and data in computer systems. Optical media utilize high concentrations of laser light as the method of recording the information on the disk platters. In records management applications, optical disks are typically utilized for the storage of high volumes of electronic documents and data requiring very rapid on-line or near-line retrieval. Optical disks are available in erasable and non-erasable formats. Initially called an Optical Digital Disk, but now most frequently referred to simply as an Optical Disk.

Optical or object (image) server A server that directs all functions of the jukebox, on an electronic imaging network.

Order of entry First unit to be considered in filing.

Organizational manual A publication that identifies the executive structure of an organization, unit, or department.

Original order A principle of archival arrangement that holds that archival materials should be arranged in the order and sequence in which they were maintained when they were in current use in the office that created them, rather than in accordance with some arbitrary scheme, provided their original order is sufficient to permit easy access and use.

Occupational Safety and Health Administration (OSHA) A federal agency supervising health and safety of workers.

Out-guide A guide to indicate what material has been taken from the file and by whom.

Outsourcing The practice of a business contracting or buying support services, supplies, or parts from outside sources rather than performing the services or manufacturing the parts themselves within their own organization and with their own employees.

Owner The originating office of a record that has been transferred to a records center.

Packing density The amount of data or images that can be recorded in a given area of a medium. See also **areal density.**

Password protection A method of providing security for computer-based records against unauthorized access using special codes or "passwords" assigned to designated users to permit them access to the records.

Pegboard forms The pegboard has a row of pegs affixed down the side of the board. The objective is to hold two or more forms in perfect alignment (registration), and to provide duplicate copies in one writing operation.

Pen plotters Fiber tip, felt tip, or ballpoint pens used for printing engineering and drafting applications.

Permanence The characteristic of a material that makes it able to last. See also *chemical stability, archivally sound.*

Permanent records Those records having sufficient historical or other value to warrant permanent or continued preservation beyond the time they are needed for administrative, legal or fiscal purposes.

Records considered so valuable or unique in documenting the history of an organization that they are preserved permanently in an archive.

Personal copier Desktop copier that produces up to 10 copies per minute. It is usually used to produce fewer than 400 copies per month.

pH In chemistry, a measure of the acidity or alkalinity of a solution. The measure is compared to a scale from 0 to 14 with 7.0 being the neutral point. Acids fall in the range below 7.0 and alkaline substances fall above 7.0.

Phonetic index Keywords (subject and name type data) are converted by the computer into a phonetic code to minimize both computer storage requirements and the occurrence of sorting errors due to spelling and terminology ambiguities.

Phonetic systems File arrangements based on a numerical code that represents certain key letter sounds in the alphabet.

Phrase searching In electronic recordkeeping systems, the ability to search two or more consecutive words within certain or all data fields of a computer database, thereby providing more precise retrieval of required data.

Pixels A word meaning "picture elements," or more frequently "bits" or "dots." The smallest segment of a document that can be digitized.

Planetary camera A type of microfilm camera in which the film and document remain stationary during filming and the lighting is from an overhead source. Sometimes referred to as an overhead (lighted) or flatbed camera.

Playscript format A format that defines procedures by identifying workers and the required action of each.

Polarity, microfilm The characteristic in a film image that is either "positive" or "negative," that is, sign reversing. A negative image is the opposite of the original and a positive is the same as the original.

Policy Broad guidelines for operating an organization. A basic guide to action that prescribes the boundaries within which activities are to take place.

Policy manual A publication that states the course of action to be followed by an organization, unit, or department in conducting its activities.

Polyester A strong, colorless, transparent plastic (polyethylene terephthalate). Commonly used in preservation and to make covers, folders, and so on. Commonly used in *encapsulation.*

Polyethylene A flexible plastic used to make covers for

photographic materials and other items. It can be transparent or translucent.

Polypropylene A hard plastic used in making stiff holders or containers.

Polyvinyl acetate A colorless transparent plastic solid used in adhesives. Abbreviated as PVA. Some PVA adhesives are commonly used in preservation.

Polyvinyl chloride (PVC) A fairly unstable plastic abbreviated PVC. Generally considered unsuitable for use in preservation.

Precise retrieval The ability of a recordkeeping system to consistently deliver to its users exactly the records and information they request—no more and no less.

Preface Includes the organization's definition, purpose of the manual, purpose of the program, advantages to be derived from the proper use of the manual, and a request for suggestions for improving the manual.

Pressboard A tough paper board with a high glaze on it for strength and stiffness. Used in notebook covers.

Primary categories Primary-level headings, the most important categories within each major heading (function).

Primary value In records appraisal, the value of information contained in records in support of the purpose(s) for which the records were created.

Printer Device used to print electronic images or data, which may be displayed on the monitor screen, onto paper using various technologies, such as ink–jet, bubble-jet, or dot matrix.

Printing on demand information is available in computer files that can be shared by any number of users

Print server A server that controls all print functions on an imaging network.

Priority mail First-class mail weighing 11 ounces or more.

Private archives An archival repository containing the records of private businesses, associations, institutions, or other organizations adjudged worthy of permanent preservation as archival materials.

Procedures A group of methods, consisting of all the steps that are taken to record, analyze, transmit, and store information needed to serve a single, specific purpose. Procedures usually provide detailed instructions of how policy is to be carried out.

Procedures audit An examination of all standard procedures used to accomplish standardized tasks.

Procedures manual A source of instruction and reference for the personnel responsible for creating, preparing, processing, storing, and disposing of records.

Processing The various procedures and chemicals required to develop the latent image on the emulsion of microfilm. Film developing.

Processing area The area set aside for accessioning, interfiling, or refiling.

Productivity The value of measurable output compared to the value of input.

Provenance A principle of arrangement of archival records that holds that archival materials should be arranged in groups that correspond to their source or office of creation, and that they should not be intermingled with records created by other offices or sources of creation.

Public archives An archival repository containing the records of agencies of government adjudged worthy of permanent preservation as archival materials.

Public data network A network that offers third–party access to large databases and serves as a clearinghouse for electronic messages of subscribers.

Random access memory (RAM) Computer memory used to process and store data that can be rapidly accessed directly rather than sequentially.

Random filing A process of storing documents as they are created in random or nonsequential order.

Range searching In electronic recordkeeping systems, the ability to limit the scope of a search of numeric, date and other fields by using range symbols, such as *greater than* or *less than* to provide more precise retrieval of required data.

Reader-printer A microimage projection device which optically enlarges and displays the image on a screen and which also prints a copy of that image on paper, using office copier technology.

Reading file An extra copy file of outgoing correspondence, usually arranged chronologically. Also call a *day file*.

Read-only memory (ROM) A solid-state memory for programs that is inflexible and unalterable.

Reciprocating file A power file where the whole file remains intact and one shelf takes the place of another in front of the worker, and rotates as in a Ferris wheel.

Record Recorded information, regardless of medium or characteristics. Any paper, book, microfilm, card, magnetic tape, disk, map, or any copy or printout that has been created or received by an organization and has been used by that organization or its successors as evidence of its activities or because of the information contained. In databases in electronic recordkeeping systems, a collection of related data fields.

Record copy The copy of a record or document that is placed on file as the official copy and therefore provides evidence of the organization's official position on a matter. In governmental organizations, a record having the legally recognized and judicially enforceable quality of establishing some fact.

Recordkeeping requirements Statements in statutes and regulations which require a regulated party to maintain certain records for some period of time.

Records analyst Specialist in the analysis and evaluation of systems and procedures involved in the creation, processing, and storing of records.

Records appraisal The analyses of records with the objective of establishing retention policy.

Records center An area in a building or a separate building for storing inactive records.

Records Disposal Act of 1943 A law enacted by the United States Congress which, for the first time in U. S. history, legally authorized the records retention schedule as a means of disposing of records of agencies of the federal government.

Records disposition The process of elimination or destruction of records, usually under a records retention program.

Records inventory An identification, description, and quantification of all of the records possessed by an organization.

Records management A professional discipline that is primarily concerned with the management of document-based information systems. The application of systematic and scientific controls to recorded information required in the operation of an organization's business. The systematic control of all organizational records during the various stages of their life cycle: from their creation or receipt, through their processing, distribution, maintenance and use, to their ultimate disposition. The purpose of records management is to promote economies and efficiencies in recordkeeping, to assure that useless records are systematically destroyed while valuable information is protected and maintained in a manner that facilitates its access and use.

Records management manual A publication that defines the scope of the records management program, its authority, the services it provides, and an introduction to the concepts to enhance its understanding and acceptance.

Records manager The individual within an organization who is assigned the responsibility of systematically managing the recorded information generated and received by the organization in accordance with accepted records management principles and practices.

Records recovery plan A plan for restoring damaged vital records to a useable condition following a disaster. Usually a part of a comprehensive vital records protection or disaster recovery plan.

Records retention The act of maintaining or holding records for future use, often under policies and procedures of a formally established records retention program.

Records retention and disposition manual A manual that includes information about controlling designated records and information so that the organization will be in compliance with government requirements.

Records retention program The component of a records and information management program which provides policies and procedures specifying the length of time that an organization's records must be retained. The program provides for the systematic destruction of records that no longer serve any useful purpose, and is implemented by effecting the destruction of records on a scheduled basis, as specified in the organization's records retention schedule. The retention program is one of the organization's major tools for controlling the growth of its records, and it also minimizes the legal risks that can be associated with maintaining and destroying business records.

Records series A group of identical or related records that are normally used and filed as a unit and which permits evaluation as a unit for retention scheduling purposes.

Recurring costs Items such as supplies, power, insurance, taxes, and direct labor.

Recurring data chart. A chart showing items common to all forms in the group; common to some, but not to all; and found only on one form in the group.

Reduction ratio The ratio of the size of an original document to its size on filing.

Reference copy A copy of a record used primarily for information purposes. The term is often used to denote records consisting of duplicate rather than official copies of documents.

Reference time Length of time taken to examine the document or file.

Refile The process of returning a record to its original place in a file after it has been withdrawn.

Register In archives management, a type of finding aid used to describe manuscript collections and other archival records in a manner that facilitates their retrieval and use.

Registered mail A mail service providing tight security from the point of mailing to the delivery office.

Relational database A database design that allows direct relationships between any two data elements.

Relative index A dictionary-like listing of all possible words and combinations by which material may be requested. Satisfactory performance reliability of equipment can be measured by the number of copies between service calls (CBSC) and service-call frequency (SCF).

Remote diagnostics A device that informs a host computer that some sort of part or supply failure will occur in the copier.

Remote encoder A device that allows any and all mail to be bar-coded and processed mechanically.

Remote storage Off-site storage of records in company-owned, commercial, or cooperative records centers.

Removable media Magnetic or optical storage devices which may be removed from and stored apart from the disk drives on which they are recorded and read.

Reports manual Provides writers of reports with standard practices and instructions in a form that is convenient and easy to use.

Reprography Facsimile reproduction of graphic material.

Requirements analysis An analysis of an organization's recordkeeping systems to determine whether and where records management automation is needed, the type of automation required, and other elements that are relevant to the process of applying various forms of computer automation to solve recordkeeping problems. Sometimes called a *needs analysis*.

Resolution, EIM A mathematical indication of a planned readability factor, such as "x" dots per inch, with 200 dots per inch (dpi) considered adequate. Image sharpness.

Resolution, microfilm A measure of the sharpness of the image, expressed in lines per millimeter, using a resolution test target as a standard.

Retention period The period of time during which records must be retained in a certain location or form because they are needed for operational, legal, fiscal, historical, or other purposes. A retention period may be stated in terms of months or years, and is sometimes expressed as contingent upon the occurrence of an event.

Retention schedule A document prepared as a part of a records retention program that lists the types of records maintained by each department of an organization, and specifies a period of time after which destruction is authorized as a matter of policy. The retention schedule also identifies the organization's archival records and mandates their permanent retention, and it may provide for the transfer of semi-active or inactive records from prime office space to a records center or other facility for continuing retention. Also called *retention and disposition schedule*.

Retrieval The process of locating and withdrawing a document from a collection of records.

Retrieval system A method or index used to locate and withdraw a record from a given group of records.

Retrieval time Time spent retrieving documents is divided by the total number of records retrieved for one month.

Reversibility The quality of being able to be undone or reversed back to its original state without any harm to the object. Used in some preservation.

Risk assessment In vital records protection and disaster recovery planning, the process of determining the risks to which an organization may be exposed in the event of loss of some or all its vital records, and whether it would be in the organization's best interest to take certain measures to reduce these risks to a level that is considered to be acceptable.

Rotary camera A microfilm camera that photographs moving documents.

Sampling test Test made to determine the scan speeds and image quality, using random samples of documents and random timings.

Scanner A device used in electronic imaging, that raster scans a document to record the image on an optical disk or tape, using binary code.

Scan/workstation server A server that processes all scanning and workstation activities.

Screening The elimination of material before it is filed.

Search The act of locating and/or withdrawing a record from a group or collection of files. In electronic filing, examination of a series of items for those that have desired properties.

Secondary categories Subdivisions of primary headings.

Secondary value In records appraisal, the value of information contained in records which reflects the actual or potential uses to which the information may be put for purposes other than the purpose for which it was created.

Second-class mail A mail service available only to publishers and registered news agents.

Server A computer on an electronic image network designed to serve a specific need.

Service report A service history of all equipment.

Sizing A substance added to paper to hold fibers together and to make it less absorbent so that inks will not bleed.

Slant file The file module is shaped like a parallelogram and is a variation of the traditional mobile aisle shelving system.

Software, applications Computer programs designed to process data and perform functions and applications required by end users, as opposed to software designed to operate the computer's basic functions. In PC computing, word processing and spreadsheet software programs are common types of applications software.

Software, document management In large, multi–user network computing environments, a family of packaged software products designed to facilitate the management of documents and files stored in the PC's and file servers connected to the local or wide area network.

Software, files management In PC-based electronic recordkeeping systems, a family of packaged software products designed to facilitate the management of the documents and files resident on the system.

Software, records management A general term which refers to a family of packaged software products designed to provide computer enhancement over a wide variety of records management functions; the major functional applications include indexing, tracking and monitoring file folders in active recordkeeping systems and storage cartons containing inactive records in records center environments.

Solid board A paper board made of one material only. Board made of two or more types of fiber in layers is called *combination board.*

Sorting Process of arranging records in the order in which they will eventually be filed.

Soundex A phonetic file arrangement based on a numerical code that represents certain key letters and consonant sounds in the alphabet.

Space planning Coordination of the physical components to provide maximum efficiency within the available floor space in the most attractive arrangement.

Special delivery A mail service that provides delivery beyond normal delivery hours and on Sundays and holidays.

Specialty forms Includes various types of forms, such as pegboard forms, bank checks, or office supplies, such as tags, labels, mailers, and envelopes.

Spirit process A process that uses alcohol as a solvent to transfer images from a carbon master. Also called "ditto," "liquid," or "fluid" process.

Stack area That portion of a records center or archive that contains the records holdings.

Staging area An area used for intermediate or temporary storage of records awaiting accessioning or disposal processing.

Standalone system A computer system that contains its own processing and memory units so that it can operate independently of other computers.

Standard A rule or principle established to measure quality or value.

Standard operating procedure (SOP) Instructions for the performance of individual tasks and jobs.

Statutes of limitations Laws containing provisions specifying the period of time during which a party can sue or be sued on a matter. Records are often considered to possess varying degrees of legal value during this time period, and decisions to retain them are often based on this value. Also referred to as *limitations of action.*

Straight numeric filing A system in which consecutively numbered folders are placed in a file in exact sequential order.

Strategic plan A plan that impacts directly on the

success of the organization's primary purpose or goal. A plan that affects substantive rather than facilitative activities.

Subdirectory A method of organizing and managing PC-based electronic records into logical subgroups under each directory, in cases where the file contents and structure of the directory become too large or cumbersome for effective processing and retrieval.

Subpoena duces tecum A court order requiring a witness to appear in court, produce relevant records, or provide testimony.

Supersession notice A notice that shows dates of revision, consolidation, or elimination.

Suspense file A file organized chronologically in which documents or data are entered or filed by a future date of recall.

Synthetical index An index that brings together like items or concepts, as in a coordinate indexing system or keyword subject index.

System An array of components that interact to achieve some objective through a network of procedures that were integrated and designed to carry out an activity.

System conversion The tasks associated with implementing a new or upgraded recordkeeping system by conversion of the existing records to the new system's format and structure. The term applies to both manual and computerized recordkeeping systems.

Tab A projection above the guide or folder body upon which the caption appears.

Tabbing The process of applying small adhesive pieces of paper (tabs) to keep the ends of folded mail pieces together.

Tape rotation backup system A method of protecting vital computer-based records by periodically storing copies of magnetic tapes containing the updated vital data in a secure facility remote from an organization's computer processing facility.

Targets and certifications Sheets of paper which are microfilmed together with documents to serve as index points or to make the certification a part of the microimages.

Teleconferencing A form of communication that permits people at different locations to conduct meetings together and includes computer conferencing and videoconferencing.

Template electronic forms Forms for which only the variable information needs to be keyed into a form

template or blank form, and a hard copy can be made of the entire record.

Terminal-digit filing A system of filing in which the numbers are read, right to left, in groups of two, three, or four digits, or in combinations of two and three digits.

Tertiary heading Subdivision of secondary heading.

Text files A collection of computer-based electronic records typically consisting of character-coded alpha-numeric and graphic symbols commonly encountered in typewritten documents. Text files may be created by word processing software programs, electronic messaging programs, or other computer software.

Thesaurus In electronic recordkeeping systems, a display of the content and structure of indexing terminology; a listing of document indexing terms designed to provide consistency in identifying documents and files so that the records can be effectively retrieved.

Third-class mail A mail service for bulk business mail or advertising mail weighing less than 16 ounces.

Tickler A memory aid; a file set up as a reminder to "tickle" the memory.

Timely retrieval The ability of a recordkeeping system to consistently deliver to its users the records and information they request within time frames sufficient to enable them to perform their work in a productive manner.

Toner Colored (usually black) carbon-like substance used to form images in copiers and printers.

Topical filing A system in which one file follows another in alphabetical order. Also known as a *dictionary* system.

Transaction set The grouping of data elements needed to provide information in the document.

Transfer list A list of the contents of a group of records that are being transferred from one holding to another, usually from active files to a records center.

Trustworthiness The degree to which records containing evidence introduced or proposed for introduction in legal proceedings may be relied upon as being factual or otherwise what they purport to be.

Turnaround ratio Average time it takes to retrieve a document and get it to the requester divided by the total number of requests.

Turnkey A sale of equipment or a system that provides for installation that is ready to use by the buyer with no further action required, except for "turning the key."

Ultraviolet (UV) filter Any material that filters out UV ultraviolet rays. Such rays are harmful to preserved materials. Some exhibition spaces use UV filters on the windows and over fluorescent lights.

Uniform file classification A classification system that preserves the set order of records and establishes common titles.

Uniform Photographic Copies of Business and Public Records as Evidence Act A United States federal statute (adopted by many of the U. S. states) which holds that duplicate copies of documents are considered to have the same legal status as the original documents from which they were reproduced, provided the duplicates are accurate reproductions of the original documents.

Unitized microform A microform that is used to display a single frame of film, such as an aperture card, or a group of related images in a jacket, thus unitizing (uniting) an image or group of images that are related.

User A patron of records center services or computers. (See also **customer**.)

User-defined reports In electronic recordkeeping systems, the ability of the user to create system–generated reports that are customized to meet specific needs. This capability is sometimes provided in applications software programs.

Vacuum drying A general term which refers to several methods (freeze drying, thermal vacuum freeze drying, vacuum drying) for removing water from wet paper records by placing them in an airless chamber which vaporizes the water, which is then expelled from the chamber as steam, leaving the records dry.

Vault A fire-resistive and highly secure enclosure constructed within an office building or other workplace and used for the protection of large quantities of vital records. Vaults are designed to provide a high level of protection against fire and other hazards and are usually designed to be structurally independent from the building in which they are located.

Vaulting, electronic A method of protecting vital computer-based records by periodically transmitting updated data to a remote computer or tape drive. The transmission occurs in an on-line, electronic mode over telecommunications links.

Video conferencing A type of telecommunication. It is a variation of computer conferencing with cameras so that participants are visible to each other and the conference is on videotape.

Videodisc A laser disk which records and plays motion pictures.

Vinyl A group of plastics generally considered inappropriate for used in preservation. Often refers to *polyvinyl chloride (PVC)*.

Virus, computer A computer program that is capable of inserting a copy of itself into another computer program, thereby corrupting the integrity of the data in the program.

Visible file Arrangement of strips, cards, or other documents in specially designed equipment so that one line of each record is visible to serve as an index.

Vital records Records containing information required to re-establish or continue an organization in the event of a disaster; records containing unique and irreplaceable information necessary to recreate an organization's legal and financial position and preserve the rights of the organization and its employees, customers, shareholders and other constituent groups. Vital records include records whose informational value to the organization is so great, and the consequences of loss are so severe, that special protection is justified in order to reduce the risk of loss.

Vital records center A commercial or user-owned facility dedicated to the storage and protection of vital records. The facility is usually equipped with special fire detection, suppression and other security systems, and is generally located remote from the organization's primary place of business.

Vital records manual Includes procedures of the vital records protection program, explains the vital records master list, and provides instructions for reconstructing vital records in the event of a disaster.

Vital records master list A document that provides each department with a listing of all vital records for which it is responsible.

Vital records program That component of a records and information management program that manages the protection of vital records from loss or damage.

Voice mail A message that is digitized and can be reconstructed in audio or visual format.

Wheel file Usually an upright file which rotates like a Ferris wheel and holds cards.

Wild-card searching In electronic recordkeeping systems, the ability to use wild card symbols to represent multiple prefixes or suffixes of words (e.g. *automate*, *automation*), or alternate word spellings (e.g. *labor*, *labour*), thereby providing more precise retrieval of required data.

Workflow program A multi-step procedure of processing documents or completing transactions, where a document flows from station to station.

WORM A type of optical disk that permits recording only once while having the capability of being read many times. An Acronym meaning "Write Once, Read Many".

X–Y grid A coordinate used to locate a specific area on a plane or map. X representing the vertical columns and Y representing the Horizontal Rows.

ZIP code A five-digit number designed to expedite mail delivery in the United States

ZIP code + 4 A nine-digit number that identifies a geographic segment within the 5-digit area, such as city block, an office building, or a high-volume mailer.

Index

Please return or renew this item **East Sussex**
by the last date shown. You may County Council
return items to any East Sussex
Library. You may renew books
by telephone or the internet.

0345 60 80 196 for enquiries

Library and Information Services
eastsussex.gov.uk/libraries

04606658

Calm the
F**k Down

Calm the
F**k Down

How to control what you can
and accept what you can't
so you can stop freaking out
and get on with your life

Sarah Knight

Quercus

First published in 2018 in Great Britain by

Quercus Editions Ltd
Carmelite House
50 Victoria Embankment
London EC4Y 0DZ

An Hachette UK company

A CIP catalogue record for this book is available
from the British Library.

HB ISBN 978 1 78747 619 6
TPB ISBN 978 1 78747 620 2

Illustrations and hand lettering by Lauren Harms

6

Printed and bound in Great Britain by Clays Ltd, Elcograf S.p.A.

Contents

II

CALM THE FUCK DOWN: Identify what you can control, accept what you can't, and let that shit go   67

|||

DEAL WITH IT: Address what you *can* control **155**

IV

CHOOSE YOUR OWN ADVENTURE: When shit happens, how will *you* calm the fuck down and deal with it? **211**

Calm the
F**k Down

A note on the title

This is a book about anxiety — from the white noise of what-ifs to the white-hot terror of a full-blown crisis. As such, you'd be forgiven for thinking I'm the world's biggest asshole for titling it as I have, since everyone knows that the first entry on a long list of Unhelpful Things to Say to a Person Experiencing Anxiety is "Calm the fuck down."

Indeed, when I'm upset and somebody tells me to calm down, I want to murder them in swift and decisive fashion. So I see where you'd be coming from.

But this is also a book about problems — we've all got 'em — and **calming down is exactly what you need to do if you want to *solve* those problems.** It is what it is. So if it keeps you from wanting to murder the messenger, know that in these pages I'm saying "Calm the fuck down" the same way I said "Get your shit together" in the <cough> *New York Times* bestseller of the same name — not to shame or criticize you, but to offer motivation and encouragement.

I promise that's all I'm going for. (And that I'm not the world's biggest asshole; that honor belongs to whoever invented the vuvuzela.)

We cool? Excellent.

One more thing before we dive into all of that anxiety-reducing, problem-solving goodness: **I understand the difference between *anxiety,* the mental illness, and *anxiety,* the temporary state of mind.** I understand it because I myself happen to possess a diagnosis of Generalized Anxiety and Panic Disorder. (Write what you know, folks!)

So although a profanity-riddled self-help book is no substitute for professional medical care, if you picked up *Calm the Fuck Down* because you're perennially, clinically anxious like me, in it you will find plenty of tips, tricks, and techniques to help you manage that shit, which will allow you to **move on to the business of solving the problems that are feeding your anxiety in the first place.**

But maybe you don't have — or don't realize you have, or aren't ready to admit you have — *anxiety,* the mental illness. Maybe you just get temporarily anxious when the situation demands it (see: the white-hot terror of a full-blown crisis). Never fear! ***Calm the Fuck Down* will provide you with ample calamity management tools for stressful times.**

Plus maybe some tips, tricks, and techniques for dealing with that thing you don't realize or aren't ready to admit you have.

Just sayin'.

Introduction

I'd like to kick things off with a few questions:

- How many times a day do you ask yourself *What if?* As in: *What if X happens? What if Y goes wrong? What if Z doesn't turn out like I want/need/expect it to?*

- How much time do you spend worrying about something that hasn't happened yet? Or about something that not only hasn't happened, but probably won't?

- And how many hours have you wasted freaking out about something that has *already* happened (or avoiding it, as a quiet panic infests your soul) instead of just dealing with it?

It's okay to be honest — I'm not trying to shame you. In fact, I'll go first!

My answer is: *Too many, too much, and a LOT.* I assume yours is too, because if the answer is *Never, none, and ZERO*, then you have no reason to be reading this book (nor, I might add, the hard-won qualifications to have written it).

Well, I come bearing good news.

When we're finished, the next time you come down with a case of the what-ifs — and whether they remain theoretical anxieties or turn into real, live problems that need solvin' — instead of worrying yourself into a panic attack, crying the day away, punching a wall, or avoiding things until they get even worse, you'll have learned to replace the open-ended nature of that unproductive question with one that's much more **logical, realistic, and actionable:**

OKAY, NOW WHAT?

Then, you'll deal with it, whatever it is.

But let's not get ahead of ourselves — for now, we start with the basics.

Shit happens

Boy, does it. And when I think about all the shit that could or probably will happen to me on any given day, I'm reminded of a lyric from departed musical genius and spiritual gangsta, the one, the only, Prince (RIP):

"Dearly Beloved, we are gathered here today to get through this thing called life."

The Purple One had suspect opinions about a lot of things — among them religion, tasteful fabrics, and age-appropriate relationships — but in this regard he was spot-on. Each morning that we wake up and lurch across this rotating time bomb called Earth, our baseline goal is to get through the day. Some of us are angling for more — like success, a bit of relaxation, or a kind word from a loved one. Others are just hoping not to get arrested for treason. (While every day, some of us are hoping someone *else* gets arrested for treason!)

And though each twenty-four-hour cycle brings the potential for good things to happen — your loan gets approved, your girl-friend proposes, your socks match — **there's also the chance that a big steaming pile of shit will land in your lap.** Your house could get repossessed, your girlfriend might break up with you, your socks may become wooly receptacles for cat vomit. Not to mention the potential for earthquakes, tornados, military coups, nuclear accidents, the world wine output falling to record lows, and all manner of disasters that could strike at any time and really fuck up your shit. Especially the wine thing.

That's just how life works. Prince knew it. You know it. And that is literally all you and Prince have in common.

So here's another question for you: **When shit happens, how do you react?** Do you freeze or do you freak out? Do you lock the bathroom door and cry or do you howl at the sky with rage? Personally, I've been known to pretend shit is *not* happening, bury my head in a pillow, and stick my ass in the air in a move I call "ostriching."

Unfortunately, while these coping mechanisms can be comforting, none are especially productive (and I say that having invented one of them). Eventually you have to stop freaking out and start dealing with your shit, and — shocker — **it's hard to make decisions and solve problems when you're panicking or sobbing or shouting, or when all the blood is rushing to your head.**

Which is why what you really need to do, first and foremost, is **calm the fuck down.**

Yes, you.*

---

* If you're having an A-plus day, the sun is shining, the birds are singing, and all is right with your minuscule slice of rotating time bomb, you probably

We've all been there. I simply maintain that most of us could learn how to handle it better. Related: most of us also have a friend, relative, or partner whose inevitable reaction to our every crisis is "Don't worry, everything's going to be okay." Or worse: "Aw, it's not so bad."

On that, I call bullshit. Well-meaning platitudes are easy to offer for someone with no skin in the game. **In this book, we'll be dealing in reality, not nicety.**

The truth is:

Yes, sometimes things will be okay. You pass the test, the tumor comes back benign, Linda returns your text.

But sometimes they won't. Investments go south, friendships fall away, in an election of monumental consequence millions of people cast their vote for an ingrown toenail in a cheap red hat.

In some cases, it's really not so bad, and you *are* overreacting. You've built an imagined crisis up in your head and let it feed your anxiety like a mogwai after dark. If you've seen *Gremlins*, you know how this ends.

But in other cases IT'S REAL BAD BRO, and you? You're *under*reacting. You're like that cartoon dog who sits at a table

---

don't need to calm the fuck down. Congrats. Go outside, enjoy. Things will turn to shit soon enough, and I'll be waiting.

drinking coffee while the house burns down around him thinking *It's fine. This is fine.*

And sure, by saying "everything's going to be okay," your friend/relative/partner is probably just trying to help you. But whether you're making a Taj Mahal out of a teepee, or ignoring a problem for so long that it sets your metaphorical house on fire, I'm *actually* going to help you. That's just how I roll.

Thus begins your education in calming the fuck down:

Lesson #1: Merely *believing* that things will be okay or aren't so bad may make you feel better in the moment, but it won't solve the problem. (And a lot of times it doesn't even feel good in the moment — it feels like you're being condescended to by the Happy Industrial Complex. Don't get me started.)

Either way, it doesn't change a goddamn thing!

Lesson #2: When shit happens, circumstances are what they are: tires are flat, wrists are broken, files are deleted, hamsters are dead. You may be frustrated, anxious, hurt, angry, or sad — but you are right there in the thick of it and the only thing you can control in this equation is YOU, and your reaction.

Lesson #3: To survive and thrive in these moments, you need to ACKNOWLEDGE what's happened, ACCEPT the parts you can't control, and ADDRESS the parts you can.

Per that last one, have you heard of the Serenity Prayer — you know, the one about **accepting the things you cannot change and having the wisdom to know the difference?** *Calm the Fuck Down* is essentially a blasphemous, long-form version of that, with flowcharts 'n' stuff.

If you're into that sort of thing, we're going to get along just fine.

What, me worry?

I'm guessing that if you came to this book for guidance, then worrying about shit — either before or after it happens — is a problem for you. So here's a mini-lesson: **"worrying" has two separate but related meanings.** In addition to the act of anxiously fretting about one's problems, "worrying" also means constantly fiddling with something, rubbing at it, tearing it open, and making it worse.

It's like noticing that your sweater has a dangling thread, maybe the beginnings of a hole. And it's natural to want to pull on it. You're getting a feel for the problem, measuring its potential impact. *How bad is it already? What can I do about it?*

But if you keep pulling — and then tugging, yanking, and fiddling **instead of taking action to fix it** — suddenly you're down a whole sleeve, you're freaking out, and both your state of mind and your sweater are in tatters. I've seen smaller piles of yarn at a cat café.

When you get into this state of mind, you're not just worried *about* something; you're actually *worrying it*. **And in both senses, worrying makes the problem worse.**

This series of unfortunate events applies across the board, **from worries that bring on low-level anxiety to those that precede full-bore freakouts.** Some of that anxiety and freaking out is warranted — like *What if my car runs out of gas in the middle of a dark desert highway?* But some of it isn't — like *What if Linda is mad at me? I know she saw that text I sent yesterday and she hasn't replied. WHY HAVEN'T YOU REPLIED, LINDA???*

Luckily, I'm going to show you how to get a handle on ALL of your worries — **how to accept the ones you can't control, and how to act in a productive way on the ones you can.**

I call it the **NoWorries Method.** It's based on the same concept that anchors all of my work — **"mental decluttering"** — and it has two steps:

Step 1: Calm the fuck down

Step 2: Deal with it

Sounds promising, no?

Or does it sound overly reductive and like it couldn't possibly help you in any way? I hear that, but "overly reductive *yet* extremely helpful" is kind of my thing, so maybe give it another page or two before you decide.

For now, let's circle back to those questions you already admitted you can't stop asking yourself:

What if X happens?
What if Y goes wrong?
What if Z doesn't turn out like I want/need/
expect it to?

The "X" you're worried about could be anything from getting your period on a first date to the untimely death of a loved one. "Y" could be your dissertation defense or the landing gear on your connecting flight to Milwaukee. "Z" might be a job interview, a driving test, or the rather large wager you placed on the latest Royal baby name. (It's a four-thousand-pound shame they didn't go with Gary, I know.)

In the end, it doesn't matter precisely what your what-ifs are — only that they exist and they're occupying some/a lot/too much of your mental space on any given day, unraveling your metaphorical sweater bit by bit. You would therefore do well to note the following:

Lesson #4: A bunch of this shit is unlikely to happen at all.

Lesson #5: You can prevent some of it and mitigate the effects of some of the rest.

Lesson #6: Some of it is and has always been completely out of your hands and locked in the steely grip of Her Majesty, Queen Elizabeth II. You need to take your licks, learn the lesson, and let this one go.

And hey, no judgments. I'm right there with you (hence the hard-won qualifications to have written this book).

For most of my life, I've been a champion worrier. *What-ifs* swirl inside my skull like minnows on a meth bender. I fret about shit that hasn't happened. I obsess over shit that may or may not happen. And when shit does happen, I possess an astounding capacity for freaking out about it.

But over the last few years I've found ways to keep that stuff to a minimum. I'm not completely worry-free, but I have become less anxious and am no longer, shall we say, paralyzed by dread and/or driven to the brink of madness by unmet expectations and a boiling sense of injustice. It's an improvement.

I'm amazed at how good it feels and how much I've been able to accomplish with a relatively simple change in mind-set — **accepting the shit I can't control** — which allows me to focus on dealing with the shit I *can* control, leaving me better equipped to make decisions and solve problems both in the moment and after the fact.

And even to prevent some of them from happening in the first place. Nifty!

I've learned how to stop dwelling on unlikely outcomes in

favor of acting to create more likely ones. How to plow forward rather than agonize backward. And crucially, **how to separate my anxiety about what** *might* **occur from the act of handling it when it** *does* **occur.**

You can learn to do all of that too. *Calm the Fuck Down* will help you—

Stop freaking out about shit you can't control.

AND

Enable yourself to make rational decisions.

SO YOU CAN

Solve problems instead of making them worse.

Here's what that process looked like for me during the last few years, and a little taste of how it can work for you.

I can't deal with this shit. (Or can I?)

The beginnings of my change in mind-set happened to coincide with a change of location when my husband and I moved from bustling Brooklyn, New York, to a tranquil fishing village on the north coast of the Dominican Republic.

I know, shut the fuck up, right? But I swear this isn't a story about idyllic, sun-drenched days full of coco locos and aquamarine vistas. I do enjoy those, but the primary benefit of living where I

do is that it has forced me — like, aquamarine waterboarded me —
to calm down.

During the previous sixteen years in New York, I'd had a lot
going on: I climbed the corporate ladder; planned and executed a
wedding; bought real estate; and orchestrated the aforementioned
move to the Dominican Republic. I was always good at getting
shit done, yes, but I was not especially calm while doing it.*

And when anything happened to alter the course of my carefully cultivated expectations — well, *fughetaboutit*.

You might think that a high-functioning, high-achieving,
highly organized person would be able to adjust if the situation
demanded it. But back then, I couldn't deviate from the plan
without experiencing a major freakout — such as when a down-
pour on the day of my husband's thirtieth-birthday picnic sent
me into a fit of *Goodbye, cruel world!*

In those days I had a tendency to melt down faster than a half
pound of raclette at a bougie Brooklyn dinner party — **making all
of the shit I had to do far more difficult and anxiety-inducing
than it needed to be.** Two steps forward, one step back. All. The.
Damn. Time.

Something had to give; but I didn't know what, or how to
give it.

Which brings us to that tranquil fishing village on the north

---

* Where "not especially calm" equals "a total fucking lunatic."

coast of the Dominican Republic. Three years ago I moved to a place where you might as well abandon planning altogether. Here, the tropical weather shifts faster than the Real Housewives' loyalties; stores close for unspecified periods of time on random days of the week; and the guy who is due to fix the roof *"mañana"* is just as likely to arrive "a week from *mañana*" — possibly because of thunderstorms, or because he couldn't buy the materials he needed from the hardware store that is only periodically and inconsistently open.

Or both. Or neither. Who knows?

Caribbean life may look seductively slow-paced and groovy when you've called in sick from your demanding job to lie on the couch bingeing on chicken soup and HGTV — and in lots of ways it is; I AM NOT COMPLAINING — but it can also be **frustrating for those of us who thrive on reliability and structure, or who don't deal particularly well with the unexpected.**

After a few weeks of hanging out in Hispaniola, I began to realize that if I clung to my old ways in our new life, I would wind up in a perpetual panic about *something,* because *nothing* goes according to plan around here. And THAT would negate the entire purpose of having gotten the hell out of New York in the first place.

So for me, landing in the DR was a shot of exposure therapy with a coconut rum chaser. I've been forced to relax and go with the flow, which has done wonders for my attitude and my Xanax supply.

AGAIN, NOT COMPLAINING.

But through observation and practice, I've also determined that one doesn't need to uproot to an island in the middle of the Atlantic to calm the fuck down.

Anyone can do it — including you.

You just need to shift your mind-set, like I did, to react to problems in a different way. In doing so, you'll also learn that **you actually *can* prepare for the unexpected,** which helps a lot with that whole "one step back" thing.

How is that possible? Wouldn't preparing for every potential outcome drive you crazy in a totally different way?

Well yes, yes it would. But I'm not talking about securing multiple locations for your husband's thirtieth-birthday party because "what if" it rains; or preparing three different versions of a presentation because "what if" the client seems to be in less of a pie chart and more of a bar graph mood that day; or erecting a complicated system of moats around your property because "what if" your neighbor's frisky cows get loose someday. That could definitely drive you crazy in a different way. And possibly to bankruptcy.

I'm talking about **preparing *mentally.***

That's what this book helps you do, so that when shit happens, you'll have the tools to handle it — **whoever you are, wherever you live, and whenever things get hairy.**

(Pssst: that's what we in the biz call "foreshadowing.")

✻ ✳ ✽

A few months ago after a pleasant night out at a local tiki bar, my husband and I arrived home to an unexpected visitor.

I had opened our gate and was slowly picking my way across the flagstone path to our deck (it was dark, I was tipsy) when a larger-than-usual leaf caught my eye. It seemed to be not so much fluttering on the breeze as...scuttling on it. A quick beam of my iPhone flashlight confirmed that the presumptive almond leaf was in fact a tarantula the size of a honeydew melon.

Yup. I'll give you a moment to recover. Lord knows I needed one.

Now, assuming you haven't thrown the book across the room in disgust (or that you have at least picked it back up), may I continue?

Having previously declared my intention to BURN THE MOTHERFUCKER DOWN if we ever spotted such a creature in our house, I was faced with a quandary. By this time, I had grown fond of my house. And technically, the creature was not *in* it. Just *near* it.

What to do? Stand frozen in place until the thing wandered back to the unknowable depths from whence it came? Sleep with one eye open for eternity? Politely ask the tarantula to skedaddle?

None of those were realistic options. As it turned out, apart from shouting at my husband to "Pleasecomedealwiththetarantula!"

there wasn't much I *could* do. We live in the jungle, baby. And no matter how many real estate agents and fellow expats had told us "those guys stay up in the mountains — you'll never see one," there was no denying the seven-legged fact that one had found its way to our humble sea-level abode.

(You read that correctly. This gent was missing one of his furry little limbs — a fact that will become important later in this story.)

What we *did* do was this: my husband grabbed a broom and used it to guide the uninvited guest off our property and into the neighbors' bushes, and I fled into the house muttering "Everything is a tarantula" under my breath until I was safely upstairs and sufficiently drugged to sleep.

It wasn't totally calming the fuck down, but it was a step in the right direction.

The next morning we got up early to go on an all-day, rum-guzzling boat trip with some friends. (I know, I know, shut the fuck up.) I staggered downstairs in a pre-8:00-a.m. haze and as I turned at the landing toward the bottom of the stairs, I saw it.

Hiding behind the floor-length curtain in the living room was the very same tarantula that had previously been shooed a good hundred feet away from its current position. I knew it was the same one because it had only seven legs. And lest you think I got close enough to count them, I will remind you that *this spider was so fucking big you did not have to get close to it to count its legs* — with which it had, overnight, crossed an expanse of grass, climbed back up onto the deck, and then CLIMBED AGAIN UP TO THE TERRACE AND SQUEEZED IN BETWEEN THE CRACKS OF OUR SLIDING DOORS TO GET INSIDE THE HOUSE.

I know what you're thinking. *THIS is when you burn the motherfucker down, right?*

And yes, my instinctive reaction was *I can't deal with this shit.*

But you know what? Upon second viewing, the tarantula was not so bad. **Or rather, it was still bad, but *I* was better.**

If we'd found a spider like that inside our Brooklyn apartment, I would have lit a match right then and there. But now it seemed I'd been trained by all those unpredictable monsoon rains and unreliable roof guys: Expect the unexpected! Nothing goes according to plan! *SURPRIIIISE!!!*

From our practice run the night before, I knew it wasn't going to move very fast or, like, start growling at me. And I had to admit that a honeydew-sized spider operating one leg short was a lot smaller and less nimble than a five-foot-tall person with both her legs intact. (It turns out that exposure therapy is clinically sanctioned for a reason.)

By activating the logical part of my brain, I was able to one-up that instinctive *I can't deal with this shit* with a more productive *Okay, well, what are we going to do about this because I have a boat to catch and vast quantities of rum to imbibe.* This was no time for hysterics; **freaking out was not going to solve the problem.**

Recall, if you would, my jacked-up version of the Serenity Prayer:

ACKNOWLEDGE what has happened (a tarantula is in my house)

ACCEPT what you can't control (tarantulas can get into my house?!?)

ADDRESS what you *can* control (get the tarantula out of my house)

I had officially calmed the fuck down — now it was time to deal with it.

Fine, it was time for my husband to deal with it. I helped.

Using an empty plastic pitcher, a broom, a piece of cardboard, and nerves of steel, he trapped the thing humanely and secured it on the dining table while I rounded up sunscreen, towels, portable speakers, and an extra pint of Barceló because last time the boat captain underestimated and really, who wants to hang out on a deserted beach with an infinite supply of coconuts and a finite supply of rum? YOU CAN CONTROL THE RUM.

Then we drove a mile down the road with our new pal Lucky (ensconced in his plastic jug), released the wayward spider into a vacant lot, and boarded the SS *Mama Needs Her Juice*.

✳ ✴ ✳

So what do my newfound Caribbean calm and tales of tarantulian derring-do have to do with acknowledging, accepting, and addressing **your overactive what-ifs, worries, anxiety, and freakouts?**

A fair question.

In addition to spending many years as a professional worrier, I am currently a professional writer of self-help books, including *The Life-Changing Magic of Not Giving a Fuck, Get Your Shit Together,* and *You Do You.* Each has recounted aspects of my personal trek toward becoming a happier and mentally healthier person, combined with practical, profanity-riddled tips re: accomplishing same.

They call me **"the Anti-Guru."** Not gonna lie, it's a pretty sweet gig.

Collectively, the No Fucks Given Guides—NFGGs, for short—have helped millions of people cast off burdensome obligations, organize their lives, and be their authentic selves. If you are one of those people, I want to thank you for enabling this supersweet gig. If you're new to the party: Welcome! And sorry about the spider stuff. I know that was off-putting, but the NFGGs are like that sometimes. You'll get used to it.

Anyway, I'm glad you're here. And between us, I believe you

are holding in your hands the most useful No Fucks Given Guide of them all, since, as I think we've agreed, everyone has problems.

That's right: You cannot get through life without shit happening to you!

But also: HEREWITH, A MANUAL FOR LEARNING HOW TO COPE!

In *Calm the Fuck Down,* you'll learn about:

- The Four Faces of Freaking Out (and their Flipsides)
- Managing your freakout funds
- Mental decluttering
- The One Question to Rule Them All
- How to sort your problems by probability and prioritize them by urgency
- "Sleight of mind"
- Ostrich Mode and how to avoid it
- Productive Helpful Effective Worrying (PHEW)
- The Three Principles of Dealing With It
- Realistic ideal outcomes (RIOs)
- And much, much more...

So if you're like me — if you've ever thought *I can't deal with this shit*, or if you're asking *What if?* more than you ought to be, worrying too much, freaking out too often, and wasting time and energy obsessing over things you can't control — I can help.

Remember: I'm not here to invalidate or minimize your anxiety or your problems. I just want to assist you in dealing with them, and calming the fuck down is the first step. Along the way, I swear I'll never tell you "everything's going to be okay" or push the narrative that "it's not so bad."

Whatever's going on in your life sucks as hard as you think it does. No arguments here.

But I will say this:

I am 100 percent positive that if I can spend ten minutes in a car with a tarantula on my lap, **you can calm the fuck down and deal with your shit, too.**

1

SO YOU'RE FREAKING OUT:

Acknowledge the real problem and rein in your reaction

In part I, we'll establish some parameters, beginning with what your problems are, exactly, and what variations of havoc they're wreaking on your life.

Could you BE any more excited???

Then we'll study **the evolution of a freakout: how it happens, what it looks like, and what it costs you.** I'll introduce the **Four Faces of Freaking Out and their Flipsides,** and show you how to transition from one to the other. This section includes a primer on a little something known in our household as Mexican Airport Syndrome. Pay attention, amigos.

Next, we'll talk **freakout funds.** These are the resources you have at your disposal to forestall or combat a freakout: **time, energy, and money** — they make the world go round, especially when shit is going down. Plus, there's **the Fourth Fund,** which you may have unknowingly been overdrawing for far too long. We'll discuss.

I'll wrap up part I by explaining the concept of **mental decluttering** (both in general and as it pertains to calming the fuck down); introducing you to **the One Question to Rule Them All;** and finally, walking you through a technique I call **"emotional puppy crating."**

All of this may sound a little wacky (especially the emotional puppy crating), but give it a chance. The way I see it, there are thousands of self-improvement methods on the market that peddle far more suspect solutions to life's problems. At least I know the stuff in this book works, because it works on ME—and in addition to being very logical and rational, I am also, at times, a Bona Fide Basket Case.

Anti-gurus: they're just like us!

Now, let's freak out—together.

What seems to be the problem?

Forgive me for saying so, but you seem a little anxious.

Perhaps it's about something small, like wrapping up the last thing on your to-do list or the niggling concern that you should be calling your parents more often. Maybe you're worried about something bigger or more complicated, like you want to apply to grad school but you're not sure if you can fit it around your day job and budget. The source of your anxiety might be hard to pinpoint, or it could be pretty fucking obvious — like you just totaled your bike, or discovered your house was built on top of an active gopher colony.

Or, and this is just a wild guess, maybe it's all of the above?

Yeah, I kinda thought so.

Well get ready to drop a jaw, because I have news for you: **IT'S ALL CONNECTED.** That low hum of background anxiety, your worries about Shit That Hasn't Happened Yet and Shit That Already Has, the little stuff and the big. All of it is related and **all of it can be attacked with the realism, pragmatism, and logical thinking** that I'll be preaching throughout *Calm the Fuck Down.*

But before you can attack your anxiety *about* it, **you must identify and isolate the specific, underlying problem.** One at a time, please.

Sometimes that's easier said than done. If we're talking about a smashed-up Raleigh or a gopher colony, then I trust you know what's what.* But there may also be days when **you feel *blah* and *blech* for no reason,** and those feelings send you spiraling into the Bad Place.

I can't fall asleep at night.

I woke up in a panic.

I can't relax.

I'm so distracted.

No reason, huh? INCORRECT.

There *is* a reason for your anxiety, a what-if behind your worry. And if you can name it, you'll be in a much better position to calm the fuck down about and deal with it. For example:

I can't fall asleep at night because what if I get bad news from the doctor tomorrow?

I woke up in a panic because what if my presentation goes badly today?

I can't relax because what if I don't study enough to pass the test?

I'm so distracted because what if I forget to do everything I'm supposed to do?

---

* Gopher colonies being a prime example of an underlying problem.

Everything is a tarantula

I'm familiar with waking up in a panic. I'm also familiar with feeling *blah* and *blech* for "no reason." It can come upon me in the morning, late at night, or even at the stroke of 4:00 p.m., my cherished "spritz o'clock." I liken it to being stalked by a hidden tarantula; I know there's something out there, but if it refuses to show its fuzzy little face, how can I be expected to deal with it? When I find myself actually muttering "Everything is a tarantula" out loud — as I have taken to doing since oh, about six months ago — I've learned to stop and ask myself *No, what is it really?* Because everything is not a hidden tarantula. Everything is right out there in the open, with a name and a form of its own: *My book is due. My parents are coming to visit. The roof is leaking. I'm planning a party. I have a new boss. Did I pay the phone bill?* Only when you take the time to identify what's truly bothering you, can you start to address it. And anything is better than a tarantula, which means this technique works on multiple levels.

First, you need to figure out *why* you feel this way, so you can figure out *what to do* about it. ACKNOWLEDGE the problem. You do that part, and I'll help with the rest. I think it's a more-than-fair trade for a few minutes of introspection on your part, don't you?

If you woke up in a panic this morning or you're feeling *blah* or *blech* in this very moment, take ten minutes right now to give your tarantulas a name. You don't have to calm down about or deal with them just yet, but get 'em out of the shadows and onto the page.

(If you are not currently experiencing "everything is a tarantula" anxiety, skip this part — but keep it in mind for the future.)

MY TARANTULAS:

_____

_____

_____

_____

Next up, I'll show you **what happens when your worries and what-ifs leave you not merely distracted or unable to sleep, but barreling toward a full-fledged freakout.**

Why am I taking you deep into the Bad Place? Because understanding how freaking out works will help you understand how to *avoid it*.

The evolution of a freakout

Imagine you're hosting your daughter's high school graduation party this weekend. She's headed off to the University of Texas; you're very proud. And although you tallied the RSVPs thrice and calculated your provisions accordingly, what if more people show up than you expected?

You start to worry that you don't have enough food and drink to serve all of your guests, plus the inevitable plus-ones, *plus* a half dozen teenage boys who will undoubtedly show up unannounced and decimate the hot dog supplies, leaving you with a subpar grilled-meat-to-potato-salad ratio far too early in the day.

This is normal. Show me someone who's planned a big event and hasn't been plagued by what-ifs and worries and I'll show you a superhuman who runs on Klonopin and hubris.

It's what you do (or don't do) next that counts.

You could run out and grab an extra pack of dogs, and just throw them in the freezer if they don't get eaten. By taking action — tying a knot in that loose thread — you can prevent this worry from destroying your metaphorical sweater.

Or, instead of acknowledging the problem (potential meat shortage), accepting what you can't control (uninvited guests), and addressing what you can (dog quantities), you could just keep worrying.

Let's say you do that.

What if the citronella torches don't keep the mosquitos away as advertised? What if it rains? What if the UT novelty coasters I ordered don't get here in time?

Uh-oh. Your sweater is unraveling knit one by purl two — and those are just the logistical what-ifs! You can't help yourself. You keep pulling and tugging and adding more to the mix:

What if people take one look at my yard decorations and think I'm trying too hard? (Or not hard enough?) What if the neighbors are annoyed by all the cars parked along the street? What if we did all this work and everybody cancels at the last minute?

Now your sweater is more of a midriff top, you can't stop to breathe, let alone take action, and you're no longer merely worried — you're officially freaking out.

EVOLUTION OF A FREAKOUT:

WHAT-IF
↓
WORRY
↓
INACTION
↓
FREAKOUT!

This is how it happens. And with the proper training, you should be able to prevent it.

In part II, for example, we'll practice **identifying what you can control** (investing in a few cans of industrial-strength bug spray, a tent, and expedited shipping) **and accepting what you can't** (next-door neighbor Debbie's disdain for orange-and-white floral arrangements; everyone you invited gets chicken pox) **so you can prepare for some outcomes and let go of your worries about others.** Go Longhorns!

But for the moment, and for the sake of a good ol' cautionary tale, let's stick to diagnostics. **Because whether it's bubbling up or already boiling over, it helps to know which *type* of freakout you're experiencing.**

They all look different and there are different ways to defuse each of them.

The Four Faces of Freaking Out

In my previous books, I've been known to offer a neat taxonomy of the different types of readers who could benefit from taking my advice. I do this because I find that encountering a somewhat personalized profile helps one feel seen, which is comforting when one is about to be smacked upside the head with some decidedly uncomfortable truths.

Which makes it unfortunate for you and me both that **Freak-**

ing Out, How Everybody Does It and Why, is all over the god-damn map.

Some of us don't blink an eye when our septic tanks back up, but hyperventilate if Starbucks runs out of almond croissants. Others pull a Cool Hand Luke when the car gets towed or the test results come back positive, but reach our own personal DEFCON 1 when the cable goes out during *America's Next Top Model*.

Furthermore, **freaking out manifests in different strokes for different folks.** For some it's the openmouthed, panic-sweating countenance of a *Cathy* cartoon from the eighties ("Ack!"); but for others, freaking out is more about tears than tremors. Or black moods. Or blank stares.

And to top it all off — any one of us might experience a different form of freakout on a different day, for a different reason.

For example, *you* may not be a big dumb crybaby like your friend Ted who spends all day posting "feeling emotional" emoji on Facebook, but if you lose your wedding ring or your grandma, you're liable to get a little weepy. And *I* don't typically waste my breath screaming and shouting, but one time in 2001 I opened the refrigerator door on my foot and the resulting spittle-filled tirade was not unlike Jack Nicholson's turn on the stand in *A Few Good Men*.

As I said, all over the map.

So instead of trying to fit you, as an individual freaker-outer, into one tidy category, I've winnowed the types of freakouts themselves into four big, messy categories — any one or more of which you might fall into at any given time:

Anxiety

Sadness

Anger

Avoidance (aka "Ostrich Mode")

These are the Four Faces of Freaking Out — the masks we wear when we worry obsessively — and *ooh, mama* it's getting hard to breathe up in this piece. Your job is to learn how to recognize them, so you can fight back.

Know your enemy and all that.

😬 ANXIOUS

What it looks like: Anxiety comes in many forms, and for the uninitiated it can sometimes be hard to label. For example, you may think you've got a touch of food poisoning, when your upset stomach is actually due to anxiety. Or you might think you've *been poisoned* when really you're just having an old-fashioned panic attack. (Been there, thought that.) Other indicators include but are not limited to: nervousness, headaches, hot flashes, shortness of breath, light-headedness, insomnia, indecision, the runs, and compulsively checking your email to see if your editor has responded to those pages you sent an hour ago.

(And remember, you don't have to be diagnosed with capital-A Anxiety Disorder to experience lowercase-a anxiety. Plenty of calm, rational, almost-always-anxiety-free people go through occasional bouts of situational anxiety. Good times.)

Why it's bad: Apart from the symptoms I listed above, one of the most toxic and insidious side effects of being anxious is **OVER-THINKING.** It's like that buzzy black housefly that keeps dipping and swooping in and out of your line of vision, and every time you think you've drawn a bead on it, it changes direction. Up in the corner! No, wait! Over there by the stairs! Uh-oh, too slow! Now it's hovering three feet above your head, vibrating like the physical manifestation of your brain about to explode. WHERE DO YOU WANT TO BE, HOUSEFLY??? MAKE UP YOUR MIND.

Overthinking is the antithesis of productivity. I mean, have you ever seen a fly land anywhere for more than three seconds? How much could they possibly be getting accomplished in any given day?

What can you do about it? You need to Miyagi that shit. Focus. One problem at a time, one *part* of that problem at a time. And most important: one *solution* to that problem at a time. Lucky for you, part II contains many practical tips for accomplishing just that.

Keep reading, is what I'm saying.

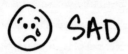 **SAD**

What it looks like: Weeping, moping, rumpled clothes, running mascara, the scent of despair, and heaving breathless heaving breaths. It can also lead to a condition I call Social Media Self-Pity, which is tiring not only for you, but also for your friends and followers. Cut it out, Ted. Nobody wants to watch you have an emotional breakdown in *Garfield* memes.

Why it's bad: Listen, I've got absolutely nothing against a good cry. You're worried that your childhood home is going to be bull-dozed by evil city planners or that your hamster, Ping-Pong, might not make it out of surgery? By all means, bawl it out. I do it all the time. Catharsis!

Just try not to, you know, *wallow.*

When worrying becomes wallowing — letting sadness over-take you for long periods of time — you've got bigger problems. Ongoing sadness is **EXHAUSTING.** As energy flags, you might stop eating or leaving the house, which compounds the encroach-ing lethargy. You'll get less and less productive. And all of *that* can lead to feeling depressed and giving up on dealing with your shit altogether.

But to be clear, being sad — even for a messy, depressing stretch — is one thing. Having clinical depression is another. If you think you might not be merely sad, but fully in the grip of depression, I urge you to seek help beyond the pages of a twenty-dollar book written by a woman whose literal job is to come up with new ways to work "fuck" into a sentence.

Though if that woman may be so bold: depression, like anxiety, can be hard to suss out when you're the detective and your own head is the case. Do yourself a favor and listen to people around you when they say "Hey, you seem not merely sad, but fully in the grip of depression. Maybe you should talk to a professional?" And don't be ashamed about it. All kinds of people — even ones with objectively hunky-dory lives — can suffer from depression. Mental illness is a bitch.*

All of this is to say, I may not be qualified to diagnose or treat you for depression (the disease); but under the auspices of *Calm the Fuck Down,* I think feeling depressed (the state of mind) is fair game. And to my mind, that state is *exhausted.*

What can you do about it? Patience, my pretties. We're gonna get you up and out of bed sooner rather than later. It's what Ping-Pong would have wanted.

---

* Welp, looks like I found a title for my next book!

 # ANGRY

What it looks like: Painful encounters with fridge doors not-withstanding, I don't tend to get angry. Maybe it's because my parents didn't fight in front of me. Maybe it's just my natural temperament. Or maybe it's because I'm a stone-cold bitch who skips getting mad and goes straight to getting even. But even though I don't do a lot of yelling, screaming, wishing poxes on people, or setting fire to their prized possessions myself, that doesn't mean I don't know the drill. Those in the throes of anger experience unhealthy side effects such as rising blood pressure and body temperature, the desire to inflict physical violence and the injuries sustained upon doing so, splotchy faces, clenched jaws, and unsightly bulging neck tendons.

But an invisible — though no less damaging — result of an angry freakout is that it impedes good judgment. **IT MAKES THINGS WORSE.**

Why it's bad: In the age of smartphone cameras, every meltdown is a potential fifteen minutes of infamy. Do you want to wind up on the evening news spewing regrettable epithets or on Facebook Live destroying public property because you couldn't calm the fuck down? No, you do not. Behold: Mexican Airport Syndrome.

Mexican Airport Syndrome

Once upon a time my husband and I were returning from a family vacation that had been organized by a travel agent. Somehow, when the thirteen of us got to our connecting flight in Mexico City, I didn't have a ticket. Not a seat assignment, mind you, but *a fucking ticket*. Who knows what had happened, but you know what doesn't fix it? Getting all up in the face of the airline employee manning the check-in desk. My [sweet, generous, kind, typically very calm] husband nearly learned this lesson the hard way when he lost his shit on one of said employees for about three-point-two seconds before I elbowed him in the ribs and communicated *I don't want to get detained overnight — or forever — in Mexico City* with my eyes. Also saving his *tocineta* that day was the Long Island mom who was having the same problem and dealing with it in an exponentially worse way. Do you know that she has a Very Important Bar Mitzvah to attend tomorrow?!? Right. I got on the plane. She didn't.

What can you do about it? Well, you could take an anger management class, but that doesn't sound very pleasant. I have a few stimulating alternatives I think you're going to like. (Especially page 115. That's a good one.)

PS If I'm being honest, I'm curious about what it'll take to activate my Anger face. It's been a good fifteen years since the Refrigerator Incident and ya girl is only human.

 # AVOIDANCE
(aka Ostrich Mode)

What it looks like: The tricky thing about Ostrich Mode is that you may not even realize you're doing it, because "doing it" is quite literally "doing nothing." You're just ignoring or dismissing warnings and pretending like shit isn't happening. Nothing to see here, folks! Head firmly in the sand.

(BTW, I know these giant birds do not really bury their disproportionately tiny heads in the sand to escape predators, but I need you to lighten up a little when it comes to the accuracy of my metaphors; otherwise this book will be no fun for either of us.)

Now, sometimes the 'strich stands alone — if you're merely putting off a mundane chore, that's pure, unadulterated avoidance. Other times, ostriching is the result of having *already* succumbed to anxiety, sadness, and/or anger. In those moments it feels like your brain is a pot of boiling lobsters, and if you can just keep the lid tamped down tightly enough, maybe you'll never have to confront their silent screams. (This is typically when I dive headfirst for the couch pillows.)

Why it's bad: First of all, un-dealt-with shit begets *more shit*. Ignoring a jury summons can lead to fines, a bench warrant, and a misdemeanor on your permanent record. Pretending like you haven't developed late-life lactose intolerance can lead to embarrassing dinner party fallout. And refusing to tend to that pesky wound you got while chopping down your Christmas tree may mean spending the New Year learning to operate a prosthetic hand better than you operate an axe.

And second, while I concede that willfully ignoring whatever shit may be happening to you is a shrewd means of getting around having to acknowledge, accept, or address it — guess what? If your worries have sent you into Ostrich Mode, you haven't actually escaped them. They'll be sitting right outside your hidey-hole the next time you lift your head. (Hi, guys. Touché.) Avoidance means **NEVER, EVER SOLVING YOUR PROBLEM.**

What can you do about it? Great question. Just by asking, you're already making progress.

Survey says: y'all are a bunch of freaks

As part of my research for *Calm the Fuck Down*, I conducted an anonymous online survey asking people to name their go-to freakout reaction. It revealed that most folks (38.6 percent) fall into the "Anxious/Panicky" category; 10.8 percent each cop to "I get angry" and "I avoid things"; and another 8.3 percent pledge allegiance to "Sad/Depressed." As for the rest? Nearly one third of respondents (30.3 percent) said "I can't pick just one. I do all of these things," which was when I knew this book would be a hit. And a mere 1.2 percent said "I never do any of these things." Sure you don't.

Welcome to the Flipside

Okay, I was saving the nitty-gritty practical stuff for part II, but you've been so patient with all these parameters that I want to give you a sneak peek at **how we're going to flip the script** on whichever Freakout Face you're experiencing.

I've based my method on a little gem called Newton's Third Law of Motion, which states that **"for every action, there is an equal and opposite reaction."**

You don't have to have taken high school physics (which I didn't, as may be obvious from my forthcoming interpretation of this law) to understand the idea that you can counteract a bad thing with a good thing. Laughing is the opposite of crying. Deep breaths are the opposite of lung-emptying screams. The pendulum swings both ways, et cetera, et cetera.

Ergo, one simple route to calming down pre-, mid-, or post-freakout is to — cue Gloria Estefan — **turn the beat around.**

FREAKOUT FACES: THE FLIPSIDES

Anxious and overthinking?	**FOCUS**: Which of these worries takes priority? Which can you actually control? Zero in on those and set the others aside. (A bit of a recurring theme throughout the book.)

Sad and exhausted?	**REPAIR WITH SELF-CARE:** Treat yourself the way you would treat a sad friend in need. Be kind. Naps, chocolate, baths, cocktails, a *South Park* marathon; whatever relieves your funk or puts a spring back in your step and a giggle in your wiggle.
Angry and making shit worse?	**PEACE OUT WITH PERSPECTIVE:** You can't elbow yourself in the ribs like I did to my husband in the Mexico City airport (seriously, elbows don't bend in that direction). But when you're getting hot under the collar, you can *imagine* what it would be like to live out your days in a south-of-the-border airport holding pen. Visualize the consequences and adjust your attitude accordingly.
Avoiding and prolonging the agony?	**ACT UP:** Take one step, no matter how small, toward acknowledging your problem. Say it out loud. Write it in steam on the bathroom mirror. Fashion its likeness into a voodoo doll. If you can do that, you're on your way to calming the fuck down.

So there you have it: **a simple framework for acknowledging your worries, recognizing your unhealthy reactions, and beginning to reverse them.**

I mean, I didn't become an internationally bestselling anti-guru by making this shit *hard* for you guys.

Freakout funds

In *The Life-Changing Magic of Not Giving a Fuck* I introduced the concept of "fuck bucks," which are the resources — **time, energy, and money** — that you spend on everything you care about, from activities and appointments to friends, family, and more. Conversely, you can choose to *not* spend those resources on things you *don't* care about. Managing them is called "making a Fuck Budget," a concept that is on track to become my most enduring legacy. A *Lemonade* for anti-gurus, if you will.

Since you don't fix what ain't broke, I carried fuck bucks and the budgeting thereof through the next book, *Get Your Shit Together* — the premise being that you also have to spend time, energy, and/or money on things you MUST do, even if you don't really WANT to do them — like, say, going to work so you can earn money so you can pay your rent. In the epilogue, I warned (presciently, as it turns out) that **"shit happens"** and **"you might want to reserve a little time, energy, and money for that scenario, just in case."**

Thus, in *Calm the Fuck Down* — because I am nothing if not a maker-upper of catchy names for commonsense concepts that we should all be employing even if we didn't have catchy names for them — I give you **freakout funds (FFs)**.

These are the fuck bucks you access when shit happens. You could spend them exacerbating all the delightful behavior I went over in the previous section. **Or you could spend them calming the fuck down and dealing with the shit that caused said freakout.**

Ideally, you've read *Get Your Shit Together* and saved up for this scenario. If not, you're in even more need of the following tutorial. But any way you slice it, their quantities are limited and **every freakout fund spent is time, energy, or money deducted from your day.**

TIME

Time has been in finite supply since, well, since the beginning. They're not making any more of it. Which means that eventually you're going to run out of time to spend doing everything — including freaking out about or dealing with whatever is about to happen/is happening/just happened to you. Why waste it on the former when spending it on the latter would vastly improve the quality of your entire remaining supply of minutes?

ENERGY

You will also eventually run out of energy, because although Jeff Bezos is trying really hard, he has not yet programmed Alexa to suck out your mortal soul while you're sleeping and recharge you on Wi-Fi. At some point, you have to eat, rest, and renew the old-fashioned way — and if the shit does hit the fan, you'll wish you'd spent less energy freaking out about it and had more left in the tank to devote to dealing with it.

MONEY

This one's more complex, since some people have a lot and some people have none, and everyone's ability to replenish their coffers varies. But if you're broke, then stress-shopping while you freak out about passing the bar exam is obviously poor form. Whereas if you've got a bottomless bank account, you might argue that cleaning out the J.Crew clearance rack is at least contributing to the improvement of your overall mood. I'm not one to pooh-pooh anyone's version of self-care, but all that money you spent on khaki short-shorts and wicker belts is definitely not *solving the underlying problem* of your LSAT scores. Hiring a tutor would probably be a better use of funds. (And to all my billionaire doomsday preppers out there with money to burn: you do you, but I have a hunch neither your guns nor your bitcoin will be worth shit on the Zombie Exchange.)

In sum: **Worrying is wasteful.** It costs you time, energy, and/ or money and gives you nothing useful in return. Whereas if you spend your freakout funds actually dealing with something, you've, you know — actually dealt with it.

My goal is to help you minimize your worrying and spend your FFs wisely along the way.

Nice try, Knight. If I could stop worrying and retain a viselike grip over my time, energy, and money, I'd BE Jeff Bezos by now.

Hey, calm the fuck down — I said "minimize." I personally hold the Women's World Record for Worrying Every Day About Dying of Cancer. Nobody's perfect. **But when you find yourself worrying to the point of freaking out, you should consider the resources you're wasting on that futile pursuit.**

Anxious? Overthinking is overspending.

Sad? After you've spent all that energy on crying, wailing, beating your chest, and feeding the depressive beast, you've got nothing left with which to deal.

Angry? This might be the biggest misuse of freakout funds, since it usually *adds* to your debt. Like when you get so mad at the amount of time you've

---

3 ways in which overthinking wastes time, energy, and money

If you change your outfit seven times before you go out, you'll be late.

If you spend more time fiddling with fonts than writing your term paper, you'll never turn it in.

If you keep second-guessing him, your interior decorator will fire you and you'll lose your deposit.

spent on hold with Home Depot Customer Service that you throw your iPhone at the wall, crack the screen, dent the Sheetrock, and drop the call—which means you haven't solved your original problem (faulty birdbath), AND you've added two new line items to your real and metaphorical bills.

Ostriching? Don't think you guys are getting away with anything. Even by avoiding your shit, you're depleting your FFs. You've wasted a lot of valuable time—a nonrenewable resource that could have been put toward solutions—doing a whole lot of nothing. You've also wasted energy contorting yourself into pretending *EVERYTHINGISFINEJUSTFINE*.

Remember that cartoon dog? He's a pile of cartoon embers now.

No matter which type of freakout you're experiencing or trying to avoid, **there are wiser ways to deploy your funds.** For example:

- Instead of wasting TIME worrying about failing your physics class, you could spend it mocking up some quantum flash cards.
- Instead of wasting ENERGY pacing around the apartment worrying about what's going to happen when your roommate gets home and sees that the dog, Meatball, has

had his way with someone's favorite Air Jordans, you could spend that energy researching obedience schools for Meatball.

- And instead of spending MONEY on quacky products that will supposedly prevent you from going bald but don't actually work, you could buy yourself a few really cool hats and become Really Cool Hat Guy.

Welcome to the Flipside, stranger. Fancy meeting you here.

(In other news, I'm pretty sure at least three readers and one dog have already gotten their money's worth out of this book.)

The Fourth Fund

Curtis "50 Cent" Jackson had *The 50th Law*. I have the Fourth Fund, an offshoot of fuck bucks that I developed exclusively for *Calm the Fuck Down*. This is HOT HOT ORIGINAL CONTENT right here, folks.

We all have that friend or family member or coworker or fellow volunteer at the food co-op who seems to be in **Constant Crisis Mode**, don't we? I'll call her Sherry. There isn't a date that hasn't stood Sherry up, an asshole that hasn't rear-ended her in the parking lot, a deadline that hasn't been COMPLETELY BLOWN by one of her clients, or a bucket of compost that hasn't been upended on her lap by a careless stoner wearing those godaw-ful TOMS shoes that make your feet look like mummified remains.

You want to be sympathetic when Sherry kvetches about her latest catastrophe or shows up to the morning meeting all sweaty and blinking rapidly and going on and on about *Would you believe the shit I have to deal with?!*

But the thing is, she does this all the time. So you also kind of want to be like, *What's your problem now, you freakshow? Just calm the fuck down and deal with it. Jesus.* (If you can't relate to this sentiment at all, you're a better person than I am. Enjoy your priority seating in the Afterlife.)

This brings us to the **Fourth Fund: Goodwill.**

GOODWILL

Unlike time, energy, and money, the goodwill account is not held by you. It is funded by the sympathy and/or assistance of *others,* and is theirs to dole out or withhold as they see fit. Your job is to keep your account in good standing by not being a fucking freakshow all the time like Sherry.

What Sherry doesn't realize is **how much sympathy she erodes when she brings her constant crises to your front door.** At some point you'll start shutting it in her face like you do with Jehovah's Witnesses or little kids looking for their ball.

What? They shouldn't have kicked it in my yard. It's my ball now.

Anyway, now let's turn the tables and say *you're* the one looking for sympathy from your fellow man. That's cool. It's human nature to commiserate. Like making conversation about the weather, we all do it — we bitch, we moan, we casually remark on how warm it's gotten lately as though we don't know a ninety-degree summer in Ireland foretells the death of our planet.

When you're feeling overcome by the sheer magnitude of your personal misfortune, it's understandable to cast about for and feel buoyed by the sympathy of others.

Sometimes you just want a friend to agree with you that you shouldn't have had to wait around forty-five minutes for the cable guy to show up and then realize he didn't have the part he needed to connect your box, causing you to get so mad that you broke a tooth chomping down in frustration on the complimentary pen he left behind. What good is a fucking *pen* going to do you when all you want is to be able to watch Bravo and now you have to go to the fucking *dentist,* which is undoubtedly going to ruin another entire day! Or maybe you just need to let someone — anyone — know that Jeremy the Assistant Marketing VP is the absolute, goddamn *worst!*

I hear ya. (So does everybody in a fifty-foot radius. You might want to tone it down just a touch.) And when your friends, family, and fellow volunteers see you in distress, their first reaction will probably be to sympathize with you. They wouldn't be working at a food co-op if they weren't bleeding-heart socialists.

But this is where the Fourth Fund comes into play: **if you freak out *all* the time, about *everything,* you're spending heavily against your account of goodwill.** You're in danger of overdrawing it faster than they drain the aquarium after a kid falls into the shark tank, resulting in the classic Boy Who Cried Shark conundrum:

When you need the help and sympathy for something worthy, it may no longer be there.

\<hums *Jaws* theme song>

\<sees self out>

Hot take, coming right up!

If you'll indulge me in a brief tangent, I have some real talk for my fellow Anxiety-with-a-capital-A sufferers who find themselves in Constant Crisis Mode more often than not.

Due to my then-undiagnosed Generalized Anxiety Disorder, I spent years treating my friends, family, colleagues, and husband to all of my mysterious stomachaches and last-minute cancellations and office crying and whirling-dervish-like propensity for reorganizing other people's homes without permission.

Most of them couldn't understand why I was freaking out all

the time. To them, the majority of my worries didn't seem worthy of such chaos and insanity.

What's your problem now, you freakshow? Just calm the fuck down and deal with it. Jesus.

Sound familiar?

Some of these peeps began to withdraw, withholding their sympathy and support — and they weren't always able to hide their annoyance or frustration with me, either. At the time, I was confused. A little bit hurt. Righteously indignant, even. But today, with the benefit of both hindsight and therapeutic intervention, you know what?

I DON'T BLAME THEM. It's not the rest of the world's job to deal with my shit.

Harsh? Maybe, but I get paid to tell it like it is.

As I've said, I know exactly how badly *anxiety,* the mental illness, can fuck with us — and it's awesome when our family and friends can learn about it and help us through it. I'm eternally grateful to my husband for putting up with a few years of extreme unpleasantness before beginning to understand and accept my anxiety. It's still unpleasant sometimes, but at least he knows that **now *I* know what the underlying problem is,** and that I'm trying to keep it in check — which deposits a lot more goodwill into my account than when I spent most of my time sleeping and crying and not doing anything to change my situation.

So if I may make a potentially controversial argument:

Some of us get dealt worse hands than others, and deserve a little overdraft protection, but the Bank of Goodwill shouldn't extend lifetime credit just because *you* have some issues to work through.

If not a day goes by when you don't don your Anxious Freak-out Face — and consequently get all up in other people's faces with your problems — then it may be time to consider that You. Are. Part. Of. Your. Problem.

Am I a monster? I don't think so. A blunt-ass bitch maybe, but you already knew that. And this blunt-ass bitch thinks that **we actually-clinically-anxious people need to take some personal responsibility.** We need to acknowledge our tendencies, do some soul-searching, and maybe go to a doctor or therapist or Reiki healer or something and sort out our shit, **lest we risk alienating our entire support system.**

To put it another way: If you had chronic diarrhea, you'd be looking into ways to stop having chronic diarrhea, right? And what if it was affecting your relationships because you couldn't go to parties or you were always canceling dates at the last minute or when you *were* at other people's houses you were so distracted by your own shit (literally) that you weren't being very good company anyway? You wouldn't want to continue shitting all over your friends (figuratively), would you?

I thought so. Moving on.

Mental decluttering and the One Question to Rule Them All

We're getting down to the last of the brass tacks here in part I. We've gone over **the importance of naming your problems, understanding your reaction to those problems, and valuing your response.** It's time to segue into *how*, exactly, you're supposed to put all of those lessons into action and begin calming the fuck down.

Enter: **mental decluttering.**

If you've read any of the NFGGs or watched my TEDx Talk, you're familiar with the concept; I'll try to explain it succinctly enough to first-timers that it won't send the rest of you flocking to Amazon to complain that "Knight repeats herself."*

Here's how it works:

Just like the physical decluttering made popular in recent years by Japanese tidying expert and author of *The Life-Changing Magic of Tidying Up* Marie Kondo, **mental decluttering** (made popular by anti-guru, sometime parodist, and author of *The Life-Changing Magic of Not Giving a Fuck* Sarah Knight) has two steps:

DISCARDING and ORGANIZING

---

* It's a series, guys. Cut a bitch some slack.

The difference is, my version of discarding and organizing happens entirely in your mind, not in your drawers or closets or garage.

There is no physical exertion involved. You won't catch me chanting, ohm-ing, or downward dogging my way through this shit. You're free to engage in those activities if you wish, whether it's to calm the fuck down or just to pick up nice single moms named Beth at the YMCA. But it's not required.

(Will mental decluttering eventually leave you feeling physically refreshed? It sure will! After all, fewer panic attacks and rage-gasms are good for your heart, your lungs, and the tiny bones in your feet that tend to break when you kick things that are not meant to be kicked. But that's not the primary focus, just a snazzy by-product.)

The two steps of mental decluttering align not at all coincidentally with the two steps of the NoWorries Method.

Step 1: DISCARD your worries (aka calm the fuck down)

Step 2: ORGANIZE your response to what's left (aka deal with it)

That's it. Discard, then organize. And the way you begin is by looking at whatever problem you're worried about and asking yourself a very simple question.

Mental decluttering and the One Question to Rule Them All really shine in part II, but before we get there, I have one last parameter I want to parametate, which is this:

When what-ifs become worries and worries become freakouts and freakouts make everything harder and more miserable than it ever had to be, **one of the things you can control right away is your *emotional response.***

With that, I'll turn it over to man's best friend…who is also sometimes man's worst enemy.

(Please don't tell John Wick I said that.)

This is your brain on puppies

Emotions are like puppies. Sometimes they're purely fun and diverting; sometimes they're comforting or distracting; sometimes they just peed on your mother-in-law's carpet and aren't allowed in the house anymore.

In any case, **puppies are good for short periods of time until you have to get something accomplished,** and then you need to coax them into a nice, comfy crate because you cannot — I repeat: CANNOT — deal with your shit while those little fuckers are on the loose.*

It doesn't even matter if these are "bad" puppies/emotions or "good" puppies/emotions. (Emuppies? Pupmotions?) ALL puppies/emotions are distracting. It's in their nature. You can totally get derailed by positive emotions — like if you're so excited that the Oreo McFlurry is back, you go straight to the drive-through having forgotten that it was your turn to pick up your kid at preschool. Oops.

But I think we both know that happy and excited to make digestive love to diabetes in a cup aren't the emotions *Calm the Fuck Down* is here to help you corral.

What we're trying to do is take the freakout-inducing puppies/emotions and:

Grant them a reasonable visitation period in which to healthily acknowledge their existence;

---

* Please don't email me about the detriments of crate-training your dog. Please. I'm sitting up and begging you.

Give them a chance to wear themselves out with a short burst of activity;

And then exile them while we get to work on solving the problems that brought them out to play in the first place.

Quick reminder

Hi, it's me, not a doctor or psychologist! Nor am I a behavioral therapist! Honestly, I can't even be trusted to drink eight glasses of water every day and I consider Doritos a mental health food. But what I do have is the learned ability to relegate emotions to the sidelines as needed, so that I can focus on logical solutions. This is my thing; it's what works for me and it's why I have written four No Fucks Given Guides and not the *Let's All Talk About Our Feelings Almanac*. If you *do* happen to be a doctor, psychologist, or therapist and you don't approve of sidelining one's emotions in order to calm the fuck down and deal with one's shit, first of all, thanks for reading. I appreciate the work you do, I respect your game, and I hope my Olympic-level floor routine of caveats makes it clear that I'm presenting well-intentioned, empirically proven suggestions, not medical fact. If you could take this into consideration before clicking that one-star button, I would greatly appreciate it.

Alright, just to be sure we're all on the same emotionally healthy page, let me be superduper clear:

- **It's okay to have emotions.** Or as another guru might put it: "*You've* got emotions! And *you've* got emotions! And *you've* got emotions!" Having them is not the problem; it's when you let emotions run rampant *at the expense of taking action* that you start having problems (see: The evolution of a freakout).

- **In fact, there's a lot of science that says you must allow yourself to "feel the feels" about the bad stuff — that you have to go *through* it to get *past* it.** This is especially true when it comes to trauma, and I'm not advising you to ignore those problems/emotions. Just to sequester them periodically like you would an unruly puppy. (See: I am not a doctor.)

- **It's even okay to freak out a little bit.** To yell and scream and ostrich every once in a while. We're not aiming for "vacant-eyed emotionless husk." That's some prelude-to-going-on-a-killing-spree shit, right there, and not an outcome I wish to promote to my readership.

That said — and in my decidedly nonscientific opinion — when your emuppies are running amok, it's time to lock 'em up and at least temporarily misplace the key. What I will henceforth refer to as **emotional puppy crating** has been useful to me in the following scenarios:

It's how I continued to enjoy my wedding reception after the train of my dress caught on fire, instead of going on a champagne rampage against the culprit. Love you, Mom!

It's how I managed to write and deliver a eulogy for my uncle's funeral instead of being incapacitated by grief.

It's how we decided to call an emergency plumbing hotline at 2:00 a.m. when the upstairs neighbor's toilet went Niagara Falls into our bathroom, instead of succumbing to despair (and sleep) and making everything that much worse (and wet) for ourselves the next day.

First, I acknowledge the emotion — be it anxiety, anger, sadness, or one of their many tributaries (e.g., fear) — and then I sort of mentally pick it up by the scruff of the neck and quarantine it in a different part of my brain than the part that I need to use to deal with the problem at hand. **If you practice mindfulness, you might know this trick as "Teflon mind," so termed because negative thoughts aren't allowed to stick.** I think the puppy analogy is more inviting than the image of an eight-inch frying pan anywhere near my skull, but tomato, tomahto.

Am I successful every time? Of course not! In addition to being not a doctor, I am also not an all-powerful goddess. (Or a liar.) Emotional puppy crating isn't always feasible, and even when it is, it takes practice and concerted effort. Much like herding a twenty-pound package of muscle and saliva into a five-by-five cage, if you don't fasten the lock firmly enough, your emuppies could escape for a potentially destructive/exhausting scamper around your mental living room, scratching mental floors, chewing mental furniture, and further distracting you from calming the fuck down and dealing with your shit.

Who let the dogs out? You. You let them out.

That's okay. **You can always wrestle or gently lead or even trick them back in** — all tactics I'll explore and explain in part II. Like I said, *practice*. But it's worth it.

And don't forget: in the same way that you can lock those rascals up, you can also let them back out whenever you want.

Whenever you must.

Whenever their precious puppy faces will make you feel *better*, not worse.

It's not like you've sent your emotions to live with an elderly couple on a nice farm upstate. They're just chillin' in their crate until such time as they are once again invited to roam freely. When that time comes, go ahead, open the door. Let them romp around and entertain you for a spell, distract you from your woes, nuzzle your face, lick your toes. Whatever, I don't even have a dog, I'm just spitballing here.

But oh, hey! Once you've had your emotional puppy time, back in the crate they go.

Now be a good boy, and let's calm the fuck down.

11

CALM THE FUCK DOWN:
Identify what you can control,
accept what you can't,
and let that shit go

If part I was all about parameters, part II is all about practical application — the **how-tos for converting the what-ifs into the now-whats,** so to speak.

To ease you in, I'm going to focus mainly on **Shit That Hasn't Happened Yet** — the still-theoretical what-ifs, the kind of stuff that worries you whether or not it's even likely to occur. I'll help you determine if those worries are justified and if so, **how to prepare for and mitigate the damage** should the problems they stem from come to fruition.

And in some cases, **how to prevent those problems from happening at all.**

We'll start by **classifying your what-ifs by category,** much like the National Weather Service classifies hurricanes. Except in your case we're not dealing with hurricanes; we're dealing with...**shitstorms.**

Oh come on, you saw that pun coming a mile away.

Next, we'll assign a status — **prioritizing not only** *what* **needs dealing with, but** *how soon* — a calculation based on my very favorite factor: urgency.

At the end of part II, we'll use all of these tools to **mentally declutter your worryscape,** one hypothetical shitstorm at a time. And by practicing it on Shit That Hasn't Happened Yet, it'll be even easier to employ the NoWorries Method on Shit That Has Already Happened (coming right up in part III, natch).

Soon **you'll be turning what-ifs into now-whats like a pro.**

You won't even need me anymore. *Sniff.*

Pick a category, any category

As you probably know, hurricanes are categorized on a scale of 1 to 5. This is called the Saffir-Simpson Hurricane Wind Scale.

Those numbers are then used by meteorologists to forecast (and convey to you) the level of damage the storm is likely to inflict along its path, 1 being least severe, 5 being most. Of course, weatherpeople are not always correct—there are many unpredictable variables that determine the scope of the actual post-storm damage, such as the relative stability of the roofs, power lines, trees, awnings, boat docks, and lawn furniture in the affected area. (This is why weatherpeople have the best job security in all the land; it barely matters if they get it right all the time, because they *can't* get it right all the time and they seem totally okay with that. I would be a very bad weatherperson.)

But anyway, the 1–5 categories themselves are indisputable. They reflect the hurricane's strength in terms of its maximum sustained wind speed, which is a totally objective measurement. The anemometer don't lie.

Shitstorms are different in the sense that there is no "-ometer" that can measure the precise strength of any single event; **its strength, or what we'll term "severity," is informed solely by how the individual person affected** *experiences it.*

For example, say you've dreamt of playing Blanche Devereaux in *Thank You for Being a Friend: The Golden Girls Musical* for your entire life, but after a successful three-week run, you were unceremoniously kicked to the curb in favor of the director's new cougar girlfriend. You're devastated. On the other hand, your friend Guillermo is positively jubilant to have been let go from the funeral home where he was in charge of applying rouge and eye makeup to the clientele.

Same objective shitstorm, different subjective experience.

(Though maybe you could hook G up with the director's girlfriend? It would be a shame to let his talent for reanimating corpses go to waste.)

Further, you cannot compare your experience of any given shitstorm to anyone else's experience of a *different* shitstorm. Is your broken heart more or less "major" than my broken tooth? WHO CAN SAY.

Therefore, shitstorm categories are based not on *how severe* they might be — but simply *how likely* they are to actually hit you. One to five, on a scale of least to most probable. For example, if you're a popular person, then "What if nobody comes to my birthday party?" would be a **Category 1 Highly Unlikely,** whereas "What if two of my friends are having parties on the same weekend and I have to choose between them?" is a **Category 5 Inevitable.** Or vice versa, if you're a hermit.

From here on out, probability is your barometer. We'll call it, I don't know, your **probometer.**

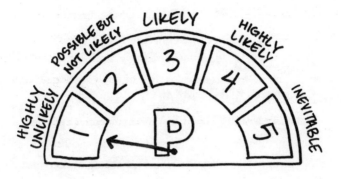

And instead of having one weatherperson for the entire tri-state area charged with forecasting the accurate potential damage of a Category 3 storm passing over a thirteen-thousand-square-mile radius, who may or may not get it right when it comes to your house — we'll have one weatherperson focused *solely* on your house.

Oh, and your house is your life, and you are that weatherperson.

Actually, you're the "whetherperson," **because you and only you get to predict *whether* this shitstorm is likely to land on YOU.***

---

* These are the jokes, people.

The five categories on the Sarah Knight Shitstorm Scale are as follows:

Category 1: HIGHLY UNLIKELY

Category 2: POSSIBLE BUT NOT LIKELY

Category 3: LIKELY

Category 4: HIGHLY LIKELY

Category 5: INEVITABLE

Again, note that this scale indicates nothing of the "strength" or "severity" of the storm, merely the **probability of its occurrence.** When it comes to boarding up your metaphorical windows and battening down your metaphorical hatches, **your probometer rating will help you budget your freakout funds effectively.** Fewer FFs on less likely stuff, more on more likely stuff.

(And sometimes you won't need to spend any FFs at all on preparation; you can save them exclusively for cleanup. More on that later.)

To familiarize you with the category system, let's look at some potential shitstorms in action.

For example, do you ski? I don't, so it's HIGHLY UNLIKELY that I will break my leg skiing. Category 1, all the way. (Though if I *did* ski it would be Category 4 HIGHLY LIKELY that I would break my leg. I know my limits.)

Now consider Olympic gold medalist and nineties superhunk Alberto Tomba. Breaking his leg skiing might also be a HIGHLY UNLIKELY Category 1, because he's just that good. Or it might be a HIGHLY LIKELY Category 4 because he skis often, at high speeds, threading his obscenely muscled thighs between unforgiving metal structures. I leave it to Alberto in his capacity as his own personal whetherman to decide how likely *he* thinks it is that he'll break his leg skiing, and therefore how many (or few) freakout funds he needs to budget for that outcome on any given day.

Or, let's look at earthquakes. Those are fun.

People who live in Minnesota, which Wikipedia tells me is "not a very tectonically active state," are Category 1 HIGHLY UNLIKELY to experience a major earthquake; whereas homeowners along North America's Cascadia subduction zone are flirting with Category 5 every day. (Did you read that *New Yorker* article back in 2015, because I sure did. Sorry, Pacific Northwest, it was nice knowing you.) But that said, keep in mind that a Category 5 shitstorm doesn't have to be a catastrophic, earth-shaking event. **It is not necessarily all that *severe*; it is simply INEVITABLE.**

For example, if you're a parent, getting thrown up on is fully in the cards. If you're a female candidate for office, you'll be unfairly judged for your vocal timbre and wardrobe choices. And if you're a frequent flier, one of these days your connection will be delayed and leave you stranded in the Shannon, Ireland, airport for six hours with nothing but a complimentary ham sandwich and your laptop, on which you will watch *The Hateful Eight* and think, *Eh, it was just okay.*

Oh, and death is obviously a Category 5. It's gonna happen to all of us, our cats, dogs, hamsters, and annual plants.

Can I get a downgrade?

Each what-if is like a tropical cyclone brewing on the radar screen of your mind. A shitclone, as it were. Some will turn into full-fledged shitstorms and some won't — but unlike tropical cyclones, you may have control over the direction your shitclones take. Especially the Category 1s, since they're highly unlikely as it is. For example, if I continue to never go skiing, I will NEVER break my leg skiing. Crisis completely and totally averted! Yeah, yeah, I heard you groan, but that was a freebie. I can't give away my best stuff this early. Later in part II, we'll discuss less ridiculously restrictive but equally effective ways to send a shitstorm out to sea. Promise.

Mulling the likelihood of a potential shitstorm actually coming to pass is a useful exercise. Consulting your probometer helps you focus on the reality of your situation instead of obsessing over what-ifs that are often as unrealistic as the "after" photos in an ad for cut-rate diet pills. You know she just went for a spray tan, sucked in her stomach, and tricked out the tatas in a more flattering bra. Stop falling for that shit, will ya?

And by the way, I apologize if all this talk of impending doom is triggering a freakout, but it's for the best. **Because when you start thinking about shitstorms based on probability, you'll begin to realize you don't have nearly as much to worry about as you thought you did.**

Soon, when a what-if pops up on your radar screen you'll be able to say, "Total Cat. One. Not worth worrying about." Or "Category Two, no need to spend those freakout funds quite yet."

LOGIC CAN BE VERY SOOTHING.

Logicats, ho!

Speaking of logic, from here on out, I'm going to see your emotional puppies and raise you some cold, hard logical cats. Think about it: a puppy will flail around in the yard trying to scratch his back on a busted Frisbee, whereas cats can reach their own backs and, generally speaking, they're not much for flailing. Dogs are players — giddily chasing a ball one minute, then getting distracted by a body of water that needs splashing in. Cats are hunters — approaching their target with laser focus and pouncing (it must be said) with catlike reflexes. They are the official spirit animal of *Calm the Fuck Down*.

The gathering shitstorms: a list

You may already know this about me, but I fucking love a list.

In this section, and in keeping with what I asked you to do back in part I, I'm going to **name some of my what-ifs — the** things that wake me up in a panic or keep me from fully enjoying my afternoon spritz — so I can figure out which resultant worries deserve my attention and which ones I can discard, then start organizing my response to the rest.

Lists, man. Lists give me life!

For now, I'll stick with **Shit That Hasn't Happened Yet** because it's easier to practice on a theoretical. Fear not, though — we'll deal with **Shit That Has Already Happened** a bit later in the book.

10 WHAT-IFS I MAY OR MAY NOT NEED TO WORRY ABOUT

- My house key gets stuck in the door
- A palm tree falls on my roof
- More tarantulas appear in my house
- I get into a car accident on the winding mountain road to the airport
- It rains on my day off that I wanted to spend at the beach
- My cats die
- I order a different pizza than usual and it isn't very good
- My editor hates this chapter
- I show up for a speaking gig and totally bomb

- I ruin my favorite pineapple-print shorts by sitting in something nasty

Now I'm going to ask you to make your own list of what-ifs. Like mine, they should be drawn from **Shit That Hasn't Happened Yet.**

If you are a generally anxious person who has also been known to gaze into a clear blue sky and imagine a plane falling out of it and onto your hammock, this should be an easy exercise.

If you consider yourself merely **situationally anxious — worrying about shit only if and when it happens** — I envy you, buddy. But I still want you to make a list, because it doesn't really matter whether every time you sit in the chair you're worried the barber is going to cut it too short. One of these days, he may slip up and give you an unintentional asymmetrical fade, and you'll have to calm the fuck down and deal with it — the strategy for which is the same for all of us. Use your imagination.

10 WHAT-IFS I MAY OR MAY NOT
NEED TO WORRY ABOUT

_____ _____

_____ _____

_____ _____

_____   _____

_____   _____

Next, we're going to bust out our probometers and **categorize each of these potential shitstorms by probability.** Looking at problems rationally and based on all available data — like your friendly neighborhood weatherperson would look at them — helps you budget your freakout funds effectively.

I'll annotate my list/categorizations so you can follow my train of thought.

10 WHAT-IFS I MAY OR MAY NOT NEED TO WORRY ABOUT: RANKED BY PROBABILITY

- **My house key gets stuck in the door**
  Cat. 2 — POSSIBLE BUT NOT LIKELY

It may seem trivial, but I worry about this because it happened once before and my husband had to climb a ladder and go in through a window, which made us realize how unsecured our windows were, so now we've installed locks on those. Therefore, if my key gets stuck in the door again, I'*ll* be stuck outside with the mosquitos waiting for a locksmith, which, per earlier, is a dangerous game in this town. Since we never figured out why it got stuck that one time, I have to assume it could happen again. However, the ratio is like, one thousand door unlockings to one stuck key, so probability remains low.*

- **A palm tree falls on my roof**
  Cat. 2 — POSSIBLE BUT NOT LIKELY

There are only two palm trees within striking distance of our house, and we had two *actual* Category 5 hurricanes pass over our town in two weeks last summer. So far, so good. Then again, climate change. I'll give it a 2.

- **More tarantulas appear in my house**
  Cat. 1 — HIGHLY UNLIKELY

I've been here several years and seen exactly one tarantula. On a day-to-day basis, this is a technical 1, even if it's an emotional 5. Emuppies, in the crate you go. Logicats, be on the lookout, 'kay?

- **I get into a car accident on the winding mountain road to the airport**
  Cat. 2 — POSSIBLE BUT NOT LIKELY

I had to think a little harder about this one — you often do, when the worries are about really bad potential shit. My first instinct was to call it a Cat. 4 Highly Likely simply because every single time I get in that taxi I fear for my life. But I'm a nervous passenger,

---

* I guess I technically broke my own rule about Shit That Hasn't Happened Yet. Whatever, it's my book.

equally terrified on third world dirt roads and well-maintained five-lane highways in developed countries. And if we've all been paying attention, we know that our level of anxiety *about* the problem doesn't predict the *probability of the problem occurring.* I can't bring myself to call it "highly unlikely" (I've seen, um, a few accidents on the way to the airport); however, "possible but not likely" feels both accurate and manageably stressful.

- **It rains on my day off that I wanted to spend at the beach**
  Cat. 4 — HIGHLY LIKELY

I'm not making this up for effect — it is currently raining (and has been all morning) *while* the sun is shining brightly. I will never understand this form of tropical shower. WHERE IS THE RAIN COMING FROM?

- **My cats die**
  Cat. 5 — INEVITABLE

Cats are fascinating, crafty beasts, but they are not immortal. (I suppose there's a small chance that Gladys and/or Mister Stussy will outlive *me,* but that's a Category 1.)

- **I order a different pizza than usual and it isn't very good**
  Cat. 1 — HIGHLY UNLIKELY

I'm a creature of habit *and* I'm very good at predicting what toppings will work in harmony on a pizza. Get to know me.

- **My editor hates this chapter**
  Cat. 1 — HIGHLY UNLIKELY

Like driving the winding mountain road, this is a situation where my innate anxiety initially compels me to forecast a more severe shitstorm than is on the radar. When in truth, it is neither inevitable nor even highly likely that my editor will hate this chapter. We must use all available data to make our predictions. And Mike? He's a lover, not a hater.

- **I show up for a speaking gig and totally bomb**
  Cat. 2 — POSSIBLE BUT NOT LIKELY

Again, setting aside the anxious emotions and focusing on the raw data, I have done a fair amount of public speaking and I have never once bombed. But there's no point in jinxing it, so we'll call this a 2.

- **I ruin my favorite pineapple-print shorts by sitting in something nasty**
  Cat. 3 — LIKELY

In my new hometown, it's nearly impossible not to sit in something nasty at one point or another — be it dirt, sand, a squashed bug, animal poop, motor oil, or an old wet cigar. With indoor/outdoor living comes schmutz. With tourists comes litter. With drunk people and children come spills. Ah, island life. I used to think I could keep this brand of shitstorm to a Category 1 if I just didn't wear my favorite shorts whenever I went to…oh, right. Everywhere I go is schmutz waiting to happen. Sigh. On the bright side, I have a washing machine and I know how to use it! Category 3 it is.

<table>
<tr><td>

Category key

1. HIGHLY
   UNLIKELY
2. POSSIBLE BUT
   NOT LIKELY
3. LIKELY
4. HIGHLY LIKELY
5. INEVITABLE

</td></tr>
</table>

Looking over my annotated list, you'll see that out of ten random things I have been known to worry about— **and that haven't even happened yet**— three of them are Category 1 Highly Unlikely. That's 33.3 percent of my shit off the screens, right there.

Another four of them are Category 2 Possible But Not Likely. We are now more than halfway through my what-ifs and they're dropping like flies in the champagne room.

I don't know about you, but I'm feeling calmer already.

So, are you hip to categorizing your own list? I'll give you extra space to jot down your thought process like I did—because sometimes you have to explain yourself *to* yourself before either of you can understand where you're coming from.

10 WHAT-IFS I MAY OR MAY NOT NEED TO WORRY ABOUT: RANKED BY PROBABILITY

Category: _____   Category: _____

Category: _____   Category: _____

Category: _____   Category: _____

Category: _____   Category: _____

Category: _____   Category: _____

Without being there to look over your shoulder or knowing you personally (Well, most of you. Hi, Dave!), I'm guessing that a solid chunk of your what-if list is populated by Category 1s and 2s like mine was, which you can and should stop worrying about post-haste. Later in part II, I'll show you how to do just that. (Hint: it involves the One Question to Rule Them All.)

And even if you're a little heavier on the 3s, 4s, and 5s, you're about to pick up a whole lotta new strategies for weathering shit-storms by *discarding* **unproductive worries and** *organizing* **a productive response.**

Mental decluttering. I'm telling you, it's the tits.

What's your status?

Once you have logically, rationally determined that a what-if is a probable shitstorm, a useful follow-up question is **"How *soon* is it going to land?"**

There are three levels of urgency:

OUTLYING

An outlying shitstorm not only hasn't happened, you can't even be sure if it will. Theoretically, these should be the easiest to stop worrying about because they are both unlikely *and* distant — low pressure and low priority. Ironic, since low-pressure situations are what create legit rainstorms, but once again, metaphors and the anti-gurus who employ them are imperfect.

IMMINENT

Imminent shitstorms also haven't happened yet, but they're more solidly formed and you're likely to know if and when they'll hit. You still might be

---

Examples of outlying shitstorms

You might lose the election next year.

You might not get promoted as fast as you wanted to.

You might hurt yourself training for a marathon.

You might never hear back from that girl you met at the bar.

You might not lose the weight in time for the class reunion.

You might follow in your parents' footsteps and need cataract surgery someday.

You might get beaten to that patent by a fellow inventor.

---

able to prevent an imminent shitstorm, but if not, at least you can prep for impact and mitigate the fallout.

TOTAL

A total shitstorm is one that is already upon you. You might've seen it coming when it was still imminent, or it may have appeared out of nowhere like some twelve-year-old YouTuber who has more followers than Islam and Christianity combined. It matters not whether the effects of the storm would be considered mild or severe (by you or anyone else) — it's here, and you have to deal with it.

Whether the shitstorm is a Highly Unlikely Category 1 or an Inevitable 5 — **if it hasn't happened yet, you can worry about it less urgently than if it's just about to or if it just did.**

Got it?

Examples of imminent shitstorms

You might lose the election *tomorrow*.

You might not hit your 5:00 p.m. deadline.

You might fail your history exam on Monday.

You might get in trouble for that inappropriate joke you made in the meeting.

You might not qualify for the mortgage.

You might miss your tight connection in Philly.

If she sees you leaving the building on her way in, your sister might find out you slept with her boyfriend.

Examples of total shitstorms

Examples of total shitstorms

You got red wine on your wedding dress.

You got red wine on someone else's wedding dress.

You received a scary diagnosis.

Your company downsized you.

Your car got towed.

You lost a bet. A big bet.

Your kid broke his leg.

Your wife told you she's pregnant...with someone else's baby.

The more the hairier

Okay, but what happens if you have *multiple* storms on the radar and you're reasonably confident you're going to need to spend time, energy, and/or money worrying about/dealing with all of them?

There's a reason the phrase is "mo' money, mo' problems," not "mo' problems, mo' money." You don't get a magical influx of freakout funds just because you've had a magical influx of shit land in your lap. **Keep using urgency as a tool for determining the prioritization of withdrawals.**

Here's a little quiz:

1. **You fucked up at work, but your boss doesn't know it yet because she's on vacation for two weeks.**

   Category: _____
   Status: _____

2. **Your wife is 9.2 months pregnant.**

   Category: _____
   Status: _____

3. **This is a two-parter:**

a. **Your car is a relatively new make and reliable model. What if it breaks down?**

    Category: _____

    Status: _____

b. **Surprise! It just broke down.**

    Category: _____

    Status: _____

ANSWERS:

1. **Category 4 Highly Likely / Outlying Shitstorm
    (Also acceptable: Category 3 Likely / Outlying)**

You're pretty sure your boss is going to tear you a new one when she gets back. However, it's going to be at least two weeks, which is in no way "imminent." So much other shit could happen in two weeks—including your boss acquiring more urgent fires to put out than yelling at or firing *you*. (I'm not saying go full ostrich—just pointing out that the time to deal with your boss being mad at you is if/when you know your boss is actually mad at you. Maybe she'll be too blissed out from her Peruvian ayahuasca retreat to even notice what you did.)

Save your freakout funds for now. Especially since (a) you can't do anything about the fact that you already fucked up and (b) you might need that time and energy later to beg for-giveness or update your résumé.

2. Category 5 Inevitable / Imminent Shitstorm

That baby is coming soon and you know it. You have no con-trol over when or how, but you can do a little prep to make life easier in the eventual moment.

A prudent withdrawal of FFs is in order. Prepare for landfall by spending some time, energy, and money putting together a go bag, stocking the freezer with ready-made meals, and sleeping — because once that kid arrives it's all over between you and Mr. Sandman.

3a. Category 1 Highly Unlikely / Outlying Shitstorm

3b. Category 1 Highly Unlikely / Total Shitstorm

Based on the information contained in the first part of the question, this should have been an easy Category 1. But as we know, SHIT HAPPENS — even, sometimes, the highly unlikely shit — and when its status leaps from outlying to total, you have to deal with it in a *higher-priority* fashion than either of the other two storms on the radar.

Prioritizing based on urgency. BOOM.

You're going to need a car to drive yourself to work for the last two weeks that you definitely still have a job, and to drive Margaret to the hospital sometime, well, imminently.

Withdraw FFs immediately. Call a mechanic and see about getting your Volvo towed over to the garage, then call Hertz to see about a rental to tide you over.

Oh, wait, what was that? Margaret's water just broke? Fuck. Another total shitstorm! In this particular case it doesn't take a genius to determine that the one raining down amniotic fluid upon you and your sofa is the one you need to worry about first. Margaret's comfort takes priority, and you can deal with your car sitch whenever there's a break in the action.*

Time to reprioritize. Instead of a mechanic, you're calling an Uber. And a cleaning service.

Choose it or lose it

When more than one shitstorm is vying for top priority, pick one to focus on *for now*. You can always switch back and forth, but if you try to do simultaneous double duty, you'll blow through your freakout funds faster than Johnny Depp through a pile of Colombian marching powder, and lose your goddamn mind while you're at it. I can see it now — you'll be trying to change Margaret's fan belt and begging the mechanic for an epidural in an absurd Cockney pirate accent. If you want to stay sane, pick a lane.

---

* Hahaha you're about to have a baby. There won't be a break in the action for eighteen years.

EXTRA CREDIT QUIZ QUESTION: You get lost while hiking in the Sierra Madres (total shitstorm) and then you break your toe on a big stupid rock (total shitstorm *numero dos*) just as a rescue helicopter is circling overhead. Do you spend your time and energy wrapping your broken toe, or jumping up and down on it waving your only survival flare in hopes of flagging down your ride to the nearest ER?

Answer: P-R-I-O-R-I-T-I-Z-E. Jump for your life! Signal the chopper! (And carry more than one survival flare, kids. Safety first.)

To recap: When it comes to outlying, imminent, or total shitstorms, how do you prepare?

- Make like a weatherperson and forecast outcomes based on all available data.

- Ask yourself not only *How likely is this to happen to me?* but also *How soon?*

- And before you spend your freakout funds, ask yourself the One Question to Rule Them All: *Can I control it?*

Get ur control freak on

In this section I'll take you through a practice round of "Can I control it?" But first, I want to examine **the different _kinds_ of control you may or may not be able to exert on any given situation.** It's a sliding scale, and you'd be well served to understand the nuances.

> **Out of your hands:** These are the things you can't control at all — such as the weather, other people's actions, the number of hours in a day, and the number of chances your boyfriend is going to give you before he gets sick of your _What if he's cheating on me_ bullshit and dumps you anyway because you're needy and untrusting.*

> **Make a contribution:** You can't control the larger underlying problem, but you can do your part to minimize its effects. For example, in terms of the weather, you can't control the rain, but you can control _whether_ or not you suffer its effects to the fullest if you bring an umbrella. You can't control the number of hours in a day, but you can control _whether_ you spend too many of them watching online contouring tutorials instead of hand-washing your delicates like you should be. And you

---

* This Category 4 goes out to a Twitter follower who seems both admirably self-aware and destined to remain single forever.

can't control Randy's ultimate level of tolerance for your "WHO IS SHE???" comments on his Facebook page, but you can control *whether* you keep using your fingers to tap out those three little words. (Or you could just break up with Randy because, let's face it, where there's smoke there's fire.)

Under your influence: This stuff, you can *heavily influence* if not completely control — such as "not oversleeping," by way of setting an alarm. Is it possible that something will prevent your alarm from going off (like a power outage or a mouse gnawing through the wire), or you from heeding its siren song (like accidentally pressing OFF instead of SNOOZE)? Sure, but that's a Category 1 Highly Unlikely Shitstorm and you know it. Or…am I to infer from this line of questioning that you don't really *want* to calm the fuck down?

Uh-huh. Carry on.

Complete control: This is shit you are always 100 percent in control of, such as "the words that come out of your mouth" and "whether or not you are wearing pants."

As I have stated and will continue to drill into your skull like an old-timey lobotomist, **worrying is a waste of your precious time, energy, and money. And worrying about things you CAN'T CONTROL is the biggest waste of all.** This is true of low-level anxieties and high-probability shitstorms, from existential angst to all-out catastrophes. Whether they be problems with your friends, family, boss, coworkers, car, bank account, boyfriend, girlfriend, or tarantulas — the ones you have the power to solve, the worries YOU can discard and the responses YOU can organize are the ones to focus on.

The One Question to Rule Them All, in action

- **What if I tell my bestie Rachel what I really think of her new bangs and she never forgives me?**

Can I control it? Completely. Keep your trap shut and your friendship intact.

Or:

- **What if I accidentally shout another woman's name in bed with my new girlfriend?**

Can I control it? Yes. For God's sake, Randy, get ahold of yourself. No wonder your new girlfriend doesn't trust you.

How about:

- **What if rumors of a union dispute come to pass and force the cancellation of that monster truck rally next Wednesday that I was all excited about?**

Can I control it? Unless you also happen to be the Monster Truckers Union president, unequivocally no. Which means that this is a worry you should ideally DISCARD. (I'll move on to "Okay, but *how* do I discard it?" in a few. Be patient — it's not like you have a monster truck rally to attend.)

Or:

- **What if something bad happens to people I give incorrect directions to?**

Can I control it? Yes, by telling the next nice young couple from Bismarck that you have a terrible sense of geography and they'd be better off querying a fire hydrant. This what-if is supremely easy to snuff out in its inception — take it from someone who thinks turning right automatically means going "east."

And sometimes, you might have to **break a big worry down into smaller components** — some of which you can control and some of which you can't.

- **What if I laugh so hard I pee my pants during my friend's stand-up gig?**

Can I control it? First of all, lucky you if your stand-up comedian friend is actually that funny. If you're prone to laugh-leaks, you may not be able to control the bladder, but you can make a contribution to your overall preparedness. There are many options in the personal hygiene aisle that were invented expressly to assist you in dealing with this issue.

This is so much fun, I think we should try a few more — this time, on what-ifs pulled directly from the pulsating brains of my Twitter followers.

Shit people in my Twitter feed are worried about. Can they control it?

- **I'm happy and in a good relationship, but what if we wait too long to get married and never have kids?**

Can I control it? This is one you can heavily influence. You don't necessarily have full control over whether you get pregnant, but in terms of this specific what-if, you *can* control "not waiting too long" to start trying. You know how this whole aging eggs thing works, and if you have to, you can explain it to Dan. However, if you have to explain it to Dan…maybe Dan should have paid more attention in tenth-grade bio.

- **What if I never find the escape hatch from my soul-sucking day job?**

Can I control it? Yes. You can only never find what you stop looking for. I think it was Yoda who said that. Bit of an anti-guru himself, that guy.

- **What if I'm failing as an adult?**

Can I control it? Yes. Adults do things like pay taxes, take responsibility for their actions, make their own dinner, and show up on time for prostate exams. Do these things and you will be succeeding as an adult. If your what-if is more existential in nature, perhaps you should get a hobby. Adults have those, too.

- **What if I choose not to go home and visit my family this weekend and something bad happens to them and then I regret it forever?**

Can I control it? Yes. If your goal is not to have to worry about this, go visit them. If what you're really asking for is permission to not drive six hours to DC in holiday-weekend traffic and you *also* don't want to worry about the consequences of that decision, bust out your trusty probometer. How likely is it that something bad is going to happen to your family, this weekend of all weekends? It's a Category 1, isn't it? You know what to do.

- **What if my son doesn't have the developmental problems his doctors think he has and he's just a budding sociopath?**

Can I control it? Yikes. I'm sorry to say, you can't control *whether* the kid's a sociopath. You can't even heavily influence it, if we're talking a DNA-level shitstorm. But you can contribute to the overall cause by continuing to seek help for him.

(And maybe a second opinion while you're at it. Seems prudent in this case.)

- **What if all my friends secretly hate me and I don't know it?**

Can I control it? I refer you to your internal whetherperson to determine the probability of this scenario. Assemble all the available data. If your friends are nice to you on a regular basis and don't avoid your calls or talk shit about you in group chats that they think you're not going to see except they don't know that Sondra is always leaving her phone unlocked and sitting on the table when she goes to pee, then they probably don't hate you. If they *do* do these things, I don't think they're keeping it much of a secret? I'm not sure I understand the question.

- **What if I have an ugly baby?**

Can I control it? No. And besides, all babies are ugly. You're not going to get a real sense of how that thing turned out until much later in life, and even then, puberty does terrible things to a human.

- **What if democracy is failing and my kids are in mortal danger because of that?**

Can I control it? Not really. But please vote. Or run for office. We all need you.

- **What if I get laid off without warning?**

Can I control it? Being laid off? As in not fired, but rather let go without cause, and as you said, "without warning"? No. (Come on, the answer was right there in the question!) On the other hand, if you're asking what if you get *fired* without warning, well, I bet that if your boss plans on firing you, he or she has actually given you plenty of warning — you just weren't listening.

- **What if my aging parents start to fall apart?**

Can I control it? Ultimately, no. You can encourage them to get checkups and fill prescriptions and maybe sign up for a light water aerobics class to stay limber, but you're not in control of anyone else's health or related decision-making. If they do go ahead and fall apart, you can worry about it then.

- **What if I get bitten by a raccoon?**

Can I control it? Yes. By not hanging out with raccoons. Who are you, Davy Crockett?

Last but not least, a query that stood out to me for an oddly personal reason:

- **What if my teeth fall out?**

Can I control it? You can heavily influence your teeth staying put by brushing regularly, swigging mouthwash, flossing (eh), going to the dentist, wearing a night guard, and steering clear of ice hockey and guys named Wonka. However, this particular tweet gave me pause not because I'm consciously worried about the fate of my bicuspids, but because I happen to have a teeth-falling-out dream every few months. And when I looked it up in one of those dream interpretation books I learned that lost or crumbling teeth in your dream indicates a feeling of powerlessness in real life. In other words, a loss of control. Apparently my anxiety runs so deep, I'm what-iffing in my sleep. So meta!

If the answer is no, this is how you let it go

What may come as a surprise to you after reading the previous section is that NONE OF THIS SHOULD COME AS A SURPRISE TO YOU.

Can you control it (or aspects of it) — yes or no? You already have the answers, friend.

We've established that you cannot, for example, *control* being suddenly laid off. But if you're worried about this, I understand where you're coming from. Throughout my twenties, my ability to perform my job well was not in question. I was not in danger of getting fired for cause. Still, I worried passionately about losing my job due to cutbacks or other factors at the corporate level that I definitely could not control.

I remember having these worries. I remember people telling me that everything would be fine and that I couldn't control it anyway, so I should let it go and stop freaking out about it.

And I remember thinking EASY FOR YOU TO SAY, JERK-FACE McGEE.

Or, as one of my Twitter followers more politely articulated, **"How do I get from understanding that worry is pointless to *actually not worrying?*"**

Excellent question. Once you've ACKNOWLEDGED the problem, you begin to let go of your worries about said problem by ACCEPTING the things you can't control — a skill that over 60 percent of my anonymous survey takers have yet to master, by the by.

I hope that the same 60 percent are reading, because it's actually easier to do than they — or you — might think.

Reality check, please!

Please note: I am not using the word "acceptance" in the sense that you're supposed to suddenly become *happy* about whatever shit has happened that you can't control. It's totally understandable — especially in the short term — to be very fucking upset by shit we can't control, as Ross was when Rachel broke up with him on *Friends* using the very words "Accept that."*

But if you've been dumped, duped, or dicked over, facts are facts. Continuing to spend time, energy, and/or money — in the long term — being anxious, sad, or angry about it (or avoiding it) is a waste of freakout funds.

Girl, don't act like you don't know this. We've been over it multiple times.

For the purposes of this book and execution of the NoWorries Method, **I'm using the word "accept" to mean "understand the reality of the situation."**

That's not so hard, is it? If you can accept that the sky is blue and water is wet and macarons are disappointing and borderline fraudulent as a dessert, you can accept the things you can't control.

And when you answer the One Question to Rule Them All with a *No*, you have *already* accepted reality. You have admitted that you can't control something — it's that simple. HUZZAH! Sarah Knight, dropping commonsense knowledge bombs since 2015.

---

* From "The One the Morning After."

Let's be real

A frequent precursor to the Freakout Faces is an inability to accept reality. In one sense, you may be worrying about something that hasn't even happened yet, which means it is literally not yet "real." A what-if exists in your imagination; only when it becomes real is it a problem you can acknowledge, accept, and address. Or you may be freaking out because you can't force the outcome you want, e.g., one that is not "realistic." I'll go over that more in part III, in the section aptly titled "Identify your realistic ideal outcome." Meanwhile, chew on this:

The path from what-ifs and worrying to calming the fuck down is a straight line from "things that exist in your imagination" to "things that exist in reality" and then "accepting those things as reality."

Maybe reread that a few times just to be sure you're smelling what I'm cooking. In fact, see the next page for a graphic you can photocopy and keep in your wallet or bring down to Spike at the Sweet Needle so he can tattoo it across your chest for daily reaffirmation.

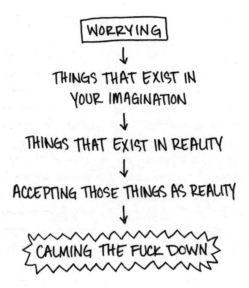

And just like that, you've nearly calmed the fuck down — all that remains to complete Step 1 of the NoWorries Method is to DISCARD that unrealistic, unproductive worry like the good little mental declutterer I know you can be.

To do that, you have a couple of options.

Option 1: Just fucking let it go

You still think it's easier said than done? Fine. But I encourage you to consider everything we've talked about so far and apply your new tools and perspective on a case-by-case basis.

For example, if you're working those shitstorm categories like I taught you, you should be able to reduce your worry load immediately, and significantly.

If something is highly unlikely to happen, why are you worrying about it?

And if it's far off in the distance, why are you worrying about it NOW?

Oh, and is this something you can control? No? Hm. Then there's no reason you should be spending your precious time, energy, and money on it at all.

Seems pretty straightforward, doesn't it? Like...maybe the kind of stuff you should already know?

Well, I think you DO know it, somewhere in your palpitating heart of hearts—I'm just helping you access that knowledge. No shame in a little teamwork. I've found that in times of stress, people can't always make the commonsense connections that others can make *for* them, if others are granted a reasonable deadline and unlimited Doritos to sit down at their laptop and spell it all out.

It's a symbiotic relationship, yours and mine.

Which is to say, I'm not at all surprised that you couldn't just fucking let go of any of your worries before you picked up this book—but I'd be really surprised if by now, you can't just fucking let go of, like, a bunch of them.

Option 2: Houdini that shit

Unlike Bryan Cranston, whose character starts out enraged by but eventually comes to like the guy who's trying to marry his onscreen daughter in the criminally underrated movie *Why Him?*, you cannot count on becoming happy about the thing that, right now, has you very fucking upset.

But you CAN become happy (or calm or proactive, etc.), right now, about *something else* entirely — which in turn causes you to stop worrying about the original thing.

Ta-daaa! I call this technique **"sleight of mind."**

It's like when I'm freaking out about a deadline, so I go for a bracing dip in the pool to clear my head. That doesn't change the fact of five thousand words being due in someone's inbox tomorrow, but it does temporarily change my focus from *I'm a fraud and will never write another syllable* to *Ooh, that feels nice.*

Just like sleight of hand enables a magician to perform his thrilling act, sleight of mind is how we'll make your worries disappear — at least temporarily, and maybe even for good. (And don't come at me with "That's cheating!" I promised you tricks all the way back on page one. You should really start taking me at my word.)

Now, recall, if you would, the Flipsides of the Four Faces of Freaking Out:

ANXIOUS?	→	FOCUS
SAD?	→	REPAIR WITH SELF-CARE
ANGRY?	→	PEACE OUT WITH PERSPECTIVE
AVOIDING?	→	ACT UP

This is where the magic happens, people. I now present you with a collection of simple, elegant tricks you can tuck up your voluminous sleeve for when the worrying gets tough and the tough need to STOP WORRYING.*

How to stop being anxious about something

The what-ifs are multiplying on the radar screen. Your nerves are frayed, your teeth are ground to nubs, and you can't stop overthinking whatever shit is about to go or has gone down.

You need to FOCUS, Jim! (On something else.)

GIVE ANXIETY THE FINGER(S)

When I'm anxious, I walk around the house wiggling my digits like I'm playing air piano or doing low-key jazz hands. My hus-

---

* For linguistic continuity with the NoWorries Method, I use "worrying" here to mean "any way in which you are exhibiting the signs of a freakout."

band calls them my "decluttering fingers" since they always signal a prelude to some semimanic tidying. But in addition to clearing out the kitchen cabinets or denuding the coffee table of old magazines, what I'm doing is temporarily channeling my anxiety into something productive and, to me, comforting.

You may not be as into tidying-as-therapy, but surely there's another hands-on task you enjoy that you could turn to when you feel your Anxious face settling in around the temples. Perhaps industriously restringing your guitar, mending a pair of pants, or repairing the teeny-tiny trundle bed in your kid's dollhouse. (It's probably time to admit it's *your* dollhouse, Greg.)*

GET DOWN WITH O.P.P.

Other people's problems, that is. Maybe you don't have an on-call therapist — but you've got friends, family, neighbors, and the guy down at the post office with the beard that looks like it rehomes geese who got lost on their way south for the winter. Chat 'em up. Ask your sister how she's doing and listen to *her* shit. Release some of your anxiety by giving her advice that you should probably be taking your own damn self.

It's harder to stay anxious about any particular thing when you don't allow yourself the mental space to dwell on it — and a darn good

---

* Someone who was anxious about finishing her book on time may also have pruned a gigantic papyrus bush with a pair of kitchen scissors today.

way to accomplish that is by filling said space with conversation, human interaction, and *other people's* problems. How do you think I stay so calm these days? I spend all year giving you advice.

Tonight You, meet Tomorrow You

This seems like a good place to address the tarantula in the room, which is that when anxiety is keeping you up at night, you may be able to name your problem (Good job!), but you can't necessarily solve it in the moment.

I get that, which is why I want to take a moment to introduce you to one of my favorite mental magician-and-assistant duos: **Tonight You and Tomorrow You.**

Let's say it is currently 3:00 a.m. on Friday, and you can't sleep because on Tuesday you made an offhand comment to your coworker Ruth that you're worried she may have interpreted as an insult even though she didn't give any indication of such at the time and even though not one single word that came out of your mouth could possibly, by any sentient being, be thought of as a criticism.

Still. *What if?!?*

Well, if it's 3:00 a.m., then Tonight You CAN'T call Ruth and CAN'T tell her you hope she wasn't offended by that thing you said and CAN'T feel better about it when she replies, "What? I don't even remember you saying that, so obviously I was not offended, you silly goose."

But **Tonight You CAN set Tomorrow You up for success** — by getting some goddamn sleep, Chief.

You may think it's impossible to fall asleep when you're anxious about making things right with Ruth or when your to-do list is scrolling through your mind on endless loop like the NASDAQ on Times Square, **but hear me out — this might be the single most useful nugget in this entire compendium of calm.**

First, think of the problem in terms of what we've discussed thus far:

Falling asleep is the more urgent issue, so it should be your priority, right? *Check.*

Furthermore, it's the only part of this equation you have some control over now, *and* it's one you can actually solve, correct? *Check plus.*

This is reality. Can you accept it? *Checkmate.*

Ah, but not so fast, eh? I can smell your annoyance from here — a heady musk of *Fuck you* with a hint of *Don't patronize me, lady.* Do you feel like you're being bullied into doing something you simply cannot do, even though you know it's good for you? I get that, too. For whatever reason, sometimes taking good, solid advice from other people is impossible. Definitely an occupational hazard for *moi.*

So let's look at your problem another way. Say, through the lens of my early twenties — a time when my then-boyfriend, now-husband's entreaties for me to hydrate after every third cocktail felt more like a scolding than a suggestion, and when *even though I knew he was right,* I didn't like feeling pressured, condescended to, or preshamed for tomorrow's hangover. Nope, there was no better way to activate the You-Can't-Make-Me Face than to tell Sarah Knight a few V&Ts in that she "should drink some water."

Did I regret it in the morning? Yes. Did I take his advice next time? No. 'Twas a vicious cycle, with extra lime.

Then one blessed day, a friend introduced me to the concept of a "spacer," and everything changed. This was not a stupid glass of stupid water that somebody else *told* me to drink. No, it's a spacer! It has a fun name! And I get to control my own narrative by sidling up to the bar and ordering one. My spacer, my choice.

Where the fuck, you may by now be thinking, *is she going with this?*

Well, besides having just introduced you to the second-most-useful nugget in this entire book, I would argue that deciding to have oneself a spacer is similar to deciding to go to sleep. In terms of being in a state where you know what you should be doing but don't appreciate being told to do it, "intoxicated" is quite similar to "whipped into an anxious, insomniac frenzy," is it not?

I take your point. But what if I just can't fall asleep, even though I agree that it's best for me?

Good, I'm glad we're getting somewhere. Because I think—based on extensive personal experience—that you CAN drift off to dreamland if you approach the task differently than you have been thus far. If you take control of the narrative. If you treat "going to sleep" like ordering a spacer or checking off an item on that scrolling to-do list. Set your mind to accomplishing it and therefore to *feeling accomplished* instead of feeling like a very tired failure.

But you're not going to be there to remind me of this helpful nugget every night when my brain goes into overdrive—and even if you were, you still sound kind of smugly self-satisfied about the whole thing, tbh.

Noted. But remember Tonight You and Tomorrow You? They've been waiting in the wings for the grand finale...

One night as I was tossing and turning like one of those Chinese fortune-telling fish, my husband looked at me and said, **"Tonight Sarah's job is to go to sleep. Tomorrow Sarah can deal with this shit tomorrow."**

So I thought about it that way, and I gave Tonight Me her marching orders.

And it worked!

Maybe he adapted it from the spacer trick when he saw how well that penetrated my defenses, or maybe I married a goddamn wizard, but I don't care either way because ever since, I've been able to reframe the I-can't-fall-asleep conversation—with MYSELF—and **shift my focus from not being able to do the only thing I so badly *want* to do, to doing the only thing I *can* do.**

> **Other ways to reduce anxiety that I didn't invent but that have been known to work**
>
> Deep breaths. In through the nose, out through the mouth.
> Yoga
> Sex
> Bubble baths
> Counting slowly to one hundred
> Magnesium supplements
> Adult coloring books

And you know, I've always trusted Tomorrow Me to handle tomorrow's tasks, assuming she gets enough shut-eye. Now I recognize that it's Tonight Me's job to get her to the starting line in fine fettle.

Talk about sleight of mind. Yep. Definitely married a wizard.

But hey, you don't have to take it from us. Take it from Tonight You — Tomorrow You will thank you tomorrow.

How to stop being sad about something

What's another word for grieving, blue, mopey, forlorn, despondent, and depressed? HURTING. You're hurting. So you need to heal. Grant yourself a reasonable amount of time and energy to be sad about whatever shit has you worried and weepy.

Then, crate your emotional puppies and stave off the prolonged wallowing with a shot of SELF-CARE.

LAUGHTER IS THE BEST MEDICINE

Much like "Calm the fuck down," the phrase "Turn that frown upside down" is advice not often well received by a person who is midfreakout. I know that, but I'll say it anyway, because that shit *works*. For example, when I'm feeling utterly dejected, a certain someone's patented C + C Music Factory tribute dance/lip sync always brings me back from the brink. If something has you down, seek help from things that reliably cheer you up. Cat pics. Videos of people coming out of anesthesia. Perhaps an aptly termed "feel-good movie"? Anything in the *Pitch Perfect* oeuvre applies.

Even if this trick stops you worrying for only the length of one song (in my case, "Things That Make You Go Hmmm...") — you've stopped, haven't you? Progress!

YOU'RE IN FOR A TREAT

When someone else is sad, be they grieving or recuperating, you might stop by with some prepared food to get them over the hump — casserole, cookies, a fruit basket. Why not show yourself the same kindness? Your treat doesn't have to be food-based — some of us like to eat our feelings, some of us prefer to have them massaged away by a bulky Salvadoran named Javier. So do unto yourself as you would do unto others, and trade those worries for a trip to Cupcakes "R" Us, or an hour of shoulder work from Javi. Yummy either way.

> **5 things I have stopped worrying about while eating a king-sized Snickers bar**
>
> Final exams
> Thunder
> Credit card debt
> Nuclear proliferation
> That rat I saw outside the deli where I bought the Snickers

How to stop being angry about something

Exhaling bitchily, shouting "Shut the fuck up!" every five minutes, and jabbing a broom through the hole in the fence that separates your yard from the neighbor's new pet rooster is one way to pass the time, but it's not a good long-term use of freakout funds. Trust me on this.

Instead, calm the fuck down by redirecting that time and energy into more PEACEFUL pursuits.

WORK IT OUT

I said I wouldn't make you get physical with your mental decluttering, but sometimes I fib, like the lady who waxed my bikini area for the first time ever and told me the worst part was over *and then she did the middle.*

But I digress.

Serotonin, known as "the happiness hormone," can be naturally boosted in many ways, including by exercise. But that doesn't have to mean dragging ass to the gym, *per se.* Sure, you can run out your rage on the treadmill or crunch your way to calm—if that works for you, so be it. Even I sometimes enjoy a low-impact stroll on the beach to clear my mind of rooster-cidal thoughts. Got a stairwell in your office? Walk up and down it until you no longer want to tear your boss a new asshole with his own tie pin. Empty lot down the street? Cartwheels! Empty lot down the street, under cover of night? NAKED CARTWHEELS.

PLOT YOUR REVENGE

Hopefully they won't revoke my guru card for this one, but let's just say you live downstairs from Carl and his all-night drug parties, and every morning your anger rises just as he and his crew finally drop off into a cracked-out slumber. Instead of seething into your dark roast, you might consider perking up by mentally cataloguing the ways in which you could repay your neighbors' kindness. You don't have to follow through—merely thinking about the mayhem you *could* visit upon your enemies is a terrific mood booster. (Though "accidentally" upending a bottle of clam juice into Carl's open car window on your way to work is fun too.)

> ### 5 forms of revenge that are fun to think about
>
> Writing your enemy's phone number and a related "service" on the wall of a sketchy bar bathroom
>
> Or, like, fifty sketchy bar bathrooms
>
> Ordering a 4:00 a.m. wakeup call to your enemy's hotel room
>
> Mailing your enemy a box of loose black pepper
>
> Filling your enemy's pants pockets with gum right before they go into the wash

How to stop avoiding something

If anxiety sends you into overthinking, overwhelmed, overstimulation mode, then avoidance sends you in the exact opposite direction. Your worries have you paralyzed with inaction, indecision, and inability to deal. You may *think* you're saving freakout funds with all this inactivity, but you're actually wasting a lot of time that could otherwise be spent shoveling shit off your plate. It's the difference between napping as healthy self-care and napping as unhealthy coping mechanism. Let's not ruin napping for ourselves, okay?

Instead, try these ACTIVE alternatives on for size:

GET ALARMED

If you're putting something off — say, having "the talk" with your teenage son — use the alarm feature on your smartphone or watch to remind you about it ten times a day until you'd rather unroll a condom onto a banana than listen to that infernal jingle-jangle ONE MORE TIME. Even if you chicken out yet again, you'll have forced yourself to acknowledge the situation with every beep of your alarm, and that's half the battle.

(Actually, if you've been paying attention, it's one third of the battle. The middle third is *accepting* that you can't control a fifteen-year-old's libido, and the final third is *addressing* the part you can control — teaching safe sex — with prophylactics and phallic produce. You're welcome.)

PROPOSE A TRADE

If you're the ostriching type, I bet you're avoiding a few things at once. Oh, I'm right? Funny how that works. Well, just like focusing on one anxiety-inducing shitstorm at a time helps clear the deck of another set of worries (see: Choose it or lose it), you could make a deal with yourself that you only get to *avoid* one thing at a time. For example, if you're avoiding going to the doctor to get that suspicious mole checked out, you're not allowed to ALSO avoid balancing your checkbook.

And while you might be avoiding each of these activities because you additionally wish to avoid "getting bad news," I should point out that closing your eyes, plugging your ears, and singing "Nah nah nah nah" never stopped a hurricane from making land-fall, and it's not going to halt the total shitstorm of skin cancer or bankruptcy. Confront the fear behind the worry now, so at least you have a *chance* to deal with it if it turns out to be warranted.

Is sleight of mind a little sneaky? Maybe. But you have to admit, it's hard to freak out while you're enjoying yourself — whether that's laughing at a silly movie, savoring a tasty treat, or focusing on getting every last drop of clam juice out of the bottle and absorbed deep into a Subaru's upholstery.

And if you ostriches took my advice and sprang into action, well, you may still be worrying a little as you sit in your derma-tologist's waiting room, but you're also not avoiding it anymore. I call that a win.

Secret Option C

"Just fucking let it go" and "sleight of mind" are two excellent paths forward to a calmer, happier you. Highly recommended.

But depending on the person and worry and related shitstorm in question, these two methods alone are not always enough. I understand. And I'm not here to set you up for failure; if I wanted to do that, I would have called the book *How to Reason with a Toddler*.

As such, it's time for me to make a confession. **Despite its powerful cross-branding with my NotSorry Method from** *The Life-Changing Magic of Not Giving a Fuck* **and a very strong hashtag, the "NoWorries" Method may be a slight misnomer.**

No worries — like actually zero? Ever? That's probably not strictly possible. Sometimes your probometer is in the shop and your worries remain omnipresent and all-consuming. Sometimes you really just can't stop worrying or focus on other things.

It's okay, we can work with that.

Much like the "responsible procrastination" I detailed in *Get Your Shit Together*, or the "good selfish" discussed in *You Do You*, **there is such a thing as "useful worrying."**

You might engage in it in order to prevent the thing you're worried about from ever happening — as with a Category 1 Highly Unlikely Shitstorm that could be blown out to sea with a preemptive strike on your part.

Or, you might do some useful worrying to help yourself be in better shape when the shitstorm lands — as in the case of a Category 5 Inevitable. There's bound to be a lot less cleanup if you've adequately prepped the metaphorical house and grounds. (PS Have you made that dermatologist appointment yet?)

Wait, both of those sound like "dealing with it." Did you skip ahead?

Good on you for paying attention! But I really try not to skip ahead; it sets a bad example for my readers. No, what I'm about to teach you isn't quite "dealing with it," which we will cover in the aptly titled part III: Deal With It. This is sort of an in-between step.

Ladies and Gentlemen of the Worry, I give you…

Productive Helpful Effective Worrying (PHEW)

Up to this point, our goal has been to discard worries about shit you can't control, saving your time, energy, and money for dealing with the shit you can. We've been **CONSERVING freakout funds.**

That's one way to do it.

If you can't bring yourself to discard your worries altogether, another way to calm the fuck down is to **CONVERT those worries into productive, beneficial action — ensuring that any FFs you dole out in advance of a shitstorm are spent wisely.** They will (at least) help *prepare* you for surviving it; and (at best) help *prevent* it altogether.

That's what makes it PRODUCTIVE, HELPFUL, and EFFECTIVE worrying. The awesome acronym is just a side benefit. Here's how it plays out:

- Once a shitstorm has been classified and prioritized, the **NoWorries Method** dictates that you ask yourself *Can I control it?*

- If the answer is no, ideally you ACCEPT that you can't control it, and discard said worry. That's **Step 1: Calm the fuck down.**

- If the answer is yes, I can control it, then YAY! You may proceed directly to **Step 2: Deal with it,** organizing your response.

- However, if the answer is *No, I can't control it, BUT I ALSO CAN'T STOP WORRYING ABOUT IT OR DISTRACT MYSELF WITH OTHER THINGS!* then it's time to do some **Productive Helpful Effective Worrying.**

As an example, let's examine a perpetually outlying shitstorm offered by an anxious parent in my Twitter feed:

- **What if I fuck up my kids and turn them into bad people?**

This is a big, complex worry that causes many parents low-level anxiety every day, plus occasional bouts of hard-core freaking out.

Challenge accepted!

First, I absolutely understand why lots of them might not be able to "just fucking let it go." And I understand that it might be hard to employ sleight of mind and focus on other things while parenting. In fact, maybe you shouldn't get too distracted. Especially at the playground. Accidents happen.

But I humbly suggest that what you *could* do if you are constantly worried about fucking up your kids and turning them into bad people — and you are unable to let that worry go — is to spend your time, energy, and money on being the best parent you, personally, can be.

You don't have complete control over whether your kid turns out to be a bad person. At some point, that's on them. **But you can indulge your worries and *at the same time* contribute to the cause** by engaging in child-rearing tactics that are objectively proven to result in positives — such as reading to your kids, telling your kids you love them and are proud of them, and teaching them to say please and thank you and to not kick sand on me at the beach.

At least if you're taking these actions — **actions that are not shifting your focus via sleight of mind, but rather are *directly related* to the worry at hand** — you may still be yanking your metaphorical yarn, but you also know you're doing what you can to help your kids become good people.

That's PHEW in a nutshell. Not the worst advice you've ever received, if I do say so myself. (It's also not the first time I've given it here in this very book. Remember Really Cool Hat Guy? That was PHEW — you just didn't know it yet.)

You can't stop worrying? Fine. Worry away! But make it count for something.

Sending a shitstorm out to sea

As someone who once sat glued to the Weather Channel for ten days as two Category 5 hurricanes charted a collision course with my home on a fragile Caribbean peninsula, I know there is no greater relief than watching a seemingly inevitable monster storm veer away at the eleventh hour.

But of course, those near misses were due to sheer luck. (As Puerto Ricans know all too well, both Mother Nature and a certain world leader are capricious when it comes to visiting chaos and destruction upon a people.)

When it's a *shitstorm* on the radar, however — and a low-probability one at that — **you may be able to engineer a downgrade.** Sometimes you can gin that probometer readout from a 2 or 1 down to a harmless little tropical shitclone that potters off the grid before you can say "I presided over and directly contributed to the worst humanitarian crisis America has seen since the Civil War."

There are two different ways to prevent an already unlikely shitstorm from making landfall:

1. Take action (PHEW)
2. Do nothing (Counterintuitive, I know. Bear with me.)

Each has its place; deciding to implement one or the other is simply a matter of recognizing what you can control, and then acting (or not acting) accordingly. For example:

- **What if I spend thousands of dollars to paint my house and on a large scale the color turns out to be ugly?**

Action you could take: They have apps and online simulators for this. Do your research. (Same goes for drastic haircuts, BTW.)
Outcome: No surprises.

- **What if my wife doesn't like the gift I bought her for our 25th anniversary?**

Action you could take: You're so sweet! Ask your wife's most trusted friend to help you shop, or to slyly solicit ideas from her BFF over coffee. Also: DIAMONDS.
Outcome: Happy wife, happy life.

- **What if I get seasick on my first-ever boat ride, which also happens to be my best chance to impress a client on his private catamaran?**

Action you could take: Dramamine, for the win.

Outcome: Your cookies remain untossed.

In each of the above scenarios, the total shitstorm is unlikely to evolve, but if you know you're going to be worrying about it anyway, you can take action to prevent it.

If you like that shade of blue on a small scale, chances are you'll like it at split-level size, but it pays to make sure beforehand. If you've been married for twenty-five years, you probably have a pretty good sense of your beloved's taste, but calling for reinforcements can only improve your chances of a tearful "Oh my God, how did you know?!?" (Maybe improve your chances of a little something else, too, *if* you know what I mean…) And not everyone experiences motion sickness, but there's no point in finding out you're susceptible the moment you're attempting to close a deal. "Barfs on clients" doesn't look good on your LinkedIn profile.

Sure, these happen to be somewhat low-level problems with fairly easy, self-evident solutions, but that's what made them unlikely to begin with. If you're the kind of person who worries about unlikely shit happening, you just gained the perspective to wipe a few Category 1s and 2s off the screen before breakfast. Not too shabby.

Your other option to stave off a shitstorm is to do nothing at all.

Yes, I know, I've previously advocated for taking action in order to prevent a freakout, but now we're talking about *the problem itself*, not *your reaction to it*. If you can blow the shitstorm out to sea by taking ZERO action, the freakout is rendered moot anyway.

Like, let's say you're hella concerned about the prospect of an unwanted pregnancy. If you use birth control regularly (and properly), then *What if I get pregnant?* should already be a Cat. 1 Highly Unlikely — but if you really can't afford any room for error, I know just the thing to nip that fetus in the bud.

Abstinence! I'm talking about abstinence, guys. Jesus.

Hey, if you care as much about sex as I do about skiing, then doing nothing totally works. Groan away, but it's true, isn't it? In fact, there's really no limit to the things you could *never* do if you *never* want to risk a potential bad outcome — **as long as whatever you're giving up is worth the sacrifice.**

For example:

You could never go canoeing so that you never flip over in a canoe and drown. There are other ways to transport oneself across water. Like bridges.

You could never handle fireworks, so that you never get into a freak Roman candle accident. You know what they say: it's all fun and games until someone has to be fitted for a glass eye.

Or you could never agree to retrieve the sacred sivalinga stone for the villagers of Mayapore and therefore never be forced to drink the blood of Kali and almost die at the hands of a prepubescent maharaja in a faraway temple of doom. Easy-peasy.

Are you sensing a little sarcasm here? Good. You sense correctly. Because what's not useful is *never doing something* because you're afraid of an outcome so unlikely in its own right that you'd actually be doing yourself a bigger disservice by avoiding the original thing entirely.

Or to put it another way, **being crippled by anxiety is no way to live.**

Houston, we have an irrational fear

I'd like to treat you to a bonus what-if scenario that's near and dear to my own heart, and that **might give you a new way of looking at something you may have long considered an insurmountable problem.** Or this could be the point in the book where you snort derisively, proclaim me a fucking idiot, and go on your merry way. It's your world, squirrel.

For the sake of argument, let's imagine that you're traveling from New York to New Mexico, and you're worried that this Delta Death Blimp is destined to go down over the Great Lakes and take you and 114 other easy marks along with it.

The first step toward staving off a freakout in Terminal A is to categorize the potential shitstorm in question (dying in a plane crash), and **acknowledge that it's not *probable*.**

To wit: the odds of dying in a plane crash are one in eleven million, which makes it less likely than being killed by a shark (one in eight million), dying on a cruise ship (one in 6.25 million), or getting hit by lightning (one in twelve thousand).

You are dealing with a Category 1 Highly Unlikely here. No two ways about it. Furthermore, even if your 747 *is* destined to fall out of the sky like a drone operated by your drunk uncle Ronnie at a Freemasons' picnic, **what the fuck are you going to do about it?***

Unless you plan to abandon your current career to spend a couple of years in flight school and become a pilot, which you would have to overcome your fear of flying to do in the first place, **you cannot control the situation. It is 100 percent out of your hands.**

Which means what?

---

* At this time, I would like to apologize to anyone who bought this book at the airport for a bit of light travel reading.

THAT'S RIGHT. It's a waste of time and energy to worry about it.

If you still want to play devil's advocate, I suppose you could also control the situation by never flying anywhere, ever — but then you should stop driving, riding, sailing, walking, or roller-blading anywhere too, because the probability of death goes way up the closer to Earth you travel.

Let's stop talking about it.

The thing is, I know that the irrational fear of flying (or irrational fear of anything, for that matter) is very upsetting. I myself am terrified of air travel for all kinds of reasons that, when examined in the weak glow of the overhead light, do not hold up.

So when I'm settled into seat 5A staring down the barrel of a cross-country hop to give a lecture at Marriott Corporate on getting your shit together, I counter this pernicious what-if with a big ol' dose of *Is there one single goddamn thing you can do to prevent this plane from exploding, falling apart, or dropping out of the sky? No? Then calm the fuck down and worry about something you* can *control, like writing out your speech all professional-like on some index cards and then not spilling your miniature vodka tonic on them.*

I also treat this particular case of the what-ifs with .25 milligrams of Xanax, but that's beside the point. I didn't even have a Xanax prescription for the first thirty years of my life and I still got on planes when I was feeling wicked anxious because it's just not logical or rational to avoid them for eternity — and, as mentioned previously, I am a very logical and rational person.

Most of the time.

Hi, I'm Sarah and I have a mental illness (More than one, actually!)

As you may have gleaned, I'm a proponent of better living not only through logic and reason and emotional puppy crating, but also through pharmaceuticals. In addition to employing nonchemical techniques like deep breathing and walking on the beach and balancing pineapples on my head, I take different daily and situational prescription medications to keep a lid on my anxiety and keep panic attacks at bay. And I TAKE THEM BECAUSE THEY WORK. Pills aren't for everyone, of course, and neither is meditation or electroconvulsive therapy. But I want to talk about this stuff to do my small part to help eradicate the stigma surrounding mental health issues and getting treatment for them. Mental illness is a disease like any other and if *that's* your underlying problem, you don't deserve to be shamed for or feel shame about it.

There, I said it. Now back to our regularly scheduled menu of absurd hypotheticals, dirty jokes, and meteorological metaphors.

The calm before the shitstorm

At this point in our journey — a word I use with the utmost sarcasm — I hope you're feeling really good about your prospects for calming the fuck down.

- You've been armed with the knowledge and tools to **prioritize.**
- You understand the concept of **control** and **what it means to accept that which you cannot.**
- And I've presented you with many techniques for **discarding, distracting yourself from, or converting your what-ifs and worries** like a boss — and **steering clear of freakouts** along the way.

As such, now is the time on *Sprockets* when we put everything you've learned into action.*

To show you how it's done, I'm returning to the what-ifs from the list I made at the beginning of part II. I already gave you my thought process for categorizing each of those potential shitstorms. That's where I **ACKNOWLEDGED** them. Here, I'll go

---

* To those of you who got that reference, congrats on being at least forty.

further, asking myself which parts of these potential shitstorms I can control — and then **ACCEPTING** the answers, aka the reality of my situation(s).

We'll start at the bottom of the Shitstorm Scale with my Category 1s & 2s, and work our way up.

10 WHAT-IFS I MAY OR MAY NOT NEED TO WORRY ABOUT: CAN I CONTROL THEM?

CATEGORY 1 — HIGHLY UNLIKELY

What if...

- **More tarantulas appear in my house**

Can I control it? Nope. On the sliding scale of control, this is an "out of my hands" for the ages. When it comes to worrying about tarantulas, I'm going to just fucking let it go. (And if Lucky comes back a third time, I think he's officially our pet.)

- **I order a different pizza than usual and it isn't very good**

Can I control it? Yes, but that's exactly why it's highly unlikely to happen in the first place. Every practice test has a trick question.

- **My editor hates this chapter**

Can I control it? I can definitely heavily influence this outcome by not sending Mike a piece of shit, but then again, his opinion is his alone. However, one's thing's for sure: if I'm sitting here obsessing over what he might think about something I sent him, then I'm taking time away from finishing the rest of the book — arguably a worse outcome, since I'm on a bit of a deadline here. So I've elected to press SEND and **convert those worries** (productively, helpfully, and effectively) into "writing more chapters." Then on the off chance that he *does* hate this one, I'll spend my FFs ordering a perfectly topped large pizza, calming the fuck down, and dealing with the revisions.

CATEGORY 2 — POSSIBLE BUT NOT LIKELY

What if…

- **My house key gets stuck in the door**

Can I control it? Since I don't know why it happened the first time, there's nothing I can do to ensure it doesn't happen again — except stop locking the house altogether, which invites a shitstorm of a different stripe. Nope, can't control it, so I'll discard that worry and save my freakout funds for conducting a little light B&E if necessary.

- **A palm tree falls on my roof**

Can I control it? Nope. (Technically, I could spend some time, energy, and money on Productive Helpful Effective Worrying and have the two trees within spitting distance cut down before they can fuck with us, but they grow out of the neighbor's yard and I don't think she'd appreciate it; plus then I wouldn't get to look at them every day while I bob in my pool.) The freakout funds remains untouched...for now.

- **I get into a car accident on the winding mountain road to the airport**

Can I control it? This is a "contribute to the cause" situation. The reasons for the difference between the amount of freakout funding I give to speaking gigs (a lot) vs. the Return of Lucky (none) vs. airport transport (some) are simple: My relative preparedness for a speech, I can heavily influence. But I can't do anything about keeping the tarantula out. Spiders gonna spider. Whereas on the airport road, although I'm not driving the car myself and *directly* influencing the ride, I can control *whether* we only book flights that have us traveling that stretch during daylight hours, and I'm not shy about asking the driver to slow down or pull over if it starts pouring rain. Control what you can, accept what you can't, and wear your seat belt.

- I show up for a speaking gig and totally bomb

Can I control it? Again, yes, but the way to control this outcome is *not* by worrying about failing. It's by spending my time and energy preparing a great talk and rehearsing the shit out of it. PHEW. So productive! So helpful! So effective! (And sure, there's a first time for everything, but if I worried about that I would have used up all my freakout funds on *What if aliens invade Earth and make us their space bitches?* a long time ago.)

Et voilà! With seven unlikely what-ifs on my radar, I've **CONSERVED** freakout funds by discarding my worries about four of them (tarantulas, bad pizza, stuck keys, fallen palms), and **CONVERTED** funds via Productive Helpful Effective Worrying for three more (speaking gig fails, seat belts, subsequent chapters).

I've still got plenty of FFs in reserve for total shitstorms, if (Categories 3 and 4) and when (Category 5) they occur.

CATEGORY 3 — LIKELY

What if...

- I ruin my favorite pineapple-print shorts by sitting in something nasty

Can I control it? Eh. I can heavily influence this outcome by watching where I sit, but I don't want that to be my full-time job, so I've decided to let this one go. Thus far, club soda and dish soap have staved off ruination, but one day it's likely that the shorts will be unsalvageable, at which time I will spend $16 in freakout funds to get another pair from Target and restart the clock. Discard that worry for now.

CATEGORY 4 — HIGHLY LIKELY

What if...

- **It rains on my day off that I wanted to spend at the beach**

Can I control it? That's a big "no" to the weather itself and "barely" in terms of predicting it. Weather apps might as well be made of old soup cans and string for all the good they do me here. This is a perfect example of a shitstorm that — despite its high level of probability — is pointless to worry about. (In this case, a nice tall piña colada does wonders for my attitude.)

CATEGORY 5 — INEVITABLE

What if...

- **My cats die**

Can I control it? Nope. That's the thing about "average lifespans." Should I spend FFs worrying about it? Hell nope! I've suffered through the deaths of a couple of pets in my time, and it's horrible. When it happens again, I'll be really sad, but I'll deal with it then. What I'm not going to do is preemptively freak out and stop surrounding myself with feline friends just because one day I'm going to have to decide where to display their ashes or whether to have them stuffed and mounted above the dining table over my husband's strenuous objections.

Now you try, with that same list of what-ifs you made on page 77 and that you already sorted by category. Use these questions as your guide:

- Can I **control** it?

- If not, can I **accept** that reality, **stop worrying about it,** and **conserve** freakout funds?

- If I can't stop worrying about it, can I **convert** freakout funds to **productive, helpful, effective worrying** that will prevent or mitigate it?

10 WHAT-IFS I MAY OR MAY NOT NEED TO WORRY ABOUT: CAN I CONTROL THEM?

_____

Category: _____

Can I control it? [Y] [N]

_____

Category: _____

Can I control it? [Y] [N]

_____

Category: _____

Can I control it? [Y] [N]

_____

Category: _____

Can I control it? [Y] [N]

_____

Category: _____

Can I control it? [Y] [N]

_____

Category: _____

Can I control it? [Y] [N]

_____

Category: _____

Can I control it? [Y] [N]

_____

Category: _____

Can I control it? [Y] [N]

_____

Category: _____

Can I control it? [Y] [N]

_____

Category: _____

Can I control it? [Y] [N]

Are you feeling a little more — dare I say it — in control? I hope so, and I hope asking the One Question to Rule Them All becomes a vibrant element of your daily process.

It certainly has for me; I estimate that I'm 75 percent less basket case-y as a result.

In fact, lately it's been especially helpful being able to categorize my what-ifs and let go of stuff I can't control. Have you been watching CNN? I'm surprised the chyron below Jake Tapper's skeptical mug doesn't just run "THIS SHIT IS BANANAS" on infinite loop. When nearly every hour of every day brings to light some further debasement America and/or the rest of the world has endured at the tiny paws of a D-list wannabe Mafioso — well, it's useful to have some defense mechanisms firmly in place.

I read the news today, oh boy

It did not take a master's in guruing to discern that as of the time of this writing, people around the world are more in need than ever of calming the fuck down.

The United States of America, as mentioned, is a total shitshow. The president is an unhinged narcissist, the ruling political party is composed largely of simpering cowards, and affordable health care is nothing more than a collective hallucination — treatment for which is not covered by your insurance company.

England and the rest of the United [for now] Kingdom: not doing so hot either. Perhaps you've noticed? In fact, if you watch the news, or even just scroll through Twitter, it seems like every continent is seeing fascism, xenophobia, and sea levels on the rise — or icebergs, honeybees, and civil liberties on the decline.

Ugh.

I don't know if there's actually *more* war, pestilence, extreme weather, or dismaying cultural regression going on than ever before, but I do know we're more *aware of it,* because technology has seen to it that humans can't go a millisecond without finding out about the latest school shooting, terror attack, election meddling, or rendezvous between evil dictators hell-bent on destroying Western civilization.

Double UGH.

It's a problem, and one I hope this book will help you address in some small but significant way, she writes, as women's right to bodily autonomy hangs perpetually in the balance.

ROE V. *UGHHH.*

What to do? Well, because I still believe in the benefits of an informed/enraged citizenry, I'm afraid I cannot personally advocate for Total Ostrich Mode, aka "not consuming the news at all." But a few minor bouts of ostriching in service to shit you can't control? I'll allow it. Go on, get that face in the pillows and that ass in the air!

As to anger, you're entitled. Letting loose a full-throated howl *while* your face is in the pillows can be satisfying. You know, if the mood strikes. And if you can channel your anger into something productive, so much the better — like, after hurling every glass container in your home against a wall as though it were an old white man trying to steal your children's future, you could take out the recycling. Smash the patriarchy, save the planet.

When you're done — and apart from just hoping things will improve or that you can primal scream them into submission — **there are other ways to counteract the feelings of helplessness** you might have when being bombarded daily with the worst the media has to offer. Rather than scrolling through your newsfeeds each night before bed and giving yourself teeth-falling-out dreams, perhaps you could try one of the following **calming, control-regaining techniques?**

They work for me, and I'm about as despondent over crumbling democracy and devastating climate crisis as it gets!

5 TIPS FOR CALMING THE FUCK DOWN
ABOUT THE WORLD FALLING APART

LIMIT YOUR EXPOSURE

An informed citizen doesn't have to be gathering information over breakfast, on the toilet, astride an exercise bike, during their commute, AND right before going to sleep (or trying to go to sleep, anyway). A once-per-day news dump should be sufficient to keep you in the know without also keeping your blood pressure higher than Snoop Dogg.

BALANCING ACT

If you can't dodge the twenty-four-hour news cycle, for every @WashingtonPost you follow, add a palliative account to the mix. I recommend @PepitoTheCat, which is just time-stamped black-and-white footage of some cat in France coming and going through his cat door, accompanied by the captions "Pépito is out" or "Pépito is back home." I like to scroll through Pépito's feed before bed. It's like counting sheep, but instead you're counting the same French cat over and over again. *Trés* relaxing.

BONE UP

It may seem counterintuitive, but doing a deep dive into whatever single current event is giving you the biggest case of the what-ifs can help you vanquish some of your more paranoid fantasies. For example, researching how the "nuclear football" actually works and learning that a certain feeble-minded president would have to memorize certain information in order to launch an attack may have done wonders for a certain someone's ability to stop worrying [quite so much] about the prospect of this particular mushroom shitcloud sprouting anytime soon.

TAKE A MEMO

Drafting an angry letter — to a global leader, a local representative, or, say, morally repugnant NRA spokeswoman Dana

Loesch — can really get the mad out of you. Journaling is scientifically proven to help calm you down by moving all those burning, churning thoughts out of your head and onto the page. And you don't even have to send your angry missive to reap the in-the-moment benefit, but for the cost of a stamp it might be nice to know it'll reach its intended target. Or at least clutter their inbox, which in my opinion is a fate worse than death.

DO GOOD

When I'm feeling powerless about the state of the world, one thing that brings me comfort is donating to a cause — be it a natural disaster relief fund, a local charity, or just a single person who needs a hand. Is this my economic privilege talking? Sure, but if spending my freakout funds this way makes me feel better *and* helps someone less fortunate, all I see is a two-for-one special on good deeds. And "giving" needn't require a cash outlay — you have other FFs at your disposal. Time and energy spent calling your reps to protest inhumane immigration practices, volunteering at Planned Parenthood, or mocking up some zesty protest signs and taking a brisk walk around your nearest city center will help you sleep better in more ways than one.

Now if you'll excuse me, while my husband is watching the orange howler monkey's latest antics on MSNBC, I have a French cat's whereabouts to monitor.

(Pépito is out.)

Stirring the shit

Okay, folks. We are neck-deep in part II. I trust you're starting to see that, **logically and rationally, much of the shit you worry about is unlikely to happen** — and that you can do enough PHEW-ing to ensure that even the likely stuff can be made less terrible with some effort on your part. Just don't get cocky.

I would be remiss if I didn't warn you that **it is possible to trick yourself into *thinking* you're PHEW-ing, when what you are really doing is WILLING A SHITSTORM INTO EXISTENCE.**

In psychological terms, **"catastrophizing"** is the belief that a situation is worse than it actually is. And I promised I wouldn't argue with you about how hard things suck for you right now. I fucking hate it when people do that. But **if you *do* happen to be catastrophizing, you may also be *creating your own catastrophe*** — something I can and will caution you against.

That's right: you have the ability to send a shitstorm out to sea, but also to conjure a Category 5 out of thin air.

For example, if your friend Andy hasn't gotten back to you about you taking his extra ticket for the Cubs game tomorrow night and you're paranoid that he's mad at you even though he hasn't said anything specific, you might text him to be like, "Hey dude, are you pissed because I wrote your email address on that

Church of Scientology sign-up sheet? Sorry, they surrounded me when I was leaving the gym and I panicked. My bad."

And maybe he wasn't mad at you (just busy getting off the Church of Scientology mailing list). BUT NOW HE IS.

If you'd stopped to study all available data you would have realized there was no way Andy could have known you were the clipboard culprit. If you hadn't panic-texted, he never would have put two and Xenu together and you'd be slammin' deep dish in the box seats — no harm, no foul.

Instead, you overthought it and you're watching the game on TV with your good friend Papa John.

Other times, when a shitstorm is already tracking as "inevitable," your actions may significantly hasten its arrival and amplify its effects.

Historically, this has been a bit of a problem for yours truly. On the one hand, and as I wrote about in *You Do You*, my natural tendency toward anxiety can in some ways be a good thing. It helps me plan ahead, because I can envision the perils and consequences of not doing so. It helps me be prepared, be on time, and generally stay on top of my shit.

But every once in a while, the anxiety, and the overthinking it enables, knocks over a domino that might never have fallen on its own.

And then I'm left picking up the whole damn pile.

That was not a chill pill

It was finals week during my junior year of college. I had exams to study for and papers to write, and both time and energy were running low. I'd done all the research for my last remaining essay, but it was already early evening the night before it was due. My late-nineties desktop computer sat there judging me like Judy.

I was mentally and physically exhausted, at the end of an already frayed rope. I knew I didn't have the juice — let alone the hours on the clock — to pull this one out. But as a classic over-achiever and rule-follower, the prospect of not handing in an assignment on time was simply off the table. I couldn't fail to show up at my professor's office at 9:00 a.m. with dot-matrix printout in hand, and I for damn sure couldn't beg for an extension on a *final paper*. That would be madness!

Speaking of which, I had started to go a little nutso myself worrying about what would happen when I blew this assignment — and in the throes of the ensuing freakout I made a Very Bad Decision in service to what I *thought* was Productive Helpful Effective Worrying.

Can't stay awake for the limited number of hours left in which to craft a piece of writing that will account for 25 percent of your final grade in a Harvard undergraduate seminar?

Accept two mystery pills from a friend who tells you "This will keep you up and help you focus!"

NARRATOR: It kept her up. It did not help her focus.

By dawn I was thoroughly cracked out, defeated, and dehydrated from an hour or so of inconsolable sobbing triggered by the realization that I was *definitely* not going to finish this paper on time. Since swallowing the mystery pills I'd spent ten hours growing increasingly frantic, my heart thumping in my chest, fingers shaking over my keyboard, and pacing my dorm room like an extra in *Orange Is the New Black*.

Now it was time to swallow something else: my pride.

Still huffing and snuffling, I pecked out an email to my professor. Rather than compound my sins by concocting a dead grandmother or severe tendinitis, I decided to tell her the truth — that I had backed myself into a corner time-wise and attempted to rectify my [first] mistake with an influx of energy-by-what-was-probably-Adderall. I was sorry and ashamed and had generated four pages of gobbledygook instead of fifteen pages of cogent argument. I needed an extra day.

Then I collapsed onto my futon and waited for the other Doc Marten to fall. (As mentioned, it was the late nineties.)

My professor didn't curse or rage or threaten to have me expelled. She was matter-of-fact about the whole situation. She granted me the bonus time and said whatever grade I received on merit would have to be taken down a point for lateness.

Well, that was... easier than I thought it would be.

I still had to deal with the original task, sure. But in the meantime, I'd had to deal with the total shitstorm I'd summoned by freaking out about the original task and making a Very Bad Decision fueled by anxiety. Had I been able to calm the fuck down in the first place, I might have missed my deadline, but I would have asked for the extension up front; gotten a good night's sleep; spent the following day writing my paper with a fresh brain; and avoided the ten-hour interlude of weeping, shaking, and pacing.

Also: I would have avoided emailing my professor at six in the morning to tell her I TOOK SPEED. So there's that.

I love it when a plan comes together

Before we round the corner to part III: Deal With It, I feel a pressing urge to drive home the power of all of the tips and techniques from part II. What can I say? Sometimes I just can't stop guruing.

In the next few pages, I'm going to take a sample what-if and help you calm the fuck down about it. We will:

- Assign a category and status to this potential shitstorm
- Determine what (if any) control you might have over the outcome
- Accept the reality of the situation
- Discard worries stemming from the parts you can't control

- Spend your freakout funds wisely to prevent, prepare for, or mitigate the results of the rest.

I'll even throw in a preview of dealing with it, because I'm a full-service anti-guru and I respect a seamless transition.

Categorizin' cousins

Let's say, hypothetically, you have two cousins named Renée and Julie. Recently Renée posted something nasty on Facebook that was oblique-yet-clearly-aimed-at-Julie, and now the two of them are about to cross paths...at your wedding.

Do you feel a freakout coming on?

Assuming for the sake of our hypothetical that the answer is yes (or that you can imagine how it would be a yes for some people, given that weddings are traditionally known to be intrafamilial hotbeds of stress and strife), you have a decision to make.

You could spend time and energy worrying about your cousins getting into a parking lot fistfight during the reception, working yourself into a double-whammy Anxious/Angry Freakout Face — but that's neither going to prevent it from happening nor help you deal with it.

Instead, let's **activate your inner whetherperson and assemble all the available data.** Such as:

- What's Renée and Julie's history?
- Has this kind of thing happened before?
- How well do they hold their liquor?

Asking logical, rational questions like these will help you determine whether it's HIGHLY UNLIKELY, POSSIBLE BUT NOT LIKELY, LIKELY, HIGHLY LIKELY, or INEVITABLE that these bitches are getting ready to rumble.

And who knows? Maybe they'll be so inspired by your vows that they will "vow" to stop being so nasty to each other. Maybe they'll hug and make up in the photo booth, before the pigs in blankets hit the buffet. Maybe at least one of them will take the high road as her wedding gift to you.

I certainly don't know, because I don't know them — but *you* do. **Check your probometer** and make a reasonable guess as to which category this potential shitstorm falls under. Then earmark your freakout funds accordingly.

SCENARIO 1

Trolling each other online is Renée and Julie's standard MO and so far, it hasn't resulted in a parking lot fistfight. They tend to circle each other like wary cats, bond over their shared passion for twerking to Nicki Minaj, and then all is forgiven over the third SoCo-and-lime shot of the night.

Probometer Readout: Cat. 1 / 2 — Highly Unlikely or Possible But Not Likely

- Worrying about something that's unlikely to happen is a risky use of valuable freakout funds. You know this. If the storm never comes to pass, you've wasted time, energy, and/or money; and if it *does* happen, you'll be forced to pay double — having freaked out about it then + having to deal with it now. **Conclusion:** Your FFs are better reserved for other potential wedding day snafus. We all know your friend Travis is a loose cannon.

SCENARIO 2

Your cousins always had a complicated relationship, but it's gotten more volatile in the last year, ever since Julie dropped Renée from their *RuPaul's Drag Race* recap WhatsApp group. Ice cold. Of course you can never be 100 percent sure what she's thinking, but Renée is not one to let sleeping drag queens lie.

Probometer Readout: Cat. 3 / 4 — Likely or Highly Likely

- If you're that much more convinced the shitstorm is coming, you also have that much of a better idea about when it will land. **If it's a 3 or 4, you should do a status check.** Are we talking merely OUTLYING (it's a few weeks before the wedding) or IMMINENT (it's the morning of the wedding)? The status informs **how *soon* you need to spend your freakout funds on prevention or mitigation.**

- But before you dole out any FFs to a Category 3 or 4 shitstorm, you should ask yourself ***Can I control it?***

If the answer is "Nope, out of my hands" (e.g., your cousins have never listened to you a day in their lives; why would they start now?), then discard that worry like Travis will undoubtedly discard his bow tie when the first bars of "Hot in Herre" infiltrate the dance floor. Don't waste time, energy, and/or money *freaking out about it.* Consequently, if/when the girls do decide to take out their earrings and their aggression, you'll have that time, energy, and/or money to spend *dealing with it.*

(Still feeling anxious? Try a little sleight of mind. I hear calligraphy is relaxing, and if you start practicing now, maybe you can save some money on your invites.)

If the answer is a hearty *Yes, I can control or heavily influence this outcome!* (e.g., you believe your cousins will respond well to the threat of being cut off from the Southern Comfort if they misbehave), then by all means, whip out your worry wallet and peel off a thoughtfully composed email to Renée and Julie warning them that wedding day shenanigans will result in them being *personae non gratae* at the open bar. That's **Productive Helpful Effective Worrying** in action. Phew.

SCENARIO 3

Renée and Julie came to blows at your brother's state championship football game three years ago and dragged each other into the pond at their own mother's seventieth-birthday party. There is no reason to believe your wedding will count as sacred ground. These broads are out for blood. Their husbands are selling tickets and taking bets. The forecast is clear. It is ON.*

> *Probometer Readout: Cat. 5 — Inevitable*
>
> - I understand why you'd worry about something like this, which you believe is inevitable — it's human nature, and it's also YOUR FUCKING WEDDING DAY. On the other hand, **if it's inevitable and you can't control it,** perhaps you could accept that and let go of your worries unless/until you absolutely *must* spend some freakout funds dealing with the fallout?

---

* This is assuming you didn't disinvite them already, which would count as PHEW to the MAX but also leave me unable to follow this hypothetical to its messiest conclusion, and that's no fun.

- Furthermore, if you believe a conflagration of cousins is past the point of being staved off by PHEW on your part — then I'd suggest a big, fat **"Just fucking let it go."** You're about to embark on one of the most momentous occasions of your life. And whether it's in three months' or three hours' time, you do not need this shit.

- **ACKNOWLEDGE** that no matter what you do, your flesh and blood are gearing up for Parking Lot Grudge Match 3; **ACCEPT the reality;** and **ADDRESS it** when and only when it becomes a textbook total shitstorm.

  Do NOT spend freakout funds now. You're going to need that time, energy, and money when the total shitstorm makes landfall — time to collect yourself in the ladies' room; energy to kick some ass of your own; and money to post Julie's bail. Renée started it. Let her rot.

  But DO put fifty bucks on Julie. She spent the last six months taking jujitsu, which Renée would know if she weren't such a self-absorbed cunt.

Aaaaand that's a wrap on part II!

Or, well, not quite. There's a smidge more overly reductive yet extremely helpful content left to be had, and if you're a seasoned NFGG reader, you know what's coming…

OH YEAH, IT'S FLOWCHART TIME.

HOW DO I CALM THE FUCK DOWN?

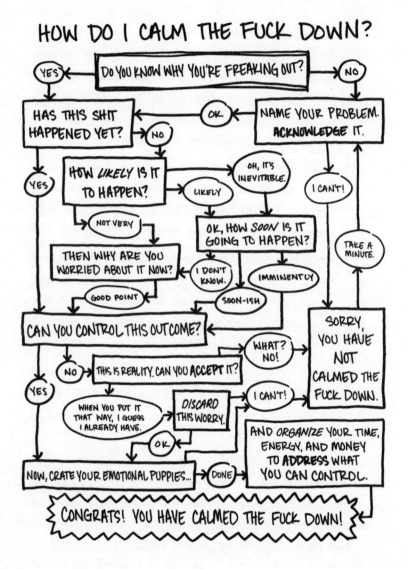

||||

DEAL WITH IT:
Address what you *can* control

Hey, hey, hey, look at you! You made it to part III, where all of your rigorous training in calming the fuck down will be put to the ultimate test: **dealing with the shit you're worried about.**

And for the purposes of this section, we're going to assume this is **Shit That Has Already Happened.** Congrats, you're really moving up in the world.

Thus far, we've **dissected freaking out** — making you more aware of the symptoms and consequences of doing so. We've **wrestled with worrying** — not doing it with regard to things you can't control, and/or doing it more effectively. Those are the initial steps toward both **combating existential anxiety** and **surviving any shitstorm** that well and truly comes to pass.

You've already done a shit-ton of **mental decluttering, Step 1: Discarding.** You've rid yourself of so many unproductive worries that you should have a healthy supply of freakout funds left to move on to **Step 2: Organizing** — aka dealing with whatever's left, now or in the future.

Mental decluttering is like hanging up on telemarketers; learn it once and it's a skill that sticks with you for life.

Now it's time to introduce my **Three Principles of Dealing With It** — developed to help you and the 75 percent of people who responded to my survey by saying **they wish they had better coping mechanisms for when shit happens.**

Baby, I've got the only three you'll ever need.

I'll also help you identify your **RIOs (realistic ideal out-**

comes). These ensure that you don't waste time, energy, money, or goodwill dealing yourself down a rabbit hole of dubious destination.

Prescriptive pragmatism: learn it, live it.

Finally, we'll put it all into practice. The last section of part III functions like a catalogue of terror. In it, **I'll take you through a bunch of total shitstorm scenarios to illustrate how a logical, rational mind-set can help you deal with them.** We'll cover work mishaps, family feuds, missed opportunities, natural disasters, broken limbs, broken hearts, and broken dreams.

It'll be a hoot, I promise.

Of course, no single book or catalogue of terror can prepare you for each and every potential trauma life has to offer. But just like *Get Your Shit Together* offered a simple toolkit for proactively setting goals and achieving them, *Calm the Fuck Down* gives you the tools to **productively *react to* all the shit you didn't want and didn't choose** but that happened to you anyway because life isn't fair.

You just have to **ACKNOWLEDGE, ACCEPT,** and **ADDRESS** it.

If I have anything to say about it, by the time you turn the final page of part III you will be fully equipped to do just that.

Deal me in

"Dealing with it" encompasses a range of actions taken — and outcomes achieved — in response to shit happening.

At the top of the outcomes scale you've got the **FULL FIX**. Like, you left your iPhone X on the city bus, but realized it just in time to take off running like a bipedal cocker spaniel until a divinely placed red light allowed you time to catch up to the bus, rap on the door, indicate "I left my cell phone!" and reclaim your property.

Done. Like it never happened.

Below that, there are **SALVAGE JOBS**. You left your iPhone X on the bus and you didn't get it back, so you had to buy a new one. You dealt with it, but you spent a lot of freakout funds on that mistake. No Chinese takeout for you for the next two years, give or take.

Or maybe you can't afford a new iPhone X right now, so you curse your carelessness, learn a lesson, get a refurbished 5se off eBay, and go on with your life.* If you can't afford a replacement smartphone at all, you pick up a cheapie burner at Radio Shack that doesn't connect to the cloud and spend the next week asking

_____
* I've been rocking a 5se since 2016. No complaints.

all your Facebook friends to resend you their contact info via smoke signal.

More FFs withdrawn, plus a smidgen of goodwill, but at least you're back in the game.

Below that, you've got **BASIC SURVIVAL.** You're between jobs and on a strict budget. You can't afford a new phone of any sort. You're anxious about missing a callback for an interview and angry that you put yourself in this position, but now that you've read this book, you're able to practice some sleight of mind and pull yourself together. **Focus, peace out, act up. You know the drill.**

Instead of letting this costly error further erode your fragile state of both mind and finances, you find a workaround, perhaps making a few withdrawals from the Fourth Fund (which is topped up, since you haven't been freaking the fuck out all the time lately like Sherry). Maybe you ask a friend or relative if they have a spare old phone lying around that they could activate for you. Definitely reach out to prospective employers to let them know you're temporarily without access to the number on your résumé and request that they make contact by email if they have news for you. You could start a GoFundMe page. Or sell your used panties on Craigslist. It's honest work.

Of course, a lost phone is just one example out of a million possibilities of shit happening that you then have to deal with. It may not apply to you (in fact, if you've read *Get Your Shit Together*, I hope you've been conditioned to never lose your phone under any circumstances).

Or maybe you could never afford an iPhone X in the first place, or you think I'm being cavalier in the face of something that, for you, would be a Really Fucking Big Problem that's Not So Easy to Solve. I understand; everyone's situation is different and their resource levels vary. Maybe no matter how much you want to, you can't run after that bus because you're still recovering from hip surgery.

I'm sorry about that. Get well soon.

My point is, this or any of the 999,999 thousand examples I could give totally sucks — yes indeedy — but there ARE ways to deal with it that don't involve purchasing a replacement iPhone X and that *also* don't involve crying into your pillow until such time as the ghost of Steve Jobs appears to grant you three wishes.

This entire book is about *finding a way*. It's about calming down, making decisions, taking action, and solving problems — or at least not making them worse with freaking out and *in*action.

So get used to it, m'kay? There's more where that came from.

The Three Principles of Dealing With It

At this point, you may be wondering why I don't simply refer you to *Get Your Shit Together,* which lays out **three easy, actionable steps for accomplishing anything: strategize, focus, commit.** *Bada-bing.* And yes, my GYST Theory is simple and effective — but it's primarily concerned with goals you have *time* to strategize about, habits you can focus on *slowly* forming, and commitments you can budget for *well in advance.*

> *Getting your shit together* is **PROACTIVE.** It's an ongoing process.
>
> *Dealing with shit that has already happened* is **REACTIVE.** It's something you have to do in the heat of the moment.

"Dealing with it" could mean anything from having the wherewithal to get online and rebook your tickets when you oversleep and miss a flight, or applying pressure to a gushing wound because you stupidly used the wrong tool to cut cheese and you're alone in the apartment while your husband makes a quick run to the deli for ice before your friends arrive for dinner and it would be bad to lose so much blood that you pass out in your kitchen and add a concussion to the mix.

Not that I would know anything about that.

Step 2 of the NoWorries Method requires its own set of skills and tools — busted out in the moment and honed in the blink of an eye — whether they're used to engender a Full Fix or simply to survive.

THE THREE PRINCIPLES OF DEALING WITH IT

TAKE STOCK

Imagine you just landed in enemy territory and you have precious little time to assess the situation before it goes from bad to worse. You're going to have to grit your teeth and gather the facts. Emotional puppies in the crate, logical cats on the prowl.

IDENTIFY YOUR REALISTIC IDEAL OUTCOME (RIO)

When shit happens, an ideal Full Fix may or may not be possible, which means that accepting what you can't control isn't just for calming the fuck down anymore — it's for dealing with it, too! Running full-tilt boogie down a dead-end street literally gets you nowhere, fast. Better to start with a realistic, achievable end goal in mind.

TRIAGE

If the storm is upon you, your probometer has outlived its usefulness, but you can still prioritize based on urgency. Like an ER nurse, the faster you determine which patients are in the direst straits and which have the best chance of survival — i.e., which problems will get worse without your intercession and which stand the best chance of getting solved — the sooner you can minister effectively to each of them.

Now let's go over each of these principles in a bit more detail and accompanied by illustrative anecdotes, as is my wont.

Take stock

I mentioned the idea of "landing in enemy territory" because that's what it feels like every time I find myself in a bad-shit-just-happened situation. Are you familiar with this feeling? **It's equal parts terror and adrenaline** — like, I know I'm down, but perhaps not yet out. My next move is pivotal. If I choose wisely, I may be able to escape clean (i.e., the **Full Fix**); get away injured but intact (i.e., a **Salvage Job**); or at least elude my adversaries long enough to try again tomorrow (i.e., **Basic Survival**).

I felt this feeling when a car I was riding in was hit broadside, deploying its airbags along with an acrid smell that apparently accompanies deployed airbags and which I assumed was an indicator that the vehicle was going to explode with me in it if I didn't get out of there ASAP.

Reader, I got out of there ASAP.

But I've also felt it under circumstances of less immediate, less physical danger — such as when the new boss who had just lured me away from a good, stable job stepped into my five-days-old office to tell me *he'd* been fired, but that he was "sure the CEO had taken that into consideration" when she approved my hire the week before.

The logicats leaped into action. Should I set up a preemptive chat with HR rather than sitting around waiting for a potential axe to fall? Was I entitled to any severance or health insurance if I became a casualty of the outgoing administration? Was it too early to start drinking?*

The ability to assess a situation swiftly and to identify your next best steps is really important in a crisis. Why do you think flight attendants are always yapping about knowing where the emergency exits are? (Anxious fliers: forget I said that.) And as I said in the introduction, you don't have to be born with this skill; you can practice and develop it over time like I did.

HOWEVER: note that I said to swiftly "identify" your next best steps — not necessarily to swiftly *take* them.

Taking immediate action can occasionally be good, such as frantically searching for the "undo send" option in Gmail upon realizing you just directed an off-color joke about your boss, to your boss. But acting without having taken the lay of the land is far more likely to exacerbate your original problem. Like, just because you've

---

* Full disclosure: there was some delayed-onset freaking out on that one, but at least I had already asked and answered the important questions before I started sobbing into my Amstel Light.

parachuted into the villain's compound and don't want to be fed to his pet bobcat for breakfast doesn't mean you should be making any rash moves. (For one thing, bobcats are nocturnal, so I would tread real lightly overnight and make a break for it *at* breakfast.)

Rash moves can get you served up as human hash browns just as easily as if you had succumbed to Ostrich Mode. And if that last sentence doesn't get me a Pulitzer nomination, then I don't know what will.

Just make a simple, immediate *assessment* of the situation. Nuts and bolts. Pros and cons. Taking stock not only helps calm you down (What's the Flipside to anxiety? Focus!); it gives you a rough blueprint for dealing with it, when the time is right.

What-iffing for good instead of evil

If you're adept at imagining the worst before it even happens, you can apply that same obsessive creativity to dealing with it when it does! For example, say your backpack gets stolen from the sidelines while you're playing a heated cornhole tournament in the park. You're already programmed to take a mental inventory of what was in it and visualize the consequences of being without those items. **Credit cards**: What if the thief is headed straight for a shopping spree at Best Buy? **Medication**: What if you're stuck without your inhaler or your birth control pills indefinitely?? **Eight tubes of cherry ChapStick**: What if your lips get dry while you're on the phone with Customer Service trying to cancel your Mastercard??? **Library book**:

> What if you have to pay a fine for losing the new John Grisham *and* you don't get to find out what happens????
>
> Go ahead and survey the damage. But then make a plan for dealing with it efficiently and effectively. (Pro tip: canceling cards and requesting an emergency refill from your doctor should take precedence over lip care, library fees, and legal thrillers.)

Identify your realistic ideal outcome (RIO)

WHAT'S REALISTIC?

Looking again at the backpack scenario, if the thief is apprehended ten minutes away with all of your stuff intact and unpawned — what ho, it's a Full Fix!

But assuming that isn't the case, then dealing with it will be annoying, but probably a pretty decent Salvage Job. Most of your crap can be replaced, and it was time to dump that loose Blueberry Bliss LUNA Bar anyway. It was getting hard to tell if those were blueberries or ants.

On the other hand, if you were to, say, drop Great-Grandpa Eugene's antique watch overboard in the middle of the Pacific, a Full Fix would definitely be off the table. Obviously you could buy a new watch, but you can't bring your father's grandfather back from the dead to break it in for you for sixty years before you start wearing it. All you can hope for is a swift and substantial insurance claim — filling out the paperwork for which is the best and only thing you can do to ensure the manifestation of your RIO on this particular Salvage Job.

WHAT'S IDEAL?

Every shitstorm harbors a range of realistic outcomes, and what makes any one of them an *ideal* outcome depends on the preferences of the person afflicted.

For example, if you just discovered your fiancée's very active online dating profile a month before your wedding, there are plenty of realistic outcomes. You may be ready to call the whole thing off, or you may decide to kiss and make up (and personally delete her Tinder account). You'll take stock of the situation by confronting her (or not), believing her (or not), and deciding whether you're through with her (or not), and then proceed to solve for X.

Or for "your ex," as the case may be. Whatever is ideal, for YOU.

HOW DO I FIGURE IT OUT?

The key to determining your RIO is to be honest with yourself. Honest about what's possible and what you want, honest about what you're capable of doing to get there, and honest about what's out of your control.

Think of it like buying a pair of shoes. When you try them on, no matter how much you like them, if they don't fit, they don't fit. Do not go to the cash register. Do not drop $200 on a pair of sweet-but-uncomfortable kicks. You cannot will your size 10s to shrink overnight, and if the shoes pinch your feet now, imagine how your poor toes are going to feel after you walk around in them all day tomorrow. You'll be blistered and bleeding, relegating your expensive mistakes to the bottom of your IKEA MACKAPÄR cupboard as soon as you hobble in the door.

Dealing with it becomes exponentially more difficult if you're chasing improbable outcomes and handicapping yourself with subpar tools.

Be realistic. Be honest with yourself. And be ready to walk away. Comfortably.

Triage

Prioritizing is at the core of all the advice I give — for determining what you give a fuck about, for getting your shit together, and for calming the fuck down.

Dealing with it is more of the same. **Triage is just a fancy word for prioritizing.** I like to mix it up every once in a while and create a sense of DRAMA for my readers.

You've probably heard them talk about triaging on *Grey's Anatomy*. And like an emergency room only has so many beds to go around and its staff so many hands with which to compress chests, dispense morphine, and change bedpans — **you only have so many resources to devote to your personal emergencies.** You need to learn to do *mental triage* so you'll be prepared to deal when a total shitstorm blows through the swinging doors of your mental ER with little or no warning.

I gave you a taste with the Case of the Stolen Backpack, but let's look at a few different shitstorms in action, and practice prioritizing in terms of "dealing with it."

- **On your way to your best friend's surprise thirtieth-birthday party in Boston, your flight gets canceled.**

TAKE STOCK

What time is it now, what time do the festivities begin, and are there any other flights (or perhaps trains, buses, or nonthreatening guys named Ben who are headed in that direction) that could get you there?

RIO

Depending on the answers to the above, you may still realistically be able to land in time for dinner, or at least for after-hours club-hopping—and you may want to try. Or if booking a substitute flight means missing the party completely and showing up just as your pals are stumbling home from Whisky Saigon at 5:00 a.m. (and about five hours before they decide to bail on the planned postbirthday brunch), you may decide to cut your losses. It's up to you, boo. What's your ideal outcome?

TRIAGE

Your priorities should be set in service to your RIO. It's a matter of time and money if you can find and afford another flight out, or energy and money if you decide that instead of making a personal appearance, you'll be calling the club and putting the $ from your canceled ticket toward bottle service for your besties and a cab back to your own bed. Either way, the clock is ticking, which is why we prioritize — once more, with feeling — BASED ON URGENCY.

(Or you could decide your most realistic ideal outcome is to find another flight to Boston but *pretend* that you couldn't, taking in a game at Fenway while your friends are busy regretting their life choices. Go Sox!)

- **Grades are in. You're failing.**

TAKE STOCK

What does this mean? Are we talking one exam or an entire course? High school or traffic school? Did you lose your scholarship or just a little respect from your professor?

For the sake of this example, let's say you have not yet failed an entire class in oh, how about Science A-35: Matter in the Universe, but as you approach the midterm, you're well on your way.*

---

* 1998 was a tough year for me, okay?

RIO

An *ideal* outcome would be that you improve both your study habits and your capacity for comprehending "science" and ace every assignment from here on out to bring your grade to the minimum passing level. Alas, that is not *realistic*. Your best bet is probably to cut your losses and drop the class before it drops you down a point on your GPA.

TRIAGE

Alright, Einstein, time is of the essence. University rules say that any grade achieved after the midterm stands on your permanent record, so you need to get that course-droppin' paperwork submitted ASAP. Then consult the master class schedule and see where you can fit this bitch of a required science credit in next semester — and which easier, more palatable elective you'll have to sacrifice in its place. Sorry, English 110FF: Medieval Fanfiction, I hardly knew ye.

Is it distressing to discover that you are failing at something at which you need to succeed in order to get a diploma, a driver's license, or an A grade from the city health inspector? Yes, it is. Are there plenty of logical, rational ways to deal with it? Yes, there are.

- **A big, bad storm blows through town.**

TAKE STOCK

Walk around your home (and property, if you have it), assessing the scope of destruction.

RIO

Secure the place from further damage, repair whatever's broken, and don't go bankrupt while doing it.

TRIAGE

Here's a secret top priority — take photos. You're going to need them for your insurance claim, which means they can't wait until you've already started fixing the place up. Then put a stop to any leaks and get rid of standing water and soaked rugs if you can. Mold is some vile shit and you don't want it growing in your hall closet. Any busted doors and windows should be closed off to further rain and opportunistic thieves/raccoons. And if the power looks to be out for a while, empty the contents of your fridge into a cooler to save what food you can. After five hours of wet rug lugging, you'll die for some leftover chicken pot pie.

That's just off the top of my head — obviously there could be much more or much less or much different stuff to deal with in the aftermath of a shitstorm/actual storm of this variety. But no matter what, **you can't do it all FIRST.** At least if you prioritize based on urgency, **you're going to get the *right* things done first.**

For example, you may want to get a tarp over that hole in the roof before you start saving the pot plants you've been hobby-growing in the basement. Just a thought.

Get bent! (a bonus principle)

If *Get Your Shit Together* was about bending life to your will, this book helps you not get broken by it. How? **By being flexible when the situation demands it.**

When shit happens (e.g., sudden monsoon rains, absentee roof guys, early-a.m. spider wrangling), it puts a minor-to-major dent in your plans. And while maintaining a rigid stance in the face of unwelcome developments such as these is good for, say, culling surprise Trump supporters from your Facebook feed, it's not terribly useful otherwise.

You gotta be flexible.

I'm not talking about touching your nose to your hamstring (although that is impressive and the logicats would surely approve). **No, it's not so much contorting like a cat as it is *thinking* like one.**

As an example, when my Gladys discovers that the terrace is crowded with humans and therefore feels she cannot eat her dinner in peace and at the stroke of five as she is accustomed, she saunters over to the side of the house and waits for clearance. Grabs a snack lizard to tide her over.

Gladys is no dummy. She's not going to meow "Fuck this shit!" and foolishly strike out for parts unknown just because her schedule got thrown off a little bit. She knows there are other ways to get food (wait for it, hunt for it), and all she has to do is chill (or kill) if she wants to eat. A logicat after my own heart.

Like Gladys, you can't afford to freak out (alienate or abandon your food source) and not accomplish your end goal (eating dinner) just because some shit happened (rude humans changed the rules).

You gotta be flexible. **Regroup. Reimagine. Reattack.**

Unfortunately, flexibility doesn't come naturally to everyone — including me. I'm a literal thinker, which is great for writing and editing books but not so great for adapting when the landscape shifts. For most of my life, if you gave me rules, I would follow them. Rigid was good. I knew what I was dealing with.

But if you *changed* the rules? OH HELL NO. That was bound to trigger a freakout.

How do I move forward? Now I feel like I'm breaking the very rules I so carefully observed and internalized for so long. This doesn't feel right. I can't do this. I'm trapped!

And more specifically:

But-but-but YOU told me to do it one way and now you're telling me to do it another and WHICH WAY IS IT, GARY?!? Clearly my resulting confusion and paralysis are ALL YOUR FAULT.

This doesn't end well for anybody.

Here's a lesson I learned rather too late in my corporate tenure (mea culpa old bosses, coworkers, and assistants), but have since been able to apply in my professional and personal relationships to great effect: **it really doesn't matter why this shit happened or who "changed the rules."**

All that matters is that it happened, they've changed, and you have to be flexible and deal with it. And THAT means being less concerned about *Why?* and more with *Okay, now what?*

Whose fault is it anyway?

Placing blame is a classic impediment to dealing with whatever shit has happened. So much time wasted. So much energy. Why don't you take a unicycle ride across Appalachia while you're at it? Determining once and for all who was at fault doesn't fix your problem, and it won't make you feel better about it, either. How much satisfaction are you really going to get from browbeating your coworker Sven into admitting that he was the one who left the laptop with the presentation slides in the back of the taxi you shared last night? It's 7:00 a.m., your client is expecting a PowerPoint bonanza in two hours, and you and Sven *both* smell like the back room at Juicy Lucy's. Put a pin in the blame game, hit the shower, and send Sven to the Staples in downtown Phoenix for some poster board and a pack of markers.

Remember: when options seem to be closing off all around you, the ability to be flexible opens up new ones. **If you're still bending, you're not broken.***

---

* That's a Sarah Knight original inspirational quote. Slap it on a throw pillow and sell it on Etsy if you're so inclined. You have my blessing.

Incoming!

Listen, I know you're kinda busy reading an awesome book, but your mother, Gwen, just called from the airport. SURPRISE — she'll be here in forty-five minutes, she's staying for a week, and oh, can you order her an Uber-thingy? Thanks, doll.

Can you calm the fuck down? I hope so, because otherwise I've failed you and I will have to "get a real vocation," as a helpful online reviewer recently suggested. (Thank you, Dorothy — your input is valued.) If you're struggling, consult the flowchart on page 154 and meet me back here in five.

No need to panic — this is a solid Salvage Job. You're not getting your afternoon back, but you do have the power to minimize the fallout from Hurricane Gwen. If your home is not exactly camera-ready and you don't give a fuck what your mother thinks about this sort of thing, congrats! "Dealing with it" just got a whole lot easier. But if you *do* care what she thinks about this sort of thing, then you've got a wee window in which to tidy up and a lot of places you might start.

Take stock of them all, identify your **RIO,** and then it's time for some **triage.**

If it were me, the RIO would be to give Gwen a good first impression and then keep her from inspecting anything too closely.

- I'd begin with the guest room/sofa bed. Make sure you have clean sheets or put them in the wash N-O-W so they'll be fresh when it comes time for Gwen to rest her weary, immaculately coiffed head.

- Next, stow all of your stray shoes, sports equipment, broken umbrellas, and half-empty duffel bags from your last vacation that you haven't unpacked yet in a closet or under your bed.

- Wipe down visible surfaces. Leave higher shelves and ledges alone — dragging the step stool all over the joint is just going to aggravate your bad back, and you *really* don't need more aggravation right now. (**Realistic** + **ideal** = **WINNING**)

- Then take out the trash, light a few scented candles, and chill some Pinot Grigio if you have it. Gwen loves that shit, and after two glasses she won't be able to tell the difference between dust bunnies and her grandkids.

Oh, and you may have to cancel or put off a couple of less urgent things you were planning to do this week in favor of tending to your surprise houseguest.

Good thing you're so **flexible.**

It's all in your head

The foregoing example may have been an exercise in physical decluttering—but where did it start? Why, IN YOUR MIND, of course. Recall that the NoWorries Method has its roots in *mental* decluttering.

Step 1: Calm the fuck down. DISCARD unproductive worries.

(Gwen's already here; don't waste freakout funds on stuff you can't control.)

Step 2: Deal with it. ORGANIZE your response.

(Spend your FFs on stuff you *can* control. Like Febrezing the pull-out couch. Maybe there just isn't enough time to do those sheets.)

Lots of shit happens with no warning. Parental sneak attacks, birds pooping from above, or that crack in the sidewalk that caused you to faceplant on the cement and now you're hunting for an emergency dental clinic in the middle of your Haunted Sites tour vacation in Charleston. Damn sidewalk ghosts. They'll get you every time.

Which means that often you'll need to be able to organize

with little or no advance notice: taking stock, deciding on a real-istic ideal outcome, triaging the elements, and, sometimes, getting your Gumby on.

And you'll be doing all of this *mentally* before you attempt any of it *physically*.

(No rash moves, remember? That bobcat be hungry.)

In the case of Sudden-Onset Houseguest, you had virtually no time to solve a problem, you had already learned how to not waste it freaking out, and you were able to alter the course of your afternoon, not to mention the rest of your week, to accommodate your new reality.

- All of that was mental decluttering in action.

- All of it was accomplished after you put down the phone but before you ever picked up a dustcloth — by knowing your limits, focusing on what you could control vs. what you couldn't, and prioritizing.

- All of it was the NoWorries Method helping you calm the fuck down and deal with it.

So tell me: are you ready to take it to the next level?
BECAUSE I AM.

Total shitstorms: a catalogue of terror

In my anonymous online survey, I asked **"What's the most recent shit that happened to you?"***

I've fashioned a bunch of those responses into a lightning round of total shitstorms spanning health, finances, family, work, relationships, and more. From bad hair days to broken bones, **I'll offer my quick-and-dirty take on each entry from a logical, rational point of view.**

Now, to be clear — I don't necessarily have personal experience in all of the following situations. (I would never be caught dead wearing a Fitbit, for one.) But if my methods are sound, that shouldn't matter. I should be able to work the steps just like I've been asking you to throughout this whole book.

The idea behind *Calm the Fuck Down* is to **apply universal truths to the whole universe of problems.** Probability. Urgency. Control (or lack thereof). Learning to prioritize. Crating your emotional puppies. Keeping your eye on the Flipside.

And anyway, quick-and-dirty advice aside, in the end none of

---

* I also asked "How did you deal with it?" and given the responses, I'm more confident than ever that you and your family, friends, enemies, neighbors, bosses, coworkers, underlings, significant other, and especially someone's sister-in-law Courtney really need this book. I hope it's working out for you so far.

this is really about me and what I would do. **It's about YOU, and changing your mind-set to change your life.**

YOU take stock of what you see laid out before you.

YOU determine your own realistic ideal outcome.

YOU set your priorities and plans in motion.

I'm just the foulmouthed, commonsense lady who's lighting the way. Let's see what I got.

Relatively painless shit

This is the kind of stuff that puts a kink in or all-out ruins your day, but not so much your week, month, or life. It's not the end of the world, but it's at least mildly annoying. The good news is—there's a lot of potential here for Full Fixes, or for high-level Salvage Jobs. Like I said, I'm easing you in slowly. Think of this section like a warm bath.

In fact, why not run yourself a temperate tub to enjoy while you read? If you don't have a bathtub, a shot of tequila will produce roughly the same effect. Or so I'm told.

- **The restaurant lost my reservation.**

Take stock. Are they offering to seat you at the next available time, and is that time acceptable to you? If so, do you know how to pronounce the words "Might you spot us a round of gin and tonics while we wait?" Good, you're all set. If it's more of a "Sorry, we can't accommodate you at all this evening," then your time, energy, and money are better spent patronizing another establishment, not sticking around this one just to have a word with the manager. (Plus, remember what we talked about earlier—you don't want to wind up an unwitting star in somebody's viral "Customer Does Unspeakable Things with a Breadstick, Gets Banned for Life from Local Olive Garden" YouTube video.)

- **I couldn't fit 10,000 steps into one day.**

Shit happens. You got stuck in an endless series of meetings, you tweaked your hip flexor, or that darn ankle monitor won't let you go more than fifty feet from the house, and walking back and forth two hundred times would really start to chafe the Achilles. If you've heretofore been anally committed to an exercise regimen, this could be a big deal—but in that case, you've also been anally committed to an exercise regimen. Nice work! Maybe your magnificent calves could use a break?

Or, if you've just gotten into this whole "exercise" thing, you may be feeling depressed because you can't seem to establish a routine. Either way, if it bothers you that much, just carry over the negative balance to tomorrow's goal. I won't tell your Fitbit.

- **I got a bad haircut.**

Welcome to my early teens. Lacking either a time machine or an on-call custom wigmaker, your realistic ideal outcome is probably to mask the damage until it grows back. May I introduce you to hats, headbands, bobby pins, barrettes, bandanas, scarves, weaves, and/or the concept of not giving a fuck?

- **My boss yelled at me.**

Did you mess up? If yes, then it's unfortunate that you work for a screamer, but dealing with it should be focused on whatever you can do to ensure that you don't provoke his ire in the future. If you did not deserve it and you're gunning for total vindication, first assess whether your boss is the type of person to change his mind and apologize when calmly presented with evidence of his miscalculations. If you determine that he is not this type of person, then I refer you back to page 115, "Plot your revenge." That'll calm you down and enable you to organize your response — maybe in the form of a complaint to HR, or a letter of resignation. Or just carrying out your revenge plot. Totally worth it.

- **I went trampolining and the next day my body hurt so bad I legit could not move.**

Well, this is a pickle. Much like a soldier who parachutes behind enemy lines, gets tangled in her gear, and breaks a few nonnegotiable bones — it's time for you to draw on the Fourth

Fund and call in reinforcements. In this case, dealing with it means getting someone else to *help you* deal with it, possibly in the form of a burly pal who can carry you to the car and drive you to the chiropractor. On the bright side, you probably got those 10,000 steps in.

- **I sent a work email to more than one hundred people and forgot to use bcc.**

Ladies and gentlemen, forget the inventor of the vuvuzela, we have found the world's biggest asshole! No, I'm sorry, I'm sorry, that was a joke. I'm not being fair. You do at least seem to understand the concept *of* bcc, so I'll give you a pass here. We all make mistakes. There are two paths forward. (1) You could send another email to the same list (bcc'd this time, of course), apologizing and begging people not to reply-all to the original—although in my experience, by this point the seven people in your office who are clueless enough to reply-all will have done so already. (2) You could sit quietly at your desk and think about what you've done. Up to you.

- **I shat my pants (as an adult).**

Ouch. One hopes that as an adult you also have the wherewithal to get cleaned up, dispose of your befouled undergarments, and if necessary, tie a sweater around your waist and head on down to Old Navy for a new pair of khakis. Oh well, at least you didn't fail to bcc more than one hundred people on a work email.

- **The printer isn't working.**

This one—again, straight from the survey—reminds me of my very first day at my very first job as an editorial assistant in New York City. It was 10:30 a.m. and the big scary boss-of-*my*-boss asked me to photocopy something and return the copies to her "before eleven," and it was then that I became acquainted with the Xerox Machine from Hell. It beeped. It jammed. It stapled indiscriminately. It jammed some more. As I was standing in the Xerox room contemplating whether it was better to confess to the Big Boss that I, a recent college graduate, could not operate a copy machine, or to tender my immediate resignation, another assistant took pity on me and showed me where the "better" copier was located.*

5 things you might do accidentally that are still not as bad as failing to bcc more than 100 people on a work email

Ruin the series finale of *House of Cards* before your boyfriend sees it

Bite into a rotten peach

Get drunk and French-kiss your cousin

Make an own goal to lose your team the World Cup final

Run over your neighbor's puppy

---

* To this day I wonder if the Big Boss threw me into the lion's den on purpose. I would not put it past her.

Anyway, what I'm saying is — there's probably another printer you could use. Though I also cosign the actions of the anonymous survey taker whose response to this problem was "on our LAN network, I renamed it 'littlefuckbox.'"

- **I drank too much at the office Christmas party and...
well, I don't remember.**

Easy there, Tiger. Crack open an ice-cold Gatorade and listen to me close: *nobody else remembers either.* And if they do, the best way to deal with this is to pretend nothing happened and in doing so, cultivate an air of mystery even more intriguing than your nogged-up karaoke rendition of "Shape of You." Then use the next office shindig as an opportunity to get your nemesis blind drunk and pass the torch.

Tedious Shit

Here we have your mid-to-high-level annoying, unexpected, and unwelcome shit. It's poised to cramp your style for the foreseeable future; it's going to take more time, energy, and/or money to recover from; and the Full Fixes will be fewer and further between. Luckily, if you've conserved a goodly amount of freakout funds — calming the fuck down in a timely, low-impact fashion as per my instructions in part II — you'll be well situated to deal with it.

For now, though, let's see if I can offer inspiration.

- **My car was towed.**

Depending on how soon you need your wheels back, you may have to shuffle a few items on ye olde calendar — and maybe even drain ye olde vacation fund (or max out ye olde credit card) to get it out of hock. So let's survey the landscape here: Where is the car? How soon do you need it back? How much is it going to cost? And in terms of outcome, would you *ideally* prefer to get it back sooner, with greater adverse impact on your schedule, or at a more convenient time, but accumulating additional fines per day? Triage accordingly.

- **I found out that I owe back taxes to the government.**

Without knowing the details of your particular situation, I'm confident that the Three Principles of Dealing With It will apply. Take stock: How much do you owe? By when are you supposed to pay it off? Is that timetable realistic — yes or no? If you have the money now, just write the check and be done with it. It'll hurt, but not as much as a $100,000 fine and up to five years in prison. If you don't have the means with which to settle your debt on a tight deadline, there's always a payment plan. If you're never going to have those means, it may be time to consult a tax lawyer (or Google, if you can't afford a lawyer either) and figure out your best next move. Triage that shit, and stop hemorrhaging late fees.

You snooze, you lose (your car)

I personally know SEVERAL people who have let a manageable debt (a parking ticket, credit card bill, tax lien, etc.) turn into the worst possible outcome simply by avoidance. In some cases the avoidance was due to serious mental health issues, and as I've said, I'm not an authority when it comes to treating an illness that could cause someone to blow up their financial life via inaction. But I *am* an authority on slapping some sense into the rest of you. And I'm not talking about people who avoid paying a bill they cannot afford, either — that's a whole other pooch to screw. I'm talking about people who can afford it but don't recognize that paying said bill *needs to be prioritized* above a half dozen other daily tasks, the putting off of which would not result in losing their car, their good credit score, or their split-level ranch. I consider it my sworn duty to help you prevent such outcomes, and if I have to call you out on your shit to get the job done, then so be it. No fucks given.

Maybe Google Lawyer will reveal an extension you can file for or some kind of aid for which you can apply. All I know is, the longer you wait, the more interest and penalties you'll accrue — and if you think the government is bleeding you dry now, just wait till they pronounce you DOA in federal court.*

———
* You could also say *Fuck it* and move so far off the grid that Uncle Sam couldn't find you with an army-issue Mark V HD Long-Range scope. Good luck! I'm sure that'll be easier than paying your taxes.

- **My girlfriend told me I'm bad in bed.**

You have every right to be hurt, miffed, or purely puzzled, but nothing good will come of indulging those emotional puppies for more than an afternoon's romp. Once you've recovered from what was undoubtedly the Greatest Shock of Your Life and taken stock, you'll find that you have a couple of options — it's up to you to decide which one wears the RIO crown. You could break up with her and await your introduction to a woman more appreciative of your conjugal talents. Or you could take her criticisms to heart and make some changes to your technique.

(Here I feel the need to once more underscore the simplicity that is "dealing with it." In so many problem-solving situations, we are working within a binary — do either this, or that, to begin righting the ship. Pick one and run with it. Or pick one and handcuff yourself to the bed with it. Whatever works, Fabio.)

- **I broke a semi-important bone.**

Clearly the first thing you should do is seek medical treatment, but on your way to the ER (or once the anesthesia wears off), you can spend some time cataloguing the consequences and making/changing your plans according to your projected recovery time. Can you still go to work? What other daily responsibilities may be hampered by your tetchy tibia? Be flexible! For example, my husband does all of our grocery shopping and dinner cooking, so when he broke his collarbone on an ill-advised motorbike outing, we had to make alternate eating arrangements for the next four to six weeks. They're called Eggos; I suggest you look into them.

- **I can't fit into my bridesmaid dress/tuxedo for this wedding I'm in...today.**

Assuming your RIO is to appear as a member of the bridal or groomal party and fête your friends whilst wearing the official wedding frock of their choosing, you may have to resign yourself to looking a bit overstuffed in the photos, then "accidentally" spill some red wine on your duds during dinner and change into that roomy-yet-wedding-appropriate outfit you "totally forgot you had in your trunk!"

- **I failed my driving test.**

Same. The way I dealt with it was to silently curse the trick stop sign, moan about it for a day, then retake the test at the earliest possible opportunity. If you fail again (and again), maybe you should practice more. Or take public transportation. Or commit to making enough money that you can afford a chauffeur for life. #GOALS.

- **The pipes in my house froze and burst.**

As a relatively new homeowner myself, I am continually amazed by the volume of shit that can go wrong in, under, around, and on top of one's house. That any domicile-based fail is happening in the place where you also need to sleep — let alone potentially work and parent — makes it potentially triply frustrating. As such, you might be tempted to waste freakout funds shaking your fists at the sky gods when you realize what went down behind your kitchen walls. But you need to quell that impulse and direct your energies instead to the much more urgent task of finding a good plumber who can show up on short notice.

- **Recently I decided to get a Whopper with cheese at 6:30 a.m. While driving, I dropped my cheeseburger and rear-ended someone at a stoplight.**

Who among us hasn't had the urge to consume processed meat in the wee hours? "Have it your way" indeed, anonymous survey taker. I hope that after you had a good chuckle at the absurdity of your predicament, you swiftly and responsibly checked both cars for damage and, if necessary, contacted the respective insurance companies. I also hope you went back for a replacement Whopper. You'll need your strength to explain to your boss why you're an hour late to work and covered in special sauce.

- **My best friend is pissed at me.**

Is it because you spilled red wine on that bridesmaid dress she so lovingly selected a year ago and in which you now resemble a lilac taffeta sausage? No? Okay, well, whatever the reason is, run a quick assessment of what you may need to apologize for and how soon you can fit that into your busy schedule of reading profane self-help books. If you're in the wrong and your RIO is to remain besties, then get on with it. Or if this incident provides you a convenient path toward dialing back your and Marsha's codependent tendencies, that's fine too. See who blinks first.

- **I've had to go on a severely limited diet due to health issues.**

Remember when I said that everything that's going on in your life sucks exactly as hard as you think it does, and that I'll never be the one to tell you "It's going to be okay" or "Aw, it's not so bad?"

WELL, CONSIDER ME A WOMAN OF MY MOTHER-FUCKING *WORD*.

If you're going down this road, you have my deepest sympathies. And please know that by taking a logical look at the problem I am in no way invalidating your emotional distress. Dietary restrictions are awful and shitty. They rob us of one of the greatest of life's pleasures and are often onerous and expensive to follow through on. Suckage of the highest order.

> FUN FACT: In my anonymous survey I asked "Do you hate it when something bad happens and people tell you 'Everything's going to be okay?'" 77.4 percent of respondents answered "Yes, that bugs the shit out of me."

Calming the fuck down will be challenging, but you do have some fancy new tools now to help you get started. Can you plot revenge on gluten? I don't see why not.

Dealing with it will be a combo of planning ahead and in-the-moment coping when faced with a brunch menu, passed hors d'oeuvres, or a hospital cafeteria. Besides traveling everywhere with appropriate snacks, what do you do? Take stock: What's on offer and what won't aggravate your condition? Realistic ideal outcome: Getting enough to eat and not getting sick. Triage: Depending on your situation, this may be the time to deploy your pocket snacks to ensure you don't get hangry, then seek out a waiter to ask about ingredients and substitutions. Also, for what it's worth, I've heard oat milk is nice.

Really Heavy Shit

Oof. To be honest, I've been dreading this part ever since I started writing *Calm the Fuck Down* — not because it's chock-full of the stuff of nightmares (although, that too), but because I'm apprehensive about claiming to be an authority on dealing with the absolute worst that life has to offer. It's a lot of responsibility for a potty-mouthed anti-guru, and while I have experienced some really heavy shit in my time, I've by no means cornered the market.

The problems I'll be addressing in the last segment of our

lightning round are among the most painful and difficult — if not impossible — for anyone to solve. In most cases I doubt they're even the problems you came to *Calm the Fuck Down* for help with; certainly there are more thorough tomes written by more qualified persons than me on subjects like divorce, disease, and death that you could lay your hands on if you were so inclined.*

As you read this section, you may wonder who the fuck I think I am to tell *you* how to cope with your marriage falling apart or prep for chemotherapy. What right do I have to natter on about the productive aftermath of a home invasion or getting through the emotionally and physically devastating trials of infertility? Not to mention advising you re: nuclear fallout and bedbugs, two things with which I have exactly zero experience. (So far, at least. Thanks Obama!)

You're entitled to wonder these things. As I said, I've wondered them too. But I believe in the power of the NoWorries Method to help you even in your darkest moments, precisely **because it's a different way to look at those dark moments than you may be used to getting from friends and family, or even from your therapist.**

Which is to say that if you find the next few pages of advice brutally pragmatic and emotionless — well, that's kind of the point.

I wrote *Calm the Fuck Down* in service to the notion that nobody else in your life is giving you brutally pragmatic, emotionless advice

---

* There definitely are.

about your anxiety and stress and problems because they're too busy telling you EVERYTHING IS GOING TO BE OKAY and glossing over the nuts and bolts of exactly how to get there.

And much like 77.4 percent of my survey respondents, that bugs the shit out of me.

That said, my suggestions for dealing with your really heavy shit come with the same qualifier I've supplied a few times in this book: **anxiety, panic, depression, and trauma may be candidates for the NoWorries treatment, but they are also NoJoke.** If you are going through any of the stuff I'm about to give a pithy paragraph's worth of advice on dealing with, it would mean a lot to me if you would *also* talk to a professional about what you can do to feel better and move forward, okay?

Thank you in advance for humoring me.

With that, we enter the third and final phase of total shit-storms: a catalogue of terror. If the first of these sections was like easing into a warm bath, this one is more like waking up in a tub full of ice and discovering you're down a kidney.

And although I don't necessarily have all the answers, hopefully I can get you pointed in the right fucking direction.

Meow.

- **I got robbed.**

Whether your pocket was picked, your safe was cracked, or your car was jacked, you're bound to be spooked. And depending on the thieves' haul, you could be a little or a lot inconvenienced. Throw in any grievous bodily harm and we've got a trifecta of shit to deal with — and that's AFTER you've managed to calm the fuck down. But solely in terms of dealing with it — first, secure your personal safety. Call the cops. Think you might be concussed? Call an ambulance.

A friend of mine's house was robbed recently, with his kids in it. He was meant to be performing in a concert that night, but instead he bailed on the gig, got the bashed-in front door boarded up, and stood guard over his family until morning.

Priorities, pals. Priorities.

You can apply the same triage process to getting reimbursed for the things you lost, and replacing the most urgent ones first, if you can afford it and/or your insurance comes through.

NOTE: If you meant "I got robbed" in the sense that your Pork Niblets came in first runner-up in the Elks' Club Annual Smoked Meat Challenge, that belongs a few pages back in the catalogue. Next time, may I suggest smoking an actual elk? TV food show judges always give extra points for adherence to theme. Couldn't hurt.

You should also start making the rounds of "So *this* happened." By that I mean — tell people what's up, so they can help you out or at least assuage some of your more pressing concerns. For example, if you've got a deadline looming, you'll feel a million-and-two percent better once you inform whomever needs informing that your laptop was stolen and they undoubtedly grant you an extension, because whomever they are is not an asshole.

This is a terrible, awful, no-good, very bad situation — no doubt about it — but neither a prolonged freakout nor a haphazard effort at dealing with it is going to help you salvage your shit. Take stock, identify your ideal outcome, and then pursue it one concentrated, most-urgent step at a time.

• I'm getting divorced.

This could be happening *to* you or it could be at your behest, but either way it's probably awful for all concerned. I'm not trying to minimize the emotional turmoil you're going through when I say "One thing you could do is get logical and prioritize."

But, um, maybe give it a shot?

If divorce is in the offing and there's nothing more you can do to stop your marriage from dissolving, now's a good time to focus on what you *can* control and on achieving your realistic ideal outcome. Maybe that RIO is to part ways as amicably as possible. Maybe it's to get the house, the cars, and full custody of the Instant Pot. Maybe it's just to get through the whole process without letting your kids see you cry. It won't be easy, but if you can crate your emotional puppies — for short stretches, even — in service to those concrete goals, at least you'll be "dealing with it" in a more productive way.

Plus: lamb tagine in just thirty-five minutes!

- **We're struggling to have a baby.**

Jesus, I'm sorry. I told you it was about to get dark up in this piece.

I know virtually nothing about pregnancy except that I never want to experience it, which probably makes me the least-qualified guru, anti- or otherwise, to field advice on this topic. In fact, I'm reminded of a conversation I had with a dear friend several years ago, well before I developed the NoWorries Method. She and her husband had been trying and failing to conceive for a long time, and over a plate of Middle Eastern apps I confidently told her "It'll be okay. I'm sure you guys will work it out." (In the spirit of full disclosure, I *may* have even said something along the lines of "You just need to relax.")

In other words, I responded in the EXACT WRONG WAY. The look on her face was part misery, part second-degree murder.

Admittedly, it's possible that I'm about to overcompensate in the other direction, but in for a penny, in for a round of IVF, amirite?* If you're experiencing that same mix of anguish and anger at your circumstances as my friend was, I wonder now — *very respectfully* — if it might help to crate your emuppies for a little while and send the logicats out to do recon.

---

* Yes, I know I'm pushing my luck here. It's part of my charm.

Take a deep breath and take stock: Where are you in terms of your or your partner's child-bearing years? Where are you in the process of trying? Have you done everything you can or are there still stones left unturned? How much more time, energy, and money can you afford to spend?

After confronting these questions, you may not have the answers you *want,* and you will almost surely still be sad and angry—but at least you'll have some clarity about where you stand and what your options are for moving forward.

Clarity is good.

Whatever remains *realistic and ideal* for you is where you can continue to spend time, energy, and money in a productive way—whether it's to keep doing what you're doing, or to look into alternatives. In this way, you're working hard and smart toward reaching your goal of becoming a parent, and you can feel good about that even when you can't help but feel bad about the parts of the process you simply can't control.

If you're dealing with this, I know you've been through the fucking wringer, as have so many of my friends and family. And I know that a rational approach might seem devoid of empathy. But it also might help you to accept where you are and get to where you want to be.

- **France has run out of butter.**

FACT: There was a butter shortage in French supermarkets in late 2017 and I'm not going to say it caused me heart palpitations when I read the headlines but I'm not going to say it didn't, either. Stay vigilant out there, people. If it happens again you'll need to bone up on best hoarding practices *tout de suite*. (And if you think this qualifies as merely "tedious" shit, then you, Monsieur, have never eaten a decent croissant.)

- **A natural disaster just hit.**

I riffed a little on hurricanes earlier in the book, but you've also got your tornados, floods, wildfires, volcanic eruptions, earthquakes, and—the star of my most terrifying nightmares—tsunamis. I hesitate to make generalizations (let alone jokes) about this stuff when my husband's family lived through Hurricane Katrina; my friend's mom lost her home to Harvey; and just the other day, an earthquake 300 miles away rumbled our house, causing the couch I was sitting on to vibrate like a by-the-hour hotel bed—and killing at least fifteen people at its epicenter in Haiti. This shit is fucked up. But if you are lucky enough to wake up the morning after a megacalamity and you still have breath in your lungs, well, you are knee-deep in dealing with it. And before you can hope to achieve a Full Fix or get started on some Salvage Jobs, you'll be starting from a place of Basic Survival. Water, food, shelter. You need 'em, so it's time to find 'em.

But you know that. This is really just me giving voice to your lizard brain, reminding you that your instincts for preserving your personal safety are in and of themselves your best blueprint for "dealing with it."

- **I was diagnosed with [insert something terrible].**

Folks, I've already accepted the reality that come publication, I will be savaged by no small number of readers accusing me of playing fast and loose with tragedy, travesty, and heartbreak. All I can say is, the book isn't called *Feel Better Sweetie, This Too Shall Pass.*

As I have stressed repeatedly, and undoubtedly to my editor's [though not to the legal department's] irritation, I AM NOT A DOCTOR. I'm not an expert in anything, really, unless you count "hating the New York Yankees with a fiery passion." In these very pages I have admitted that anxiety, panic, and ostriching are my own instinctual coping mechanisms and that I often rely on the wonder of prescription pharmaceuticals to calibrate my freakout-prone brain and body.

And yet, also in these very pages, I've tried to show that it's possible to calm the fuck down and deal with things in a more effective, efficient way than by remaining committed to the anxious, sad, angry, avoid-y, flailing processes you and I have both heretofore "enjoyed."

With regard to a major-league health problem, I harbor no illusions that either one of us could just calmly accept something like a chronic or — dear God — potentially fatal illness. But personally, I would try really, really hard to do as much productive, helpful, effective worrying as I could.

Also, who are we kidding? I would ugly-cry, emotionally eat, and request a medical marijuana prescription, stat.

- **Nuclear war just broke out.**

HAHAHAHAHAHA. I know when I'm beat.

- **Bedbugs.**

I've never had bedbugs, but my friends did and their lives became a months-long blur of toxic chemicals, mattress bags, and dry cleaning receipts. Maybe I can get them to do a guest post on my website. Stay tuned.

Meanwhile, I can tell you that we had termites last year and I'm proud to say I bypassed freaking out entirely. Once we discovered their happy little piles of "frass"* collecting in the closet under the stairs, I went into the Deal With It *Zone,* I

---

* The technical term for termite poop. Maybe you'll win a game of Trivial Pursuit with it someday.

tell you. Vacuumed up the leavings, removed all the food and dishes and contaminable shit from the house, called an exterminator to fumigate, then stripped every stitch of treated fabric and had it laundered. Twice. Then, advised by the exterminator to go the extra and deeply annoying step of removing the affected wood entirely—which would require rebuilding said closet under the stairs—said HELL YES GIT 'ER DONE. A week later we were footloose and frass-free.

Those motherfuckers never saw me coming.

• Death.

You've probably been wondering when I was going to get to death. Not hamster or cat death, either, but full-blown human-beings-ceasing-to-be. You've been whiling away the hours, waiting for me to walk out into the mother of all shitstorms, wondering how—just exactly *how*—Little Miss Anti-Guru proposes to *calm the fuck down about* and *deal with* D-E-A-T-H.

And maybe I should've stopped short of including this section, to avoid tarnishing what precious authority and goodwill I've earned thus far. But we all have to deal with death eventually—our own or the mortality of our loved ones—and ignoring that would make me either willfully ignorant or a dirty rotten cheater, neither of which I'd want as my epitaph. Additionally, I think about death ALL THE

TIME, so I might as well exploit my own overactive imagination for fun and profit.

To get the full effect, let's back up a bit to Shit That Hasn't Happened Yet and talk about anxiety over the mere *prospect* of death.

For me, this is the Mother of Tarantulas. It's where almost all of my smaller anxieties lead—like, *I just saw the bus driver yawn* easily metastasizes into *what if we die in a highway pileup and my parents have to clean out our house which means my night table drawer which means...uh oh.* Then once I get that far, there's nowhere worse to go. It winds up being a relief to stare this terrifying what-if directly in the kisser so I can defang it with my trusty CTFD toolkit and move on.

Yawning bus drivers? Think about *probability.* This guy drives the 7:00 a.m. route between New York and Maine five days a week. He's entitled to be a little tired, but this is not his first rodeo and he's packing a 20-ounce Americano with sugar, so.

A heavily reported article by a trusted news source that predicts the world will become uninhabitable by 2040? Ask: *Is this something I can control?* I accept what I can't change about this situation (most of it) and turn my focus to what I can (vote for legislators who believe in climate science, reduce my own carbon footprint, move further inland in ten years). I discard. I organize. I calm the fuck down. Again, I'm not going to claim it *always* works; anxiety, panic, and despondence are bad enough — when you add pain and suffering to the mix, you can get overwhelmed fast. But these techniques do work for me *a lot* of the time, and that's way better than *never*.

Someone I know is terminally ill or inching ever closer to simply terminally old? Acknowledge the *inevitability*. This Category 5 is already formed; it's going to be excruciating when I have to face it, so why torture myself when I don't yet? When I'm gripped by the pointy little teeth of these particular emotional puppies, I pry them loose — logically, rationally, and methodically. I bargain with myself. I'll avoid freaking out about this now, and focus on something I *can* control — like picking up the phone and calling my ailing friend or grandmother — before the day comes that I have to take my fine feathered head out of the sand to mourn them. That these mental negotiations actually succeed in tamping down my anxious flare-ups is almost as much of a miracle as someone beating stage-five cancer. I think that alone renders them worthy of your consideration.

But, of course, there's also the kind of death you don't see coming. The sudden, unpredictable, unfathomable news that takes you from anxious worrying to devastating reality: Shit That Has Already Happened. I could try to soften the blow by saying I hope you never have reason to take my advice on this front, but we both know you will, and insincerity is not my forte.

So when that total shitstorm lands, how do you deal with it?

My doctor once told me that a sense of injustice is one of the biggest triggers of anxiety and panic, and I can think of no greater injustice than the death of someone you love, whether anticipated or unexpected. When it happens, you're likely to experience a range of prolonged, chaotic emotions. Sadness, certainly. Even rage. But while depression and anger are among the five stages of grief made famous in Elisabeth Kübler-Ross's seminal book *On Death and Dying,* I will also gently point out that acceptance is the final stage.

And by now, you know a little something about finding your way there. Not necessarily to accepting the outcome itself, but simply accepting the *reality of it,* enabling you to move through it, past it, and on with *your* life.

I've been there — getting the call, crying for hours, stumbling through days, wondering if anything would ever hurt more or if this would ever hurt less — and in those moments, I remind myself that I'll get to acceptance someday because *this is what humans do.* None of us live forever, which means that every day, whether we know it or not, we encounter someone in the process of surviving someone else's death. For me in recent years it's been a friend who lost her brother, a colleague who lost his husband, and each member of my family who lost in one man their partner, father, sibling, uncle, and grandfather. Watching all of them get through their days and move forward with their lives shows me that it's possible to do the same.

It won't be easy and it's going to hurt like all fuck, but it's possible.

And where do you go from there? Apart from grief, which is nearly impossible to control with anything other than the march of time, what are the practicalities of "dealing with" death? Often, we inherit responsibilities such as organizing a funeral, emptying a loved one's house, or executing a will. And morbid though these tasks are, in some ways they can also be helpful. In addressing them, you'll recognize elements of sleight of mind — such as refocusing your foggy brain on detail-oriented plans that require all logicians on deck, or occupying your wringing hands on mindless chores that allow you to zone out for a little while.

At some point, you'll have been practicing calming the fuck down without realizing it. And once you experience the benefit of that a few times, you may even get better at doing it on purpose.

However, and as Kübler-Ross describes it, grieving is a nonlinear process. You may feel better one day and far worse the next. I'm not saying it will be okay. But it will *be*. As the one left behind, you're in charge of what that means for you.

And just remember: anytime you need to let those emotional puppies run free, you've got the keys to the crate. There's no shame in using them.

Woof.

Over to you, Bob

Whoa. That was intense.

But...would you agree that the catalogue of terror becomes a little less scary and a little-to-a-lot more manageable when you confront each entry rationally instead of emotionally, with a pragmatic outlook on outcomes?

And that these techniques can actually be applied across a pretty wide range of what-ifs and worries?

I hope so.

Calm the Fuck Down was always intended to offer you one set of tools for all kinds of problems. I mean, despite my relatively low-impact tropical existence, it's not like I had the time or wherewithal to write a book that covers every possible iteration of all the shit that might and/or probably will happen to every single reader, and how to handle it.

But you don't need that book anyway.

What you need is a mental toolkit that you can *apply* to every possible iteration of all the shit that might and/or probably will happen to you.

That, I think I have provided. And in just a moment, it will be time to let you flex your brand-new decision-making, problem-solving skills in a ski-jump finish worthy of our old friend, Italian superhunk Alberto Tomba.

Before you turn the page, though, I just want to say two more things:

1. I have faith in you.

2. Immediately following the next section, there's an epilogue on page 269. Don't forget to check it out for the final word on my own personal quest to calm the fuck down. It involves a feral cat, some coconut oil, and a shitstorm the probometer could never have predicted.

And now, onward to the next...ADVENTURE!

IV

CHOOSE YOUR OWN ADVENTURE:

When shit happens, how will *you* calm the fuck down and deal with it?

Part IV is going to be so much fun! In an effort to put everything I've taught you throughout *Calm the Fuck Down* into practice in one zany, interactive section, I'll present you with a totally plausible shitstorm and YOU get to react to and solve it your own damn self.

Ready?

Good. Because shit just *happened,* yo.

You're traveling far from home. Far enough that you had to fly, and for a duration long enough that you couldn't fit everything into a carry-on and had to check some luggage. Also, you're traveling for an occasion that required you to pack a few specific, very important items *in* your luggage. Now that luggage is lost somewhere between your point of origin and your final destination.

What was in your bag? Well, I want to make sure this whole Choose Your Own Adventure deal works for everyone, so let's say **you're missing one or more of the following:**

- An important article of clothing you are supposed to wear on this trip — such as your Spock ears for the Trekkie convention; a custom T-shirt for your BFF's birthday bonanza (I SHOWED UP AT RASHIDA'S 40TH AND ALL I GOT WAS PERIMENOPAUSE); a tuxedo for a work trip awards ceremony; or your lucky bowling shoes for the Northeastern Regional League Championships.

- Your favorite pajamas.

- A difficult-to-replace specialty item.
- All of your charging cords and cables. Every single one.
- The framed photo of your cat that you always travel with. (What? I would be shocked if not a *single* reader relates to this example.)
- A really great sex toy.

How do you react?

Hey, don't look at me. I don't know your life. But for the sake of this complicated gimmick I'm about to embark on, let's say your first instinct is to freak out. Pick whichever one of the Four Faces seems most likely to descend upon you in this time of extreme duress and shittiness, and then follow it on an illuminating adventure into calming the fuck down and dealing with it. (Or not, depending on which choices you make.)

Then, just to be thorough, pick another one and see it through.

Actually, you know what? Read 'em all. What the hell else do you have to do tonight?

Ready, set, FREAK OUT!

If you pick **ANXIOUS,** go to page 214.

If you pick **SAD,** go to page 250.

If you pick **ANGRY,** go to page 255.

If you pick **AVOIDANCE,** go to page 261.

You picked 😬 ANXIOUS

For what it's worth, I'm totally with you on this one. Although I do not know your life, I know *my* life — and if I'd lost every stitch of beachwear I'd brought with me to Bermuda for Spring Break '00, plus the copy of *The Odyssey* I was supposed to be studying for my world lit final, PLUS the Advil bottle full of weed that I forgot I had in my toiletry kit, I would have been seriously anxious. My potential tan and GPA in jeopardy, and, if they *did* locate my bag, the threat of a Bermudian SWAT team banging down my hotel room door — and me without my "calming herbs"? Yikes.

Back to you.

I totally understand why you're feeling anxious. But anxiety is not going to solve the Mystery of the Missing Luggage nor get your Spock ears and Magic Wand™ back in good working order. You need to calm the fuck down.

But how?

We went over this in part II. FOCUS, JIM!

Give anxiety the finger(s): Go to page 215.

Get down with O.P.P. (Other People's Problems): Go to page 216.

Nah, I'm just going to panic. Go to page 217.

You picked "Give anxiety the finger(s)."

As you'll recall, this coping mechanism finds you doing something constructive with your hands to give your brain a rest. Such as:

If you're standing at baggage claim being hypnotized into a panic attack by the rotations of an empty luggage carousel, you need to snap out of it. Why not literally? Try snapping your fingers a hundred times and when you're done, it's time to walk away.

Or, head to the nearest airport tchotchke shop and scope out their wares. If they sell stress balls — huzzah! — you're in business. But if not, buy a container of dental floss. While in the taxi en route to your hotel, unspool the whole thing and then play that Cat's Cradle game until your fingers bleed, minty fresh. There, now you have something different to worry about.

Finally, once you arrive at your hotel and it sinks in that your vibrator may never get out of Denver International — well, there are ways to lull yourself to sleep that don't require batteries. All hands on deck.

Whew. Feeling a little calmer, all things considered? Good, good. Would you like to give that second coping mechanism a whirl as well, or just go straight to dealing with it?

You know what? I think I will try "Getting down with O.P.P. (Other People's Problems)." Why the hell not? Lovely. Go to page 216.

I'm ready to deal with it! Go to page 218.

You elected to "Get down with O.P.P. (Other People's Problems)"

You're having a hard day, pookie. One way to distract from or make yourself feel better about your own problems is to focus on someone else's.

Like the lady with the screaming toddler who was sitting a few rows ahead of you. I bet she *wishes* that human vuvuzela was hanging out in Denver International Lost & Found right about now. Then there's the flight crew, who have the privilege of capping off an eight-hour shift by probing the crevices between every cushion on this two-hundred-seat airplane looking for crumbs, loose pretzels, and lost pacifiers. **BONUS:** If you're getting a taxi to the TrekFest convention hotel, this is the one and only time you may *want* to engage the driver in conversation by asking "Hey, what's the worst thing that happened to you this week? Tell me all about it!" In my experience with loquacious cabbies, your current predicament is likely to seem mild in comparison to tales of greedy landlords, student loan debt, stabby ex-wives, and "that time Eric Trump got a BJ in my backseat."

Feeling a little better? Oh come on — admit it, you temporarily forgot about your lost luggage as you pictured that poor cabdriver catching sight of Eric's O-face in the rearview mirror. That was all you needed — distraction with a side of schadenfreude. But if you want to go back and try giving anxiety the finger(s), feel free.

That was helpful, but I want to see what else you got. Go to page 215.

I'm ready to deal with it! Go to page 218.

Uh-oh, you decided to PANIC!

You're hyperventilating so hard you can barely explain to the desk agent why it is TERRIBLY URGENT that Delta retrieves your suitcase AS SOON AS POSSIBLE because you will NEVER BE ABLE TO GET A NEW PAIR OF CUSTOM-FIT SPOCK EARS DELIVERED IN TIME TO EMCEE TOMORROW'S BATTLE OF THE BANDS: "THE SEARCH FOR ROCK."

Friend, you are boldly going nowhere with this shit. Or as Spock himself might put it, "Your illogic and foolish emotions are a constant irritant." Are you absolutely sure you don't want to see what's happening over on the Flipside?

YES, YES I WOULD LIKE TO TRY GIVING ANXIETY THE FINGER(S), PLEASE. Good choice. Go to page 215.

I have erred. Please redirect me to "Getting down with O.P.P." In retrospect, that seems much more prudent than the course I have thus far taken. Go to page 216.

Fuck it. I've already wasted too much time. Take me straight to dealing with it. Go to page 226. (But don't say I didn't warn you...)

Dealing with it after you've calmed the fuck down (from ANXIETY)

My, how well you're holding up in this time of crisis! You're a beacon of hope and light to us all. You recognized the creeping Freakout Face and you resisted. You returned your heart rate to normal and staved off a full-blown panic attack, so now you can focus on solving (or at least mitigating) your problem in time to enjoy the rest of your trip. You've been looking forward to TrekFest for an entire year — now's the time to be *enterprising* in your efforts to deal with this shit.

TAKE STOCK:

You already know what you're missing. Now think about where you are and how easy/difficult it might be to shop for or order replacement gear, in whatever time you have to get that done. Ruminate, too, on your other resources. How much energy do you really want to expend running around an unfamiliar city all night when it's *possible* your bags will arrive on the early flight into Kansas City tomorrow? And how likely are you to find Spock ears on short notice? Furthermore, if you already tested the limits of your Amex card on the Fest tickets, you may not have a lot of spare cash (or credit) to replace all your AWOL electronics in one go. Survey the damage, assess the recovery potential, and then make some game-time decisions. You got this.

WHAT'S YOUR REALISTIC IDEAL OUTCOME?
PICK ONE:

RIO #1: Assuming your bags won't show up of their own volition, you want to make as many inquiries as you can, then get a good night's sleep and muster the will to carry on in the morning. Go to page 233.

RIO #2: The specialty items must be replaced ASAP; your whole trip is meaningless without them. Go to page 241.

Dealing with it after you've calmed the fuck down (from SADNESS)

My, how well you're holding up in this time of crisis! You're a beacon of hope and light to us all. You recognized the creeping Freakout Face and you resisted. You dried your tears, practiced some emergency self-care, and now you can focus on dealing with this shit and solving (or at least mitigating) your problem in time to enjoy the rest of your trip.

TAKE STOCK:

You already know what you're missing. Now think about where you are and how easy/difficult it might be to shop for or order replacement gear, in whatever time you have to get that done. Ruminate, too, on your other resources. How much energy do you really want to expend running around an unfamiliar town all night when it's *possible* your bags will arrive on the early flight tomorrow? (And if they don't, you're going to need all the energy you have to deal with Rashida when she finds out you lost the custom birthday T-shirt AND her gift.)

Evaluate your gumption levels! And your cash reserves: if you already tested the limits of your Amex card on the plane tickets, you may not have a lot of spare cash (or credit) to replace all your AWOL electronics. Survey the damage, assess the recovery potential, and then make some game-time decisions. You got this.

WHAT'S YOUR REALISTIC IDEAL OUTCOME? PICK ONE:

RIO #1: Assuming your bags won't show up of their own volition, you want to make as many inquiries as you can, then get a good night's sleep and muster the will to carry on tomorrow. Go to page 235.

RIO #2: The specialty items must be replaced ASAP; your whole trip is meaningless without them. Go to page 243.

Dealing with it after you've calmed the fuck down (from ANGER)

My, how well you're holding up in this time of crisis! You're a beacon of hope and light to us all. You recognized the creeping Freakout Face and you resisted. You channeled your energy into more fruitful, peaceful pursuits, and Mexican Airport Syndrome failed to claim another inmate. Now you can focus on dealing with this shit and solving (or at least mitigating) your problem in time to enjoy the rest of your trip. Though I suppose "enjoy" might be a strong word for it; this is a work conference and the best part about it is going to be the unlimited shrimp cocktail at the awards ceremony.

TAKE STOCK:

You already know what you're missing. Now think about where you are and how easy/difficult it might be to shop for or order replacement gear, in whatever time you have to get that done. Assuming you've landed in a city known to host conventions requiring formalwear, tuxedos probably aren't tough to rent, but ruminate, too, on your other resources. How much energy do you really want to expend running around an unfamiliar town all night when it's *possible* your bags will arrive on the early flight tomorrow? And if you already tested the limits of your corporate Amex this month, you probably shouldn't be using it to replace all your AWOL electronics — unless you're looking forward to a stern email from Helen in HR come Monday. Survey the damage, assess the recovery potential, and then make some game-time decisions. You got this.

WHAT'S YOUR REALISTIC IDEAL OUTCOME?
PICK ONE:

RIO #1: Assuming your bags won't show up of their own volition, you want to make as many inquiries as you can, then get a good night's sleep and muster the will to carry on tomorrow. Go to page 237.

RIO #2: The specialty items must be replaced ASAP; your whole trip is meaningless without them. Go to page 245.

Dealing with it after you've calmed the fuck down (from OSTRICH MODE)

My, how well you're holding up in this time of crisis! You're a beacon of hope and light to us all. You recognized the creeping Freakout Face and you resisted. You cast off your cloak of avoidance and actually managed to make some headway. Perhaps all is not lost (where "all" equals "your luggage"). Now you can focus on dealing with this shit and solving — or at least mitigating — your problem in time to kick the crap out of Reverend Paul from Pittsburgh and his team, the Holy Rollers.

TAKE STOCK:

You already know what you're missing. Now think about where you are and how easy/difficult it might be to shop for or order replacement gear, in whatever time you have to get that done. Ruminate, too, on your other resources. How much energy do you want to spend running around looking for a pair of KR Strikeforce size 11 Titans vs. holding in reserve for the tournament itself? And if you already tested the limits of your Amex card on three nights at the Econo Lodge, you may not have a lot of spare cash (or credit) to replace all your AWOL electronics *and* fancy shoes in one go. Survey the damage, assess the recovery potential, and then make some game-time decisions. You got this.

WHAT'S YOUR REALISTIC IDEAL OUTCOME?
PICK ONE:

RIO #1: Assuming your bags won't show up of their own volition, you want to make as many inquiries as you can, then get a good night's sleep and muster the will to carry on tomorrow. Go to page 239.

RIO #2: The specialty items must be replaced ASAP; your whole trip is meaningless without them. Go to page 247.

Dealing with it when you are FREAKING THE FUCK OUT (with ANXIETY)

This is so much harder than it had to be. Not only have you started to panic, your brain is now cycling through worst-case scenarios like that girl next to you at Flywheel last Sunday who was obviously working out her dating-life aggression on the bike. You're not just overwhelmed, you're OVERTHINKING — and this nemesis will *Klingon* to you for the duration of your trip. Look, I know that was an egregious pun, but you brought it on yourself.

TAKE STOCK:

Oh shit. You can't think clearly about any of this, can you? In fact, you've added a few new line items to the Captain's Log since you first discovered your bags wouldn't be joining you in Kansas City for TrekFest. For one, you posted your woes to the whole Slack group and now Cory from Indianapolis is gunning for your spot as emcee of tomorrow's festivities, and two, you ran down the battery of your phone in doing so, so your lack of charging cords is now just as critical as your lack of silicone ear tips.

WHAT'S YOUR REALISTIC IDEAL OUTCOME?

Before you freaked out, it would have been to call the only friend you have who has the right size ears and *isn't* at this convention using them himself, and beg him to get up and go to the nearest FedEx location to overnight them to you. (Pledging your firstborn Tribble in gratitude, of course.) But now that you've wasted a bunch of time FFs, Gordon is fast asleep, and—realistically—the best you can hope for is to buy a new cord, charge your phone overnight, and manage the fallout on Slack tomorrow while you prowl KC for Silly Putty and Super Glue.

Go to page 249.

Dealing with it when you are FREAKING THE FUCK OUT (with SADNESS)

This is so much harder than it had to be. Not only did you wear yourself out with all that crying, your makeup is a *shambles* and you're without your toiletry kit. Even if you felt like going out tonight, you look like Robert Smith after a tennis match in hot weather. And of course, that's cause for further wallowing. Why does this shit always happen to YOU? How come Brenda and Traci never lose THEIR luggage??

To top it all off, your phone battery died while you were posting a flurry of vague, sad memes intended to generate concern from your Facebook friends and now you can't even see who commented. God, this is so depressing.

TAKE STOCK:

Ugh. You'll *never* be able to replace the AMAZING birthday gift you had lined up for Rashida on such short notice. (The Je Joue Mio was for her.) At this point all you want to do is lie down on the bed and sleep this ruined weekend away. Except — *oh nooooo* — you just remembered you're in South Beach and your favorite jammies are lost somewhere over the Bermuda Triangle.

WHAT'S YOUR REALISTIC IDEAL OUTCOME?

Before you freaked out, it would have been to get your suitcase back at all costs, or at least squeeze Southwest for a free ticket — and barring that, get shoppin'! But now that you've wasted so many freakout funds sniffling, moaning, and vaguebooking, the best you can hope for is to call in depressed to welcome drinks and hope one of the girls can lend you an outfit for tomorrow. *If* you even feel like getting out of bed tomorrow, that is.

Go to page 254.

Dealing with it when you are FREAKING THE FUCK OUT (with ANGER)

God-fucking-*dammit*. It turns out that asinine comments and rude gestures neither win friends nor influence people at airport security. Thankfully you didn't get arrested, but your blood pressure is soaring, your mind is racing, and you're t-h-i-s-c-l-o-s-e to making a lifelong enemy of the United customer service helpline.

Also, you rage-ate a Big Mac and got yellow mustard all over the only shirt you currently possess. Smooth move, Mr. Hyde.

TAKE STOCK:

This whole situation got a lot more complicated when you decided to give in to your anger. Now you've got time-sensitive shit to deal with, you have to do damage control on that YouTube video, add another dress shirt to your shopping list, AND you can barely see straight, you're so agitated. (You may also want to think about how you're going to explain the video to Helen from HR when you see her at the awards banquet. It has 300,000 views and counting.)

WHAT'S YOUR REALISTIC IDEAL OUTCOME?

Before you wasted all that time, energy, money, and goodwill tarnishing both your shirt and your reputation, your RIO would have been to get to the hotel, plug in at the Business Center, put out a few feelers on the stuff you need to replace, and wind down with some Will Ferrell on Pay-Per-

View. However, realistically the best you can hope for now is to not get fired for conduct unbecoming a regional sales manager, and (if you're even still invited to the banquet) scoring a rental tux that doesn't smell like cheese.

Go to page 260.

Dealing with it when you are FREAKING THE FUCK OUT (via AVOIDANCE)

I'm afraid that the end result of succumbing to Ostrich Mode is that you NEVER, EVER DEAL WITH IT. Sorry, game over. Better luck next time.

However, if you decide to change your mind and take my advice to calm the fuck down *before* you try to deal with shit in the future, I recommend turning to page 262 or 264.

I also recommend reading this book over again, cover to cover, because — and I say this with love — I don't think you were paying attention the first time through.

> To choose a different adventure, go back to page 213.
> Or, skip ahead to the Epilogue on 269.

TrekFest

RIO #1: Assuming your bags won't show up of their own volition, you want to make as many inquiries as you can, then get a good night's sleep and muster the will to carry on in the morning.

TRIAGE AND TACKLE:

The most urgent element is to get through to a human being at the airline — ideally one in each of your departure and arrival cities — to lodge your complaint and ask if there are any other human beings who might be able to track down your bags and find a way to get them to you. It would be much better to be reunited with your custom Spock ears than to have to canvass Kansas City for a new pair.

If your phone battery is low, move "buy a new phone charger" up in the queue. If you're still at the airport, this should be easy. If you didn't manage to calm the fuck down until you were already outta there, that's okay — just ask your taxi driver to reroute to the nearest Target or comparable store and pay them to wait fifteen minutes while you perform a one-person version of *Supermarket Sweep,* grabbing the bare essentials off the shelves.

If you're driving a rental car or got picked up by a friend, this step is even easier. You'll have a bit more time and may be able to replace a few other lost items there too — as much as your energy and money FFs allow.

Plus your hotel probably has complimentary toiletries; for now, get the stuff that's only available in-store.

And if the only nearby shop is a gas station 7-Eleven, give it a shot — the teenage cashier is almost certainly charging their phone behind the counter and might be willing to sell you their cord at a markup. (If they sell Snickers bars, buy yourself a Snickers bar. You need it.)

AND THERE YOU HAVE IT!

Shit happened, but you calmed the fuck down, took stock of the situation, determined your realistic ideal outcome, and triaged the elements — and in doing so, set yourself up for the best-case scenario in this worst-case suitcase debacle. Winner, winner, Kansas City BBQ dinner.

To choose a different adventure, go back to page 213. Or, skip ahead to the Epilogue on 269.

Rashida's Birthday Bash

RIO #1: Assuming your bags won't show up of their own volition, you want to make as many inquiries as you can, then get a good night's sleep and muster the will to carry on tomorrow.

TRIAGE AND TACKLE:

The most urgent element is to get through to a human being at the airline — ideally one in each of your departure and arrival cities — to lodge your complaint and ask if there are any other human beings who might be able to track down your bags and find a way to get them to you. Life will be a LOT easier if Rashida never has to know how close you came to ruining her birthday photo op.

If your phone battery is low, move "buy a new phone charger" up in the queue. If you're still at the airport, this should be easy. If you didn't manage to calm the fuck down until you were already outta there, that's okay — just ask your taxi driver to reroute to the nearest Target or comparable store and pay them to wait fifteen minutes while you perform a one-person version of *Supermarket Sweep,* grabbing the bare essentials off the shelves.

If you're driving a rental car or got picked up by a friend, this step is even easier. You'll have a bit more time and may be able to replace a few other lost items there too — as much as your energy and money FFs allow.

Plus, your hotel probably has complimentary toiletries; for now, get the stuff that's only available in-store.

And if the only nearby shop is a gas station 7-Eleven, give it a shot—the teenage cashier is almost certainly charging their phone behind the counter and might be willing to sell you their cord at a markup. (If they sell Snickers bars, buy yourself a Snickers bar. You need it.)

AND THERE YOU HAVE IT!

Shit happened, but you calmed the fuck down, took stock of the situation, determined your realistic ideal outcome, and triaged the elements—and in doing so, set yourself up for the best-case scenario in this worst-case suitcase debacle. Winner, winner, Cuba libres with dinner.

To choose a different adventure, go back to page 213.
Or, skip ahead to the Epilogue on 269.

The Business Trip

RIO #1: Assuming your bags won't show up of their own volition, you want to make as many inquiries as you can, then get a good night's sleep and muster the will to carry on tomorrow.

TRIAGE AND TACKLE:

The most urgent element is to get through to a human being at the airline — ideally in each of your departure and arrival cities — to lodge your complaint and ask if there are any other human beings who might be able to track down your shit and get it delivered to you.

If your phone battery is low, move "buy a new phone charger" up in the queue. If you're still at the airport, this should be easy. If you didn't manage to calm the fuck down until you were already outta there, that's okay — just ask your taxi driver to reroute to the nearest Target or comparable store and pay them to wait fifteen minutes while you perform a one-person version of *Supermarket Sweep,* grabbing the bare essentials off the shelves.

(PSA: Don't forget underwear — if you end up having to wear a rented tux, you have no idea whose crotch has rubbed up inside that thing.)

If you're driving a rental car, this step is even easier. You'll have a bit more time and may be able to replace a few other lost items there too — as much as your energy and money FFs allow. Plus, your hotel probably has complimentary toiletries; for now, get the stuff that's only available in-store.

Finally, use your recharged phone to call your wife and ask her if she knows your jacket size, because you sure don't.

AND THERE YOU HAVE IT!

Shit happened, but you calmed the fuck down, took stock of the situation, determined your realistic ideal outcome, and triaged the elements — and in doing so, set yourself up for the best-case scenario in this worst-case suitcase debacle. Winner, winner, room service dinner.

To choose a different adventure, go back to page 213.
Or, skip ahead to the Epilogue on 269.

Northeastern Regionals

RIO #1: Assuming your bags won't show up of their own volition, you want to make as many inquiries as you can, then get a good night's sleep and muster the will to carry on in the morning.

TRIAGE AND TACKLE:

The most urgent element is to get through to a human being at the airline — ideally one in each of your departure and arrival cities — to lodge your complaint and ask if there are any other human beings who might be able to track down your bags and get them to you.

If your phone battery is low, move "buy a new phone charger" up in the queue. If you're still at the airport, this should be easy. If you didn't manage to calm the fuck down until you were already outta there, that's okay — just ask your taxi driver to reroute to the nearest Target or comparable store and pay them to wait fifteen minutes while you perform a one-person version of *Supermarket Sweep,* grabbing the bare essentials off the shelves.

If you're driving a rental car or got picked up by a friend, this step is even easier. You'll have a bit more time and may be able to replace a few other lost items there too — as much as your energy and money FFs allow. I wouldn't count on the Econo Lodge having complimentary toiletries, so don't forget the toothpaste and deodorant.

And, rural though it may be, if this town is hosting the Northeastern Regionals, they probably have a decent bowling shoe store. Google it now and hoof it over there first thing tomorrow. (And make sure you pick up clean socks at Target; you don't need to add athlete's foot to your list of shit to deal with.)

AND THERE YOU HAVE IT!

Shit happened, but you calmed the fuck down, took stock of the situation, determined your realistic ideal outcome, and triaged the elements — and in doing so, set yourself up for the best-case scenario in this worst-case suitcase debacle. Winner, winner, cheesesteak dinner.

To choose a different adventure, go back to page 213.
Or, skip ahead to the Epilogue on 269.

TrekFest

RIO #2: The specialty items must be replaced ASAP; your whole trip is meaningless without them.

TRIAGE AND TACKLE:

You have zero faith in the airline to straighten this out in a timely fashion, so rather than waste precious hours (and battery life) on the horn to Customer Service, you make a list of the most urgent, replaceable items in your suitcase and a plan to acquire them.

For example:

Chargers first — Good luck finding your way around without the official convention app. You'll be drifting through Bartle Hall Convention Center like one of Wesley Crusher's neutrinos.

Spock ears — Your best bet is probably to hop on the TrekFest Slack channel and ask if anyone brought spares (for which you still need internet connectivity, hence a charged phone/laptop).

Febreze — Luckily, you wore your Federation blues on the plane, but they could use a little freshening up before you put them on again tomorrow.

Too bad about your favorite pj's and that cat pic, but you can sleep naked, and now that your phone is charged, you can FaceTime the cat-sitter to say hi to Chairman Meow when you wake up tomorrow. Just keep the sheets pulled up tight; the Chairman doesn't need to see all that.

CONGRATS!

Shit happened, but you calmed the fuck down, took stock of the situation, determined your realistic ideal outcome, and triaged the elements — and in doing so, set yourself up for the best-case scenario in this worst-case suitcase debacle. Live long and prosper.

To choose a different adventure, go back to page 213. Or, skip ahead to the Epilogue on 269.

Rashida's Birthday Bash

RIO #2: The specialty items must be replaced ASAP; your whole trip is meaningless without them.

TRIAGE AND TACKLE:

You have zero faith in the airline to straighten this out in a timely fashion, so rather than waste precious hours (and battery life) on the horn to Customer Service, you make a list of the most urgent, replaceable items in your suitcase and a plan to acquire them. For example:

> **Chargers first** — This whole debacle basically *exists* to be chronicled on Instagram Stories.
>
> **Rashida's birthday gift** — You're already going to be in trouble for misplacing your party T-shirt; they're all going to think you made up the whole "lost luggage" story just to get out of wearing it — which, come to think of it... Well, anyway, you CANNOT show up empty-handed. The Je Joue Mio was for her, by the way, so that's one more reason to get your smartphone up and running — you'll need to find the closest sex shop *and* summon a Lyft to get you there.
>
> **Next stop: the mall** — At a bare minimum, you need a party dress and a pair of shoes; the Uggs you wore on the flight won't cut it. Depending on how much those and the replacement gift run you,

you might try to pick up a cheap bikini and a sundress to get you through the weekend. The hotel will have toiletries, but don't forget to buy sunscreen. Skin care is important.

It's too bad about your pj's; that twenty-four-year-old shirt was the longest, most faithful relationship you've had. Oh well, with your new dress and attitude adjustment, maybe you'll meet another twenty-four-year-old this weekend who can take your mind off it.

CONGRATS!

Shit happened, but you calmed the fuck down, took stock of the situation, determined your realistic ideal outcome, and triaged the elements — and in doing so, set yourself up for the best-case scenario in this worst-case suitcase debacle. Margaritas on me!

To choose a different adventure, go back to page 213. Or, skip ahead to the Epilogue on 269.

The Business Trip

RIO #2: The specialty items must be replaced ASAP; your whole trip is meaningless without them.

You have zero faith in the airline to straighten this out in a timely fashion, so rather than waste precious hours (and battery life) on the horn to Customer Service, you make a list of the most urgent, replaceable items in your suitcase and a plan to acquire them. For example:

Chargers first — It's not just your phone; your laptop cord was in that suitcase too, and if you don't get up and running soon, your boss will see to it that you get the business end of this business trip.

Specialty item #1 — If you can't find a replacement ugly Lucite statue thingy, what are you going to stare at on Helen's desk during your extremely awkward exit interview?

Specialty item #2 — Assuming you manage to source the award, you're going to have to bring it with you to the black-tie dinner in Ballroom A, for which you need a temporary tuxedo and all the trimmings.

Sadly, the awesome martini-glasses bow tie and olive cuff links you packed are MIA, so you'll have to make do with standard-issue rentals.

On the bright side, this will make it easier to blend into the crowd while you drown your lost-suitcase sorrows in unlimited shrimp cocktail.

CONGRATS!

Shit happened, but you calmed the fuck down, took stock of the situation, determined your realistic ideal outcome, and triaged the elements — and in doing so, set yourself up for the best-case scenario in this worst-case suitcase debacle. Helen from HR would be proud.

To choose a different adventure, go back to page 213. Or, skip ahead to the Epilogue on 269.

Northeastern Regionals

RIO #2: The specialty items must be replaced ASAP; your whole trip is meaningless without them.

TRIAGE AND TACKLE:

You have zero faith in the airline to straighten this out in a timely fashion, so — newly invigorated — and rather than waste precious hours (and battery life) on the horn to Customer Service, you make a list of the most urgent, replaceable items in your suitcase and a plan to acquire them.

For example:

Chargers first — You'll be even more helpless trying to navigate rural Pennsylvania without Google Maps.

Bowling shoes — You're unlikely to find another pair as loyal and lucky as the ones you packed, but it's against league rules to bowl barefoot, and you're not leaving your fate as the Hook Ball King to a set of rentals.

The team mascot — "Strike" the taxidermied rattlesnake joins you at every road tournament, and it was your turn to pack her. (Come to think of it, it's possible your bag has been confiscated by airport authorities for this very reason.) To be honest, you're unlikely to solve this problem — but at least you're no longer trying to pretend it never happened. Strike deserves better than that.

You're still down your favorite pj's, but if you win this weekend, the prize money will more than cover a new set of Dude-inspired sleepwear.

CONGRATS!

Shit happened, but you calmed the fuck down, took stock of the situation, determined your realistic ideal outcome, and triaged the elements — and in doing so, set yourself up for the best-case scenario in this worst-case suitcase debacle. Doesn't it feel good to abide?

To choose a different adventure, go back to page 213. Or, skip ahead to the Epilogue on 269.

TrekFest

RIO #3: Silly Putty and Super Glue

Neither desperation nor silicone polymers are a good look for anyone. It may be time to admit defeat, cede your emcee duties to Cory from Indianapolis, and focus your dwindling freakout funds on getting a good night's sleep. If nothing else, you want to be well rested for the Holodeck Hoedown on Sunday.

Oh, and if you decide you want to take my advice and calm the fuck down *before* you try to deal with shit next time, please feel free to revert to pages 215 or 216.

As a wise Vulcan once said, change is the essential process of all existence.

To choose a different adventure, go back to page 213.
Or, skip ahead to the Epilogue on 269.

You picked 😢 SAD

I know, this is a real blow — especially after you just spent two hours watching *Lion* on the plane. People might think you're sobbing at baggage claim because of that final scene, but really it's because tears are your go-to reaction when shit happens. It's cool. We all have our tells; some of them are just more mucusy than others.

So what exactly was in your bag, the loss of which has brought on the waterworks? Among other things, that "I Showed Up at Rashida's 40th and All I Got Was Perimenopause" T-shirt is going to be tough to replace. And your favorite pajamas? I sense another sob session coming on. And I fully support a quick confab with the emotional puppies, but if you have any hope of salvaging this trip (and maybe being reunited with your Samsonite), now you need to crate 'em up and calm the fuck down.

Bu-bu-bu-but h-h-how?

We need to reboot your mood. Choose one of the self-care techniques from pages 112 and 113 and see where it takes you.

Laughter is the best medicine. Go to page 251.

You're in for a treat. Go to page 252.

Nah, I'm just going to wallow. Suit yourself. Go to page 253.

You picked "Laughter is the best medicine."

On the face of it, there is nothing funny about the pickle in which you find yourself — and far be it from me to make light of your situation in an effort to cheer you up — but…might it be just a *teensy* bit amusing to think about the look on the face of the insurance adjuster who has to Google a "Je Joue Mio" in order to approve your claim?

When you realized the baggage carousel was empty, your mind leapt immediately to that Hard Rock Daytona Beach XXL T-shirt you've been sleeping in since 1994. You got a little choked up, sure. But I suggest digging a little deeper, and recalling the story *behind* the shirt? THAT might bring a smile to your face.

Now take a deep breath. Connect to the airport Wi-Fi. Go to YouTube and search for the following:

"Hey cat. Hey."

"Alan, Alan, Alan."

"Dogs: 1 Nash: 0"

(If none of these do it for you, I give up. You're dead inside.)

Alright, feeling a smidge better? Did you, at the very least, stop crying? Good. Baby steps. Now, would you like to give that other coping mechanism a shot to help you calm down even more — or just go straight to dealing with it?

It probably wouldn't hurt to get yet more calm. Go to page 252.

I feel like I can deal with it now. Go to page 220.

You picked "You're in for a treat."

This would be my go-to as well. I don't know what it is about stress or feeling sad that makes me want to engage in some balls-to-the-wall emotional eating, drinking, and shopping, but there you have it, sports fans — if I'm leaving the airport without my suitcase, I'm ALSO leaving it with three Cinnabons, a novelty shot glass, and the latest *Us Weekly*.

Furthermore, there are worse places to hang out for an hour while the Southwest rep "double-checks the baggage carts" than an airport bar/restaurant that serves alcohol, dessert, and alcoholic dessert. A Baileys-infused Brownie Sundae never hurt nobody. If you're teetotal, or if savory treats are more your bag, I have it on good authority that at any given time an airport contains more Cheddar Cheese Pretzel Combos than you are capable of eating. I smell a challenge!

And think about it this way: on one hand, if your bag doesn't materialize, you'll be the odd woman out at Rashida's birthday party. But on the other hand, you have an excuse to shop for a sexy replacement outfit, and while everyone else is wearing their PERIMENOPAUSE tees, you'll be — as Robin Thicke maintains — "the hottest bitch in this place."

Smiling yet? I hope so. But if you want to get additional self-care on, there's more where this came from — or you can go straight to dealing with it. Your choice.

I am feeling better, but I could still use a laugh. Go to page 251.

I'm ready to deal with it! Go to page 220.

You decided to WALLOW...

Did you hear that? I think it was a sad trombone. This doesn't bode well for your vacation.

You moped through the taxi line, did the "Woe Is Me" dance up to your hotel room, and are considering skipping Rashida's welcome drinks to sit on your bed and cry into the minibar, waiting for Southwest to call. Right now, you're more focused on feeling sorry for yourself than you are on enjoying the girls' weekend you spent good money on (not to mention got waxed for). I'd tell you to snap out of it, but you already sealed your fate when you turned to this page.

Can we all agree that this is no way to fly? Are you *sure* you wouldn't like to see what's happening over on the Flipside?

I know when I'm beat. Gimme some of that "laughter is the best medicine" shit. It's got to be better than this. Word. Go to page 251.

Yes, I would like to try the treats. You won't be sorry. Go to page 252.

Nope, I'm a martyr for the cause. Time to deal with it. Go to page 228.

Rashida's Birthday Bash

RIO #3: Call in depressed to welcome drinks and hope one of the girls can lend you an outfit for tomorrow.

Well, that's just sad. If you were going to let something like lost luggage send you this deep into the doldrums, I'm not sure you ever had a fighting chance. If, someday, you get tired of being so easily brought to tears and wish to instead calm the fuck down *before* you try to deal with shit — and then, you know, actually deal with it — I humbly direct you to pages 251 or 252.

Or — and this is a novel idea! — you might just want to reread the whole book. A little refresher course never hurt anyone.

To choose a different adventure, go back to page 213.
Or, skip ahead to the Epilogue on 269.

You picked 😠 ANGRY

Simmer down there, Hulk Hogan. I know you're upset, but ramming your [empty] luggage cart into a wall is not going to win you any points with airport security.

What exactly was in your bag that's worth the scene you're about to cause at the United Help Desk? Are you really getting this worked up over a tuxedo for a work trip awards ceremony? Ah, or is it because you were in charge of transporting Helen from HR's lifetime achievement award to this annual shareholders' meeting and now you need a replacement ugly Lucite statue thingy by 5:00 p.m. Thursday?

Gotcha. This is bullshit. You were literally the first one at the gate for this flight — how the fuck did they lose your *and only your* bag? I don't know. But I do know this: you need to calm the fuck down.

Oh yeah? And how the hell am I supposed to do that?

Well, you have a couple of options, both of which I outlined on pages 114–115 of this very book. Pick one.

Work it out. Go to page 256. (And maybe do some stretches first.)

Plot your revenge. Go to page 257.

Actually, I've been looking for an excuse to punch a wall. Suit yourself. Go to page 259.

You decided to work it out!

Good choice. And although Terminal B at LaGuardia is probably not the *most* opportune place to do a naked cartwheel, there do happen to be endless roomy corridors in which you could hop, skip, or jump your way to calming the fuck down.

Or you could try walking in the wrong direction on one of those people movers. It might get you some dirty looks from your fellow travelers, but at this point, they're lucky they're not getting far worse from you. In addition to physical exertion, this activity requires focus and coordination—two more things that are better employed in service of calming down than they are directed from your fist to the face of the United rep who is wholly blameless but unlucky enough to be on duty tonight.

Now, with the remaining charge left on your phone (why you didn't pack your chargers in your carry-on, I'll never understand, but we'll deal with that later), may I suggest locating the nearest restroom, locking yourself in a stall, and completing a ten-minute meditation app before you continue on with your evening?

You're getting there. The angry juices have exited your body by way of perspiration or deep breathing, and you're feeling pretty calm, all things considered. Did you want to plot some revenge as well, or just go straight to dealing with it?

Ooh, plotting my revenge sounds fun. And so it is. Go to page 257.

Nope, I'm ready to rip off the Band-Aid. Let's deal with it! Go to page 222.

You decided to plot your revenge.

Excellent. <makes Dr. Evil fingers>

You're still well and truly pissed off, but you recognize that getting up in anyone's face — directly, at least — will probably not serve and may actually impede your end goal of getting your stuff back and/or getting out of this airport *not* in handcuffs. So once you do manage to exit LGA without a felony assault charge, in what ways might you direct your vengeance? (Hypothetically, of course.) You can't be sure precisely who mislaid your bag, but that doesn't matter in a hypothetical. Let's say it was the dude at the check-in desk whose brain freeze sent your stuff to Newark instead of New York. You could:

Find out his home address and sign him up for a lifetime subscription to *Girls and Corpses* magazine.*

Or

Have an exact replica of your suitcase delivered to his front door, but instead of your stuff, it's full of glitter. And a remote-controlled wind turbine.

That was fun, wasn't it? Now it's time to have a calm conversation with the gate agent, hand over your details in case they can locate and

---

* http://www.girlsandcorpses.com/

deliver your stuff in time for it to be of any use to you, and get in the taxi line.

Unless — did you want to try "Working it out" as well — just in case it suits you even better? Or shall we go straight to dealing with it?

I'm still a little peeved, to be honest. Let's try to work it out. Go to page 256.

I'm ready to deal with it! Go to page 222.

Uh-oh. You decided to MAKE IT WORSE.

Although you fell short of being thrown in airport jail (barely), you did not conduct yourself in a manner becoming a Platinum Rewards member, that's for sure. You whined, you snarked, you said "You've got to be kidding me" about fifteen times — each progressively louder than the last — and then you demanded to speak to a supervisor. A request to take your grievance up the chain is not in and of itself a terrible idea, but you (and it physically pains me to type this), you preceded that entreaty with the words "Whose friendly skies do I have to fly to get somebody who knows what they're doing around here, Caroline?" and made, um, a *very rude gesture* to the gate agent.

Plus, the nine-year-old kid across the way was taking video. You're going viral in — oh, wait, you already have. Your boss, your wife, and your own nine-year-old kid are going to see exactly what you've been up to since you landed. And Caroline? She's going to "locate" your missing suitcase in the trash room behind the food court MexiJoe's. Good luck getting the cumin smell out of your tux.

Now, are you sure you wouldn't like to see what's up on the Flipside?

YES, YES I SHOULD PROBABLY TRY TO "WORK IT OUT."
Go to page 256.

Politely and silently plotting my revenge is a better use of my time and energy. I see that now. Go to page 257.

Fuck it. Take me straight to dealing with it. Okeydokey then. Go to page 230.

The Business Trip

RIO #3: Try to not get fired or smell like cheese.

TRIAGE AND TACKLE:

Remember when life was simpler and you didn't just put your job and reputation on the line for the sake of venting your frustrations at a perfectly nice gate agent named Caroline who was just following Lost Luggage/Angry Customer protocol? Those were the days.

Also: I just saw the YouTube video. It's not looking good for you, bud. You may want to save your pennies on that tux rental — you'll need them to supplement your unemployment benefits.

Next time, if you decide you do want to take my advice and calm the fuck down *before* you try to deal with shit, give page 256 or 257 a shot. (Or maybe just go back to the beginning of the book and start over. Yeah, maybe that.)

To choose a different adventure, go back to page 213.
Or, skip ahead to the Epilogue on 269.

You picked  **AVOIDANCE** *(aka Ostrich Mode)*

Tempting. Very tempting. If you close your eyes and pretend like this isn't happening, maybe it will resolve itself like these kinds of things ~~often~~ NEVER do. Which is why you've decided your best defense is no offense at all, and that is the hill you're prepared to die on/bury your head in. Okay.

And I know you've already stopped listening, but can we talk for just a sec about what was in your bag? Your chargers and cables, the team mascot you were babysitting, and your lucky bowling shoes for the Northeastern Regional League Championships aren't going to replace themselves, and avoidance is neither going to solve the Mystery of the Missing Luggage nor help you defend your league-leading five-bagger from last year's Semis.

You need to calm the fuck down.

I REFUSE TO ENGAGE WITH ANY OF THIS SHIT. DOES THAT COUNT AS BEING CALM?

We've been over this. Avoidance is still a form of freaking out, and you *are* going to have to deal with all of it at some point. For now, can I at least convince you to choose a better coping mechanism and see where it takes you?

Get alarmed. Go to page 262.

Propose a trade. Go to page 264.

I'll just be over here with my head in the sand. Fine. Be that way. Go to page 266.

You decided to "get alarmed."

Your initial instinct was to treat this debacle like the Republican establishment treated Donald Trump in the 2016 primary—just ignore it and hope it'll go away. And we all know how that turned out. THANKS GUYS. Instead, you need to take *action*. Even if it's just a small step forward, it's better than standing by as a limp-dicked man-child destroys the world. Or, you know, as your lucky bowling shoes get rerouted to Tampa.

You may recall from my tip on page 116 that one surefire way to shock yourself into action is by way of an incessant noise. As such, here are some ideas to get your head out of the sand and back into the game:

Set a deadline. Give yourself, say, twenty minutes to pretend this isn't happening. Set an alarm on your watch or phone and when it goes off, spring into action like one of Pavlov's pooches. Get thee to the Help Desk!

Or, dial up the Econo Lodge right now and request a 7:00 a.m. wakeup call. Quick, before you can think too hard about it. You can spend the intervening hours in blissful ignorance, but when the handset starts squawking, that's your cue to get a move on.

Talk to yourself. Not to be confused with sobbing uncontrollably or screaming at airline employees, a midvolume mantra can do wonders for your mind-set. Resist the urge to retreat inward, and repeat after me (out loud): I CAN DEAL WITH THIS SHIT. I *WILL* DEAL WITH THIS SHIT.

Well, would you look at that? You might have some life in you yet. Did you want to try my "propose a trade" tip too, or just go straight to dealing with it?

You know what? I think I could use a little more motivation. Go to page 264.

I'm totally ready to deal with it! Go to page 224.

You decided to "propose a trade."

I know you, and I know this latest shitstorm isn't the only thing on your must-avoid list these days. So how about we make a deal? If you bite the bullet and march yourself over to the gate agent to start the torturous process of SPEAKING TO ANOTHER HUMAN BEING in hopes of tracking down your bag and getting it delivered to the Econo Lodge in a timely fashion (such that you can avoid having to avoid OTHER EXTREMELY ENERVATING ACTIVITIES like "shopping for new bowling shoes"), then I hereby grant you permission to *continue* avoiding any one of the following:

- Investigating those scratching noises coming from behind the wall in the kitchen.

- Opening that card from your ex. It might not be a birth announcement. (It is definitely a birth announcement.)

- Booking a root canal.

- RSVP'ing to Steve's Chili Cook-off. (Steve's famous recipe is less "chili" and more "hot dog smoothie.")

What say you? Rapping with Delta Customer Service seems practically pleasant in comparison to some of those other tasks, eh? So come on—put one foot in front of the other and let's go see a guy about a suitcase, shall we? (Then maybe when you get back from the Regionals, it'll be time to let Steve down gently while you avoid unpacking said suitcase.)

But I don't want to rush you. Would you like to try "getting alarmed," just to see what that's all about? Or go straight to dealing with it?

If trying another coping mechanism means I get to avoid dealing with it for a little longer, sign me up. Fair enough. Go to page 262.

No, you know what? I am totally ready to deal with it! Go to page 224.

Northeastern Regionals

You decided to do absolutely nothing.

Which is why you find yourself wondering what the heck you're supposed to do in Doylestown, PA, for the next four days if you can't compete in Regionals because you don't really feel like having to go out and buy new bowling shoes (and you certainly don't want to wear *rentals* like some kind of *amateur*), but you also don't have the gumption to rebook your return flight home any earlier.

Actually, you're probably not even wondering any of that...yet. You're the type who waits for the shitstorm to pause directly overhead and deposit its metaphorical deluge before you even think about reaching for a metaphorical umbrella.

Let me tell you how I think this is going to go. (I'm trying really hard not to be judgy, but we've come a long way together and I hate to see you reverting to your ostrichy ways.) I think you're going to fall asleep in this lumpy hotel bed and wake up tomorrow with a dead cell phone and no toothbrush. I *hope* that one of those outcomes compels you to take action and at least cadge a mini-bottle of Scope from the sundries shop in the lobby. If they sell phone chargers, so much the better — you do love the path of least resistance! But this is the Econo Lodge, so don't get your hopes up. If they don't, you're either going to keep avoiding dealing with any part of this shitshow and waste four days eating the best the vending machine has to offer before you can go home and continue pretending like it never happened; OR one of your teammates will notice you haven't been replying to his trash-talking texts, come looking for you, lend you some clean socks, and physically drag you to Barry's House of Bowling-wear. You may be hopeless when it comes to dealing with shit, but you're the Hook Ball King. The team needs you.

No matter how it plays out, you still don't have your luggage back because you totally gave up on that, which means your lucky shoes, your favorite pajamas, and the team mascot (long story) are lost to the same sands of time under which you buried your head for four days. Are you *sure* you wouldn't like to see what's up over on the Flipside?

On second thought, yes. I'm interested in "getting alarmed." Go to page 262.

I'm willing to "propose a trade." Go to page 264.

Gumption levels dangerously low. Better just go straight to dealing with it. Go to page 232.

Epilogue

I'm so pleased to see you made it all the way to the end of *Calm the Fuck Down*. Cheers! And I really hope you had fun choosing your own adventures because that section was a bitch to put together.

I also hope you feel like you're walking away with a host of practical, actionable methods with which to turn yourself into a calmer and more productive version of yourself, when shit happens.

Because it will. *OH, IT WILL*. Shit will happen both predictably and unpredictably, each time with the potential to throw your day, month, or life off course. Such as, for example, when the first draft of your book is due in one week and you break your hand on a cat.

Yes. A *cat*.

In fact, this epilogue was going in a totally different direction until such time as I found myself squatting over Mister Stussy — one of my two feral rescue kitties, affectionately dubbed #trashcatsofavenidaitalia over on Instagram — ready to surprise him with a paper towel soaked in organic coconut oil.

He's very scabby. I'm just trying to help.

Unfortunately, just as I descended with hands outstretched, Mister Stussy spooked. And instead of running away from me like he usually does when I try to medicate him, he launched himself up and backward into my outstretched fingers.

Crunch!

I've been asked many times since that fateful day to explain — in both English and Spanish — the physics of how a cat manages to break a human hand. I'm not sure I fully understand it myself, though I'm told Mercury was in retrograde, which may have been a factor. The closest I can get to describing what happened is that it was like someone had hurled a large, furry brick as hard as they could, at close range and exactly the wrong angle, and scored a direct hit on my fifth metacarpal.

And remember, before I met him, Mister Stussy had long been surviving on garbage and mud puddles. Dude is a bony motherfucker.

I was momentarily stunned by the pain, and then by the deep, visceral knowledge that finishing this book was about to get a whole lot more difficult. The leftmost digits on my thankfully nondominant hand were — and I believe this is the technical term — *fuuuuuuucked.*

Would you like to know how I reacted?

First, I told my husband, "I need to go be upset about this for a little bit." Then I went upstairs and cried, out of both pain and dismay. My emuppies were on struggle mode. Then I started to feel a little anxious on top of it, so I took a shower. Focusing on shampooing and soaping myself without doing further damage to my throbbing hand provided a goodly distraction and by the time I was finished, I was no longer sad/anxious.

I was *angry*.

Yes, for those of you keeping track at home, this is how my "I don't really get angry" streak was broken. By a fucking CAT, to whom I have been nothing but KIND and SOLICITOUS, and who repaid me with ASSAULT AND CATTERY.

For the rest of the night I walked around the house muttering "I am very *angry* with Mister Stussy" like Richard Gere when he was very angry with his father in *Pretty Woman*. I imagined wreaking vengeance upon him — picture the ALS Ice Bucket Challenge, with coconut oil — and that gave me some time and space to remember that Tim Stussert (as I sometimes call him) is just a fucking trash cat who doesn't want coconut oil rubbed into his scabs. It wasn't his fault.

Sigh.

In taking stock of my situation, I realized that in addition to finishing writing this book, I had my husband's boat-based birthday party to sort out; a takeover of the Urban Oufitters Instagram Stories to film; a haircut to schedule *before* I took over the Urban Outfitters Instagram Stories; and then I was supposed to pack for a three-week, three-state trip to the US.

If you started the clock at that sickening *Crunch!,* I needed to do all of it in thirteen days. Hmm.

At this point, I didn't know that my hand was broken. I thought it was a bad sprain and not worth spending untold hours in what passes for an "emergency" room in this town when I had so little time to finish my work. In the immediate aftermath of the cat attack, my ideal and, I believed, still-realistic outcome was to finish the book on schedule so I would have six days left to deal with the rest of my shit.

So I took a bunch of Advil and got back to work.

For the next week, I pounded awkwardly away at the last 5 percent of the manuscript with my right hand (and three fifths of the left) while the affected fingers cuddled in a homemade splint fashioned out of an Ace bandage and two emery boards. The look was sort of Captain Hook meets Keyboard Cat.

Was there an anxious voice in the back of my head saying *What if you* tore *something? What if you regret not getting that looked at right away?* Of course there was. It just lost out to the other total shitstorm on the docket.

(BTW, I'd hate to be seen as promoting cavalier attitudes toward your health, so please rest assured, I am nothing if not a GIANT pussy. If the pain had been unbearable, I would have asked my editor for an extension and gone to get an X-ray. At the time, on a scale of relatively painless to unbearable, I gave it a "tedious.")

I was able to ice, elevate, and type (with Righty), and my husband started picking up my slack on chores. I missed out on a couple fun dinners with friends because the last 5 percent of the writing process was taking five times as long as it was supposed to, and when unwrapped, my pinky finger had a disconcerting tendency to jerk in and out of formation like James Brown live at the Apollo, but overall things seemed...okay.

When I finished the book, I decided a leisurely afternoon at the clinic was in order. That's when I found out it was a break, not a sprain. Score one for Mister Stussy.

The next several weeks were challenging. (You may recall that multistate trip I had to pack for. Blurf.) But along the way, I calmed the fuck down and dealt with it. It's almost as if writing this book for the past six months had been preparing me for this very situation — like some kind of Rhonda Byrne *The Secret* manifestation crap, except I manifested a shitstorm instead of untold riches.

I suppose that's what I get for being an anti-guru.

On the bright side: when the storm hit without warning, I emoted, then crated the puppies and gave anxiety the finger. I plotted revenge against him who had wronged me and in doing so released my aggression in a way that didn't make anything worse. I took stock, I identified my RIO, and I've been triaging ever since.

I don't want to alarm you, but think I might be onto something here.

Remember in the introduction when I said I'd always had a problem "dealing with it" when unexpected shit cropped up? In fact, readers of *Get Your Shit Together* know that the writing of that book ended on a similarly chaotic note — we'd been living nomadically for months and the Airbnb we moved into just when I was ready to make the final push on the manuscript turned out to be more of a Bugbnb. I fully freaked out and I did not calm down even a little bit. (I also drew heavily on the Fourth Fund, both at the Bank of My Husband and of the Friends We Subsequently Moved In With).

Eventually, I got over and through and past it — I know how to get my shit together, after all — but not without wasting an enormous amount of time, energy, money, and goodwill in the process.

Whereas if we fast-forward a couple years, in the wake of a much more damaging (and painful) shitstorm, I seem to have become rather capable of dealing under duress.

Fancy that!

I'm still no Rhonda Byrne, but I do have a little secret for you: I don't spend all this time writing No Fucks Given Guides just for shits and giggles, or to make money, or to improve your life (although these are all sound justifications). I do it because each book, each writing process, and each hour I spend chatting away about my wacky ideas on someone else's podcast provides ME with an opportunity for personal growth.

I'm giving fewer, better fucks than ever, and I'm much happier as a result. In teaching others to get their shit together, I discovered new ways of keeping mine in line. And holy hell, was *You Do You* exactly the book I needed to write to heal myself of a bunch of unhealthy trauma and resentment I didn't even know I'd been carrying around for thirty years.

But I have to say that for me, *Calm the Fuck Down* is going in the annals as the most self-fulfilling titular prophecy of them all. I know how hard it was for me to handle unexpected mayhem just a few years ago, so I also know how remarkable it is to have been able to get this far in training myself to chill the fuck out about it. Yes, a move to the tropics and a massive cultural paradigm shift helped jump-start my education, but I took to it like a feral cat to a pile of trash — and then I wrote a book about it so you can get your own jump start at a much more reasonable and sweet-smelling price point.

So my final hope is this: that if you internalize all of my tips and techniques for changing your mind-set, and implement the lessons I've striven to impart — you'll realize that most of the shit that happens to you (even failing to bcc more than one hundred people on a work email) doesn't have to be as freakout-inducing as it might have seemed before you read this book. And that you can deal with it.

I mean, that's *my* realistic ideal outcome for you, and I'm feeling pretty good about it.

CALM

THE

FUCK

DOWN

AND DEAL WITH IT.

Acknowledgments

As a publishing insider for many years, I know how rare and special it is to work with the same team, book after book after book after book. It means we're all having fun and enjoying the fruits of our collective labor, and that nobody has accepted a better job elsewhere. So I really hope I haven't jinxed that by saying how grateful I am to have been supported by Jennifer Joel at ICM Partners, Michael Szczerban at Little, Brown, and Jane Sturrock at Quercus Books since day one.

Jenn — my hero in heels, my tireless champion, and the calmest of us all. I don't think she even needs this book, but I sure needed her to make it happen. And so she did.

Mike — the original Alvin to my Simon and the Tom to my Foolery. He has tended to these books like a mother hen and made them better with every peck and cluck.

And Jane — effortlessly co-steering the ship from across the Pond. Her enthusiasm for the very first No Fucks Given Guide has carried us close to the million-copy mark in the UK alone, not to mention given me a regular excuse to both say and be "chuffed."

Thanks also to *their* respective comrades-in-arms, including Loni Drucker, Lindsay Samakow, and Nic Vivas at ICM; Ben Allen (production editor and saint), Reagan Arthur, Ira Boudah, Martha Bucci, Sabrina Callahan, Nicky Guerreiro, Lauren Harms, Lauren Hesse, Brandon Kelley, Nel Malikova, Laura Mamelok, Katharine Meyers, Barbara Perris (copyeditor and saint), Jennifer Shaffer, and Craig Young at Little, Brown; and Olivia Allen, Charlotte Fry, Ana McLaughlin, Katie Sadler, and Hannah Winter at Quercus. Also: David Smith, the designer who supplied the UK versions of all the graphics for my new website, is both patient and quick on the draw, two qualities I love in a person; Alana Kelly at Hachette Australia has moved mountains and time zones to get me publicity Down Under; my friends at Hachette Canada have helped us crack the bestseller list book after book; and, finally, thanks to Lisa Cahn from Hachette Audio and Aybar Aydin, Callum Plews, Gavin Skal, and director Patrick Smith at Audiomedia Production.

Of course, the fourth NFGG would never have been possible without all y'all who read installments one, two, and/or three. A bigly thank-you goes out to my readers worldwide, as well as to anyone who's bought a copy for someone else as either a sincere or a passive-aggressive gift. (I'm looking at you, Sir Anthony Hopkins!) And thank you to the dysfunctional families, terrible bosses, fair-weather friends, and schoolyard bullies who built my audience from the ground up. Much appreciated.

Speaking of building from the ground up, I also want to thank my parents, Tom and Sandi Knight. They never once told me to calm the fuck down, even though they probably thought it *frequently.*

Finally, even when the topic is calming down, writing a book is a struggle. The following individuals all did their part to soothe me in my time of need: Pépito, Sir Steven Jay Catsby, Steinbeck, Millay, Baloo, Ferris Mewler, Mittens, Marcello, Benjamin, Steve Nash (Steve), The Matterhorn (Matty), Joni, Edgar, Misko, Hammie, Mushka, Dashiell, Moxie, Gladys, and [begrudgingly] Mister Stussy.

But it must be said that no one, human or feline, did more to help *Calm the Fuck Down* come to fruition than my husband, Judd Harris. Not only did he build my new website — a Herculean undertaking on behalf of a persnickety client — he made my coffee throughout and tended to my broken hand and bruised psyche at the end, and he was there for the nineteen years that preceded the writing of this book, including both the best and the worst stretches that inspired it. He is my favorite.

Index

Page numbers of illustrations appear in italics

About the Author

Sarah Knight's first book, *The Life-Changing Magic of Not Giving a Fuck,* has been published in more than twenty languages, and her TEDx talk, "The Magic of Not Giving a Fuck," has more than four million views. All of the books in her No Fucks Given Guides series have been international bestsellers, including *Get Your Shit Together,* which was on the *New York Times* bestseller list for sixteen weeks. Her writing has also appeared in *Glamour, Harper's Bazaar, Marie Claire, Red, Refinery29,* and elsewhere. After quitting her corporate job to pursue a freelance life, she moved from Brooklyn, New York, to the Dominican Republic, where she currently resides with her husband, two feral rescue cats, and a shitload of lizards.

You can learn more and sign up for her newsletter at nofucks givenguides.com, follow Sarah on Twitter and Instagram @MCSnugz, and follow the books @NoFucksGivenGuides (Facebook and Instagram) and @NoFucksGiven (Twitter).

Also available

The
*Life-Changing
Magic of
Not Giving
a* F**k

How to stop spending time you don't have
doing things you don't want to do
with people you don't like

Sarah Knight

'Genius'
Cosmopolitan

'Works a charm'
Sunday Times Magazine

'Life-affirming'
Guardian

Get Your
Sh•t Together

How to stop worrying about what you should do
so you can finish what you need to do
and start doing what you want to do

Sarah Knight

'Genius'
Vogue

'I love Knight'
Sunday Times Magazine

'The anti-guru'
Observer

You Do You

how to be who you are
and use what you've got
to get what you want

Sarah Knight

The bestselling author of
*The Life-Changing Magic of Not Giving a F***k*
and *Get Your Sh*t Together*

Get Your
Sh•t Together
Journal

Practical ways to cut the
bullsh•t and win at life

Sarah Knight

Bestselling author of *The Life-Changing Magic
of Not Giving a F**k*

Praise for Sarah Knight

"Genius" —*Cosmopolitan*

"Life-affirming" —*Guardian*

"Absolutely blinding. Read it. Do it." —*Daily Mail*